Spon's Architects' and Builders' Price Book

2006

Spon's Architects' and Builders' Price Book

Edited by

DAVIS LANGDON

2006

One hundred and thirty-first edition

Taylor & Francis
Taylor & Francis Group

LONDON AND NEW YORK

First edition 1873
One hundred and thirty-first edition published 2006
by Taylor & Francis
2 Park Square, Milton Park, Abingdon, Oxon OX14 4RN

Simultaneously published in the USA and Canada
by Taylor & Francis
270 Madison Avenue, New York, NY 10016

Taylor & Francis is an imprint of the Taylor & Francis Group

Printed and bound in Great Britain by
TJ International Ltd, Padstow, Cornwall

Publisher's note
This book has been produced from camera-ready copy supplied by the authors.

British Library Cataloguing in Publication Data
A catalogue record for this book is available from the British Library

ISBN 0-415-37030-2
ISSN 0306-3046

Contents

PART III - PRICES FOR MEASURED WORKS - cont'd

Prices for Measured Works - Minor Works

PART IV - APPROXIMATE ESTIMATING

PART V - TABLES AND MEMORANDA

Preface to the One Hundred and Thirty First edition

Following the May 2005 election, when Labour was returned for a third successive term, the outlook for the construction industry continues to look rosy. Public sector procurement is set to continue and private commercial work in the offices and entertainment sectors continues to pick up, though the retail sector may be entering a period of retrenchment. Although the housing market is remarkably flat for the time of year, pundits are predicting a soft landing for house prices, rather than a slump, following 9 years of successive increases.

Tender prices in Greater London, measured by Davis Langdon's Tender Price Index, showed a rise of 1.5% in the first quarter of 2005, continuing an increase of 4% since mid 2004. Over the past twelve months, there has been a 6% increase in tender prices in London, compared with other regions, where increases of up to 9% have been observed.

Market Conditions

The construction industry and the associated housing market have always been regarded as two of the key barometers of the UK economy. They are driven by a multitude of factors such as work volumes, inflation and borrowing levels, profitability, labour availability and cost, and a general confidence to invest in the future. The current view is that construction and housing are underpinned by low interest rates and relatively strong market conditions, and that these should prevail. Problems are only expected to occur if the economy slows markedly and unemployment starts to rise significantly. The Chancellor, as always, remains dedicated to low inflation and using interest rates as the main 'stick' to control matters. 2004 saw huge steel price hikes in building and construction, fed by an insationable demand from an active Chinese economy. However, few commentators foresee this re-occurring in 2005. There are already signs of a 'softening' of previous increases early in 2005. There are also conflicting signs that other metal prices may have peaked, although some copper and aluminium price increases may still be working their way up the supply chain. Analysts are also uncertain as to the direction oil prices are heading. At the time of writing, the price is $55.00 per barrel, but many believe that the price might climb even higher; certainly for the fore-seeable future. At current high levels, oil prices continue to impact on manufacturing, energy and transport costs. Numerous building materials have also risen in price since the beginning of 2005, and ever-rising oil and transportation costs, as well as increases in raw material prices, are thought to be one of the key factors behind such increases.

Prices

The price level of Spon's A&B 2006 has been indexed at 480, an increase of 5.5% over the index of 455 in the 2005 edition. Readers of Spon's A&B are reminded that Spon is the only known price book in which key rates are checked against current tender prices.

From 27 June 2005, the third and final part of a 2002 Construction Industry Joint Council three-year agreement on pay and conditions came into effect, raising wage rates from last year by approximately 9.5%. The revised labour rates provide basic hourly rates of £6.77 for general operatives and £9.00 for the craft rate, and have been taken into account in the preparation of this year's book, along with material prices, generally applicable as at April/May 2005.

Davis Langdon's forecast of tender price inflation over the next twelve months to 1st quarter 2006 is that prices will rise by 4 to 5% in Greater London as workload continues to pick up but already high capacity usage in some regions will see further inflation rises up to 6%. Over the following year to 1st quarter 2007, construction activity in Greater London is expected to have increased as more large commercial developments reach site, enabling certain sectors where prices have been restrained such as curtain walling and office fit-out, to re-establish margins and recoup cost increases.

This Edition

In the New Items sections, the 2006 edition includes Minipile piling, Grade 316 stainless steel rebar, Movable acoustic walls, Panel fire partitions, additional steel cladding and decking items and Bathroom Pods.

Substantive overhauls have also been undertaken on Asphalt and tarmacadam roads, Building prices per square metre, Diamond drilling and sawing, Ironmongery, including specification changes to comply with BS 8300 and Approved Document M and Sanitary fittings.

Profits and Overheads

The 2005 edition includes a 5% mark-up for overheads and 2½% mark-up for profit on built-up labour rates and material prices in the Measured Major Works section and a 7½% mark-up for overheads and a 5% mark-up for profit in the Measured Minor Works section. For non-analysed sub-contractor prices, only a 2½% mark-up for profit has been included, in both Major and Minor Works sections.

Preliminaries

Preliminaries costs have grown steadily over the last year and this year we have raised our example provision from 11% to 12%. Management and supervisory staff salaries have risen in response to demand, insurance premiums have suffered well publicised hikes, scaffolding costs rose more than most other trades and, in some areas, security costs have risen substantially. For Inner London, the congestion charge has also affected costs.

Value Added Tax

Since 1989 all non-domestic building work, refurbishment and alterations, has been subject VAT, currently at 17½ %. In the March 2001 Budget VAT payable on residential conversions was cut from 17½ % to 5%.

Prices included within this edition do not include for VAT, which must be added if appropriate.

The book is divided into five parts as follows:

Part I: Fees and Daywork

This section contains Fees for Professional Services, Daywork and Prime Cost.

Part II: Rates of Wages

This section includes authorised wage agreements applicable to the Building and associated Industries.

Part III: Prices for Measured Work

This section contains Prices for Measured Work - Major Works, and Prices for Measured Work - Minor Works (on coloured paper).

Part IV: Approximate Estimating

This section contains the Building Cost and Tender Price Index, information on regional price variations, prices per functional unit and square metre for various types of buildings, approximate estimates, cost limits and allowances for 'public sector' building work and a procedure for valuing property for insurance purposes.

Part V: Tables and Memoranda

This section contains general formulae, weights and quantities of materials, other design criteria and useful memoranda associated with each trade, and a list of useful Trade Associations.

While every effort is made to ensure the accuracy of the information given in this publication, neither the Editors nor Publishers in any way accept liability for loss of any kind resulting from the use made by any person of such information.

DAVIS LANGDON
MidCity Place
71 High Holborn
London
WC1V 6QS

Acknowledgements

Abbey Building Supplies Company
213 Stourbridge Road
Halesowen
West Midlands
B63 3QY
Building Fixings and Fastenings
Tel: 0121 550 7674
Fax: 0121 585 5031

ACO Technologies Ltd
ACO Business Park
Hitchin Road
Shefford
Bedfordshire
SG17 5TE
Drainage Channels
Tel: 01462 816 666
Fax: 01462 815 895
E-mail: drainsales@aco.co.uk
Website: www.aco.co.uk

Akzo Nobel Decorative Coatings Ltd
PO Box 37
Crown House
Hollins Road
Darwen
Lancashire
BB3 0BG
Paints, Varnishes etc.
Tel: 01254 704 951
Fax: 01245 870 155
E-mail: spicer@darwen.deconorth.com

Albion Concrete Products Ltd
Pipe House Wharf
Morfa Road
Swansea
West Glamorgan
SA1 1TD
Precast Concrete Pipes and Manhole Rings, etc.
Tel: 01792 655 968
Fax: 01792 644 461
E-mail: sales@albionc.co.uk

Alexander Adams Ltd
Hylton Bridge Farm
West Boldon
Tyne and Wear
NE36 0BB
Raised Access Floors and Accessories
Tel: 0191 519 0707
Fax: 0191 519 2121

Alfred McAlpine Slate Ltd
Penrhyn Quarry
Bethesda
Bangor
Gwynedd
LL57 4YG
Natural Welsh Slates
Tel: 01248 600 656
Fax: 01248 602 447
E-mail: slate@alfred-mcalpine.com
Website: www.amslate.com

Allgood PLC
297 Euston Road
London
NW1 3AQ
Ironmongery
Tel: 020 7387 9951
Fax: 020 7380 1232
E-mail: info@allgood.co.uk
Website: www.allgood.co.uk

Altro Floors
Works Road
Letchworth
Hertfordshire
SG6 1NW
"Altro" Sheet and Tile Flooring and Stair Nosings
Tel: 0870 548 0480
Fax: 0870 511 3388
E-mail: info@altro.co.uk
Website: www.altro.co.uk

Alumasc Exterior Building Products Ltd
White House Works
Bold Road
Sutton
St Helens
WA9 4JG
Aluminium Rainwater Goods
Tel: 01744 648 400
Fax: 01744 648 401
E-mail: info@alumasc-exteriors.co.uk
Website: alumasc-exteriors.co.uk

Andrews Marble Tiles
324 – 330, Meanwood Road
Leeds
LS7 2JE
Tel: 0113 262 4751
Fax: 0113 262 3337
E-mail: contracts@andrews-tiles.co.uk
Website: www.andrews-tiles.co.uk

A-Plant
Unit E
Kingsbridge Wharf
Barking
Essex
IG11 0BD
Site Plant
Tel: 0208 507 8111
Fax: 0208 591 2036

Armitage Shanks Group Ltd
Armitage
Rugeley
Staffordshire
WS15 4BT
Sanitary Fittings
Tel: 0870 122 8822
Fax: 0870 122 8282
Website: www.armitage-shanks.co.uk

Artex-Rawlplug Ltd
Skibo Drive
Thronliebank Industrial Estate
Glasgow
Scotland
G46 8JR
Tel: 0141 638 7961
Fax: 0141 273 2333
E-mail: rawlinfo@bpb.com
Website: www.bpb.com

Ash Resources
West Burton
Retford
Nottinghamshire
DN22 9BL
Lytag
Tel: 01427 881 234
Fax: 01788 567 546
E-mail: sales@ashresources.co.uk
Website: www.ashresources.co.uk

Astec Projects Ltd
Astec House
187-9, Kings Road
Reading
Berkshire
RG1 4EX
Suspended Ceiling Systems
Tel: 0118 958 1333
Fax: 0118 958 1337
E-mail: astec@astecprojects.co.uk
Website: www.astecprojects.co.uk

Bison Concrete Products Ltd
Millennium Court
First Avenue
Burton Upon Trent
DE14 2WR
Precast Concrete Flooring Systems
Tel: 01283 495 000
Fax: 01283 544 900
E-mail: concrete@bison.co.uk
Website: www.bison.co.uk

Bolton Gate Company
Waterloo Street
Bolton
Lancashire
BL1 2SP
Roller Shutters
Tel: 01204 871 000
Fax: 01204 871 049
E-mail: boltongate@dial.pipex.com
Web: www.boltongate.co.uk

Bonar Floors (Nuway)
High Holburn Road
Ripley
Derbyshire
DE5 3NT
Entrance Matting and Aluminium Matwell Frames
Tel: 01773 744 121
Fax: 01773 744 142
E-mail: infouk@bonarfloors.com
Website: www.bonarfloors.com

BRC Building Products
Carver Road
Astonfields Industrial Estate
Staffordshire
ST16 3BP
Brick Reinforcement
Tel: 01785 222 288
Fax: 01785 240 029
E-mail: email@brc-special-products.co.uk
Website: www.brc-uk.co.uk

B R Hodgson Ltd
Ability House
121, Brooker Road
Waltham Abbey
Essex
EN9 1JH
Plastering and screeding
Tel: 01992 766777
Fax: 01992 766888
Website: www.brhodgson.co.uk

British Gypsum Ltd
Technical Services Department
East Leake, Loughborough
Leicestershire
LE12 6JT
Plasterboard and Plaster Products
Tel: 0870 456 123
Fax   0870 456 356
E-mail: BGTechnical.Enquiries@bpb.com
Website: www.british-gypsum.com

Burlington Slate Ltd
Cavendish House
Kirkby-in-Furness
Cumbria
LA17 7UN
"Westmoreland" Slating
Tel: 01229 889 661
Fax: 01229 889 466
E-mail: sales@burlingtonstone.co.uk
Website: www.burlingtonstone.co.uk

Callenders Construction Products
Harvey Road
Burnt Mills Industrial Estate
Basildon
Essex
SS13 1QJ
Flooring, Roofing and Damp Proofing Products
Tel: 01268 591 155
Fax: 01268 591 165
E-mail: email@callenders.co.uk
Website: www.callenders.co.uk

Charcon
Hulland Ward
Ashbourne
Derbyshire
DE6 3ET
Reconstructed Stone Roofing/Kerbs etc.
Tel: 01335 372 222
Fax: 01335 370 074
E-mail: sales@bradstone.com
Website: www.bradstone.com

Cape Calsil Systems Ltd
Iver Lane
Uxbridge
Middlesex
UB8 2JQ
Boarding and TRADA Firecheck Panelling
Tel: 01895 463 000
Fax: 01895 259 262
Website: www.capecalisil.com

Catnic Ltd
Pontypandy Industrial Estate
Caerphilly
Mid Glamorgan
CF83 3GL
Steel Lintels
Tel: 02920 337 900
Fax: 02920 867 796
Website: www.catnic.com

Cavity Trays Ltd
Administration Centre
Lufton Trading Estate
Yeovil
Somerset
BA22 8HU
Cavity Trays, Closers and Associated Products
Tel: 01935 474 769
Fax: 01935 428 223
E-mail: sales@cavitytrays.co.uk
Website: www.cavitytrays.com

Cementation Foundations Skanska Ltd
Maple Cross House
Denham Way
Maple Cross
Rickmansworth
Hertfordshire
WD3 2SW
Piling
Tel: 01923 423 100
Fax: 01923 777 834
E-mail: cementation.foundations@skanska.co.uk
Website:www.cementationfoundations.skanska.co.uk

Custom Metal Fabricators
Central Way
Feltham
Middlesex
TW14 0XJ
Metalwork and balustrading
Tel: 0208 844 0940
Fax: 0208 751 5793
E-mail: dgibbs@cmf.co.uk
Website: www.cmf.co.uk

CF Anderson & Son Ltd
228 London Road
Marks Tey
Colchester
Essex
C06 1HD
Wrought Softwood Boarding and Panel Products
Tel: 01206 211 666
Fax: 01206 212 450
E-mail: gec@ndirect.co.uk

Colour Centre
29a Offord Road
London
N1 1AE
Paints, varnishes, stains
Tel: 020 7609 1164
Fax: 020 7700 1345
Website: www.colourcentre.com

Cordek Ltd
Spring Copse Business Park
Slinfold
West Sussex
RH13 7SZ
Trough Moulds
Tel: 01403 799 600
Fax: 01403 791 718
E-mail: sales@cordek.com
Website: www.cordek.com

Corus UK Ltd
PO Box 1
Brigg Road
Scunthorpe
North Lincolnshire
DN16 1BP
Structural Steel
Tel: 01724 404040
Fax: 01724 405600
Website: www.corusconstructionandindustrial.com

Cox Building Products
Unit 1
Shaw Road
Bishbury
Wolverhampton
WV10 9LA
Rooflights
Tel: 01902 371 800
Fax: 01902 371 810
E-mail: enquiries@coxdome.co.uk
Website: www.coxbp.com

Crittall Steel Windows
Springwood Drive
Braintree
Essex
CM7 2YN
Aluminium and Steel Windows
Tel: 01376 324 106
Fax: 01376 349 662
E-mail: hp@crittall-windows.co.uk
Website: www.crittall-windows.co.uk

Daniel Platt Ltd
Brownhills Tileries
Tunstall
Stoke-on-Trent
Staffordshire
ST6 4NY
Quarry & Ceramic Floor Tiles
Tel: 01782 577 187
Fax: 01782 577 877
E-mail: sale@danielplatt.co.uk
Website: www.danielplatt.co.uk

Decra Roof Systems (UK) Ltd
Unit 3
Faraday Centre
Faraday Road
Crawley
West Sussex
RH10 9PX
"Decra Stratos" Roofing System and Accessories
Tel: 01293 545 058
Fax: 01293 562 709
E-mail: sales@decra.co.uk
Website: www.decra.co.uk

Dennis Ruabon Ltd
Hafod Tileries
Ruabon
Wrexham
Clywdd
LL14 6ET
Quarry Floor Tiles
Tel: 01978 843 484
Fax: 01978 843 276
E-mail: sales@dennisruabon.co.uk
Website: www.dennisruabon.co.uk

Dow Construction Products
2 Heathrow Boulevard
284 Bath Road
West Drayton
Middlesex
UB7 0DQ
Insulation Products
Tel: 0208 917 5050
Fax: 0208 917 5413
E-mail: Styrofoam-uk@dow.com
Website: www.styrofoameurope.com

Dreadnought Clay Roof Tiles
(Hinton, Perry & Davenhill Ltd)
Dreadnought Works
Pensnett
Brierley Hill
Staffordshire
DY5 4TH
Clay Roof Tiling
Tel: 01384 774 05
Fax: 01384 745 53
E-mail: sales@dreadnought-tiles.co.uk
Website: www.dreadnought-tiles.co.uk

Essex Insulation Ltd
Essex House
Josselin Road
Burnt Mills
Basildon
Essex
SS13 1EL
Insulation products
Tel: 01268 724455
Fax: 01268 727963
E-mail: info@essexinsulation.co.uk
Website: www.essexinsulation.co.uk

Eternit Building Materials
Ridgehill Drive
Maddely Heath
Crewe
Cheshire
CW3 9LY
Slates, Tiles and Cladding
Tel: 01782 758 800
Fax: 01782 750 901
E-mail: marketing@eternit.co.uk
Website: www.eternit.co.uk

Eurobrick Systems Ltd
Unit 6
Bonville Business Centre
Dixon Road
Brislington
Bristol
BS4 5QW
Insulated Brick Cladding System
Tel: 0117 971 7117
Fax: 0117 971 7217
E-mail: info@eurobrick.co.uk
Website: www.eurobrick.co.uk

Expamet Building Products
PO Box 52
Longhill Industrial Estate (North)
Hartlepool
Cleveland
TS25 1PR
Expanded Metal Building Products
Tel: 01429 866 611
Fax: 01429 866 633
E-mail: expamet@compuserve.com

Forbo-Nairn Ltd
PO Box 1
Den Road
Kirkcaldy
Fife
KY1 2SB
Tiles and Sheet Flooring
Tel: 01592 643 777
Fax: 01592 643 999
E-mail: info@forbo-linoleum.co.uk
Website: www.forbo-linoleum.co.uk

Forticrete Architectural Products
8 Buckingham Street
London
WC2 6BX
Concrete, Stone Faced and "Astra" Glazed Blocks
Tel: 0207 723 4329
Fax: 0207 723 4339
E-mail: Info@forticrete.co.uk
Website: www.forticrete.co.uk

Forticrete Ltd
Heath Road
Leighton Buzzard
Bedfordshire
LU7 8ER
"Hardrow" Slating
Tel: 01525 244 900
Fax: 01525 850 432
E-mail: technical@forticrete.co.uk
Website: www.forticrete.co.uk

Fosroc Ltd
Coleshill Road
Tamworth
Staffordshire
B78 3TL
Admixtures, Expansion Joint Fillers etc
Tel: 01827 262 222
Fax: 01827 262 444
Website: www.fosrocuk.com

Franklin + Andrews
3 Tythe Barn
Brumstead Road
Stalham
Norwich
NR12 9DH
Griffiths Building Materials
Price Guides
Tel: 01692 581 545
Fax: 01692 582 893
Website: www.franklinandrews.com

Garador Ltd
Bunford Lane
Yeovil
Somerset
BA20 2YA
Garage Doors
Tel: 01935 443 700
Fax: 01935 443 744
Website: www.garador.co.uk

Geberit Ltd
Wedgenock House
Wedgenock Lane
Aylesford
Kent
ME20 7PJ
Above and Below Ground Drainage Goods
Tel: 01622 717 811
Fax: 01622 716 920
E-mail: technical@geberit-terrain.demon.co.uk
Website: www.geberit.co.uk

Gerfloor Ltd
Rothwell Road
Warwick
Warwickshire
CV34 5PY
Sheet and Tile Flooring
Tel: 01926 401 500
Fax: 01926 401 650
E-mail: gerflor@gerfloor.com
Website: www.gerfloor.com

Grace Servicised
Expansion Jointing and Waterproofing Division
Ajax Avenue
Slough
Berkshire
SL1 4BH
Expansion Joint Fillers and Waterbars
Tel: 01753 692 929
Fax: 01753 691 623
E-mail: uksales@grace.com
Website: www.graceconstruction.com

Gradus Wall Protection
Park Green
Macclesfield
Cheshire
SK11 7LZ
Stair edgings and floor trims
Tel: 01625 428922
Fax: 01625 433949
E-mail: sales@gradusworld.com
Website: www.gradusworld.com

Hallgate Timber
Red Maze Farm
Sevenoaks
Linewalk
Long Sutton
Nr Spalding
Lincolnshire
PE12 9HG
Carcassing softwood
Tel: 01406 363 9878
Fax: 01406 363 5689
E-mail: sales@hallgate.co.uk
Website: www.hallgate.co.uk

H&H Celcon Ltd
Celcon House
Ightham
Sevenoaks
Kent
TN15 9HZ
Concrete Blocks
Tel: 01732 886 333
Fax: 01732 886 810
E-mail: marketing@celcon.co.uk
Website: www.celcon.co.uk

Halfen-Deha
Humphrys Road
Woodside Estate
Dunstable
Bedfordshire
LU5 4TP
Building Fixings and Fastenings
Tel: 01582 470 300
Fax: 08705 316 304
E-mail: info@halfen.co.uk
Website: www.halfen.co.uk

Hanson Building Products
Stewartby
Bedford
MK43 9LZ
"London Brand" Facing Bricks
Tel: 0870 525 8258
Fax: 01234 762 040
E-mail: info@hansonbrick.com
Website: www.hanson-brickeurope.com

Hanson Bath & Portland Stone
Bumpers Lane
Wakeham
Portland
Dorset
DT5 1HY
Cotswold Stone
Tel: 01305 820 207
Fax: 01305 860 275
Website: www.hanson-quarryproduct.com

Hanson Conbloc
Mells Road
Mells
Frome
Somerset
BA11 3PD
Building Block Products
Tel: 01179 812 791
Fax: 01179 814 516
E-mail: drainage@hanson-concreteprods.com
Website: www.hanson-conbloc.com

Hanson Southern
Garston Road
Frome
Somerset
BA11 1RS
Cotswold Stone
Tel: 01373 453 333
Fax: 01373 452 964

Hanson Thermalite
Pembroke Road
Sevenoaks
TN13 1XR
"Thermalite" blocks
Tel: 08705 626500
Fax: 08705 626550

Harvey Fabrication Ltd
Hancock Road
London
E3 3DA
Galvanised Tank & Water Cylinders
Tel: 0208 981 7811
Fax: 0208 981 7815

Hathaway Roofing Ltd
Tindale Crescent
Bishop Auckland
County Durham
DL14 9TL
Sheet Wall and Roof Claddings
Tel: 01388 605 636
Fax: 01388 608 841
E-mail: mark.watson@hathaway-roofing.co.uk
Website: www.hathaway-roofing.co.uk

Hepworth Drainage
Hazelhead
Crow Edge
Sheffield
South Yorkshire
S36 4HG
Clay Drainage Goods
Tel: 01226 763 561
Fax: 01226 764 827
E-mail: info@hepworthdrainage.co.uk
Website: www.hepworthdrainage.co.uk

Hillaldam Coburn Ltd
Unit 6
Wyvern Estate
Beverly Way
New Malden
Surrey
KT3 4PH
Sliding and Folding Door Gear
Tel: 0208 336 1515
Fax: 0208 336 1414
E-mail: sales@hillaldam.co.uk
Website: www.coburn.co.uk

Hilti (Great Britain) Ltd
1 Trafford Wharf Road
Trafford Park
Manchester
M17 1BY
Fixings
Tel: 0800 886 100
Fax: 0800 886 200
Website: www.hilti.com

Hudevad Britain
Bridge House
Bridge Street
Walton-on-Thames
Surrey
KT12 1AL
Hot Water Radiators and Fittings
Tel: 01932 247 835
Fax: 01932 247 694
E-mail: sales@hudevad.co.uk

Hunter Plastics Ltd
Nathan Way
London
SE28 0AE
Plastic Rainwater Goods
Tel: 0208 855 9851
Fax: 0208 317 7764
E-mail: hunplas@hunterplastics.co.uk
Website: www.hunterplastics.co.uk

Ibstock Building Products Ltd
Leicester Road
Ibstock
Leicestershire
LE67 6HS
Facing Bricks
Tel: 01530 261 999
Fax: 01530 261 888
E-mail: marketing@ibstock.co.uk
Website: www.ibstock.co.uk

IG Ltd
Avondale Road
Cwmbran
Gwent
NP44 1XY
"Weatherbeater" Doors & Frames
Tel: 01633 486 486
Fax: 01633 486 465
E-mail: info@igltd.co.uk
Website: www.igltd.co.uk

IMI Yorkshire Copper Tube Ltd
East Lancashire Road
Kirkby
Liverpool
Merseyside
L33 7TU
Copper Piping
Tel: 0151 546 2700
Fax: 0151 549 2139

IMI Yorkshire Fittings Ltd
PO Box 166
Haigh Park Road
Leeds
LS1 1RD
"Yorkshire" & "Kuterlite" Fittings
Tel: 0113 270 6945
Fax: 0113 270 5644
E-mail: info@yorkshirefittings.co.uk
Website: www.yorkshirefittings.co.uk

Instafoam and Fibre Ltd
Hogwood Basin
Ivanhoe Road
Finchampstead
Wokingham
RG40 4PZ
Cavity Wall Insulation
Tel: 0118 932 8811
Fax: 0118 932 8314
Website: www.instagroup.co.uk

James Halstead Ltd
PO Box 3
Radcliffe New Road
Whitefield
Manchester
M45 7NR
"Polyflor" Contract Flooring
Tel: 0161 767 1111
Fax: 0161 767 1128
Website: www.polyflor.com

James Latham (Western)
Badminton Road
Yate
Bristol
Avon
BS37 5JX
Softwood, Hardwood and Panel Products
Tel: 01454 315 421
Fax: 01454 323 488
E-mail: plywood.west@lathams.co.uk
Website: www.lathamtimber-co.uk

Jeld-Wen Ltd
Watch House Lane
Doncaster
South Yorkshire
DN5 9LR
Tel: 0870 126 0000
Fax: 0870 126 0006
Website: www.jeld-wen.co.uk

John Newton & Co Ltd
12 Verney Road
London
SE16 3DH
Waterproofing Lathing
Tel: 0207 237 1217
Fax: 0207 252 2769

Junckers Ltd
Unit A
1 Wheaton Road
Whitham
Essex
CM8 3UJ
Hardwood Flooring
Tel: 01376 534 700
Fax: 01376 514 401
E-mail: sales@junkers.co.uk
Website: www.junkers.com

Keymer Tiles Ltd
Nye Road
Burgess Hill
West Sussex
NE11 0SZ
Hand made clay tiles
Tel: 01444 232931
Fax: 01444 871852
E-mail: info@keymer.co.uk
Website: www.keymer.co.uk

Kingspan Group PLC
Dublin Road
Kingscourt
County Cavan
Ireland
Cladding panels and purlins
Tel: 035342 969 8000
Fax: 035342 966 7501
E-mail: info.uk@insulation.kingspan.com
Website: www.insulation.kingspan.com

Klargester Environmental Engineering Ltd
College Road
Aston Clinton
Aylesbury
Buckinghamshire
HP22 5EW
Petrol Interceptors and Septic Tanks
Tel: 01296 633 000
Fax: 01296 633 001
E-mail: uksales@klargester.co.uk
Website: www.klargester.co.uk

Lafarge Cement
The Shore
Northfleet
Kent
DA11 9AN
Cement, Lime and Flintag
Tel: 01474 564 344
Fax: 01474 531 281
Website: www.bluecircle.co.uk

Lafarge Contracting
Pesthouse Lane
Barham
Suffolk
IP6 0PF
Tarmacadam and Asphalte Roads
Tel: 01473 833146
Fax: 01473 833114
Website: www.lafarge.co.uk

Lafarge Roofing Ltd
Mile Tree Road
Leighton Buzzard
Bedfordshire
LU7 9LA
"Redland" roofing tiles
Tel: 0870 601 000
Fax;   0870 642 742
E-mail: roofing@lafarge-roofing.co.uk
Website: www.lafarge-roofing.co.uk

Lamatherm Products Ltd
Forge Industrial Estate
Maesteg
Bridgend
Mid Glamorgan
CF34 0AU
Under Floor Cavity Barriers
Tel: 01656 730 833
Fax: 01656 730 115
E-mail: sales@lamatherm.co.uk
Website: www.lamatherm.co.uk

Langley Waterproofing Systems Ltd
Bishop Crewe House
North Street
Daventry
Northamptonshire
NN11 5PN
Roof Tiling
Tel: 01327 704 778
Fax: 01327 704 845
E-mail: sales@langleywaterproofing.co.uk
Website: www.langleywaterproofing.co.uk

LS Leaderflush Shapland
PO Box 5404
Nottingham
Nottinghamshire
NG16 4BU
Internal Doors
Tel: 0870 240 0666
Fax: 0870 240 0777
E-mail: marketing@lsleaderflushshapland.co.uk
Website: www.lsleaderflushshapland.co.uk

Light Alloy Ltd
Dales Road
Ipswich
Suffolk
IP1 4R J
"Zig Zag" Loft Ladders
Tel: 01473 740 445
Fax: 01473 240 002

Lignacite
Meadgate Works
Nazeing
Essex
EN9 2PD
Concrete Blocks
Tel: 01992 464441
Fax: 01992 445713
E-mail: info@lignacite.co.uk
Website: www.lignacite.co.uk/

Luxaflex UK
Swanscombe Business Centre
17 London Road
Swanscombe
Kent
DA10 0LH
Roller and Vertical Blinds
Tel: 01322 624 580
Fax: 01322 624 558
E-mail: sales@luxaflex.com
Website: www.luxaflex.com

Magrini Ltd
Unit 5, Maybrook Industrial Estate
Brownhills
Walsall
West Midlands
WS8 7DG
Baby Equipment
Tel: 01543 375 311
Fax: 01543 361 172
mail:sales@magrini.co.uk
Website: www.magrini.co.uk

Marley Building Materials
Station Road
Coleshill
Birmingham
B46 1HP
Roof Tiles, Pavings and "Thermalite" Blocks
Tel: 01675 468 400
Fax: 01675 468 485
E-mail:roofing/thermalitesales@mbm-marley.co.uk
Website: www.marley.co.uk

Marley Floors Ltd
Dickley Lane
Lenham
Maidstone
Kent
ME17 2QX
Sheet and Tile Flooring
Tel: 01622 854 000
Fax: 01622 854 219
E-mail: info@marley.com
Website: www.marleyfloors.com

Manhole Covers Ltd
College Road
Aston Clinton
Bucks
HP22 5EZ
Manhole Covers
Tel: 01296 632 775
Fax: 01296 632 799
Website: www.manholecovers.com

Marshalls Mono Ltd
Brier Lodge
Southowram
Halifax
West Yorkshire
HX3 9SY
Concrete Block Paving
Tel: 01422 306 000
Fax: 01422 330 185
Website: www.marshall.co.uk

Metalwood Fencing Contracts Ltd
Hutton House
Soot House Spring
Valley Road Industrial Estate
St Albans
Hertfordshire
AL4 6PG
Fencing
Tel: 01727 861 141
Fax: 01727 846 018
Email: metalwood@msn.com

Metsec Plc
Broadwell Road
Oldbury
Warley
West Midlands
B69 4HE
Lattice Beams
Tel: 0121 601 6000
Fax: 0121 601 6119
E-mail: lattice-joists@metsec.com
Website: www.metsec.com

Moelven Laminated Timber Structures Ltd
Unit 10
Vicarage Farm
Winchester Road
Fair Oak
Eastleigh
Hampshire
SO50 7HD
"Glulam" Laminated Timber Beams
Tel: 02380 695 566
Fax: 02380 695 577
E-mail: moelvenlts@aol.com
Website: www.moelven.co.uk

Parker Sussex Ltd
46 Station Road
Worthing
West Sussex
BN11 1JP
Purpose made Joinery
Tel: 01903 237 613
Fax: 01903 820 253
E-mail: sales@parker-joinery.co.uk
Website: www.parker-joinery.co.uk

Parkwood Mellowes Ltd
Ridcare Road
West Bromwich
West Midlands
B71 1BB
Patent Glazing
Tel: 0121 553 4011
Fax: 0121 553 4019

PD Edenhall Ltd
Danycraig Works
Danycraig Road
Risca
Newport
Monmouthshire
NP1 6DP
Flue Linings and Blocks
Tel: 01633 612 671
Fax: 01633 601 280
E-mail: sales@pdbricks.co.uk

Pilkington Glazing
26, Bermondsey Trading Estate
Rotherhithe New Road
London
SE16 3LE
Glazing
Tel: 0207 231 3181
Fax: 0207 394 3836
E-mail: info@pilkington.com
Website: www.pilkington.co.uk

Pressalit Ltd
Riverside Business Park
Dansk Way
Leeds Road
Ilkley
West Yorkshire
LS29 8JZ
Grab Rails
Tel: 01943 607 651
Fax: 01943 607 214
E-mail: ltd@pressalit.com
Website: www.pressalitcare.com

Proctor Group Ltd
The Haugh
Blairgowrie
Perthshire
PH10 7ER
British Sisalkraft paper and Insulation
Tel: 01250 872261
Fax: 01250 872727
E-mail: insulation@proctorgroup.com
Website: www.proctorgroup.com

Promat UK
The Stirling Centre
Eastern Road
Bracknell
Berkshire
RG12 2ST
Fireproofing Materials
Tel: 01344 381 301
Fax: 01344 381 300
E-mail: promat@promat.co.uk
Website: www.promat.co.uk

Quelfire
PO Box 35
Caspian RoadAltrincham
Cheshire
WA14 5QA
Fire Protection Compound
Tel: 0161 928 7308
Fax: 0161 941 2635

Rentokil Ltd
Industrial Products
Felcourt
East Grinstead
West Sussex
H19 2JY
Flame Retardant Products
Tel: 01342 833 022
Fax: 01342 326 229
E-mail: tstephens@rentokil-initial.co.uk
Website: www.rentokil-initial.com

Richard Lees Steel Decking ltd
Moor Farm Road West
The Airfield
Ashbourne
Derbyshire
DE6 1HD
Structural Steel Deck Flooring
Tel: 01335 300 999
Fax: 01335 300 888
E-mail: rsld-general@kvaerner.com

RMC Specialist Products (Cemex)
Waldorf Way, Denby Dale Road
Wakefield
West Yorkshire
WF2 8DH
Thermabate
Tel: 01924 262 081
Fax: 01924 290 126
E-mail: thermabate.sales@rmc-group.com
Website: www.rmc-group.com

Rockwool Ltd
Pencoed
Bridgend
Mid Glamorgan
CF35 6NY
Cavity Wall Batts
Tel: 01656 863 210
Fax: 01656 863 611
E-mail: sales@rockpanel.co.uk
Website: www.rockpanel.co.uk

Roger Wilde Ltd
Chareau House
1 Miles Street
Oldham
OL1 3NW
Glass blocks
Tel: 0161 624 6824
Fax: 0161 627 3770
Website: www.rogerwilde.com

Rom Ltd
Eastern Avenue
Trent Valley
Lichfield
Staffordshire
WS13 6DN
Reinforcement
Tel: 01543 414 111
Fax: 01543 268 221
E-mail: enquiries@rom-co.uk
Website: www.rom.co.uk

Ruberoid Building Products
Appley Lane North
Appley Bridge
WIgan
Lancashire
WN6 9AB
Roofing Felts, DPC's
Tel: 0800 028 5573
Fax: 0800 013 5574
E-mail: marketing@ruberoid.co.uk
Website: www.ruberoid.co.uk

Ryton's Building Products Ltd
Design House
Orion Way
Kettering Business Park
Kettering
Northamptonshire
NN15 6NL
Roof Ventilation Products
Tel: 01536 511 874
Fax: 01536 310 455
E-mail: vents@rytons.com
Website: www.rytons.co.uk

Safeguard Europe
Redkiln Close
Redkiln Way
Horsham
Sussex
RH13 5QL
Tel: 01403 210 204
Fax: 01403 217 529
E-mail: info@safeguardchecn.com
Website: www.safeguardchecm.com

Saint-Gobain-Pipelines
Lows Lane
Stanton-by-Dale
Ilkeston
Derbyshire
DE7 4QU
Cast Iron Drainage Pipes, Fittings & Water Pipes
Tel: 0115 932 9513
Fax: 0115 930 5000E-mail: sales@saint-gobain-pipelines.co.uk
Website: www.saint-gobain-pipelines.co.uk

Sandtoft Roof Tiles
Sandtoft
Doncaster
South Yorkshire
DN8 5SY
Clay Roof Tiling
Tel: 01427 871200
Fax: 01427 871222
E-mail: info@sandtoft.co.uk
Website: www.sandtoft.co.uk

Screeduct Ltd
Unit 8
Northcot Business Park
Blockley
Nr Moreton-in-Marsh
Gloucestershire
GL56 9LH
Trunking Systems and Conduits
Tel: 01386 701372
Fax: 01386 701571
E-mail: sales@screeduct.com
Website: www.screeduct.com

Sealmaster
Brewery Road
Pampisford
Cambridge
Cambridgeshire
CB2 4HG
Intumescent Strips and Glazing Compound
Tel: 01223 832851
Fax: 01223 837215
E-mail: sales@sealmaster.co.uk
Website: www.sealmaster.co.uk

Sealocrete Pla Ltd
Greenfield Lane
Rochdale
Lancashire
OL11 2LD
Building Aids, Repair and Maintenance Materials
Tel: 01706 352255
Fax: 01706 860880
E-mail: bestproducts@sealocrete.co.uk

Stainless UK Ltd
Unit 1a, Newhall Road Works
Sheffield
S9 2QL
Stainless steel rebar
Tel: 0114 244 1333
Fax: 0114 244 1333
E-mail: sales@stainless-uk.co.uk
Website: www.stainless-uk.co.uk

Stone Firms Ltd
Bumpers Lane
Wakeham
Portland
Dorset
DT5 1HY
Portland Stone
Tel: 01305 820 207
Fax: 01305 860 275

Stowell Concrete Ltd
Arnolds Way
Yatton
Bristol
BS49 4QN
Precast Concrete Lintols
Tel: 01934 834 000
Tel: 01934 835 474
Website: www.stowellconcrete.co.uk

Tarmac Topblock Ltd
Wergs Hall
Wergs Hall Road
Wolverhampton
West Midlands
WV8 2HZ
Concrete Blocks
Tel: 01902 754131
Fax: 01902 743171

Tarmac Southern Ltd
Topmix
Pudding Mill Lane
Bow
London
E15 2PJ
Ready mixed concrete
Tel: 0208 555 2415
Fax: 0208 555 2593

Terram Ltd
Mamhillad Park
Pontypool
NP4 0YR
Tel: 01495 757722
Fax: 01495762383
E-mail: shancock@email.msn.com
Website: www.terram.co.uk

Tor Coatings Ltd
Portobello Industrial Estate
Birtley
Chester-le-Street
County Durham
DH3 2RE
Solignum etc.
Tel: 0191 410 6611
Fax: 0191 492 0125
Website: www.tor-coatings.com

Vandex (UK) Ltd
PO Box 88
Leatherhead
KT22 7YF
"Vandex Super" & "Premix"
Tel: 01372 363040
Fax: 01372 363373
E-mail: info@vandex.co.uk
Website: www.vandex.co.uk

Velux Co Ltd
Wellington Road
Kettering Parkway
Kettering
Northamptonshire
NN15 6XR
"Velux" Roof Windows & Flashings
Tel: 0870 166 7676
E-mail: enquiries@velux.co.uk
Website: www.velux.co.uk

Wavin Plastics Ltd
Parsonage Way
Chippenham
Wiltshire
SN15 5PN
UPVC Drainage Goods
Tel: 01249 766 600
Fax: 01249 443 286
E-mail: genenqy@wavin.co.uk
Website: www.wavin.co.uk

Welconstruct Distribution
Woodgate Business Park
Kettles Wood Drive
Birmingham
B32 3GH
Lockers and Shelving Systems
Tel: 0121 4219000
Fax: 0121 4219888
E-mail: mail@welconstruct.co.uk
Website: www.welconstruct.co.uk

Wicanders (Amorim House)
Amorim House
Star Road
Partridge Green
Horsham
West Sussex
RH13 8RA
Floor Coverings
Tel: 01403 710001
Fax: 01403 710003
Website: www.amorim.com

William Hare Ltd
Brandlesholme House
Brandlesholme Road
Bury
Lancashire
BL8 1JJ
Structural Steelwork
Tel: 0161 609 0000
Fax: 0161 609 0409
E-mail: http://www.hare.co.uk/
Website: www.hare.co.uk

WP Metals Ltd
Westgate
Aldridge
WS9 8DJ
Rainwater Goods
Tel: 01922 743111
Fax: 01922 743344
E-mail: enquiries@wpl-limited.co.uk
Website: www.wpl-limited.co.uk

Yeoman Aggregates Ltd
Stone Terminal
Horn Lane
Acton
London
W3 9EH
Hardcore, Gravels etc
Tel: 0208 8966800
Fax: 0208 8966811

How to use this Book

First-time users of *Spon's Architects' and Builders' Price Book* and others who may not be familiar with the way in which prices are compiled may find it helpful to read this section before starting to calculate the costs of building work. The level of information on a scheme and availability of detailed specifications will determine which section of the book and which level of prices users should refer to.

For preliminary estimates/indicative costs before drawings are prepared, refer to the average overall *Building Prices per Functional Units* (see Part IV) and multiply this by the proposed number of units to be contained within the building (i.e. number of bedrooms etc.) or *Building Prices per Square Metre* rates (see Part IV) and multiply this by the gross internal floor area of the building (the sum of all floor areas measured within external walls) to arrive at an overall preliminary cost. These rates include Preliminaries (the Contractors' costs) but make no allowance for the cost of External Works or VAT.

For budget estimates where preliminary drawings are available, one should be able to measure approximate quantities for all the major components of a building and multiply these by individual rates contained in the *Approximate Estimating* section (see Part IV). This should produce a more accurate estimate of cost than using overall prices per square metre. Labour and other incidental associated items, although normally measured separately within Bills of Quantities, are deemed included within approximate estimate rates.

For more detailed estimates or documents such as Bills of Quantities (Quantities of supplied and fixed components in a building, measured from drawings), either use rates from *Prices for Measured Work - Major Works* or *Prices for Measured Work - Minor Works*, depending upon the overall value of the contract. All such prices used may need adjustment for size, site constraints, local conditions location and time, etc., and users are referred to page 780 for an example of how to adjust an estimate for some of these factors. Items within the Measured Works sections are made up of many components: the cost of the material or product; any additional materials needed to carry out the work; the labour involved in unloading and fixing, etc. These components are usually broken down into:

Prime Cost

Commonly known as the "PC", Prime Cost is the actual price of the material such as bricks, blocks, tiles or paint, as sold by suppliers. Prime Cost is given "per square metre", "per 100 bags" or "each" according to the way the supplier sells the product. Unless otherwise stated, prices in *Spon's Architects' and Builders' Price Book* (hereafter referred to as *Spon's A & B*), are deemed to be "delivered to site", (in which case transport costs will be included) and also take account of trade and quantity discounts. Part loads generally cost more than whole loads but, unless otherwise stated, Prime Cost figures are based on average prices for full loads delivered to a hypothetical site in Acton, London W3. Actual prices for "live" tenders will depend on the distance from the supplier, the accessibility of the site, whether the whole quantity ordered is to be supplied in one delivery or at specified dates and market conditions prevailing at the time. Prime Cost figures for commonly-used alternative materials are supplied in listed form at the beginning of some work sections. As stated later, these prices are mainly at "list" prices before deduction of quantity discounts, and therefore require 'discount' adjustment before they can be substituted in place of "PC" figures given for Measured Work items.

Labour

This figure covers the cost of the operation and is calculated on the gang wage rate (skilled or unskilled) and the time needed for the job. A full explanation and build-up is provided on page 83. Particular shortages have been noted in the Bricklaying, Carpentry, Joinery and Shuttering trades. In response to these pressures and corresponding hikes in daily rates/measured prices, basic labour rates for Bricklayers, Carpenters and Joiners have been enhanced by using the plus 5% bonus payment figures for these trades as outlined on page 84. Extras such as highly skilled craft work, difficult access, intermittent working and the need for additional labourers to back up the craftsman (e.g. for handling heavy concrete blocks etc.) all add to the cost. Large regular or continuous areas of work are cheaper to install than smaller intricate areas, since less labour time is wasted moving from one area to another.

Materials

Material prices include the cost of any ancillary materials, nails, screws, waste, etc., which may be needed in association with the main material product/s. If the material being priced varies from a standard measured rate, then identify the difference between the original PC price and the material price and add this to your alternative material price before adding to the labour cost to produce a new overall Total rate. Alternative material prices, where given, are largely based upon "list" prices, before the deduction of quantity discounts etc., and therefore require 'discount' adjustment before they can be substituted in place of "PC" figures given for Measured Work items.

Example:

	PC £	Labour hours	Labour £	Material £	Unit	Total Rate £
100 mm Thermalite Turbo block (see page 160)	6.48	0.46	10.01	8.06	m²	**18.07**
100 mm Toplite standard block (see page 169 - £8.01 less 20% discount)	7.00					
Calculation: £8.06/1.075 (O&P) – 6.48 = 1.02 + 7.00 x 1.075 (O&P) = £8.55						
100 mm Toplite block	7.00	0.46	10.01	8.55	m²	**18.56**

Plant

Plant covers the use of machinery ranging from JCB's to shovels and static plant including running costs such as fuel, water supply (which is metered on a construction site), electricity and rubbish disposal. Some items of plant are included within the Measured Works sections e.g. "Groundwork", under a Material/Plant column. Other items are included within the Preliminaries section.

Unit

The Unit is generally based upon measurement guidelines laid out in the Standard Method of Measurement of Building Works – Seventh Edition, published by the Royal Institution of Chartered Surveyors and The Building Employers Confederation.

Total Rate

Prices in the Total Rate column generally include for the supply and fix of items, unless otherwise described.

Overheads and profit

The general overheads of the Contractor's business, the head office overheads and any profit sought on capital and turnover employed, is usually covered under a general item of overheads and profit which is applied either to all measured rates as a percentage, or alternatively added to the tender summary or included within Preliminaries (site specific overhead costs). At the present time, we are including an allowance of 5% for overheads and 2½% for profit on built-up labour rates and material prices in the Measured Major Works section and 7½% for overheads and 5% for profit on built-up labour rates and material prices in the Minor Works section. For non-analysed sub-contractor prices, only a 2½% mark-up for profit has been included, in both Major and Minor Works sections.

Preliminaries

Site specific overheads on a contract, such as insurance, site huts, security, temporary roads and the statutory health and welfare of the labour force, are not directly assignable to individual items so they are generally added as a percentage or calculated allowance after all building component items have been costed and summed. Preliminaries will vary from contract to contract according to the type of construction, difficulties of the site, labour shortage, inclement weather or involvement with other contractors, etc. The overall Preliminary addition for a scheme should be adjusted to allow for these factors. As in the last edition we have retained Preliminary costs at 12%.

The first seven of these eight items combine to form the **Price for Measured Works** sections. It will be appreciated that a variation in any one item in any group will affect the final Measured Work price. Any cost variation must be weighed against the total cost of the contract, and a small variation in Prime Cost where the items are ordered in thousands may have more effect on the total cost than a large variation on a few items, while a change in design which introduces the need to use, e.g. earth-moving equipment, which must be brought to the site for that one task, will cause a dramatic rise in the contract cost. Similarly, a small saving on multiple items will provide a useful reserve to cover unforeseen extras.

Maximising value and reducing risk for clients investing in
infrastructure, construction and property

managed
solutions

DAVIS LANGDON

EUROPE & MIDDLE EAST
office locations

Spon's International Construction Costs Handbook

This practical series of five easy-to-use Handbooks gathers together all the essential overseas price information you need. The Hand-books provide data on a country and regional basis about economic trends and construction indicators, basic data about labour and materials' costs, unit rates (in local currency), approximate estimates for building types and plenty of contact information.

Spon's African Construction Costs Handbook 2nd Edition
Countries covered: Algeria, Cameroon, Chad, Cote d'Ivoire, Gabon, The Gambia, Ghana, Kenya, Liberia, Nigeria, Senegal, South Africa, Zambia
2005: 234x156: 368 pp Hb: 0-415-36314-4: £170.00

Spon's Latin American Construction Costs Handbook
Countries covered: Argentina, Brazil, Chile, Colombia, Ecuador, French Guiana, Guyana, Mexico, Paraguay, Peru, Suriname, Uruguay, Venezuela
2000: 234x156: 332 pp Hb: 0-415-23437-9: £85.00

Spon's Middle East Construction Costs Handbook 2nd Edition
Countries covered: Bahrain, Eqypt, Iran, Jordan, Kuwait, Lebanon, Oman, Quatar, Saudi Arabia, Syria, Turkey, UAE
2005: 234x156: 384 pp Hb: 0-415-36315-2: £170.00

Spon's European Construction Costs Handbook 3rd Edition
Countries covered: Austria, Belgium, Cyprus, Czek Republic, Finland, France, Greece, Germany, Italy, Ireland, Netherlands, Portugal, Poland, Slovak Republic, Spain, Turkey
2000: 234x156: 332 pp Hb: 0-419-25460-9: £170.00

Spon's Asia Pacific Construction Costs Handbook 3rd Edition
Countries covered: Australia, Brunei Darassalem, China, Hong Kong, India, Japan, New Zealand, Indonesia, Malaysia, Philippines, Singapore, South Korea, Sri Lanka, Taiwan, Thailand, Vietnam
2000: 234x156: 332 pp Hb: 0-419-25470-6: £170.00

PART I

Fees and Daywork

This part of the book contains the following sections:

Free Updates

with three easy steps...

1. Register today on
   www.pricebooks.co.uk/updates

2. We'll alert you by email when new
   updates are posted on our website

3. Then go to
   www.pricebooks.co.uk/updates
   and download.

All four Spon Price Books – *Architects' and Builders'*, *Civil Engineering and Highway Works*, *Landscape and External Works* and *Mechanical and Electrical Services* – are supported by an updating service. Three updates are loaded on our website during the year, in November, February and May. Each gives details of changes in prices of materials, wage rates and other significant items, with regional price level adjustments for Northern Ireland, Scotland and Wales and regions of England. The updates terminate with the publication of the next annual edition.

As a purchaser of a Spon Price Book you are entitled to this updating service for the 2006 edition – free of charge. Simply register via the website www.pricebooks.co.uk/updates and we will send you an email when each update becomes available.

If you haven't got internet access we can supply the updates by an alternative means. Please write to us for details: Spon Price Book Updates, Spon Press, 2 Park Square, Milton Park, Abingdon, Oxfordshire, OX14 4RN.

Find out more about spon books
Visit www.sponpress.com for more details.

New books from Spon

The following books can be ordered directly from Spon or from your nearest good bookstore

Spon's Irish Construction Price Book 2nd edition, Franklin + Andrews
    hbk 0415344093
Spon's Estimating Costs Guide to Roofing, B. Spain
    pbk 0415344123
Spon's Estimating Costs Guide to Finishings, B. Spain
    pbk 0415344115
Spon's Estimating Costs Guide to Minor Landscaping, Gardening and External Works, B. Spain
    pbk 0415344107
Spon's Middle East Construction Costs Handbook 2nd ed., Franklin + Andrews
    hbk 0415363152
Spon's African Construction Costs Handbook 2nd ed., Franklin + Andrews
    hbk 0415363144
Construction Sector in Asian Economies, M Anson *et al.*
    hbk 0415286131
Construction Project Management, P Fewings
    hbk 0415359058, pbk 0415359066
Spon's Manual for Educational Premises 3rd edition, D Barnsley
    hbk 041528077X
Building Regulations Explained 7th edition, LDSA *et al.*
    hbk 0415308623
Understanding the Building Regulations 3rd edition, S Polley
    pbk 0415349176
Presentation and Settlement of Contractors' Claims 2nd ed., M Hackett *et al.*
    hbk 0419205004
Understanding JCT Standard Building Contracts 7th edition, D. Chappell
    pbk 0415306310
Project Planning and Control, D. Carmichael
    hbk 0415347262
Practical Construction Management 2nd edition, R Ranns *et al.*
    hbk 0415362571
Risk Management in Projects 2nd edition, J Raftery et al.
    hbk 0415260558, pbk 0415260566

Please send your order to:
Marketing Department, Spon Press, 2 Park Square, Milton Park Abingdon, Oxfordshire, OX14 4RN.
or visit www.sponpress.com for more details.

Fees for Professional Services

Extracts from the scales of fees for architects, quantity surveyors and consulting engineers are given together with extracts from the Town and Country Planning Regulations 2005 and Building Regulation Charges. These extracts are reproduced by kind permission of the bodies concerned, in the case of Building Regulation Charges, by kind permission of the London Borough of Ealing. Attention is drawn to the fact that the full scales are not reproduced here and that the extracts are given for guidance only. The full authority scales should be studied before concluding any agreement and the reader should ensure that the fees quoted here are still current at the time of reference.

ARCHITECTS' FEES

Standard Form of Agreement for the Appointment of an Architect (SFA/99), page 4 (brief notes only)
Conditions of Engagement for the Appointment of an Architect (CE/99), page 4 (brief notes only)
Small Works (SW/99), page 4 (brief notes only)
Employer's Requirements (DB1/99), page 4 (brief notes only)
Contractor's Proposals (DB2/99), page 4 (brief notes only)
Form of Appointment as Planning Supervisor (PS/99), page 4 (brief notes only)
Form of Appointment as Sub-Consultant (SC/99), page 4 (brief notes only)
Form of Appointment as Project Manager (PM/99), page 4 (brief notes only)

QUANTITY SURVEYORS' FEES

Scale 36, inclusive scale of professional charges, page 6
Scale 37, itemised scale of professional charges, page 10
Scale 40, professional charges for housing schemes for Local Authorities, page 28
Scale 44, professional charges for improvements to existing housing and environmental improvement works, page 32
Scale 45, professional charges for housing schemes financed by the Housing Corporation, page 34
Scale 46, professional charges for the assessment of damage to buildings from fire etc., page 39
Scale 47, professional charges for the assessment of replacement costs for insurance purposes, page 41

CONSULTING ENGINEERS' FEES

Guidance on Fees, page 42

PLANNING REGULATION FEES

Part I: General provisions, page 46
Part II: Scale of Fees, page 47

THE BUILDING (LOCAL AUTHORITY CHARGES) REGULATIONS 1998

Charge Schedules, page 51
Charges for erection of one or more small new domestic buildings and connected work, page 52
Charges for erection of certain small domestic buildings, garages, carports and extensions, page 52
Charges for building work other than to which tables 1 and 2 apply, page 53

ARCHITECTS' FEES

RIBA Forms of Appointment 1999
- include forms to cover all aspects of an Architect's practice;
- identify the traditional roles of an Architect;
- reflect or take into account recent legislation such as the Housing Grants, Construction and Regeneration Act 1996, the Arbitration Act 1996 (applies to England and Wales only), the Unfair Terms in Consumer Contracts Regulations 1994, Latham issues etc;
- update the Outline Plan of Work Stage titles and descriptions;
- are sufficiently flexible for use with English or Scottish Law (1); the building projects of any size (except small works); other professional services (2); different project procedures.

    (1)   The Royal Incorporation of Architects in Scotland will publish appropriate replacement pages for use where the law of Scotland applies to the Agreement.

    (2)   Excluding acting as adjudicator, arbitrator, expert witness, conciliator, party wall surveyor etc.

All forms require the Architect to agree with the Client the amount of professional indemnity insurance cover for the project.

Standard Form of Agreement for the Appointment of an Architect (SFA/99)
The core document from which all other forms are derived. Suitable for use where an Architect is to provide professional services for a fully designed building project in a wide range of size or complexity and/or to provide other professional services. Used with Articles of Agreement. Includes optional Services Supplement.

Conditions for Engagement for the Appointment of an Architect (CE/99)
Suitable for use where an Architect is to provide services for a fully designed building project and/or to provide other professional services where a Letter of Appointment is preferred in lieu of Articles of Agreement. Includes optional (modified) Services Supplement and draft Model letter.

Small Works (SW/99)
Suitable for the provision of professional services where the cost of construction is not expected to exceed £150,000 and use of the JCT Agreement for Minor Works is appropriate. The appointment is made by a specially drafted Letter of Appointment, the Conditions and an optional Schedule of Services.

Employer's Requirements (DB1/99)
A supplement to amend SFA/99 and CE/99 where an Architect is appointed by the Employer Client to prepare Employer's Requirements for a Design and Build contract. Includes replacement Services Supplement and notes on completion for initial appointment, where a change to Design and Build occurs later or where "consultant switch" is contemplated.

Contractor's Proposals (DB2/99)
A supplement to amend SFA/99 where an Architect is appointed by the Contractor Client to prepare Contractor's Proposals under a Design and Build contract. Includes replacement Services Supplement and notes on completion for initial appointment and for "consultant switch".

Form of Appointment as Planning Supervisor (PS/99)
Used with Articles of Agreement. Provides for the Planning Supervisor to prepare the Health and Safety File and the pre-tender Health and Safety Plan.

Form of Appointment as Sub-Consultant (SC/99)
Suitable for use where a Consultant wishes (another Consultant (Sub-Consultant) or Specialist) to perform a part of his responsibility but not for use where the intention is for the Client to appoint Consultants or Specialists directly. Used with Articles of Agreement. Includes draft form of Warranty to the Client.

Form of Appointment as Project Manager (PM/99)
Suitable for a wide range of projects where the Client wishes to appoint a Project Manager to provide a management service and/or other professional service. Used with Articles of Agreement. Does not duplicate or conflict with the Architect's services under other RIBA forms.

ARCHITECTS' FEES

Of the above documents, SFA/99 is the core document, which is used as the basis for all the documents in the RIBA 1999 suite. It should be suitable for any Project to be procured in the 'traditional' manner. Supplements are available for use with Design and Build procurement. It is used with Articles of Agreement and formal attestation underhand or as a deed.

Guides

A newly guide, 'A Client's Guide to Engaging an Architect: May 2004', has recently been published by:

RIBA Publications,
Construction House,
56-64 Leonard Street,
London. EC2A 4LT.
Telephone: 0207 251 0791
Fax: 0207 608 2375

This guide includes an introduction to the services an Architect can be expected to provide, advice on the forms to use, linking the RIBA Plan of work Stages with fees (which are a matter of negotiation) and classifying buildings according to three levels of complexity.

Generally, the more complex the building, the higher the level of fee. Example categories include:

Simple: for buildings such as car parks, warehouses, factories and speculative retail schemes

Average: for buildings such as offices, most retail outlets, general housing, schools etc., and

Complex: for multi-purpose developments, specialist buildings e.g. hospitals, research laboratories etc.

Typical proportions of the total fee for work stages C to L are shown in the following table which excludes additional fees for work stages A and B (Appraisal and Strategic Brief), which are normally carried out on a time charge basis.

RIBA Plan of Work Stages C – L		Proportion of 100% fee (stages C – L)
C	Outline proposals	10% - 15%
D	Detailed proposals	15% - 20%
E	Final proposals	20%
F	Production Information	20%
G-L	Tender and Construction	25% - 35%

The latest edition of this client's guide includes a fee scale graph based upon Architect's fees for services based on stages C to L, collected by survey between July 2002 and July 2003.

From this graph, the range of average fees for traditional contracts with a construction cost of up to £3m in value was:

Construction cost £	Percentage of construction cost	
	lower range*	higher range*
100,000	8.5%	11%
500,000	5.8%	8.5%
1,000,000	4.5%	7.8%
2,000,000	4%	7.3%
3,000,000	3.8%	7%

* some collected data lies beyond these ranges

Certain qualifications and other advice are associated with these figures, and readers are advised to refer to the source document for further information.

QUANTITY SURVEYORS' FEES

Author's Note:

The Royal Institution of Chartered Surveyors formally abolished the standard Quantity Surveyors' fee scales with effect from 31 December 1998. However, in the absence of any alternative guideline and for the benefit of readers, the following fee scales have been reproduced with the permission of the Royal Institution of Chartered Surveyors, which owns the copyright.

SCALE 36   INCLUSIVE OF PROFESSIONAL CHARGES FOR QUANTITY SURVEYING SERVICES FOR BUILDING WORKS ISSUED BY THE ROYAL INSTITUTION OF CHARTERED SURVEYORS. This scale has been abolished. See Author's Note on page 6.

EFFECTIVE FROM JULY 1988

1.0.   GENERALLY

     1.1   This scale is for the use when an inclusive scale of professional charges is considered to appropriate by mutual agreement between the employer and the quantity surveyor.

     1.2.   This scale does not apply to civil engineering works, housing schemes financed by local authorities and the Housing Corporation and housing improvement work for which separate scales of fees have been published.

     1.3.   The fees cover quantity surveying services as may be required in connection with a building project irrespective of the type of contract from initial appointment to final certification of the contractor's account such as:

         (a)   Budget estimating; cost planning and advice on tendering procedures and contract arrangements.

         (b)   Preparing tendering documents for main contract and specialist sub-contracts; examining tenders received and reporting thereon or negotiating tenders and pricing with a selected contractor and/or sub-contractors.

         (c)   Preparing recommendations for interim payments on account to the contractor; preparing periodic assessments of anticipated final cost and reporting thereon; measuring work and adjusting variations in accordance with the terms of the contract and preparing final account, pricing same and agreeing totals with the contractor.

         (d)   Providing a reasonable number of copies of bills of quantities and other documents; normal travelling and other expenses. Additional copies of documents, abnormal travelling and other expenses (e.g. in remote areas or overseas) and the provision of checkers on site shall be charged in addition by prior arrangement with the employer.

     1.4.   If any of the materials used in the works are supplied by the employer or charged at a preferential rate, then the actual or estimated market value thereof shall be included in the amounts upon which fees are to be calculated.

     1.5.   If the quantity surveyor incurs additional costs due to exceptional delays in building operations or any other cause beyond the control of the quantity surveyor then the fees may be adjusted by agreement between the employer and the quantity surveyor to cover the reimbursement of these additional costs.

     1.6.   The fees and charges are in all cases exclusive of value added tax which will be applied in accordance with legislation.

     1.7.   Copyright in bills of quantities and other documents prepared by the quantity surveyor is reserved to the quantity surveyor.

QUANTITY SURVEYORS' FEES

2.0. INCLUSIVE SCALE

2.1. The fees for the services outlined in para.1.3, subject to the provision of para. 2.2, shall be as follows:

(a) Category A: Relatively complex works and/or works with little or no repetition.

Examples:
Ambulance and fire stations; banks; cinemas; clubs; computer buildings; council offices; crematoria; fitting out of existing buildings; homes for the elderly; hospitals and nursing homes; laboratories; law courts; libraries; "one off" houses; petrol stations; places of religious worship; police stations; public houses, licensed premises; restaurants; sheltered housing; sports pavilions; theatres; town halls; universities, polytechnics and colleges of further education (other than halls of residence and hostels); and the like.

Value of work £		Category A fee	
		£	£
Up to	150 000	380 + 6.0% (Minimum fee £3 380)	
150 000 -	300 000	9 380 + 5.0% on balance over	150 000
300 000 -	600 000	16 880 + 4.3% on balance over	300 000
600 000 - 1 500 000		29 780 + 3.4% on balance over	600 000
1 500 000 - 3 000 000		60 380 + 3.0% on balance over	1 500 000
3 000 000 - 6 000 000		105 380 + 2.8% on balance over	3 000 000
Over	6 000 000	189 380 + 2.4% on balance over	6 000 000

(b) Category B: Less complex works and/or works with some element of repetition.

Examples:
Adult education facilities; canteens; church halls; community centres; departmental stores; enclosed sports stadia and swimming baths; halls of residence; hostels; motels; offices other than those included in Categories A and C; railway stations; recreation and leisure centres; residential hotels; schools; self-contained flats and maisonettes; shops and shopping centres; supermarkets and hypermarkets; telephone exchanges; and the like.

Value of work £		Category B fee	
		£	£
Up to	150 000	360 + 5.8% (Minimum fee £3 260)	
150 000 -	300 000	9 060 + 4.7% on balance over	150 000
300 000 -	600 000	16 110 + 3.9% on balance over	300 000
600 000 - 1 500 000		27 810 + 2.8% on balance over	600 000
1 500 000 - 3 000 000		53 010 + 2.6% on balance over	1 500 000
3 000 000 - 6 000 000		92 010 + 2.4% on balance over	3 000 000
Over	6 000 000	164 101 + 2.0% on balance over	6 000 000

(c) Category C: Simple works and/or works with a substantial element of repetition.

Examples:
Factories; garages; multi-storey car parks; open-air sports stadia; structural shell offices not
Fitted out; warehouses; workshops; and the like.

Fees for Professional Services

QUANTITY SURVEYORS' FEES

Value of work	£		Category C fee	£
		£		
Up to	150 000	300 + 4.9% (Minimum fee £2 750)		
150 000 -	300 000	7 650 + 4.1% on balance over		150 000
300 000 -	600 000	13 800 + 3.3% on balance over		300 000
600 000 - 1 500 000		23 700 + 2.5% on balance over		600 000
1 500 000 - 3 000 000		46 200 + 2.2% on balance over		1 500 000
3 000 000 - 6 000 000		79 200 + 2.0% on balance over		3 000 000
Over	6 000 000	139 200 + 1.6% on balance over		6 000 000

(d)   Fees shall be calculated upon the total of the final account for the whole of the work including all nominated sub-contractors' and nominated supplier's accounts. When work normally included in a building contract is the subject of a separate contract for which the quantity surveyor has not been paid fees under any other clause hereof, the value of such work shall be included in the amount upon which fees are charged.

(e)   When a contract comprises buildings which fall into more than one category, the fee shall be calculated as follows:

    (i)   The amount upon which fees are chargeable shall be allocated to the categories of work applicable and the amounts so allocated expressed as percentages of the total amount upon which fees are chargeable.

    (ii)   Fees shall then be calculated for each category on the total amount upon which fees are chargeable.

    (iii)   The fee chargeable shall then be calculated by applying the percentages of work in each category to the appropriate total fee and adding the resultant amounts.

    (iv)   A consolidated percentage fee applicable to the total value of the work may be charged by prior agreement between the employer and the quantity surveyor. Such a percentage shall be based on this scale and on the estimated cost of the various categories of work and calculated in accordance with the principles stated above.

(f)   When a project is subject to a number of contracts then, for the purpose of calculating fees, the values of such contracts shall not be aggregated but each contract shall be taken separately and the scale of charges (paras. 2.1 (a) to (e)) applied as appropriate.

2.2.   Air conditioning, heating, ventilating and electrical services

    (a)   When the services outlined in para. 1.3 are provided by the quantity surveyor for the air conditioning, heating, ventilating and electrical services there shall be a fee for these services in addition to the fee calculated in accordance with para. 2.1 as follows:

Value of work	£		Additional fee	£
		£		
Up to	120 000	5.0%		
120 000 -	240 000	6 000 + 4.7% on balance over		120 000
240 000 -	480 000	11 640 + 4.0% on balance over		240 000
480 000 -	750 000	21 240 + 3.6% on balance over		480 000
750 000 -	1 000 000	30 960 + 3.0% on balance over		750 000
1 000 000 -	4 000 000	38 460 + 2.7% on balance over		1 000 000
Over	4 000 000	119 200 + 2.4% on balance over		4 000 000

QUANTITY SURVEYORS' FEES

(b) The value of such services, whether the subject of separate tenders or not, shall be aggregated and the total value of work so obtained used for the purpose of calculating the additional fee chargeable in accordance with para. (a). (Except that when more than one firm of consulting engineers is engaged on the design of these services, the separate values for which each such firm is responsible shall be aggregated and the additional fees charged shall be calculated independently on each such total value so obtained.)

(c) Fees shall be calculated upon the basis of the account for the whole of the air conditioning, heating, ventilating and electrical services for which bills of quantities and final accounts have been prepared by the quantity surveyor.

2.3 Works of alteration
On works of alteration or repair, or on those sections of the work which are mainly works of alteration or repair, there shall be a fee of 1.0% in addition to the fee calculated in accordance with paras. 2.1 and 2.2.

2.4. Works of redecoration and associated minor repairs
On works of redecoration and associated minor repairs, there shall be a fee of 1.5% in addition to the fee calculated in accordance with paras. 2.1 and 2.2.

2.5. Generally
If the works are substantially varied at any stage or if the quantity surveyor is involved in an excessive amount of abortive work, then the fees shall be adjusted by agreement between the employer and the quantity surveyor.

3.0. ADDITIONAL SERVICES

3.1. For additional services not normally necessary, such as those arising as a result of the termination of a contract before completion, liquidation, fire damage to the buildings, services in connection with arbitration, litigation and investigation of the validity of contractors' claims, services in connection with taxation matters, and all similar services where the employer specifically instructs the quantity surveyor, the charges shall be in accordance with para. 4.0.

4.0. TIME CHARGES

4.1. (a) For consultancy and other services performed by a principal, a fee by arrangement according to the circumstances including the professional status and qualifications of the quantity surveyor.

(b) When a principal does work which would normally be done by a member of staff, the charge shall be calculated as para. 4.2 below.

4.2. (a) For services by a member of staff, the charges for which are to be based on the time involved, such charges shall be calculated on the hourly cost of the individual involved plus 145%.

(b) A member of staff shall include a principal doing work normally done by an employee (as para. 4.1 (b) above), technical and supporting staff, but shall exclude secretarial staff or staff engaged upon general administration.

(c) For the purpose of para. 4.2 (b) above, a principal's time shall be taken at the rate applicable to a senior assistant in the firm.

(d) The supervisory duties of a principal shall be deemed to be included in the addition of 145% as para. 4.2 (a) above and shall not be charged separately.

(e) The hourly cost to the employer shall be calculated by taking the sum of the annual cost of the member of staff of:

(i) Salary and bonus but excluding expenses;

(ii) Employer's contributions payable under any Pension and Life Assurance Schemes;

QUANTITY SURVEYORS' FEES

  (iii) Employer's contributions made under the National Insurance Acts, the Redundancy Payments Act and any other payments made in respect of the employee by virtue of any statutory requirements; and

  (iv) Any other payments or benefits made or granted by the employer in pursuance of the terms of employment of the member of staff;

and dividing by 1,650.

5.0. INSTALMENT PAYMENTS

5.1 In the absence of agreement to the contrary, fees shall be paid by instalments as follows:

  (a) Upon acceptance by the employer of a tender for the works, one half of the fee calculated on the amount of the accepted tender.

  (b) The balance by instalments at intervals to be agreed between the date of the first certificate and one month after final certification of the contractor's account.

5.2. (a) In the event of no tender being accepted, one half of the fee shall be paid within three months of completion of the tender documents. The fee shall be calculated upon the basis of the lowest original bona fide tender received. In the event of no tender being received, the fee shall be calculated upon a reasonable valuation of the works based upon the tender documents.

  (b) In the event of the project being abandoned at any stage other than those covered by the foregoing, the proportion of fee payable shall be by agreement between the employer and the quantity surveyor.

  NOTE: In the foregoing context "bona fide tender" shall be deemed to mean a tender submitted in good faith without major errors of computation and not subsequently withdrawn by the tenderer.

SCALE 37 ITEMISED SCALE OF PROFESSIONAL CHARGES FOR QUANTITY SURVEYING SERVICES FOR BUILDING WORK ISSUED BY THE ROYAL INSTITUTION OF CHARTERED SURVEYORS.
The scale is recommended and not mandatory.

EFFECTIVE FROM JULY 1988

1.0. GENERALLY

1.1. The fees are in all cases exclusive of travelling and other expenses (for which the actual disbursement is recoverable unless there is some prior arrangement for such charges) and of the cost of reproduction of bills of quantities and other documents, which are chargeable in addition at net cost.

1.2. The fees are in all cases exclusive of services in connection with the allocation of the cost of the works for purposes of calculating value added tax for which there shall be an additional fee based on the time involved (see paras. 19.1 and 19.2).

1.3. If any of the materials used in the works are supplied by the employer or charged at a preferential rate, then the actual or estimated market value thereof shall be included in the amounts upon which fees are to be calculated.

1.4. The fees are in all cases exclusive of preparing a specification of the materials to be used and the works to be done, but the fees for preparing bills of quantities and similar documents do include for incorporating preamble clauses describing the materials and workmanship (from instructions given by the architect and/or consulting engineer).

QUANTITY SURVEYORS' FEES

1.5. If the quantity surveyor incurs additional costs due to exceptional delays in building operations or any other cause beyond the control of the quantity surveyor then the fees may be adjusted by agreement between the employer and the quantity surveyor to cover the reimbursement of these additional costs.

1.6. The fees and charges are in all cases exclusive of value added tax which will be applied in accordance with legislation.

1.7. Copyright in bills of quantities and other documents prepared by the quantity surveyor is reserved to the quantity surveyor.

CONTRACTS BASED ON BILLS OF QUANTITIES: PRE-CONTRACT SERVICES

2.0. BILLS OF QUANTITIES

2.1. Basic scale

For preparing bills of quantities and examining tenders received and reporting thereon.

(a) Category A: Relatively complex works and/or works with little or no repetition.

Examples:
Ambulance and fire stations; banks; cinemas; clubs; computer buildings; council offices; crematoria; fitting out of existing buildings; homes for the elderly; hospitals and nursing homes; laboratories; law courts; libraries; "one off" houses; petrol stations; places of religious worship; police stations; public houses; licensed premises; restaurants; sheltered housing; sports pavilions; theatres; town halls; universities, polytechnics and colleges of further education (other than halls of residence and hostels); and the like.

Value of work £		Category A fee	
		£	£
Up to	150 000	230 + 3.0% (Minimum fee £1730)	
150 000 -	300 000	4 730 + 2.3% on balance over	150 000
300 000 -	600 000	8 180 + 1.8% on balance over	300 000
600 000 -	1 500 000	13 580 + 1.5% on balance over	600 000
1 500 000 - 3 000 000		27 080 + 1.2% on balance over	1 500 000
3 000 000 - 6 000 000		45 080 + 1.1% on balance over	3 000 000
Over	6 000 000	78 080 + 1.0% on balance over	6 000 000

(b) Category B: Less complex works and/or works with some element of repetition.

Examples:
Adult education facilities; canteens; church halls; community centres; departmental stores; enclosed sports stadia and swimming baths; halls of residence; hostels; motels; offices other than those included in Categories A and C; railway stations; recreation and leisure centres; residential hotels; schools; self-contained flats and maisonettes; shops and shopping centres; supermarkets and hypermarkets; telephone exchanges; and the like.

Fees for Professional Services

QUANTITY SURVEYORS' FEES

Value of work	£	Category B fee		£
		£		
Up to	150 000	210 + 2.8% (Minimum fee £1 680)		
150 000 -	300 000	4 410 + 2.0% on balance over	150 000	
300 000 -	600 000	7 410 + 1.5% on balance over	300 000	
600 000 -	1 500 000	11 910 + 1.1% on balance over	600 000	
1 500 000 - 3 000 000		21 810 + 1.0% on balance over	1 500 000	
3 000 000 - 6 000 000		36 810 + 0.9% on balance over	3 000 000	
Over	6 000 000	63 810 + 0.8% on balance over	6 000 000	

(c)   Category C: Simple works and/or works with a substantial element of repetition

Examples:
Factories; garages; multi-storey car parks; open-air sports stadia; structural shell offices not fitted out; warehouses; workshops and the like.

Value of work	£	Category C fee		£
		£		
Up to	150 000	180 + 2.5% (Minimum fee £1 430)		
150 000 -	300 000	3 930 + 1.8% on balance over	150 000	
300 000 -	600 000	6 630 + 1.2% on balance over	300 000	
600 000 -	1 500 000	10 230 + 0.9% on balance over	600 000	
1 500 000 - 3 000 000		18 330 + 0.8% on balance over	1 500 000	
3 000 000 - 6 000 000		30 330 + 0.7% on balance over	3 000 000	
Over	6 000 000	51 330 + 0.6% on balance over	6 000 000	

(d)   The scales of fees for preparing bills of quantities (paras. 2.1 (a) to (c)) are overall scales based upon the inclusion of all provisional and prime cost items, subject to the provision of para. 2.1 (g). When work normally included in a building contract is the subject of a separate contract for which the quantity surveyor has not been paid fees under any other clause hereof, the value of such work shall be included in the amount upon which fees are charged.

(e)   Fees shall be calculated upon the accepted tender for the whole of he work subject to the provisions of para. 2.6. In the event of no tender being accepted, fees shall be calculated upon the basis of the lowest original bona fide tender received. In the event of no such tender being received, the fees shall be calculated upon a reasonable valuation of the works based upon the original bills of quantities.

NOTE: In the foregoing context "bona fide tender" shall be deemed to mean a tender submitted in good faith without major errors of computation and not subsequently withdrawn by the tenderer.

(f)   In calculating the amount upon which fees are charged the total of any credits and the totals of any alternative bills shall be aggregated and added to the amount described above. The value of any omission or addition forming part of an alternative bill shall not be added unless measurement or abstraction from the original dimension sheets was necessary.

(g)   Where the value of the air conditioning, heating, ventilating and electrical services included in the tender documents together exceeds 25% of the amount calculated as described in paras. 2.1 (d) and (e), then, subject to the provisions of para. 2.2, no fee is chargeable on the amount by which the value of these services exceeds the said 25%. In this context the term "value" excludes general contractor's profit, attendance, builder's work in connection with the services, preliminaries and any similar additions.

QUANTITY SURVEYORS' FEES

(h)   When a contract comprises buildings which fall into more than one category, the fee shall be calculated as follows:

    (i)   The amount upon which fees are chargeable shall be allocated to the categories of work applicable and the amounts so allocated expressed as percentages of the total amount upon which fees are chargeable.

    (ii)   Fees shall then be calculated for each category on the total amount upon which fees are chargeable.

    (iii)   The fee chargeable shall then be calculated by applying the percentages of work in each category to the appropriate total fee and adding the resultant amounts.

(j)   When a project is the subject of a number of contracts then, for the purpose of calculating fees, the values of such contracts shall not be aggregated but each contract shall be taken separately and the scale of charges (paras. 2.1 (a) to (h)) applied as appropriate.

(k)   Where the quantity surveyor is specifically instructed to provide cost planning services the fee calculated in accordance with paras. 2.1 (a) to (j) shall be increased by a sum calculated in accordance with the following table and based upon the same value of work as that upon which the aforementioned fee has been calculated:

Categories A & B: (as defined in paras. 2.1 (a) and (b)).

Value of work	£	Fee		
		£		£
Up to	600 000	0.70%		
600 000 -	3 000 000	4 200 + 0.40%	on balance over	600 000
3 000 000 -	6 000 000	13 800 + 0.35%	on balance over	3 000 000
Over	6 000 000	24 300 + 0.30%	on balance over	6 000 000

Category C: (as defined in paras. 2.1 (c))

Value of work	£	Fee		
		£		£
Up to	600 000	0.50%		
600 000	3 000 000	3 000 + 0.30%	on balance over	600 000
3 000 000	6 000 000	10 200 + 0.25%	on balance over	3 000 000
Over	6 000 000	17 700 + 0.20%	on balance over	6 000 000

2.2.   Air conditioning, heating, ventilating and electrical services

(a)   Where bills of quantities are prepared by the quantity surveyor for the air conditioning, heating, ventilating and electrical services there shall be a fee for these services (which shall include examining tenders received and reporting thereon), in addition to the fee calculated in accordance with para. 2.1, as follows:

Value of work	£	Additional fee		
		£		£
Up to	120 000	2.50%		
120 000 -	240 000	3 000 + 2.25%	on balance over	120 000
240 000 -	480 000	5 700 + 2.00%	on balance over	240 000
480 000 -	750 000	10 500 + 1.75%	on balance over	480 000
750 000 -	1 000 000	15 225 + 1.25%	on balance over	750 000
Over	1 000 000	18 350 + 1.15%	on balance over	1 000 000

QUANTITY SURVEYORS' FEES

(b)   The values of such services, whether the subject of separate tenders or not, shall be aggregated and the total value of work so obtained used for the purpose of calculating the additional fee chargeable in accordance with para. (a). (Except that when more than one firm of consulting engineers is engaged on the design of these services, the separate values for which each such firm is responsible shall be aggregated and the additional fees charged shall be calculated independently on each such total value so obtained.)

(c)   Fees shall be calculated upon the accepted tender for the whole of the air conditioning, heating, ventilating and electrical services for which bills of quantities have been prepared by the quantity surveyor. In the event of no tender being accepted, fees shall be calculated upon the basis of the lowest original bona fide tender received. In the event of no such tender being received, the fees shall be calculated upon a reasonable valuation of the services based upon the original bills of quantities.

NOTE   In the foregoing context "bona fide tender"' shall be deemed to mean a tender submitted in good faith without major errors of computation and not subsequently withdrawn by the tenderer.

(d)   When cost planning services are provided by the quantity surveyor for air conditioning, heating, ventilating and electrical services (or for any part of such services) there shall be an additional fee based on the time involved (see paras. 19.1 and 19.2). Alternatively the fee may be on a lump sum or percentage basis agreed between the employer and the quantity surveyor.

NOTE   The incorporation of figures for air conditioning, heating, ventilating and electrical services provided by the consulting engineer is deemed to be included in the quantity surveyor's services under para. 2.1.

2.3.   Works of alteration
On works of alteration or repair, or on those sections of the works which are mainly works of alteration or repair, there shall be a fee of 1.0% in addition to the fee calculated in accordance with paras. 2.1 and 2.2.

2.4.   Works of redecoration and associated minor repairs,
On works of redecoration and associated minor repairs, there shall be a fee of 1.5% in addition to the fee calculated in accordance with paras. 2.1 and 2.2.

2.5.   Bills of quantities prepared in special forms
Fees calculated in accordance with paras. 2.1, 2.2, 2.3 and 2.4 include for the preparation of bills of quantities on a normal trade basis. If the employer requires additional information to be provided in the bills of quantities or the bills to be prepared in an elemental, operational or similar form, then the fee may be adjusted by agreement between the employer and the quantity surveyor.

2.6.   Reduction of tenders

(a) When cost planning services have been provided by the quantity surveyor and a tender, when received, is reduced before acceptance, and if the reductions are not necessitated by amended instructions of the employer or by the inclusion in the bills of quantities of items which the quantity surveyor has indicated could not be contained within the approved estimate, then in such a case no charge shall be made by the quantity surveyor for the preparation of bills of reductions and the fee for the preparation of the bills of quantities shall be based on the amount of the reduced tender.

(b) When cost planning services have not been provided by the quantity surveyor and if a tender, when received, is reduced before acceptance, fees are to be calculated upon the amount of the unreduced tender. When the preparation of bills of reductions is required, a fee is chargeable for preparing such bills of reductions as follows:

QUANTITY SURVEYORS' FEES

    (i)   2.0% upon the gross amount of all omissions requiring measurement or abstraction from original dimensional sheets.

    (ii)   3.0% upon the gross amount of all additions requiring measurement.

    (iii)   0.5% upon the gross amount of all remaining additions.

NOTE: The above scale for the preparation of bills of reductions applies to work in all categories.

2.7   Generally

If the works are substantially varied at any stage or if the quantity surveyor is involved in an excessive amount of abortive work, then the fees shall be adjusted by agreement between the employer and the quantity surveyor.

3.0.   NEGOTIATING TENDERS

3.1.   (a)   For negotiating and agreeing prices with a contractor:

Value of work	£	Fee	£
		£	
Up to	150 000	0.5%	
150 000	600 000	750 + 0.3% on balance over	150 000
600 000	1 200 000	2 100 + 0.2% on balance over	600 000
Over	1 200 000	3 300 + 0.1% on balance over	1 200 000

    (b)   The fee shall be calculated on the total value of the works as defined in paras. 2.1 (d), (e), (f), (g) and (j).

    (c)   For negotiating and agreeing prices with a contractor for air conditioning, heating, ventilating and electrical services there shall be an additional fee as para. 3.1 (a) calculated on the total value of such services as defined in para. 2.2 (b).

4.0.   CONSULTATIVE SERVICES AND PRICING BILLS OF QUANTITIES

4.1.   Consultative services

Where the quantity surveyor is appointed to prepare approximate estimates, feasibility studies or submissions for the approval of financial grants or similar services, then the fee shall be based on the time involved (see paras. 19.1 and 19.2) or alternatively, on a lump sum or percentage basis agreed between the employer and the quantity surveyor.

4.2.   Pricing bills of quantities

    (a)   For pricing bills of quantities, if instructed, to provide an estimate comparable with tenders, the fee shall be one-third (33.33%) of the fee for negotiating and agreeing prices with a contractor, calculated in accordance with paras. 3.1 (a) and (b).

    (b)   For pricing bills of quantities, if instructed, to provide an estimate comparable with tenders for air conditioning, heating, ventilating and electrical services the fee shall be one-third (33.33%) of the fee calculated in accordance with para. 3.1. (c).

CONTRACTS BASED ON BILLS OF QUANTITIES: POST-CONTRACT SERVICES

Alternative scales (I and II) for post-contract services are set out below to be used at the quantity surveyor's discretion by prior agreement with the employer.

5.0.   ALTERNATIVE I: OVERALL SCALE OF CHARGES FOR POST-CONTRACT SERVICES

5.1.   If the quantity surveyor appointed to carry out the post-contract services did not prepare the bills of quantities then the fees in paras. 5.2 and 5.3 shall be increased to cover the additional services undertaken by the quantity surveyor.

QUANTITY SURVEYORS' FEES

5.2.   Basic scale
For taking particulars and reporting valuations for interim certificates for payments on account to the contractor, preparing periodic assessments of anticipated final cost and reporting thereon, measuring and making up bills of variations including pricing and agreeing totals with the contractor, and adjusting fluctuations in the cost of labour and materials if required by the contract.

(a)   Category A: Relatively complex works and/or works with little or no repetition.

Examples:
Ambulance and fire stations; banks; cinemas; clubs; computer buildings; council offices; crematoria; fitting out existing buildings; homes for the elderly; hospitals and nursing homes; laboratories; law courts; libraries; "one-off" houses; petrol stations; places of religious worship; police stations; public houses; licensed premises; restaurants; sheltered housing; sports pavilions; theatres; town halls; universities, polytechnics and colleges of further education (other than halls of residence and hostels); and the like.

Value of work	£	Category A fee £		£
Up to	150 000	150 + 2.0%	(Minimum fee £1 150)	
150 000 -	300 000	3 150 + 1.7%	on balance over	150 000
300 000 -	600 000	5 700 + 1.6%	on balance over	300 000
600 000 -	1 500 000	10 500 + 1.3%	on balance over	600 000
1 500 000 -	3 000 000	22 200 + 1.2%	on balance over	1 500 000
3 000 000 -	6 000 000	40 200 + 1.1%	on balance over	3 000 000
Over	6 000 000	73 200 + 1.0%	on balance over	6 000 000

(b)   Category B: Less complex works and/or works with some element of repetition.

Examples:
Adult education facilities; canteens; church halls; community centres; departmental stores; enclosed sports stadia and swimming baths; halls of residence; hostels; motels; offices other than those included in Categories A and C; railway stations; recreation and leisure centres; residential hotels; schools; self-contained flats and maisonettes; shops and shopping centres; supermarkets and hypermarkets; telephone exchanges; and the like.

Value of work	£	Category B fee £		£
Up to	150 000	150 + 2.0%	(Minimum fee £1 150)	
150 000 -	300 000	3 150 + 1.7%	on balance over	150 000
300 000 -	600 000	5 700 + 1.5%	on balance over	300 000
600 000 -	1 500 000	10 200 + 1.1%	on balance over	600 000
1 500 000 -	3 000 000	20 100 + 1.0%	on balance over	1 500 000
3 000 000 -	6 000 000	35 100 + 0.9%	on balance over	3 000 000
Over	6 000 000	62 100 + 0.8%	on balance over	6 000 000

QUANTITY SURVEYORS' FEES

(c)   Category C: Simple works and/or works with a substantial element of repetition.

Examples:
Factories; garages; multi-storey car parks; open-air sports stadia; structural shell offices not fitted out; warehouses; workshops; and the like.

Value of work	£	Category C fee	£
		£	
Up to	150 000	120 + 1.6% (Minimum fee £920)	
150 000 -	300 000	2 520 + 1.5% on balance over	150 000
300 000 -	600 000	4 770 + 1.4% on balance over	300 000
600 000 -	1 500 000	8 970 + 1.1% on balance over	600 000
1 500 000 -	3 000 000	18 870 + 0.9% on balance over	1 500 000
3 000 000 -	6 000 000	32 370 + 0.8% on balance over	3 000 000
Over	6 000 000	56 370 + 0.7% on balance over	6 000 000

(d)   The scales of fees for post-contract services (paras. 5.2 (a) to (c)) are overall scales based upon the inclusion of all nominated sub-contractors' and nominated suppliers' accounts, subject to the provision of para. 5.2 (g). When work normally included in a building contract is the subject of a separate contract for which the quantity surveyor has not been paid fees under any other clause hereof, the value of such work shall be included in the amount on which fees are charged.

(e)   Fees shall be calculated upon the basis of the account for the whole of the work, subject to the provisions of para. 5.3.

(f)   In calculating the amount on which fees are charged the total of any credits is to be added to the amount described above.

(g)   Where the value of air conditioning, heating, ventilating and electrical services included in the tender documents together exceeds 25% of the amount calculated as described in paras. 5.2. (d) and (e) above, then, subject to provisions of para. 5.3, no fee is chargeable on the amount by which the value of these services exceeds the said 25%. In this context the term "value" excludes general contractors' profit, attendance, builders work in connection with the services, preliminaries and other similar additions.

(h)   When a contract comprises buildings which fall into more than one category, the fee shall be calculated as follows:

(i)   The amount upon which fees are chargeable shall be allocated to the categories of work applicable and the amounts so allocated expressed as percentages of the total amount upon which fees are chargeable.

(ii)   Fees shall then be calculated for each category on the total amount upon which fees are chargeable.

(iii)   The fee chargeable shall then be calculated by applying the percentages of work in each category to the appropriate total fee and adding the resultant amounts.

(j)   When a project is the subject of a number of contracts then, for the purposes of calculating fees, the values of such contracts shall not be aggregated but each contract shall be taken separately and the scale of charges (paras. 5.2 (a) to (h)), applied as appropriate.

(k)   When the quantity surveyor is required to prepare valuations of materials or goods off site, an additional fee shall be charged based on the time involved (see paras. 19.1 and 19.2).

(l)   The basic scale for post-contract services includes for a simple routine of periodically estimating final costs. When the employer specifically requests a cost monitoring service which involves the quantity surveyor in additional or abortive measurement an additional fee shall be charged based on the time involved (see paras. 19.1 and 19.2),

QUANTITY SURVEYORS' FEES

or alternatively on a lump sum or percentage basis agreed between the employer and the quantity surveyor.

(m)   The above overall scales of charges for post-contract services assume normal conditions when the bills of quantities are based on drawings accurately depicting the building work the employer requires. If the works are materially varied to the extent that substantial re-measurement is necessary then the fee for post contract services shall be adjusted by agreement between the employer and the quantity surveyor.

5.3. Air conditioning, heating, ventilating and electrical services

(a)   Where final accounts are prepared by the quantity surveyor for the air conditioning, heating, ventilating and electrical services there shall be a fee for these services, in addition to the fee calculated in accordance with para. 5.2, as follows:

Value of work	£	Additional fee		£
		£		
Up to	120 000	2.00%		
120 000 -	240 000	2 400 + 1.60%	on balance over	120 000
240 000 -	1 000 000	4 320 + 1.25%	on balance over	240 000
1 000 000 -	4 000 000	13 820 + 1.00%	on balance over	1 000 000
Over	4 000 000	43 820 + 0.90%	on balance over	4 000 000

(b)   The values of such services, whether the subject of separate tenders or not, shall be aggregated and the total value of work so obtained used for the purpose of calculating the additional fee chargeable in accordance with para. (a). (Except that when more than one firm of consulting engineers is engaged on the design of these services the separate values for which each such firm is responsible shall be aggregated and the additional fee charged shall be calculated independently on each such total value so obtained.)

(c)   The scope of the services to be provided by the quantity surveyor under para. (a) above shall be deemed to be equivalent to those described for the basic scale for post-contract services.

(d)   When the quantity surveyor is required to prepare periodic valuations of materials or goods off site, an additional fee shall be charged based on the time involved (see paras. 19.1 and 19.2).

(e)   The basic scale for post-contract services includes for a simple routine of periodically estimating final costs. When the employer specifically requests a cost monitoring service which involves the quantity surveyor in additional or abortive measurement an additional fee shall be based on the time involved (see paras. 19.1 and 19.2), or alternatively on a lump sum or percentage basis agreed between the employer and the quantity surveyor.

(f)   Fees shall be calculated upon the basis of the account for the whole of the air conditioning, heating, ventilating and electrical services for which final accounts have been prepared by the quantity surveyor.

6.0.   ALTERNATIVE II: SCALE OF CHARGES FOR SEPARATE STAGES OF POST-CONTRACT SERVICES

6.1.   If the quantity surveyor appointed to carry out the post-contract services did not prepare the bills of quantities then the fees in paras. 6.2 and 6.3 shall be increased to cover the additional services undertaken by the quantity surveyor.

NOTE: The scales of fees in paras. 6.2 and 6.3 apply to work in all categories (including air conditioning, heating, ventilating and electrical services).

QUANTITY SURVEYORS' FEES

6.2.   Valuations for interim certificates

(a)   For taking particulars and reporting valuations for interim certificates for payments on account to the contractor.

Total of valuations £		Fee	£	£
Up to	300 000	0.5%		
300 000 -	1 000 000	1 500 + 0.4% on balance over		300 000
1 000 000 -	6 000 000	4 300 + 0.3% on balance over		1 000 000
Over	6 000 000	19 300 + 0.2% on balance over		6 000 000

NOTES:

1.   Subject to note 2 below, the fees are to be calculated on the total of all interim valuations (i.e. the amount of the final account less only the net amount of the final valuation).

2.   When consulting engineers are engaged in supervising the installation of air conditioning, heating, ventilating and electrical services and their duties include reporting valuations for inclusion in interim certificates for payments on account in respect of such services, then valuations so reported shall be excluded from any total amount of valuations used for calculating fees.

(b)   When the quantity surveyor is required to prepare valuations of materials or goods off site, an additional fee shall be charged based on the time involved (see paras. 19.1 and 19.2).

6.3.   Preparing accounts of variation upon contracts
For measuring and making up bills of variations including pricing and agreeing totals with the contractor:

(a)   An initial lump sum of £600 shall be payable on each contract.
(b)   2.0% upon the gross amount of omissions requiring measurement or abstraction from the original dimension sheets.
(c)   3.0% upon the gross amount of additions requiring measurement and upon dayworks.
(d)   0.5% upon the gross amount of remaining additions which shall be deemed to include all nominated sub-contractors' and nominated suppliers' accounts which do not involve measurement or checking of quantities but only checking against lump sum estimates.
(e)   3.0% upon the aggregate of the amounts of the increases and/or decreases in the cost of labour and materials in accordance with any fluctuations clause in the conditions of contract, except where a price adjustment formula applies.
(f)   On contracts where fluctuations are calculated by the use of a price adjustment formula method the following scale shall be applied to the account for the whole of the work:

Value of work £		Fee	£	£
Up to	300 000	300 + 0.5%		
300 000 -	1 000 000	1 800 + 0.3% on balance over		300 000
Over	1 000 000	3 900 + 0.1% on balance over		1 000 000

(g)   When consulting engineers are engaged in supervising the installation of air conditioning, heating, ventilating and electrical services and their duties include for the adjustment of accounts and pricing and agreeing totals with the sub-contractors for inclusion in the measured account, then any totals so agreed shall be excluded from any amounts used for calculating fees.

QUANTITY SURVEYORS' FEES

6.4.   Cost monitoring services
The fee for providing all approximate estimates of final cost and/or a cost monitoring service shall be based on the time involved (see paras. 19.1 and 19.2), or alternatively on a lump sum or percentage basis agreed between the employer and the quantity surveyor.

7.0.   BILLS OF APPROXIMATE QUANTITIES, INTERIM CERTIFICATES AND FINAL ACCOUNTS

7.1.   Basic scale
For preparing bills of approximate quantities suitable for obtaining competitive tenders which will provide a schedule of prices and a reasonably close forecast of the cost of the works, but subject to complete re-measurement, examining tenders and reporting thereon, taking particulars and reporting valuations for interim certificates for payments on account to the contractor, preparing periodic assessments of anticipated final cost and reporting thereon, measuring and preparing final account, including pricing and agreeing totals with the contractor and adjusting fluctuations in the cost of labour and materials if required by the contract:

(a)   Category A: Relatively complex works and/or works with little or no repetition.
Examples:
Ambulance and fire stations; banks; cinemas; clubs; computer buildings; council offices; crematoria; fitting out existing buildings; homes for the elderly; hospitals and nursing homes; laboratories; law courts; libraries; "one-off" houses; petrol stations; places of religious worship; police stations; public houses; licensed premises; restaurants; sheltered housing; sports pavilions; theatres; town halls; universities, polytechnics and colleges of further education (other than halls of residence and hostels); and the like.

Value of work	£	Category A fee	
		£	£
Up to	150 000	380 + 5.0% (Minimum fee £2 880)	
150 000 -	300 000	7 880 + 4.0% on balance over	150 000
300 000 -	600 000	13 880 + 3.4% on balance over	300 000
600 000 -	1 500 000	24 080 + 2.8% on balance over	600 000
1 500 000 -	3 000 000	49 280 + 2.4% on balance over	1 500 000
3 000 000 -	6 000 000	85 280 + 2.2% on balance over	3 000 000
Over	6 000 000	151 280 + 2.0% on balance over	6 000 000

(b)   Category B: Less complex works and/or works with some element of repetition
Examples:
Adult education facilities; canteens; church halls; community centres; departmental stores; enclosed sports stadia and swimming baths; halls of residence; hostels; motels; offices other than those included in Categories A and C; railway stations; recreation and leisure centres; residential hotels; schools; self-contained flats and maisonettes; shops and shopping centres; supermarkets and hypermarkets; telephone exchanges; and the like.

Value of work	£	Category B fee	
		£	£
Up to	150 000	360 + 4.8% (Minimum fee £2 760)	
150 000 -	300 000	7 560 + 3.7% on balance over	150 000
300 000 -	600 000	13 110 + 3.0% on balance over	300 000
600 000 -	1 500 000	22 110 + 2.2% on balance over	600 000
1 500 000 -	3 000 000	41 910 + 2.0% on balance over	1 500 000
3 000 000 -	6 000 000	71 910 + 1.8% on balance over	3 000 000
Over	6 000 000	125 910 + 1.6% on balance over	6 000 000

QUANTITY SURVEYORS' FEES

(c)   Category C: Simple works and/or works with a substantial element of repetition.
Examples:
Factories; garages; multi-storey car parks; open air sports stadia; structural shell offices not fitted out; warehouses; workshops; and the like.

Value of work	£	Category C fee	£
		£	
Up to	150 000	300 + 4.1% (Minimum fee £2 350)	
150 000 -	300 000	6 450 + 3.3% on balance over	150 000
300 000 -	600 000	11 400 + 2.6% on balance over	300 000
600 000 -	1 500 000	19 200 + 2.0% on balance over	600 000
1 500 000 -	3 000 000	37 200 + 1.7% on balance over	1 500 000
3 000 000 -	6 000 000	62 700 + 1.5% on balance over	3 000 000
Over	6 000 000	107 700 + 1.3% on balance over	6 000 000

(d)   The scales of fees for pre-contract and post-contract services (paras. 7.1 (a) to (c)) are overall scales based upon the inclusion of all nominated sub-contractors' and nominated suppliers' accounts, subject to the provision of para. 7.1. (g). When work normally included in a building contract is the subject of a separate contract for which the quantity surveyor has not been paid fees under any other clause hereof, the value of such work shall be included in the amount on which fees are charged.

(e)   Fees shall be calculated upon the basis of the account for the whole of the work, subject to the provisions of para. 7.2.

(f)   In calculating the amount on which fees are charged the total of any credits is to be added to the amount described above.

(g)   Where the value of air conditioning, heating, ventilating and electrical services included in tender documents together exceeds 25% of the amount calculated as described in paras. 7.1. (d) and (e), then, subject to the provisions of para. 7.2 no fee is chargeable on the amount by which the value of these services exceeds the said 25%. In this context the term "value" excludes general contractors' profit, attendance, builders' work in connection with the services, preliminaries and any other similar additions.

(h)   When a contract comprises buildings which fall into more than one category, the fee shall be calculated as follows.

(i)   The amount upon which fees are chargeable shall be allocated to the categories of work applicable and the amount so allocated expressed as percentages of the total amount upon which fees are chargeable.

(ii)   Fees shall then be calculated for each category on the total amount upon which fees are chargeable.

(iii)   The fee chargeable shall then be calculated by applying the percentages of work in each category to the appropriate total fee adding the resultant amounts.

(j)   When a project is the subject of a number of contracts then, for the purpose of calculating fees, the values of such contracts shall not be aggregated but each contract shall be taken separately and the scale of charges (paras. 7.1(a) to (h)) applied as appropriate.

QUANTITY SURVEYORS' FEES

(k)   Where the quantity surveyor is specifically instructed to provide cost planning services, the fee calculated in accordance with paras. 7.1 (a) to (j) shall be increased by a sum calculated in accordance with the following table and based upon the same value of work as that upon which the aforementioned fee has been calculated:

Categories A & B: (as defined in paras. 7.1 (a) and (b))

Value of work	£	Fee		£
		£		
Up to	600 000	0.70%		
600 000 -	3 000 000	4 200 + 0.40%	on balance over	600 000
3 000 000 -	6 000 000	13 800 + 0.35%	on balance over	3 000 000
Over	6 000 000	24 300 + 0.30%	on balance over	6 000 000

Category C: (as defined in para. 7.1 (c))

Value of work	£	Fee		£
		£		
Up to	600 000	0.50%		
600 000 -	3 000 000	3 000 + 0.30%	on balance over	600 000
3 000 000 -	6 000 000	10 200 + 0.25%	on balance over	3 000 000
Over	6 000 000	17 700 + 0.20%	on balance over	6 000 000

(l)   When the quantity surveyor is required to prepare valuations of materials or goods off site, an additional fee shall be charged based on the time involved (see paras. 19.1 and 19.2).

(m)   The basic scale for post-contract services includes for a simple routine of periodically estimating final costs. When the employer specifically requests a cost monitoring service which involves the quantity surveyor in additional or abortive measurement an additional fee shall be charged based on the time involved (see paras. 19.1 and 19.2), or alternatively on a lump sum or percentage basis agreed between the employer and the quantity surveyor.

7.2.   Air conditioning, heating, ventilating and electrical services

(a)   Where bills of approximate quantities and final accounts are prepared by the quantity surveyor for the air conditioning, heating, ventilating and electrical services there shall be a fee for these services in addition to the fee calculated in accordance with para. 7.1 as follows:

Value of work	£	Category A fee		£
		£		
Up to	120 000	4.50%		
120 000 -	240 000	5 400 + 1.85%	on balance over	120 000
240 000 -	480 000	10 020 + 3.25%	on balance over	240 000
480 000 -	750 000	17 820 + 3.00%	on balance over	480 000
750 000 - 1 000 000		25 920 + 2.50%	on balance over	750 000
1 000 000 - 4 000 000		32 170 + 2.15%	on balance over	1 000 000
Over	4 000 000	96 670 + 2.05%	on balance over	4 000 000

QUANTITY SURVEYORS' FEES

(b)   The value of such services, whether the subject of separate tenders or not, shall be aggregated and the value of work so obtained used for the purpose of calculating the additional fee chargeable in accordance with para. (a). (Except that when more than one firm of consulting engineers is engaged on the design of these services, the separate values for which each such firm is responsible shall be aggregated and the additional fees charged shall be calculated independently on each such total value so obtained.)

(c)   The scope of the services to be provided by the quantity surveyor under para. (a) above shall be deemed to be equivalent to those described for the basic scale for pre-contract and post-contract services.

(d)   When the quantity surveyor is required to prepare valuations of materials or goods off site, an additional fee shall be charged based on the time involved (see paras. 19.1 and 19.2).

(e)   The basic scale for post-contract services includes for a simple routine of periodically estimating final costs. When the employer specifically requests a cost monitoring service, which involves the quantity surveyor in additional or abortive measurement, an additional fee shall be charged based on the time involved (see paras. 19.1 and 19.2), or alternatively on a lump sum or percentage basis agreed between the employer and the quantity surveyor.

(f)   Fees shall be calculated upon the basis of the account for the whole of the air conditioning, heating, ventilating and electrical services for which final accounts have been prepared by the quantity surveyor.

(g)   When cost planning services are provided by the quantity surveyor for air conditioning, heating, ventilating and electrical services (or for any part of such services) there shall be an additional fee based on the time involved (see paras. 19.1 and 19.2) or alternatively on a lump sum or percentage basis agreed between the employer and quantity surveyor.

NOTE: The incorporation of figures for air conditioning, heating, ventilating and electrical services provided by the consulting engineer is deemed to be included in the quantity surveyor's services under para 7.1.

7.3.   Works of alteration
On works of alteration or repair, or on those sections of the work which are mainly works of alteration or repair, there shall be a fee of 1.0% in addition to the fee calculated in accordance with paras. 7.1 and 7.2

7.4.   Works of redecoration and associated minor repairs
On works of redecoration and associated minor repairs, there shall be a fee of 1.5% in addition to the fee calculated in accordance with paras. 7.1 and 7.2.

7.5.   Bills of quantities and/or final accounts prepared in special forms
Fees calculated in accordance with paras. 7.1, 7.2, 7.3 and 7.4 include for the preparation of bills of quantities and/or final accounts on a normal trade basis. If the employer requires additional information to be provided in the bills of quantities and/or final accounts or the bills and/or final accounts to be prepared in an elemental, operational or similar form, then the fee may be adjusted by agreement between the employer and the quantity surveyor.

7.6.   Reduction of tenders

(a)   When cost planning services have been provided by the quantity surveyor and a tender, when received, is reduced before acceptance and if the reductions are not necessitated by amended instructions of the employer or by the inclusion in the bills of approximate quantities of items which the quantity surveyor has indicated could not be contained within the approved estimate, then in such a case no charge shall be made by the quantity surveyor for the preparation of bills of reductions and the fee for the preparation of bills of approximate quantities shall be based on the amount of the reduced tender.

QUANTITY SURVEYORS' FEES

(b)   When cost planning services have not been provided by the quantity surveyor and if a tender, when received, is reduced before acceptance, fees are to be calculated upon the amount of the unreduced tender. When the preparation of bills of reductions is required, a fee is chargeable for preparing such bills of reductions as follows:

(i)   2.0% upon the gross amount of all omissions requiring measurement or abstraction from original dimension sheets.

(ii)   3.0% upon the gross amount of all additions requiring measurement.

(iii)   0.5% upon the gross amount of all remaining additions.

NOTE: The above scale for the preparation of bills of reductions applies to work in all categories.

7.7.   Generally

If the works are substantially varied at any stage or if the quantity surveyor is involved in an excessive amount of abortive work, then the fees shall be adjusted by agreement between the employer and the quantity surveyor.

8.0.   NEGOTIATING TENDERS

8.1   (a)   For negotiating and agreeing prices with a contractor:

Value of work £	Fee	
	£	£
Up to 150 000	0.5%	
150 000 - 600 000	750 + 0.3% on balance over	150 000
600 000 - 1 200 000	2 100 + 0.2% on balance over	600 000
Over 1 200 000	3 300 + 0.1% on balance over	1 200 000

(b)   The fee shall be calculated on the total value of the works as defined in paras. 7.1 (d), (e), (f), (g) and (j).

(c)   For negotiating and agreeing prices with a contractor for air conditioning, heating, ventilating and electrical services there shall be an additional fee as para. 8.1 (a) calculated on the total value of such services as defined in para. 7.2 (b).

9.0.   CONSULTATIVE SERVICES AND PRICING BILLS OF APPROXIMATE QUANTITIES

9.1.   Consultative services

Where the quantity surveyor is appointed to prepare approximate estimates, feasibility studies or submissions for the approval of financial grants or similar services, then the fee shall be based on the time involved (see paras. 19.1 and 19.2) or alternatively, on a lump sum or percentage basis agreed between the employer and the quantity surveyor.

9.2.   Pricing bills of approximate quantities

For pricing bills of approximate quantities, if instructed, to provide an estimate comparable with tenders, the fees shall be the same as for the corresponding services in paras. 4.2 (a) and (b).

10.0.   INSTALMENT PAYMENTS

10.1.   For the purpose of instalment payments the fee for preparation of bills of approximate quantities only shall be the equivalent of forty per cent (40%) of the fees calculated in accordance with the appropriate sections of paras. 7.1 to 7.5, and the fee for providing cost planning services shall be in accordance with the appropriate sections of para. 7.1 (k); both fees shall be based on the total value of the bills of approximate quantities ascertained in accordance with the provisions of para. 2.1 (e).

QUANTITY SURVEYORS' FEES

10.2.   In the absence of agreement to the contrary, fees shall be paid by instalments as follows:

(a)   Upon acceptance by the employer of a tender for the works the above defined fees for the preparation of bills of approximate quantities and for providing cost planning services.

(b)   In the event of no tender being accepted, the aforementioned fees shall be paid within three months of completion of the bills of approximate quantities.

(c)   The balance by instalments at intervals to be agreed between the date of the first certificate and one month after certification of the contractor's account.

10.3.   In the event of the project being abandoned at any stage other than those covered by the foregoing, the proportion of fee payable shall be by agreement between the employer and the quantity surveyor.

11.0.   SCHEDULES OF PRICES

11.1.   The fee for preparing, pricing and agreeing schedules of prices shall be based on the time involved (see paras. 19.1 and 19.2). Alternatively, the fee may be on a lump sum or percentage basis agreed between the employer and the quantity surveyor.

12.0.   COST PLANNING AND APPROXIMATE ESTIMATES

12.1.   The fee for providing cost planning services or for preparing approximate estimates shall be based on the time involved (see paras. 19.1 and 19.2). Alternatively, the fee may be on a lump sum or percentage basis agreed between the employer and the quantity surveyor.

CONTRACTS BASED ON SCHEDULES OF PRICES: POST-CONTRACT SERVICES

13.0.   FINAL ACCOUNTS

13.1.   Basic Scale

(a)   For taking particulars and reporting valuations for interim certificates for payments on account to the contractor, preparing periodic assessments of anticipated final cost and reporting thereon, measuring and preparing final account including pricing and agreeing totals with the contractor, and adjusting fluctuations in the cost of labour and materials if required by the contract, the fee shall be equivalent to sixty per cent (60%) of the fee calculated in accordance with paras. 7.1 (a) to (j).

(b)   When the quantity surveyor is required to prepare valuations of materials or goods off site, an additional fee shall be charged on the basis of the time involved (see paras. 19.1 and 19.2).

(c)   The basic scale for post-contract services includes for a simple routine of periodically estimating final costs. When the employer specifically requests a cost monitoring service which involves the quantity surveyor in additional or abortive measurement an additional fee shall be charged based on the time involved (see paras. 19.1 and 19.2), or alternatively on a lump sum or percentage basis agreed between the employer and the quantity surveyor.

13.2.   Air conditioning, heating, ventilating and electrical services
Where final accounts are prepared by the quantity surveyor for the air conditioning, heating, ventilating and electrical services there shall be a fee for these services, in addition to the fee calculated in accordance with para. 13.1, equivalent to sixty per cent (60%) of the fee calculated in accordance with paras. 7.2 (a) to (f).

13.3.   Works of alterations
On works of alteration or repair, or on those sections of the work which are mainly works of alteration or repair, there shall be a fee of 1.0% in addition to the fee calculated in accordance with paras. 13.1 and 13.2.

Fees for Professional Services

QUANTITY SURVEYORS' FEES

13.4.   Works of redecoration and associated minor repairs
On works of redecoration and associated minor repairs, there shall be a fee of 1.5% in addition to the fee calculated in accordance with paras. 13.1 and 13.2.

13.5.   Final accounts prepared in special forms
Fees calculated in accordance with paras. 13.1,13.2,13.3 and 13.4 include for the preparation of final accounts on a normal trade basis. If the employer requires additional information to be provided in the final accounts or the accounts to be prepared in an elemental, operational or similar form, then the fee may be adjusted by agreement between the employer and the quantity surveyor.

PRIME COST CONTRACTS: PRE-CONTRACT AND POST-CONTRACT SERVICES

14.0.   COST PLANNING

14.1.   The fee for providing a cost planning service shall be based on the time involved (see paras. 19.1 and 19.2). Alternatively, the fee may be on a lump sum or percentage basis agreed between the employer and the quantity surveyor.

15.0.   ESTIMATES OF COST

15.1.   (a)   For preparing an approximate estimate, calculated by measurement, of the cost of work, and, if required under the terms of the contract, negotiating, adjusting and agreeing the estimate:

Value of work	£	Fee	
		£	£
Up to	30 000	1.25%	
30 000 -	150 000	375 + 1.00% on balance over	30 000
150 000 -	600 000	1 575 + 0.75% on balance over	150 000
Over	600 000	4 950 + 0.50% on balance over	600 000

(b)   The fee shall be calculated upon the total of the approved estimates.

16.0.   FINAL ACCOUNTS

16.1.   (a)   For checking prime costs, reporting for interim certificates for payments on account to the contractor and preparing final accounts:

Value of work	£	Fee	
		£	£
Up to	30 000	2.50%	
150 000 -	150 000	750 + 2.00% on balance over	30 000
150 000 -	600 000	3 150 + 1.50% on balance over	150 000
Over	600 000	9 900 + 1.25% on balance over	600 000

(b)   The fee shall be calculated upon the total of the final account with the addition of the value of credits received for old materials removed and less the value of any work charged for in accordance with para. 16.1 (c).

(c)   On the value of any work to be paid for on a measured basis, the fee shall be 3%.

(d)   When the quantity surveyor is required to prepare valuations of materials or goods off site, an additional fee shall be charged based on the time involved (see paras. 19.1 and 19.2).

(e)   The above charges do not include the provision of checkers on the site. If the quantity surveyor is required to provide such checkers an additional charge shall be made by arrangement.

QUANTITY SURVEYORS' FEES

17.0. COST REPORTING AND MONITORING SERVICES

17.1. The fee for providing cost reporting and/or monitoring services (e.g. preparing periodic assessments of anticipated final costs and reporting thereon) shall be based on the time involved (see paras. 19.1 and 19.2) or alternatively, on a lump sum or percentage basis agreed between the employer and the quantity surveyor.

18.0. ADDITIONAL SERVICES

18.1. For additional services not normally necessary, such as those arising as a result of the termination of a contract before completion, liquidation, fire damage to the buildings, services in connection with arbitration, litigation and investigation of the validity of contractors' claims, services in connection with taxation matters and all similar services where the employer specifically instructs the quantity surveyor, the charges shall be in accordance with paras. 19.1 and 19.2.

19.0. TIME CHARGES

19.1. (a) For consultancy and other services performed by a principal, a fee by arrangement according to the circumstances including the professional status and qualifications of the quantity surveyor.

(b) When a principal does work which would normally be done by a member of staff, the charge shall be calculated as para. 19.2 below.

19.2. (a) For services by a member of staff, the charges for which are to be based on the time involved, such charges shall be calculated on the hourly cost of the individual involved plus 145%.

(b) A member of staff shall include a principal doing work normally done by an employee (as para. 19.1 (b) above), technical and supporting staff, but shall exclude secretarial staff or staff engaged upon general administration.

(c) For the purpose of para. 19.2 (b) above, a principal's time shall be taken at the rate applicable to a senior assistant in the firm.

(d) The supervisory duties of a principal shall be deemed to be included in the addition of 145% as para. 19.2 (a) above and shall not be charged separately.

(e) The hourly cost to the employer shall be calculated by taking the sum of the annual cost of the member of staff of:

(i) Salary and bonus but excluding expenses;

(ii) Employer's contributions payable under any Pension and Life Assurance Schemes;

(iii) Employer's contributions made under the National Insurance Acts, the Redundancy Payments Act and any other payments made in respect of the employee by virtue of any statutory requirements; and

(iv) Any other payments or benefits made or granted by the employer in pursuance of the terms of employment of the member of staff;

and dividing by 1,650.

19.3. The foregoing Time Charges under paras. 19.1 and 19.2 are intended for use where other paras. of the Scale (not related to Time Charges) form a significant proportion of the overall fee. In all other cases an increased time charge may be agreed.

20.0. INSTALMENT PAYMENTS

20.1. In the absence of agreement to the contrary, payments to the quantity surveyor shall be made by instalments by arrangement between the employer and the quantity surveyor.

Fees for Professional Services

QUANTITY SURVEYORS' FEES

SCALE 40   PROFESSIONAL CHARGES FOR QUANTITY SURVEYING SERVICES IN CONNECTION
              WITH HOUSING SCHEMES FOR LOCAL AUTHORITIES
              This scale has been abolished. See Author's Note on page 6.

EFFECTIVE FROM FEBRUARY 1983

1.0   GENERALLY

   1.1   The scale is applicable to housing schemes of self-contained dwellings regardless of type (e.g.
           houses, maisonettes, bungalows or flats) and irrespective of the amount of repetition of identical
           types or blocks within an individual housing scheme and shall also apply to all external works
           forming part of the contract for the housing scheme. This scale does not apply to improvement
           to existing dwellings.

   1.2   The fees set out below cover the following quantity surveying services as may be required:

           (a)   Preparing bills of quantities or other tender documents; checking tenders received or
                   negotiating tenders and pricing with a selected contractor; reporting thereon.
           (b)   Preparing recommendations for interim payments on account to the contractor;
                   measuring work and adjusting variations in accordance with the terms of the contract
                   and preparing the final account; pricing same and agreeing totals with the contractor;
                   adjusting fluctuations in the cost of labour and materials if required by the contract.
           (c)   Preparing periodic financial statements showing the anticipated final cost by means of
                   a simple routine of estimating final costs and reporting thereon, but excluding cost
                   monitoring (see para. 1.4).

   1.3   Where the quantity surveyor is appointed to prepare approximate estimates to establish and
           substantiate the economic viability of the scheme and to obtain the necessary approvals and
           consents, or to enable the scheme to be designed and constructed within approved cost criteria
           an additional fee shall be charged based on the time involved (see para. 7.0) or, alternatively, on
           a lump sum or percentage basis agreed between the employer and the quantity surveyor. (Cost
           planning services, see para. 3.0).

   1.4   When the employer specifically requests a post-contract cost monitoring service which involves
           the quantity surveyor in additional or abortive work an additional fee shall be charged based on
           the time involved (see para. 7.0) or, alternatively, on a lump sum or percentage basis agreed
           between the employer and the quantity surveyor.

   1.5   The fees are in all cases exclusive of travelling and other expenses (for which the actual
           disbursement is recoverable unless there is some prior arrangement for such charges) and of
           the cost of reproduction of bills of quantities and other documents, which are chargeable in
           addition at net cost.

   1.6   The fees are in all cases exclusive of services in connection with the allocation of the cost of the
           works for purposes of calculating value added tax for which there shall be an additional fee
           based on the time involved (see para. 7.0).

   1.7   When work normally included in a building contract is the subject of a separate contract for
           which the quantity surveyor has not been paid fees under any other clause thereof, the value of
           such work shall be included in the amount upon which fees are charged.

   1.8   If any of the materials used in the works are supplied by the employer or charged at a
           preferential rate, then the estimated or actual value thereof shall be included in the amount upon
           which fees are to be calculated.

QUANTITY SURVEYORS' FEES

1.9   The fees are in all cases exclusive of preparing a specification of the materials to be used and the works to be done, but the fees for preparing bills of quantities and similar documents do include for incorporating preamble clauses describing the materials and workmanship (from information given by the architect and/or consulting engineer).

1.10   If the quantity surveyor incurs additional costs due to exceptional delays in building operations or any other cause beyond the control of the quantity surveyor, then the fees shall be adjusted by agreement between the employer and the quantity surveyor to cover the reimbursement of these additional costs.

1.11   When a project is the subject of a number of contracts then for the purposes of calculating fees, the values of such contracts shall not be aggregated but each contract shall be taken separately and the scale of charges applied as appropriate.

1.12   The fees and charges are in all cases exclusive of value added tax which will be applied in accordance with legislation.

1.13   Copyright in bills of quantities and other documents prepared by the quantity surveyor is reserved to the quantity surveyor.

2.0   BASIC SCALE

2.1   The basic fee for the services outlined in para. 1.2 shall be as follows:-

Value of work		Fee		
		£		£
Up to	75 000	250 + 4.6%		
75 000 -	150 000	3 700 + 3.6%	on balance over	75 000
150 000 -	750 000	6 400 + 2.3%	on balance over	150 000
750 000 -	1 500 000	20 200 + 1.7%	on balance over	750 000
Over	1 500 000	32 950 + 1.5%	on balance over	1 500 000

2.2   Fees shall be calculated upon the total of the final account for the whole of the work including all nominated sub-contractors' and nominated suppliers' accounts.

2.3   For services in connection with accommodation designed for the elderly or the disabled or other special category occupants for whom special facilities are required an addition of 10% shall be made to the fee calculated in accordance with para. 2.1.

2.4   When additional fees under para. 2.3 are chargeable on a part or parts of a scheme, the value of basic fee to which the additional percentages shall be applied shall be determined by the proportion that the values of the various types of accommodation bear to the total of those values.

2.5   When the quantity surveyor is required to prepare an interim valuation of materials or goods off site, an additional fee shall be charged based on the time involved (see para. 7.0).

2.6   If the works are substantially varied at any stage and if the quantity surveyor is involved in an excessive amount of abortive work, then the fee shall be adjusted by agreement between the employer and the quantity surveyor.

2.7   The fees payable under paras. 2.1 and 2.3 include for the preparation of bills of quantities or other tender documents on a normal trade basis. If the employer requires additional information to be provided in bills of quantities, or bills of quantities to be prepared in an elemental, operational or similar form, then the fee may be adjusted by agreement between the employer and the quantity surveyor.

Fees for Professional Services

QUANTITY SURVEYORS' FEES

3.0   COST PLANNING

3.1   When the quantity surveyor is specifically instructed to provide cost planning services, the fee calculated in accordance with paras. 2.1 and 2.3 shall be increased by a sum calculated in accordance with the following table and based upon the amount of the accepted tender.

Value of work £		Fee		
		£		£
Up to	150 000	0.45%		
150 000 -	750 000	675 + 0.35%	on balance over	150 000
Over	750 000	2 775 + 0.25%	on balance over	750 000

3.2   Cost planning is defined as the process of ascertaining a cost limit, where necessary, within the guidelines set by any appropriate Authority, and thereafter checking the cost of the project within that limit throughout the design process. It includes the preparation of a cost plan (based upon elemental analysis or other suitable criterion) checking and revising it where required and effecting the necessary liaison with other consultants employed.

3.3   (a)   When cost planning services have been provided by the quantity surveyor and bills of reductions are required, then no charge shall be made by the quantity surveyor for the bills of reductions unless the reductions are necessitated by amended instructions of the employer or by the inclusion in the bills of quantities of items which the quantity surveyor has indicated could not be contained within the approved estimate.

   (b)   When cost planning services have not been provided by the quantity surveyor and bills of reductions are required, a fee is chargeable for preparing such bills of reductions:

   (i)   2.0% upon the gross amount of all omissions requiring measurement or abstraction from original dimension sheets.
   (ii)   3.0% upon the gross amount of all additions requiring measurement.
   (iii) 0.5% upon the gross amount of all remaining additions.

4.0   HEATING, VENTILATING AND ELECTRICAL SERVICES

(a)   When bills of quantities and the final account are prepared by the quantity surveyor for the heating, ventilating and electrical services, there shall be a fee for these services in addition to the fee calculated in accordance with paras. 2.1 and 2.3 as follows:

Value of work £		Fee		
		£		£
Up to	60 000	4.50%		
60 000 -	120 000	2 700 + 3.85%	on balance over	60 000
120 000 -	240 000	5 010 + 3.25%	on balance over	120 000
240 000 -	375 000	8 910 + 3.00%	on balance over	240 000
375 000 -	500 000	12 960 + 2.50%	on balance over	375 000
Over	500 000	16 085 + 2.15%	on balance over	500 000

(b)   The value of such services, whether the subject of separate tenders or not shall be aggregated and the total value of work so obtained used for the purpose of calculating the additional fee chargeable in accordance with para. (a). (Except that when more than one firm of consulting engineers is engaged on the design of these services, the separate values for which each such firm is responsible shall be aggregated and the additional fees charged shall be calculated independently on each such total value so obtained).

QUANTITY SURVEYORS' FEES

(c) The scope of the services to be provided by the quantity surveyor under para. (a) above shall be deemed to be equivalent to those outlined in para. 1.2.

(d) Fee shall be calculated upon the basis of the account for the whole of the heating, ventilating and electrical services for which final accounts have been prepared by the quantity surveyor.

5.0   INSTALMENT PAYMENTS

5.1   In the absence of agreement to the contrary, fees shall be paid by instalments as follows:

(a) Upon receipt by the employer of a tender for the works sixty per cent (60%) of the fees calculated in accordance with paras. 2.0 and 4.0 in the amount of the accepted tender plus the appropriate recoverable expenses and the full amount of the fee for cost planning services if such services have been instructed by the employer.

(b) The balance of fees and expenses by instalments at intervals to be agreed between the date of the first certificate and one month after final certification of the contractor's account.

5.2   In the event of no tender being accepted, sixty per cent (60%) of the fees, plus the appropriate recoverable expenses, and the full amount of the fee for cost planning services if such services have been instructed by the employer, shall be paid within three months of the completion of the tender documents. The fee shall be calculated on the amount of the lowest original bona fide tender received. In the event of no tender being received, the fee shall be calculated on a reasonable valuation of the work based upon the tender documents.

NOTE: In the foregoing context "bona fide tender" shall be deemed to mean a tender submitted in good faith without major errors of computation and not subsequently withdrawn by the tenderer.

5.3   In the event of the project being abandoned at any stage other than those covered by the foregoing, the proportion of fee payable shall be by agreement between the employer and the quantity surveyor.

5.4   When the quantity surveyor is appointed to carry out post-contract services only and has not prepared the bills of quantities then the fees shall be agreed between the employer and the quantity surveyor as a proportion of the scale set out in paras. 2.0 and 4.0 with an allowance for the necessary familiarisation and any additional services undertaken by the quantity surveyor. The percentages stated in paras. 5.1 and 5.2 are not intended to be used as a means of calculating the fees payable for post-contract services only.

6.0   ADDITIONAL SERVICES

6.1   For additional services not normally necessary such as those arising as a result of the termination of a contract before completion, liquidation, fire damage to the buildings, services in connection with arbitration, litigation and investigation of the validity of contractors' claims, services in connection with taxation matters, and all similar services where the employer specifically instructs the quantity surveyor, the charge shall be in accordance with para. 7.0.

7.0   TIME CHARGES

7.1   (a) For consultancy and other services performed by a principal, a fee by arrangement according to the circumstances, including the professional status and qualifications of the quantity surveyor.

(b) When a principal does work which would normally be done by a member of staff, the charge shall be calculated as para. 7.2.

Fees for Professional Services

QUANTITY SURVEYORS' FEES

7.2   (a)   For services by a member of staff, the charges for which are to be based on the time involved, such hourly charges shall be calculated on the basis of annual salary (including bonus and any other payments or benefits previously agreed with the employer) multiplied by a factor of 2.5, plus reimbursement of payroll costs, all divided by 1600. Payroll costs shall include inter alia employer's contributions payable under any Pension and Life Assurance Schemes, employer's contributions made under the National Insurance Acts, the Redundancy Payments Act and any other payments made in respect of the employee by virtue of any statutory requirements. In this connection it would not be unreasonable in individual cases to take account of the cost of providing a car as part of the "salary" of staff engaged on time charge work when considering whether the salaries paid to staff engaged on such work are reasonable.

    (b)   A member of staff shall include a principal doing work normally done by an employee (as para. 7.1 (b) above), technical and supporting staff, but shall exclude secretarial staff or staff engaged upon general administration.

    (c)   For the purpose of para. 7.2 (b) above a principal's time shall be taken at the rate applicable to a senior assistant in the firm.

    (d)   The supervisory duties of a principal shall be deemed to be included in the multiplication factor as para. 7.2 (a) above and shall not be charged separately.

7.3   The foregoing Time Charges under paras. 7.1 and 7.2 are intended for use where other paras. of the scale (not related to Time Charges) form a significant proportion of the overall fee. In all other cases an increased Time Charge may be agreed.

SCALE 44   PROFESSIONAL CHARGES FOR QUANTITY SURVEYING SERVICES IN CONNECTION WITH IMPROVEMENTS TO EXISTING HOUSING AND ENVIRONMENTAL IMPROVEMENT WORKS
This scale has been abolished. See Author's Note on page 6.

EFFECTIVE FROM FEBRUARY 1973

1.   This scale of charges is applicable to all works of improvement to existing housing for local authorities, development corporations, housing associations and the like and to environmental improvement works associated therewith or of a similar nature.

2.   The fees set out below cover such quantity surveying services as may be required in connection with an improvement project irrespective of the type of contract or contract documentation from initial appointment to final certification of the contractor's account such as:

    (a)   Preliminary cost exercises and advice on tendering procedures and contract arrangements.

    (b)   Providing cost advice to assist the design and construction of the project within approved cost limits.

    (c)   Preliminary inspection of a typical dwelling of each type.

    (d)   Preparation of tender documents; checking tenders received and reporting thereon or negotiating tenders and agreeing prices with a selected contractor.

    (e)   Making recommendations for and, where necessary, preparing bills of reductions except in cases where the reductions are necessitated by amended instructions of the employer or by the inclusion in the bills of quantities of items which the quantity surveyor has indicated could not be contained within the approved estimate.

    (f)   Analysing tenders and preparing details for submission to a Ministry or Government Department and attending upon the employer in any negotiations with such Ministry or Government Department.

    (g)   Recording the extent of work required to every dwelling before work commences.

    (h)   Preparing recommendations for interim payments on account to the contractor; preparing periodic assessments of the anticipated final cost of the works and reporting thereon

    (j)   Measurement of work and adjustment of variations and fluctuations in the cost of labour and materials in accordance with the terms of the contract and preparing final account, pricing same and agreeing totals with the contractor.

QUANTITY SURVEYORS' FEES

3.   The services listed in para. 2 do not include the carrying out of structural surveys.

4.   The fees set out below have been calculated on the basis of experience that all of the services described above will not normally be required and in consequence these scales shall not be abated if, by agreement, any of the services are not required to be provided by the quantity surveyor.

IMPROVEMENT WORKS TO HOUSING

5.   The fee for quantity surveying services in connection with improvement works to existing housing and external works in connection therewith shall be calculated from a sliding scale based upon the total number of houses or flats in a project divided by the total number of types substantially the same in design and plan as follows:

Total number of houses or flats divided by total number of types substantially the same in design and plan	Fee
not exceeding 1	see note below
exceeding 1 but not exceeding 2	7.0%
exceeding 2 but not exceeding 3	5.0%
exceeding 3 but not exceeding 4	4.5%
exceeding 4 but not exceeding 20	4.0%
exceeding 20 but not exceeding 50	3.6%
exceeding 50 but not exceeding 100	3.2%
exceeding 100	3.0%

and to the result of the computation shall be added 12.5%

NOTE: For schemes of only one house or flat per type an appropriate fee is to be agreed between the employer and the quantity surveyor on a percentage, lump sum or time basis.

ENVIRONMENTAL IMPROVEMENT WORKS

6.   The fee for quantity surveying services in connection with environmental improvement works associated with improvements to existing housing or environmental improvement works of a similar nature shall be as follows:

Value of work £		Fee		
		£		£
Up to	50 000	4.5%		
50 000 -	200 000	2 250 + 3.0%	on balance over	50 000
200 000 -	500 000	6 750 + 2.1%	on balance over	200 000
Over	500 000	13 050 + 2.0%	on balance over	500 000

and to the result of that computation shall be added 12.5%

GENERALLY

7.   When tender documents prepared by a quantity surveyor for an earlier scheme are re-used without amendment by the quantity surveyor for a subsequent scheme or part thereof for the same employer, the percentage fee in respect of such subsequent scheme or the part covered by such reused documents shall be reduced by 20%.

8.   The foregoing fees shall be calculated upon the separate totals of the final account for improvement works to housing and environmental Government works respectively including all nominated sub-contractors' and nominated suppliers' accounts and (subject to para. 5 above) regardless of the amount of repetition within the scheme. When environmental improvement works are the subject of a number of contracts then for the purpose of calculating fees, the values of such contracts shall not be aggregated but each contract shall be taken separately and the scale of charges in para. 6 above applied as appropriate.

QUANTITY SURVEYORS' FEES

9.   In cases where any of the materials used in the works are supplied by the employer, the estimated or actual value thereof is to be included in the total on which the fee is calculated.

10.   In the absence of agreement to the contrary, fees shall be paid by instalments as follows:

       (a)   Upon acceptance by the employer of a tender for the works, one half of the fee calculated on the amount of the accepted tender.

       (b)   The balance by instalments at intervals to be agreed between the date of the first certificate and one month after final certification of the contractor's account.

11.   (a)   In the event of no tender being accepted, one half of the fee shall be paid within three months of completion of the tender documents. The fee shall be calculated on the amount of the lowest original bona fide tender received. If no such tender has been received, the fee shall be calculated upon a reasonable valuation of the work based upon the tender documents.

       (b)   In the event of the project being abandoned at any stage other than those covered by the foregoing, the proportion of fee payable shall be by agreement between the employer and the quantity surveyor.

12.   If the works are substantially varied at any stage or if the quantity surveyor is involved in an excessive amount of abortive work, then the fee shall be adjusted by agreement between the employer and the quantity surveyor.

13.   When the quantity surveyor is required to perform additional services in connection with the allocation of the costs of the works for purposes of calculating value added tax there shall be an additional fee based on the time involved.

14.   For additional services not normally necessary such as those arising as a result of the termination of the contract before completion, liquidation, fire damage to the buildings, services in connection with arbitration, litigation and claims on which the employer specifically instructs the surveyor to investigate and report, there shall be an additional fee to be agreed between the employer and the quantity surveyor.

15.   Copyright in the bills of quantities and other documents prepared by the quantity surveyor is reserved to the quantity surveyor.

16.   The foregoing fees are in all cases exclusive of travelling expenses and lithography or other charges for copies of documents, the net amount of such expenses and charges to be paid for in addition. Subsistence expenses, if any, to be charged by arrangement with the employer.

17.   The foregoing fees and charges are in all cases exclusive of value added tax which shall be applied in accordance with legislation current at the time the account is rendered.

SCALE 45   PROFESSIONAL CHARGES FOR QUANTITY SURVEYING SERVICES IN CONNECTION WITH HOUSING SCHEMES FINANCED BY THE HOUSING CORPORATION EFFECTIVE FROM JANUARY 1982 - reprinted 1989

1.   (a)   This scale of charges has been agreed between The Royal Institution of Chartered Surveyors and the Housing Corporation and shall apply to housing schemes of self-contained dwellings financed by the Housing Corporation regardless of type (e.g. houses, maisonettes, bungalows or flats) and irrespective of the amount of repetition of identical types or blocks within an individual housing scheme.

       (b)   This scale does not apply to services in connection with improvements to existing dwellings.

2.   The fees set out below cover the following quantity surveying services as may be required in connection with the particular project:

       (a)   Preparing such estimates of cost as are required by the employer to establish and substantiate the economic viability of the scheme and to obtain the necessary approvals and consents from the Housing Corporation but excluding cost planning services (see para. 10)

       (b)   Providing pre-contract cost advice (e.g. approximate estimates on a floor area or similar basis) to enable the scheme to be designed and constructed within the approved cost criteria but excluding cost planning services (see para. 10).

QUANTITY SURVEYORS' FEES

(c)   Preparing bills of quantities or other tender documents; checking tenders received or negotiating tenders and pricing with a selected contractor; reporting thereon.

(d)   Preparing an elemental analysis of the accepted tender (RICS/BCIS Detailed Form of Cost Analysis excluding the specification notes or equivalent).

(e)   Preparing recommendations for interim payments on account to the contractor; measuring the work and adjusting variations in accordance with the terms of the contract and preparing the final account, pricing same and agreeing totals with the contractor; adjusting fluctuations in the cost of labour and materials if required by the contract.

(f)   Preparing periodic post-contract assessments of the anticipated final cost by means of a simple routine of periodically estimating final costs and reporting thereon, but excluding a cost monitoring service specifically required by the employer.

3.   The fees set out below are exclusive of travelling and of other expenses (for which the actual disbursement is recoverable unless there is some special prior arrangement for such charges) and the cost of reproduction of bills of quantities and other documents, which are chargeable in addition at net cost.

4.   Copyright in the bills of quantities and other documents prepared by the quantity surveyor is reserved to the quantity surveyor.

5.   (a)   The basic fee for the services outlined in para. 2 (regardless of the extent of services described in para. 2) shall be as follows:

Value of work £		Fee	
		£	£
Up to	75 000	210 + 3.8%	
75 000 -	150 000	3 060 + 3.0% on balance over	75 000
150 000 -	750 000	5 310 + 2.0% on balance over	150 000
750 000 -	1 500 000	17 310 + 1.5% on balance over	750 000
Over	1 500 000	28 560 + 1.3% on balance over	1 500 000

(b)   (i)   For services in connection with Categories 1 and 2 Accommodation designed for Old People in accordance with the standards described in Ministry of Housing and Local Government Circulars 82/69 and 27/70 (Welsh Office Circulars 84/69 & 30/70), there shall be a fee in addition to that in accordance with para. 5 (a), calculated as follows:

Category 1   An addition of five per cent (5%) to the basic fee calculated in accordance with para. 5 (a)

Category 2   An addition of twelve and a half per cent (12.5%) to the basic fee calculated in accordance with para. 5 (a).

(ii)   For services in connection with Accommodation designed for the Elderly in Scotland in accordance with the standards described in Scottish Housing Handbook Part 5, Housing for the Elderly, the fee shall be calculated as follows:

Mainstream and Amenity Housing	Basic fee in accordance with para. 5 (a)
Basic Sheltered Housing (i.e. Amenity Housing plus Warden's accommodation and alarm system)	An addition of five per cent (5%) to the basic fee calculated in accordance with para. 5 (a)
Sheltered Housing, including optional facilities	An addition of twelve and a half per cent (12.5%) of the basic fee calculated in accordance with para. 5 (a)

QUANTITY SURVEYORS' FEES

(c)   (i)   For services in connection with Accommodation designed for Disabled People in accordance with the standards described in Department of Environment Circular 92/75 (Welsh Office Circular 163/75), there shall be an addition of fifteen per cent (15%) to the fee calculated in accordance with paragraph 5 (a).

       (ii)   For services in connection with Accommodation designed for the Disabled in Scotland in accordance with the standards described in Scottish Housing Handbook Part 6, Housing for the Disabled, there shall be an addition of fifteen per cent (15%) to the fee calculated in accordance with para. 5 (a).

(d)   For services in connection with Accommodation designed for Disabled Old People, the fee shall be calculated in accordance with para. 5 (c).

(e)   For services in connection with Subsidised Fair Rent New Build Housing, there shall be a fee, in addition to that in accordance with paras. 5 (a) to (d), calculated as follows:

Value of work £		Category A fee	
		£	£
Up to	75 000	20 + 0.40%	
75 000 -	150 000	320 + 0.20% on balance over	75 000
150 000 -	500 000	470 + 0.07% on balance over	150 000
Over	500 000	715	

6.   (a)   Where additional fees under paras. 5 (b) to (d) are chargeable on a part or parts of a scheme, the value of basic fee to which the additional percentages shall be applied shall be determined by the proportion that the values of the various types of accommodation bear to the total of those values.

       (b)   Fees shall be calculated upon the total of the final account for the whole of the work including all nominated sub-contractors' and nominated suppliers' accounts.

       (c)   If any of the materials used in the works are supplied free of charge to the contractor, the estimated or actual value thereof shall be included in the amount upon which fees are to be calculated.

       (d)   When a project is the subject of a number of contracts then, for the purpose of calculating fees, the values of such contracts shall not be aggregated but each contract shall be taken separately and the scale of charges applied as appropriate.

7.   If bills of quantities and final accounts are prepared by the quantity surveyor for the heating, ventilating or electrical services, there shall be an additional fee by agreement between the employer and the quantity surveyor subject to the approval of the Housing Corporation.

8.   In the absence of agreement to the contrary, fees shall be paid by instalments as follows:

       (a)   Upon receipt by the employer of a tender for the works, or when the employer certifies to the Housing Corporation that the tender documents have been completed, a sum on account representing ninety per cent (90%) of the anticipated sum under para. 8 (b) below.

       (b)   Upon acceptance by the employer of a tender for the works, sixty per cent (60%) of the fee calculated on the amount of the accepted tender, plus the appropriate recoverable expenses.

       (c)   The balance of fees and expenses by instalments at intervals to be agreed between the date of the first certificate and one month after final certification of the contractor's account.

9.   (a)   In the event of no tender being accepted, sixty per cent (60%) of the fee and the appropriate recoverable expenses shall be paid within six months of completion of the tender documents. The fee shall be calculated on the amount of the lowest original bona fide tender received. In the event of no tender being received, the fee shall be calculated upon a reasonable valuation of the work based upon the tender documents.

     NOTE: In the foregoing context "bona fide tender" shall be deemed to mean a tender submitted in good faith without major errors of computation and not subsequently withdrawn by the tenderer.

QUANTITY SURVEYORS' FEES

(b)   In the event of part of the project being postponed or abandoned after the preparation of the bills of quantities or other tender documents, sixty per cent (60%) of the fee on this part shall be paid within three months of the date of postponement or abandonment.

(c)   In the event of the project being postponed or abandoned at any stage other than those covered by the foregoing, the proportion of fee payable shall be by agreement between the employer and the quantity surveyor.

10.   (a)   Where with the approval of the Housing Corporation the employer instructs the quantity surveyor to carry out cost planning services there shall be a fee additional to that charged under para. 5 as follows:

Value of work	£	Category A fee	
		£	£
Up to	150 000	0.45%	
150 000 - 750 000		675 + 0.35% on balance over	150 000
Over	750 000	2 775 + 0.25% on balance over	750 000

(b)   Cost planning is defined as the process of ascertaining a cost limit where necessary, within guidelines set by any appropriate Authority, and thereafter checking the cost of the project within that limit throughout the design process. It includes the preparation of a cost plan (based upon elemental analysis or other suitable criterion) checking and revising it where required and effecting the necessary liaison with the other consultants employed.

11.   If the quantity surveyor incurs additional costs due to exceptional delays in building operations or any other cause beyond the control of the quantity surveyor, then the fees shall be adjusted by agreement between the employer and the quantity surveyor to cover reimbursement of costs.

12.   When the quantity surveyor is required to prepare an interim valuation of materials or goods off site, an additional fee shall be charged based on the time involved (see paras. 15 and 16) in respect of each such valuation.

13.   If the Works are materially varied to the extent that substantial re-measurement is necessary, then the fee may be adjusted by agreement between the employer and the quantity surveyor.

14.   For additional services not normally necessary, such as those arising as a result of the termination of a contract before completion, fire damage to the buildings, cost monitoring (see para. 2 (f)), services in connection with arbitration, litigation and investigation of the validity of contractors' claims, services in connection with taxation matters and similar all services where the employer specifically instructs the quantity surveyor, the charges shall be in accordance with paras. 15 & 16.

15.   (a)   For consultancy and other services performed by a principal, a fee by arrangement according to the circumstances, including the professional status and qualifications of the quantity surveyor.

(b)   When a principal does work which would normally be done by a member of staff, the charge shall be calculated as para. 16.

16.   (a)   For services by a member of staff, the charges for which are to be based on the time involved, such hourly charges shall be calculated on the basis of annual salary (including bonus and any other payments or benefits previously agreed with the employer) multiplied by a factor of 2.5, plus reimbursement of payroll costs, all divided by 1600. Payroll costs shall include inter alia employer's contributions payable under any Pension and Life Assurance Schemes, employer's contributions made under the National Insurance Acts, the Redundancy Payments Act and any other payments made in respect of the employee by virtue of any statutory requirements in this connection it would not be unreasonable in individual cases to take account of the cost of providing a car as part of the "salary" of staff engaged on time charge work when considering whether the salaries paid to staff engaged on such work are reasonable.

(b)   A member of staff shall include a principal doing work normally done by an employee (as para. 15 (b) above), technical and supporting staff, but shall exclude secretarial staff or staff engaged upon general administration.

Fees for Professional Services

QUANTITY SURVEYORS' FEES

(c)   For the purpose of para. 16 (b) above a principal's time shall be taken at the rate applicable to a senior assistant in the firm.

(d)   The supervisory duties of a principal shall be deemed to be included in the multiplication factor as para. 16 (a) above and shall not be charged separately.

17.   The foregoing Time Charges under paras. 15 and 16 are intended for use where other paras. of the scale (not related to Time Charges) form a significant proportion of the overall fee. In all other cases an increased time charge may be agreed.

18.   (a)   In the event of the employment of the contractor being determined due to bankruptcy or liquidation, the fee for the services outlined in para. 2, and for the additional services required, shall be recalculated to the aggregate of the following:

(i)   Fifty per cent (50%) of the fee in accordance with paragraphs 5 and 6 calculated upon the total of the Notional Final Account in accordance with the terms of the original contracts.

(ii)   Fifty per cent (50%) of the fee in accordance with paragraphs 5 and 6 calculated upon the aggregate of the total value (which may differ from the total of interim valuations) of work up to the date of determination in accordance with the terms of the original contract plus the total of the final account for the completion contract;

(iii)   A charge based upon time involved (in accordance with paragraphs 15 and 16) in respect of dealing with those matters specifically generated by the liquidation (other than normal post-contract services related to the completion contract), which may include (inter alia):

Site inspection and (where required) security (initial and until the replacement contractor takes possession);
Taking instructions from and/or advising the employer;
Representing the employer at meeting(s) of creditors;
Making arrangements for the continued employment of sub-contractors and similar related matters;
Preparing bills of quantities or other appropriate documents for the completion contract, obtaining tenders, checking and reporting thereon;
The additional cost (over and above the preparation of the final account for the completion contract) of pre-paring the Notional Final Account; pricing the same;
Negotiations with the liquidator (trustee or receiver).

(b)   In calculating fees under para. 18 (a) (iii) above, regard shall be taken of any services carried out by the quantity surveyor for which a fee will ultimately be chargeable under para. 18 (a) (i) and (ii) above in respect of which a suitable abatement shall be made from the fee charged (e.g. measurement of variations for purposes of the completion contract where such would contribute towards the preparation of the contract final account).

(c)   Any interim instalments of fees paid under para. 8 in respect of services outlined in para. 2 shall be deducted from the overall fee computed as outlined herein.

(d)   In the absence of agreement to the contrary fees and expenses in respect of those services outlined in para. 18 (a) (iii) above up to acceptance of a completion tender shall be paid upon such acceptance; the balance of fees and expenses shall be paid in accordance with para. 8 (c).

(e)   For the purpose of this Scale the term "Notional Final Account" shall be deemed to mean an account indicating that which would have been payable to the original contractor had he completed the whole of the works and before deduction of interim payments to him.

19.   The fees and charges are in all cases exclusive of Value Added Tax which will be applied in accordance with legislation.

QUANTITY SURVEYORS' FEES

EXPLANATORY NOTE:
(Source: Chartered Quantity Surveyor, August 1986)

For rehabilitation projects the basic fee set out in paragraph 5 (a) of the scale will apply with the addition of a further 1% fee calculated upon the total of the final account for rehabilitation works including all nominated sub-contractors' and nominated suppliers' accounts.

In the case of special housing categories (e.g., elderly people) the additional percentage should be applied before the application of the additional percentage set out in paragraph 5 (b). The provisions of paragraph 6 (a) of the scale will also apply.

There is no longer any distinction between "hostel" and "cluster dwellings" which now have a single category of shared housing.

For shared housing new build projects other than those specified below the fee should be calculated in accordance with paragraph 5 (a) plus an enhancement of 10%.

For shared housing rehabilitation projects other than those specified below the fee should be calculated in accordance with paragraph 5 (a) of the scale plus 1% plus an enhancement of 10%.

For shared housing projects comprising wheelchair accommodation (as described in the Housing Corporation's Design and Contract Criteria) or frail elderly accommodation (as described in Housing Corporation circular HCO1/85) the fee should be calculated in accordance with paragraph 5 (a), (plus 1% for rehabilitation schemes where applicable) plus an enhancement of 15%.

The additional percentage set out in paragraph 5 (b) does not apply to shared housing projects, but the provisions of paragraph 6 (a) are applicable.

SCALE 46   PROFESSIONAL CHARGES FOR QUANTITY SURVEYING SERVICES IN CONNECTION WITH LOSS ASSESSMENT OF DAMAGE TO BUILDINGS FROM FIRE, ETC ISSUED BY THE ROYAL INSTITUTION OF CHARTERED SURVEYORS.
This scale has been abolished. See Author's Note on page 6.

EFFECTIVE FROM JULY 1988

1.   This scale of professional charges is for use in assessing loss resulting from damage to buildings by fire etc., under the "building" section of an insurance policy and is applicable to all categories of buildings.

2.   The fees set out below cover the following quantity surveying services as may be required in connection with the particular loss assessment:
(a)   Examining the insurance policy.
(b)   Visiting the building and taking all necessary site notes.
(c)   Measuring at site and/or from drawings and preparing itemised statement of claim and pricing same.
(d)   Negotiating and agreeing claim with the loss adjuster.

3.   The fees set out below are exclusive of the following:
(a)   Travelling and other expenses (for which the actual disbursement is recoverable unless there is some special prior arrangement for such charge.)
(b)   Cost of reproduction of all documents, which are chargeable in addition at net cost.

4.   Copyright in all documents prepared by the quantity surveyor is reserved.
5.   (a)   The fees for the services outlined in paragraph 2 shall be as follows:

Agreed Amount of £		Fee		
		£		£
Up to	60 000	see note 5(c) below		
60 000 -	180 000	2.5%		
180 000 -	360 000	4 500 + 2.3%	on balance over	180 000
360 000 -	720 000	8 640 + 2.0%	on balance over	360 000
Over	720 000	15 840 + 1.5%	on balance over	720 000

and to the result of that computation shall be added 12.5%

QUANTITY SURVEYORS' FEES

(b)   The sum on which the fees above shall be calculated shall be arrived at after having given effect to the following:

        (i)   The sum shall be based on the amount of damage, including such amounts in respect of architects', surveyors and other consultants' fees for reinstatement, as admitted by the loss adjuster.

        (ii)   When a policy is subject to an average clause, the sum shall be the agreed amount before the adjustment for "average".

        (iii)   When, in order to apply the average clause, the reinstatement value of the whole subject is calculated and negotiated an additional fee shall be charged commensurate with the work involved.

(c)   Subject to 5 (b) above, when the amount of the sum on which fees shall be calculated is under £60,000 the fee shall be based on time involved as defined in Scale 37 (July 1988) para. 19 or on a lump sum or percentage basis agreed between the building owner and the quantity surveyor.

6.   The foregoing scale of charges is exclusive of any services in connection with litigation and arbitration.

7.   The fees and charges are in all cases exclusive of value added tax which shall be applied in accordance with legislation.

QUANTITY SURVEYORS' FEES

SCALE 47   PROFESSIONAL CHARGES FOR THE ASSESSMENT OF REPLACEMENT COSTS BUILDINGS FOR INSURANCE, CURRENT COST ACCOUNTING AND OTHER PURPOSES ISSUED BY THE ROYAL INSTITUTION OF CHARTERED SURVEYORS
This scale has been abolished. See Author's Note on page 6.

EFFECTIVE FROM JULY 1988

1.0   GENERALLY

1.1.   The fees are in all cases exclusive of travelling and other expenses (for which the actual disbursement is recoverable unless there is some prior arrangement for such charges).

1.2.   The fees and charges are in all cases exclusive of value added tax which will be applied in accordance with legislation.

2.0   ASSESSMENT OF REPLACEMENT COSTS OF BUILDINGS FOR INSURANCE PURPOSES

2.1.   Assessing the current replacement cost of buildings where adequate drawings for the purpose are available.

Assessed current costs	Fee		
	£		£
Up to 700 000	0.2%		
140 000 - 700 000	280 + 0.075%	on balance over	140 000
700 000 - 4 200 000	700 + 0.025%	on balance over	700 000
Over 4 200 000	1 575 + 0.01%	on balance over	4 200 000

2.2.   Fees to be calculated on the assessed cost, i.e. base value, for replacement purposes including allowances for demolition and the clearance but excluding inflation allowances and professional fees.

2.3.   Where drawings adequate for the assessment of costs are not available or where other circumstances require that measurements of the whole or part of the buildings are taken, an additional fee shall be charged based on the time involved or alternatively on a lump sum basis agreed between the employer and the surveyor.

2.4   when the assessment is for buildings of different character or on more than one site, the costs shall not be aggregated for the purpose of calculating fees.

2.5   For current cost accounting purposes this scale refers only to the assessment of replacement cost of buildings.

2.6   The scale is appropriate for initial assessments but for annual review or a regular reassessment the fee should be by arrangement having regard to the scale and to the amount of work involved and the time taken.

2.7.   The fees are exclusive of services in connection with negotiations with brokers, accountants or insurance companies for which there shall be an additional fee based upon the time involved.

CONSULTING ENGINEERS' FEES

INTRODUCTION

A scale of professional charges for consulting engineering services is published by the Association of Consulting Engineers (ACE)

Copies of the document can be obtained direct from : -

> The Association of Consulting Engineers
> Alliance House
> Caxton Street
> London SW1H OQL
> Tel   0207 222 6557
> Fax 0207 222 0750

Comparisons

Instead of the previous arrangement of having different agreements designed for each major discipline of engineering, these new agreements have been developed primarily to suit the different roles that Consulting Engineers may be required to perform, with variants of some of them for different disciplines. The agreements have been standardised as far as possible whilst retaining essential differences.

Greater attention is required than with previous agreements to ensure the documents are completed properly. This is because of the perceived need to allow for a wider choice of arrangements, particularly of methods of payment.

The agreements are not intended to be used as unsigned reference material with the details of an engagement being covered in an exchange of letters, although much of their content could be used as a basis for drafting such correspondence.

Forms of Agreement

The initial agreements are for use where a Consulting Engineer is engaged as follows :

> Agreement as a Lead Consultant
>
> Agreement directly by the Client, but not as Lead Consultant
>
> Agreement to provide design services for a design and construct Contractor
>
> Short Form Agreement (Report and Advisory Services)
>
> Agreement as a Project Manager
>
> Agreement as Planning Supervisor in accordance with the Construction (Design and Management) Regulations 1994

Each of Agreements A, B and C are published in two variants

> Variant 1 Civil and Structural Engineering
>
> Variant 2 The Engineering of Electrical and Mechanical Services in Buildings

Each agreement comprises the following :-

> Memorandum of Agreement
>
> Conditions of Engagement
>
> Appendix I - Services of the Consulting Engineer
>
> Appendix II - Remuneration of the Consulting Engineer

CONSULTING ENGINEERS' FEES

Memorandum of Agreement

There is a different memorandum for each agreement, reflecting in each instance the particular relationships between the parties. It is essential that the memorandum be fully completed. Spaces are provided for entry of important and specific details relevant to each commission, such as nominated individuals, limits of liability, requirements for professional indemnity insurance, the frequency of site visits and meetings, and requirements for collateral warranties. All the memoranda are arranged for execution under hand; some also have provision for execution as deeds.

Conditions of Engagement

These have been standardised as far as possible and thus contain much that is common between the agreements, but parts differ and are peculiar to individual agreements to reflect the responsibilities applying. The conditions can normally stand as drafted but clauses may be deleted and others be added should the circumstances so require for a particular commission.

Appendix I - Services

This appendix, which has significant differences between the agreements and variants, describes the services to be performed. These services include both standard Normal Services, the majority of which will usually be required, and standard Additional Services of which only some will be required. Standard Normal Services may be deleted if not required or not relevant to a particular commission; further Services, both Normal and Additional may be added in spaces provided. It may be agreed in advance, when known that certain of the Additional Services will clearly be required, that these will be treated and paid for as Normal Services for a particular commission.

Appendix II - Remuneration / Fees and Disbursements

This appendix provides alternate means of assessing the consulting engineer's fees and disbursements. It identifies, when completed, which of those services listed in Appendix I are to be performed within the overall fee applicable for Normal Services. Figures need to be entered on such details as time charge rates, fee percentages and interest rates on delayed payments. Alternatives which do not apply require deletion and those remaining completion, so that the appendix when incorporated within an engagement contract describes the exact arrangements applicable to that commission.

Collateral Warranties

The association is convinced that collateral warranties are generally unnecessary and should only be used in exceptional circumstances. The interests of clients, employers and others are better protected by taking out project or BUILD type latent defects insurance. Nevertheless, in response to observations raised when the pilot editions excluded any mention of warranties, references and arrangements have been included in the Memorandum and elsewhere by which Consulting Engineers may agree to enter into collateral warranty agreements; these should however only be given when the format and requirements thereof have been properly defined and recorded in advance of undertaking the commission.

Requirements for the provision of collateral warranties will be justified even less with commissions under Agreement D than with those under the other ACE agreements. Occasional calls may be made for them, such as when a client intends to dispose of property and needs evidence of a duty of care being owed to specific third parties, but these will be few and far between.

Remuneration

Guidance on appropriate levels of fees to be charged is given at the end of each agreement. Firms and their clients may use this or other sources, including their own records, to determine suitable fee arrangements.

Fees for Professional Services

CONSULTING ENGINEERS' FEES

Need for formal documentation

The Association of Consulting Engineers recommends that formal written documentation should be executed to record the details of each commission awarded to a Consulting Engineer. These Conditions are published as model forms of agreement suitable for the purpose. However, even if these particular Conditions are not used, it is strongly recommended that, whenever a Consulting Engineer is appointed, there should be at least an exchange of letters defining the duties to be performed and the terms of payment.

Appointments outside the United Kingdom

These conditions of Engagement are designed for use within the UK. For work overseas it is impracticable to give definite recommendations; circumstances differ too widely between countries. There are added complications in documentation relating to local legislation, import customs, conditions of payment, insurance, freight, etc. Furthermore, it is often necessary to arrange for visits to be made by principals and senior staff whose absence abroad during such periods represents a serious reduction of their earning power. The additional duties, responsibilities and non-recoverable costs involved, and the extra work on general co-ordination, should be reflected in the levels of fees. Special arrangements are also necessary to cover travelling and other out-of-pocket expenses in excess of those normally incurred on similar work in the UK, including such matters as local cost-of-living allowances and the cost of providing home-leave facilities for expatriate staff.

CONDITIONS OF ENGAGEMENT

Obligations

The following is a brief summary of the conditions of engagement. It is recommended that reference should be made to the full document of the Association of Consulting Engineers Conditions of Engagement, 1995 before making an engagement.

Obligations of the Consulting Engineer

The responsibilities of the Consultant Engineer for the works are as set out in the actual agreement The various standard clauses in the Conditions relate to such matters as differentiating between Normal and Additional services, the duty to exercise skill and care, the need for Client's written consent to the assignment or transfer of any benefit or obligation of the agreement, the rendering of advice if requested on the appointment of other consultants and specialist sub- consultants, any recommendations for design of any part of the Works by Contractors or Sub-contractors (with the proviso that the Consulting Engineer is not responsible for detailed design of contractors or for defects or omissions in such design), the designation of a Project Leader, the need for timeliness in requests to the Client for information etc., freezing the design once it has been given Client approval and the specific exclusion of any duty to advise on the actual or possible presence of pollution or contamination or its consequences.

Obligations of the Client

The Consultant Engineer shall be supplied with all necessary data and information in good time. The Client shall designate a Representative authorised to make decisions on his behalf and ensure that all decisions, instructions, and approvals are given in time so as not to delay or disrupt the Consultant Engineer.

Site Staff

The Consulting Engineer may employ site staff he feels are required to perform the task, subject to the prior written agreement of the Client. The Client shall bear the cost of local office accommodation, equipment and running costs.

CONSULTING ENGINEERS' FEES

Commencement, Determination, Postponement, Disruption and Delay

The Consulting Engineer's appointment commences at the date of the execution of the Memorandum of Agreement or such earlier date when the Consulting Engineer first commenced the performance of the Services, subject to the right of the Client to determine or postpone all or any of the Services at any time by Notice.

The Client or the Consulting Engineer may determine the appointment in the event of a breach of the Agreement by the other party after two weeks notice. In addition, the Consulting Engineer may determine his appointment after two weeks notice in the event of the Client failing to make proper payment.

The Consulting Engineer may suspend the performance of all or any of the Services for up to twenty-six weeks if he is prevented or significantly impeded from performance by circumstances outside his control. The appointment may be determined by either party in the event of insolvency subject to the issue of notice of determination.

Payments

The Client shall pay fees for the performance of the agreed service(s) together with all fees and charges to the local or other authorities for seeking and obtaining statutory permissions, for all site staff on a time basis, together with additional payments for any variation or the disruption of the Consulting Engineer's work due to the Client varying the task list or brief or to delay caused by the Client, others or unforeseeable events.

If any part of any invoice submitted by the Consulting Engineer is contested, payment shall be made in full of all that is not contested.

Payments shall be made within 28 days of the date of the Consulting Engineer's invoice; interest shall be added to all amounts remaining unpaid thereafter.

Ownership of Documents and Copyright

The Consulting Engineer retains the copyright in all drawings, reports, specifications, calculations etc. prepared in connection with the Task; with the agreement of the Consulting Engineer and subject to certain conditions, the Client may have a licence to copy and use such intellectual property solely for his own purpose on the Task in hand, subject to reservations.

The Consulting Engineer must obtain the client's permission before he publishes any articles, photographs or other illustrations relating to the Task, nor shall he disclose to any person any information provided by the Client as private and confidential unless so authorised by the Client.

Liability, Insurance and Warranties

The liability of the Consulting Engineer is defined, together with the duty of the Client to indemnify the Consulting Engineer against all claims etc. in excess of the agreed liability limit.

The Consulting Engineer shall maintain Professional Indemnity Insurance for an agreed amount and period at commercially reasonable rates, together with Public Liability Insurance and shall produce the brokers' certificates for inspection to show that the required cover is being maintained as and when requested by the Client.

The Consulting Engineer shall enter into and provide collateral warranties for the benefit of other parties if so agreed.

Disputes and Differences

Provision is made for mediation to solve disputes, subject to a time limit of six weeks of the appointment of the mediator at which point it should be referred to an independent adjudicator. Further action could be by referring the dispute to an arbitrator.

THE TOWN AND COUNTRY PLANNING (FEES FOR APPLICATIONS AND DEEMED APPLICATIONS) (AMENDMENT) (ENGLAND) REGULATIONS 2005

S.I. 2005/843 – operative from 1st April 2005

The following extracts from the Town and Country Planning Fees Regulations, available from HMSO, relate only to those applications which meet the "deemed to qualify clauses" laid down in regulations 1 to 12 of S.I. No. 1989/193, amended by S.I. 1990/2473, 1991/2735, 1992/1817, 1992/3052, 1993/3170, 1997/37, 2001/2719 and 2002/768.

These regulations apply in relation to England only.

Further advice on the interpretation of these regulations can be found in the 1990 Town and Country Planning Acts and S.I. 1989/193.

General increase in fees
   2. - (1) The Town and Country Planning (Fees for Applications and Deemed Applications) Regulations 1989[2] are amended as follows.

    (2) In regulation 10A (fees for applications for certificates of lawful use or development) –

      (a) in paragraph (5)(b), for "£110" substitute "£135"; and

      (b) for paragraph (6) substitute-

        " (6) Where a use specified in an application under section 191(1)(a) is use as one or more separate dwellinghouses, the fee payable in respect of that use shall be:

          (a) where the use so specified is use as 50 or fewer dwellinghouses, £265 for each dwellinghouse;

          (b) where the use so specified is use as more than 50 dwellinghouses, £13,250, and an additional £80 for each dwellinghouse in excess of 50, subject to a maximum in total of £50,000.".

    (3) In regulation 11A (fees for certain applications under the General Permitted Development Order)

      (a) in paragraph (1)(a), for "£40" substitute "£50"; and

      (b) in paragraph (1)(b), for "£220" substitute "£265".

    (4) In Part I of Schedule 1 (general provisions)

      (a) in paragraphs 4(1) and 6(2), for "£220" substitute "£265"; and

      (b) in paragraphs 7, 7A] and 7B, for "£110" substitute "£135".

      (c) for paragraph 15(2) substitute

        " (2) Where an application is for outline planning permission and relates to development which is within more than one of the categories specified in that table, the fee payable in respect of the application shall be:

          (a) where the site area does not exceed 2.5 hectares, £265 for each 0.1 hectare of the site area;

          (b) where the site area exceeds 2.5 hectares £6,625, and an additional £80 for each 0.1 hectare in excess of 2.5 hectares, subject to a maximum in total of £25,000.".

    (5) For Part II of Schedule 1 (scale of fees), substitute the new Part II set out in Schedule 1 to these Regulations.

    (6) For Schedule 2 (scale of fees for advertisement applications), substitute the new Schedule 2 set out in Schedule 2 to these Regulations

THE TOWN AND COUNTRY PLANNING (FEES FOR APPLICATIONS AND DEEMED APPLICATIONS) (AMENDMENT) (ENGLAND) REGULATIONS 2005

PART II: SCALE OF FEES

Category of development	Fee payable

I. Operations
  1. The erection of dwellinghouses (other than development within category 6 below).
	(a) Where the application is for outline planning permission and -
	  (i) the site area does not exceed 2.5 hectares, £265 for each 0.1 hectare of the site area;
	  (ii) the site area exceeds 2.5 hectares, £6,625 and an additional £80 for each 0.1 hectare in excess of 2.5 hectares, subject to a maximum in total of £25,000.
	
	(b) in other cases -
	  (i) where the number of dwellinghouses to be created by the development is 50 or fewer, £265 for each dwellinghouse;
	
	  (ii) where the number of dwellinghouses to be created by the development exceeds 50, £13,250, and an additional £80 for each dwellinghouse in excess of 50 dwellinghouses, subject to a maximum in total of £50,000.

2. The erection of buildings (other than buildings in categories 1,3,4,5 or 7).	(a) Where the application is for outline planning permission and -
	  (i) the site area does not exceed 2.5 hectares, £265 for each 0.1 hectare of the site area;
	
	  (ii) the site area exceeds 2.5 hectares, £6,625, and an additional £80 for each 0.1 hectare in excess of 2.5 hectares, subject to a maximum in total of £25,000.
	
	(b) in other cases -
	  (i) where no floor space is to be created by the development, £135;
	
	  (ii) where the area of gross floor space to be created by the development does not exceed 40 square metres, £135;
	
	  (iii) where the area of the gross floor space to be created by the development exceeds 40 square metres, but does not exceed 75 square metres, £265;
	
	  (iv) where the area of the gross floor space to be created by the development exceeds 75 square metres, but does not exceed 3750 square metres, £265 for each 75 square metres of that area;
	
	  (v) where the area of gross floor space to be created by the development exceeds 3750 square metres, £13,250, and an additional £80 for each 75 square metres in excess of 3750 square metres, subject to a maximum in total of £50,000.

THE TOWN AND COUNTRY PLANNING (FEES FOR APPLICATIONS AND DEEMED APPLICATIONS) (AMENDMENT) (ENGLAND) REGULATIONS 2005

Category of development	Fee payable
3. The erection, on land used for the purposes of agriculture, of buildings to be used for agricultural purposes (other than buildings in category 4).	(a) Where the application is for outline planning permission and - (i) the site area does not exceed 2.5 hectares, £265 for each 0.1 hectare of the site area; (ii) the site area exceeds 2.5 hectares, £6,625, and an additional £80 for each additional 0.1 hectare in excess of 2.5 hectares, subject to a maximum in total of £25,000. (b) in other cases - (i) where the area of gross floor space to be created by the development does not exceed 465 square metres, £50; (ii) where the area of gross floor space to be created by the development exceeds 465 square metres but does not exceed 540 square metres, £265; (iii) where the area of the gross floor space to be created by the development exceeds 540 square metres but does not exceed 4215 square metres, £265 for the first 540 square metres, and an additional £265 for each 75 square metres in excess of 540 square metres; and (iv) where the area of gross floor space to be created by the development exceeds 4215 square metres, £13,250, and an additional £80 for each 75 square metres in excess of 4215 square metres, subject to a maximum in total of £50,000.
4. The erection of glasshouses on land used for the purposes of agriculture.	(a) Where the gross floor space to be created by the development does not exceed 465 square metres, £50; (b) where the gross floor space to be created by the development exceeds 465 square metres, £1,495.
5. The erection, alteration or replacement of plant or machinery.	(a) Where the site area does not exceed 5 hectares, £265 for each 0.1 hectare of the site area; (b) where the site area exceeds 5 hectares, £13,250, and an additional £80 for each 0.1 hectare in excess of 5 hectares, subject to a maximum in total of £50,000.
6. The enlargement, improvement or other alteration of existing dwellinghouses.	(a) Where the application relates to one dwellinghouse, £135; (b) where the application relates to 2 or more dwellinghouses, £265.

THE TOWN AND COUNTRY PLANNING (FEES FOR APPLICATIONS AND DEEMED APPLICATIONS) (AMENDMENT) (ENGLAND) REGULATIONS 2005

Category of development	Fee payable
7. (a) The carrying out of operations (including the erection of a building) within the curtilage of an existing dwellinghouse, for purposes ancillary to the enjoyment of the dwellinghouse as such, or the erection or construction of gates, fences, walls or other means of enclosure along a boundary of the curtilage of an existing dwellinghouse; or (b) the construction of carparks, service roads and other means of access on land used for the purposes of a single undertaking, where the development is required for a purpose incidental to the existing use of the land.	£135.
8. The carrying out of any operations connected with exploratory drilling for oil or natural gas.	(a) Where the site area does not exceed 7.5 hectares, £265 for each 0.1 hectares of the site area; (b) where the site area exceeds 7.5 hectares, £19,875, and an additional £80 for each 0.1 hectare in excess of 7.5 hectares, subject to a maximum in total of £50,000.
9. The carrying out of any operations not coming within any of the above categories.	(a) In the case of operations for the winning and working of minerals - 　　(i) where the site area does not exceed 15 hectares, £135 for each 0.1 hectare of the site area; 　　(ii) where the site area exceeds 15 hectares, £20,250, and an additional £80 for each 0.1 hectare in excess of 15 hectares, subject to a maximum in total of £50,000; (b) in any other case, £135 for each 0.1 hectare of the site area, subject to a maximum of £1,350.
II. Uses of land **10.** The change of use of a building to use as one or more separate dwellinghouses.	(a) Where the change of use is from a previous use as a single dwellinghouse to use as two or more single dwellinghouses- 　　(i) where the change of use is to use as 50 or fewer dwellinghouses, £265 for each additional dwellinghouse; 　　(ii) where the change of use is to use as more than 50 dwellinghouses £13,250, and an additional £80 for each dwellinghouse in excess of 50 dwellinghouses, subject to a maximum in total of £50,000; (b) in all other cases- 　　(i) where the change of use is to use as 50 or fewer dwellinghouses, £265 for each dwellinghouse; 　　(ii) where the change of use is to use as more than 50 dwellinghouses £13,250, and an additional £80 for each dwellinghouse in excess of 50 dwellinghouses, subject to a maximum in total of £50,000.

THE TOWN AND COUNTRY PLANNING (FEES FOR APPLICATIONS AND DEEMED APPLICATIONS) (AMENDMENT) (ENGLAND) REGULATIONS 2005

Category of development	Fee payable
11. (a) The use of land for the disposal of refuse or waste materials or for the deposit of material remaining after minerals have been extracted from land; or (b) for use of land for the storage of minerals in the open.	(a) Where the site area does not exceed 15 hectares, £135 for each 0.1 hectare of the site area; (b) where the site area exceeds 15 hectares £20,250, and an additional £80 for each 0.1 hectare in excess of 15 hectares, subject to a maximum in total of £50,000.
12. The making of a material change in the use of a building or land (other than a material change of use coming within any of the above categories).	£265.

SCHEDULE 2

SCALE OF FEES IN RESPECT OF APPLICATIONS FOR CONSENT TO DISPLAY ADVERTISEMENTS

Category of advertisement	Fee payable
1. Advertisements displayed on business premises, on the forecourt of business premises or on other land within the curtilage of business premises, wholly with reference to all or any of the following matters: (a) the nature of the business or other activity carried out on the premises; (b) the goods sold or the services provided on the premises; or (c) the name and qualifications of the person carrying on such business or activity or supplying such goods or services.	£75.
2. Advertisements for the purpose of directing members of the public to, or otherwise drawing attention to the existence of, business premises which are in the same locality as the site on which the advertisement is to be displayed but which are not visible from that site.	£75.
3. All other advertisements.	£265.

THE BUILDING (LOCAL AUTHORITY CHARGES) REGULATIONS 1998

Author's Note:

On the 31st July 1998 the Minister for Construction, announced his intention of improving the flexibility with which local authorities responsible for building control in England and Wales could respond to competition from the private sector by devolving to individual authorities the setting of charges for building control functions carried out in respect of the Building Regulations 1991.

The Building (Local Authority Charges) Regulations 1998 (the Charges Regulations) require each local authority to prepare a Scheme within which they are to fix their charges. They came into effect on the 1st April 1999. In a number of major cities, uniform levels of fees have been adopted. In some local authorities charges have fallen a third in comparison to those prescribed within the 1991 Regulations. A number of authorities have adopted the Local Government Association (LGA) Model Fee Scheme 2000, which is for local authority distribution only.

Consultation should be made to each local authority for their Charges, however as guidance we have kindly been given permission by the London Borough of Ealing to publish the Charges for their district, which includes Acton W3.

CHARGE SCHEDULES

With effect from 1st April 2002, there are three main charge Schedule Tables:

Table 1, For erection of one or more small new domestic buildings and connected work, ie. houses and flats up to 3 storeys in height with an internal floor area not exceeding 300 m²;

Table 2, For erection of certain small domestic building, and extensions, ie detached garages and carports not exceeding 40 m² and not exempt, and extensions including all new loft conversions up to a total of 60 m² at the same time;

Table 3, For building work other than where Tables 1 and 2 apply. Charges relate to estimated cost of the works.

EXEMPTIONS

No fees are charged, where we are satisfied **work** is **solely** for the purpose of providing means of access **for disabled persons** or within a building, or for providing facilities designed to secure greater health, safety, welfare or convenience and is carried out in relation to a building to which members of the public are admitted or is a dwelling occupied by a disabled person.

CHARGE BANDS

Charges, based upon the Total Estimated Costs of the Works, vary from one local authority to another, based on the following bands. Readers should approach the relevant local authority to ascertain their charge rates for projects under consideration. Under table 3, we have shown the published fees for projects in Ealing up to £100,000.

No.	Band	Fee up to bottom of band value	Example calculation for extra value
i.	Up to £100,000	£120	(see table)
ii.	£100,001 to £1,000,000	£1,032	£3.52 per £1,000
iii.	£1,000,001 to £10,000,000	£4,200	£2.59 per £1,000
iv.	Over £10,000,000	£27,510	£1.65 per £1,000

THE BUILDING (LOCAL AUTHORITY CHARGES) REGULATIONS 1998

TABLE 1

CHARGES FOR ERECTION OF ONE OF MORE SMALL NEW DOMESTICBUILDINGS AND CONNECTED WORK

Building Notice submissions are mainly for residential/small domestic where the full **Charge** must be paid at time of notification. These are mainly used for small domestic alterations and not house extensions. Where structural work is involved calculations need to be provided. Upon satisfactory completion of works on site a Completion Certificate may be issued.

NOTES

Table 1 is no longer a separate table and now refers users to Tables 2 and 3.
Dwellings in excess of 300 m² in floor area (excluding garage or carport) are to be calculated on estimated cost on accordance with Table 3.
Buildings in excess of 3 storeys (including any basements) to be calculated on estimated cost in accordance with Table 3.

The Charges in this table includes for works of drainage in connection with erection of a building(s), even where those drainage works are commenced in advance of the plans for the building being deposited.
The charges include for an integral garage and where a garage or carport shares at least one wall of the domestic building. Detached garages are not included in this Table (see Notes Table 2).
Where a Plan or Inspection Charge exceeds £5,000.00 the Council may agree payment in instalments.

Where all dwellings on a site or an estate are substantially the same, it may be possible to offer a discount of 30% reduction on PLAN Charge OR equivalent reduction on the BUILDING NOTICE Charge.

TABLE 2

CHARGES FOR ERECTION OF CERTAIN SMALL DOMESTIC BUILDINGS, GARAGES, CARPORTS AND EXTENSIONS

Table 2: Flat Rate Charges

	Charge £	VAT £	Total £
Detached garages or carport with floor area under 40m²	157.50	27.56	185.06
Detached garages or carport between 40m² & 60m² floor area	283.50	49.61	333.11
Extension's of a dwelling with floor area under 10m²	283.50	49.61	333.11
Extension's of a dwelling with floor area between 10m² & 40m²	413.70	72.40	486.10
Extension's of a dwelling with floor area between 40m² & 60m²	539.70	94.45	634.15

NOTES

Detached garages and carports having an internal floor area not exceeding 30 m² are 'exempt buildings', providing that in the case of a garage it is sited at least 1.0 m away from the boundary or is constructed substantially of non-combustible materials.
A carport extension having an internal floor area not exceeding 30 m² would be exempt if it is fully open on at least 2 sides.

THE BUILDING (LOCAL AUTHORITY CHARGES) REGULATIONS 1998

Detached garages in excess of 40 m² and extensions in excess of 60 m² in floor area use Table 3.
A new Dormer Windows which does not increase the usable floor area would be an alteration so use Table 3.
If the total floor area of all extensions being done at the same time exceeds 60 m² use Table 3.
Loft conversions with new internal useable floor area in roof space are to be treated as an extension in this Table 2.
Extensions more than three storeys high (including any basement) should use Table 3.
Chargeable installations of Cavity Fill Insulation, and Unvented Hot Water Systems should use Table 3 (see Table 3 notes).
Extensions to a building that is **NOT wholly domestic** should use **Table 3**.

Where on an estate erections of garages or extensions are substantially the same, it may be possible to offer a discount of 30% reduction on PLAN Charge OR a 7½% reduction on the BUILDING NOTICE Charge.

TABLE 3

CHARGES FOR BUILDING WORK OTHER THAN TO WHICH TABLES 1 AND 2 APPLY.
CHARGES RELATE TO ESTIMATED COST.

Full Plan applications apply to designated use projects, where the **Plan Charge,** equivalent to 25% of the **Full Charge** must be paid in the deposit of plans. A subsequent re-submission, further to a Rejection of Plans, will NOT attract an additional fee for essentially the same work. If the inspection charge is not paid upon the deposit of plans, an invoice will be raised after the first inspection on site as this is when **Inspection Charge** becomes payable. Where work is to be done to Shops, Factories, Offices, Railway Premises, Hotels and Boarding Houses, and Non-domestic Workplaces a Full Application should be made. It is also appropriate for Domestic Loft Conversions and other Extensions and Erections of Domestic Buildings. It is important to start work before 3 years have expired or the Plan Approval may be withdrawn. Upon satisfactory completion of the works on site a Completion Certificate may be issued.

See Table 3 example, for applications up to £100,000, on following page

NOTES

If some building work is covered by Table 2 and some by Table 3, both fees are payable.
Estimated cost of work should not include any professional fees (e.g. Architect, Quantity Surveyor, etc) nor any VAT.
Installation of cavity fill insulation in accordance with Part D of Schedule 1 to the Principle Regulations where installation is not certified to an approved standard or is not installed by an approved installer, or is part of a larger project this Table Building Notice Charge is payable.
Installation of an unvented hot water system in accordance with Part G3 of Schedule 1 to the Principle Regulations where the installation is not part of a larger project and where the authority carry out an inspection, this Table Building Notice Charge is payable.

If application is for erection of work substantially the same type under current regulations, it may be possible to offer a discount of PLAN CHARGE by 30% OR BUILDING NOTICE Charge by 7½%.

Fees for Professional Services

THE BUILDING (LOCAL AUTHORITY CHARGES) REGULATIONS 1998

TABLE 3 EXAMPLE: Total Estimated Cost of Works – up to £100,000

	Charge	VAT	Total		Charge	VAT	Total
*2,000 or less	120.00	21.00	141.00	52,001 to 53,000	618.40	108.22	726.62
*2,001 to 5,000	187.00	32.73	219.73	53,001 to 54,000	627.20	109.76	736.96
5,001 to 6,000	192.00	33.60	225.60	54,001 to 55,000	636.00	111.30	747.30
6,001 to 7,000	200.00	35.00	235.00	55,001 to 56,000	644.80	112.84	757.64
7,001 to 8,000	212.00	37.10	249.10	56,001 to 57,000	653.60	114.38	767.98
8,001 to 9,000	220.00	38.50	258.50	57,001 to 58,000	662.40	115.92	778.32
9,001 to 10,000	232.00	40.60	272.60	58,001 to 59,000	671.20	117.46	788.66
10,001 to 11,000	240.00	42.00	282.00	59,001 to 60,000	680.00	119.00	799.00
11,001 to 12,000	252.00	44.10	296.10	60,001 to 61,000	688.80	120.54	809.34
12,001 to 13,000	260.00	45.50	305.50	61,001 to 62,000	697.60	122.08	819.68
13,001 to 14,000	268.00	46.90	314.90	62,001 to 63,000	706.40	123.62	830.02
14,001 to 15,000	280.00	49.00	329.00	63,001 to 64,000	715.20	125.16	840.36
15,001 to 16,000	292.00	51.10	343.10	64,001 to 65,000	724.00	126.70	850.70
16,001 to 17,000	300.00	52.50	352.50	65,001 to 66,000	732.80	128.24	861.04
17,001 to 18,000	312.00	54.60	366.60	66,001 to 67,000	741.60	129.78	871.38
18,001 to 19,000	320.00	56.00	376.00	67,001 to 68,000	750.40	131.32	881.72
19,001 to 20,000	328.00	57.40	385.40	68,001 to 69,000	759.20	132.86	892.06
20,001 to 21,000	336.80	58.94	395.74	69,001 to 70,000	768.00	134.40	902.40
21,001 to 22,000	345.60	60.48	406.08	70,001 to 71,000	776.80	135.94	912.74
22,001 to 23,000	354.40	62.02	416.42	71,001 to 72,000	785.60	137.48	923.08
23,001 to 24,000	363.20	63.56	426.76	72,001 to 73,000	794.40	139.02	933.42
24,001 to 25,000	372.00	65.10	437.10	73,001 to 74,000	803.20	140.56	943.76
25,001 to 26,000	380.80	66.64	447.44	74,001 to 75,000	812.00	142.10	954.10
26,001 to 27,000	389.60	68.18	457.78	75,001 to 76,000	820.80	143.64	964.44
27,001 to 28,000	398.40	69.72	468.12	76,001 to 77,000	829.60	145.18	974.78
28,001 to 29,000	407.20	71.26	478.46	77,001 to 78,000	838.40	146.72	985.12
29,001 to 30,000	416.00	72.80	488.80	78,001 to 79,000	847.20	148.26	995.46
30,001 to 31,000	424.80	74.34	499.14	79,001 to 80,000	856.00	149.80	1005.80
31,001 to 32,000	433.60	75.88	509.48	80,001 to 81,000	864.80	151.34	1016.14
32,001 to 33,000	442.40	77.42	519.82	81,001 to 82,000	873.60	152.88	1026.48
33,001 to 34,000	451.20	78.96	530.16	82,001 to 83,000	882.40	154.42	1036.82
34,001 to 35,000	460.00	80.50	540.50	83,001 to 84,000	891.20	155.96	1047.16
35,001 to 36,000	468.80	82.04	550.84	84,001 to 85,000	900.00	157.50	1057.50
36,001 to 37,000	477.60	83.58	561.18	85,001 to 86,000	908.80	159.04	1067.84
37,001 to 38,000	486.40	85.12	571.52	86,001 to 87,000	917.60	160.58	1078.18
38,001 to 39,000	495.20	86.66	581.86	87,001 to 88,000	926.40	162.12	1088.52
39,001 to 40,000	504.00	88.20	592.20	88,001 to 89,000	935.20	163.66	1098.86
40,001 to 41,000	512.80	89.74	602.54	89,001 to 90,000	944.00	165.20	1109.20
41,001 to 42,000	521.60	91.28	612.88	90,001 to 91,000	952.80	166.74	1119.54
42,001 to 43,000	530.40	92.82	623.22	91,001 to 92,000	961.60	168.28	1129.88
43,001 to 44,000	539.20	94.36	633.56	92,001 to 93,000	970.40	169.82	1140.22
44,001 to 45,000	548.00	95.90	643.90	93,001 to 94,000	979.20	171.36	1150.56
45,001 to 46,000	556.80	97.44	654.24	94,001 to 95,000	988.00	172.90	1160.90
46,001 to 47,000	565.60	98.98	664.58	95,001 to 96,000	996.80	174.44	1171.24
47,001 to 48,000	574.40	100.52	674.92	96,001 to 97,000	1005.60	175.98	1181.58
48,001 to 49,000	583.20	102.06	685.26	97,001 to 98,000	1014.40	177.52	1191.92
49,001 to 50,000	592.00	103.60	695.60	98,001 to 99,000	1023.20	179.06	1202.26
50,001 to 51,000	600.80	105.14	705.94	99,001 to 100,000	1032.00	180.60	1212.60
51,001 to 52,000	609.60	106.68	716.28				

Daywork and Prime Cost

When work is carried out which cannot be valued in any other way it is customary to assess the value on a cost basis with an allowance to cover overheads and profit. The basis of costing is a matter for agreement between the parties concerned, but definitions of prime cost for the building industry have been prepared and published jointly by the Royal Institution of Chartered Surveyors and the National Federation of Building Trades Employers (now the Building Employers Confederation) for the convenience of those who wish to use them. These documents are reproduced on the following pages with the permission of the Royal Institution of Chartered Surveyors, which owns the copyright.

The daywork schedule published by the Civil Engineering Contractors Association is included in the A & B's companion title, *"Spons Civil Engineering and Highway Works Price Book"*.

For larger Prime Cost contracts the reader is referred to the form of contract issued by the Royal Institute of British Architects.

BUILDING INDUSTRY

DEFINITION OF PRIME COST OF DAYWORK CARRIED OUT UNDER A BUILDING CONTRACT (DECEMBER 1975 EDITION)

This definition of Prime Cost is published by the Royal Institution of Chartered Surveyors and the National Federation of Building Trades Employers, for convenience and for use by people who choose to use it. Members of the National Federation of Building Trades Employers are not in any way debarred from defining Prime Cost and rendering their accounts for work carried out on that basis in any way they choose. Building owners are advised to reach agreement with contractors on the Definition of Prime Cost to be used prior to issuing instructions.

SECTION 1 - APPLICATION

1.1.   This definition provides a basis for the valuation of daywork executed under such building contracts as provide for its use (e.g. contracts embodying the Standard Forms issued by the Joint Contracts Tribunal).

1.2.   It is not applicable in any other circumstances, such as jobbing or other work carried out as a separate or main contract, nor in the case of daywork executed during the Defects Liability Period of contracts embodying the above mentioned Standard Forms.

SECTION 2 - COMPOSITION OF TOTAL CHARGES

2.1.   The prime cost of daywork comprises the sum of the following costs:
    (a)   Labour as defined in Section 3.
    (b)   Material and goods as defined in Section 4.
    (c)   Plant as defined in Section 5.

2.2.   Incidental costs, overheads and profit as defined in Section 6, as provided in the building contract and expressed therein as percentage adjustments are applicable to each of 2.1 (a)-(c).

Daywork and Prime Cost

BUILDING INDUSTRY

SECTION 3 - LABOUR

3.1.   The standard wage rates, emoluments and expenses referred to below and the standard working hours referred to in 3.2 are those laid down for the time being in the rules or decisions of the National Joint Council for the Building Industry and the terms of the Building and Civil Engineering Annual and Public Holiday Agreements applicable to the works, or the rules or decisions or agreements of such body, other than the National Joint Council for the Building Industry, as may be applicable relating to the class of labour concerned at the time when and in the area where the daywork is executed.

3.2.   Hourly base rates for labour are computed by dividing the annual prime cost of labour, based upon standard working hours and as defined in 3.4 (a)-(l), by the number of standard working hours per annum.

3.3.   The hourly rates computed in accordance with 3.2 shall be applied in respect of the time spent by operatives directly engaged on daywork, including those operating mechanical plant and transport and erecting and dismantling other plant (unless otherwise expressly provided in the building contract).

3.4.   The annual prime cost of labour comprises the following:

    (a)   Guaranteed minimum weekly earnings (e.g. Standard Basic Rate of Wages, Joint Board Supplement and Guaranteed Minimum Bonus Payment in the case of NJCBI rules).

    (b)   All other guaranteed minimum payments (unless included in Section 6).

    (c)   Differentials or extra payments in respect of skill, responsibility, discomfort, inconvenience or risk (excluding those in respect of supervisory responsibility - see 3.5).

    (d)   Payments in respect of public holidays.

    (e)   Any amounts which may become payable by the Contractor to or in respect of operatives arising from the operation of the rules referred to in 3.1 which are not provided for in 3.4 (a)-(d) or in Section 6.

    (f)   Employer's National Insurance contributions applicable to 3.4 (a)-(e).

    (g)   Employer's contributions to annual holiday credits.

    (h)   Employer's contributions to death benefit scheme.

    (i)   Any contribution, levy or tax imposed by statute, payable by the contractor in his capacity as an employer.

3.5.   **Note:**   Differentials or extra payments in respect of supervisory responsibility are excluded from the annual prime cost (see Section 6). The time of principals, foremen, gangers, leading hands and similar categories, when working manually, is admissible under this Section at the appropriate rates for the trades concerned.

SECTION 4 - MATERIALS AND GOODS

4.1.   The prime cost of materials and goods obtained from stockists or manufacturers is the invoice cost after deduction of all trade discounts but including cash discounts not exceeding 5 per cent and includes the cost of delivery to site.

4.2.   The prime cost of materials and goods supplied from the Contractor's stock is based upon the current market prices plus any appropriate handling charges.

4.3.   Any Value Added Tax which is treated, or is capable of being treated, as input tax (as defined in the Finance Act, 1972) by the Contractor is excluded.

BUILDING INDUSTRY

SECTION 5 - PLANT

5.1.   The rates for plant shall be as provided in the building contract.

5.2.   The costs included in this Section comprise the following:

    (a)   Use of mechanical plant and transport for the time employed on daywork.
    (b)   Use of non-mechanical plant (excluding non-mechanical hand tools) for the time employed on daywork.

5.3.   **Note:**   The use of non-mechanical hand tools and of erected scaffolding, staging, trestles or the like is excluded (see Section 6).

SECTION 6 - INCIDENTAL COSTS, OVERHEADS AND PROFIT

6.1.   The percentage adjustments provided in the building contract, which are applicable to each of the totals of Sections 3, 4 and 5, comprise the following:

    (a)   Head Office charges.
    (b)   Site staff, including site supervision.
    (c)   The additional cost of overtime (other than that referred to in 6.2).
    (d)   Time lost due to inclement weather.
    (e)   The additional cost of bonuses and all other incentive payments in excess of any guaranteed minimum included in 3.4. (a).
    (f)   Apprentices study time.
    (g)   Subsistence and periodic allowances.
    (h)   Fares and travelling allowances.
    (i)   Sick pay or insurance in respect thereof.
    (j)   Third-party and employers' liability insurance.
    (k)   Liability in respect of redundancy payments to employees.
    (l)   Employers' National Insurance contributions not included in Section 3.4.
    (m)   Tool allowances.
    (n)   Use, repair and sharpening of non-mechanical hand tools.
    (o)   Use of erected scaffolding, staging, trestles or the like.
    (p)   Use of tarpaulins, protective clothing, artificial lighting, safety and welfare facilities, storage and the like that may be available on the site.
    (q)   Any variation to basic rates required by the Contractor in cases where the building contract provides for the use of a specified schedule of basic plant charges (to the extent that no other provision is made for such variation).
    (r)   All other liabilities and obligations whatsoever not specifically referred to in this Section nor chargeable under any other Section.
    (s)   Profit.

6.2.   **Note:**   The additional cost of overtime, where specifically ordered by the Architect/Supervising Officer shall only be chargeable in the terms of prior written agreement between the parties to the building contract.

BUILDING INDUSTRY

Example of calculation of typical standard hourly base rate (as defined in Section 3) for NJCBI building craftsman and labourer in Grade A areas at 1st July, 1975.

		Rate £	Craftsman £	Rate £	Labourer £
Guaranteed minimum weekly earnings					
Standard Basic Rate	49 wks	37.00	1813.00	31.40	1538.60
Joint Board Supplement	49 wks	5.00	245.00	4.20	205.80
Guaranteed Minimum Bonus	49 wks	4.00	196.00	3.60	176.40
			2254.00		1920.00
Employer's National Insurance Contribution at 8.5%			191.59		163.27
			2445.59		2084.07
Employer's Contribution to :					
CITB annual levy			15.00		3.00
Annual holiday credits	49 wks	2.80	137.20	2.80	137.20
Public holidays (included in guaranteed minimum weekly earnings above)					
Death benefit scheme	49 wks	0.10	4.90	0.10	4.90
Annual labour cost as defined in section 3		£	**2602.69**	£	**2229.17**

Hourly rate of labour as defined in section 3, Clause 3.02 (Annual cost/hours per annum) $\dfrac{2602.69}{1904}$ **= £ 1.37** $\dfrac{2229.17}{1904}$ **= £ 1.17**

Note:

1.   Standard working hours per annum calculated as follows:

52 weeks @ 39 hours		2080
Less		
3 weeks holiday @ 40 hours	120	
7 days public holidays @ 8 hours	56	-176
		1904

2.   It should be noted that all labour costs incurred by the Contractor in his capacity as an employer other than those contained in the hourly rate, are to be taken into account under section 6.

3.   The above example is for the convenience of users only and does not form part of the Definition; all basic costs are subject to re-examination according to the time when and in the area where the daywork is executed.

BUILDING INDUSTRY

For the convenience of readers the example which appears on the previous page has been updated by the Editors for London and Liverpool rates as at 27 June, 2005.

		Rate £	Craftsman £	Rate £	Labourer £
Guaranteed minimum weekly earnings					
Standard Basic Rate	46.2 wks	351.00	16,216.20	264.03	12,198.19
Guaranteed minimum bonus	46.2 wks	0.00	0.00	0.00	0.00
			16,216.20		12,198.19
Employer's National Insurance Contribution			1,500.48		986.18
(12.8% after the first £91.01 pre week)					
Employer's Contribution to :					
CITB annual levy at 0.50% of payroll			91.26		68.65
Holiday pay	4.2 wks	351.00	1,474.20	264.03	1,108.93
Public holidays	1.6 wks	351.00	561.60	264.03	422.45
Retirement cover scheme (Death and accident cover is provided free)	52.0 wks	3.50	182.00	3.50	182.00

Annual labour cost as defined in section 3	£ **20,025.74**	£ **14,966.40**
	20,025.74	14,966.40
Hourly rate of labour as defined in section 3,	1904 = **£11.11**	1904 = **£8.31**
Clause **3.02 (Annual cost/hours per annum)**		

Note:

1. Calculated following Definition of Prime Cost of Daywork carried out under a Building Contract, published by the Royal Institution of Chartered Surveyors and the Construction Confederation.

2. Standard basic rate effective from 27 June 2005.

3. Standard working hours per annum calculated as follows

52 weeks @ 39 hours		2028.00
Less		
4.2 weeks holiday @ 39 hours	163.8	
8 days public holidays @ 7.8 hours	62.4	-226.2
		1801.8

4. All labour costs incurred by the Contractor in his capacity as an employer other than those contained in the hourly rate, are to be taken into account under Section 6.

5. The above examples is for guidance only and does not form part of the Definition; all the basic costs are subject to re-examination according to the time when and in the area where the daywork is executed.

6. All N.I. payments are at non-contracted out rates applicable from 5 April 2005.

7. In basic rate & GMB 47.8 wks = 52.0 working - 4.2 annual holidays.

BUILDING INDUSTRY

DEFINITION OF PRIME COST OF BUILDING WORKS OF A JOBBING OR MAINTENANCE CHARACTER (1980 EDITION)

This definition of Prime Cost is published by the Royal Institution of Chartered Surveyors and the National Federation of Building Trades Employers, for convenience and for use by people who choose to use it. Members of the National Federation of Building Trades Employers are not in any way debarred from defining Prime Cost and rendering their accounts for work carried out on that basis in any way they choose. Building owners are advised to reach agreement with contractors on the Definition of Prime Cost to be used prior to issuing instructions.

SECTION 1 - APPLICATION

1.1.   This definition provides a basis for the valuation of work of a jobbing or maintenance character executed under such building contracts as provide for its use.

1.2.   It is not applicable in any other circumstances, such as daywork executed under or incidental to a building contract.

SECTION 2 - COMPOSITION OF TOTAL CHARGES

2.1.   The prime cost of jobbing work comprises the sum of the following costs:

(a)	Labour as defined in Section 3.
(b)	Materials and goods as defined in Section 4.
(c)	Plant, consumable stores and services as defined in Section 5.
(d)	Sub-contracts as defined in Section 6.

2.2.   Incidental costs, overhead and profit as defined in Section 7 and expressed as percentage adjustments are applicable to each of 2.1 (a)-(d).

SECTION 3 - LABOUR

3.1.   Labour costs comprise all payments made to or in respect of all persons directly engaged upon the work, whether on or off the site, except those included in Section 7.

3.2.   Such payments are based upon the standard wage rates, emoluments and expenses as laid down for the time being in the rules or decisions of the National Joint Council for the Building Industry and the terms of the Building and Civil Engineering Annual and Public Holiday Agreements applying to the works, or the rules of decisions or agreements of such other body as may relate to the class of labour concerned, at the time when and in the area where the work is executed, together with the Contractor's statutory obligations, including:

(a)	Guaranteed minimum weekly earnings (e.g. Standard Basic Rate of Wages and Guaranteed Minimum Bonus Payment in the case of NJCBI rules).
(b)	All other guaranteed minimum payments (unless included in Section 7).
(c)	Payments in respect of incentive schemes or productivity agreements applicable to the works.
(d)	Payments in respect of overtime normally worked; or necessitated by the particular circumstances of the work; or as otherwise agreed between the parties.
(e)	Differential or extra payments in respect of skill, responsibility, discomfort or inconvenience.
(f)	Tool allowance.
(g)	Subsistence and periodic allowances.
(h)	Fares, travelling and lodging allowances.
(j)	Employer's contributions to annual holiday credits.
(k)	Employer's contributions to death benefit schemes.
(l)	Any amounts which may become payable by the Contractor to or in respect of operatives arising from the operation of the rules referred to in 3.2 which are not provided for in 3.2 (a)-(k) or in Section 7.

BUILDING INDUSTRY

(m)   Employer's National Insurance contributions and any contribution, levy or tax imposed by statute, payable by the Contractor in his capacity as employer.

Note:

Any payments normally made by the Contractor which are of a similar character to those described in 3.2 (a)-(c) but which are not within the terms of the rules and decisions referred to above are applicable subject to the prior agreement of the parties, as an alternative to 3.2 (a)-(c).

3.3.   The wages or salaries of supervisory staff, timekeepers, storekeepers, and the like, employed on or regularly visiting site, where the standard wage rates, etc., are not applicable, are those normally paid by the Contractor together with any incidental payments of a similar character to 3.2 (c) - (k).

3.4.   Where principals are working manually their time is chargeable, in respect of the trades practised, in accordance with 3.2.

SECTION 4 - MATERIALS AND GOODS

4.1.   The prime cost of materials and goods obtained by the Contractor from stockists or manufacturers is the invoice cost after deduction of all trade discounts but including cash discounts not exceeding 5 per cent, and includes the cost of delivery to site.

4.2.   The prime cost of materials and goods supplied from the Contractor's stock is based upon the current market prices plus any appropriate handling charges.

4.3.   The prime cost under 4.1 and 4.2 also includes any costs of:

(a)   non-returnable crates or other packaging.
(b)   returning crates and other packaging less any credit obtainable.

4.4.   Any Value Added Tax which is treated, or is capable of being treated, as input tax (as defined in the Finance Act, 1972 or any re-enactment thereof) by the Contractor is excluded.

SECTION 5 - PLANT, CONSUMABLE STORES AND SERVICES

5.1.   The prime cost of plant and consumable stores as listed below is the cost at hire rates agreed between the parties or in the absence of prior agreement at rates not exceeding those normally applied in the locality at the time when the works are carried out, or on a use and waste basis where applicable:

(a)   Machinery in workshops.
(b)   Mechanical plant and power-operated tools.
(c)   Scaffolding and scaffold boards.
(d)   Non-mechanical plant excluding hand tools.
(e)   Transport including collection and disposal of rubbish.
(f)   Tarpaulins and dust sheets.
(g)   Temporary roadways, shoring, planking and strutting, hoarding, centering, formwork, temporary fans, partitions or the like.
(h)   Fuel and consumable stores for plant and power-operated tools unless included in 5.1 (a), (b), (d) or (e) above.
(j)   Fuel and equipment for drying out the works and fuel for testing mechanical services.

BUILDING INDUSTRY

5.2.   The prime cost also includes the net cost incurred by the Contractor of the following services, excluding any such cost included under Sections 3, 4 or 7:

    (a)   Charges for temporary water supply including the use of temporary plumbing and storage.

    (b)   Charges for temporary electricity or other power and lighting including the use of temporary installations.

    (c)   Charges arising from work carried out by local authorities or public undertakings.

    (d)   Fees, royalties and similar charges.

    (e)   Testing of materials.

    (f)   The use of temporary buildings including rates and telephone and including heating and lighting not charged under (b) above.

    (g)   The use of canteens, sanitary accommodation, protective clothing and other provision for the welfare of persons engaged in the work in accordance with the current Working Rule Agreement and any Act of Parliament, statutory instrument, rule, order, regulation or bye-law.

    (h)   The provision of safety measures necessary to comply with any Act of Parliament.

    (j)   Premiums or charges for any performance bonds or insurances which are required by the Building Owner and which are not referred to elsewhere in this Definition.

SECTION 6 - SUB-CONTRACTS

6.1.   The prime cost of work executed by sub-contractors, whether nominated by the Building Owner or appointed by the Contractor, is the amount which is due from the Contractor to the sub-contractors in accordance with the terms of the sub-contracts after deduction of all discounts except any cash discount offered by any sub-contractor to the Contractor not exceeding 2.5%.

SECTION 7 - INCIDENTAL COSTS, OVERHEADS AND PROFIT

7.1.   The percentage adjustments provided in the building contract, which are applicable to each of the totals of Sections 3-6, provide for the following:

    (a)   Head Office charges.

    (b)   Off-site staff including supervisory and other administrative staff in the Contractor's workshops and yard.

    (c)   Payments in respect of public holidays.

    (d)   Payments in respect of apprentices' study time.

    (e)   Sick pay or insurance in respect thereof.

    (f)   Third party employer's liability insurance.

    (g)   Liability in respect of redundancy payments made to employees.

    (h)   Use, repair and sharpening of non-mechanical hand tools.

    (j)   Any variations to basic rates required by the Contractor in cases where the building contract provides for the use of a specified schedule of basic plant charges (to the extent that no other provision is made for such variation).

    (k)   All other liabilities and obligations whatsoever not specifically referred to in this Section nor chargeable under any other section.

    (l)   Profit.

BUILDING INDUSTRY

SPECIMEN ACCOUNT FORMAT

If this Definition of Prime Cost is followed the Contractor's account could be in the following format:

£

Labour (as defined in Section 3)
  Add ____ % (see Section 7)

Materials and goods (as defined in Section 4)
  Add ____ % (see Section 7)

Plant, consumable stores and services
(as defined in Section 5)
  Add ____ % (see Section 7)

Sub-contracts (as defined in Section 6)
  Add ____ % (see Section 7)   _____

£ _____

VAT to be added if applicable.

SCHEDULE OF BASIC PLANT CHARGES (1st MAY 2001 ISSUE)

This Schedule is published by the Royal Institution of Chartered and is for use in connection with Dayworks under a Building Contract.

EXPLANATORY NOTES

1. The rates in the Schedule are intended to apply solely to daywork carried out under and incidental to a Building Contract. They are NOT intended to apply to:
  (i) Jobbing or any other work carried out as a main or separate contract; or
  (ii) Work carried out after the date of commencement of the Defects Liability Period.

2. The rates apply only to plant and machinery already on site, whether hired or owned by the Contractor.

3. The rates, unless otherwise stated, include the cost of fuel and power of every description, lubricating oils, grease, maintenance, sharpening of tools, replacement of spare parts, all consumable stores and for licences and insurances applicable to items of plant.

4. The rates, unless otherwise stated, do not include the costs of drivers and attendants.

5. The rates are base costs and may be subject to the overall adjustment for price movement, overheads and profit, quoted by the Contractor prior to the placing of the Contract.

6. The rates should be applied to the time during which the plant is actually engaged in daywork.

7. Whether or not plant is chargeable on daywork depends on the daywork agreement in use and the inclusion of an item of plant in this schedule does not necessarily indicate that the item is chargeable.

8. Rates for plant not included in the Schedule or which is not already on site and is specifically provided or hired for daywork shall be settled at prices which are reasonably related to the rates in the Schedule having regard to any overall adjustment quoted by the Contractor in the Conditions of Contract.

Daywork and Prime Cost

BUILDING INDUSTRY

MECHANICAL PLANT AND TOOLS			Rate per
Item of plant	Size/Rating	Unit	Hour £
PUMPS			
Mobile Pumps			
Including pump hoses, values and strainers etc.			
Diaphragm	50 mm diameter	Each	0.87
Diaphragm	76 mm diameter	Each	1.29
Submersible	50 mm diameter	Each	1.18
Induced Flow	50 mm diameter	Each	1.54
Induced Flow	76 mm diameter	Each	2.05
Centrifugal self priming	50 mm diameter	Each	1.96
Centrifugal self priming	102 mm diameter	Each	2.52
Centrifugal self priming	152 mm diameter	Each	3.87
SCAFFOLDING, SHORING, FENCING			
Complete Scaffolding			
Mobile working towers, single width	1.80 m x 0.80 m x 7.00 m high	Each	2.00
Mobile working towers, single width	1.80 m x 0.80 m x 9.00 m high	Each	2.80
Mobile working towers, double width	1.80 m x 1.40 m x 7.00 m high	Each	2.15
Mobile working towers, double width	1.80 m x 1.40 m x 15.00 m high	Each	5.10
Chimney scaffold, single unit		Each	1.79
Chimney scaffold, twin unit		Each	2.05
Chimney scaffold, four unit		Each	3.59
Trestles			
Trestle, adjustable	Any height	Pair	0.10
Trestle, painters	1.80 m high	Pair	0.21
Trestle, painters	2.40 m high	Pair	0.26
Shoring, Planking and Strutting			
'Acrow' adjustable prop	Sizes up to 4.90 m (open)	Each	0.10
'Strong boy' support attachment		Each	0.15
Adjustable trench struts	Sizes up to 1.67m (open)	Each	0.10
Trench sheet		Metre	0.01
Backhole trench box		Each	1.00
Temporary Fencing			
Including block and coupler			
Site fencing steel grid panel	3.50 m x 2.00 m	Each	0.08
Anti-climb site steel grid fence panel	3.50 m x 2.00 m	Each	0.08
LIFTING APPLIANCES AND CONVEYORS			
Cranes			
<u>Mobile Cranes</u>			
Rates are inclusive of drivers			
Lorry mounted, telescopic jib			
Two wheel drive	6 tonnes	Each	24.40
Two wheel drive	7 tonnes	Each	25.00
Two wheel drive	8 tonnes	Each	25.62
Two wheel drive	10 tonnes	Each	26.90
Two wheel drive	12 tonnes	Each	28.25
Two wheel drive	15 tonnes	Each	29.66
Two wheel drive	18 tonnes	Each	31.14
Two wheel drive	20 tonnes	Each	32.70
Two wheel drive	25 tonnes	Each	34.33

BUILDING INDUSTRY

Item of plant	Size/Rating	Unit	Rate per Hour £
Cranes – cont'd			
Mobile cranes – cont'd			
Rates are inclusive of divers			
Lorry mounted telescopic jib – cont'd			
Four wheel drive	10 tonnes	Each	27.44
Four wheel drive	12 tonnes	Each	28.81
Four wheel drive	15 tonnes	Each	30.25
Four wheel drive	20 tonnes	Each	33.35
Four wheel drive	25 tonnes	Each	35.19
Four wheel drive	30 tonnes	Each	37.12
Four wheel drive	45 tonnes	Each	39.16
Four wheel drive	50 tonnes	Each	41.32

Track-mounted tower crane

Rates are inclusive of divers

Note: Capacity equals maximum lift in Tonnes times maximum radius at which it Can be lifted

Item of plant	Capacity (Metre/tonnes) Up to	Height under hook above Ground (m) Up to	Unit	Rate per Hour £
Tower crane	10	17	Each	7.99
Tower crane	15	17	Each	8.59
Tower crane	20	18	Each	9.18
Tower crane	25	20	Each	11.56
Tower crane	30	22	Each	13.78
Tower crane	40	22	Each	18.09
Tower crane	50	22	Each	22.20
Tower crane	60	22	Each	24.32
Tower crane	70	22	Each	23.00
Tower crane	80	22	Each	25.91
Tower crane	110	22	Each	26.45
Tower crane	125	30	Each	29.38
Tower crane	125	30	Each	32.35

Static tower cranes

Rates inclusive of driver

To be charged at 90% of the above rates for tower mounted tower cranes

Crane Equipment

Item of plant	Size/Rating	Unit	Rate per Hour £
Mucking tipping skip	Up to 0.25 m³	Each	0.56
Muck tipping skip	0.5 m³	Each	0.67
Muck tipping skip	0.75 m³	Each	0.82
Muck tipping skip	1.00 m³	Each	1.03
Muck tipping skip	1.50 m³	Each	1.18
Muck tipping skip	2.00 m³	Each	1.38
Mortar skips	Up to 0.38 m³	Each	0.41
Boat skips	1.00 m³	Each	1.08
Boat skips	1.50 m³	Each	1.33
Boat skips	2.00 m³	Each	1.59
Concrete skips, hand levered	0.50 m³	Each	1.00
Concrete skips, hand levered	0.75 m³	Each	1.10
Concrete skips, hand levered	1.00 m³	Each	1.25
Concrete skips, hand levered	1.50 m³	Each	1.50
Concrete skips, hand levered	2.00 m³	Each	1.65

Daywork and Prime Cost

BUILDING INDUSTRY

LIFTING APPLIANCES AND CONVEYORS – cont'd			Rate per
Item of plant	Size/Rating	Unit	Hour £

Cranes – cont'd

Static tower cranes – cont'd

Rates are inclusive of driver – cont'd

To be charged at 90% of the above rates

For tower mounted tower cranes – cont'd

	Size/Rating	Unit	Rate per Hour £
Crane Equipment – cont'd			
Concrete skips, geared	0.50 m³	Each	1.30
Concrete skips, geared	0.75 m³	Each	1.40
Concrete skips, geared	1.00 m³	Each	1.55
Concrete skips, geared	1.50 m³	Each	1.80
Concrete skips, geared	2.00 m³	Each	2.05
Hoists			
Scaffold hoists	200 kg	Each	1.92
Rack and pinion (goods only)	500 kg	Each	3.31
Rack and pinion (goods only)	1100 kg	Each	4.28
Rack and pinion goods and passenger	15 person, 1200 kg	Each	5.62
Wheelbarrow chain sling		Each	0.31
Conveyors			
Belt conveyors			
Conveyor	7.50 m long x 400 mm wide	Each	6.41
Miniveyor, control box and loading hopper	3.00 m unit	Each	3.59
Other Conveying Equipment			
Wheelbarrow		Each	0.21
Hydraulic superlift		Each	2.95
Pavac slab lifter		Each	1.03
Hand pad and hose attachment		Each	0.26
Lifting Trucks			
Fork lift	Payload	Maximum Lift	
Fork lift, two wheel drive	1100 kg	up to 3.00 m	Each	4.87
Fork lift, two wheel drive	2540 kg	up to 3.70 m	Each	5.12
Fork lift, two wheel drive	1524 kg	up to 6.00 m	Each	6.04
Fork lift, two wheel drive	2600 kg	up to 5.40 m	Each	7.69
Lifting Platforms			
Hydraulic platform (Cherry picker)	7.50 m	Each	4.23
Hydraulic platform (Cherry picker)	13.00 m	Each	9.23
Scissors lift	7.80 m	Each	7.56
Telescopic handlers	7.00 m, 2 tonne	Each	7.18
Telescopic handlers	13.00 m, 3 tonne	Each	8.72
Lifting and Jacking Gear			
Pipe winch including gantry	1.00 tonne	Sets	1.92
Pipe winch including gantry	3.00 tonne	Sets	3.21
Chain block	1.00 tonne	Each	0.45
Chain block	2.00 tonne	Each	0.71
Chain block	5.00 tonne	Each	1.22
Pull lift (Tirfor winch)	1.00 tonne	Each	0.64
Pull lift (Tirfor winch)	1.60 tonne	Each	0.90
Pull lift (Tirfor winch)	3.20 tonne	Each	1.15
Brother or chain slings, two legs	not exceeding 4.20 tonnes	Set	0.35
Brother or chain slings, two legs	not exceeding 5.50 tonnes	Set	0.45
Brother or chain slings, four legs	not exceeding 3.10 tonnes	Set	0.41
Brother or chain slings, four legs	not exceeding 11.20 tonnes	Set	1.28

BUILDING INDUSTRY

CONSTRUCTION VEHICLES			Rate per
Item of plant	**Size/Rating**	**Unit**	**Hour £**
Lorries			
Plated lorries			
Rates are inclusive of driver			
Platform lorries	7.50 tonnes	Each	19.00
Platform lorries	17.00 tonnes	Each	21.00
Platform lorries	24.00 tonnes	Each	26.00
Platform lorries with winch and skids	7.50 tonnes	Each	21.40
Platform lorries with crane	17.00 tonnes	Each	27.50
Platform lorries with crane	24.00 tonnes	Each	32.10
Tipper Lorries			
Rates are inclusive of driver			
Tipper lorries	15.00/17.00 tonnes	Each	19.50
Tipper lorries	24.00 tonnes	Each	21.40
Tipper lorries	30.00 tonnes	Each	27.10
Dumpers			
Site use only (excluding tax, insurance			
and extra cost of DEFV etc. when			
operating on highway)	Makers capacity		
Two wheel drive	0.80 tonnes	Each	1.20
Two wheel drive	1.00 tonnes	Each	1.30
Two wheel drive	1.20 tonnes	Each	1.60
Four wheel drive	2.00 tonnes	Each	2.50
Four wheel drive	3.00 tonnes	Each	3.00
Four wheel drive	4.00 tonnes	Each	3.50
Four wheel drive	5.00 tonnes	Each	4.00
Four wheel drive	6.00 tonnes	Each	4.50
Dumper Trucks			
Rates are inclusive of drivers			
Dumper trucks	10.00/13.00 tonnes	Each	20.00
Dumper trucks	18.00/20.00 tonnes	Each	20.40
Dumper trucks	22.00/25.00 tonnes	Each	26.30
Dumper trucks	35.00/40.00 tonnes	Each	36.60
Tractors			
<u>Agricultural Type</u>			
Wheeled, rubber-clad tyred			
Light	48 h.p.	Each	4.65
Heavy	65 h.p.	Each	5.15
<u>Crawler Tractors</u>			
With bull or angle dozer	80/90 h.p.	Each	21.40
With bull or angle dozer	115/130 h.p.	Each	25.10
With bull or angle dozer	130/150 h.p.	Each	26.00
With bull or angle dozer	155/175 h.p.	Each	27.74
With bull or angle dozer	210/230 h.p.	Each	28.00
With bull or angle dozer	300/340 h.p.	Each	31.10
With bull or angle dozer	400/440 h.p.	Each	46.90
With loading shovel	0.80 m³	Each	25.00
With loading shovel	1.00 m³	Each	28.00
With loading shovel	1.20 m³	Each	32.00
With loading shovel	1.40 m³	Each	36.00
With loading shovel	1.80 m³	Each	45.00

Daywork and Prime Cost

BUILDING INDUSTRY

CONSTRUCTION VEHICLES – cont'd

Item of plant	Size/Rating	Unit	Rate per Hour £
Light vans			
Ford escort or the like		Each	4.74
Ford transit or the like	1.00 tonnes	Each	6.79
Luton Box Van or the like	1.80 tonnes	Each	8.33
Water/Fuel Storage			
Mobile water container	110 litres	Each	0.28
Water bowser	1100 litres	Each	0.55
Water bowser	3000 litres	Each	0.74
Mobile fuel container	110 litres	Each	0.28
Fuel bowser	1100 litres	Each	0.65
Fuel bowser	3000 litres	Each	1.02
EXCAVATIONS AND LOADERS			
Excavators			
Wheeled, hydraulic	7.00/10.00 tonnes	Each	12.00
Wheeled, hydraulic	11.00/13.00 tonnes	Each	12.70
Wheeled, hydraulic	15.00/16.00 tonnes	Each	14.80
Wheeled, hydraulic	17.00/18.00 tonnes	Each	16.70
Wheeled, hydraulic	20.00/23.00 tonnes	Each	14.70
Crawler, hydraulic	12.00/14.00 tonnes	Each	12.00
Crawler, hydraulic	15.00/17.50 tonnes	Each	14.00
Crawler, hydraulic	20.00/23.00 tonnes	Each	16.00
Crawler, hydraulic	25.00/30.00 tonnes	Each	21.00
Crawler, hydraulic	30.00/35.00 tonnes	Each	30.00
Mini excavators	1000/1500 kg	Each	4.50
Mini excavators	2150/2400 kg	Each	5.50
Mini excavators	2700/3500 kg	Each	6.50
Mini excavators	3500/4500 kg	Each	8.50
Mini excavators	4500/6000 kg	Each	9.50
Loaders			
Wheeled skip loader		Each	4.50
Shovel loaders, four wheel drive	1.60 kg	Each	12.00
Shovel loaders, four wheel drive	2.40 kg	Each	19.00
Shovel loaders, four wheel drive	3.60 kg	Each	22.00
Shovel loaders, four wheel drive	4.40 kg	Each	23.00
Shovel loaders, crawlers	0.80 kg	Each	11.00
Shovel loaders, crawlers	1.20 kg	Each	14.00
Shovel loaders, crawlers	1.60 kg	Each	16.00
Shovel loaders, crawlers	2.00 kg	Each	17.00
Skid steer loaders wheeled	300/400 kg payload	Each	6.00
Excavator Loaders			
Wheeled tractor type with black-hoe			
Excavator			
Four wheel drive	2.50/3.50 tonnes	Each	7.00
Four wheel drive, 2 wheel steer	7.00/8.00 tonnes	Each	9.00
Four wheel drive, 4 wheel steer	7.00/8.00 tonnes	Each	10.00
Crawler, hydraulic	12 tonnes	Each	20.00
Crawler, hydraulic	20 tonnes	Each	16.00
Crawler, hydraulic	30 tonnes	Each	35.00
Crawler, hydraulic	40 tonnes	Each	38.00

BUILDING INDUSTRY

COMPACTION EQUIPMENT			Rate per
Item of plant	**Size/Rating**	**Unit**	**Hour £**
Attachments			
Breakers for excavators		Each	7.50
Breakers for mini excavators		Each	3.60
Breakers for back-hoe excavator/loaders		Each	6.00
Rollers			
Vibrating roller	368 – 430 kg	Each	1.68
Single roller	533 kg	Each	1.92
Single roller	750 kg	Each	2.41
Twin roller	698 kg	Each	1.93
Twin roller	851 kg	Each	2.41
Twin roller with seat and steering wheel	1067 kg	Each	3.03
Twin roller with seat and steering wheel	1397 kg	Each	3.17
Pavement rollers	3.00 – 4.00 tonnes dead weight	Each	3.18
Pavement rollers	4.00 – 6.00 tonnes	Each	4.13
Pavement rollers	6.00 – 10.00 tonnes	Each	4.84
Rammers			
Tamper rammer 2 stoke-petrol	225 mm – 275 mm	Each	1.59
Soil Compactors			
Plate compactor	375 mm – 400 mm	Each	1.20
Plate compactor rubber pad	375 mm – 1400 mm	Each	0.33
Plate compactor reversible plate-petrol	400 mm	Each	2.20
CONCRETE EQUIPEMENT			
Concrete/Mortar Mixers			
Open drum without hopper	0.90/0.06 m³	Each	0.62
Open drum without hopper	0.12/0.09 m³	Each	0.68
Open drum without hopper	0.15/0.10 m³	Each	0.72
Open drum with hopper	0.20/0/15 m³	Each	0.80
Concrete/Mortar Transport Equipment			
Concrete pump including hose, valve and couplers			
Lorry mounted concrete pump	23 m maximum distance	Each	36.00
Lorry mounted concrete pump	50 m maximum distance	Each	46.00
Concrete Equipment			
Vibrator, poker, petrol type	Up to 75 mm diameter	Each	1.62
Air vibrator (excluding compressor and hose)	Up to 75 mm diameter	Each	0.79
Extra poker heads	25/36/60 mm diameter	Each	0.77
Vibrating Screed unit with beam	5.00 m	Each	1.77
Vibrating Screed unit with adjusting beam	3.00 – 5.00 m	Each	2.18
Power float	725 mm – 900 mm	Each	1.72
Power grouter		Each	0.92
TESTING EQUIPMENT			
Pipe Testing Equipment			
Pressure testing pump, electric		Sets	1.87
Pipe pressure testing equipment, hydraulic		Sets	2.46
Pressure test pump		Sets	0.64

BUILDING INDUSTRY

SITE ACCOMODATION AND TEMPORARY SERVICES

Item of plant	Size/Rating	Unit	Rate per Hour £
Heating equipment			
Space heaters – propane	80,000 Btu/hr	Each	0.77
Space heaters – propane/electric	125,000 Btu/hr	Each	1.56
Space heaters – propane/electric	250,000 Btu/hr	Each	1.79
Space heaters – propane	125,000 Btu/hr	Each	1.33
Space heaters – propane	260,000 Btu/hr	Each	1.64
Cabinet headers		Each	0.41
Cabinet heater catalytic		Each	0.46
Electric halogen heaters		Each	1.28
Ceramic heaters	3kW	Each	0.79
Fan heaters	3kW	Each	0.41
Cooling fan		Each	1.15
Mobile cooling unit – small		Each	1.38
Mobile cooling unit – large		Each	1.54
Air conditioning unit		Each	2.62
Site Lighting and Equipment			
Tripod floodlight	500W	Each	0.36
Tripod floodlight	1000W	Each	0.34
Towable floodlight	4 x 1000W	Each	2.00
Hand held floodlight	500W	Each	0.22
Rechargeable light		Each	0.62
Inspection light		Each	0.15
Plasterers light		Each	0.56
Lighting mast		Each	0.92
Festoon light string	33.00 m	Each	0.31
Site Electrical Equipment			
Extension leads	240V/14.00 m	Each	0.20
Extension leads	110V/14.00 m	Each	0.20
Cable reel	25.00 m 110V/240V	Each	0.28
Cable reel	50.00 m 110V240V	Each	0.33
4 way junction box	110V	Each	0.17
Power Generating Units			
Generator – petrol	2kVA	Each	1.08
Generator – silenced petrol	2kVA	Each	1.54
Generator – petrol	3kVA	Each	1.38
Generator – diesel	5kVA	Each	1.92
Generator – silenced diesel	8kVA	Each	3.59
Generator – silenced diesel	15kVA	Each	7.69
Trail adaptor	240V	Each	0.20
Transformers			
Transformer	3kVA	Each	0.36
Transformer	5kVA	Each	0.51
Transformer	7.50kVA	Each	0.82
Transformer	10kVA	Each	0.87
Rubbish Collection and Disposal Equipment			
Rubbish Chutes			
Standard plastic module	1.00 m section	Each	0.18
Steel liner insert		Each	0.26
Steel top hopper		Each	0.20
Plastic side entry hopper		Each	0.20

BUILDING INDUSTRY

Item of plant	Size/Rating	Unit	Rate per Hour £
Plastic side entry hopper line		Each	0.20
Dust Extraction Plant			
Dust extraction unit, light duty		Each	1.03
Dust extraction unit, heavy duty		Each	1.64
SITE EQUIPMENT			
Welding Equipment			
Arc-(Electric) Complete With Leads			
Welder generator – petrol	200 amp	Each	2.26
Welder generator – diesel	300/350 amp	Each	3.33
Welder generator – diesel	400 amp	Each	4.74
Extra welding lead sets		Each	0.29
Gas-Oxy Welder			
Welding and cutting set (including oxygen And acetylene, excluding underwater Equipment and thermic boring)			
Small		Each	1.41
Large		Each	2.00
Mig welder		Each	1.00
Fume extractor		Each	0.92
Road Works Equipment			
Traffic lights, main/generator	2-way	Set	4.01
Traffic lights, main/generator	3-way	Set	7.92
Traffic lights, main/generator	4-way	Set	9.81
Traffic lights, main/generator – trailer Mounted	2-way	Set	3.98
Flashing light		Each	0.20
Road safety cone	450 mm	10	0.26
Safety cone	750 mm	10	0.38
Safety barrier plank	1.25 m	Each	0.03
Safety barrier plank	2.00 m	Each	0.04
Road sign		Each	0.26
DPC Equipment			
Damp proofing injection machine		Each	1.49
Cleaning Equipment			
Vacuum cleaner (industrial wet) single motor		Each	0.62
Vacuum cleaner (industrial wet) twin motor		Each	1.23
Vacuum cleaner (industrial wet) triple motor		Each	1.44
Vacuum cleaner (industrial wet) back Pack		Each	0.97
Pressure washer, light duty, electric	1450 PSI	Each	0.97
Pressure washer, heavy duty, diesel	2500 PSI	Each	2.69
Cold pressure washer, electric		Each	1.79
Hot pressure washer, petrol		Each	2.92
Cold pressure washer, petrol		Each	2.00
Sandblast attachment to last washer		Each	0.54
Drain cleaning attachment to last washer		Each	0.31
Surface Preparation Equipment			
Rotavators	5 h.p.	Each	1.67

BUILDING INDUSTRY

SITE EQUIPMENT – cont'd			**Rate per**
Item of plant	**Size/Rating**	**Unit**	**Hour £**
Scrabbler, up to three heads		Each	1.15
Scrabbler, pole		Each	1.50
Scrabbler, multi-headed floor		Each	4.00
Floor preparation machine		Each	2.82
Compressors and Equipment			
Portable Compressors			
Compressors – electric	0.23 m³/min	Each	1..59
Compressors – petrol	0.28 m³/min	Each	1.74
Compressors – petrol	0.71 m³/min	Each	2.00
Compressors – diesel	up to 2.83 m³/min	Each	1.24
Compressors – diesel	up to 3.68 m³/min	Each	1.49
Compressors – diesel	up to 4.25 m³/min	Each	1.60
Compressors – diesel	up to 4.81 m³/min	Each	1.92
Compressors – diesel	up to 7.64 m³/min	Each	3.08
Compressors – diesel	up to 11.32 m³/min	Each	4.23
Compressors – diesel	up to 18.40 m³/min	Each	5.73
Mobile Compressors			
Lorry mounted compressors	2.86 – 4.24 m³/min	Each	12.50
(machine plus lorry only)			
Tractor mounted compressors	2.86 – 3.40 m³/min	Each	13.50
(machine plus rubber tyred tractor			
Accessories (Pneumatic Tools)			
(with and including up to 15.00 m of air			
hose)			
Demolition pick		Each	1.03
Breakers (with six steels) light	up to 150 kg	Each	0.79
Breakers (with six steels) medium	295 kg	Each	1.08
Breakers (with six steels) heavy	386 kg	Each	1.44
Rock drill (for use with compressor)			
Hand held		Each	0.90
Additional hoses	15.00 m	Each	0.16
Muffer, tool silencer		Each	0.14
Breakers			
Demolition hammer drill, heavy duty,			
Electric		Each	1.00
Road breaker, electric		Each	1.65
Road breaker, 2 stroke, petrol		Each	2.05
Hydraulic breaker unit, light duty, petrol		Each	2.05
Hydraulic breaker unit, heavy duty, petrol		Each	2.60
Hydraulic breaker unit, heavy duty, diesel		Each	2.95
Quarrying and Tooling Equipment			
Block and stone splitter, hydraulic	600 mm x 600 mm	Each	1.35
Block and stone splitter, manual		Each	1.10
Steel Reinforcement Equipment			
Bar bending machine – manual	up to 13 mm diameter rods	Each	0.90
Bar bending machine – manual	up to 20 mm diameter rods	Each	1.28
Bar bending machine – electric	up to 38 mm diameter rods	Each	2.82
Bar bending machine – electric	up to 40 mm diameter rods	Each	3.85
Bar bending machine – electric	up to 13 mm diameter rods	Each	1.54
Bar bending machine – electric	up to 20 mm diameter rods	Each	2.05
Bar bending machine – electric	up to 40 mm diameter rods	Each	2.82
Bar bending machine – 3 phase	up to 40 mm diameter rods	Each	3.85

BUILDING INDUSTRY

Item of plant	Size/Rating	Unit	Rate per Hour £
Dehumidifiers			
110/240v Water	68 litres extraction per 24 hours	Each	1.28
110/240v Water	90 litres extraction per 24 hours	Each	1.85
SMALL TOOLS			
Saws			
Masonry saw bench	350 mm – 500 mm diameter	Each	2.80
Floor saw	350 mm diameter, 125 mm max. cut	Each	1.90
Floor saw	450 mm diameter, 150 mm max. cut	Each	2.60
Floor saw, reversible	Max. Cut 300 mm	Each	13.00
Chop/cut saw, electric	350 mm diameter	Each	1.33
Circular saw, electric	230 mm diameter	Each	0.60
Tyrannosaw		Each	1.20
Reciprocating saw		Each	0.60
Door trimmer		Each	0.90
Chainsaw, petrol	500 mm	Each	2.13
Full chainsaw safety kit		Each	0.50
Working jig		Each	0.60
Pipework Equipment			
Pipe bender	15 mm – 22 mm	Each	0.33
Pipe bender, hydraulic	50 mm	Each	0.60
Pipe bender, electric	50 mm – 150 mm diameter	Each	1.35
Pipe cutter, hydraulic		Each	1.84
Tripod pipe vice		Set	0.40
Ratchet threader	12 mm – 32 mm	Each	0.55
Pipe threading machine, electric	12 mm – 75 mm	Each	2.40
Pipe threading machine, electric	12 mm – 100 mm	Each	3.00
Impact wrench, electric		Each	0.54
Impact wrench, two stroke, petrol		Each	4.49
Impact wrench, heavy duty, electric		Each	1.13
Plumber's furnace, calor gas or similar		Each	2.16
Hand-held Drills and equipment			
Impact or hammer drill	Up to 25 mm diameter	Each	0.50
Impact or hammer drill	35 mm diameter	Each	0.90
Angle heads drill		Each	0.70
Stirrer, mixed drills		Each	0.70
Paint, Insulation Application Equipment			
Airless spray unit		Each	4.20
Portaspray unit		Each	1.65
HPVL turbine spray unit		Each	1.65
Compressor and spray gun		Each	2.20
Other Handtools			
Screwing machine	13 mm – 50 mm diameter	Each	0.77
Screwing machine	25 mm – 100 mm diameter	Each	1.57
Staple gun		Each	0.33
Air nail gun	110V	Each	3.33
Cartridge hammer		Each	1.00
Tongue and groove nailer complete			
With mallet		Each	0.93
Chasing machine	152 mm	Each	1.72
Chasing machine	76 mm – 203 mm	Each	5.99
Floor grinder		Each	3.00

BUILDING INDUSTRY

SMALL TOOLS – cont'd

Item of plant	Size/Rating	Unit	Rate per Hour £
Other Handtools – cont'd			
Floor plane		Each	3.67
Diamond concrete planer		Each	2.05
Autofeed screwdriver, electric		Each	1.13
Laminate trimmer		Each	0.64
Biscuit jointer		Each	0.87
Random orbital sander		Each	0.73
Floor sander		Each	1.33
Palm, delta, flap or belt sander		Each	0.38
Saw cutter, two strokes, petrol	300 mm	Each	1.26
Grinder, angle or cutter	Up to 225 mm	Each	0.60
Grinder, angle or cutter	300 mm	Each	1.10
Mortar raking tool attachment		Each	0.15
Floor/polish scrubber	325 mm	Each	1.03
Floor tile stripper		Each	1.74
Wallpaper stripper, electric		Each	0.56
Electric scraper		Each	0.51
Hot air paint stripper		Each	0.38
Electric diamond tile cutter	All sizes	Each	1.38
Hand tile cutter		Each	0.36
Electric needle gun		Each	1.08
Needle chipping gun		Each	0.72
Pedestrian floor sweeper	1.2 m wide	Each	0.87

Rates of Wages

BUILDING INDUSTRY - ENGLAND, WALES AND SCOTLAND

The Building and Civil Engineering Joint Negotiating Committee have agreed a new three year agreement on pay and conditions for building and civil engineering operatives.

The Working Rule Agreement includes a pay structure with a general operative and additional skilled rates of pay as well as craft rate. Plus rates and additional payments will be consolidated into basic pay to provide the following rates (for a normal 39 hour week) which will come into effect from the following dates:

Effective from 27 June 2005

The following basic rates of pay will apply:

	Rate per 39-hour week (£)	Rate per hour (£)
Craft Rate	351.00	9.00
Skill Rate 1	334.62	8.58
Skill Rate 2	322.14	8.26
Skill Rate 3	301.47	7.73
Skill Rate 4	284.31	7.29
General operative	264.03	6.77

Holidays with Pay and Benefits Schemes

The Building and Civil Engineering benefits scheme has unveiled a new holiday pay plan following the introduction of the Working Time Directive. From 2 August 1999 there are no fixed holiday credits, instead employers will calculate appropriate sums to fund operatives' holiday pay entitlement and make regular monthly payments into the B&CE scheme.

For full details contact B&CE on 01293 526911.

Employers contribution towards retirement benefit is paid at £2.50 per week, effective from August 2003.

Death and accident cover is provided free.

Young Labourers

Effective from 26 June 2000

The rates of wages for young labourers shall be the following proportions of the labourers' rates:

> At 16 years of age 50%*
> At 17 years of age 70%
> At 18 years of age 100%

* Note: Under the National Minimum Wage, this cannot be currently less than £3.00 per hour.

Apprentices/Trainees

The Construction Apprenticeship Scheme (CAS) operates throughout Great Britain from 1 August 1998 it is open to all young people from the age of 16 years. For further information telephone CAS helpline - 01485 578 333.

BUILDING INDUSTRY - ENGLAND, WALES AND SCOTLAND

Apprentice rates - effective from 27 June 2005

Please note that the rates below are for guidance only:

	Rate per 39-hour week (£)	Rate per hour (£)
Year 1	146.25	3.75
Year 2	188.76	4.84*
Year 3 without NVQ2	220.74	5.66
Year 3 With NVQ2	280.80	7.20
Year 3 With NVQ3	351.00	9.00
On Completion of Apprenticeship With NVQ2	351.00	9.00

* Note: If an apprentice is 22 years and over, and in his/her second year of training, then the National Minimum Wage of £4.85 per hour currently applies, and will increase to £5.05 per hour, as from 1 October 2005.

BUILDING AND ALLIED TRADES JOINT INDUSTRIAL COUNCIL

Authorised rates of wages in the building industry in England and Wales agreed by the Building and Allied Trades Joint Industrial Council.

Effective from 13 June 2005

Subject to the conditions prescribed in the Working Rule Agreement the standard weekly rates of wages shall be as follows:

	Rate per 39-hour week (£)	Rate per hour (£)
Craft operative (NQV3)	360.75	9.25
Craft operative (NQV2)	310.05	7.95
Adult general operative	265.20	6.80

ROAD HAULAGE WORKERS EMPLOYED IN THE BUILDING INDUSTRY

Authorised rates of pay for road haulage workers in the building industry recommended by the Builders Employers Confederation.

Effective from 27 June 2005

Employers

Construction Confederation
Union
56 - 64 Leonard Street
London
EC2A 4JX

Tel: 0207 608 5039
Fax: 0207 608 5001
E-mail: enquiries@constructionconfederation.co.uk

Operatives

The Transport and General Workers

Transport House
128 Theobold's Road
London
WC1X 8TN

Tel: 0207 611 2500
Fax: 0207 611 2555
E-mail: pgwu@tgwu.org.uk

£

Lorry Drivers (irrespective of the gross weight of the vehicle driven)   351.00

PLUMBING AND MECHANICAL ENGINEERING SERVICES INDUSTRY

PLUMBING AND MECHANICAL ENGINEERING SERVICES INDUSTRY

Authorised rates of wages agreed by the Joint Industry Board for the Plumbing and Mechanical Engineering Services Industry in England and Wales

Second part effective from 3 January 2005

The Joint Industry Board for Plumbing and Mechanical Engineering Services in England and Wales
Brook House
Brook Street
St Neots
Huntingdon
Cambridgeshire
PE19 2HW

Tel: 01480 476 925
Fax: 01480 403 081
E-mail: info@jib-pmes.org.uk

	Rate per hour 03/01/2005 £
Operatives	
Technical Plumber and Gas Service Technician	12.02
Advanced Plumber and Gas Service Engineer	10.82
Trained plumber and Gas Service Fitter	9.28
Apprentices (see Note below)*	
1st year of Training	4.51
2nd year of Training	5.16
3rd year of Training	5.82
3rd year of Training with NVQ Level 2	7.08
4th year of Training	7.16
4th year of Training with NVQ Level 2	8.13
4th year of Training with NVQ Level 3	8.99
Adult Trainees	
1st 6 months of Employment	7.25
2nd 6 months of Employment	7.76
3rd 6 months of Employment	8.10

* Note: Where Apprentices have achieved NVQs, the appropriate rate is payable from the date of attainment except that it shall not be any earlier than the commencement of the promulgated year of Training in which it applies.

Rates of Wages

PLUMBING AND MECHANICAL ENGINEERING SERVICES INDUSTRY

Authorised rates of wages agreed by the Joint Industry Board for the Plumbing Industry in Scotland and Northern Ireland.

Effective from 30th May 2005

The Joint Industry Board for the Plumbing Industry in Scotland and Northern Ireland
2 Walker Street
Edinburgh
EH3 7LB

Tel: 0131 225 2255
Fax: 0131 226 7638

	Rate per hour 30/05/2005 £
Operatives Plumbers & Gas Service Operatives	
Plumber and Gas Service Fitter	9.51
Advanced Plumber and Gas Service Engineer	10.82
Technician Plumber and Gas Service Technician	11.99
Plumbing Labourer	8.47
Apprentice Plumbers and Fitters	
1st Year Apprentice	2.75
2nd Year Apprentice	4.05
3rd Year Apprentice	4.94
4th Year Apprentice	6.38
Adult Trainees	
Year 1	5.03
Year 2	5.81
Year 3	7.24

PART III

Prices for Measured Works

This part of the book contains the following sections:

Prices for Measured Works
- Major Works

INTRODUCTION

The rates contained in "Prices for Measured Works - Major Works" are intended to apply to a project in the outer London area costing about £2,500,000 (including Preliminaries) and assume that reasonable quantities of all types of work are required. Similarly it has been necessary to assume that the size of the project warrants the sub-letting of all types of work normally sub-let. Adjustments should be made to standard rates for time, location, local conditions, site constraints and any other factors likely to affect costs of a specific scheme.

The distinction between builders' work and work normally sub-let is stressed because prices for work which can be sub-let may well be quite inadequate for the contractor who is called upon to carry out relatively small quantities of such work himself.

As explained in more detail later, Measured Works prices are generally based upon wage rates which came into force on 27 June 2005, and material costs from April/May 2005. Built-up prices include an allowance of 5% for overheads and 2½% for profit, whereas non-analysed sub-contractor prices only include mark-up of 2½% for profit. They do not allow for preliminary items that are dealt with under a separate heading (see page 87) or for any Value Added Tax.

The format of this section is so arranged that, in the case of work normally undertaken by the Main Contractor, the constituent parts of the total rate are shown enabling the reader to make such adjustments as may be required in particular circumstances. Similar details have also been given for work normally sub-let although it has not been possible to provide this in all instances.

As explained in the Preface, there is a facility available to readers, which enables a comparison to be made between the level of prices in this section and current tenders by means of a tender index. The tender index for this Major Works section of Spon's is 480 (as shown on the front cover) which is close to our forecast tender price index for the outer London region for the second quarter of 2006.

To adjust prices for other regions/times, the reader is recommended to refer to the explanations and examples on how to apply these tender indices, given on page 704.

There follow explanations and definitions of the basis of costs in the "Prices for Measured Work" section under the following headings:

- Overhead charges and profit
- Labour hours and Labour £ column
- Material £ column
- Material/Plant £ columns
- Total rate £ column

OVERHEAD CHARGES AND PROFIT

All rates checked against winning tenders include overhead charges and profit at current levels.

LABOUR HOURS AND LABOUR £ COLUMNS

"Labour rates" are based upon typical gang costs divided by the number of primary working operatives for the trade concerned, and for general building work include an allowance for trade supervision (see below). "Labour hours" multiplied by "Labour rate" with the appropriate addition for overhead charges and profit (currently zero) gives "Labour £". In some instances, due to variations in gangs used, "Labour rate" figures have not been indicated, but can be calculated by dividing "Labour £" by "Labour hours".

Building craft operatives and labourers

From 27 June 2005 guaranteed minimum weekly earnings in the London area for craft operatives and general operatives are £351.00 and £264.03 respectively; to these rates have been added allowances for the items below in accordance with the recommended procedure of the Institute of Building in its "Code of Estimating Practice". The resultant hourly rates on which the "Prices for Measured Work" have generally been based are £12.44 and £9.31 for craft operatives and labourers, respectively.

- Lost time
- Construction Industry Training Board Levy
- Holidays with pay
- Accidental injury, retirement and death benefits scheme
- Sick pay
- National Insurance
- Severance pay and sundry costs
- Employer's liability and third party insurance

NOTE: For travelling allowances and site supervision see "Preliminaries" section.

The table which follows illustrates how the "all-in" hourly rates referred to on page77 have been calculated. Productive time has been based on a total of 1954 hours worked per year.

			Craft Operatives		General Operatives	
			£	£	£	£
Wages at standard basic rate						
productive time	44.30wks	351.00	15,547.86	264.03	11,695.45	
Lost time allowance	0.904wks	351.00	317.30	264.03	238.68	
Non-productive overtime	5.80 wks	526.50	3,053.70	396.05	2,297.06	
			18,918.86		14,231.19	
Extra payments under						
National Working Rules	45.2 wks		-		-	
Sick Pay	1 wk		-		-	
CITB Allowance (0.50% of payroll)	1 year		106.73		80.29	
Holiday pay	4.20 wks	418.56	1,757.95	314.85	1,322.37	
Public Holiday pay	1.60 wks	418.56	669.70	314.85	503.76	
Employer's contribution to retirement cover scheme (death and accident cover is provided free)	52.0 wks	3.50	182.00	3.50	182.00	
National Insurance (average weekly payment)	48 wks	38.42	1,844.16	25.92	1,244.16	
			23,479.41		17,563.77	
Severance pay and sundry costs	Plus	1.5%	352.19	1.5%	263.46	
			23,831.60		17,827.23	
Employer's Liability and Third Party Insurance						
	Plus	2.0%	476.63	2.0%	356.54	
Total cost per annum			**£24,308.23**		**£18,183.77**	
Total cost per hour			**£12.44**		**£9.31**	

NOTES:

1 Absence due to sickness has been assumed to be for periods not exceeding 3 days for which no payment is due (Working Rule 20.7.3).

2 EasyBuild Stakeholder Pension effective from 1 July 2002. Death and accident benefit cover is provided free of charge. Taken as £3.50/week average as range increased for 2005 wage award

3 All N.I. Payments are at not-contracted out rates applicable from April 2005. National Insurance is paid for 48 complete weeks (52wks-4.2wks) is based on employer making regular monthly payments into the Template holiday pay scheme and by doing so the employer achieves National Insurance savings on holiday wages.

The "labour rates" used in the Measured Work sections have been based on the following gang calculations which generally include an allowance for supervision by a foreman or ganger. Alternative labour rates are given showing the effect of various degrees of bonus.

Gang	Total Gang rate £/hour	Productive unit rate £/hour	Alternative labour rates £/hour			
			Normal	+5%	+15%	+25%
Groundwork Gang						
1 Ganger	1 x 10.04 =	10.04				
6 Labourers	6 x 9.31 =	55.86				
		65.90	÷ 6.5 =	10.14	10.65	11.70	12.73
Concreting gang						
1 Foreman	1 x 13.17 =	13.17				
4 Skilled Labourers	4 x 10.04 =	40.16				
		53.33	÷ 4.5 =	11.85	12.45	13.67	14.87
Steelfixing Gang						
1 Foreman	1 x 13.17 =	13.17				
4 Steelfixers	4 x 12.44 =	49.76				
		62.93	÷ 4.5 =	13.98	14.70	16.12	17.55
Formwork Gang						
1 Foreman	1 x 13.17 =	13.17				
10 Carpenters	10 x 12.44 =	124.40				
1 Labourer	1 x 9.31 =	9.31				
		146.88	÷ 10.5 =	13.99	14.71	16.13	17.55
Bricklaying/Lightweight Blockwork Gang						
1 Foreman	1 x 13.17 =	13.17				
6 Bricklayers	6 x 12.44 =	74.64				
4 Labourers	4 x 9.31 =	37.24				
		125.05	÷ 6.5 =	19.24	20.22	22.18	24.14
Dense Blockwork Gang						
1 Foreman	1 x 13.17 =	13.17				
6 Bricklayers	6 x 12.44 =	74.64				
6 Labourers	6 x 9.31 =	55.86				
		143.67	÷ 6.5 =	22.10	23.23	25.49	27.74
Carpentry/Joinery Gang						
1 Foreman	1 x 13.17 =	13.17				
5 Carpenters	5 x 12.44 =	62.20				
1 Labourer	1 x 9.31 =	9.31				
		84.68	÷ 5.5 =	15.40	16.19	17.75	19.32
Craft Operative (Painter, Wall and Floor Tiler, Slater)	1 x 12.44 =	12.44	÷ 1 =	12.44	13.08	14.34	15.61
1 and 1 Gang						
1 Craft Operative	1 x 12.44 =	12.44				
1 Skilled Labourer	1 x 10.04 =	10.04				
		22.48	÷ 1 =	22.48	23.63	25.92	28.21
2 and 1 Gang						
2 Craft Operatives	2 x 12.44 =	24.88				
1 Skilled Labourer	1 x 10.04 =	10.04				
		34.92	÷ 2 =	17.46	18.36	20.13	21.91
Small Labouring Gang (making good)						
1 Foreman	1 x 13.17 =	13.17				
4 Skilled Labourers	4 x 10.04 =	40.16				
		53.33	÷ 4.5 =	11.85	12.45	13.67	14.87
Drain Laying Gang/Clayware						
2 Skilled Labourers	2 x 10.04 =	20.08	÷ 2 =	10.04	10.55	11.58	12.60

Sub-Contractor's operatives
Similar labour rates are shown in respect of sub-let trades where applicable.

Plumbing operatives
From 3 January 2005 the hourly earnings for technical and trained plumbers are £12.02 and £9.28, respectively; to these rates have been added allowances similar to those added for building operatives (see below). The resultant average hourly rate on which the "Prices for Measured Work" have been based is £14.79. The items referred to above for which allowance has been made are:

Tool allowance
Plumbers' welding supplement
Holidays with pay
Pension and welfare stamp
National Insurance "contracted out"
Severance pay and sundry costs
Employer's liability and third party insurance

No allowance has been made for supervision as we have assumed the use of a team of technical or trained plumbers who are able to undertake such relatively straightforward plumbing works, e.g. on housing schemes, without supervision.

The table which follows shows how the average hourly rate referred to above has been calculated. Productive time has been based on a total of 1912.50 hours worked per year.

			Technical Plumber		Trained Plumber	
			£	£	£	£
Wages at standard basic rate						
productive time	1687.5hrs	12.02		20,283.75	9.28	15,660.00
Overtime (paid at standard basic rate)	226.0hrs	12.02		2,704.50	9.28	2,088.00
Overtime	0.0hrs	18.03		0.00	13.92	0.00
Plumber's welding supplement (gas and arc)	1912.4hrs	0.46		879.75		0.00
				23,868.00		17,748.00
Employer's contribution to						
holiday credit/welfare						
stamps (to provide for 29 days)	52.0wks	62.50		3,250.00	48.20	2,506.40
pension (6.5% of earnings)	46.2wks	38.16		1,762.99	28.50	1,316.70
Holiday top-up funding	52.0wks	0.04		2.08	0.01	0.52
(Provided by employer)						
National Insurance	47.0wks	52.97		2,489.59	36.30	1,706.10
				31,372.66		23,277.17
Severance pay and sundry costs	Plus	1.5%		470.59	1.5%	349.17
				31,843.25		23,626.89
Employer's Liability and Third Party Insurance	Plus	2.0%		636.87	2.0%	472.54
Total cost per annum				**£32,480.120**		**£24,099.43**
Total cost per hour				**£16.98**		**£12.60**
Average all-in rate per hour					**£14.79**	

MATERIAL £ COLUMN

Many items have reference to a "PC" value. This indicates the prime cost of the principal material delivered to site in the outer London area assuming maximum discounts for large quantities. When obtaining material prices from other sources, it is important to identify any discounts that may apply. Some manufacturers only offer 5 to 10% discount for the largest of orders; or "firm" orders (as distinct from quotations). For other materials, discounts of 30% to 40% may be obtained, depending on value of order, preferential position of the purchaser or state of the market.

The "Material £" column indicates the total materials cost including delivery, waste, sundry materials and an allowance (currently 7½%) for overhead charges and profit for the unit of work concerned. Alternative material prices are listed, excluding discount, at the beginning of many sections. If these are used they require 'discount' adjustment before they can be substituted in place of "PC" figures given for Measured Work items. All material prices quoted are exclusive of Value Added Tax.

MATERIAL PLANT £ COLUMN

Plant costs have been based on current weekly hire charges and estimated weekly cost of oil, grease, ropes (where necessary), site servicing and cartage charges. The total amount is divided by 30 (assuming 25% idle time) to arrive at a cost per working hour of plant. To this hourly rate is added one hour fuel consumption and one hour for an operator where indicated; the rate to be calculated in accordance with the principles set out earlier in this section, i.e. with an allowance for plus rates, etc.

For convenience the all-in rates per hour used in the calculations of "Prices for Measured Work" are shown below and where included in Material/Plant £ column.

Plant	Labour	"All-in" rate per hour £
Excavator (4 wheeled - 0.76 m^3 shovel, 0.24 m^3 bucket)	Driver	23.50
Excavator (JCB 3C - 0.24 m^3 bucket)	Driver	19.00
Excavator (JCB 3C off centre - 0.24 m^3 bucket)	Driver	22.00
Excavator (Hitachi EX120 - 0.53 m^3 bucket)	Driver	25.00
Dumper (2.30 m^3)	Driver	13.50
Two tool portable compressor (125 cfm)*		
per breaking tool		2.00
per punner foot and stem rammer		1.65
Roller		
Bomag BW75S - pedestrian double drum		2.75
Bomag BW120AD - tandem		4.00
5/3.50 cement mixer		0.90
Kango heavy duty breaker		0.67
Power float		0.67
Light percussion drill		0.65

* Operation of compressor by tool operator

TOTAL RATE £ COLUMN

"Total rate £" column is the sum of "Labour £" and "Material £" columns. This column excludes any allowance for "Preliminaries" which must be taken into account if one is concerned with the total cost of work.

The example of "Preliminaries" in the following section indicates that in the absence of detailed calculations currently 12% should be added to all prices for measured work to arrive at total cost.

A PRELIMINARIES

The number of items priced in the "Preliminaries" section of Bills of Quantities and the manner in which they are priced vary considerably between Contractors. Some Contractors, by modifying their percentage factor for overheads and profit, attempt to cover the costs of "Preliminary" items in their "Prices for Measured Work". However, the cost of "Preliminaries" will vary widely according to job size and complexity, site location, accessibility, degree of mechanisation practicable, position of the Contractor's head office and relationships with local labour/domestic Sub-Contractors. It is therefore usually far safer to price "Preliminary" items separately on their merits according to the job.

In amending the Preliminaries/General Conditions section for SMM7, the Joint Committee stressed that the preliminaries section of a bill should contain two types of cost significant item:

1. Items which are not specific to work sections but which have an identifiable cost which is useful to consider separately in tendering e.g. contractual requirements for insurances, site facilities for the employer's representative and payments to the local authority.

2. Items for fixed and time-related costs which derive from the contractor's expected method of carrying out the work, e.g. bringing plant to and from site, providing temporary works and supervision.

A fixed charge is for work the cost of which is to be considered as independent of duration. A time related charge is for work the cost of which is to be considered as dependent on duration. The fixed and time-related subdivision given for a number of preliminaries items will enable tenderers to price the elements separately should they so desire. Tenderers also have the facility at their discretion to extend the list of fixed and time-related cost items to suit their particular methods of construction.

The opportunity for Tenderers to price fixed and time-related items in A30-A37, A40-A44 and A51-A52 have been noted against the following appropriate items although we have not always provided guidance as costs can only be assessed in the light of circumstances of a particular job.

Works of a temporary nature are deemed to include rates, fees and charges related thereto in Sections A36, A41, A42, and A44, all of which will probably be dealt with as fixed charges.

In addition to the cost significant items required by the method, other preliminaries items which are important from other points of view, e.g. quality control requirements, administrative procedures, may need to be included to complete the Preliminaries/General conditions as a comprehensive statement of the employer's requirements.

Typical clause descriptions from a "Preliminaries/General Conditions" section are given below together with details of those items that are usually priced in detail in tenders.

An example in pricing "Preliminaries" follows, and this assumes the form of contract used is the Standard Form of Building Contract 1998 Edition and the value, including "Preliminaries", is £2,500 000. The contract is estimated to take 80 weeks to complete and the value is built up as follows:

	£
Labour value	800,000
Material value	685,000
Provisional sums and all Sub-Contractors	765,000
£	2,250,000

At the end of the section the examples are summarised to give a total value of "Preliminaries" for the project.

A PRELIMINARIES

A PRELIMINARIES/GENERAL CONDITIONS

Preliminary particulars

A10   **Project particulars** - Not priced

A11   **Drawings** - Not priced

A12   **The Site/Existing buildings** - Generally not priced

The reference to existing buildings relates only to those buildings that could have an influence on cost. This could arise from their close proximity making access difficult, their heights relative to the possible use of tower cranes or the fragility of, for example, an historic building necessitating special care.

A13   **Description of the work** - Generally not priced

A20   **The Contract/Sub-contract**
           (The Standard Form of Building Contract 1998 Edition is assumed)

Clause no
1.   **Interpretation, definitions, etc.** - Not priced
2.   **Contractor's obligations** - Not priced
3.   **Contract Sum - adjustment - Interim certificates** - Not priced
4.   **Architect's Instructions** - Not priced
5.   **Contract documents - other documents - issue of certificates**
        The contract conditions may require a master programme to be prepared. This will normally form part of head office overheads and therefore is not priced separately here.
6.   **Statutory obligations, notices, fees and charges** - Not priced. Unless the Contractor is specifically instructed to allow for these items.
7.   **Level and setting out of the works** - Not priced
8.   **Materials, goods and workmanship to conform to description, testing and inspection** - Not priced
9.   **Royalties and patent rights** - Not priced

NOTE: The term "Not priced" or "Generally not priced" where used throughout this section means either that the cost implication is negligible or that it is usually included elsewhere in the tender.

10.   **Person-in-charge**
        Under this heading are usually priced any staff that will be required on site. The staff required will vary considerably according to the size, layout and complexity of the scheme, from one foreman-in-charge to a site agent, general foreman, assistants, checkers and storemen, etc. The costs included for such people should include not only their wages, but also their total cost to the site including statutory payments, pension, expenses, holiday relief, overtime, etc. Part of the foreman's time, together with that of an assistant, will be spent on setting out the site. Allow, say, £3.00 per day for levels, staff, pegs and strings, plus the assistant's time if not part of the general management team. Most sites usually include for one operative to clean up generally and do odd jobs around the site.
        Cost of other staff, such as buyers, and quantity surveyors, are usually part of head office overhead costs, but alternatively, may now be covered under A40 Management and staff.

A PRELIMINARIES

A20   **The Contract/Sub-contract** - cont'd

A typical build-up of a site manager's costs might be:

	£
Annual salary	25,000.00
Expenses	2,000.00
Bonus – say	2,500.00
Employer's National Insurance contribution	
(12.8% on £25,000.00) say	2,800.00
Training levy @ 0.25% say	140.00
Pension scheme	
(say 7.5% of salary and bonus) say	2,062.50
Sundries, including Employer's Liability and Third	
Party (say 3.5% of salary and bonus) say	962.50
	£ 35,465.00

Divide by 47 to allow for holidays:

per week	754.58
Say	£ 750.00

Corresponding costs for other site staff should be calculated in a similar manner, e.g.

Site administration	£
Site Manager 80 weeks @ £750	60,000.00
Holiday relief 4 weeks @ £750	3,000.00
Assistant foreman 60 weeks @ £375	22,500.00
Storemen/checker 60 weeks @ £275	16,500.00
	£ 102,000.00

11.   **Access for Architect to the Works** - Not priced
12.   **Clerk of Works** - Not priced
13.   **Variations and provisional sums** - Not priced
14.   **Contract Sum** -Not priced
15.   **Value Added Tax - supplemental provisions**
Major changes to the VAT status of supplies of goods and services by Contractors came into effect on 1 April 1989. It is clear that on and from that date the majority of work supplied under contracts on JCT Forms will be chargeable on the Contractor at the standard rate of tax. In April 1989, the JCT issued Amendment 8 and a guidance note dealing with the amendment to VAT provisions. This involves a revision to clause 15 and the Supplemental Provisions (the VAT agreement). Although the standard rating of most supplies should reduce the amount of VAT analysing previously undertaken by contractors, he should still allow for any incidental costs and expenses which may be incurred.
16.   **Materials and goods unfixed or off-site** - Not priced

A PRELIMINARIES

A20   **The Contract/Sub-contract** - cont'd.

17.   **Practical completion and Defects Liability**
        Inevitably some defects will arise after practical completion and an allowance will often be made
        to cover this. An allowance of say 0.25 to 0.50% should be sufficient, e.g. Example

        Defects after completion

        Based on 0.25% of the contract sum
                                                                    _____
        £2,250,000 x 0.25%   £   5,625.00
                                                                    _____
18.   **Partial possession by Employer** - Not priced
19.   **Assignment and Sub-Contracts** - Not priced

19A   **Fair wages** - Not priced
20.   **Injury to persons and property and Employers indemnity**
        (See Clause no 21)
21.   **Insurance against injury to persons and property**
        The Contractor's Employer's Liability and Public Liability policies (which would both be involved
        under this heading) are often in the region of 0.50 to 0.60% on the value of his own contract
        work (excluding provisional sums and work by Sub-Contractors whose prices should allow for
        these insurances). However, this allowance can be included in the all-in hourly rate used in the
        calculation of "Prices for Measured Work" (see page 99).
        Under Clause 21.2 no requirement is made upon the Contractor to insure as stated by the
        clause unless a provisional sum is allowed in the Contract Bills.
22.   **Insurance of the works against Clause 22 Perils**
        If, at the Contractor's risk, the insurance cover must be sufficient to include the full cost of
        reinstatement, all increases in cost, professional fees and any consequential costs such as
        demolition. The average provision for fire risk is 0.10% of the value of the work after adding for
        increased costs and professional fees.

        Contractor's Liability - Insurance of works against fire, etc.   £

        Contract value (including "Preliminaries"), say   2,500,000.00
        Estimated increased costs during contract period, say 6%   150,000.00
                                                                                      _____
                                                                                    2,650,000.00
        Estimated increased costs incurred during period of reinstatement, say 3%   80,000.00
                                                                                      _____
                                                                                    2,730,000.00
        Professional fees @ 15%   410,000.00
                                                                                      _____
                                                                                    3,140,000.00
                                                                                      _____
                                                        Allow 0.1%   3,140.00
                                                                                      _____

NOTE: Insurance premiums are liable to considerable variation, depending on the Contractor, the
        nature of the work and the market in which the insurance is placed.

23.   **Date of possession, completion and postponement** - Not priced
24.   **Damages for non-completion** - Not priced

A PRELIMINARIES

A20   The Contract/Sub-contract - cont'd.

25.   **Extension of time** - Not priced
26.   **Loss and expense caused by matters materially affecting regular progress of the works** - Not priced
27.   **Determination by Employer** - Not priced
28.   **Determination by Contractor** -Not priced
29.   **Works by Employer or persons employed or engaged by Employer** - Not priced
30.   **Certificates and payments** - Not priced
31.   **Finance (No.2) Act 1975 - Statutory tax deduction scheme** - Not priced
32.   **Outbreak of hostilities** -Not priced
33.   **War damage** - Not priced
34.   **Antiquities** - Not priced
35.   **Nominated Sub-Contractors** - Not priced here. An amount should be added to the relevant PC sums, if required, for profit and a further sum for special attendance.
36.   **Nominated Suppliers** - Not priced here. An amount should be added to the relevant PC sums, if required, for profit.
37.   **Choice of fluctuation provisions - entry in Appendix**
        The amount which the Contractor may recover under the fluctuations clauses (Clause nos 38, 39 and 40) will vary depending on whether the Contract is "firm", i.e. Clause no 38 is included, or "fluctuating", whether the traditional method of assessment is used, i.e. Clause no 39 or the formula method, i.e. Clause no 40. An allowance should be made for any shortfall in reimbursement under fluctuating contracts.
38.   **Contribution Levy and Tax Fluctuations** (see Clause no 37)
39.   **Labour and Materials Cost and Tax Fluctuations** (see Clause no 37)
40.   **Use of Price Adjustment Formulae** (see Clause no 37)
        Details should include special conditions or amendments to standard conditions, the Appendix insertions and the Employer's insurance responsibilities. Additional obligations may include the provision of a performance bond. If the Contractor is required to provide sureties for the fulfilment of the work the usual method of providing this is by a bond provided by one or more insurance companies. The cost of a performance bond depends largely on the financial standing of the applying Contractor. Figures tend to range from 0.25 to 0.50% of the contract sum.

A30-A37 EMPLOYERS' REQUIREMENTS

These include the following items but costs can only be assessed in the light of circumstances on a particular job. Details should be given for each item and the opportunity for the Tenderer to separately price items related to fixed charges and time related charges.

A30   **Tendering/Sub-letting/Supply**

A31   **Provision, content and use of documents**

A32   **Management of the works**

A33   **Quality standards/control**

A34   **Security/Safety/Protection**

This includes noise and pollution control, maintaining adjoining buildings, public and private roads, live services, security and the protection of work in all sections.
(i)   Control of noise, pollution and other obligations
        The Local Authority, Landlord or Management Company may impose restrictions on the timing of certain operations, particularly noisy of dust-producing operations, which may necessitate the carrying out of these works outside normal working hours or using special tools and equipment. The situation is most likely to occur in built-up areas such as city centres, shopping malls etc., where the site is likely to be in close proximity to offices, commercial or residential property.

A PRELIMINARIES

A34   **Security/Safety/Protection** – cont'd.

(ii)   Maintenance of public and private roads
Some additional value or allowance may be required against this item to insure/protect against damage to entrance gates, kerbs or bridges caused by extraordinary traffic in the execution of the works.

A35   **Specific limitations on method/sequence/timing**

This includes design constraints, method and sequence of work, access, possession and use of the site, use or disposal of materials found, start of work, working hours, employment of labour and sectional possession or partial possession etc.

A36   **Facilities/Temporary work/Services**

This includes offices, sanitary accommodation, temporary fences, hoardings, screens and roofs, name boards, technical and surveying equipment, temperature and humidity, telephone/facsimile installation and rental/maintenance, special lighting and other general requirements, etc. The attainment and maintenance of suitable levels necessary for satisfactory completion of the work including the installation of joinery, suspended ceilings, lift machinery, etc. is the responsibility of the contractor.
The following is an example how to price a mobile office for a Clerk of Works

		£
(a)	Fixed charge	
	Haulage to and from site - say	200.00
(b)	Time related charge	
	Hire charge - 15m^2 x 76 weeks @ £3.00/m^2	3,420.00
	Lighting, heating and attendance on office,	
	say 76 weeks @ £35.00	2,660.00
	Rates on temporary building based on £20.00/m^2 per annum	450.00
		6,530.00
(c)	Combined charge £	6,730.00

The installation of telephones or facsimiles for the use of the Employer, and all related charges therewith, shall be given as a provisional sum.

A37   **Operation/Maintenance of the finished building**

A40-A44 CONTRACTORS GENERAL COST ITEMS

For items A41-A44 it shall be clearly indicated whether such items are to be "Provided by the Contractor" or "Made available (in any part) by the Employer".

A40 Management and staff (Provided by the Contractor)

NOTE: The cost of site administrative staff has previously been included against Clause 10 of the Conditions of Contract, where Readers will find an example of management and staff costs.

A PRELIMINARIES

A40 Management and staff (Provided by the Contractor) – cont'd.

When required allow for the provision of a watchman or inspection by a security organization. Other general administrative staff costs, e.g. Engineering, Programming and production and Quantity Surveying could be priced as either fixed or time related charges, under this section. For the purpose of this example allow, say, 1% of measured work value for other administrative staff costs.

    (a)   Time related charge

    Based on 1% of £2,250,000 - say   £   22,500.00

A41 Site accommodation (Provided by the Contractor or made available by the Employer)

This includes all temporary offices laboratories, cabins, stores, compounds, canteens, sanitary facilities and the like for the Contractor's and his domestic sub-contractors' use (temporary office for a Clerk of Works is covered under obligations and restrictions imposed by the Employer).

Typical costs for jack-type offices are as follows, based upon a twelve months minimum hire period they exclude furniture which could add a further £14.00 - £16.00 per week.

Size	Rate per week £
12 ft x 9 ft (10.03 m^2)	30.00 (£2.90/m^2)
16 ft x 9 ft (13.37 m^2)	35.00 (£2.60/m^2)
24 ft x 9 ft (20.06 m^2)	46.00 (£2.30/m^2)
32 ft x 12 ft (35.67 m^2)	70.00 (£2.00/m^2)

Typical rates for security units are as follows:

Size	Rate per week £
12 ft x 8 ft (8.92 m²)	30.00 (£3.36/m^2)
16 ft x 8 ft (11.89 m^2)	35.00 (£2.95/m^2)
24 ft x 8 ft (17.84 m^2)	48.00 (£2.70/m^2)
32 ft x 8 ft (23.78 m^2)	60.00 (£2.52/m^2)

The following example is for one Foreman's office and two security units.

		£
(a)	Fixed charge	
	Haulage to and from site – Site Manager's Office, say	200.00
	Haulage to and from site - Storage sheds, say	400.00
		600.00
(b)	Time related charge	
	Hire charge – Site Manager's office 15 m^2 x 76 weeks @ £2.60/m^2	2,964.00
	Hire charge - Storage sheds 40 m^2 x 70 weeks @ £2.60/m^2	7,280.00
	Lighting, heating and attendance on office, 76 weeks @ £35.00	2,660.00
	Rates on temporary building based on £20.00/m^2 per annum	1,650.00
		14,554.00
(c)	Combined charge	£ 15,154.00

A PRELIMINARIES

A42 Services and facilities (Provided by the Contractor or made available by the Employer)

This generally includes the provision of all of the Contractor's own services, power, lighting, fuels, water, telephone and administration, safety, health and welfare, storage of materials, rubbish disposal, cleaning, drying out, protection of work in all sections, security, maintaining public and private roads, small plant and tools and general attendance on nominated sub-contractors.

However, this section does not cover fuel for testing and commissioning permanent installations, which would be measured under Sections Y51 and Y81. Examples of build-ups/allowances for some of the major items are provided below:

(i)   Lighting and power for the works
The Contractor is usually responsible for providing all temporary lighting and power for the works and all charges involved. On large sites this could be expensive and involve sub-stations and the like, but on smaller sites it is often limited to general lighting (depending upon time of year) and power for power operated tools for which a small diesel generator and some transformers usually proves adequate.

Typical costs are:

Low voltage diesel generator	£140.00 - £150.00 per week
2.20 to 10 kVA transformer	£30.00 - £70.00 per week

A typical allowance, including charges, installation and fitting costs could be 1% of contract value.

Example
Lighting and power for the works
Combined charge
The fixed charge would normally represent a proportion of the following allowance applicable to connection and supply charges. The residue would be allocated to time related charges.

Dependant on the nature of the work, time of year
and incidence of power operated tools

based on 1% of £2,250,000 – say   £   22,500.00

(ii)   Water for the works

Charges should properly be ascertained from the local Water Authority. If these are not readily available, an allowance of 0.33% of the value of the contract is probably adequate, providing water can be obtained directly from the mains. Failing this, each case must be dealt with on its merits. In all cases an allowance should also be made for temporary plumbing including site storage of water if required.

Useful rates for temporary plumbing include:

Piping	£7.00 per metre
Connection	£200.00
Standpipe	£75.00

Plus an allowance for barrels and hoses.

A PRELIMINARIES

A42 Services and facilities - cont'd

    Example

    Water for the works
    Combined charge
    The fixed charge would normally represent a proportion of the following allowance applicable to connection and supply charges. The residue would be allocated to time related charges.

	£
0.33% of £2,250,000	7,425.00
Temporary plumbing, say	500.00
£	7,925.00

(iii)   Temporary telephones for the use of the Contractor

    Against this item should be included the cost of installation, rental and an assessment of the cost of calls made during the contract.

Installation costs	£99.00
Rental	£28.67 Initial Monthly Payment
	£14.33 Monthly Payment Thereafter
Cost of calls	For sites with one telephone allow about £22.00 per week.

    Example
    Temporary telephones   £

			£
(a)	Fixed charge		
	Connection charges		
	line with socket outlet		99.00
	external ringing device		10.00
			109.00
(b)	Time related charge		
	line rental - 6 quarters - 1 Month @ £28.67		28.67
	17 Months @ £14.33		243.61
	external ringing device rental - 6 quarters @ £2.50		15.00
	call charges - 76 weeks @ £22.00		1,672.00
			1,959.28
(c)	Combined charges, say		£ 2,070.00

(iv)   Safety, health and welfare of workpeople
    The Contractor is required to comply with the Code of Welfare Conditions for the Building Industry which sets out welfare requirements for the following: Shelter from inclement weather; Accommodation for clothing; Accommodation and provision for meals; Provision of drinking water; Sanitary conveniences; Washing facilities; First aid; Site conditions

A PRELIMINARIES

A42 Services and facilities - cont'd

A variety of self-contained mobile or jack-type units are available for hire and a selection of rates is given below:

Kitchen with cooker, fridge, sink unit, water heater and basin

32 ft x 10 ft jack-type	£100.00 per week

Mess room with water heater, wash basin and seating

16 ft x 7 ft 6 in mobile	£55.00 per week
16 ft x 9 ft jack-type	£50.00 per week

Welfare unit with drying rack, lockers, tables, seating, cooker, heater, sink and basin

22 ft x 7 ft 6 in mobile	£70.00 per week

Toilets (mains type)

One pan unit	£20.00 per week
Two pan unit mobile	£55.00 per week
Four pan unit jack-type	£70.00 per week

Allowance must be made in addition for transport costs to and from site, setting up costs, connection to mains, fuel supplies and attendance

Site first aid kit	£ 5.00 per week

A general provision to comply with the above code is often 0.1 to 0.5% of the measured work value. The costs of safety supervisors (required for firms employing more than 20 people) are usually part of head office overhead costs.

Example
Safety, health and welfare
Combined charge
The fixed charge would normally represent a proportion of the following allowance, with the majority allocated to time related charges.

Based on 0.1% of £2,250,000 - say	£ 2,250.00

(v)   Removing rubbish, protective casings and coverings and cleaning the works on completion. This includes removing surplus materials and final cleaning of the site prior to handover. Allow for sufficient "bins" for the site throughout the contract duration and for some operatives time at the end of the contract for final clearing and cleaning ready for handover.

Cost of "bins" - approx. £50.00 each
A general allowance of 0.4% to 0.5% of measured work value is probably sufficient.

Example
Removing rubbish, etc., and cleaning
Combined charge
The fixed charge would normally represent an allowance for final clearing of the works on completion with the residue for cleaning throughout the contract period

Based on 0.4% of £2,250,000 – say	£ 9,000.00

A PRELIMINARIES

A42   Services and facilities - cont'd

(vi)   Drying the works
Use or otherwise of an installed heating system will probably determine the value to be placed against this item. Dependent upon the time of year, say allow 0.1% to 0.2% of the contract value to cover this item.

Example
Drying of the works
Combined charge
Generally this cost is likely to be related to a fixed charge only

Based on 0.1% of £2,250,000 - say   £   2,250.00

(vii)   Protecting the works from inclement weather
In areas likely to suffer particularly inclement weather, some nominal allowance should be included for tarpaulins, polythene sheeting, battening, etc., and the effect of any delays in concreting or brickwork by such weather.

(viii)   Small plant and tools
Small plant and hand tools are usually assessed as between 0.5% and 1.5% of total labour value.
Combined charge

Based on 0.5% of labour cost of £800,000 - say   £   4,000.00

(ix)   General attendance on nominated sub-contractors
In the past this item was located after each PC sum. Under SMM7 it is intended that two composite items (one for fixed charges and the other for time related charges) should be provided in the preliminaries bill for general attendance on all nominated sub-contractors.

A43   Mechanical plant

This includes for cranes, hoists, personnel transport, transport, earthmoving plant, concrete plant, piling plant, paving and surfacing plant, etc. SMM6 required that items for protection or for plant be given in each section, whereas SMM7 provides for these items to be covered under A34, A42 and A43, as appropriate.

(i)   Plant and transport
Quite often, the Contractors own plant and plant employed by sub-contractors are included in measured rates, (e.g. for earthmoving, concrete or piling plant) and the Editors have adopted this method of pricing where they believe it to be appropriate. As for other items of plant e.g. cranes, hoists, site vans etc., these tend to be used by a variety of trades and are therefore often priced in the preliminaries section. An example of such an item might be:

A PRELIMINARIES

A43   **Mechanical Plant** - cont'd

Example
Tower crane - static 30 m radius - 4/5 tonne max. load

			£
(a)	Fixed charge		
	Haulage of crane to and from site, erection, testing, commissioning & dismantling - say		5,000.00
(b)	Time related charge		
	Hire of crane, say 30 weeks @ 600.00		18,000.00
	electricity fuel and oil - say		5,000.00
	operator 30 weeks x 40 hours @ £10.00		12,000.00
			35,000.00
(c)	Combined charge, say		£ 40,000.00

For the purpose of this example in pricing of Preliminaries, the Editors have assumed that the costs of the above tower crane are included in with "Measured Rates" items and have not therefore carried this total to the Sample Summary.

(ii)   Personnel transport
The labour rates per hour on which "Prices for Measured Work" have been based do not cover travel and lodging allowances, which must be assessed according to the appropriate working rule agreement.

Example
Personnel transport

Assuming all labour can be found within the London region, the labour value of £800,000 represents approximately 750 man weeks. Assume each man receives an allowance of £2.30 per day or £11.50 per week of five days.

Combined/time related charge

750 man weeks @ £11.50, say   £   8,600.00

A44   **Temporary works** (Provided by the Contractor or made available by the Employer)

This includes for temporary roads, temporary walkways, access scaffolding, support scaffolding and propping, hoardings, fans, fencing etc., hardstanding and traffic regulations etc. The Contractor should include maintaining any temporary works in connection with the items, adapting, clearing away and making good, and all notices and fees to Local Authorities and public undertakings. On fluctuating contracts, i.e. where Clause 39 or 40 is incorporated there Is no allowance for fluctuations in respect of plant and temporary works and in such instances allowances must be made for any increases likely to occur over the contract period.

Examples of build-ups/allowances for some items are provided below:

A PRELIMINARIES

A44   **Temporary works** (Provided by the Contractor or made available by the Employer) – cont'd.

(i)   Temporary roads, hardstandings, crossings and similar items
Quite often consolidated bases of eventual site roads are used throughout a contract to facilitate movement of materials around the site. However, during the initial setting up of a site, with drainage works outstanding, this is not always possible and occasionally temporary roadways have to be formed and ground levels later reinstated.

Typical costs are:

Removal of topsoil and provision of a 225 mm thick stone/hardcore base blinded with ashes as a temporary roadway 3.50 m wide and subsequent reinstatement:

on level ground	£30.00 per metre
on sloping ground (including 1m of cut or fill)	£37.50 per metre

Removal of topsoil and provision of 225 mm thick stone/hardcore base blinded with ashes as a temporary hardstanding   £9.00 per m^2

Provision of "Aluminium Trakway"; Eve Trakway or equal and approved; portable road system laid directly onto existing surface or onto compacted removable granular base to protect existing surface (Note: most systems are based on a weekly hire charge and laid and removed by the supplier):

Heavy Duty Trakpanel (3.00 m x 2.50 m)	£5.00 per m²/per week
Delivery charge for Trakpanel	£2.50 per m²
Outrigger mats for use in conjunction with Heavy Duty Trakpanel - per set of 4 mats	£100.00 per set/per week
Single Trak Roadway (3.90 m x 1.22 m)	£3.60 per m²/per week
LD20 Evolution - Light Duty Trakway (roll out system - minimum delivery 75 m)	£6.50 per m²/per first week £2.00 per m²/per week thereafter
Terraplas Walkways (turf protection system) - per section (1.00 m x 1.00 m)	£7.00 per m²/per week

NOTE: Any allowance for special hardcore hardstandings for piling Sub-Contractors is usually priced against the "special attendance" clause after the relevant Prime Cost sum.

(ii)   Scaffolding
The General Contractor's standing scaffolding is usually undertaken by specialist Sub-Contractors who will submit quotations based on the specific requirements of the works. It is not possible to give rates here for the various types of scaffolding that may be required but for the purposes of this section it is assumed that the cost of supplying, erecting, maintaining and subsequently dismantling the scaffolding required would amount to £50,000.00 inclusive of overheads and profit.

A PRELIMINARIES

A44   **Temporary works** (Provided by the Contractor or made available by the Employer) – cont'd.

(iii)   Temporary fencing, hoarding, screens, fans, planked footways, guardrails, gantries, and similar items.
This item must be considered in some detail as it is dependant on site perimeter, phasing of the work, work within existing buildings, etc.

Useful rates include:

Hoarding 2.30 m high of 18 mm thick plywood with 50 mm x 100 mm sawn softwood studding, rails and posts, including later dismantling

undecorated	£75.00/m (£32.60/m^2)
decorated one side	£85.00/m (£37.00/m^2)
Pair of gates for hoarding	extra £300.00 per pair
Cleft Chestnut fencing 1.20 m high	
including dismantling	£9.50/m
Morarflex "T-Plus" scaffold sheeting	£4.50/m^2

Example
Temporary hoarding
Combined fixed charge

Decorated plywood hoarding	£
100m @ £85.00	8,500.00
extra for one pair of gates	300.00
	£ 8,800.00

(iv)   Traffic regulations
Waiting and unloading restrictions can occasionally add considerably to costs, resulting in forced overtime or additional weekend working. Any such restrictions must be carefully assessed for the job in hand.

A50   Work/Materials by the Employer

A description shall be given of works by others directly engaged by the Employer and any attendance that is required shall be priced in the same way as works by nominated sub-contractors.

A51   Nominated sub-contractors

This section governs how nominated sub-contractors should be covered in the bills of quantities for main contracts. Bills of quantities used for inviting tenders from potential nominated sub-contractors should be drawn up in accordance with SMM7 as a whole as if the work was main contractor's work. This means, for example, that bills issued to potential nominated sub-contractors should include preliminaries and be accompanied by the drawings.
As much information as possible should be given in respect of nominated sub-contractors' work in order that tenderers can make due allowance when assessing the overall programme and establishing the contract period if not already laid down. A simple list of the component elements of the work might not be sufficient, but a list describing in addition the extent and possible value of each element would be more helpful. The location of the main plant, e.g. whether in the basement or on the roof, would clearly have a bearing on tenderers' programmes. It would be good practice to seek programme information when obtaining estimates from sub-contractors so that this can be incorporated in the bills of quantities for the benefit of tenderers.
A percentage should be added for the main contractor's profit together with items for fixed and time related charges for special attendances required by nominated sub-contractors. Special attendances to include scaffolding (additional to the Contractor's standing scaffolding), access roads, hardstandings, positioning (including unloading, distributing, hoisting or placing in position items of significant weight or size), storage, power, temperature and humidity etc.

A PRELIMINARIES

A52   **Nominated suppliers**

Goods and materials which are required to be obtained from a nominated supplier shall be given as a prime cost sum to which should be added, if required, a percentage for profit.

A53   **Work by statutory authorities**

Works which are to be carried out by a Local Authority or statutory undertakings shall be given as provisional sums.

A54   **Provisional work**

One of the more significant revisions in SMM7 is the requirement to identify provisional sums as being for either defined or undefined work.
The new rules require that each sum for defined work should be accompanied in the bills of quantities by a description of the work sufficiently detailed for the tenderer to make allowance for its effect in the pricing of relevant preliminaries. The information should also enable the length of time required for execution of the work to be estimated and its position in the sequence of construction to be determined and incorporated into the programme. Where Provisional Sums are given for undefined work the Contractor will be deemed not to have made any allowance in programming, planning and pricing preliminaries. Any provision for Contingencies shall be given as a provisional sum for undefined work.

A55   **Dayworks**

To include provisional sums for: Labour, Materials and Goods and Plant

Items		**£**
A20.10	Site administration	102,000.00
A20.17	Defects after completion	6,250.00
A20.22	Insurance of the works against fire, etc.	3,140.00
A36	Clerk of Work's Office	5,625.00
A40	Additional management and staff	22,500.00
A41	Contractor's accommodation	15,154.00
A42(i)	Lighting and power for the works	22,500.00
A42(ii)	Water for the works	7,925.00
A42(iii)	Temporary telephones	2,070.00
A42(iv)	Safety, health and welfare	2,250.00
A42(v)	Removing rubbish, etc., and cleaning	9,000.00
A42(vi)	Drying the works	2,250.00
A42(viii)	Small plant and tools	4,000.00
A43(ii)	Personnel transport	8,600.00
A44(ii)	Scaffolding	50,000.00
A44(iii)	Temporary hoarding	8,800.00
	TOTAL £	272,064.00

It is emphasized that the above is an example only of the way in which Preliminaries may be priced and it is essential that for any particular contract or project the items set out in Preliminaries should be assessed on their respective values. The value of the Preliminaries items in the above example represents approximately an 12% addition to the value of measured work.

A PRELIMINARIES

NEW ITEMS

The One Hundred and Thirtieth edition of Spon's Architects' and Builders' Price Book introduces a number of new items into both the Measured Works sections. These new items, as part of a rolling programme of improvements, compliment and expand the existing information that makes Spon's the most detailed, professionally relevant source of construction price data. Pages 103 to 108 and 413 to 419 separately identify the new items also introduced into the relevant Major and Minor Works sections of the book, respectively. Any suggestions for further suitable new items in future editions should be addressed to the authors.

B NEW ITEMS

Item	PC £	Labour hours	Labour £	Material £	Unit	Total rate £
NEW ITEMS are also included in their appropriate Work section						
D30 CAST IN PLACE PILING						
Minipile cast-in-place concrete piles						
Provision of all plant (2 nr rigs) ; including bringing to and removing from site; maintenance, erection and dismantling at each pile position for 100 nr						
piles	-	-	-	-	item	20756.25
Bored piles						
450 mm diameter piles; reinforced; 10 m long	-	-	-	-	nr	1107.00
add for additional piles length up to 15 m	-	-	-	-	m	110.70
deduct for reduction in pile length	-	-	-	-	m	11.07
Cutting off tops of piles*	-	1.20	22.55	-	m	22.55
Blind bored piles						
500 mm diameter	-	-	-	-	m	99.63
Delays						
rig standing time	-	-	-	-	hour	230.63
Extra over piling						
breaking through obstructions	-	-	-	-	hour	276.75
Pile tests						
working to 600 kN/t; using tension piles as reaction; first pile	-	-	-	-	nr	5535.00
working to 600 kN/t; using tension piles as reaction; subsequent piles	-	-	-	-	nr	5304.38
E05 IN SITU CONCRETE CONSTRUCTION						
Grouting with "Conbextra HF" flowable cementitious grout						
Stanchion bases						
10 mm thick	-	1.16	14.79	1.52	nr	16.31
25 mm thick	-	1.39	17.73	3.88	nr	21.61
E30 REINFORCEMENT FOR IN SITU CONCRETE						
Bar; BS 6744; stainless steel bars; grade 316						
32 mm diameter nominal size						
straight	3375.00	17.00	255.78	3774.44	tonne	4030.22
bent	3475.00	21.00	311.38	3884.75	tonne	4196.13
25 mm diameter nominal size						
straight	3375.00	18.00	270.83	3771.80	tonne	4042.63
bent	3475.00	18.00	270.83	3882.12	tonne	4152.95
20 mm diameter nominal size						
straight	3450.00	20.00	300.92	3858.07	tonne	4158.99
bent	3550.00	20.00	300.92	3968.39	tonne	4269.31
16 mm diameter nominal size						
straight	3575.00	22.00	331.01	4002.49	tonne	4333.50
bent	3675.00	22.00	331.01	4112.80	tonne	4443.81
12 mm diameter nominal size						
straight	3675.00	24.00	361.10	4119.33	tonne	4480.43
bent	3775.00	24.00	361.10	4229.64	tonne	4590.74
10 mm diameter nominal size						
straight	3780.00	26.00	391.20	4242.58	tonne	4633.77
bent	3880.00	26.00	391.20	4352.89	tonne	4744.09
8 mm diameter nominal size						
straight	3675.00	28.00	419.00	4133.27	tonne	4552.26
bent	3775.00	28.00	419.00	4243.58	tonne	4662.58

B NEW ITEMS

Item	PC £	Labour hours	Labour £	Material £	Unit	Total rate £
E40 DESIGNED JOINTS IN IN SITU CONCRETE						
Hydrophilic strip water stop; lapped joints; cast into concrete						
5 x 20 mm "Servistrip AH 205"	-	0.30	3.83	5.93	m	9.76
50 x 20 mm "Adcor 500S"	-	0.30	3.83	7.83	m	11.66
F30 ACCESSORIES / SUNDRY ITEMS						
FOR BRICK / STONE WALLING						
Joint reinforcement						
"Brickforce" galvanised steel joint reinforcement or other equal and approved						
width 60 mm; ref GBF40W60B	-	0.05	1.09	0.45	m	1.54
width 100 mm; ref GBF40W100B	-	0.07	1.52	0.53	m	2.06
width 150 mm; ref GBF40W150B	-	0.09	1.85	0.66	m	2.51
width 175 mm; ref GBF40W175B	-	0.10	2.18	0.79	m	2.96
"Brickforce" stainless steel joint reinforcement or other equal and approved						
width 60 mm; ref SBF40W60	-	0.06	1.20	1.23	m	2.43
width 100 mm; ref SBF40W100	-	0.07	1.52	1.26	m	2.79
width 150 mm; ref SBF40W150	-	0.09	1.85	1.29	m	3.14
width 175 mm; ref SBF40W175	-	0.10	2.18	1.39	m	3.57
"Wallforce" stainless steel joint reinforcement or other equal and approved						
width 240 mm; ref SWF40W240	-	0.12	2.61	3.84	m	6.45
width 260 mm; ref SWF40W260	-	0.13	2.83	4.01	m	6.84
width 275 mm; ref SWF40W275	-	0.14	3.05	4.15	m	7.20
G10 STRUCTURAL STEEL FRAMING						
Surface treatment						
On site						
intumescent paint fire protection (30 minutes) to circular columns etc.; spray applied	-	-	-	-	m^2	11.54
intumescent paint fire protection (60 minutes) to circular columns etc.; spray applied	-	-	-	-	m^2	14.64
H31 METAL PROFILED / FLAT SHEET						
CLADDING / COVERING / SIDING						
Galvanised steel strip troughed sheets;						
Corus Products or other equal and						
approved						
Roof cladding or decking; sloping not exceeding 50 degrees; fixing to steel purlins with plastic headed self-tapping screws						
0.7 mm thick; 46 profile	-	-	-	-	m^2	11.30
0.7 mm thick; 60 profile	-	-	-	-	m^2	12.38
0.7 mm thick; 100 profile	-	-	-	-	m^2	13.45
Galvanised steel strip troughed sheets;						
PMF Strip Mill Products or other equal						
and approved						
Roof cladding; sloping not exceeding 50 degrees; fixing to steel purlins with plastic headed self-tapping screws						
0.7 mm thick type HPS200 13.5/3 corrugated	-	-	-	-	m^2	12.75
0.7 mm thick type HPS200 R32/1000	-	-	-	-	m^2	11.57
0.7 mm thick type Arcline 40; plasticol finished	-	-	-	-	m^2	17.02
Extra over for aluminium cladding or decking	-	-	-	-	m^2	6.46

B NEW ITEMS

Item	PC £	Labour hours	Labour £	Material £	Unit	Total rate £
Accessories for roof cladding						
HPS200 Drip flashing; 250 mm girth	-	-	-	-	m	3.96
HPS200 Ridge flashing; 375 mm girth	-	-	-	-	m	5.18
HPS200 Gable flashing; 500 mm girth	-	-	-	-	m	6.58
HPS200 Internal angle; 625 mm girth	-	-	-	-	m	7.59
Extra over steel roofing for						
roof penetration; 150 mm dia. opening; with top hat flashing and collar 150 mm high; and silicone joint to roofsheet	-	-	-	-	nr	53.30
roof penetration; 250 mm dia. opening; with top hat flashing and collar 150 mm high; and silicone joint to roofsheet	-	-	-	-	nr	75.85
H72 ALUMINIUM SHEET COVERINGS / FLASHINGS						
Aluminium Alumasc "Skyline" coping system; polyester powder coated						
Coping; fixing straps plugged and screwed to brickwork						
362 mm wide; for parapet wall 271 - 300 mm wide	-	0.50	9.14	17.95	m	27.08
Extra for						
90 degree angle	-	0.25	4.57	42.76	nr	47.33
90 degree tee junction	-	0.35	6.40	45.87	nr	52.27
stop end	-	0.15	2.74	25.28	nr	28.03
stop end upstand	-	0.20	3.65	27.43	nr	31.08
J40 FLEXIBLE SHEET / TANKING / DAMP PROOF MEMBRANES						
Tanking and damp proofing						
Visqueen self-adhesive damp proof membrane						
over 300 mm wide; horizontal	-	-	-	-	m²	6.46
not exceeding 300 mm wide; horizontal	-	-	-	-	m	2.48
Tanking primer for self-adhesive dpm						
over 300 mm wide; horizontal	-	-	-	-	m²	4.47
not exceeding 300 mm wide; horizontal	-	-	-	-	m	2.04
Ruberoid "Plasfrufe 2000SA" self-adhesive damp proof membrane						
over 300 mm wide; horizontal	-	-	-	-	m²	12.30
not exceeding 300 mm wide; horizontal	-	-	-	-	m	4.71
Extra for 50 mm thick sand blinding	-	-	-	-	m²	2.15
K10 PLASTERBOARD DRY LINING / PARTITIONS / CEILINGS						
Gypsum cladding; Glasroc "Firecase s" board or other equal and approved; fixed with adhesive; joints pointed in adhesive						
25 mm thick column linings, faces - 4; 2 hour fire protection rating						
not exceeding 600 mm girth	-	0.30	5.23	13.09	m	18.32
600 mm - 1200 mm girth	-	0.45	7.84	19.92	m	27.76
1200 mm - 1800 mm girth	-	0.60	10.45	26.75	m	37.20
30 mm thick beam linings, faces - 3; 2 hour fire protection rating						
not exceeding 600 mm girth	-	0.60	10.45	12.63	m	23.09
600 mm - 1200 mm girth	-	0.90	15.68	20.35	m	36.03
1200 mm - 1800 mm girth	-	1.20	20.91	28.06	m	48.97

B NEW ITEMS

Item	PC £	Labour hours	Labour £	Material £	Unit	Total rate £
K30 DEMOUNTABLE PARTITIONS						
Insulated panel and two-hour fire wall system for warehouses etc., comprising white polyester coated galvanised steel frame and 0.55 mm galv. steel panels either side of rockwool infill						
100 mm thick wall: 31 Rw dB acoustic rating	-	-	-	-	m²	41.00
150 mm thick wall: 31 Rw dB acoustic rating	-	-	-	-	m²	44.08
intumescent mastic sealant; bedding frames at perimeters of metal fire walls	-	-	-	-	m	3.59
Getalit laminated both sides top hung movable acoustic panel wall with concealed uPVC vertical edge profiles, 9 nr 1106 m x 3000 mm panels and type K two point panel support system						
105 mm thick wall: 47 Rw dB acoustic rating	-	-	-	-	m²	379.25
105 mm thick wall: 50 Rw dB acoustic rating	-	-	-	-	m²	410.00
105 mm thick wall: 53 Rw dB acoustic rating	-	-	-	-	m²	440.75
K40 DEMOUNTABLE SUSPENDED CEILINGS						
Edge treatments						
20 x 20 mm SAS perimeter shadow gap; screwed to plasterboard	-	-	-	-	m	5.64
20 x 20 mm SAS shadow gap around 450 mm dia. column; including 15 x 44 mm batten plugged and screwed to concrete	-	-	-	-	nr	28.19
M10 SAND CEMENT SCREEDS						
Early drying floor screed; RMC Mortars "Readyscreed"; steel trowlelled						
Work to floors; one coat; level; to concrete base; over 300 mm wide						
100 mm thick	-	-	-	-	m²	20.50
Extra over last for galvanised chicken wire anticrack reinforcement	-	-	-	-	m²	0.97
Extra for isolation joint to perimeter	-	-	-	-	m	1.27
M60 PAINTING / CLEAR FINISHING - INTERNALLY						
Two coats of epoxy anti-slip floor paint; on screeded concrete surfaces						
General surfaces						
over 300 mm girth	-	0.25	3.35	11.08	m²	14.42
M60 PAINTING / CLEAR FINISHING - EXTERNALLY						
One coat sealer and two coats of anti-graffiti paint (spray applied)						
Brick or block walls						
over 300 mm girth	-	0.23	3.08	2.47	m²	5.55
Cement render or concrete walls						
over 300 mm girth	-	0.26	3.48	3.67	m²	7.15
2.5 mm of "Vandalene" anti-climb paint (spray applied)						
General surfaces						
over 300 mm girth	-	0.30	4.02	3.49	m²	7.51

B NEW ITEMS

Item	PC £	Labour hours	Labour £	Material £	Unit	Total rate £
N20 HOTEL BATHROOM PODS						
Fully fitted out, finished and furnished bathroom pods; installed						
standard pod (4.5 m² on plan)	-	-	-	-	nr	3690.00
accessible pod (4.5 m² on plan)	-	-	-	-	nr	5125.00
P10 SUNDRY INSULATION / PROOFING WORK / FIRE STOPS						
Expanded polystyrene board standard grade SD/N or other equal and approved; fixed with adhesive						
20 mm thick	-	0.14	2.44	3.28	m²	5.72
30 mm thick	-	0.14	2.44	4.49	m²	6.93
60 mm thick	-	0.17	2.96	8.11	m²	11.07
75 mm thick	-	0.18	3.14	9.93	m²	13.07
Corofil C144 fire barrier to edge of slab; fixed with non-flammable contact adhesive						
to suit void 30 mm wide x 100 mm deep; one hour	-	-	-	-	m	12.56
P31 HOLES / CHASES / COVERS / SUPPORTS FOR SERVICES						
Builder's work for other services						
Cutting or forming holes for pipes or the like; not exceeding 55 mm nominal size; making good						
reinforced concrete; not exceeding 100 mm deep	-	0.75	9.57	0.65	nr	10.21
reinforced concrete; 100 mm - 200 mm deep	-	1.15	14.67	0.99	nr	15.66
reinforced concrete; 200 mm - 300 mm deep	-	1.50	19.13	1.29	nr	20.42
plasterboard partition or suspended ceiling	-	0.35	4.46	-	nr	4.46
Cutting or forming holes for pipes or the like; 55 mm - 110 mm nominal size; making good						
reinforced concrete; not exceeding 100 mm deep	-	0.95	12.12	0.82	nr	12.93
reinforced concrete; 100 mm - 200 mm deep	-	1.45	18.49	1.25	nr	19.74
reinforced concrete; 200 mm - 300 mm deep	-	1.90	24.23	1.64	nr	25.87
plasterboard partition or suspended ceiling	-	0.40	5.10	-	nr	5.10
Cutting or forming holes for pipes or the like; exceeding 110 mm nominal size; making good						
reinforced concrete; not exceeding 100 mm deep	-	1.15	14.67	0.99	nr	15.66
reinforced concrete; 100 mm - 200 mm deep	-	1.75	22.32	1.51	nr	23.83
reinforced concrete; 200 mm - 300 mm deep	-	2.25	28.70	1.94	nr	30.64
plasterboard partition or suspended ceiling	-	0.45	5.74	-	nr	5.74
Add for fixing one-hour intumescent sleeve						
for pipe; small	-	0.25	3.19	9.23	nr	12.42
for pipe; large	-	0.28	3.57	11.84	nr	15.41
for pipe; extra large	-	0.30	3.83	15.61	nr	19.43
Cutting or forming holes for ducts; girth not exceeding 1.00 m; making good						
plasterboard partition or suspended ceiling	-	0.65	8.29	-	nr	8.29
Cutting or forming holes for ducts; girth 1.00 m - 2.00 m; making good						
plasterboard partition or suspended ceiling	-	0.75	9.57	-	nr	9.57
Cutting or forming holes for ducts; girth 2.00 m - 3.00 m; making good						
plasterboard partition or suspended ceiling	-	1.00	12.75	-	nr	12.75
Cutting or forming holes for ducts; girth 3.00 m - 4.00 m; making good						
plasterboard partition or suspended ceiling	-	1.25	15.94	-	nr	15.94

B NEW ITEMS

Item	PC £	Labour hours	Labour £	Material £	Unit	Total rate £
NOTE: The following rates for cutting holes and mortices in brickwork or blockwork etc. allow for diamond drilling						
Cutting holes and mortices in brickwork; per 25 mm depth						
25 mm diameter	-	-	-	-	nr	1.08
32 mm diameter	-	-	-	-	nr	1.08
52 mm diameter	-	-	-	-	nr	1.28
76 mm diameter	-	-	-	-	nr	1.44
107 mm diameter	-	-	-	-	nr	1.54
127 mm diameter	-	-	-	-	nr	1.84
152 mm diameter	-	-	-	-	nr	2.15
200 mm diameter	-	-	-	-	nr	2.87
250 mm diameter	-	-	-	-	nr	4.82
300 mm diameter	-	-	-	-	nr	5.74
Diamond chasing; per 25 x 25 mm section						
in facing or common brickwork	-	-	-	-	m	2.82
in semi-engineering brickwork	-	-	-	-	m	5.89
in engineering brickwork	-	-	-	-	m	8.20
in lightweight blockwork	-	-	-	-	m	2.31
in heavyweight blockwork	-	-	-	-	m	4.61
in render/screed	-	-	-	-	m	8.97
Forming boxes; per 25 mm depth (per m of perimeter)						
in facing or common brickwork	-	-	-	-	m	2.82
in semi-engineering brickwork	-	-	-	-	m	5.89
in engineering brickwork	-	-	-	-	m	8.20
in lightweight blockwork	-	-	-	-	m	2.31
in heavyweight blockwork	-	-	-	-	m	4.61
in render/screed	-	-	-	-	m	8.97
Other items						
diamond track mount or ring sawing brickwork	-	-	-	-	m	4.36
diamond floor sawing asphalte	-	-	-	-	m	0.92
stitch drilling 107 mm diameter hole in brickwork	-	-	-	-	nr	1.13

D GROUNDWORKS

Item	PC £	Labour hours	Labour £	Material /Plant £	Unit	Total rate £
D20 EXCAVATING AND FILLING						
Prices are applicable to excavation in firm soil. Multiplying factors for other soils are as follows:						
Mechanical **Hand**						
Clay x 2.00 x 1.20						
Compact gravel x 3.00 x 1.50						
Soft chalk x 4.00 x 2.00						
Hard rock x 5.00 x 6.00						
Running sand or silt x 6.00 x 2.00						
Site preparation						
Removing trees						
girth 600 mm - 1.50 m	-	18.50	201.89	-	nr	**201.89**
girth 1.50 - 3.00 m	-	32.50	354.68	-	nr	**354.68**
girth exceeding 3.00 m	-	46.50	507.46	-	nr	**507.46**
Removing tree stumps						
girth 600 mm - 1.50 m	-	0.93	10.15	35.17	nr	**45.32**
girth 1.50 - 3.00 m	-	0.93	10.15	51.42	nr	**61.57**
girth exceeding 3.00 m	-	0.93	10.15	70.41	nr	**80.56**
Clearing site vegetation						
bushes, scrub, undergrowth, hedges and trees and tree stumps not exceeding 600 mm girth	-	0.03	0.33	-	m²	**0.33**
Lifting turf for preservation						
stacking	-	0.32	3.49	-	m²	**3.49**
Excavating; by machine						
Topsoil for preservation						
average depth 150 mm	-	0.02	0.22	0.98	m²	**1.20**
add or deduct for each 25 mm variation in average depth	-	0.01	0.11	0.23	m²	**0.34**
To reduce levels						
maximum depth not exceeding 0.25 m	-	0.05	0.55	1.28	m³	**1.83**
maximum depth not exceeding 1.00 m	-	0.03	0.33	0.90	m³	**1.23**
maximum depth not exceeding 2.00 m	-	0.05	0.55	1.28	m³	**1.83**
maximum depth not exceeding 4.00 m	-	0.07	0.76	1.58	m³	**2.35**
Basements and the like; commencing level exceeding 0.25 m below existing ground level						
maximum depth not exceeding 1.00 m	-	0.07	0.76	1.05	m³	**1.81**
maximum depth not exceeding 2.00 m	-	0.05	0.55	0.81	m³	**1.35**
maximum depth not exceeding 4.00 m	-	0.07	0.76	1.05	m³	**1.81**
maximum depth not exceeding 6.00 m	-	0.09	0.98	1.37	m³	**2.35**
maximum depth not exceeding 8.00 m	-	0.12	1.31	1.61	m³	**2.92**
Pits						
maximum depth not exceeding 0.25 m	-	0.31	3.38	4.28	m³	**7.66**
maximum depth not exceeding 1.00 m	-	0.33	3.60	3.79	m³	**7.40**
maximum depth not exceeding 2.00 m	-	0.39	4.26	4.28	m³	**8.53**
maximum depth not exceeding 4.00 m	-	0.47	5.13	4.84	m³	**9.97**
maximum depth not exceeding 6.00 m	-	0.49	5.35	5.09	m³	**10.43**
Extra over pit excavating for commencing level exceeding 0.25 m below existing ground level						
1.00 m below	-	0.03	0.33	0.56	m³	**0.89**
2.00 m below	-	0.05	0.55	0.81	m³	**1.35**
3.00 m below	-	0.06	0.65	1.05	m³	**1.70**
4.00 m below	-	0.09	0.98	1.37	m³	**2.35**

D GROUNDWORKS

Item	PC £	Labour hours	Labour £	Material /Plant £	Unit	Total rate £
D20 EXCAVATING AND FILLING – cont'd						
Excavating; by machine – cont'd						
Trenches; width not exceeding 0.30 m						
maximum depth not exceeding 0.25 m	-	0.26	2.84	3.47	m^3	**6.31**
maximum depth not exceeding 1.00 m	-	0.28	3.06	2.99	m^3	**6.04**
maximum depth not exceeding 2.00 m	-	0.33	3.60	3.47	m^3	**7.07**
maximum depth not exceeding 4.00 m	-	0.40	4.37	4.28	m^3	**8.64**
maximum depth not exceeding 6.00 m	-	0.46	5.02	5.09	m^3	**10.11**
Trenches; width exceeding 0.30 m						
maximum depth not exceeding 0.25 m	-	0.23	2.51	3.23	m^3	**5.74**
maximum depth not exceeding 1.00 m	-	0.25	2.73	2.66	m^3	**5.39**
maximum depth not exceeding 2.00 m	-	0.30	3.27	3.23	m^3	**6.50**
maximum depth not exceeding 4.00 m	-	0.35	3.82	3.79	m^3	**7.61**
maximum depth not exceeding 6.00 m	-	0.43	4.69	4.84	m^3	**9.54**
Extra over trench excavating for commencing level exceeding 0.25 m below existing ground level						
1.00 m below	-	0.03	0.33	0.56	m^3	**0.89**
2.00 m below	-	0.05	0.55	0.81	m^3	**1.35**
3.00 m below	-	0.06	0.65	1.05	m^3	**1.70**
4.00 m below	-	0.09	0.98	1.37	m^3	**2.35**
For pile caps and ground beams between piles						
maximum depth not exceeding 0.25 m	-	0.39	4.26	5.65	m^3	**9.91**
maximum depth not exceeding 1.00 m	-	0.35	3.82	5.09	m^3	**8.90**
maximum depth not exceeding 2.00 m	-	0.39	4.26	5.65	m^3	**9.91**
To bench sloping ground to receive filling						
maximum depth not exceeding 0.25 m	-	0.09	0.98	1.37	m^3	**2.35**
maximum depth not exceeding 1.00 m	-	0.07	0.76	1.61	m^3	**2.38**
maximum depth not exceeding 2.00 m	-	0.09	0.98	1.37	m^3	**2.35**
Extra over any types of excavating irrespective of depth						
excavating below ground water level	-	0.13	1.42	1.86	m^3	**3.28**
next existing services	-	2.55	27.83	1.05	m^3	**28.88**
around existing services crossing excavation	-	5.80	63.30	2.99	m^3	**66.28**
Extra over any types of excavating irrespective of depth for breaking out existing materials						
rock	-	2.95	32.19	13.12	m^3	**45.32**
concrete	-	2.55	27.83	9.57	m^3	**37.39**
reinforced concrete	-	3.60	39.29	14.19	m^3	**53.48**
brickwork, blockwork or stonework	-	1.85	20.19	7.21	m^3	**27.40**
Extra over any types of excavating irrespective of depth for breaking out existing hard pavings, 75 mm thick						
coated macadam or asphalt	-	0.19	2.07	0.50	m^2	**2.58**
Extra over any types of excavating irrespective of depth for breaking out existing hard pavings, 150 mm thick						
concrete	-	0.39	4.26	1.52	m^2	**5.77**
reinforced concrete	-	0.58	6.33	2.04	m^2	**8.37**
coated macadam or asphalt and hardcore	-	0.26	2.84	0.55	m^2	**3.39**
Working space allowance to excavations						
reduce levels, basements and the like	-	0.07	0.76	1.05	m^2	**1.81**
pits	-	0.19	2.07	2.99	m^2	**5.06**
trenches	-	0.18	1.96	2.66	m^2	**4.63**
pile caps and ground beams between piles	-	0.20	2.18	2.99	m^2	**5.17**
Extra over excavating for working space for backfilling in with special materials						
hardcore	-	0.13	1.42	15.46	m^2	**16.88**
sand	-	0.13	1.42	16.72	m^2	**18.14**

D GROUNDWORKS

Item	PC £	Labour hours	Labour £	Material /Plant £	Unit	Total rate £
40 mm - 20 mm gravel	-	0.13	1.42	17.60	m²	19.02
plain in situ ready mixed designated concrete						
C7.5 - 40 mm aggregate	-	0.93	11.86	45.41	m²	57.27
Excavating; by hand						
Topsoil for preservation						
average depth 150 mm	-	0.23	2.51	-	m²	2.51
add or deduct for each 25 mm variation in						
average depth	-	0.03	0.33	-	m²	0.33
To reduce levels						
maximum depth not exceeding 0.25 m	-	1.44	15.71	-	m³	15.71
maximum depth not exceeding 1.00 m	-	1.63	17.79	-	m³	17.79
maximum depth not exceeding 2.00 m	-	1.80	19.64	-	m³	19.64
maximum depth not exceeding 4.00 m	-	1.99	21.72	-	m³	21.72
Basements and the like; commencing level						
exceeding 0.25 m below existing ground level						
maximum depth not exceeding 1.00 m	-	1.90	20.74	-	m³	20.74
maximum depth not exceeding 2.00 m	-	2.04	22.26	-	m³	22.26
maximum depth not exceeding 4.00 m	-	2.73	29.79	-	m³	29.79
maximum depth not exceeding 6.00 m	-	3.33	36.34	-	m³	36.34
maximum depth not exceeding 8.00 m	-	4.02	43.87	-	m³	43.87
Pits						
maximum depth not exceeding 0.25 m	-	2.13	23.25	-	m³	23.25
maximum depth not exceeding 1.00 m	-	2.75	30.01	-	m³	30.01
maximum depth not exceeding 2.00 m	-	3.30	36.01	-	m³	36.01
maximum depth not exceeding 4.00 m	-	4.18	45.62	-	m³	45.62
maximum depth not exceeding 6.00 m	-	5.17	56.42	-	m³	56.42
Extra over pit excavating for commencing level						
exceeding 0.25 m below existing ground level						
1.00 m below	-	0.42	4.58	-	m³	4.58
2.00 m below	-	0.88	9.60	-	m³	9.60
3.00 m below	-	1.30	14.19	-	m³	14.19
4.00 m below	-	1.71	18.66	-	m³	18.66
Trenches; width not exceeding 0.30 m						
maximum depth not exceeding 0.25 m	-	1.85	20.19	-	m³	20.19
maximum depth not exceeding 1.00 m	-	2.76	30.12	-	m³	30.12
maximum depth not exceeding 2.00 m	-	3.24	35.36	-	m³	35.36
maximum depth not exceeding 4.00 m	-	3.96	43.22	-	m³	43.22
maximum depth not exceeding 6.00 m	-	5.10	55.66	-	m³	55.66
Trenches; width exceeding 0.30 m						
maximum depth not exceeding 0.25 m	-	1.80	19.64	-	m³	19.64
maximum depth not exceeding 1.00 m	-	2.46	26.85	-	m³	26.85
maximum depth not exceeding 2.00 m	-	2.88	31.43	-	m³	31.43
maximum depth not exceeding 4.00 m	-	3.66	39.94	-	m³	39.94
maximum depth not exceeding 6.00 m	-	4.68	51.07	-	m³	51.07
Extra over trench excavating for commencing						
level exceeding 0.25 m below existing ground						
level						
1.00 m below	-	0.42	4.58	-	m³	4.58
2.00 m below	-	0.88	9.60	-	m³	9.60
3.00 m below	-	1.30	14.19	-	m³	14.19
4.00 m below	-	1.71	18.66	-	m³	18.66
For pile caps and ground beams between piles						
maximum depth not exceeding 0.25 m	-	2.78	30.34	-	m³	30.34
maximum depth not exceeding 1.00 m	-	2.96	32.30	-	m³	32.30
maximum depth not exceeding 2.00 m	-	3.52	38.41	-	m³	38.41
To bench sloping ground to receive filling						
maximum depth not exceeding 0.25 m	-	1.30	14.19	-	m³	14.19
maximum depth not exceeding 1.00 m	-	1.48	16.15	-	m³	16.15
maximum depth not exceeding 2.00 m	-	1.67	18.23	-	m³	18.23

D GROUNDWORKS

Item	PC £	Labour hours	Labour £	Material /Plant £	Unit	Total rate £
D20 EXCAVATING AND FILLING – cont'd						
Excavating; by hand – cont'd						
Extra over any types of excavating irrespective of depth						
excavating below ground water level	-	0.32	3.49	-	m^3	3.49
next existing services	-	0.93	10.15	-	m^3	10.15
around existing services crossing excavation	-	1.85	20.19	-	m^3	20.19
Extra over any types of excavating irrespective of depth for breaking out existing materials						
rock	-	4.63	50.53	6.46	m^3	56.99
concrete	-	4.16	45.40	5.38	m^3	50.78
reinforced concrete	-	5.55	60.57	7.54	m^3	68.10
brickwork, blockwork or stonework	-	2.78	30.34	3.23	m^3	33.57
Extra over any types of excavating irrespective of depth for breaking out existing hard pavings, 60 mm thick						
precast concrete paving slabs	-	0.28	3.06	-	m^2	3.06
Extra over any types of excavating irrespective of depth for breaking out existing hard pavings, 75 mm thick						
coated macadam or asphalt	-	0.37	4.04	0.43	m^2	4.47
Extra over any types of excavating irrespective of depth for breaking out existing hard pavings, 150 mm thick						
concrete	-	0.65	7.09	0.76	m^2	7.85
reinforced concrete	-	0.83	9.06	1.08	m^2	10.14
coated macadam or asphalt and hardcore	-	0.46	5.02	0.54	m^2	5.56
Working space allowance to excavations						
reduce levels, basements and the like	-	2.13	23.25	-	m^2	23.25
pits	-	2.22	24.23	-	m^2	24.23
trenches	-	1.94	21.17	-	m^2	21.17
pile caps and ground beams between piles	-	2.31	25.21	-	m^2	25.21
Extra over excavation for working space for backfilling with special materials						
hardcore	-	0.74	8.08	13.73	m^2	21.81
sand	-	0.74	8.08	14.99	m^2	23.06
40 mm - 20 mm gravel	-	0.74	8.08	15.87	m^2	23.94
plain in situ concrete ready mixed designated concrete; C7.5 - 40 mm aggregate	-	1.02	13.01	43.68	m^2	56.69
Earthwork support (average "risk" prices)						
Maximum depth not exceeding 1.00 m						
distance between opposing faces not exceeding 2.00 m	-	0.10	1.09	0.39	m^2	1.48
distance between opposing faces 2.00 - 4.00 m	-	0.11	1.20	0.46	m^2	1.66
distance between opposing faces exceeding 4.00 m	-	0.12	1.31	0.58	m^2	1.89
Maximum depth not exceeding 2.00 m						
distance between opposing faces not exceeding 2.00 m	-	0.12	1.31	0.46	m^2	1.77
distance between opposing faces 2.00 - 4.00 m	-	0.13	1.42	0.58	m^2	2.00
distance between opposing faces exceeding 4.00 m	-	0.14	1.53	0.73	m^2	2.26
Maximum depth not exceeding 4.00 m						
distance between opposing faces not exceeding 2.00 m	-	0.16	1.75	0.58	m^2	2.33
distance between opposing faces 2.00 - 4.00 m	-	0.16	1.75	0.73	m^2	2.48

D GROUNDWORKS

Item	PC £	Labour hours	Labour £	Material /Plant £	Unit	Total rate £
distance between opposing faces exceeding 4.00 m	-	0.18	1.96	0.92	m²	**2.89**
Maximum depth not exceeding 6.00 m						
distance between opposing faces not exceeding 2.00 m	-	0.18	1.96	0.69	m²	**2.66**
distance between opposing faces 2.00 - 4.00 m	-	0.19	2.07	0.92	m²	**3.00**
distance between opposing faces exceeding 4.00 m	-	0.22	2.40	1.15	m²	**3.55**
Maximum depth not exceeding 8.00 m						
distance between opposing faces not exceeding 2.00 m	-	0.23	2.51	0.92	m²	**3.43**
distance between opposing faces 2.00 - 4.00 m	-	0.28	3.06	1.15	m²	**4.21**
distance between opposing faces exceeding 4.00 m	-	0.33	3.60	1.38	m²	**4.98**
Earthwork support (open boarded)						
Maximum depth not exceeding 1.00 m						
distance between opposing faces not exceeding 2.00 m	-	0.28	3.06	0.81	m²	**3.87**
distance between opposing faces 2.00 - 4.00 m	-	0.31	3.38	0.92	m²	**4.30**
distance between opposing faces exceeding 4.00 m	-	0.35	3.82	1.15	m²	**4.97**
Maximum depth not exceeding 2.00 m						
distance between opposing faces not exceeding 2.00 m	-	0.35	3.82	0.92	m²	**4.74**
distance between opposing faces 2.00 - 4.00 m	-	0.39	4.26	1.11	m²	**5.37**
distance between opposing faces exceeding 4.00 m	-	0.44	4.80	1.38	m²	**6.18**
Maximum depth not exceeding 4.00 m						
distance between opposing faces not exceeding 2.00 m	-	0.44	4.80	1.04	m²	**5.85**
distance between opposing faces 2.00 - 4.00 m	-	0.50	5.46	1.29	m²	**6.74**
distance between opposing faces exceeding 4.00 m	-	0.56	6.11	1.61	m²	**7.72**
Maximum depth not exceeding 6.00 m						
distance between opposing faces not exceeding 2.00 m	-	0.56	6.11	1.15	m²	**7.26**
distance between opposing faces 2.00 - 4.00 m	-	0.61	6.66	1.45	m²	**8.11**
distance between opposing faces exceeding 4.00 m	-	0.70	7.64	1.84	m²	**9.48**
Maximum depth not exceeding 8.00 m						
distance between opposing faces not exceeding 2.00 m	-	0.74	8.08	1.50	m²	**9.58**
distance between opposing faces 2.00 - 4.00 m	-	0.83	9.06	1.73	m²	**10.79**
distance between opposing faces exceeding 4.00 m	-	0.97	10.59	2.30	m²	**12.89**
Earthwork support (close boarded)						
Maximum depth not exceeding 1.00 m						
distance between opposing faces not exceeding 2.00 m	-	0.74	8.08	1.61	m²	**9.69**
distance between opposing faces 2.00 - 4.00 m	-	0.81	8.84	1.84	m²	**10.68**
distance between opposing faces exceeding 4.00 m	-	0.90	9.82	2.30	m²	**12.13**
Maximum depth not exceeding 2.00 m						
distance between opposing faces not exceeding 2.00 m	-	0.93	10.15	1.84	m²	**11.99**
distance between opposing faces 2.00 - 4.00 m	-	1.02	11.13	2.21	m²	**13.34**
distance between opposing faces exceeding 4.00 m	-	1.11	12.11	2.76	m²	**14.88**

D GROUNDWORKS

Item	PC £	Labour hours	Labour £	Material /Plant £	Unit	Total rate £
D20 EXCAVATING AND FILLING – cont'd						
Earthwork support (close boarded) – cont'd						
Maximum depth not exceeding 4.00 m						
distance between opposing faces not exceeding						
2.00 m	-	1.16	12.66	2.07	m²	14.73
distance between opposing faces 2.00 - 4.00 m	-	1.30	14.19	2.58	m²	16.76
distance between opposing faces exceeding						
4.00 m	-	1.43	15.61	3.23	m²	18.83
Maximum depth not exceeding 6.00 m						
distance between opposing faces not exceeding						
2.00 m	-	1.44	15.71	2.30	m²	18.02
distance between opposing faces 2.00 - 4.00 m	-	1.57	17.13	2.90	m²	20.03
distance between opposing faces exceeding						
4.00 m	-	1.76	19.21	3.69	m²	22.89
Maximum depth not exceeding 8.00 m						
distance between opposing faces not exceeding						
2.00 m	-	1.76	19.21	3.00	m²	22.20
distance between opposing faces 2.00 - 4.00 m	-	1.94	21.17	3.46	m²	24.63
distance between opposing faces exceeding						
4.00 m	-	2.22	24.23	4.15	m²	28.37
Extra over earthwork support for						
Curved	-	0.02	0.22	0.39	m²	0.61
Below ground water level	-	0.28	3.06	0.35	m²	3.41
Unstable ground	-	0.46	5.02	0.69	m²	5.71
Next to roadways	-	0.37	4.04	0.58	m²	4.62
Left in	-	0.60	6.55	16.13	m²	22.68
Earthwork support (average "risk" prices						
- inside existing buildings)						
Maximum depth not exceeding 1.00 m						
distance between opposing faces not exceeding						
2.00 m	-	0.18	1.96	0.58	m²	2.55
distance between opposing faces 2.00 - 4.00 m	-	0.19	2.07	0.66	m²	2.74
distance between opposing faces exceeding						
4.00 m	-	0.22	2.40	0.81	m²	3.21
Maximum depth not exceeding 2.00 m						
distance between opposing faces not exceeding						
2.00 m	-	0.22	2.40	0.66	m²	3.06
distance between opposing faces 2.00 - 4.00 m	-	0.24	2.62	0.88	m²	3.50
distance between opposing faces exceeding						
4.00 m	-	0.32	3.49	0.98	m²	4.47
Maximum depth not exceeding 4.00 m						
distance between opposing faces not exceeding						
2.00 m	-	0.28	3.06	0.88	m²	3.94
distance between opposing faces 2.00 - 4.00 m	-	0.31	3.38	1.04	m²	4.43
distance between opposing faces exceeding						
4.00 m	-	0.34	3.71	1.22	m²	4.93
Maximum depth not exceeding 6.00 m						
distance between opposing faces not exceeding						
2.00 m	-	0.34	3.71	0.99	m²	4.70
distance between opposing faces 2.00 - 4.00 m	-	0.38	4.15	1.22	m²	5.37
distance between opposing faces exceeding						
4.00 m	-	0.43	4.69	1.45	m²	6.14
Disposal; by machine						
Excavated material						
off site; to tip not exceeding 13 km (using lorries)						
including Landfill Tax based on inactive waste	-	-	-	16.36	m³	16.36

D GROUNDWORKS

Item	PC £	Labour hours	Labour £	Material /Plant £	Unit	Total rate £
on site; depositing in spoil heaps; average 25 m distance	-	-	-	0.75	m³	0.75
on site; spreading; average 25 m distance	-	0.20	2.18	0.53	m³	2.71
on site; depositing in spoil heaps; average 50 m distance	-	-	-	1.28	m³	1.28
on site; spreading; average 50 m distance	-	0.20	2.18	0.98	m³	3.16
on site; depositing in spoil heaps; average 100 m distance	-	-	-	2.26	m³	2.26
on site; spreading; average 100 m distance	-	0.20	2.18	1.51	m³	3.69
on site; depositing in spoil heaps; average 200 m distance	-	-	-	2.86	m³	2.86
on site; spreading; average 200 m distance	-	0.20	2.18	2.03	m³	4.22
Disposal; by hand						
Excavated material						
off site; to tip not exceeding 13 km (using lorries) including Landfill Tax based on inactive waste	-	0.74	8.08	22.28	m³	30.35
on site; depositing in spoil heaps; average 25 m distance	-	1.02	11.13	-	m³	11.13
on site; spreading; average 25 m distance	-	1.34	14.62	-	m³	14.62
on site; depositing in spoil heaps; average 50 m distance	-	1.34	14.62	-	m³	14.62
on site; spreading; average 50 m distance	-	1.62	17.68	-	m³	17.68
on site; depositing in spoil heaps; average 100 m distance	-	1.94	21.17	-	m³	21.17
on site; spreading; average 100 m distance	-	2.22	24.23	-	m³	24.23
on site; depositing in spoil heaps; average 200 m distance	-	2.87	31.32	-	m³	31.32
on site; spreading; average 200 m distance	-	3.15	34.38	-	m³	34.38
Filling to excavations; by machine						
Average thickness not exceeding 0.25 m						
arising from the excavations	-	0.17	1.86	2.03	m³	3.89
obtained off site; hardcore	23.63	0.19	2.07	29.37	m³	31.45
obtained off site; granular fill type one	22.11	0.19	2.07	29.35	m³	31.42
obtained off site; granular fill type two	20.84	0.19	2.07	27.88	m³	29.95
Average thickness exceeding 0.25 m						
arising from the excavations	-	0.14	1.53	1.51	m³	3.03
obtained off site; hardcore	20.25	0.16	1.75	24.94	m³	26.69
obtained off site; granular fill type one	22.11	0.16	1.75	28.60	m³	30.34
obtained off site; granular fill type two	20.84	0.16	1.75	27.12	m³	28.87
Filling to make up levels; by machine						
Average thickness not exceeding 0.25 m						
arising from the excavations	-	0.24	2.62	2.26	m³	4.88
obtained off site; imported topsoil	10.51	0.24	2.62	14.09	m³	16.71
obtained off site; hardcore	23.63	0.28	3.06	29.48	m³	32.54
obtained off site; granular fill type one	22.11	0.28	3.06	29.46	m³	32.51
obtained off site; granular fill type two	20.84	0.28	3.06	27.99	m³	31.04
obtained off site; sand	22.43	0.28	3.06	29.83	m³	32.88
Average thickness exceeding 0.25 m						
arising from the excavations	-	0.20	2.18	1.61	m³	3.79
obtained off site; imported topsoil	10.51	0.20	2.18	13.44	m³	15.62
obtained off site; hardcore	20.25	0.24	2.62	24.94	m³	27.56
obtained off site; granular fill type one	22.11	0.24	2.62	28.59	m³	31.21
obtained off site; granular fill type two	20.84	0.24	2.62	27.12	m³	29.74
obtained off site; sand	22.43	0.24	2.62	28.96	m³	31.58

D GROUNDWORKS

Item	PC £	Labour hours	Labour £	Material /Plant £	Unit	Total rate £
D20 EXCAVATING AND FILLING – cont'd						
Filling to excavations; by hand						
Average thickness not exceeding 0.25 m						
arising from the excavations	-	1.16	12.66	-	m³	12.66
obtained off site; hardcore	23.63	1.25	13.64	27.34	m³	40.98
obtained off site; granular fill type one	22.11	1.48	16.15	25.58	m³	41.73
obtained off site; granular fill type two	20.84	1.48	16.15	24.11	m³	40.26
obtained off site; sand	22.43	1.48	16.15	25.95	m³	42.10
Average thickness exceeding 0.25 m						
arising from the excavations	-	0.93	10.15	-	m³	10.15
obtained off site; hardcore	20.25	1.02	11.13	23.43	m³	34.57
obtained off site; granular fill type one	22.11	1.20	13.10	25.58	m³	38.68
obtained off site; granular fill type two	20.84	1.20	13.10	24.11	m³	37.21
obtained off site; sand	22.43	1.20	13.10	25.95	m³	39.05
Filling to make up levels; by hand						
Average thickness not exceeding 0.25 m						
arising from the excavations	-	1.25	13.64	3.87	m³	17.52
obtained off site; imported soil	10.51	1.25	13.64	15.18	m³	28.82
obtained off site; hardcore	23.63	1.39	15.17	31.64	m³	46.81
obtained off site; granular fill type one	22.11	1.54	16.81	30.34	m³	47.15
obtained off site; granular fill type two	20.84	1.54	16.81	28.87	m³	45.68
obtained off site; sand	22.43	1.54	16.81	30.71	m³	47.52
Average thickness exceeding 0.25 m						
arising from the excavations	-	1.02	11.13	3.16	m³	14.29
arising from on site spoil heaps; average 25 m						
distance; multiple handling	-	2.22	24.23	6.89	m³	31.12
obtained off site; imported soil	10.51	1.02	11.13	14.47	m³	25.60
obtained off site; hardcore	20.25	1.34	14.62	27.59	m³	42.22
obtained off site; granular fill type one	22.11	1.43	15.61	30.03	m³	45.64
obtained off site; granular fill type two	20.84	1.43	15.61	28.56	m³	44.17
obtained off site; sand	22.43	1.43	15.61	30.40	m³	46.01
Surface packing to filling						
To vertical or battered faces	-	0.17	1.86	0.09	m²	1.95
Surface treatments						
Compacting						
filling; blinding with sand	-	0.04	0.44	1.41	m²	1.85
bottoms of excavations	-	0.04	0.44	0.02	m²	0.45
Trimming						
sloping surfaces	-	0.17	1.86	-	m²	1.86
sloping surfaces; in rock	-	0.93	9.32	1.50	m²	10.82
Filter membrane; one layer; laid on earth to receive granular material						
"Terram 500" filter membrane or other equal and approved; one layer; laid on earth	-	0.04	0.44	0.37	m²	0.80
"Terram 700" filter membrane or other equal and approved; one layer; laid on earth	-	0.04	0.44	0.39	m²	0.83
"Terram 1000"; filter membrane or other equal and approved; one layer; laid on earth	-	0.04	0.44	0.41	m²	0.85
"Terram 2000"; filter membrane or other equal and approved; one layer; laid on earth	-	0.04	0.44	0.88	m²	1.31

D GROUNDWORKS

Item	PC £	Labour hours	Labour £	Material £	Unit	Total rate £
D30 CAST IN PLACE PILING						
NOTE: The following approximate prices, for the quantities of piling quoted, are for work on clear open sites with reasonable access. They are based on 500 mm nominal diameter piles, normal concrete mix 20.00 N/mm2 reinforced for loading up to 40,000 kg depending upon ground conditions and include up to 0.16 m of projecting reinforcement at top of pile. The prices do not allow for removal of spoil.						
NOTE: *indicates work normally carried out by the Main Contractor						
Minipile cast-in-place concrete piles						
Provision of all plant (2 nr rigs) ; including bringing to and removing from site; maintenance, erection and dismantling at each pile position for 100 nr piles	-	-	-	-	item	20756.25
Bored piles						
450 mm diameter piles; reinforced; 10 m long	-	-	-	-	nr	1107.00
add for additional piles length up to 15 m	-	-	-	-	m	110.70
deduct for reduction in pile length	-	-	-	-	m	11.07
Cutting off tops of piles*	-	1.20	22.55	-	m	22.55
Blind bored piles						
500 mm diameter	-	-	-	-	m	99.63
Delays						
rig standing time	-	-	-	-	hour	230.63
Extra over piling						
breaking through obstructions	-	-	-	-	hour	276.75
Pile tests						
working to 600 kN/t; using tension piles as reaction; first pile	-	-	-	-	nr	5535.00
working to 600 kN/t; using tension piles as reaction; subsequent piles	-	-	-	-	nr	5304.38
Rotary bored cast-in-place concrete piles						
Provision of all plant (1 nr rig); including bringing to and removing from site; maintenance, erection and dismantling at each pile position for 100 nr piles	-	-	-	-	item	9225.00
Bored piles						
500 mm diameter piles; reinforced; 10 m long	-	-	-	-	nr	415.13
add for additional piles length up to 15 m	-	-	-	-	m	41.51
deduct for reduction in pile length	-	-	-	-	m	20.30
Cutting off tops of piles*	-	1.20	22.55	-	m	22.55
Blind bored piles						
500 mm diameter	-	-	-	-	m	21.22
Delays						
rig standing time	-	-	-	-	hour	184.50
Extra over piling						
breaking through obstructions	-	-	-	-	hour	230.63
Pile tests						
working to 600 kN/t; using tension piles as reaction; first pile	-	-	-	-	nr	4381.88
working to 600 kN/t; using tension piles as reaction; subsequent piles	-	-	-	-	nr	4151.25

D GROUNDWORKS

Item	PC £	Labour hours	Labour £	Material £	Unit	Total rate £
D32 STEEL PILING						
"Frodingham" steel sheeting piling or other equal and approved; grade 43A; pitched and driven						
Provision of all plant; including bringing to and removing from site; maintenance, erection and dismantling; assuming one rig for 1500 m^2 of piling	-	-	-	-	item	4772.90
Driven shell piles						
type 1N; 99.10 kg/m^2	-	-	-	-	m^2	107.89
type 2N; 112.30 kg/m^2	-	-	-	-	m^2	124.23
type 3N; 137.10 kg/m^2	-	-	-	-	m^2	137.30
type 4N; 170.80 kg/m^2	-	-	-	-	m^2	169.99
type 5N; 236.90 kg/m^2	-	-	-	-	m^2	222.30
Burning off tops of piles	-	-	-	-	m	14.38
"Frodingham" steel sheet piling or other equal or approved; extract only						
Provision of all plant; including bringing to and removing from site; maintenance, erection and dismantling; assuming one rig as before	-	-	-	-	nr	4249.84
Driven sheet piling; extract only						
type 1N; 99.10 kg/m^2	-	-	-	-	m^2	20.92
type 2N; 112.30 kg/m^2	-	-	-	-	m^2	20.92
type 3N; 137.10 kg/m^2	-	-	-	-	m^2	20.92
type 4N; 170.80 kg/m^2	-	-	-	-	m^2	20.92
type 5N; 236.90 kg/m^2	-	-	-	-	m^2	22.23
D40 EMBEDDED RETAINING WALLING						
Diaphragm walls; contiguous panel construction; panel lengths not exceeding 5 m						
Provision of all plant; including bringing to and removing from site; maintenance, erection and dismantling; assuming one rig for 1000 m^2 of walling	-	-	-	-	item	115312.50
Excavation for diaphragm wall; excavated material removed from site; Bentonite slurry supplied and disposed of						
600 mm thick walls	-	-	-	-	m^3	230.63
1000 mm thick walls	-	-	-	-	m^3	230.63
Ready mixed reinforced in situ concrete; normal portland cement; C30 - 10 mm aggregate in walls	-	-	-	-	m^3	96.86
Reinforcement bar; BS 4449 cold rolled deformed square high yield steel bars; straight or bent						
25 mm - 40 mm diameter	-	-	-	-	t	622.69
20 mm diameter	-	-	-	-	t	622.69
16 mm diameter	-	-	-	-	t	622.69
Formwork 75 mm thick to form chases	-	-	-	-	m^2	55.35
Construct twin guide walls in reinforced concrete; together with reinforcement and formwork along the axis of the diaphragm wall	-	-	-	-	m	258.30
Delays						
rig standing	-	-	-	-	hour	738.00

D GROUNDWORKS

Item	PC £	Labour hours	Labour £	Material £	Unit	Total rate £
D41 CRIB WALLS/GABIONS/REINFORCED EARTH						
Gabion baskets						
Wire mesh gabion baskets; Maccaferri Ltd or other equal and approved; galvanised mesh 80 mm x 100 mm; filling with broken stones 125 mm - 200 mm size						
2.00 x 1.00 x 0.50 m	-	1.46	27.44	83.29	nr	**110.72**
2.00 x 1.00 x 1.00 m	-	1.39	26.12	149.68	nr	**175.80**
3.00 x 1.00 x 0.50 m	-	1.94	36.46	115.52	nr	**151.98**
3.00 x 1.00 x 1.00 m	-	3.89	73.10	205.04	nr	**278.14**
"Reno" mattress gabion baskets or other equal and approved; Maccaferri Ltd; filling with broken stones 125 mm - 200 mm size						
6.00 x 2.00 x 0.17 m	-	0.46	8.64	194.11	nr	**202.76**
6.00 x 2.00 x 0.23 m	-	0.62	11.65	238.07	nr	**249.72**
6.00 x 2.00 x 0.30 m	-	0.69	12.97	294.71	nr	**307.68**
D50 UNDERPINNING						
Excavating; by machine						
Preliminary trenches						
maximum depth not exceeding 1.00 m	-	0.23	2.51	5.81	m^3	**8.32**
maximum depth not exceeding 2.00 m	-	0.28	3.06	7.00	m^3	**10.05**
maximum depth not exceeding 4.00 m	-	0.32	3.49	8.18	m^3	**11.68**
Extra over preliminary trench excavating for breaking out existing hard pavings, 150 mm thick						
concrete	-	0.65	7.09	0.76	m^2	**7.85**
Excavating; by hand						
Preliminary trenches						
maximum depth not exceeding 1.00 m	-	2.68	29.25	-	m^3	**29.25**
maximum depth not exceeding 2.00 m	-	3.05	33.29	-	m^3	**33.29**
maximum depth not exceeding 4.00 m	-	3.93	42.89	-	m^3	**42.89**
Extra over preliminary trench excavating for breaking out existing hard pavings, 150 mm thick						
concrete	-	0.28	3.06	1.73	m^2	**4.78**
Underpinning pits; commencing from 1.00 m below existing ground level						
maximum depth not exceeding 0.25 m	-	4.07	44.42	-	m^3	**44.42**
maximum depth not exceeding 1.00 m	-	4.44	48.45	-	m^3	**48.45**
maximum depth not exceeding 2.00 m	-	5.32	58.06	-	m^3	**58.06**
Underpinning pits; commencing from 2.00 m below existing ground level						
maximum depth not exceeding 0.25 m	-	5.00	54.57	-	m^3	**54.57**
maximum depth not exceeding 1.00 m	-	5.37	58.60	-	m^3	**58.60**
maximum depth not exceeding 2.00 m	-	6.24	68.10	-	m^3	**68.10**
Underpinning pits; commencing from 4.00 m below existing ground level						
maximum depth not exceeding 0.25 m	-	5.92	64.61	-	m^3	**64.61**
maximum depth not exceeding 1.00 m	-	6.29	68.64	-	m^3	**68.64**
maximum depth not exceeding 2.00 m	-	7.17	78.25	-	m^3	**78.25**
Extra over any types of excavating irrespective of depth						
excavating below ground water level	-	0.32	3.49	-	m^3	**3.49**

D GROUNDWORKS

Item	PC £	Labour hours	Labour £	Material £	Unit	Total rate £
Earthwork support to preliminary trenches (open boarded - in 3.00 m lengths)						
Maximum depth not exceeding 1.00 m						
distance between opposing faces not exceeding 2.00 m	-	0.37	4.04	1.50	m^2	5.54
Maximum depth not exceeding 2.00 m						
distance between opposing faces not exceeding 2.00 m	-	0.46	5.02	1.84	m^2	6.86
Maximum depth not exceeding 4.00 m						
distance between opposing faces not exceeding 2.00 m	-	0.59	6.44	2.30	m^2	8.74
Earthwork support to underpinning pits (open boarded - in 3.00 m lengths)						
Maximum depth not exceeding 1.00 m						
distance between opposing faces not exceeding 2.00 m	-	0.41	4.47	1.61	m^2	6.09
Maximum depth not exceeding 2.00 m						
distance between opposing faces not exceeding 2.00 m	-	0.51	5.57	2.07	m^2	7.64
Maximum depth not exceeding 4.00 m						
distance between opposing faces not exceeding 2.00 m	-	0.65	7.09	2.53	m^2	9.63
Earthwork support to preliminary trenches (closed boarded - in 3.00 m lengths)						
Maximum depth not exceeding 1.00 m						
1.00 m deep	-	0.93	10.15	2.53	m^2	12.68
Maximum depth not exceeding 2.00 m						
distance between opposing faces not exceeding 2.00 m	-	1.16	12.66	3.23	m^2	15.88
Maximum depth not exceeding 4.00 m						
distance between opposing faces not exceeding 2.00 m	-	1.43	15.61	3.92	m^2	19.52
Earthwork support to underpinning pits (closed boarded - in 3.00 m lengths)						
Maximum depth not exceeding 1.00 m						
distance between opposing faces not exceeding 2.00 m	-	1.02	11.13	2.76	m^2	13.90
Maximum depth not exceeding 2.00 m						
distance between opposing faces not exceeding 2.00 m	-	1.28	13.97	3.46	m^2	17.42
Maximum depth not exceeding 4.00 m						
distance between opposing faces not exceeding 2.00 m	-	1.57	17.13	4.38	m^2	21.51
Extra over earthwork support for						
Left in	-	0.69	7.53	16.13	m^2	23.66

D GROUNDWORKS

Item	PC £	Labour hours	Labour £	Material £	Unit	Total rate £
D50 UNDERPINNING – cont'd						
Cutting away existing projecting foundations						
Concrete						
maximum width 150 mm; maximum depth 150 mm	-	0.15	1.64	0.14	m	**1.78**
maximum width 150 mm; maximum depth 225 mm	-	0.22	2.40	0.22	m	**2.62**
maximum width 150 mm; maximum depth 300 mm	-	0.30	3.27	0.29	m	**3.56**
maximum width 300 mm; maximum depth 300 mm	-	0.58	6.33	0.56	m	**6.89**
Masonry						
maximum width one brick thick; maximum depth one course high	-	0.04	0.44	0.05	m	**0.48**
maximum width one brick thick; maximum depth two courses high	-	0.13	1.42	0.13	m	**1.55**
maximum width one brick thick; maximum depth three courses high	-	0.25	2.73	0.24	m	**2.97**
maximum width one brick thick; maximum depth four courses high	-	0.42	4.58	0.40	m	**4.99**
Preparing the underside of existing work to receive the pinning up of the new work						
Width of existing work						
380 mm wide	-	0.56	6.11	-	m	**6.11**
600 mm wide	-	0.74	8.08	-	m	**8.08**
900 mm wide	-	0.93	10.15	-	m	**10.15**
1200 mm wide	-	1.11	12.11	-	m	**12.11**
Disposal; by hand						
Excavated material						
off site; to tip not exceeding 13 km (using lorries) including Landfill Tax based on inactive waste	-	0.74	8.08	27.85	m^3	**35.92**
Filling to excavations; by hand						
Average thickness exceeding 0.25 m						
arising from the excavations	-	0.93	10.15	-	m^3	**10.15**
Surface treatments						
Compacting						
bottoms of excavations	-	0.04	0.44	0.02	m^2	**0.45**
Plain in situ ready mixed designated concrete; C10 - 40 mm aggregate; poured against faces of excavation						
Underpinning						
thickness not exceeding 150 mm	-	3.42	43.62	80.52	m^3	**124.14**
thickness 150 - 450 mm	-	2.87	36.60	80.52	m^3	**117.12**
thickness exceeding 450 mm	-	2.50	31.88	80.52	m^3	**112.41**
Plain in situ ready mixed designated concrete; C20 - 20 mm aggregate; poured against faces of excavation						
Underpinning						
thickness not exceeding 150 mm	-	3.42	43.62	82.84	m^3	**126.46**
thickness 150 - 450 mm	-	2.87	36.60	82.84	m^3	**119.44**
thickness exceeding 450 mm	-	2.50	31.88	82.84	m^3	**114.72**
Extra for working around reinforcement	-	0.28	3.57	-	m^3	**3.57**

D GROUNDWORKS

Item	PC £	Labour hours	Labour £	Material £	Unit	Total rate £
Sawn formwork; sides of foundations in underpinning						
Plain vertical						
height exceeding 1.00 m	-	1.48	23.43	5.76	m²	29.19
height not exceeding 250 mm	-	0.51	8.07	1.65	m²	9.73
height 250 - 500 mm	-	0.79	12.51	3.08	m²	15.58
height 500 mm - 1.00 m	-	1.20	19.00	5.76	m²	24.76
Reinforcement bar; BS4449; hot rolled plain round mild steel bars						
20 mm diameter nominal size						
bent	344.00	24.00	356.52	398.80	tonne	755.31
16 mm diameter nominal size						
bent	344.00	26.00	386.61	401.21	tonne	787.82
12 mm diameter nominal size						
bent	346.00	28.00	416.70	405.83	tonne	822.53
10 mm diameter nominal size						
bent	349.00	30.00	446.80	412.45	tonne	859.24
8 mm diameter nominal size						
bent	357.00	32.00	474.59	423.69	tonne	898.28
Reinforcement bar; BS 4461; cold worked deformed square high yield steel bars						
20 mm diameter nominal size						
bent	344.00	24.00	356.52	398.80	tonne	755.31
16 mm diameter nominal size						
bent	344.00	26.00	386.61	401.21	tonne	787.82
12 mm diameter nominal size						
bent	346.00	28.00	416.70	405.83	tonne	822.53
10 mm diameter nominal size						
bent	349.00	30.00	446.80	412.45	tonne	859.24
8 mm diameter nominal size						
bent	357.00	32.00	474.59	423.69	tonne	898.28
Common bricks; PC £200.00/1000; in cement mortar (1:3)						
Walls in underpinning						
one brick thick	-	2.22	48.31	31.25	m²	79.56
one and a half brick thick	-	3.05	66.37	46.54	m²	112.91
two brick thick	-	3.79	82.48	64.57	m²	147.05
Class A engineering bricks; PC £345.00/1000; in cement mortar (1:3)						
Walls in underpinning						
one brick thick	-	2.22	48.31	51.32	m²	99.63
one and a half brick thick	-	3.05	66.37	76.65	m²	143.02
two brick thick	-	3.79	82.48	104.72	m²	187.19
Class B engineering bricks; PC £246.00/1000; in cement mortar (1:3)						
Walls in underpinning						
one brick thick	-	2.22	48.31	37.65	m²	85.96
one and a half brick thick	-	3.05	66.37	56.13	m²	122.51
two brick thick	-	3.79	82.48	77.37	m²	159.85
Add or deduct for variation of £10.00/1000 in PC of bricks						
one brick thick	-	-	-	1.39	m²	1.39
one and a half bricks thick	-	-	-	2.09	m²	2.09
two bricks thick	-	-	-	2.79	m²	2.79

D GROUNDWORKS

Item	PC £	Labour hours	Labour £	Material £	Unit	Total rate £
D50 UNDERPINNING – cont'd						
"Pluvex" (hessian based) damp proof course or similar; 200 mm laps; in cement mortar (1:3)						
Horizontal						
width exceeding 225 mm	6.52	0.23	5.01	7.54	m²	12.55
width not exceeding 225 mm	6.67	0.46	10.01	7.72	m²	17.73
"Hyload" (pitch polymer) damp proof course or similar; 150 mm laps; in cement mortar (1:3)						
Horizontal						
width exceeding 225 mm	5.75	0.23	5.01	6.65	m²	11.66
width not exceeding 225 mm	5.88	0.46	10.01	6.81	m²	16.82
"Ledkore" grade A (bitumen based lead cored) damp proof course or other equal and approved; 200 mm laps; in cement mortar (1:3)						
Horizontal						
width exceeding 225 mm	18.02	0.31	6.75	20.84	m²	27.59
width not exceeding 225 mm	18.44	0.61	13.27	21.33	m²	34.60
Two courses of slates in cement mortar (1:3)						
Horizontal						
width exceeding 225 mm	-	1.39	30.25	23.02	m²	53.27
width not exceeding 225 mm	-	2.31	50.27	23.54	m²	73.81
Wedging and pinning						
To underside of existing construction with slates in cement mortar (1:3)						
width of wall - half brick thick	-	1.02	22.20	5.47	m	27.66
width of wall - one brick thick	-	1.20	26.11	10.93	m	37.05
width of wall - one and a half brick thick	-	1.39	30.25	16.40	m	46.65

E IN SITU CONCRETE/LARGE PRECAST CONCRETE

Item	PC £	Labour hours	Labour £	Material £	Unit	Total rate £
BASIC MIXED CONCRETE PRICES						
DESIGNED MIXES						
Definition: "Mix for which the purchaser is responsible for specifying the required performances and the producer is responsible for selecting the mix proportions to produce the required performance".						
NOTE: The following prices are for designed mix concrete ready for placing excluding any allowance for waste, discount or overheads and profit. Prices are based upon delivery to site within a 5 mile (8 km) radius of concrete mixing plant, using full loads.						
Grade C7.5; cement to BS12; 10 mm aggregate	-	-	-	65.62	m³	-
Grade C7.5; cement to BS12; 20 mm aggregate	-	-	-	63.93	m³	-
Grade C7.5; cement to BS12; 40 mm aggregate	-	-	-	63.39	m³	-
Grade C7.5; sulphate resistant cement; 10 mm aggregate	-	-	-	68.10	m³	-
Grade C7.5; sulphate resistant cement; 20 mm aggregate	-	-	-	66.34	m³	-
Grade C7.5; sulphate resistant cement; 40 mm aggregate	-	-	-	65.77	m³	-
Grade C10; cement to BS12; 10 mm aggregate	-	-	-	66.46	m³	-
Grade C10; cement to BS12; 20 mm aggregate	-	-	-	64.74	m³	-
Grade C10; cement to BS12; 40 mm aggregate	-	-	-	63.80	m³	-
Grade C10; sulphate resistant cement; 10 mm aggregate	-	-	-	70.71	m³	-
Grade C10; sulphate resistant cement; 20 mm aggregate	-	-	-	67.19	m³	-
Grade C10; sulphate resistant cement; 40 mm aggregate	-	-	-	66.20	m³	-
Grade C15; cement to BS12; 10 mm aggregate	-	-	-	66.90	m³	-
Grade C15; cement to BS12; 20 mm aggregate	-	-	-	65.18	m³	-
Grade C15; cement to BS12; 40 mm aggregate	-	-	-	64.20	m³	-
Grade C15; sulphate resistant cement; 10 mm aggregate	-	-	-	69.45	m³	-
Grade C15; sulphate resistant cement; 20 mm aggregate	-	-	-	67.63	m³	-
Grade C15; sulphate resistant cement; 40 mm aggregate	-	-	-	66.62	m³	-
Grade C20; cement to BS12; 10 mm aggregate	-	-	-	67.33	m³	-
Grade C20; cement to BS12; 20 mm aggregate	-	-	-	65.58	m³	-
Grade C20; cement to BS12; 40 mm aggregate	-	-	-	64.62	m³	-
Grade C20; sulphate resistant cement; 10 mm aggregate	-	-	-	69.90	m³	-
Grade C20; sulphate resistant cement; 20 mm aggregate	-	-	-	68.06	m³	-
Grade C20; sulphate resistant cement; 40 mm aggregate	-	-	-	67.06	m³	-
Grade C25; cement to BS12; 10 mm aggregate	-	-	-	67.76	m³	-
Grade C25; cement to BS12; 20 mm aggregate	-	-	-	66.01	m³	-
Grade C25; cement to BS12; 40 mm aggregate	-	-	-	65.02	m³	-
Grade C25; sulphate resistant cement; 10 mm aggregate	-	-	-	70.35	m³	-
Grade C25; sulphate resistant cement; 20 mm aggregate	-	-	-	68.52	m³	-

E IN SITU CONCRETE/LARGE PRECAST CONCRETE

Item	PC £	Labour hours	Labour £	Material £	Unit	Total rate £
Grade C25; sulphate resistant cement; 40 mm aggregate	-	-	-	67.48	m³	-
Grade C30; cement to BS12; 10 mm aggregate	-	-	-	68.19	m³	-
Grade C30; cement to BS12; 20 mm aggregate	-	-	-	66.42	m³	-
Grade C30; cement to BS12; 40 mm aggregate	-	-	-	65.45	m³	-
Grade C30; sulphate resistant cement; 10 mm aggregate	-	-	-	70.81	m³	-
Grade C30; sulphate resistant cement; 20 mm aggregate	-	-	-	68.95	m³	-
Grade C30; sulphate resistant cement; 40 mm aggregate	-	-	-	67.93	m³	-
Grade C40; cement to BS12; 10 mm aggregate	-	-	-	72.62	m³	-
Grade C40; cement to BS12; 20 mm aggregate	-	-	-	71.16	m³	-
Grade C40; sulphate resistant cement; 10 mm aggregate	-	-	-	75.42	m³	-
Grade C40; sulphate resistant cement; 20 mm aggregate	-	-	-	73.43	m³	-
Grade C50; cement to BS12; 10 mm aggregate	-	-	-	73.09	m³	-
Grade C50; cement to BS12; 20 mm aggregate	-	-	-	71.17	m³	-
Grade C50; sulphate resistant cement; 10 mm aggregate	-	-	-	75.92	m³	-
Grade C50; sulphate resistant cement; 20 mm aggregate	-	-	-	73.90	m³	-

DESIGNATED MIXES

Definition "Mix produced in accordance with the Specification given in section 5 of BS 5328: 2 : 1991 and requiring the producer to hold current Product conformity certification based on product Testing and surveillance coupled with approval of His quality system to BS 5750 : 1 (En 29001)".

NOTE: The following prices are for designated mix concrete ready for placing excluding any allowance for waste, discount or overheads and profit. Prices are based upon delivery to site within a 5 mile (8 km) radius of concrete mixing plant, using full loads.

Item	PC £	Labour hours	Labour £	Material £	Unit	Total rate £
Grade C7.5; cement to BS12; 10 mm aggregate	-	-	-	65.12	m³	-
Grade C7.5; cement to BS12; 20 mm aggregate	-	-	-	63.46	m³	-
Grade C7.5; cement to BS12; 40 mm aggregate	-	-	-	62.92	m³	-
Grade C7.5; sulphate resistant cement; 10 mm aggregate	-	-	-	67.58	m³	-
Grade C7.5; sulphate resistant cement; 20 mm aggregate	-	-	-	65.87	m³	-
Grade C7.5; sulphate resistant cement; 40 mm aggregate	-	-	-	65.27	m³	-
Grade C10; cement to BS12; 10 mm aggregate	-	-	-	65.96	m³	-
Grade C10; cement to BS12; 20 mm aggregate	-	-	-	64.26	m³	-
Grade C10; cement to BS12; 40 mm aggregate	-	-	-	63.27	m³	-
Grade C10; sulphate resistant cement; 10 mm aggregate	-	-	-	70.17	m³	-
Grade C10; sulphate resistant cement; 20 mm aggregate	-	-	-	66.68	m³	-
Grade C10; sulphate resistant cement; 40 mm aggregate	-	-	-	65.70	m³	-
Grade C15; cement to BS12; 10 mm aggregate	-	-	-	66.39	m³	-
Grade C15; cement to BS12; 20 mm aggregate	-	-	-	64.68	m³	-
Grade C15; cement to BS12; 40 mm aggregate	-	-	-	63.72	m³	-

E IN SITU CONCRETE/LARGE PRECAST CONCRETE

Item	PC £	Labour hours	Labour £	Material £	Unit	Total rate £
BASIC MIXED CONCRETE PRICES – cont'd						
DESIGNATED MIXES – cont'd						
Grade C15; sulphate resistant cement; 10 mm aggregate	-	-	-	68.92	m³	-
Grade C15; sulphate resistant cement; 20 mm aggregate	-	-	-	67.08	m³	-
Grade C15; sulphate resistant cement; 40 mm aggregate	-	-	-	66.07	m³	-
Grade C20; cement to BS12; 10 mm aggregate	-	-	-	66.82	m³	-
Grade C20; cement to BS12; 20 mm aggregate	-	-	-	65.09	m³	-
Grade C20; cement to BS12; 40 mm aggregate	-	-	-	64.13	m³	-
Grade C20; sulphate resistant cement; 10 mm aggregate	-	-	-	69.37	m³	-
Grade C20; sulphate resistant cement; 20 mm aggregate	-	-	-	67.55	m³	-
Grade C20; sulphate resistant cement; 40 mm aggregate	-	-	-	66.55	m³	-
Grade C25; cement to BS12; 10 mm aggregate	-	-	-	67.24	m³	-
Grade C25; cement to BS12; 20 mm aggregate	-	-	-	65.50	m³	-
Grade C25; cement to BS12; 40 mm aggregate	-	-	-	64.54	m³	-
Grade C25; sulphate resistant cement; 10 mm aggregate	-	-	-	69.81	m³	-
Grade C25; sulphate resistant cement; 20 mm aggregate	-	-	-	67.99	m³	-
Grade C25; sulphate resistant cement; 40 mm aggregate	-	-	-	66.98	m³	-
Grade C30; cement to BS12; 10 mm aggregate	-	-	-	67.67	m³	-
Grade C30; cement to BS12; 20 mm aggregate	-	-	-	65.88	m³	-
Grade C30; cement to BS12; 40 mm aggregate	-	-	-	64.96	m³	-
Grade C30; sulphate resistant cement; 10 mm aggregate	-	-	-	70.27	m³	-
Grade C30; sulphate resistant cement; 20 mm aggregate	-	-	-	68.42	m³	-
Grade C30; sulphate resistant cement; 40 mm aggregate	-	-	-	67.41	m³	-
Grade C35; cement to BS12; 10 mm aggregate	-	-	-	71.55	m³	-
Grade C35; cement to BS12; 20 mm aggregate	-	-	-	69.70	m³	-
Grade C35; sulphate resistant cement; 10 mm aggregate	-	-	-	74.30	m³	-
Grade C35; sulphate resistant cement; 20 mm aggregate	-	-	-	72.30	m³	-
Grade C40; cement to BS12; 10 mm aggregate	-	-	-	72.06	m³	-
Grade C40; cement to BS12; 20 mm aggregate	-	-	-	70.19	m³	-
Grade C40; sulphate resistant cement; 10 mm aggregate	-	-	-	74.84	m³	-
Grade C40; sulphate resistant cement; 20 mm aggregate	-	-	-	72.87	m³	-
Grade C50; cement to BS12; 10 mm aggregate	-	-	-	72.53	m³	-
Grade C50; cement to BS12; 20 mm aggregate	-	-	-	70.64	m³	-
Grade C50; sulphate resistant cement; 10 mm aggregate	-	-	-	75.33	m³	-
Grade C50; sulphate resistant cement; 20 mm aggregate	-	-	-	73.34	m³	-

E IN SITU CONCRETE/LARGE PRECAST CONCRETE

Item	PC £	Labour hours	Labour £	Material £	Unit	Total rate £
STANDARD MIXES						
Definition "Mix selected from the restricted list given in section 4 of BS 5328 : 2 : 1991 and made with a restricted range of materials".						
NOTE: The following prices are for standard mix concrete ready for placing excluding any allowance for waste, discount or overheads and profit. Prices are based upon delivery to site within a 5 mile (8 km) radius of concrete mixing plant, using full loads.	-	-	-			-
Standard mix; GEN 0	-	-	-	59.79	m^3	-
Standard mix; GEN 1	-	-	-	60.91	m^3	-
Standard mix; GEN 2	-	-	-	62.04	m^3	-
Standard mix; GEN 3	-	-	-	63.15	m^3	-
Standard mix; GEN 4	-	-	-	64.29	m^3	-
Standard mix; ST 1	-	-	-	62.04	m^3	-
Standard mix; ST 2	-	-	-	63.40	m^3	-
Standard mix; ST 3	-	-	-	64.75	m^3	-
Standard mix; ST 4	-	-	-	66.09	m^3	-
Standard mix; ST 5	-	-	-	67.89	m^3	-
LIGHTWEIGHT CONCRETE						
Grade 25; pumped; Lytag medium and natural sand	-	-	-	90.00	m^3	-
Grade 30; pumped; Lytag medium and natural sand	-	-	-	92.00	m^3	-
Grade 35; pumped; Lytag medium and natural sand	-	-	-	94.10	m^3	-
Reduction for un-pumped concrete	-	-	-	-1.30	m^3	-
SITE MIXED CONCRETE						
Mix 7.50 N/mm2; cement to BS12 (1:8); 40 mm aggregate	-	-	-	74.78	m^3	-
Mix 7.50 N/mm2; sulphate resisting cement (1:8) 40 mm aggregate	-	-	-	76.65	m^3	-
Mix 10.00 N/mm2; cement to BS12 (1:8): 40 mm aggregate	-	-	-	74.78	m^3	-
Mix 10.00 N/mm2; sulphate resisting cement (1:8): 40 mm aggregate.	-	-	-	76.65	m^3	-
Mix 20.00 N/mm2; cement to BS12 (1:2:4); 20 mm aggregate	-	-	-	77.57	m^3	-
Mix 20.00 N/mm2; sulphate resisting cement (1:2:4); 20 mm aggregate	-	-	-	79.79	m^3	-
Mix 25.00 N/mm2; cement to BS12 (1:1:5:3); 20 mm aggregate	-	-	-	83.91	m^3	-
Mix 25.00 N/mm2; sulphate resisting cement (1:1:5:3); 20 mm aggregate	-	-	-	86.92	m^3	-
Add to preceding prices						
Rapid-hardening cement to BS 12	-	-	-	3.84	m^3	-
Polypropylene fibre additive	-	-	-	1.10	m^3	-
Air entraned concrtete	-	-	-	3.84	m^3	-
Water repellant additive	-	-	-	4.10	m^3	-
Distance per mile in excess of 5 miles (8 km)	-	-	-	0.86	m^3	-
Part loads per m3 below full load	-	-	-	19.76	m^3	-

E IN SITU CONCRETE/LARGE PRECAST CONCRETE

Item	PC £	Labour hours	Labour £	Material £	Unit	Total rate £
OTHER MATERIAL PRICES						
CEMENTS						
Ordinary portland to BS12	-	-	-	111.90	tonne	-
Lighting high alumina	-	-	-	374.02	tonne	-
Sulfacrete sulphate resisting	-	-	-	136.74	tonne	-
Ferrocrete rapid hardening	-	-	-	124.67	tonne	-
Snowcrete white cement	-	-	-	261.41	tonne	-
CEMENT ADMIXTURES						
Febtone colourant - red, marigold, yellow, brown, black	-	-	-	9.45	kg	-
Febproof waterproof	-	-	-	9.97	5 litre	-
Febond PVA bonding agent	-	-	-	17.23	5 litre	-
Febspeed frostproofer and hardener	-	-	-	6.12	5 litre	-
E05 IN SITU CONCRETE CONSTRUCTION						
SUPPLY AND FIX PRICES						
NOTE: The following concrete material prices include an allowance for shrinkage factors at plus 2½% (or 5% when poured against earth or unblinded hardcore) and waste at plus 7½%, together with overheads and profit at plus 5% and 2.5% respectively. PC Sums are designated Basic mixed concrete prices						
Plain in situ ready mixed designated concrete; C7.5 - 40 mm aggregate						
Foundations	62.92	1.20	15.30	74.62	m^3	89.92
Isolated foundations	-	1.39	17.73	74.62	m^3	92.35
Beds						
thickness not exceeding 150 mm	-	1.62	20.66	74.62	m^3	95.28
thickness 150 - 450 mm	-	1.16	14.79	74.62	m^3	89.41
thickness exceeding 450 mm	-	0.93	11.86	74.62	m^3	86.48
Screeded beds; protection to compressible formwork						
50 mm thick	-	0.10	1.28	3.64	m^2	4.92
75 mm thick	-	0.15	1.91	5.46	m^2	7.37
100 mm thick	-	0.20	2.55	7.28	m^2	9.83
Filling hollow walls						
thickness not exceeding 150 mm	-	3.15	40.17	74.62	m^3	114.79
Column casings						
stub columns beneath suspended ground slabs	-	4.50	57.39	74.62	m^3	132.01
Plain in situ ready mixed designated concrete; C10 - 40 mm aggregate						
Foundations	63.27	1.20	15.30	75.03	m^3	90.34
Isolated foundations	-	1.39	17.73	75.03	m^3	92.76
Beds						
thickness not exceeding 150 mm	-	1.62	20.66	75.03	m^3	95.69
thickness 150 - 450 mm	-	1.16	14.79	75.03	m^3	89.83
thickness exceeding 450 mm	-	0.93	11.86	75.03	m^3	86.89
Filling hollow walls						
thickness not exceeding 150 mm	-	3.15	40.17	75.03	m^3	115.21

E IN SITU CONCRETE/LARGE PRECAST CONCRETE

Item	PC £	Labour hours	Labour £	Material £	Unit	Total rate £
Plain in situ ready mixed designated concrete; C10 - 40 mm aggregate; poured on or against earth or unblinded hardcore						
Foundations	63.27	1.25	15.94	76.86	m^3	92.81
Isolated foundations	-	1.48	18.88	76.86	m^3	95.74
Beds						
thickness not exceeding 150 mm	-	1.71	21.81	76.86	m^3	98.67
thickness 150 - 450 mm	-	1.25	15.94	76.86	m^3	92.81
thickness exceeding 450 mm	-	0.97	12.37	76.86	m^3	89.24
Plain in situ ready mixed designated concrete; C20 - 20 mm aggregate						
Foundations	65.09	1.20	15.30	77.19	m^3	92.50
Isolated foundations	-	1.39	17.73	77.19	m^3	94.92
Beds						
thickness not exceeding 150 mm	-	1.76	22.45	77.19	m^3	99.64
thickness 150 - 450 mm	-	1.20	15.30	77.19	m^3	92.50
thickness exceeding 450 mm	-	0.93	11.86	77.19	m^3	89.05
Filling hollow walls						
thickness not exceeding 150 mm	-	3.15	40.17	77.19	m^3	117.37
Plain in situ ready mixed designated concrete; C20 - 20 mm aggregate; poured on or against earth or unblinded hardcore						
Foundations	65.09	1.25	15.94	79.08	m^3	95.02
Isolated foundations	-	1.48	18.88	79.08	m^3	97.95
Beds						
thickness not exceeding 150 mm	-	1.85	23.59	79.08	m^3	102.67
thickness 150 - 450 mm	-	1.30	16.58	79.08	m^3	95.66
thickness exceeding 450 mm	-	0.97	12.37	79.08	m^3	91.45
Reinforced in situ ready mixed designated concrete; C25 - 20 mm aggregate						
Foundations	65.50	1.30	16.58	77.68	m^3	94.26
Ground beams	-	2.59	33.03	77.68	m^3	110.71
Isolated foundations	-	1.57	20.02	77.68	m^3	97.70
Beds						
thickness not exceeding 150 mm	-	2.04	26.02	77.68	m^3	103.70
thickness 150 - 450 mm	-	1.48	18.88	77.68	m^3	96.55
thickness exceeding 450 mm	-	1.20	15.30	77.68	m^3	92.98
Slabs						
thickness not exceeding 150 mm	-	3.24	41.32	77.68	m^3	119.00
thickness 150 - 450 mm	-	2.59	33.03	77.68	m^3	110.71
thickness exceeding 450 mm	-	2.31	29.46	77.68	m^3	107.14
Coffered and troughed slabs						
thickness 150 - 450 mm	-	2.96	37.75	77.68	m^3	115.43
thickness exceeding 450 mm	-	2.59	33.03	77.68	m^3	110.71
Extra over for sloping						
not exceeding 15 degrees	-	0.23	2.93	-	m^3	2.93
over 15 degrees	-	0.46	5.87	-	m^3	5.87
Walls						
thickness not exceeding 150 mm	-	3.42	43.62	77.68	m^3	121.30
thickness 150 - 450 mm	-	2.73	34.82	77.68	m^3	112.50
thickness exceeding 450 mm	-	2.41	30.74	77.68	m^3	108.41

E IN SITU CONCRETE/LARGE PRECAST CONCRETE

Item	PC £	Labour hours	Labour £	Material £	Unit	Total rate £
E05 IN SITU CONCRETE CONSTRUCTION						
– cont'd						
Reinforced in situ ready mixed designated						
concrete; C25 - 20 mm aggregate – cont'd						
Beams						
isolated	-	3.70	47.19	77.68	m^3	124.87
isolated deep	-	4.07	51.91	77.68	m^3	129.59
attached deep	-	3.70	47.19	77.68	m^3	124.87
Beam casings						
isolated	-	4.07	51.91	77.68	m^3	129.59
isolated deep	-	4.44	56.63	77.68	m^3	134.30
attached deep	-	4.07	51.91	77.68	m^3	129.59
Columns	-	4.44	56.63	77.68	m^3	134.30
Column casings	-	4.90	62.49	77.68	m^3	140.17
Staircases	-	5.55	70.78	77.68	m^3	148.46
Upstands	-	3.56	45.40	77.68	m^3	123.08
Reinforced in situ ready mixed						
designated concrete; C35 -20 mm						
aggregate						
Foundations	69.70	1.30	16.58	82.66	m^3	99.24
Ground beams	-	2.59	33.03	82.66	m^3	115.69
Isolated foundations	-	1.57	20.02	82.66	m^3	102.68
Beds						
thickness not exceeding 150 mm	-	2.04	26.02	82.66	m^3	108.68
thickness 150 - 450 mm	-	1.48	18.88	82.66	m^3	101.53
thickness exceeding 450 mm	-	1.20	15.30	82.66	m^3	97.96
Slabs						
thickness not exceeding 150 mm	-	3.24	41.32	82.66	m^3	123.98
thickness 150 - 450 mm	-	2.59	33.03	82.66	m^3	115.69
thickness exceeding 450 mm	-	2.31	29.46	82.66	m^3	112.12
Coffered and troughed slabs						
thickness 150 - 450 mm	-	2.96	37.75	82.66	m^3	120.41
thickness exceeding 450 mm	-	2.59	33.03	82.66	m^3	115.69
Extra over for sloping						
not exceeding 15 degrees	-	0.23	2.93	-	m^3	2.93
over 15 degrees	-	0.46	5.87	-	m^3	5.87
Walls						
thickness not exceeding 150 mm	-	3.42	43.62	82.66	m^3	126.28
thickness 150 - 450 mm	-	2.73	34.82	82.66	m^3	117.48
thickness exceeding 450 mm	-	2.41	30.74	82.66	m^3	113.39
Beams						
isolated	-	3.70	47.19	82.66	m^3	129.85
isolated deep	-	4.07	51.91	82.66	m^3	134.57
attached deep	-	3.70	47.19	82.66	m^3	129.85
Beam casings						
isolated	-	4.07	51.91	82.66	m^3	134.57
isolated deep	-	4.44	56.63	82.66	m^3	139.28
attached deep	-	4.07	51.91	82.66	m^3	134.57
Columns	-	4.44	56.63	82.66	m^3	139.28
Column casings	-	4.90	62.49	82.66	m^3	145.15
Staircases	-	5.55	70.78	82.66	m^3	153.44
Upstands	-	3.56	45.40	82.66	m^3	128.06

E IN SITU CONCRETE/LARGE PRECAST CONCRETE

Item	PC £	Labour hours	Labour £	Material £	Unit	Total rate £
Reinforced in situ ready mixed designed concrete; C40 -20 mm aggregate						
Foundations	70.19	1.30	16.58	83.24	m^3	99.82
Ground beams	-	2.59	33.03	83.24	m^3	116.27
Isolated foundations	-	1.57	20.02	83.24	m^3	103.26
Beds						
thickness not exceeding 150 mm	-	2.04	26.02	83.24	m^3	109.26
thickness 150 - 450 mm	-	1.48	18.88	83.24	m^3	102.11
thickness exceeding 450 mm	-	1.20	15.30	83.24	m^3	98.54
Slabs						
thickness not exceeding 150 mm	-	3.24	41.32	83.24	m^3	124.56
thickness 150 - 450 mm	-	2.59	33.03	83.24	m^3	116.27
thickness exceeding 450 mm	-	2.31	29.46	83.24	m^3	112.70
Coffered and troughed slabs						
thickness 150 - 450 mm	-	2.96	37.75	83.24	m^3	120.99
thickness exceeding 450 mm	-	2.59	33.03	83.24	m^3	116.27
Extra over for sloping						
not exceeding 15 degrees	-	0.23	2.93	-	m^3	2.93
over 15 degrees	-	0.46	5.87	-	m^3	5.87
Walls						
thickness not exceeding 150 mm	-	3.42	43.62	83.24	m^3	126.86
thickness 150 - 450 mm	-	2.73	34.82	83.24	m^3	118.06
thickness exceeding 450 mm	-	2.41	30.74	83.24	m^3	113.98
Beams						
isolated	-	3.70	47.19	83.24	m^3	130.43
isolated deep	-	4.07	51.91	83.24	m^3	135.15
attached deep	-	3.70	47.19	83.24	m^3	130.43
Beam casings						
isolated	-	4.07	51.91	83.24	m^3	135.15
isolated deep	-	4.44	56.63	83.24	m^3	139.87
attached deep	-	4.07	51.91	83.24	m^3	135.15
Columns	-	4.44	56.63	83.24	m^3	139.87
Column casings	-	4.90	62.49	83.24	m^3	145.73
Staircases	-	5.55	70.78	83.24	m^3	154.02
Upstands	-	3.56	45.40	83.24	m^3	128.64
Extra over vibrated concrete for						
Reinforcement content over 5%	-	0.51	6.50	-	m^3	6.50
Grouting with cement mortar (1:1)						
Stanchion bases						
10 mm thick	-	0.93	11.86	0.11	nr	11.97
25 mm thick	-	1.16	14.79	0.29	nr	15.08
Grouting with epoxy resin						
Stanchion bases						
10 mm thick	-	1.16	14.79	8.32	nr	23.12
25 mm thick	-	1.39	17.73	21.27	nr	38.99
Grouting with "Conbextra GP" cementitious grout						
Stanchion bases						
10 mm thick	-	1.16	14.79	1.23	nr	16.03
25 mm thick	-	1.39	17.73	3.15	nr	20.88

E IN SITU CONCRETE/LARGE PRECAST CONCRETE

Item	PC £	Labour hours	Labour £	Material £	Unit	Total rate £
E05 IN SITU CONCRETE CONSTRUCTION – cont'd						
Grouting with "Conbextra HF" flowable cementitious grout						
Stanchion bases						
10 mm thick	-	1.16	14.79	1.52	nr	**16.31**
25 mm thick	-	1.39	17.73	3.88	nr	**21.61**
Filling; plain in situ designated concrete; C20 - 20 mm aggregate						
Mortices	-	0.09	1.15	0.42	nr	**1.57**
Holes	-	0.23	2.93	87.66	m³	**90.59**
Chases exceeding 0.01 m²	-	0.19	2.42	87.66	m³	**90.08**
Chases not exceeding 0.01 m²	-	0.14	1.79	0.88	m	**2.66**
Sheeting to prevent moisture loss						
Building paper; lapped joints						
subsoil grade 410; horizontal on foundations	-	0.02	0.26	0.46	m²	**0.71**
standard grade 420; horizontal on slabs	-	0.04	0.51	0.77	m²	**1.28**
Polythene sheeting; lapped joints; horizontal on slabs						
250 microns; 0.25 mm thick	-	0.04	0.51	0.39	m²	**0.90**
"Visqueen" sheeting or other equal and approved; lapped joints; horizontal on slabs						
250 microns; 0.25 mm thick	-	0.04	0.51	0.33	m²	**0.84**
300 microns; 0.30 mm thick	-	0.05	0.64	0.40	m²	**1.04**
E20 FORMWORK FOR IN SITU CONCRETE						
NOTE: Generally all formwork based on four uses unless otherwise stated.						
Sides of foundations; basic finish						
Plain vertical						
height exceeding 1.00 m	-	1.48	23.43	5.83	m²	**29.26**
height exceeding 1.00 m; left in	-	1.30	20.58	14.35	m²	**34.93**
height not exceeding 250 mm	-	0.42	6.65	2.42	m	**9.07**
height not exceeding 250 mm; left in	-	0.42	6.65	4.23	m	**10.88**
height 250 - 500 mm	-	0.79	12.51	4.89	m	**17.40**
height 250 - 500 mm; left in	-	0.69	10.92	9.84	m	**20.77**
height 500 mm - 1.00 m	-	1.11	17.57	5.83	m	**23.40**
height 500 mm - 1.00 m; left in	-	1.06	16.78	14.35	m	**31.13**
Sides of foundations; polystyrene sheet formwork; Cordek "Claymaster" or other equal and approved; 50 mm thick						
Plain vertical						
height exceeding 1.00 m; left in	-	0.30	4.75	8.47	m²	**13.22**
height not exceeding 250 mm; left in	-	0.10	1.58	2.12	m	**3.70**
height 250 - 500 mm; left in	-	0.16	2.53	4.24	m	**6.77**
height 500 mm - 1.00 m; left in	-	0.24	3.80	8.47	m	**12.27**
Sides of foundations; polystyrene sheet formwork; Cordek "Claymaster" or other equal and approved; 75 mm thick						
Plain vertical						
height exceeding 1.00 m; left in	-	0.30	4.75	12.69	m²	**17.44**
height not exceeding 250 mm; left in	-	0.10	1.58	3.17	m	**4.76**
height 250 - 500 mm; left in	-	0.16	2.53	6.35	m	**8.88**
height 500 mm - 1.00 m; left in	-	0.24	3.80	12.69	m	**16.49**

E IN SITU CONCRETE/LARGE PRECAST CONCRETE

Item	PC £	Labour hours	Labour £	Material £	Unit	Total rate £
Sides of foundations; polystyrene sheet formwork; Cordek "Claymaster" or other equal and approved; 100 mm thick						
Plain vertical						
height exceeding 1.00 m; left in	-	0.30	4.75	16.90	m²	**21.65**
height not exceeding 250 mm; left in	-	0.10	1.58	4.23	m	**5.81**
height 250 - 500 mm; left in	-	0.16	2.53	8.45	m	**10.98**
height 500 mm - 1.00 m; left in	-	0.24	3.80	16.90	m	**20.70**
Combined heave presssure relief insulation and compressible board substructure formwork; Cordeck "Cellcore CP" or other equal and approved; butt joints; securely fixed in place						
Plain horizontal						
200 mm thick; beneath slabs; left in	-	0.60	9.50	17.72	m²	**27.22**
250 mm thick; beneath slabs; left in	-	0.65	10.29	19.55	m²	**29.84**
300 mm thick; beneath slabs; left in	-	0.70	11.08	21.26	m²	**32.34**
Sides of ground beams and edges of beds; basic finish						
Plain vertical						
height exceeding 1.00 m	-	1.53	24.22	5.79	m²	**30.01**
height not exceeding 250 mm	-	0.46	7.28	2.38	m	**9.66**
height 250 - 500 mm	-	0.83	13.14	4.85	m	**17.99**
height 500 mm - 1.00 m	-	1.16	18.36	5.79	m	**24.15**
Edges of suspended slabs; basic finish						
Plain vertical						
height not exceeding 250 mm	-	0.69	10.92	2.47	m	**13.39**
height 250 - 500 mm	-	1.02	16.15	3.93	m	**20.08**
height 500 mm - 1.00 m	-	1.62	25.65	5.87	m	**31.52**
Sides of upstands; basic finish						
Plain vertical						
height exceeding 1.00 m	-	1.85	29.29	7.29	m²	**36.58**
height not exceeding 250 mm	-	0.58	9.18	2.55	m	**11.73**
height 250 - 500 mm	-	0.93	14.72	5.02	m	**19.74**
height 500 mm - 1.00 m	-	1.62	25.65	7.29	m	**32.94**
Steps in top surfaces; basic finish						
Plain vertical						
height not exceeding 250 mm	-	0.46	7.28	2.59	m	**9.88**
height 250 - 500 mm	-	0.74	11.72	5.06	m	**16.78**
Steps in soffits; basic finish						
Plain vertical						
height not exceeding 250 mm	-	0.51	8.07	1.99	m	**10.07**
height 250 - 500 mm	-	0.81	12.82	3.56	m	**16.38**
Machine bases and plinths; basic finish						
Plain vertical						
height exceeding 1.00 m	-	1.48	23.43	5.79	m²	**29.22**
height not exceeding 250 mm	-	0.46	7.28	2.38	m	**9.66**
height 250 - 500 mm	-	0.79	12.51	4.85	m	**17.36**
height 500 mm - 1.00 m	-	1.16	18.36	5.79	m	**24.15**

E IN SITU CONCRETE/LARGE PRECAST CONCRETE

Item	PC £	Labour hours	Labour £	Material £	Unit	Total rate £
E20 FORMWORK FOR IN SITU CONCRETE						
– cont'd						
Soffits of slabs; basic finish						
Slab thickness not exceeding 200 mm						
horizontal; height to soffit not exceeding 1.50 m	-	1.67	26.44	5.31	m^2	**31.75**
horizontal; height to soffit 1.50 - 3.00 m	-	1.62	25.65	5.40	m^2	**31.05**
horizontal; height to soffit 1.50 - 3.00 m (based						
on 5 uses)	-	1.53	24.22	4.49	m^2	**28.71**
horizontal; height to soffit 1.50 - 3.00 m (based						
on 6 uses)	-	1.48	23.43	3.89	m^2	**27.32**
horizontal; height to soffit 3.00 - 4.50 m	-	1.57	24.86	5.61	m^2	**30.47**
horizontal; height to soffit 4.50 - 6.00 m	-	1.67	26.44	5.83	m^2	**32.27**
Slab thickness 200 - 300 mm						
horizontal; height to soffit 1.50 - 3.00 m	-	1.67	26.44	7.16	m^2	**33.60**
Slab thickness 300 - 400 mm						
horizontal; height to soffit 1.50 - 3.00 m	-	1.71	27.07	8.04	m^2	**35.12**
Slab thickness 400 - 500 mm						
horizontal; height to soffit 1.50 - 3.00 m	-	1.80	28.50	8.93	m^2	**37.42**
Slab thickness 500 - 600 mm						
horizontal; height to soffit 1.50 - 3.00 m	-	1.94	30.71	8.93	m^2	**39.64**
Extra over soffits of slabs for						
sloping not exceeding 15 degrees	-	0.19	3.01	-	m^2	**3.01**
sloping exceeding 15 degrees	-	0.37	5.86	-	m^2	**5.86**
Soffits of slabs; Expamet "Hy-Rib"						
permanent shuttering and reinforcement						
or other equal and approved; ref. 2411						
Slab thickness not exceeding 200 mm						
horizontal; height to soffit 1.50 - 3.00 m	-	1.39	22.01	19.21	m^2	**41.21**
Soffits of slabs; Richard Lees galvanised						
steel permanent shuttering; or other						
equal and approved						
Slab thickness not exceeding 200 mm						
0.9 mm S350 'Holorib' decking; height to soffit						
1.50 - 3.00 m	12.64	0.25	3.96	14.01	m^2	**17.97**
0.9 mm S350 'Holorib' decking; height to soffit						
3.00 - 4.50 m	12.64	0.30	4.75	14.01	m^2	**18.76**
1.2 mm S350 'Holorib' decking; height to soffit						
3.00 - 4.50 m	15.22	0.30	4.75	16.88	m^2	**21.62**
0.9 mm S350 'Ribdeck E60' decking; height to						
soffit 3.00 - 4.50 m	9.87	0.30	4.75	10.94	m^2	**15.69**
1.2 mm S350 'Ribdeck E60' decking; height to						
soffit 3.00 - 4.50 m	11.85	0.30	4.75	13.14	m^2	**17.89**
0.9 mm S350 'Ribdeck AL' decking; height to						
soffit 3.00 - 4.50 m	10.22	0.30	4.75	11.33	m^2	**16.08**
1.2 mm S350 'Ribdeck AL' decking; height to						
soffit 3.00 - 4.50 m	12.28	0.30	4.75	13.61	m^2	**18.36**
1.2 mm S350 'Ribdeck 80' decking; height to						
soffit 3.00 - 4.50 m	15.27	0.30	4.75	16.93	m^2	**21.68**
Edge trim and restraints to decking						
Edge trim 1.2 mm x 300 mm girth	-	0.12	1.90	4.93	m	**6.83**
Edge trim 1.2 mm x 350 mm girth	-	0.12	1.90	5.56	m	**7.46**
Edge trim 1.2 mm x 400 mm girth	-	0.12	1.90	6.16	m	**8.06**

E IN SITU CONCRETE/LARGE PRECAST CONCRETE

Item	PC £	Labour hours	Labour £	Material £	Unit	Total rate £
Bearings to decking; connection to steel work with 'thru-deck' welded shear studs						
19 mm dia x 95 mm high studs at 100 mm c/cs	-	-	-	13.01	m	**13.01**
19 mm dia x 95 mm high studs at 200 mm c/cs	-	-	-	6.51	m	**6.51**
19 mm dia x 95 mm high studs at 300 mm c/cs	-	-	-	4.33	m	**4.33**
19 mm dia x 120 mm high studs at 100 mm centres	-	-	-	15.07	m	**15.07**
19 mm dia x 120 mm high studs at 200 mm centres	-	-	-	7.53	m	**7.53**
19 mm dia x 120 mm high studs at 300 mm centres	-	-	-	5.02	m	**5.02**
Soffits of landings; basic finish						
Slab thickness not exceeding 200 mm						
horizontal; height to soffit 1.50 - 3.00 m	-	1.67	26.44	5.75	m²	**32.19**
Slab thickness 200 - 300 mm						
horizontal; height to soffit 1.50 - 3.00 m	-	1.76	27.86	7.69	m²	**35.55**
Slab thickness 300 - 400 mm						
horizontal; height to soffit 1.50 - 3.00 m	-	1.80	28.50	8.66	m²	**37.16**
Slab thickness 400 - 500 mm						
horizontal; height to soffit 1.50 - 3.00 m	-	1.90	30.08	9.63	m²	**39.71**
Slab thickness 500 - 600 mm						
horizontal; height to soffit 1.50 - 3.00 m	-	2.04	32.30	9.63	m²	**41.93**
Extra over soffits of landings for						
sloping not exceeding 15 degrees	-	0.19	3.01	-	m²	**3.01**
sloping exceeding 15 degrees	-	0.37	5.86	-	m²	**5.86**
Soffits of coffered or troughed slabs; basic finish						
Cordek "Correx" trough mould or other equal and approved; 300 mm deep; ribs of mould at 600 mm centres and cross ribs at centres of bay; slab thickness 300 - 400 mm						
horizontal; height to soffit 1.50 - 3.00 m	-	2.31	36.57	10.10	m²	**46.68**
horizontal; height to soffit 3.00 - 4.50 m	-	2.41	38.15	10.32	m²	**48.47**
horizontal; height to soffit 4.50 - 6.00 m	-	2.50	39.58	10.45	m²	**50.03**
Top formwork; basic finish						
Sloping exceeding 15 degrees	-	1.39	22.01	3.85	m²	**25.86**
Walls; basic finish						
Vertical	-	1.67	26.44	7.16	m²	**33.60**
Vertical; height exceeding 3.00 m above floor level	-	2.04	32.30	7.38	m²	**39.67**
Vertical; interrupted	-	1.94	30.71	7.38	m²	**38.09**
Vertical; to one side only	-	3.24	51.29	9.35	m²	**60.65**
Battered	-	2.59	41.00	7.76	m²	**48.77**
Beams; basic finish						
Attached to slabs						
regular shaped; square or rectangular; height to soffit 1.50 - 3.00 m	-	2.04	32.30	6.90	m²	**39.20**
regular shaped; square or rectangular; height to soffit 3.00 - 4.50 m	-	2.13	33.72	7.16	m²	**40.88**
regular shaped; square or rectangular; height to soffit 4.50 - 6.00 m	-	2.22	35.15	7.38	m²	**42.52**
Attached to walls						
regular shaped; square or rectangular; height to soffit 1.50 - 3.00 m	-	2.13	33.72	6.90	m²	**40.63**

E IN SITU CONCRETE/LARGE PRECAST CONCRETE

Item	PC £	Labour hours	Labour £	Material £	Unit	Total rate £
E20 FORMWORK FOR IN SITU CONCRETE – cont'd						
Beams; basic finish – cont'd						
Isolated						
regular shaped; square or rectangular; height to soffit 1.50 - 3.00 m	-	2.22	35.15	6.90	m²	42.05
regular shaped; square or rectangular; height to soffit 3.00 - 4.50 m	-	2.31	36.57	7.16	m²	43.73
regular shaped; square or rectangular; height to soffit 4.50 - 6.00 m	-	2.41	38.15	7.38	m²	45.53
Extra over beams for						
regular shaped; sloping not exceeding 15 degrees	-	0.28	4.43	0.84	m²	5.27
regular shaped; sloping exceeding 15 degrees	-	0.56	8.87	1.68	m²	10.54
Beam casings; basic finish						
Attached to slabs						
regular shaped; square or rectangular; height to soffit 1.50 - 3.00 m	-	2.13	33.72	6.90	m²	40.63
regular shaped; square or rectangular; height to soffit 3.00 - 4.50 m	-	2.22	35.15	7.16	m²	42.31
Attached to walls						
regular shaped; square or rectangular; height to soffit 1.50 - 3.00 m	-	2.22	35.15	6.90	m²	42.05
Isolated						
regular shaped; square or rectangular; height to soffit 1.50 - 3.00 m	-	2.31	36.57	6.90	m²	43.48
regular shaped; square or rectangular; height to soffit 3.00 - 4.50 m	-	2.41	38.15	7.16	m²	45.32
Extra over beam casings for						
regular shaped; sloping not exceeding 15 degrees	-	0.28	4.43	0.84	m²	5.27
regular shaped; sloping exceeding 15 degrees	-	0.56	8.87	1.68	m²	10.54
Columns; basic finish						
Attached to walls						
regular shaped; square or rectangular; height to soffit 1.50 - 3.00 m	-	2.04	32.30	5.83	m²	38.13
Isolated						
regular shaped; square or rectangular; height to soffit 1.50 - 3.00 m	-	2.13	33.72	5.83	m²	39.55
regular shaped; circular; not exceeding 300 mm diameter; height to soffit 1.50 - 3.00 m	-	3.70	58.58	10.26	m²	68.84
regular shaped; circular; 300 - 600 mm diameter; height to soffit 1.50 - 3.00 m	-	3.47	54.94	8.93	m²	63.86
regular shaped; circular; 600 - 900 mm diameter; height to soffit 1.50 - 3.00 m	-	3.24	51.29	8.71	m²	60.01
Column casings; basic finish						
Attached to walls						
regular shaped; square or rectangular; height to soffit 1.50 - 3.00 m	-	2.13	33.72	5.83	m²	39.55
Isolated						
regular shaped; square or rectangular; height to soffit 1.50 - 3.00 m	-	2.22	35.15	5.83	m²	40.97

E IN SITU CONCRETE/LARGE PRECAST CONCRETE

Item	PC £	Labour hours	Labour £	Material £	Unit	Total rate £
Recesses or rebates						
12 x 12 mm	-	0.06	0.95	0.07	m	1.02
25 x 25 mm	-	0.06	0.95	0.09	m	1.04
25 x 50 mm	-	0.06	0.95	0.13	m	1.08
50 x 50 mm	-	0.06	0.95	0.21	m	1.16
Nibs						
50 x 50 mm	-	0.51	8.07	0.74	m	8.82
100 x 100 mm	-	0.72	11.40	0.90	m	12.30
100 x 200 mm	-	0.96	15.20	2.12	m	17.32
Extra over a basic finish for fine formed finishes						
Slabs	-	0.30	4.75	-	m²	4.75
Walls	-	0.30	4.75	-	m²	4.75
Beams	-	0.30	4.75	-	m²	4.75
Columns	-	0.30	4.75	-	m²	4.75
Add to prices for basic formwork for						
Curved radius 6.00 m - 50%						
Curved radius 2.00 m - 100%						
Coating with retardant agent	-	0.01	0.16	0.29	m²	0.45
Wall kickers; basic finish						
Height 150 mm	-	0.46	7.28	1.66	m	8.94
Height 225 mm	-	0.60	9.50	1.94	m	11.44
Suspended wall kickers; basic finish						
Height 150 mm	-	0.58	9.18	1.88	m	11.06
Wall ends, soffits and steps in walls; basic finish						
Plain						
width exceeding 1.00 m	-	1.76	27.86	7.16	m²	35.03
width not exceeding 250 mm	-	0.56	8.87	1.78	m	10.64
width 250 - 500 mm	-	0.88	13.93	4.01	m	17.94
width 500 mm - 1.00 m	-	1.39	22.01	7.16	m	29.17
Openings in walls						
Plain						
width exceeding 1.00 m	-	1.94	30.71	7.16	m²	37.88
width not exceeding 250 mm	-	0.60	9.50	1.78	m	11.28
width 250 - 500 mm	-	1.02	16.15	4.01	m	20.16
width 500 mm - 1.00 m	-	1.57	24.86	7.16	m	32.02
Stairflights						
Width 1.00 m; 150 mm waist; 150 mm undercut risers						
string, width 300 mm	-	4.63	73.30	15.21	m	88.51
Width 2.00 m; 200 mm waist; 150 mm undercut risers						
string, width 350 mm	-	8.33	131.88	26.74	m	158.62
Mortices						
Girth not exceeding 500 mm						
depth not exceeding 250 mm; circular	-	0.14	2.22	0.45	nr	2.66

E IN SITU CONCRETE/LARGE PRECAST CONCRETE

Item	PC £	Labour hours	Labour £	Material £	Unit	Total rate £
E20 FORMWORK FOR IN SITU CONCRETE – cont'd						
Holes						
Girth not exceeding 500 mm						
depth not exceeding 250 mm; circular	-	0.19	3.01	0.67	nr	3.67
depth 250 - 500 mm; circular	-	0.28	4.43	1.90	nr	6.33
Girth 500 mm - 1.00 m						
depth not exceeding 250 mm; circular	-	0.23	3.64	1.04	nr	4.68
depth 250 - 500 mm; circular	-	0.35	5.54	3.31	nr	8.85
Girth 1.00 - 2.00 m						
depth not exceeding 250 mm; circular	-	0.42	6.65	3.31	nr	9.96
depth 250 - 500 mm; circular	-	0.62	9.82	7.08	nr	16.90
Girth 2.00 - 3.00 m						
depth not exceeding 250 mm; circular	-	0.56	8.87	6.60	nr	15.47
depth 250 - 500 mm; circular	-	0.83	13.14	13.79	nr	26.93
E30 REINFORCEMENT FOR IN SITU CONCRETE						
Bar; BS 4449; hot rolled deformed high steel bars; grade 460						
40 mm diameter nominal size						
straight	349.00	16.00	240.74	401.90	tonne	642.63
bent	389.00	16.00	240.74	446.02	tonne	686.76
32 mm diameter nominal size						
straight	346.00	17.00	255.78	400.10	tonne	655.89
bent	386.00	17.00	255.78	444.23	tonne	700.01
25 mm diameter nominal size						
straight	344.00	18.00	270.83	397.32	tonne	668.15
bent	384.00	18.00	270.83	441.45	tonne	712.27
20 mm diameter nominal size						
straight	344.00	20.00	300.92	398.80	tonne	699.72
bent	384.00	18.00	270.83	442.92	tonne	713.75
16 mm diameter nominal size						
straight	344.00	22.00	331.01	401.21	tonne	732.22
bent	384.00	22.00	331.01	445.34	tonne	776.35
12 mm diameter nominal size						
straight	346.00	24.00	361.10	405.83	tonne	766.93
bent	386.00	24.00	361.10	449.96	tonne	811.06
10 mm diameter nominal size						
straight	349.00	26.00	391.20	412.45	tonne	803.64
bent	389.00	26.00	391.20	456.57	tonne	847.77
8 mm diameter nominal size						
straight	357.00	28.00	419.00	423.69	tonne	842.68
links	357.00	31.00	464.13	426.72	tonne	890.85
bent	408.00	28.00	419.00	479.95	tonne	898.94
6 mm diameter nominal size						
straight	367.00	31.00	464.13	434.72	tonne	898.85
links	408.00	34.00	509.27	479.95	tonne	989.22
bent	408.00	31.00	464.13	479.95	tonne	944.08
Bar; BS 6744; stainless steel bars; grade 304						
32 mm diameter nominal size						
straight	2250.00	17.00	255.78	2533.39	tonne	2789.17
bent	2350.00	21.00	311.38	2643.70	tonne	2955.08
25 mm diameter nominal size						
straight	2250.00	18.00	270.83	2530.75	tonne	2801.58
bent	2350.00	18.00	270.83	2641.07	tonne	2911.90

E IN SITU CONCRETE/LARGE PRECAST CONCRETE

Item	PC £	Labour hours	Labour £	Material £	Unit	Total rate £
20 mm diameter nominal size						
straight	2300.00	20.00	300.92	2589.44	tonne	2890.36
bent	2400.00	20.00	300.92	2699.76	tonne	3000.68
16 mm diameter nominal size						
straight	2390.00	22.00	331.01	2695.25	tonne	3026.26
bent	2490.00	22.00	331.01	2805.56	tonne	3136.57
12 mm diameter nominal size						
straight	2450.00	24.00	361.10	2767.96	tonne	3129.06
bent	2550.00	24.00	361.10	2878.27	tonne	3239.38
10 mm diameter nominal size						
straight	2520.00	26.00	391.20	2852.60	tonne	3243.80
bent	2620.00	26.00	391.20	2962.91	tonne	3354.11
8 mm diameter nominal size						
straight	2450.00	28.00	419.00	2781.90	tonne	3200.90
bent	2550.00	28.00	419.00	2892.22	tonne	3311.21
Bar; BS 6744; stainless steel bars; grade 316						
32 mm diameter nominal size						
straight	3375.00	17.00	255.78	3774.44	tonne	4030.22
bent	3475.00	21.00	311.38	3884.75	tonne	4196.13
25 mm diameter nominal size						
straight	3375.00	18.00	270.83	3771.80	tonne	4042.63
bent	3475.00	18.00	270.83	3882.12	tonne	4152.95
20 mm diameter nominal size						
straight	3450.00	20.00	300.92	3858.07	tonne	4158.99
bent	3550.00	20.00	300.92	3968.39	tonne	4269.31
16 mm diameter nominal size						
straight	3575.00	22.00	331.01	4002.49	tonne	4333.50
bent	3675.00	22.00	331.01	4112.80	tonne	4443.81
12 mm diameter nominal size						
straight	3675.00	24.00	361.10	4119.33	tonne	4480.43
bent	3775.00	24.00	361.10	4229.64	tonne	4590.74
10 mm diameter nominal size						
straight	3780.00	26.00	391.20	4242.58	tonne	4633.77
bent	3880.00	26.00	391.20	4352.89	tonne	4744.09
8 mm diameter nominal size						
straight	3675.00	28.00	419.00	4133.27	tonne	4552.26
bent	3775.00	28.00	419.00	4243.58	tonne	4662.58
Fabric; BS 4483						
Ref A98 (1.54 kg/m^2)						
400 mm minimum laps	0.95	0.12	1.81	1.12	m^2	2.93
strips in one width; 600 mm width	0.95	0.15	2.26	1.12	m^2	3.38
strips in one width; 900 mm width	0.95	0.14	2.11	1.12	m^2	3.23
strips in one width; 1200 mm width	0.95	0.13	1.96	1.12	m^2	3.08
Ref A142 (2.22 kg/m^2)						
400 mm minimum laps	0.98	0.12	1.81	1.16	m^2	2.97
strips in one width; 600 mm width	0.98	0.15	2.26	1.16	m^2	3.42
strips in one width; 900 mm width	0.98	0.14	2.11	1.16	m^2	3.27
strips in one width; 1200 mm width	0.98	0.13	1.96	1.16	m^2	3.12
Ref A193 (3.02 kg/m^2)						
400 mm minimum laps	1.34	0.12	1.81	1.59	m^2	3.39
strips in one width; 600 mm width	1.34	0.15	2.26	1.59	m^2	3.84
strips in one width; 900 mm width	1.34	0.14	2.11	1.59	m^2	3.69
strips in one width; 1200 mm width	1.34	0.13	1.96	1.59	m^2	3.54

E IN SITU CONCRETE/LARGE PRECAST CONCRETE

Item	PC £	Labour hours	Labour £	Material £	Unit	Total rate £
E30 REINFORCEMENT FOR IN SITU CONCRETE – cont'd						
Fabric; BS 4483– cont'd						
Ref A252 (3.95 kg/m²)						
400 mm minimum laps	1.74	0.13	1.96	2.06	m²	**4.02**
strips in one width; 600 mm width	1.74	0.16	2.41	2.06	m²	**4.47**
strips in one width; 900 mm width	1.74	0.15	2.26	2.06	m²	**4.32**
strips in one width; 1200 mm width	1.74	0.14	2.11	2.06	m²	**4.17**
Ref A393 (6.16 kg/m²)						
400 mm minimum laps	2.72	0.15	2.26	3.22	m²	**5.48**
strips in one width; 600 mm width	2.72	0.18	2.71	3.22	m²	**5.93**
strips in one width; 900 mm width	2.72	0.17	2.56	3.22	m²	**5.78**
strips in one width; 1200 mm width	2.72	0.16	2.41	3.22	m²	**5.63**
Ref B196 (3.05 kg/m²)						
400 mm minimum laps	1.35	0.12	1.81	1.60	m²	**3.40**
strips in one width; 600 mm width	1.35	0.15	2.26	1.60	m²	**3.86**
strips in one width; 900 mm width	1.35	0.14	2.11	1.60	m²	**3.70**
strips in one width; 1200 mm width	1.35	0.13	1.96	1.60	m²	**3.55**
Ref B283 (3.73 kg/m²)						
400 mm minimum laps	1.66	0.12	1.81	1.97	m²	**3.77**
strips in one width; 600 mm width	1.66	0.15	2.26	1.97	m²	**4.22**
strips in one width; 900 mm width	1.66	0.14	2.11	1.97	m²	**4.07**
strips in one width; 1200 mm width	1.66	0.13	1.96	1.97	m²	**3.92**
Ref B385 (4.53 kg/m²)						
400 mm minimum laps	2.00	0.13	1.96	2.37	m²	**4.32**
strips in one width; 600 mm width	2.00	0.16	2.41	2.37	m²	**4.78**
strips in one width; 900 mm width	2.00	0.15	2.26	2.37	m²	**4.62**
strips in one width; 1200 mm width	2.00	0.14	2.11	2.37	m²	**4.47**
Ref B503 (5.93 kg/m²)						
400 mm minimum laps	2.63	0.15	2.26	3.11	m²	**5.37**
strips in one width; 600 mm width	2.63	0.18	2.71	3.11	m²	**5.82**
strips in one width; 900 mm width	2.63	0.17	2.56	3.11	m²	**5.67**
strips in one width; 1200 mm width	2.63	0.16	2.41	3.11	m²	**5.52**
Ref B785 (8.14 kg/m²)						
400 mm minimum laps	3.60	0.17	2.56	4.26	m²	**6.82**
strips in one width; 600 mm width	3.60	0.20	3.01	4.26	m²	**7.27**
strips in one width; 900 mm width	3.60	0.19	2.86	4.26	m²	**7.12**
strips in one width; 1200 mm width	3.60	0.18	2.71	4.26	m²	**6.97**
Ref B1131 (10.90 kg/m²)						
400 mm minimum laps	4.82	0.18	2.71	5.71	m²	**8.41**
strips in one width; 600 mm width	4.82	0.24	3.61	5.71	m²	**9.32**
strips in one width; 900 mm width	4.82	0.22	3.31	5.71	m²	**9.02**
strips in one width; 1200 mm width	4.82	0.20	3.01	5.71	m²	**8.72**
Ref C385 (3.41 kg/m²)						
400 mm minimum laps	1.51	0.12	1.81	1.79	m²	**3.59**
strips in one width; 600 mm width	1.51	0.15	2.26	1.79	m²	**4.04**
strips in one width; 900 mm width	1.51	0.14	2.11	1.79	m²	**3.89**
strips in one width; 1200 mm width	1.51	0.13	1.96	1.79	m²	**3.74**
Ref C503 (4.34 kg/m²)						
400 mm minimum laps	1.92	0.13	1.96	2.27	m²	**4.23**
strips in one width; 600 mm width	1.92	0.16	2.41	2.27	m²	**4.68**
strips in one width; 900 mm width	1.92	0.15	2.26	2.27	m²	**4.53**
strips in one width; 1200 mm width	1.92	0.14	2.11	2.27	m²	**4.38**
Ref C636 (5.55 kg/m²)						
400 mm minimum laps	2.46	0.14	2.11	2.91	m²	**5.02**
strips in one width; 600 mm width	2.46	0.17	2.56	2.91	m²	**5.47**
strips in one width; 900 mm width	2.46	0.16	2.41	2.91	m²	**5.32**
strips in one width; 1200 mm width	2.46	0.15	2.26	2.91	m²	**5.17**

E IN SITU CONCRETE/LARGE PRECAST CONCRETE

Item	PC £	Labour hours	Labour £	Material £	Unit	Total rate £
Ref C785 (6.72 kg/m^2)						
400 mm minimum laps	2.96	0.14	2.11	3.50	m^2	5.61
strips in one width; 600 mm width	2.96	0.17	2.56	3.50	m^2	6.06
strips in one width; 900 mm width	2.96	0.16	2.41	3.50	m^2	5.91
strips in one width; 1200 mm width	2.96	0.15	2.26	3.50	m^2	5.76
Ref D49 (0.77 kg/m^2)						
100 mm minimum laps; bent	1.04	0.24	3.61	1.23	m^2	4.84
Ref D98 (1.54 kg/m^2)						
200 mm minimum laps; bent	1.16	0.24	3.61	1.37	m^2	4.98
E40 DESIGNED JOINTS IN IN SITU CONCRETE						
Formed; Fosroc impregnated fibreboard joint filler or other equal and approved						
Width not exceeding 150 mm						
12.50 mm thick	-	0.14	2.22	1.26	m	3.47
20 mm thick	-	0.19	3.01	1.92	m	4.93
25 mm thick	-	0.23	3.64	2.00	m	5.64
Width 150 - 300 mm						
12.50 mm thick	-	0.23	3.64	1.97	m	5.61
20 mm thick	-	0.23	3.64	3.08	m	6.72
25 mm thick	-	0.23	3.64	3.64	m	7.28
Width 300 - 450 mm						
12.50 mm thick	-	0.28	4.43	2.77	m	7.20
20 mm thick	-	0.28	4.43	4.29	m	8.72
25 mm thick	-	0.28	4.43	5.06	m	9.50
Formed; Grace Servicised "Kork-pak" waterproof bonded cork joint filler board or other equal and approved						
Width not exceeding 150 mm						
10 mm thick	-	0.14	2.22	2.39	m	4.60
13 mm thick	-	0.14	2.22	2.42	m	4.64
19 mm thick	-	0.14	2.22	3.14	m	5.36
25 mm thick	-	0.14	2.22	3.59	m	5.81
Width 150 - 300 mm						
10 mm thick	-	0.19	3.01	4.38	m	7.39
13 mm thick	-	0.19	3.01	4.46	m	7.46
19 mm thick	-	0.19	3.01	5.90	m	8.91
25 mm thick	-	0.19	3.01	6.80	m	9.81
Width 300 - 450 mm						
10 mm thick	-	0.23	3.64	6.69	m	10.33
13 mm thick	-	0.23	3.64	6.80	m	10.44
19 mm thick	-	0.23	3.64	8.96	m	12.61
25 mm thick	-	0.23	3.64	10.31	m	13.95
Sealants; Fosroc"Pliastic 77" hot poured rubberized bituminous compound or other equal and approved						
Width 10 mm						
25 mm depth	-	0.17	2.69	0.89	m	3.58
Width 12.50 mm						
25 mm depth	-	0.18	2.85	1.09	m	3.94
Width 20 mm						
25 mm depth	-	0.19	3.01	1.78	m	4.78
Width 25 mm						
25 mm depth	-	0.20	3.17	2.18	m	5.35

E IN SITU CONCRETE/LARGE PRECAST CONCRETE

Item	PC £	Labour hours	Labour £	Material £	Unit	Total rate £
E40 DESIGNED JOINTS IN IN SITU CONCRETE – cont'd						
Sealants; Fosroc "Thioflex 600" gun grade two part polysulphide or other equal and approved						
Width 10 mm						
25 mm depth	-	0.05	0.79	3.37	m	**4.17**
Width 12.50 mm						
25 mm depth	-	0.06	0.95	4.22	m	**5.17**
Width 20 mm						
25 mm depth	-	0.07	1.11	6.75	m	**7.86**
Width 25 mm						
25 mm depth	-	0.08	1.27	8.44	m	**9.70**
Sealants; Grace Servicised "Paraseal" polysulphide compound or other equal and approved; priming with Grace Servicised "Primer P"						
Width 10 mm						
25 mm depth	-	0.19	2.42	2.20	m	**4.62**
Width 13 mm						
25 mm depth	-	0.19	2.42	2.81	m	**5.24**
Width 19 mm						
25 mm depth	-	0.23	2.93	4.05	m	**6.99**
Width 25 mm						
25 mm depth	-	0.23	2.93	5.29	m	**8.22**
Waterstops; Grace Servicised or other equal and approved;						
Hydrophilic strip water stop; lapped joints; cast into concrete						
5 x 20 mm "Servistrip AH 205"	-	0.30	3.83	5.93	m	**9.76**
50 x 20 mm "Adcor 500S"	-	0.30	3.83	7.83	m	**11.66**
"Servitite" Internal 10mm thick pvc water stop; flat dumbell type; heat welded joints; cast into concrete						
Servitite 150; 150mm wide	4.93	0.23	3.46	5.72	m	**9.18**
flat angle	9.81	0.28	4.21	13.12	nr	**17.34**
vertical angle	9.74	0.28	4.21	13.05	nr	**17.27**
flat three way intersection	14.14	0.37	5.57	19.06	nr	**24.63**
vertical three way intersection	16.38	0.37	5.57	21.53	nr	**27.10**
four way intersection	17.33	0.46	6.92	23.73	nr	**30.65**
Servitite 230; 230mm wide	6.93	0.23	3.46	7.98	m	**11.44**
flat angle	11.63	0.28	4.21	16.03	nr	**20.25**
vertical angle	14.23	0.28	4.21	18.91	nr	**23.12**
flat three way intersection	16.86	0.37	5.57	23.42	nr	**28.99**
vertical three way intersection	32.17	0.37	5.57	40.31	nr	**45.88**
four way intersection	20.96	0.46	6.92	29.54	nr	**36.46**
Servitite AT200; 200 mm wide	10.70	0.23	3.46	12.25	m	**15.71**
flat angle	13.33	0.28	4.21	19.62	nr	**23.83**
vertical angle	14.72	0.28	4.21	21.15	nr	**25.37**
flat three way intersection	23.85	0.37	5.57	33.69	nr	**39.25**
vertical three way intersection	17.65	0.37	5.57	26.85	nr	**32.42**
four way intersection	27.59	0.46	6.92	40.27	nr	**47.19**

E IN SITU CONCRETE/LARGE PRECAST CONCRETE

Item	PC £	Labour hours	Labour £	Material £	Unit	Total rate £
Servitite K305; 305 mm wide	11.94	0.28	4.21	13.64	m	17.85
flat angle	19.03	0.32	4.81	27.82	nr	32.63
vertical angle	20.93	0.32	4.81	29.91	nr	34.72
flat three way intersection	26.75	0.42	6.32	39.74	nr	46.06
vertical three way intersection	32.68	0.42	6.32	46.28	nr	52.60
four way intersection	36.41	0.51	7.67	53.81	nr	61.48
"Serviiseal" External pvc water stop; PVC water stop; centre bulb type; heat welded joints; cast into concrete						
Serviseal 195; 195mm wide	3.16	0.23	3.46	3.72	m	7.18
flat angle	6.08	0.28	4.21	8.21	nr	12.42
vertical angle	10.91	0.28	4.21	13.54	nr	17.75
flat three way intersection	10.42	0.37	5.57	13.76	nr	19.33
vertical three way intersection	7.57	0.37	5.57	10.61	nr	16.18
four way intersection	15.72	0.46	6.92	20.35	nr	27.27
Serviseal 240; 240 mm wide	3.85	0.23	3.46	4.50	m	7.96
flat angle	6.91	0.28	4.21	9.44	nr	13.65
vertical angle	11.41	0.28	4.21	14.40	nr	18.62
flat three way intersection	11.68	0.37	5.57	15.62	nr	21.19
vertical three way intersection	7.64	0.37	5.57	11.16	nr	16.73
four way intersection	17.39	0.46	6.92	22.82	nr	29.74
Serviseal AT240; 240 mm wide	12.63	0.23	3.46	14.42	m	17.88
flat angle	12.42	0.28	4.21	19.48	nr	23.70
vertical angle	11.70	0.28	4.21	18.70	nr	22.91
flat three way intersection	19.12	0.37	5.57	29.78	nr	35.35
vertical three way intersection	15.15	0.37	5.57	21.77	nr	27.33
four way intersection	28.80	0.46	6.92	43.34	nr	50.26
Serviseal K320; 320 mm wide	5.39	0.28	4.21	6.24	m	10.46
flat angle	15.56	0.32	4.81	20.29	nr	25.10
vertical angle	3.23	0.32	4.81	11.04	nr	15.85
flat three way intersection	22.79	0.42	6.32	29.83	nr	36.14
vertical three way intersection	4.85	0.42	6.32	10.95	nr	17.27
four way intersection	28.38	0.51	7.67	37.55	nr	45.22
E41 WORKED FINISHES/CUTTING TO IN SITU CONCRETE						
Worked finishes						
Tamping by mechanical means	-	0.02	0.26	0.04	m²	0.29
Power floating	-	0.16	2.04	0.12	m²	2.16
Trowelling	-	0.31	3.95	-	m²	3.95
Hacking						
by mechanical means	-	0.31	3.95	0.30	m²	4.25
by hand	-	0.65	8.29	-	m²	8.29
Lightly shot blasting surface of concrete	-	0.37	4.72	-	m²	4.72
Blasting surface of concrete	-	0.65	8.29	2.15	m²	10.44
to produce textured finish	-	0.65	8.29	0.63	m²	8.92
Sand blasting (blast and vac method)	-	-	-	-	m²	24.09
Wood float finish	-	0.12	1.53	-	m²	1.53
Tamped finish						
level or to falls	-	0.06	0.77	-	m²	0.77
to falls	-	0.09	1.15	-	m²	1.15
Spade finish	-	0.14	1.79	-	m²	1.79

E IN SITU CONCRETE/LARGE PRECAST CONCRETE

Item	PC £	Labour hours	Labour £	Material £	Unit	Total rate £
E41 WORKED FINISHES/CUTTING TO IN SITU CONCRETE – cont'd						
Cutting chases						
Depth not exceeding 50 mm						
width 10 mm	-	0.31	3.95	0.48	m	4.43
width 50 mm	-	0.46	5.87	0.63	m	6.50
width 75 mm	-	0.61	7.78	0.78	m	8.56
Depth 50 - 100 mm						
width 75 mm	-	0.83	10.59	1.22	m	11.80
width 100 mm	-	0.93	11.86	1.30	m	13.17
width 100 mm; in reinforced concrete	-	1.39	17.73	2.06	m	19.78
Depth 100 - 150 mm						
width 100 mm	-	1.20	15.30	1.52	m	16.83
width 100 mm; in reinforced concrete	-	1.85	23.59	2.64	m	26.24
width 150 mm	-	1.48	18.88	1.79	m	20.67
width 150 mm; in reinforced concrete	-	2.22	28.31	2.97	m	31.28
Cutting rebates						
Depth not exceeding 50 mm						
width 50 mm	-	0.46	5.87	0.63	m	6.50
Depth 50 - 100 mm						
width 100 mm	-	0.93	11.86	1.30	m	13.17
NOTE: The following rates for cutting holes and mortices in concrete allow for diamond drilling.						
Cutting holes and mortices in concrete; per 25 mm depth						
25 mm diameter	-	-	-	-	nr	1.33
32 mm diameter	-	-	-	-	nr	1.33
52 mm diameter	-	-	-	-	nr	1.64
76 mm diameter	-	-	-	-	nr	1.90
107 mm diameter	-	-	-	-	nr	2.05
127 mm diameter	-	-	-	-	nr	2.20
152 mm diameter	-	-	-	-	nr	2.67
200 mm diameter	-	-	-	-	nr	3.54
250 mm diameter	-	-	-	-	nr	5.28
300 mm diameter	-	-	-	-	nr	6.97
Cutting holes and mortices in reinforced concrete; per 25 mm depth						
25 mm diameter	-	-	-	-	nr	1.95
32 mm diameter	-	-	-	-	nr	1.95
52 mm diameter	-	-	-	-	nr	1.90
76 mm diameter	-	-	-	-	nr	2.00
107 mm diameter	-	-	-	-	nr	2.31
127 mm diameter	-	-	-	-	nr	2.67
152 mm diameter	-	-	-	-	nr	3.18
200 mm diameter	-	-	-	-	nr	4.51
250 mm diameter	-	-	-	-	nr	6.92
300 mm diameter	-	-	-	-	nr	8.92
Other items in reinforced concrete						
diamond chasing; per 25 x 25 mm section	-	-	-	-	m	11.69
forming box; per 25 mm depth (per m of perimeter)	-	-	-	-	m	11.79
diamond floor sawing; per 25 mm depth	-	-	-	-	m	3.38
diamond track mount or ring sawing; per 25 mm depth	-	-	-	-	m	7.69
stitch drilling 107 mm diameter hole; per25 mm depth	-	-	-	-	nr	2.05

E IN SITU CONCRETE/LARGE PRECAST CONCRETE

Item	PC £	Labour hours	Labour £	Material £	Unit	Total rate £
E42 ACCESSORIES CAST INTO IN SITU CONCRETE						
Foundation bolt boxes						
Temporary plywood; for group of 4 nr bolts						
75 x 75 x 150 mm	-	0.42	6.65	0.78	nr	7.43
75 x 75 x 250 mm	-	0.42	6.65	0.99	nr	7.64
Expanded metal; Expamet Building Products Ltd or other equal and approved						
75 mm diameter x 150 mm long	-	0.28	4.43	1.03	nr	5.46
75 mm diameter x 300 mm long	-	0.28	4.43	1.49	nr	5.92
100 mm diameter x 450 mm long	-	0.28	4.43	1.78	nr	6.21
Foundation bolts and nuts						
Black hexagon						
10 mm diameter x 100 mm long	-	0.23	3.64	0.55	nr	4.19
12 mm diameter x 120 mm long	-	0.23	3.64	0.83	nr	4.47
16 mm diameter x 160 mm long	-	0.28	4.43	2.31	nr	6.74
20 mm diameter x 180 mm long	-	0.28	4.43	2.70	nr	7.13
Masonry slots						
Galvanised steel; dovetail slots; 1.20 mm thick; 18G						
75 mm long	-	0.07	1.11	0.22	nr	1.33
100 mm long	-	0.07	1.11	0.24	nr	1.35
150 mm long	-	0.08	1.27	0.29	nr	1.56
225 mm long	-	0.09	1.42	0.41	nr	1.84
Galvanised steel; metal insert slots; Halfen Ltd or other equal and approved; 2.50 mm thick; end caps and foam filling						
41 x 41 mm; ref P3270	-	0.37	5.86	5.96	m	11.81
41 x 41 x 75 mm; ref P3249	-	0.09	1.42	0.73	nr	2.16
41 x 41 x 100 mm; ref P3250	-	0.09	1.42	0.80	nr	2.23
41 x 41 x 150 mm; ref P3251	-	0.09	1.42	1.03	nr	2.46
Cramps						
Mild steel; once bent; one end shot fired into concrete; other end fanged and built into brickwork joint						
200 mm girth	-	0.14	2.44	0.54	nr	2.98
Column guards						
White nylon coated steel; "Rigifix" or other equal and approved; Huntley and Sparks Ltd; plugging; screwing to concrete; 1.50 mm thick						
75 x 75 x 1000 mm	-	0.74	11.72	18.52	nr	30.24
Galvanised steel; "Rigifix" or other equal and approved; Huntley and Sparks Ltd; 3 mm thick						
75 x 75 x 1000 mm	-	0.56	8.87	13.23	nr	22.10
Galvanised steel; "Rigifix" or other equal and approved; Huntley and Sparks Ltd; 4.50 mm thick						
75 x 75 x 1000 mm	-	0.56	8.87	17.79	nr	26.66
Stainless steel; "HKW" or other equal and approved; Halfen Ltd; 5 mm thick						
50 x 50 x 1200 mm	-	0.93	14.72	56.49	nr	71.21
50 x 50 x 2000 mm	-	1.11	17.57	75.31	nr	92.89

E IN SITU CONCRETE/LARGE PRECAST CONCRETE

Item	PC £	Labour hours	Labour £	Material £	Unit	Total rate £
E42 ACCESSORIES CAST INTO IN SITU CONCRETE – cont'd						
Channels						
Stainless steel; Halfen Ltd or other equal and approved						
ref 38/17/HTA	-	0.32	5.07	52.96	m	58.03
ref 41/22/HZA; 80 mm long; including "T" headed bolts and plate washers	-	0.09	1.42	8.12	nr	9.54
Channel ties						
Stainless steel; Halfen Ltd or other equal and approved						
ref HTS - B12; 150 mm projection; including insulation retainer	-	0.03	0.65	0.42	nr	1.07
ref HTS - B12; 200 mm projection; including insulation retainer	-	0.03	0.65	0.58	nr	1.23
E60 PRECAST/COMPOSITE CONCRETE DECKING						
Prestressed precast flooring planks; Bison "Drycast" or other equal and approved; cement and sand (1:3) grout between planks and on prepared bearings						
100 mm thick suspended slabs; horizontal						
600 mm wide planks	-	-	-	-	m^2	35.73
1200 mm wide planks	-	-	-	-	m^2	33.89
150 mm thick suspended slabs; horizontal						
1200 mm wide planks	-	-	-	-	m^2	35.33
Prestressed precast concrete beam and block floor; Bison "Housefloor" or other equal and approved; in situ concrete 30.00 N/mm2 - 10 mm aggregate in filling at wall abutments; cement and sand (1:6) grout brushed in between beams and blocks						
155 mm thick suspended slab at ground level; 440 mm x 215 mm x 100 mm blocks; horizontal						
beams at 510 mm centres; up to 3.30 m span with a superimposed load of 5.00 kN/m^2	-	-	-	-	m^2	19.35
beams at 285 mm centres; up to 4.35 m span with a superimposed load of 5.00 kN/m^2	-	-	-	-	m^2	22.60

E IN SITU CONCRETE/LARGE PRECAST CONCRETE

Item	PC £	Labour hours	Labour £	Material £	Unit	Total rate £
Prestressed precast concrete structural suspended floors; Bison "Hollowcore" or other equal and approved; supplied and fixed on hard level bearings, to areas of 500 m² per site visit; top surface screeding and ceiling finishes by others						
Floors to dwellings, offices, car parks, shop retail floors, hospitals, school teaching rooms, staff rooms and the like; superimposed load of 5.00 kN/m²						
floor spans up to 3.00 m; 1200 mm x 150 mm	-	-	-	-	m²	39.42
floor spans 3.00 m - 6.00 m; 1200 mm x 150 mm	-	-	-	-	m²	40.14
floor spans 6.00 m - 7.50 m; 1200 mm x 200 mm	-	-	-	-	m²	41.42
floor spans 7.50 m - 9.50 m; 1200 mm x 250 mm	-	-	-	-	m²	46.85
floor spans 9.50 m - 12.00 m; 1200 mm x 300 mm	-	-	-	-	m²	49.52
floor spans 12.00 m - 13.00 m; 1200 mm x 350 mm	-	-	-	-	m²	51.90
floor spans 13.00 m - 14.00 m; 1200 mm x 400 mm	-	-	-	-	m²	56.85
floor spans 14.00 m - 15.00 m; 1200 mm x 450 mm	-	-	-	-	m²	57.75
Floors to shop stockrooms, light warehousing, schools, churches or similar places of assembly, light factory accommodation, laboratories and the like; superimposed load of 8.50 kN/m²						
floor spans up to 3.00 m; 1200 mm x 150 mm	-	-	-	-	m²	39.66
floor spans 3.00 m - 6.00 m; 1200 mm x 200 mm	-	-	-	-	m²	41.24
floor spans 6.00 m - 7.50 m; 1200 mm x 250 mm	-	-	-	-	m²	46.90
floors to heavy warehousing, factories, stores and the like; superimposed load of 12.50 kN/m²						
floor spans up to 3.00 m; 1200 mm x 150 mm	-	-	-	-	m²	39.91
floor spans 3.00 m - 6.00 m; 1200 mm x 250 mm	-	-	-	-	m²	47.10
Prestressed precast concrete staircase, supplied and fixed in conjunction with Bison "Hollowcore" flooring system or similar; comprising 2 nr 1100 mm wide flights with 7 nr 275 mm treads, 8 nr 185 mm risers and 150 mm waist; 1 nr 2200 mm x 1400 mm x 150 mm half landing and 1 nr top landing						
3.00 m storey height	-	-	-	-	nr	1963.42
Composite floor comprising reinforced in situ ready-mixed concrete 30.00 N/mm²; on and including 1.20 mm thick "Super Holorib" steel deck permanent shutting; complete with reinforcement to support imposed loading and A142 anti-crack mesh						
150 mm thick suspended slab; 5.00 kN/m² loading						
1.50 m - 3.00 m high to soffit	-	1.43	20.54	36.91	m²	57.44
3.00 m - 4.50 m high to soffit	-	1.43	20.54	38.26	m²	58.80
4.50 m - 6.00 m high to soffit	-	1.67	24.34	38.78	m²	63.11
200 mm thick suspended slab; 7.50 kN/m² loading						
1.50 m - 3.00 m high to soffit	-	1.47	21.05	40.71	m²	61.76
3.00 m - 4.50 m high to soffit	-	1.47	21.05	42.07	m²	63.12
4.50 m - 6.00 m high to soffit	-	1.70	24.69	42.58	m²	67.27

F MASONRY

Item	PC £	Labour hours	Labour £	Material £	Unit	Total rate £
BASIC MORTAR PRICES						
Coloured mortar materials (£/tonne); (excluding cement)						
light	-	-	-	48.99	tonne	-
medium	-	-	-	50.96	tonne	-
dark	-	-	-	61.64	tonne	-
extra dark	-	-	-	61.64	tonne	-
Mortar materials (£/tonne)						
cement	-	-	-	95.47	tonne	-
sand	-	-	-	17.00	tonne	-
lime	-	-	-	151.77	tonne	-
white cement	-	-	-	177.05	tonne	-
Mortar materials (£/5 litres)						
"Cemplas Super" mortar plasticiser	-	-	-	5.22	5 litre	-
F10 BRICK/BLOCK WALLING						
SUPPLY AND FIX PRICES						
Common bricks; PC £200.00/1000; in gauged mortar (1:1:6)						
Walls						
half brick thick	-	0.93	20.24	15.68	m²	35.92
half brick thick; building against other work;						
concrete	-	1.02	22.20	16.88	m²	39.08
half brick thick; building overhand	-	1.16	25.24	15.68	m²	40.93
half brick thick; curved; 6.00 m radii	-	1.20	26.11	15.68	m²	41.80
half brick thick; curved; 1.50 m radii	-	1.57	34.17	18.00	m²	52.16
one brick thick	-	1.57	34.17	31.36	m²	65.53
one brick thick; curved; 6.00 m radii	-	2.04	44.39	33.68	m²	78.07
one brick thick; curved; 1.50 m radii	-	2.54	55.27	34.28	m²	89.55
one and a half brick thick	-	2.13	46.35	47.05	m²	93.40
one and a half brick thick; battering	-	2.45	53.32	47.05	m²	100.36
two brick thick	-	2.59	56.36	62.73	m²	119.09
two brick thick; battering	-	3.05	66.37	62.73	m²	129.10
337 average thick; tapering, one side	-	2.68	58.32	47.05	m²	105.37
450 average thick; tapering, one side	-	3.47	75.51	62.73	m²	138.24
337 average thick; tapering, both sides	-	3.10	67.46	47.05	m²	114.51
450 average thick; tapering, both sides	-	3.89	84.65	63.33	m²	147.98
facework one side, half brick thick	-	1.02	22.20	15.68	m²	37.88
facework one side, one brick thick	-	1.67	36.34	31.36	m²	67.71
facework one side, one and a half brick thick	-	2.22	48.31	47.05	m²	95.36
facework one side, two brick thick	-	2.68	58.32	62.73	m²	121.05
facework both sides, half brick thick	-	1.11	24.16	15.68	m²	39.84
facework both sides, one brick thick	-	1.76	38.30	31.36	m²	69.67
facework both sides, one and a half brick thick	-	2.31	50.27	47.05	m²	97.32
facework both sides, two brick thick	-	2.78	60.50	62.73	m²	123.23
Isolated piers						
one brick thick	-	2.36	51.36	31.36	m²	82.72
two brick thick	-	3.70	80.52	63.33	m²	143.85
three brick thick	-	4.67	101.63	95.29	m²	196.92
Isolated casings						
half brick thick	-	1.20	26.11	15.68	m²	41.80
one brick thick	-	2.04	44.39	31.36	m²	75.76
Chimney stacks						
one brick thick	-	2.36	51.36	31.36	m²	82.72
two brick thick	-	3.70	80.52	63.33	m²	143.85
three brick thick	-	4.67	101.63	95.29	m²	196.92

F MASONRY

Item	PC £	Labour hours	Labour £	Material £	Unit	Total rate £
Projections						
225 mm width; 112 mm depth; vertical	-	0.28	6.09	3.30	m	**9.39**
225 mm width; 225 mm depth; vertical	-	0.56	12.19	6.59	m	**18.78**
337 mm width; 225 mm depth; vertical	-	0.83	18.06	9.89	m	**27.95**
440 mm width; 225 mm depth; vertical	-	0.93	20.24	13.18	m	**33.42**
Closing cavities						
width of cavity 50 mm, closing with common brickwork half brick thick; vertical	-	0.28	6.09	0.80	m	**6.89**
width of cavity 50 mm, closing with common brickwork half brick thick; horizontal	-	0.28	6.09	2.44	m	**8.53**
width of cavity 50 mm, closing with common brickwork half brick thick; including damp proof course; vertical	-	0.37	8.05	1.57	m	**9.62**
width of cavity 50 mm, closing with common brickwork half brick thick; including damp proof course; horizontal	-	0.32	6.96	3.00	m	**9.97**
width of cavity 75 mm, closing with common brickwork half brick thick; vertical	-	0.28	6.09	1.17	m	**7.26**
width of cavity 75 mm, closing with common brickwork half brick thick; horizontal	-	0.28	6.09	3.60	m	**9.69**
width of cavity 75 mm, closing with common brickwork half brick thick; including damp proof course; vertical	-	0.37	8.05	1.94	m	**9.99**
width of cavity 75 mm, closing with common brickwork half brick thick; including damp proof course; horizontal	-	0.32	6.96	4.16	m	**11.12**
Bonding to existing						
half brick thick	-	0.28	6.09	0.86	m	**6.95**
one brick thick	-	0.42	9.14	1.72	m	**10.86**
one and a half brick thick	-	0.65	14.15	2.58	m	**16.73**
two brick thick	-	0.88	19.15	3.45	m	**22.60**
Arches						
height on face 102 mm, width of exposed soffit 102 mm, shape of arch - segmental, one ring	-	1.57	26.63	5.45	m	**32.08**
height on face 102 mm, width of exposed soffit 215 mm, shape of arch - segmental, one ring	-	2.04	36.86	7.23	m	**44.09**
height on face 102 mm, width of exposed soffit 102 mm, shape of arch - semi-circular, one ring	-	1.99	35.77	5.45	m	**41.22**
height on face 102 mm, width of exposed soffit 215 mm, shape of arch - semi-circular, one ring	-	2.50	46.87	7.23	m	**54.10**
height on face 215 mm, width of exposed soffit 102 mm, shape of arch - segmental, two ring	-	1.99	35.77	7.11	m	**42.88**
height on face 215 mm, width of exposed soffit 215 mm, shape of arch - segmental, two ring	-	2.45	45.78	10.56	m	**56.34**
height on face 215 mm, width of exposed soffit 102 mm, shape of arch - semi-circular, two ring	-	2.68	50.79	7.11	m	**57.90**
height on face 215 mm, width of exposed soffit 215 mm, shape of arch - semi-circular, two ring	-	3.05	58.84	10.56	m	**69.39**
ADD or DEDUCT to walls for variation of £10.00/1000 in PC of common bricks						
half brick thick	-	-	-	0.70	m²	**0.70**
one brick thick	-	-	-	1.39	m²	**1.39**
one and a half brick thick	-	-	-	2.09	m²	**2.09**
two brick thick	-	-	-	2.79	m²	**2.79**

F MASONRY

Item	PC £	Labour hours	Labour £	Material £	Unit	Total rate £
F10 BRICK/BLOCK WALLING – cont'd						
Class B engineering bricks; PC						
£246.00/1000; in cement mortar (1:3)						
Walls						
half brick thick	-	1.02	22.20	19.09	m^2	41.29
one brick thick	-	1.67	36.34	38.18	m^2	74.52
one brick thick; building against other work	-	1.99	43.31	40.18	m^2	83.49
one brick thick; curved; 6.00 m radii	-	2.22	48.31	38.18	m^2	86.49
one and a half brick thick	-	2.22	48.31	57.27	m^2	105.58
one and a half brick thick; building against other work	-	2.68	58.32	57.27	m^2	115.59
two brick thick	-	2.78	60.50	76.36	m^2	136.86
337 mm thick; tapering, one side	-	2.87	62.46	57.27	m^2	119.73
450 mm thick; tapering, one side	-	3.70	80.52	76.36	m^2	156.88
337 mm thick; tapering, both sides	-	3.33	72.47	57.27	m^2	129.74
450 mm thick; tapering, both sides	-	4.21	91.62	77.03	m^2	168.65
facework one side, half brick thick	-	1.11	24.16	19.09	m^2	43.25
facework one side, one brick thick	-	1.76	38.30	38.18	m^2	76.48
facework one side, one and a half brick thick	-	2.31	50.27	57.27	m^2	107.54
facework one side, two brick thick	-	2.87	62.46	76.36	m^2	138.82
facework both sides, half brick thick	-	1.20	26.11	19.09	m^2	45.20
facework both sides, one brick thick	-	1.85	40.26	38.18	m^2	78.44
facework both sides, one and a half brick thick	-	2.41	52.45	57.27	m^2	109.72
facework both sides, two brick thick	-	2.96	64.41	76.36	m^2	140.78
Isolated piers						
one brick thick	-	2.59	56.36	38.18	m^2	94.54
two brick thick	-	4.07	88.57	77.03	m^2	165.60
three brick thick	-	5.00	108.81	115.88	m^2	224.69
Isolated casings						
half brick thick	-	1.30	28.29	19.09	m^2	47.38
one brick thick	-	2.22	48.31	38.18	m^2	86.49
Projections						
225 mm width; 112 mm depth; vertical	-	0.32	6.96	4.03	m	10.99
225 mm width; 225 mm depth; vertical	-	0.60	13.06	8.06	m	21.12
337 mm width; 225 mm depth; vertical	-	0.88	19.15	12.09	m	31.24
440 mm width; 225 mm depth; vertical	-	1.02	22.20	16.12	m	38.32
Bonding to existing						
half brick thick	-	0.32	6.96	1.05	m	8.01
one brick thick	-	0.46	10.01	2.10	m	12.11
one and a half brick thick	-	0.65	14.15	3.15	m	17.29
two brick thick	-	0.97	21.11	4.20	m	25.31
ADD or DEDUCT to walls for variation of £10.00/1000 in PC of bricks						
half brick thick	-	-	-	0.70	m^2	0.70
one brick thick	-	-	-	1.39	m^2	1.39
one and a half brick thick	-	-	-	2.09	m^2	2.09
two brick thick	-	-	-	2.79	m^2	2.79
ALTERNATIVE FACING BRICK PRICES						
(£/1000)						
Discounts of 10 - 20% available depending on quantity / status.						
Ibstock facing bricks; 215 x 102.5 x 65 mm						
Aldridge Brown Blend	-	-	-	313.00	1000nr	-
Aldridge Leicester Anglican Red Rustic	-	-	-	266.00	1000nr	-
Ashdown Cottage Mixture	-	-	-	259.00	1000nr	-
Ashdown Crowborough Multi	-	-	-	334.00	1000nr	-

F MASONRY

Item	PC £	Labour hours	Labour £	Material £	Unit	Total rate £
Ashdown Pevensey Multi	-	-	-	313.00	1000nr	-
Cattybrook Gloucester Golden	-	-	-	280.00	1000nr	-
Chailey Stock	-	-	-	341.00	1000nr	-
Dorking Multi	-	-	-	253.00	1000nr	-
Funton Second Hard Stock	-	-	-	364.00	1000nr	-
Holbook Smooth Red	-	-	-	283.00	1000nr	-
Leicester Red Stock	-	-	-	279.00	1000nr	-
Roughdales Red Multi Rustic	-	-	-	254.00	1000nr	-
Roughdales Trafford Multi Rustic	-	-	-	281.00	1000nr	-
Stourbridge Himley Mixed Russet	-	-	-	253.00	1000nr	-
Stourbridge Kenilworth Multi	-	-	-	243.00	1000nr	-
Stourbridge Pennine Pastone	-	-	-	297.00	1000nr	-
Strattford Red Rustic	-	-	-	249.00	1000nr	-
Swanage Handmade Restoration	-	-	-	582.00	1000nr	-
Tonbridge Handmade Multi	-	-	-	556.00	1000nr	-
Hanson Brick Limited, London brand; 215 x 102.5 x 65 mm						
Autumn leaf	-	-	-	243.40	1000nr	-
Burghley Red Rustic	-	-	-	255.80	1000nr	-
Dawn Red	-	-	-	254.70	1000nr	-
Hathaway Brindled	-	-	-	280.90	1000nr	-
Honey Buff	-	-	-	244.50	1000nr	-
Sunset Red	-	-	-	261.90	1000nr	-
Georgian	-	-	-	220.40	1000nr	-
Regency	-	-	-	277.70	1000nr	-
Saxon Gold	-	-	-	284.40	1000nr	-
Tudor	-	-	-	291.90	1000nr	-
Chiltern	-	-	-	296.40	1000nr	-
Heather	-	-	-	296.40	1000nr	-
Hereward Light	-	-	-	263.50	1000nr	-
Sandfaced	-	-	-	285.00	1000nr	-
Claydon Red Multi	-	-	-	258.00	1000nr	-
Delph Autumn	-	-	-	252.30	1000nr	-
Longville Stone	-	-	-	249.40	1000nr	-
Muirfield Mixture	-	-	-	371.50	1000nr	-
Nene Valley Stone	-	-	-	249.40	1000nr	-
Old English Brindled Red	-	-	-	270.50	1000nr	-
Brecken Grey	-	-	-	249.20	1000nr	-
Ironstone	-	-	-	254.70	1000nr	-
Milton Buff	-	-	-	270.50	1000nr	-
Windsor	-	-	-	257.60	1000nr	-
SUPPLY AND FIX PRICES						
Facing bricks; machine made facings; PC £275.00/1000 (unless otherwise stated); in gauged mortar (1:1:6)						
Walls						
facework one side, half brick thick; stretcher bond	16.47	1.20	26.11	20.85	m²	**46.96**
facework one side, half brick thick, flemish bond with snapped headers	-	1.39	30.25	20.89	m²	**51.14**
facework one side, half brick thick, stretcher bond; building against other work; concrete	-	1.30	28.29	22.08	m²	**50.37**
facework one side, half brick thick; flemish bond with snapped headers; building against other work; concrete	-	1.48	32.21	22.08	m²	**54.29**
facework one side, half brick thick, stretcher bond; building overhand	-	1.48	32.21	20.89	m²	**53.09**

F MASONRY

Item	PC £	Labour hours	Labour £	Material £	Unit	Total rate £
F10 BRICK/BLOCK WALLING – cont'd						
Facing bricks; PC £275.00/1000 – cont'd						
Walls – cont'd						
facework one side, half brick thick; flemish bond with snapped headers; building overhand	-	1.67	36.34	20.89	m²	**57.23**
facework one side, half brick thick; stretcher bond; curved; 6.00 m radii	-	1.76	38.30	20.89	m²	**59.19**
facework one side, half brick thick; flemish bond with snapped headers; curved; 6.00 m radii	-	1.99	43.31	20.89	m²	**64.19**
facework one side, half brick thick; stretcher bond; curved; 1.50 m radii	-	2.22	48.31	24.07	m²	**72.38**
facework one side, half brick thick; flemish bond with snapped headers; curved; 1.50 m radii	-	2.59	56.36	24.07	m²	**80.43**
facework both sides, one brick thick; two stretcher skins tied together	-	2.08	45.26	43.15	m²	**88.42**
facework both sides, one brick thick; flemish bond	-	2.13	46.35	41.77	m²	**88.13**
facework both sides, one brick thick; two stretcher skins tied together; curved; 6.00 m radii	-	2.87	62.46	46.33	m²	**108.79**
facework both sides, one brick thick; flemish bond; curved; 6.00 m radii	-	2.96	64.41	44.96	m²	**109.37**
facework both sides, one brick thick; two stretcher skins tied together; curved; 1.50 m radii	-	3.56	77.47	50.11	m²	**127.59**
facework both sides, one brick thick; flemish bond; curved; 1.50 m radii	-	3.70	80.52	48.74	m²	**129.26**
Isolated piers						
facework both sides, one brick thick; two stretcher skins tied together	-	2.45	53.32	43.94	m²	**97.26**
facework both sides, one brick thick; flemish bond	-	2.50	54.40	43.94	m²	**98.34**
Isolated casings						
facework one side, half brick thick; stretcher bond	-	1.85	40.26	20.89	m²	**61.15**
facework one side, half brick thick; flemish bond with snapped headers	-	2.04	44.39	20.89	m²	**65.28**
Projections						
225 mm width; 112 mm depth; stretcher bond; vertical	-	0.28	6.09	4.45	m	**10.55**
225 mm width; 112 mm depth; flemish bond with snapped headers; vertical	-	0.37	8.05	4.45	m	**12.50**
225 mm width; 225 mm depth; flemish bond; vertical	-	0.60	13.06	8.90	m	**21.96**
328 mm width; 112 mm depth; stretcher bond; vertical	-	0.56	12.19	6.68	m	**18.87**
328 mm width; 112 mm depth; flemish bond with snapped headers; vertical	-	0.65	14.15	6.68	m	**20.83**
328 mm width; 225 mm depth; flemish bond; vertical	-	1.11	24.16	13.33	m	**37.48**
440 mm width; 112 mm depth; stretcher bond; vertical	-	0.83	18.06	8.90	m	**26.97**
440 mm width; 112 mm depth; flemish bond with snapped headers; vertical	-	0.88	19.15	8.90	m	**28.05**
440 mm width; 225 mm depth; flemish bond; vertical	-	1.62	35.25	17.81	m	**53.06**
Arches						
height on face 215 mm, width of exposed soffit 102 mm, shape of arch - flat	-	0.93	16.89	5.91	m	**22.79**
height on face 215 mm, width of exposed soffit 215 mm, shape of arch - flat	-	1.39	26.90	10.52	m	**37.42**

F MASONRY

Item	PC £	Labour hours	Labour £	Material £	Unit	Total rate £
height on face 215 mm, width of exposed soffit 102 mm, shape of arch - segmental, one ring	-	1.76	29.93	8.27	m	38.20
height on face 215 mm, width of exposed soffit 215 mm, shape of arch segmental, one ring	-	2.13	37.98	12.63	m	50.61
height on face 215 mm, width of exposed soffit 102 mm, shape of arch - semi-circular, one ring	-	2.68	49.95	8.27	m	58.22
height on face 215 mm, width of exposed soffit 215 mm, shape of arch - semi-circular, one ring	-	3.61	70.19	12.63	m	82.82
height on face 215 mm, width of exposed soffit 102 mm, shape of arch - segmental, two ring	-	2.17	38.85	8.27	m	47.12
height on face 215 mm, width of exposed soffit 215 mm, shape of arch - segmental; two ring	-	2.82	52.99	12.63	m	65.63
height on face 215 mm, width of exposed soffit 102 mm, shape of arch - semi-circular, two ring	-	3.61	70.19	8.27	m	78.46
height on face 215 mm, width of exposed soffit 215 mm, shape of arch - semi-circular, two ring	-	5.00	100.44	12.63	m	113.07
Arches; cut voussoirs; PC £3000.00/1000						
height on face 215 mm, width of exposed soffit 102 mm, shape of arch - segmental, one ring	-	1.80	30.80	50.31	m	81.10
height on face 215 mm, width of exposed soffit 215 mm, shape of arch - segmental, one ring	-	2.27	41.03	96.70	m	137.73
height on face 215 mm, width of exposed soffit 102 mm, shape of arch - semi-circular, one ring	-	2.04	36.02	50.31	m	86.33
height on face 215 mm, width of exposed soffit 215 mm, shape of arch - semi-circular, one ring	-	2.59	47.99	96.70	m	144.69
height on face 320 mm, width of exposed soffit 102 mm, shape of arch - segmental, one and a half ring	-	2.41	44.07	96.70	m	140.78
height on face 320 mm, width of exposed soffit 215 mm, shape of arch - segmental, one and a half ring	-	3.15	60.18	196.20	m	256.38
Arches; bullnosed specials; PC £1700.00/1000						
height on face 215 mm, width of exposed soffit 102 mm, shape of arch - flat	22.67	0.97	17.76	27.89	m	45.65
height on face 215 mm, width of exposed soffit 215 mm, shape of arch - flat	-	1.43	27.77	55.04	m	82.81
Bullseye windows; 600 mm diameter						
height on face 215 mm, width of exposed soffit 102 mm, two rings	-	4.63	92.38	10.91	nr	103.29
height on face 215 mm, width of exposed soffit 215 mm, two rings	-	6.48	132.64	20.50	nr	153.14
Bullseye windows; 600 mm; cut voussoirs; PC £3000.00/1000						
height on face 215 mm, width of exposed soffit 102 mm, one ring	-	3.89	76.28	123.48	nr	199.76
height on face 215 mm, width of exposed soffit 215 mm, one ring	-	5.37	108.49	245.64	nr	354.13
Bullseye windows; 1200 mm diameter						
height on face 215 mm, width of exposed soffit 102 mm, two rings	-	7.22	148.75	23.76	nr	172.51
height on face 215 mm, width of exposed soffit 215 mm, two rings	-	10.36	217.08	43.49	nr	260.57
Bullseye windows; 1200 mm diameter; cut voussoirs; PC £3000.00/1000						
height on face 215 mm, width of exposed soffit 102 mm, one ring	-	6.11	124.59	214.79	nr	339.38
height on face 215 mm, width of exposed soffit 215 mm, one ring	-	8.70	180.95	424.35	nr	605.31
ADD or DEDUCT for variation of £10.00/1000 in PC of facing bricks in 102 mm high arches	-	-	-	0.31	m	0.31

F MASONRY

Item	PC £	Labour hours	Labour £	Material £	Unit	Total rate £
F10 BRICK/BLOCK WALLING – cont'd						
Facing bricks; machine made facings; **PC £275.00/1000** – cont'd						
Facework sills						
150 mm x 102 mm; headers on edge; pointing top and one side; set weathering; horizontal	-	0.51	11.10	4.45	m	**15.55**
150 mm x 102 mm; cant headers on edge; PC £1700.00/1000; pointing top and one side; set weathering; horizontal	-	0.56	12.19	26.43	m	**38.62**
150 mm x 102 mm; bullnosed specials; PC £1700.00/1000; headers on flat; pointing top and one side; horizontal	-	0.46	10.01	26.43	m	**36.44**
Facework copings						
215 mm x 102 mm; headers on edge; pointing top and both sides; horizontal	-	0.42	9.14	4.54	m	**13.68**
260 mm x 102 mm; headers on edge; pointing top and both sides; horizontal	-	0.65	14.15	6.74	m	**20.89**
215 mm x 102 mm; double bullnose specials; PC £1700.00/1000; headers on edge; pointing top and both sides; horizontal	-	0.46	10.01	26.52	m	**36.53**
260 mm x 102 mm; single bullnose specials; PC £1700.00/1000; headers on edge; pointing top and both sides; horizontal	-	0.65	14.15	52.83	m	**66.97**
ADD or DEDUCT for variation of £10.00/1000 in PC of facing bricks in copings 215 mm wide, 102 mm high	-	-	-	0.15	m	**0.15**
Extra over facing bricks for; facework ornamental bands and the like, plain bands; PC £305.00/1000						
flush; horizontal; 225 mm width; entirely of stretchers	-	0.19	4.13	0.46	m	**4.60**
Extra over facing brick for; facework quoins; PC £305.00/1000						
flush; mean girth 320 mm	0.40	0.28	6.09	0.46	m	**6.56**
Bonding to existing						
facework one side, half brick thick; stretcher bond	-	0.46	10.01	1.15	m	**11.16**
facework one side, half brick thick; flemish bond with snapped headers	-	0.46	10.01	1.15	m	**11.16**
facework both sides, one brick thick; two stretcher skins tied together	-	0.65	14.15	2.30	m	**16.45**
facework both sides, one brick thick; flemish bond	-	0.65	14.15	2.30	m	**16.45**
ADD or DEDUCT for variation of £10.00/1000 in PC of facing bricks; in walls built entirely of facings; in stretcher or flemish bond						
half brick thick	-	-	-	0.70	m²	**0.70**
one brick thick	-	-	-	1.39	m²	**1.39**
Facing bricks; hand made; PC **£450.00/1000 (unless otherwise stated);** **in gauged mortar (1:1:6)**						
Walls						
facework one side, half brick thick; stretcher bond	27.00	1.20	26.11	33.03	m²	**59.15**
facework one side, half brick thick; flemish bond with snapped headers	-	1.39	30.25	33.03	m²	**63.28**
facework one side; half brick thick; stretcher bond; building against other work; concrete	-	1.30	28.29	34.23	m²	**62.52**

F MASONRY

Item	PC £	Labour hours	Labour £	Material £	Unit	Total rate £
facework one side, half brick thick; flemish bond with snapped headers; building against other work; concrete	-	1.48	32.21	34.23	m²	**66.44**
facework one side, half brick thick; stretcher bond; building overhand	-	1.48	32.21	33.03	m²	**65.24**
facework one side, half brick thick; flemish bond with snapped headers; building overhand	-	1.67	36.34	33.03	m²	**69.37**
facework one side, half brick thick; stretcher bond; curved; 6.00 m radii	-	1.76	38.30	33.03	m²	**71.33**
facework one side, half brick thick; flemish bond with snapped headers; curved; 6.00 m radii	-	1.99	43.31	36.94	m²	**80.24**
facework one side, half brick thick; stretcher bond; curved 1.50 m radii	-	2.22	48.31	33.03	m²	**81.34**
facework one side, half brick thick; flemish bond with snapped headers; curved; 1.50 m radii	-	2.59	56.36	39.54	m²	**95.90**
facework both sides, one brick thick; two stretcher skins tied together	-	2.08	45.26	67.44	m²	**112.71**
facework both sides, one brick thick; flemish bond	-	2.13	46.35	66.07	m²	**112.42**
facework both sides; one brick thick; two stretcher skins tied together; curved; 6.00 m radii	-	2.87	62.46	72.65	m²	**135.11**
facework both sides, one brick thick; flemish bond; curved; 6.00 m radii	-	2.96	64.41	71.27	m²	**135.69**
facework both sides, one brick thick; two stretcher skins tied together; curved; 1.50 m radii	-	3.56	77.47	78.45	m²	**155.93**
facework both sides, one brick thick; flemish bond; curved; 1.50 m radii	-	3.70	80.52	77.08	m²	**157.60**
Isolated piers						
facework both sides, one brick thick; two stretcher skins tied together	-	2.45	53.32	68.23	m²	**121.55**
facework both sides, one brick thick; flemish bond	-	2.50	54.40	68.23	m²	**122.63**
Isolated casings						
facework one side, half brick thick; stretcher bond	-	1.85	40.26	33.03	m²	**73.29**
facework one side, half brick thick; flemish bond with snapped headers	-	2.04	44.39	33.03	m²	**77.43**
Projections						
225 mm width; 112 mm depth; stretcher bond; vertical	-	0.28	6.09	7.15	m	**13.24**
225 mm width; 112 mm depth; flemish bond with snapped headers; vertical	-	0.37	8.05	7.15	m	**15.20**
225 mm width; 225 mm depth; flemish bond; vertical	-	0.60	13.06	14.30	m	**27.36**
328 mm width; 112 mm depth; stretcher bond; vertical	-	0.56	12.19	10.74	m	**22.92**
328 mm width; 112 mm depth; flemish bond with snapped headers; vertical	-	0.65	14.15	10.74	m	**24.88**
328 mm width; 225 mm depth; flemish bond; vertical	-	1.11	24.16	21.42	m	**45.58**
440 mm width; 112 mm depth; stretcher bond; vertical	-	0.83	18.06	14.30	m	**32.36**
440 mm width; 112 mm depth; flemish bond with snapped headers; vertical	-	0.88	19.15	14.30	m	**33.45**
440 mm width; 225 mm depth; flemish bond; vertical	-	1.62	35.25	28.60	m	**63.86**

F MASONRY

Item	PC £	Labour hours	Labour £	Material £	Unit	Total rate £
F10 BRICK/BLOCK WALLING – cont'd						
Facing bricks; machine made facings; PC £450.00/1000 – cont'd						
Arches						
height on face 215 mm, width of exposed soffit 102 mm, shape of arch - flat	-	0.93	16.89	8.60	m	**25.49**
height on face 215 mm, width of exposed soffit 215 mm, shape of arch - flat	-	1.39	26.90	15.99	m	**42.89**
height on face 215 mm, width of exposed soffit 102 mm, shape of arch - segmental, one ring	-	1.76	29.93	10.97	m	**40.90**
height on face 215 mm, width of exposed soffit 215 mm, shape of arch - segmental, one ring	-	2.13	37.98	18.03	m	**56.01**
height on face 215 mm, width of exposed soffit 102 mm, shape of arch - semi-circular, one ring	-	2.68	49.95	10.97	m	**60.92**
height on face 215 mm, width of exposed soffit 215 mm, shape of arch - semi-circular, one ring	-	3.61	70.19	18.03	m	**88.22**
height on face 215 mm, width of exposed soffit 102 mm, shape of arch - segmental, two ring	-	2.17	38.85	10.97	m	**49.82**
height on face 215 mm, width of exposed soffit 215 mm, shape of arch - segmental, two ring	-	2.82	52.99	18.03	m	**71.02**
height on face 215 mm, width of exposed soffit 102 mm, shape of arch - semi-circular, two ring	-	3.61	70.19	10.97	m	**81.16**
height on face 215 mm, width of exposed soffit 215 mm, shape of arch - semi-circular, two ring	-	5.00	100.44	18.03	m	**118.46**
Arches; cut voussoirs; PC £3000.00/1000						
height on face 215 mm, width of exposed soffit 102 mm, shape of arch - segmental, one ring	-	1.80	30.80	50.31	m	**81.10**
height on face 215 mm, width of exposed soffit 215 mm, shape of arch - segmental, one ring	-	2.27	41.03	96.70	m	**137.73**
height on face 215 mm, width of exposed soffit 102 mm, shape of arch - semi-circular, one ring	-	2.04	36.02	50.31	m	**86.33**
height one face 215 mm, width of exposed soffit 215 mm, shape of - arch semi-circular, one ring	-	2.59	47.99	96.70	m	**144.69**
height on face 320 mm, width of exposed soffit 102 mm, shape of arch - segmental, one and a half ring	-	2.41	44.07	96.70	m	**140.78**
height on face 320 mm, width of exposed soffit 215 mm, segmental arch -, one and a half ring	-	3.15	60.18	196.20	m	**256.38**
Arches; bullnosed specials; PC £1700.00/1000						
height on face 215 mm, width of exposed soffit 102 mm, shape of arch - flat	-	0.97	17.76	27.89	m	**45.65**
height on face 215 mm, width of exposed soffit 215 mm, shape of arch - flat	-	1.43	27.77	55.04	m	**82.81**
Bullseye windows; 600 mm diameter						
height on face 215 mm, width of exposed soffit 102 mm, two ring	-	4.63	92.38	16.58	nr	**108.96**
height on face 215 mm, width of exposed soffit 215 mm, two ring	-	6.48	132.64	42.61	nr	**175.25**
Bullseye windows; 600 mm diameter; cut voussoirs; PC £3000.00/1000						
height on face 215 mm, width of exposed soffit 102 mm, one ring	-	3.89	76.28	123.48	nr	**199.76**
height on face 215 mm, width of exposed soffit 215 mm, one ring	-	5.37	108.49	245.64	nr	**354.13**
Bullseye windows; 1200 mm diameter						
height on face 215 mm, width of exposed soffit 102 mm, two ring	-	7.22	148.75	35.09	nr	**183.84**
height on face 215 mm, width of exposed soffit 215 mm, two ring	-	10.36	217.08	66.16	nr	**283.24**

F MASONRY

Item	PC £	Labour hours	Labour £	Material £	Unit	Total rate £
Bullseye windows; 1200 mm diameter; cut voussoirs; PC £3000.00/1000						
height on face 215 mm, width of exposed soffit 102 mm, one ring	-	6.11	124.59	214.79	nr	**339.38**
height on face 215 mm, width of exposed soffit 215 mm, one ring	-	8.70	180.95	424.35	nr	**605.31**
ADD or DEDUCT for variation of £10.00/1000 in PC of facing bricks in 102 mm high arches with 215 mm soffit	-	-	-	0.31	m	**0.31**
Facework sills						
150 mm x 102 mm; headers on edge; pointing top and one side; set weathering; horizontal	-	0.51	11.10	7.15	m	**18.25**
150 mm x 102 mm; cant headers on edge; PC £1700.00/1000; pointing top and one side; set weathering; horizontal	-	0.56	12.19	26.43	m	**38.62**
150 mm x 102 mm; bullnosed specials; PC £1700.00/1000; headers on edge; pointing top and one side; horizontal	-	0.46	10.01	26.43	m	**36.44**
Facework copings						
215 mm x 102 mm; headers on edge; pointing top and both sides; horizontal	-	0.42	9.14	7.24	m	**16.38**
260 mm x 102 mm; headers on edge; pointing top and both sides; horizontal	-	0.65	14.15	10.79	m	**24.93**
215 mm x 102 mm; double bullnose specials; PC £1700.00/1000; headers on edge; pointing top and both sides; horizontal	-	0.46	10.01	26.52	m	**36.53**
260 mm x 102 mm; single bullnose specials; PC £1700.00/1000; headers on edge; pointing top and both sides; horizontal	-	0.65	14.15	52.83	m	**66.97**
ADD or DEDUCT for variation of £10.00/1000 in PC of facing bricks in copings 215 mm wide, 102 mm high	-	-	-	0.15	m	**0.15**
Extra over facing bricks for; facework ornamental bands and the like, plain bands; PC £480.00/1000						
flush; horizontal; 225 mm width; entirely of stretchers	-	0.19	4.13	0.46	m	**4.60**
Extra over facing bricks for; facework quoins; PC £480.00/1000						
flush mean girth 320 mm	-	0.28	6.09	0.46	m	**6.56**
Bonding ends to existing						
facework one side, half brick thick; stretcher bond	-	0.46	10.01	1.83	m	**11.84**
facework one side, half brick thick; flemish bond with snapped headers	-	0.46	10.01	1.83	m	**11.84**
facework both sides, one brick thick; two stretcher skins tied together	-	0.65	14.15	3.65	m	**17.80**
facework both sides, one brick thick; flemish bond	-	0.65	14.15	3.65	m	**17.80**
ADD or DEDUCT for variation of £10.00/1000 in PC of facing bricks; in walls built entirely of facings; in stretcher or flemish bond						
half brick thick	-	-	-	0.70	m²	**0.70**
one brick thick	-	-	-	1.39	m²	**1.39**

F MASONRY

Item	PC £	Labour hours	Labour £	Material £	Unit	Total rate £
F10 BRICK/BLOCK WALLING – cont'd						
Facing bricks; slips 50 mm thick; PC £1100.00/1000; in gauged mortar (1:1:6) built up against concrete including flushing up at back (ties not included)						
Walls	66.00	1.85	40.26	78.16	m²	118.42
Edges of suspended slabs; 200 mm wide	-	0.56	12.19	15.63	m	27.82
Columns; 400 mm wide	-	1.11	24.16	31.26	m	55.42
Engineering bricks; PC £345.00/1000; and specials at PC £1700.00/1000; in cement mortar (1:3)						
Facework steps						
215 mm x 102 mm; all headers-on-edge; edges set with bullnosed specials; pointing top and one side; set weathering; horizontal	-	0.51	11.10	26.46	m	37.56
returned ends pointed	-	0.14	3.05	4.98	nr	8.03
430 mm x 102 mm; all headers-on-edge; edges set with bullnosed specials; pointing top and one side; set weathering; horizontal	-	0.74	16.10	32.01	m	48.11
returned ends pointed	-	0.19	4.13	6.38	nr	10.51
Facing tile bricks; Ibstock "Tilebrick" or other equal and approved; in gauged mortar (1:1:6)						
Walls						
facework one side; half brick thick; stretcher bond	-	0.87	18.93	59.65	m²	78.58
Extra over facing tile bricks for						
fair ends; 79 mm long	-	0.28	6.09	18.94	m	25.03
fair ends; 163 mm long	-	0.28	6.09	20.72	m	26.82
fair ends; 247 mm long	-	0.28	6.09	26.97	m	33.06
90° internal returns	-	0.28	6.09	51.98	m	58.08
45° external returns	-	0.28	6.09	43.51	m	49.60
45° internal returns	-	0.28	6.09	43.51	m	49.60
angled verges	-	0.28	6.09	24.30	m	30.40
ALTERNATIVE BLOCK PRICES						
Discounts of 0 - 20% available depending on quantity / status.						
Aerated concrete Durox "Supablocs"; 630 mm x 225 mm						
100 mm	-	-	-	9.54	m²	-
130 mm	-	-	-	13.46	m²	-
140 mm	-	-	-	15.56	m²	-
150 mm	-	-	-	15.93	m²	-
215 mm	-	-	-	22.76	m²	-
Hanson Conbloc blocks: 450 x 225 mm						
Cream fair faced						
100 mm hollow	-	-	-	8.30	m²	-
100 mm solid	-	-	-	8.99	m²	-
140mm hollow	-	-	-	12.30	m²	-
140 mm solid	-	-	-	14.64	m²	-
190 mm hollow	-	-	-	17.53	m²	-
190 mm solid	-	-	-	19.31	m²	-
215 mm hollow	-	-	-	17.48	m²	-

F MASONRY

Item	PC £	Labour hours	Labour £	Material £	Unit	Total rate £
Fenlite						
100 mm solid; 3.50 N/mm^2	-	-	-	6.91	m^2	-
100 mm solid; 7.00 N/mm^2	-	-	-	7.28	m^2	-
140 mm solid; 3.50 N/mm^2	-	-	-	10.33	m^2	-
Standard Dense	-	-	-	-	m^2	-
100 mm solid	-	-	-	6.45	m^2	-
140 mm solid	-	-	-	9.64	m^2	-
140 mm hollow	-	-	-	9.58	m^2	-
190 mm hollow	-	-	-	13.78	m^2	-
190 mm solid	-	-	-	13.51	m^2	-
215 mm hollow	-	-	-	14.45	m^2	-
Celcon "Standard" blocks; 450 mm x 225 mm						
100 mm	-	-	-	12.55	m^2	-
125 mm	-	-	-	15.47	m^2	-
140 mm	-	-	-	17.75	m^2	-
215 mm	-	-	-	29.78	m^2	-
Forticrete painting quality blocks; 450 mm x 225 mm						
100 mm hollow	-	-	-	11.82	m^2	-
100 mm solid	-	-	-	13.16	m^2	-
140 mm hollow	-	-	-	16.31	m^2	-
140 mm solid	-	-	-	19.05	m^2	-
190 mm hollow	-	-	-	21.66	m^2	-
190 mm solid	-	-	-	24.70	m^2	-
215 mm hollow	-	-	-	22.73	m^2	-
215 mm solid	-	-	-	27.32	m^2	-
Tarmac "Topblocks"; 450 mm x 225 mm; 3.50 N/mm2 "Hemelite"						
100 mm solid	-	-	-	5.71	m^2	-
190 mm solid	-	-	-	11.70	m^2	-
215 mm solid	-	-	-	12.59	m^2	-
Tarmac "Topblocks"; 450 mm x 225 mm; 7.00 N/mm2 "Hemelite"						
100 mm solid	-	-	-	6.13	m^2	-
140 mm solid	-	-	-	8.78	m^2	-
190 mm solid	-	-	-	12.54	m^2	-
215 mm solid	-	-	-	13.50	m^2	-
Tarmac "Toplite" standard blocks; 450 mm x 225 mm						
100 mm	-	-	-	8.76	m^2	-
140 mm	-	-	-	12.27	m^2	-
150 mm	-	-	-	13.14	m^2	-
215 mm	-	-	-	18.86	m^2	-
Tarmac "Toplite" GTI (thermal) blocks; 450 mm x 225 mm						
115 mm	-	-	-	10.38	m^2	-
125 mm	-	-	-	11.30	m^2	-
130 mm	-	-	-	11.74	m^2	-
140 mm	-	-	-	12.65	m^2	-
150 mm	-	-	-	13.56	m^2	-
215 mm	-	-	-	19.43	m^2	-

Prices for Measured Works – Major Works

F MASONRY

Item	PC £	Labour hours	Labour £	Material £	Unit	Total rate £
F10 BRICK/BLOCK WALLING – cont'd						
SUPPLY AND FIX PRICES						
Lightweight aerated concrete blocks;						
Thermalite "Turbo" blocks or other equal						
and approved; in gauged mortar (1:2:9)						
Walls						
100 mm thick	6.48	0.46	10.01	8.06	m²	18.07
115 mm thick	7.46	0.46	10.01	9.27	m²	19.28
125 mm thick	8.10	0.46	10.01	10.07	m²	20.08
130 mm thick	8.42	0.46	10.01	10.47	m²	20.48
140 mm thick	9.07	0.51	11.10	11.28	m²	22.38
150 mm thick	9.72	0.51	11.10	12.09	m²	23.19
190 mm thick	12.31	0.56	12.19	15.30	m²	27.49
200 mm thick	12.96	0.56	12.19	16.11	m²	28.30
215 mm thick	13.94	0.56	12.19	17.33	m²	29.51
Isolated piers or chimney stacks						
190 mm thick	-	0.83	18.06	15.30	m²	33.37
215 mm thick	-	0.83	18.06	17.33	m²	35.39
Isolated casings						
100 mm thick	-	0.51	11.10	8.06	m²	19.16
115 mm thick	-	0.51	11.10	9.27	m²	20.37
125 mm thick	-	0.51	11.10	10.07	m²	21.17
140 mm thick	-	0.56	12.19	11.28	m²	23.47
Extra over for fair face; flush pointing						
walls; one side	-	0.04	0.87	-	m²	0.87
walls; both sides	-	0.09	1.96	-	m²	1.96
Closing cavities						
width of cavity 50 mm, closing with lightweight blockwork 100 mm thick; vertical	-	0.23	5.01	0.45	m	5.46
width of cavity 50 mm, closing with lightweight blockork 100 mm thick; including damp proof course; vertical	-	0.28	6.09	1.22	m	7.32
width of cavity 75 mm, closing with lightweight blockwork 100 mm thick; vertical	-	0.23	5.01	0.65	m	5.66
width of cavity 75 mm, closing with lightweight blockwork 100 mm thick; including damp proof course; vertical	-	0.28	6.09	1.42	m	7.52
Bonding ends to common brickwork						
100 mm thick	-	0.14	3.05	0.93	m	3.97
115 mm thick	-	0.14	3.05	1.07	m	4.11
125 mm thick	-	0.23	5.01	1.16	m	6.17
130 mm thick	-	0.23	5.01	1.21	m	6.22
140 mm thick	-	0.23	5.01	1.31	m	6.31
150 mm thick	-	0.23	5.01	1.39	m	6.40
190 mm thick	-	0.28	6.09	1.76	m	7.86
200 mm thick	-	0.28	6.09	1.86	m	7.95
215 mm thick	-	0.32	6.96	2.01	m	8.97
Lightweight aerated concrete blocks;						
Thermalite "Shield" blocks or other						
equal and approved; in gauged mortar (1:2:9)						
Walls						
75 mm thick	5.45	0.42	9.14	6.16	m²	15.30
90 mm thick	5.77	0.42	9.14	6.56	m²	15.70
100 mm thick	6.42	0.46	10.01	7.29	m²	17.30
140 mm thick	8.98	0.51	11.10	10.21	m²	21.31
150 mm thick	9.63	0.51	11.10	10.94	m²	22.04
190 mm thick	12.19	0.56	12.19	13.85	m²	26.03

F MASONRY

Item	PC £	Labour hours	Labour £	Material £	Unit	Total rate £
Walls – cont'd						
200 mm thick	12.83	0.56	12.19	14.58	m²	**26.77**
Isolated piers or chimney stacks						
190 mm thick	-	0.83	18.06	13.85	m²	**31.91**
Isolated casings						
75 mm thick	-	0.51	11.10	6.16	m²	**17.26**
90 mm thick	-	0.51	11.10	6.56	m²	**17.66**
100 mm thick	-	0.51	11.10	7.29	m²	**18.39**
140 mm thick	-	0.56	12.19	10.21	m²	**22.39**
Extra over for fair face; flush pointing						
walls; one side	-	0.04	0.87	-	m²	**0.87**
walls; both sides	-	0.09	1.96	-	m²	**1.96**
Closing cavities						
width of cavity 50 mm, closing with lightweight blockwork 100 mm thick; vertical	-	0.23	5.01	0.41	m	**5.42**
width of cavity 50 mm, closing with lightweight blockork 100 mm thick; including damp proof course; vertical	-	0.28	6.09	1.19	m	**7.28**
width of cavity 75 mm, closing with lightweight blockwork 100 mm thick; vertical	-	0.23	5.01	0.59	m	**5.60**
width of cavity 75 mm, closing with lightweight blockwork 100 mm thick; including damp proof course; vertical	-	0.28	6.09	1.36	m	**7.46**
Bonding ends to common brickwork						
75 mm thick	-	0.09	1.96	0.71	m	**2.67**
90 mm thick	-	0.09	1.96	0.76	m	**2.72**
100 mm thick	-	0.14	3.05	0.84	m	**3.89**
140 mm thick	-	0.23	5.01	1.19	m	**6.20**
150 mm thick	-	0.23	5.01	1.27	m	**6.27**
190 mm thick	-	0.28	6.09	1.60	m	**7.70**
200 mm thick	-	0.28	6.09	1.69	m	**7.78**
Lightweight smooth face aerated concrete blocks; Thermalite "Smooth Face" blocks or other equal and approved; in gauged mortar (1:2:9); flush pointing one side						
Walls						
100 mm thick	10.18	0.56	12.19	12.44	m²	**24.63**
140 mm thick	14.25	0.65	14.15	17.41	m²	**31.55**
150 mm thick	15.27	0.65	14.15	18.66	m²	**32.80**
190 mm thick	19.34	0.74	16.10	23.62	m²	**39.73**
200 mm thick	20.36	0.74	16.10	24.87	m²	**40.98**
215 mm thick	21.89	0.74	16.10	26.74	m²	**42.84**
Isolated piers or chimney stacks						
190 mm thick	-	0.93	20.24	23.62	m²	**43.86**
200 mm thick	-	0.93	20.24	24.87	m²	**45.11**
215 mm thick	-	0.93	20.24	26.74	m²	**46.98**
Isolated casings						
100 mm thick	-	0.69	15.02	12.44	m²	**27.45**
140 mm thick	-	0.74	16.10	17.41	m²	**33.51**
Extra over for fair face flush pointing						
walls; both sides	-	0.04	0.87	-	m²	**0.87**
Bonding ends to common brickwork						
100 mm thick	-	0.23	5.01	1.41	m	**6.42**
140 mm thick	-	0.23	5.01	1.99	m	**7.00**
150 mm thick	-	0.28	6.09	2.12	m	**8.22**
190 mm thick	-	0.32	6.96	2.69	m	**9.65**
200 mm thick	-	0.32	6.96	2.83	m	**9.80**
215 mm thick	-	0.32	6.96	3.05	m	**10.02**

F MASONRY

Item	PC £	Labour hours	Labour £	Material £	Unit	Total rate £
F10 BRICK/BLOCK WALLING – cont'd						
Lightweight smooth face aerated concrete blocks; Thermalite "Party Wall" blocks or other equal and approved; in gauged mortar (1:2:9); flush pointing one side						
Walls						
100 mm thick	6.42	0.56	12.19	7.29	m²	19.48
215 mm thick	13.79	0.74	16.10	15.67	m²	31.78
Isolated piers or chimney stacks						
215 mm thick	-	0.93	20.24	15.67	m²	35.91
Isolated casings						
100 mm thick	-	0.69	15.02	7.29	m²	22.31
Extra over for fair face flush pointing						
walls; both sides	-	0.04	0.87	-	m²	0.87
Bonding ends to common brickwork						
100 mm thick	-	0.23	5.01	0.84	m	5.85
215 mm thick	-	0.32	6.96	1.82	m	8.79
Lightweight aerated high strength concrete blocks (7.00 N/mm2); Thermalite "High Strength" blocks or other equal and approved; in cement mortar (1:3)						
Walls						
100 mm thick	6.83	0.46	10.01	8.53	m²	18.54
140 mm thick	10.62	0.51	11.10	13.20	m²	24.29
150 mm thick	11.38	0.51	11.10	14.14	m²	25.24
190 mm thick	14.41	0.56	12.19	17.90	m²	30.09
200 mm thick	15.17	0.56	12.19	18.85	m²	31.04
215 mm thick	16.31	0.56	12.19	20.26	m²	32.45
Isolated piers or chimney stacks						
190 mm thick	-	0.83	18.06	17.90	m²	35.96
200 mm thick	-	0.83	18.06	18.85	m²	36.91
215 mm thick	-	0.83	18.06	20.26	m²	38.32
Isolated casings						
100 mm thick	-	0.51	11.10	8.53	m²	19.63
140 mm thick	-	0.56	12.19	13.20	m²	25.38
150 mm thick	-	0.56	12.19	14.14	m²	26.33
190 mm thick	-	0.69	15.02	17.90	m²	32.92
200 mm thick	-	0.69	15.02	18.85	m²	33.86
215 mm thick	-	0.69	15.02	20.26	m²	35.28
Extra over for flush pointing						
walls; one side	-	0.04	0.87	-	m²	0.87
walls; both sides	-	0.09	1.96	-	m²	1.96
Bonding ends to common brickwork						
100 mm thick	-	0.23	5.01	0.98	m	5.99
140 mm thick	-	0.23	5.01	1.53	m	6.54
150 mm thick	-	0.28	6.09	1.63	m	7.72
190 mm thick	-	0.32	6.96	2.06	m	9.03
200 mm thick	-	0.32	6.96	2.18	m	9.14
215 mm thick	-	0.32	6.96	2.35	m	9.31

F MASONRY

Item	PC £	Labour hours	Labour £	Material £	Unit	Total rate £
Lightweight aerated high strength concrete blocks; Thermalite "Trenchblock" blocks or other equal and approved; in cement mortar (1:4)						
Walls						
255 mm thick	16.85	0.74	16.10	19.16	m²	35.27
275 mm thick	18.18	0.79	17.19	20.67	m²	37.86
305 mm thick	19.83	0.83	18.06	22.57	m²	40.63
355 mm thick	23.46	0.93	20.24	26.63	m²	46.87
Medium dense smoth faced concrete blocks; Lignacite grey common 3.50N/mm2 blocks or other equal and approved; in gauged mortar (1:2:9); flush pointing one side						
Walls						
100 mm thick	6.91	0.62	13.49	8.57	m²	22.07
140 mm thick	9.51	0.72	15.67	11.80	m²	27.47
150 mm thick	10.54	0.74	16.10	13.06	m²	29.16
190 mm thick	12.74	0.86	18.72	15.81	m²	34.53
215 mm thick	15.18	0.95	20.67	18.80	m²	39.47
Isolated piers or chimney stacks						
190 mm thick	-	1.14	24.81	15.81	m²	40.62
215 mm thick	-	1.26	27.42	18.80	m²	46.22
Isolated casings						
100 mm thick	-	0.78	16.97	8.57	m²	25.55
140 mm thick	-	0.90	19.59	11.80	m²	31.38
Extra over for fair face flush pointing						
walls; both sides	-	0.04	0.87	-	m²	0.87
Bonding ends to common brickwork						
100 mm thick	-	0.23	5.01	0.98	m	5.99
140 mm thick	-	0.23	5.01	1.37	m	6.37
150 mm thick	-	0.28	6.09	1.50	m	7.60
190 mm thick	-	0.32	6.96	1.82	m	8.78
215 mm thick	-	0.32	6.96	2.17	m	9.13
Medium dense smoth faced concrete blocks; Lignacite grey common 7.00N/mm2 blocks or other equal and approved; in gauged mortar (1:2:9); flush pointing one side						
Walls						
100 mm thick	7.12	0.62	13.49	8.81	m²	22.31
140 mm thick	10.41	0.72	15.67	12.87	m²	28.54
150 mm thick	11.47	0.74	16.10	14.16	m²	30.26
190 mm thick	14.67	0.86	18.72	18.10	m²	36.81
215 mm thick	16.02	0.95	20.67	19.79	m²	40.47
Isolated piers or chimney stacks						
190 mm thick	-	1.14	24.81	18.10	m²	42.91
215 mm thick	-	1.26	27.42	19.79	m²	47.21
Isolated casings						
100 mm thick	-	0.78	16.97	8.81	m²	25.79
140 mm thick	-	0.90	19.59	12.87	m²	32.45

F MASONRY

Item	PC £	Labour hours	Labour £	Material £	Unit	Total rate £
F10 BRICK/BLOCK WALLING – cont'd						
Dense aggregate concrete blocks; "ARC Conbloc" or other equal and approved; in cement mortar (1:2:9)						
Walls or partitions or skins of hollow walls						
75 mm thick; solid	5.09	0.56	14.00	6.32	m²	**20.32**
100 mm thick; solid	5.63	0.69	17.25	7.06	m²	**24.31**
140 mm thick; solid	11.08	0.83	20.75	13.66	m²	**34.41**
140 mm thick; hollow	10.63	0.74	18.50	13.13	m²	**31.63**
190 mm thick; hollow	12.56	0.93	23.25	15.59	m²	**38.84**
215 mm thick; hollow	13.09	1.02	25.50	16.33	m²	**41.83**
Isolated piers or chimney stacks						
140 mm thick; hollow	-	1.02	25.50	13.13	m²	**38.63**
190 mm thick; hollow	-	1.34	33.50	15.59	m²	**49.10**
215 mm thick; hollow	-	1.53	38.25	16.33	m²	**54.58**
Isolated casings						
75 mm thick; solid	-	0.69	17.25	6.32	m²	**23.57**
100 mm thick; solid	-	0.74	18.50	7.06	m²	**25.56**
140 mm thick; solid	-	0.93	23.25	13.66	m²	**36.91**
Extra over for fair face; flush pointing						
walls; one side	-	0.09	2.25	-	m²	**2.25**
walls; both sides	-	0.14	3.50	-	m²	**3.50**
Bonding ends to common brickwork						
75 mm thick solid	-	0.14	3.50	0.73	m	**4.23**
100 mm thick solid	-	0.23	5.75	0.82	m	**6.57**
140 mm thick solid	-	0.28	7.00	1.57	m	**8.57**
140 mm thick hollow	-	0.28	7.00	1.51	m	**8.51**
190 mm thick hollow	-	0.32	8.00	1.80	m	**9.80**
215 mm thick hollow	-	0.37	9.25	1.90	m	**11.15**
Dense aggregate concrete blocks; (7.00 N/mm2) Forticrete "Shepton Mallet Common" blocks or other equal and approved; in cement mortar (1:3)						
Walls						
75 mm thick; solid	6.73	0.56	14.00	8.30	m²	**22.30**
100 mm thick; hollow	7.84	0.69	17.25	9.73	m²	**26.99**
100 mm thick; solid	5.07	0.69	17.25	6.44	m²	**23.70**
140 mm thick; hollow	10.84	0.74	18.50	13.46	m²	**31.96**
140 mm thick; solid	7.77	0.83	20.75	9.82	m²	**30.57**
190 mm thick; hollow	14.39	0.93	23.25	17.88	m²	**41.13**
190 mm thick; solid	10.61	1.02	25.50	13.41	m²	**38.91**
215 mm thick; hollow	11.44	1.02	25.50	14.50	m²	**40.00**
215 mm thick; solid	11.32	1.16	29.00	14.35	m²	**43.35**
Dwarf support wall						
140 mm thick; solid	-	1.16	29.00	9.82	m²	**38.82**
190 mm thick; solid	-	1.34	33.50	13.41	m²	**46.91**
215 mm thick; solid	-	1.53	38.25	14.35	m²	**52.61**
Isolated piers or chimney stacks						
140 mm thick; hollow	-	1.02	25.50	13.46	m²	**38.96**
190 mm thick; hollow	-	1.34	33.50	17.88	m²	**51.38**
215 mm thick; hollow	-	1.53	38.25	14.50	m²	**52.75**
Isolated casings						
75 mm thick; solid	-	0.69	17.25	8.30	m²	**25.55**
100 mm thick; solid	-	0.74	18.50	6.44	m²	**24.95**
140 mm thick; solid	-	0.93	23.25	9.82	m²	**33.07**
Extra over for fair face; flush pointing						
walls; one side	-	0.09	2.25	-	m²	**2.25**
walls; both sides	-	0.14	3.50	-	m²	**3.50**

F MASONRY

Item	PC £	Labour hours	Labour £	Material £	Unit	Total rate £
Bonding ends to common brickwork						
75 mm thick solid	-	0.14	3.50	0.94	m	4.44
100 mm thick solid	-	0.23	5.75	0.74	m	6.49
140 mm thick solid	-	0.28	7.00	1.14	m	8.14
190 mm thick solid	-	0.32	8.00	1.54	m	9.54
215 mm thick solid	-	0.37	9.25	1.66	m	10.91
Dense aggregate coloured concrete blocks; Forticrete "Shepton Mallet Bathstone" or other equal and approved; in coloured gauged mortar (1:1:6); flush pointing one side						
Walls						
100 mm thick hollow	17.52	0.74	18.50	20.30	m²	38.80
100 mm thick solid	21.23	0.74	18.50	24.49	m²	42.99
140 mm thick hollow	23.06	0.83	20.75	26.75	m²	47.50
140 mm thick solid	30.92	0.93	23.25	35.64	m²	58.89
190 mm thick hollow	29.31	1.02	25.50	34.06	m²	59.56
190 mm thick solid	42.46	1.16	29.00	48.92	m²	77.92
215 mm thick hollow	30.93	1.16	29.00	36.02	m²	65.02
215 mm thick solid	45.00	1.20	30.00	51.92	m²	81.92
Isolated piers or chimney stacks						
140 mm thick solid	-	1.25	31.25	35.64	m²	66.89
190 mm thick solid	-	1.39	34.75	48.92	m²	83.67
215 mm thick solid	-	1.57	39.25	51.92	m²	91.17
Extra over blocks for						
100 mm thick half lintel blocks; ref D14	-	0.23	5.75	18.78	m	24.53
140 mm thick half lintel blocks; ref H14	-	0.28	7.00	23.88	m	30.88
140 mm thick quoin blocks; ref H16	-	0.32	8.00	27.27	m	35.27
140 mm thick cavity closer blocks; ref H17	-	0.32	8.00	32.71	m	40.71
140 mm thick cill blocks; ref H21	-	0.28	7.00	19.41	m	26.41
190 mm thick half lintel blocks; ref A14	-	0.32	8.00	27.42	m	35.42
"Astra-Glaze" satin-gloss glazed finish blocks or other equal and approved; Forticrete Ltd; standard colours; in gauged mortar (1:1:6); joints raked out; gun applied latex grout to joints						
Walls or partitions or skins of hollow walls						
100 mm thick; glazed one side	74.84	0.93	23.25	84.98	m²	108.23
extra; glazed square end return	48.37	0.37	9.25	28.59	m	37.84
150 mm thick; glazed one side	85.54	1.02	25.50	97.26	m²	122.76
extra; glazed square end return	77.37	0.46	11.50	57.73	m	69.23
200 mm thick; glazed one side	96.23	1.16	29.00	109.54	m²	138.54
extra; glazed square end return	-	0.51	12.75	81.51	m	94.26
100 mm thick; glazed both sides	106.92	1.11	27.75	121.23	m²	148.98
150 mm thick; glazed both sides	117.61	1.20	30.00	133.51	m²	163.51
100 mm thick lintel 200 mm high; glazed one side	-	0.83	14.94	23.38	m	38.33
150 mm thick lintel 200 mm high; glazed one side	-	0.93	17.44	28.34	m	45.78
200 mm thick lintel 200 mm high; glazed one side	-	1.25	22.54	26.93	m	49.47
"Fireborn" terracotta blocks or other equal and approved; Ibstock Brick Ltd; in coloured gauged mortar (1:1:6); flush pointing one side						
Walls or partitions or skins of hollow walls						
102.50 mm thick; stretcher bond	47.25	0.33	8.25	54.04	m²	62.29
102.50 mm thick; stack bond	47.25	0.35	8.75	54.00	m²	62.75

F MASONRY

Item	PC £	Labour hours	Labour £	Material £	Unit	Total rate £
F11 GLASS BLOCK WALLING						
NOTE: The following specialist prices for glass block walling; supplied by Roger Wilde Ltd; assume standard blocks in panels of 50 m2; no fire rating; work in straight walls at ground level; and all necessary ancillary fixing; strengthening; easy access; pointing and expansion materials etc.						
Hollow glass block walling; Pittsburgh Corning sealed "Thinline" or other equal and approved; in cement mortar joints; reinforced with 6 mm diameter stainless steel rods; pointed both sides with mastic or other equal and approved						
Walls; facework both sides						
115 mm x 115 mm x 80 mm flemish blocks	-	-	-	-	m²	414.82
190 mm x 190 mm x 80 mm flemish; cross reeded or clear blocks	-	-	-	-	m²	188.91
240 mm x 240 mm x 80 mm flemish; cross reeded or clear blocks	-	-	-	-	m²	185.99
240 mm x 115 mm x 80 mm flemish or clear blocks	-	-	-	-	m²	222.01
F20 NATURAL STONE RUBBLE WALLING						
Cotswold Guiting limestone or other equal and approved ; laid dry						
Uncoursed random rubble walling						
275 mm thick	-	2.07	45.05	68.81	m²	113.86
350 mm thick	-	2.46	53.11	87.56	m²	140.67
425 mm thick	-	2.81	60.21	106.33	m²	166.53
500 mm thick	-	3.15	67.06	125.10	m²	192.16
Cotswold Guiting limestone or other equal and approved; bedded; jointed and pointed in cement:lime mortar (1:2:9)						
Uncoursed random rubble walling; faced and pointed; both sides						
275 mm thick	-	1.98	42.87	72.31	m²	115.19
350 mm thick	-	2.18	46.34	92.02	m²	138.35
425 mm thick	-	2.39	50.04	111.74	m²	161.79
500 mm thick	-	2.59	53.51	131.47	m²	184.98
Coursed random rubble walling; rough dressed; faced and pointed one side						
114 mm thick	-	1.48	31.13	44.85	m²	75.97
150 mm thick	-	1.76	40.75	45.31	m²	86.06
Fair returns on walling						
114 mm wide	-	0.02	0.44	-	m	0.44
150 mm wide	-	0.03	0.65	-	m	0.65
275 mm wide	-	0.06	1.31	-	m	1.31
350 mm wide	-	0.08	1.74	-	m	1.74
425 mm wide	-	0.10	2.18	-	m	2.18
500 mm wide	-	0.12	2.61	-	m	2.61
Fair raking cutting or circular cutting						
114 mm wide	-	0.20	4.40	6.51	m	10.91
150 mm wide	-	0.25	5.51	6.51	m	12.02

F MASONRY

Item	PC £	Labour hours	Labour £	Material £	Unit	Total rate £
Level uncoursed rubble walling for damp proof courses and the like						
275 mm wide	-	0.19	4.60	7.78	m	12.38
350 mm wide	-	0.20	4.84	9.82	m	14.66
425 mm wide	-	0.21	5.08	11.93	m	17.01
500 mm wide	-	0.22	5.32	14.00	m	19.33
Copings formed of rough stones; faced and pointed all round						
275 mm x 200 mm (average) high	-	0.56	12.52	28.42	m	40.93
350 mm x 250 mm (average) high	-	0.75	16.54	39.90	m	56.44
425 mm x 300 mm (average) high	-	0.97	21.18	56.19	m	77.37
500 mm x 300 mm (average) high	-	1.23	26.56	76.40	m	102.95
F22 CAST STONE ASHLAR WALLING DRESSINGS						
Reconstructed limestone walling; Bradstone 100 bed weathered "Cotswold" or "North Cerney" masonry blocks or other equal and approved; laid to pattern or course recommended; bedded; jointed and pointed in approved coloured cement:lime mortar (1:2:9)						
Walls; facing and pointing one side						
masonry blocks; random uncoursed	-	1.04	22.63	40.07	m²	62.70
extra; returned ends	-	0.37	8.05	22.22	m	30.27
extra; plain L shaped quoins	-	0.12	2.61	34.75	m	37.37
traditional walling; coursed squared	-	1.30	28.29	40.07	m²	68.36
squared random rubble	-	1.30	28.29	40.97	m²	69.26
squared coursed rubble (large module)	-	1.20	26.11	40.82	m²	66.94
squared coursed rubble (small module)	-	1.25	27.20	41.12	m²	68.33
squared and pitched rock faced walling; coursed	-	1.34	29.16	40.97	m²	70.13
rough hewn rockfaced walling; random	-	1.39	30.25	40.82	m²	71.07
extra; returned ends	-	0.15	3.26	-	m	3.26
Isolated piers or chimney stacks; facing and pointing one side						
masonry blocks; random uncoursed	-	1.43	31.12	40.07	m²	71.19
traditional walling; coursed squared	-	1.80	39.17	40.07	m²	79.24
squared random rubble	-	1.80	39.17	40.97	m²	80.14
squared coursed rubble (large module)	-	1.67	36.34	40.82	m²	77.16
squared coursed rubble (small module)	-	1.76	38.30	41.12	m²	79.42
squared and pitched rock faced walling; coursed	-	1.90	41.35	40.97	m²	82.32
rough hewn rockfaced walling; random	-	1.94	42.22	40.82	m²	83.04
Isolated casings; facing and pointing one side						
masonry blocks; random uncoursed	-	1.25	27.20	40.07	m²	67.27
traditional walling; coursed squared	-	1.57	34.17	40.07	m²	74.24
squared random rubble	-	1.57	34.17	40.97	m²	75.14
squared coursed rubble (large module)	-	1.43	31.12	40.82	m²	71.94
squared coursed rubble (small module)	-	1.53	33.30	41.12	m²	74.42
squared and pitched rock faced walling; coursed	-	1.62	35.25	40.97	m²	76.23
rough hewn rockfaced walling; random	-	1.67	36.34	40.82	m²	77.16
Fair returns 100 mm wide						
masonry blocks; random uncoursed	-	0.11	2.39	-	m²	2.39
traditional walling; coursed squared	-	0.14	3.05	-	m²	3.05
squared random rubble	-	0.14	3.05	-	m²	3.05
squared coursed rubble (large module)	-	0.13	2.83	-	m²	2.83
squared coursed rubble (small module)	-	0.13	2.83	-	m²	2.83
squared and pitched rock faced walling; coursed	-	0.14	3.05	-	m²	3.05
rough hewn rockfaced walling; random	-	0.15	3.26	-	m²	3.26
Fair raking cutting or circular cutting						
100 mm wide	-	0.17	3.70	-	m	3.70

F MASONRY

Item	PC £	Labour hours	Labour £	Material £	Unit	Total rate £
F22 CAST STONE ASHLAR WALLING DRESSINGS – cont'd						
Reconstructed limestone dressings; "Bradstone Architectural" dressings in weathered "Cotswold" or "North Cerney" shades or other equal and approved; bedded, jointed and pointed in approved coloured cement:lime mortar (1:2:9)						
Copings; twice weathered and throated						
152 mm x 76 mm; type A	-	0.31	6.75	11.04	m	17.78
178 mm x 64 mm; type B	-	0.31	6.75	10.71	m	17.46
305 mm x 76 mm; type A	-	0.37	8.05	20.93	m	28.99
Extra for						
fair end	-	-	-	4.55	nr	4.55
returned mitred fair end	-	-	-	4.55	nr	4.55
Copings; once weathered and throated						
191 mm x 76 mm	-	0.31	6.75	11.90	m	18.64
305 mm x 76 mm	-	0.37	8.05	20.61	m	28.66
365 mm x 76 mm	-	0.37	8.05	22.05	m	30.10
Extra for						
fair end	-	-	-	4.55	nr	4.55
returned mitred fair end	-	-	-	4.55	nr	4.55
Chimney caps; four times weathered and throated; once holed						
553 mm x 553 mm x 76 mm	-	0.37	8.05	25.69	nr	33.75
686 mm x 686 mm x 76 mm	-	0.37	8.05	42.10	nr	50.15
Pier caps; four times weathered and throated						
305 mm x 305 mm	-	0.23	5.01	9.25	nr	14.26
381 mm x 381 mm	-	0.23	5.01	12.83	nr	17.83
457 mm x 457 mm	-	0.28	6.09	17.39	nr	23.48
533 mm x 533 mm	-	0.28	6.09	24.56	nr	30.65
Splayed corbels						
479 mm x 100 mm x 215 mm	-	0.14	3.05	11.92	nr	14.96
665 mm x 100 mm x 215 mm	-	0.19	4.13	19.15	nr	23.29
Air bricks						
300 mm x 140 mm x 76 mm	-	0.07	1.52	6.79	nr	8.31
100 mm x 140 mm lintels; rectangular; reinforced with mild steel bars						
not exceeding 1.22 m long	-	0.22	4.79	18.78	m	23.57
1.37 m - 1.67 m long	-	0.24	5.22	18.78	m	24.01
1.83 m - 1.98 m long	-	0.26	5.66	18.78	m	24.44
100 mm x 215 mm lintels; rectangular; reinforced with mild steel bars						
not exceeding 1.67 m long	-	0.24	5.22	25.28	m	30.50
1.83 m - 1.98 m long	-	0.26	5.66	25.28	m	30.94
2.13 m - 2.44 m long	-	0.28	6.09	25.28	m	31.37
2.59 m - 2.90 m long	-	0.30	6.53	25.28	m	31.81
197 mm x 67 mm sills to suit standard softwood windows; stooled at ends						
not exceeding 2.54 m long	-	0.28	6.09	29.44	m	35.53
Window surround; traditional with label moulding; for single light; sill 146 mm x 133 mm; jambs 146 mm x 146 mm; head 146 mm x 105 mm; including all dowels and anchors						
overall size 508 mm x 1479 mm	137.90	0.83	18.06	149.91	nr	167.97

F MASONRY

Item	PC £	Labour hours	Labour £	Material £	Unit	Total rate £
Window surround; traditional with label moulding; three light; for windows 508 mm x 1219 mm; sill 146 mm x 133 mm; jambs 146 mm x 146 mm; head 146 mm x 103 mm; mullions 146 mm x 108 mm; including all dowels and anchors						
overall size 1975 mm x 1479 mm	294.82	2.17	47.22	321.05	nr	368.27
Door surround; moulded continuous jambs and head with label moulding; including all dowels and anchors						
door 839 mm x 1981 mm in 102 mm x 64 mm frame	252.02	1.53	33.30	271.98	nr	305.28
F30 ACCESSORIES/SUNDRY ITEMS FOR BRICKS/BLOCKS						
Forming cavities						
In hollow walls						
width of cavity 50 mm; polypropylene ties; three wall ties per m²	-	0.05	1.09	0.20	m²	1.29
width of cavity 50 mm; galvanised steel butterfly wall ties; three wall ties per m²	-	0.05	1.09	0.19	m²	1.28
width of cavity 50 mm; galvanised steel twisted wall ties; three wall ties per m²	-	0.05	1.09	0.39	m²	1.48
width of cavity 50 mm; stainless steel butterfly wall ties; three wall ties per m²	-	0.05	1.09	0.41	m²	1.50
width of cavity 50 mm; stainless steel twisted wall ties; three wall ties per m²	-	0.05	1.09	0.80	m²	1.89
width of cavity 75 mm; polypropylene ties; three wall ties per m²	-	0.05	1.09	0.20	m²	1.29
width of cavity 75 mm; galvanised steel butterfly wall ties; three wall ties per m²	-	0.05	1.09	0.25	m²	1.33
width of cavity 75 mm; galvanised steel twisted wall ties; three wall ties per m²	-	0.05	1.09	0.43	m²	1.52
width of cavity 75 mm; stainless steel butterfly wall ties; three wall ties per m²	-	0.05	1.09	0.58	m²	1.67
width of cavity 75 mm; stainless steel twisted wall ties; three wall ties per m²	-	0.05	1.09	0.88	m²	1.96
Damp proof courses						
"Pluvex No 1" (hessian based) damp proof course or other equal and approved; 200 mm laps; in gauged morter (1:1:6)						
width exceeding 225 mm; horizontal	6.07	0.23	5.01	7.02	m²	12.02
width exceeding 225 mm; forming cavity gutters in hollow walls; horizontal	-	0.37	8.05	7.02	m²	15.07
width not exceeding 225 mm; horizontal	-	0.46	10.01	7.02	m²	17.03
width not exceeding 225 mm; vertical	-	0.69	15.02	7.02	m²	22.03
"Pluvex No 2" (fibre based) damp proof course or other equal and approved; 200 mm laps; in gauged mortar (1:1:6)						
width exceeding 225 mm; horizontal	4.07	0.23	5.01	4.71	m²	9.72
width exceeding 225 mm wide; forming cavity gutters in hollow walls; horizontal	-	0.37	8.05	4.71	m²	12.76
width not exceeding 225 mm; horizontal	-	0.46	10.01	4.71	m²	14.72
width not exceeding 225 mm; vertical	-	0.69	15.02	4.71	m²	19.73

F MASONRY

Item	PC £	Labour hours	Labour £	Material £	Unit	Total rate £
F30 ACCESSORIES/SUNDRY ITEMS FOR BRICKS/BLOCKS – cont'd						
Damp proof courses – cont'd						
"Ruberthene" polythylene damp proof course or other equal and approved; 200 mm laps; in gauged mortar (1:1:6)						
width exceeding 225 mm; horizontal	0.94	0.23	5.01	1.09	m^2	6.10
width exceeding 225 mm; forming cavity gutters in hollow walls; horizontal	-	0.37	8.05	1.09	m^2	9.14
width not exceeding 225 mm; horizontal	-	0.46	10.01	1.09	m^2	11.10
width not exceeding 225 mm; vertical	-	0.69	15.02	1.09	m^2	16.11
"Permabit" bitumen polymer damp proof course or other equal and approved; 150 mm laps; in gauged mortar (1:1:6)						
width exceeding 225 mm; horizontal	5.35	0.23	5.01	6.19	m^2	11.19
width exceeding 225 mm; forming cavity gutters in hollow walls; horizontal	-	0.37	8.05	6.19	m^2	14.24
width not exceeding 225 mm; horizontal	-	0.46	10.01	6.19	m^2	16.20
width not exceeding 225 mm; vertical	-	0.69	15.02	6.19	m^2	21.20
"Hyload" (pitch polymer) damp proof course or other equal and approved; 150 mm laps; in gauged mortar (1:1:6)						
width exceeding 225 mm; horizontal	5.35	0.23	5.01	6.19	m^2	11.19
width exceeding 225 mm; forming cavity gutters in hollow walls; horizontal	-	0.37	8.05	6.19	m^2	14.24
width not exceeding 225 mm; horizontal	-	0.46	10.01	6.19	m^2	16.20
width not exceeding 225 mm	-	0.69	15.02	6.19	m^2	21.20
"Ledkore" grade A (bitumen based lead cored); damp proof course or other equal and approved; 200 mm laps; in gauged mortar (1:1:6)						
width exceeding 225 mm; horizontal	16.76	0.31	6.75	19.39	m^2	26.14
width exceeding 225 mm; forming cavity gutters in hollow walls; horizontal	-	0.49	10.66	19.39	m^2	30.05
width not exceeding 225 mm; horizontal	-	0.60	13.06	19.39	m^2	32.45
width not exceeding 225 mm; vertical	-	0.83	18.06	19.39	m^2	37.45
Milled lead damp proof course; BS 1178; 1.80 mm thick (code 4), 175 mm laps; in cement:lime mortar (1:2:9)						
width exceeding 225 mm; horizontal	15.51	1.85	40.26	17.52	m^2	57.78
width not exceeding 225 mm; horizontal	-	2.78	60.50	17.52	m^2	78.02
Two courses slates in cement:mortar (1:3)						
width exceeding 225 mm; horizontal	-	1.39	30.25	10.27	m^2	40.51
width exceeding 225 mm; vertical	-	2.08	45.26	10.27	m^2	55.53
"Synthaprufe" damp proof membrane or other equal and approved; PC £45.65/25 litres; three coats brushed on						
width not exceeding 150 mm; vertical	-	0.31	3.11	6.15	m^2	9.26
width 150 mm - 225 mm; vertical	-	0.30	3.01	6.15	m^2	9.16
width 225 mm - 300 mm; vertical	-	0.28	2.81	6.15	m^2	8.96
width exceeding 300 mm wide; vertical	-	0.26	2.61	6.15	m^2	8.76
Joint reinforcement						
"Brickforce" galvanised steel joint reinforcement or other equal and approved						
width 60 mm; ref GBF40W60B	-	0.05	1.09	0.45	m	1.54
width 100 mm; ref GBF40W100B	-	0.07	1.52	0.53	m	2.06
width 150 mm; ref GBF40W150B	-	0.09	1.85	0.66	m	2.51
width 175 mm; ref GBF40W175B	-	0.10	2.18	0.79	m	2.96

F MASONRY

Item	PC £	Labour hours	Labour £	Material £	Unit	Total rate £
"Brickforce" stainless steel joint reinforcement or other equal and approved						
width 60 mm; ref SBF35W60	-	0.05	1.09	0.95	m	2.04
width 100 mm; ref SBF35W100	-	0.07	1.52	0.97	m	2.50
width 150 mm; ref SBF35W150	-	0.09	1.85	1.07	m	2.92
width 175 mm; ref SBF35W175	-	0.10	2.18	1.07	m	3.25
width 60 mm; ref SBF40W60	-	0.06	1.20	1.23	m	2.43
width 100 mm; ref SBF40W100	-	0.07	1.52	1.26	m	2.79
width 150 mm; ref SBF40W150	-	0.09	1.85	1.29	m	3.14
width 175 mm; ref SBF40W175	-	0.10	2.18	1.39	m	3.57
"Wallforce" stainless steel joint reinforcement or other equal and approved						
width 240 mm; ref SWF35W240	-	0.12	2.61	2.74	m	5.35
width 260 mm; ref SWF35W260	-	0.13	2.83	2.87	m	5.70
width 275 mm; ref SWF35W275	-	0.14	3.05	2.90	m	5.95
width 240 mm; ref SWF40W240	-	0.12	2.61	3.84	m	6.45
width 260 mm; ref SWF40W260	-	0.13	2.83	4.01	m	6.84
width 275 mm; ref SWF40W275	-	0.14	3.05	4.15	m	7.20
Weather fillets						
Weather fillets in cement:mortar (1:3)						
50 mm face width	-	0.11	2.39	0.04	m	2.43
100 mm face width	-	0.19	4.13	0.17	m	4.30
Angle fillets						
Angle fillets in cement:mortar (1:3)						
50 mm face width	-	0.11	2.39	0.04	m	2.43
100 mm face width	-	0.19	4.13	0.17	m	4.30
Pointing in						
Pointing with mastic						
wood frames or sills	-	0.09	1.21	0.49	m	1.70
Pointing with polysulphide sealant						
wood frames or sills	-	0.09	1.21	1.55	m	2.76
Wedging and pinning						
To underside of existing construction with slates in cement mortar (1:3)						
width of wall - one brick thick	-	0.74	16.10	2.20	m	18.30
width of wall - one and a half brick thick	-	0.93	20.24	4.40	m	24.64
width of wall - two brick thick	-	1.11	24.16	6.60	m	30.75
Joints						
Hacking joints and faces of brickwork or blockwork						
to form key for plaster	-	0.24	2.40	-	m²	2.40
Raking out joint in brickwork or blockwork for turned-in edge of flashing						
horizontal	-	0.14	3.05	-	m	3.05
stepped	-	0.19	4.13	-	m	4.13
Raking out and enlarging joint in brickwork or blockwork for nib of asphalt						
horizontal	-	0.19	4.13	-	m	4.13
Cutting grooves in brickwork or blockwork						
for water bars and the like	-	0.23	2.30	0.30	m	2.60
for nib of asphalt; horizontal	-	0.23	2.30	0.30	m	2.60
Preparing to receive new walls						
top existing 215 mm wall	-	0.19	4.13	-	m	4.13

F MASONRY

Item	PC £	Labour hours	Labour £	Material £	Unit	Total rate £
F30 ACCESSORIES/SUNDRY ITEMS FOR BRICKS/BLOCKS – cont'd						
Joints – cont'd						
Cleaning and priming both faces; filling with pre-formed closed cell joint filler and pointing one side with polysulphide sealant; 12 mm deep						
expansion joints; 12 mm wide	-	0.23	4.17	3.09	m	7.26
expansion joints; 20 mm wide	-	0.28	4.84	4.52	m	9.36
expansion joints; 25 mm wide	-	0.32	5.29	5.46	m	10.75
Fire resisting horizontal expansion joints; filling with joint filler; fixed with high temperature slip adhesive; between top of wall and soffit						
wall not exceeding 215 mm wide; 10 mm wide joint with 30 mm deep filler (one hour fire seal)	-	0.23	5.01	4.89	m	9.90
wall not exceeding 215 mm wide; 10 mm wide joint with 30 mm deep filler (two hour fire seal)	-	0.23	5.01	4.89	m	9.90
wall not exceeding 215 mm wide; 20 mm wide joint with 45 mm deep filler (two hour fire seal)	-	0.28	6.09	7.35	m	13.44
wall not exceeding 215 mm wide; 30 mm wide joint with 75 mm deep filler (three hour fire seal)	-	0.32	6.96	18.29	m	25.26
Fire resisting vertical expansiojn joints; filling with joint filler; fixed with high temperature slip adhesive; with polysulphide sealant one side; between end of wall and concrete						
wall not exceeding 215 mm wide; 20 mm wide joint with 45 mm deep filler (two hour fire seal)	-	0.37	7.21	10.45	m	17.67
Slate and tile sills						
Sills; two courses of machine made plain roofing tiles						
set weathering; bedded and pointed	-	0.56	12.19	4.48	m	16.67
Sundries						
Weep holes						
Perpend units; plastic	-	0.02	0.44	0.11	nr	0.54
Chimney pots; red terracotta; plain or cannon-head; setting and flaunching in cement mortar (1:3)						
185 mm diameter x 300 mm long	10.22	1.67	36.34	12.34	nr	48.68
185 mm diameter x 600 mm long	18.13	1.85	40.26	20.85	nr	61.11
185 mm diameter x 900 mm long	33.04	1.85	40.26	36.90	nr	77.15
Air bricks						
Air bricks; red terracotta; building into prepared openings						
215 mm x 65 mm	-	0.07	1.52	1.09	nr	2.61
215 mm x 140 mm	-	0.07	1.52	1.51	nr	3.03
215 mm x 215 mm	-	0.07	1.52	4.09	nr	5.62
Gas flue blocks						
Gas flue system; Marflex "HP"or other equal and approved; concrete blocks built in; in flue joint mortar mix; cutting brickwork or blockwork around						
recess unit; ref HP1	-	0.09	1.96	1.70	nr	3.66
cover block; ref HP2	-	0.09	1.96	3.80	nr	5.76
222 mm standard block with nib; ref HP3	-	0.09	1.96	2.68	nr	4.64
112 mm standard block with nib; ref HP3112	-	0.09	1.96	2.10	nr	4.06
72 mm standard block with nib; ref HP372	-	0.09	1.96	2.10	nr	4.06
222 mm standard block without nib; ref HP4	-	0.09	1.96	2.63	nr	4.59

F MASONRY

Item	PC £	Labour hours	Labour £	Material £	Unit	Total rate £
112 mm standard block without nib; ref HP4112	-	0.09	1.96	2.10	nr	4.06
72 mm standard block without nib; ref HP472	-	0.09	1.96	2.10	nr	4.06
120 mm side offset block; ref HP5	-	0.09	1.96	2.82	nr	4.78
70 mm back offset block; ref HP6	-	0.09	1.96	8.28	nr	10.24
vertical exit block; ref HP7	-	0.09	1.96	5.43	nr	7.39
angled entry/exit block; ref HP8	-	0.09	1.96	5.43	nr	7.39
reverse rebate block; ref HP9	-	0.09	1.96	3.90	nr	5.85
corbel block; ref HP10	-	0.09	1.96	5.22	nr	7.18
lintel unit; ref HP11	-	0.09	1.96	4.92	nr	6.88
Flue linings						
Flue linings; Marflex "ML 200" square refractory concrete flue linings or other equal and approved; rebated joints in flue joint mortar mix						
linings; ref MLS1U	-	0.28	6.09	10.31	m	16.40
bottom swivel unit; ref MLS2U	-	0.09	1.96	8.28	nr	10.24
45 degree bend; ref MLS4U	-	0.09	1.96	6.05	nr	8.01
90 mm offset liner; ref MLS5U	-	0.09	1.96	4.01	nr	5.96
70 mm offset liner; ref MLS6U	-	0.09	1.96	3.61	nr	5.57
57 mm offset liner; ref MLS7U	-	0.09	1.96	8.78	nr	10.74
pot; ref MLS9UR	-	0.09	1.96	15.58	nr	17.54
single cap unit; ref MLS10U	-	0.23	5.01	19.84	nr	24.85
double cap unit; ref MLS11U	-	0.28	6.09	18.25	nr	24.35
combined gather lintel; ref MLSUL4	-	0.28	6.09	18.55	nr	24.65
Proprietary items						
External Door and window cavity closers; "Thermabate" or equivalent; inclusive of flange clips; jointing strips; wall fixing ties and adhesive tape						
closing cavities; width of cavity 50 mm	-	0.14	3.05	3.09	m	6.14
closing cavities; width of cavity 75 mm	-	0.14	3.05	3.29	m	6.34
closing cavities; width of cavity 100 mm	-	0.14	3.05	3.71	m	6.75
"Westbrick" cavity closers or other equal and approved; Manthorpe Building Products Ltd						
closing cavities; width of cavity 50 mm	-	0.14	3.05	4.83	m	7.87
"Type H cavicloser" or other equal and approved; uPVC universal cavity closer, insulator and damp proof course by Cavity Trays Ltd; built into cavity wall as work proceeds, complete with face closer and ties						
closing cavities; width of cavity 50 mm - 100 mm	-	0.07	1.52	5.19	m	6.71
"Type L" durropolyethelene lintel stop ends or other equal and approved; Cavity Trays Ltd; fixing with butyl anchoring strip; building in as the work proceeds						
adjusted to lintel as required	-	0.04	0.87	0.52	nr	1.39
"Type W" polypropylene weeps/vents or other equal and approved; Cavity Trays Ltd; built into cavity wall as work proceeds						
100/115 mm x 65 mm x 10 mm including lock fit wedges	-	0.04	0.87	0.40	nr	1.27
extra; extension duct 200/225 mm x 65 mm x 10 mm	-	0.07	1.52	0.67	nr	2.19

F MASONRY

Item	PC £	Labour hours	Labour £	Material £	Unit	Total rate £
F30 ACCESSORIES/SUNDRY ITEMS FOR BRICKS/BLOCKS – cont'd						
Proprietary items – cont'd						
"Type X" polypropylene abutment cavity tray or other equal and approved; Cavity Trays Ltd; built into facing brickwork as the work proceeds; complete with Code 4 flashing; intermediate/catchment tray with short leads (requiring soakers); to suit roof of						
17 - 20 degree pitch	-	0.05	1.09	4.40	nr	5.49
21 - 25 degree pitch	-	0.05	1.09	4.09	nr	5.17
26 - 45 degree pitch	-	0.05	1.09	3.91	nr	5.00
"Type X" polypropylene abutment cavity tray or other equal and approved; Cavity Trays Ltd; built into facing brickwork as the work proceeds; complete with Code 4 flashing; intermediate/catchment tray with long leads (suitable only for corrugated roof tiles); to suit roof of						
17 - 20 degree pitch	-	0.05	1.09	5.94	nr	7.03
21 - 25 degree pitch	-	0.05	1.09	5.46	nr	6.55
26 - 45 degree pitch	-	0.05	1.09	5.04	nr	6.13
"Type X" polypropylene abutment cavity tray or other equal and approved; Cavity Trays Ltd; built into facing brickwork as the work proceeds; complete with Code 4 flashing; ridge tray with short/long leads; to suit roof of						
17 - 20 degree pitch	-	0.05	1.09	10.00	nr	11.09
21 - 25 degree pitch	-	0.05	1.09	9.28	nr	10.36
26 - 45 degree pitch	-	0.05	1.09	8.25	nr	9.34
Servicised "Bitu-thene" self-adhesive cavity flashing or other equal and approved; type "CA"; well lapped at joints; in gauged mortar (1:1:6)						
width exceeding 225 mm wide	-	0.79	17.19	17.47	m²	34.66
"Expamet" stainless steel wall starters or other equal and approved; plugged and screwed						
to suit walls 60 mm - 75 mm thick	-	0.23	2.30	6.01	m	8.31
to suit walls 100 mm - 115 mm thick	-	0.23	2.30	6.60	m	8.91
to suit walls 125 mm - 180 mm thick	-	0.37	3.71	8.85	m	12.56
to suit walls 190 mm - 260 mm thick	-	0.46	4.61	11.31	m	15.91
Stainless steel posts, channels and ties						
Windposts; 130 x 70 x 6 mm; including one piece through ties						
1200 mm overall long	-	-	-	-	nr	112.94
3000 mm overall long	-	-	-	-	nr	169.41
4800 mm overall long	-	-	-	-	nr	248.47
Wall restraint channel ties; vertical channels; welded to steelwork. with lateral resatrint ties						
channel reference 28/15; tie reference HTS-B9; 200 mm long; one end of tie secured to channel; other end and debonding sleeve built into horizontal joint of masonry at 250 mm centres	-	0.12	2.61	9.36	m	11.97
Brickwork support angle welded to bracket reference HC6C or other equal and approved; Halfen Ltd; to suit 75 mm cavity, support to brickwork 6000 mm high						
6 mm thick; bolting with M12 x 50 mm T head bolts to cast in channel (not included)	-	0.32	5.58	59.01	m	64.59

F MASONRY

Item	PC £	Labour hours	Labour £	Material £	Unit	Total rate £
Wall restraint individually fixed ties; fixed to steelwork						
ties reference HTS-B9; 200 mm long; one end of tie secured to channel; other end and debonding sleeve built into horizontal joint of masonry at 250 mm centres	-	0.02	0.44	0.55	nr	0.98
Head restraints; sliding brick anchors reference SBA/L at 900 mm horizontal centres; 500 mm deep tying into two courses of blockwork; fixed to steelwork						
2 nr ties reference HTS-B12; 200 mm long; built into horizontal joint of masonry	-	0.05	1.09	6.84	nr	7.93
Head restraint fixings; sliding brick anchors with 500 mm long stem; 2 nr 100 mm projection HST brick anchor ties or other equal and approved; Halfen Ltd; fixing with bolts to concrete soffit (bolts not included)						
ref. SBA/L	-	0.19	3.31	6.77	nr	10.08
Ties in walls; 200 mm long butterfly type; building into joints of brickwork or blockwork						
galvanised steel or polypropylene	-	0.02	0.44	0.08	nr	0.52
stainless steel	-	0.02	0.44	0.17	nr	0.60
Ties in walls; 20 mm x 3 mm x 200 mm long twisted wall type; building into joints of brickwork or blockwork						
galvanised steel	-	0.02	0.44	0.16	nr	0.59
stainless steel	-	0.02	0.44	0.32	nr	0.76
Anchors in walls; 25 mm x 3 mm x 100 mm long; one end dovetailed; other end building into joints of brickwork or blockwork						
galvanised steel	-	0.05	1.09	0.22	nr	1.30
stainless steel	-	0.05	1.09	0.34	nr	1.43
Slotted frame cramp; Halfen Ltd or other equal and approved; fixing by bolting (bolts measured elsewhere)						
ref. HTS - FH12; 150 mm projection	-	0.07	0.89	0.46	nr	1.35
Single expansion bolt; Halfen Ltd or other equal and approved: including washer						
8 mm diameter; ref. SEB 8	-	0.11	1.92	1.94	nr	3.86
Fixing cramps; 25 mm x 3 mm x 250 mm long; once bent; fixed to back of frame; other end building into joints of brickwork or blockwork						
galvanised steel	-	0.05	1.09	0.17	nr	1.26
Lintels						
Galvanised steel lintels; "Catnic" or other equal and approved; built into brickwork or blockwork; "CN7" combined lintel; 143 mm high; for standard cavity walls						
750 mm long	24.64	0.23	5.01	26.55	nr	31.56
900 mm long	29.83	0.28	6.09	32.14	nr	38.23
1200 mm long	38.67	0.32	6.96	41.65	nr	48.62
1500 mm long	46.69	0.37	8.05	50.29	nr	58.34
1800 mm long	60.90	0.42	9.14	65.58	nr	74.72
2100 mm long	71.95	0.46	10.01	77.47	nr	87.48

F MASONRY

Item	PC £	Labour hours	Labour £	Material £	Unit	Total rate £
F30 ACCESSORIES/SUNDRY ITEMS FOR BRICKS/BLOCKS – cont'd						
Lintels – cont'd						
Galvanised steel lintels; "Catnic" or other equal and approved; built into brickwork or blockwork; "CN8" combined lintel; 219 mm high; for standard cavity walls						
2400 mm long	90.72	0.56	12.19	97.68	nr	109.87
2700 mm long	127.89	0.65	14.15	137.68	nr	151.82
3000 mm long	137.40	0.74	16.10	147.91	nr	164.02
3300 mm long	153.36	0.83	18.06	165.09	nr	183.15
3600 mm long	168.30	0.93	20.24	181.17	nr	201.40
3900 mm long	204.54	1.02	22.20	220.17	nr	242.37
4200 mm long	204.65	0.46	10.01	220.29	nr	230.30
Galvanised steel lintels; "Catnic" or other equal and approved; built into brickwork or blockwork; "CN92" single lintel; for 75 mm internal walls						
900 mm long	3.67	0.28	6.09	3.97	nr	10.06
1050 mm long	4.44	0.28	6.09	4.79	nr	10.89
1200 mm long	5.03	0.32	6.96	5.43	nr	12.39
Galvanised steel lintels; "Catnic" or other equal and approved; built into brickwork or blockwork; "CN102" single lintel; for 100 mm internal walls						
900 mm long	4.68	0.28	6.09	5.06	nr	11.15
1050 mm long	5.62	0.28	6.09	6.06	nr	12.16
1200 mm long	6.20	0.32	6.96	6.70	nr	13.66
F31 PRECAST CONCRETE SILLS/LINTELS/ COPINGS/FEATURES						
Mix 20.00 N/mm^2 - 20 mm aggregate (1:2:4)						
Lintels; plate; prestressed bedded						
100 mm x 70 mm x 750 mm long	2.86	0.37	8.05	3.09	nr	11.15
100 mm x 70 mm x 900 mm long	3.38	0.37	8.05	3.66	nr	11.71
100 mm x 70 mm x 1050 mm long	4.01	0.37	8.05	4.34	nr	12.39
100 mm x 70 mm x 1200 mm long	4.54	0.37	8.05	4.91	nr	12.96
150 mm x 70 mm x 900 mm long	4.64	0.46	10.01	5.03	nr	15.04
150 mm x 70 mm x 1050 mm long	5.42	0.46	10.01	5.86	nr	15.87
150 mm x 70 mm x 1200 mm long	6.18	0.46	10.01	6.69	nr	16.70
220 mm x 70 mm x 900 mm long	7.16	0.56	12.19	7.75	nr	19.93
220 mm x 70 mm x 1200 mm long	9.51	0.56	12.19	10.28	nr	22.47
220 mm x 70 mm x 1500 mm long	11.93	0.65	14.15	12.88	nr	27.03
265 mm x 70 mm x 900 mm long	7.64	0.56	12.19	8.27	nr	20.46
265 mm x 70 mm x 1200 mm long	10.20	0.56	12.19	11.03	nr	23.21
265 mm x 70 mm x 1500 mm long	12.71	0.65	14.15	13.73	nr	27.87
265 mm x 70 mm x 1800 mm long	15.21	0.74	16.10	16.43	nr	32.53
Lintels; rectangular; reinforced with mild steel bars; bedded						
100 mm x 145 mm x 900 mm long	6.91	0.56	12.19	7.46	nr	19.64
100 mm x 145 mm x 1050 mm long	8.12	0.56	12.19	8.76	nr	20.94
100 mm x 145 mm x 1200 mm long	9.18	0.56	12.19	9.90	nr	22.09
225 mm x 145 mm x 1200 mm long	11.65	0.74	16.10	12.58	nr	28.69
225 mm x 225 mm x 1800 mm long	22.57	1.39	30.25	24.34	nr	54.59
Lintels; boot; reinforced with mild steel bars; bedded						
250 mm x 225 mm x 1200 mm long	18.70	1.11	24.16	20.18	nr	44.33
275 mm x 225 mm x 1800 mm long	25.07	1.67	36.34	27.03	nr	63.37

F MASONRY

Item	PC £	Labour hours	Labour £	Material £	Unit	Total rate £
Padstones						
300 mm x 100 mm x 75 mm	3.82	0.28	6.09	4.13	nr	**10.22**
225 mm x 225 mm x 150 mm	5.80	0.37	8.05	6.27	nr	**14.32**
450 mm x 450 mm x 150 mm	15.32	0.56	12.19	16.62	nr	**28.80**
Mix 30.00 N/mm^2 - 20 mm aggregate (1:1:2)						
Copings; once weathered; once throated; bedded and pointed						
152 mm x 76 mm	4.64	0.65	14.15	5.31	m	**19.45**
178 mm x 64 mm	5.12	0.65	14.15	5.85	m	**20.00**
305 mm x 76 mm	8.64	0.74	16.10	9.92	m	**26.02**
extra for fair ends	-	-	-	4.26	nr	**4.26**
extra for angles	-	-	-	4.84	nr	**4.84**
Copings; twice weathered; twice throated; bedded and pointed						
152 mm x 76 mm	4.64	0.65	14.15	5.31	m	**19.45**
178 mm x 64 mm	5.08	0.65	14.15	5.80	m	**19.95**
305 mm x 76 mm	8.64	0.74	16.10	9.92	m	**26.02**
extra for fair ends	-	-	-	4.26	nr	**4.26**
extra for angles	-	-	-	4.84	nr	**4.84**

G STRUCTURAL/CARCASSING METAL/TIMBER

Item	PC £	Labour hours	Labour £	Material £	Unit	Total rate £
BASIC STEEL PRICES						
UNIVERSAL BEAMS AND COLUMNS						
NOTE: The following are January 2005 basis prices are for basic quantities of BS EN10025 1993 grade 275 JR steel (over 10 tonnes of one quantity, one serial size and one thickness in lengths between 6 m and 18½ m, for delivery to outer London). They include current end user discounts. Readers should contact Corus to check the currency of these prices.						
Universal beams (kg/m)						
1016 x 305 mm (222, 249, 272, 314, 349, 393, 438, 487)	-	-	-	684.00	tonne	-
914 x 419 mm (343, 388)	-	-	-	674.00	tonne	-
914 x 305 mm (201, 224, 253, 289)	-	-	-	669.00	tonne	-
838 x 292 mm (176, 194, 226)	-	-	-	664.00	tonne	-
762 x 267 mm (134, 147, 173, 197)	-	-	-	664.00	tonne	-
686 x 254 mm (125, 140, 152, 170)	-	-	-	664.00	tonne	-
610 x 305 mm (149, 179, 238)	-	-	-	654.00	tonne	-
610 x 229 mm (101, 113, 125, 140)	-	-	-	594.00	tonne	-
533 x 210 mm (82, 92, 101, 109, 122)	-	-	-	579.00	tonne	-
457 x 191 mm (67, 74, 82, 89, 98)	-	-	-	564.00	tonne	-
457 x 152 mm (52, 60, 67, 74, 82)	-	-	-	564.00	tonne	-
406 x 178 mm (54, 60, 67, 74)	-	-	-	569.00	tonne	-
406 x 140 mm (39, 46)	-	-	-	569.00	tonne	-
356 x 171 mm (45, 51, 57, 67)	-	-	-	569.00	tonne	-
356 x 127 mm (33, 39)	-	-	-	569.00	tonne	-
305 x 165 mm (40, 46, 54)	-	-	-	564.00	tonne	-
305 x 127 mm (37, 42, 48)	-	-	-	564.00	tonne	-
305 x 102 mm (25, 28, 33)	-	-	-	564.00	tonne	-
254 x 146 mm (31, 37, 43)	-	-	-	579.00	tonne	-
254 x 102 mm (22, 25, 28)	-	-	-	569.00	tonne	-
203 x 133 mm (25, 30)	-	-	-	579.00	tonne	-
203 x 102 mm (23)	-	-	-	579.00	tonne	-
178 x 102 mm (19)	-	-	-	579.00	tonne	-
152 x 89 mm (16)	-	-	-	589.00	tonne	-
127 x 76 mm (13)	-	-	-	589.00	tonne	-
Universal columns (kg/m)						
356 x 406 mm (235, 287, 340, 393, 467, 551, 634)	-	-	-	674.00	tonne	-
356 x 368 mm (129, 153, 177, 202)	-	-	-	674.00	tonne	-
305 x 305 mm (97, 118, 137, 158, 198, 240, 283)	-	-	-	589.00	tonne	-
254 x 254 mm (73, 89, 107, 132, 167)	-	-	-	569.00	tonne	-
203 x 203 mm (46, 52, 60, 71, 86)	-	-	-	559.00	tonne	-
152 x 152 mm (23, 30, 37)	-	-	-	579.00	tonne	-
Joists (kg/m)						
203 x 152 mm (60.2)	-	-	-	719.00	tonne	-
203 x 152 mm (52.3)	-	-	-	694.00	tonne	-
152 x 127 mm (37.3)	-	-	-	694.00	tonne	-
Channels (kg/m)						
430 x 100 mm (64.4)	-	-	-	619.00	tonne	-
380 x 100 mm (54.0)	-	-	-	619.00	tonne	-
300 x 100 mm (45.5)	-	-	-	589.00	tonne	-
300 x 90 mm (41.4)	-	-	-	589.00	tonne	-
260 x 90 mm (34.8)	-	-	-	589.00	tonne	-

G STRUCTURAL/CARCASSING METAL/TIMBER

Item	PC £	Labour hours	Labour £	Material £	Unit	Total rate £
260 x 75 mm (27.6)	-	-	-	589.00	tonne	-
230 x 90 mm (32.2)	-	-	-	589.00	tonne	-
230 x 75 mm (25.7)	-	-	-	589.00	tonne	-
200 x 90 mm (29.7)	-	-	-	589.00	tonne	-
200 x 75 mm (23.4)	-	-	-	554.00	tonne	-
180 x 90 mm (26.1)	-	-	-	589.00	tonne	-
180 x 75 mm (20.3)	-	-	-	554.00	tonne	-
150 x 90 mm (23.9)	-	-	-	589.00	tonne	-
150 x 75 mm (17.9)	-	-	-	554.00	tonne	-
125 x 65 mm (14.8)	-	-	-	554.00	tonne	-
100 x 50 mm (10.2)	-	-	-	554.00	tonne	-
Equal angles (mm)						
200 x 200 mm (16,18,20,24)	-	-	-	544.00	tonne	-
150 x 150 mm (10,12,15,18)	-	-	-	539.00	tonne	-
120 x 120 mm (8, 10, 12, 15)	-	-	-	544.00	tonne	-
100 x 100 mm (8, 10, 12, 15)	-	-	-	529.00	tonne	-
90 x 90 mm (6, 7, 8, 10, 12)	-	-	-	529.00	tonne	-
Unequal angles (mm)						
200 x 150 mm (12,15, 18)	-	-	-	559.00	tonne	-
200 x 100 mm (10, 12, 15)	-	-	-	554.00	tonne	-
150 x 90 mm (10, 12, 15)	-	-	-	539.00	tonne	-
150 x 75 mm (10, 12, 15)	-	-	-	529.00	tonne	-
125 x 75 mm (8, 10, 12)	-	-	-	529.00	tonne	-
100 x 75 mm (8, 10, 12)	-	-	-	529.00	tonne	-
100 x 65 mm (7, 8, 10)	-	-	-	529.00	tonne	-
Please refer to the Corus Price List for other extras to basis prices						
HOLLOW SECTIONS						
NOTE: The following are basis June 2004 prices are for basic quantities of 10 tonnes and over in one size, thickness, length, steelgrade and surface finish and include delivery for delivery to outer London). They include current end user discounts.						
The following lists represent only extracts for standard items and are not fully comprehensive. Readers should contact Corus for prices of alternative grades/sections and to check the currency of these prices.						
Hot formed structural circular hollow section; S355J2H Grade 50D (kg/m)						
48.30 x 3.20 mm (3.56); (approximately 281.00 metres per tonne)	-	-	-	282.04	100 m	-
48.30 x 4.00 mm (4.37); (approximately 229.00 metres per tonne)	-	-	-	349.12	100 m	-
48.30 x 5.00 mm (5.34); (approximately 188.00 metres per tonne)	-	-	-	426.61	100 m	-
60.30 x 3.20 mm (4.51); (approximately 222.00 metres per tonne)	-	-	-	357.31	100 m	-
60.30 x 4.00 mm (5.55); (approximately 181.00 metres per tonne)	-	-	-	458.15	100 m	-
60.30 x 5.00 mm (6.82); (approximately 147.00 metres per tonne)	-	-	-	562.98	100 m	-

G STRUCTURAL/CARCASSING METAL/TIMBER

Item	PC £	Labour hours	Labour £	Material £	Unit	Total rate £
BASIC STEEL PRICES – cont'd						
Hot formed structural circular hollow section S355J2H Grade 50D (kg/m) – cont'd						
76.10 x 3.20 mm (5.75); (approximately 174.00 metres per tonne)	-	-	-	455.54	100 m	-
76.10 x 4.00 mm (7.11); (approximately 141.00 metres per tonne)	-	-	-	586.92	100 m	-
76.10 x 5.00 mm (8.77); (approximately 115.00 metres per tonne)	-	-	-	723.95	100 m	-
88.90 x 3.20 mm (6.76); (approximately 148.00 metres per tonne)	-	-	-	535.56	100 m	-
88.90 x 4.00 mm (8.38); (approximately 120.00 metres per tonne)	-	-	-	663.91	100 m	-
88.90 x 5.00 mm (10.30); (approximately 97.10 metres per tonne)	-	-	-	850.26	100 m	-
114.30 x 3.60 mm (9.83); (approximately 102.00 metres per tonne)	-	-	-	811.46	100 m	-
114.30 x 5.00 mm (13.50); (approximately 74.10 metres per tonne)	-	-	-	1114.41	100 m	-
114.30 x 6.30 mm (16.80); (approximately 59.60 metres per tonne)	-	-	-	1713.33	100 m	-
139.70 x 5.00 mm (16.60); (approximately 60.30 metres per tonne)	-	-	-	1373.98	100 m	-
139.70 x 6.30 mm (20.70); (approximately 48.40 metres per tonne)	-	-	-	1713.33	100 m	-
139.70 x 8.00 mm (26.00); (approximately 38.50 metres per tonne)	-	-	-	2152.02	100 m	-
139.70 x 10.00 mm (32.00); (approximately 31.30 metres per tonne)	-	-	-	2725.01	100 m	-
168.30 x 5.00 mm (20.10); (approximately 49.80 metres per tonne)	-	-	-	1663.68	100 m	-
168.30 x 6.30 mm (25.20); (approximately 39.70 metres per tonne)	-	-	-	2085.80	100 m	-
168.30 x 8.00 mm (31.60); (approximately 31.70 metres per tonne)	-	-	-	2195.53	100 m	-
168.30 x 10.00 mm (39.00); (approximately 25.70 metres per tonne)	-	-	-	3321.10	100 m	-
193.70 x 5.00 mm (23.30); (approximately 42.90 metres per tonne)	-	-	-	1928.54	100 m	-
193.70 x 6.30 mm (29.10); (approximately 34.40 metres per tonne)	-	-	-	5908.60	100 m	-
193.70 x 8.00 mm (36.60); (approximately 27.30 metres per tonne)	-	-	-	3029.38	100 m	-
193.70 x 10.00 mm (45.30); (approximately 22.10 metres per tonne)	-	-	-	3857.59	100 m	-
219.10 x 5.00 mm (26.40); (approximately 37.90 metres per tonne)	-	-	-	2283.64	100 m	-
219.10 x 6.30 mm (33.10); (approximately 30.20 metres per tonne)	-	-	-	2863.21	100 m	-
219.10 x 8.00 mm (41.60); (approximately 24.10 metres per tonne)	-	-	-	3598.47	100 m	-
219.10 x 10.00 mm (51.60); (approximately 19.40 metres per tonne)	-	-	-	4463.48	100 m	-
219.10 x 12.50 mm (63.70); (approximately 15.70 metres per tonne)	-	-	-	5895.74	100 m	-
244.50 x 8.00 mm (46.70); (approximately 21.50 metres per tonne)	-	-	-	4039.62	100 m	-
244.50 x 10.00 mm (57.80); (approximately 17.40 metres per tonne)	-	-	-	4999.79	100 m	-

G STRUCTURAL/CARCASSING METAL/TIMBER

Item	PC £	Labour hours	Labour £	Material £	Unit	Total rate £
244.50 x 12.50 mm (71.50); (approximately 14.00 metres per tonne)	-	-	-	6450.13	100 m	-
244.50 x 16.00 mm (90.20); (approximately 11.10 metres per tonne)	-	-	-	8304.41	100 m	-
273.00 x 6.30 mm (41.40); (approximately 24.20 metres per 0tonne)	-	-	-	3581.17	100 m	-
273.00 x 8.00 mm (52.30); (approximately 19.10 metres per tonne)	-	-	-	4524.03	100 m	-
273.00 x 10.00 mm (64.90); (approximately 15.40 metres per tonne)	-	-	-	5613.96	100 m	-
273.00 x 12.50 mm (80.30); (approximately 12.50 metres per tonne)	-	-	-	7243.99	100 m	-
273.00 x 16.00 mm (101.00); (approximately 9.91 metres per tonne)	-	-	-	9298.72	100 m	-
323.90 x 6.30 mm (49.30); (approximately 20.30 metres per tonne)	-	-	-	4264.53	100 m	-
323.90 x 8.00 mm (62.30); (approximately 16.10 metres per tonne)	-	-	-	5389.05	100 m	-
323.90 x 10.00 mm (77.40); (approximately 12.90 metres per tonne)	-	-	-	6695.22	100 m	-
323.90 x 12.50 mm (96.00); (approximately 10.40 metres per tonne)	-	-	-	8660.31	100 m	-
323.90 x 16.00 mm (121.00); (approximately 8.27 metres per tonne)	-	-	-	4840.06	100 m	-
355.60 x 16.00 mm (134.00); (approximately 7.47metres per tonne)	-	-	-	12336.92	100 m	-
406.40 x 10.00 mm (97.80); (approximately 10.20 metres per tonne)	-	-	-	8459.85	100 m	-
406.40 x 12.50 mm (121.00); (approximately 8.27 metres per 0tonne)	-	-	-	10915.60	100 m	-
406.40 x 16.00 mm (154.00); (approximately 6.50 metres per tonne)	-	-	-	14178.25	100 m	-
457.00 x 10.00 mm (110.00); (approximately 9.09 metres per tonne)	-	-	-	9515.17	100 m	-
457.00 x 12.50 mm (137.00); (approximately 7.30 metres per tonne)	-	-	-	11850.72	100 m	-
457.00 x 16.00 mm (174.00); (approximately 5.75 metres per tonne)	-	-	-	16019.58	100 m	-
508.00 x 10.00 mm (123.00); (approximately 8.13 metres per tonne)	-	-	-	10639.47	100 m	-
508.00 x 12.50 mm (153.00); (approximately 6.54 metres per tonne)	-	-	-	13802.37	100 m	-
508.00 x 16.00 mm (194.00); (approximately 5.16 metres per tonne)	-	-	-	17860.55	100 m	-
Hot formed structural square hollow section; S355J2H Grade 50D (kg/m)						
40 x 40 x 3.00 mm (3.41); (approximately 293.30 metres per tonne)	-	-	-	264.32	100 m	-
40 x 40 x 3.20 mm (3.61); (approximately 277.00 metres per tonne)	-	-	-	279.82	100 m	-
40 x 40 x 4.00 mm (4.39); (approximately 227.80 metres per tonne)	-	-	-	340.28	100 m	-
40 x 40 x 5.00 mm (5.28); (approximately 189.40 metres per tonne)	-	-	-	409.27	100 m	-
50 x 50 x 3.00 mm (4.35); (approximately 229.90 metres per tonne)	-	-	-	337.18	100 m	-
50 x 50 x 3.20 mm (4.62); (approximately 216.50 metres per tonne)	-	-	-	358.11	100 m	-
50 x 50 x 4.00 mm (5.64); (approximately 216.50 metres per tonne)	-	-	-	437.17	100 m	-

G STRUCTURAL/CARCASSING METAL/TIMBER

Item	PC £	Labour hours	Labour £	Material £	Unit	Total rate £
BASIC STEEL PRICES – cont'd						
Hot formed structural square hollow section; S355J2H Grade 50D (kg/m) – cont'd						
50 x 50 x 5.00 mm (6.85); (approximately 177.30 metres per tonne)	-	-	-	530.96	100 m	-
50 x 50 x 6.30 mm (8.31); (approximately 120.30 metres per tonne)	-	-	-	644.13	100 m	-
60 x 60 x 3.00 mm (5.29); (approximately 189.00 metres per tonne)	-	-	-	410.04	100 m	-
60 x 60 x 3.20 mm (5.62); (approximately 177.90 metres per tonne)	-	-	-	435.62	100 m	-
60 x 60 x 4.00 mm (6.90); (approximately 145.00 metres per tonne)	-	-	-	556.49	100 m	-
60 x 60 x 5.00 mm (8.42); (approximately 118.80 metres per tonne)	-	-	-	679.08	100 m	-
60 x 60 x 6.30 mm (10.30); (approximately 97.10 metres per tonne)	-	-	-	830.70	100 m	-
60 x 60 x 8.00 mm (12.50); (approximately 80.00 metres per tonne)	-	-	-	1008.13	100 m	-
70 x 70 x 3.60 mm (7.40); (approximately 135.10 metres per tonne)	-	-	-	578.24	100 m	-
70 x 70 x 5.00 mm (9.99); (approximately 100.10 metres per tonne)	-	-	-	805.70	100 m	-
70 x 70 x 6.30 mm (12.30); (approximately 81.30 metres per tonne)	-	-	-	992.00	100 m	-
70 x 70 x 8.00 mm (15.00); (approximately 66.70 metres per tonne)	-	-	-	1209.76	100 m	-
80 x 80 x 3.60 mm (8.53); (approximately 117.20 metres per tonne)	-	-	-	666.54	100 m	-
80 x 80 x 5.00 mm (11.60); (approximately 86.20 metres per tonne)	-	-	-	935.55	100 m	-
80 x 80 x 6.30 mm (14.20); (approximately 70.40 metres per tonne)	-	-	-	1145.24	100 m	-
80 x 80 x 8.00 mm (17.50); (approximately 57.10 metres per tonne)	-	-	-	1411.38	100 m	-
90 x 90 x 3.60 mm (9.66); (approximately 103.50 metres per tonne)	-	-	-	754.83	100 m	-
90 x 90 x 5.00 mm (13.10); (approximately 76.30 metres per tonne)	-	-	-	1056.52	100 m	-
90 x 90 x 6.30 mm (16.20); (approximately 61.70 metres per tonne)	-	-	-	1306.54	100 m	-
90 x 90 x 8.00 mm (20.10); (approximately 49.80 metres per tonne)	-	-	-	1621.08	100 m	-
100 x 100 x 4.00 mm (11.90); (approximately 84.00 metres per tonne)	-	-	-	909.95	100 m	-
100 x 100 x 5.00 mm (14.70); (approximately 68.00 metres per tonne)	-	-	-	1185.56	100 m	-
100 x 100 x 6.30 mm (18.20); (approximately 54.90 metres per tonne)	-	-	-	1467.84	100 m	-
100 x 100 x 10.00 mm (27.40); (approximately 36.50 metres per tonne)	-	-	-	2153.46	100 m	-
120 x 120 x 5.00 mm (17.80); (approximately 56.20 metres per tonne)	-	-	-	1355.51	100 m	-
120 x 120 x 6.30 mm (22.20); (approximately 45.00 metres per tonne)	-	-	-	1690.59	100 m	-
120 x 120 x 8.00 mm (27.60); (approximately 36.20 metres per tonne)	-	-	-	2101.81	100 m	-
120 x 120 x 10.00 mm (33.70); (approximately 29.70 metres per tonne)	-	-	-	2648.60	100 m	-

G STRUCTURAL/CARCASSING METAL/TIMBER

Item	PC £	Labour hours	Labour £	Material £	Unit	Total rate £
120 x 120 x 12.50 mm (40.90); (approximately 24.40 metres per tonne)	-	-	-	3214.47	100 m	-
140 x 140 x 5.00 mm (21.00); (approximately 17.60 metres per tonne)	-	-	-	1599.20	100 m	-
140 x 140 x 6.30 mm (26.10); (approximately 38.30 metres per tonne)	-	-	-	1987.58	100 m	-
140 x 140 x 8.00 mm (32.60); (approximately 30.70 metres per tonne)	-	-	-	2482.58	100 m	-
140 x 140 x 10.00 mm (40.00); (approximately 25.00 metres per tonne)	-	-	-	3143.74	100 m	-
140 x 140 x 12.50 mm (48.70); (approximately 20.50 metres per tonne)	-	-	-	4935.33	100 m	-
150 x 150 x 5.00 mm (21.00); (approximately 44.20 metres per tonne)	-	-	-	1721.05	100 m	-
150 x 150 x 6.30 mm (28.10); (approximately 35.60 metres per tonne)	-	-	-	2139.89	100 m	-
150 x 150 x 8.00 mm (35.10); (approximately 28.50 metres per tonne)	-	-	-	2672.96	100 m	-
150 x 150 x 10.00 mm (43.10); (approximately 23.20 metres per tonne)	-	-	-	3387.38	100 m	-
150 x 150 x 12.50 mm (52.70); (approximately 19.00 metres per tonne)	-	-	-	5340.70	100 m	-
160 x 160 x 5.00 mm (24.10); (approximately 41.50 metres per tonne)	-	-	-	1905.34	100 m	-
160 x 160 x 6.30 mm (30.10); (approximately 33.20 metres per tonne)	-	-	-	2379.70	100 m	-
160 x 160 x 8.00 mm (37.60); (approximately 26.60 metres per tonne)	-	-	-	2972.65	100 m	-
160 x 160 x 10.00 mm (46.30); (approximately 21.60 metres per tonne)	-	-	-	3660.47	100 m	-
160 x 160 x 12.50 mm (56.60); (approximately 17.70 metres per tonne)	-	-	-	4656.53	100 m	-
180 x 180 x 6.30 mm (34.00); (approximately 29.40 metres per tonne)	-	-	-	2688.03	100 m	-
180 x 180 x 8.00 mm (42.70); (approximately 23.40 metres per tonne)	-	-	-	3375.86	100 m	-
180 x 180 x 10.00 mm (52.50); (approximately 19.00 metres per tonne)	-	-	-	4150.64	100 m	-
180 x 180 x 12.50 mm (64.40); (approximately 15.50 metres per tonne)	-	-	-	5298.24	100 m	-
180 x 180 x 16.00 mm (80.20); (approximately 12.50 metres per tonne)	-	-	-	7224.53	100 m	-
200 x 200 x 5.00 mm (30.40); (approximately 32.90 metres per tonne)	-	-	-	2403.42	100 m	-
200 x 200 x 6.30 mm (38.00); (approximately 26.30 metres per tonne)	-	-	-	3004.28	100 m	-
200 x 200 x 8.00 mm (47.70); (approximately 21.00 metres per tonne)	-	-	£	3771.16	100 m	-
200 x 200 x 10.00 mm (58.80); (approximately 17.00 metres per tonne)	-	-	-	4648.72	100 m	-
200 x 200 x 12.50 mm (72.30); (approximately 13.80 metres per tonne)	-	-	-	5948.19	100 m	-
200 x 200 x 16.00 mm (90.30); (approximately 11.10 metres per tonne)	-	-	-	8134.35	100 m	-
250 x 250 x 6.30 mm (47.90); (approximately 20.90 metres per tonne)	-	-	-	3786.97	100 m	-
250 x 250 x 8.00 mm (60.30); (approximately 16.60 metres per tonne)	-	-	-	4767.31	100 m	-
250 x 250 x 10.00 mm (74.50); (approximately 13.40 metres per tonne)	-	-	-	5889.96	100 m	-

G STRUCTURAL/CARCASSING METAL/TIMBER

Item	PC £	Labour hours	Labour £	Material £	Unit	Total rate £
BASIC STEEL PRICES – cont'd						
Hot formed structural square hollow section; S355J2H Grade 50D (kg/m) – cont'd						
250 x 250 x 12.50 mm (91.90); (approximately 10.90 metres per tonne)	-	-	-	7560.69	100 m	-
250 x 250 x 16.00 mm (115.00); (approximately 8.70 metres per tonne)	-	-	-	10359.36	100 m	-
300 x 300 x 6.30 mm (57.80); (approximately 17.30 metres per tonne)	-	-	-	4569.66	100 m	-
300 x 300 x 8.00 mm (72.80); (approximately 13.70 metres per tonne)	-	-	-	5755.56	100 m	-
300 x 300 x 10.00 mm (90.20); (approximately 11.10 metres per tonne)	-	-	-	7131.20	100 m	-
300 x 300 x 12.50 mm (112.00); (approximately 8.93 metres per tonne)	-	-	-	9214.34	100 m	-
300 x 300 x 16.00 mm (141.00); (approximately 7.09 metres per tonne)	-	-	-	12701.48	100 m	-
350 x 350 x 8.00 mm (85.40); (approximately 11.70 metres per tonne)	-	-	-	6751.71	100 m	-
350 x 350 x 10.00 mm (106.00); (approximately 9.43 metres per tonne)	-	-	-	8380.35	100 m	-
350 x 350 x 12.50 mm (131.00); (approximately 7.63 metres per onne)	-	-	-	10777.49	100 m	-
350 x 350 x 16.00 mm (166.00); (approximately 6.02 metres per tonne)	-	-	-	14953.51	100 m	-
400 x 400 x 10.00 mm (122.00); (approximately 8.20 metres per tonne)	-	-	-	9645.31	100 m	-
400 x 400 x 12.50 mm (151.00); (approximately 6.62 metres per tonne)	-	-	-	1242.50	100 m	-
400 x 400 x 16.00 mm (191.00); (approximately 5.24 metres per tonne)	-	-	-	17205.55	100 m	-
Hot formed structural rectangular hollow section; S355J2H Grade 50D (kg/m)						
50 x 30 x 3.20 mm (3.61); (approximately 277.00 metres per tonne)	-	-	-	279.82	100 m	-
60 x 40 x 3.00 mm (4.35); (approximately 229.90 metres per tonne)	-	-	-	337.18	100 m	-
60 x 40 x 4.00 mm (5.64); (approximately 177.30 metres per tonne)	-	-	-	437.17	100 m	-
60 x 40 x 5.00 mm (6.85); (approximately 146.00 metres per tonne)	-	-	-	530.96	100 m	-
80 x 40 x 3.20 mm (5.62); (approximately 177.90 metres per tonne)	-	-	-	435.62	100 m	-
80 x 40 x 4.00 mm (6.90); (approximately 144.90 metres per tonne)	-	-	-	556.49	100 m	-
80 x 40 x 5.00 mm (8.42); (approximately 118.80 metres per tonne)	-	-	-	679.08	100 m	-
80 x 40 x 6.30 mm (10.30); (approximately 97.10 metres per tonne)	-	-	-	830.70	100 m	-
80 x 40 x 8.00 mm (12.50); (approximately 80.00 metres per tonne)	-	-	-	1008.13	100 m	-
90 x 50 x 3.60 mm (7.40); (approximately 135.10 metres per tonne)	-	-	-	578.24	100 m	-
90 x 50 x 5.00 mm (9.99); (approximately 100.10 metres per tonne)	-	-	-	805.70	100 m	-
90 x 50 x 6.30 mm (12.30); (approximately 81.30 metres per tonne)	-	-	-	992.20	100 m	-
100 x 50 x 3.00 mm (6.71); (approximately 149.00 metres per tonne)	-	-	-	503.96	100 m	-

G STRUCTURAL/CARCASSING METAL/TIMBER

Item	PC £	Labour hours	Labour £	Material £	Unit	Total rate £
100 x 50 x 3.20 mm (7.13); (approximately 140.30 metres per tonne)	-	-	-	535.51	100 m	-
100 x 50 x 4.00 mm (8.78); (approximately 113.90 metres per tonne)	-	-	-	686.07	100 m	-
100 x 50 x 5.00 mm (10.80); (approximately 92.60 metres per tonne)	-	-	-	871.03	100 m	-
100 x 50 x 6.30 mm (13.30); (approximately 75.20 metres per tonne)	-	-	-	1072.66	100 m	-
100 x 60 x 3.60 mm (8.53); (approximately 117.20 metres per tonne)	-	-	-	666.54	100 m	-
100 x 60 x 5.00 mm (11.60); (approximately 86.20 metres per tonne)	-	-	-	935.55	100 m	-
100 x 60 x 6.30 mm (14.20); (approximately 70.40 metres per tonne)	-	-	-	1145.24	100 m	-
100 x 60 x 8.00 mm (17.50); (approximately 57.10 metres per tonne)	-	-	-	1411.38	100 m	-
120 x 60 x 3.60 mm (9.66); (approximately 103.50 metres per tonne)	-	-	-	757.96	100 m	-
120 x 60 x 5.00 mm (13.10); (approximately 76.30 metres per tonne)	-	-	-	1056.52	100 m	-
120 x 60 x 6.30 mm (16.20); (approximately 61.70 metres per tonne)	-	-	-	1306.54	100 m	-
120 x 60 x 8.00 mm (20.10); (approximately 49.80 metres per tonne)	-	-	-	1621.08	100 m	-
120 x 80 x 5.00 mm (14.70); (approximately 68.00 metres per tonne)	-	-	-	1185.56	100 m	-
120 x 80 x 6.30 mm (18.20); (approximately 54.90 metres per tonne)	-	-	-	1467.84	100 m	-
120 x 80 x 8.00 mm (22.60); (approximately 44.20 metres per tonne)	-	-	-	1888.90	100 m	-
120 x 80 x 10.00 mm (27.40); (approximately 36.50 metres per tonne)	-	-	-	2307.28	100 m	-
150 x 100 x 5.00 mm (18.60); (approximately 53.80 metres per tonne)	-	-	-	1416.44	100 m	-
150 x 100 x 6.30 mm (23.10); (approximately 43.30 metres per tonne)	-	-	-	1759.12	100 m	-
150 x 100 x 8.00 mm (28.90); (approximately 34.60 metres per tonne)	-	-	-	2200.81	100 m	-
150 x 100 x 10.00 mm (35.30); (approximately 28.30 metres per tonne)	-	-	-	2774.35	100 m	-
150 x 100 x 12.50 mm (42.80); (approximately 23.40 metres per tonne)	-	-	-	3363.80	100 m	-
160 x 80 x 4.00 mm (14.40); (approximately 69.40 metres per tonne)	-	-	-	1096.60	100 m	-
160 x 80 x 5.00 mm (17.80); (approximately 56.20 metres per tonne)	-	-	-	1355.51	100 m	-
160 x 80 x 6.30 mm (22.20); (approximately 45.00 metres per tonne)	-	-	-	1690.59	100 m	-
160 x 80 x 8.00 mm (27.60); (approximately 36.20 metres per tonne)	-	-	-	2101.81	100 m	-
160 x 80 x 10.00 mm (33.70); (approximately 29.70 metres per tonne)	-	-	-	2648.60	100 m	-
200 x 100 x 5.00 mm (22.60); (approximately 44.20 metres per tonne)	-	-	-	1721.05	100 m	-
200 x 100 x 6.30 mm (28.10); (approximately 35.60 metres per tonne)	-	-	-	2139.89	100 m	-
200 x 100 x 8.00 mm (35.10); (approximately 28.50 metres per tonne)	-	-	-	2672.96	100 m	-
200 x 100 x 10.00 mm (43.10); (approximately 23.20 metres per tonne)	-	-	-	3387.38	100 m	-

G STRUCTURAL/CARCASSING METAL/TIMBER

Item	PC £	Labour hours	Labour £	Material £	Unit	Total rate £
BASIC STEEL PRICES – cont'd						
Hot formed structural rectangular hollow section; S355J2H Grade 50D (kg/m) – cont'd						
200 x 100 x 12.50 mm (52.70); (approximately 19.00 metres per tonne)	-	-	-	5340.70	100 m	-
250 x 150 x 5.00 mm (30.40); (approximately 32.90 metres per tonne)	-	-	-	2403.42	100 m	-
250 x 150 x 6.30 mm (38.00); (approximately 26.30 metres per tonne)	-	-	-	3004.28	100 m	-
250 x 150 x 8.00 mm (47.70); (approximately 21.00 metres per tonne)	-	-	-	3771.16	100 m	-
250 x 150 x 10.00 mm (58.80); (approximately 17.00 metres per tonne)	-	-	-	4648.72	100 m	-
250 x 150 x 12.50 mm (72.30); (approximately 13.80 metres per tonne)	-	-	-	5948.19	100 m	-
250 x 150 x 16.00 mm (90.30); (approximately 11.10 metres per tonne)	-	-	-	8134.35	100 m	-
300 x 200 x 6.30 mm (47.90); (approximately 20.90 metres per tonne)	-	-	-	3786.97	100 m	-
300 x 200 x 8.00 mm (60.30); (approximately 16.60 metres per tonne)	-	-	-	4767.31	100 m	-
300 x 200 x 10.00 mm (74.50); (approximately 13.40 metres per tonne)	-	-	-	5889.96	100 m	-
300 x 200 x 12.50 mm (91.90); (approximately 10.90 metres per tonne)	-	-	-	7560.69	100 m	-
300 x 200 x 16.00 mm (115.00); (approximately 8.70 metres per tonne)	-	-	-	10359.36	100 m	-
400 x 200 x 8.00 mm (72.80); (approximately 13.70 metres per tonne)	-	-	-	5755.56	100 m	-
400 x 200 x 10.00 mm (90.20); (approximately 11.10 metres per tonne)	-	-	-	7131.20	100 m	-
400 x 200 x 12.50 mm (112.00); (approximately 8.93 metres per tonne)	-	-	-	9214.34	100 m	-
400 x 200 x 16.00 mm (141.00); (approximately 7.09 metres per tonne)	-	-	-	12701.48	100 m	-
450 x 250 x 8.00 mm (85.40); (approximately 11.70 metres per tonne)	-	-	-	6751.71	100 m	-
450 x 250 x 10.00 mm (106.00); (approximately 9.43 metres per tonne)	-	-	-	8380.35	100 m	-
450 x 250 x 12.50 mm (131.00); (approximately 7.63 metres per tonne)	-	-	-	10777.49	100 m	-
450 x 250 x 16.00 mm (166.00); (approximately 6.02 metres per tonne)	-	-	-	14953.51	100 m	-
500 x 300 x 10.00 mm (122.00); (approximately 8.20 metres per tonne)	-	-	-	9650.91	100 m	-
500 x 300 x 12.50 mm (151.00); (approximately 6.62 metres per tonne)	-	hours	-	12422.90	100 m	-
500 x 300 x 16.00 mm (191.00); (approximately 5.24 metres per tonne)	-	-	-	17205.55	100 m	-

G STRUCTURAL/CARCASSING METAL/TIMBER

Item	PC £	Labour hours	Labour £	Material £	Unit	Total rate £
G10 STRUCTURAL STEEL FRAMING						
SUPPLY AND FIX PRICES						
Framing, fabrication; weldable steel; BS EN 10025: 1993 Grade S275; hot rolled structural steel sections; welded fabrication						
Columns						
weight not exceeding 40 kg/m	-	-	-	-	tonne	1281.35
weight not exceeding 40 kg/m; castellated	-	-	-	-	tonne	1516.59
weight not exceeding 40 kg/m; curved	-	-	-	-	tonne	1704.78
weight not exceeding 40 kg/m; square hollow section	-	-	-	-	tonne	1533.19
weight not exceeding 40 kg/m; circular hollow section	-	-	-	-	tonne	1620.83
weight 40 - 100 kg/m	-	-	-	-	tonne	1108.85
weight 40 - 100 kg/m; castellated	-	-	-	-	tonne	1297.04
weight 40 - 100 kg/m; curved	-	-	-	-	tonne	1438.18
weight 40 - 100 kg/m; square hollow section	-	-	-	-	tonne	1387.44
weight 40 - 100 kg/m; circular hollow section	-	-	-	-	tonne	1466.78
weight exceeding 100 kg/m	-	-	-	-	tonne	996.30
weight exceeding 100 kg/m; castellated	-	-	-	-	tonne	1137.44
weight exceeding 100 kg/m; curved	-	-	-	-	tonne	1278.59
weight exceeding 100 kg/m; square hollow section	-	-	-	-	tonne	1334.86
weight exceeding 100 kg/m; circular hollow section	-	-	-	-	tonne	1428.95
Beams						
weight not exceeding 40 kg/m	-	-	-	-	tonne	1334.86
weight not exceeding 40 kg/m; castellated	-	-	-	-	tonne	1570.10
weight not exceeding 40 kg/m; curved	-	-	-	-	tonne	1758.29
weight not exceeding 40 kg/m; square hollow section	-	-	-	-	tonne	1797.95
weight not exceeding 40 kg/m; circular hollow section	-	-	-	-	tonne	2134.66
weight 40 - 100 kg/m	-	-	-	-	tonne	1062.72
weight 40 - 100 kg/m; castellated	-	-	-	-	tonne	1250.91
weight 40 - 100 kg/m; curved	-	-	-	-	tonne	1392.05
weight 40 - 100 kg/m; square hollow section	-	-	-	-	tonne	1683.56
weight 40 - 100 kg/m; circular hollow section	-	-	-	-	tonne	1975.07
weight exceeding 100 kg/m	-	-	-	-	tonne	1011.06
weight exceeding 100 kg/m; castellated	-	-	-	-	tonne	1152.20
weight exceeding 100 kg/m; curved	-	-	-	-	tonne	1293.35
weight exceeding 100 kg/m; square hollow section	-	-	-	-	tonne	1631.90
weight exceeding 100 kg/m; circular hollow section	-	-	-	-	tonne	1867.14
Bracings						
weight not exceeding 40 kg/m	-	-	-	-	tonne	1560.87
weight not exceeding 40 kg/m; square hollow section	-	-	-	-	tonne	1796.11
weight not exceeding 40 kg/m; circular hollow section	-	-	-	-	tonne	1796.11
weight 40 - 100 kg/m	-	-	-	-	tonne	1448.33
weight 40 - 100 kg/m; square hollow section	-	-	-	-	tonne	1683.56
weight 40 - 100 kg/m; circular hollow section	-	-	-	-	tonne	1683.56
weight exceeding 100 kg/m	-	-	-	-	tonne	1368.07
weight exceeding 100 kg/m; square hollow section	-	-	-	-	tonne	1603.31
weight exceeding 100 kg/m; circular hollow section	-	-	-	-	tonne	1603.31

G STRUCTURAL/CARCASSING METAL/TIMBER

Item	PC £	Labour hours	Labour £	Material £	Unit	Total rate £
G10 STRUCTURAL STEEL FRAMING – cont'd						
Framing, fabrication; structural steel – cont'd						
Purlins and cladding rails						
weight not exceeding 40 kg/m	-	-	-	-	tonne	1193.71
weight not exceeding 40 kg/m; square hollow section	-	-	-	-	tonne	2003.67
weight not exceeding 40 kg/m; circular hollow section	-	-	-	-	tonne	2003.67
weight 40 - 100 kg/m	-	-	-	-	tonne	1058.11
weight 40 - 100 kg/m; square hollow section	-	-	-	-	tonne	1796.11
weight 40 - 100 kg/m; circular hollow section	-	-	-	-	tonne	1796.11
weight exceeding 100 kg/m	-	-	-	-	tonne	973.24
weight exceeding 100 kg/m; square hollow section	-	-	-	-	tonne	1735.22
weight exceeding 100 kg/m; circular hollow section	-	-	-	-	tonne	1735.22
Grillages						
weight not exceeding 40 kg/m	-	-	-	-	tonne	1334.86
weight 40 - 100 kg/m	-	-	-	-	tonne	1062.72
weight exceeding 100 kg/m	-	-	-	-	tonne	1011.06
Trestles, towers and built up columns						
straight	-	-	-	-	tonne	1786.88
Trusses and built up girders						
straight	-	-	-	-	tonne	1786.88
curved	-	-	-	-	tonne	2210.31
Fittings	-	-	-	-	tonne	1786.88
Add to the aforementioned prices for:						
grade 355 steelwork	-	-	-	-	%	8.03
Framing, erection						
Trial erection	-	-	-	-	tonne	276.75
Permanent erection on site	-	-	-	-	tonne	276.75
Surface preparation						
At works						
blast cleaning	-	-	-	-	m²	2.30
Surface treatment						
At works						
galvanising	-	-	-	-	m²	10.18
shotblasting and priming to SA 2.5	-	-	-	-	m²	6.15
touch up primer and one coat of two pack epoxy zinc phosphate primer	-	-	-	-	m²	4.23
intumescent paint fire protection (30 minutes); spray applied	-	-	-	-	m²	9.18
intumescent paint fire protection (60 minutes); spray applied	-	-	-	-	m²	13.77
Extra over for decorative sealer top coat	-	-	-	-	m²	2.76
On site						
intumescent paint fire protection (30 minutes); spray applied	-	-	-	-	m²	6.89
intumescent paint fire protection (30 minutes) to circular columns etc.; spray applied	-	-	-	-	m²	11.54
intumescent paint fire protection (60 minutes) to UBs etc.; spray applied	-	-	-	-	m²	8.72
intumescent paint fire protection (60 minutes) to circular columns etc.; spray applied	-	-	-	-	m²	14.64
Extra over for decorative sealer top coat	-	-	-	-	m²	2.29

G STRUCTURAL/CARCASSING METAL/TIMBER

Item	PC £	Labour hours	Labour £	Material £	Unit	Total rate £
Cold formed galvanised steel; Kingspan "Multibeam" or other equal and approved						
Cold rolled purlins and cladding rails						
175 x 60 x 1.40 mm gauge purlins or rails; fixed to steelwork	-	0.04	0.63	6.00	m	6.63
175 x 60 x 1.65 mm gauge purlins or rails; fixed to steelwork	-	0.04	0.63	6.53	m	7.17
175 x 60 x 2.00 mm gauge purlins or rails; fixed to steelwork	-	0.04	0.63	7.93	m	8.57
205 x 60 x 1.45 mm gauge purlins or rails; fixed to steelwork	-	0.04	0.63	6.89	m	7.52
205 x 60 x 1.65 mm gauge purlins or rails; fixed to steelwork	-	0.04	0.63	7.59	m	8.22
205 x 60 x 2.00 mm gauge purlins or rails; fixed to steelwork	-	0.04	0.63	8.47	m	9.11
Heavy duty Zed section spacers						
vertically; across cladding rails; fixed to steelwork	-	0.05	0.79	6.54	m	7.33
Cleats						
weld-on for 175 mm purlin or rail	-	0.10	1.58	1.77	nr	3.35
bolt-on for 175 mm purlin or rail; including fixing bolts	-	0.02	0.32	3.67	m	3.99
weld-on for 205 mm purlin or rail	-	0.10	1.58	2.01	nr	3.59
bolt-on for 205 mm purlin or rail; including fixing bolts	-	0.02	0.32	3.97	m	4.28
Tubular ties						
1500 mm long; bolted diagonally across purlins or cladding rails	-	0.02	0.32	3.95	m	4.26
G12 ISOLATED STRUCTURAL METAL MEMBERS						
Isolated structural member; weldable steel; BS EN 10025: 1993 Grade S275; hot rolled structural steel sections						
Plain member; beams						
weight not exceeding 40 kg/m	-	-	-	-	tonne	944.64
weight 40 - 100 kg/m	-	-	-	-	tonne	916.97
weight exceeding 100 kg/m	-	-	-	-	tonne	892.98
Metsec open web steel lattice beams or other equal and approved; in single members; raised 3.50 m above ground; ends built in						
Beams; one coat zinc phosphate primer at works						
200 mm deep; to span 5.00 m (7.69 kg/m); ref B22	-	0.19	4.60	38.78	m	43.38
200 mm deep; to span 5.00 m (7.64 kg/m); ref B27	-	0.19	4.60	35.19	m	39.79
300 mm deep; to span 7.00 m (10.26 kg/m); ref B30	-	0.23	5.56	42.36	m	47.93
350 mm deep; to span 8.50 m (10.60 kg/m); ref B35	-	0.23	5.56	45.95	m	51.52
350 mm deep; to span 10.00 m (12.76 kg/m); ref D35	-	0.28	6.77	63.88	m	70.65
450 mm deep; to span 11.50 m (17.08 kg/m); ref D50	-	0.32	7.74	71.05	m	78.79
450 mm deep; to span 13.00 m (25.44 kg/m); ref G50		0.46	11.13	102.56	m	113.69

G STRUCTURAL/CARCASSING METAL/TIMBER

Item	PC £	Labour hours	Labour £	Material £	Unit	Total rate £
G12 ISOLATED STRUCTURAL METAL MEMBERS – cont'd						
Metsec open web steel lattice beams – cont'd						
Beams; galvanised						
200 mm deep; to span 5.00 m (7.69 kg/m); ref B22	-	0.19	4.60	39.95	m	**44.55**
200 mm deep; to span 5.00 m (7.64 kg/m); ref B27	-	0.19	4.60	36.25	m	**40.84**
300 mm deep; to span 7.00 m (10.26 kg/m); ref B30	-	0.23	5.56	43.65	m	**49.21**
350 mm deep; to span 8.50 m (10.60 kg/m); ref B35	-	0.23	5.56	47.35	m	**52.91**
350 mm deep; to span 10.00 m (12.76 kg/m); ref D35	-	0.28	6.77	65.86	m	**72.64**
450 mm deep; to span 11.50 m (17.08 kg/m); ref D50	-	0.32	7.74	73.26	m	**81.01**
450 mm deep; to span 13.00 m (25.44 kg/m); ref G50	-	0.46	11.13	105.81	m	**116.94**
G20 CARPENTRY/TIMBER FRAMING/ FIRST FIXING						
BASIC TIMBER PRICES						
Hardwood; Joinery quality (£/wall m^3)						
Agba	-	-	-	1069.94	m^3	-
American White Ash	-	-	-	1085.99	m^3	-
Beech	-	-	-	1176.94	m^3	-
Brazilian Mahogany	-	-	-	1620.96	m^3	-
European Oak	-	-	-	2006.14	m^3	-
Iroko	-	-	-	968.30	m^3	-
Maple	-	-	-	1925.90	m^3	-
Sapele	-	-	-	893.40	m^3	-
Teak	-	-	-	2353.88	m^3	-
Utile	-	-	-	1134.14	m^3	-
West African Mahogany	-	-	-	829.21	m^3	-
Softwood; Carcassing quality (£/m^3)						
2.00 m - 4.80 m lengths	-	-	-	278.00	m^3	-
4.80 m - 6.00 m lengths	-	-	-	262.26	m^3	-
6.00 m - 9.00 m lengths	-	-	-	288.50	m^3	-
G.S. Grade	-	-	-	16.79	m^3	-
S.S. Grade	-	-	-	31.99	m^3	-
Softwood; Joinery quality (£/m^3)	-	-	-	203.80	m^3	-
Timber Treatment (£/m^3)						
Pre-treatment of timber by vacuum/pressure impregnation, excluding transport costs and any subsequent seasoning:						
interior work; min. salt retention 4.00 kg/ m^3	-	-	-	56.39	m^3	-
exterior work; min. salt retention 5.30 kg/ m^3	-	-	-	64.44	m^3	-
Pre-treatment of timber including flame proofing						-
all purposes; min. salt retention 36.00 kg/ m^3	-	-	-	-	m^3	-
"Aquaseal" timber treatments - (£/25 litres)						
"Timbershield"	-	-	-	28.00	25 litre	-
"Longlife Wood Protector"	-	-	-	75.65	25 litre	-

G STRUCTURAL/CARCASSING METAL/TIMBER

Item	PC £	Labour hours	Labour £	Material £	Unit	Total rate £
SUPPLY AND FIX PRICES						
Sawn softwood; untreated						
Floor members						
38 mm x 100 mm	-	0.11	1.92	0.90	m	2.82
38 mm x 150 mm	-	0.13	2.27	1.35	m	3.61
50 mm x 75 mm	-	0.11	1.92	0.84	m	2.75
50 mm x 100 mm	-	0.13	2.27	1.03	m	3.30
50 mm x 125 mm	-	0.13	2.27	1.35	m	3.61
50 mm x 150 mm	-	0.14	2.44	1.59	m	4.03
50 mm x 175 mm	-	0.14	2.44	1.93	m	4.37
50 mm x 200 mm	-	0.15	2.61	2.09	m	4.70
50 mm x 225 mm	-	0.15	2.61	2.37	m	4.98
50 mm x 250 mm	-	0.16	2.79	2.63	m	5.42
75 mm x 125 mm	-	0.15	2.61	2.25	m	4.87
75 mm x 150 mm	-	0.15	2.61	2.70	m	5.32
75 mm x 175 mm	-	0.15	2.61	3.08	m	5.69
75 mm x 200 mm	-	0.16	2.79	3.56	m	6.34
75 mm x 225 mm	-	0.16	2.79	3.96	m	6.75
75 mm x 250 mm	-	0.17	2.96	4.40	m	7.36
100 mm x 150 mm	-	0.20	3.48	3.61	m	7.09
100 mm x 200 mm	-	0.21	3.66	4.82	m	8.48
100 mm x 250 mm	-	0.23	4.01	5.97	m	9.98
100 mm x 300 mm	-	0.25	4.36	7.17	m	11.53
Wall or partition members						
25 mm x 25 mm	-	0.06	1.05	0.25	m	1.30
25 mm x 38 mm	-	0.06	1.05	0.28	m	1.33
25 mm x 75 mm	-	0.08	1.39	0.49	m	1.89
38 mm x 38 mm	-	0.08	1.39	0.43	m	1.82
38 mm x 50 mm	-	0.08	1.39	0.49	m	1.89
38 mm x 75 mm	-	0.11	1.92	0.73	m	2.65
38 mm x 100 mm	-	0.14	2.44	0.90	m	3.34
50 mm x 50 mm	-	0.11	1.92	0.62	m	2.54
50 mm x 75 mm	-	0.14	2.44	0.86	m	3.30
50 mm x 100 mm	-	0.17	2.96	1.06	m	4.02
50 mm x 125 mm	-	0.18	3.14	1.37	m	4.51
75 mm x 75 mm	-	0.17	2.96	1.37	m	4.33
75 mm x 100 mm	-	0.19	3.31	1.81	m	5.12
100 mm x 100 mm	-	0.19	3.31	2.48	m	5.79
Joist strutting; herringbone						
50 mm x 50 mm; depth of joist 150 mm	-	0.46	8.02	1.47	m	9.48
50 mm x 50 mm; depth of joist 175 mm	-	0.46	8.02	1.50	m	9.51
50 mm x 50 mm; depth of joist 200 mm	-	0.46	8.02	1.52	m	9.54
50 mm x 50 mm; depth of joist 225 mm	-	0.46	8.02	1.55	m	9.57
50 mm x 50 mm; depth of joist 250 mm	-	0.46	8.02	1.58	m	9.59
Joist strutting; block						
50 mm x 150 mm; depth of joist 150 mm	-	0.28	4.88	1.88	m	6.76
50 mm x 175 mm; depth of joist 175 mm	-	0.28	4.88	2.22	m	7.10
50 mm x 200 mm; depth of joist 200 mm	-	0.28	4.88	2.38	m	7.26
50 mm x 225 mm; depth of joist 225 mm	-	0.28	4.88	2.66	m	7.54
50 mm x 250 mm; depth of joist 250 mm	-	0.28	4.88	2.92	m	7.80
Cleats						
225 mm x 100 mm x 75 mm	-	0.19	3.31	0.42	nr	3.73
Extra for stress grading to above timbers						
structural (SC3) grade	-	-	-	8.56	%	8.56
structural (SC4) grade	-	-	-	14.27	%	14.27
structural (SC16) grade	-	-	-	25.69	%	25.69

G STRUCTURAL/CARCASSING METAL/TIMBER

Item	PC £	Labour hours	Labour £	Material £	Unit	Total rate £
G20 CARPENTRY/TIMBER FRAMING/ FIRST FIXING – cont'd						
Sawn softwood; untreated – cont'd						
Extra for protecting and flameproofing timber with "Celgard CF" protection or other equal and approved						
small sections	-	-	-	105.80	m³	105.80
large sections	-	-	-	101.57	m³	101.57
Wrot surfaces						
plain; 50 mm wide	-	0.02	0.35	-	m	0.35
plain; 100 mm wide	-	0.03	0.52	-	m	0.52
plain; 150 mm wide	-	0.04	0.70	-	m	0.70
Sawn softwood; "Tanalised"						
Floor members						
38 mm x 75 mm	-	0.11	1.92	0.85	m	2.77
38 mm x 100 mm	-	0.11	1.92	1.06	m	2.97
38 mm x 150 mm	-	0.13	2.27	1.58	m	3.85
50 mm x 75 mm	-	0.11	1.92	0.99	m	2.91
50 mm x 100 mm	1.03	0.13	2.27	1.24	m	3.51
50 mm x 125 mm	-	0.13	2.27	1.61	m	3.87
50 mm x 150 mm	-	0.14	2.44	1.90	m	4.34
50 mm x 175 mm	-	0.14	2.44	2.30	m	4.74
50 mm x 200 mm	-	0.15	2.61	2.50	m	5.12
50 mm x 225 mm	-	0.15	2.61	2.84	m	5.45
50 mm x 250 mm	-	0.16	2.79	3.15	m	5.93
75 mm x 125 mm	-	0.15	2.61	2.65	m	5.26
75 mm x 150 mm	-	0.15	2.61	3.17	m	5.78
75 mm x 175 mm	-	0.15	2.61	3.62	m	6.24
75 mm x 200 mm	-	0.16	2.79	4.18	m	6.97
75 mm x 225 mm	-	0.16	2.79	4.67	m	7.45
75 mm x 250 mm	-	0.17	2.96	5.18	m	8.14
100 mm x 150 mm	-	0.20	3.48	4.23	m	7.72
100 mm x 200 mm	-	0.21	3.66	5.65	m	9.31
100 mm x 250 mm	-	0.23	4.01	7.01	m	11.02
100 mm x 300 mm	-	0.25	4.36	8.42	m	12.78
Wall or partition members						
25 mm x 25 mm	-	0.06	1.05	0.28	m	1.32
25 mm x 38 mm	-	0.06	1.05	0.33	m	1.37
25 mm x 75 mm	-	0.08	1.39	0.57	m	1.96
38 mm x 38 mm	-	0.08	1.39	0.49	m	1.88
38 mm x 50 mm	-	0.08	1.39	0.57	m	1.96
38 mm x 75 mm	-	0.11	1.92	0.85	m	2.77
38 mm x 100 mm	-	0.14	2.44	1.06	m	3.50
50 mm x 50 mm	-	0.11	1.92	0.72	m	2.64
50 mm x 75 mm	-	0.14	2.44	1.02	m	3.46
50 mm x 100 mm	-	0.17	2.96	1.27	m	4.23
50 mm x 125 mm	-	0.18	3.14	1.63	m	4.77
75 mm x 75 mm	-	0.17	2.96	1.60	m	4.56
75 mm x 100 mm	-	0.19	3.31	2.12	m	5.43
100 mm x 100 mm	-	0.19	3.31	2.89	m	6.20
Roof members; flat						
38 mm x 75 mm	-	0.13	2.27	0.85	m	3.12
38 mm x 100 mm	-	0.13	2.27	1.06	m	3.32
38 mm x 125 mm	-	0.13	2.27	1.38	m	3.65
38 mm x 150 mm	-	0.13	2.27	1.58	m	3.85
50 mm x 100 mm	-	0.13	2.27	1.24	m	3.51
50 mm x 125 mm	-	0.13	2.27	1.61	m	3.87
50 mm x 150 mm	-	0.14	2.44	1.90	m	4.34

G STRUCTURAL/CARCASSING METAL/TIMBER

Item	PC £	Labour hours	Labour £	Material £	Unit	Total rate £
50 mm x 175 mm	-	0.14	2.44	2.30	m	**4.74**
50 mm x 200 mm	-	0.15	2.61	2.50	m	**5.12**
50 mm x 225 mm	-	0.15	2.61	2.84	m	**5.45**
50 mm x 250 mm	-	0.16	2.79	3.15	m	**5.93**
75 mm x 150 mm	-	0.15	2.61	3.17	m	**5.78**
75 mm x 175 mm	-	0.15	2.61	3.62	m	**6.24**
75 mm x 200 mm	-	0.16	2.79	4.18	m	**6.97**
75 mm x 225 mm	-	0.16	2.79	4.67	m	**7.45**
75 mm x 250 mm	-	0.17	2.96	5.18	m	**8.14**
Roof members; pitched						
25 mm x 100 mm	-	0.11	1.92	0.73	m	**2.65**
25 mm x 125 mm	-	0.11	1.92	0.89	m	**2.81**
25 mm x 150 mm	-	0.14	2.44	1.06	m	**3.50**
25 mm x 175 mm	-	0.16	2.79	1.26	m	**4.05**
25 mm x 200 mm	-	0.17	2.96	1.42	m	**4.38**
38 mm x 100 mm	-	0.14	2.44	1.06	m	**3.50**
38 mm x 125 mm	-	0.14	2.44	1.38	m	**3.82**
38 mm x 150 mm	-	0.14	2.44	1.58	m	**4.02**
50 mm x 50 mm	-	0.11	1.92	0.70	m	**2.62**
50 mm x 75 mm	-	0.14	2.44	0.99	m	**3.43**
50 mm x 100 mm	-	0.17	2.96	1.24	m	**4.21**
50 mm x 125 mm	-	0.17	2.96	1.61	m	**4.57**
50 mm x 150 mm	-	0.19	3.31	1.90	m	**5.21**
50 mm x 175 mm	-	0.19	3.31	2.30	m	**5.61**
50 mm x 200 mm	-	0.19	3.31	2.50	m	**5.81**
50 mm x 225 mm	-	0.19	3.31	2.84	m	**6.15**
75 mm x 100 mm	-	0.23	4.01	2.08	m	**6.08**
75 mm x 125 mm	-	0.23	4.01	2.65	m	**6.65**
75 mm x 150 mm	-	0.23	4.01	3.17	m	**7.18**
100 mm x 150 mm	-	0.28	4.88	4.25	m	**9.13**
100 mm x 175 mm	-	0.28	4.88	4.98	m	**9.86**
100 mm x 200 mm	-	0.28	4.88	5.65	m	**10.53**
100 mm x 225 mm	-	0.31	5.40	6.34	m	**11.74**
100 mm x 250 mm	-	0.31	5.40	7.01	m	**12.42**
Plates						
38 mm x 75 mm	-	0.11	1.92	0.89	m	**2.81**
38 mm x 100 mm	-	0.14	2.44	1.06	m	**3.50**
50 mm x 75 mm	-	0.14	2.44	0.99	m	**3.43**
50 mm x 100 mm	-	0.17	2.96	1.24	m	**4.21**
75 mm x 100 mm	-	0.19	3.31	2.08	m	**5.39**
75 mm x 125 mm	-	0.22	3.83	2.62	m	**6.46**
75 mm x 150 mm	-	0.25	4.36	3.15	m	**7.50**
Plates; fixing by bolting						
38 mm x 75 mm	-	0.20	3.48	0.85	m	**4.34**
38 mm x 100 mm	-	0.23	4.01	1.06	m	**5.07**
50 mm x 75 mm	-	0.23	4.01	0.99	m	**5.00**
50 mm x 100 mm	-	0.26	4.53	1.24	m	**5.77**
75 mm x 100 mm	-	0.29	5.05	2.08	m	**7.13**
75 mm x 125 mm	-	0.31	5.40	2.62	m	**8.02**
75 mm x 150 mm	-	0.34	5.92	3.15	m	**9.07**
Joist strutting; herringbone						
50 mm x 50 mm; depth of joist 150 mm	-	0.46	8.02	1.68	m	**9.70**
50 mm x 50 mm; depth of joist 175 mm	-	0.46	8.02	1.72	m	**9.73**
50 mm x 50 mm; depth of joist 200 mm	-	0.46	8.02	1.75	m	**9.76**
50 mm x 50 mm; depth of joist 225 mm	-	0.46	8.02	1.78	m	**9.79**
50 mm x 50 mm; depth of joist 250 mm	-	0.46	8.02	1.81	m	**9.83**

G STRUCTURAL/CARCASSING METAL/TIMBER

Item	PC £	Labour hours	Labour £	Material £	Unit	Total rate £
G20 CARPENTRY/TIMBER FRAMING/ FIRST FIXING – cont'd						
Sawn softwood; "Tanalised" – cont'd						
Joist strutting; block						
50 mm x 150 mm; depth of joist 150 mm	-	0.28	4.88	2.19	m	7.07
50 mm x 175 mm; depth of joist 175 mm	-	0.28	4.88	2.59	m	7.47
50 mm x 200 mm; depth of joist 200 mm	-	0.28	4.88	2.80	m	7.67
50 mm x 225 mm; depth of joist 225 mm	-	0.28	4.88	3.13	m	8.01
50 mm x 250 mm; depth of joist 250 mm	-	0.28	4.88	3.44	m	8.32
Cleats						
225 mm x 100 mm x 75 mm	-	0.19	3.31	0.49	nr	3.80
Extra for stress grading to above timbers						
general structural (GS) grade	-	-	-	17.92	m^3	17.92
special structural (SS) grade	-	-	-	34.47	m^3	34.47
Extra for protecting and flameproofing timber with "Celgard CF" protection or other equal and approved						
small sections	-	-	-	105.80	m^3	105.80
large sections	-	-	-	101.57	m^3	101.57
Wrot surfaces						
plain; 50 mm wide	-	0.02	0.35	-	m	0.35
plain; 100 mm wide	-	0.03	0.52	-	m	0.52
plain; 150 mm wide	-	0.04	0.70	-	m	0.70
Trussed rafters, stress graded sawn softwood pressure impregnated; raised through two storeys and fixed in position						
"W" type truss (Fink); 22.5 degree pitch; 450 mm eaves overhang						
5.00 m span	-	1.48	25.79	27.91	nr	53.70
7.60 m span	-	1.62	28.23	35.18	nr	63.41
10.00 m span	-	1.85	32.24	45.81	nr	78.04
"W" type truss (Fink); 30 degree pitch; 450 mm Eaves overhang						
5.00 m span	-	1.48	25.79	27.70	nr	53.49
7.60 m span	-	1.62	28.23	36.15	nr	64.38
10.00 m span	-	1.85	32.24	51.83	nr	84.06
"W" type truss (Fink); 45 degree pitch; 450 mm eaves overhang						
4.60 m span	-	1.48	25.79	29.75	nr	55.54
7.00 m span	-	1.62	28.23	40.06	nr	68.28
"Mono" type truss; 17.5 degree pitch; 450 mm eaves overhang						
3.30 m span	-	1.30	22.65	22.52	nr	45.17
5.60 m span	-	1.48	25.79	31.89	nr	57.68
7.00 m span	-	1.71	29.80	40.06	nr	69.85
"Mono" type truss; 30 degree pitch; 450 mm eaves overhang						
3.30 m span	-	1.30	22.65	24.19	nr	46.84
5.60 m span	-	1.48	25.79	34.52	nr	60.31
7.00 m span	-	1.71	29.80	45.49	nr	75.28
"Attic" type truss; 45 degree pitch; 450 mm eaves overhang						
5.00 m span	-	2.91	50.71	60.31	nr	111.01
7.60 m span	-	3.05	53.14	97.85	nr	151.00
9.00 m span	-	3.24	56.46	125.30	nr	181.76

G STRUCTURAL/CARCASSING METAL/TIMBER

Item	PC £	Labour hours	Labour £	Material £	Unit	Total rate £
Moelven Toreboda" glulam timber beams or other equal and approved; Moelven Laminated Timber Structures; LB grade whitewood; pressure impregnated; phenbol resorcinal adhesive; clean planed finish; fixed						
Laminated roof beams						
56 mm x 225 mm	-	0.51	8.89	6.91	m	15.80
66 mm x 315 mm	-	0.65	11.33	11.41	m	22.74
90 mm x 315 mm	-	0.83	14.46	15.56	m	30.03
90 mm x 405 mm	-	1.06	18.47	20.02	m	38.49
115 mm x 405 mm	-	1.34	23.35	25.58	m	48.92
115 mm x 495 mm	-	1.67	29.10	31.26	m	60.36
115 mm x 630 mm	-	2.04	35.55	39.79	m	75.34
"Masterboard" or other equal and approved; 6 mm thick						
Eaves, verge soffit boards, fascia boards and the like						
over 300 mm wide	5.29	0.65	11.33	6.57	m²	17.90
75 mm wide	-	0.19	3.31	0.50	m	3.81
150 mm wide	-	0.22	3.83	0.99	m	4.82
225 mm wide	-	0.26	4.53	1.47	m	6.00
300 mm wide	-	0.28	4.88	1.95	m	6.83
Plywood; external quality; 12 mm thick						
Eaves, verge soffit boards, fascia boards and the like						
over 300 mm wide	4.76	0.76	13.24	5.96	m²	19.20
75 mm wide	-	0.23	4.01	0.46	m	4.47
150 mm wide	-	0.27	4.70	0.89	m	5.60
225 mm wide	-	0.31	5.40	1.33	m	6.73
300 mm wide	-	0.34	5.92	1.76	m	7.69
Plywood; external quality; 15 mm thick						
Eaves, verge soffit boards, fascia boards and the like						
over 300 mm wide	5.80	0.76	13.24	7.16	m²	20.40
75 mm wide	-	0.23	4.01	0.55	m	4.56
150 mm wide	-	0.27	4.70	1.07	m	5.78
225 mm wide	-	0.31	5.40	1.60	m	7.00
300 mm wide	-	0.34	5.92	2.13	m	8.05
Plywood; external quality; 18 mm thick						
Eaves, verge soffit boards, fascia boards and the like						
over 300 mm wide	6.72	0.76	13.24	8.22	m²	21.46
75 mm wide	-	0.23	4.01	0.63	m	4.64
150 mm wide	-	0.27	4.70	1.23	m	5.94
225 mm wide	-	0.31	5.40	1.84	m	7.24
300 mm wide	-	0.34	5.92	2.44	m	8.37
Plywood; marine quality; 18 mm thick						
Gutter boards; butt joints						
over 300 mm wide	8.82	0.86	14.99	10.65	m²	25.64
150 mm wide	-	0.31	5.40	1.60	m	7.00
225 mm wide	-	0.34	5.92	2.41	m	8.33
300 mm wide	-	0.38	6.62	3.20	m	9.82

G STRUCTURAL/CARCASSING METAL/TIMBER

Item	PC £	Labour hours	Labour £	Material £	Unit	Total rate £
G20 CARPENTRY/TIMBER FRAMING/ **FIRST FIXING** – cont'd						
Plywood; marine quality; 18 mm thick – cont'd						
Eaves, verge soffit boards, fascias boards and the like						
over 300 mm wide	-	0.76	13.24	10.65	m²	**23.90**
75 mm wide	-	0.23	4.01	0.81	m	**4.82**
150 mm wide	-	0.27	4.70	1.60	m	**6.30**
225 mm wide	-	0.31	5.40	2.39	m	**7.79**
300 mm wide	-	0.34	5.92	3.17	m	**9.10**
Plywood; marine quality; 25 mm thick						
Gutter boards; butt joints						
over 300 mm wide	12.25	0.93	16.20	14.62	m²	**30.82**
150 mm wide	-	0.32	5.58	2.19	m	**7.77**
225 mm wide	-	0.37	6.45	3.30	m	**9.75**
300 mm wide	-	0.42	7.32	4.39	m	**11.70**
Eaves, verge soffit boards, fascia baords and the like						
over 300 mm wide	-	0.81	14.11	14.62	m²	**28.73**
75 mm wide	-	0.24	4.18	1.11	m	**5.29**
150 mm wide	-	0.29	5.05	2.19	m	**7.25**
225 mm wide	-	0.29	5.05	3.28	m	**8.33**
300 mm wide	-	0.37	6.45	4.36	m	**10.81**
Sawn softwood; untreated						
Gutter boards; butt joints						
19 mm thick; sloping	-	1.16	20.21	5.92	m²	**26.13**
19 mm thick; 75 mm wide	-	0.32	5.58	0.48	m	**6.06**
19 mm thick; 150 mm wide	-	0.37	6.45	0.86	m	**7.31**
19 mm thick; 225 mm wide	-	0.42	7.32	1.29	m	**8.61**
25 mm thick; sloping	-	1.16	20.21	6.48	m²	**26.69**
25 mm thick; 75 mm wide	-	0.32	5.58	0.51	m	**6.09**
25 mm thick; 150 mm wide	-	0.37	6.45	0.94	m	**7.39**
25 mm thick; 225 mm wide	-	0.42	7.32	1.41	m	**8.73**
Cesspools with 25 mm thick sides and bottom						
225 mm x 225 mm x 150 mm	-	1.11	19.34	1.21	nr	**20.56**
300 mm x 300 mm x 150 mm	-	1.30	22.65	1.60	nr	**24.26**
Individual supports; firrings						
50 mm wide x 36 mm average depth	-	0.14	2.44	0.82	m	**3.26**
50 mm wide x 50 mm average depth	-	0.14	2.44	0.96	m	**3.40**
50 mm wide x 75 mm average depth	-	0.14	2.44	1.38	m	**3.82**
Individual supports; bearers						
25 mm x 50 mm	-	0.09	1.57	0.43	m	**2.00**
38 mm x 50 mm	-	0.09	1.57	0.54	m	**2.11**
50 mm x 50 mm	-	0.09	1.57	0.64	m	**2.21**
50 mm x 75 mm	-	0.09	1.57	0.88	m	**2.45**
Individual supports; angle fillets						
38 mm x 38 mm	-	0.09	1.57	0.38	m	**1.95**
50 mm x 50 mm	-	0.09	1.57	0.51	m	**2.07**
75 mm x 75 mm	-	0.11	1.92	1.07	m	**2.99**
Individual supports; tilting fillets						
19 mm x 38 mm	-	0.09	1.57	0.38	m	**1.95**
25 mm x 50 mm	-	0.09	1.57	0.35	m	**1.92**
38 mm x 75 mm	-	0.09	1.57	0.61	m	**2.18**
50 mm x 75 mm	-	0.09	1.57	0.54	m	**2.11**
75 mm x 100 mm	-	0.14	2.44	1.63	m	**4.07**

G STRUCTURAL/CARCASSING METAL/TIMBER

Item	PC £	Labour hours	Labour £	Material £	Unit	Total rate £
Individual supports; grounds or battens						
13 mm x 19 mm	-	0.04	0.70	0.23	m	0.93
13 mm x 32 mm	-	0.04	0.70	0.25	m	0.95
25 mm x 50 mm	-	0.04	0.70	0.39	m	1.09
Individual supports; grounds or battens; plugged and screwed						
13 mm x 19 mm	-	0.14	2.44	0.27	m	2.71
13 mm x 32 mm	-	0.14	2.44	0.29	m	2.73
25 mm x 50 mm	-	0.14	2.44	0.43	m	2.87
Framed supports; open-spaced grounds or battens; at 300 mm centres one way						
25 mm x 50 mm	-	0.14	2.44	1.28	m²	3.72
25 mm x 50 mm; plugged and screwed	-	0.42	7.32	1.42	m²	8.74
Framed supports; at 300 mm centres one way and 600 mm centres the other way						
25 mm x 50 mm	-	0.69	12.02	1.92	m²	13.94
38 mm x 50 mm	-	0.69	12.02	2.44	m²	14.46
50 mm x 50 mm	-	0.69	12.02	2.96	m²	14.98
50 mm x 75 mm	-	0.69	12.02	4.16	m²	16.18
75 mm x 75 mm	-	0.69	12.02	6.71	m²	18.73
Framed supports; at 300 mm centres one way and 600 mm centres the other way; plugged and screwed						
25 mm x 50 mm	-	1.16	20.21	2.31	m²	22.52
38 mm x 50 mm	-	1.16	20.21	2.83	m²	23.04
50 mm x 50 mm	-	1.16	20.21	3.35	m²	23.57
50 mm x 75 mm	-	1.16	20.21	4.55	m²	24.76
75 mm x 75 mm	-	1.16	20.21	7.10	m²	27.31
Framed supports; at 500 mm centres both ways						
25 mm x 50 mm; to bath panels	-	0.83	14.46	2.50	m²	16.96
Framed supports; as bracketing and cradling around steelwork						
25 mm x 50 mm	-	1.30	22.65	2.72	m²	25.37
50 mm x 50 mm	-	1.39	24.22	4.18	m²	28.40
50 mm x 75 mm	-	1.48	25.79	5.85	m²	31.64
Sawn softwood; "Tanalised"						
Gutter boards; butt joints						
19 mm thick; sloping	-	1.16	20.21	6.71	m²	26.92
19 mm thick; 75 mm wide	-	0.32	5.58	0.54	m	6.12
19 mm thick; 150 mm wide	-	0.37	6.45	0.98	m	7.43
19 mm thick; 225 mm wide	-	0.42	7.32	1.47	m	8.79
25 mm thick; sloping	-	1.16	20.21	7.52	m²	27.73
25 mm thick; 75 mm wide	-	0.32	5.58	0.59	m	6.17
25 mm thick; 150 mm wide	-	0.37	6.45	1.10	m	7.55
25 mm thick; 225 mm wide	-	0.42	7.32	1.65	m	8.96
Cesspools with 25 mm thick sides and bottom						
225 mm x 225 mm x 150 mm	-	1.11	19.34	1.42	nr	20.76
300 mm x 300 mm x 150 mm	-	1.30	22.65	1.89	nr	24.54
Individual supports; firrings						
50 mm wide x 36 mm average depth	-	0.14	2.44	0.90	m	3.33
50 mm wide x 50 mm average depth	-	0.14	2.44	1.07	m	3.51
50 mm wide x 75 mm average depth	-	0.14	2.44	1.54	m	3.98
Individual supports; bearers						
25 mm x 50 mm	-	0.09	1.57	0.49	m	2.06
38 mm x 50 mm	-	0.09	1.57	0.61	m	2.18
50 mm x 50 mm	-	0.09	1.57	0.75	m	2.31
50 mm x 75 mm	-	0.09	1.57	1.04	m	2.61

G STRUCTURAL/CARCASSING METAL/TIMBER

Item	PC £	Labour hours	Labour £	Material £	Unit	Total rate £
G20 CARPENTRY/TIMBER FRAMING/ FIRST FIXING – cont'd						
Sawn softwood; "Tanalised" – cont'd						
Individual supports; angle fillets						
38 mm x 38 mm	-	0.09	1.57	0.41	m	**1.98**
50 mm x 50 mm	-	0.09	1.57	0.56	m	**2.13**
75 mm x 75 mm	-	0.11	1.92	1.18	m	**3.10**
Individual supports; tilting fillets						
19 mm x 38 mm	-	0.09	1.57	0.40	m	**1.96**
25 mm x 50 mm	-	0.09	1.57	0.37	m	**1.94**
38 mm x 75 mm	-	0.09	1.57	0.67	m	**2.24**
50 mm x 75 mm	-	0.09	1.57	0.61	m	**2.18**
75 mm x 100 mm	-	0.14	2.44	1.79	m	**4.23**
Individual supports; grounds or battens						
13 mm x 19 mm	-	0.04	0.70	0.24	m	**0.94**
13 mm x 32 mm	-	0.04	0.70	0.27	m	**0.97**
25 mm x 50 mm	-	0.04	0.70	0.44	m	**1.14**
Individual supports; grounds or battens; plugged and screwed						
13 mm x 19 mm	-	0.14	2.44	0.28	m	**2.72**
13 mm x 32 mm	-	0.14	2.44	0.31	m	**2.75**
25 mm x 50 mm	-	0.14	2.44	0.48	m	**2.92**
Framed supports; open-spaced grounds or battens; at 300 mm centres one way						
25 mm x 50 mm	-	0.14	2.44	1.45	m²	**3.89**
25 mm x 50 mm; plugged and screwed	-	0.42	7.32	1.59	m²	**8.91**
Framed supports; at 300 mm centres one way and 600 mm centres the other way						
25 mm x 50 mm	-	0.69	12.02	2.18	m²	**14.21**
38 mm x 50 mm	-	0.69	12.02	2.84	m²	**14.86**
50 mm x 50 mm	-	0.69	12.02	3.48	m²	**15.50**
50 mm x 75 mm	-	0.69	12.02	4.94	m²	**16.96**
75 mm x 75 mm	-	0.69	12.02	7.88	m²	**19.90**
Framed supports; at 300 mm centres one way and 600 mm centres the other way; plugged and screwed						
25 mm x 50 mm	-	1.16	20.21	2.57	m²	**22.79**
38 mm x 50 mm	-	1.16	20.21	3.23	m²	**23.44**
50 mm x 50 mm	-	1.16	20.21	3.87	m²	**24.08**
50 mm x 75 mm	-	1.16	20.21	5.33	m²	**25.55**
75 mm x 75 mm	-	1.16	20.21	8.27	m²	**28.48**
Framed supports; at 500 mm centres both ways						
25 mm x 50 mm; to bath panels	-	0.83	14.46	2.84	m²	**17.30**
Framed supports; as bracketing and cradling around steelwork						
25 mm x 50 mm	-	1.30	22.65	3.09	m²	**25.74**
50 mm x 50 mm	-	1.39	24.22	4.91	m²	**29.13**
50 mm x 75 mm	-	1.48	25.79	6.95	m²	**32.74**
Wrought softwood						
Gutter boards; tongued and grooved joints						
19 mm thick; sloping	-	1.39	24.22	10.73	m²	**34.95**
19 mm thick; 75 mm wide	-	0.37	6.45	1.04	m	**7.49**
19 mm thick; 150 mm wide	-	0.42	7.32	1.58	m	**8.90**
19 mm thick; 225 mm wide	-	0.46	8.02	2.58	m	**10.59**
25 mm thick; sloping	-	1.39	24.22	12.94	m²	**37.16**
25 mm thick; 75 mm wide	-	0.37	6.45	1.04	m	**7.49**
25 mm thick; 150 mm wide	-	0.42	7.32	1.86	m	**9.18**
25 mm thick; 225 mm wide	-	0.46	8.02	2.83	m	**10.84**

G STRUCTURAL/CARCASSING METAL/TIMBER

Item	PC £	Labour hours	Labour £	Material £	Unit	Total rate £
Eaves, verge soffit boards, fascia boards and the like						
19 mm thick; over 300 mm wide	-	1.15	20.04	9.52	m²	29.56
19 mm thick; 150 mm wide; once grooved	-	0.19	3.31	1.66	m	4.97
25 mm thick; 150 mm wide; once grooved	-	0.19	3.31	1.66	m	4.97
25 mm thick; 175 mm wide; once grooved	-	0.19	3.31	1.91	m	5.22
32 mm thick; 225 mm wide; once grooved	-	0.23	4.01	2.48	m	6.48
Wrought softwood; "Tanalised"						
Gutter boards; tongued and grooved joints						
19 mm thick; sloping	-	1.39	24.22	11.52	m²	35.74
19 mm thick; 75 mm wide	-	0.37	6.45	1.10	m	7.54
19 mm thick; 150 mm wide	-	0.42	7.32	1.70	m	9.02
19 mm thick; 225 mm wide	-	0.46	8.02	2.75	m	10.77
25 mm thick; sloping	-	1.39	24.22	13.98	m²	38.20
25 mm thick; 75 mm wide	-	0.37	6.45	1.12	m	7.56
25 mm thick; 150 mm wide	-	0.42	7.32	2.02	m	9.33
25 mm thick; 225 mm wide	-	0.46	8.02	3.06	m	11.08
Eaves, verge soffit boards, fascia boards and the like						
19 mm thick; over 300 mm wide	-	1.15	20.04	10.31	m²	30.35
19 mm thick; 150 mm wide; once grooved	-	0.19	3.31	1.78	m	5.09
25 mm thick; 150 mm wide; once grooved	-	0.19	3.31	1.82	m	5.13
25 mm thick; 175 mm wide; once grooved	-	0.20	3.48	2.09	m	5.58
32 mm thick; 225 mm wide; once grooved	-	0.23	4.01	2.77	m	6.78
Straps; mild steel; galvanised						
Standard twisted vertical restraint; fixing to softwood and brick or blockwork						
30 mm x 2.5 mm x 400 mm girth	-	0.23	4.01	0.74	nr	4.75
30 mm x 2.5 mm x 600 mm girth	-	0.24	4.18	1.04	nr	5.23
30 mm x 2.5 mm x 800 mm girth	-	0.25	4.36	1.47	nr	5.83
30 mm x 2.5 mm x 1000 mm girth	-	0.28	4.88	1.90	nr	6.78
30 mm x 2.5 mm x 1200 mm girth	-	0.29	5.05	2.27	nr	7.32
Hangers; mild steel; galvanised						
Joist hangers 0.90 mm thick; The Expanded Metal Company Ltd "Speedy" or other equal and approved; for fixing to softwood; joist sizes						
50 mm wide; all sizes to 225 mm deep	0.87	0.11	1.92	1.09	nr	3.00
75 mm wide; all sizes to 225 mm deep	0.91	0.14	2.44	1.18	nr	3.62
100 mm wide; all sizes to 225 mm deep	0.98	0.17	2.96	1.31	nr	4.28
Joist hangers 2.50 mm thick; for building in; joist sizes						
50 mm x 100 mm	1.68	0.07	1.31	1.97	nr	3.28
50 mm x 125 mm	1.69	0.07	1.31	1.98	nr	3.28
50 mm x 150 mm	1.59	0.09	1.65	1.89	nr	3.55
50 mm x 175 mm	1.67	0.09	1.65	1.99	nr	3.65
50 mm x 200 mm	1.85	0.11	2.00	2.23	nr	4.23
50 mm x 225 mm	1.96	0.11	2.00	2.36	nr	4.36
75 mm x 150 mm	2.45	0.09	1.65	2.87	nr	4.53
75 mm x 175 mm	2.31	0.09	1.65	2.71	nr	4.37
75 mm x 200 mm	2.45	0.11	2.00	2.91	nr	4.91
75 mm x 225 mm	2.62	0.11	2.00	3.10	nr	5.10
75 mm x 250 mm	2.78	0.13	2.35	3.31	nr	5.67
100 mm x 200 mm	3.06	0.11	2.00	3.59	nr	5.59

G STRUCTURAL/CARCASSING METAL/TIMBER

Item	PC £	Labour hours	Labour £	Material £	Unit	Total rate £
G20 CARPENTRY/TIMBER FRAMING/ FIRST FIXING – cont'd						
Metal connectors; mild steel; galvanised						
Round toothed plate; for 10 mm or 12 mm diameter bolts						
50 mm diameter; single sided	-	0.01	0.17	0.28	nr	0.46
50 mm diameter; double sided	-	0.01	0.17	0.32	nr	0.49
63 mm diameter; single sided	-	0.01	0.17	0.41	nr	0.59
63 mm diameter; double sided	-	0.01	0.17	0.46	nr	0.63
75 mm diameter; single sided	-	0.01	0.17	0.61	nr	0.78
75 mm diameter; double sided	-	0.01	0.17	0.63	nr	0.81
framing anchor	-	0.14	2.44	0.42	nr	2.86
Bolts; mild steel; galvanised						
Fixing only bolts; 50 mm - 200 mm long						
6 mm diameter	-	0.03	0.52	-	nr	0.52
8 mm diameter	-	0.03	0.52	-	nr	0.52
10 mm diameter	-	0.04	0.70	-	nr	0.70
12 mm diameter	-	0.04	0.70	-	nr	0.70
16 mm diameter	-	0.05	0.87	-	nr	0.87
20 mm diameter	-	0.05	0.87	-	nr	0.87
Bolts						
Expanding bolts; "Rawlbolt" projecting type or other equal and approved; The Rawlplug Company; plated; one nut; one washer						
6 mm diameter; ref M6 10P	-	0.09	1.57	0.67	nr	2.24
6 mm diameter; ref M6 25P	-	0.09	1.57	0.75	nr	2.32
6 mm diameter; ref M6 60P	-	0.09	1.57	0.79	nr	2.36
8 mm diameter; ref M8 25P	-	0.09	1.57	0.89	nr	2.46
8 mm diameter; ref M8 60P	-	0.09	1.57	0.95	nr	2.52
10 mm diameter; ref M10 15P	-	0.09	1.57	1.16	nr	2.73
10 mm diameter; ref M10 30P	-	0.09	1.57	1.22	nr	2.79
10 mm diameter; ref M10 60P	-	0.09	1.57	1.27	nr	2.84
12 mm diameter; ref M12 15P	-	0.09	1.57	1.85	nr	3.42
12 mm diameter; ref M12 30P	-	0.10	1.74	0.18	nr	1.92
12 mm diameter; ref M12 75P	-	0.09	1.57	2.48	nr	4.05
16 mm diameter; ref M16 35P	-	0.09	1.57	4.73	nr	6.30
16 mm diameter; ref M16 75P	-	0.09	1.57	4.96	nr	6.53
Expanding bolts; "Rawlbolt" loose bolt type or other equal and approved; The Rawlplug Company; plated; one bolt; one washer						
6 mm diameter; ref M6 10L	-	0.09	1.57	0.67	nr	2.24
6 mm diameter; ref M6 25L	-	0.09	1.57	0.71	nr	2.28
6 mm diameter; ref M6 40L	-	0.09	1.57	0.72	nr	2.28
8 mm diameter; ref M8 25L	-	0.09	1.57	0.87	nr	2.44
8 mm diameter; ref M8 40L	-	0.09	1.57	0.93	nr	2.50
10 mm diameter; ref M10 10L	-	0.09	1.57	1.12	nr	2.69
10 mm diameter; ref M10 25L	-	0.09	1.57	1.15	nr	2.72
10 mm diameter; ref M10 50L	-	0.09	1.57	1.22	nr	2.79
10 mm diameter; ref M10 75L	-	0.09	1.57	1.26	nr	2.83
12 mm diameter; ref M12 10L	-	0.09	1.57	1.68	nr	3.25
12 mm diameter; ref M12 25L	-	0.09	1.57	1.85	nr	3.42
12 mm diameter; ref M12 40L	-	0.09	1.57	1.93	nr	3.50
12 mm diameter; ref M12 60L	-	0.09	1.57	2.03	nr	3.60
16 mm diameter; ref M16 30L	-	0.09	1.57	4.50	nr	6.07
16 mm diameter; ref M16 60L	-	0.09	1.57	4.87	nr	6.43

G STRUCTURAL/CARCASSING METAL/TIMBER

Item	PC £	Labour hours	Labour £	Material £	Unit	Total rate £
Truss clips						
Truss clips; fixing to softwood; joist size						
38 mm wide	0.15	0.14	2.44	0.37	nr	**2.81**
50 mm wide	0.16	0.14	2.44	0.39	nr	**2.83**
Sole plate angles; mild steel galvanised						
Sole plate angle; fixing to softwood and concrete						
112 mm x 40 mm x 76 mm	0.39	0.19	3.31	1.33	nr	**4.64**
Chemical anchors						
"Kemfix" capsules and standard studs or other						
equal and approved; The Ramplug Company;						
with nuts and washers; drilling masonry						
capsule ref 60-408; stud ref 60-448	-	0.25	4.36	1.25	nr	**5.60**
capsule ref 60-410; stud ref 60-454	-	0.28	4.88	1.41	nr	**6.29**
capsule ref 60-412; stud ref 60-460	-	0.31	5.40	1.72	nr	**7.12**
capsule ref 60-416; stud ref 60-472	-	0.34	5.92	2.71	nr	**8.63**
capsule ref 60-420; stud ref 60-478	-	0.36	6.27	4.41	nr	**10.68**
capsule ref 60-424; stud ref 60-484	-	0.40	6.97	6.77	nr	**13.74**
"Kemfix" capsules and stainless steel studs or						
other equal and approved; The Rawlplug						
Company; with nuts and washers; drilling masonry						
capsule ref 60-408; stud ref 60-905	-	0.25	4.36	2.27	nr	**6.63**
capsule ref 60-410; stud ref 60-910	-	0.28	4.88	3.06	nr	**7.93**
capsule ref 60-412; stud ref 60-915	-	0.31	5.40	4.22	nr	**9.62**
capsule ref 60-416; stud ref 60-920	-	0.34	5.92	7.21	nr	**13.13**
capsule ref 60-420; stud ref 60-925	-	0.36	6.27	11.41	nr	**17.68**
capsule ref 60-424; stud ref 60-930	-	0.40	6.97	18.65	nr	**25.62**
"Kemfix" capsules and standard internal						
threaded sockets or other equal and approved;						
The Rawlpug Company; drilling masonry						
capsule ref 60-408; socket ref 60-650	-	0.25	4.36	1.51	nr	**5.87**
capsule ref 60-410; socket ref 60-656	-	0.28	4.88	1.58	nr	**6.46**
capsule ref 60-412; socket ref 60-662	-	0.31	5.40	1.97	nr	**7.37**
capsule ref 60-416; socket ref 60-668	-	0.34	5.92	2.69	nr	**8.61**
capsule ref 60-420; socket ref 60-674	-	0.36	6.27	3.46	nr	**9.74**
capsule ref 60-424; socket ref 60-676	-	0.40	6.97	5.85	nr	**12.82**
"Kemfix" capsules and stainless steel internal						
threaded sockets or other equal and approved;						
The Rawlplug Company; drilling masonry						
capsule ref 60-408; socket ref 60-943	-	0.25	4.36	2.79	nr	**7.15**
capsule ref 60-410; socket ref 60-945	-	0.28	4.88	2.86	nr	**7.73**
capsule ref 60-412; socket ref 60-947	-	0.31	5.40	3.30	nr	**8.70**
capsule ref 60-416; socket ref 60-949	-	0.34	5.92	4.67	nr	**10.60**
capsule ref 60-420; socket ref 60-951	-	0.36	6.27	5.86	nr	**12.14**
capsule ref 60-424; socket ref 60-955	-	0.40	6.97	10.95	nr	**17.92**
"Kemfix" capsules, perforated sleeves and						
standard studs or other equal and approved; The						
Rawlplug Company; in low density material; with						
nuts and washers; drilling masonry						
capsule ref 60-408; sleeve ref 60-538; stud						
ref 60-448	-	0.25	4.36	1.87	nr	**6.22**
capsule ref 60-410; sleeve ref 60-544; stud						
ref 60-454	-	0.28	4.88	2.06	nr	**6.93**
capsule ref 60-412; sleeve ref 60-550; stud						
ref 60-460	-	0.31	5.40	2.47	nr	**7.87**
capsule ref 60-416; sleeve ref 60-562; stud						
ref 60-472	-	0.34	5.92	3.62	nr	**9.55**

Prices for Measured Works – Major Works

G STRUCTURAL/CARCASSING METAL/TIMBER

Item	PC £	Labour hours	Labour £	Material £	Unit	Total rate £
G20 CARPENTRY/TIMBER FRAMING/ FIRST FIXING – cont'd						
Chemical anchors – cont'd						
"Kemfix" capsules, perforated sleeves and stainless steel studs or other equal and approved; The Rawlplug Company; in low density material; with nuts and washers; drilling masonry						
capsule ref 60-408; sleeve ref 60-538; stud ref 60-905	-	0.25	4.36	2.89	nr	7.25
capsule ref 60-410; sleeve ref 60-544; stud ref 60-910	-	0.28	4.88	3.70	nr	8.58
capsule ref 60-412; sleeve ref 60-550; stud ref 60-915	-	0.31	5.40	4.97	nr	10.37
capsule ref 60-416; sleeve ref 60-562; stud ref 60-920	-	0.34	5.92	8.12	nr	14.05
"Kemfix" capsules, perforated sleeves and standard internal threaded sockets or other equal and approved; The Rawlplug Company; in low density material; with nuts and washers; drilling masonry						
capsule ref 60-408; sleeve ref 60-538; socket ref 60-650	-	0.25	4.36	2.13	nr	6.49
capsule ref 60-410; sleeve ref 60-544; socket ref 60-656	-	0.28	4.88	2.23	nr	7.10
capsule ref 60-412; sleeve ref 60-550; socket ref 60-662	-	0.31	5.40	2.72	nr	8.12
capsule ref 60-416; sleeve ref 60-562; socket ref 60-668	-	0.34	5.92	3.60	nr	9.53
"Kemfix" capsules, perforated sleeves and stainless steel internal threaded sockets or other equal and approved; The Rawlplug Company; in low density material; drilling masonry						
capsule ref 60-408; sleeve ref 60-538; socket ref 60-943	-	0.25	4.36	3.41	nr	7.77
capsule ref 60-410; sleeve ref 60-544; socket ref 60-945	-	0.28	4.88	3.50	nr	8.38
capsule ref 60-412; sleeve ref 60-550; socket ref 60-947	-	0.31	5.40	4.05	nr	9.45
capsule ref 60-416; sleeve ref 60-562; socket ref 60-949	-	0.34	5.92	5.59	nr	11.51

H CLADDING/COVERING

Item	PC £	Labour hours	Labour £	Material £	Unit	Total rate £
H10 PATENT GLAZING						
Patent glazing; aluminium alloy bars 2.55 m long at 622 mm centres; fixed to supports						
Roof cladding						
glazing with 7 mm thick Georgian wired cast glass	-	-	-	-	m²	119.56
Associated code 4 lead flashings						
top flashing; 210 mm girth	-	-	-	-	m	38.04
bottom flashing; 240 mm girth	-	-	-	-	m	30.98
end flashing; 300 mm girth	-	-	-	-	m	70.65
Wall cladding						
glazing with 7 mm thick Georgian wired cast glass	-	-	-	-	m²	125.00
glazing with 6 mm thick plate glass	-	-	-	-	m²	114.13
Extra for aluminium alloy members						
38 mm x 38 mm x 3 mm angle jamb	-	-	-	-	m	16.30
pressed cill member	-	-	-	-	m	35.33
pressed channel head and PVC case	-	-	-	-	m	29.89
"Kawneer" window frame system or other equal and approved; polyester powder coated glazing bars; glazed with double hermetically sealed units in toughened safety glass; one 6 mm thick air space; overall 18 mm thick						
Vertical surfaces						
single tier; aluminium glazing bars at 850 mm centres x 890 mm long; timber supports at 890 mm centres	-	-	-	-	m²	205.11
"Kawneer" window frame system or other equal and approved; polyester powder coated glazing bars; glazed with clear toughened safety glass; 10.70 mm thick						
Vertical surfaces						
single tier; aluminium glazing bars at 850 mm centres x 890 mm long; timber supports at 890 mm centres	-	-	-	-	m²	194.86
H11 CURTAIN WALLING						
Curtain walling; Senior Aluminium System SMR 900 System or equal and approved						
Curtain walling; powder coated aluminium; single glazed with 6 mm clear toughened glass						
flat; drilling and screwing; to metal	-	-	-	-	m²	245.17
Curtain walling; powder coated aluminium; double glazed with 6 mm clear toughened glass outer pane and 6.40 mm laminated inner pane						
flat; drilling and screwing; to metal	-	-	-	-	m²	290.61
Extra over for						
Low 'E' glass to inner leaf	-	-	-	-	m²	29.97
high performance glass to inner leaf	-	-	-	-	m²	24.98
body tinted anti-sun glass to outer leaf	-	-	-	-	m²	49.97

H CLADDING/COVERING

Item	PC £	Labour hours	Labour £	Material £	Unit	Total rate £
H20 RIGID SHEET CLADDING						
"Resoplan" sheet or other equal and approved; Eternit UK Ltd; flexible neoprene gasket joints; fixing with stainless steel screws and coloured caps 6 mm thick cladding to walls						
over 300 mm wide	-	1.94	33.80	52.62	m²	86.42
not exceeding 300 mm wide	-	0.65	11.33	20.18	m	31.50
Eternit 2000 "Glasal" sheet or other equal and approved; Eternit UK Ltd; flexible neoprene gasket joints; fixing with stainless steel screws and coloured caps 7.50 mm thick cladding to walls						
over 300 mm wide	-	1.94	33.80	46.59	m²	80.40
not exceeding 300 mm wide	-	0.65	11.33	18.37	m	29.70
external angle trim	-	0.09	1.57	8.63	m	10.19
7.50 mm thick cladding to eaves, verge soffit boards, fascia boards or the like						
100 mm wide	-	0.46	8.02	10.19	m	18.21
200 mm wide	-	0.56	9.76	14.28	m	24.04
300 mm wide	-	0.65	11.33	18.37	m	29.70
H21 TIMBER WEATHERBOARDING						
Prodema Lignum weatherboarding; Eurocom Enterprise Ltd or equal and approved; 8 mm thick; including secondary supports Walls						
over 300 mm wide; fixing with screws; to timber	-	1.30	22.65	54.43	m²	77.08
over 300 mm wide; fixing with adhesive; to timber	-	1.45	25.27	58.02	m²	83.28
over 300 mm wide; fixing with rivets; to aluminium	-	1.35	23.52	61.97	m²	85.49
over 300 mm wide; fixing with adhesive; to aluminium	-	1.50	26.14	67.33	m²	93.47
Prodema Lignum weatherboarding; Eurocom Enterprise Ltd or equal and approved; 8 mm thick; including adjustable grid support Walls						
over 300 mm wide; fixing with rivets; to aluminium	-	1.55	27.01	73.64	m²	100.65
over 300 mm wide; fixing with adhesive; to aluminium	-	1.50	26.14	76.71	m²	102.85
over 300 mm wide; secret fixing; to aluminium	-	2.20	38.33	92.38	m²	130.71
H30 FIBRE CEMENT PROFILED SHEET CLADDING						
Asbestos-free corrugated sheets; Eternit "2000" or other equal and approved Roof cladding; sloping not exceeding 50 degrees; fixing to timber purlins with drive screws						
"Profile 3"; natural grey	12.10	0.19	4.99	15.97	m²	20.96
"Profile 3"; coloured	14.52	0.19	4.99	18.70	m²	23.69
"Profile 6"; natural grey	9.31	0.23	6.04	12.74	m²	18.78
"Profile 6"; coloured	10.34	0.23	6.04	13.91	m²	19.95
"Profile 6"; natural grey; insulated 60 glass fibre infill; lining panel	-	0.42	11.03	30.95	m²	41.98

H CLADDING/COVERING

Item	PC £	Labour hours	Labour £	Material £	Unit	Total rate £
Roof cladding; sloping not exceeding 50 degrees; fixing to steel purlins with hook bolts						
"Profile 3"; natural grey	-	0.23	6.04	17.27	m²	23.31
"Profile 3"; coloured	-	0.23	6.04	20.01	m²	26.05
"Profile 6"; natural grey	-	0.28	7.35	14.05	m²	21.40
"Profile 6"; coloured	-	0.28	7.35	15.22	m²	22.57
"Profile 6"; natural grey; insulated 60 glass fibre infill; lining panel	-	0.46	12.08	28.51	m²	40.59
Wall cladding; vertical; fixing to steel rails with hook bolts						
"Profile 3"; natural grey	-	0.28	7.35	17.27	m²	24.63
"Profile 3"; coloured	-	0.28	7.35	20.01	m²	27.36
"Profile 6"; natural grey	-	0.32	8.40	14.05	m²	22.45
"Profile 6"; coloured	-	0.32	8.40	15.22	m²	23.62
"Profile 6"; natural grey; insulated 60 glass fibre infill; lining panel	-	0.51	13.39	28.51	m²	41.91
raking cutting	-	0.14	3.68	-	m	3.68
holes for pipe and the like	-	0.14	3.68	-	nr	3.68
Accessories; to "Profile 3" cladding; natural grey						
eaves filler	-	0.09	2.36	11.75	m	14.11
vertical corrugation closer	-	0.11	2.89	11.75	m	14.64
apron flashing	-	0.11	2.89	11.75	m	14.64
plain wing or close fitting two piece adjustable capping to ridge	-	0.16	4.20	11.02	m	15.22
ventilating two piece adjustable capping to ridge	-	0.16	4.20	16.53	m	20.73
Accessories; to "Profile 3" cladding; coloured						
eaves filler	-	0.09	2.36	14.36	m	16.72
vertical corrugation closer	-	0.11	2.89	14.36	m	17.25
apron flashing	-	0.11	2.89	14.36	m	17.25
plain wing or close fitting two piece adjustable capping to ridge	-	0.16	4.20	13.14	m	17.34
ventilating two piece adjustable capping to ridge	-	0.16	4.20	20.34	m	24.54
Accessories; to "Profile 6" cladding; natural grey						
eaves filler	-	0.09	2.36	7.63	m	9.99
vertical corrugation closer	-	0.11	2.89	7.63	m	10.52
apron flashing	-	0.11	2.89	8.48	m	11.36
underglazing flashing	-	0.11	2.89	7.63	m	10.52
plain cranked crown to ridge	-	0.16	4.20	16.78	m	20.98
plain wing or close fitting two piece adjustable capping to ridge	-	0.16	4.20	15.26	m	19.46
ventilating two piece adjustable capping to ridge	-	0.16	4.20	19.49	m	23.70
Accessories; to "Profile 6" cladding; coloured						
eaves filler	-	0.09	2.36	9.75	m	12.11
vertical corrugation closer	-	0.11	2.89	9.75	m	12.64
apron flashing	-	0.11	2.89	10.59	m	13.48
underglazing flashing	-	0.11	2.89	9.32	m	12.21
plain cranked crown to ridge	-	0.16	4.20	20.51	m	24.71
plain wing or close fitting two piece adjustable capping to ridge	-	0.16	4.20	18.65	m	22.85
ventilating two piece adjustable capping to ridge	-	0.16	4.20	24.58	m	28.78

H CLADDING/COVERING

Item	PC £	Labour hours	Labour £	Material £	Unit	Total rate £
H31 METAL PROFILED/FLAT SHEET CLADDING/COVERING/SIDING						
Lightweight galvanised steel roof tiles; Decra Roof Systems (UK) Ltd or other equal and approved; coated finish						
Roof coverings	-	0.23	6.04	13.23	m²	**19.27**
Accessories for roof cladding						
pitched "D" ridge	-	0.09	2.36	7.14	m	**9.50**
barge cover (handed)	-	0.09	2.36	7.68	m	**10.05**
in line air vent	-	0.09	2.36	33.14	nr	**35.51**
in line soil vent	-	0.09	2.36	51.80	nr	**54.16**
gas flue terminal	-	0.19	4.99	72.20	nr	**77.19**
Galvanised steel strip troughed sheets; Corus Products or other equal and approved						
Roof cladding or decking; sloping not exceeding 50 degrees; fixing to steel purlins with plastic headed self-tapping screws						
0.7 mm thick; 46 profile	-	-	-	-	m²	**11.30**
0.7 mm thick; 60 profile	-	-	-	-	m²	**12.38**
0.7 mm thick; 100 profile	-	-	-	-	m²	**13.45**
Galvanised steel strip troughed sheets; PMF Strip Mill Products or other equal and approved						
Roof cladding; sloping not exceeding 50 degrees; fixing to steel purlins with plastic headed self-tapping screws						
0.7 mm thick type HPS200 13.5/3 corrugated	-	-	-	-	m²	**12.75**
0.7 mm thick type HPS200 R32/1000	-	-	-	-	m²	**11.57**
0.7 mm thick type Arcline 40; plasticol finished	-	-	-	-	m²	**17.02**
Extra over last for aluminium roof cladding or decking	-	-	-	-	m²	**6.46**
Accessories for roof cladding						
HPS200 Drip flashing; 250 mm girth	-	-	-	-	m	**3.96**
HPS200 Ridge flashing; 375 mm girth	-	-	-	-	m	**5.18**
HPS200 Gable flashing; 500 mm girth	-	-	-	-	m	**6.58**
HPS200 Internal angle; 625 mm girth	-	-	-	-	m	**7.59**
Zalutite coated steel flat composite panel cladding; Kingspan or other equal and approved; outer panel 0.7 mm gauge HPS200 colourcoated; HCFC free LPCB FM/FW core and 0.4 mm stucco embossed lining panel with bright white ployester paint finish						
Roof cladding; vertical fixing to steel rails (measured elsewhere)						
80 mm wall panel; ref. KS1000RW	-	-	-	-	m²	**33.90**
Wall cladding; vertical fixing to steel rails (measured elsewhere)						
60 mm wall panel; ref. KS1000RW	-	-	-	-	m²	**32.61**
70 mm wall panel; ref. KS1000RW	-	-	-	-	m²	**33.36**
80 mm wall panel; ref. KS1000RW	-	-	-	-	m²	**34.12**
70 mm wall panel; ref. KS1000MR	-	-	-	-	m²	**46.71**
80 mm wall panel; ref. KS1000MR	-	-	-	-	m²	**47.46**
70 mm wall panel; ref. KS900MR	-	-	-	-	m²	**49.72**
80 mm wall panel; ref. KS900MR	-	-	-	-	m²	**50.48**

H CLADDING/COVERING

Item	PC £	Labour hours	Labour £	Material £	Unit	Total rate £
70 mm wall panel ; ref. KS600MR	-	-	-	-	m²	68.66
80 mm wall panel ; ref. KS600MR	-	-	-	-	m²	69.31
Extra over for						
raking cutting to 60 mm KS1000RW panel including waste	-	-	-	-	m	17.22
raking cutting to 70 mm KS1000RW panel including waste	-	-	-	-	m	17.58
raking cutting to 80 mm KS1000RW panel including waste	-	-	-	-	m	17.94
raking cutting to 70 mm KS1000MR panel including waste	-	-	-	-	m	24.43
raking cutting to 80 mm KS1000MR panel including waste	-	-	-	-	m	24.75
raking cutting to 70 mm KS900MR panel including waste	-	-	-	-	m	25.83
raking cutting to 80 mm KS900MR panel including waste	-	-	-	-	m	26.19
raking cutting to 70 mm KS600MR panel including waste	-	-	-	-	m	34.44
raking cutting to 80 mm KS600MR panel including waste	-	-	-	-	m	34.80
panel bearers ' 1500 mm centres	-	-	-	-	m	5.95
vertical tophat joint in HPS200	-	-	-	-	m	10.19
vertical tophat joint with cap in HPS200	-	-	-	-	m	13.24
cranked KS1000MR panel	-	-	-	-	m	99.04
cranked KS900MR panel	-	-	-	-	m	110.04
cranked KS600MR panel	-	-	-	-	m	165.06
roof penetration; 150 mm dia. opening; with top hat flashing and collar 150 mm high; and silicone joint to roofsheet	-	-	-	-	nr	53.30
roof penetration; 250 mm dia. opening; with top hat flashing and collar 150 mm high; and silicone joint to roofsheet	-	-	-	-	nr	75.85
GRP Transluscent rooflights; factory assembled						
Rooflight; vertical fixing to steel purlins (measured elsewhere)						
double skin; class 3 over 1	-	-	-	-	m²	50.81
triple skin; class 3 over 1	-	-	-	-	m²	53.27
Wall cladding; Gasell Profiles Ltd or equal and approved; steel GA50-30 profiled sheeting to outer face; stee; GA600 lining to inner face; including profile fillers; sealing						
Coverings; fixing to and including vertical and horizontal secondary supports						
250 mm girth	-	-	-	-	m²	69.10

H CLADDING/COVERING

Item	PC £	Labour hours	Labour £	Material £	Unit	Total rate £
H32 PLASTICS PROFILED SHEET CLADDING/ COVERING/SIDING						
Extended, hard skinned, foamed PVC-UE profiled sections; Swish Celuka or other equal and approved; Class 1 fire rated to BS 476; Part 7; 1987; in white finish						
Wall cladding; vertical; fixing to timber						
100 mm shiplap profiles; Code 001	-	0.35	6.10	17.22	m²	**23.32**
150 mm shiplap profiles; Code 002	-	0.32	5.58	22.66	m²	**28.24**
125 mm feather-edged profiles; Code C208	-	0.34	5.92	20.64	m²	**26.56**
Vertical angles	-	0.19	3.31	3.57	m	**6.89**
Raking cutting	-	0.14	2.44	-	m	**2.44**
Holes for pipes and the like	-	0.03	0.52	-	nr	**0.52**
H41 GLASS REINFORCED PLASTICS PANEL CLADDING FEATURES						
Glass fibre translucent sheeting grade AB class 3						
Roof cladding; sloping not exceeding 50 degrees; fixing to timber purlins with drive screws; to suit						
"Profile 3" or other equal and approved	10.62	0.18	4.73	13.72	m²	**18.45**
"Profile 6" or other equal and approved	9.96	0.23	6.04	12.97	m²	**19.01**
Roof cladding; sloping not exceeding 50 degrees; fixing to timber purlins with hook bolts; to suit						
"Profile 3" or other equal and approved	10.62	0.23	6.04	15.03	m²	**21.07**
"Profile 6" or other equal and approved	9.96	0.28	7.35	14.28	m²	**21.63**
"Longrib 1000" or other equal and approved	9.79	0.28	7.35	14.09	m²	**21.44**
H51 NATURAL STONE SLAB CLADDING FEATURES						
BASIC NATURAL STONE BLOCK PRICES						
Block prices (£/m³)						
Bath Stone						
Monks Park bed height not exceeding 300 mm	-	-	-	135.00	m³	-
Monks Park bed height 300 – 599 mm	-	-	-	423.00	m³	-
Monks Park bed height exceeding 600 mm	-	-	-	423.00	m³	-
Westwood Ground not exceeding 0.60 m³	-	-	-	326.70	m³	-
Westwood Ground 0.60 - 0.99 m³	-	-	-	381.15	m³	-
Westwood Ground exceeding 1.00 m³	-	-	-	381.15	m³	-
Hatham Park not exceeding 0.39 m³	-	-	-	288.00	m³	-
Hatham Park 0.40 - 0.59 m³	-	-	-	343.35	m³	-
Hatham Park 0.60 - 0.99 m³	-	-	-	400.05	m³	-
Hatham Park 1.00 - 1.99 m³	-	-	-	403.20	m³	-
Hatham Park exceeding 2.00 m³	-	-	-	436.95	m³	-
Portland Stone						
not exceeding 0.60 m³	-	-	-	266.33	m³	-
0.60 - 0.99 m³	-	-	-	405.00	m³	-
exceeding 1.00 m³	-	-	-	522.00	m³	-

H CLADDING/COVERING

Item	PC £	Labour hours	Labour £	Material £	Unit	Total rate £
SUPPLY AND FIX PRICES						
Portland Whitbed limestone bedded and jointed in cement - lime - mortar (1:2:9); slurrying with weak lime and stone dust mortar; flush pointing and cleaning on completion (cramps etc. not included)						
Facework; one face plain and rubbed; bedded against backing						
50 mm thick stones	-	-	-	-	m^2	276.75
63 mm thick stones	-	-	-	-	m^2	328.00
75 mm thick stones	-	-	-	-	m^2	358.75
100 mm thick stones	-	-	-	-	m^2	410.00
Fair returns on facework						
50 mm wide	-	-	-	-	m	1.20
63 mm wide	-	-	-	-	m	1.70
75 mm wide	-	-	-	-	m	1.70
100 mm wide	-	-	-	-	m	2.22
Fair raking cutting on facework						
50 mm thick	-	-	-	-	m	17.68
63 mm thick	-	-	-	-	m	20.08
75 mm thick	-	-	-	-	m	22.47
100 mm thick	-	-	-	-	m	26.98
Copings; once weathered; and throated; rubbed; set horizontal or raking						
250 mm x 50 mm	-	-	-	-	m	125.49
extra for external angle	-	-	-	-	nr	19.17
extra for internal angle	-	-	-	-	nr	29.38
300 mm x 50 mm	-	-	-	-	m	131.20
extra for external angle	-	-	-	-	nr	23.95
extra for internal angle	-	-	-	-	nr	35.94
350 mm x 75 mm	-	-	-	-	m	182.53
extra for external angle	-	-	-	-	nr	26.98
extra for internal angle	-	-	-	-	nr	40.72
400 mm x 100 mm	-	-	-	-	m	211.06
extra for external angle	-	-	-	-	nr	31.14
extra for internal angle	-	-	-	-	nr	46.72
450 mm x 100 mm	-	-	-	-	m	228.16
extra for external angle	-	-	-	-	nr	35.94
extra for internal angle	-	-	-	-	nr	53.90
500 mm x 125 mm	-	-	-	-	m	285.21
extra for external angle	-	-	-	-	nr	39.52
extra for internal angle	-	-	-	-	nr	59.90
Band courses; plain; rubbed; horizontal						
225 mm x 112 mm	-	-	-	-	m	89.84
300 mm x 112 mm	-	-	-	-	m	107.80
extra for stopped ends	-	-	-	-	nr	0.79
extra for external angles	-	-	-	-	nr	0.79
Band courses; moulded 100 mm girth on face; rubbed; horizontal						
125 mm x 75 mm	-	-	-	-	m	114.08
extra for stopped ends	-	-	-	-	nr	0.79
extra for external angles	-	-	-	-	nr	10.83
extra for internal angles	-	-	-	-	nr	21.68
150 mm x 75 mm	-	-	-	-	m	125.49
extra for stopped ends	-	-	-	-	nr	0.79
extra for external angles	-	-	-	-	nr	14.37
extra for internal angles	-	-	-	-	nr	29.09

H CLADDING/COVERING

Item	PC £	Labour hours	Labour £	Material £	Unit	Total rate £
H51 NATURAL STONE SLAB CLADDING FEATURES – cont'd						
Portland Whitbed limestone – cont'd						
200 mm x 100 mm	-	-	-	-	m	159.72
extra for stopped ends	-	-	-	-	nr	0.79
extra for external angles	-	-	-	-	nr	24.52
extra for internal angles	-	-	-	-	nr	46.77
250 mm x 150 mm	-	-	-	-	m	205.35
extra for stopped ends	-	-	-	-	nr	0.79
extra for external angles	-	-	-	-	nr	32.35
extra for internal angles	-	-	-	-	nr	57.60
300 mm x 250 mm	-	-	-	-	m	302.31
extra for stopped ends	-	-	-	-	nr	0.79
extra for external angles	-	-	-	-	nr	43.92
extra for internal angles	-	-	-	-	nr	77.86
Coping apex block; two sunk faces; rubbed						
650 mm x 450 mm x 225 mm	-	-	-	-	nr	325.13
Coping kneeler block; three sunk faces; rubbed						
350 mm x 350 mm x 375 mm	-	-	-	-	nr	239.57
450 mm x 450 mm x 375 mm	-	-	-	-	nr	342.25
Corbel; turned and moulded; rubbed						
225 mm x 225 mm x 375 mm	-	-	-	-	nr	171.12
Slab surrounds to openings; one face splayed; rubbed						
75 mm x 100 mm	-	-	-	-	m	65.89
75 mm x 200 mm	-	-	-	-	m	89.84
100 mm x 100 mm	-	-	-	-	m	77.86
125 mm x 100 mm	-	-	-	-	m	83.84
125 mm x 150 mm	-	-	-	-	m	101.81
175 mm x 175 mm	-	-	-	-	m	131.20
225 mm x 175 mm	-	-	-	-	m	148.31
300 mm x 175 mm	-	-	-	-	m	182.53
300 mm x 225 mm	-	-	-	-	m	228.16
Slab surrounds to openings; one face sunk splayed; rubbed						
75 mm x 100 mm	-	-	-	-	m	79.58
75 mm x 200 mm	-	-	-	-	m	103.54
100 mm x 100 mm	-	-	-	-	m	91.55
125 mm x 100 mm	-	-	-	-	m	97.54
125 mm x 150 mm	-	-	-	-	m	115.51
175 mm x 175 mm	-	-	-	-	m	144.89
225 mm x 175 mm	-	-	-	-	m	162.00
300 mm x 175 mm	-	-	-	-	m	196.23
300 mm x 225 mm	-	-	-	-	m	241.86
extra for throating	-	-	-	-	m	6.90
extra for rebates and grooves	-	-	-	-	m	21.11
extra for stooling	-	-	-	-	m	19.39
Sundries - stone walling						
Coating backs of stones with brush applied cold bitumen solution; two coats						
limestone facework	-	0.19	2.42	2.05	m²	4.47
Cutting grooves in limestone masonry for						
water bars or the like	-	-	-	-	m	6.62
Mortices in limestone masonry for						
metal dowel	-	-	-	-	nr	0.63
metal cramp	-	-	-	-	nr	1.20

H CLADDING/COVERING

Item	PC £	Labour hours	Labour £	Material £	Unit	Total rate £
"Eurobrick" insulated brick cladding systems or other equal and approved ; extruded polystyrene foam insulation; brick slips bonded to insulation panels with "Eurobrick" gun applied adhesive or other equal and approved; pointing with formulated mortar grout						
25 mm insulation to walls						
over 300 mm wide; fixing with proprietary screws and plates to timber	-	1.39	28.08	43.68	m²	**71.76**
50 mm insulation to walls						
over 300 mm wide; fixing with proprietary screws and plates; to timber	-	1.39	28.08	47.75	m²	**75.83**
Cramps and dowels; Harris and Edgar's "Hemax" range or other equal and approved; one end built into brickwork or set in slot in concrete; stainless steel						
Dowel						
8 mm diameter x 75 mm long	0.20	0.04	0.87	0.22	nr	**1.09**
10 mm diameter x 150 mm long	0.58	0.04	0.87	0.65	nr	**1.52**
Pattern "J" tie						
25 mm x 3 mm x 100 mm	0.43	0.06	1.31	0.48	nr	**1.79**
Pattern "S" cramp; with two 20 mm turndowns (190 mm girth)						
25 mm x 3 mm x 150 mm	0.60	0.06	1.31	0.68	nr	**1.98**
Pattern "B" anchor; with 8 mm x 75 mm loose dowel						
25 mm x 3 mm x 150 mm	0.74	0.09	1.96	0.83	nr	**2.79**
Pattern "Q" tie						
25 mm x 3 mm x 200 mm	0.74	0.06	1.31	0.84	nr	**2.14**
38 mm x 3 mm x 250 mm	1.51	0.06	1.31	1.70	nr	**3.01**
Pattern "P" half twist tie						
25 mm x 3 mm x 200 mm	0.80	0.06	1.31	0.91	nr	**2.21**
38 mm x 3 mm x 250 mm	1.27	0.06	1.31	1.43	nr	**2.74**
H53 CLAY SLAB/CLADDING/FEATURES						
Terracotta cladding and panels; LockClad or equal and approved; 240 mm x 390 mm x 14½ mm thick terracotta panels; including horizontal rails, clips and vertical spacers, insulation, structural liner trays and fixings						
Walls						
over 300 mm wide	-	-	-	-	m²	**199.95**

H CLADDING/COVERING

Item	PC £	Labour hours	Labour £	Material £	Unit	Total rate £
H60 PLAIN ROOF TILING						
ALTERNATIVE TILE PRICES (£/1000)						
Discounts of 5 - 25% available depending on quantity / status.						
Clay tiles; plain, interlocking and pantiles						
Langleys "Sterreberg" pantiles						
Anthracite	-	-	-	1072.00	1000	-
Glazed brown	-	-	-	1476.00	1000	-
Natural red/rustic	-	-	-	920.00	1000	-
Sandtoft pantiles						
Bridgewater Double Roman	-	-	-	3602.00	1000	-
"Gaelic"	-	-	-	1444.00	1000	-
Arcadia	-	-	-	1029.00	1000	-
William Blyth pantiles	-	-	-	-	-	
"Barco bold Roll"	-	-	-	838.00	1000	-
"Celtic (french)"	-	-	-	940.00	1000	-
Concrete tiles; plain and interlocking						
Marley roof tiles						
"Anglia Plus"	-	-	-	536.40	1000	-
"Ludlow Major"	-	-	-	751.40	1000	-
"Ludlow Plus"	-	-	-	536.40	1000	-
"Plain"	-	-	-	310.70	1000	-
Redland roof tiles						
"Redland 49"	-	-	-	499.00	1000	-
"50 Double Roman"	-	-	-	700.00	1000	-
"Mini Stoneworld"	-	-	-	744.00	1000	-
"Grovebury"	-	-	-	724.00	1000	-
SUPPLY AND FIX PRICES						
NOTE: The following items of tile roofing unless otherwise described, include for conventional fixing assuming normal exposure with appropriate nails and/or rivets or clips to pressure impregnated softwood battens fixed with galvanised nails; prices also include for all bedding and pointing at verges, beneath ridge tiles, etc.						
Clay interlocking plain tiles; Sandtoft "20/20" natural red faced or other equal and approved; PC £867.00/1000; 370 mm x 223 mm; to 75 mm lap; on 25 mm x 38 mm battens and type 1F reinforced underlay						
Roof coverings	-	0.42	11.03	10.17	m²	**21.20**
Extra over coverings for						
fixing every tile	-	0.02	0.53	1.45	m²	**1.97**
double course at eaves	-	0.28	7.35	9.71	m	**17.06**
verges; extra single undercloak course of plain tiles	-	0.28	7.35	3.79	m	**11.15**
open valleys; cutting both sides	-	0.17	4.46	2.94	m	**7.40**
dry ridge tiles	-	0.56	14.71	10.15	m	**24.86**
dry hips; cutting both sides	-	0.69	18.12	14.23	m	**32.35**
holes for pipes and the like	-	0.19	4.99	-	nr	**4.99**

H CLADDING/COVERING

Item	PC £	Labour hours	Labour £	Material £	Unit	Total rate £
Clay pantiles; Sandtoft Goxhill "Old English"; red sand faced or other equal and approved; PC £967.00/1000; 342 mm x 241 mm; to 75 mm lap; on 25 mm x 38 mm battens and type 1F reinforced underlay						
Roof coverings	-	0.42	11.03	16.66	m^2	27.69
Extra over coverings for						
fixing every tile	-	0.02	0.53	3.62	m^2	4.14
other colours	-	-	-	0.48	m^2	0.48
double course at eaves	-	0.31	8.14	4.48	m	12.63
verges; extra single undercloak course of plain tiles	-	0.28	7.35	9.22	m	16.57
open valleys; cutting both sides	-	0.17	4.46	3.28	m	7.74
ridge tiles; tile slips	-	0.56	14.71	23.09	m	37.79
hips; cutting both sides	-	0.69	18.12	26.37	m	44.49
holes for pipes and the like	-	0.19	4.99	-	nr	4.99
Clay pantiles; William Blyth's "Lincoln" natural or other equal and approved; 343 mm x 280 mm; to 75 mm lap; PC £1,135.00/1000; on 19 mm x 38 mm battens and type 1F reinforced underlay						
Roof coverings	-	0.42	11.03	18.99	m^2	30.02
Extra over coverings for						
fixing every tile	-	0.02	0.53	3.62	m^2	4.14
other colours	-	-	-	1.36	m^2	1.36
double course at eaves	-	0.31	8.14	5.19	m	13.33
verges; extra single undercloak course of plain tiles	-	0.28	7.35	11.57	m	18.92
open valleys; cutting both sides	-	0.17	4.46	3.99	m	8.45
ridge tiles; tile slips	-	0.56	14.71	20.22	m	34.93
hips; cutting both sides	-	0.69	18.12	24.21	m	42.33
holes for pipes and the like	-	0.19	4.99	-	nr	4.99
Clay plain tiles; Hinton, Perry and Davenhill "Dreadnought" smooth red machine-made or other equal and approved; PC £315.00/1000; 265 mm x 165 mm; on 19 mm x 38 mm battens and type 1F reinforced underlay						
Roof coverings; to 64 mm lap	14.76	0.97	25.47	22.37	m^2	47.84
Wall coverings; to 38 mm lap	-	1.16	30.46	19.01	m^2	49.47
Extra over coverings for						
other colours	-	-	-	1.94	m^2	1.94
ornamental tiles	-	-	-	13.28	m^2	13.28
double course at eaves	-	0.23	6.04	2.72	m	8.76
verges	-	0.28	7.35	1.03	m	8.39
swept valleys; cutting both sides	-	0.60	15.76	29.90	m	45.66
bonnet hips; cutting both sides	-	0.74	19.43	29.97	m	49.40
external vertical angle tiles; supplementary nail fixings	-	0.37	9.72	34.00	m	43.72
half round ridge tiles	-	0.56	14.71	9.89	m	24.60
holes for pipes and the like	-	0.19	4.99	-	nr	4.99

H CLADDING/COVERING

Item	PC £	Labour hours	Labour £	Material £	Unit	Total rate £
H60 PLAIN ROOF TILING – cont'd						
Concrete interlocking tiles; Marley "Bold Roll" granule finish tiles or other equal and approved; PC £715.00/1000; 420 mm x 330 mm; to 75 mm lap; on 25 mm x 38 mm battens and type 1F reinforced underlay						
Roof coverings	-	0.32	8.40	8.70	m^2	17.11
Extra over coverings for						
fixing every tile	-	0.02	0.53	0.60	m^2	1.13
eaves; eaves filler	-	0.04	1.05	0.96	m	2.01
verges; 150 mm wide asbestos free strip						
undercloak	-	0.21	5.51	1.28	m	6.79
valley trough tiles; cutting both sides	-	0.51	13.39	17.37	m	30.76
segmental ridge tiles; tile slips	-	0.51	13.39	9.84	m	23.23
segmental hip tiles; tile slips; cutting both sides	-	0.65	17.07	11.80	m	28.86
dry ridge tiles; segmental including batten						
sections; unions and filler pieces	-	0.28	7.35	13.71	m	21.07
segmental mono-ridge tiles	-	0.51	13.39	13.73	m	27.12
gas ridge terminal	-	0.46	12.08	53.88	nr	65.96
holes for pipes and the like	-	0.19	4.99	-	nr	4.99
Concrete interlocking tiles; Marley "Ludlow Major" granule finish tiles or other equal and approved; PC £699.00/1000; 420 mm x 330 mm; to 75 mm lap; on 25 mm x 38 mm battens and type 1F reinforced underlay						
Roof coverings	-	0.32	8.40	8.63	m^2	17.03
Extra over coverings for						
fixing every tile	-	0.02	0.53	0.60	m^2	1.13
eaves; eaves filler	-	0.04	1.05	0.44	m	1.49
verges; 150 mm wide asbestos free strip						
undercloak	-	0.21	5.51	1.28	m	6.79
dry verge system; extruded white pvc	-	0.14	3.68	6.80	m	10.48
segmental ridge cap to dry verge	-	0.02	0.53	2.49	m	3.01
valley trough tiles; cutting both sides	-	0.51	13.39	17.34	m	30.73
segmental ridge tiles	-	0.46	12.08	6.78	m	18.86
segmental hip tiles; cutting both sides	-	0.60	15.76	8.69	m	24.45
dry ridge tiles; segmental including batten						
sections; unions and filler pieces	-	0.28	7.35	13.71	m	21.07
segmental mono-ridge tiles	-	0.46	12.08	11.94	m	24.02
gas ridge terminal	-	0.46	12.08	53.88	nr	65.96
holes for pipes and the like	-	0.19	4.99	-	nr	4.99
Concrete interlocking tiles; Marley "Mendip" granule finish double pantiles or other equal and approved; PC £715.00/1000; 420 mm x 330 mm; to 75 mm lap; on 22 mm x 38 mm battens and type 1F reinforced underlay						
Roof coverings	5.59	0.32	8.40	8.70	m^2	17.11
Extra over coverings for						
fixing every tile	-	0.02	0.53	0.60	m^2	1.13
eaves; eaves filler	-	0.02	0.53	0.59	m	1.12
verges; 150 mm wide asbestos free strip						
undercloak	-	0.21	5.51	1.28	m	6.79
dry verge system; extruded white pvc	-	0.14	3.68	6.80	m	10.48
segmental ridge cap to dry verge	-	0.02	0.53	2.49	m	3.01

H CLADDING/COVERING

Item	PC £	Labour hours	Labour £	Material £	Unit	Total rate £
valley trough tiles; cutting both sides	-	0.51	13.39	17.37	m	30.76
segmental ridge tiles	-	0.51	13.39	9.84	m	23.23
segmental hip tiles; cutting both sides	-	0.65	17.07	11.80	m	28.86
dry ridge tiles; segmental including batten						
sections; unions and filler pieces	-	0.28	7.35	13.71	m	21.07
segmental mono-ridge tiles	-	0.46	12.08	13.47	m	25.55
gas ridge terminal	-	0.46	12.08	53.88	nr	65.96
holes for pipes and the like	-	0.19	4.99	-	nr	4.99
Concrete interlocking tiles; Marley "Modern" smooth finish tiles or other equal and approved; PC £735.00/1000; 420 mm x 220 mm; to 75 mm lap; on 25 mm x 38 mm battens and type 1F reinforced underlay						
Roof coverings	-	0.32	8.40	9.09	m²	17.50
Extra over coverings for						
fixing every tile	-	0.02	0.53	0.60	m²	1.13
verges; 150 wide asbestos free strip undercloak	-	0.21	5.51	1.28	m	6.79
dry verge system; extruded white pvc	-	0.19	4.99	6.80	m	11.79
"Modern" ridge cap to dry verge	-	0.02	0.53	2.49	m	3.01
valley trough tiles; cutting both sides	-	0.51	13.39	17.40	m	30.80
"Modern" ridge tiles	-	0.46	12.08	7.08	m	19.16
"Modern" hip tiles; cutting both sides	-	0.60	15.76	9.09	m	24.85
dry ridge tiles; "Modern"; including batten						
sections; unions and filler pieces	-	0.28	7.35	14.02	m	21.37
"Modern" mono-ridge tiles	-	0.46	12.08	11.94	m	24.02
gas ridge terminal	-	0.46	12.08	53.88	nr	65.96
holes for pipes and the like	-	0.19	4.99	-	nr	4.99
Concrete interlocking tiles; Marley "Wessex" smooth finish tiles or other equal and approved; PC £1,202.00/1000; 413 mm x 330 mm; to 75 mm lap; on 25 mm x 38 mm battens and type 1F reinforced underlay						
Roof coverings	-	0.32	8.40	13.31	m²	21.71
Extra over coverings for						
fixing every tile	-	0.02	0.53	0.60	m²	1.13
verges; 150 mm wide asbestos free strip						
undercloak	-	0.21	5.51	1.28	m	6.79
dry verge system; extruded white pvc	-	0.19	4.99	6.80	m	11.79
"Modern" ridge cap to dry verge	-	0.02	0.53	2.49	m	3.01
valley trough tiles; cutting both sides	-	0.51	13.39	18.25	m	31.65
"Modern" ridge tiles	-	0.46	12.08	7.08	m	19.16
"Modern" hip tiles; cutting both sides	-	0.60	15.76	10.37	m	26.12
dry ridge tiles; "Modern"; including batten						
sections; unions and filler pieces	-	0.28	7.35	14.02	m	21.37
"Modern" mono-ridge tiles	-	0.46	12.08	11.94	m	24.02
gas ridge terminal	-	0.46	12.08	53.88	nr	65.96
holes for pipes and the like	-	0.19	4.99	-	nr	4.99

H CLADDING/COVERING

Item	PC £	Labour hours	Labour £	Material £	Unit	Total rate £
H60 PLAIN ROOF TILING – cont'd						
Concrete interlocking slates; Redland "Richmond" smooth finish tiles or other equal and approved; PC £980.00/1000; 430 x 380; to 75 mm lap; on 25 mm x 38 mm battens and type 1F reinforced underlay						
Roof coverings	-	0.32	8.40	10.52	m²	18.93
Extra over coverings for						
fixing every tile	-	0.02	0.53	0.60	m²	1.13
eaves; eaves filler	-	0.02	0.53	5.10	m	5.63
verges; extra single undercloak course of plain tiles	-	0.23	6.04	3.43	m	9.47
ambi-dry verge system	-	0.19	4.99	9.70	m	14.69
ambi-dry verge eave/ridge end piece	-	0.02	0.53	3.46	m	3.98
valley trough tiles; cutting both sides	-	0.56	14.71	30.11	m	44.82
"Richmond" ridge tiles	-	0.46	12.08	10.44	m	22.52
"Richmond" hip tiles; cutting both sides	-	0.60	15.76	13.43	m	29.19
"Richmond" mono-ridge tiles	-	0.46	12.08	20.30	m	32.38
gas ridge terminal	-	0.46	12.08	62.26	nr	74.34
ridge vent with 110 mm diameter flexible adaptor	-	0.46	12.08	74.16	nr	86.24
holes for pipes and the like	-	0.19	4.99	-	nr	4.99
Concrete interlocking tiles; Redland "Norfolk" smooth finish pantiles or other equal and approved; PC £548.00/1000; 381 mm x 229 mm; to 75 mm lap; on 25 mm x 38 mm battens and type 1F reinforced underlay						
Roof coverings	-	0.42	11.03	12.60	m²	23.63
Extra over coverings for						
fixing every tile	-	0.04	1.05	0.26	m²	1.31
eaves; eaves filler	-	0.04	1.05	1.09	m	2.14
verges; extra single undercloak course of plain tiles	-	0.28	7.35	5.91	m	13.27
valley trough tiles; cutting both sides	-	0.56	14.71	28.91	m	43.62
universal ridge tiles	-	0.46	12.08	11.06	m	23.14
universal hip tiles; cutting both sides	-	0.60	15.76	13.84	m	29.60
universal gas flue ridge tile	-	0.46	12.08	62.92	nr	75.00
universal ridge vent tile with 110 mm diameter adaptor	-	0.50	13.13	74.82	nr	87.95
holes for pipes and the like	-	0.19	4.99	-	nr	4.99
Concrete interlocking tiles; Redland "Regent" granule finish bold roll tiles or other equal and approved; PC £774.00/1000; 418 mm x 332 mm; to 75 mm lap; on 25 mm x 38 mm battens and type 1F reinforced underlay						
Roof coverings	-	0.32	8.40	10.20	m²	18.60
Extra over coverings for						
fixing every tile	-	0.03	0.79	0.64	m²	1.43
eaves; eaves filler	-	0.04	1.05	0.82	m	1.87
verges; extra single undercloak course of plain tiles	-	0.23	6.04	2.86	m	8.90
cloaked verge system	-	0.14	3.68	6.52	m	10.20
valley trough tiles; cutting both sides	-	0.51	13.39	28.49	m	41.88
universal ridge tiles	-	0.46	12.08	11.06	m	23.14
universal hip tiles; cutting both sides	-	0.60	15.76	13.42	m	29.18

H CLADDING/COVERING

Item	PC £	Labour hours	Labour £	Material £	Unit	Total rate £
dry ridge system; universal ridge tiles	-	0.23	6.04	36.81	m	42.85
universal half round mono-pitch ridge tiles	-	0.51	13.39	23.19	m	36.59
universal gas flue ridge tile	-	0.46	12.08	62.92	nr	75.00
universal ridge vent tile with 110 mm diameter adaptor	-	0.46	12.08	74.82	nr	86.90
holes for pipes and the like	-	0.19	4.99	-	nr	4.99
Concrete interlocking tiles; Redland "Renown" granule finish tiles or other equal and approved; PC £750.00/1000; 418 mm x 330 mm; to 75 mm lap; on 25 mm x 38 mm battens and type 1F reinforced underlay						
Roof coverings	-	0.32	8.40	9.96	m²	18.37
Extra over coverings for						
fixing every tile	-	0.02	0.53	0.32	m²	0.84
verges; extra single undercloak course of plain tiles	-	0.23	6.04	3.43	m	9.47
cloaked verge system	-	0.14	3.68	6.59	m	10.27
valley trough tiles; cutting both sides	-	0.51	13.39	28.42	m	41.81
universal ridge tiles	-	0.46	12.08	11.06	m	23.14
universal hip tiles; cutting both sides	-	0.60	15.76	13.35	m	29.10
dry ridge system; universal ridge tiles	-	0.23	6.04	36.81	m	42.85
universal half round mono-pitch ridge tiles	-	0.51	13.39	23.19	m	36.59
universal gas flue ridge tile	-	0.46	12.08	62.92	nr	75.00
universal ridge vent tile with 110 mm diameter adaptor	-	0.46	12.08	74.82	nr	86.90
holes for pipes and the like	-	0.19	4.99	-	nr	4.99
Concrete interlocking tiles; Redland "Stonewold II" smooth finish tiles or other equal and approved; PC £1,470.00/1000; 430 mm x 380 mm; to 75 mm lap; on 25 mm x 38 mm battens and type 1F reinforced underlay						
Roof coverings	-	0.32	8.40	17.29	m²	25.70
Extra over coverings for						
fixing every tile	-	0.02	0.53	1.20	m²	1.72
verges; extra single undercloak course of plain tiles	-	0.28	7.35	3.43	m	10.78
ambi-dry verge system	-	0.19	4.99	9.70	m	14.69
ambi-dry verge eave/ridge end piece	-	0.02	0.53	3.46	m	3.98
valley trough tiles; cutting both sides	-	0.51	13.39	30.61	m	44.01
universal angle ridge tiles	-	0.46	12.08	8.21	m	20.29
universal hip tiles; cutting both sides	-	0.60	15.76	12.70	m	28.45
dry ridge system; universal angle ridge tiles	-	0.23	6.04	22.36	m	28.40
universal mono-pitch angle ridge tiles	-	0.51	13.39	15.76	m	29.15
universal gas flue angle ridge tile	-	0.46	12.08	75.74	nr	87.82
universal angle ridge vent tile with 110 mm diameter adaptor	-	0.46	12.08	33.33	nr	45.41
holes for pipes and the like	-	0.19	4.99	-	nr	4.99

H CLADDING/COVERING

Item	PC £	Labour hours	Labour £	Material £	Unit	Total rate £
H60 PLAIN ROOF TILING – cont'd						
Concrete plain tiles; EN 490 and 491						
group A; PC £315.00/1000; 267 mm x						
165 mm; on 25 mm x 38 mm battens and						
type 1F reinforced underlay						
Roof coverings; to 64 mm lap	-	0.97	25.47	24.92	m²	50.39
Wall coverings; to 38 mm lap	-	1.16	30.46	21.26	m²	51.72
Extra over coverings for						
ornamental tiles	-	-	-	15.86	m²	15.86
double course at eaves	-	0.23	6.04	2.98	m	9.02
verges	-	0.31	8.14	1.28	m	9.42
swept valleys; cutting both sides	-	0.60	15.76	27.95	m	43.71
bonnet hips; cutting both sides	-	0.74	19.43	28.03	m	47.46
external vertical angle tiles; supplementary nail						
fixings	-	0.37	9.72	19.84	m	29.55
half round ridge tiles	-	0.46	12.08	7.12	m	19.20
third round hip tiles; cutting both sides	-	0.46	12.08	9.04	m	21.12
holes for pipes and the like	-	0.19	4.99	-	nr	4.99
Sundries						
Hip irons						
galvanised mild steel; fixing with screws	-	0.09	2.36	1.70	nr	4.06
"Rytons Clip strip" or other equal and approved;						
continuous soffit ventilator						
51 mm wide; plastic; code CS351	-	0.28	7.35	1.05	m	8.40
"Rytons over fascia ventilator" or other equal						
and approved; continuous eaves ventilator						
40 mm wide; plastic; code OFV890	-	0.09	2.36	1.61	m	3.98
"Rytons roof ventilator" or other equal and						
approved; to suit rafters at 600 mm centres						
250 mm deep x 43 mm high; plastic; code TV600	-	0.09	2.36	1.62	m	3.98
"Rytons push and lock ventilators" or other equal						
and approved; circular						
83 mm diameter; plastic; code PL235	-	0.04	0.70	0.28	nr	0.98
Fixing only						
lead soakers (supply cost not included)	-	0.07	1.28	-	nr	1.28
Pressure impregnated softwood counter battens;						
25 mm x 50 mm						
450 mm centres	-	0.06	1.58	1.07	m²	2.64
600 mm centres	-	0.04	1.05	0.81	m²	1.86
Underlay; BS 747 type 1B; bitumen felt						
weighing 14 kg/10 m2; 75 mm laps						
To sloping or vertical surfaces	0.51	0.02	0.53	1.10	m²	1.63
Underlay; BS 747 type 1F; reinforced						
bitumen felt weighing 22.50 kg/10 m2;						
75 mm laps						
To sloping or vertical surfaces	0.94	0.02	0.53	1.60	m²	2.12
Underlay; Visqueen "Tilene 200P" or						
other equal and approved;						
micro-perforated sheet; 75 mm laps						
To sloping or vertical surfaces	0.53	0.02	0.53	1.15	m²	1.68
Underlay; "Powerlon 250 BM" or other						
equal and approved; reinforced breather						
membrane; 75 mm laps						
To sloping or vertical surfaces	0.56	0.02	0.53	1.19	m²	1.72

H CLADDING/COVERING

Item	PC £	Labour hours	Labour £	Material £	Unit	Total rate £
Underlay; "Anticon" or other equal and approved sarking membrane; Euroroof Ltd; polyethylene; 75 mm laps						
To sloping or vertical surfaces	-	0.02	0.53	1.54	m²	2.06
H61 FIBRE CEMENT SLATING						
Asbestos-free artificial slates; Eternit "Garsdale/E2000T" or other equal and approved; to 75 mm lap; on 19 mm x 50 mm battens and type 1F reinforced underlay						
Coverings; 400 mm x 200 mm slates						
roof coverings	-	0.74	19.43	26.48	m²	45.92
wall coverings	-	0.97	25.47	26.48	m²	51.96
Coverings; 500 mm x 250 mm slates						
roof coverings	-	0.60	15.76	17.70	m²	33.45
wall coverings	-	0.74	19.43	17.70	m²	37.13
Coverings; 600 mm x 300 mm slates						
roof coverings	-	0.46	12.08	14.69	m²	26.77
wall coverings	-	0.60	15.76	14.69	m²	30.44
Extra over slate coverings for						
double course at eaves	-	0.23	6.04	3.58	m	9.62
verges; extra single undercloak course	-	0.31	8.14	0.78	m	8.92
open valleys; cutting both sides	-	0.19	4.99	3.11	m	8.10
valley gutters; cutting both sides	-	0.51	13.39	19.14	m	32.53
half round ridge tiles	-	0.46	12.08	21.00	m	33.08
stop end	-	0.09	2.36	7.46	nr	9.82
roll top ridge tiles	-	0.56	14.71	47.41	m	62.12
stop end	-	0.09	2.36	9.57	nr	11.93
mono-pitch ridge tiles	-	0.46	12.08	26.57	m	38.65
stop end	-	0.09	2.36	28.85	nr	31.21
duo-pitch ridge tiles	-	0.46	12.08	21.51	m	33.59
stop end	-	0.09	2.36	21.15	nr	23.51
mitred hips; cutting both sides	-	0.19	4.99	3.11	m	8.10
half round hip tiles; cutting both sides	-	0.19	4.99	24.11	m	29.10
holes for pipes and the like	-	0.19	4.99	-	nr	4.99
H62 NATURAL SLATING						
NOTE: The following items of slate roofing unless otherwise described, include for conventional fixing assuming "normal exposure" with appropriate nails and/or rivets or clips to pressure impregnated softwood battens fixed with galvanised nails; prices also include for all bedding and pointing at verges; beneath verge tiles etc.						
Natural slates; BS 680 Part 2; Welsh blue; uniform size; to 75 mm lap; on 25 mm x 50 mm battens and type 1F reinforced underlay						
Coverings; 400 mm x 250 mm slates						
roof coverings	-	0.83	21.80	31.97	m²	53.77
wall coverings	-	1.06	27.84	31.97	m²	59.81
Coverings; 500 mm x 300 mm slates						
roof coverings	-	0.69	18.12	42.83	m²	60.95
wall coverings	-	0.83	21.80	42.83	m²	64.63

H CLADDING/COVERING

Item	PC £	Labour hours	Labour £	Material £	Unit	Total rate £
H62 NATURAL SLATING – cont'd						
Natural Welsh slates – cont'd						
Coverings; 600 mm x 300 mm slates						
roof coverings	-	0.56	14.71	56.09	m²	70.80
wall coverings	-	0.69	18.12	56.09	m²	74.21
Extra over coverings for						
double course at eaves	-	0.28	7.35	14.75	m	22.10
verges; extra single undercloak course	-	0.39	10.24	8.62	m	18.86
open valleys; cutting both sides	-	0.20	5.25	34.01	m	39.26
blue/black glazed ware 152 mm half round ridge tiles	-	0.46	12.08	6.82	m	18.90
blue/black glazed ware 125 mm x 125 mm plain angle ridge tiles	-	0.46	12.08	17.41	m	29.49
mitred hips; cutting both sides	-	0.20	5.25	34.01	m	39.26
blue/black glazed ware 152 mm half round hip tiles; cutting both sides	-	0.65	17.07	40.83	m	57.90
blue/black glazed ware 125 mm x 125 mm plain angle hip tiles; cutting both sides	-	0.65	17.07	51.42	m	68.49
holes for pipes and the like	-	0.19	4.99	-	nr	4.99
Natural slates; Westmoreland green; PC £2,331.00/tonne; random lengths; 457 mm - 229 mm proportionate widths to 75 mm lap; in diminishing courses; on 25 mm x 50 mm battens and type 1F underlay						
Roof coverings	-	1.06	27.84	138.91	m²	166.75
Wall coverings	-	1.34	35.19	138.91	m²	174.10
Extra over coverings for						
double course at eaves	-	0.61	16.02	25.67	m	41.69
verges; extra single undercloak course slates 152 mm wide	-	0.69	18.12	22.50	m	40.62
holes for pipes and the like	-	0.28	7.35	-	nr	7.35
H63 RECONSTRUCTED STONE SLATING/ TILING						
Reconstructed stone slates; "Hardrow Slates" or other equal and approved; standard colours; or similar; PC £1,029.00/1000 75 mm lap; on 25 mm x 50 mm battens and type 1F reinforced underlay						
Coverings; 457 mm x 305 mm slates						
roof coverings	-	0.74	19.43	20.94	m²	40.37
wall coverings	-	0.93	24.42	20.94	m²	45.36
Coverings; 457 mm x 457 mm slates						
roof coverings	-	0.60	15.76	20.60	m²	36.35
wall coverings	-	0.79	20.75	20.60	m²	41.34
Extra over 457 mm x 305 mm coverings for						
double course at eaves	-	0.28	7.35	3.79	m	11.15
verges; pointed	-	0.39	10.24	0.06	m	10.30
open valleys; cutting both sides	-	0.20	5.25	9.11	m	14.37
ridge tiles	-	0.46	12.08	23.13	m	35.21
hip tiles; cutting both sides	-	0.65	17.07	19.51	m	36.58
holes for pipes and the like	-	0.19	4.99	-	nr	4.99

H CLADDING/COVERING

Item	PC £	Labour hours	Labour £	Material £	Unit	Total rate £
Reconstructed stone slates; "Hardrow Slates" or other equal and approved; green/oldstone colours; PC £1,029.00/1000; to 75 mm lap; on 25 mm x 50 mm battens and type 1F reinforced underlay						
Coverings; 457 mm x 305 mm slates						
roof coverings	-	0.74	19.43	20.94	m²	40.37
wall coverings	-	0.93	24.42	20.94	m²	45.36
Coverings; 457 mm x 457 mm slates						
roof coverings	-	0.60	15.76	20.60	m²	36.35
wall coverings	-	0.79	20.75	20.60	m²	41.34
Extra over 457 mm x 305 mm coverings for						
double course at eaves	-	0.28	7.35	3.79	m	11.15
verges; pointed	-	0.39	10.24	0.06	m	10.30
open valleys; cutting both sides	-	0.20	5.25	9.11	m	14.37
ridge tiles	-	0.46	12.08	23.13	m	35.21
hip tiles; cutting both sides	-	0.65	17.07	19.51	m	36.58
holes for pipes and the like	-	0.19	4.99	-	nr	4.99
Reconstructed stone slates; Bradstone "Cotswold" stye or other equal and approved; random lengths 550 mm - 300 mm; proportional widths; to 80 mm lap; in diminishing courses; on 25 mm x 50 mm battens and type 1F reinforced underlay						
Roof coverings (all-in rate inclusive of eaves and verges)	24.12	0.97	25.47	32.52	m²	57.99
Extra over coverings for						
open valleys/mitred hips; cutting both sides	-	0.42	11.03	12.26	m²	23.29
ridge tiles	-	0.61	16.02	16.31	m	32.32
hip tiles; cutting both sides	-	0.97	25.47	27.72	m	53.19
holes for pipes and the like	-	0.28	7.35	-	nr	7.35
Reconstructed stone slates; Bradstone "Moordale" style or other equal and approved; random lengths 550 mm - 450 mm; proportional widths; to 80 mm lap; in diminishing course; on 25 mm x 50 mm battens and type 1F reinforced underlay						
Roof coverings (all-in rate inclusive of eaves and verges)	22.69	0.97	25.47	30.91	m²	56.38
Extra over coverings for						
open valleys/mitred hips; cutting both sides	-	0.42	11.03	11.54	m²	22.57
ridge tiles	-	0.61	16.02	16.31	m	32.32
holes for pipes and the like	-	0.28	7.35	-	nr	7.35
H64 TIMBER SHINGLING						
Red cedar sawn shingles preservative treated; PC £36.92/bundle; uniform length 400 mm; to 125 mm gauge; on 25 mm x 38 mm battens and type 1F reinforced underlay						
Roof coverings; 125 mm gauge, 2.28 m²/bundle	-	0.97	25.47	18.68	m²	44.16
Wall coverings; 190 mm gauge, 3.47 m²/bundle	-	0.74	19.43	12.71	m²	32.14
Extra over coverings for						
double course at eaves	-	0.19	4.99	1.84	m	6.83
open valleys; cutting both sides	-	0.19	4.99	3.43	m	8.42

H CLADDING/COVERING

Item	PC £	Labour hours	Labour £	Material £	Unit	Total rate £
H64 TIMBER SHINGLING – cont'd						
Red cedar sawn shingles – cont'd						
Extra over coverings for						
pre-formed ridge capping	-	0.28	7.35	6.14	m	13.50
pre-formed hip capping; cutting both sides	-	0.46	12.08	9.57	m	21.65
double starter course to cappings	-	0.09	2.36	0.65	m	3.01
holes for pipes and the like	-	0.14	3.68	-	nr	3.68
H71 LEAD SHEET COVERINGS/FLASHINGS						
Milled lead; BS 1178; PC £765.00/tonne						
1.32 mm thick (code 3) roof coverings						
flat	-	2.50	45.69	12.85	m^2	58.53
sloping 10 - 50 degrees	-	2.78	50.80	12.85	m^2	63.65
vertical or sloping over 50 degrees	-	3.05	55.74	12.85	m^2	68.58
1.80 mm thick (code 4) roof coverings						
flat	-	2.68	48.98	17.52	m^2	66.50
sloping 10 - 50 degrees	-	2.96	54.09	17.52	m^2	71.61
vertical or sloping over 50 degrees	-	3.24	59.21	17.52	m^2	76.73
1.80 mm thick (code 4) dormer coverings						
flat	-	3.15	57.57	17.52	m^2	75.09
sloping 10 - 50 degrees	-	3.61	65.97	17.52	m^2	83.49
vertical or sloping over 50 degrees	-	3.89	71.09	17.52	m^2	88.61
2.24 mm thick (code 5) roof coverings						
flat	-	2.87	52.45	23.36	m^2	75.81
sloping 10 - 50 degrees	-	3.15	57.57	23.36	m^2	80.93
vertical or sloping over 50 degrees	-	3.42	62.50	23.36	m^2	85.86
2.24 mm thick (code 5) dormer coverings						
flat	-	3.42	62.50	23.36	m^2	85.86
sloping 10 - 50 degrees	-	3.79	69.26	23.36	m^2	92.62
vertical or sloping over 50 degrees	-	4.16	76.02	23.36	m^2	99.38
2.65 mm thick (code 6) roof coverings						
flat	-	3.05	55.74	25.79	m^2	81.53
sloping 10 - 50 degrees	-	3.33	60.85	25.79	m^2	86.65
vertical or sloping over 50 degrees	-	3.61	65.97	25.79	m^2	91.77
2.65 mm thick (code 6) dormer coverings						
flat	-	3.70	67.62	25.79	m^2	93.41
sloping 10 - 50 degrees	-	3.98	72.73	25.79	m^2	98.53
vertical or sloping over 50 degrees	-	4.35	79.49	25.79	m^2	105.29
3.15 mm thick (code 7) roof coverings						
flat	-	3.24	59.21	30.66	m^2	89.87
sloping 10 - 50 degrees	-	3.52	64.33	30.66	m^2	94.99
vertical or sloping over 50 degrees	-	3.79	69.26	30.66	m^2	99.92
3.15 mm thick (code 7) dormer coverings						
flat	-	3.89	71.09	30.66	m^2	101.75
sloping 10 - 50 degrees	-	4.16	76.02	30.66	m^2	106.68
vertical or sloping over 50 degrees	-	4.53	82.78	30.66	m^2	113.45
3.55 mm thick (code 8) roof coverings						
flat	-	3.42	62.50	34.56	m^2	97.05
sloping 10 - 50 degrees	-	3.70	67.62	34.56	m^2	102.17
vertical or sloping over 50 degrees	-	3.98	72.73	34.56	m^2	107.29
3.55 mm thick (code 8) dormer coverings						
flat	-	4.16	76.02	34.56	m^2	110.58
sloping 10 - 50 degrees	-	4.44	81.14	34.56	m^2	115.69
vertical or sloping over 50 degrees	-	4.81	87.90	34.56	m^2	122.46
Dressing over glazing bars and glass	-	0.31	5.67	-	m	5.67
Soldered dot	-	0.14	2.56	-	nr	2.56
Copper nailing; 75 mm centres	-	0.19	3.47	0.36	m	3.83

H CLADDING/COVERING

Item	PC £	Labour hours	Labour £	Material £	Unit	Total rate £
1.80 mm thick (code 4) lead flashings, etc.						
Flashings; wedging into grooves						
150 mm girth	-	0.74	13.52	3.85	m	17.38
240 mm girth	-	0.83	15.17	6.14	m	21.31
Stepped flashings; wedging into grooves						
180 mm girth	-	0.83	15.17	4.58	m	19.75
270 mm girth	-	0.93	17.00	6.87	m	23.87
Linings to sloping gutters						
390 mm girth	-	1.11	20.28	10.00	m	30.28
450 mm girth	-	1.20	21.93	11.45	m	33.38
Cappings to hips or ridges						
450 mm girth	-	1.39	25.40	11.45	m	36.86
600 mm girth	-	1.48	27.05	15.31	m	42.35
Soakers						
200 mm x 200 mm	-	0.14	2.56	0.70	nr	3.26
300 mm x 300 mm	-	0.19	3.47	1.58	nr	5.05
Saddle flashings; at intersections of hips and ridges; dressing and bossing						
450 mm x 600 mm	-	1.67	30.52	6.87	nr	37.39
Slates; with 150 mm high collar						
450 mm x 450 mm; to suit 50 mm diameter pipe	-	1.57	28.69	5.93	nr	34.62
450 mm x 450 mm; to suit 100 mm diameter pipe	-	1.85	33.81	6.50	nr	40.31
2.24 mm thick (code 5) lead flashings, etc.						
Flashings; wedging into grooves						
150 mm girth	-	0.74	13.52	4.79	m	18.31
240 mm girth	-	0.83	15.17	7.60	m	22.77
Stepped flashings; wedging into grooves						
180 mm girth	-	0.83	15.17	5.73	m	20.89
270 mm girth	-	0.93	17.00	8.54	m	25.53
Linings to sloping gutters						
390 mm girth	-	1.11	20.28	12.39	m	32.68
450 mm girth	-	1.20	21.93	14.27	m	36.20
Cappings to hips or ridges						
450 mm girth	-	1.39	25.40	14.27	m	39.67
600 mm girth	-	1.48	27.05	19.06	m	46.10
Soakers						
200 mm x 200 mm	-	0.14	2.56	0.93	nr	3.49
300 mm x 300 mm	-	0.19	3.47	2.10	nr	5.57
Saddle flashings; at intersections of hips and ridges; dressing and bossing						
450 mm x 600 mm	-	1.67	30.52	8.56	nr	39.08
Slates; with 150 mm high collar						
450 mm x 450 mm; to suit 50 mm diameter pipe	-	1.57	28.69	7.38	nr	36.07
450 mm x 450 mm; to suit 100 mm diameter pipe	-	1.85	33.81	8.10	nr	41.90
H72 ALUMINIUM SHEET COVERINGS/ FLASHINGS						
Aluminium roofing; commercial grade						
0.90 mm thick roof coverings						
flat	5.89	2.78	50.80	6.65	m²	57.46
sloping 10 - 50 degrees	-	3.05	55.74	6.65	m²	62.39
vertical or sloping over 50 degrees	-	3.33	60.85	6.65	m²	67.51
0.90 mm thick dormer coverings						
flat	-	3.33	60.85	6.65	m²	67.51
sloping 10 - 50 degrees	-	3.70	67.62	6.65	m²	74.27
vertical or sloping over 50 degrees	-	4.07	74.38	6.65	m²	81.03
Aluminium nailing; 75 spacing	-	0.19	3.47	0.26	m	3.74

H CLADDING/COVERING

Item	PC £	Labour hours	Labour £	Material £	Unit	Total rate £
H72 ALUMINIUM SHEET COVERINGS/ FLASHINGS – cont'd						
0.90 mm commercial grade aluminium flashings, etc.						
Flashings; wedging into grooves						
150 mm girth	-	0.74	13.52	1.03	m	14.56
240 mm girth	-	0.82	14.99	1.68	m	16.67
300 mm girth	-	0.97	17.73	2.05	m	19.77
Stepped flashings; wedging into grooves						
180 mm girth	-	0.83	15.17	1.22	m	16.39
270 mm girth	-	0.93	17.00	1.91	m	18.91
1.20 mm commercial grade aluminium flashings; polyester powder coated						
Flashings; fixed with self tapping screws						
170 mm girth	-	0.83	15.17	1.42	m	16.59
200 mm girth	-	0.88	16.08	1.89	m	17.97
280 mm girth	-	1.02	18.64	2.48	m	21.12
Aluminium Alumasc "Skyline" coping system; polyester powder coated						
Coping; fixing straps plugged and screwed to brickwork						
362 mm wide; for parapet wall						
271 - 300 mm wide	-	0.50	9.14	17.95	m	27.08
Extra for						
90 degree angle	-	0.25	4.57	42.76	nr	47.33
90 degree tee junction	-	0.35	6.40	45.87	nr	52.27
stop end	-	0.15	2.74	25.28	nr	28.03
stop end upstand	-	0.20	3.65	27.43	nr	31.08
Standing seam aluminium roof cladding; "Kal-zip" Hoogovens Aluminium Building Systems Ltd or other equal and approved; ref AA 3004 A1 Mn1 Mg1; standard natural aluminium stucco embossed finish						
Roof coverings (lining sheets not included); sloping not exceeding 50 degrees; 305 mm wide units						
0.90 mm thick	-	-	-	-	m^2	18.33
1.00 mm thick	-	-	-	-	m^2	20.89
1.20 mm thick	-	-	-	-	m^2	26.02
extra over for	-	-	-	-	-	-
polyester coating	-	-	-	-	m^2	5.54
PVF2 coating	-	-	-	-	m^2	6.83
smooth curved	-	-	-	-	m^2	33.16
factory formed tapered sheets	-	-	-	-	m^2	28.19
raking cutting	-	-	-	-	m	14.61
Accessories for roof coverings						
thermal insulation quilt; 60 mm thick	-	-	-	-	m^2	1.26
thermal insulation quilt; 80 mm thick	-	-	-	-	m^2	2.88
thermal insulation quilt; 100 mm thick	-	-	-	-	m^2	3.18
thermal insulation quilt; 150 mm thick	-	-	-	-	m^2	5.76
semi-rigid insulation slab; 30 mm thick; tissue faced	-	-	-	-	m^2	6.79
semi-rigid insulation slab; 50 mm thick	-	-	-	-	m^2	7.60
"Kal-Foil" vapour check	-	-	-	-	m^2	3.09

H CLADDING/COVERING

Item	PC £	Labour hours	Labour £	Material £	Unit	Total rate £
Lining sheets; "Kal-bau" aluminium ref TR 30/150; natural aluminium stucco embossed finish; fixed to steel purlins with stainless steel screws						
0.90 mm gauge	-	-	-	-	m²	14.94
Lining sheets; profiled steel; 1000 mm cover; bright white polyester paint finish; fixed to steel purlins with stainless steel screws						
0.70 mm gauge; ref TRS30/150S	-	-	-	-	m²	9.91
0.70 mm gauge; ref TRS35/200S	-	-	-	-	m²	8.75
extra over for						
crimped curve	-	-	-	-	m²	19.28
perforated sheet	-	-	-	-	m²	3.65
tapered 0.70 mm plain galvanised steel liner	-	-	-	-	m²	16.71
plastisol coating on external liners	-	-	-	-	m²	2.14
Eaves detail for 305 mm wide "Kal-zip" roof cladding units; including high density polythylene foam fillers; 2 mm extruded alloy drip angle; fixed to Kalzip sheet using stainless steel blind rivets						
40 mm x 20 mm angle: single skin	-	-	-	-	m	13.36
70 mm x 30 mm angle: single skin	-	-	-	-	m	14.49
40 mm x 20 mm angle: double skin	-	-	-	-	m	20.55
70 mm x 30 mm angle: double skin	-	-	-	-	m	22.17
Verge detail for 305 mm wide "Kal-zip" roof cladding units						
2 mm extruded aluminium alloy gable closure section; fixed with stainless steel blind sealed rivets; gable end hook/verge clip fixed to ST clip with stainless steel screws and 2 mm extruded aluminium tolerance clip	-	-	-	-	m	11.53
Ridge detail for 305 mm wide "Kal-zip" roof cladding units						
abutment ridge including natural aluminium stucco embossed "U" type ridge closures fixed with stainless steel blind steel rivets; "U" type polythylene ridge fillers and 2 mm extruded aluminium aluminium alloy support Zed fixed with stainless steel blind sealed rivets; fixing with rivets through small seam of "Kal-zip" into ST clip using stainless steel blind sealed rivets	-	-	-	-	m	41.41
duo ridge including natural aluminium stucco embossed "U" type ridge closures fixed with stainless steel blind sealed rivets; "U" type polythylene ridge fillers and 2 mm extruded aluminium alloy support Zed fixed with stainless steel blind sealed rivets; fixing with rivets through small seam of "Kal-zip" into ST clip using stainless steel blind steel rivets	-	-	-	-	m	62.20
0.9 mm Roof accessories						
Eaves closure; 200 mm girth	-	-	-	-	m	6.83
Ridge; 600 mm girth	-	-	-	-	m	13.22
Verge; 700 mm girth	-	-	-	-	m	17.47
1.0 mm Flashings etc.; fixing/wedging into grooves						
Flashing; 500 mm girth	-	-	-	-	m	13.22
Flashing; 750 mm girth	-	-	-	-	m	17.47
Flashing; 1000 mm girth	-	-	-	-	m	24.57

H CLADDING/COVERING

Item	PC £	Labour hours	Labour £	Material £	Unit	Total rate £
H72 ALUMINIUM SHEET COVERINGS/ FLASHINGS – cont'd						
"Kal-zip" Standing seam aluminium roof Cladding – cont'd						
1.2 mm Flashings etc.; fixing/wedging into grooves						
Flashing; 500 mm girth	-	-	-	-	m	14.54
Flashing; 750 mm girth	-	-	-	-	m	19.21
Flashing; 1000 mm girth	-	-	-	-	m	24.27
1.4 mm Flashings etc.; fixing/wedging into grooves						
Flashing; 500 mm girth	-	-	-	-	m	16.73
Flashing; 750 mm girth	-	-	-	-	m	22.09
Flashing; 1000 mm girth	-	-	-	-	m	33.19
H73 COPPER STRIP SHEET COVERINGS/ FLASHINGS						
Copper roofing; BS 2870						
0.56 mm thick (24 swg) roof coverings						
flat	20.72	2.96	54.09	23.41	m²	77.51
sloping 10 - 50 degrees	-	3.24	59.21	23.41	m²	82.62
vertical or sloping over 50 degrees	-	3.52	64.33	23.41	m²	87.74
0.56 mm thick (24 swg) dormer coverings						
flat	20.72	3.52	64.33	23.41	m²	87.74
sloping 10 - 50 degrees	-	3.89	71.09	23.41	m²	94.50
vertical or sloping over 50 degrees	-	4.26	77.85	23.41	m²	101.26
0.61 mm thick (23 swg) roof coverings						
flat	22.65	2.96	54.09	25.59	m²	79.69
sloping 10 - 50 degrees	-	3.24	59.21	25.59	m²	84.80
vertical or sloping over 50 degrees	-	3.52	64.33	25.59	m²	89.92
0.61 mm thick (23 swg) dormer coverings						
flat	22.65	3.52	64.33	25.59	m²	89.92
sloping 10 - 50 degrees	-	3.89	71.09	25.59	m²	96.68
vertical or sloping over 50 degrees	-	4.26	77.85	25.59	m²	103.44
Copper nailing; 75 mm spacing	-	0.19	3.47	0.36	m	3.83
0.56 mm thick copper flashings, etc.						
Flashings; wedging into grooves						
150 mm girth	-	0.74	13.52	3.67	m	17.20
240 mm girth	-	0.83	15.17	5.90	m	21.07
300 mm girth	-	0.97	17.73	7.41	m	25.13
Stepped flashings; wedging into grooves						
180 mm girth	-	0.83	15.17	4.46	m	19.62
270 mm girth	-	0.93	17.00	6.65	m	23.64
0.61 mm thick copper flashings, etc.						
Flashings; wedging into grooves						
150 mm girth	-	0.74	13.52	4.00	m	17.52
240 mm girth	-	0.83	15.17	6.44	m	21.61
300 mm girth	-	0.97	17.73	8.05	m	25.78
Stepped flashings; wedging into grooves						
180 mm girth	-	0.83	15.17	4.83	m	20.00
270 mm girth	-	0.93	17.00	7.23	m	24.23

H CLADDING/COVERING

Item	PC £	Labour hours	Labour £	Material £	Unit	Total rate £
H74 ZINC STRIP SHEET COVERINGS/ FLASHINGS						
Zinc; BS 849						
0.80 mm thick roof coverings						
flat	13.61	2.96	54.09	15.38	m²	**69.48**
sloping 10 - 50 degrees	-	3.24	59.21	15.38	m²	**74.59**
vertical or sloping over 50 degrees	-	3.52	64.33	15.38	m²	**79.71**
0.80 mm thick (23 swg) dormer coverings						
flat	-	3.52	64.33	15.38	m²	**79.71**
sloping 10 - 50 degrees	-	3.89	71.09	15.38	m²	**86.47**
vertical or sloping over 50 degrees	-	4.26	77.85	15.38	m²	**93.23**
0.80 mm thick zinc flashings, etc.						
Flashings; wedging into grooves						
150 mm girth	-	0.74	13.52	2.38	m	**15.91**
240 mm girth	-	0.83	15.17	3.86	m	**19.03**
300 mm girth	-	0.97	17.73	4.86	m	**22.59**
Stepped flashings; wedging into grooves						
180 mm girth	-	0.83	15.17	2.91	m	**18.08**
270 mm girth	-	0.93	17.00	4.35	m	**21.35**
H75 STAINLESS STEEL SHEET COVERINGS/ FLASHINGS						
Terne coated stainless steel roofing; Ugine & Alz (UK) Ltd or other equal and approved						
Roof coverings; "Uginox AME"; 0.40 mm thick						
flat; fixing with stainless steel screws to timber	28.57	0.93	24.42	34.73	m²	**59.15**
flat; including batten rolls; fixing with stainless steel screws to timber	-	0.93	24.42	37.30	m²	**61.73**
Roof coverings; "Uginox AE"; 0.40 mm thick						
flat; fixing with stainless steel screws to timber	23.98	0.93	24.42	29.78	m²	**54.21**
flat; including batten rolls; fixing with stainless steel screws to timber	-	0.93	24.42	32.28	m²	**56.70**
Wall coverings; "Uginox AME"; 0.40 mm thick						
vertical; coulisseau joints; fixing with stainless steel screws; to timber	-	0.83	21.80	32.83	m²	**54.63**
Wall coverings; "Uginox AE"; 0.40 mm thick						
vertical; coulisseau joints; fixing with stainless steel screws; to timber	-	0.83	21.80	28.01	m²	**49.80**
Flashings						
head abutments; swiss fold and cover flashings 150 mm girth	-	0.37	9.72	6.88	m	**16.60**
head abutments; manchester fold and cover flashings 150 mm girth	-	0.46	12.08	6.88	m	**18.96**
head abutments; soldered saddle flashings 150 mm girth	-	0.46	12.08	7.82	m	**19.90**
head abutments; into brick wall with timber infill; cover flashings 150 mm girth	-	0.74	19.43	10.77	m	**30.21**
head abutments; into brick wall with soldered apron; cover flashings 150 mm girth	-	0.88	23.11	12.07	m	**35.18**
side abutments; "Uginox" stepped flashings 170 mm girth	-	1.48	38.87	8.65	m²	**47.52**
eaves flashings 140 mm girth; approned with single lock welts	-	0.32	8.40	12.40	m	**20.80**
eaves flashings 190 mm girth; approned with flashings and soldered strips	-	0.46	12.08	15.20	m	**27.28**
verge flashings 150 mm girth	-	0.23	6.04	12.77	m	**18.81**

H CLADDING/COVERING

Item	PC £	Labour hours	Labour £	Material £	Unit	Total rate £
H75 STAINLESS STEEL SHEET COVERINGS/ FLASHINGS – cont'd						
Terne coated stainless steel roofing – cont'd						
Aprons						
fan aprons 250 mm girth	-	0.28	7.35	10.68	m	18.03
Ridges						
ridge with coulisseau closures	-	0.56	14.71	4.99	m	19.70
monoridge flanged apex (AME)	-	0.28	7.35	7.39	m	14.74
ridge with tapered timber infill and flat saddles	-	0.93	24.42	10.09	m	34.51
monoridge with timber infill and flat saddles	-	0.51	13.39	15.81	m	29.21
ventilated ridge with timber kerb and flat saddles	-	1.11	29.15	26.90	m	56.05
ventilated ridge with stainless steel brackets	-	0.83	21.80	46.65	m	68.45
Edges						
downstand	-	0.28	7.35	9.93	m	17.29
flanged	-	0.23	6.04	10.68	m	16.72
Gutters						
double lock welted valley gutters	-	0.97	25.47	16.42	m	41.89
eaves gutters; against masonry work	-	1.11	29.15	22.34	m	51.49
recessed valley gutters	-	0.83	21.80	31.55	m	53.35
recessed valley gutters with laplocks	-	1.02	26.79	37.15	m	63.94
secret	-	0.93	24.42	38.81	m	63.23
saddle expansion joints in gutters	-	0.93	24.42	13.35	m	37.77
H76 FIBRE BITUMEN THERMOPLASTIC SHEET COVERINGS/FLASHINGS						
Glass fibre reinforced bitumen strip slates; "Ruberglas 105" or other equal and approved; 1000 mm x 336 mm mineral finish; to external quality plywood boarding (boarding not included)						
Roof coverings	10.00	0.23	6.04	11.78	m^2	17.82
Wall coverings	-	0.37	9.72	11.78	m^2	21.50
Extra over coverings for						
double course at eaves; felt soaker	-	0.19	4.99	7.93	m	12.92
verges; felt soaker	-	0.14	3.68	6.57	m	10.25
valley slate; cut to shape; felt soaker and cutting both sides	-	0.42	11.03	10.40	m	21.43
ridge slate; cut to shape	-	0.28	7.35	6.57	m	13.92
hip slate; cut to shape; felt soaker and cutting both sides	-	0.42	11.03	10.30	m	21.33
holes for pipes and the like	-	0.48	12.61	-	nr	12.61
"Evode Flashband Original" sealing strips and flashings or other equal and approved; special grey finish						
Flashings; wedging at top if required; pressure bonded; flashband primer before application; to walls						
75 mm girth	-	0.17	3.11	1.01	m	4.12
100 mm girth	-	0.23	4.20	1.38	m	5.59
150 mm girth	-	0.31	5.67	2.07	m	7.73
225 mm girth	-	0.37	6.76	3.24	m	10.00
300 mm girth	-	0.42	7.68	4.07	m	11.74

J WATERPROOFING

Item	PC £	Labour hours	Labour £	Material £	Unit	Total rate £
J10 SPECIALIST WATERPROOF RENDERING						
"Sika" waterproof rendering or other equal and approved; steel trowelled						
20 mm work to walls; three coat; to concrete base						
over 300 mm wide	-	-	-	-	m²	38.02
not exceeding 300 mm wide	-	-	-	-	m²	57.61
25 mm work to walls; three coat; to concrete base						
over 300 mm wide	-	-	-	-	m²	44.93
not exceeding 300 mm wide	-	-	-	-	m²	69.13
40 mm work to walls; four coat; to concrete base						
over 300 mm wide	-	-	-	-	m²	66.25
not exceeding 300 mm wide	-	-	-	-	m²	103.70
J20 MASTIC ASPHALT TANKING/DAMP PROOF MEMBRANES						
Mastic asphalt to BS 6925 Type T 1097						
13 mm thick one coat coverings to concrete base; flat; subsequently covered						
over 300 mm wide	-	-	-	-	m²	8.90
225 mm - 300 mm wide	-	-	-	-	m²	21.13
150 mm - 225 mm wide	-	-	-	-	m²	23.24
not exceeding 150 mm wide	-	-	-	-	m²	28.99
20 mm thick two coat coverings to concrete base; flat; subsequently covered						
over 300 mm wide	-	-	-	-	m²	12.87
225 mm - 300 mm wide	-	-	-	-	m²	23.52
150 mm - 225 mm wide	-	-	-	-	m²	25.68
not exceeding 150 mm wide	-	-	-	-	m²	31.39
30 mm thick three coat coverings to concrete base; flat; subsequently covered						
over 300 mm wide	-	-	-	-	m²	18.40
225 mm - 300 mm wide	-	-	-	-	m²	26.72
150 mm - 225 mm wide	-	-	-	-	m²	28.99
not exceeding 150 mm wide	-	-	-	-	m²	34.58
13 mm thick two coat coverings to brickwork base; vertical; subsequently covered						
over 300 mm wide	-	-	-	-	m²	35.75
225 mm - 300 mm wide	-	-	-	-	m²	43.62
150 mm - 225 mm wide	-	-	-	-	m²	51.53
not exceeding 150 mm wide	-	-	-	-	m²	66.78
20 mm thick three coat coverings to brickwork base; vertical; subsequently covered						
over 300 mm wide	-	-	-	-	m²	55.95
225 mm - 300 mm wide	-	-	-	-	m²	60.20
150 mm - 225 mm wide	-	-	-	-	m²	63.94
not exceeding 150 mm wide	-	-	-	-	m²	82.68
Turning into groove 20 mm deep	-	-	-	-	m	0.70
Internal angle fillets; subsequently covered	-	-	-	-	m	4.13

J WATERPROOFING

Item	PC £	Labour hours	Labour £	Material £	Unit	Total rate £
J21 MASTIC ASPHALT ROOFING/ INSULATION/FINISHES						
Mastic asphalt to BS 6925 Type R 988						
20 mm thick two coat coverings; felt isolating membrane; to concrete (or timber) base; flat or to falls or slopes not exceeding 10 degrees from horizontal						
over 300 mm wide	-	-	-	-	m²	12.69
225 mm - 300 mm wide	-	-	-	-	m²	23.29
150 mm - 225 mm wide	-	-	-	-	m²	25.80
not exceeding 150 mm wide	-	-	-	-	m²	31.15
Add to the above for covering with:						
10 mm thick limestone chippings in hot bitumen	-	-	-	-	m²	2.50
coverings with solar reflective paint	-	-	-	-	m²	2.27
300 mm x 300 mm x 8 mm g.r.p. tiles in hot bitumen	-	-	-	-	m²	33.25
Cutting to line; jointing to old asphalt	-	-	-	-	m	5.59
13 mm thick two coat skirtings to brickwork base						
not exceeding 150 mm girth	-	-	-	-	m	9.96
150 mm - 225 mm girth	-	-	-	-	m	11.47
225 mm - 300 mm girth	-	-	-	-	m	12.87
13 mm thick three coat skirtings; expanded metal lathing reinforcement nailed to timber base						
not exceeding 150 mm girth	-	-	-	-	m	15.78
150 mm - 225 mm girth	-	-	-	-	m	18.63
225 mm - 300 mm girth	-	-	-	-	m	21.73
13 mm thick two coat fascias to concrete base						
not exceeding 150 mm girth	-	-	-	-	m	9.96
150 mm - 225 mm girth	-	-	-	-	m	11.47
20 mm thick two coat linings to channels to concrete base						
not exceeding 150 mm girth	-	-	-	-	m	24.34
150 mm - 225 mm girth	-	-	-	-	m	25.80
225 mm - 300 mm girth	-	-	-	-	m	29.12
20 mm thick two coat lining to cesspools						
250 mm x 150 mm x 150 mm deep	-	-	-	-	nr	23.64
Collars around pipes, standards and like members	-	-	-	-	nr	11.47
Accessories						
Eaves trim; extruded aluminium alloy; working asphalt into trim						
"Alutrim"; type A roof edging or other equal and approved	-	-	-	-	m	11.06
extra; angle	-	-	-	-	nr	6.17
Roof screed ventilator - aluminium alloy "Extr-aqua-vent" or other equal and approved; set on screed over and including dished sinking; working collar around ventilator	-	-	-	-	nr	21.42
J30 LIQUID APPLIED TANKING/DAMP PROOF MEMBRANES						
Tanking and damp proofing						
"Synthaprufe" or other equal and approved; blinding with sand; horizontal on slabs						
two coats	-	0.19	2.42	2.83	m²	5.26
three coats	-	0.26	3.32	4.20	m²	7.52

J WATERPROOFING

Item	PC £	Labour hours	Labour £	Material £	Unit	Total rate £
"Tretolastex 202T" or other equal and approved; on vertical surfaces of concrete						
two coats	-	0.19	2.42	0.51	m^2	2.93
three coats	-	0.26	3.32	0.76	m^2	4.08
One coat Vandex "Super" 0.75 kg/m^2 slurry or other equal and approved; one consolidating coat of Vandex "Premix" 1 kg/m2 slurry or other equal and approved; horizontal on beds						
over 225 mm wide	-	0.32	4.08	2.95	m^2	7.03
J40 FLEXIBLE SHEET TANKING/DAMP PROOF MEMBRANES						
Tanking and damp proofing						
Visqueen self-adhesive damp proof membrane						
over 300 mm wide; horizontal	-	-	-	-	m^2	6.46
not exceeding 300 mm wide; horizontal	-	-	-	-	m	2.48
Tanking primer for self-adhesive dpm						
over 300 mm wide; horizontal	-	-	-	-	m^2	4.47
not exceeding 300 mm wide; horizontal	-	-	-	-	m	2.04
"Bituthene" sheeting or other equal and approved; lapped joints; horizontal on slabs						
3000 grade	-	0.09	1.15	3.62	m^2	4.77
8000 grade	-	0.10	1.28	5.03	m^2	6.30
5000HD heavy duty grade	-	0.12	1.53	4.78	m^2	6.31
"Bituthene" sheeting or other equal and approved; lapped joints; dressed up vertical face of concrete						
8000 grade	-	0.17	2.17	5.03	m^2	7.20
RIW "Structureseal" tanking and damp proof membrane; or other equal and approved						
over 300 mm wide; horizontal	-	-	-	-	m^2	5.54
"Structureseal" Fillet						
40mm x 40mm	-	-	-	-	m	4.06
Ruberoid "Plasfrufe 2000SA" self-adhesive damp proof membrane						
over 300 mm wide; horizontal	-	-	-	-	m^2	12.30
not exceeding 300 mm wide; horizontal	-	-	-	-	m	4.71
Extra for 50 mm thick sand blinding	-	-	-	-	m^2	2.15
"Servi-pak" protection board or other equal and approved; butt jointed; taped joints; to horizontal surfaces;						
3 mm thick	-	0.14	1.79	3.84	m^2	5.63
6 mm thick	-	0.14	1.79	5.75	m^2	7.53
12 mm thick	-	0.19	2.42	10.15	m^2	12.58
"Servi-pak" protection board or other equal and approved; butt jointed; taped joints; to vertical surfaces						
3 mm thick	-	0.19	2.42	3.84	m^2	6.26
6 mm thick	-	0.19	2.42	5.75	m^2	8.17
12 mm thick	-	0.23	2.93	10.15	m^2	13.09
"Bituthene" reinforcing strip or other equal and approved; 70 mm wide						
Bitutape 4000	-	0.09	1.15	0.40	m	1.54
Expandite "Famflex" hot bitumen bonded waterproof tanking or other equal and approved; 150 mm laps						
horizontal; over 300 mm wide	-	0.37	4.72	13.23	m^2	17.95
vertical; over 300 mm wide	-	0.60	7.65	13.23	m^2	20.88

J WATERPROOFING

Item	PC £	Labour hours	Labour £	Material £	Unit	Total rate £
J41 BUILT UP FELT ROOF COVERINGS						
NOTE: The following items of felt roofing, unless otherwise described, include for conventional lapping, laying and bonding between layers and to base; and laying flat or to falls, crossfalls or to slopes not exceeding 10 degrees - but exclude any insulation etc.						
Felt roofing; BS 747; suitable for flat roofs						
Three layer coverings first layer type 3G; subsequent layers type 3B bitumen glass fibre based felt	-	-	-	-	m²	8.29
Extra over felt for covering with and bedding in hot bitumen						
13 mm thick stone chippings	-	-	-	-	m²	2.67
300 mm x 300 mm x 8 mm g.r.p. tiles	-	-	-	-	m²	45.69
working into outlet pipes and the like	-	-	-	-	m²	11.25
Skirtings; three layer; top layer mineral surfaced; dressed over tilting fillet; turned into groove						
not exceeding 200 mm girth	-	-	-	-	m	8.36
200 mm - 400 mm girth	-	-	-	-	m	10.00
Coverings to kerbs; three layer						
400 mm - 600 mm girth	-	-	-	-	m	21.09
Linings to gutters; three layer						
400 mm - 600 mm girth	-	-	-	-	m	14.32
Collars around pipes and the like; three layer mineral surface; 150 mm high						
not exceeding 55 mm nominal size	-	-	-	-	nr	9.38
55 mm - 110 mm nominal size	-	-	-	-	nr	9.38
Three layer coverings; two base layers type 5U bitumen polyester based felt; top layer type 5B polyester based mineral surfaced felt; 10 mm stone chipping covering; bitumen bonded	-	-	-	-	m²	17.45
Coverings to kerbs						
not exceeding 200 mm girth	-	-	-	-	m	11.02
200 mm - 400 mm girth	-	-	-	-	m	13.75
Outlets and dishing to gullies						
300 mm diameter	-	-	-	-	nr	11.25
"Andersons" high performance polyester-based roofing system or other equal and approved						
Two layer coverings; first layer HT 125 underlay; second layer HT 350; fully bonded to wood; fibre or cork base	-	-	-	-	m²	12.50
Extra over for						
top layer mineral surfaced	-	-	-	-	m²	2.44
13 mm thick stone chippings	-	-	-	-	m²	2.67
third layer of type 3B as underlay for concrete or screeded base	-	-	-	-	m²	2.44
working into outlet pipes and the like	-	-	-	-	nr	11.25
Skirtings; two layer; top layer mineral surfaced; dressed over tilting fillet; turned into groove						
not exceeding 200 mm girth	-	-	-	-	m	8.87
200 mm - 400 mm girth	-	-	-	-	m	10.69

J WATERPROOFING

Item	PC £	Labour hours	Labour £	Material £	Unit	Total rate £
Coverings to kerbs; two layer						
400 mm - 600 mm girth	-	-	-	-	m	24.89
Linings to gutters; three layer						
400 mm - 600 mm girth	-	-	-	-	m	18.19
Collars around pipes and the like; two layer; 150 mm high						
not exceeding 55 mm nominal size	-	-	-	-	nr	9.38
55 mm - 110 mm nominal size	-	-	-	-	nr	9.38
"Ruberglas 120 GP" high performance roofing or other equal and approved						
Two layer coverings; first and second layers "Ruberglas 120 GP"; fully bonded to wood, fibre or cork base	-	-	-	-	m²	7.73
Extra over for						
top layer mineral surfaced	-	-	-	-	m²	2.44
13 mm thick stone chippings	-	-	-	-	m²	2.67
third layer of "Rubervent 3G" as underlay for concrete or screeded base	-	-	-	-	m²	2.44
working into outlet pipes and the like	-	-	-	-	nr	11.25
Skirtings; two layer; top layer mineral surfaced; dressed over tilting fillet; turned into groove						
not exceeding 200 mm girth	-	-	-	-	m	7.73
200 mm - 400 mm girth	-	-	-	-	m	8.97
Coverings to kerbs; two layer						
400 mm - 600 mm girth	-	-	-	-	m	15.46
Linings to gutters; three layer						
400 mm - 600 mm girth	-	-	-	-	m	12.84
Collars around pipes and the like; two layer, 150 mm high						
not exceeding 55 mm nominal size	-	-	-	-	nr	9.38
55 mm - 110 mm nominal size	-	-	-	-	nr	9.38
"Ruberfort HP 350" high performance roofing or other equal and approved						
Two layer coverings; first layer "Ruberfort HP 180"; second layer "Ruberfort HP 350"; fully bonded; to wood; fibre or cork base	-	-	-	-	m²	12.00
Extra over for						
top layer mineral surfaced	-	-	-	-	m²	2.44
13 mm thick stone chippings	-	-	-	-	m²	2.67
third layer of "Rubervent 3G"; as underlay for concrete or screeded base	-	-	-	-	m²	2.49
working into outlet pipes and the like	-	-	-	-	nr	11.25
Skirtings; two layer; top layer mineral surface; dressed over tilting fillet; turned into groove						
not exceeding 200 mm girth	-	-	-	-	m	8.53
200 mm - 400 mm girth	-	-	-	-	m	10.12
Coverings to kerbs; two layer						
400 mm - 600 mm girth	-	-	-	-	m	23.93
Linings to gutters; three layer						
400 mm - 600 mm girth	-	-	-	-	m	17.28
Collars around pipes and the like; two layer; 150 mm high						
not exceeding 55 mm nominal size	-	-	-	-	nr	9.38
55 mm - 110 mm nominal size	-	-	-	-	nr	9.38

J WATERPROOFING

Item	PC £	Labour hours	Labour £	Material £	Unit	Total rate £
J41 BUILT UP FELT ROOF COVERINGS – cont'd						
"Polybit 350" elastomeric roofing or						
other equal and approved						
Two layer coverings; first layer "Polybit 180";						
second layer "Polybit 350"; fully bonded to wood;						
fibre or cork base	-	-	-	-	m²	12.28
Extra over for						
top layer mineral surfaced	-	-	-	-	m²	2.44
13 mm thick stone chippings	-	-	-	-	m²	2.67
third layer of "Rubervent 3G" as underlay for						
concrete or screeded base	-	-	-	-	m²	2.44
working into outlet pipes and the like	-	-	-	-	nr	11.25
Skirtings; two layer; top layer mineral surfaced;						
dressed over tilting fillet; turned into groove						
not exceeding 200 mm girth	-	-	-	-	m	8.76
200 mm - 400 mm girth	-	-	-	-	m	11.71
Coverings to kerbs; two layer						
400 mm - 600 mm girth	-	-	-	-	m	24.49
Linings to gutters; three layer						
400 mm - 600 mm girth	-	-	-	-	m	17.73
Collars around pipes and the like; two layer; 150						
mm high						
not exceeding 55 mm nominal size	-	-	-	-	nr	9.38
55 mm - 110 mm nominal size	-	-	-	-	nr	9.38
"Hyload 150 E" elastomeric roofing or						
other equal and approved						
Two layer coverings; first layer "Ruberglas 120						
GHP"; second layer "Hyload 150 E" fully bonded						
to wood; fibre or cork base	-	-	-	-	m²	25.00
Extra over for						
13 mm thick stone chippings	-	-	-	-	m²	2.67
third layer of "Rubervent 3G" as underlay for						
concrete or screeded base	-	-	-	-	m²	2.44
working into outlet pipes and the like	-	-	-	-	nr	11.20
Skirtings; two layer; dressed over tilting fillet;						
turned into groove						
200 mm - 400 mm girth	-	-	-	-	m	22.90
Coverings to kerbs; two layer						
400 mm - 600 mm girth	-	-	-	-	m	46.66
Linings to gutters; three layer						
400 mm - 600 mm girth	-	-	-	-	m	30.86
Collars around pipes and the like; two layer; 150						
mm high						
not exceeding 55 mm nominal size	-	-	-	-	nr	9.38
55 mm - 110 mm nominal size	-	-	-	-	nr	9.38
Accessories						
Eaves trim; extruded aluminium alloy; working felt						
into trim						
"Alutrim"; type F roof edging or other equal and						
approved	-	-	-	-	m	7.86
extra over for; external angle	-	-	-	-	nr	10.57
Roof screed ventilator - aluminium alloy						
"Extr-aqua-vent" or other equal and approved -						
set on screed over and including dished sinking						
and collar	-	-	-	-	nr	23.48

J WATERPROOFING

Item	PC £	Labour hours	Labour £	Material £	Unit	Total rate £
Insulation board underlays						
Vapour barrier						
reinforced; metal lined	-	-	-	-	m²	11.34
Cork boards; density 112 - 125 kg/ m³						
60 mm thick	-	-	-	-	m²	14.75
Rockwool; slab RW4 or other equal and approved						
60 mm thick	-	-	-	-	m²	17.97
Perlite boards or other equal and approved; density 170 - 180 kg/ m³						
60 mm thick	-	-	-	-	m²	23.48
Polyurethane boards; density 32 kg/ m³						
30 mm thick	-	-	-	-	m²	9.29
35 mm thick	-	-	-	-	m²	9.90
50 mm thick	-	-	-	-	m²	10.77
Wood fibre boards; impregnated; density 220 - 350 kg/ m³						
12.70 mm thick	-	-	-	-	m²	4.13
Insulation board overlays						
Dow "Roofmate SL" extruded polystyrene foam boards or other equal and approved						
50 mm thick	-	0.28	7.35	13.60	m²	20.96
75 mm thick	-	0.28	7.35	18.61	m²	25.96
Dow "Roofmate LG" extruded polystyrene foam boards or other equal and approved						
60 mm thick	-	0.28	7.35	24.40	m²	31.76
90 mm thick	-	0.28	7.35	27.70	m²	35.05
110 mm thick	-	0.28	7.35	30.62	m²	37.97
Dow "Roofmate PR" extruded polystyrene foam boards or other equal and approved						
90 mm thick	-	0.28	7.35	20.96	m²	28.31
120 mm thick	-	0.28	7.35	27.92	m²	35.28
J42 SINGLE LAYER PLASTICS ROOF COVERINGS						
"Trocal S" PVC roofing or other equal and approved						
Coverings	-	-	-	-	m²	16.60
Skirtings; dressed over metal upstands						
not exceeding 200 mm girth	-	-	-	-	m	12.89
200 mm - 400 mm girth	-	-	-	-	m	15.85
Coverings to kerbs						
400 mm - 600 mm girth	-	-	-	-	m	29.01
Collars around pipes and the like; 150 mm high						
not exceeding 55 mm nominal size	-	-	-	-	nr	8.87
55 mm - 110 mm nominal size	-	-	-	-	nr	8.87
"Trocal" metal upstands or other equal and approved						
not exceeding 200 mm girth	-	-	-	-	m	9.40
200 mm - 400 mm girth	-	-	-	-	m	12.20

J WATERPROOFING

Item	PC £	Labour hours	Labour £	Material £	Unit	Total rate £
J42 SINGLE LAYER PLASTICS ROOF COVERINGS – cont'd						
Sarnafil G410 - 12ELF light grey ployester reinforced fleece lined single layer roofing material fully adhered to and including SarnaTherm 90mm insulation board on Sarnavap 1000 gauge polythene vapour control layer						
Roof coverings; flat; to concrete base						
1.2 mm gauge	-	-	-	-	m^2	31.15
1.5 mm gauge	-	-	-	-	m^2	34.44
1.8 mm gauge	-	-	-	-	m^2	37.38
Extra over for						
welded pvc cord to perimeters	-	-	-	-	m	0.97
Sarnabars for direct fixing to trapezoidal metal decking centrally at 3.22 m spacings one way and at 1.61 m spacings at perimeters	-	-	-	-	m	5.95
movement joint	-	-	-	-	m	25.18
Sarnatred walkway tiles	-	-	-	-	m^2	41.87
Standard details						
hip or valley	-	-	-	-	m	8.81
gutter edge	-	-	-	-	m	31.66
parapet	-	-	-	-	m	31.94
J43 PROPRIETARY ROOF DECKING WITH FELT FINISH						
"Bitumetal" flat roof construction or other equal and approved; fixing to timber, steel or concrete; flat or sloping; vapour check; 32 mm thick polyurethane insulation; 3G perforated felt underlay; two layers of glass fibre base felt roofing; stone chipping finish						
0.70 mm thick galvanized steel						
35 mm deep profiled decking; 2.38 m span	-	-	-	-	m^2	34.40
46 mm deep profiled decking; 2.96 m span	-	-	-	-	m^2	34.77
60 mm deep profiled decking; 3.74 m span	-	-	-	-	m^2	35.83
100 mm deep profiled decking; 5.13 m span	-	-	-	-	m^2	36.97
0.90 mm thick aluminium; mill finish						
35 mm deep profiled decking; 1.79 m span	-	-	-	-	m^2	36.09
60 mm deep profiled decking; 2.34 m span	-	-	-	-	m^2	36.40
"Bitumetal" flat roof construction or other equal and approved; fixing to timber, steel or concrete; flat or sloping; vapour check; 32 mm polyurethane insulation; 3G perforated felt underlay; two layers of polyester based roofing; stone chipping finish						
0.70 mm thick galvanised steel						
35 mm deep profiled decking; 2.38 m span	-	-	-	-	m^2	38.61
46 mm deep profiled decking; 2.96 m span	-	-	-	-	m^2	38.97
60 mm deep profiled decking; 3.74 m span	-	-	-	-	m^2	40.04
100 mm deep profiled decking; 5.13 m span	-	-	-	-	m^2	41.18
0.90 mm thick aluminium; mill finish						
35 mm deep profiled decking; 1.79 m span	-	-	-	-	m^2	40.29
60 mm deep profiled decking; 2.34 m span	-	-	-	-	m^2	40.61

K LININGS/SHEATHING/DRY PARTITIONING

Item	PC £	Labour hours	Labour £	Material £	Unit	Total rate £
ALTERNATIVE SHEET LINING MATERIAL PRICES						
Discounts of 0 - 20% available depending on quantity/status						
Fibreboard; 19 mm Decorative faced (£/10 m²)						
Ash	-	-	-	78.75	10 m²	-
Beech	-	-	-	91.90	10 m²	-
Oak	-	-	-	92.90	10 m²	-
Teak	-	-	-	126.50	10 m²	-
Edgings; self adhesive (£/50 m roll)						
22 mm Ash	-	-	-	17.50	50 m	-
22 mm Beech	-	-	-	17.50	50 m	-
22 mm Oak	-	-	-	17.50	50 m	-
Chipboard Standard Grade (£/10m²)						
12 mm	-	-	-	16.80	10 m²	-
16 mm	-	-	-	21.00	10 m²	-
22 mm	-	-	-	27.50	10 m²	-
25 mm	-	-	-	31.25	10 m²	-
Chipboard; melamine faced (£/10m²)						
12 mm	-	-	-	33.05	10 m²	-
18 mm	-	-	-	38.20	10 m²	-
Laminboard; Birch faced (£/10m²)						
19 mm	-	-	-	128.23	10 m²	-
22 mm	-	-	-	149.60	10 m²	-
25 mm	-	-	-	149.58	10 m²	-
Medium density fibreboard; external quality (£/10m²)						
6 mm	-	-	-	46.43	10 m²	-
9 mm	-	-	-	61.86	10 m²	-
19 mm	-	-	-	101.02	10 m²	-
25 mm	-	-	-	140.61	10 m²	-
Plasterboards						
Wallboard plank (£/100m²)						
9.5 mm	-	-	-	152.00	100 m²	-
12.5 mm	-	-	-	163.00	100 m²	-
15 mm	-	-	-	198.00	100 m²	-
Industrial board (£/100 m²)						
12.5 mm	-	-	-	468.00	100 m²	-
Moisture resistant board (£/100 m²)						
9.5 mm	-	-	-	258.00	100 m²	-
Fireline board (£/100 m²)						
12.5 mm	-	-	-	203.00	100m²	-
15 mm	-	-	-	248.00	100 m²	-

K LININGS/SHEATHING/DRY PARTITIONING

Item	PC £	Labour hours	Labour £	Material £	Unit	Total rate £
K10 PLASTERBOARD DRY LINING/ PARTITIONS/CEILINGS						
SUPPLY AND FIX PRICES						
Linings; "Gyproc GypLyner" metal framed wall lining system; or other equal and approved; floor and ceiling channels plugged and screwed to concrete Tapered edge panels; joints filled with joint filler and joint tape to receive direct decoration; one layer of 12.5 mm thick Gyproc Wallboard; or other equal and approved						
height 2.10 m - 2.40 m	-	1.05	18.71	11.63	m	30.33
height 2.40 m - 2.70 m	-	1.15	20.52	13.00	m	33.51
height 2.70 m - 3.00 m	-	1.27	22.70	14.19	m	36.90
height 3.00 m - 3.30 m	-	1.45	25.95	15.40	m	41.35
height 3.30 m - 3.60 m	-	1.63	29.19	16.40	m	45.59
height 3.60 m - 3.90 m	-	1.88	33.69	17.82	m	51.51
height 3.90 m - 4.20 m	-	2.11	37.80	19.03	m	56.83
Linings; "Gyproc GypLyner IWL" independent walling system or other equal and approved; comprising 48 mm wide metal I stud frame; 50 mmm wide metal C stud floor and ceiling channels; plugged and screwed to concrete 62.5 mm partition; outer skin of 12.50 mm thick tapered edge wallboard one side; joints filled with joint filler and joint tape to receive direct decoration						
height 2.10 m - 2.40 m	-	3.05	54.24	7.93	m	62.17
height 2.40 m - 2.70 m	-	3.56	63.67	9.60	m	73.28
height 2.70 m - 3.00 m	-	3.94	70.57	10.51	m	81.08
height 3.00 m - 3.30 m	-	4.58	81.99	11.46	m	93.45
height 3.30 m - 3.60 m	-	4.95	88.71	12.42	m	101.14
height 3.60 m - 3.90 m	-	5.65	101.18	13.39	m	114.58
height 3.90 m - 4.20 m	-	6.20	111.04	14.37	m	125.41
62.5 mm partition; outer skin of 12.50 mm thick tapered edge wallboard one side; filling cavity with "Isowool high performance slab (2405); wallboard joints filled with joint filler and joint tape to receive direct decoration						
height 2.10 m - 2.40 m	-	3.05	54.24	19.22	m	73.45
height 2.40 m - 2.70 m	-	3.56	63.67	22.30	m	85.97
height 2.70 m - 3.00 m	-	3.94	70.57	24.62	m	95.18
height 3.00 m - 3.30 m	-	4.58	81.99	26.97	m	108.96
height 3.30 m - 3.60 m	-	4.95	88.71	29.35	m	118.06
height 3.60 m - 3.90 m	-	5.65	101.18	31.73	m	132.91
height 3.90 m - 4.20 m	-	6.20	111.04	34.11	m	145.15

K LININGS/SHEATHING/DRY PARTITIONING

Item	PC £	Labour hours	Labour £	Material £	Unit	Total rate £
"Gyproc" laminated proprietary partitions or other equal and approved; two skins of gypsum plasterboard bonded to a centre core of plasterboard square edge plank 19 mm thick; fixing with nails to softwood perimeter battens (not included); joints filled with filler and joint tape; to receive direct decoration						
50 mm partition; two outer skins of 12.50 mm thick tapered edge wallboard						
height 2.10 m - 2.40 m	-	1.85	33.33	13.61	m	**46.94**
height 2.40 m - 2.70 m	-	2.41	43.63	15.81	m	**59.44**
height 2.70 m - 3.00 m	-	2.68	48.61	17.25	m	**65.87**
height 3.00 m - 3.30 m	-	2.96	53.76	18.71	m	**72.47**
height 3.30 m - 3.60 m	-	3.24	58.92	20.24	m	**79.15**
65 mm partition; two outer skins of 19 mm thick tapered edge planks						
height 2.10 m - 2.40 m	-	2.04	36.64	19.24	m	**55.88**
height 2.40 m - 2.70 m	-	2.59	46.77	21.79	m	**68.56**
height 2.70 m - 3.00 m	-	2.87	51.92	23.59	m	**75.51**
height 3.00 m - 3.30 m	-	3.19	57.77	25.39	m	**83.16**
height 3.30 m - 3.60 m	-	3.47	62.92	27.27	m	**90.20**
"Gypwall Rapid/db Plus" metal stud housing partitioning system; or other equal and approved; floor and ceiling channels plugged and screwed to concrete						
75 mm partition; 43/44 mm studs and channels; one layer of 15 mm SoundBloc Rapid each side; joints filled with joint filler and joint tape to receive direct decoration						
height 2.10 m - 2.40 m; studs at 900 mm centres	-	2.70	48.69	16.35	m	**65.03**
height 2.10 m - 2.40 m; studs at 900 mm centres; with 25 mm Isowool 1200 insulation in cavity	-	2.70	48.69	18.18	m	**66.87**
height 2.10 m - 2.40 m; studs at 450 mm centres	-	3.70	66.11	17.96	m	**84.07**
height 2.10 m - 2.40 m; studs at 450 mm centres; with 25 mm Isowool 1200 insulation in cavity	-	3.70	66.11	19.80	m	**85.91**
height 2.40 m - 2.70 m; studs at 450 mm centres	-	4.07	72.72	19.97	m	**92.69**
height 2.40 m - 2.70 m; studs at 450 mm centres; with 25 mm Isowool 1200 insulation in cavity	-	4.07	72.72	21.81	m	**94.53**
102 mm partition; 70/72 mm studs and channels; one layer of 15 mm SoundBloc Rapid each side; joints filled with joint filler and joint tape to receive direct decoration						
height 2.10 m - 2.40 m; studs at 900 mm centres	-	3.00	53.91	18.15	m	**72.07**
height 2.10 m - 2.40 m; studs at 900 mm centres; with 25 mm Isowool 1200 insulation in cavity	-	3.00	53.91	19.99	m	**73.90**
height 2.10 m - 2.40 m; studs at 450 mm centres	-	4.00	71.34	20.80	m	**92.14**
height 2.10 m - 2.40 m; studs at 450 mm centres; with 25 mm Isowool 1200 insulation in cavity stud cavity	-	4.00	71.34	22.64	m	**93.98**
height 2.40 m - 2.70 m; studs at 900 mm centres	-	3.32	59.65	19.98	m	**79.63**
height 2.40 m - 2.70 m; studs at 900 mm centres; with 25 mm Isowool 1200 insulation in cavity	-	3.32	59.65	21.81	m	**81.47**
height 2.40 m - 2.70 m; studs at 450 mm centres	-	4.32	77.08	23.11	m	**100.19**
height 2.40 m - 2.70 m; studs at 450 mm centres; with 25 mm Isowool 1200 insulation in cavity	-	4.32	77.08	24.95	m	**102.02**

K LININGS/SHEATHING/DRY PARTITIONING

Item	PC £	Labour hours	Labour £	Material £	Unit	Total rate £
K10 PLASTERBOARD DRY LINING/ PARTITIONS/CEILINGS – cont'd						
"Gyproc" metal stud proprietary partitions or other equal and approved; comprising 48 mm wide metal stud frame; 50 mm wide floor channel plugged and screwed to concrete through 38 mm x 48 mm tanalised softwood sole plate						
Tapered edge panels; joints filled with joint filler and joint tape to receive direct decoration; 80 mm thick partition; one hour; one layer of 15 mm thick "Fireline" board or other equal and approved each side						
height 2.10 m - 2.40 m	-	3.89	68.87	15.55	m	84.42
height 2.40 m - 2.70 m	-	4.49	79.88	18.10	m	97.98
height 2.70 m - 3.00 m	-	5.00	89.04	19.90	m	108.94
height 3.00 m - 3.30 m	-	5.78	102.90	21.88	m	124.78
height 3.30 m - 3.60 m	-	6.34	112.93	23.58	m	136.52
height 3.60 m - 3.90 m	-	7.59	134.99	25.44	m	160.43
height 3.90 m - 4.20 m	-	8.14	144.84	27.30	m	172.14
angles	-	0.19	3.45	1.02	m	4.47
T-junctions	-	0.09	1.57	-	m	1.57
fair ends	-	0.19	3.45	0.40	m	3.85
Tapered edge panels; joints filled with joint filler and joint tape to receive direct decoration; 100 mm thick partition; two hour; two layers of 12.50 mm thick "Fireline" board or other equal and approved both sides						
height 2.10 m - 2.40 m	-	4.81	84.91	21.21	m	106.12
height 2.40 m - 2.70 m	-	5.53	98.00	24.49	m	122.49
height 2.70 m - 3.00 m	-	6.15	109.07	26.99	m	136.06
height 3.00 m - 3.30 m	-	6.13	109.00	29.68	m	138.68
height 3.30 m - 3.60 m	-	7.72	136.98	32.08	m	169.06
height 3.60 m - 3.90 m	-	7.59	134.99	34.76	m	169.74
height 3.90 m - 4.20 m	-	9.76	173.07	37.21	m	210.28
angles	-	0.28	5.02	1.09	m	6.11
T-junctions	-	0.09	1.57	-	m	1.57
fair ends	-	0.28	5.02	0.47	m	5.49
Gypsum plasterboard; BS 1230; plain grade tapered edge wallboard; fixing with nails; joints left open to receive "Artex" finish or other equal and approved; to softwood base						
9.50 mm board to ceilings						
over 300 mm wide	-	0.23	4.01	1.20	m²	5.21
9.50 mm board to beams						
girth not exceeding 600 mm	-	0.28	4.88	0.74	m²	5.62
girth 600 mm - 1200 mm	-	0.37	6.45	1.46	m²	7.90
12.50 mm board to ceilings						
over 300 mm wide	-	0.31	5.40	1.35	m²	6.75
12.50 mm board to beams						
girth not exceeding 600 mm	-	0.28	4.88	0.84	m²	5.71
girth 600 mm - 1200 mm	-	0.37	6.45	1.62	m²	8.07

K LININGS/SHEATHING/DRY PARTITIONING

Item	PC £	Labour hours	Labour £	Material £	Unit	Total rate £
Gypsum plasterboard to BS 1230; fixing with nails; joints filled with joint filler and joint tape to receive direct decoration; to softwood base						
Plain grade tapered edge wallboard						
9.50 mm board to walls						
wall height 2.40 m - 2.70 m	-	0.93	17.02	4.33	m	21.35
wall height 2.70 m - 3.00 m	-	1.06	19.43	4.81	m	24.24
wall height 3.00 m - 3.30 m	-	1.20	22.00	5.30	m	27.30
wall height 3.30 m - 3.60 m	-	1.39	25.45	5.82	m	31.27
9.50 mm board to reveals and soffits of openings and recesses						
not exceeding 300 mm wide	-	0.19	3.45	0.98	m	4.43
300 mm - 600 mm wide	-	0.37	6.72	1.34	m	8.06
9.50 mm board to faces of columns - 4 nr						
not exceeding 600 mm total girth	-	0.46	8.36	2.00	m	10.36
600 mm - 1200 mm total girth	-	0.93	16.96	2.71	m	19.66
1200 mm - 1800 mm total girth	-	1.20	22.00	3.41	m	25.41
9.50 mm board to ceilings						
over 300 mm wide	-	0.39	7.07	1.60	m²	8.67
9.50 mm board to faces of beams - 3 nr						
not exceeding 600 mm total girth	-	0.56	10.17	1.97	m	12.14
600 mm - 1200 mm total girth	-	1.02	18.59	2.67	m	21.27
1200 mm - 1800 mm total girth	-	1.30	23.81	3.38	m	27.19
12.50 mm board to walls						
wall height 2.40 m - 2.70 m	-	0.97	17.72	4.66	m	22.38
wall height 2.70 m - 3.00 m	-	1.11	20.30	5.18	m	25.48
wall height 3.00 m - 3.30 m	-	1.25	22.87	5.70	m	28.58
wall height 3.30 m - 3.60 m	-	1.43	26.15	6.26	m	32.41
12.50 mm board to reveals and soffits of openings and recesses						
not exceeding 300 mm wide	-	0.19	3.45	1.04	m	4.49
300 mm - 600 mm wide	-	0.37	6.72	1.42	m	8.14
12.50 mm board to faces of columns - 4 nr						
not exceeding 600 mm total girth	-	0.46	8.36	2.12	m	10.47
600 mm - 1200 mm total girth	-	0.93	16.96	2.89	m	19.84
1200 mm - 1800 mm total girth	-	1.20	22.00	3.65	m	25.66
12.50 mm board to ceilings						
over 300 mm wide	-	0.41	7.42	1.73	m²	9.14
12.50 mm board to faces of beams - 3 nr						
not exceeding 600 mm total girth	-	0.56	10.17	2.07	m	12.23
600 mm - 1200 mm total girth	-	1.02	18.59	2.84	m	21.43
1200 mm - 1800 mm total girth	-	1.30	23.81	3.60	m	27.42
external angle; with joint tape bedded and covered with "Jointex" or other equal and approved	-	0.11	2.07	0.30	m	2.37
Tapered edge wallboard TEN						
12.50 mm board to walls						
wall height 2.40 m - 2.70 m	-	0.97	17.72	5.35	m	23.08
wall height 2.70 m - 3.00 m	-	1.11	20.30	5.95	m	26.25
wall height 3.00 m - 3.30 m	-	1.25	22.87	6.55	m	29.43
wall height 3.30 m - 3.60 m	-	1.43	26.15	7.18	m	33.33
12.50 mm board to reveals and soffits of openings and recesses						
not exceeding 300 mm wide	-	0.19	3.45	1.12	m	4.57
300 mm - 600 mm wide	-	0.37	6.72	1.57	m	8.29

K LININGS/SHEATHING/DRY PARTITIONING

Item	PC £	Labour hours	Labour £	Material £	Unit	Total rate £
K10 PLASTERBOARD DRY LINING/ PARTITIONS/CEILINGS – cont'd						
Tapered edge wallboard TEN – cont'd						
12.50 mm board to faces of columns - 4 nr						
not exceeding 600 mm total girth	-	0.46	8.36	2.27	m	10.63
600 mm - 1200 mm total girth	-	0.93	16.96	3.19	m	20.15
1200 mm - 1800 mm total girth	-	1.20	22.00	4.12	m	26.12
12.50 mm board to ceilings						
over 300 mm wide	-	0.41	7.42	1.98	m²	9.40
12.50 mm board to faces of beams - 3 nr						
not exceeding 600 mm total girth	-	0.56	10.17	2.22	m	12.39
600 mm - 1200 mm total girth	-	1.02	18.59	3.14	m	21.74
1200 mm - 1800 mm total girth	-	1.30	23.81	4.07	m	27.88
external angle; with joint tape bedded and covered with "Jointex" or other equal and approved	-	0.11	2.07	0.30	m	2.37
Tapered edge plank						
19 mm plank to walls						
wall height 2.40 m - 2.70 m	-	1.02	18.59	7.83	m	26.43
wall height 2.70 m - 3.00 m	-	1.20	21.87	8.71	m	30.57
wall height 3.00 m - 3.30 m	-	1.30	23.75	9.58	m	33.33
wall height 3.30 m - 3.60 m	-	1.53	27.89	10.49	m	38.38
19 mm plank to reveals and soffits of openings and recesses						
not exceeding 300 mm wide	-	0.20	3.62	1.39	m	5.02
300 mm - 600 mm wide	-	0.42	7.59	2.12	m	9.71
19 mm plank to faces of columns - 4 nr						
not exceeding 600 mm total girth	-	0.51	9.23	2.82	m	12.05
600 mm - 1200 mm total girth	-	0.97	17.65	4.30	m	21.95
1200 mm - 1800 mm total girth	-	1.25	22.87	5.77	m	28.64
19 mm plank to ceilings						
over 300 mm wide	-	0.43	7.77	2.90	m²	10.67
19 mm plank to faces of beams - 3 nr						
not exceeding 600 mm total girth	-	0.60	10.86	2.77	m	13.64
600 mm - 1200 mm total girth	-	1.06	19.29	4.25	m	23.54
1200 mm - 1800 mm total girth	-	1.34	24.51	5.72	m	30.23
Thermal Board						
27 mm board to walls						
wall height 2.40 m - 2.70 m	-	1.06	19.29	13.03	m	32.32
wall height 2.70 m - 3.00 m	-	1.23	22.39	14.48	m	36.87
wall height 3.00 m - 3.30 m	-	1.34	24.37	15.93	m	40.31
wall height 3.30 m - 3.60 m	-	1.62	29.46	17.42	m	46.88
27 mm board to reveals and soffits of openings and recesses						
not exceeding 300 mm wide	-	0.21	3.80	1.97	m	5.77
300 mm - 600 mm wide	-	0.43	7.77	3.28	m	11.04
27 mm board to faces of columns - 4 nr						
not exceeding 600 mm total girth	-	0.52	9.40	3.98	m	13.38
600 mm - 1200 mm total girth	-	1.02	18.52	6.61	m	25.13
1200 mm - 1800 mm total girth	-	1.30	23.75	9.23	m	32.98
27 mm board to ceilings						
over 300 mm wide	-	0.46	8.29	4.83	m²	13.12
27 mm board to faces of beams - 3 nr						
not exceeding 600 mm total girth	-	0.56	10.10	3.93	m	14.03
600 mm - 1200 mm total girth	-	1.06	19.22	6.56	m	25.78
1200 mm - 1800 mm total girth	-	1.43	26.08	9.18	m	35.26

K LININGS/SHEATHING/DRY PARTITIONING

Item	PC £	Labour hours	Labour £	Material £	Unit	Total rate £
50 mm board to walls						
wall height 2.40 m - 2.70 m	-	1.06	19.29	13.68	m	**32.98**
wall height 2.70 m - 3.00 m	-	1.30	23.61	15.22	m	**38.83**
wall height 3.00 m - 3.30 m	-	1.43	25.94	16.75	m	**42.69**
wall height 3.30 m - 3.60 m	-	1.71	31.03	18.31	m	**49.34**
50 mm board to reveals and soffits of openings and recesses						
not exceeding 300 mm wide	-	0.23	4.14	2.05	m	**6.19**
300 mm - 600 mm wide	-	0.46	8.29	3.43	m	**11.72**
50 mm board to faces of columns - 4 nr						
not exceeding 600 mm total girth	-	0.56	10.10	4.17	m	**14.27**
600 mm - 1200 mm total girth	-	1.11	20.09	6.94	m	**27.03**
1200 mm - 1800 mm total girth	-	1.43	26.01	9.70	m	**35.71**
50 mm board to ceilings						
over 300 mm wide	-	0.49	8.81	5.07	m²	**13.89**
50 mm board to faces of beams - 3 nr						
not exceeding 600 mm total girth	-	0.58	10.45	4.20	m	**14.65**
600 mm - 1200 mm total girth	-	1.17	21.14	7.00	m	**28.14**
1200 mm - 1800 mm total girth	-	1.57	28.52	9.80	m	**38.32**
White plastic faced gypsum plasterboard to BS 1230; industrial grade square edge wallboard; fixing with screws; butt joints; to softwood base						
12.50 mm board to walls						
wall height 2.40 m - 2.70 m	-	0.69	12.02	9.40	m	**21.43**
wall height 2.70 m - 3.00 m	-	0.83	14.46	10.44	m	**24.90**
wall height 3.00 m - 3.30 m	-	0.97	16.90	11.48	m	**28.38**
wall height 3.30 m - 3.60 m	-	1.11	19.34	12.52	m	**31.86**
12.50 mm board to reveals and soffits of openings and recesses						
not exceeding 300 mm wide	-	0.15	2.61	1.06	m	**3.67**
300 mm - 600 mm wide	-	0.30	5.23	2.09	m	**7.32**
12.50 mm board to faces of columns - 4 nr						
not exceeding 600 mm total girth	-	0.39	6.80	2.17	m	**8.97**
600 mm - 1200 mm total girth	-	0.78	13.59	4.30	m	**17.89**
1200 mm - 1800 mm total girth	-	1.02	17.77	6.39	m	**24.16**
Plasterboard jointing system; filling joint with jointing compounds						
To ceilings						
to suit 9.50 mm or 12.50 mm thick boards	-	0.09	1.57	1.91	m	**3.48**
Angle trim; plasterboard edge support system						
To ceilings						
to suit 9.50 mm or 12.50 mm thick boards	-	0.09	1.57	1.78	m	**3.35**
Gyproc SoundBloc plasterboard with higher density core; fixing with nails; joints filled with joint filler and joint tape to receive direct decoration; to softwood base						
Tapered edge board						
12.50 mm board to walls						
wall height 2.40 m - 2.70 m	-	0.97	17.72	5.95	m	**23.67**
wall height 2.70 m - 3.00 m	-	1.11	20.30	6.62	m	**26.92**
wall height 3.00 m - 3.30 m	-	1.24	22.70	7.28	m	**29.98**
wall height 3.30 m - 3.60 m	-	1.43	26.15	7.99	m	**34.13**

K LININGS/SHEATHING/DRY PARTITIONING

Item	PC £	Labour hours	Labour £	Material £	Unit	Total rate £
K10 PLASTERBOARD DRY LINING/ PARTITIONS/CEILINGS – cont'd						
Gyproc SoundBloc plasterboard – cont'd						
12.50 mm board to ceilings						
over 300 mm wide	-	0.41	7.42	2.21	m^2	9.62
15.00 mm board to walls						
wall height 2.40 m - 2.70 m	-	1.00	18.24	6.64	m	24.89
wall height 2.70 m - 3.00 m	-	1.14	20.82	7.38	m	28.21
wall height 3.00 m - 3.30 m	-	1.27	23.22	8.13	m	31.35
wall height 3.30 m - 3.60 m	-	1.46	26.67	8.90	m	35.57
15.00 mm board to reveals and soffits of openings and recesses						
not exceeding 300 mm wide	-	0.20	3.62	1.26	m	4.88
300 mm - 600 mm wide	-	0.38	6.89	1.86	m	8.75
15.00 mm board to ceilings						
over 300 mm wide	-	0.43	7.77	2.46	m^2	10.23
Two layers of gypsum plasterboard to BS 1230; plain grade square and tapered edge wallboard; fixing with nails; joints filled with joint filler and joint tape; top layer to receive direct decoration; to softwood base						
19 mm two layer board to walls						
wall height 2.40 m - 2.70 m	-	1.30	23.47	7.67	m	31.15
wall height 2.70 m - 3.00 m	-	1.48	26.75	8.54	m	35.28
wall height 3.00 m - 3.30m	-	1.67	30.19	9.40	m	39.59
wall height 3.30 m - 3.60m	-	1.94	35.03	10.29	m	45.32
19 mm two layer board to reveals and soffits of openings and recesses						
not exceeding 300 mm wide	-	0.28	5.02	1.40	m	6.42
300 mm - 600 mm wide	-	0.56	10.03	2.11	m	12.14
19 mm two layer board to faces of columns - 4 nr						
not exceeding 600 mm total girth	-	0.69	12.36	2.87	m	15.24
600 mm - 1200 mm total girth	-	1.34	24.10	4.30	m	28.40
1200 mm - 1800 mm total girth	-	1.67	30.19	5.72	m	35.91
25 mm two layer board to walls						
wall height 2.40 m - 2.70 m	-	1.39	25.04	8.23	m	33.27
wall height 2.70 m - 3.00 m	-	1.57	28.31	9.15	m	37.46
wall height 3.00 m - 3.30 m	-	1.76	31.76	10.07	m	41.83
wall height 3.30 m - 3.60 m	-	2.04	36.78	11.02	m	47.80
25 mm two layer board to reveals and soffits of openings and recesses						
not exceeding 300 mm wide	-	0.28	5.02	1.48	m	6.50
300 mm - 600 mm wide	-	0.56	10.03	2.24	m	12.27
25 mm two layer board to faces of columns - 4 nr						
not exceeding 600 mm total girth	-	0.69	12.36	3.04	m	15.40
600 mm - 1200 mm total girth	-	1.34	24.10	4.57	m	28.67
1200 mm - 1800 mm total girth	-	1.67	30.19	6.11	m	36.30
Gyproc Dri-Wall dry lining system or other equal or approved; plain grade tapered edge wallboard; fixed to walls with adhesive; joints filled with joint filler and joint tape; to receive direct decoration						
9.50 mm board to walls						
wall height 2.40 m - 2.70 m	-	1.11	20.16	5.67	m	25.83
wall height 2.70 m - 3.00 m	-	1.28	23.26	6.29	m	29.55

K LININGS/SHEATHING/DRY PARTITIONING

Item	PC £	Labour hours	Labour £	Material £	Unit	Total rate £
9.50 mm board to walls						
wall height 3.00 m - 3.30 m	-	1.43	26.01	6.91	m	**32.92**
wall height 3.30 m - 3.60 m	-	1.67	30.33	7.57	m	**37.90**
9.50 mm board to reveals and soffits of openings						
and recesses						
not exceeding 300 mm wide	-	0.23	4.14	1.10	m	**5.24**
300 mm - 600 mm wide	-	0.46	8.29	1.59	m	**9.88**
9.50 mm board to faces of columns - 4 nr						
not exceeding 600 mm total girth	-	0.58	10.45	2.19	m	**12.64**
600 mm - 1200 mm total girth	-	1.14	20.62	3.30	m	**23.91**
1200 mm - 1800 mm total girth	-	1.43	26.01	4.18	m	**30.19**
Angle; with joint tape bedded and covered with						
"Jointex" or other equal and approved						
internal	-	0.05	0.94	0.30	m	**1.24**
external	-	0.11	2.07	0.30	m	**2.37**
Gyproc Dri-Wall M/F dry lining system or						
other equal or approved; mild steel						
furrings fixed to walls with adhesive;						
tapered edge wallboard screwed to						
furrings; joints filled with joint filler and						
joint tape						
12.50 mm board to walls						
wall height 2.40 m - 2.70 m	-	1.48	26.61	8.54	m	**35.15**
wall height 2.70 m - 3.00 m	-	1.69	30.40	9.48	m	**39.89**
wall height 3.00 m - 3.30 m	-	1.90	34.20	10.44	m	**44.64**
wall height 3.30 m - 3.60 m	-	2.22	39.91	11.43	m	**51.34**
12.50 mm board to reveals and soffits of						
openings and recesses						
not exceeding 300 mm wide	-	0.23	4.14	0.97	m	**5.12**
300 mm - 600 mm wide	-	0.46	8.29	1.35	m	**9.64**
add for one coat of "Drywall" top coat or other						
equal and approved	-	0.04	0.75	0.67	m²	**1.42**
Lafarge plasterboard to BS 1230; fixing						
with screws; joints filled with joint filler						
and joint tape to receive direct						
decortaion; to softwood						
Megadeco wallboard						
12.50 mm board to walls						
wall height 2.40 m - 2.70 m	-	0.97	17.72	10.43	m	**28.16**
wall height 2.70 m - 3.00 m	-	1.11	20.30	11.60	m	**31.90**
wall height 3.00 m - 3.30 m	-	1.25	22.87	12.76	m	**35.63**
wall height 3.30 m - 3.60 m	-	1.43	26.15	13.92	m	**40.06**
12.50 mm board to ceilings						
over 300 mm wide	-	0.41	7.42	3.87	m²	**11.28**
Gypsum cladding; Glasroc "Firecase s"						
board or other equal and approved; fixed						
with adhesive; joints pointed in adhesive						
25 mm thick column linings, faces - 4; 2 hour fire						
protection rating						
not exceeding 600 mm girth	-	0.30	5.23	13.09	m	**18.32**
600 mm - 1200 mm girth	-	0.45	7.84	19.92	m	**27.76**
1200 mm - 1800 mm girth	-	0.60	10.45	26.75	m	**37.20**
30 mm thick beam linings, faces - 3; 2 hour fire						
protection rating						
not exceeding 600 mm girth	-	0.60	10.45	12.63	m	**23.09**
600 mm - 1200 mm girth	-	0.90	15.68	20.35	m	**36.03**
1200 mm - 1800 mm girth	-	1.20	20.91	28.06	m	**48.97**

K LININGS/SHEATHING/DRY PARTITIONING

Item	PC £	Labour hours	Labour £	Material £	Unit	Total rate £
K10 PLASTERBOARD DRY LINING/ PARTITIONS/CEILINGS – cont'd						
Vermiculite gypsum cladding; "Vermiculux" board or other equal and approved; fixed with adhesive; joints pointed in adhesive						
25 mm thick column linings, faces - 4; 2 hour fire protection rating						
not exceeding 600 mm girth	-	0.30	5.23	14.49	m	**19.72**
600 mm - 1200 mm girth	-	0.45	7.84	28.76	m	**36.60**
1200 mm - 1800 mm girth	-	0.60	10.45	43.02	m	**53.48**
30 mm thick beam linings, faces - 3; 2 hour fire protection rating						
not exceeding 600 mm girth	-	0.60	10.45	19.05	m	**29.51**
600 mm - 1200 mm girth	-	0.90	15.68	37.88	m	**53.56**
1200 mm - 1800 mm girth	-	1.20	20.91	56.71	m	**77.62**
55 mm thick column linings, faces - 4 ; 4 hour fire protection rating						
not exceeding 600 mm girth	-	0.35	6.10	40.56	m	**46.66**
600 mm - 1200 mm girth	-	0.50	8.71	80.90	m	**89.61**
1200 mm - 1800 mm girth	-	0.65	11.33	121.23	m	**132.56**
60 mm thick beam linings, faces - 3; 4 hour fire protection rating						
not exceeding 600 mm girth	-	0.70	12.20	43.83	m	**56.03**
600 mm - 1200 mm girth	-	1.00	17.42	87.44	m	**104.86**
1200 mm - 1800 mm girth	-	1.02	17.77	129.43	m	**147.21**
Add to the above for						
plus 3% for work 3.50 m - 5.00 m high						
plus 6% for work 5.00 m - 6.50 m high						
plus 12% for work 6.50 m - 8.00 m high						
plus 18% for work over 8.00 m high						
Cutting and fitting around steel joints, angles, trunking, ducting, ventilators, pipes, tubes, etc						
over 2 m girth	-	0.42	7.32	-	m	**7.32**
not exceeding 0.30 m girth	-	0.28	4.88	-	nr	**4.88**
0.30 m - 1 m girth	-	0.37	6.45	-	nr	**6.45**
1 m - 2 m girth	-	0.51	8.89	-	nr	**8.89**
K11 RIGID SHEET FLOORING/SHEATHING/ LININGS/CASINGS						
Blockboard (Birch faced)						
Linings to walls 12 mm thick						
over 300 mm wide	-	0.43	7.49	5.65	m²	**13.14**
not exceeding 300 mm wide	-	0.29	5.05	1.71	m	**6.76**
holes for pipes and the like	-	0.03	0.52	-	nr	**0.52**
Two-sided 12 mm thick pipe casing; to softwood framing (not included)						
300 mm girth	-	0.69	12.02	1.77	m	**13.80**
600 mm girth	-	0.83	14.46	3.41	m	**17.88**
Three-sided 12 mm thick pipe casing; to softwood framing (not included)						
450 mm girth	-	0.93	16.20	2.66	m	**18.87**
900 mm girth	-	1.11	19.34	5.14	m	**24.49**
extra for 400 mm x 400 mm removable access panel; brass cups and screws; additional framing	-	1.00	17.42	0.72	nr	**18.15**

K LININGS/SHEATHING/DRY PARTITIONING

Item	PC £	Labour hours	Labour £	Material £	Unit	Total rate £
Lining to walls 18 mm thick						
over 300 wide	5.50	0.46	8.02	6.54	m²	14.56
not exceeding 300 wide	-	0.30	5.23	1.98	m	7.20
holes for pipes and the like	-	0.04	0.70	-	nr	0.70
Lining to walls 25 mm thick						
over 300 wide	9.12	0.50	8.71	10.78	m²	19.49
not exceeding 300 wide	-	0.32	5.58	3.23	m	8.81
holes for pipes and the like	-	0.05	0.87	-	nr	0.87
Chipboard (plain)						
Lining to walls 12 mm thick						
over 300 mm wide	1.01	0.35	6.10	1.35	m²	7.44
not exceeding 300 mm wide	-	0.20	3.48	0.42	m	3.90
holes for pipes and the like	-	0.02	0.35	-	nr	0.35
Lining to walls 15 mm thick						
over 300 mm wide	1.26	0.37	6.45	1.64	m²	8.08
not exceeding 300 mm wide	-	0.22	3.83	0.50	m	4.34
holes for pipes and the like	-	0.03	0.52	-	nr	0.52
Two-sided 15 mm thick pipe casing; to softwood framing (not included)						
300 mm girth	-	0.56	9.76	0.57	m	10.33
600 mm girth	-	0.65	11.33	1.01	m	12.34
Three-sided 15 mm thick pipe casing; to softwood framing (not included)						
450 mm girth	-	1.16	20.21	0.86	m	21.07
900 mm girth	-	1.39	24.22	1.54	m	25.76
extra for 400 mm x 400 mm removable access panel; brass cups and screws; additional framing	-	0.93	16.20	0.72	nr	16.93
Lining to walls 18 mm thick						
over 300 mm wide	1.51	0.39	6.80	1.97	m²	8.77
not exceeding 300 mm wide	-	0.25	4.36	0.59	m	4.95
holes for pipes and the like	-	0.04	0.70	-	nr	0.70
Fire-retardent chipboard; Antivlam or other equal and approved; Class 1 spread of flame						
Lining to walls 12 mm thick						
over 300 mm wide	-	0.35	6.10	7.89	m²	13.99
not exceeding 300 mm wide	-	0.20	3.48	2.38	m	5.87
holes for pipes and the like	-	0.02	0.35	-	nr	0.35
Lining to walls 18 mm thick						
over 300 mm wide	-	0.39	6.80	10.41	m²	17.21
not exceeding 300 mm wide	-	0.25	4.36	3.14	m	7.49
holes for pipes and the like	-	0.04	0.70	-	nr	0.70
Lining to walls 22 mm thick						
over 300 mm wide	-	0.41	7.14	13.21	m²	20.36
not exceeding 300 mm wide	-	0.28	4.88	3.98	m	8.86
holes for pipes and the like	-	0.05	0.87	-	nr	0.87
Chipboard Melamine faced; white matt finish; laminated masking strips						
Lining to walls 15 mm thick						
over 300 mm wide	2.23	0.97	16.90	3.01	m²	19.91
not exceeding 300 mm wide	-	0.63	10.98	1.01	m	11.98
holes for pipes and the like	-	0.06	1.05	-	nr	1.05

K LININGS/SHEATHING/DRY PARTITIONING

Item	PC £	Labour hours	Labour £	Material £	Unit	Total rate £
K11 RIGID SHEET FLOORING/SHEATHING/ LININGS/CASINGS – cont'd						
Chipboard boarding and flooring						
Boarding to floors; butt joints						
18 mm thick	2.09	0.28	4.88	2.64	m²	7.52
22 mm thick	2.72	0.31	5.40	3.37	m²	8.77
Boarding to floors; tongued and grooved joints						
18 mm thick	2.07	0.30	5.23	2.62	m²	7.84
22 mm thick	2.57	0.32	5.58	3.20	m²	8.77
Boarding to roofs; butt joints						
18 mm thick	2.35	0.31	5.40	2.95	m²	8.35
Durabella "Westbourne" flooring system or other equal and approved; comprising 19 mm thick tongued and grooved chipboard panels secret nailed to softwood MK 10X-profiled foam backed battens at 600 mm centres; on concrete floor						
Flooring tongued and grooved joints						
63 mm thick overall; 44 mm x 54 mm nominal size battens	-	-	-	-	m²	20.10
75 mm thick overall; 56 mm x 54 mm nominal size battens	-	-	-	-	m²	22.07
Plywood flooring						
Boarding to floors; tongued and grooved joints						
15 mm thick	15.72	0.37	6.45	18.41	m²	24.86
18 mm thick	20.20	0.41	7.14	23.59	m²	30.74
Plywood; external quality; 18 mm thick						
Boarding to roofs; butt joints						
flat to falls	6.72	0.37	6.45	7.99	m²	14.44
sloping	6.72	0.40	6.97	7.99	m²	14.96
vertical	6.72	0.53	9.23	7.99	m²	17.23
Plywood; external quality; 12 mm thick						
Boarding to roofs; butt joints						
flat to falls	4.76	0.37	6.45	5.73	m²	12.18
sloping	4.76	0.40	6.97	5.73	m²	12.70
vertical	4.76	0.53	9.23	5.73	m²	14.97
Glazed hardboard to BS 1142; on and including 38 mm x 38 mm sawn softwood framing						
3.20 mm thick panel						
to side of bath	-	1.67	29.10	3.89	nr	32.98
to end of bath	-	0.65	11.33	1.11	nr	12.43
Insulation board to BS 1142						
Lining to walls 12 mm thick						
over 300 mm wide	1.76	0.22	3.83	2.21	m²	6.05
not exceeding 300 mm wide	-	0.13	2.27	0.68	m	2.94
holes for pipes and the like	-	0.01	0.17	-	nr	0.17
Lining to walls 18 mm thick						
over 300 mm wide	2.76	0.24	4.18	3.37	m²	7.55
not exceeding 300 mm wide	-	0.15	2.61	1.03	m	3.64
holes for pipes and the like	-	0.01	0.17	-	nr	0.17

K LININGS/SHEATHING/DRY PARTITIONING

Item	PC £	Labour hours	Labour £	Material £	Unit	Total rate £
Non-asbestos board; "Masterboard" or other equal and approved; sanded finish						
Lining to walls 6 mm thick						
over 300 mm wide	5.29	0.31	5.40	6.26	m²	11.66
not exceeding 300 mm wide	-	0.19	3.31	1.88	m	5.19
Lining to ceilings 6 mm thick						
over 300 mm wide	5.29	0.41	7.14	6.26	m²	13.40
not exceeding 300 mm wide	-	0.25	4.36	1.88	m	6.24
holes for pipes and the like	-	0.02	0.35	-	nr	0.35
Lining to walls 9 mm thick						
over 300 mm wide	11.18	0.33	5.75	13.07	m²	18.82
not exceeding 300 mm wide	-	0.19	3.31	3.93	m	7.24
Lining to ceilings 9 mm thick						
over 300 mm wide	11.18	0.42	7.32	13.07	m²	20.39
not exceeding 300 mm wide	-	0.27	4.70	3.93	m	8.63
holes for pipes and the like	-	0.03	0.52	-	nr	0.52
Non-asbestos board; "Supalux" or other equal and approved; sanded finish						
Lining to walls 6 mm thick						
over 300 mm wide	8.39	0.31	5.40	9.84	m²	15.24
not exceeding 300 mm wide	-	0.19	3.31	2.96	m	6.27
Lining to ceilings 6 mm thick						
over 300 mm wide	8.39	0.41	7.14	9.84	m²	16.98
not exceeding 300 mm wide	-	0.25	4.36	2.96	m	7.31
holes for pipes and the like	-	0.03	0.52	-	nr	0.52
Lining to walls 9 mm thick						
over 300 mm wide	12.48	0.33	5.75	14.57	m²	20.32
not exceeding 300 mm wide	-	0.19	3.31	4.38	m	7.69
Lining to ceilings 9 mm thick						
over 300 mm wide	12.48	0.42	7.32	14.57	m²	21.89
not exceeding 300 mm wide	-	0.27	4.70	4.38	m	9.08
holes for pipes and the like	-	0.03	0.52	-	nr	0.52
Lining to walls 12 mm thick						
over 300 mm wide	16.53	0.37	6.45	19.26	m²	25.70
not exceeding 300 mm wide	-	0.22	3.83	5.78	m	9.61
Lining to ceilings 12 mm thick						
over 300 mm wide	16.53	0.49	8.54	19.26	m²	27.79
not exceeding 300 mm wide	-	0.30	5.23	5.78	m	11.01
holes for pipes and the like	-	0.04	0.70	-	nr	0.70
Non-asbestos board; "Monolux 40" or other equal and approved; 6 mm x 50 mm "Supalux" cover fillets or other equal and approved one side						
Lining to walls 19 mm thick						
over 300 mm wide	29.54	0.65	11.33	35.82	m²	47.15
not exceeding 300 mm wide	-	0.46	8.02	12.18	m	20.19
Lining to walls 25 mm thick						
over 300 mm wide	35.42	0.69	12.02	42.62	m²	54.64
not exceeding 300 mm wide	10.63	0.49	8.54	14.22	m	22.75
Plywood (Far Eastern); internal quality						
Lining to walls 4 mm thick						
over 300 mm wide	1.69	0.34	5.92	2.14	m²	8.06
not exceeding 300 mm wide	-	0.22	3.83	0.65	m	4.49
Lining to ceilings 4 mm thick						
over 300 mm wide	1.69	0.46	8.02	2.14	m²	10.15
not exceeding 300 mm wide	-	0.30	5.23	0.65	m	5.88
holes for pipes and the like	-	0.02	0.35	-	nr	0.35

K LININGS/SHEATHING/DRY PARTITIONING

Item	PC £	Labour hours	Labour £	Material £	Unit	Total rate £
K11 RIGID SHEET FLOORING/SHEATHING/ LININGS/CASINGS - cont'd						
Plywood (Far Eastern); internal quality - cont'd						
Lining to walls 6 mm thick						
over 300 mm wide	2.35	0.37	6.45	2.90	m²	9.34
not exceeding 300 mm wide	-	0.24	4.18	0.88	m	5.06
Lining to ceilings 6 mm thick						
over 300 mm wide	2.35	0.49	8.54	2.90	m²	11.43
not exceeding 300 mm wide	-	0.32	5.58	0.88	m	6.46
holes for pipes and the like	-	0.02	0.35	-	nr	0.35
Two-sided 6 mm thick pipe casings; to softwood framing (not included)						
300 mm girth	-	0.74	12.89	0.95	m	13.84
600 mm girth	-	0.93	16.20	1.76	m	17.97
Three-sided 6 mm thick pipe casing; to softwood framing (not included)						
450 mm girth	-	1.06	18.47	1.42	m	19.89
900 mm girth	-	1.25	21.78	2.67	m	24.45
Lining to walls 9 mm thick						
over 300 mm wide	3.17	0.40	6.97	3.85	m²	10.82
not exceeding 300 mm wide	-	0.26	4.53	1.17	m	5.70
Lining to ceilings 9 mm thick						
over 300 mm wide	3.17	0.53	9.23	3.85	m²	13.08
not exceeding 300 mm wide	-	0.34	5.92	1.17	m	7.09
holes for pipes and the like	-	0.03	0.52	-	nr	0.52
Lining to walls 12 mm thick						
over 300 mm wide	3.99	0.43	7.49	4.80	m²	12.29
not exceeding 300 mm wide	-	0.28	4.88	1.45	m	6.33
Lining to ceilings 12 mm thick						
over 300 mm wide	3.99	0.56	9.76	4.80	m²	14.55
not exceeding 300 mm wide	-	0.37	6.45	1.45	m	7.90
holes for pipes and the like	-	0.03	0.52	-	nr	0.52
Plywood (Far Eastern); external quality						
Lining to walls 4 mm thick						
over 300 mm wide	1.97	0.34	5.92	2.46	m²	8.39
not exceeding 300 mm wide	-	0.22	3.83	0.75	m	4.59
Lining to ceilings 4 mm thick						
over 300 mm wide	1.97	0.46	8.02	2.46	m²	10.48
not exceeding 300 mm wide	-	0.30	5.23	0.75	m	5.98
holes for pipes and the like	-	0.02	0.35	-	nr	0.35
Lining to walls 6 mm thick						
over 300 mm wide	2.54	0.37	6.45	3.12	m²	9.57
not exceeding 300 mm wide	-	0.24	4.18	0.95	m	5.13
Lining to ceilings 6 mm thick						
over 300 mm wide	2.54	0.49	8.54	3.12	m²	11.66
not exceeding 300 mm wide	-	0.32	5.58	0.95	m	6.53
holes for pipes and the like	-	0.02	0.35	-	nr	0.35
Two-sided 6 mm thick pipe casings; to softwood framing (not included)						
300 mm girth	-	0.74	12.89	1.02	m	13.91
600 mm girth	-	0.93	16.20	1.90	m	18.11
Three-sided 6 mm thick pipe casing; to softwood framing (not included)						
450 mm girth	-	1.06	18.47	1.53	m	20.00
900 mm girth	-	1.25	21.78	2.87	m	24.65
Lining to walls 9 mm thick						
over 300 mm wide	3.65	0.40	6.97	4.40	m²	11.37
not exceeding 300 mm wide	-	0.26	4.53	1.33	m	5.87

K LININGS/SHEATHING/DRY PARTITIONING

Item	PC £	Labour hours	Labour £	Material £	Unit	Total rate £
Lining to ceilings 9 mm thick						
over 300 mm wide	3.65	0.53	9.23	4.40	m²	**13.64**
not exceeding 300 mm wide	-	0.34	5.92	1.33	m	**7.26**
holes for pipes and the like	-	0.03	0.52	-	nr	**0.52**
Lining to walls 12 mm thick						
over 300 mm wide	4.74	0.43	7.49	5.66	m²	**13.16**
not exceeding 300 mm wide	-	0.28	4.88	1.71	m	**6.59**
Lining to ceilings 12 mm thick						
over 300 mm wide	4.74	0.56	9.76	5.66	m²	**15.42**
not exceeding 300 mm wide	-	0.37	6.45	1.71	m	**8.16**
holes for pipes and the like	-	0.03	0.52	-	nr	**0.52**
Extra over wall linings fixed with nails for screwing	-	-	-	-	m²	**1.71**
Preformed white melamine faced						
plywood casings; Pendock Profiles Ltd						
or other equal and approved; to						
softwood battens (not included)						
Skirting trunking profile; plain butt joints in the running length						
45 mm x 150 mm; ref TK150	-	0.11	1.92	9.31	m	**11.23**
extra for stop end	-	0.04	0.70	7.77	nr	**8.46**
extra for external corner	-	0.09	1.57	9.56	nr	**11.13**
extra for internal corner	-	0.09	1.57	7.15	nr	**8.72**
Casing profiles						
150 mm x 150 mm; ref MX150/150; 5 mm thick	-	0.11	1.92	14.89	m	**16.81**
extra for stop end	-	0.04	0.70	6.07	nr	**6.76**
extra for external corner	-	0.09	1.57	22.55	nr	**24.12**
extra for internal corner	-	0.09	1.57	7.15	nr	**8.72**
Internal quality American Cherry						
veneered plywood; 6 mm thick						
Lining to walls						
over 300 mm wide	4.65	0.41	7.14	5.51	m²	**12.65**
not exceeding 300 mm wide	-	0.27	4.70	1.68	m	**6.38**
"Tacboard" or other equal and						
approved; Eternit UK Ltd; fire resisting						
boards; butt joints; to softwood base						
Lining to walls; 6 mm thick						
over 300 mm wide	-	0.31	5.40	9.24	m²	**14.64**
not exceeding 300 mm wide	-	0.19	3.31	2.80	m	**6.11**
Lining to walls; 9 mm thick						
over 300 mm wide	-	0.33	5.75	16.92	m²	**22.67**
not exceeding 300 mm wide	-	0.20	3.48	5.10	m	**8.59**
Lining to walls; 12 mm thick						
over 300 wide	-	0.37	6.45	21.99	m²	**28.43**
not exceeding 300 mm wide	-	0.22	3.83	6.62	m	**10.46**
"Tacfire" or other equal and approved;						
Eternit UK Ltd; fire resisting boards						
Lining to walls; 6 mm thick						
over 300 mm wide	-	0.31	5.40	12.37	m²	**17.77**
not exceeding 300 mm wide	-	0.19	3.31	3.74	m	**7.05**
Lining to walls; 9 mm thick						
over 300 mm wide	-	0.33	5.75	18.88	m²	**24.63**
not exceeding 300 mm wide	-	0.20	3.48	5.69	m	**9.17**
Lining to walls; 12 mm thick						
over 300 mm wide	-	0.37	6.45	24.86	m²	**31.31**
not exceeding 300 mm wide	-	0.22	3.83	7.48	m	**11.32**

K LININGS/SHEATHING/DRY PARTITIONING

Item	PC £	Labour hours	Labour £	Material £	Unit	Total rate £
K14 GLASS REINFORCED GYPSUM LININGS/ PANELLING/CASINGS/MOULDINGS						
Glass reinforced gypsum Glasroc Multi-board or other equal and approved; fixing with nails; joints filled with joint filler and joint tape; finishing with "Jointex" or other equal and approved to receive decoration; to softwood base						
10 mm board to walls						
wall height 2.40 m - 2.70 m	-	0.93	17.02	30.27	m	**47.29**
wall height 2.70 m - 3.00 m	-	1.06	19.43	33.64	m	**53.06**
wall height 3.00 m - 3.30 m	-	1.20	22.00	37.00	m	**59.00**
wall height 3.30 m - 3.60 m	-	1.39	25.45	40.41	m	**65.86**
12.50 mm board to walls						
wall height 2.40 m - 2.70 m	-	0.97	17.72	39.51	m	**57.23**
wall height 2.70 m - 3.00 m	-	1.11	20.30	43.90	m	**64.20**
wall height 3.00 m - 3.30 m	-	1.25	22.87	48.29	m	**71.17**
wall height 3.30 m - 3.60 m	-	1.43	26.15	52.72	m	**78.87**
K20 TIMBER BOARD FLOORING/SHEATHING/ LININGS/CASINGS						
Sawn softwood; untreated						
Boarding to roofs; 150 mm wide boards; butt joints						
19 mm thick; flat; over 300 mm wide	-	0.42	7.32	5.59	m²	**12.90**
19 mm thick; flat; not exceeding 300 mm wide	-	0.28	4.88	1.70	m	**6.58**
19 mm thick; sloping; over 300 mm wide	-	0.46	8.02	5.59	m²	**13.60**
19 mm thick; sloping; not exceeding 300 mm wide	-	0.31	5.40	1.70	m	**7.10**
19 mm thick; sloping; laid diagonally; over 300 mm wide	-	0.58	10.11	5.59	m²	**15.69**
19 mm thick; sloping; laid diagonally; not exceeding 300 mm wide	-	0.37	6.45	1.70	m	**8.15**
25 mm thick; flat; over 300 mm wide	-	0.42	7.32	6.14	m²	**13.46**
25 mm thick; flat; not exceeding 300 mm wide	-	0.28	4.88	1.86	m	**6.74**
25 mm thick; sloping; over 300 mm wide	-	0.46	8.02	6.14	m²	**14.16**
25 mm thick; sloping; not exceeding 300 mm wide	-	0.31	5.40	1.86	m	**7.27**
25 mm thick; sloping; laid diagonally; over 300 mm wide	-	0.58	10.11	6.14	m²	**16.25**
25 mm thick; sloping; laid diagonally; not exceeding 300 mm wide	-	0.37	6.45	1.86	m	**8.31**
Boarding to tops or cheeks of dormers; 150 mm wide boards; butt joints						
19 mm thick; laid diagonally; over 300 mm wide	-	0.74	12.89	5.59	m²	**18.48**
19 mm thick; laid diagonally; not exceeding 300 mm wide	-	0.46	8.02	1.70	m	**9.71**
19 mm thick; laid diagonally; area not exceeding 1.00 m2 irrespective of width	-	0.93	16.20	5.29	nr	**21.50**
Sawn softwood; "Tanalised"						
Boarding to roofs; 150 wide boards; butt joints						
19 mm thick; flat; over 300 mm wide	-	0.42	7.32	6.38	m²	**13.69**
19 mm thick; flat; not exceeding 300 mm wide	-	0.28	4.88	1.93	m	**6.81**
19 mm thick; sloping; over 300 mm wide	-	0.46	8.02	6.38	m²	**14.39**
19 mm thick; sloping; not exceeding 300 mm wide	-	0.31	5.40	1.93	m	**7.34**

K LININGS/SHEATHING/DRY PARTITIONING

Item	PC £	Labour hours	Labour £	Material £	Unit	Total rate £
19 mm thick; sloping; laid diagonally; over 300 mm wide	-	0.58	10.11	6.38	m²	16.48
19 mm thick; sloping; laid diagonally; not exceeding 300 mm wide	-	0.37	6.45	1.93	m	8.38
25 mm thick; flat; over 300 mm wide	-	0.42	7.32	7.18	m²	14.50
25 mm thick; flat; not exceeding 300 mm wide	-	0.28	4.88	2.18	m	7.06
25 mm thick; sloping; over 300 mm wide	-	0.46	8.02	7.18	m²	15.20
25 mm thick; sloping; not exceeding 300 mm wide	-	0.31	5.40	2.18	m	7.58
25 mm thick; sloping; laid diagonally; over 300 mm wide	-	0.58	10.11	7.18	m²	17.29
25 mm thick; sloping; laid diagonally; not exceeding 300 mm wide	-	0.37	6.45	2.18	m	8.63
Boarding to tops or cheeks of dormers; 150 mm wide boards; butt joints						
19 mm thick; laid diagonally; over 300 mm wide	-	0.74	12.89	6.38	m²	19.27
19 mm thick; laid diagonally; not exceeding 300 mm wide	-	0.46	8.02	1.93	m	9.95
19 mm thick; laid diagonally; area not exceeding 1.00 m2 irrespective of width	-	0.93	16.20	6.08	nr	22.29
Wrought softwood						
Boarding to floors; butt joints						
19 mm x 75 mm boards	-	0.56	9.76	7.38	m²	17.14
19 mm x 125 mm boards	-	0.51	8.89	8.16	m²	17.05
22 mm x 150 mm boards	-	0.46	8.02	8.75	m²	16.77
25 mm x 100 mm boards	-	0.51	8.89	9.45	m²	18.34
25 mm x 150 mm boards	-	0.46	8.02	10.15	m²	18.17
Boarding to floors; tongued and grooved joints						
19 mm x 75 mm boards	-	0.65	11.33	8.07	m²	19.40
19 mm x 125 mm boards	-	0.60	10.45	8.84	m²	19.30
22 mm x 150 mm boards	-	0.56	9.76	9.45	m²	19.21
25 mm x 100 mm boards	-	0.60	10.45	10.15	m²	20.60
25 mm x 150 mm boards	-	0.56	9.76	10.84	m²	20.60
Boarding to internal walls; tongued and grooved and V-jointed						
12 mm x 100 mm boards	-	0.74	12.89	7.62	m²	20.52
16 mm x 100 mm boards	-	0.74	12.89	10.26	m²	23.15
19 mm x 100 mm boards	-	0.74	12.89	11.53	m²	24.42
19 mm x 125 mm boards	-	0.69	12.02	12.17	m²	24.20
19 mm x 125 mm boards; chevron pattern	-	1.11	19.34	12.17	m²	31.51
25 mm x 125 mm boards	-	0.69	12.02	15.72	m²	27.74
12 mm x 100 mm boards; knotty pine	-	0.74	12.89	7.08	m²	19.98
Boarding to internal ceilings						
12 mm x 100 mm boards	-	0.93	16.20	7.62	m²	23.83
16 mm x 100 mm boards	-	0.93	16.20	10.26	m²	26.47
19 mm x 100 mm boards	PC	0.93	16.20	11.53	m²	27.73
19 mm x 125 mm boards	-	0.88	15.33	12.17	m²	27.51
19 mm x 125 mm boards; chevron pattern	-	1.30	22.65	12.17	m²	34.83
25 mm x 125 mm boards	-	0.88	15.33	15.72	m²	31.05
12 mm x 100 mm boards; knotty pine	-	0.93	16.20	7.08	m²	23.29
Boarding to roofs; tongued and grooved joints						
19 mm thick; flat to falls	-	0.51	8.89	10.39	m²	19.28
19 mm thick; sloping	-	0.56	9.76	10.39	m²	20.15
19 mm thick; sloping; laid diagonally	-	0.72	12.55	10.39	m²	22.94
25 mm thick; flat to falls	-	0.51	8.89	12.38	m²	21.27
25 mm thick; sloping	-	0.56	9.76	12.38	m²	22.14
Boarding to tops or cheeks of dormers; tongued and grooved joints						
19 mm thick; laid diagonally	-	0.93	16.20	10.39	m²	26.60

K LININGS/SHEATHING/DRY PARTITIONING

Item	PC £	Labour hours	Labour £	Material £	Unit	Total rate £
K20 TIMBER BOARD FLOORING/SHEATHING/ LININGS/CASINGS – cont'd						
Wrought softwood; "Tanalised"						
Boarding to roofs; tongued and grooved joints						
19 mm thick; flat to falls	-	0.51	8.89	11.18	m²	20.07
19 mm thick; sloping	-	0.56	9.76	11.18	m²	20.94
19 mm thick; sloping; laid diagonally	-	0.72	12.55	11.18	m²	23.73
25 mm thick; flat to falls	-	0.51	8.89	13.42	m²	22.31
25 mm thick; sloping	-	0.56	9.76	13.42	m²	23.18
Boarding to tops or cheeks of dormers; tongued and grooved joints						
19 mm thick; laid diagonally	-	0.93	16.20	11.18	m²	27.39
Wood strip; 22 mm thick; "Junckers" pre-treated or other equal and approved; tongued and grooved joints; pre-finished boards; level fixing to cement and sand base						
Strip flooring; over 300 mm wide						
Sylvasport Premium on 57 mm deep BluBat battens	-	-	-	-	m²	48.43
unsealed Sylvasport Premium on 57 mm deep BluBat battens	-	-	-	-	m²	53.27
beech Classic on battens	-	-	-	-	m²	58.12
oak Harmony on battens	-	-	-	-	m²	58.12
oak Harmony on polylay and clips	-	-	-	-	m²	61.99
Wrought hardwood						
Strip flooring to floors; 25 mm thick x 75 mm wide; tongue and grooved joints; secret fixing; surface sanded after laying						
american oak	-	-	-	-	m²	53.22
canadian maple	-	-	-	-	m²	56.55
gurjun	-	-	-	-	m²	49.89
iroko	-	-	-	-	m²	46.56
K30 DEMOUNTABLE PARTITIONS						
Insulated panel and two-hour fire wall system for warehouses etc., comprising white polyester coated galvanised steel frame and 0.55 mm galvanised steel panels either side of rockwool infill						
100 mm thick wall: 31 Rw dB acoustic rating	-	-	-	-	m²	41.00
150 mm thick wall: 31 Rw dB acoustic rating	-	-	-	-	m²	44.08
intumescent mastic sealant; bedding frames at perimeter of metal fire walls	-	-	-	-	m	3.59
Getalit laminated both sides top hung movable acoustic panel wall with concealed uPVC vertical edge profiles, 9 nr 1106 m x 3000 mm panels and type K two point panel support system						
105 mm thick wall: 47 Rw dB acoustic rating	-	-	-	-	m²	379.25
105 mm thick wall: 50 Rw dB acoustic rating	-	-	-	-	m²	410.00
105 mm thick wall: 53 Rw dB acoustic rating	-	-	-	-	m²	440.75

K LININGS/SHEATHING/DRY PARTITIONING

Item	PC £	Labour hours	Labour £	Material £	Unit	Total rate £
K32 FRAMED PANEL CUBICLE PARTITIONS						
Cubicle partitions; Armitage Shanks "Rapide" range or other equal and approved; standard colours; standard ironmongery; assembling; screwing to floor and wall						
Cubicle sets complete with doors						
range of 1 nr open ended cubicles; 1 nr panel; 1 nr door	-	2.08	36.24	288.20	nr	**324.44**
range of 3 nr open ended cubicles; 3 nr panel; 3 nr door	-	6.24	108.73	775.90	nr	**884.63**
range of 6 nr open ended cubicles; 6 nr panel; 6 nr door	-	12.50	217.81	1496.38	nr	**1714.19**
K33 CONCRETE/TERRAZZO PARTITIONS						
Terrazzo faced partitions; polished on two faces						
Pre-cast reinforced terrazzo faced WC partitions						
38 mm thick; over 300 mm wide	-	-	-	-	m²	**236.95**
50 mm thick; over 300 mm wide	-	-	-	-	m²	**246.55**
Wall post; once rebated						
64 mm x 102 mm	-	-	-	-	m	**109.47**
64 mm x 152 mm	-	-	-	-	m	**119.91**
Centre post; twice rebated						
64 mm x 102 mm	-	-	-	-	m	**114.26**
64 mm x 152 mm	-	-	-	-	m	**124.70**
Lintel; once rebated						
64 mm x 102 mm	-	-	-	-	m	**109.47**
Pair of brass topped plates or sockets cast into posts for fixings (not included)	-	-	-	-	nr	**27.63**
Brass indicator bolt lugs cast into posts for fixings (not included)	-	-	-	-	nr	**13.30**
K40 DEMOUNTABLE SUSPENDED CEILINGS						
Suspended ceilings; Donn Products exposed suspended ceiling system or other equal and approved; hangers plugged and screwed to concrete soffit; 600 mm x 600 mm x 15 mm Cape TAP Ceilings Ltd; "Solitude" tegular fissured tile						
Lining to ceilings; hangers average 400 mm long						
over 300 mm wide	-	0.32	6.07	9.50	m²	**15.57**
Suspended ceilings, Gyproc M/F suspended ceiling system or other equal and approved; hangers plugged and screwed to concrete soffit, 900 mm x 1800 mm x 12.50 mm tapered edge wallboard infill; joints filled with joint filler and taped to receive direct direction						
Lining to ceilings; hangers average 400 mm long						
over 300 mm wide	-	1.30	23.06	10.22	m²	**33.28**
not exceeding 300 mm wide in isolated strips	-	0.52	9.22	5.44	m	**14.66**
300 mm - 600 mm wide in isolated strips	-	0.82	14.53	6.07	m	**20.60**

Prices for Measured Works – Major Works

K LININGS/SHEATHING/DRY PARTITIONING

Item	PC £	Labour hours	Labour £	Material £	Unit	Total rate £
K40 DEMOUNTABLE SUSPENDED CEILINGS - cont'd						
Gyproc M/F suspended ceiling - cont'd						
Edge treatments						
20 x 20 mm SAS perimeter shadow gap; screwed to plasterboard	-	-	-	-	m	5.64
20 x 20 mm SAS shadow gap around 450 mm dia. column; including 15 x 44 mm batten plugged and screwed to concrete	-	-	-	-	nr	28.19
Vertical bulkhead; including additional hangers						
over 300 mm wide	-	1.50	26.62	10.81	m^2	37.43
not exceeding 300 mm wide in isolated strips	-	0.60	10.65	6.04	m	16.68
300 mm - 600 mm wide in isolated strips	-	0.95	16.84	6.67	m	23.51
Suspended ceilings; "Z" demountable suspended ceiling system or other equal and approved; hangers plugged and screwed to concrete soffit, 600 mm x 600 mm x 19 mm "Echostop" glass reinforced fibrous plaster lightweight plain bevelled edge tiles						
Lining to ceilings; hangers average 400 mm long						
over 300 mm wide	-	-	-	-	m^2	66.67
not exceeding 300 mm wide in isolated strips	-	-	-	-	m	31.78
Suspended ceilings; concealed galvanised steel suspension system; hangers plugged and screwed to concrete soffit, "Burgess" white stove enamelled perforated mild steel tiles 600 mm x 600 mm						
Lining to ceilings; hangers average 400 mm long						
over 300 mm wide	-	-	-	-	m^2	24.34
not exceeding 300 mm wide; in isolated strips	-	-	-	-	m	21.96
Suspended ceilings; concealed galvanised steel "Trulok" suspension system or other equal and approved; hangers plugged and screwed to concrete; Armstrong "Ultima Microlok BE Plain" 300 mm x 300 mm x 18 mm mineral ceiling tiles						
Linings to ceilings; hangers average 700 mm long						
over 300 mm wide	-	-	-	-	m^2	22.70
over 300 mm wide; 3.50 m - 5.00 m high	-	-	-	-	m^2	28.26
over 300 mm wide; in staircase areas or plant rooms	-	-	-	-	m^2	33.02
not exceeding 300 mm wide; in isolated strips	-	-	-	-	m	15.50
300 mm - 600 mm wide; in isolated strips	-	-	-	-	m	17.26
Extra for cutting and fitting around modular downlighter including yoke	-	-	-	-	nr	11.62
Vertical bulkhead; including additional hangers						
over 300 mm wide	-	-	-	-	m^2	43.91
not exceeding 300 mm wide; in isolated strips	-	-	-	-	m	34.07
300 mm - 600 mm wide; in isolated strips	-	-	-	-	m	39.15
24 mm x 19 mm white finished angle edge trim	-	-	-	-	m	2.68
Cutting and fitting around pipes; not exceeding 0.30 m girth	-	-	-	-	nr	3.58

K LININGS/SHEATHING/DRY PARTITIONING

Item	PC £	Labour hours	Labour £	Material £	Unit	Total rate £
Suspended ceilings; galvanised steel suspension system; hangers plugged and screwed to concrete soffit, "Luxalon" stove enamelled aluminium linear panel ceiling, type 80B or other equal and approved, complete with mineral insulation; PC £19.00/m2						
Linings to ceilings; hangers average 700 mm long						
over 300 mm wide	-	-	-	-	m^2	58.90
not exceeding 300 mm wide; in isolated strips	-	-	-	-	m	32.71
K41 RAISED ACCESS FLOORS						
Raised flooring system; laid on or fixed to concrete floor						
Full access system; 150 mm high overall; pedestal supports						
PSA light grade; steel finish	-	-	-	-	m^2	45.23
PSA medium grade; steel finish	-	-	-	-	m^2	51.67
PSA heavy grade; steel finish	-	-	-	-	m^2	58.12
Extra for						
factory applied needlepunch carpet	-	-	-	-	m^2	14.88
factory applied anti-static vinyl	-	-	-	-	m^2	32.28
factory applied black PVC edge strips	-	-	-	-	m	3.86
ramps; 3.00 m x 1.40 m (no finish)	-	-	-	-	nr	708.92
steps (no finish)	-	-	-	-	m	38.85
forming cut-out for electrical boxes	-	-	-	-	nr	8.72

L WINDOWS/DOORS/STAIRS

Item	PC £	Labour hours	Labour £	Material £	Unit	Total rate £
L10 WINDOWS/ROOFLIGHTS/SCREENS/ LOUVRES						
Standard windows; "treated" wrought softwood; Jeld-Wen or other equal and approved						
Side hung casement windows; factory glazed with low E 24mm double glazing; with 140 mm wide softwood sills; opening casements and ventilators hung on rustproof hinges; fitted with aluminized lacquered finish casement stays and fasteners						
500 mm x 750 mm; ref N07V	97.46	0.65	11.33	105.12	nr	**116.45**
500 mm x 900 mm; ref N09V	99.09	0.74	12.89	106.88	nr	**119.78**
600 mm x 750 mm; ref 107V	108.00	0.74	12.89	116.47	nr	**129.37**
600 mm x 750 mm; ref 107C	88.07	0.74	12.89	95.02	nr	**107.91**
600 mm x 900 mm; ref 109V	111.91	0.83	14.46	120.67	nr	**135.14**
600 mm x 900 mm; ref 109C	94.97	0.74	12.89	102.44	nr	**115.34**
600 mm x 1050 mm; ref 109V	117.09	0.74	12.89	126.33	nr	**139.22**
600 mm x 1050 mm; ref 110V	98.44	0.93	16.20	106.26	nr	**122.47**
915 mm x 900 mm; ref 2NO9W	134.63	1.02	17.77	145.13	nr	**162.90**
915 mm x 1050 mm; ref 2N1OW	141.44	1.06	18.47	152.53	nr	**171.00**
915 mm x 1200 mm; ref 2N12W	153.05	1.11	19.34	165.03	nr	**184.37**
915 mm x 1350 mm; ref 2N13W	160.45	1.25	21.78	173.00	nr	**194.78**
915 mm x 1500 mm; ref 2N15W	182.06	1.30	22.65	196.33	nr	**218.98**
1200 mm x 750 mm; ref 2O7C	138.38	1.06	18.47	149.24	nr	**167.71**
1200 mm x 750 mm; ref 2O7CV	175.02	1.06	18.47	188.67	nr	**207.14**
1200 mm x 900 mm; ref 2O9C	147.21	1.11	19.34	158.74	nr	**178.08**
1200 mm x 900 mm; ref 2O9W	154.91	1.11	19.34	167.03	nr	**186.37**
1200 mm x 900 mm; ref 2O9CV	182.88	1.11	19.34	197.14	nr	**216.48**
1200 mm x 1050 mm; ref 210C	155.83	1.25	21.78	168.10	nr	**189.88**
1200 mm x 1050 mm; ref 210W	164.20	1.25	21.78	177.11	nr	**198.89**
1200 mm x 1050 mm; ref 210T	193.74	1.25	21.78	208.90	nr	**230.68**
1200 mm x 1050 mm; ref 210CV	190.00	1.25	21.78	204.88	nr	**226.66**
1200 mm x 1200 mm; ref 212C	162.71	1.34	23.35	175.59	nr	**198.93**
1200 mm x 1200 mm; ref 212W	173.67	1.34	23.35	187.38	nr	**210.73**
1200 mm x 1200 mm; ref 212TX	225.69	1.34	23.35	243.37	nr	**266.72**
1200 mm x 1200 mm; ref 212CV	200.14	1.34	23.35	215.87	nr	**239.22**
1200 mm x 1350 mm; ref 213W	186.44	1.43	24.92	201.13	nr	**226.04**
1200 mm x 1350 mm; ref 213CV	221.36	1.43	24.92	238.71	nr	**263.63**
1200 mm x 1500 mm; ref 215W	216.21	1.57	27.36	233.24	nr	**260.60**
1770 mm x 750 mm; ref 307CC	203.23	1.30	22.65	219.19	nr	**241.85**
1770 mm x 900 mm; ref 309CC	216.23	1.57	27.36	233.19	nr	**260.54**
1770 mm x 1050 mm; ref 310C	204.93	1.62	28.23	221.02	nr	**249.25**
1770 mm x 1050 mm; ref 310T	270.13	1.57	27.36	291.19	nr	**318.55**
1770 mm x 1050 mm; ref 310CC	226.90	1.30	22.65	244.67	nr	**267.32**
1770 mm x 1050 mm; ref 310WW	238.94	1.30	22.65	257.63	nr	**280.28**
1770 mm x 1200 mm; ref 312C	218.85	1.67	29.10	236.08	nr	**265.18**
1770 mm x 1200 mm; ref 312T	262.37	1.67	29.10	282.92	nr	**312.02**
1770 mm x 1200 mm; ref 312CC	244.55	1.67	29.10	263.74	nr	**292.84**
1770 mm x 1200 mm; ref 312WW	253.29	1.67	29.10	273.14	nr	**302.24**
1770 mm x 1200 mm; ref 312CVC	285.33	1.67	29.10	307.64	nr	**336.73**
1770 mm x 1350 mm; ref 313CC	276.92	1.76	30.67	298.58	nr	**329.25**
1770 mm x 1350 mm; ref 313WW	275.80	1.76	30.67	297.38	nr	**328.04**
1770 mm x 1350 mm; ref 313CVC	310.67	1.76	30.67	334.90	nr	**365.57**
1770 mm x 1500 mm; ref 315T	329.48	1.85	32.24	355.14	nr	**387.38**
2340 mm x 1050 mm; ref 410CWC	315.18	1.80	31.36	339.76	nr	**371.12**
2340 mm x 1200 mm; ref 412CWC	334.82	1.90	33.11	360.98	nr	**394.08**
2340 mm x 1350 mm; ref 413CWC	368.16	2.04	35.55	396.94	nr	**432.48**

L WINDOWS/DOORS/STAIRS

Item	PC £	Labour hours	Labour £	Material £	Unit	Total rate £
Top hung casement windows; factory glazed with low E 24mm double glazing; with 140 mm wide softwood sills; opening casements and ventilators hung on rustproof hinges; fitted with aluminized lacquered finish casement stays						
600 mm x 750 mm; ref 107A	94.95	0.74	12.89	102.42	nr	115.31
600 mm x 900 mm; ref 109A	100.21	0.83	14.46	108.08	nr	122.55
600 mm x 1050 mm; ref 110A	106.16	0.93	16.20	114.57	nr	130.77
915 mm x 750 mm; ref 2N07A	115.30	0.97	16.90	124.33	nr	141.23
915 mm x 900 mm; ref 2N09A	129.37	1.02	17.77	139.47	nr	157.24
915 mm x 1050 mm; ref 2N10A	137.63	1.06	18.47	148.44	nr	166.91
915 mm x 1350 mm; ref 2N13AS	174.17	1.25	21.78	187.84	nr	209.62
1200 mm x 750 mm; ref 207A	135.67	1.06	18.47	146.32	nr	164.79
1200 mm x 900 mm; ref 209A	148.07	1.11	19.34	159.67	nr	179.01
1200 mm x 1050 mm; ref 210A	158.30	1.25	21.78	170.76	nr	192.54
1200 mm x 1200 mm; ref 212A	171.57	1.34	23.35	185.04	nr	208.39
1200 mm x 1350 mm; ref 213AS	200.33	1.43	24.92	216.07	nr	240.99
1200 mm x 1500 mm; ref 215AS	218.61	1.57	27.36	235.74	nr	263.10
1770 mm x 1050 mm; ref 310AE	219.18	1.57	27.36	236.35	nr	263.71
1770 mm x 1200 mm; ref 312A	233.57	1.67	29.10	251.84	nr	280.94
High performance single light with canopy sash windows; factory glazed with low E 24mm double glazing; ventilators; weather stripping; opening sashes and fanlights hung on rustproof hinges; fitted with aluminized lacquered espagnolette bolts						
600 mm x 900 mm; ref AL0609	140.35	0.83	14.46	151.29	nr	165.75
900 mm x 900 mm; ref AL0909	145.61	1.02	17.77	156.94	nr	174.72
900 mm x 1050 mm; ref AL0910	146.38	1.06	18.47	157.78	nr	176.25
900 mm x 1200 mm; ref AL0912	149.29	1.16	20.21	160.98	nr	181.19
900 mm x 1500 mm; ref AL0915	157.30	1.30	22.65	169.61	nr	192.26
1200 mm x 1050 mm; ref AL1210	169.66	1.25	21.78	182.91	nr	204.69
1200 mm x 1200 mm; ref AL1212	170.74	1.34	23.35	184.15	nr	207.50
1200 mm x 1500 mm; ref AL1215	192.76	1.57	27.36	207.93	nr	235.29
1500 mm x 1050 mm; ref AL1510	169.94	1.53	26.66	183.29	nr	209.95
1500 mm x 1200 mm; ref AL1512	178.46	1.57	27.36	192.46	nr	219.81
1500 mm x 1500 mm; ref AL1515	192.19	1.67	29.10	207.39	nr	236.48
1500 mm x 1650 mm; ref AL1516	198.36	1.76	30.67	213.96	nr	244.62
High performance double hung sash windows with glazing bars; factory glazed with low E 24mm double glazing; solid frames; 63 mm x 175 mm softwood sills; standard flush external linings; spiral spring balances and sash catch						
635 mm x 1050 mm; ref VS0610B	265.06	1.85	32.24	285.58	nr	317.81
635 mm x 1350 mm; ref VS0613B	274.98	2.04	35.55	296.33	nr	331.88
635 mm x 1650 mm; ref VS0616B	293.09	2.27	39.55	315.90	nr	355.46
860 mm x 1050 mm; ref VS0810B	278.22	2.13	37.11	299.75	nr	336.86
860 mm x 1350 mm; ref VS0813B	293.33	2.41	41.99	316.09	nr	358.08
860 mm x 1650 mm; ref VS0816B	323.17	2.78	48.44	348.28	nr	396.72
1085 mm x 1050 mm; ref VS1010B	298.15	2.41	41.99	321.20	nr	363.19
1085 mm x 1350 mm; ref VS1013B	322.21	2.78	48.44	347.16	nr	395.60
1085 mm x 1650 mm; ref VS1016B	350.31	3.42	59.59	377.49	nr	437.08
1725 mm x 1050 mm; ref VS1710B	484.18	3.42	59.59	521.48	nr	581.08
1725 mm x 1350 mm; ref VS1713B	515.54	4.26	74.23	555.31	nr	629.54
1725 mm x 1650 mm; ref VS1716B	574.56	4.35	75.80	618.92	nr	694.71

L WINDOWS/DOORS/STAIRS

Item	PC £	Labour hours	Labour £	Material £	Unit	Total rate £
L10 WINDOWS/ROOFLIGHTS/SCREENS/ LOUVRES – cont'd						
Standard windows; Jeld-Wen Hardwood or other equal and approved; factory applied preservative stain base coat						
Side hung casement windows; factory glazed with low E 24mm double glazing; 45 mm x 140 mm hardwood sills; weather stripping; opening sashes on canopy hinges; fitted with fasteners; brown finish ironmongery						
630 mm x 750 mm; ref LEW107CH	173.06	0.88	15.33	186.49	nr	**201.82**
630 mm x 900 mm; ref LEW109CH	183.00	1.11	19.34	197.18	nr	**216.52**
630 mm x 900 mm; ref LEW109VH	201.26	0.88	15.33	216.84	nr	**232.17**
630 mm x 1050 mm; ref LEW110VH	209.34	1.20	20.91	225.54	nr	**246.45**
915 mm x 900 mm; ref LEW2N09WH	247.36	1.39	24.22	266.53	nr	**290.75**
915 mm x 1050 mm; ref LEW2N10WH	257.13	1.48	25.79	277.13	nr	**302.91**
915 mm x 1200 mm; ref LEW2N12WH	268.46	1.57	27.36	289.32	nr	**316.68**
915 mm x 1350 mm; ref LEW2N13WH	279.53	1.67	29.10	301.24	nr	**330.33**
915 mm x 1550 mm; ref LEW2N15WH	308.19	1.76	30.67	332.16	nr	**362.83**
1200 mm x 900 mm; ref LEW209CH	269.52	1.57	27.36	290.30	nr	**317.66**
1200 mm x 900 mm; ref LEW209WH	339.46	1.57	27.36	365.58	nr	**392.93**
1200 mm x 1050 mm; ref LEW210CH	278.33	1.67	29.10	299.78	nr	**328.88**
1200 mm x 1050 mm; ref LEW210CVH	355.35	1.67	29.10	382.68	nr	**411.78**
1200 mm x 1200 mm; ref LEW212CH	305.61	1.80	31.36	329.22	nr	**360.59**
1200 mm x 1200 mm; ref LEW212CVH	372.54	1.80	31.36	401.25	nr	**432.62**
1200 mm x 1350 mm; ref LEW213CVH	457.52	1.94	33.80	492.72	nr	**526.52**
1200 mm x 1550 mm; ref LEW215CVH	426.46	2.04	35.55	459.29	nr	**494.83**
1770 mm x 1050 mm; ref LEW310CCH	425.17	2.08	36.24	457.98	nr	**494.22**
1770 mm x 1200 mm ; ref LEW312CCH	452.80	2.22	38.68	487.72	nr	**526.40**
2339 mm x 1200 mm; ref LEW412CMCH	584.93	2.41	41.99	630.00	nr	**671.99**
Top hung casement windows; factory glazed with low E 24mm double glazing; 45 mm x 140 mm hardwood sills; weather stripping; opening sashes on canopy hinges; fitted with fasteners; brown finish ironmongery						
630 mm x 900 mm; ref LEW109AH	192.22	0.88	15.33	207.12	nr	**222.45**
630 mm x 1050 mm; ref LEW110AH	201.65	1.20	20.91	217.34	nr	**238.25**
915 mm x 900 mm; ref LEW2N09AH	248.46	1.39	24.22	267.64	nr	**291.86**
915 mm x 1050 mm; ref LEW2N10AH	262.44	1.48	25.79	282.77	nr	**308.55**
915 mm x 1350 mm; ref LEW2N13ASH	302.38	1.67	29.10	325.83	nr	**354.93**
1200 mm x 1050 mm; ref LEW210AH	299.41	1.57	27.36	322.55	nr	**349.91**
1200 mm x 1350 mm; ref LEW212 ASH	318.88	1.67	29.10	343.51	nr	**372.61**
1770 mm x 1050 mm; ref LEW310AEH	403.23	1.80	31.36	434.37	nr	**465.73**
Purpose made window casements; "treated" wrought softwood						
Casements; rebated; moulded - supply only						
44 mm thick	-	-	-	48.33	m²	**48.33**
57 mm thick	-	-	-	50.75	m²	**50.75**
Casements; rebated; moulded; in medium panes - supply only						
44 mm thick	-	-	-	77.26	m²	**77.26**
57 mm thick	-	-	-	80.50	m²	**80.50**

L WINDOWS/DOORS/STAIRS

Item	PC £	Labour hours	Labour £	Material £	Unit	Total rate £
Casements; rebated; moulded; with semi-circular head - supply only						
44 mm thick	-	-	-	101.02	m^2	101.02
57 mm thick	-	-	-	104.18	m^2	104.18
Casements; rebated; moulded; to bullseye window - supply only						
44 mm thick; 600 mm diameter	-	-	-	160.12	nr	160.12
44 mm thick; 900 mm diameter	-	-	-	190.75	nr	190.75
57 mm thick; 600 mm diameter	-	-	-	167.66	nr	167.66
57 mm thick; 900 mm diameter	-	-	-	23.07	nr	23.07
Fitting and hanging casements						
square or rectangular	-	-	-	11.30	nr	11.30
semi-circular	-	-	-	18.36	nr	18.36
bullseye	-	-	-	23.07	nr	23.07
Purpose made window casements; selected Sapele						
Casements; rebated; moulded - supply only						
44 mm thick	-	-	-	54.94	m^2	54.94
57 mm thick	-	-	-	60.19	m^2	60.19
Casements; rebated; moulded; in medium panes - supply only						
44 mm thick	-	-	-	88.96	m^2	88.96
57 mm thick	-	-	-	95.99	m^2	95.99
Casements; rebated; moulded with semi-circular head - supply only						
44 mm thick	-	-	-	112.07	m^2	112.07
57 mm thick	-	-	-	118.93	m^2	118.93
Casements; rebated; moulded; to bullseye window - supply only						
44 mm thick; 600 mm diameter	-	-	-	198.07	nr	198.07
44 mm thick; 900 mm diameter	-	-	-	238.37	nr	238.37
57 mm thick; 600 mm diameter	-	-	-	214.41	nr	214.41
57 mm thick; 900 mm diameter	-	-	-	259.18	nr	259.18
Fitting and hanging casements						
square or rectangular	-	-	-	12.24	nr	12.24
semi-circular	-	-	-	20.25	nr	20.25
bullseye	-	-	-	25.90	nr	25.90
Purpose made window frames; "treated" wrought softwood; prices indicated are for supply only as part of a complete window frame; the reader is referred to the previous pages for fixing costs for frames based on the overall window size						
Frames; rounded; rebated check grooved						
44 mm x 69 mm	-	-	-	13.14	m	13.14
44 mm x 94 mm	-	-	-	13.77	m	13.77
44 mm x 119 mm	-	-	-	14.40	m	14.40
57 mm x 94 mm	-	-	-	14.43	m	14.43
69 mm x 144 mm	-	-	-	19.02	m	19.02
90 mm x 140 mm	-	-	-	26.99	m	26.99
Mullions and transoms; twice rounded, rebated and check grooved						
57 mm x 69 mm	-	-	-	15.30	m	15.30
57 mm x 94 mm	-	-	-	16.08	m	16.08
69 mm x 94 mm	-	-	-	18.18	m	18.18
69 mm x 144 mm	-	-	-	26.70	m	26.70

L WINDOWS/DOORS/STAIRS

Item	PC £	Labour hours	Labour £	Material £	Unit	Total rate £
L10 WINDOWS/ROOFLIGHTS/SCREENS/ LOUVRES – cont'd						
Purpose made softwood window frames – cont'd						
Sill; sunk weathered, rebated and grooved						
69 mm x 94 mm	-	-	-	31.92	m	**31.92**
69 mm x 144 mm	-	-	-	33.79	m	**33.79**
Add 5% to the above material prices for "selected" softwood for staining						**5%**
Purpose made window frames; selected Sapele; prices given are for supply only as part of a complete window frame; the reader is referred to the previous pages for fixing costs for frames based on the overall window size						
Frames; rounded; rebated check grooved						
44 mm x 69 mm	-	-	-	16.77	m	**16.77**
44 mm x 94 mm	-	-	-	18.05	m	**18.05**
44 mm x 119 mm	-	-	-	19.31	m	**19.31**
57 mm x 94 mm	-	-	-	21.12	m	**21.12**
69 mm x 144 mm	-	-	-	30.26	m	**30.26**
90 mm x 140 mm	-	-	-	42.98	m	**42.98**
Mullions and transoms; twice rounded, rebated and check grooved						
57 mm x 69 mm	-	-	-	19.06	m	**19.06**
57 mm x 94 mm	-	-	-	22.18	m	**22.18**
69 mm x 94 mm	-	-	-	26.60	m	**26.60**
69 mm x 144 mm	-	-	-	40.42	m	**40.42**
Sill; sunk weathered, rebated and grooved						
69 mm x 94 mm	-	-	-	37.67	m	**37.67**
69 mm x 144 mm	-	-	-	41.76	m	**41.76**
Purpose made double hung sash windows; "treated" wrought softwood						
Cased frames of 100 mm x 25 mm grooved inner linings; 114 mm x 25 mm grooved outer linings; 125 mm x 38 mm twice rebated head linings; 125 mm x 32 mm twice rebated grooved pulley stiles; 150 mm x 13 mm linings; 50 mm x 19 mm parting slips; 25 mm x 19 mm inside beads; 150 mm x 75 mm Oak twice sunk weathered throated sill; 50 mm thick rebated and moulded sashes and horns.						
over 1.25 m² each; both sashes in medium panes; including spiral spring balances	338.05	2.08	36.24	429.90	m²	**466.14**
As above but with cased mullions	384.24	2.31	40.25	479.61	m²	**519.86**
Purpose made double hung sash windows; selected Sapele						
Cased frames of 100 mm x 25 mm grooved inner linings; 114 mm x 25 mm grooved outer linings; 125 mm x 38 mm twice rebated head linings; 125 mm x 32 mm twice rebated grooved pulley stiles; 150 mm x 13 mm linings; 50 mm x 19 mm parting slips; 25 mm x 19 mm inside beads; 150 mm x 75 mm Oak twice sunk weathered throated sill; 50 mm thick rebated and moulded sashes and horns.						
over 1.25 m² each; both sashes in medium panes; including spiral sash balances	376.28	2.78	48.44	471.04	m²	**519.48**
As above but with cased mullions	403.75	3.08	53.67	500.61	m²	**554.28**

L WINDOWS/DOORS/STAIRS

Item	PC £	Labour hours	Labour £	Material £	Unit	Total rate £
uPVC windows; Jeld-Wen or other equal and approved; reinforced where appropriate with aluminium alloy; including standard ironmongery; cills and factory glazed with low E 24mm double glazing; fixed in position; including lugs plugged and screwed to brickwork or blockwork						
Casement/fixed light; including e.p.d.m. glazing gaskets and weather seals						
630 mm x 900 mm; ref P109C	79.05	1.39	24.22	85.39	nr	109.61
630 mm x 1200 mm; ref P112V	99.67	1.62	28.23	107.66	nr	135.89
1200 mm x 1200 mm; ref P212C	115.71	1.85	32.24	125.00	nr	157.24
1770 mm x 1200 mm; ref P312CC	187.89	1.85	32.24	202.68	nr	234.92
Casement/fixed light; including vents; e.p.d.m. glazing gaskets and weather seals						
630 mm x 900 mm; ref P109V	90.51	1.39	24.22	97.72	nr	121.94
630 mm x 1200 mm; ref P112C	88.22	1.62	28.23	95.33	nr	123.56
1200 mm x 1200 mm; ref P212W	115.71	1.85	32.24	125.00	nr	157.24
1200 mm x 1200 mm; ref P212CV	165.55	1.85	32.24	178.64	nr	210.87
1770 mm x 1200 mm; ref P312WW	198.20	1.85	32.24	213.78	nr	246.01
1770 mm x 1200 mm; ref P312CV	225.69	1.85	32.24	243.37	nr	275.60
Galvanised steel fixed, casement and fanlight windows; Crittall "Homelight" range or other equal and approved; site glazing not included; fixed in position including lugs plugged and screwed to brickwork or blockwork						
Basic fixed lights; including easy-glaze beads						
628 mm x 292 mm; ref ZNG5	19.73	1.11	19.34	21.39	nr	40.73
628 mm x 923 mm; ref ZNC5	27.08	1.11	19.34	29.38	nr	48.72
628 mm x 1513 mm; ref ZNDV5	38.68	1.11	19.34	42.02	nr	61.36
1237 mm x 292 mm; ref ZNG13	30.94	1.11	19.34	33.46	nr	52.80
1237 mm x 923 mm; ref ZNC13	38.68	1.62	28.23	41.86	nr	70.09
1237 mm x 1218 mm; ref ZND13	46.41	1.62	28.23	50.26	nr	78.49
1237 mm x 1513 mm; ref ZNDV13	50.28	1.62	28.23	54.50	nr	82.73
1846 mm x 292 mm; ref ZNG14	38.68	1.11	19.34	41.86	nr	61.20
1846 mm x 923 mm; ref ZNC14	46.41	1.62	28.23	50.34	nr	78.57
1846 mm x 1513 mm; ref ZNDV14	58.01	2.04	35.55	62.98	nr	98.53
Basic opening lights; including easy-glaze beads and weatherstripping						
628 mm x 292 mm; ref ZNG1	50.28	1.11	19.34	54.27	nr	73.61
1237 mm x 292 mm; ref ZNG13G	73.48	1.11	19.34	79.24	nr	98.58
1846 mm x 292 mm; ref ZNG4	123.76	1.11	19.34	133.51	nr	152.85
One piece composites; including easy-glaze beads and weatherstripping						
628 mm x 923 mm; ref ZNC5F	69.62	1.11	19.34	75.16	nr	94.50
628 mm x 1513 mm; ref ZNDV5F	81.22	1.11	19.34	87.81	nr	107.15
1237 mm x 923 mm; ref ZNC2F	131.50	1.62	28.23	141.76	nr	169.99
1237 mm x 1218 mm; ref ZND2F	154.71	1.62	28.23	166.81	nr	195.04
1237 mm x 1513 mm; ref ZNDV2V	181.78	1.62	28.23	196.03	nr	224.26
1846 mm x 923 mm; ref ZNC4F	201.12	1.62	28.23	216.84	nr	245.07
1846 mm x 1218 mm; ref ZND10F	193.39	2.04	35.55	208.60	nr	244.14
Reversible windows; including easy-glaze beads						
997 mm x 923 mm; ref NC13R	174.04	1.43	24.92	187.55	nr	212.46
997 mm x 1067 mm; ref NCO13R	181.78	1.43	24.92	195.88	nr	220.80
1237 mm x 923 mm; ref ZNC13R	189.52	2.13	37.11	204.20	nr	241.32
1237 mm x 1218 mm; ref ZND13R	204.99	2.13	37.11	220.93	nr	258.04
1237 mm x 1513 mm; ref ZNDV13RS	232.06	2.13	37.11	250.14	nr	287.25

L WINDOWS/DOORS/STAIRS

Item	PC £	Labour hours	Labour £	Material £	Unit	Total rate £
L10 WINDOWS/ROOFLIGHTS/SCREENS/ LOUVRES – cont'd						
Galvanised steel windows – cont'd						
Pressed steel sills; to suit above window widths						
628 mm long	12.00	0.32	5.58	12.91	nr	18.49
997 mm long	15.47	0.42	7.32	16.65	nr	23.97
1237 mm long	19.73	0.51	8.89	21.23	nr	30.12
1846 mm long	27.08	0.69	12.02	29.14	nr	41.16
Factory finished steel fixed light; casement and fanlight windows; Crittall polyester powder coated "Homelight" range or other equal and approved; site glazing not included; fixed in position; including lugs plugged and screwed to brickwork or blockwork						
Basic fixed lights; including easy-glaze beads						
628 mm x 292 mm; ref ZNG5	25.13	1.11	19.34	27.21	nr	46.55
628 mm x 923 mm; ref ZNC5	34.81	1.11	19.34	37.70	nr	57.04
628 mm x 1513 mm; ref ZNDV5	50.28	1.11	19.34	54.50	nr	73.84
1237 mm x 292 mm; ref ZNG13	38.68	1.11	19.34	41.78	nr	61.12
1237 mm x 923 mm; ref ZNC13	50.28	1.62	28.23	54.35	nr	82.58
1237 mm x 1218 mm; ref ZND13	58.01	1.62	28.23	62.75	nr	90.98
1237 mm x 1513 mm; ref ZNDV13	61.88	1.62	28.23	66.99	nr	95.22
1846 mm x 292 mm; ref ZNG14	50.28	1.11	19.34	54.27	nr	73.61
1846 mm x 923 mm; ref ZNC14	61.88	1.62	28.23	66.83	nr	95.06
1846 mm x 1513 mm; ref ZNDV14	73.48	2.04	35.55	79.48	nr	115.02
Basic opening lights; including easy-glaze beads and weatherstripping						
628 mm x 292 mm; ref ZNG1	59.94	1.11	19.34	64.67	nr	84.01
1237 mm x 292 mm; ref ZNG13G	85.09	1.11	19.34	91.74	nr	111.08
1846 mm x 292 mm; ref ZNG4	146.97	1.11	19.34	158.34	nr	177.68
One piece composites; including easy-glaze beads and weatherstripping						
628 mm x 923 mm; ref ZNC5F	81.22	1.11	19.34	87.65	nr	106.99
628 mm x 1513 mm; ref ZNDV5F	100.56	1.11	19.34	108.62	nr	127.96
1237 mm x 923 mm; ref ZNC2F	162.44	1.62	28.23	175.06	nr	203.29
1237 mm x 1218 mm; ref ZND2F	185.65	1.62	28.23	200.04	nr	228.27
1237 mm x 1513 mm; ref ZNDV2V	216.59	1.62	28.23	233.49	nr	261.72
1846 mm x 923 mm; ref ZNC4F	243.67	1.62	28.23	262.48	nr	290.71
1846 mm x 1218 mm; ref ZND10F	232.06	2.04	35.55	250.14	nr	285.69
Reversible windows; including easy-glaze beads						
997 mm x 923 mm; ref NC13R	224.32	1.43	24.92	241.66	nr	266.58
997 mm x 1218 mm; ref NCO13R	235.93	1.43	24.92	254.15	nr	279.07
1237 mm x 923 mm; ref ZNC13R	243.67	2.13	37.11	262.48	nr	299.59
1237 mm x 1218 mm; ref ZND13R	266.87	2.13	37.11	287.53	nr	324.64
1237 mm x 1513 mm; ref ZNDV13RS	297.81	2.13	37.11	320.91	nr	358.02
Pressed steel sills; to suit above window widths						
628 mm long	15.47	0.32	5.58	16.65	nr	22.22
997 mm long	20.89	0.42	7.32	22.48	nr	29.80
1237 mm long	24.75	0.51	8.89	26.64	nr	35.53
1846 mm long	34.81	0.69	12.02	37.47	nr	49.49

L WINDOWS/DOORS/STAIRS

Item	PC £	Labour hours	Labour £	Material £	Unit	Total rate £
Rooflights, skylights, roof windows and frames; pre-glazed; "treated" Nordic Red Pine and aluminium trimmed "Velux" windows or other equal and approved; type U flashings and soakers (for tiles and pantiles), and sealed double glazing unit (trimming opening not included)						
Roof windows						
550 mm x 780 mm; ref GGL-3000-C02	105.68	1.85	32.24	114.00	nr	146.23
550 mm x 980 mm; ref GGL-3000-C04	116.42	2.08	36.24	125.56	nr	161.80
660 mm x 1180 mm; ref GGL-3000-F06	137.94	2.31	40.25	148.77	nr	189.02
780 mm x 980 mm; ref GGL-3000-M04	131.59	2.31	40.25	141.93	nr	182.18
780 mm x 1180 mm; ref GGL-3000-M06	147.52	2.78	48.44	159.23	nr	207.67
780 mm x 1400 mm; ref GGL-3000-M08	159.00	2.31	40.25	171.54	nr	211.79
940 mm x 1600 mm; ref GGL-3000-P10	190.34	2.78	48.44	205.32	nr	253.76
1140 mm x 1180 mm; ref GGL-3000-S06	175.60	2.78	48.44	189.46	nr	237.90
1340 mm x 980 mm; ref GGL-3000-U04	181.36	2.78	48.44	195.66	nr	244.10
Rooflights, skylights, roof windows and frames; uPVC; plugged and screwed to concrete; or screwed to timber						
Rooflight; Cox "Suntube" range or other equal and approved; double skin polycarbonate dome						
230 mm dia.; for flat roof using felt or membrane	220.15	2.50	43.56	237.47	nr	281.03
230 mm dia.; for up to 30 degree pitch roof with standard tiles	220.15	3.00	52.27	237.37	nr	289.64
230 mm dia.; for up to 30 degree pitch roof with bold roll tiles	279.65	3.00	52.27	301.46	nr	353.73
Rooflight; Cox "Galaxy" range or other equal and approved; double skin polycarbonate dome						
600 mm x 600 mm	94.35	1.50	26.14	101.83	nr	127.97
900 mm x 900 mm	174.25	1.75	30.49	187.92	nr	218.42
1200 mm x 1200 mm	266.90	2.00	34.85	287.73	nr	322.58
Rooflight; Cox "Trade" range or other equal and approved; double skin polycarbonate dome on 150mm PVCU upstand						
600 mm x 600 mm	207.40	2.00	34.85	223.55	nr	258.40
900 mm x 900 mm	328.10	2.25	39.21	353.55	nr	392.76
1200 mm x 1200 mm	464.10	2.50	43.56	500.02	nr	543.58
Rooflight; Cox "2000" range or other equal and approved; double skin polycarbonate dome on 235mm PVCU upstand						
900 mm x900 mm	826.20	2.50	43.56	889.54	nr	933.10
1200 mm x 1200 mm	1134.75	3.00	52.27	1221.66	nr	1273.93
Louvres and frames; polyester powder coated aluminium; fixing in position including brackets						
Louvre; Gil Airvac "Plusaire 75SP" weatherlip or other equal and approved						
1250 mm x 675 mm	-	-	-	-	nr	494.81
2000 mm x 530 mm	-	-	-	-	nr	494.81

L WINDOWS/DOORS/STAIRS

Item	PC £	Labour hours	Labour £	Material £	Unit	Total rate £
L20 DOORS/SHUTTERS/HATCHES						
Doors; standard matchboarded; wrought softwood						
Matchboarded, ledged and braced doors; 25 mm thick ledges and braces; 19 mm thick tongued, grooved and V-jointed boarding; one side vertical boarding						
762 mm x 1981mm	51.39	1.39	24.22	55.31	nr	**79.53**
838 mm x 1981mm	51.39	1.39	24.22	55.31	nr	**79.53**
Matchboarded, framed, ledged and braced doors; 44 mm thick overall; 19 mm thick tongued, grooved and V-jointed boarding; one side vertical boarding						
762 mm x 1981mm	63.57	1.67	29.10	68.42	nr	**97.52**
838 mm x 1981mm	63.57	1.67	29.10	68.42	nr	**97.52**
Doors; standard flush; softwood composition						
Flush door; internal quality; skeleton or cellular core; hardboard faced both sides; lipped on two long edges; Jeld-Wen "Carrwood" or other equal and approved						
457 mm x 1981 mm x 35 mm	16.28	1.16	20.21	17.52	nr	**37.73**
533 mm x 1981 mm x 35 mm	16.28	1.16	20.21	17.52	nr	**37.73**
610 mm x 1981 mm x 35 mm	16.28	1.16	20.21	17.52	nr	**37.73**
686 mm x 1981 mm x 35 mm	16.59	1.16	20.21	17.86	nr	**38.07**
762 mm x 1981 mm x 35 mm	16.83	1.16	20.21	18.11	nr	**38.33**
838 mm x 1981 mm x 35 mm	17.72	1.16	20.21	19.07	nr	**39.28**
626 mm x 2040 mm x 40 mm	17.58	1.16	20.21	18.92	nr	**39.14**
726 mm x 2040 mm x 40 mm	17.92	1.16	20.21	19.29	nr	**39.50**
Flush door; internal quality; skeleton or cellular core; chipboard veneered; faced both sides; lipped on two long edges; Jeld-Wen "Paint grade veneeed" or other equal and approved						
457 mm x 1981 mm x 35 mm	22.03	1.16	20.21	23.71	nr	**43.92**
533 mm x 1981 mm x 35 mm	22.03	1.16	20.21	23.71	nr	**43.92**
610 mm x 1981 mm x 35 mm	22.03	1.16	20.21	23.71	nr	**43.92**
686 mm x 1981 mm x 35 mm	22.03	1.16	20.21	23.71	nr	**43.92**
762 mm x 1981 mm x 35 mm	22.58	1.16	20.21	24.30	nr	**44.52**
838 mm x 1981 mm x 35 mm	23.61	1.16	20.21	25.41	nr	**45.62**
526 mm x 2040 mm x 40 mm	23.46	1.16	20.21	25.25	nr	**45.46**
626 mm x 2040 mm x 40 mm	23.46	1.16	20.21	25.25	nr	**45.46**
726 mm x 2040 mm x 40 mm	23.97	1.16	20.21	25.80	nr	**46.02**
826 mm x 2040 mm x 40 mm	24.77	1.16	20.21	26.65	nr	**46.87**
Flush door; internal quality; skeleton or cellular core; chipboard veneered; faced both sides; lipped on two long edges; Jeld-Wen "Sapele veneered" or other equal and approved						
457 mm x 1981 mm x 35 mm	28.81	1.25	21.78	31.01	nr	**52.79**
533 mm x 1981 mm x 35 mm	28.81	1.25	21.78	31.01	nr	**52.79**
610 mm x 1981 mm x 35 mm	28.81	1.25	21.78	31.01	nr	**52.79**
686 mm x 1981 mm x 35 mm	28.95	1.25	21.78	31.16	nr	**52.94**
762 mm x 1981 mm x 35 mm	29.11	1.25	21.78	31.33	nr	**53.11**
838 mm x 1981 mm x 35 mm	30.22	1.25	21.78	32.52	nr	**54.30**
526 mm x 2040 mm x 40 mm	30.22	1.25	21.78	32.52	nr	**54.30**
626 mm x 2040 mm x 40 mm	30.22	1.25	21.78	32.52	nr	**54.30**
726 mm x 2040 mm x 40 mm	30.39	1.25	21.78	32.71	nr	**54.49**
826 mm x 2040 mm x 40 mm	31.32	1.25	21.78	33.71	nr	**55.49**

L WINDOWS/DOORS/STAIRS

Item	PC £	Labour hours	Labour £	Material £	Unit	Total rate £
Flush door; half-hour fire resisting (FD30); hardboard faced both sides; Jeld-Wen "Silverwood" or other equal and approved						
762 mm x 1981 mm x 44 mm	37.30	1.62	28.23	40.14	nr	68.37
838 mm x 1981 mm x 44 mm	38.95	1.62	28.23	41.92	nr	70.14
726 mm x 2040 mm x 44 mm	38.04	1.62	28.23	40.94	nr	69.17
826 mm x 2040 mm x 44 mm	39.84	1.62	28.23	42.88	nr	71.11
Flush door; half-hour fire resisting (FD30); chipboard veneered; faced both sides; lipped on two long edges; Jeld-Wen "Paint grade veneeed" or other equal and approved						
610 mm x 1981 mm x 44 mm	37.30	1.62	28.23	40.14	nr	68.37
686 mm x 1981 mm x 44 mm	37.30	1.62	28.23	40.14	nr	68.37
762 mm x 1981 mm x 44 mm	37.30	1.62	28.23	40.14	nr	68.37
838 mm x 1981 mm x 44 mm	38.82	1.62	28.23	41.78	nr	70.01
526 mm x 2040 mm x 44 mm	39.14	1.62	28.23	42.12	nr	70.35
626 mm x 2040 mm x 44 mm	39.14	1.62	28.23	42.12	nr	70.35
726 mm x 2040 mm x 44 mm	39.14	1.62	28.23	42.12	nr	70.35
826 mm x 2040 mm x 44 mm	40.82	1.62	28.23	43.93	nr	72.16
Flush door; half-hour fire resisting (FD30); faced both sides; lipped on two long edges; Jeld-Wen "Sapele veneered" or other equal and approved						
610 mm x 1981 mm x 44 mm	59.34	1.71	29.80	63.86	nr	93.66
686 mm x 1981 mm x 44 mm	59.34	1.71	29.80	63.86	nr	93.66
762 mm x 1981 mm x 44 mm	59.34	1.71	29.80	63.86	nr	93.66
838 mm x 1981 mm x 44 mm	61.46	1.71	29.80	66.14	nr	95.94
726 mm x 2040 mm x 44 mm	60.14	1.71	29.80	64.73	nr	94.52
826 mm x 2040 mm x 44 mm	62.22	1.71	29.80	66.97	nr	96.76
Flush door; half-hour fire resisting; chipboard for painting; hardwood lipping two long edges; "Leaderflush" type B30 or other equal and approved;						
526 mm x 2040 mm x 44 mm	83.23	1.71	29.80	89.58	nr	119.37
626 mm x 2040 mm x 44 mm	85.09	1.71	29.80	91.58	nr	121.38
726 mm x 2040 mm x 44 mm	86.45	1.71	29.80	93.05	nr	122.84
826 mm x 2040 mm x 44 mm	92.46	1.71	29.80	99.51	nr	129.30
Flush door; half-hour fire resisting; American light oak veneer; hardwood lipping all edges; "Leaderflush" type B30 or other equal and approved;						
526 mm x 2040 mm x 44 mm	112.16	1.71	29.80	120.71	nr	150.51
626 mm x 2040 mm x 44 mm	115.56	1.71	29.80	124.37	nr	154.17
726 mm x 2040 mm x 44 mm	117.72	1.71	29.80	126.70	nr	156.49
826 mm x 2040 mm x 44 mm	125.21	1.71	29.80	134.76	nr	164.55
Flush door; one-hour fire resisting (FD60); plywood faced both sides; lipped on two long edges; Jeld-Wen "Paint grade veneeed faced" or other equal and approved						
762 mm x 1981 mm x 54 mm	132.59	1.85	32.24	142.70	nr	174.93
838 mm x 1981 mm x 54 mm	140.94	1.85	32.24	151.68	nr	183.92
726 mm x 2040 mm x 54 mm	139.21	1.85	32.24	149.83	nr	182.06
826 mm x 2040 mm x 54 mm	148.22	1.85	32.24	159.52	nr	191.76
Flush door; one-hour fire resisting (FD60); lipped on two long edges; Jeld-Wen "Carrsilk veneered faced" or other equal and approved						
762 mm x 1981 mm x 54 mm	89.37	1.94	33.80	96.18	nr	129.99
838 mm x 1981 mm x 54 mm	92.93	1.94	33.80	100.02	nr	133.82

L WINDOWS/DOORS/STAIRS

Item	PC £	Labour hours	Labour £	Material £	Unit	Total rate £
L20 DOORS/SHUTTERS/HATCHES – cont'd						
Doors; standard flush; softwood						
Composition – cont'd						
Flush door; one-hour fire resisting; Iroko veneer; hardwood lipping all edges; Leaderflush" type B60 or other equal and approved; including groove and "Leaderseal" intumescent strip						
457 mm x 1981 mm x 54 mm	136.46	1.94	33.80	146.86	nr	**180.67**
533 mm x 1981 mm x 54 mm	137.97	1.94	33.80	148.49	nr	**182.29**
610 mm x 1981 mm x 54 mm	142.26	1.94	33.80	153.11	nr	**186.91**
686 mm x 1981 mm x 54 mm	143.32	1.94	33.80	154.25	nr	**188.06**
762 mm x 1981 mm x 54 mm	153.41	1.94	33.80	165.11	nr	**198.92**
838 mm x 1981 mm x 54 mm	154.69	1.94	33.80	166.49	nr	**200.29**
526 mm x 2040 mm x 54 mm	138.14	1.94	33.80	148.67	nr	**182.48**
626 mm x 2040 mm x 54 mm	142.97	1.94	33.80	153.87	nr	**187.67**
726 mmx 2040 mm x 54 mm	144.56	1.94	33.80	155.58	nr	**189.38**
826 mm x 2040 mm x 54 mm	155.18	1.94	33.80	167.01	nr	**200.81**
Flush door; external quality; skeleton or cellular core; plywood faced both sides; lipped on all four edges						
762 mm x 1981 mm x 54 mm	37.08	1.62	28.23	39.90	nr	**68.13**
838 mm x 1981 mm x 54 mm	38.41	1.62	28.23	41.34	nr	**69.56**
Flush door; external quality with standard glass opening; skeleton or cellular core; plywood faced both sides; lipped on all four edges; including glazing beads						
762 mm x 1981 mm x 54 mm	46.59	1.62	28.23	50.14	nr	**78.36**
838 mm x 1981 mm x 54 mm	47.81	1.62	28.23	51.45	nr	**79.68**
Doors; purpose made panelled; wrought softwood						
Panelled doors; one open panel for glass; including glazing beads						
686 mm x 1981 mm x 44 mm	81.90	1.62	28.23	88.14	nr	**116.37**
762 mm x 1981 mm x 44 mm	82.58	1.62	28.23	88.88	nr	**117.11**
838 mm x 1981 mm x 44 mm	83.27	1.62	28.23	89.61	nr	**117.84**
Panelled doors; two open panel for glass; including glazing beads						
686 mm x 1981 mm x 44 mm	114.51	1.62	28.23	123.24	nr	**151.47**
762 mm x 1981 mm x 44 mm	115.50	1.62	28.23	124.31	nr	**152.53**
838 mm x 1981 mm x 44 mm	116.49	1.62	28.23	125.37	nr	**153.60**
Panelled doors; four 19 mm thick plywood panels; mouldings worked on solid both sides						
686 mm x 1981 mm x 44 mm	173.89	1.62	28.23	187.15	nr	**215.38**
762 mm x 1981 mm x 44 mm	176.14	1.62	28.23	189.57	nr	**217.80**
838 mm x 1981 mm x 44 mm	178.39	1.62	28.23	191.99	nr	**220.22**
Panelled doors; six 25 mm thick panels raised and fielded; mouldings worked on solid both sides						
686 mm x 1981 mm x 44 mm	319.96	1.94	33.80	344.36	nr	**378.16**
762 mm x 1981 mm x 44 mm	323.15	1.94	33.80	347.80	nr	**381.60**
838 mm x 1981 mm x 44 mm	326.35	1.94	33.80	351.23	nr	**385.04**
rebated edges beaded	-	-	-	2.07	m	**2.07**
rounded edges or heels	-	-	-	0.47	m	**0.47**
weatherboard fixed to bottom rail	-	0.23	4.01	7.35	m	**11.36**
stopped groove for weatherboard	-	-	-	2.35	m	**2.35**

L WINDOWS/DOORS/STAIRS

Item	PC £	Labour hours	Labour £	Material £	Unit	Total rate £
Doors; purpose made panelled; selected Sapele						
Panelled doors; one open panel for glass; including glazing beads						
686 mm x 1981 mm x 44 mm	110.88	2.31	40.25	119.33	nr	159.59
762 mm x 1981 mm x 44 mm	112.38	2.31	40.25	120.94	nr	161.20
838 mm x 1981 mm x 44 mm	113.88	2.31	40.25	122.56	nr	162.82
686 mm x 1981 mm x 57 mm	118.52	2.54	44.26	127.56	nr	171.81
762 mm x 1981 mm x 57 mm	120.30	2.54	44.26	129.48	nr	173.74
838 mm x 1981 mm x 57 mm	122.08	2.54	44.26	131.39	nr	175.65
Panelled doors; 250 mm wide cross tongued intermediate rail; two open panels for glass; mouldings worked on the solid one side; 19 mm x 13 mm beads one side; fixing with brass cups and screws						
686 mm x 1981 mm x 44 mm	169.52	2.31	40.25	182.45	nr	222.70
762 mm x 1981 mm x 44 mm	172.38	2.31	40.25	185.52	nr	225.77
838 mm x 1981 mm x 44 mm	180.75	2.31	40.25	194.53	nr	234.78
686 mm x 1981 mm x 57 mm	180.75	2.54	44.26	194.53	nr	238.79
762 mm x 1981 mm x 57 mm	184.14	2.54	44.26	198.18	nr	242.44
838 mm x 1981 mm x 57 mm	187.61	2.54	44.26	201.91	nr	246.17
Panelled doors; four panels; (19 mm thick for 44 mm doors, 25 mm thick for 57 mm doors); mouldings worked on solid both sides						
686 mm x 1981 mm x 44 mm	238.20	2.31	40.25	256.36	nr	296.61
762 mm x 1981 mm x 44 mm	256.77	2.31	40.25	276.35	nr	316.60
838 mm x 1981 mm x 44 mm	269.46	2.31	40.25	290.00	nr	330.25
686 mm x 1981 mm x 57 mm	243.01	2.54	44.26	261.54	nr	305.80
762 mm x 1981 mm x 57 mm	263.11	2.54	44.26	283.17	nr	327.43
838 mm x 1981 mm x 57 mm	247.84	2.54	44.26	266.73	nr	310.99
Panelled doors; 150 mm wide stiles in one width; 430 mm wide cross tongued bottom rail; six panels raised and fielded one side; (19 mm thick for 44 mm doors, 25 mm thick for 57 mm doors); mouldings worked on solid both sides						
686 mm x 1981 mm x 44 mm	406.62	2.31	40.25	437.63	nr	477.88
762 mm x 1981 mm x 44 mm	448.73	2.31	40.25	482.94	nr	523.19
838 mm x 1981 mm x 44 mm	457.25	2.31	40.25	492.11	nr	532.36
686 mm x 1981 mm x 57 mm	432.99	2.54	44.26	466.01	nr	510.27
762 mm x 1981 mm x 57 mm	477.44	2.54	44.26	513.84	nr	558.10
838 mm x 1981 mm x 57 mm	488.30	2.54	44.26	525.54	nr	569.79
rebated edges beaded	-	-	-	2.64	m	2.64
rounded edges or heels	-	-	-	0.71	m	0.71
weatherboard fixed to bottom rail	-	0.31	5.40	9.94	m	15.35
stopped groove for weatherboard	-	-	-	2.45	m	2.45
Doors; galvanised steel "up and over" type garage doors; Catnic "Horizon 90" or other equal and approved; spring counter balanced; fixed to timber frame (not included)						
Garage door						
2135 mm x 1980 mm	166.54	3.70	64.47	179.54	nr	244.02
2135 mm x 2135 mm	190.91	3.70	64.47	205.77	nr	270.25
2400 mm x 2135 mm	233.56	3.70	64.47	251.73	nr	316.20
3965 mm x 2135 mm	576.78	5.55	96.71	621.49	nr	718.19

L WINDOWS/DOORS/STAIRS

Item	PC £	Labour hours	Labour £	Material £	Unit	Total rate £
L20 DOORS/SHUTTERS/HATCHES – cont'd						
Doorsets; Anti-Vandal Security door and frame units; Bastion Security Ltd or other equal and approved; to BS 5051; factory primed; fixing with frame anchors to masonry; cutting mortices; external 46 mm thick insulated door with birch grade plywood; sheet steel bonded into door core; 2 mm thick polyester coated laminate finish; hardwood lippings all edges; 95 mm x 65 mm hardwood frame; polyester coated standard ironmongery; weather stripping all round; low projecting aluminium threshold; plugging; screwing						
for 980 mm x 2100 mm structural opening; single door sets; panic bolt	-	-	-	-	nr	1400.18
for 1830 mm x 2100 mm structural opening; double door sets; panic bolt	-	-	-	-	nr	2369.54
Doorsets; galvanised steel IG "Weatherbeater Original" door and frame units or other equal and approved; treated softwood frame, primed hardwood sill; fixing in position; plugged and screwed to brickwork or blockwork Door and frame						
762 mm x 1981 mm; ref IGD01	129.86	2.78	48.44	140.08	nr	188.52
Doorsets; steel door and frame units; Jandor Architectural Ltd or other equal and approved; polyester powder coated; ironmongery Single action door set; "Metset MD01" doors and "Metset MF" frames						
900 mm x 2100 mm	-	-	-	-	nr	2014.18
pair 1800 mm x 2100 mm	-	-	-	-	nr	2782.35
Rolling shutters and collapsible gates; steel counter shutters; Bolton Brady Ltd or other equal and approved; push-up, self-coiling; polyester power coated; fixing by bolting Shutters						
3000 mm x 1000 mm	-	-	-	-	nr	1174.23
4000 mm x 1000 mm; in two panels	-	-	-	-	nr	2042.14
Rolling shutters and collapsible gates; galvanised steel; Bolton Brady Type 474 or other equal and approved; one hour fire resisting; self-coiling; activated by fusible link; fixing with bolts Rolling shutters and collapsible gates						
1000 mm x 2750 mm	-	-	-	-	nr	1403.97
1500 mm x 2750 mm	-	-	-	-	nr	1474.17
2400 mm x 2750 mm	-	-	-	-	nr	1742.20

L WINDOWS/DOORS/STAIRS

Item	PC £	Labour hours	Labour £	Material £	Unit	Total rate £
Rolling shutters and collapsible gates; GRP vertically opening insulated panel shutter doors; electrically operated; Envirodoor Markus Ltd; type HT40 or other equal and approved; manual over-ride, lock interlock, stop and return safety cage, "deadmans" down button, anti-flip device, photo-electric cell and beam deflectors; fixing by bolting						
Shutter doors						
3000 mm x 3000 mm; windows - 2 nr	-	-	-	-	nr	7705.41
4000 mm x 4000 mm; windows - 2 nr	-	-	-	-	nr	9527.64
5000 mm x 5000 mm; windows - 2 nr	-	-	-	-	nr	11349.86
Sliding/folding partitions; aluminium double glazed sliding patio doors; Crittal "Luminaire" or equal and approved; white acrylic finish; with and including 18 thick annealed double glazing; fixed in position; including lugs plugged and screwed to brickwork or blockwork						
Patio doors						
1800 mm x 2100 mm; ref PF1821	1032.80	2.31	40.25	1112.32	nr	1152.58
2400 m x 2100 mm; ref PF2421	1239.36	2.78	48.44	1334.61	nr	1383.05
2700 mm x 2100 mm; ref PF2721	1377.06	3.24	56.46	1482.79	nr	1539.25
Grilles; "Galaxy" nylon rolling counter grille or other equal and approved; Bolton Brady Ltd; colour, off-white; self-coiling; fixing by bolting						
Grilles						
3000 mm x 1000 mm	-	-	-	-	nr	928.23
4000 mm x 1000 mm	-	-	-	-	nr	1397.95
Sliding/folding partitions; Alco Beldan Ltd or equal and approved						
Sliding/folding partitions						
ref. NW100 Moveable Wall; 5000 mm (wide) x 2495 mm (high)l comrpising 4 nr. 954 mm (wide) standard panels and 1 nr. 954 mm (wide) telescopic panel; sealing; fixing	-	-	-	-	nr	8932.88
External softwood door frame composite standard joinery sets						
External door frame composite set; 56 mm x 78mm wide (finished); for external doors						
686 mm x 1981 mm x 44mm	28.83	0.75	13.07	31.34	nr	44.41
762 mm x 1981 mm x 44mm	29.28	0.75	13.07	31.82	nr	44.89
838 mm x 1981 mm x 44mm	30.61	0.75	13.07	33.26	nr	46.33
External door frame composite set; 56 mm x 78mm wide (finished); with 45 mm x 140 mm (finished) hardwood cill; for external doors						
686 mm x 1981 mm x 44mm	47.51	1.00	17.42	51.45	nr	68.87
762 mm x 1981 mm x 44mm	49.00	1.00	17.42	53.05	nr	70.47
838 mm x 1981 mm x 44mm	50.96	1.00	17.42	55.16	nr	72.58
826 mm x 2040 mm x 44mm	52.51	1.00	17.42	56.83	nr	74.25

L WINDOWS/DOORS/STAIRS

Item	PC £	Labour hours	Labour £	Material £	Unit	Total rate £
L20 DOORS/SHUTTERS/HATCHES – cont'd						
Internal white foiled moisture-resistant MDF door lining composite standard joinery set						
22 mm x 77mm wide (finished) set; with loose stops; for internal doors						
610 mm x 1981 mm x 35mm	12.73	0.70	12.20	14.01	nr	26.21
686 mm x 1981 mm x 35mm	12.71	0.70	12.20	13.99	nr	26.19
762 mm x 1981 mm x 35mm	12.71	0.70	12.20	13.99	nr	26.19
838 mm x 1981 mm x 35mm	17.28	0.70	12.20	18.91	nr	31.11
864 mm x 1981 mm x 35mm	13.31	0.70	12.20	14.64	nr	26.83
22 mm x 150mm wide (finished) set; with loose stops; for internal doors						
610 mm x 1981 mm x 35mm	16.48	0.70	12.20	18.05	nr	30.25
686 mm x 1981 mm x 35mm	16.48	0.70	12.20	18.05	nr	30.25
762 mm x 1981 mm x 35mm	16.48	0.70	12.20	18.05	nr	30.25
838 mm x 1981 mm x 35mm	17.28	0.70	12.20	18.91	nr	31.11
864 mm x 1981 mm x 35mm	17.28	0.70	12.20	18.91	nr	31.11
Mitred architrave set; 22 mm x 59mm wide (finished); ogee or torus; to one side of internal door						
610 mm x 1981 mm x 35mm	5.48	0.30	5.23	6.10	nr	11.33
686 mm x 1981 mm x 35mm	5.48	0.30	5.23	6.10	nr	11.33
762 mm x 1981 mm x 35mm	5.48	0.30	5.23	6.10	nr	11.33
838 mm x 1981 mm x 35mm	5.69	0.30	5.23	6.33	nr	11.56
864 mm x 1981 mm x 35mm	5.69	0.30	5.23	6.33	nr	11.56
Mitred architrave sets; 22 mm x 69 mm wide (finished); ogee or torus; to one side of internal door						
610 mm x 1981 mm x 35mm	5.75	0.30	5.23	6.40	nr	11.63
686 mm x 1981 mm x 35mm	5.75	0.30	5.23	6.40	nr	11.63
762 mm x 1981 mm x 35mm	5.75	0.30	5.23	6.40	nr	11.63
838 mm x 1981 mm x 35mm	6.01	0.30	5.23	6.67	nr	11.90
864 mm x 1981 mm x 35mm	6.01	0.30	5.23	6.67	nr	11.90
Door frames and door linings, sets; purpose made; wrought softwood						
Jambs and heads; as linings						
32 mm x 63 mm	-	0.16	2.79	5.11	m	7.89
32 mm x 100 mm	-	0.16	2.79	5.75	m	8.53
32 mm x 140 mm	-	0.16	2.79	6.15	m	8.94
Jambs and heads; as frames; rebated, rounded and grooved						
44 mm x 75 mm	-	0.16	2.79	8.20	m	10.98
44 mm x 100 mm	-	0.16	2.79	8.82	m	11.60
44 mm x 115 mm	-	0.16	2.79	8.89	m	11.68
44 mm x 140 mm	-	0.19	3.31	9.32	m	12.63
57 mm x 100 mm	-	0.19	3.31	9.45	m	12.76
57 mm x 125 mm	-	0.19	3.31	9.98	m	13.29
69 mm x 88 mm	-	0.19	3.31	9.59	m	12.90
69 mm x 100 mm	-	0.19	3.31	10.30	m	13.61
69 mm x 125 mm	-	0.20	3.48	10.93	m	14.41
69 mm x 150 mm	-	0.20	3.48	11.57	m	15.05
94 mm x 100 mm	-	0.23	4.01	15.58	m	19.59
94 mm x 150 mm	-	0.23	4.01	18.15	m	22.16
Mullions and transoms; in linings						
32 mm x 63 mm	-	0.11	1.92	6.76	m	8.68
32 mm x 100 mm	-	0.11	1.92	7.40	m	9.32
32 mm x 140 mm	-	0.11	1.92	7.72	m	9.64

L WINDOWS/DOORS/STAIRS

Item	PC £	Labour hours	Labour £	Material £	Unit	Total rate £
Mullions and transoms; in frames; twice rebated, rounded and grooved						
44 mm x 75 mm	-	0.11	1.92	10.25	m	12.16
44 mm x 100 mm	-	0.11	1.92	10.67	m	12.59
44 mm x 115 mm	-	0.11	1.92	10.67	m	12.59
44 mm x 140 mm	-	0.13	2.27	11.09	m	13.36
57 mm x 100 mm	-	0.13	2.27	11.23	m	13.49
57 mm x 125 mm	-	0.13	2.27	11.75	m	14.02
69 mm x 88 mm	-	0.13	2.27	11.09	m	13.36
69 mm x 100 mm	-	0.13	2.27	11.73	m	14.00
Add 5% to the above material prices for selected softwood for staining						
Door frames and door linings, sets; purpose made; selected Sapele						
Jambs and heads; as linings						
32 mm x 63 mm	5.53	0.21	3.66	6.03	m	9.69
32 mm x 100 mm	8.99	0.21	3.66	9.76	m	13.42
32 mm x 140 mm	9.84	0.21	3.66	10.75	m	14.41
Jambs and heads; as frames; rebated, rounded and grooved						
44 mm x 75 mm	11.93	0.21	3.66	12.91	m	16.57
44 mm x 100 mm	13.59	0.21	3.66	14.70	m	18.36
44 mm x 115 mm	14.04	0.21	3.66	15.27	m	18.93
44 mm x 140 mm	14.72	0.25	4.36	16.00	m	20.35
57 mm x 100 mm	15.05	0.25	4.36	16.35	m	20.71
57 mm x 125 mm	16.47	0.25	4.36	17.88	m	22.23
69 mm x 88 mm	15.03	0.25	4.36	16.26	m	20.61
69 mm x 100 mm	16.72	0.25	4.36	18.15	m	22.51
69 mm x 125 mm	18.41	0.28	4.88	19.97	m	24.85
69 mm x 150 mm	20.10	0.28	4.88	21.79	m	26.67
94 mm x 100 mm	23.48	0.28	4.88	25.42	m	30.30
94 mm x 150 mm	28.80	0.28	4.88	31.15	m	36.03
Mullions and transoms; in linings						
32 mm x 63 mm	9.13	0.15	2.61	9.83	m	12.45
32 mm x 100 mm	10.84	0.15	2.61	11.67	m	14.28
32 mm x 140 mm	11.70	0.15	2.61	12.59	m	15.20
Mullions and transoms; in frames; twice rebated, rounded and grooved						
44 mm x 75 mm	14.68	0.15	2.61	15.80	m	18.42
44 mm x 100 mm	15.80	0.15	2.61	17.01	m	19.62
44 mm x 115 mm	16.26	0.15	2.61	17.50	m	20.11
44 mm x 140 mm	16.93	0.17	2.96	18.22	m	21.18
57 mm x 100 mm	17.27	0.17	2.96	18.59	m	21.55
57 mm x 125 mm	18.69	0.17	2.96	20.12	m	23.08
69 mm x 88 mm	16.93	0.17	2.96	18.22	m	21.18
69 mm x 100 mm	19.06	0.17	2.96	20.51	m	23.47
Sills; once sunk weathered; once rebated, three times grooved						
63 mm x 175 mm	42.18	0.31	5.40	45.40	m	50.80
75 mm x 125 mm	40.63	0.31	5.40	43.72	m	49.13
75 mm x 150 mm	42.54	0.31	5.40	45.79	m	51.19
Door frames and door linings, sets; European Oak						
Sills; once sunk weathered; once rebated, three times grooved						
63 mm x 175 mm	69.33	0.31	5.40	74.62	m	80.02
75 mm x 125 mm	68.45	0.31	5.40	73.67	m	79.07
75 mm x 150 mm	74.84	0.31	5.40	80.55	m	85.95

L WINDOWS/DOORS/STAIRS

Item	PC £	Labour hours	Labour £	Material £	Unit	Total rate £
L20 DOORS/SHUTTERS/HATCHES – cont'd						
Bedding and pointing frames						
Pointing wood frames or sills with mastic						
one side	-	0.09	1.21	0.49	m	**1.70**
both sides	-	0.19	2.54	0.98	m	**3.52**
Pointing wood frames or sills with polysulphide sealant						
one side	-	0.09	1.21	1.55	m	**2.76**
both sides	-	0.19	2.54	3.11	m	**5.65**
Bedding wood frames in cement mortar (1:3) and point						
one side	-	0.07	1.52	0.07	m	**1.59**
both sides	-	0.09	1.96	0.09	m	**2.05**
one side in mortar; other side in mastic	-	0.19	3.38	0.56	m	**3.94**
L30 STAIRS/WALKWAYS/BALUSTRADES						
Standard staircases; wrought softwood (parana pine)						
Stairs; 25 mm thick treads with rounded nosings; 9 mm thick plywood risers; 32 mm thick strings; bullnose bottom tread; 50 mm x 75 mm hardwood handrail; 32 mm square plain balusters; 100 mm square plain newel posts						
straight flight; 838 mm wide; 2676 mm going; 2600 mm rise; with two newel posts	-	6.48	112.91	289.84	nr	**402.75**
straight flight with turn; 838 mm wide; 2676 mm going; 2600 mm rise; with two newel posts; three top treads winding	-	6.48	112.91	366.58	nr	**479.49**
dogleg staircase; 838 mm wide; 2676 mm going; 2600 mm rise; with two newel posts; quarter space landing third riser from top	-	6.48	112.91	308.11	nr	**421.02**
dogleg staircase; 838 mm wide; 2676 mm going; 2600 mm rise; with two newel posts; half space landing third riser from top	-	7.40	128.94	326.38	nr	**455.32**
Standard balustrades; wrought softwood						
Landing balustrade; 50 mm x 75 mm hardwood handrail; three 32 mm x 140 mm balustrade kneerails; two 32 mm x 50 mm stiffeners; one end of handrail jointed to newel post; other end built into wall; (newel post and mortices both not included)						
3.00 m long	-	2.54	44.26	98.67	nr	**142.93**
Landing balustrade; 50 mm x 75 mm hardwood handrail; 32 mm square plain balusters; one end of handrail jointed to newel post; other end built into wall; balusters housed in at bottom (newel post and mortices both not included)						
3.00 m long	-	3.70	64.47	62.13	nr	**126.60**
Hardwood staircases; purpose made; assembled at works						
Fixing only complete staircase including landings, balustrades, etc.						
plugging and screwing to brickwork or blockwork	-	13.88	241.85	1.90	nr	**243.75**

L WINDOWS/DOORS/STAIRS

Item	PC £	Labour hours	Labour £	Material £	Unit	Total rate £
The following are supply only prices for purpose made staircase components in selected Sapele supplied as part of an assembled staircase and may be used to arrive at a guide price for a complete hardwood staircase						
Board landings; cross-tongued joints; 100 mm x 50 mm sawn softwood bearers						
25 mm thick	-	-	-	89.24	m²	89.24
32 mm thick	-	-	-	100.32	m²	100.32
Treads; cross-tongued joints and risers; rounded nosings; tongued, grooved, glued and blocked together; one 175 mm x 50 mm sawn softwood carriage						
25 mm treads; 19 mm risers	-	-	-	85.17	m²	85.17
ends; quadrant	-	-	-	54.64	nr	54.64
ends; housed to hardwood	-	-	-	1.01	nr	1.01
32 mm treads; 25 mm risers	-	-	-	185.81	m²	185.81
ends; quadrant	-	-	-	70.22	nr	70.22
ends; housed to hardwood	-	-	-	1.01	nr	1.01
Winders; cross-tongued joints and risers in one width; rounded nosings; tongued, grooved glued and blocked together; one 175 mm x 50 mm sawn softwood carriage						
25 mm treads; 19 mm risers	-	-	-	249.32	m²	249.32
32 mm treads; 25 mm risers	-	-	-	255.18	m²	255.18
wide ends; housed to hardwood	-	-	-	2.02	nr	2.02
narrow ends; housed to hardwood	-	-	-	1.52	nr	1.52
Closed strings; in one width; 230 mm wide; rounded twice						
32 mm thick	-	-	-	32.84	m	32.84
38 mm thick	-	-	-	35.76	m	35.76
50 mm thick	-	-	-	39.83	m	39.83
Closed strings; cross-tongued joints; 280 mm wide; once rounded						
32 mm thick	-	-	-	42.62	m	42.62
extra for short ramp	-	-	-	21.89	nr	21.89
38 mm thick	-	-	-	46.49	m	46.49
extra for short ramp	-	-	-	24.89	nr	24.89
50 mm thick	-	-	-	51.89	m	51.89
extra for short ramp	-	-	-	30.82	nr	30.82
The following labours are irrespective of timber width						
ends; fitted	-	-	-	1.30	nr	1.30
ends; framed	-	-	-	7.63	nr	7.63
extra for tongued heading joint	-	-	-	3.77	nr	3.77
Closed strings; ramped; crossed tongued joints 280 mm wide; once rounded						
32 mm thick	-	-	-	42.62	m	42.62
44 mm thick	-	-	-	46.49	m	46.49
57 mm thick	-	-	-	51.89	m	51.89
Apron linings; in one width 230 mm wide						
19 mm thick	-	-	-	11.34	m	11.34
25 mm thick	-	-	-	13.35	m	13.35
Handrails; rounded						
40 mm x 50 mm	-	-	-	12.31	m	12.31
50 mm x 75 mm	-	-	-	14.84	m	14.84
57 mm x 87 mm	-	-	-	17.41	m	17.41
69 mm x 100 mm	-	-	-	21.64	m	21.64

L WINDOWS/DOORS/STAIRS

Item	PC £	Labour hours	Labour £	Material £	Unit	Total rate £
L30 STAIRS/WALKWAYS/BALUSTRADES						
– cont'd						
Sapele purpose made staircase – cont'd						
Handrails; moulded						
40 mm x 50 mm	-	-	-	13.69	m	13.69
50 mm x 75 mm	-	-	-	16.23	m	16.23
57 mm x 87 mm	-	-	-	18.81	m	18.81
69 mm x 100 mm	-	-	-	23.02	m	23.02
Add to above for						
grooved once	-	-	-	0.61	m	0.61
ends; framed	-	-	-	5.75	nr	5.75
ends; framed on rake	-	-	-	7.06	nr	7.06
Heading joints to handrail; mitred or raked						
overall size not exceeding 50 mm x 75 mm	-	-	-	28.25	nr	28.25
overall size not exceeding 69 mm x 100 mm	-	-	-	35.31	nr	35.31
Knee piece to handrail; mitred or raked						
overall size not exceeding 69 mm x 100 mm	-	-	-	75.34	nr	75.34
Balusters; stiffeners						
25 mm x 25 mm	-	-	-	3.15	m	3.15
32 mm x 32 mm	-	-	-	3.59	m	3.59
44 mm x 44 mm	-	-	-	4.71	m	4.71
ends; housed	-	-	-	1.41	nr	1.41
Sub rails						
32 mm x 63 mm	-	-	-	7.26	m	7.26
ends; framed joint to newel	-	-	-	6.12	nr	6.12
Knee rails						
32 mm x 140 mm	-	-	-	12.04	m	12.04
ends; framed joint to newel	-	-	-	6.12	nr	6.12
Newel posts						
44 mm x 94 mm; half newel	-	-	-	8.35	m	8.35
69 mm x 69 mm	-	-	-	9.07	m	9.07
94 mm x 94 mm	-	-	-	18.54	m	18.54
Newel caps; splayed on four sides						
62.50 mm x 125 mm x 50 mm	-	-	-	8.84	nr	8.84
100 mm x 100 mm x 50 mm	-	-	-	9.03	nr	9.03
125 mm x 125 mm x 50 mm	-	-	-	9.48	nr	9.48
The following are supply only prices for						
purpose made staircase components in						
selected American Oak; supplied as part						
of an assembled staircase						
Board landings; cross-tongued joints; 100 mm x						
50 mm sawn softwood bearers						
25 mm thick	-	-	-	131.65	m²	131.65
32 mm thick	-	-	-	158.98	m²	158.98
Treads; cross-tongued joints and risers; rounded						
nosings; tongued, grooved, glued and blocked;						
one 175 mm x 50 mm sawn softwood carriage						
25 mm treads; 19 mm risers	-	-	-	218.55	m²	218.55
ends; quadrant	-	-	-	109.17	nr	109.17
ends; housed to hardwood	-	-	-	1.34	nr	1.34
32 mm treads; 25 mm risers	-	-	-	250.43	m²	250.43
ends; quadrant	-	-	-	134.39	nr	134.39
ends; housed to hardwood	-	-	-	1.34	nr	1.34
Winders; cross-tongued joints and risers; rounded						
Nosings etc.; as above						
25 mm treads; 19 mm risers	-	-	-	277.04	m²	277.04
32 mm treads; 25 mm risers	-	-	-	302.28	m²	302.28
wide ends; housed to hardwood	-	-	-	2.69	nr	2.69

L WINDOWS/DOORS/STAIRS

Item	PC £	Labour hours	Labour £	Material £	Unit	Total rate £
narrow ends; housed to hardwood	-	-	-	2.02	nr	2.02
Closed strings; in one width; 230 mm wide; rounded twice						
32 mm thick	-	-	-	51.63	m	51.63
44 mm thick	-	-	-	59.59	m	59.59
57 mm thick	-	-	-	81.82	m	81.82
Closed strings; cross-tongued joints; 280 mm wide; once rounded						
32 mm thick	-	-	-	65.60	m	65.60
extra for short ramp	-	-	-	37.51	nr	37.51
38 mm thick	-	-	-	76.03	m	76.03
extra for short ramp	-	-	-	42.73	nr	42.73
50 mm thick	-	-	-	104.24	m	104.24
extra for short ramp	-	-	-	56.83	nr	56.83
Closed strings; ramped; crossed tongued joints 280 mm wide; once rounded						
32 mm thick	-	-	-	75.44	m	75.44
44 mm thick	-	-	-	87.44	m	87.44
57 mm thick	-	-	-	119.87	m	119.87
Apron linings; in one width 230 mm wide						
19 mm thick	-	-	-	17.58	m	17.58
25 mm thick	-	-	-	21.55	m	21.55
Handrails; rounded						
40 mm x 50 mm	-	-	-	14.25	m	14.25
50 mm x 75 mm	-	-	-	18.26	m	18.26
57 mm x 87 mm	-	-	-	27.40	m	27.40
69 mm x 100 mm	-	-	-	36.90	m	36.90
Handrails; moulded						
40 mm x 50 mm	-	-	-	15.63	m	15.63
50 mm x 75 mm	-	-	-	19.64	m	19.64
57 mm x 87 mm	-	-	-	28.79	m	28.79
69 mm x 100 mm	-	-	-	38.28	m	38.28
Add to above for						
grooved once	-	-	-	0.71	m	0.71
ends; framed	-	-	-	7.06	nr	7.06
ends; framed on rake	-	-	-	8.95	nr	8.95
Heading joints to handrail; mitred or raked						
overall size not exceeding 50 mm x 75 mm	-	-	-	37.67	nr	37.67
overall size not exceeding 69 mm x 100 mm	-	-	-	44.73	nr	44.73
Knee piece to handrail; mitred or raked						
overall size not exceeding 69 mm x 100 mm	-	-	-	80.05	nr	80.05
Balusters; stiffeners						
25 mm x 25 mm	-	-	-	3.24	m	3.24
32 mm x 32 mm	-	-	-	4.10	m	4.10
44 mm x 44 mm	-	-	-	6.47	m	6.47
ends; housed	-	-	-	1.65	nr	1.65
Sub rails						
32 mm x 63 mm	-	-	-	8.77	m	8.77
ends; framed joint to newel	-	-	-	7.06	nr	7.06
Knee rails						
32 mm x 140 mm	-	-	-	15.24	m	15.24
ends; framed joint to newel	-	-	-	7.06	nr	7.06
Newel posts						
44 mm x 94 mm; half newel	-	-	-	11.43	m	11.43
69 mm x 69 mm	-	-	-	19.47	m	19.47
94 mm x 94 mm	-	-	-	48.61	m	48.61
Newel caps; splayed on four sides						
62.50 mm x 125 mm x 50 mm	-	-	-	9.80	nr	9.80
100 mm x 100 mm x 50 mm	-	-	-	10.36	nr	10.36
125 mm x 125 mm x 50 mm	-	-	-	11.39	nr	11.39

L WINDOWS/DOORS/STAIRS

Item	PC £	Labour hours	Labour £	Material £	Unit	Total rate £
L20 DOORS/SHUTTERS/HATCHES – cont'd						
Spiral staircases, balustrades and handrails; mild steel; galvanised and polyester powder coated						
Staircase						
2080 mm diameter x 3695 mm high; 18 nr treads ;16 mm diameter intermediate balusters; 1040 x 1350 mm landing unit with matching balustrade both sides; fixing with 16 mm diameter resin anchors to masonry at landing and with 12 mm diameter expanding bolts to concrete at base	-	-	-	-	nr	5811.75
Aluminium alloy folding loft ladders; "Zig Zag" stairways, model B or other equal and approved; Light Alloy Ltd; on and including plywood backboard; fixing with screws to timber lining (not included)						
Loft ladders						
ceiling height not exceeding 2500 mm; model 888801	-	0.93	16.20	419.46	nr	435.67
ceiling height not exceeding 2750 mm; model 888802	-	0.93	16.20	459.93	nr	476.13
ceiling height not exceeding 3000 mm; model 888803	-	0.93	16.20	513.31	nr	529.52
ceiling height not exceeding 3250 mm; model 888804	-	0.93	16.20	539.14	nr	555.35
Access ladders; mild steel						
Ladders						
400 mm wide; 3850 mm long (overall); 12 mm diameter rungs; 65 mm x 15 mm strings; 50 mm x 5 mm safety hoops; fixing with expanded bolts; To masonry; mortices; welded fabrication	-	-	-	-	nr	1383.75
Flooring, balustrades and handrails; mild steel						
Chequer plate flooring; galvanised; over 300 mm wide; bolted to steel supports						
6 mm thick	-	-	-	-	m²	129.15
8 mm thick	-	-	-	-	m²	156.82
Open grid steel flooring; Eurogrid Ltd; "Safeway" type D38 diamond pattern flooring or other equal and approved to steel supports at 1200 mm centres; galvanised; to BS 729 part 1						
30 mm x 5 mm sections; in one mat; fixing to 10 mm thick channels with type F5 clamps	-	-	-	-	m²	120.02
Balustrades; welded construction; 1070 mm high; galvanized; 50 mm x 50 mm x 3.20 mm rhs top rail; 38 mm x 13 mm bottom rail, 50 mm x 50 mm x 3.20 mm rhs standards at 1830 mm centres with base plate drilled and bolted to concrete; 13 mm x 13 mm balusters at 102 mm centres	-	-	-	-	m	249.07
Balustrades; welded construction; 1300 mm high; galvanized; 42 mm diameter stainless steel top rail; 45 mm diameter bottom rail; 50 mm x 50 mm x 3.20 mm rhs standards at 1800 mm centres with fixing lugs, base plate drilled and bolted to concrete; pressed grating Type 'R' infill panels, Arco Gratings or equal and approved	-	-	-	-	m	207.56

L WINDOWS/DOORS/STAIRS

Item	PC £	Labour hours	Labour £	Material £	Unit	Total rate £
Balusters; isolated; one end ragged and cemented in; one 76 mm x 25 mm x 6 mm flange plate welded on; ground to a smooth finish; countersunk drilled and tap screwed to underside of handrail						
19 mm square; 914 mm long bar	-	-	-	-	nr	22.14
Core-rails; joints prepared, welded and ground to a smooth finish; fixing on brackets (not included)						
38 mm x 10 mm flat bar	-	-	-	-	m	22.14
50 mm x 8 mm flat bar	-	-	-	-	m	24.91
Handrails; joints prepared, welded and ground to a smooth finish; fixing on brackets (not included)						
38 mm x 12 mm half oval bar	-	-	-	-	m	23.98
44 mm x 13 mm half oval bar	-	-	-	-	m	27.68
Handrail bracket; comprising 40 mm x 5 mm plate with mitred and welded angle; one end welded to 100 mm diameter x 5 mm backplate; three times holed and plugged and screwed to brickwork; other end scribed and welded to underside of handrail						
140 mm girth	-	-	-	-	nr	59.04
Holes						
Holes; countersunk; for screws or bolts						
6 mm diameter; 3 mm thick	-	-	-	-	nr	0.65
6 mm diameter; 6 mm thick	-	-	-	-	nr	0.88
8 mm diameter; 6 mm thick	-	-	-	-	nr	0.88
10 mm diameter; 6 mm thick	-	-	-	-	nr	1.09
12 mm diameter; 8 mm thick	-	-	-	-	nr	1.29
Balustrades; stainless steel BS 970 grade 316; TIG welded joints; satin polished finish						
Raking balustrade; comprising 40 mm handrail on 40 mm standards at 1 m centres with two 16 mm diameter intermediate rails						
1.10 m high	-	-	-	-	m	221.40
L40 GENERAL GLAZING						
BASIC GLASS PRICES						
Prices displayed include discounts						
Ordinary transluscent/patterned glass						
3 mm	-	-	-	13.25	m²	-
4 mm	-	-	-	14.06	m²	-
5 mm	-	-	-	17.10	m²	-
6 mm	-	-	-	18.76	m²	-
Obscured ground sheet glass - patterned						
4 mm white	-	-	-	19.87	m²	-
6 mm white	-	-	-	21.88	m²	-
Rough cast						
6 mm	-	-	-	15.89	m²	-
Ordinary Georgian wired						
7 mm cast	-	-	-	16.15	m²	-
6 mm polish	-	-	-	25.08	m²	-

L WINDOWS/DOORS/STAIRS

Item	PC £	Labour hours	Labour £	Material £	Unit	Total rate £
L40 GENERAL GLAZING – cont'd						
BASIC GLASS PRICES– cont'd						
"Cetuff" toughened; float						
4 mm	-	-	-	14.11	m²	-
5 mm	-	-	-	18.71	m²	-
6 mm	-	-	-	20.60	m²	-
10 mm	-	-	-	34.20	m²	-
Clear laminated; safety						
4.40 mm	-	-	-	22.58	m²	-
6.40 mm	-	-	-	26.96	m²	-
SUPPLY AND FIX PRICES						
NOTE: The following "measured rates" are provided by a glazing sub-contractor and assume in excess of 500 m², within 20 miles of the suppliers branch.						
Standard plain glass; BS 952; clear float; panes area 0.15 m² - 4.00 m²						
3 mm thick; glazed with						
screwed beads	-	-	-	-	m²	24.70
4 mm thick; glazed with						
screwed beads	-	-	-	-	m²	26.19
5 mm thick; glazed with						
screwed beads	-	-	-	-	m²	31.90
6 mm thick; glazed with						
screwed beads	-	-	-	-	m²	34.95
Standard plain glass; BS 952; obscure patterned; panes area 0.15 m² - 4.00 m²						
4 mm thick; glazed with						
screwed beads	-	-	-	-	m²	37.04
6 mm thick; glazed with						
screwed beads	-	-	-	-	m²	40.77
Standard plain glass; BS 952; rough cast; panes area 0.15 m² - 4.00 m²						
6 mm thick; glazed with						
screwed beads	-	-	-	-	m²	29.61
Standard plain glass; BS 952; Georgian wired cast; panes area 0.15 m² - 4.00 m²						
7 mm thick; glazed with						
screwed beads	-	-	-	-	m²	30.13
Extra for lining up wired glass	-	-	-	-	m²	3.01
Standard plain glass; BS 952; Georgian wired polished; panes area 0.15 m² - 4.00 m²						
6 mm thick; glazed with						
screwed beads	-	-	-	-	m²	46.74
Extra for lining up wired glass	-	-	-	-	m²	3.01

L WINDOWS/DOORS/STAIRS

Item	PC £	Labour hours	Labour £	Material £	Unit	Total rate £
Special glass; BS 952; toughened clear float; panes area 0.15 m² - 4.00 m²						
4 mm thick; glazed with						
screwed beads	-	-	-	-	m²	26.27
5 mm thick; glazed with						
screwed beads	-	-	-	-	m²	34.89
6 mm thick; glazed with						
screwed beads	-	-	-	-	m²	38.38
10 mm thick; glazed with						
screwed beads	-	-	-	-	m²	63.68
Special glass; BS 952; clear laminated safety glass; panes area 0.15 m² - 4.00 m²						
4.40 mm thick; glazed with						
screwed beads	-	-	-	-	m²	42.09
6.40 mm thick; glazed with						
screwed beads	-	-	-	-	m²	50.34
Special glass; BS 952; "Pyran" half-hour fire resisting glass or other equal or approved						
6.50 mm thick rectangular panes; glazed with screwed hardwood beads and Sealmaster "Fireglaze" intumescent compound or other equal and approved to rebated frame						
300 mm x 400 mm pane	-	0.37	9.72	33.93	nr	43.65
400 mm x 800 mm pane	-	0.46	12.08	82.81	nr	94.89
500 mm x 1400 mm pane	-	0.74	19.43	173.12	nr	192.55
600 mm x 1800 mm pane	-	0.93	24.42	286.34	nr	310.76
Special glass; BS 952; "Pyrostop" one-hour fire resisting glass or other equal and approved						
15 mm thick regular panes; glazed with screwed hardwood beads and Sealmaster "Fireglaze" intumescent liner and compound or other equal and approved both sides						
300 mm x 400 mm pane	-	1.11	29.15	69.79	nr	98.94
400 mm x 800 mm pane	-	1.39	36.50	136.62	nr	173.12
500 mm x 1400 mm pane	-	1.85	48.58	270.65	nr	319.23
600 mm x 1800 mm pane	-	2.31	60.66	395.42	nr	456.09
Special glass; BS 952; clear laminated security glass						
7.50 mm thick regular panes; glazed with screwed hardwood beads and Intergens intumescent strip						
300 mm x 400 mm pane	-	0.37	9.72	21.71	nr	31.43
400 mm x 800 mm pane	-	0.46	12.08	50.69	nr	62.77
500 mm x 1400 mm pane	-	0.74	19.43	102.99	nr	122.43
600 mm x 1800 mm pane	-	0.93	24.42	177.20	nr	201.62
Mirror panels; BS 952; silvered; insulation backing						
4 mm thick float; fixing with adhesive						
1000 mm x 1000 mm	-	-	-	-	nr	29.49
1000 mm x 2000 mm	-	-	-	-	nr	59.04
1000 mm x 4000 mm	-	-	-	-	nr	215.18

L WINDOWS/DOORS/STAIRS

Item	PC £	Labour hours	Labour £	Material £	Unit	Total rate £
L40 GENERAL GLAZING – cont'd						
Glass louvres; BS 952; with long edges ground or smooth						
6 mm thick float						
150 mm wide	-	-	-	-	m	13.01
7 mm thick Georgian wired cast						
150 mm wide	-	-	-	-	m	18.05
6 mm thick Georgian wire polished						
150 mm wide	-	-	-	-	m	25.75
Factory made double hermetically sealed units; to wood or metal with screwed or clipped beads						
Two panes; BS 952; clear float glass; 4 mm thick; 6 mm air space						
0.35 m^2 - 2.00 m^2	-	-	-	-	m^2	66.23
Two panes; BS 952; clear float glass; 6 mm thick; 6 mm air space						
0.35 m^2 - 2.0 m^2	-	-	-	-	m^2	77.13
2.00 m^2 - 4.00 m^2	-	-	-	-	m^2	115.97

M SURFACE FINISHES

Item	PC £	Labour hours	Labour £	Material £	Unit	Total rate £
M10 CEMENT SAND/CONCRETE/ GRANOLITHIC SCREEDS/FLOORING						
Cement and sand (1:3) screeds; steel trowelled						
Work to floors; one coat; level and to falls not exceeding 15 degrees from horizontal; to concrete base; over 300 mm wide						
25 mm thick	-	0.35	6.58	1.76	m²	8.33
32 mm thick	-	0.36	6.76	2.24	m²	9.01
40 mm thick	-	0.37	6.95	2.81	m²	9.76
48 mm thick	-	0.38	7.14	3.37	m²	10.51
50 mm thick	-	0.39	7.33	3.51	m²	10.84
60 mm thick	-	0.40	7.52	4.21	m²	11.73
65 mm thick	-	0.41	7.70	4.56	m²	12.27
70 mm thick	-	0.43	8.08	4.91	m²	12.99
75 mm thick	-	0.45	8.46	5.26	m²	13.72
100 mm thick	-	0.50	9.40	7.01	m²	16.41
Add to the above for work to falls and crossfalls and to slopes						
not exceeding 15 degrees from horizontal	-	0.02	0.38	-	m²	0.38
over 15 degrees from horizontal	-	0.09	1.69	-	m²	1.69
water repellent additive incorporated in the mix	-	0.02	0.38	4.80	m²	5.18
oil repellent additive incorporated in the mix	-	0.07	1.32	3.85	m²	5.17
Fine concrete (1:4-5) levelling screeds; steel trowelled						
Work to floors; one coat; level; to concrete base; over 300 mm wide						
50 mm thick	-	-	-	-	m²	10.06
75 mm thick	-	-	-	-	m²	13.32
Extra over last for isolation joint to perimeter	-	-	-	-	m	1.27
Early drying floor screed; RMC Mortars "Readyscreed"; or other equal and approved; steel trowelled						
Work to floors; one coat; level; to concrete base; over 300 mm wide						
100 mm thick	-	-	-	-	m²	20.50
Extra over last for galvanised chicken wire anticrack reinforcement	-	-	-	-	m²	0.97
Granolithic paving; cement and granite chippings 5 to dust (1:1:2); steel trowelled						
Work to floors; one coat; level; laid on concrete while green; bonded; over 300 mm wide						
25 mm thick	-	-	-	-	m²	22.90
38 mm thick	-	-	-	-	m²	25.50
Work to floors; two coat; laid on hacked concrete with slurry; over 300 mm wide						
50 mm thick	-	-	-	-	m²	28.20
75 mm thick	-	-	-	-	m²	34.70
Work to landings; one coat; level; laid on concrete while green; bonded; over 300 mm wide						
25 mm thick	-	-	-	-	m²	34.27
38 mm thick	-	-	-	-	m²	38.24

M SURFACE FINISHES

Item	PC £	Labour hours	Labour £	Material £	Unit	Total rate £
M10 CEMENT SAND/CONCRETE/ GRANOLITHIC SCREEDS/FLOORING - cont'd						
Granolithic paving - cont'd						
Work to landings; two coat; laid on hacked concrete with slurry; over 300 mm wide						
50 mm thick	-	-	-	-	m²	42.29
75 mm thick	-	-	-	-	m²	52.05
Add to the above over 300 mm wide for						
liquid hardening additive incorporated in the mix	-	0.04	0.75	0.55	m²	1.30
oil-repellent additive incorporated in the mix	-	0.07	1.32	3.85	m²	5.17
25 mm work to treads; one coat; to concrete base						
225 mm wide	-	0.83	20.08	8.92	m	29.00
275 mm wide	-	0.83	20.08	9.99	m	30.07
returned end	-	0.17	4.11	-	nr	4.11
13 mm skirtings; rounded top edge and coved bottom junction; to brickwork or blockwork base						
75 mm wide on face	-	0.51	12.34	0.43	m	12.77
150 mm wide on face	-	0.69	16.69	7.85	m	24.54
ends; fair	-	0.04	0.97	-	nr	0.97
angles	-	0.06	1.45	-	nr	1.45
13 mm outer margin to stairs; to follow profile of and with rounded nosing to treads and risers; fair edge and arris at bottom, to concrete base						
75 mm wide	-	0.83	20.08	4.28	m	24.36
angles	-	0.06	1.45	-	nr	1.45
13 mm wall string to stairs; fair edge and arris on top; coved bottom junction with treads and risers; to brickwork or blockwork base						
275 mm (extreme) wide	-	0.74	17.90	7.49	m	25.39
ends	-	0.04	0.97	-	nr	0.97
angles	-	0.06	1.45	-	nr	1.45
ramps	-	0.07	1.69	-	nr	1.69
ramped and wreathed corners	-	0.09	2.18	-	nr	2.18
13 mm outer string to stairs; rounded nosing on top at junction with treads and risers; fair edge and arris at bottom; to concrete base						
300 mm (extreme) wide	-	0.74	17.90	9.27	m	27.18
ends	-	0.04	0.97	-	nr	0.97
angles	-	0.06	1.45	-	nr	1.45
ramps	-	0.07	1.69	-	nr	1.69
ramps and wreathed corners	-	0.09	2.18	-	nr	2.18
19 mm thick skirtings; rounded top edge and coved bottom junction; to brickwork or blockwork base						
75 mm wide on face	-	0.51	12.34	7.85	m	20.19
150 mm wide on face	-	0.69	16.69	12.13	m	28.82
ends; fair	-	0.04	0.75	-	nr	0.75
angles	-	0.06	1.45	-	nr	1.45
19 mm riser; one rounded nosing; to concrete base						
150 mm high; plain	-	0.83	20.08	6.78	m	26.86
150 mm high; undercut	-	0.83	20.08	6.78	m	26.86
180 mm high; plain	-	0.83	20.08	9.27	m	29.36
180 mm high; undercut	-	0.83	20.08	9.27	m	29.36

M SURFACE FINISHES

Item	PC £	Labour hours	Labour £	Material £	Unit	Total rate £
M11 MASTIC ASPHALT FLOORING/FLOOR UNDERLAYS						
Mastic asphalt flooring to BS 6925 Type F 1076; black						
20 mm thick; one coat coverings; felt isolating membrane; to concrete base; flat						
over 300 mm wide	-	-	-	-	m²	12.91
225 mm - 300 mm wide	-	-	-	-	m²	23.98
150 mm - 225 mm wide	-	-	-	-	m²	26.34
not exceeding 150 mm wide	-	-	-	-	m²	32.25
25 mm thick; one coat coverings; felt isolating membrane; to concrete base; flat						
over 300 mm wide	-	-	-	-	m²	14.99
225 mm - 300 mm wide	-	-	-	-	m²	25.58
150 mm - 225 mm wide	-	-	-	-	m²	27.89
not exceeding 150 mm wide	-	-	-	-	m²	33.81
20 mm three coat skirtings to brickwork base						
not exceeding 150 mm girth	-	-	-	-	m	13.19
150 mm - 225 mm girth	-	-	-	-	m	16.12
225 mm - 300 mm girth	-	-	-	-	m	19.05
Mastic asphalt flooring; acid-resisting; black						
20 mm thick; one coat coverings; felt isolating membrane; to concrete base flat						
over 300 mm wide	-	-	-	-	m²	15.12
225 mm - 300 mm wide	-	-	-	-	m²	27.66
150 mm - 225 mm wide	-	-	-	-	m²	28.56
not exceeding 150 mm wide	-	-	-	-	m²	34.46
25 mm thick; one coat coverings; felt isolating membrane; to concrete base; flat						
over 300 mm wide	-	-	-	-	m²	17.86
225 mm - 300 mm wide	-	-	-	-	m²	28.43
150 mm - 225 mm wide	-	-	-	-	m²	30.77
not exceeding 150 mm wide	-	-	-	-	m²	36.68
20 mm thick; three coat skirtings to brickwork base						
not exceeding 150 mm girth	-	-	-	-	m	13.32
150 mm - 225 mm girth	-	-	-	-	m	15.52
225 mm - 300 mm girth	-	-	-	-	m	17.62
Mastic asphalt flooring to BS 6925 Type F 1451; red						
20 mm thick; one coat coverings; felt isolating membrane; to concrete base; flat						
over 300 mm wide	-	-	-	-	m²	21.15
225 mm - 300 mm wide	-	-	-	-	m²	34.94
150 mm - 225 mm wide	-	-	-	-	m²	37.75
not exceeding 150 mm wide	-	-	-	-	m²	45.16
20 mm thick; three coat skirtings to brickwork base						
not exceeding 150 mm girth	-	-	-	-	m	16.61
150 mm - 225 mm girth	-	-	-	-	m	21.15

M SURFACE FINISHES

Item	PC £	Labour hours	Labour £	Material £	Unit	Total rate £
M12 TROWELLED BITUMEN/RESIN/RUBBER LATEX FLOORING						
Latex cement floor screeds; steel trowelled						
Work to floors; level; to concrete base; over 300 mm wide						
3 mm thick; one coat	-	-	-	-	m²	3.93
5 mm thick; two coats	-	-	-	-	m²	5.54
Epoxy resin flooring; Altro "Altroflow 3000" or other equal and approved; steel trowelled						
Work to floors; level; to concrete base; over 300 mm wide						
3 mm thick; one coat	-	-	-	-	m²	25.67
Isocrete K screeds or other equal and approved; steel trowelled						
Work to floors; level; to concrete base; over 300 mm wide						
35 mm thick; plus polymer bonder coat	-	-	-	-	m²	13.96
40 mm thick	-	-	-	-	m²	12.88
45 mm thick	-	-	-	-	m²	13.62
50 mm thick	-	-	-	-	m²	14.35
Work to floors; to falls or cross-falls; to concrete base; over 300 mm wide						
55 mm (average) thick	-	-	-	-	m²	15.08
60 mm (average) thick	-	-	-	-	m²	15.81
65 mm (average) thick	-	-	-	-	m²	16.54
75 mm (average) thick	-	-	-	-	m²	18.01
90 mm (average) thick	-	-	-	-	m²	20.20
Bituminous lightweight insulating roof screeds						
"Bit-Ag" or similar roof screed or other equal and approved; to falls or cross-falls; bitumen felt vapour barrier; over 300 mm wide						
75 mm (average) thick	-	-	-	-	m²	33.93
100 mm (average) thick	-	-	-	-	m²	43.01
M20 PLASTERED/RENDERED/ROUGHCAST COATINGS						
Cement and sand (1:3) beds and backings						
10 mm thick work to walls; one coat; to brickwork or blockwork base						
over 300 mm wide	-	-	-	-	m²	11.39
not exceeding 300 mm wide	-	-	-	-	m	5.70
13 mm thick; work to walls; two coats; to brickwork or blockwork base						
over 300 mm wide	-	-	-	-	m²	13.70
not exceeding 300 mm wide	-	-	-	-	m	6.86
15 mm thick work to walls; two coats; to brickwork or blockwork base						
over 300 mm wide	-	-	-	-	m²	14.78
not exceeding 300 mm wide	-	-	-	-	m	7.40

M SURFACE FINISHES

Item	PC £	Labour hours	Labour £	Material £	Unit	Total rate £
Cement and sand (1:3); steel trowelled						
13 mm thick work to walls; two coats; to						
brickwork or blockwork base						
over 300 mm wide	-	-	-	-	m²	11.93
not exceeding 300 mm wide	-	-	-	-	m	5.96
16 mm thick work to walls; two coats; to						
brickwork or blockwork base						
over 300 mm wide	-	-	-	-	m²	13.36
not exceeding 300 mm wide	-	-	-	-	m	6.70
19 mm thick work to walls; two coats; to						
brickwork or blockwork base						
over 300 mm wide	-	-	-	-	m²	15.46
not exceeding 300 mm wide	-	-	-	-	m	7.73
ADD to above						
over 300 mm wide in water repellant cement	-	-	-	-	m²	3.16
finishing coat in colour cement	-	-	-	-	m²	6.74
Cement-lime-sand (1:2:9); steel trowelled						
19 mm thick work to walls; two coats; to						
brickwork or blockwork base						
over 300 mm wide	-	-	-	-	m²	14.99
not exceeding 300 mm wide	-	-	-	-	m	7.50
Cement-lime-sand (1:1:6); steel trowelled						
13 mm thick work to walls; two coats; to						
brickwork or blockwork base						
over 300 mm wide	-	-	-	-	m²	12.26
not exceeding 300 mm wide	-	-	-	-	m	6.04
Add to the above over 300 mm wide for						
waterproof additive	-	-	-	-	m²	2.07
19 mm thick work to ceilings; three coats; to						
metal lathing base						
over 300 mm wide	-	-	-	-	m²	14.42
not exceeding 300 mm wide	-	-	-	-	m	8.43
Sto External Render System; StoRend						
Cote or other equal and approved; CCS						
Scotseal Ltd						
12 mm thick StoLevell Cote; one coat Sto primer;						
to brickwork or blockwork base						
over 300 mm wide	-	0.62	20.02	16.67	m²	36.69
Sto External Render System; StoRend						
Fibre or other equal and approved; CCS						
Scotseal Ltd						
12 mm thick Sto Fibrecoat; one coat Sto primer;						
to brickwork or blockwork base						
over 300 mm wide	-	0.62	20.02	23.51	m²	43.53
Sto External Render System; StoRend						
Fibre Plus or other equal and approved;						
CCS Scotseal Ltd						
10 mm thick Sto Fibrecoat; glassfibre reinforcing						
mesh; one coat Sto primer; to brickwork or						
blockwork base						
over 300 mm wide	-	0.69	22.28	23.36	m²	45.64

M SURFACE FINISHES

Item	PC £	Labour hours	Labour £	Material £	Unit	Total rate £
M20 PLASTERED/RENDERED/ROUGHCAST COATINGS – cont'd						
Sto External Render System; StoRend Flex or other equal and approved; CCS Scotseal Ltd 2 mm Sto RFP reinforcing coat; glassfibre reinforcing mesh; one coat Sto primer; to existing rendered brickwork or blockwork base						
over 300 mm wide	-	0.54	17.44	17.20	m²	34.64
Sto External Render System; StoRend Flex Cote or other equal and approved; CCS Scotseal Ltd 12 mm StoLevell Cote; 2 mm Sto RFP reinforcing coat; glassfibre reinforcing mesh; to brickwork or blockwork base						
over 300 mm wide	-	0.85	27.44	26.96	m²	54.40
Plaster; first 11 mm coat of "Thistle Hardwall" plaster; second 2 mm finishing coat of "Thistle Multi Finish" plaster; steel trowelled 13 mm thick work to walls; two coats; to brickwork or blockwork base						
over 300 mm wide	-	-	-	-	m²	9.46
over 300 mm wide; in staircase areas or plant rooms	-	-	-	-	m²	11.36
not exceeding 300 mm wide	-	-	-	-	m	5.03
13 mm thick work to isolated brickwork or blockwork columns; two coats						
over 300 mm wide	-	-	-	-	m²	17.82
not exceeding 300 mm wide	-	-	-	-	m	8.91
Plaster; first 11 mm coat of "Thistle Browning" plaster; second 2 mm finishing coat of "Thistle Multi Finish" plaster; steel trowelled 13 mm thick; work to walls; two coats; to brickwork or blockwork base						
over 300 mm wide	-	-	-	-	m²	9.46
over 300 mm wide; in staircase areas or plant rooms	-	-	-	-	m²	11.35
not exceeding 300 mm wide	-	-	-	-	m	5.03
13 mm thick work to isolated brickwork or blockwork columns; two coats						
over 300 mm wide	-	-	-	-	m²	17.82
not exceeding 300 mm wide	-	-	-	-	m	7.90
Plaster; first 8 mm or 11 mm coat of "Thistle Bonding" plaster; second 2 mm finishing coat of "Thistle Multi Finish" plaster;steel trowelled 13 mm thick work to walls; two coats; to concrete base						
over 300 mm wide	-	-	-	-	m²	10.59
over 300 mm wide; in staircase areas or plant rooms	-	-	-	-	m²	12.54
not exceeding 300 mm wide	-	-	-	-	m	4.85

M SURFACE FINISHES

Item	PC £	Labour hours	Labour £	Material £	Unit	Total rate £
13 mm thick work to isolated piers or columns; two coats; to concrete base						
over 300 mm wide	-	-	-	-	m²	18.92
not exceeding 300 mm wide	-	-	-	-	m	8.86
10 mm thick work to ceilings; two coats; to concrete base						
over 300 mm wide	-	-	-	-	m²	9.06
over 300 wide; 3.50 m - 5.00 m high	-	-	-	-	m²	10.87
over 300 mm wide; in staircase areas or plant rooms	-	-	-	-	m²	12.03
not exceeding 300 mm wide	-	-	-	-	m	5.06
10 mm thick work to isolated beams; two coats; to concrete base						
over 300 mm wide	-	-	-	-	m²	18.12
over 300 mm wide; 3.50 m - 5.00 m high	-	-	-	-	m²	19.32
not exceeding 300 mm wide	-	-	-	-	m	9.11
Plaster; one coat "Snowplast" plaster or other equal and approved; steel trowelled						
13 mm thick work to walls; one coat; to brickwork or blockwork base						
over 300 mm wide	-	-	-	-	m²	10.46
over 300 mm wide; in staircase areas or plant rooms	-	-	-	-	m²	12.43
not exceeding 300 mm wide	-	-	-	-	m	5.24
13 thick work to isolated columns; one coat						
over 300 mm wide	-	-	-	-	m²	12.66
not exceeding 300 mm wide	-	-	-	-	m	6.35
Plaster; first coat of "Limelite" renovating plaster; finishing coat of "Limelite" finishing plaster; or other equal and approved; steel trowelled						
13 mm thick work to walls; two coats; to brickwork or blockwork base						
over 300 mm wide	-	-	-	-	m²	14.50
over 300 mm wide; in staircase areas or plant rooms	-	-	-	-	m²	15.92
not exceeding 300 mm wide	-	-	-	-	m	7.25
Dubbing out existing walls with undercoat plaster; average 6 mm thick						
over 300 mm wide	-	-	-	-	m²	4.35
not exceeding 300 mm wide	-	-	-	-	m	2.20
Dubbing out existing walls with undercoat plaster; average 12 mm thick						
over 300 mm wide	-	-	-	-	m²	8.70
not exceeding 300 mm wide	-	-	-	-	m	4.35
Plaster; first coat of "Thistle X-ray" plaster or other equal and approved; finishing coat of "Thistle X-ray" finishing plaster or other equal and approved; steel trowelled						
17 mm thick work to walls; two coats; to brickwork or blockwork base						
over 300 mm wide	-	-	-	-	m²	47.06
over 300 mm wide; in staircase areas or plant rooms	-	-	-	-	m²	50.57
not exceeding 300 mm wide	-	-	-	-	m	18.82

M SURFACE FINISHES

Item	PC £	Labour hours	Labour £	Material £	Unit	Total rate £
M20 PLASTERED/RENDERED/ROUGHCAST COATINGS – cont'd						
Thistle X-ray plaster – cont'd						
17 mm thick work to isolated columns; two coats						
over 300 mm wide	-	-	-	-	m²	76.35
not exceeding 300 mm wide	-	-	-	-	m	30.51
Plaster; one coat "Thistle" projection plaster or other equal and approved; steel trowelled						
13 mm thick work to walls; one coat; to brickwork or blockwork base						
over 300 mm wide	-	-	-	-	m²	10.09
over 300 mm wide; in staircase areas or plant rooms	-	-	-	-	m²	11.54
not exceeding 300 mm wide	-	-	-	-	m	5.04
10 mm thick work to isolated columns; one coat						
over 300 mm wide	-	-	-	-	m²	12.28
not exceeding 300 mm wide	-	-	-	-	m	6.13
Plaster; first 11 mm coat of "Thistle Bonding" plaster; second 2 mm finishing coat of "Thistle Multi Finish" plaster;steel trowelled						
13 mm thick work to ceilings; three coats to metal lathing base						
over 300 mm wide	-	-	-	-	m²	10.99
over 300 mm wide; in staircase areas or plant rooms	-	-	-	-	m²	13.19
not exceeding 300 mm wide	-	-	-	-	m	5.93
13 mm thick work to swept soffit of metal lathing arch former						
not exceeding 300 mm wide	-	-	-	-	m	7.92
300 mm - 400 mm wide	-	-	-	-	m	10.58
13 mm thick work to vertical face of metal lathing arch former						
not exceeding 0.50 m² per side	-	-	-	-	nr	11.24
0.50 m2 - 1 m² per side	-	-	-	-	nr	16.86
Squash court plaster, Prodorite Ltd; first coat "Formula Base" screed or other equal and approved; finishing coat "Formula 90" finishing plaster or other equal and approved; steel trowelled and finished with sponge float						
12 mm thick work to walls; two coats; to brickwork or blockwork base						
over 300 mm wide	-	-	-	-	m²	32.14
not exceeding 300 mm wide	-	-	-	-	m	15.80
demarcation lines on battens	-	-	-	-	m	4.56
"Cemrend" self-coloured render or other equal and approved; one coat; to brickwork or blockwork base						
20 mm thick work to walls; to brickwork or blockwork base						
over 300 mm wide	-	-	-	-	m²	32.27
not exceeding 300 mm wide	-	-	-	-	m	18.82

M SURFACE FINISHES

Item	PC £	Labour hours	Labour £	Material £	Unit	Total rate £
Tyrolean decorative rendering or similar; 13 mm thick first coat of cement-lime-sand (1:1:6); finishing three coats of "Cullamix"' or other equal and approved; applied with approved hand operated machine external						
To walls; four coats; to brickwork or blockwork base						
over 300 mm wide	-	-	-	-	m²	24.12
not exceeding 300 mm wide	-	-	-	-	m	12.05
Drydash (pebbledash) finish of Derbyshire Spar chippings or other equal and approved on and including cement-lime-sand (1:2:9) backing						
18 mm thick work to walls; two coats; to brickwork or blockwork base						
over 300 mm wide	-	-	-	-	m²	20.91
not exceeding 300 mm wide	-	-	-	-	m	10.46
Plaster; one coat "Thistle" board finish or other equal and approved; steel trowelled (prices included within plasterboard rates)						
3 mm thick work to walls or ceilings; one coat; to plasterboard base						
over 300 mm wide	-	-	-	-	m²	4.26
over 300 mm wide; in staircase areas or plant rooms	-	-	-	-	m²	5.12
not exceeding 300 mm wide	-	-	-	-	m	1.71
Plaster; one coat "Thistle" board finish or other and approved; steel trowelled 3 mm work to walls or ceilings; one coat on and including gypsum plasterboard; BS 1230; fixing with nails; 3 mm joints filled with plaster and jute scrim cloth; to softwood base; plain grade baseboard or lath with rounded edges						
9.50 mm thick boards to walls						
over 300 mm wide	-	0.97	12.14	2.14	m²	14.28
not exceeding 300 mm wide	-	0.37	4.95	0.60	m	5.56
9.50 mm thick boards to walls; in staircase areas or plant rooms						
over 300 mm wide	-	1.06	13.35	2.14	m²	15.49
not exceeding 300 mm wide	-	0.46	6.16	0.60	m	6.76
9.50 mm thick boards to isolated columns						
over 300 mm wide	-	1.06	13.35	2.14	m²	15.49
not exceeding 300 mm wide	-	0.56	7.50	0.60	m	8.10
9.50 mm thick boards to ceilings						
over 300 mm wide	-	0.89	11.07	2.14	m²	13.21
over 300 mm wide; 3.50 m - 5.00 m high	-	1.03	12.95	2.14	m²	15.09
not exceeding 300 mm wide	-	0.43	5.76	0.60	m	6.36
9.50 mm thick boards to ceilings; in staircase areas or plant rooms						
over 300 mm wide	-	0.98	12.28	2.14	m²	14.42
not exceeding 300 mm wide	-	0.47	6.29	0.60	m	6.90
9.50 mm thick boards to isolated beams						
over 300 mm wide	-	1.05	13.22	2.14	m²	15.35
not exceeding 300 mm wide	-	0.50	6.69	0.60	m	7.30

M SURFACE FINISHES

Item	PC £	Labour hours	Labour £	Material £	Unit	Total rate £
M20 PLASTERED/RENDERED/ROUGHCAST COATINGS – cont'd						
Thistle Plaster on gypsum plasterboard – cont'd						
12.50 mm thick boards to walls; in staircase areas or plant rooms						
over 300 mm wide	-	1.12	14.15	2.22	m^2	16.37
not exceeding 300 mm wide	-	0.50	6.69	0.63	m	7.32
12.50 mm thick boards to isolated columns						
over 300 mm wide	-	1.12	14.15	2.22	m^2	16.37
not exceeding 300 mm wide	-	0.59	7.90	0.63	m	8.53
12.50 mm thick boards to ceilings						
over 300 mm wide	-	0.95	11.88	2.22	m^2	14.10
over 300 mm wide; 3.50 m - 5.00 m high	-	1.06	13.35	2.22	m^2	15.57
not exceeding 300 mm wide	-	0.45	6.02	0.63	m	6.65
12.50 mm thick boards to ceilings; in staircase areas or plant rooms						
over 300 mm wide	-	1.06	13.35	2.22	m^2	15.57
not exceeding 300 mm wide	-	0.51	6.83	0.63	m	7.46
12.50 mm thick boards to isolated beams						
over 300 mm wide	-	1.15	14.55	2.22	m^2	16.77
not exceeding 300 mm wide	-	0.56	7.50	0.63	m	8.13
Accessories						
"Expamet" render beads or other equal and approved; white PVC nosings; to brickwork or blockwork base						
external stop bead; ref 573	-	0.07	0.94	1.30	m	2.24
"Expamet" render beads or other equal and approved; stainless steel; to brickwork or blockwork base						
stop bead; ref 546	-	0.07	0.94	2.29	m	3.23
stop bead; ref 547	-	0.07	0.94	2.29	m	3.23
"Expamet" plaster beads or other equal and approved; galvanised steel; to brickwork or blockwork base						
angle bead; ref 550	-	0.08	1.07	0.55	m	1.62
architrave bead; ref 579	-	0.10	1.34	1.48	m	2.82
stop bead; ref 562	-	0.07	0.94	0.68	m	1.62
stop beads; ref 563	-	0.07	0.94	0.68	m	1.62
movement bead; ref 588	-	0.09	1.21	5.29	m	6.50
"Expamet" plaster beads or other equal and approved; stainless steel; to brickwork or blockwork base						
angle bead; ref 545	-	0.08	1.07	2.57	m	3.65
stop bead; ref 534	-	0.07	0.94	2.29	m	3.23
stop bead; ref 533	-	0.07	0.94	2.29	m	3.23
"Expamet" thin coat plaster beads or other equal and approved; galvanised steel; to timber base						
angle bead; ref 553	-	0.07	0.94	0.52	m	1.45
angle bead; ref 554	-	0.07	0.94	0.43	m	1.37
stop bead; ref 560	-	0.06	0.80	0.78	m	1.59
stop bead; ref 561	-	0.06	0.80	0.78	m	1.59

M SURFACE FINISHES

Item	PC £	Labour hours	Labour £	Material £	Unit	Total rate £
M21 INSULATION WITH RENDERED FINISH						
"StoTherm" mineral external wall insulation system or other equal and approved; CCS Scotseal Ltd						
70 mm thick expanded polystyrene; Sto RFP reinforcing coat; glassfibre reinforcing mesh; one coat Sto Primer; mechanical fixing using PVC intermediate tracks and T-splines; to brickwork or blockwork base						
over 300 mm wide	-	1.23	39.71	34.48	m²	74.19
70 mm thick expanded polystyrene; Sto RFP reinforcing coat; glassfibre reinforcing mesh; fixing using adhesive; to brickwork or blockwork base						
over 300 mm wide	-	1.00	32.29	30.43	m²	62.72
70 mm thick mineral wool; Sto RFP reinforcing coat; glassfibre reinforcing mesh; one coat Sto Primer; mechanical fixing using PVC intermediate tracks and T-splines; to brickwork or blockwork base						
over 300 mm wide	-	1.54	49.72	44.74	m²	94.46
70 mm thick mineral wool; StoLevell Uni reinforcing coat; glassfibre reinforcing mesh; one coat Sto Primer; fixing using adhesive; to brickwork or blockwork base						
over 300 mm wide	-	1.39	44.88	39.02	m²	83.90
M22 SPRAYED MINERAL FIBRE COATINGS						
Prepare and apply by spray "Mandolite CP2" fire protection or other equal and approved on structural steel/metalwork						
16 mm thick (one hour) fire protection						
to walls and columns	-	-	-	-	m²	9.10
to ceilings and beams	-	-	-	-	m²	10.05
to isolated metalwork	-	-	-	-	m²	20.02
22 mm thick (one and a half hour) fire protection						
to walls and columns	-	-	-	-	m²	10.58
to ceilings and beams	-	-	-	-	m²	11.74
to isolated metalwork	-	-	-	-	m²	23.48
28 mm thick (two hour) fire protection						
to walls and columns	-	-	-	-	m²	12.41
to ceilings and beams	-	-	-	-	m²	13.56
to isolated metalwork	-	-	-	-	m²	27.10
52 mm thick (four hour) fire protection						
to walls and columns	-	-	-	-	m²	18.77
to ceilings and beams	-	-	-	-	m²	20.90
to isolated metalwork	-	-	-	-	m²	41.59
Prepare and apply by spray; cementitious "Pyrok WF26" render or other equal and approved; on expanded metal lathing (not included)						
15 mm thick						
to ceilings and beams	-	-	-	-	m²	28.81

M SURFACE FINISHES

Item	PC £	Labour hours	Labour £	Material £	Unit	Total rate £
M30 METAL MESH LATHING/ANCHORED REINFORCEMENT FOR PLASTERED COATING						
Accessories						
Pre-formed galvanised expanded steel arch-frames; "Simpson's Strong-Tie" or other equal and approved; semi-circular; to suit walls up to 230 mm thick						
375 mm radius; for 800 mm opening; ref SC 750	21.07	0.46	5.38	23.24	nr	28.63
425 mm radius; for 850 mm opening; ref SC 850	20.12	0.46	5.38	22.20	nr	27.58
450 mm radius; for 900 mm opening; ref SC 900	20.81	0.46	5.38	22.96	nr	28.34
600 mm radius; for 1200 mm opening; ref SC 1200	24.07	0.46	5.38	26.56	nr	31.94
Lathing; Expamet "BB" expanded metal lathing or other equal and approved; BS 1369; 50 mm laps						
6 mm thick mesh linings to ceilings; fixing with staples; to softwood base; over 300 mm wide						
ref BB263; 0.500 mm thick	3.09	0.56	6.55	3.49	m^2	10.04
ref BB264; 0.675 mm thick	4.32	0.56	6.55	4.88	m^2	11.44
6 mm thick mesh linings to ceilings; fixing with wire; to steelwork; over 300 mm wide						
ref BB263; 0.500 mm thick	-	0.59	6.92	3.49	m^2	10.41
ref BB264; 0.675 mm thick	-	0.59	6.92	4.88	m^2	11.80
6 mm thick mesh linings to ceilings; fixing with wire; to steelwork; not exceeding 300 mm wide						
ref BB263; 0.500 mm thick	-	0.37	4.31	3.49	m^2	7.80
ref BB264; 0.675 mm thick	-	0.37	4.31	4.88	m^2	9.20
raking cutting	-	0.19	2.54	-	m	2.54
cutting and fitting around pipes; not exceeding 0.30 m girth	-	0.28	3.75	-	nr	3.75
Lathing; Expamet "Riblath" or "Spraylath" or other equal and approved stiffened expanded metal lathing or similar; 50 mm laps						
10 mm thick mesh lining to walls; fixing with nails; to softwood base; over 300 mm wide						
"Riblath" ref 269; 0.30 mm thick	5.10	0.46	5.38	5.87	m^2	11.25
"Riblath" ref 271; 0.50 mm thick	5.88	0.46	5.38	6.74	m^2	12.12
10 mm thick mesh lining to walls; fixing with nails; to softwood base; not exceeding 300 mm wide						
"Riblath" ref 269; 0.30 mm thick	-	0.28	3.28	1.80	m^2	5.07
"Riblath" ref 271; 0.50 mm thick	-	0.28	3.28	2.06	m^2	5.34
10 mm thick mesh lining to walls; fixing to brick or blockwork; over 300 mm wide						
"Red-rib" ref 274; 0.50 mm thick	6.49	0.37	4.31	7.97	m^2	12.29
Stainless steel "Riblath" ref 267; 0.30 mm thick	13.71	0.37	4.31	16.14	m^2	20.45
10 mm thick mesh lining to ceilings; fixing with wire; to steelwork; over 300 mm wide						
"Riblath" ref 269; 0.30 mm thick	-	0.59	6.92	6.32	m^2	13.24
"Riblath" ref 271; 0.50 mm thick	-	0.59	6.92	7.19	m^2	14.11

M SURFACE FINISHES

Item	PC £	Labour hours	Labour £	Material £	Unit	Total rate £
M31 FIBROUS PLASTER						
Fibrous plaster; fixing with screws;						
plugging; countersinking; stopping;						
filling and pointing joints with plaster						
16 mm thick plain slab coverings to ceilings						
over 300 mm wide	-	-	-	-	m^2	118.14
not exceeding 300 mm wide	-	-	-	-	m	39.74
Coves; not exceeding 150 mm girth						
per 25 mm girth	-	-	-	-	m	5.70
Coves; 150 mm - 300 mm girth						
per 25 mm girth	-	-	-	-	m	6.98
Cornices						
per 25 mm girth	-	-	-	-	m	7.09
Cornice enrichments						
per 25 mm girth; depending on degree of						
enrichments	-	-	-	-	m	8.37
Fibrous plaster; fixing with plaster						
wadding filling and pointing joints with						
plaster; to steel base						
16 mm thick plain slab coverings to ceilings						
over 300 mm wide	-	-	-	-	m^2	118.14
not exceeding 300 mm wide	-	-	-	-	m	39.74
16 mm thick plain casings to stanchions						
per 25 mm girth	-	-	-	-	m	3.54
16 mm thick plain casings to beams						
per 25 mm girth	-	-	-	-	m	3.54
Gyproc cove or other equal and						
approved; fixing with adhesive; filling						
and pointing joints with plaster						
Cove						
125 mm girth	-	0.19	2.54	0.75	m	3.30
Angles	-	0.03	0.40	0.48	nr	0.88
M40 STONE/CONCRETE/QUARRY/						
CERAMIC TILING						
ALTERNATIVE TILE MATERIALS						
Discounts of 10 - 30% available depending on						
quantity/status						
Dennis Ruabon clay floor quarries (£/1000);						
Heather Brown						
150 mm x 150 mm x 12.5 mm	-	-	-	468.50	1000nr	-
194 mm x 94 mm x 12.5 mm	-	-	-	541.40	1000nr	-
194 mm x 194 mm x 12.5 mm	-	-	-	832.90	1000nr	-
Red						
150 mm x 150 mm x 12.50 mm; square	-	-	-	364.40	1000nr	-
150 mm x 150 mm x 12.50 mm; hexagonal	-	-	-	593.40	1000nr	-
Daniel Platt heavy duty floor tiles (£/m^2)						
"Ferrolite" flat; 100 mm x 100 mm x 9 mm						
black	-	-	-	17.48	m^2	-
cream mingled	-	-	-	17.48	m^2	-
red	-	-	-	17.48	m^2	-

M SURFACE FINISHES

Item	PC £	Labour hours	Labour £	Material £	Unit	Total rate £
M40 STONE/CONCRETE/QUARRY/ CERAMIC TILING – cont'd						
ALTERNATIVE TILE MATERIALS – cont'd						
"Ferrolite" flat; 152 mm x 152 mm x 12 mm						
black	-	-	-	30.41	m²	-
chocolate	-	-	-	30.41	m²	-
cream mingled (M29)	-	-	-	25.77	m²	-
red	-	-	-	24.47	m²	-
"Ferrundum" anti-slip; 152 x 152 x 12 mm						
black	-	-	-	32.77	m²	-
cream mingled (M29)	-	-	-	27.52	m²	-
Marley floor tiles; 300 mm x 300 mm						
"Marleyflex"						
series 2 - 2.50 mm	-	-	-	5.85	m²	-
series 4 - 2.50 mm	-	-	-	6.15	m²	-
"Europa - Through Clip - semi-flexible"						
2.00 mm	-	-	-	6.69	m²	-
2.50 mm	-	-	-	8.16	m²	-
"Conductive"; 608 mm x 608 mm						
2.00 mm	-	-	-	16.28	m²	-
"Vylon Plus"; 300 mm x 300 mm					-	
2.00 mm	-	-	-	5.57	m²	-
SUPPLY AND FIX PRICES						
Clay floor quarries; BS 6431; class 1; Daniel Platt "Crown" tiles or other equal and approved; level bedding 10 mm thick and jointing in cement and sand (1:3); butt joints; straight both ways; flush pointing with grout; to cement and sand base						
Work to floors; over 300 mm wide						
150 mm x 150 mm x 12.50 mm thick; red	-	0.74	13.91	17.54	m²	**31.45**
150 mm x 150 mm x 12.50 mm thick; brown	-	0.74	13.91	21.25	m²	**35.15**
200 mm x 200 mm x 19 mm thick; brown	-	0.60	11.27	29.64	m²	**40.92**
Works to floors; in staircase areas or plant rooms						
150 mm x 150 mm x 12.50 mm thick; red	-	0.83	15.60	17.54	m²	**33.14**
150 mm x 150 mm x 12.50 mm thick; brown	-	0.83	15.60	21.25	m²	**36.84**
200 mm x 200 mm x 19 mm thick; brown	-	0.69	12.97	29.64	m²	**42.61**
Work to floors; not exceeding 300 mm wide						
150 mm x 150 mm x 12.50 mm thick; red	-	0.37	6.95	3.93	m	**10.88**
150 mm x 150 mm x 12.50 mm thick; brown	-	0.37	6.95	5.04	m	**11.99**
200 mm x 200 mm x 19 mm thick; brown	-	0.31	5.83	7.56	m	**13.38**
fair square cutting against flush edges of existing finishes	-	0.11	1.37	0.87	m	**2.24**
raking cutting	-	0.19	2.43	0.98	m	**3.40**
cutting around pipes; not exceeding 0.30 m girth	-	0.14	1.87	-	nr	**1.87**
extra for cutting and fitting into recessed manhole cover 600 mm x 600 mm	-	0.93	12.45	-	nr	**12.45**
Work to sills; 150 mm wide; rounded edge tiles						
150 mm x 150 mm x 12.50 mm thick; red	2.88	0.31	5.83	3.46	m	**9.28**
150 mm x 150 mm x 12.50 mm thick; brown	-	0.31	5.83	4.57	m	**10.40**
fitted end	-	0.14	1.87	-	nr	**1.87**
Coved skirtings; 138 mm high; rounded top edge						
150 mm x 138 mm x 12.50 mm thick; red	2.57	0.23	4.32	4.24	m	**8.57**
150 mm x 138 mm x 12.50 mm thick; brown	2.93	0.23	4.32	4.64	m	**8.96**
ends	-	0.04	0.54	-	nr	**0.54**
angles	-	0.14	1.87	1.60	nr	**3.47**

M SURFACE FINISHES

Item	PC £	Labour hours	Labour £	Material £	Unit	Total rate £
Glazed ceramic wall tiles; BS 6431;						
fixing with adhesive; butt joints; straight						
both ways; flush pointing with white						
grout; to plaster base						
Work to walls; over 300 mm wide						
152 mm x 152 mm x 5.50 mm thick; white	10.89	0.56	13.55	16.81	m²	**30.36**
152 mm x 152 mm x 5.50 mm thick; light colours	13.29	0.56	13.55	19.52	m²	**33.07**
152 mm x 152 mm x 5.50 mm thick; dark colours	14.53	0.56	13.55	20.92	m²	**34.47**
extra for RE or REX tile	-	-	-	6.31	m²	**6.31**
200 mm x 100 mm x 6.50 mm thick; white and						
light colours	10.89	0.56	13.55	16.81	m²	**30.36**
250 mm x 200 mm x 7 mm thick; white and light						
colours	11.80	0.56	13.55	17.84	m²	**31.39**
Work to walls; in staircase areas or plant rooms						
152 mm x 152 mm x 5.50 mm thick; white	-	0.62	15.00	16.81	m²	**31.81**
Work to walls; not exceeding 300 mm wide						
152 mm x 152 mm x 5.50 mm thick; white	-	0.28	6.77	4.99	m	**11.77**
152 mm x 152 mm x 5.50 mm thick; light colours	-	0.28	6.77	7.95	m	**14.72**
152 mm x 152 mm x 5.50 mm thick; dark colours	-	0.28	6.77	8.37	m	**15.14**
200 mm x 100 mm x 6.50 mm thick; white and						
light colours	-	0.28	6.77	4.99	m	**11.77**
250 mm x 200 mm x 7 mm thick; white and light						
colours	-	0.23	5.56	5.30	m	**10.86**
cutting around pipes; not exceeding 0.30 m girth	-	0.09	1.21	-	nr	**1.21**
Work to sills; 150 mm wide; rounded edge tiles						
152 mm x 152 mm x 5.50 mm thick; white	-	0.23	5.56	2.50	m	**8.06**
fitted end	-	0.09	1.21	-	nr	**1.21**
198 mm x 64.50 mm x 6 mm thick wall						
tiles; fixing with adhesive; butt joints;						
straight both ways; flush pointing with						
white grout; to plaster base						
Work to walls						
over 300 mm wide	23.06	1.67	40.40	30.56	m²	**70.96**
not exceeding 300 mm wide	-	0.65	15.73	9.11	m	**24.84**
20 mm x 20 mm x 5.50 mm thick glazed						
mosaic wall tiles; fixing with adhesive;						
butt joints; straight both ways; flush						
pointing with white grout; to plaster base						
Work to walls						
over 300 mm wide	28.30	1.76	42.58	37.27	m²	**79.86**
not exceeding 300 mm wide	-	0.69	16.69	13.17	m	**29.86**
50 mm x 50 mm x 5.50 mm thick slip						
resistant mosaic floor tiles, Series 2 or						
other equal and approved; Langley						
London Ltd; fixing with adhesive; butt						
joints; straight both ways; flush pointing						
with white grout; to cement and sand						
base						
Work to floors						
over 300 mm wide	28.33	1.76	33.07	38.24	m²	**71.32**
not exceeding 300 mm wide	-	0.69	12.97	13.18	m	**26.15**

M SURFACE FINISHES

Item	PC £	Labour hours	Labour £	Material £	Unit	Total rate £
M40 STONE/CONCRETE/QUARRY/ **CERAMIC TILING** – cont'd						
Dakota mahogany granite cladding; **polished finish; jointed and pointed in** **coloured mortar (1:2:8)**						
20 mm work to floors; level; to cement and sand base						
over 300 mm wide	-	-	-	-	m²	280.45
20 mm x 300 mm treads; plain nosings	-	-	-	-	m	159.60
raking, cutting	-	-	-	-	m	28.62
polished edges	-	-	-	-	m	35.98
birdsmouth	-	-	-	-	m	37.13
20 mm thick work to walls; to cement and sand base						
over 300 mm wide	-	-	-	-	m²	286.09
not exceeding 300 mm wide	-	-	-	-	m	128.74
40 mm thick work to walls; to cement and sand base						
over 300 mm wide	-	-	-	-	m²	475.04
not exceeding 300 mm wide	-	-	-	-	m	213.75
Riven Welsh slate floor tiles; level; **bedding 10 mm thick and jointing in** **cement and sand (1:3); butt joints;** **straight both ways; flush pointing with** **coloured mortar; to cement and sand** **base**						
Work to floors; over 300 mm wide						
250 mm x 250 mm x 12 mm - 15 mm thick	-	0.56	13.55	36.40	m²	49.95
Work to floors; not exceeding 300 mm wide						
250 mm x 250 mm x 12 mm - 15 mm thick	-	0.28	6.77	11.00	m	17.77
Roman Travertine marble cladding; **polished finish; jointed and pointed in** **coloured mortar (1:2:8)**						
20 mm thick work to floors; level; to cement and sand base						
over 300 mm wide	-	-	-	-	m²	183.15
20 mm x 300 mm treads; plain nosings	-	-	-	-	m	110.33
raking cutting	-	-	-	-	m	21.39
polished edges	-	-	-	-	m	19.67
birdsmouth	-	-	-	-	m	39.43
20 mm thick work to walls; to cement and sand base						
over 300 mm wide	-	-	-	-	m²	217.78
not exceeding 300 mm wide	-	-	-	-	m	97.86
40 mm thick work to walls; to cement and sand base						
over 300 mm wide	-	-	-	-	m²	299.79
not exceeding 300 mm wide	-	-	-	-	m	134.90
M41 TERRAZZO TILING/IN SITU TERRAZZO						
Terrazzo tiles; BS 4131; aggregate size **random ground grouted and polished to** **80's grit finish; standard colour range; 3** **mm joints symmetrical layout; bedding in** **42 mm cement semi-dry mix (1:4);** **grouting with neat matching cement**						

M SURFACE FINISHES

Item	PC £	Labour hours	Labour £	Material £	Unit	Total rate £
300 mm x 300 mm x 28 mm (nominal) Terrazzo tile units; hydraulically pressed, mechanically vibrated, steam cured; to floors on concrete base (not included); sealed with penetrating case hardener or other equal and approved; 2 coats applied immediately after final polishing						
plain; laid level	-	-	-	-	m²	36.79
plain; to slopes exceeding 15 degrees from horizontal	-	-	-	-	m²	43.99
to small areas/toilets	-	-	-	-	m²	80.28
Accessories						
plastic division strips; 6 mm x 38 mm; set into floor tiling above crack inducing joints, to the nearest full tile module	-	-	-	-	m	2.49
Specially made terrazzo precast units; BS 4387; aggregate size random; standard colour range; 3 mm joints; grouting with neat matching cement						
Standard tread and riser square combined terrazzo units (with riser cast down) or other equal and approved; 280 mm wide; 150 mm high; 40 mm thick; machine made; vibrated and fully machine polished; incorporating 1 nr. "Ferodo" anti-slip insert ref. OT/D or other equal and approved cast-in during manufacture; one end polished only						
fixed with cement:sand (1:4) mortar on prepared backgrounds (not included); grouted in neat tinted cement; wiped clean on completion of fixing	-	-	-	-	m	175.46
Standard tread square terrazzo units or other equal and approved; 40 mm thick; 280 mm wide; factory polished; incorporating 1 nr. "Ferodo" anti-slip insert ref. OT/D or other equal and approved						
fixed with cement:sand (1:4) mortar on prepared backgrounds (not included); grouted in neat tinted cement; wiped clean on completion of fixing	-	-	-	-	m	105.58
Extra over for 55 x 55 mm contrasting colour To step nosing	-	-	-	-	m	38.46
Standard riser square terrazzo units or other equal and approved; 40 mm thick; 150 mm high; factory polished						
fixed with cemnt:sand (1:4) mortar on prepared backgrounds (not included); grouted in neat tinted cement; wiped clean on completion of fixing	-	-	-	-	m	65.52
Standard coved terrazzo skirting units or other equal and approved; 904 mm long; 150 mm high; nominal finish; 23 mm thick; with square top edge						
fixed with cement:sand (1:4) mortar on prepared backgrounds (by others); grouted in neat tinted cement; wiped clean on completion of fixing	-	-	-	-	m	61.54
extra over for special internal/external angle pieces to match	-	-	-	-	m	17.48
extra over for special polished ends	-	-	-	-	nr	5.76

M SURFACE FINISHES

Item	PC £	Labour hours	Labour £	Material £	Unit	Total rate £
M42 WOOD BLOCK/COMPOSITION BLOCK/ PARQUET FLOORING						
Wood block; Vigers, Stevens & Adams "Vigerflex" or other equal and approved; 7.50 mm thick; level; fixing with adhesive; to cement:sand base						
Work to floors; over 300 mm wide						
"Maple 7"	-	0.46	8.64	17.63	m²	26.28
Wood blocks 25 mm thick; tongued and grooved joints; herringbone pattern; level; fixing with adhesive; to cement:sand base						
Work to floors; over 300 mm wide						
iroko	-	-	-	-	m²	49.23
"Maple 7"	-	-	-	-	m²	53.22
french Oak	-	-	-	-	m²	73.17
american oak	-	-	-	-	m²	66.52
fair square cutting against flush edges of existing finishings	-	-	-	-	m	6.33
extra for cutting and fitting into recessed duct covers 450 mm wide; lining up with adjoining work	-	-	-	-	nr	16.22
cutting around pipes; not exceeding 0.30 m girth	-	-	-	-	nr	2.66
extra for cutting and fitting into recessed manhole covers 600 mm x 600 mm; lining up with adjoining work	-	-	-	-	nr	11.97
Add to wood block flooring over 300 wide for						
sanding; one coat sealer; one coat wax polish	-	-	-	-	m²	5.32
sanding; two coats sealer; buffing with steel wool	-	-	-	-	m²	5.18
sanding; three coats polyurethane lacquer; buffing down between coats	-	-	-	-	m²	7.98
M50 RUBBER/PLASTICS/CORK/LINO/ CARPET TILING/SHEETING						
Linoleum sheet; Forbo-Nairn "Marmoleum Real" or other equal and approved; level; fixing with adhesive; butt joints; to cement and sand base						
Work to floors; over 300 mm wide						
2.50 mm thick	-	0.37	6.95	9.29	m²	16.24
3.20 mm thick; marbled	-	0.37	6.95	11.52	m²	18.47
Linoleum sheet; Forbo-Nairn "Walton" or other equal and approved; level; with welded seams; fixing with adhesive; to cement and sand base						
Work to floors; over 300 mm wide						
2.50 mm thick; plain	-	0.46	8.64	10.66	m²	19.31
Vinyl sheet; Altro "Safety" range or other equal and approved; with welded seams; level; fixing with adhesive; to cement and sand base						
Work to floors; over 300 mm wide						
2.00 mm thick; "Marine T20"	-	0.56	10.52	13.85	m²	24.38
2.50 mm thick; "Classic D25"	-	0.65	12.21	15.57	m²	27.79
3.50 mm thick; "Stronghold"	-	0.74	13.91	20.62	m²	34.53

M SURFACE FINISHES

Item	PC £	Labour hours	Labour £	Material £	Unit	Total rate £
Slip resistant vinyl sheet; Forbo-Nairn "Surestep" or other equal and approved; level with welded seams; fixing with adhesive; to cement and sand base Work to floors; over 300 mm wide						
2.00 mm thick	-	0.46	8.64	11.43	m²	**20.08**
Vinyl sheet; heavy duty; Marley "HD" or other equal and approved; level; with welded seams; fixing with adhesive; level; to cement and sand base Work to floors; over 300 mm wide						
2.00 mm thick	-	0.42	7.89	5.74	m²	**13.64**
2.50 mm thick	-	0.46	8.64	6.99	m²	**15.64**
2.00 mm thick skirtings						
100 mm high	-	0.11	2.07	1.76	m	**3.83**
Vinyl sheet; Marley "Sport" or other equal and approved; level; with welded seams; fixing with adhesive; level; to cement and sand base Work to floors; over 300 mm wide						
6.70 mm thick	-	0.90	16.91	19.70	m²	**36.61**
8.00 mm thick	-	1.00	18.79	22.94	m²	**41.73**
Vinyl sheet; Gerflor "Gerflex" standard sheet; "Classic" range or other equal and approved; level; with welded seams; fixing with adhesive; to cement and sand base Work to floors; over 300 mm wide						
2.00 mm thick	-	0.46	8.64	6.19	m²	**14.84**
Vinyl sheet; Armstrong "Rhino Contract" or other equal and approved; level; with welded seams; fixing with adhesive; to cement and sand base Work to floors; over 300 mm wide						
2.50 mm thick	-	0.46	8.64	7.28	m²	**15.92**
Vinyl tiles; Armstrong "Accoflex" or other equal and approved; level; fixing with adhesive; butt joints; straight both ways; to cement and sand base Work to floors; over 300 mm wide						
608 mm x 608 mm x 2.00 mm thick	-	0.23	4.32	4.42	m²	**8.74**
Vinyl semi-flexible tiles; Armstrong "Arlon" or other equal and approved; level; fixing with adhesive; butt joints; straight both ways; to cement and sand base Work to floors; over 300 mm wide						
250 mm x 250 mm x 2.00 mm thick	-	0.23	4.32	4.49	m²	**8.81**

M SURFACE FINISHES

Item	PC £	Labour hours	Labour £	Material £	Unit	Total rate £
M50 RUBBER/PLASTICS/CORK/LINO/ CARPET TILING/SHEETING – cont'd						
Vinyl semi-flexible tiles; Marley "Marleyflex" or other equal and approved; level; fixing with adhesive; butt joints; straight both ways; to cement and sand base						
Work to floors; over 300 mm wide						
300 mm x 300 mm x 2.00 mm thick	-	0.23	4.32	4.95	m²	**9.28**
300 mm x 300 mm x 2.50 mm thick	-	0.23	4.32	5.97	m²	**10.30**
Vinyl semi-flexible tiles; Marley "Vylon" or other equal and approved; level; fixing with adhesive; butt joints; straight both ways; to cement and sand base						
Work to floors; over 300 mm wide						
250 mm x 250 mm x 2.00 mm thick	-	0.26	4.89	4.71	m²	**9.59**
Vinyl tiles; James Halstead "Polyflex" or other equal and approved; level; fixing with adhesive; butt joints; straight both ways; to cement and sand base						
Work to floors; over 300 mm wide						
300 mm x 300 mm x 1.50 mm thick	-	0.23	4.32	4.08	m²	**8.40**
300 mm x 300 mm x 2.00 mm thick	-	0.23	4.32	4.51	m²	**8.83**
Vinyl tiles; "Polyflor XL" or other equal and approved; level; fixing with adhesive; butt joints; straight both ways; to cement and sand base						
Work to floors; over 300 mm wide						
300 mm x 300 mm x 2.00 mm thick	-	0.32	6.01	5.56	m²	**11.58**
Vinyl tiles; James Halstead "Polyflor"anti-static; level; fixing with adhesive; butt joints; straight both ways; to cement and sand base						
Work to floors; over 300 mm wide						
457 mm x 457 mm x 2.00 mm thick	-	0.42	7.89	9.45	m²	**17.34**
Vinyl tiles; Marley "HD" or other equal and approved; level; fixing with adhesive; butt joints; straight both ways; to cement and sand base						
Work to floors; over 300 mm wide						
300 mm x 300 mm x 2.00 mm thick	-	0.32	6.01	5.74	m²	**11.76**
Thermoplastic tiles; Marley "Marleyflex" or other equal and approved; level; fixing with adhesive; butt joints; straight both ways; to cement and sand base						
Work to floors; over 300 mm wide						
300 mm x 300 mm x 2.00 mm thick; series 2	-	0.21	3.95	4.37	m²	**8.31**
300 mm x 300 mm x 2.00 mm thick; series 4	-	0.21	3.95	4.69	m²	**8.64**

M SURFACE FINISHES

Item	PC £	Labour hours	Labour £	Material £	Unit	Total rate £
Linoleum tiles; BS 6826; Forbo-Nairn Floors or other equal and approved; level; fixing with adhesive; butt joints; straight both ways; to cement and sand base						
Work to floors; over 300 mm wide						
2.50 mm thick (marble pattern)	-	0.28	5.26	10.42	m²	**15.68**
Cork tiles Wicanders "Cork-Master" or other equal and approved; level; fixing with adhesive; butt joints; straight both ways; to cement and sand base						
Work to floors; over 300 mm wide						
300 mm x 300 mm x 4.00 mm thick	-	0.37	6.95	20.77	m²	**27.72**
Rubber studded tiles; Altro "Mondopave" or other equal and approved; level; fixing with adhesive; butt joints; straight to cement and sand base						
Work to floors; over 300 mm wide						
500 mm x 500 mm x 2.50 mm thick; type MRB; black	-	0.56	10.52	24.45	m²	**34.97**
500 mm x 500 mm x 4.00 mm thick; type MRB; black	-	0.56	10.52	23.41	m²	**33.93**
Work to landings; over 300 mm wide						
500 mm x 500 mm x 4.00 mm thick; type MRB; black	-	0.74	13.91	23.41	m²	**37.31**
4.00 mm thick to tread						
275 mm wide	-	0.46	8.64	6.96	m	**15.60**
4.00 mm thick to riser						
180 mm wide	-	0.56	10.52	4.95	m	**15.47**
Sundry floor sheeting underlays						
For floor finishings; over 300 mm wide						
building paper to BS 1521; class A; 75 mm lap (laying only)	-	0.05	0.50	-	m²	**0.50**
3.20 mm thick hardboard	-	0.19	4.60	1.23	m²	**5.83**
6.00 mm thick plywood	-	0.28	6.77	4.18	m²	**10.96**
Skirtings; plastic; Gradus or equivalent						
Set-in skirtings						
100 mm high; ref. SI1002.5P	-	0.11	2.07	1.91	m	**3.98**
150 mm high; ref. SI1502P	-	0.22	4.13	2.87	m	**7.00**
Set-on skirtings						
100 mm high; ref. SO100P	-	0.22	4.13	1.26	m	**5.40**
Stair nosings						
Light duty hard aluminium alloy stair tread nosings; plugged and screwed in concrete						
57 mm x 32 mm	6.28	0.23	3.08	7.04	m	**10.12**
84 mm x 32 mm	8.69	0.28	3.75	9.70	m	**13.45**
Heavy duty aluminium alloy stair tread nosings; plugged and screwed to concrete						
60 mm x 32 mm	7.46	0.28	3.75	8.35	m	**12.10**
92 mm x 32 mm	10.23	0.32	4.28	11.40	m	**15.68**

M SURFACE FINISHES

Item	PC £	Labour hours	Labour £	Material £	Unit	Total rate £
M50 RUBBER/PLASTICS/CORK/LINO/ CARPET TILING/SHEETING – cont'd						
Heavy duty carpet tiles; "Heuga 580 Olympic" or other equal and approved; to cement and sand base Work to floors						
over 300 mm wide	17.07	0.28	5.26	19.29	m²	24.55
M51 EDGE FIXED CARPETING						
Fitted carpeting; Wilton wool/nylon or other equal and approved; 80/20 velvet pile; heavy domestic plain Work to floors						
over 300 mm wide	34.46	0.37	4.72	40.80	m²	45.52
Work to treads and risers						
over 300 mm wide	-	0.74	9.44	40.80	m²	50.24
Underlay to carpeting Work to floors						
over 300 mm wide	3.36	0.07	0.89	3.80	m²	4.69
raking cutting	-	0.07	0.70	-	m	0.70
Sundries Carpet gripper fixed to floor; standard edging						
22 mm wide	-	0.04	0.40	0.23	m	0.63
M52 DECORATIVE PAPERS/FABRICS						
Lining paper; PC £1.95/roll; and hanging Plaster walls or columns						
over 300 mm girth	-	0.19	2.54	0.35	m²	2.90
Plaster ceilings or beams						
over 300 mm girth	-	0.23	3.08	0.35	m²	3.43
Decorative paper-backed vinyl wallpaper; PC £10.35/roll; and hanging Plaster walls or columns						
over 300 mm girth	-	0.23	3.08	1.97	m²	5.05
M60 PAINTING/CLEAR FINISHING						
BASIC PAINT PRICES						
Discounts of 10 - 40% available depending on quantity/status						
Paints						
matt emulsion	-	-	-	17.99	5 litre	-
gloss	-	-	-	20.94	5 litre	-
eggshell gloss	-	-	-	36.50	5 litre	-
oil based undercoat	-	-	-	20.94	5 litre	-
"Weathershield" gloss	-	-	-	42.18	5 litre	-
"Weathershield" undercoat	-	-	-	45.09	5 litre	-
"Sandtex" masonry paint						
brilliant white	-	-	-	12.99	5 litre	-
coloured	-	-	-	21.99	5 litre	-

M SURFACE FINISHES

Item	PC £	Labour hours	Labour £	Material £	Unit	Total rate £
Primer/undercoats						
acrylic	-	-	-	29.70	5 litre	-
red oxide	-	-	-	25.98	5 litre	-
water based	-	-	-	21.99	5 litre	-
zinc phosphate	-	-	-	34.50	5 litre	-
masonry sealer	-	-	-	21.99	5 litre	-
knotting solution	-	-	-	40.70	5 litre	-
Special paints						
solar reflective aluminium	-	-	-	40.35	5 litre	-
anti-graffiti	-	-	-	155.73	5 litre	-
bituminous emulsion	-	-	-	13.05	5 litre	-
"Hammerite"	-	-	-	47.99	5 litre	-
"Smoothrite"	-	-	-	47.99	5 litre	-
fire retardant						
undercoat	-	-	-	55.13	5 litre	-
top coat	-	-	-	73.43	5 litre	-
Stains and Preservatives						
Cuprinol	-	-	-	-	-	-
"Clear"	-	-	-	25.36	5 litre	-
Boiled linseed oil	-	-	-	19.55	5 litre	-
Sadolin						
"Extra"	-	-	-	68.28	5 litre	-
"New Base"	-	-	-	38.17	5 litre	-
Sikkens						
"Cetol HLS"	-	-	-	57.00	5 litre	-
"Cetol TS"	-	-	-	82.00	5 litre	-
"Cetol Filter 7"	-	-	-	86.72	5 litre	-
Protim Solignum						
"Architectural"	-	-	-	63.60	5 litre	-
"Brown"	-	-	-	25.62	5 litre	-
"Cedar"	-	-	-	30.25	5 litre	-
Varnishes						
polyurethane	-	-	-	35.65	5 litre	-

SUPPLY AND FIX PRICES

NOTE: The following prices include for preparing surfaces. Painting woodwork also includes for knotting prior to applying the priming coat and for all stopping of nail holes etc.

M60 PAINTING/CLEAR FINISHING - INTERNALLY

Item	PC £	Labour hours	Labour £	Material £	Unit	Total rate £
One coat primer; on wood surfaces before fixing						
General surfaces						
over 300 mm girth	-	0.08	1.07	0.76	m^2	1.83
isolated surfaces not exceeding 300 mm girth	-	0.02	0.27	0.27	m	0.54
isolated areas not exceeding 0.50 m^2						
irrespective of girth	-	0.06	0.80	0.30	nr	1.11
One coat polyurethane sealer; on wood surfaces before fixing						
General surfaces						
over 300 mm girth	-	0.10	1.34	0.76	m^2	2.10
isolated surfaces not exceeding 300 mm girth	-	0.03	0.40	0.27	m	0.67
isolated areas not exceeding 0.50 m^2;						
irrespective of girth	-	0.08	1.07	0.37	nr	1.44

M SURFACE FINISHES

Item	PC £	Labour hours	Labour £	Material £	Unit	Total rate £
M60 PAINTING/CLEAR FINISHING **– INTERNALLY** – cont'd						
One coat of Sikkens "Cetol HLS" stain **or other equal and approved; on wood** **surfaces before fixing**						
General surfaces						
over 300 mm girth	-	0.11	1.47	0.82	m²	2.29
isolated surfaces not exceeding 300 mm girth	-	0.03	0.40	0.32	m	0.72
isolated areas not exceeding 0.50 m²;						
irrespective of girth	-	0.08	1.07	0.40	nr	1.47
One coat of Sikkens "Cetol TS" interior **stain or other equal and approved; on** **wood surfaces before fixing**						
General surfaces						
over 300 mm girth	-	0.11	1.47	1.15	m²	2.63
isolated surfaces not exceeding 300 mm girth	-	0.03	0.40	0.44	m	0.84
isolated areas not exceeding 0.50 m²:						
irrespective of girth	-	0.08	1.07	0.56	nr	1.63
One coat Cuprinol clear wood **preservative or other equal and** **approved; on wood surfaces before** **fixing**						
General surfaces						
over 300 mm girth	-	0.08	1.07	0.51	m²	1.58
isolated surfaces not exceeding 300 mm girth	-	0.02	0.27	0.18	m	0.45
isolated areas not exceeding 0.50 m²;						
irrespective of girth	-	0.05	0.67	0.24	nr	0.91
One coat HCC Protective Coatings Ltd **"Permacor" urethane alkyd gloss** **finishing coat or other equal and** **approved; on previously primed** **steelwork**						
Members of roof trusses						
over 300 mm girth	-	0.06	0.80	1.52	m²	2.33
Two coats emulsion paint						
Brick or block walls						
over 300 mm girth	-	0.21	2.81	0.76	m²	3.57
Cement render or concrete						
over 300 mm girth	-	0.20	2.68	0.67	m²	3.35
isolated surfaces not exceeding 300 mm girth	-	0.10	1.34	0.21	m	1.55
Plaster walls or plaster/plasterboard ceilings						
over 300 mm girth	-	0.18	2.41	0.65	m²	3.06
over 300 mm girth; in multi colours	-	0.24	3.21	0.78	m²	4.00
over 300 mm girth; in staircase areas	-	0.21	2.81	0.75	m²	3.56
cutting in edges on flush surfaces	-	0.08	1.07	-	m	1.07
Plaster/plasterboard ceilings						
over 300 mm girth; 3.50 m - 5.00 m high	-	0.21	2.81	0.66	m²	3.47
One mist and two coats emulsion paint						
Brick or block walls						
over 300 mm girth	-	0.19	2.54	0.99	m²	3.53
Cement render or concrete						
over 300 mm girth	-	0.19	2.54	0.92	m²	3.46

M SURFACE FINISHES

Item	PC £	Labour hours	Labour £	Material £	Unit	Total rate £
Plaster walls or plaster/plasterboard ceilings						
over 300 mm girth	-	0.18	2.41	0.92	m²	3.33
over 300 mm girth; in multi colours	-	0.25	3.35	0.93	m²	4.28
over 300 mm girth; in staircase areas	-	0.21	2.81	0.92	m²	3.73
cutting in edges on flush surfaces	-	0.09	1.21	-	m	1.21
Plaster/plasterboard ceilings						
over 300 mm girth; 3.50 m - 5.00 m high	-	0.21	2.81	0.92	m²	3.73
One mist Supermatt; one full Supermatt and one full coat of quick drying Acrylic Eggshell						
Brick or block walls						
over 300 mm girth	-	0.19	2.54	1.71	m²	4.25
Cement render or concrete						
over 300 mm girth	-	0.19	2.54	1.57	m²	4.12
Plaster walls or plaster/plasterboard ceilings						
over 300 mm girth	-	0.18	2.41	1.57	m²	3.98
over 300 mm girth; in multi colours	-	0.25	3.35	1.57	m²	4.92
over 300 mm girth; in staircase areas	-	0.21	2.81	1.57	m²	4.38
cutting in edges on flush surfaces	-	0.09	1.21	-	m	1.21
Plaster/plasterboard ceilings						
over 300 mm girth; 3.50 m - 5.00 m high	-	0.21	2.81	1.57	m²	4.38
One coat "Tretol No 10 Sealer" or other equal and approved; two coats "Tretol sprayed Supercover Spraytone" emulsion paint or other equal and approved						
Plaster walls or plaster/plasterboard ceilings						
over 300 mm girth	-	-	-	-	m²	4.92
Textured plastic; "Artex" or other equal and approved finish						
Plasterboard ceilings						
over 300 mm girth	-	0.19	2.54	1.67	m²	4.21
Concrete walls or ceilings						
over 300 mm girth	-	0.23	3.08	1.55	m²	4.63
Touch up primer; one undercoat and one finishing coat of gloss oil paint; on wood surfaces						
General surfaces						
over 300 mm girth	-	0.23	3.08	1.71	m²	4.79
isolated surfaces not exceeding 300 mm girth	-	0.09	1.21	0.57	m	1.78
isolated areas not exceeding 0.50 m²;						
irrespective of girth	-	0.18	2.41	0.88	nr	3.29
Glazed windows and screens						
panes; area not exceeding 0.10 m²	-	0.38	5.09	1.36	m²	6.45
panes; area 0.10 m² - 0.50 m²	-	0.31	4.15	1.02	m²	5.17
panes; area 0.50 m² - 1.00 m²	-	0.26	3.48	0.83	m²	4.31
panes; area over 1.00 m²	-	0.23	3.08	0.71	m²	3.79
Knot; one coat primer; stop; one undercoat and one finishing coat of gloss oil paint; on wood surfaces						
General surfaces						
over 300 mm girth	-	0.33	4.42	1.73	m²	6.15
isolated surfaces not exceeding 300 mm girth	-	0.13	1.74	0.57	m	2.32
isolated areas not exceeding 0.50 m²;						
irrespective of girth	-	0.25	3.35	1.14	nr	4.49

M SURFACE FINISHES

Item	PC £	Labour hours	Labour £	Material £	Unit	Total rate £
M60 PAINTING/CLEAR FINISHING – INTERNALLY – cont'd						
Glazed windows and screens						
panes; area not exceeding 0.10 m^2	-	0.56	7.50	1.73	m^2	9.23
panes; area 0.10 m^2 - 0.50 m^2	-	0.45	6.02	1.44	m^2	7.46
panes; area 0.50 m^2 - 1.00 m^2	-	0.40	5.36	1.44	m^2	6.79
panes; area over 1.00 m^2	-	0.33	4.42	1.06	m^2	5.48
One coat primer; one undercoat and one finishing coat of gloss oil paint						
Plaster surfaces						
over 300 mm girth	-	0.30	4.02	2.19	m^2	6.21
One coat primer; two undercoats and one finishing coat of gloss oil paint						
Plaster surfaces						
over 300 mm girth	-	0.40	5.36	2.98	m^2	8.33
One coat primer; two undercoats and one finishing coat of eggshell paint						
Plaster surfaces						
over 300 mm girth	-	0.40	5.36	3.27	m^2	8.62
Touch up primer; one undercoat and one finishing coat of gloss paint; on iron or steel surfaces						
General surfaces						
over 300 mm girth	-	0.23	3.08	1.33	m^2	4.40
isolated surfaces not exceeding 300 mm girth	-	0.09	1.21	0.45	m	1.65
isolated areas not exceeding 0.50 m^2;						
irrespective of girth	-	0.18	2.41	0.71	nr	3.12
Glazed windows and screens						
panes; area not exceeding 0.10 m^2	-	0.38	5.09	1.35	m^2	6.44
panes; area 0.10 m^2 - 0.50 m^2	-	0.31	4.15	1.02	m^2	5.17
panes; area 0.50 m^2 - 1.00 m^2	-	0.26	3.48	0.81	m^2	4.29
panes; area over 1.00 m^2	-	0.23	3.08	0.69	m^2	3.77
Structural steelwork						
over 300 mm girth	-	0.25	3.35	1.36	m^2	4.71
Members of roof trusses						
over 300 mm girth	-	0.34	4.55	1.56	m^2	6.11
Ornamental railings and the like; each side measured overall						
over 300 mm girth	-	0.40	5.36	1.69	m^2	7.05
Iron or steel radiators						
over 300 mm girth	-	0.23	3.08	1.43	m^2	4.51
Pipes or conduits						
over 300 mm girth	-	0.34	4.55	1.48	m^2	6.03
not exceeding 300 mm girth	-	0.13	1.74	0.49	m	2.23
One coat primer; one undercoat and one finishing coat of gloss oil paint; on iron or steel surfaces						
General surfaces						
over 300 mm girth	-	0.30	4.02	1.33	m^2	5.34
isolated surfaces not exceeding 300 mm girth	-	0.12	1.61	0.78	m	2.38
isolated areas not exceeding 0.50 m^2;						
irrespective of girth	-	0.23	3.08	1.28	nr	4.36

M SURFACE FINISHES

Item	PC £	Labour hours	Labour £	Material £	Unit	Total rate £
Glazed windows and screens						
panes; area not exceeding 0.10 m^2	-	0.50	6.69	2.10	m^2	**8.79**
panes; area 0.10 m^2 - 0.50 m^2	-	0.40	5.36	1.67	m^2	**7.02**
panes; area 0.50 m^2 - 1.00 m^2	-	0.34	4.55	1.44	m^2	**5.99**
panes; area over 1.00 m^2	-	0.30	4.02	1.28	m^2	**5.29**
Structural steelwork						
over 300 mm girth	-	0.33	4.42	2.05	m^2	**6.47**
Members of roof trusses						
over 300 mm girth	-	0.45	6.02	2.14	m^2	**8.17**
Ornamental railings and the like; each side measured overall						
over 300 mm girth	-	0.51	6.83	2.55	m^2	**9.38**
Iron or steel radiators						
over 300 mm girth	-	0.30	4.02	2.14	m^2	**6.16**
Pipes or conduits						
over 300 mm girth	-	0.45	6.02	2.14	m^2	**8.17**
not exceeding 300 mm girth	-	0.18	2.41	0.70	m	**3.11**
Two coats of bituminous paint; on iron or steel surfaces						
General surfaces						
over 300 mm girth	-	0.23	3.08	0.53	m^2	**3.61**
Inside of galvanized steel cistern						
over 300 mm girth	-	0.34	4.55	0.64	m^2	**5.19**
Two coats bituminous paint; first coat blinded with clean sand prior to second coat; on concrete surfaces						
General surfaces						
over 300 mm girth	-	0.79	10.58	1.40	m^2	**11.98**
Mordant solution; one coat HCC Protective Coatings Ltd "Permacor Alkyd MIO" or other equal and approved; one coat "Permatex Epoxy Gloss" finishing coat or other equal and approved on galvanised steelwork						
Structural steelwork						
over 300 mm girth	-	0.44	5.89	2.51	m^2	**8.40**
One coat HCC Protective Coatings Ltd "Epoxy Zinc Primer" or other equal and approved; two coats "Permacor Alkyd MIO" or other equal and approved; one coat "Permacor Epoxy Gloss" finishing coat or other equal and approved on steelwork						
Structural steelwork						
over 300 mm girth	-	0.63	8.43	4.58	m^2	**13.01**
Steel protection; HCC Protective Coatings Ltd "Unitherm" or other equal and approved; two coats to steelwork						
Structural steelwork						
over 300 mm girth	-	0.99	13.25	1.56	m^2	**14.82**
Two coats of epoxy anti-slip floor paint; on screeded concrete surfaces						
General surfaces						
over 300 mm girth	-	0.25	3.35	11.08	m^2	**14.42**

M SURFACE FINISHES

Item	PC £	Labour hours	Labour £	Material £	Unit	Total rate £
M60 PAINTING/CLEAR FINISHING **– INTERNALLY** – cont'd						
Fosroc Expandite's "Nitoflor Lithurin" floor **hardener and dust proofer or other equal and** **approved; two coats; on concrete surfaces** General surfaces						
over 300 mm girth	-	0.24	2.40	0.49	m²	2.89
Two coats of boiled linseed oil; on **hardwood surfaces** General surfaces						
over 300 mm girth	-	0.18	2.41	1.27	m²	3.68
isolated surfaces not exceeding 300 mm girth	-	0.07	0.94	0.41	m	1.35
isolated areas not exceeding 0.50 m²; irrespective of girth	-	0.13	1.74	0.74	nr	2.48
Two coats polyurethane varnish; on **wood surfaces** General surfaces						
over 300 mm girth	-	0.18	2.41	1.34	m²	3.75
isolated surfaces not exceeding 300 mm girth	-	0.07	0.94	0.49	m	1.43
isolated areas not exceeding 0.50 m²; irrespective of girth	-	0.13	1.74	0.16	nr	1.90
Three coats polyurethane varnish; on **wood surfaces** General surfaces						
over 300 mm girth	-	0.26	3.48	2.06	m²	5.54
isolated surfaces not exceeding 300 mm girth	-	0.10	1.34	0.62	m	1.96
isolated areas not exceeding 0.50 m²; irrespective of girth	-	0.19	2.54	1.14	nr	3.69
One undercoat; and one finishing coat; **of "Albi" clear flame retardant surface** **coating or other equal and approved; on** **wood surfaces** General surfaces						
over 300 mm girth	-	0.34	4.55	2.30	m²	6.85
isolated surfaces not exceeding 300 mm girth	-	0.14	1.87	0.80	m	2.68
isolated areas not exceeding 0.50 m²; irrespective of girth	-	0.19	2.54	1.76	nr	4.31
Two undercoats; and one finishing coat; **of "Albi" clear flame retardant surface** **coating or other equal and approved; on** **wood surfaces** General surfaces						
over 300 mm girth	-	0.40	5.36	3.24	m²	8.60
isolated surfaces not exceeding 300 mm girth	-	0.20	2.68	1.17	m	3.85
isolated areas not exceeding 0.50 m²; irrespective of girth	-	0.33	4.42	1.79	nr	6.21
Seal and wax polish; dull gloss finish on **wood surfaces** General surfaces						
over 300 mm girth	-	-	-	-	m²	9.33
isolated surfaces not exceeding 300 mm girth	-	-	-	-	m	4.22
isolated areas not exceeding 0.50m²; irrespective of girth	-	-	-	-	nr	6.51

M SURFACE FINISHES

Item	PC £	Labour hours	Labour £	Material £	Unit	Total rate £
One coat of "Sadolin Extra" or other equal and approved; clear or pigmented; one further coat of "Holdex" clear interior silk matt lacquer or similar						
General surfaces						
over 300 mm girth	-	0.25	3.35	4.47	m^2	7.81
isolated surfaces not exceeding 300 mm girth	-	0.10	1.34	2.09	m	3.43
isolated areas not exceeding 0.50 m^2;						
irrespective of girth	-	0.20	2.68	2.17	nr	4.85
Glazed windows and screens						
panes; area not exceeding 0.10 m^2	-	0.42	5.62	2.55	m^2	8.18
panes; area 0.10 m^2 - 0.50 m^2	-	0.33	4.42	2.38	m^2	6.80
panes; area 0.50 m^2 - 1.00 m^2	-	0.29	3.88	2.20	m^2	6.09
panes; area over 1.00 m^2	-	0.25	3.35	2.09	m^2	5.44
Two coats of "Sadolin Extra" or other equal and approved; clear or pigmented; two further coats of "Holdex" clear interior silk matt lacquer or similar						
General surfaces						
over 300 mm girth	-	0.40	5.36	8.25	m^2	13.61
isolated surfaces not exceeding 300 mm girth	-	0.16	2.14	4.13	m	6.27
isolated areas not exceeding 0.50 m^2;						
irrespective of girth	-	0.30	4.02	4.71	nr	8.73
Glazed windows and screens						
panes; area not exceeding 0.10 m^2	-	0.66	8.84	5.06	m^2	13.90
panes; area 0.10 m^2 - 0.50 m^2	-	0.52	6.96	4.71	m^2	11.67
panes; area 0.50 m^2 - 1.00 m^2	-	0.45	6.02	4.36	m^2	10.38
panes; area over 1.00 m^2	-	0.40	5.36	4.13	m^2	9.48
Two coats of Sikkens "Cetol TS" interior stain or other equal and approved; on wood surfaces						
General surfaces						
over 300 mm girth	-	0.19	2.54	2.08	m^2	4.63
isolated surfaces not exceeding 300 mm girth	-	0.08	1.07	0.73	m	1.80
isolated areas not exceeding 0.50 m^2;						
irrespective of girth	-	0.13	1.74	1.13	nr	2.87
Body in and wax polish; dull gloss finish; on hardwood surfaces						
General surfaces						
over 300 mm girth	-	-	-	-	m^2	10.73
isolated surfaces not exceeding 300 mm girth	-	-	-	-	m	4.87
isolated areas not exceeding 0.50 m^2;						
irrespective of girth	-	-	-	-	nr	7.50
Stain; body in and wax polish; dull gloss finish; on hardwood surfaces						
General surfaces						
over 300 mm girth	-	-	-	-	m^2	14.84
isolated surfaces not exceeding 300 mm girth	-	-	-	-	m	6.69
isolated areas not exceeding 0.50 m^2;						
irrespective of girth	-	-	-	-	nr	10.44

M SURFACE FINISHES

Item	PC £	Labour hours	Labour £	Material £	Unit	Total rate £
M60 PAINTING/CLEAR FINISHING – INTERNALLY – cont'd						
Seal; two coats of synthetic resin lacquer; decorative flatted finish; wire down, wax and burnish; on wood surfaces						
General surfaces						
over 300 mm girth	-	-	-	-	m²	17.83
isolated surfaces not exceeding 300 mm girth	-	-	-	-	m	8.03
isolated areas not exceeding 0.50 m²;						
irrespective of girth	-	-	-	-	nr	12.50
Stain; body in and fully French polish; full gloss finish; on hardwood surfaces						
General surfaces						
over 300 mm girth	-	-	-	-	m²	20.52
isolated surfaces not exceeding 300 mm girth	-	-	-	-	m	9.26
isolated areas not exceeding 0.50 m²;						
irrespective of girth	-	-	-	-	nr	14.37
Stain; fill grain and fully French polish; full gloss finish; on hardwood surfaces						
General surfaces						
over 300 mm girth	-	-	-	-	m²	28.15
isolated surfaces not exceeding 300 mm girth	-	-	-	-	m	12.66
isolated areas not exceeding 0.50 m²;						
irrespective of girth	-	-	-	-	nr	19.71
Stain black; body in and fully French polish; ebonized finish; on hardwood surfaces						
General surfaces						
over 300 mm girth	-	-	-	-	m²	35.18
isolated surfaces not exceeding 300 mm girth	-	-	-	-	m	14.66
isolated areas not exceeding 0.50 m²;						
irrespective of girth	-	-	-	-	nr	24.63
M60 PAINTING/CLEAR FINISHING - EXTERNALLY						
Two coats of cement paint, "Sandtex Matt" or other equal and approved						
Brick or block walls						
over 300 mm girth	-	0.26	3.48	1.34	m²	4.82
Cement render or concrete walls						
over 300 mm girth	-	0.23	3.08	0.89	m²	3.97
Roughcast walls						
over 300 mm girth	-	0.40	5.36	0.89	m²	6.24
One coat sealer and two coats of external grade emulsion paint, Dulux "Weathershield" or other equal and approved						
Brick or block walls						
over 300 mm girth	-	0.43	5.76	6.12	m²	11.88
Cement render or concrete walls						
over 300 mm girth	-	0.35	4.69	4.08	m²	8.77
Concrete soffits						
over 300 mm girth	-	0.40	5.36	4.08	m²	9.44

M SURFACE FINISHES

Item	PC £	Labour hours	Labour £	Material £	Unit	Total rate £
One coat sealer (applied by brush) and two coats of external grade emulsion paint, Dulux "Weathershield" or other equal and approved (spray applied)						
Roughcast						
over 300 mm girth	-	0.29	3.88	8.26	m^2	**12.15**
One coat sealer and two coats of anti-graffiti paint (spray applied)						
Brick or block walls						
over 300 mm girth	-	0.23	3.08	2.47	m^2	**5.55**
Cement render or concrete walls						
over 300 mm girth	-	0.26	3.48	3.67	m^2	**7.15**
2.5 mm of "Vandalene" anti-climb paint (spray applied)						
General surfaces						
over 300 mm girth	-	0.30	4.02	3.49	m^2	**7.51**
Two coats solar reflective aluminium paint; on bituminous roofing						
General surfaces						
over 300 mm girth	-	0.44	5.89	11.02	m^2	**16.91**
over 300 mm girth	-	0.44	5.89	11.02	m^2	**16.91**
Touch up primer; two undercoats and one finishing coat of gloss oil paint; on wood surfaces						
General surfaces						
over 300 mm girth	-	0.35	4.69	1.74	m^2	**6.42**
isolated surfaces not exceeding 300 mm girth	-	0.15	2.01	0.46	m	**2.47**
isolated areas not exceeding 0.50 m^2;						
irrespective of girth	-	0.27	3.61	0.92	nr	**4.53**
Glazed windows and screens						
panes; area not exceeding 0.10 m^2	-	0.59	7.90	1.53	m^2	**9.43**
panes; area 0.10 m^2 - 0.50 m^2	-	0.59	7.90	1.29	m^2	**9.19**
panes; area 0.50 m^2 - 1.00 m^2	-	0.47	6.29	1.12	m^2	**7.41**
panes; area over 1.00 m^2	-	0.35	4.69	0.92	m^2	**5.60**
Glazed windows and screens; multi-coloured work						
panes; area not exceeding 0.10 m^2	-	0.68	9.10	1.53	m^2	**10.63**
panes; area 0.10 m^2 - 0.50 m^2	-	0.55	7.36	1.33	m^2	**8.69**
panes; area 0.50 m^2 - 1.00 m^2	-	0.47	6.29	1.12	m^2	**7.41**
panes; area over 1.00 m^2	-	0.41	5.49	0.92	m^2	**6.41**
Knot; one coat primer; two undercoats and one finishing coat of gloss oil paint; on wood surfaces						
General surfaces						
over 300 mm girth	-	0.46	6.16	1.80	m^2	**7.96**
isolated surfaces not exceeding 300 mm girth	-	0.19	2.54	0.64	m	**3.19**
isolated areas not exceeding 0.50 m^2;						
irrespective of girth	-	0.35	4.69	1.26	nr	**5.94**
Glazed windows and screens						
panes; area not exceeding 0.10 m^2	-	0.78	10.44	2.01	m^2	**12.46**
panes; area 0.10 m^2 - 0.50 m^2	-	0.62	8.30	1.79	m^2	**10.09**
panes; area 0.50 m^2 - 1.00 m^2	-	0.55	7.36	1.37	m^2	**8.73**
panes; area over 1.00 m^2	-	0.46	6.16	0.94	m^2	**7.10**

M SURFACE FINISHES

Item	PC £	Labour hours	Labour £	Material £	Unit	Total rate £
M60 PAINTING/CLEAR FINISHING - EXTERNALLY – cont'd						
Two undercoats and one finishing coat of gloss oil paint on wood surfaces – cont'd						
Glazed windows and screens; multi-coloured work						
panes; area not exceeding 0.10 m²	-	0.89	11.92	2.01	m²	**13.93**
panes; area 0.10 m² - 0.50 m²	-	0.72	9.64	1.80	m²	**11.44**
panes; area 0.50 m² - 1.00 m²	-	0.64	8.57	1.37	m²	**9.94**
panes; area over 1.00 m²	-	0.54	7.23	0.94	m²	**8.17**
Touch up primer; two undercoats and one finishing coat of gloss oil paint; on iron or steel surfaces						
General surfaces						
over 300 mm girth	-	0.35	4.69	1.30	m²	**5.99**
isolated surfaces not exceeding 300 mm girth	-	0.14	1.87	0.35	m	**2.23**
isolated areas not exceeding 0.50 m²;						
irrespective of girth	-	0.26	3.48	0.73	nr	**4.21**
Glazed windows and screens						
panes; area not exceeding 0.10 m²	-	0.59	7.90	1.32	m²	**9.22**
panes; area 0.10 m² - 0.50 m²	-	0.47	6.29	1.14	m²	**7.43**
panes; area 0.50 m² - 1.00 m²	-	0.41	5.49	0.96	m²	**6.45**
panes; area over 1.00 m²	-	0.35	4.69	0.78	m²	**5.46**
Structural steelwork						
over 300 mm girth	-	0.40	5.36	1.35	m²	**6.70**
Members of roof trusses						
over 300 mm girth	-	0.54	7.23	1.53	m²	**8.76**
Ornamental railings and the like; each side measured overall						
over 300 mm girth	-	0.60	8.03	1.58	m²	**9.62**
Eaves gutters						
over 300 mm girth	-	0.64	8.57	1.74	m²	**10.31**
not exceeding 300 mm girth	-	0.25	3.35	0.73	m	**4.07**
Pipes or conduits						
over 300 mm girth	-	0.54	7.23	1.74	m²	**8.97**
not exceeding 300 mm girth	-	0.21	2.81	0.60	m	**3.41**
One coat primer; two undercoats and one finishing coat of gloss oil paint; on iron or steel surfaces						
General surfaces						
over 300 mm girth	-	0.43	5.76	1.51	m²	**7.27**
isolated surfaces not exceeding 300 mm girth	-	0.18	2.41	0.39	m	**2.80**
isolated areas not exceeding 0.50 m²;						
irrespective of girth	-	0.32	4.28	0.78	nr	**5.06**
Glazed windows and screens						
panes; area not exceeding 0.10 m²	-	0.71	9.51	1.38	m²	**10.88**
panes; area 0.10 m² - 0.50 m²	-	0.56	7.50	1.19	m²	**8.69**
panes; area 0.50 m² - 1.00 m²	-	0.50	6.69	1.01	m²	**7.71**
panes; area over 1.00 m²	-	0.43	5.76	0.78	m²	**6.54**
Structural steelwork						
over 300 mm girth	-	0.48	6.43	1.56	m²	**7.99**
Members of roof trusses						
over 300 mm girth	-	0.64	8.57	1.74	m²	**10.31**
Ornamental railings and the like; each side measured overall						
over 300 mm girth	-	0.72	9.64	1.74	m²	**11.38**

M SURFACE FINISHES

Item	PC £	Labour hours	Labour £	Material £	Unit	Total rate £
Eaves gutters						
over 300 mm girth	-	0.76	10.18	1.98	m²	12.15
not exceeding 300 mm girth	-	0.31	4.15	0.68	m	4.83
Pipes or conduits						
over 300 mm girth	-	0.64	8.57	1.98	m²	10.55
not exceeding 300 mm girth	-	0.25	3.35	0.66	m	4.00
One coat of Andrews "Hammerite" paint or other equal and approved; on iron or steel surfaces						
General surfaces						
over 300 mm girth	-	0.15	2.01	1.19	m²	3.20
isolated surfaces not exceeding 300 mm girth	-	0.08	1.07	0.37	m	1.44
isolated areas not exceeding 0.50 m²;						
irrespective of girth	-	0.11	1.47	0.68	nr	2.16
Glazed windows and screens						
panes; area not exceeding 0.10 m²	-	0.25	3.35	0.90	m²	4.25
panes; area 0.10 m² - 0.50 m²	-	0.19	2.54	0.99	m²	3.53
panes; area 0.50 m² - 1.00 m²	-	0.18	2.41	0.89	m²	3.30
panes; area over 1.00 m²	-	0.15	2.01	0.89	m²	2.90
Structural steelwork						
over 300 mm girth	-	0.17	2.28	1.09	m²	3.37
Members of roof trusses						
over 300 mm girth	-	0.23	3.08	1.19	m²	4.27
Ornamental railings and the like; each side measured overall						
over 300 mm girth	-	0.26	3.48	1.19	m²	4.67
Eaves gutters						
over 300 mm girth	-	0.27	3.61	1.29	m²	4.90
not exceeding 300 mm girth	-	0.08	1.07	0.59	m	1.66
Pipes or conduits						
over 300 mm girth	-	0.26	3.48	1.09	m²	4.57
not exceeding 300 mm girth	-	0.08	1.07	0.49	m	1.57
Two coats of creosote; on wood surfaces						
General surfaces						
over 300 mm girth	-	0.16	2.14	0.31	m²	2.45
isolated surfaces not exceeding 300 mm girth	-	0.05	0.67	0.18	m	0.85
Two coats of "Solignum" wood preservative or other equal and approved; on wood surfaces						
General surfaces						
over 300 mm girth	-	0.14	1.87	0.95	m²	2.83
isolated surfaces not exceeding 300 mm girth	-	0.05	0.67	0.29	m	0.96
Three coats of polyurethane; on wood surfaces						
General surfaces						
over 300 mm girth	-	0.29	3.88	2.28	m²	6.16
isolated surfaces not exceeding 300 mm girth	-	0.11	1.47	1.12	m	2.59
isolated areas not exceeding 0.50 m²;						
irrespective of girth	-	0.21	2.81	1.30	nr	4.11

M SURFACE FINISHES

Item	PC £	Labour hours	Labour £	Material £	Unit	Total rate £
M60 PAINTING/CLEAR FINISHING - EXTERNALLY – cont'd						
Two coats of "New Base" primer or other equal and approved; and two coats of "Extra" or other equal and approved; Sadolin Ltd; pigmented; on wood surfaces						
General surfaces						
over 300 mm girth	-	0.43	5.76	4.28	m²	**10.03**
isolated surfaces not exceeding 300 mm girth	-	0.26	3.48	1.46	m	**4.94**
Glazed windows and screens						
panes; area not exceeding 0.10 m²	-	0.71	9.51	3.04	m²	**12.55**
panes; area 0.10 m² - 0.50 m²	-	0.57	7.63	2.87	m²	**10.50**
panes; area 0.50 m² - 1.00 m²	-	0.50	6.69	2.69	m²	**9.39**
panes; area over 1.00 m²	-	0.43	5.76	2.16	m²	**7.92**
Two coats Sikkens "Cetol Filter 7" exterior stain or other equal and approved; on wood surfaces						
General surfaces						
over 300 mm girth	-	0.20	2.68	3.49	m²	**6.17**
isolated surfaces not exceeding 300 mm girth	-	0.09	1.21	1.20	m	**2.40**
isolated areas not exceeding 0.50 m²; irrespective of girth	-	0.14	1.87	1.77	nr	**3.64**

N FURNITURE/EQUIPMENT

Item	PC £	Labour hours	Labour £	Material £	Unit	Total rate £
N10/11 GENERAL FIXTURES/ KITCHEN FITTINGS						
SUPPLY ONLY PRICES						
NOTE: The fixing of general fixtures will vary considerably dependent upon the size of the fixture and the method of fixing employed. Prices for fixing like sized kitchen fittings may be suitable for certain fixtures, although adjustment to those rates will almost invariably be necessary and the reader is directed to section "G20" for information on bolts, plugging brickwork and blockwork, etc. which should prove useful in building up a suitable rate.						
The following supply only prices are for purpose made fittings components in various materials supplied as part of an assembled fitting and therefore may be used to arrive at a guide price for a complete fitting.						
Fitting components; medium density fibreboard						
Backs, fronts, sides or divisions; over 300 mm wide						
12 mm thick	-	-	-	21.81	m²	**21.81**
18 mm thick	-	-	-	23.12	m²	**23.12**
25 mm thick	-	-	-	25.73	m²	**25.73**
Shelves or worktops; over 300 mm wide						
18 mm thick	-	-	-	23.12	m²	**23.12**
25 mm thick	-	-	-	25.73	m²	**25.73**
Flush doors; lipped on four edges						
450 mm x 750 mm x 18 mm	-	-	-	33.48	nr	**33.48**
450 mm x 750 mm x 25 mm	-	-	-	34.12	nr	**34.12**
600 mm x 900 mm x 18 mm	-	-	-	39.51	nr	**39.51**
600 mm x 900 mm x 25 mm	-	-	-	40.55	nr	**40.55**
Fitting components; moisture-resistant medium density fibreboard						
Backs, fronts, sides or divisions; over 300 mm wide						
12 mm thick	-	-	-	24.42	m²	**24.42**
18 mm thick	-	-	-	27.03	m²	**27.03**
25 mm thick	-	-	-	29.64	m²	**29.64**
Shelves or worktops; over 300 mm wide						
18 mm thick	-	-	-	27.03	m²	**27.03**
25 mm thick	-	-	-	29.64	m²	**29.64**
Flush doors; lipped on four edges						
450 mm x 750 mm x 18 mm	-	-	-	34.12	nr	**34.12**
450 mm x 750 mm x 25 mm	-	-	-	35.08	nr	**35.08**
600 mm x 900 mm x 18 mm	-	-	-	40.55	nr	**40.55**
600 mm x 900 mm x 25 mm	-	-	-	42.11	nr	**42.11**

N FURNITURE/EQUIPMENT

Item	PC £	Labour hours	Labour £	Material £	Unit	Total rate £
N10/11 GENERAL FIXTURES/ KITCHEN FITTINGS – cont'd						
Fitting components; medium density fibreboard; melamine faced both sides						
Backs, fronts, sides or divisions; over 300 mm wide						
12 mm thick	-	-	-	28.78	m²	28.78
18 mm thick	-	-	-	32.05	m²	32.05
Shelves or worktops; over 300 mm wide						
18 mm thick	-	-	-	32.05	m²	32.05
Flush doors; lipped on four edges						
450 mm x 750 mm x 18 mm	-	-	-	23.95	nr	23.95
600 mm x 900 mm x 25 mm	-	-	-	30.38	nr	30.38
Fitting components; medium density fibreboard; formica faced both sides						
Backs, fronts, sides or divisions; over 300 mm wide						
12 mm thick	-	-	-	87.64	m²	87.64
18 mm thick	-	-	-	91.12	m²	91.12
Shelves or worktops; over 300 mm wide						
18 mm thick	-	-	-	91.12	m²	91.12
Flush doors; lipped on four edges						
450 mm x 750 mm x 18 mm	-	-	-	48.25	nr	48.25
600 mm x 900 mm x 25 mm	-	-	-	491.91	nr	491.91
Fitting components; wrought softwood						
Backs, fronts, sides or divisions; cross-tongued joints; over 300 mm wide						
25 mm thick	-	-	-	41.88	m²	41.88
Shelves or worktops; cross-tongued joints; over 300 mm wide						
25 mm thick	-	-	-	41.88	m²	41.88
Bearers						
19 mm x 38 mm	-	-	-	2.19	m	2.19
25 mm x 50 mm	-	-	-	2.43	m	2.43
44 mm x 44 mm	-	-	-	2.59	m	2.59
44 mm x 75 mm	-	-	-	2.99	m	2.99
Bearers; framed; to backs, fronts or sides						
19 mm x 38 mm	-	-	-	5.01	m	5.01
25 mm x 50 mm	-	-	-	5.42	m	5.42
50 mm x 50 mm	-	-	-	7.01	m	7.01
50 mm x 75 mm	-	-	-	8.04	m	8.04
Add 5% to the above material prices for selected softwood staining						
Fitting components; selected Sapele						
Backs, fronts, sides or divisions; cross-tongued joints; over 300 mm wide						
25 mm thick	-	-	-	65.92	m²	65.92
Shelves or worktops; cross-tongued joints; over 300 mm wide						
25 mm thick	-	-	-	65.92	m²	65.92
Bearers						
19 mm x 38 mm	-	-	-	3.31	m	3.31
25 mm x 50 mm	-	-	-	4.12	m	4.12
50 mm x 50 mm	-	-	-	4.62	m	4.62
50 mm x 75 mm	-	-	-	6.02	m	6.02

N FURNITURE/EQUIPMENT

Item	PC £	Labour hours	Labour £	Material £	Unit	Total rate £
Bearers; framed; to backs, fronts or sides						
19 mm x 38 mm	-	-	-	6.38	m	6.38
25 mm x 50 mm	-	-	-	7.08	m	7.08
50 mm x 50 mm	-	-	-	9.49	m	9.49
50 mm x 75 mm	-	-	-	11.90	m	11.90
Fitting components; Iroko						
Backs, fronts, sides or divisions; cross-tongued joints; over 300 mm wide						
25 mm thick	-	-	-	72.66	m²	72.66
Shelves or worktops; cross-tongued joints; over 300 mm wide						
25 mm thick	-	-	-	72.66	m²	72.66
Draining boards; cross-tongued joints; over 300 mm wide						
25 mm thick	-	-	-	91.05	m²	91.05
stopped flutes	-	-	-	4.71	m	4.71
grooves; cross-grain	-	-	-	0.71	m	0.71
Bearers						
19 mm x 38 mm	-	-	-	3.62	m	3.62
25 mm x 50 mm	-	-	-	4.61	m	4.61
50 mm x 50 mm	-	-	-	5.25	m	5.25
50 mm x 75 mm	-	-	-	6.91	m	6.91
Bearers; framed; to backs, fronts or sides						
19 mm x 38 mm	-	-	-	6.60	m	6.60
25 mm x 50 mm	-	-	-	7.35	m	7.35
50 mm x 50 mm	-	-	-	9.93	m	9.93
50 mm x 75 mm	-	-	-	12.89	m	12.89
SUPPLY AND FIX PRICES						
NOTE: Kitchen fittings vary considerably. PC supply prices for reasonable quantities for a moderately priced range of kitchen fittings have been shown.						
Supplying and fixing to backgrounds requiring plugging; including any pre-assembly						
Wall units						
300 mm x 300 mm x 720 mm	50.01	1.11	14.86	54.03	nr	68.89
500 mm x 300 mm x 720 mm	58.92	1.16	15.53	63.63	nr	79.16
600 mm x 300 mm x 720 mm	66.04	1.30	17.41	71.29	nr	88.69
800 mm x 300 mm x 720 mm	100.48	1.48	19.82	108.36	nr	128.17
Floor units with drawers						
500 mm x 600 mm x 870 mm	87.76	1.16	15.53	94.66	nr	110.19
600 mm x 600 mm x 870 mm	97.69	1.30	17.41	105.34	nr	122.75
1000 mm x 600 mm x 870 mm	150.56	1.57	21.02	162.25	nr	183.27
Sink units (excluding sink top)						
1000 mm x 600 mm x 870 mm	152.85	1.48	19.82	164.72	nr	184.54
Laminated plastics worktops; single rolled edge; prices include for fixing						
38 mm thick; 600 mm wide	23.77	0.37	4.95	26.96	m	31.92
extra for forming hole for inset sink	-	0.69	9.24	-	nr	9.24
extra for jointing strip at corner intersection of worktops	-	0.14	1.87	5.61	nr	7.48
extra for butt and scribe joint at corner intersection of worktops	-	4.16	55.70	-	nr	55.70

N FURNITURE/EQUIPMENT

Item	PC £	Labour hours	Labour £	Material £	Unit	Total rate £
N10/11 GENERAL FIXTURES/ KITCHEN FITTINGS – cont'd						
Lockers; Welconstruct Distribution or other equal and approved						
Standard clothes lockers; steel body and door within reinforced 19G frame, powder coated finish, cam locks						
1 compartment; placing in position						
300 mm x 300 mm x 1800 mm	-	0.23	2.30	50.61	nr	52.92
380 mm x 380 mm x 1800 mm	-	0.23	2.30	61.22	nr	63.52
450 mm x 450 mm x 1800 mm	-	0.28	2.81	71.87	nr	74.68
610 mm x 450 mm x 1800 mm	-	0.28	2.81	98.12	nr	100.93
Compartment lockers; steel body and door within reinforced 19G frame, powder coated finish, cam locks						
2 compartments; placing in position						
300 mm x 300 mm x 1800 mm	-	0.23	2.30	68.29	nr	70.59
380 mm x 380 mm x 1800 mm	-	0.23	2.30	76.33	nr	78.63
450 mm x 450 mm x 1800 mm	-	0.28	2.81	94.34	nr	97.15
4 compartments; placing in position						
300 mm x 300 mm x 1800 mm	-	0.23	2.30	79.33	nr	81.63
380 mm x 380 mm x 1800 mm	-	0.23	2.30	89.40	nr	91.71
450 mm x 450 mm x 1800 mm	-	0.28	2.81	109.45	nr	112.26
Wet area lockers; stainless steel; cam locks						
1 compartment; placing in position						
305 mm x 305 mm x 1780 mm	-	0.23	2.30	342.89	nr	345.20
2 compartments; placing in position						
305 mm x 305 mm x 1780 mm	-	0.23	2.30	416.51	nr	418.81
305 mm x 460 mm x 1780 mm	-	0.23	2.30	476.56	nr	478.87
4 compartments; placing in position						
305 mm x 305 mm x 1780 mm	-	0.23	2.30	495.94	nr	498.24
305 mm x 460 mm x 1780 mm	-	0.23	2.30	568.58	nr	570.89
Extra for						
coin operated lock; coin returned	-	-	-	49.59	nr	49.59
coin operated lock; coin retained	-	-	-	77.01	nr	77.01
Timber clothes lockers; veneered MDF finish, routed door, cam locks						
1 compartment; placing in position						
380 mm x 380 mm x 1830 mm	-	0.28	2.81	185.49	nr	188.30
4 compartments; placing in position						
380 mm x 380 mm x 1830 mm	-	0.28	2.81	344.83	nr	347.64
Shelving support systems; Welconstruct Distribution or other equal and approved						
Shelving support systems; steel body; stove enamelled finish; assembling						
open initial bay; 5 shelves; placing in position						
915 mm x 305 mm x 1905 mm	-	0.69	8.80	117.69	nr	126.49
915 mm x 460 mm x 1905 mm	-	0.69	8.80	161.76	nr	170.56
open extension bay; 5 shelves; placing in position						
915 mm x 305 mm x 1905 mm	-	0.83	10.59	86.50	nr	97.08
915 mm x 460 mm x 1905 mm	-	0.83	10.59	108.29	nr	118.88
closed initial bay; 5 shelves; placing in position						
915 mm x 305 mm x 1905 mm	-	0.69	8.80	148.68	nr	157.48
915 mm x 460 mm x 1905 mm	-	0.69	8.80	192.76	nr	201.56

N FURNITURE/EQUIPMENT

Item	PC £	Labour hours	Labour £	Material £	Unit	Total rate £
closed extension bay; 5 shelves; placing in position						
915 mm x 305 mm x 1905 mm	-	0.83	10.59	123.11	nr	**133.70**
915 mm x 460 mm x 1905 mm	-	0.83	10.59	152.56	nr	**163.14**
extra for pair of doors; fixing in position						
1000 mm x 1850 mm	-	0.75	9.57	157.89	nr	**167.45**
Cloakroom racks; Welconstruct						
Distribution or other equal and approved						
Cloakroom racks; 40 mm x 40 mm square tube framing, polyester powder coated finish; beech slatted seats and rails to one side only; placing in position						
1675 mm x 325 mm x 1500 mm; 5 nr coat hooks	-	0.30	3.83	341.92	nr	**345.75**
1825 mm x 325 mm x 1500 mm; 15 nr coat hangers	-	0.30	3.83	378.73	nr	**382.56**
Extra for						
shoe baskets	-	-	-	64.61	nr	**64.61**
mesh bottom shelf	-	-	-	50.95	nr	**50.95**
Cloakroom racks; 40 mm x 40 mm square tube framing, polyester powder coated finish; beech slatted seats and rails to both sides; placing in position						
1675 mm x 600 mm x 1500 mm; 10 nr coat hooks	-	0.40	5.10	392.29	nr	**397.39**
1825 mm x 600 mm x 1500 mm; 30 nr coat hangers	-	0.40	5.10	449.44	nr	**454.54**
Extra for						
shoe baskets	-	-	-	109.65	nr	**109.65**
mesh bottom shelf	-	-	-	61.31	nr	**61.31**
6 mm thick rectangular glass mirrors; silver backed; fixed with chromium plated domed headed screws; to background requiring plugging						
Mirror with polished edges						
365 mm x 254 mm	4.83	0.74	9.91	6.19	nr	**16.09**
400 mm x 300 mm	6.30	0.74	9.91	8.01	nr	**17.92**
560 mm x 380 mm	10.92	0.83	11.11	13.72	nr	**24.83**
640 mm x 460 mm	14.28	0.93	12.45	17.88	nr	**30.33**
Mirror with bevelled edges						
365 mm x 254 mm	8.61	0.74	9.91	10.86	nr	**20.77**
400 mm x 300 mm	10.08	0.74	9.91	12.68	nr	**22.59**
560 mm x 380 mm	16.80	0.83	11.11	21.00	nr	**32.11**
640 mm x 460 mm	21.00	0.93	12.45	26.20	nr	**38.65**
Door mats						
Entrance mats; "Tuftiguard type C" or other equal and approved; laying in position; 12 mm thick						
900 mm x 550 mm	101.25	0.46	4.61	108.97	nr	**113.58**
1200 mm x 750 mm	182.25	0.46	4.61	196.15	nr	**200.76**
2400 mm x 1200 mm	583.20	0.93	9.32	627.67	nr	**636.99**
Matwells						
Polished aluminium matwell; comprising 34 mm x 26 mm x 6 mm angle rim; with brazed angles and lugs brazed on; to suit mat size						
914 mm x 560 mm	28.22	0.93	9.32	30.38	nr	**39.69**
1067 mm x 610 mm	33.23	0.93	9.32	35.76	nr	**45.08**
1219 mm x 762 mm	39.28	0.93	9.32	42.27	nr	**51.59**

N FURNITURE/EQUIPMENT

Item	PC £	Labour hours	Labour £	Material £	Unit	Total rate £
N10/11 GENERAL FIXTURES/ KITCHEN FITTINGS – cont'd						
Internal blinds; Luxaflex Ltd or other equal and approved						
Roller blinds; Luxaflex "Safeweave RB"; fire resisting material; 1200 mm drop; fixing with screws						
1000 mm wide	47.23	0.93	9.32	50.83	nr	60.15
2000 mm wide	65.93	1.45	14.53	70.95	nr	85.48
3000 mm wide	81.67	1.97	19.74	87.90	nr	107.64
Roller blinds; Luxaflex "Plain RB"; plain type material; 1200 mm drop; fixing with screws						
1000 mm wide	47.23	0.93	9.32	50.83	nr	60.15
2000 mm wide	65.93	1.45	14.53	70.95	nr	85.48
3000 mm wide	81.67	1.97	19.74	87.90	nr	107.64
Roller blinds; Luxaflex "Dimout plain RB"; blackout material; 1200 mm drop; fixing with screws						
1000 mm wide	55.10	0.93	9.32	59.31	nr	68.62
2000 mm wide	83.64	1.45	14.53	90.02	nr	104.55
3000 mm wide	109.22	1.97	19.74	117.55	nr	137.29
Roller blinds; Luxaflex "Lite-master Crank Op"; 100% blackout; 1200 mm drop; fixing with screws						
1000 mm wide	226.32	1.96	19.64	243.58	nr	263.22
2000 mm wide	280.44	2.75	27.55	301.82	nr	329.38
3000 mm wide	373.92	3.53	35.37	402.43	nr	437.80
Vertical louvre blinds; 89 mm wide louvres; Luxaflex "Finessa 3430" Group 0; 1200 mm drop; fixing with screws						
1000 mm wide	65.93	0.82	8.22	70.95	nr	79.17
2000 mm wide	85.61	1.30	13.03	92.14	nr	105.16
3000 mm wide	116.11	1.77	17.74	124.97	nr	142.70
Vertical louvre blinds; 127 mm wide louvres; "Finessa 3430" Group 0; 1200 mm drop; fixing with screws						
1000 mm wide	53.14	0.88	8.82	57.19	nr	66.01
2000 mm wide	75.77	1.35	13.53	81.55	nr	95.07
3000 mm wide	100.37	1.81	18.14	108.02	nr	126.16
N13 SANITARY APPLIANCES/FITTINGS						
Sinks; Armitage Shanks or equal and approved						
Sinks; white glazed fireclay; BS 1206; pointing all round with Dow Corning Hansil silicone sealant ref 785						
Belfast sink; 455 mm x 380 mm x 205 mm ref S580001; Nuastyle 2 ½" pillar taps with anti-vandal indices ref S7106AA; ½" wall mounts ref S8331AA; 1½" slotted waste, chain and plug, screw stay ref S8766AA; aluminium alloy build-in fixing brackets ref S921967	192.31	2.78	50.80	267.46	nr	318.26
Belfast sink; 610 mm x 455 mm x 255 mm ref S580501; Nuastyle 2 ½" pillar taps with anti-vandal indices ref S7106AA; ½" wall mounts ref S8331AA; 1½" slotted waste, chain and plug, screw stay ref S8766AA; aluminium alloy build-in fixing brackets ref S921967	227.75	2.78	50.80	305.76	nr	356.56

N FURNITURE/EQUIPMENT

Item	PC £	Labour hours	Labour £	Material £	Unit	Total rate £
Belfast sink; 760 mm x 455 mm x 255 mm ref S581101; Nuastyle 2 ½" pillar taps with anti-vandal indices ref S7106AA; ½" wall mounts ref S8331AA; 1½" slotted waste, chain and plug, screw stay ref S8766AA; aluminium alloy build-in fixing brackets ref S921967	306.80	2.78	50.80	390.98	nr	**441.79**
Lavatory basins; Armitage Shanks or **equal and approved** Basins; white vitreous china; BS 5506 Part 3; pointing all round with Dow Corning Hansil silicone sealant ref 785						
Portman basin 400 mm x 350 mm ref S219001; Nuastyle 2 ½" pillar taps with anti-vandal indices ref S7106AA; 1¼" bead chain waste and plug, 80 mm slotted tail, bolt stay ref S8800AA; 1¼" plastics bottle trap with 75 mm seal ref S891067; concealed fixing bracket ref S915067; Isovalve servicing valve ref S900067; screwing	95.61	2.13	38.93	141.73	nr	**180.66**
Portman basin 500 mm x 400 mm ref S222001; Nuastyle 2 ½" pillar taps with anti-vandal indices ref S7106AA; 1¼" bead chain waste and plug, 80 mm slotted tail, bolt stay ref S8800AA; 1¼" plastics bottle trap with 75 mm seal ref S891067; concealed fixing bracket ref S915067; Isovalve servicing valve ref S900067; screwing	117.32	2.13	38.93	165.20	nr	**204.13**
Portman basin 600 mm x 450 mm ref S226001; Nuastyle 2 ½" pillar taps with anti-vandal indices ref S7106AA; 1¼" bead chain waste and plug, 80 mm slotted tail, bolt stay ref S8800AA; 1¼" plastics bottle trap with 75 mm seal ref S891067; concealed fixing bracket ref S915067; Isovalve servicing valve ref S900067; screwing	155.20	2.13	38.93	206.06	nr	**244.99**
Tiffany basin 505 mm x 410 mm ref S208001; Tiffany pedestal ref S292001; Millenia ½" monobloc mixer tap with non-return valves and 1¼" pop-up waste ref S7300AA; Millenia metal handwheels ref S8000AA; Isovalve servicing valve ref S900067; screwing	166.74	2.13	38.93	198.25	nr	**237.17**
Tiffany basin 560 mm x 455 mm ref S208301; Tiffany pedestal ref S292001; Millenia ½" monobloc mixer tap with non-return valves and 1¼" pop-up waste ref S7300AA; Millenia metal handwheels ref S8000AA; Isovalve servicing valve ref S900067; screwing	163.16	2.13	38.93	194.39	nr	**233.32**
Tiffany basin 610 mm x 470 mm ref S208601; Tiffany pedestal ref S292001; Millenia ½" monobloc mixer tap with non-return valves and 1¼" pop-up waste ref S7300AA; Millenia metal handwheels ref S8000AA; Isovalve servicing valve ref S900067; screwing	170.35	2.13	38.93	202.13	nr	**241.06**
Montana basin 510 mm x 410 mm ref S210101; Montana pedestal ref S292001; Millenia ½" monobloc mixer tap with non-return valves and 1¼" pop-up waste ref S7300AA; Millenia metal handwheels ref S8000AA; Isovalve servicing valve ref S900067; screwing	157.89	2.31	42.21	188.67	nr	**230.88**

N FURNITURE/EQUIPMENT

Item	PC £	Labour hours	Labour £	Material £	Unit	Total rate £
N13 SANITARY APPLIANCES/FITTINGS – cont'd						
Lavatory basins; Armitage Shanks – cont'd Montana basin 580 mm x 475 mm ref S210401; Montana pedestal ref S292001; Millenia ½" monobloc mixer tap with non-return valves and 1¼" pop-up waste ref S7300AA; Millenia metal handwheels ref S8000AA; Isovalve servicing valve ref S900067; screwing	161.33	2.31	42.21	192.45	nr	**234.66**
Drinking fountains; Armitage Shanks or equal and approved White vitreous china fountains; pointing all round with Dow Corning Hansil silicone selant ref 785 Aqualon drinking fountain ref 200100; ½" self closing non-conclussive valve with flow control, plastics strainer waste, concealed hanger ref 0275A00; 1¼" plastics bottle trap with 75 mm seal; screwing	58.37	2.31	42.21	192.04	nr	**234.26**
Stainless steel fountains; pointing all round with Dow Corning Hansil silicone selant ref 785 Purita drinking fountain, self closing non-conclussive valve with push button operation, flow control and 1¼" strainer waste ref 53400Z5; screwing	156.53	2.31	42.21	172.01	nr	**214.23**
Purita drinking fountain, self closing non-conclussive valve with push button operation, flow control and 1¼" strainer waste ref 53400Z5; pedestal shroud ref 5341000; screwing	344.36	2.78	50.80	381.33	nr	**432.14**
Baths; Armitage Shanks or equal and approved Bath; reinforced acrylic rectangular pattern; chromium plated overflow chain and plug; 40 mm diameter chromium plated waste; cast brass "P" trap with plain outlet and overflow connection; pair 20 mm diameter chromium plated easy clean pillar taps to BS 1010						
1700 mm long; white	190.54	3.50	63.96	205.06	nr	**269.02**
1700 mm long; coloured	211.13	3.50	63.96	227.23	nr	**291.19**
Bath; enamelled steel; medium gauge rectangular pattern; 40 mm diameter chromium plated overflow chain and plug; 40 mm diameter chromium plated waste; cast brass "P" trap with plain outlet and overflow connection; pair 20 mm diameter chromium plated easy clean pillar taps to BS 1010						
1700 mm long; white	293.53	3.50	63.96	315.91	nr	**379.87**
1700 mm long; coloured	308.97	3.50	63.96	332.53	nr	**396.49**

N FURNITURE/EQUIPMENT

Item	PC £	Labour hours	Labour £	Material £	Unit	Total rate £
Water closets; Armitage Shanks or equal and approved						
White vitreous china pans and cisterns; pointing all round base with Dow Corning Hansil silicone sealant ref 785						
Wentworth close coupled washdown pan ref S316101; Orion plastic seat and cover ref S404501; Panekta WC pan P trap connector ref S430501; Group 7½ litres capacity cistern and cover, bottom supply ballvalve, bottom overflow, close coupling fitment and lever ref S392001	161.84	3.05	55.74	181.44	nr	237.18
Tiffany back to wall washdown pan ref S341001; Saturn plastic seat and cover ref S404001; Panekta WC pan P trap connector ref S430501; Conceala 6 litres capacity cistern and cover, side supply ball valve, side overflow, flushbend and extended lever ref S361767	214.87	3.05	55.74	238.51	nr	294.25
Extra over for; Panekta WC pan S trap connector ref S430001	-	-	-	1.72	nr	1.72
Tiffany close coupled washdown pan ref S308001; Saturn plastic seat and cover ref S404001; Panekta WC pan P trap connector ref S430501; Tiffany 7½ litres capacity cistern and cover, side supply ball valve, side overflow, flushbend and extended lever ref S365001	215.37	3.05	55.74	239.05	nr	294.79
Extra over for Panekta WC pan S trap connector ref S430001	-	-	-	1.72	nr	1.72
Cameo close coupled washdown pan ref S308001; Cameo plastic seat and cover ref S402501; Panekta WC pan P trap connector ref S430501; Cameo 6 litres capactity cistern and cover, bottom supply ball valve, bottom overflow and close coupling fitment; push button fittings ref S361301	268.60	3.05	55.74	296.34	nr	352.08
Extra over for; Panekta WC pan S trap connector ref S430001	-	-	-	1.72	nr	1.72
Wall urinals; Armitage Shanks or equal and approved						
White vitreous china bowls and cisterns; pointing all round with Dow Corning Hansil silicone sealant ref 785						
single Sanura 400 mm bowl ref S610501; top inlet spreader ref S6285AA; concealed steel hangers ref S9725AA; 1½" plastics domed strainer waste ref S885067; 1½" plastics bottle trap with 75 mm seal ref S891567; Conceala 4½ litres capacity cistern and cover ref S620001; concealed flushpipes ref S6226NU; screwing	189.44	3.70	67.62	256.45	nr	324.06
single Sanura 500 mm bowl ref S610001; top inlet spreader ref S6285AA; concealed steel hangers ref S9725AA; 1½" plastics domed strainer waste ref S885067; 1½" plastics bottle trap with 75 mm seal ref S891567; Conceala 4½ litres capacity cistern and cover ref S620001; concealed flushpipes ref S6226NU; screwing	257.61	3.70	67.62	329.89	nr	397.50

N FURNITURE/EQUIPMENT

Item	PC £	Labour hours	Labour £	Material £	Unit	Total rate £
N13 SANITARY APPLIANCES/FITTINGS – cont'd						
Wall urinals; Armitage Shanks – cont'd						
range of 2 nr Sanura 400 mm bowls ref S610501; top inlet spreaders ref S6285AA; concealed steel hangers ref S9725AA; 1½" plastics domed strainer wastes ref S885067; 1½" plastics bottle traps with 75 mm seal ref S891567; Conceala 9 litres capacity cistern and cover ref S620101; concealed flushpipes ref S6226NU; screwing	307.67	6.94	126.83	436.27	nr	**563.09**
range of 2 nr Sanura 500 mm bowls ref S610001; top inlet spreaders ref S6285AA; concealed steel hangers ref S9725AA; 1½" plastics domed strainer wastes ref S885067; 1½" plastics bottle traps with 75 mm seal ref S891567; Conceala 9 litres capacity cistern and cover ref S620101; concealed flushpipes ref S6226NU; screwing	444.01	6.94	126.83	583.14	nr	**709.97**
range of 3 nr Sanura 400 mm bowls ref S610501; top inlet spreaders ref S6285AA; concealed steel hangersref S9725AA; 1½" plastics domed strainer wastes ref S885067; 1½" plastics bottle traps with 75 mm seal ref S891567; Conceala 9 litres capacity cistern and cover ref S620101; concealed flushpipes ref S6226NU; screwing	405.31	10.18	186.04	593.89	nr	**779.93**
range of 3 nr Sanura 500 mm bowls ref S610001; top inlet spreaders ref S6285AA; concealed steel hangers ref S9725AA; 1½" plastics domed strainer wastes ref S885067; 1½" plastics bottle traps with 75 mm seal ref S891567; Conceala 9 litres capacity cistern and cover ref S620101; concealed flushpipes ref S6226NU; screwing	609.80	10.18	186.04	813.99	nr	**1000.02**
range of 4 nr Sanura 400 mm bowls ref S610501; top inlet spreaders ref S6285AA; concealed steel hangers ref S9725AA; 1½" plastics domed strainer wastes ref S885067; 1½" plastics bottle traps with 75 mm seal ref S891567; Conceala 13.60 litres capacity cistern and cover ref S620201; concealed flushpipes ref S6226NU; screwing	522.70	13.41	245.06	772.82	nr	**1017.89**
range of 4 nr Sanura 500 mm bowls ref S610001; top inlet spreaders ref S6285AA; concealed steel hangers ref S9725AA 1½" plastics domed strainer wastes ref S885067; 1½" plastics bottle traps with 75 mm seal ref S891567; Conceala 13.60 litres capacity cistern and cover ref S620201; concealed flushpipes ref S6226NU; screwing	795.37	13.41	245.06	1066.58	nr	**1311.64**
range of 5 nr Sanura 400 mm bowls ref S610501; top inlet spreaders ref S6285AA; concealed steel hangers ref S9725AA; 1½" plastics domed strainer wastes ref S885067; 1½" plastics bottle traps with 75 mm seal ref S891567, Conceala 13.60 litres capacity cistern and cover ref S620201; concealed flushpipes ref S6226NU; screwing	620.33	16.65	304.27	901.71	nr	**1205.99**

N FURNITURE/EQUIPMENT

Item	PC £	Labour hours	Labour £	Material £	Unit	Total rate £
range of 5 nr Sanura 500 mm bowls ref S610001; top inlet spreaders ref S6285AA; concealed steel hangers ref S9725AA; 1½" plastics domed strainer wastes ref S885067; 1½" plastics bottle traps with 75 mm seal ref S891567, Conceala 13.60 litres capacity cistern and cover ref S620201; concealed flushpipes ref S6226NU; screwing	961.16	16.65	304.27	1268.90	nr	1573.18
White vitreous china division panels; pointing all round with Hansill silicone sealant ref 785						
625 mm long ref S612001; screwing	58.43	0.69	12.61	63.70	nr	76.31
Bidets; Armitage Shanks or equal and approved						
Bidet; vitreous china; chromium plated waste; mixer tap with hand wheels						
600 mm x 400 x x 400 mm; white	190.54	3.50	63.96	205.06	nr	269.02
Shower tray and fittings; Armitage Shanks or equal and approved						
Shower tray; glazed fireclay with outlet and grated waste; chain and plug; bedding and pointing in waterproof cement mortar						
760 mm x 760 mm x 180 mm; white	118.43	3.00	54.82	127.47	nr	182.29
760 mm x 760 mm x 180 mm; coloured	180.23	3.00	54.82	193.98	nr	248.80
Shower fitting; riser pipe with mixing valve and shower rose; chromium plated; plugging and screwing mixing valve and pipe bracket						
15 mm diameter riser pipe; 127 mm diameter shower rose	231.73	5.00	91.37	249.40	nr	340.77
Miscellaneous fittings; Magrini Ltd or equal and approved						
Vertical nappy changing unit						
ref KBCS; screwing	-	0.60	8.03	253.77	nr	261.80
Horizontal nappy changing unit						
ref KBHS; screwing	-	0.60	8.03	253.77	nr	261.80
Stay Safe baby seat						
ref KBPS; screwing	-	0.55	7.36	63.44	nr	70.81
Miscellaneous fittings; Pressalit Ltd or equal and approved						
Grab rails						
300 mm long ref RT100000; screwing	-	0.50	6.69	37.82	nr	44.52
450 mm long ref RT101000; screwing	-	0.50	6.69	44.30	nr	50.99
600 mm long ref RT102000; screwing	-	0.50	6.69	50.72	nr	57.41
800 mm long ref RT103000; screwing	-	0.50	6.69	56.90	nr	63.60
1000 mm long ref RT104000; screwing	-	0.50	6.69	65.47	nr	72.16
Angled grab rails						
900 mm long, angled 135° ref RT110000; screwing	-	0.50	6.69	82.12	nr	88.81
1300 mm long, angled 90° ref RT119000; screwing	-	0.75	10.04	128.53	nr	138.57
Hinged grab rails						
600 mm long ref R3016000 ; screwing	-	0.35	4.69	133.10	nr	137.79
600 mm long with spring counter balance ref RF016000 ; screwing	-	0.35	4.69	184.61	nr	189.30
800 mm long ref R3010000 ; screwing	-	0.35	4.69	159.34	nr	164.03
800 mm long with spring counter balance ref RF010000 ; screwing	-	0.35	4.69	196.19	nr	200.88

N FURNITURE/EQUIPMENT

Item	PC £	Labour hours	Labour £	Material £	Unit	Total rate £
N15 SIGNS/NOTICES						
Plain script; in gloss oil paint; on painted or varnished surfaces						
Capital letters; lower case letters or numerals						
per coat; per 25 mm high	-	0.09	1.21	-	nr	**1.21**
Stops						
per coat	-	0.02	0.27	-	nr	**0.27**
N20 HOTEL BATHROOM PODS						
Fully fitted out, finished and furnished bathroom pods; installed						
standard pod (4.5 m^2 on plan)	-	-	-	-	nr	**3690.00**
Accessible pod (4.5 m^2 on plan)	-	-	-	-	nr	**5125.00**

P BUILDING FABRIC SUNDRIES

Item	PC £	Labour hours	Labour £	Material £	Unit	Total rate £
P10 SUNDRY INSULATION/PROOFING WORK/ FIRE STOPS						
ALTERNATIVE INSULATION PRICES						
Discounts of 10 - 50% available depending on quantity/status						
Insulation						
"Crown Wallmate"						
25 mm	-	-	-	4.66	m²	-
30 mm	-	-	-	5.21	m²	-
40 mm	-	-	-	5.61	m²	-
50 mm	-	-	-	8.53	m²	-
"Crown Wool"						
60 mm	-	-	-	2.21	m²	-
80 mm	-	-	-	2.90	m²	-
100 mm	-	-	-	3.46	m²	-
"Crown Dritherm" - part fill						
30 mm	-	-	-	2.38	m²	-
50 mm	-	-	-	4.24	m²	-
75 mm	-	-	-	5.62	m²	-
"Crown Sound Deadening Quilt"						
13 mm	-	-	-	2.57	m²	-
25 mm	-	-	-	4.93	m²	-
"Crown Factoryclad"						
80 mm	-	-	-	3.31	m²	-
90 mm	-	-	-	3.61	m²	-
100 mm	-	-	-	3.90	m²	-
SUPPLY AND FIX PRICES						
"Sisalkraft" building papers/vapour barriers or other equal and approved						
Building paper; 150 mm laps; fixed to softwood						
"Moistop" grade 728 (class A1F)	-	0.08	1.02	0.90	m²	**1.92**
Vapour barrier/reflective insulation 150 mm laps; fixed to softwood						
"Insulex" grade 714; single sided	-	0.08	1.02	0.97	m²	**1.99**
"Insulex" grade 714; double sided	-	0.08	1.02	1.60	m²	**2.62**
Mat or quilt insulation						
Glass fibre quilt; Isowool "Modular roll" or other Equal and approved; laid loose between members At 600 mm centres						
60 mm thick	1.33	0.09	1.15	1.43	m²	**2.58**
80 mm thick	1.74	0.10	1.28	1.87	m²	**3.15**
100 mm thick	2.07	0.11	1.40	2.23	m²	**3.63**
150 mm thick	3.17	0.12	1.53	3.41	m²	**4.94**
Mineral fibre quilt; Isowool "APR 1200" or other equal and approved; pinned vertically to softwood						
25 mm thick	0.92	0.08	1.02	0.98	m²	**2.01**
50 mm thick	1.45	0.09	1.15	1.56	m²	**2.70**
Glass fibre building roll; pinned vertically to softwood						
60 mm thick	1.11	0.09	1.15	1.25	m²	**2.40**
80 mm thick	1.45	0.10	1.28	1.64	m²	**2.92**
100 mm thick	1.73	0.11	1.40	1.96	m²	**3.36**

P BUILDING FABRIC SUNDRIES

Item	PC £	Labour hours	Labour £	Material £	Unit	Total rate £
P10 SUNDRY INSULATION/PROOFING WORK/ FIRE STOPS – cont'd						
"Crown Dritherm" glass fibre semi-rigid or rigid batt or other equal and approved; as full or partial cavity fill; including cutting and fitting around wall ties and retaining discs						
50 mm thick	2.12	0.12	1.53	2.60	m²	4.13
75 mm thick	2.81	0.13	1.66	3.38	m²	5.04
100 mm thick	3.74	0.14	1.79	4.43	m²	6.21
"Crown Frametherm" glass fibre semi-rigid or rigid batt or other equal and approved; pinned vertically in timber frame construction						
80 mm thick	2.63	0.13	1.66	2.97	m²	4.63
100 mm thick	3.16	0.14	1.79	3.57	m²	5.36
150 mm thick	4.80	0.15	1.91	5.43	m²	7.34
Glass fibre flanged building roll; paper faces; pinned vertically or to slope between timber framing						
60 mm thick	2.93	0.17	2.96	3.31	m²	6.27
80 mm thick	3.65	0.18	3.14	4.12	m²	7.26
100 mm thick	4.26	0.19	3.31	4.82	m²	8.13
Glass fibre aluminium foil faced roll; pinned to softwood						
80 mm thick	-	0.17	2.96	3.48	m²	6.44
Board or slab insulation						
Expanded polystyrene board standard grade SD/N or other equal and approved; fixed with adhesive						
20 mm thick	-	0.14	2.44	3.28	m²	5.72
25 mm thick	-	0.14	2.44	3.89	m²	6.33
30 mm thick	-	0.14	2.44	4.49	m²	6.93
40 mm thick	-	0.15	2.61	5.70	m²	8.32
50 mm thick	-	0.16	2.79	6.91	m²	9.70
60 mm thick	-	0.17	2.96	8.11	m²	11.07
75 mm thick	-	0.18	3.14	9.93	m²	13.07
100 mm thick	-	0.19	3.31	12.95	m²	16.26
"Kingspan Thermawall TW50" zero ODP rigid urethene insulation board or other equal and approved; as full or partial cavity fill; including cutting and fitting around wall ties and retaining discs						
50 mm thick	5.23	0.17	2.96	6.11	m²	9.08
75 mm thick	7.72	0.18	3.14	8.93	m²	12.07
100 mm thick	10.04	0.19	3.31	11.55	m²	14.86
"Styrofoam Floormate 350" extruded polystyrene foam or other equal and approved						
50 mm thick	-	0.46	8.02	21.38	m²	29.40
75 mm thick	-	0.46	8.02	32.07	m²	40.08
100 mm thick	-	0.46	8.02	42.76	m²	50.77
Fire stops						
Cape "Firecheck" channel; intumescent coatings on cut mitres; fixing with brass cups and screws						
19 mm x 44 mm or 19 mm x 50 mm	8.46	0.56	9.76	9.93	m	19.69
"						

P BUILDING FABRIC SUNDRIES

Item	PC £	Labour hours	Labour £	Material £	Unit	Total rate £
Sealmaster" intumescent fire and smoke seals or other equal and approved; pinned into groove in timber						
type N30; for single leaf half hour door	5.01	0.28	4.88	5.66	m	10.54
type N60; for single leaf one hour door	7.62	0.31	5.40	8.61	m	14.01
type IMN or IMP; for meeting or pivot stiles of pair of one hour doors; per stile	7.62	0.31	5.40	8.61	m	14.01
intumescent plugs in timber; including boring	-	0.09	1.57	0.26	nr	1.83
Rockwool fire stops or other equal and approved; between top of brick/block wall and concrete soffit						
25 mm deep x 100 mm wide	-	0.07	1.22	2.09	m	3.31
25 mm deep x 150 mm wide	-	0.09	1.57	2.78	m	4.35
25 mm deep x 200 mm wide	-	0.11	1.92	3.48	m	5.40
50 mm deep x 100 mm wide	-	0.08	1.39	3.93	m	5.32
50 mm deep x 150 mm wide	-	0.10	1.74	5.24	m	6.98
50 mm deep x 200 mm wide	-	0.12	2.09	6.55	m	8.64
90 mm deep x 100 mm wide	-	0.10	1.74	6.87	m	8.61
90 mm deep x 150 mm wide	-	0.12	2.09	9.16	m	11.25
90 mm deep x 200 mm wide	-	0.14	2.44	11.45	m	13.89
Fire protection compound						
Quelfire QF4, fire protection compound or other equal and approved; filling around pipes, ducts and the like; including all necessary formwork						
300 mm x 300 mm x 250 mm; pipes - 2	-	0.93	13.95	9.70	nr	23.65
500 mm x 500 mm x 250 mm; pipes - 2	-	1.16	16.83	29.09	nr	45.91
Fire barriers						
Rockwool fire barrier or other equal and approved; between top of suspended ceiling and concrete soffit						
one 50 mm layer x 900 mm wide; half hour	-	0.56	9.76	5.57	m²	15.32
two 50 mm layers x 900 mm wide; one hour	-	0.83	14.46	10.90	m²	25.37
Corofil C144 fire barrier to edge of slab; fixed with non-flammable contact adhesive						
to suit void 30 mm wide x 100 mm deep; one hour	-	-	-	-	m	12.56
Lamatherm fire barrier or other equal and approved; to void below raised access floors						
75 mm thick x 300 mm high; half hour	-	0.17	2.96	12.41	m	15.37
75 mm thick x 600 mm high; half hour	-	0.17	2.96	27.96	m	30.92
90 mm thick x 300 mm high; half hour	-	0.17	2.96	14.79	m	17.75
90 mm thick x 600 mm high; half hour	-	0.17	2.96	34.57	m	37.53
Dow Chemicals "Styrofoam 1B" or other equal and approved; cold bridging insulation fixed with adhesive to brick, block or concrete base						
Insulation to walls						
25 mm thick	-	0.31	5.40	5.95	m²	11.35
50 mm thick	-	0.33	5.75	10.97	m²	16.72
75 mm thick	-	0.35	6.10	16.36	m²	22.46
Insulation to isolated columns						
25 mm thick	-	0.38	6.62	5.95	m²	12.57
50 mm thick	-	0.41	7.14	10.97	m²	18.11
75 mm thick	-	0.43	7.49	16.36	m²	23.86

P BUILDING FABRIC SUNDRIES

Item	PC £	Labour hours	Labour £	Material £	Unit	Total rate £
P10 SUNDRY INSULATION/PROOFING WORK/ FIRE STOPS – cont'd						
Dow Chemicals "Styrofoam 1B" – cont'd						
Insulation to ceilings						
25 mm thick	-	0.33	5.75	5.95	m²	11.70
50 mm thick	-	0.36	6.27	10.97	m²	17.24
75 mm thick	-	0.39	6.80	16.36	m²	23.16
Insulation to isolated beams						
25 mm thick	-	0.41	7.14	5.95	m²	13.10
50 mm thick	-	0.43	7.49	10.97	m²	18.46
75 mm thick	-	0.46	8.02	16.36	m²	24.38
P11 FOAMED/FIBRE/BEAD CAVITY WALL INSULATION						
Injected insulation						
Cavity wall insulation; injecting 65 mm cavity with						
blown EPS granules	-	-	-	-	m²	2.61
blown mineral wool	-	-	-	-	m²	2.71
P20 UNFRAMED ISOLATED TRIMS/ SKIRTINGS/SUNDRY ITEMS						
Medium density fibreboard (Sapele veneered one side); 18 mm thick						
Window boards and the like; rebated; hardwood lipped on one edge						
18 mm x 200 mm	-	0.25	4.36	14.63	m	18.98
18 mm x 250 mm	-	0.28	4.88	15.40	m	20.28
18 mm x 300 mm	-	0.31	5.40	15.78	m	21.18
18 mm x 350 mm	-	0.33	5.75	16.94	m	22.69
returned and fitted ends	-	0.20	3.48	2.85	nr	6.34
Medium density fibreboard (American White Ash veneered one side); 18 mm thick						
Window boards and the like; rebated; hardwood lipped on one edge						
18 mm x 200 mm	-	0.25	4.36	15.20	m	19.56
18 mm x 250 mm	-	0.28	4.88	16.17	m	21.05
18 mm x 300 mm	-	0.31	5.40	16.64	m	22.04
18 mm x 350 mm	-	0.33	5.75	18.08	m	23.83
returned and fitted ends	-	0.20	3.48	2.85	nr	6.34
Wrought softwood						
Skirtings, picture rails, dado rails and the like; splayed or moulded						
19 mm x 44 mm; splayed	-	0.09	1.57	2.75	m	4.32
19 mm x 44 mm; moulded	-	0.09	1.57	2.95	m	4.52
19 mm x 69 mm; splayed	-	0.09	1.57	2.99	m	4.56
19 mm x 69 mm; moulded	-	0.09	1.57	2.99	m	4.56
19 mm x 94 mm; splayed	-	0.09	1.57	3.35	m	4.92
19 mm x 94 mm; moulded	-	0.09	1.57	3.35	m	4.92
19 mm x 144 mm; moulded	-	0.11	1.92	3.95	m	5.86
19 mm x 169 mm; moulded	-	0.11	1.92	4.17	m	6.09
25 mm x 50 mm; moulded	-	0.09	1.57	2.89	m	4.46
25 mm x 69 mm; splayed	-	0.09	1.57	3.19	m	4.76
25 mm x 94 mm; splayed	-	0.09	1.57	3.58	m	5.15

P BUILDING FABRIC SUNDRIES

Item	PC £	Labour hours	Labour £	Material £	Unit	Total rate £
25 mm x 144 mm; splayed	-	0.11	1.92	4.35	m	6.27
25 mm x 144 mm; moulded	-	0.11	1.92	4.35	m	6.27
25 mm x 169 mm; moulded	-	0.11	1.92	4.84	m	6.75
25 mm x 219 mm; moulded	-	0.13	2.27	6.30	m	8.56
returned ends	-	0.14	2.44	-	nr	2.44
mitres	-	0.09	1.57	-	nr	1.57
Architraves, cover fillets and the like; half round; splayed or moulded						
13 mm x 25 mm; half round	-	0.11	1.92	2.59	m	4.51
13 mm x 50 mm; moulded	-	0.11	1.92	2.75	m	4.67
16 mm x 32 mm; half round	-	0.11	1.92	2.88	m	4.79
16 mm x 38 mm; moulded	-	0.11	1.92	2.88	m	4.79
16 mm x 50 mm; moulded	-	0.11	1.92	2.88	m	4.79
19 mm x 50 mm; splayed	-	0.11	1.92	2.88	m	4.79
19 mm x 63 mm; splayed	-	0.11	1.92	2.99	m	4.90
19 mm x 69 mm; splayed	-	0.11	1.92	3.17	m	5.09
25 mm x 44 mm; splayed	-	0.11	1.92	2.85	m	4.77
25 mm x 50 mm; moulded	-	0.11	1.92	3.58	m	5.50
25 mm x 63 mm; splayed	-	0.11	1.92	3.13	m	5.04
25 mm x 69 mm; splayed	-	0.11	1.92	3.56	m	5.48
32 mm x 88 mm; moulded	-	0.11	1.92	3.16	m	5.08
38 mm x 38 mm; moulded	-	0.11	1.92	3.69	m	5.61
50 mm x 50 mm; moulded	-	0.11	1.92	2.85	m	4.77
returned ends	-	0.14	2.44	-	nr	2.44
mitres	-	0.09	1.57	-	nr	1.57
Stops; screwed on						
16 mm x 38 mm	-	0.09	1.57	1.30	m	2.87
16 mm x 50 mm	-	0.09	1.57	1.41	m	2.98
19 mm x 38 mm	-	0.09	1.57	1.30	m	2.87
25 mm x 38 mm	-	0.09	1.57	1.42	m	2.99
25 mm x 50 mm	-	0.09	1.57	1.46	m	3.03
Glazing beads and the like						
13 mm x 16 mm	-	0.04	0.70	1.58	m	2.28
13 mm x 19 mm	-	0.04	0.70	1.58	m	2.28
13 mm x 25 mm	-	0.04	0.70	1.62	m	2.32
13 mm x 25 mm; screwed	-	0.04	0.70	4.06	m	4.76
13 mm x 25 mm; fixing with brass cups and screws	-	0.04	0.70	5.29	m	5.99
16 mm x 25 mm; screwed	-	0.04	0.70	4.06	m	4.76
16 mm quadrant	-	0.04	0.70	2.41	m	3.11
19 mm quadrant or scotia	-	0.04	0.70	2.41	m	3.11
19 mm x 36 mm; screwed	-	0.04	0.70	2.67	m	3.37
25 mm x 38 mm; screwed	-	0.04	0.70	2.79	m	3.49
25 mm quadrant or scotia	-	0.04	0.70	2.55	m	3.25
38 mm scotia	-	0.04	0.70	3.08	m	3.77
50 mm scotia	-	0.04	0.70	3.60	m	4.30
Isolated shelves, worktops, seats and the like						
19 mm x 150 mm	-	0.15	2.61	3.35	m	5.97
19 mm x 200 mm	-	0.20	3.48	4.63	m	8.11
25 mm x 150 mm	-	0.15	2.61	3.83	m	6.44
25 mm x 200 mm	-	0.20	3.48	5.43	m	8.91
32 mm x 150 mm	-	0.15	2.61	4.47	m	7.08
32 mm x 200 mm	-	0.20	3.48	6.11	m	9.60

P BUILDING FABRIC SUNDRIES

Item	PC £	Labour hours	Labour £	Material £	Unit	Total rate £
P20 UNFRAMED ISOLATED TRIMS/ **SKIRTINGS/SUNDRY ITEMS** – cont'd						
Wrought softwood – cont'd						
Isolated shelves, worktops, seats and the like; cross-tongued joints						
19 mm x 300 mm	-	0.26	4.53	13.78	m	18.31
19 mm x 450 mm	-	0.31	5.40	20.78	m	26.19
19 mm x 600 mm	-	0.37	6.45	26.89	m	33.33
25 mm x 300 mm	-	0.26	4.53	14.79	m	19.32
25 mm x 450 mm	-	0.31	5.40	22.42	m	27.82
25 mm x 600 mm	-	0.37	6.45	29.14	m	35.59
32 mm x 300 mm	-	0.26	4.53	15.66	m	20.19
32 mm x 450 mm	-	0.31	5.40	23.82	m	29.22
32 mm x 600 mm	-	0.37	6.45	31.08	m	37.53
Isolated shelves, worktops, seats and the like; slatted with 50 wide slats at 75 mm centres						
19 mm thick	-	0.60	10.45	33.56	m	44.02
25 mm thick	-	0.60	10.45	34.31	m	44.77
32 mm thick	-	0.60	10.45	34.96	m	45.41
Window boards, nosings, bed moulds and the like; rebated and rounded						
19 mm x 75 mm	-	0.17	2.96	4.17	m	7.13
19 mm x 150 mm	-	0.19	3.31	5.18	m	8.49
19 mm x 225 mm; in one width	-	0.24	4.18	6.42	m	10.60
19 mm x 300 mm; cross-tongued joints	-	0.28	4.88	14.93	m	19.81
25 mm x 75 mm	-	0.17	2.96	4.40	m	7.37
25 mm x 150 mm	-	0.19	3.31	5.69	m	9.00
25 mm x 225 mm; in one width	-	0.24	4.18	7.21	m	11.39
25 mm x 300 mm; cross-tongued joints	-	0.28	4.88	16.15	m	21.03
32 mm x 75 mm	-	0.17	2.96	4.63	m	7.59
32 mm x 150 mm	-	0.19	3.31	6.14	m	9.45
32 mm x 225 mm; in one width	-	0.24	4.18	7.89	m	12.07
32 mm x 300 mm; cross-tongued joints	-	0.28	4.88	17.19	m	22.07
38 mm x 75 mm	-	0.17	2.96	5.07	m	8.03
38 mm x 150 mm	-	0.19	3.31	7.10	m	10.41
38 mm x 225 mm; in one width	-	0.24	4.18	9.23	m	13.41
38 mm x 300 mm; cross-tongued joints	-	0.28	4.88	19.26	m	24.14
returned and fitted ends	-	0.14	2.44	-	nr	2.44
Handrails; mopstick						
50 mm diameter	-	0.23	4.01	9.62	m	13.62
Handrails; rounded						
44 mm x 50 mm	-	0.23	4.01	9.31	m	13.32
50 mm x 75 mm	-	0.25	4.36	10.18	m	14.54
63 mm x 87 mm	-	0.28	4.88	11.29	m	16.17
75 mm x 100 mm	-	0.32	5.58	13.84	m	19.41
Handrails; moulded						
44 mm x 50 mm	-	0.23	4.01	9.31	m	13.32
50 mm x 75 mm	-	0.25	4.36	10.18	m	14.54
63 mm x 87 mm	-	0.28	4.88	11.29	m	16.17
75 mm x 100 mm	-	0.32	5.58	13.84	m	19.41
Add 5% to the above material prices for selected softwood for staining						5%

P BUILDING FABRIC SUNDRIES

Item	PC £	Labour hours	Labour £	Material £	Unit	Total rate £
Medium density fibreboard						
Skirtings, picture rails, dado rails and the like;						
splayed or moulded						
18 mm x 50 mm; splayed	-	0.09	1.57	2.72	m	4.29
18 mm x 50 mm; moulded	-	0.09	1.57	2.72	m	4.29
18 mm x 75 mm; splayed	-	0.09	1.57	2.83	m	4.40
18 mm x 75 mm; moulded	-	0.09	1.57	2.83	m	4.40
18 mm x 100 mm; splayed	-	0.09	1.57	2.95	m	4.52
18 mm x 100 mm; moulded	-	0.09	1.57	2.95	m	4.52
18 mm x 150 mm; moulded	-	0.11	1.92	3.21	m	5.13
18 mm x 175 mm; moulded	-	0.11	1.92	3.33	m	5.25
22 mm x 100 mm; splayed	-	0.09	1.57	4.75	m	6.32
25 mm x 50 mm; moulded	-	0.09	1.57	2.85	m	4.42
25 mm x 75 mm; splayed	-	0.09	1.57	3.02	m	4.58
25 mm x 100 mm; splayed	-	0.09	1.57	3.20	m	4.77
25 mm x 150 mm; splayed	-	0.11	1.92	3.61	m	5.53
25 mm x 150 mm; moulded	-	0.11	1.92	3.61	m	5.53
25 mm x 175 mm; moulded	-	0.11	1.92	3.80	m	5.71
25 mm x 225 mm; moulded	-	0.13	2.27	4.06	m	6.33
returned ends	-	0.14	2.44	-	nr	2.44
mitres	-	0.09	1.57	-	nr	1.57
Architraves, cover fillets and the like; half round;						
splayed or moulded						
12 mm x 25 mm; half round	-	0.11	1.92	3.75	m	5.67
12 mm x 50 mm; moulded	-	0.11	1.92	2.67	m	4.59
15 mm x 32 mm; half round	-	0.11	1.92	2.61	m	4.53
15 mm x 38 mm; moulded	-	0.11	1.92	2.63	m	4.55
15 mm x 50 mm; moulded	-	0.11	1.92	2.67	m	4.59
18 mm x 50 mm; splayed	-	0.11	1.92	2.67	m	4.59
18 mm x 63 mm; splayed	-	0.11	1.92	2.79	m	4.71
18 mm x 75 mm; splayed	-	0.11	1.92	2.85	m	4.77
25 mm x 44 mm; splayed	-	0.11	1.92	2.85	m	4.77
25 mm x 50 mm; moulded	-	0.11	1.92	2.85	m	4.77
25 mm x 63 mm; splayed	-	0.11	1.92	2.95	m	4.86
25 mm x 75 mm; splayed	-	0.11	1.92	3.05	m	4.96
30 mm x 88 mm; moulded	-	0.11	1.92	3.96	m	5.87
38 mm x 38 mm; moulded	-	0.11	1.92	3.38	m	5.30
50 mm x 50 mm; moulded	-	0.11	1.92	3.55	m	5.47
returned ends	-	0.14	2.44	-	nr	2.44
mitres	-	0.09	1.57	-	nr	1.57
Stops; screwed on						
15 mm x 38 mm	-	0.09	1.57	1.48	m	3.05
15 mm x 50 mm	-	0.09	1.57	1.53	m	3.10
18 mm x 38 mm	-	0.09	1.57	1.52	m	3.09
25 mm x 38 mm	-	0.09	1.57	1.60	m	3.16
25 mm x 50 mm	-	0.09	1.57	1.68	m	3.24
Glazing beads and the like						
12 mm x 16 mm	-	0.04	0.70	1.71	m	2.41
12 mm x 19 mm	-	0.04	0.70	1.72	m	2.42
12 mm x 25 mm	-	0.04	0.70	1.74	m	2.44
12 mm x 25 mm; screwed	-	0.04	0.70	2.48	m	3.18
12 mm x 25 mm; brass cups and screws	-	0.04	0.70	2.86	m	3.55
15 mm x 25 mm; screwed	-	0.04	0.70	2.57	m	3.27
15 mm quadrant	-	0.04	0.70	2.46	m	3.16
18 mm quadrant or scotia	-	0.04	0.70	2.47	m	3.17
18 mm x 36 mm; screwed	-	0.04	0.70	2.62	m	3.32
25 mm x 38 mm; screwed	-	0.04	0.70	2.74	m	3.44
25 mm quadrant or scotia	-	0.04	0.70	2.58	m	3.28
38 mm scotia	-	0.04	0.70	2.45	m	3.15
50 mm scotia	-	0.04	0.70	2.85	m	3.54

P BUILDING FABRIC SUNDRIES

Item	PC £	Labour hours	Labour £	Material £	Unit	Total rate £
P20 UNFRAMED ISOLATED TRIMS/ SKIRTINGS/SUNDRY ITEMS – cont'd						
Medium density fibreboard – cont'd						
Isolated shelves, worktops, seats and the like						
18 mm x 150 mm	-	0.15	2.61	3.23	m	5.85
18 mm x 200 mm	-	0.20	3.48	3.40	m	6.89
25 mm x 150 mm	-	0.15	2.61	3.71	m	6.32
25 mm x 200 mm	-	0.20	3.48	3.97	m	7.45
30 mm x 150 mm	-	0.15	2.61	5.20	m	7.81
30 mm x 200 mm	-	0.20	3.48	5.76	m	9.25
Isolated shelves, worktops, seats and the like; cross-tongued joints						
18 mm x 300 mm	-	0.26	4.53	10.53	m	15.06
18 mm x 450 mm	-	0.31	5.40	12.04	m	17.45
18 mm x 600 mm	-	0.37	6.45	20.10	m	26.55
25 mm x 300 mm	-	0.26	4.53	11.09	m	15.62
25 mm x 450 mm	-	0.31	5.40	13.58	m	18.98
25 mm x 600 mm	-	0.37	6.45	19.60	m	26.05
30 mm x 300 mm	-	0.26	4.53	12.81	m	17.34
30 mm x 450 mm	-	0.31	5.40	15.25	m	20.65
30 mm x 600 mm	-	0.37	6.45	22.19	m	28.64
Isolated shelves, worktops, seats and the like; slatted with 50 wide slats at 75 mm centres						
18 mm thick	-	0.60	10.45	32.93	m	43.39
25 mm thick	-	0.60	10.45	34.95	m	45.40
30 mm thick	-	0.60	10.45	36.79	m	47.25
Window boards, nosings, bed moulds and the like; rebated and rounded						
18 mm x 75 mm	-	0.17	2.96	3.08	m	6.04
18 mm x 150 mm	-	0.19	3.31	3.49	m	6.80
18 mm x 225 mm	-	0.24	4.18	3.81	m	7.99
18 mm x 300 mm	-	0.28	4.88	4.19	m	9.07
25 mm x 75 mm	-	0.17	2.96	3.23	m	6.19
25 mm x 150 mm	-	0.19	3.31	3.81	m	7.12
25 mm x 225 mm	-	0.24	4.18	4.26	m	8.44
25 mm x 300 mm	-	0.28	4.88	4.80	m	9.68
30 mm x 75 mm	-	0.17	2.96	4.43	m	7.40
30 mm x 150 mm	-	0.19	3.31	5.47	m	8.78
30 mm x 225 mm	-	0.24	4.18	6.29	m	10.47
30 mm x 300 mm	-	0.28	4.88	7.25	m	12.13
38 mm x 75 mm	-	0.17	2.96	5.02	m	7.98
38 mm x 150 mm	-	0.19	3.31	6.28	m	9.59
38 mm x 225 mm	-	0.24	4.18	7.24	m	11.42
38 mm x 300 mm	-	0.28	4.88	8.39	m	13.27
returned and fitted ends	-	-	-	1.01	nr	1.01
Selected Sapele						
Skirtings, picture rails, dado rails and the like; splayed or moulded						
19 mm x 44 mm; splayed	3.67	0.13	2.27	4.23	m	6.50
19 mm x 44 mm; moulded	3.67	0.13	2.27	4.23	m	6.50
19 mm x 69 mm; splayed	4.26	0.13	2.27	4.91	m	7.17
19 mm x 69 mm; moulded	4.26	0.13	2.27	4.91	m	7.17
19 mm x 94 mm; splayed	4.98	0.13	2.27	5.72	m	7.98
19 mm x 94 mm; moulded	4.98	0.13	2.27	5.72	m	7.98
19 mm x 144 mm; moulded	6.62	0.15	2.61	7.57	m	10.18
19 mm x 169 mm; moulded	7.32	0.15	2.61	8.37	m	10.98
25 mm x 44 mm; moulded	4.12	0.13	2.27	4.75	m	7.01
25 mm x 69 mm; splayed	4.91	0.13	2.27	5.64	m	7.90

P BUILDING FABRIC SUNDRIES

Item	PC £	Labour hours	Labour £	Material £	Unit	Total rate £
25 mm x 94 mm; splayed	6.01	0.13	2.27	6.88	m	9.15
25 mm x 144 mm; splayed	7.90	0.15	2.61	9.02	m	11.63
25 mm x 144 mm; moulded	7.90	0.15	2.61	9.02	m	11.63
25 mm x 169 mm; moulded	8.85	0.15	2.61	10.09	m	12.70
25 mm x 219 mm; moulded	10.11	0.17	2.96	11.51	m	14.47
returned ends	-	0.20	3.48	-	nr	3.48
mitres	-	0.14	2.44	-	nr	2.44
Architraves, cover fillets and the like; half round; splayed or moulded						
13 mm x 25 mm; half round	2.22	0.15	2.61	2.60	m	5.21
13 mm x 50 mm; moulded	3.56	0.15	2.61	4.11	m	6.73
16 mm x 32 mm; half round	2.26	0.15	2.61	2.64	m	5.25
16 mm x 38 mm; moulded	3.43	0.15	2.61	3.97	m	6.58
16 mm x 50 mm; moulded	3.67	0.15	2.61	4.23	m	6.85
19 mm x 50 mm; splayed	3.67	0.15	2.61	4.23	m	6.85
19 mm x 63 mm; splayed	3.98	0.15	2.61	4.59	m	7.20
19 mm x 69 mm; splayed	4.26	0.15	2.61	4.91	m	7.52
25 mm x 44 mm; splayed	3.96	0.15	2.61	4.57	m	7.18
25 mm x 50 mm; moulded	4.12	0.15	2.61	4.75	m	7.36
25 mm x 63 mm; splayed	4.59	0.15	2.61	5.28	m	7.89
25 mm x 69 mm; splayed	4.91	0.15	2.61	5.64	m	8.25
32 mm x 88 mm; moulded	5.98	0.15	2.61	6.84	m	9.46
38 mm x 38 mm; moulded	4.70	0.15	2.61	5.40	m	8.01
50 mm x 50 mm; moulded	6.14	0.15	2.61	7.03	m	9.64
returned ends	-	0.20	3.48	-	nr	3.48
mitres	-	0.14	2.44	-	nr	2.44
Stops; screwed on						
16 mm x 38 mm	1.51	0.14	2.44	1.71	m	4.15
16 mm x 50 mm	1.63	0.14	2.44	1.84	m	4.28
19 mm x 38 mm	1.51	0.14	2.44	1.71	m	4.15
25 mm x 38 mm	1.91	0.14	2.44	2.16	m	4.60
25 mm x 50 mm	2.21	0.14	2.44	2.50	m	4.94
Glazing beads and the like						
13 mm x 16 mm	1.98	0.06	1.05	2.23	m	3.28
13 mm x 19 mm	1.98	0.06	1.05	2.23	m	3.28
13 mm x 25 mm	2.13	0.06	1.05	2.40	m	3.45
13 mm x 25 mm; screwed	1.98	0.06	1.05	2.23	m	3.28
13 mm x 25 mm; fixing with brass cups and screws	2.13	0.06	1.05	2.40	m	3.45
16 mm x 25 mm; screwed	4.14	0.06	1.05	4.68	m	5.72
16 mm quadrant	2.77	0.06	1.05	3.13	m	4.18
19 mm quadrant or scotia	2.77	0.06	1.05	3.13	m	4.18
19 mm x 36 mm; screwed	3.54	0.06	1.05	4.00	m	5.05
25 mm x 38 mm; screwed	3.87	0.06	1.05	4.37	m	5.42
25 mm quadrant or scotia	3.17	0.06	1.05	3.58	m	4.63
38 mm scotia	4.70	0.06	1.05	5.31	m	6.36
50 mm scotia	6.14	0.06	1.05	6.94	m	7.99
Isolated shelves; worktops, seats and the like						
19 mm x 150 mm	6.74	0.20	3.48	7.61	m	11.10
19 mm x 200 mm	7.96	0.28	4.88	9.00	m	13.88
25 mm x 150 mm	7.90	0.20	3.48	8.93	m	12.41
25 mm x 200 mm	9.48	0.28	4.88	10.71	m	15.59
32 mm x 150 mm	8.91	0.20	3.48	10.07	m	13.55
32 mm x 200 mm	10.77	0.28	4.88	12.17	m	17.05
Isolated shelves, worktops, seats and the like; cross-tongued joints						
19 mm x 300 mm	18.22	0.35	6.10	20.59	m	26.69
19 mm x 450 mm	28.52	0.42	7.32	32.23	m	39.55
19 mm x 600 mm	37.90	0.51	8.89	42.83	m	51.71

P BUILDING FABRIC SUNDRIES

Item	PC £	Labour hours	Labour £	Material £	Unit	Total rate £
P20 UNFRAMED ISOLATED TRIMS/ SKIRTINGS/SUNDRY ITEMS – cont'd						
Medium density fibreboard – cont'd						
Isolated shelves – cont'd						
25 mm x 300 mm	20.46	0.35	6.10	23.12	m	29.22
25 mm x 450 mm	32.14	0.42	7.32	36.32	m	43.64
25 mm x 600 mm	42.72	0.51	8.89	48.27	m	57.16
32 mm x 300 mm	22.37	0.35	6.10	25.28	m	31.38
32 mm x 450 mm	35.24	0.42	7.32	39.82	m	47.14
32 mm x 600 mm	46.85	0.51	8.89	52.94	m	61.83
Isolated shelves, worktops, seats and the like; slatted with 50 wide slats at 75 mm centres						
19 mm thick	51.27	0.80	13.94	59.66	m²	73.60
25 mm thick	54.90	0.80	13.94	63.85	m²	77.79
32 mm thick	57.99	0.80	13.94	67.43	m²	81.37
Window boards, nosings, bed moulds and the like; rebated and rounded						
19 mm x 75 mm	5.20	0.22	3.83	6.08	m	9.91
19 mm x 150 mm	7.53	0.25	4.36	8.72	m	13.07
19 mm x 225 mm; in one width	9.26	0.33	5.75	10.66	m	16.41
19 mm x 300 mm; cross-tongued joints	18.84	0.37	6.45	21.49	m	27.94
25 mm x 75 mm	5.71	0.22	3.83	6.66	m	10.49
25 mm x 150 mm	8.39	0.25	4.36	9.68	m	14.04
25 mm x 225 mm; in one width	11.02	0.33	5.75	12.65	m	18.40
25 mm x 300 mm; cross-tongued joints	21.89	0.37	6.45	24.94	m	31.39
32 mm x 75 mm	6.21	0.22	3.83	7.22	m	11.06
32 mm x 150 mm	9.34	0.25	4.36	10.75	m	15.11
32 mm x 225 mm; in one width	12.45	0.33	5.75	14.27	m	20.02
32 mm x 300 mm; cross-tongued joints	24.08	0.37	6.45	27.41	m	33.86
returned and fitted ends	-	0.21	3.66	-	nr	3.66
Handrails; rounded						
44 mm x 50 mm	11.44	0.31	5.40	12.92	m	18.33
50 mm x 75 mm	13.79	0.33	5.75	15.58	m	21.33
63 mm x 87 mm	16.18	0.37	6.45	18.28	m	24.73
75 mm x 100 mm	20.11	0.42	7.32	22.72	m	30.04
Handrails; moulded						
44 mm x 50 mm	12.72	0.31	5.40	14.38	m	19.78
50 mm x 75 mm	15.08	0.33	5.75	17.04	m	22.79
63 mm x 87 mm	17.47	0.37	6.45	19.75	m	26.19
75 mm x 100 mm	21.39	0.42	7.32	24.18	m	31.49
Pin-boards; medium board						
Sundeala "A" pin-board or other equal and approved; fixed with adhesive to backing (not included); over 300 mm wide						
6.40 mm thick	-	0.56	9.76	18.06	m²	27.81
Sundries on softwood/hardwood						
Extra over fixing with nails for						
gluing and pinning	-	0.01	0.17	0.06	m	0.23
masonry nails	-	-	-	-	m	0.30
steel screws	-	-	-	-	m	0.28
self-tapping screws	-	-	-	-	m	0.29
steel screws; gluing	-	-	-	-	m	0.48
steel screws; sinking; filling heads	-	-	-	-	m	0.61
steel screws; sinking; pellating over	-	-	-	-	m	1.34
brass cups and screws	-	-	-	-	m	1.65

P BUILDING FABRIC SUNDRIES

Item	PC £	Labour hours	Labour £	Material £	Unit	Total rate £
Extra over for						
countersinking	-	-	-	-	m	0.25
pellating	-	-	-	-	m	1.17
Head or nut in softwood						
let in flush	-	-	-	-	nr	0.61
Head or nut; in hardwood						
let in flush	-	-	-	-	nr	0.91
let in over; pellated	-	-	-	-	nr	2.14
Metalwork; mild steel						
Angle section bearers; for building in						
90 mm x 90 mm x 6 mm	-	0.31	5.83	5.54	m	11.37
120 mm x 120 mm x 8 mm	-	0.32	6.01	8.36	m	14.37
200 mm x 150 mm x 12 mm	-	0.37	6.95	22.49	m	29.44
Metalwork; mild steel; galvanized						
Waterbars; groove in timber						
6 mm x 30 mm	-	0.46	8.02	4.10	m	12.11
6 mm x 40 mm	-	0.46	8.02	5.38	m	13.40
6 mm x 50 mm	-	0.46	8.02	6.75	m	14.77
Angle section bearers; for building in						
90 mm x 90 mm x 6 mm	-	0.31	5.83	7.37	m	13.20
120 mm x 120 mm x 8 mm	-	0.32	6.01	11.12	m	17.13
200 mm x 150 mm x 12 mm	-	0.37	6.95	29.94	m	36.89
Dowels; mortice in timber						
8 mm diameter x 100 mm long	-	0.04	0.70	0.12	nr	0.82
10 mm diameter x 50 mm long	-	0.04	0.70	0.29	nr	0.99
Cramps						
25 mm x 3 mm x 230 mm girth; one end bent, holed and screwed to softwood; other end fishtailed for building in	-	0.06	1.05	0.70	nr	1.75
Metalwork; stainless steel						
Angle section bearers; for building in						
90 mm x 90 mm x 6 mm	-	0.31	5.83	29.12	m	34.94
120 mm x 120 mm x 8 mm	-	0.32	6.01	43.04	m	49.05
200 mm x 150 mm x 12 mm	-	0.37	6.95	112.28	m	119.24
P21 IRONMONGERY						
NOTE: Ironmongery is largely a matter of selection and prices vary considerably; indicative prices for reasonable quantities of "good quality" ironmongery are given below.						
Ironmongery; Allgood or other equal and approved; to softwood						
Bolts						
75 x 35 mm Modric anodised aluminium straight barrel bolt	-	0.30	5.23	6.20	nr	11.43
150 x 35 mm Modric anodised aluminium Modric anodised aluminium straight barrel bolt	-	0.30	5.23	9.25	nr	14.48
75 x 35 mm Modric anodised aluminium necked barrel bolt	-	0.30	5.23	8.23	nr	13.46
150 x 35 mm Modric anodised aluminium necked barrel bolt	-	0.30	5.23	10.80	nr	16.03
11 mm Easiclean socket	-	0.10	1.74	2.66	nr	4.41
Security hinge bolt chubb WS12	-	0.50	8.71	12.20	nr	20.92

P BUILDING FABRIC SUNDRIES

Item	PC £	Labour hours	Labour £	Material £	Unit	Total rate £
P21 IRONMONGERY – cont'd						
Ironmongery; Allgood; to softwood – cont'd						
Bolts – cont'd						
203 x 19 x 11 mm Complete bolt set, with floor socket and intumescent pack for FD30 and FD60 fire doors	-	0.60	10.45	30.37	nr	40.82
203/457 x 19 mm Complete bolt set, with floor socket and intumescent pack for FD30 and FD60 fire doors	-	0.60	10.45	61.27	nr	71.72
203/609 x 19 mm Complete bolt set, with floor socket and intumescent pack for FD30 and FD60 fire doors	-	0.60	10.45	71.44	nr	81.89
11 mm Dust excluding socket, satin nickel plated	-	0.10	1.74	7.99	nr	9.73
Stainless steel indicating bolt complete with outside indicator and emergency release	-	0.60	10.45	58.02	nr	68.48
Catches						
Magnetic catch	-	0.20	3.48	0.87	nr	4.36
Door closers and furniture						
13 mm Satin chrome rebate component for 7204/08/78/79/86	-	0.60	10.45	18.02	nr	28.47
90 x 90 mm Modric anodised aluminium electrically powered hold open wall magnet. CE marked to BS EN1155:1997 & A1:2002 3-5-6/3-1-1-3	-	0.40	6.97	9.88	nr	16.85
Modric anodised aluminium bathroom configuration with quadaxial assembly, turn, release and optional indicator	-	0.80	13.94	65.87	nr	79.81
Concealed overhead door restraining stay with S/S arm and aluminium channel & bracket and adjustable friction slide block, spring buffer to curtail door opening. NOT for use with concealed door closing devices	-	1.00	17.42	22.76	nr	40.19
213 x 48 x 48 mm Overhead door closers complete with fixings for fig 1 and fig 6 applications. Certifire listed. CE Marked to BS EN1154 4-8-3-1-1-3	-	1.00	17.42	49.45	nr	66.87
Concealed jamb door closer check action	-	1.00	17.42	77.54	nr	94.96
75 x 57 x 170 mm Modric anodised aluminium door co-ordinator for pairs of rebated leaves, CE Marked to BS EN1158 3-5-3/5-1-1-0	-	0.80	13.94	26.49	nr	40.43
263 x 50 x 48 mm Modric anodised aluminium overhead door closer Fig 1 available power 1-4 with adjustable backcheck, intumescent protected bracket. Certifire listed and CE Marked to BS EN1154 4-8-4-1-1-3	-	1.00	17.42	56.23	nr	73.65
290 x 48 x 50 mm Modric anodised aluminium rectangular overhead door closer with adjustable power and adjustable backcheck intumescent protected arm heavy duty U.L. & certifire listed & CE Marked to BS EN1154 4-8-2/4-1-1-3 and Kitemarked.	-	1.00	17.42	71.15	nr	88.57
Stainless steel overhead door closer Fig 1. Projecting armset, Power EN 2-5, CE marked , c/w Backcheck, Latch action and Speed control. Max door width 1100 mm, Max door weight 100kg	-	1.00	17.42	70.52	nr	87.94
Stainless steel finished track and arm to suit 9124 fully concealed door closer	-	0.80	13.94	48.29	nr	62.23

P BUILDING FABRIC SUNDRIES

Item	PC £	Labour hours	Labour £	Material £	Unit	Total rate £
92 x 45 mm Stainless steel heavy duty floor pivot set with thrust roller bearing 400kg load capacity. Complete with forged steel intumescent protected double action strap with 10 mm height adjustment, new low profile top centre, and matching cover plate	-	2.30	40.08	151.78	nr	**191.86**
92 x 45 mm Stainless steel heavy duty floor pivot set with thrust roller bearing 400kg load capacity, with stainless steel intumescent protected S/A 25 mm offset strap & top centre, matching plate	-	2.30	40.08	188.98	nr	**229.06**
Double action pivot set for door maximum width 1100 mm and maximum weight 80kg	-	2.30	40.08	73.03	nr	**113.11**
305 x 80 x 50 mm Stainless steel 'Cavalier' floor spring, intumescent protected forged steel D/A strap with 10 mm height adjustment & low profile top centre, matching covers & box. CE Marked to BS EN1154 4-8-*-1-1-3. Adjustable power 2/4	-	2.30	40.08	217.07	nr	**257.15**
305 x 80 x 50 mm Stainless steel 'Cavalier' floor spring adjustable power 2/4 stainless steel intumsecent protected S/A 16 mm offset strap & top centre, matching covers & box. Certifire listed and CE marked to BSEN1154 4-8-2/4-1-1-3	-	2.30	40.08	254.26	nr	**294.34**
Surface vertical rod push bar panic bolt, reversible, tp suit doors 2500x1100 mm maximum, silver finish, CE marked to EN1125 class 3-7-5-1-1-3-2-2-A	-	1.50	26.14	105.77	nr	**131.91**
Rim push bar panic latch, reversible, to suit doors 1100 mm wide maximum, silver finish, CE marked to EN1125 class 3-7-5-1-1-3-2-2-A	-	1.30	22.65	73.52	nr	**96.17**
76 x 51 x 13 mm Adjustable heavy roller catch satin chrome	-	0.60	10.45	5.86	nr	**16.31**
External access device for use with XX10280/2 panic hardware to suit door thickness 45-55 mm, complete with SS3006N lever, SS755 rose, SS796 profile escutcheon and spindle.For use with MA7420A51 or MA7420A55 profile cylinders	-	1.30	22.65	25.28	nr	**47.93**
142 x 22 mm Ø Concealed jamb door closer light duty	-	0.80	13.94	9.44	nr	**23.38**
112 x 42 mm Emergency release door stop for toilet doors	-	1.00	17.42	72.74	nr	**90.17**
Modric anodised aluminium quadaxial lever assembly tested to BS EN1906 4/7/-/1/1/4/0/U	-	0.80	13.94	25.86	pair	**39.80**
Modric anodised aluminium quadaxial lever assembly Tested to BS EN1906 4/7/-/1/1/4/0/U	-	0.80	13.94	26.64	pair	**40.58**
Modric anodised aluminium quadaxial lever assembly Tested to BS EN1906 4/7/-/1/1/4/0/U with Biocote® anti-bacterial protection	-	0.80	13.94	31.96	pair	**45.90**
Modric stainless steel quadaxial lever assembly Tested to BS EN1906 4/7/-/1/1/4/0/U	-	0.80	13.94	56.76	pair	**70.70**
152 x 38 x 13 mm Modric anodised aluminium security door chain leather covered	-	0.40	6.97	43.78	nr	**50.75**
50 Ø x 3 mm Modric anodised aluminium circular covered rose for profile cylinder	-	0.10	1.74	3.10	nr	**4.84**
50 Ø x 3 mm Modric anodised aluminium circular covered rose with indicator and emergency release	-	0.15	2.61	7.99	nr	**10.60**
50 Ø x 3 mm Modric anodised aluminium circular covered rose with heavy turn, 5-8 mm spindle	-	0.15	2.61	12.45	nr	**15.06**

P BUILDING FABRIC SUNDRIES

Item	PC £	Labour hours	Labour £	Material £	Unit	Total rate £
P21 IRONMONGERY – cont'd						
Ironmongery; Allgood; to softwood – cont'd						
Door closers and furniture – cont'd						
Budget lock escutcheon - satin stainless steel 316	-	0.10	1.74	4.31	nr	6.05
50 Ø x 3 mm Stainless steel circular covered rose for profile cylinder	-	0.10	1.74	5.62	nr	7.36
50 Ø x 3 mm Stainless steel circular covered rose with indicator and emergency release	-	0.15	2.61	13.71	nr	16.32
50 Ø x 3 mm Stainless steel circular covered rose with heavy turn, 5-8 mm spindle	-	0.15	2.61	19.61	nr	22.23
330 x 76 x 1.6 mm Modric anodised aluminium push plate	-	0.15	2.61	3.10	nr	5.71
330 x 76 x 1.6 mm Stainless steel push plate	-	0.15	2.61	6.01	nr	8.62
800 x 150 x 1.5 mm Modric anodised aluminium kicking plate, drilled and countersunk with screws.	-	0.25	4.36	7.07	nr	11.43
900 x 150 x 1.5 mm Modric anodised aluminium kicking plate, drilled and countersunk with screws.	-	0.25	4.36	7.89	nr	12.25
1000 x 150 x 1.5 mm Modric anodised aluminium kicking plate, drilled & countersunk with screws.	-	0.25	4.36	8.72	nr	13.07
800 x 150 x 1.5 mm Stainless steel kicking plate, drilled and countersunk with screws.	-	0.25	4.36	15.69	nr	20.05
900 x 150 x 1.5 mm Stainless steel kicking plate, drilled and countersunk with screws.	-	0.25	4.36	17.68	nr	22.03
1000 x 150 x 1.5 mm Stainless steel kicking plate, drilled & countersunk with screws.	-	0.25	4.36	19.57	nr	23.92
305 x 80 x 3 mm Stainless steel letter plate with spring loaded flap opening 250 x 45 mm only for doors up to 60 mm 316 stainless steel	-	1.25	21.78	50.71	nr	72.49
19 mm Ø straight pull handle with M8 threaded holes, fixing centres 300 mm, satin stainless steel 316	-	0.33	5.75	30.42	nr	36.17
610 x 70 x 19 mm Ø Modric anodised aluminium grab handle bolt through fixing		0.40	6.97	31.34	nr	38.30
457 x 457 x 25 mm Ø Modric anodised aluminium heavy duty grab handle 3 point fixing 70 mm projection	-	0.40	6.97	100.83	nr	107.80
Hinges						
100 x 75 x 2.5 mm Triple knuckle button tipped butt hinges satin chrome plated on steel, jig drilled CE Marked to EN1935		0.25	5.44	8.52	pair	13.96
100 x 75 x 2.5 mm Triple knuckle concealed twin Newton bearings, button tipped hinges, satin chrome plated steel, jig drilled, CE marked to EN1935 4-7-7-1-1-4-0-14	-	0.25	4.36	11.62	pair	15.98
90 x 90 x 3 mm Stainless steel triple knuckle concealed twin Newton bearings, button tipped hinges, template drilled to ANSI 156.7 and BS7352 satin stainless steel 316 CE marked to EN1935 4-7-6-1-1-4-0-13	-	0.25	4.36	20.92	pair	25.28
100 x 75 x 3 mm Stainless steel triple knuckle concealed twin Newton bearings, button tipped hinges, jig drilled, stainless steel 316 CE marked to EN1935 4-7-7-1-1-4-0-14	-	0.25	4.36	14.43	pair	18.79

P BUILDING FABRIC SUNDRIES

Item	PC £	Labour hours	Labour £	Material £	Unit	Total rate £
100 x 75 x 3 mm Stainless steel triple knuckle concealed twin Newtonbearings, button tipped butt hinges, jig drilled for metal doors/frames, complete with M6x12MT 'undercut' machine screws, stainless steel 316 CE marked to EN1935 4-7-7-1-1-4-0-14	-	0.25	4.36	21.50	pair	25.86
100 x 100 x 3 mm Stainless steel triple knuckle concealed twin Newton bearings, button tipped hinges, jig drilled, stainless steel grade 316 CE marked to EN1935 4-7-7-1-1-4-0-14	-	0.25	4.36	22.18	pair	26.54
Latches						
Modric anodised aluminium 'Advanced' round cylinder for rim night latch or locking attachment, anti-pick paracentric keyway with exclusive 'TG' pins, hardened driver and body insert, 2 keyed	-	0.40	6.97	13.03	nr	20.00
93 x 75 mm Cylinder rim non-deadlocking night latch case only 60 mm backset	-	0.40	6.97	14.63	nr	21.60
92 x 60 mm b/s Stainless steel 'HL' series mortice latch, case only, stainless steel low friction latchbolt, unique Griptight follower, heavy spring for levers, squared ended forend and strike, CE marked to BSEN 12209 3/X/8/1/0/F/1/3/0/3/0	-	0.80	13.94	15.98	nr	29.92
Satin chrome 'Advanced' round cylinder for rim night latch or locking attachment, anti-pick paracentric keyway with exclusive 'TG' pins. hardened driver and body insert, 2 keyed under Master Key	-	0.80	13.94	18.26	nr	32.20
Modric anodised aluminium latch configuration with quadaxial assembly	-	0.80	13.94	40.34	nr	54.28
Modric anodised aluminium Nightlatch configuration with quadaxial assembly and single cylinder	-	0.80	13.94	78.51	nr	92.45
Locks						
44 mm case Bright zinc plated steel mortice budget lock with slotted strike plate 33 mm backset	-	0.80	13.94	9.01	nr	22.95
76 x 58 mm b/s Stainless steel cubicle mortice deadlock with 8 mm follower	-	0.80	13.94	10.90	nr	24.84
Advanced' profile single cylinder, anti-pick paracentric keyway with exclusive "TG" pins, hardened drivers and body insert, 2 keyed, Satin Nickel finish.	-	0.80	13.94	13.66	nr	27.60
Advanced' profile single cylinder, anti-pick paracentric keyway with exclusive "TG" pins, hardened drivers and body insert, 2 keyed under Master Key, Satin Nickel finish.	-	0.80	13.94	19.13	nr	33.07
65 mm 'Advanced' profile cylinder with Allgood inside turn anti-pick paracentric keyway with exclusive "TG" pins, hardened driver and body inserts. 2 keyed. satin nickel finish.	-	0.80	13.94	21.99	nr	35.93
65 mm 'Advanced' profile cylinder with Allgood inside turn anti-pick paracentric keyway with exclusive "TG" pins, hardened driver and body insert. 2 keyed. Under master key Satin nickel finish.	-	0.80	13.94	27.80	nr	41.74
Advanced' profile double cylinder, anti-pick paracentric keyway with exclusive "TG" pins, hardened drivers and body insert, 2 keyd under Master key, Satin Nickel finish	-	0.80	13.94	30.61	nr	44.55

P BUILDING FABRIC SUNDRIES

Item	PC £	Labour hours	Labour £	Material £	Unit	Total rate £
P21 IRONMONGERY – cont'd						
Ironmongery; Allgood; to softwood – cont'd						
Locks – cont'd						
55 mm 'Advanced' cylinder hardened steel padlock, anti-pick paracentric keyway with exclusive 'TG' pins, hardened driver and body insert, 2 keyed under Master Key.	-	0.80	13.94	58.89	nr	72.83
92 x 60 mm b/s Stainless steel 'HL' series profile cylinder mortice deadlock, case only, single throw 20 mm stainless steel deadbolt, square forend and plain flat strike CE Marked to BS EN12209 3/X/8/1/0/F/1/K/A/0/0	-	0.80	13.94	15.98	nr	29.92
92 x 60 mm b/s Stainless steel 'HL' series bathroom lock, case only, stainless steel low friction latchbolt, unique Griptight follower, heavy spring for levers, twin 8 mm followers at 78 mm centres, square ended forend and strike	-	0.80	13.94	16.95	nr	30.89
92 x 60 mm b/s Stainless steel 'HL' series profile cyl mort lock, case only, stainless steel low friction l/bolt, unique Griptight follower, hvy spring for lvrs, 20 mm throw d/bolt, cyl can w/draw both bolts sq f/end & strike. CE marked to BSEN 12209 3/X/8/1/0/F/1/K/A/3/0	-	0.80	13.94	16.95	nr	30.89
92 x 60 mm b/s Stainless steel 'HL' series profile cylinder split follower entrance door lockcase with safety re-entry function. Stainless steel latch & single throw 20 mm throw deadbolt. Inside lever withdraws both bolts and unlocks outside lever.	-	0.80	13.94	56.47	nr	70.41
Modric anodised aluminium lock configuration with quadaxial assembly and cylinder with turn	-	0.80	13.94	73.81	nr	87.75
Sundries						
76 mm Ø Modric anodised aluminium circular sex symbol male	-	0.08	1.39	5.04	nr	6.43
76 mm Ø Modric anodised aluminium circular symbol fire door keep locked	-	0.08	1.39	5.04	nr	6.43
76 mm Ø Modric anodised aluminium circular symbol fire door keep shut	-	0.10	1.74	5.04	nr	6.78
38 x 47 mm Ø Modric anodised aluminium heavy circular floor door stop with cover	-	0.10	1.74	7.31	nr	9.06
38 x 47 mm Ø Stainless steel heavy circular floor door stop with cover	-	0.10	1.74	7.94	nr	9.69
102 x 25 mm Ø Modric ancdised aluminium Circular heavy duty skirting buffer with thief resistant insert	-	0.10	1.74	9.54	nr	11.28
102 x 25 mm Ø Stainless steel circular heavy duty skirting buffer with thief resistant insert	-	0.10	1.74	14.14	nr	15.88
152 mm Cabin hook satin chrome on brass	-	0.15	2.61	13.71	nr	16.32
Toilet roll holder, length 145 mm, colour white, satin stainless steel 316	-	0.15	2.61	33.95	nr	36.56
Towel rail with bushes, fixing centres 450 mm, satin stainless steel 316	-	0.25	4.36	49.93	nr	54.29
Toilet brush holder with toilet brush, with bushes, satin stainless steel 316	-	0.20	3.48	72.21	nr	75.70
Set of stainless steel rails, one lift-up, 3 straight, and one backrest for use in toilets for the disabled, to meet the requirements of Part M of the Building Regulations	-	1.50	26.14	345.61	set	371.74

P BUILDING FABRIC SUNDRIES

Item	PC £	Labour hours	Labour £	Material £	Unit	Total rate £
Ironmongery; Allgood or other equal and approved; to hardwood						
Bolts						
75 x 35 mm Modric anodised aluminium straight barrel bolt	-	0.40	6.97	6.20	nr	**13.17**
150 x 35 mm Modric anodised aluminium Modric anodised aluminium straight barrel bolt	-	0.40	6.97	9.25	nr	**16.22**
75 x 35 mm Modric anodised aluminium necked barrel bolt	-	0.40	6.97	8.23	nr	**15.20**
150 x 35 mm Modric anodised aluminium necked barrel bolt	-	0.40	6.97	10.80	nr	**17.77**
11 mm Easiclean socket	-	0.15	2.61	2.66	nr	**5.28**
Security hinge bolt chubb WS12	-	0.65	11.33	12.20	nr	**23.53**
203 x 19 x 11 mm Complete bolt set, with floor socket and intumescent pack for FD30 and FD60 fire doors	-	0.80	13.94	30.37	nr	**44.31**
203/457 x 19 mm Complete bolt set, with floor socket and intumescent pack for FD30 and FD60 fire doors	-	0.80	13.94	61.27	nr	**75.21**
203/609 x 19 mm Complete bolt set, with floor socket and intumescent pack for FD30 and FD60 fire doors	-	0.80	13.94	71.44	nr	**85.38**
11 mm Dust excluding socket, satin nickel plated	-	0.15	2.61	7.99	nr	**10.60**
Stainless steel indicating bolt complete with outside indicator and emergency release	-	0.80	13.94	58.02	nr	**71.96**
Catches						
Magnetic catch	-	0.25	4.36	0.87	nr	**5.23**
Door closers and furniture						
13 mm Satin chrome rebate component for 7204/08/78/79/86	-	0.80	13.94	18.02	nr	**31.96**
90 x 90 mm Modric anodised aluminium electrically powered hold open wall magnet. CE marked to BS EN1155:1997 & A1:2002 3-5-6/3-1-1-3	-	0.55	9.58	9.88	nr	**19.46**
Modric anodised aluminium bathroom configuration with quadaxial assembly, turn, release and optional indicator	-	1.05	18.30	65.87	nr	**84.16**
Concealed overhead door restraining stay with S/S arm and aluminium channel & bracket and adjustable friction slide block, spring buffer to curtail door opening. NOT for use with concealed door closing devices	-	1.35	23.52	22.76	nr	**46.29**
213 x 48 x 48 mm Overhead door closers complete with fixings for fig 1 and fig 6 applications. Certifire listed. CE Marked to BS EN1154 4-8-3-1-1-3	-	1.35	23.52	49.45	nr	**72.97**
Concealed jamb door closer check action	-	1.35	23.52	77.54	nr	**101.06**
75 x 57 x 170 mm Modric anodised aluminium door co-ordinator for pairs of rebated leaves, CE Marked to BS EN1158 3-5-3/5-1-1-0	-	1.05	18.30	26.49	nr	**44.79**
263 x 50 x 48 mm Modric anodised aluminium overhead door closer Fig 1 available power 1-4 with adjustable backcheck, intumescent protected bracket. Certifire listed and CE Marked to BS EN1154 4-8-4-1-1-3	-	1.35	23.52	56.23	nr	**79.75**

P BUILDING FABRIC SUNDRIES

Item	PC £	Labour hours	Labour £	Material £	Unit	Total rate £
P21 IRONMONGERY – cont'd						
Ironmongery; Allgood; to hardwood – cont'd						
Door closers and furniture – cont'd						
290 x 48 x 50 mm Modric anodised aluminium rectangular overhead door closer with adjustable power and adjustable backcheck intumescent protected arm heavy duty U.L. & certifire listed & CE Marked to BS EN1154 4-8-2/4-1-1-3 and Kitemarked.	-	1.35	23.52	71.15	nr	**94.67**
Stainless steel overhead door closer Fig 1. Projecting armset, Power EN 2-5, CE marked , c/w Backcheck, Latch action and Speed control. Max door width 1100 mm, Max door weight 100kg	-	1.35	23.52	70.52	nr	**94.04**
Stainless steel finished track and arm to suit 9124 fully concealed door closer	-	1.05	18.30	48.29	nr	**66.58**
92 x 45 mm Stainless steel heavy duty floor pivot set with thrust roller bearing 400kg load capacity. Complete with forged steel intumescent protected double action strap with 10 mm height adjustment, new low profile top centre, and matching cover plate	-	3.05	53.14	151.78	nr	**204.93**
92 x 45 mm Stainless steel heavy duty floor pivot set with thrust roller bearing 400kg load capacity, with stainless steel intumescent protected S/A 25 mm offset strap & top centre, matching plate	-	3.05	53.14	188.98	nr	**242.12**
Double action pivot set for door maximum width 1100 mm and maximum weight 80kg	-	3.05	53.14	73.03	nr	**126.18**
305 x 80 x 50 mm Stainless steel 'Cavalier' floor spring, intumescent protected forged steel D/A strap with 10 mm height adjustment & low profile top centre, matching covers & box. CE Marked to BS EN1154 4-8-*-1-1-3. Adjustable power 2/4	-	3.05	53.14	217.07	nr	**270.21**
305 x 80 x 50 mm Stainless steel 'Cavalier' floor spring adjustable power 2/4 stainless steel intumsecent protected S/A 16 mm offset strap & top centre, matching covers & box. Certifire listed and CE marked to BSEN1154 4-8-2/4-1-1-3	-	3.05	53.14	254.26	nr	**307.41**
Surface vertical rod push bar panic bolt, reversible, tp suit doors 2500x1100 mm maximum, silver finish, CE marked to EN1125 class 3-7-5-1-1-3-2-2-A	-	2.00	34.85	105.77	nr	**140.62**
Rim push bar panic latch, reversible, to suit doors 1100 mm wide maximum, silver finish, CE marked to EN1125 class 3-7-5-1-1-3-2-2-A	-	1.75	30.49	73.52	nr	**104.01**
76 x 51 x 13 mm Adjustable heavy roller catch satin chrome	-	0.80	13.94	5.86	nr	**19.80**
External access device for use with XX10280/2 panic hardware to suit door thickness 45-55 mm, complete with SS3006N lever, SS755 rose, SS796 profile escutcheon and spindle.For use with MA7420A51 or MA7420A55 profile cylinders	-	1.75	30.49	25.28	nr	**55.77**
142 x 22 mm Ø Concealed jamb door closer light duty	-	1.05	18.30	9.44	nr	**27.74**
112 x 42 mm Emergency release door stop for toilet doors	-	1.35	23.52	72.74	nr	**96.27**
Modric anodised aluminium quadaxial lever assembly tested to BS EN1906 4/7/-/1/1/4/0/U	-	1.05	18.30	25.86	pair	**44.16**

P BUILDING FABRIC SUNDRIES

Item	PC £	Labour hours	Labour £	Material £	Unit	Total rate £
Modric anodised aluminium quadaxial lever assembly Tested to BS EN1906 4/7/-/1/1/4/0/U	-	1.05	18.30	26.64	pair	**44.93**
Modric anodised aluminium quadaxial lever assembly Tested to BS EN1906 4/7/-/1/1/4/0/U with Biocote® anti-bacterial protection	-	1.05	18.30	31.96	pair	**50.26**
Modric stainless steel quadaxial lever assembly Tested to BS EN1906 4/7/-/1/1/4/0/U	-	1.05	18.30	56.76	nr	**75.06**
152 x 38 x 13 mm Modric anodised aluminium security door chain leather covered	-	0.55	9.58	43.78	nr	**53.37**
50 Ø x 3 mm Modric anodised aluminium circular covered rose for profile cylinder	-	0.15	2.61	3.10	nr	**5.71**
50 Ø x 3 mm Modric anodised aluminium circular covered rose with indicator and emergency release	-	0.20	3.48	7.99	nr	**11.48**
50 Ø x 3 mm Modric anodised aluminium circular covered rose with heavy turn, 5-8 mm spindle	-	0.20	3.48	12.45	nr	**15.93**
Budget lock escutcheon - satin stainless steel 316	-	0.15	2.61	4.31	nr	**6.92**
50 Ø x 3 mm Stainless steel circular covered rose for profile cylinder	-	0.15	2.61	5.62	nr	**8.23**
50 Ø x 3 mm Stainless steel circular covered rose with indicator and emergency release	-	0.20	3.48	13.71	nr	**17.19**
50 Ø x 3 mm Stainless steel circular covered rose with heavy turn, 5-8 mm spindle	-	0.20	3.48	19.61	nr	**23.10**
330 x 76 x 1.6 mm Modric anodised aluminium push plate	-	0.20	3.48	3.10	nr	**6.58**
330 x 76 x 1.6 mm Stainless steel push plate	-	0.20	3.48	6.01	nr	**9.49**
800 x 150 x 1.5 mm Modric anodised aluminium kicking plate, drilled and countersunk with screws.	-	0.35	6.10	7.07	nr	**13.17**
900 x 150 x 1.5 mm Modric anodised aluminium kicking plate, drilled and countersunk with screws.	-	0.35	6.10	7.89	nr	**13.99**
1000 x 150 x 1.5 mm Modric anodised aluminium kicking plate, drilled & countersunk with screws.	-	0.35	6.10	8.72	nr	**14.82**
800 x 150 x 1.5 mm Stainless steel kicking plate, drilled and countersunk with screws.	-	0.35	6.10	15.69	nr	**21.79**
900 x 150 x 1.5 mm Stainless steel kicking plate, drilled and countersunk with screws.	-	0.35	6.10	17.68	nr	**23.78**
1000 x 150 x 1.5 mm Stainless steel kicking plate, drilled & countersunk with screws.	-	0.35	6.10	19.57	nr	**25.66**
305 x 80 x 3 mm Stainless steel letter plate with spring loaded flap opening 250 x 45 mm only for doors up to 60 mm 316 stainless steel	-	1.65	28.75	50.71	nr	**79.46**
19 mm Ø straight pull handle with M8 threaded holes, fixing centres 300 mm, satin stainless steel 316	-	0.45	7.84	30.42	nr	**38.26**
610 x 70 x 19 mm Ø Modric anodised aluminium grab handle bolt through fixing	-	0.55	9.58	31.34	nr	**40.92**
457 x 457 x 25 mm Ø Modric anodised aluminium heavy duty grab handle 3 point fixing 70 mm projection	-	0.55	9.58	100.83	nr	**110.42**

P BUILDING FABRIC SUNDRIES

Item	PC £	Labour hours	Labour £	Material £	Unit	Total rate £
P21 IRONMONGERY – cont'd						
Ironmongery; Allgood; to hardwood – cont'd						
Hinges						
100 x 75 x 2.5 mm Triple knuckle button tipped butt hinges satin chrome plated on steel, jig drilled CE Marked to EN1935	-	0.35	7.62	8.52	pair	**16.14**
100 x 75 x 2.5 mm Triple knuckle concealed twin Newton bearings, button tipped hinges, satin chrome plated steel, jig drilled, CE marked to EN1935 4-7-7-1-1-4-0-14	-	0.35	6.10	11.62	pair	**17.72**
90 x 90 x 3 mm Stainless steel triple knuckle concealed twin Newton bearings, button tipped hinges, template drilled to ANSI 156.7 and BS7352 satin stainless steel 316 CE marked to EN1935 4-7-6-1-1-4-0-13	-	0.35	6.10	20.92	pair	**27.02**
100 x 75 x 3 mm Stainless steel triple knuckle concealed twin Newton bearings, button tipped hinges, jig drilled, stainless steel 316 CE marked to EN1935 4-7-7-1-1-4-0-14	-	0.35	6.10	14.43	pair	**20.53**
100 x 75 x 3 mm Stainless steel triple knuckle concealed twin Newtonbearings, button tipped butt hinges, jig drilled for metal doors/frames, complete with M6x12MT 'undercut' machine screws, stainless steel 316 CE marked to EN1935 4-7-7-1-1-4-0-14	-	0.35	6.10	21.50	pair	**27.60**
100 x 100 x 3 mm Stainless steel triple knuckle concealed twin Newton bearings, button tipped hinges, jig drilled, stainless steel grade 316 CE marked to EN1935 4-7-7-1-1-4-0-14	-	0.35	6.10	22.18	pair	**28.28**
Latches						
Modric anodised aluminium 'Advanced' round cylinder for rim night latch or locking attachment, anti-pick paracentric keyway with exclusive 'TG' pins, hardened driver and body insert, 2 keyed	-	0.55	9.58	13.03	nr	**22.61**
93 x 75 mm Cylinder rim non-deadlocking night latch case only 60 mm backset	-	0.55	9.58	14.63	nr	**24.21**
92 x 60 mm b/s Stainless steel 'HL' series mortice latch, case only, stainless steel low friction latchbolt, unique Griptight follower, heavy spring for levers, squared ended forend and strike, CE marked to BSEN 12209 3/X/8/1/0/F/1/3/0/3/0	-	1.05	18.30	15.98	nr	**34.28**
Satin chrome 'Advanced' round cylinder for rim night latch or locking attachment, anti-pick paracentric keyway with exclusive 'TG' pins. hardened driver and body insert, 2 keyed under Master Key	-	1.05	18.30	18.26	nr	**36.55**
Modric anodised aluminium latch configuration with quadaxial assembly	-	1.05	18.30	40.34	nr	**58.64**
Modric anodised aluminium Nightlatch configuration with quadaxial assembly and single cylinder	-	1.05	18.30	78.51	nr	**96.80**
Locks						
44 mm case Bright zinc plated steel mortice budget lock with slotted strike plate 33 mm backset	-	1.05	18.30	9.01	nr	**27.30**
76 x 58 mm b/s Stainless steel cubicle mortice deadlock with 8 mm follower	-	1.05	18.30	10.90	nr	**29.19**

P BUILDING FABRIC SUNDRIES

Item	PC £	Labour hours	Labour £	Material £	Unit	Total rate £
Advanced' profile single cylinder, anti-pick paracentric keyway with exclusive "TG" pins, hardened drivers and body insert, 2 keyed, Satin Nickel finish.	-	1.05	18.30	13.66	nr	**31.95**
Advanced' profile single cylinder, anti-pick paracentric keyway with exclusive "TG" pins, hardened drivers and body insert, 2 keyed under Master Key, Satin Nickel finish.	-	1.05	18.30	19.13	nr	**37.43**
65 mm 'Advanced' profile cylinder with Allgood inside turn anti-pick paracentric keyway with exclusive "TG" pins, hardened driver and body inserts. 2 keyed. satin nickel finish.	-	1.05	18.30	21.99	nr	**40.28**
65 mm 'Advanced' profile cylinder with Allgood inside turn anti-pick paracentric keyway with exclusive "TG" pins, hardened driver and body insert. 2 keyed. Under master key Satin nickel finish.	-	1.05	18.30	27.80	nr	**46.10**
Advanced' profile double cylinder, anti-pick paracentric keyway with exclusive "TG" pins, hardened drivers and body insert, 2 keyd under Master key, Satin Nickel finish	-	1.05	18.30	30.61	nr	**48.90**
55 mm 'Advanced' cylinder hardened steel padlock, anti-pick paracentric keyway with exclusive 'TG' pins, hardened driver and body insert, 2 keyed under Master Key.	-	1.05	18.30	58.89	nr	**77.19**
92 x 60 mm b/s Stainless steel 'HL' series profile cylinder mortice deadlock, case only, single throw 20 mm stainless steel deadbolt, square forend and plain flat strike CE Marked to BS EN12209 3/X/8/1/0/F/1/K/A/0/0	-	1.05	18.30	15.98	nr	**34.28**
92 x 60 mm b/s Stainless steel 'HL' series bathroom lock, case only, stainless steel low friction latchbolt, unique Griptight follower, heavy spring for levers, twin 8 mm followers at 78 mm centres, square ended forend and strike	-	1.05	18.30	16.95	nr	**35.25**
92 x 60 mm b/s Stainless steel 'HL' series profile cyl mort lock, case only, stainless steel low friction l/bolt, unique Griptight follower, hvy spring for lvrs, 20 mm throw d/bolt, cyl can w/draw both bolts sq f/end & strike. CE marked to BSEN 12209 3/X/8/1/0/F/1/K/A/3/0	-	1.05	18.30	16.95	nr	**35.25**
92 x 60 mm b/s Stainless steel 'HL' series profile cylinder split follower entrance door lockcase with safety re-entry function. Stainless steel latch & single throw 20 mm throw deadbolt. Inside lever withdraws both bolts and unlocks outside lever.	-	1.05	18.30	56.47	nr	**74.77**
Modric anodised aluminium lock configuration with quadaxial assembly and cylinder with turn	-	1.05	18.30	73.81	nr	**92.10**
Sundries						
76 mm Ø Modric anodised aluminium circular sex symbol male	-	0.10	1.74	5.04	nr	**6.78**
76 mm Ø Modric anodised aluminium circular symbol fire door keep locked	-	0.10	1.74	5.04	nr	**6.78**
76 mm Ø Modric anodised aluminium circular symbol fire door keep shut	-	0.15	2.61	5.04	nr	**7.65**
38 x 47 mm Ø Modric anodised aluminium heavy circular floor door stop with cover	-	0.15	2.61	7.31	nr	**9.93**
38 x 47 mm Ø Stainless steel heavy circular floor door stop with cover	-	0.15	2.61	7.94	nr	**10.56**

P BUILDING FABRIC SUNDRIES

Item	PC £	Labour hours	Labour £	Material £	Unit	Total rate £
P21 IRONMONGERY – cont'd						
Ironmongery; Allgood; to hardwood – cont'd						
Sundries – cont'd						
102 x 25 mm Ø Modric ancdised aluminium circular heavy duty skirting buffer with thief resistant insert	-	0.15	2.61	9.54	nr	**12.15**
102 x 25 mm Ø Stainless steel circular heavy duty skirting buffer with thief resistant insert	-	0.15	2.61	14.14	nr	**16.76**
152 mm Cabin hook satin chrome on brass	-	0.20	3.48	13.71	nr	**17.19**
Toilet roll holder, length 145 mm, colour white, satin stainless steel 316	-	0.20	3.48	33.95	nr	**37.44**
Towel rail with bushes, fixing centres 450 mm, satin stainless steel 316	-	0.35	6.10	49.93	nr	**56.03**
Toilet brush holder with toilet brush, with bushes, satin stainless steel 316	-	0.25	4.36	72.21	nr	**76.57**
Set of stainless steel rails, one lift-up, 3 straight, and one backrest for use in toilets for the disabled, to meet the requirements of Part M of the Building Regulations	-	2.00	34.85	345.61	set	**380.45**
Sliding door gear; Hillaldam Coburn Ltd or other equal and approved; Commercial/Light industrial; for top hung timber/metal doors, weight not exceeding 365 kg						
Sliding door gear						
bottom guide; fixed to concrete in groove	13.83	0.46	8.02	14.89	m	**22.90**
top track	20.48	0.23	4.01	22.04	m	**26.05**
detachable locking bar	18.34	0.31	5.40	19.74	nr	**25.14**
hangers; timber doors	38.25	0.46	8.02	41.16	nr	**49.18**
hangers; metal doors	27.27	0.46	8.02	29.35	nr	**37.37**
head brackets; open, side fixing; bolting to masonry	5.19	0.46	8.02	8.46	nr	**16.47**
head brackets; open, soffit fixing; screwing to timber	1.67	0.32	5.58	1.85	nr	**7.42**
door guide to timber door	4.56	0.23	4.01	4.91	nr	**8.92**
door stop; rubber buffers; to masonry	21.08	0.69	12.02	22.68	nr	**34.71**
drop bolt; screwing to timber	16.67	0.46	8.02	17.95	nr	**25.96**
bow handle; to timber	8.49	0.23	4.01	9.14	nr	**13.15**
Sundries						
rubber door stop; plugged and screwed to concrete	5.08	0.09	1.57	5.47	nr	**7.03**
P30 TRENCHES/PIPEWAYS/PITS FOR BURIED ENGINEERING SERVICES						
Excavating trenches; by machine; grading bottoms; earthwork support; filling with excavated material and compacting; disposal of surplus soil on site; spreading on site average 50 m						
Services not exceeding 200 mm nominal size						
average depth of run not exceeding 0.50 m	-	0.28	3.06	1.23	m	**4.28**
average depth of run not exceeding 0.75 m	-	0.37	4.04	2.02	m	**6.06**
average depth of run not exceeding 1.00 m	-	0.79	8.62	3.72	m	**12.34**
average depth of run not exceeding 1.25 m	-	1.16	12.66	5.10	m	**17.76**
average depth of run not exceeding 1.50 m	-	1.48	16.15	6.68	m	**22.83**
average depth of run not exceeding 1.75 m	-	1.85	20.19	8.53	m	**28.72**
average depth of run not exceeding 2.00 m	-	2.13	23.25	9.79	m	**33.04**

P BUILDING FABRIC SUNDRIES

Item	PC £	Labour hours	Labour £	Material £	Unit	Total rate £
Excavating trenches; by hand; grading bottoms; earthwork support; filling with excavated material and compacting; disposal; of surplus soil on site; spreading on site average 50 m						
Services not exceeding 200 mm nominal size						
average depth of run not exceeding 0.50 m	-	0.93	10.15	-	m	10.15
average depth of run not exceeding 0.75 m	-	1.39	15.17	-	m	15.17
average depth of run not exceeding 1.00 m	-	2.04	22.26	1.17	m	23.43
average depth of run not exceeding 1.25 m	-	2.87	31.32	1.61	m	32.93
average depth of run not exceeding 1.50 m	-	3.93	42.89	1.96	m	44.85
average depth of run not exceeding 1.75 m	-	5.18	56.53	2.37	m	58.90
average depth of run not exceeding 2.00 m	-	5.92	64.61	2.60	m	67.21
Stop cock pits, valve chambers and the like; excavating; half brick thick walls in common bricks in cement mortar (1:3); on in situ concrete designated mix C20 - 20 mm aggregate bed; 100 mm thick						
Pits						
100 mm x 100 mm x 750 mm deep; internal holes for one small pipe; polypropylene hinged box cover; bedding in cement mortar (1:3)	-	3.89	84.65	26.98	nr	111.63
P31 HOLES/CHASES/COVERS/SUPPORTS FOR SERVICES						
Builders' work for electrical installations; cutting away for and making good after electrician; including cutting or leaving all holes, notches, mortices, sinkings and chases, in both the structure and its coverings, for the following electrical points						
Exposed installation						
lighting points	-	0.28	3.68	-	nr	3.68
socket outlet points	-	0.46	6.36	-	nr	6.36
fitting outlet points	-	0.46	6.36	-	nr	6.36
equipment points or control gear points	-	0.65	9.14	-	nr	9.14
Concealed installation						
lighting points	-	0.37	5.02	-	nr	5.02
socket outlet points	-	0.65	9.14	-	nr	9.14
fitting outlet points	-	0.65	9.14	-	nr	9.14
equipment points or control gear points	-	0.93	12.83	-	nr	12.83
Builders' work for other services installations						
Cutting chases in brickwork						
for one pipe; not exceeding 55 mm nominal size; vertical	-	0.37	3.71	-	m	3.71
for one pipe; 55 mm - 110 mm nominal size; vertical	-	0.65	6.51	-	m	6.51
Cutting and pinning to brickwork or blockwork; ends of supports						
for pipes not exceeding 55 mm nominal size	-	0.19	4.13	-	nr	4.13
for cast iron pipes 55 mm - 110 mm nominal size	-	0.31	6.75	-	nr	6.75

P BUILDING FABRIC SUNDRIES

Item	PC £	Labour hours	Labour £	Material £	Unit	Total rate £
P31 HOLES/CHASES/COVERS/SUPPORTS FOR SERVICES – cont'd						
Builders' work for other services						
Installations – cont'd						
Cutting or forming holes for pipes or the like; not exceeding 55 mm nominal size; making good						
reinforced concrete; not exceeding 100 mm deep	-	0.75	9.57	0.65	nr	10.21
reinforced concrete; 100 mm - 200 mm deep	-	1.15	14.67	0.99	nr	15.66
reinforced concrete; 200 mm - 300 mm deep	-	1.50	19.13	1.29	nr	20.42
half brick thick	-	0.31	3.95	-	nr	3.95
one brick thick	-	0.51	6.50	-	nr	6.50
one and a half brick thick	-	0.83	10.59	-	nr	10.59
100 mm blockwork	-	0.28	3.57	-	nr	3.57
140 mm blockwork	-	0.37	4.72	-	nr	4.72
215 mm blockwork	-	0.46	5.87	-	nr	5.87
plasterboard partition or suspended ceiling	-	0.35	4.46	-	nr	4.46
Cutting or forming holes for pipes or the like; 55 mm - 110 mm nominal size; making good						
reinforced concrete; not exceeding 100 mm deep	-	1.15	14.67	0.99	nr	15.66
reinforced concrete; 100 mm - 200 mm deep	-	1.75	22.32	1.51	nr	23.83
reinforced concrete; 200 mm - 300 mm deep	-	2.25	28.70	1.94	nr	30.64
half brick thick	-	0.37	4.72	-	nr	4.72
one brick thick	-	0.65	8.29	-	nr	8.29
one and a half brick thick	-	1.02	13.01	-	nr	13.01
100 mm blockwork	-	0.32	4.08	-	nr	4.08
140 mm blockwork	-	0.46	5.87	-	nr	5.87
215 mm blockwork	-	0.56	7.14	-	nr	7.14
plasterboard partition or suspended ceiling	-	0.40	5.10	-	nr	5.10
Cutting or forming holes for pipes or the like; over 110 mm nominal size; making good						
reinforced concrete; not exceeding 100 mm deep	-	1.15	14.67	0.99	nr	15.66
reinforced concrete; 100 mm - 200 mm deep	-	1.75	22.32	1.51	nr	23.83
reinforced concrete; 200 mm - 300 mm deep	-	2.25	28.70	1.94	nr	30.64
half brick thick	-	0.46	5.87	-	nr	5.87
one brick thick	-	0.79	10.08	-	nr	10.08
one and a half brick thick	-	1.25	15.94	-	nr	15.94
100 mm blockwork	-	0.42	5.36	-	nr	5.36
140 mm blockwork	-	0.56	7.14	-	nr	7.14
215 mm blockwork	-	0.69	8.80	-	nr	8.80
plasterboard partition or suspended ceiling	-	0.45	5.74	-	nr	5.74
Add for making good fair face or facings one side						
pipe; not exceeding 55 mm nominal size	-	0.07	1.52	-	nr	1.52
pipe; 55 mm - 110 mm nominal size	-	0.09	1.96	-	nr	1.96
pipe; over 110 mm nominal size	-	0.11	2.39	-	nr	2.39
Add for fixing sleeve (supply not included)						
for pipe; small	-	0.14	3.05	-	nr	3.05
for pipe; large	-	0.19	4.13	-	nr	4.13
for pipe; extra large	-	0.28	6.09	-	nr	6.09
Add for supplying and fixing one-hour intumescent sleeve						
for pipe; small	-	0.25	3.19	9.23	nr	12.42
for pipe; large	-	0.28	3.57	11.84	nr	15.41
for pipe; extra large	-	0.30	3.83	15.61	nr	19.43

P BUILDING FABRIC SUNDRIES

Item	PC £	Labour hours	Labour £	Material £	Unit	Total rate £
Cutting or forming holes for ducts; girth not exceeding 1.00 m; making good						
half brick thick	-	0.56	7.14	-	nr	7.14
one brick thick	-	0.93	11.86	-	nr	11.86
one and a half brick thick	-	1.48	18.88	-	nr	18.88
100 mm blockwork	-	0.46	5.87	-	nr	5.87
140 mm blockwork	-	0.65	8.29	-	nr	8.29
215 mm blockwork	-	0.83	10.59	-	nr	10.59
plasterboard partition or suspended ceiling	-	0.65	8.29	-	nr	8.29
Cutting or forming holes for ducts; girth 1.00 m - 2.00 m; making good						
half brick thick	-	0.65	8.29	-	nr	8.29
one brick thick	-	1.11	14.16	-	nr	14.16
one and a half brick thick	-	1.76	22.45	-	nr	22.45
100 mm blockwork	-	0.56	7.14	-	nr	7.14
140 mm blockwork	-	0.74	9.44	-	nr	9.44
215 mm blockwork	-	0.93	11.86	-	nr	11.86
plasterboard partition or suspended ceiling	-	0.75	9.57	-	nr	9.57
Cutting or forming holes for ducts; girth 2.00 m - 3.00 m; making good						
half brick thick	-	1.02	13.01	-	nr	13.01
one brick thick	-	1.76	22.45	-	nr	22.45
one and a half brick thick	-	2.78	35.45	-	nr	35.45
100 mm blockwork	-	0.88	11.22	-	nr	11.22
140 mm blockwork	-	1.20	15.30	-	nr	15.30
215 mm blockwork	-	1.53	19.51	-	nr	19.51
plasterboard partition or suspended ceiling	-	1.00	12.75	-	nr	12.75
Cutting or forming holes for ducts; girth 3.00 m - 4.00 m; making good						
half brick thick	-	1.39	17.73	-	nr	17.73
one brick thick	-	2.31	29.46	-	nr	29.46
one and a half brick thick	-	3.70	47.19	-	nr	47.19
100 mm blockwork	-	1.02	13.01	-	nr	13.01
140 mm blockwork	-	1.39	17.73	-	nr	17.73
215 mm blockwork	-	1.76	22.45	-	nr	22.45
plasterboard partition or suspended ceiling	-	1.25	15.94	-	nr	15.94
Mortices in brickwork						
for expansion bolt	-	0.19	2.42	-	nr	2.42
for 20 mm diameter bolt; 75 mm deep	-	0.14	1.79	-	nr	1.79
for 20 mm diameter bolt; 150 mm deep	-	0.23	2.93	-	nr	2.93
Mortices in brickwork; grouting with cement mortar (1:1)						
75 mm x 75 mm x 200 mm deep	-	0.28	3.57	0.13	nr	3.70
75 mm x 75 mm x 300 mm deep	-	0.37	4.72	0.19	nr	4.91
Holes in softwood for pipes, bars, cables and the like						
12 mm thick	-	0.03	0.52	-	nr	0.52
25 mm thick	-	0.05	0.87	-	nr	0.87
50 mm thick	-	0.09	1.57	-	nr	1.57
100 mm thick	-	0.14	2.44	-	nr	2.44
Holes in hardwood for pipes, bars, cables and the like						
12 mm thick	-	0.05	0.87	-	nr	0.87
25 mm thick	-	0.08	1.39	-	nr	1.39
50 mm thick	-	0.14	2.44	-	nr	2.44
100 mm thick	-	0.20	3.48	-	nr	3.48

P BUILDING FABRIC SUNDRIES

Item	PC £	Labour hours	Labour £	Material £	Unit	Total rate £
P31 HOLES/CHASES/COVERS/SUPPORTS FOR SERVICES – cont'd						
Builders' work for other services Installations – cont'd						
NOTE: The following rates for cutting holes and mortices in brickwork or blockwork etc. allow for diamond drilling						
Cutting holes and mortices in brickwork; per 25 mm depth						
25 mm diameter	-	-	-	-	nr	**1.08**
32 mm diameter	-	-	-	-	nr	**1.08**
52 mm diameter	-	-	-	-	nr	**1.28**
76 mm diameter	-	-	-	-	nr	**1.44**
107 mm diameter	-	-	-	-	nr	**1.54**
127 mm diameter	-	-	-	-	nr	**1.84**
152 mm diameter	-	-	-	-	nr	**2.15**
200 mm diameter	-	-	-	-	nr	**2.87**
250 mm diameter	-	-	-	-	nr	**4.82**
300 mm diameter	-	-	-	-	nr	**5.74**
Diamond chasing; per 25 x 25 mm section						
in facing or common brickwork	-	-	-	-	m	**2.82**
in semi-engineering brickwork	-	-	-	-	m	**5.89**
in engineering brickwork	-	-	-	-	m	**8.20**
in lightweight blockwork	-	-	-	-	m	**2.31**
in heavyweight blockwork	-	-	-	-	m	**4.61**
in render/screed	-	-	-	-	m	**8.97**
Forming boxes; per 25 mm depth (per m of perimeter)						
in facing or common brickwork	-	-	-	-	m	**2.82**
in semi-engineering brickwork	-	-	-	-	m	**5.89**
in engineering brickwork	-	-	-	-	m	**8.20**
in lightweight blockwork	-	-	-	-	m	**2.31**
in heavyweight blockwork	-	-	-	-	m	**4.61**
in render/screed	-	-	-	-	m	**8.97**
Other items						
diamond track mount or ring sawing brickwork	-	-	-	-	m	**4.36**
diamond floor sawing asphalte	-	-	-	-	m	**0.92**
stitch drilling 107 mm diameter hole in brickwork	-	-	-	-	nr	**1.13**
"XDT Screeduct" or other equal and approved; MDT Ducting Ltd; laid within floor screed; galvanised mild steel						
Floor ducting						
100 mm wide x 50 mm deep	3.87	0.19	3.31	4.37	m	**7.68**
extra for						
bend	3.83	0.09	1.57	4.32	nr	**5.89**
tee section	3.83	0.09	1.57	4.32	nr	**5.89**
connector / stop end	0.51	0.09	1.57	0.58	nr	**2.14**
ply cover 15 mm/16 mm thick WBP exterior grade	0.53	0.09	1.57	0.60	m	**2.17**
200 mm wide x 75 mm deep	6.38	0.19	3.31	7.20	m	**10.51**
extra for						
bend	6.16	0.09	1.57	6.96	nr	**8.53**
tee section	6.16	0.09	1.57	6.96	nr	**8.53**
connector / stop end	6.80	0.09	1.57	7.68	nr	**9.25**
ply cover 15 mm/16 mm thick WBP exterior grade	0.89	0.09	1.57	1.00	m	**2.57**

P BUILDING FABRIC SUNDRIES

Item	PC £	Labour hours	Labour £	Material £	Unit	Total rate £
"SFD Screeduct" or other equal and approved; MDT Ducting Ltd; with side flanges; laid within floor screed; galvanised mild steel						
Floor ducting						
100 mm wide x 50 mm deep	6.38	0.19	3.31	7.20	m	**10.51**
extra for	-	-	-	-	-	**-**
bend	4.89	0.09	1.57	5.52	nr	**7.09**
tee section	4.89	0.09	1.57	5.52	nr	**7.09**
connector / stop end	0.51	0.09	1.57	0.58	nr	**2.14**
ply cover 15 mm/16 mm thick WBP exterior grade	0.53	0.09	1.57	0.60	m	**2.17**
200 mm wide x 75 mm deep	8.07	0.19	3.31	9.13	m	**12.44**
extra for	-	-	-	-	-	**-**
bend	6.38	0.09	1.57	7.20	nr	**8.77**
tee section	6.38	0.09	1.57	7.20	nr	**8.77**
connector / stop end	0.68	0.09	1.57	0.77	nr	**2.34**
ply cover 15 mm/16 mm thick WBP exterior grade	0.89	0.09	1.57	1.00	m	**2.57**

Q PAVING/PLANTING/FENCING/SITE FURNITURE

Item	PC £	Labour hours	Labour £	Material £	Unit	Total rate £
Q10 KERBS/EDGINGS/CHANNELS/ PAVING ACCESSORIES						
Excavating; by machine						
Excavating trenches; to receive kerb foundations; average size						
300 mm x 100 mm	-	0.02	0.22	0.31	m	0.52
450 mm x 150 mm	-	0.02	0.22	0.61	m	0.83
600 mm x 200 mm	-	0.03	0.35	0.86	m	1.21
Excavating curved trenches; to receive kerb foundations; average size						
300 mm x 100 mm	-	0.01	0.11	0.49	m	0.60
450 mm x 150 mm	-	0.03	0.33	0.74	m	1.06
600 mm x 200 mm	-	0.04	0.44	0.92	m	1.36
Excavating; by hand						
Excavating trenches; to receive kerb foundations; average size						
150 mm x 50 mm	-	0.02	0.22	-	m	0.22
200 mm x 75 mm	-	0.06	0.65	-	m	0.65
250 mm x 100 mm	-	0.10	1.09	-	m	1.09
300 mm x 100 mm	-	0.13	1.42	-	m	1.42
Excavating curved trenches; to receive kerb foundations; average size						
150 mm x 50 mm	-	0.03	0.33	-	m	0.33
200 mm x 75 mm	-	0.07	0.76	-	m	0.76
250 mm x 100 mm	-	0.11	1.20	-	m	1.20
300 mm x 100 mm	-	0.14	1.53	-	m	1.53
Plain in situ ready mixed designated concrete; C7.5 - 40 mm aggregate; poured on or against earth or unblinded hardcore						
Foundations	66.07	1.16	14.79	76.44	m³	91.23
Blinding beds						
thickness not exceeding 150 mm	66.07	1.71	21.81	76.44	m³	98.25
Plain in situ ready mixed designated concrete; C10 - 40 mm aggregate; poured on or against earth or unblinded hardcore						
Foundations	66.43	1.16	14.79	76.86	m³	91.66
Blinding beds						
thickness not exceeding 150 mm	66.43	1.71	21.81	76.86	m³	98.67
Plain in situ ready mixed designated concrete; C20 - 20 mm aggregate; poured on or against earth or unblinded hardcore						
Foundations	68.34	1.16	14.79	79.08	m³	93.87
Blinding beds						
thickness not exceeding 150 mm	68.34	1.71	21.81	79.08	m³	100.88

Q PAVING/PLANTING/FENCING/SITE FURNITURE

Item	PC £	Labour hours	Labour £	Material £	Unit	Total rate £
Precast concrete kerbs, channels, edgings, etc.; BS 340; bedded, jointed and pointed in cement mortar (1:3); including haunching up one side with in situ ready mix designated concrete C10 - 40 mm aggregate; to concrete base						
Edgings; straight; square edge, fig 12						
50 mm x 150 mm	-	0.23	4.32	2.95	m	7.28
50 mm x 200 mm	-	0.23	4.32	3.51	m	7.84
50 mm x 255 mm	-	0.23	4.32	3.77	m	8.09
Kerbs; straight						
125 mm x 255 mm; fig 7	-	0.31	5.83	5.52	m	11.35
150 mm x 305 mm; fig 6	-	0.31	5.83	7.96	m	13.79
Kerbs; curved						
125 mm x 255 mm; fig 7	-	0.46	8.64	7.15	m	15.79
150 mm x 305 mm; fig 6	-	0.46	8.64	12.96	m	21.60
Channels; 255 x 125 mm; fig 8						
straight	-	0.31	5.83	5.01	m	10.83
curved	-	0.46	8.64	6.60	m	15.25
Quadrants; fig 14						
305 mm x 305 mm x 150 mm	-	0.32	6.01	7.93	nr	13.95
305 mm x 305 mm x 255 mm	-	0.32	6.01	8.53	nr	14.54
457 mm x 457 mm x 150 mm	-	0.37	6.95	9.36	nr	16.31
457 mm x 457 mm x 255 mm	-	0.37	6.95	9.96	nr	16.92
Q20 HARDCORE/GRANULAR/CEMENT BOUND BASES/SUB-BASES TO ROADS/PAVINGS						
Filling to make up levels; by machine						
Average thickness not exceeding 0.25 m						
obtained off site; hardcore	-	0.28	3.06	28.68	m^3	31.74
obtained off site; granular fill type one	-	0.28	3.06	26.92	m^3	29.98
obtained off site; granular fill type two	-	0.28	3.06	25.45	m^3	28.51
Average thickness exceeding 0.25 m						
obtained off site; hardcore	-	0.24	2.62	24.54	m^3	27.16
obtained off site; granular fill type one	-	0.24	2.62	26.69	m^3	29.31
obtained off site; granular fill type two	-	0.24	2.62	25.22	m^3	27.84
Filling to make up levels; by hand						
Average thickness not exceeding 0.25 m						
obtained off site; hardcore	-	0.61	6.66	29.23	m^3	35.89
obtained off site; sand	-	0.71	7.75	27.34	m^3	35.08
Average thickness exceeding 0.25 m						
obtained off site; hardcore	-	0.51	5.57	25.01	m^3	30.58
obtained off site; sand	-	0.60	6.55	26.99	m^3	33.54
Surface treatments						
Compacting						
filling; blinding with sand	-	0.04	0.44	1.41	m^2	1.85
Q21 IN SITU CONCRETE ROADS/PAVINGS						
Reinforced in situ ready mixed designated concrete; C10 - 40 mm aggregate						
Roads; to hardcore base						
thickness not exceeding 150 mm	63.27	1.85	23.59	73.20	m^3	96.80
thickness 150 mm - 450 mm	63.27	1.30	16.58	73.20	m^3	89.78

Q PAVING/PLANTING/FENCING/SITE FURNITURE

Item	PC £	Labour hours	Labour £	Material £	Unit	Total rate £
Q21 IN SITU CONCRETE ROADS/PAVINGS - cont'd						
Reinforced in situ ready mixed designated concrete; C20 - 20 mm aggregate						
Roads; to hardcore base						
thickness not exceeding 150 mm	65.09	1.85	23.59	75.31	m³	**98.90**
thickness 150 mm - 450 mm	65.09	1.30	16.58	75.31	m³	**91.89**
Reinforced in situ ready mixed designated concrete; C25 - 20 mm aggregate						
Roads; to hardcore base						
thickness ot exceeding 150 mm	65.50	1.85	23.59	75.78	m³	**99.38**
thickness 150 mm - 450 mm	65.50	1.30	16.58	75.78	m³	**92.36**
Formwork; sides of foundations; basic finish						
Plain vertical						
height not exceeding 250 mm	-	0.39	6.17	1.21	m	**7.39**
height 250 mm - 500 mm	-	0.57	9.02	2.02	m	**11.05**
height 500 mm - 1.00 m	-	0.83	13.14	3.71	m	**16.85**
add to above for curved radius 6m	-	0.03	0.47	0.16	m	**0.64**
Reinforcement; fabric; BS 4483; lapped; in roads, footpaths or pavings						
Ref A142 (2.22 kg/m2)						
400 mm minimum laps	0.98	0.14	2.11	1.16	m²	**3.27**
Ref A193 (3.02 kg/m2)						
400 mm minimum laps	-	0.14	2.11	1.59	m²	**3.69**
Formed joints; Fosroc Expandite "Flexcell" impregnated joint filler or other equal and approved						
Width not exceeding 150 mm						
12.50 mm thick	-	0.14	2.22	1.56	m	**3.78**
25 mm thick	-	0.19	3.01	2.40	m	**5.41**
Width 150 - 300 mm						
12.50 mm thick	-	0.19	3.01	2.46	m	**5.46**
25 mm thick	-	0.19	3.01	3.99	m	**6.99**
Width 300 - 450 mm						
12.50 mm thick	-	0.23	3.64	3.68	m	**7.32**
25 mm thick	-	0.23	3.64	5.98	m	**9.62**
Sealants; Fosroc Expandite "Pliastic N2" hot poured rubberized bituminous compound or other equal and approved						
Width 25 mm						
25 mm depth	-	0.20	3.17	1.63	m	**4.80**
Concrete sundries						
Treating surfaces of unset concrete; grading to cambers; tamping with a 75 mm thick steel shod tamper	-	0.23	2.93	-	m²	**2.93**

Q PAVING/PLANTING/FENCING/SITE FURNITURE

Item	PC £	Labour hours	Labour £	Material £	Unit	Total rate £
Q22 COATED MACADAM/ASPHALT ROADS/ PAVINGS						
NOTE: The prices for all bitumen macadam and hot rolled asphalt materials are for individual courses to roads and footpaths and need combining to arrive at complete specifications and costs for full construction. Intermediate course thicknesses can interpolated so long as BS 594 and BS 4987 allow the material type to be compacted to the required thickness. Costs include for work to falls, crossfalls or slopes not exceeding 15 degrees from horizontal; for laying on prepared bases (prices not included) and for rolling with an appropriate roller.						
The following rates are based on black bitumen macadam. Red bitumen macadam rates are approximately 50% dearer. PSV is Polished Stone Value.						
Dense bitumen macadam base course; BS 4987 - 1:2003; bitumen penetration 100/125						
Carriageway, hardshoulder and hardstrip						
100 mm thick; one coat; with 0/32mm aggregate size; to clause 5.2	-	-	-	-	m^2	10.51
200 mm thick; one coat; with 0/32mm aggregate size; to clause 5.2	-	-	-	-	m^2	19.70
Extra over above items for increase / reduction in 10 mm increments	-	-	-	-	m^2	1.02
Hot rolled asphalt base course; BS 594 - 1:2003						
Carriageway, hardshoulder and hardstrip						
150 mm thick; one coat; 60% 0/32 mm aggregate size; to column 2/5	-	-	-	-	m^2	17.05
200 mm thick; one coat; 60% 0/32 mm aggregate size; to column 2/5	-	-	-	-	m^2	20.84
Extra over above items for increase / reduction in 10 mm increments	-	-	-	-	m^2	1.02
Dense bitumen macadam binder course; BS 4987 - 1:2003; bitumen penetration 100/125						
Carriageway, hardshoulder and hardstrip						
60 mm thick; one coat; with 0/32 mm aggregate size; to clause 6.4	-	-	-	-	m^2	6.89
60 mm thick; one coat; with 0/32 mm aggregate size; to clause 6.5	-	-	-	-	m^2	6.96
Extra over above items for increase / reduction in 10 mm increments	-	-	-	-	m^2	0.91

Q PAVING/PLANTING/FENCING/SITE FURNITURE

Item	PC £	Labour hours	Labour £	Material £	Unit	Total rate £
Q22 COATED MACADAM/ASPHALT ROADS/ PAVINGS - cont'd						
Hot rolled asphalt binder course; BS 594 - 1:2003						
Carriageway, hardshoulder and hardstrip						
40 mm thick; one coat; 50% 0/14 mm aggregate size; to column 2/2; 55 PSV	-	-	-	-	m^2	6.91
60 mm thick; one coat; 50% 0/14 mm aggregate size; to column 2/2	-	-	-	-	m^2	7.70
60 mm thick; one coat; 50% 0/20 mm aggregate size; to column 2/3	-	-	-	-	m^2	7.53
60 mm thick; one coat; 60% 0/32 mm aggregate size; to column 2/5	-	-	-	-	m^2	7.09
100 mm thick; one coat; 60% 0/32 mm aggregate size; to column 2/5	-	-	-	-	m^2	11.43
Extra over above items for increase / reduction in 10 mm increments	-	-	-	-	m^2	1.40
Macadam surface course; BS 4987 - 1:2003; bitumen penetration 100/125						
Carriageway, hardshoulder and hardstrip						
30 mm thick; one coat; medium graded with 0/6 mm nominal aggregate binder; to clause 7.6	-	-	-	-	m^2	4.51
40 mm thick; one coat; close graded with 0/14 mm nominal aggregate binder; to clause 7.3	-	-	-	-	m^2	5.43
40 mm thick; one coat; close graded with 0/10 mm nominal aggregate binder; to clause 7.4	-	-	-	-	m^2	5.43
Extra over above items for increase / reduction in 10 mm increments	-	-	-	-	m^2	1.05
Extra over above items for coarse aggregate 60-64 PSV	-	-	-	-	m^2	1.11
Extra over above items for coarse aggregate 65-67 PSV	-	-	-	-	m^2	1.22
Extra over above items for coarse aggregate 68 PSV	-	-	-	-	m^2	1.51
Hot rolled asphalt surface course; BS 594 - 1:2003; bitumen penetration 40/60						
Carriageway, hardshoulder and hardstrip						
40 mm thick; one coat; 30% mix 0/10 mm aggregate size; to column 3/2; with 20 mm pre-coated chippings 60-64 PSV	-	-	-	-	m^2	6.81
40 mm thick; one coat; 30% mix 0/10 mm aggregate size; to column 3/2; with 14 mm pre-coated chippings 60-64 PSV	-	-	-	-	m^2	6.86
Extra over above items for increase / reduction in 10 mm increments	-	-	-	-	m^2	1.11
Extra over above items for chippings with 65-67 PSV	-	-	-	-	m^2	0.05
Extra over above items for chippings with 68 PSV	-	-	-	-	m^2	0.11
Extra over above items for 6-10KN High Traffic Flows	-	-	-	-	m^2	0.51

Q PAVING/PLANTING/FENCING/SITE FURNITURE

Item	PC £	Labour hours	Labour £	Material £	Unit	Total rate £
Stone mastic asphalt surface course; BS 594 - 1:2003						
Carriageway, hardshoulder and hardstrip						
35 mm thick; one coat; with 0/14 mm nominal aggregate size; 55 PSV	-	-	-	-	m²	6.33
35 mm thick; one coat; with 0/10 mm nominal aggregate size; 55 PSV	-	-	-	-	m²	6.33
Extra over above items for increase / reduction in 10 mm increments	-	-	-	-	m²	1.40
Thin surface course with 60 PSV						
Carriageway, hardshoulder and hardstrip						
35 mm thick; one coat; with 0/10 mm nominal aggregate size	-	-	-	-	m²	6.33
Extra over above items for increase / reduction in 10 mm increments	-	-	-	-	m²	0.70
Extra over above items for coarse aggregate 60-64 PSV	-	-	-	-	m²	0.17
Extra over above items for coarse aggregate 65-67 PSV	-	-	-	-	m²	0.17
Extra over above items for coarse aggregate 68 PSV	-	-	-	-	m²	0.36
Regulating courses						
Carriageway, hardshoulder and hardstrip						
Dense Bitumen Macadam; bitumen penetration 100/125; with 0/20 mm nominal aggregate regulating course (BS 4987 - clause 6.5)	-	-	-	-	tonne	65.63
Hot rolled asphalte; 50% 0/20 mm aggregate size (BS 594 - 1:2003 column 2/3)	-	-	-	-	tonne	71.11
Stone mastic asphalte; 0/6 mm aggregate	-	-	-	-	tonne	92.43
Bitumen Emulsion tack coats						
Carriageway, hardshoulder and hardstrip						
K1-40; applied 0.35-0.45l/m2	-	-	-	-	m²	0.11
K1-70; applied 0.35-0.45l/m2	-	-	-	-	m²	0.19
Q23 GRAVEL/HOGGIN/WOODCHIP ROADS/ PAVINGS						
Two coat gravel paving; level and to falls; first layer course clinker aggregate and wearing layer fine gravel aggregate						
Pavings; over 300 mm wide						
50 mm thick	-	0.07	1.32	1.44	m²	2.75
63 mm thick	-	0.09	1.69	1.88	m²	3.57

Q PAVING/PLANTING/FENCING/SITE FURNITURE

Item	PC £	Labour hours	Labour £	Material £	Unit	Total rate £
Q25 SLAB/BRICK/BLOCK/SETT/COBBLE PAVINGS						
Artificial stone paving; Redland Aggregates "Texitone" or other equal and approved; to falls or crossfalls; bedding 25 mm thick in cement mortar (1:3); staggered joints; jointing in coloured cement mortar (1:3), brushed in; to sand base						
Pavings; over 300 mm wide						
450 mm x 600 mm x 50 mm thick; grey or coloured	11.79	0.42	7.89	16.07	m²	23.97
600 mm x 600 mm x 50 mm thick; grey or coloured	10.26	0.39	7.33	14.35	m²	21.67
750 mm x 600 mm x 50 mm thick; grey or coloured	9.57	0.36	6.76	13.57	m²	20.33
900 mm x 600 mm x 50 mm thick; grey or coloured	9.11	0.33	6.20	13.05	m²	19.25
Brick paviors; 215 mm x 103 mm x 65 mm rough stock bricks; PC £352.00/1000; to falls or crossfalls; bedding 10 mm thick in cement mortar (1:3); jointing in cement mortar (1:3); as work proceeds; to concrete base						
Pavings; over 300 mm wide; straight joints both ways						
bricks laid flat	-	0.74	16.10	17.14	m²	33.24
bricks laid on edge	-	1.04	22.63	25.38	m²	48.01
Pavings; over 300 mm wide; laid to herringbone pattern						
bricks laid flat	-	0.93	20.24	17.14	m²	37.38
bricks laid on edge	-	1.30	28.29	25.38	m²	53.67
Add or deduct for variation of £10.00/1000 in PC of brick paviours						
bricks laid flat	-	-	-	0.49	m²	0.49
bricks laid on edge	-	-	-	0.73	m²	0.73
River washed cobble paving; 50 mm -75 mm; PC £94.00/tonne; to falls or crossfalls; bedding 13 mm thick in cement mortar (1:3); jointing to a height of two thirds of cobbles in dry mortar (1:3); tightly butted, washed and brushed; to concrete						
Pavings; over 300 mm wide						
regular	-	3.70	69.53	22.71	m²	92.23
laid to pattern	-	4.63	87.00	22.71	m²	109.71
Concrete paving flags; BS 7263; to falls or crossfalls; bedding 25 mm thick in cement and sand mortar (1:4); butt joints straight both ways; jointing in cement and sand (1:3); brushed in; to sand base						
Pavings; over 300 mm wide						
450 mm x 600 mm x 50 mm thick; grey	6.18	0.42	7.89	8.33	m²	16.22
450 mm x 600 mm x 60 mm thick; coloured	7.12	0.42	7.89	9.39	m²	17.28
600 mm x 600 mm x 50 mm thick; grey	5.30	0.39	7.33	7.32	m²	14.65
600 mm x 600 mm x 50 mm thick; coloured	6.12	0.39	7.33	8.26	m²	15.59

Q PAVING/PLANTING/FENCING/SITE FURNITURE

Item	PC £	Labour hours	Labour £	Material £	Unit	Total rate £
750 mm x 600 mm x 50 mm thick; grey	4.98	0.36	6.76	6.96	m²	**13.73**
750 mm x 600 mm x 50 mm thick; coloured	5.74	0.36	6.76	7.82	m²	**14.58**
900 mm x 600 mm x 50 mm thick; grey	4.59	0.33	6.20	6.52	m²	**12.72**
900 mm x 600 mm x 50 mm thick; coloured	5.37	0.33	6.20	7.40	m²	**13.60**
Concrete rectangular paving blocks; to falls or crossfalls; bedding 50 mm thick in dry sharp sand; filling joints with sharp sand brushed in; on earth base						
Pavings; "Keyblock" or other equal and approved; over 300 mm wide; straight joints both ways						
200 mm x 100 mm x 60 mm thick; grey	7.44	0.69	12.97	11.41	m²	**24.38**
200 mm x 100 mm x 60 mm thick; coloured	8.16	0.69	12.97	12.23	m²	**25.19**
200 mm x 100 mm x 80 mm thick; grey	8.13	0.74	13.91	12.44	m²	**26.35**
200 mm x 100 mm x 80 mm thick; coloured	9.45	0.74	13.91	13.93	m²	**27.84**
Pavings; "Keyblock" or other equal and approved; over 300 mm wide; laid to herringbone pattern						
200 mm x 100 mm x 60 mm thick; grey	-	0.88	16.54	11.41	m²	**27.95**
200 mm x 100 mm x 60 mm thick; coloured	-	0.88	16.54	12.23	m²	**28.76**
200 mm x 100 mm x 80 mm thick; grey	-	0.93	17.48	12.44	m²	**29.92**
200 mm x 100 mm x 80 mm thick; coloured	-	0.93	17.48	13.93	m²	**31.41**
Extra for two row boundary edging to herringbone pavings; 200 mm wide; including a 150 mm high in situ concrete mix C10 - 40 mm aggregate haunching to one side; blocks laid breaking joint						
200 mm x 100 mm x 60 mm; coloured	-	0.28	5.26	2.11	m	**7.37**
200 mm x 100 mm x 80 mm; coloured	-	0.28	5.26	2.21	m	**7.47**
Pavings; "Mount Sorrel" or other equal and approved; over 300 mm wide; straight joints both ways						
200 mm x 100 mm x 60 mm thick; grey	6.63	0.69	12.97	10.49	m²	**23.46**
200 mm x 100 mm x 60 mm thick; coloured	7.63	0.69	12.97	11.63	m²	**24.59**
200 mm x 100 mm x 80 mm thick; grey	7.89	0.74	13.91	12.16	m²	**26.07**
200 mm x 100 mm x 80 mm thick; coloured	9.06	0.74	13.91	13.49	m²	**27.40**
Pavings; "Pedesta" or other equal and approved; over 300 mm wide; straight joints both ways						
200 mm x 100 mm x 60 mm thick; grey	9.60	0.69	12.97	13.85	m²	**26.82**
200 mm x 100 mm x 60 mm thick; coloured	9.60	0.69	12.97	13.85	m²	**26.82**
200 mm x 100 mm x 80 mm thick; grey	12.24	0.74	13.91	17.09	m²	**30.99**
200 mm x 100 mm x 80 mm thick; coloured	12.24	0.74	13.91	17.09	m²	**30.99**
Pavings; "Intersett" or other equal and approved; over 300 mm wide; straight joints both ways						
200 mm x 100 mm x 60 mm thick; grey	9.98	0.69	12.97	14.29	m²	**27.25**
200 mm x 100 mm x 60 mm thick; coloured	11.09	0.69	12.97	15.53	m²	**28.50**
200 mm x 100 mm x 80 mm thick; grey	11.94	0.74	13.91	16.75	m²	**30.66**
200 mm x 100 mm x 80 mm thick; coloured	13.26	0.74	13.91	18.24	m²	**32.15**

Q PAVING/PLANTING/FENCING/SITE FURNITURE

Item	PC £	Labour hours	Labour £	Material £	Unit	Total rate £
Q25 SLAB/BRICK/BLOCK/SETT/COBBLE PAVINGS - cont'd						
Concrete rectangular paving blocks; to falls or crossfalls; 6 mm wide joints; symmetrical layout; bedding in 15 mm semi-dry cement mortar (1:4); jointing and pointing in cement and sand (1:4); on concrete base						
Pavings; "Trafica" or other equal and approved; over 300 mm wide						
400 mm x 400 mm x 65 mm; Standard; natural	8.67	0.44	8.27	11.01	m²	**19.27**
400 mm x 400 mm x 65 mm; Standard; buff	12.49	0.44	8.27	15.32	m²	**23.59**
400 mm x 400 mm x 65 mm; Saxon textured; natural	17.03	0.44	8.27	20.46	m²	**28.73**
400 mm x 400 mm x 65 mm; Saxon textured; buff	20.13	0.44	8.27	23.95	m²	**32.22**
400 mm x 400 mm x 65 mm; Perfecta; natural	20.37	0.44	8.27	24.23	m²	**32.50**
400 mm x 400 mm x 65 mm; Perfecta; buff	24.19	0.44	8.27	28.54	m²	**36.81**
450 mm x 450 mm x 70 mm; Standard; natural	9.98	0.43	8.08	12.49	m²	**20.57**
450 mm x 450 mm x 70 mm; Standard; buff	13.24	0.43	8.08	16.17	m²	**24.25**
450 mm x 450 mm x 70 mm; Saxon textured; natural	16.75	0.43	8.08	20.13	m²	**28.21**
450 mm x 450 mm x 70 mm; Saxon textured; buff	19.82	0.43	8.08	23.60	m²	**31.68**
450 mm x 450 mm x 70 mm; Perfecta; natural	20.01	0.43	8.08	23.82	m²	**31.90**
450 mm x 450 mm x 70 mm; Perfecta; buff	23.56	0.43	8.08	27.83	m²	**35.91**
450 mm x 450 mm x 100 mm; Standard; natural	26.58	0.44	8.27	31.25	m²	**39.52**
450 mm x 450 mm x 100 mm; Standard; buff	32.91	0.44	8.27	38.40	m²	**46.67**
450 mm x 450 mm x 100 mm; Saxon textured; natural	29.99	0.44	8.27	35.10	m²	**43.37**
450 mm x 450 mm x 100 mm; Saxon textured; buff	35.41	0.44	8.27	41.22	m²	**49.49**
450 mm x 450 mm x 100 mm; Perfecta; natural	32.15	0.44	8.27	37.54	m²	**45.80**
450 mm x 450 mm x 100 mm; Perfecta; buff	37.62	0.44	8.27	43.72	m²	**51.99**
York stone slab pavings; to falls or crossfalls; bedding 25 mm thick in cement:sand mortar (1:4); 5 mm wide joints; jointing in coloured cement mortar (1:3); brushed in; to sand base						
Pavings; over 300 mm wide						
50 mm thick; random rectangular pattern	73.06	0.69	15.02	82.22	m²	**97.23**
600 mm x 600 mm x 50 mm thick	88.71	0.39	8.49	99.49	m²	**107.98**
600 mm x 900 mm x 50 mm thick	91.32	0.33	7.18	102.37	m²	**109.55**
Granite setts; BS 435; 200 mm x 100 mm x 100 mm; PC £156.50/tonne; standard "C" dressing; tightly butted to falls or crossfalls; bedding 25 mm thick in cement mortar (1:3); filling joints with dry mortar (1:6); washed and brushed; on concrete base						
Pavings; over 300 mm wide						
straight joints	-	1.48	27.81	49.80	m²	**77.61**
laid to pattern	-	1.85	34.76	49.80	m²	**84.56**
Two rows of granite setts as boundary edging; 200 mm wide; including a 150 mm high ready mixed designated concrete C10 - 40 mm aggregate; haunching to one side; blocks laid breaking joint	-	0.65	12.21	11.38	m	**23.60**

Q PAVING/PLANTING/FENCING/SITE FURNITURE

Item	PC £	Labour hours	Labour £	Material £	Unit	Total rate £
Q26 SPECIAL SURFACINGS/PAVINGS FOR SPORT/GENERAL AMENITY						
Sundries						
Line marking						
width not exceeding 300 mm	-	0.04	0.54	0.12	m	0.66
Q30 SEEDING/TURFING						
Vegetable soil						
Selected from spoil heaps; grading; prepared for turfing or seeding; to general surfaces						
average 75 mm thick	-	0.21	2.29	-	m²	2.29
average 100 mm thick	-	0.23	2.51	-	m²	2.51
average 125 mm thick	-	0.25	2.73	-	m²	2.73
average 150 mm thick	-	0.26	2.84	-	m²	2.84
average 175 mm thick	-	0.27	2.95	-	m²	2.95
average 200 mm thick	-	0.29	3.16	-	m²	3.16
Selected from spoil heaps; grading; prepared for turfing or seeding; to cuttings or embankments						
average 75 mm thick	-	0.24	2.62	-	m²	2.62
average 100 mm thick	-	0.26	2.84	-	m²	2.84
average 125 mm thick	-	0.28	3.06	-	m²	3.06
average 150 mm thick	-	0.30	3.27	-	m²	3.27
average 175 mm thick	-	0.31	3.38	-	m²	3.38
average 200 mm thick	-	0.32	3.49	-	m²	3.49
Imported vegetable soil						
Grading; prepared for turfing or seeding; to general surfaces						
average 75 mm thick	-	0.19	2.07	0.90	m²	2.97
average 100 mm thick	-	0.20	2.18	1.17	m²	3.35
average 125 thick	-	0.22	2.40	1.71	m²	4.11
average 150 mm thick	-	0.23	2.51	2.25	m²	4.76
average 175 mm thick	-	0.25	2.73	2.52	m²	5.24
average 200 mm thick	-	0.26	2.84	2.79	m²	5.62
Grading; preparing for turfing or seeding; to cuttings or embankments						
average 75 mm thick	-	0.21	2.29	0.90	m²	3.19
average 100 mm thick	-	0.23	2.51	1.17	m²	3.68
average 125 mm thick	-	0.25	2.73	1.71	m²	4.44
average 150 mm thick	-	0.26	2.84	2.25	m²	5.08
average 175 mm thick	-	0.27	2.95	2.52	m²	5.46
average 200 mm thick	-	0.29	3.16	2.79	m²	5.95
Fertilizer; PC £9.76/25 kg						
Fertilizer 0.07 kg/m2; raking in						
general surfaces	-	0.03	0.33	0.03	m²	0.36
Selected grass seed; PC £86.60/25kg						
Grass seed; sowing at a rate of 0.042 kg/m2 two applications; raking in						
general surfaces	-	0.06	0.65	0.29	m²	0.95
cuttings or embankments	-	0.07	0.76	0.29	m²	1.06
Preserved turf from stack on site						
Turfing						
general surfaces	-	0.19	2.07	-	m²	2.07
cuttings or embankments; shallow	-	0.20	2.18	-	m²	2.18
cuttings or embankments; steep; pegged	-	0.28	3.06	-	m²	3.06

Q PAVING/PLANTING/FENCING/SITE FURNITURE

Item	PC £	Labour hours	Labour £	Material £	Unit	Total rate £
Q30 SEEDING/TURFING - cont'd						
Imported turf; selected meadow turf						
Turfing						
general surfaces	1.67	0.19	2.07	1.80	m²	3.88
cuttings or embankments; shallow	1.67	0.20	2.18	1.80	m²	3.98
cuttings or embankments; steep; pegged	1.67	0.28	3.06	1.80	m²	4.86
Q31 PLANTING						
Planting only						
Hedge plants						
height not exceeding 750 mm	-	0.23	2.51	-	nr	2.51
height 750 mm - 1.50 m	-	0.56	6.11	-	nr	6.11
Saplings						
height not exceeding 3.00 m	-	1.57	17.13	-	nr	17.13
Q40 FENCING						
NOTE: The prices for all fencing include for setting posts in position, to a depth of 0.60 m for fences not exceeding 1.40 m high and of 0.76 m for fences over 1.40 m high. The prices allow for excavating post holes; filling to within 150 mm of ground level with concrete and all necessary backfilling.						
Strained wire fencing; BS 1722 Part 3; 4 mm diameter galvanized mild steel plain wire threaded through posts and strained with eye bolts						
Fencing; height 900 mm; three line; concrete posts at 2750 mm centres	-	-	-	-	m	16.06
Extra for						
end concrete straining post; one strut	-	-	-	-	nr	39.06
angle concrete straining post; two struts	-	-	-	-	nr	45.37
Fencing; height 1.07 m; six line; concrete posts at 2750 mm centres	-	-	-	-	m	16.72
Extra for						
end concrete straining post; one strut	-	-	-	-	nr	43.93
angle concrete straining post; two struts	-	-	-	-	nr	50.23
Fencing; height 1.20 m; six line; concrete posts at 2750 mm centres	-	-	-	-	m	16.81
Extra for						
end concrete straining post; one strut	-	-	-	-	nr	45.17
angle concrete straining post; two struts	-	-	-	-	nr	51.46
Fencing; height 1.40 m; eight line; concrete posts at 2750 mm centres	-	-	-	-	m	17.28
Extra for						
end concrete straining post; one strut	-	-	-	-	nr	46.14
angle concrete straining post; two struts	-	-	-	-	nr	52.43

Q PAVING/PLANTING/FENCING/SITE FURNITURE

Item	PC £	Labour hours	Labour £	Material £	Unit	Total rate £
Chain link fencing; BS 1722 Part 1; 3 mm diameter galvanized mild steel wire; 50 mm mesh; galvanized mild steel tying and line wire; three line wires threaded through posts and strained with eye bolts and winding brackets						
Fencing; height 900 mm; galvanized mild steel angle posts at 3.00 m centres	-	-	-	-	m	22.59
Extra for						
end steel straining post; one strut	-	-	-	-	nr	65.12
angle steel straining post; two struts	-	-	-	-	nr	75.10
Fencing; height 900 mm; concrete posts at 3.00 m centres	-	-	-	-	m	16.37
Extra for						
end concrete straining post; one strut	-	-	-	-	nr	34.98
angle concrete straining post; two struts	-	-	-	-	nr	41.28
Fencing; height 1.20 m; galvanized mild steel angle posts at 3.00 m centres	-	-	-	-	m	16.66
Extra for						
end steel straining post; one strut	-	-	-	-	nr	69.48
angle steel straining post; two struts	-	-	-	-	nr	88.98
Fencing; height 1.20 m; concrete posts at 3.00 m centres	-	-	-	-	m	15.97
Extra for						
end concrete straining post; one strut	-	-	-	-	nr	40.04
angle concrete straining post; two struts	-	-	-	-	nr	47.30
Fencing; height 1.80 m; galvanized mild steel angle posts at 3.00 m centres	-	-	-	-	m	18.74
Extra for						
end steel straining post; one strut	-	-	-	-	nr	70.67
angle steel straining post; two struts	-	-	-	-	nr	87.91
Fencing; height 1.80 m; concrete posts at 3.00 m centres	-	-	-	-	m	21.63
Extra for						
end concrete straining post; one strut	-	-	-	-	nr	55.99
angle concrete straining post; two struts	-	-	-	-	nr	66.05
Pair of gates and gate posts; gates to match galvanized chain link fencing, with angle framing, braces, etc., complete with hinges, locking bar, lock and bolts; two 100 mm x 100 mm angle section gate posts; each with one strut						
2.44 m x 0.90 m	-	-	-	-	nr	549.11
2.44 m x 1.20 m	-	-	-	-	nr	566.69
2.44 m x 1.80 m	-	-	-	-	nr	611.30
Chain link fencing; BS 1722 Part 1; 3 mm diameter plastic coated mild steel wire; 50 mm mesh; plastic coated mild steel tying and line wire; three line wires threaded through posts and strained with eye bolts and winding brackets						
Fencing; height 900 mm; galvanized mild steel angle posts at 3.00 m centres	-	-	-	-	m	20.72
Extra for						
end steel straining post; one strut	-	-	-	-	nr	57.42
angle steel straining post; two struts	-	-	-	-	nr	63.92

Q PAVING/PLANTING/FENCING/SITE FURNITURE

Item	PC £	Labour hours	Labour £	Material £	Unit	Total rate £
Q40 FENCING - cont'd						
Chain link fencing; plastic coated - cont'd						
Fencing; height 900 mm; concrete posts at 3.00 m centres	-	-	-	-	m	15.45
Extra for						
end concrete straining post; one strut	-	-	-	-	nr	34.98
angle concrete straining post; two struts	-	-	-	-	nr	41.28
Fencing; height 1.20 m; galvanized mild steel angle posts at 3.00 m centres	-	-	-	-	m	15.30
Extra for						
end steel straining post; one strut	-	-	-	-	nr	60.23
angle steel straining post; two struts	-	-	-	-	nr	64.34
Fencing; height 1.20 m; concrete posts at 3.00 m centres	-	-	-	-	m	15.66
Extra for						
end concrete straining post; one strut	-	-	-	-	nr	40.04
angle concrete straining post; two struts	-	-	-	-	nr	47.30
Fencing; height 1.80 m; galvanized mild steel angle posts at 3.00 m centres	-	-	-	-	m	17.35
Extra for						
end steel straining post; one strut	-	-	-	-	nr	59.61
angle steel straining post; two struts	-	-	-	-	nr	71.20
Fencing; height 1.80 m; concrete posts at 3.00 m centres	-	-	-	-	m	19.95
Extra for						
end concrete straining post; one strut	-	-	-	-	nr	55.99
angle concrete straining post; two struts	-	-	-	-	nr	66.05
Pair of gates and gate posts; gates to match plastic chain link fencing; with angle framing, braces, etc. complete with hinges, locking bar, lock and bolts; two 100 mm x 100 mm angle section gate posts; each with one strut						
2.44 m x 0.90 m	-	-	-	-	nr	480.14
2.44 m x 1.20 m	-	-	-	-	nr	492.66
2.44 m x 1.80 m	-	-	-	-	nr	530.61
Chain link fencing for tennis courts; BS 1722 Part 13; 2.5 diameter galvanised mild wire; 45 mm mesh; line and tying wires threaded through 45 mm x 45 mm x 5 mm galvanised mild steel angle standards, posts and struts; 60 mm x 60 mm x 6 mm straining posts and gate posts; straining posts and struts strained with eye bolts and winding brackets						
Fencing to tennis court 36.00 m x 18.00 m; including gate 1.07 m x 1.98 m; complete with hinges, locking bar, lock and bolts						
height 2745 mm fencing; standards at 3.00 m centres	-	-	-	-	nr	2501.55
height 3660 mm fencing; standards at 2.50 m centres	-	-	-	-	nr	3354.35

Q PAVING/PLANTING/FENCING/SITE FURNITURE

Item	PC £	Labour hours	Labour £	Material £	Unit	Total rate £
Cleft chestnut pale fencing; BS 1722 Part 4; pales spaced 51 mm apart; on two lines of galvanized wire; 64 mm diameter posts; 76 mm x 51 mm struts						
Fencing; height 900 mm; posts at 2.50 m centres	-	-	-	-	m	10.59
Extra for						
straining post; one strut	-	-	-	-	nr	28.24
corner straining post; two struts	-	-	-	-	nr	28.24
Fencing; height 1.05 m; posts at 2.50 m centres	-	-	-	-	m	12.00
Extra for						
straining post; one strut	-	-	-	-	nr	28.61
corner straining post; two struts	-	-	-	-	nr	28.61
Close boarded fencing; BS 1722 Part 5; 76 mm x 38 mm softwood rails; 89 mm x 19 mm softwood pales lapped 13 mm; 152 mm x 25 mm softwood gravel boards; all softwood "treated"; posts at 3.00 m centres						
Fencing; two rail; concrete posts						
height 1.00 m	-	-	-	-	m	32.58
height 1.20 m	-	-	-	-	m	32.88
Fencing; three rail; concrete posts						
height 1.40 m	-	-	-	-	m	36.17
height 1.60 m	-	-	-	-	m	36.25
height 1.80 m	-	-	-	-	m	37.63
Precast concrete slab fencing; 305 mm x 38 mm x 1753 mm slabs; fitted into twice grooved concrete posts at 1830 mm centres						
Fencing						
height 1.50 m	-	-	-	-	m	63.86
height 1.80 m	-	-	-	-	m	70.72
Mild steel unclimbable fencing; in rivetted panels 2440 mm long; 44 mm x 13 mm flat section top and bottom rails; two 44 mm x 19 mm flat section standards; one with foot plate; and 38 mm x 13 mm raking stay with foot plate; 20 mm diameter pointed verticals at 120 mm centres; two 44 mm x 19 mm supports 760 mm long with ragged ends to bottom rail; the whole bolted together; coated with red oxide primer; setting standards and stays in ground at 2440 mm centres and supports at 815 mm centres						
Fencing						
height 1.67 m	-	-	-	-	m	119.39
height 2.13 m	-	-	-	-	m	137.30
Pair of gates and gate posts, to match mild steel unclimbable fencing; with flat section framing, braces, etc., complete with locking bar, lock, handles, drop bolt, gate stop and holding back catches; two 102 mm x 102 mm hollow section gate posts with cap and foot plates						
2.44 m x 1.67 m	-	-	-	-	nr	1034.73
2.44 m x 2.13 m	-	-	-	-	nr	1193.92
4.88 m x 1.67 m	-	-	-	-	nr	1620.32
4.88 m x 2.13 m	-	-	-	-	nr	2029.66

Q PAVING/PLANTING/FENCING/SITE FURNITURE

Item	PC £	Labour hours	Labour £	Material £	Unit	Total rate £
Q40 FENCING - cont'd						
PVC coated, galvanised mild steel high security fencing; "Sentinal Sterling" fencing or other equal and approved; Twil Wire Products Ltd; 50 mm x 50 mm mesh; 3/3.50 mm gauge wire; barbed edge - 1; "Sentinal Bi-steel" colour coated posts or other equal and approved at 2440 mm centres						
Fencing						
1.80 m	-	0.93	10.15	32.07	m	**42.22**
2.10 m	-	1.16	12.66	35.42	m	**48.08**

R DISPOSAL SYSTEMS

Item	PC £	Labour hours	Labour £	Material £	Unit	Total rate £
R10 RAINWATER PIPEWORK/GUTTERS						
Aluminium pipes and fittings; BS 2997; ears cast on; polyester powder coated finish						
63 mm diameter pipes; plugged and screwed	8.96	0.34	5.41	10.71	m	16.12
Extra for						
fittings with one end	-	0.20	3.18	5.55	nr	8.74
fittings with two ends	-	0.39	6.21	5.74	nr	11.95
fittings with three ends	-	0.56	8.91	7.61	nr	16.53
shoe	5.49	0.20	3.18	5.55	nr	8.74
bend	5.85	0.39	6.21	5.74	nr	11.95
single branch	7.63	0.56	8.91	7.61	nr	16.53
offset 228 projection	13.49	0.39	6.80	13.48	nr	20.27
offset 304 projection	15.05	0.39	6.21	15.19	nr	21.40
access pipe	16.67	-	-	15.91	nr	15.91
connection to clay pipes; cement and sand (1:2) joint	-	0.14	2.23	0.10	nr	2.32
76.50 mm diameter pipes; plugged and screwed	10.44	0.37	5.89	12.39	m	18.28
Extra for						
shoe	7.53	0.23	3.66	7.69	nr	11.35
bend	7.39	0.42	6.69	7.33	nr	14.02
single branch	9.16	0.60	9.55	9.14	nr	18.69
offset 228 projection	14.92	0.42	6.69	14.78	nr	21.46
offset 304 projection	16.60	0.42	6.69	16.63	nr	23.32
access pipe	18.21	-	-	17.20	nr	17.20
connection to clay pipes; cement and sand (1:2) joint	-	0.16	2.55	0.10	nr	2.64
100 mm diameter pipes; plugged and screwed	17.82	0.42	6.69	20.75	m	27.43
Extra for						
shoe	9.07	0.26	4.14	8.74	nr	12.88
bend	10.30	0.46	7.32	9.91	nr	17.23
single branch	12.31	0.69	10.98	11.66	nr	22.65
offset 228 projection	17.27	0.46	7.32	15.70	nr	23.02
offset 304 projection	19.16	0.46	7.32	17.80	nr	25.12
access pipe	21.59	-	-	18.86	nr	18.86
connection to clay pipes; cement and sand (1:2) joint	-	0.19	3.02	0.10	nr	3.12
Roof outlets; circular aluminium; with flat or domed grating; joint to pipe						
50 mm diameter	49.27	0.56	14.71	53.03	nr	67.73
75 mm diameter	64.58	0.60	15.76	69.50	nr	85.26
100 mm diameter	84.09	0.65	17.07	90.50	nr	107.57
150 mm diameter	107.74	0.69	18.12	115.95	nr	134.07
Roof outlets; d-shaped; balcony; with flat or domed grating; joint to pipe						
50 mm diameter	58.35	0.56	14.71	62.80	nr	77.51
75 mm diameter	67.09	0.60	15.76	72.20	nr	87.96
100 mm diameter	82.40	0.65	17.07	88.68	nr	105.75
Galvanized wire balloon grating; BS 416 for pipes or outlets						
50 mm diameter	1.65	0.06	1.58	1.78	nr	3.36
63 mm diameter	1.68	0.06	1.58	1.80	nr	3.38
75 mm diameter	1.78	0.06	1.58	1.91	nr	3.49
100 mm diameter	1.97	0.07	1.84	2.12	nr	3.96

R DISPOSAL SYSTEMS

Item	PC £	Labour hours	Labour £	Material £	Unit	Total rate £
R10 RAINWATER PIPEWORK/GUTTERS						
- cont'd						
Aluminium gutters and fittings; BS 2997;						
polyester powder coated finish						
100 mm half round gutters; on brackets; screwed						
to timber	8.22	0.32	5.58	11.70	m	17.28
Extra for						
stop end	2.23	0.15	2.61	4.74	nr	7.35
running outlet	4.94	0.31	5.40	5.41	nr	10.81
stop end outlet	4.39	0.15	2.61	6.38	nr	9.00
angle	4.57	0.31	5.40	4.19	nr	9.60
113 mm half round gutters; on brackets; screwed						
to timber	8.61	0.32	5.58	12.17	m	17.74
Extra for						
stop end	2.34	0.15	2.61	4.88	nr	7.49
running outlet	5.38	0.31	5.40	5.87	nr	11.27
stop end outlet	5.04	0.15	2.61	7.06	nr	9.68
angle	5.14	0.31	5.40	4.73	nr	10.13
125 mm half round gutters; on brackets; screwed						
to timber	9.67	0.37	6.45	14.60	m	21.04
Extra for						
stop end	2.85	0.17	2.96	6.57	nr	9.53
running outlet	5.83	0.32	5.58	6.26	nr	11.84
stop end outlet	5.35	0.17	2.96	8.45	nr	11.41
angle	5.71	0.32	5.58	6.24	nr	11.81
100 mm ogee gutters; on brackets; screwed to						
timber	10.26	0.34	5.92	14.97	m	20.89
Extra for						
stop end	2.35	0.16	2.79	3.12	nr	5.90
running outlet	5.79	0.32	5.58	5.72	nr	11.30
stop end outlet	4.49	0.16	2.79	7.14	nr	9.93
angle	4.88	0.32	5.58	3.71	nr	9.29
112 mm ogee gutters; on brackets; screwed to						
timber	11.41	0.39	6.80	16.47	m	23.27
Extra for						
stop end	2.52	0.16	2.79	3.30	nr	6.09
running outlet	5.86	0.32	5.58	5.70	nr	11.27
stop end outlet	5.03	0.16	2.79	7.82	nr	10.60
angle	5.82	0.32	5.58	4.53	nr	10.11
125 mm ogee gutters; on brackets; screwed to						
timber	12.60	0.39	6.80	18.11	m	24.90
Extra for						
stop end	2.75	0.18	3.14	3.57	nr	6.70
running outlet	6.41	0.34	5.92	6.20	nr	12.13
stop end outlet	5.71	0.18	3.14	8.72	nr	11.86
angle	6.79	0.34	5.92	5.38	nr	11.31
Cast iron pipes and fittings; EN 1462;						
ears cast on; joints						
65 mm pipes; primed; nailed to masonry	17.36	0.48	7.64	19.95	m	27.59
Extra for						
shoe	15.23	0.30	4.78	15.52	nr	20.29
bend	9.33	0.53	8.44	9.00	nr	17.44
single branch	18.34	0.67	10.66	18.32	nr	28.98
offset 225 mm projection	16.62	0.53	8.44	15.87	nr	24.31
offset 305 mm projection	19.46	0.53	8.44	18.61	nr	27.05
connection to clay pipes; cement and sand (1:2)						
joint	-	0.14	2.23	0.11	nr	2.34

R DISPOSAL SYSTEMS

Item	PC £	Labour hours	Labour £	Material £	Unit	Total rate £
75 mm pipes; primed; nailed to masonry	17.36	0.51	8.12	20.14	m	28.26
Extra for						
shoe	15.23	0.32	5.09	15.58	nr	20.67
bend	11.32	1.11	18.57	11.26	nr	29.84
single branch	19.83	0.69	10.98	20.09	nr	31.08
offset 225 mm projection	16.62	0.56	8.91	15.94	nr	24.85
offset 305 mm projection	20.43	0.56	8.91	19.74	nr	28.66
connection to clay pipes; cement and sand (1:2)						
joint	-	0.16	2.55	0.11	nr	2.65
100 mm pipes; primed; nailed to masonry	23.32	0.56	8.91	27.08	m	35.99
Extra for						
shoe	20.23	0.37	5.89	20.68	nr	26.57
bend	15.99	0.60	9.55	16.00	nr	25.55
single branch	23.56	0.74	11.78	23.65	nr	35.42
offset 225 mm projection	32.62	0.60	9.55	32.77	nr	42.32
offset 305 mm projection	33.26	0.60	9.55	32.94	nr	42.49
connection to clay pipes; cement and sand (1:2)						
joint	-	0.19	3.02	0.10	nr	3.12
100 mm x 75 mm rectangular pipes; primed;						
nailing to masonry	67.36	0.56	8.91	76.86	m	85.77
Extra for						
shoe	57.07	0.37	5.89	57.34	nr	63.23
bend	54.34	0.60	9.55	54.32	nr	63.87
offset 225 mm projection	76.53	0.37	5.89	74.23	nr	80.12
offset 305 mm projection	81.79	0.37	5.89	78.52	nr	84.41
connection to clay pipes; cement and sand (1:2)						
joint	-	0.19	3.02	0.10	nr	3.12
Rainwater head; rectangular; for pipes						
65 mm diameter	24.70	0.53	8.44	27.53	nr	35.97
75 mm diameter	24.70	0.56	8.91	27.60	nr	36.51
100 mm diameter	34.11	0.60	9.55	38.10	nr	47.65
Rainwater head; octagonal; for pipes						
65 mm diameter	14.12	0.53	8.44	15.86	nr	24.29
75 mm diameter	16.05	0.56	8.91	18.05	nr	26.96
100 mm diameter	35.55	0.60	9.55	39.69	nr	49.24
Copper wire balloon grating; BS 416 for pipes or outlets						
50 mm diameter	2.01	0.06	0.96	2.17	nr	3.12
63 mm diameter	2.04	0.06	0.96	2.19	nr	3.15
75 mm diameter	2.29	0.06	0.96	2.47	nr	3.43
100 mm diameter	2.61	0.07	1.11	2.81	nr	3.92
Cast iron gutters and fittings; EN 1462						
100 mm half round gutters; primed; on brackets;						
screwed to timber	8.92	0.37	6.45	12.83	m	19.27
Extra for						
stop end	2.25	0.16	2.79	3.73	nr	6.52
running outlet	6.51	0.32	5.58	6.35	nr	11.93
angle	6.69	0.32	5.58	7.86	nr	13.44
115 mm half round gutters; primed; on brackets;						
screwed to timber	9.30	0.37	6.45	13.28	m	19.73
Extra for						
stop end	2.91	0.16	2.79	4.45	nr	7.24
running outlet	7.10	0.32	5.58	6.96	nr	12.53
angle	6.89	0.32	5.58	8.01	nr	13.58

R DISPOSAL SYSTEMS

Item	PC £	Labour hours	Labour £	Material £	Unit	Total rate £
R10 RAINWATER PIPEWORK/GUTTERS						
- cont'd						
Cast iron gutters and fittings – cont'd						
125 mm half round gutters; primed; on brackets;						
screwed to timber	10.88	0.42	7.32	15.07	m	**22.39**
Extra for						
stop end	2.91	0.19	3.31	4.45	nr	**7.77**
running outlet	8.12	0.37	6.45	7.91	nr	**14.36**
angle	8.12	0.37	6.45	9.03	nr	**15.48**
150 mm half round gutters; primed; on brackets;						
screwed to timber	18.44	0.46	8.02	23.28	m	**31.29**
Extra for						
stop end	4.04	0.20	3.48	7.30	nr	**10.79**
running outlet	14.06	0.42	7.32	13.70	nr	**21.02**
angle	14.83	0.42	7.32	15.54	nr	**22.86**
100 mm ogee gutters; primed; on brackets;						
screwed to timber	9.95	0.39	6.80	14.17	m	**20.97**
Extra for						
stop end	2.30	0.17	2.96	5.03	nr	**8.00**
running outlet	7.11	0.34	5.92	6.91	nr	**12.83**
angle	6.98	0.34	5.92	8.17	nr	**14.09**
115 mm ogee gutters; primed; on brackets;						
screwed to timber	10.94	0.39	6.80	15.32	m	**22.12**
Extra for						
stop end	2.98	0.17	2.96	5.77	nr	**8.73**
running outlet	7.57	0.34	5.92	7.31	nr	**13.23**
angle	7.57	0.34	5.92	8.61	nr	**14.53**
125 mm ogee gutters; primed; on brackets;						
screwed to timber	11.48	0.43	7.49	16.26	m	**23.76**
Extra for						
stop end	2.98	0.19	3.31	6.08	nr	**9.39**
running outlet	8.26	0.39	6.80	8.02	nr	**14.81**
angle	8.26	0.39	6.80	9.57	nr	**16.36**
3 mm thick galvanised heavy pressed						
steel gutters and fittings; joggle joints;						
BS 1091						
200 mm x 100 mm (400 mm girth) box gutter;						
screwed to timber	-	0.60	9.55	17.93	m	**27.48**
Extra for						
stop end	-	0.32	5.09	9.96	nr	**15.06**
running outlet	-	0.65	10.35	16.52	nr	**26.87**
stop end outlet	-	0.32	5.09	23.08	nr	**28.18**
angle	-	0.65	10.35	18.34	nr	**28.68**
381 mm boundary wall gutters (900 mm girth);						
bent twice; screwed to timber	-	0.60	9.55	29.45	m	**39.01**
Extra for						
stop end	-	0.37	5.89	16.98	nr	**22.87**
running outlet	-	0.65	10.35	22.73	nr	**33.07**
stop end outlet	-	0.32	5.09	32.04	nr	**37.13**
angle	-	0.65	10.35	26.70	nr	**37.05**
457 mm boundary wall gutters (1200 mm girth);						
bent twice; screwed to timber	-	0.69	10.98	39.29	m	**50.27**
Extra for						
stop end	-	0.37	5.89	21.79	nr	**27.67**
running outlet	-	0.74	11.78	32.86	nr	**44.63**
stop end outlet	-	0.37	5.89	34.93	nr	**40.82**
angle	-	0.74	11.78	36.07	nr	**47.85**

R DISPOSAL SYSTEMS

Item	PC £	Labour hours	Labour £	Material £	Unit	Total rate £
uPVC external rainwater pipes and fittings; BS 4576; slip-in joints						
50 mm pipes; fixing with pipe or socket brackets; plugged and screwed	4.05	0.28	4.46	6.14	m	**10.60**
Extra for						
shoe	2.39	0.19	3.02	3.27	nr	**6.29**
bend	2.79	0.28	4.46	3.71	nr	**8.17**
two bends to form offset 229 mm projection	5.59	0.28	4.46	6.02	nr	**10.47**
connection to clay pipes; cement and sand (1:2) joint	-	0.12	1.91	0.11	nr	**2.02**
68 mm pipes; fixing with pipe or socket brackets; plugged and screwed	3.13	0.31	4.93	5.39	m	**10.33**
Extra for						
shoe	2.39	0.20	3.18	3.55	nr	**6.73**
bend	3.66	0.31	4.93	4.94	nr	**9.88**
single branch	7.36	0.41	6.53	9.03	nr	**15.56**
two bends to form offset 229 mm projection	7.32	0.31	4.93	8.38	nr	**13.31**
loose drain connector; cement and sand joint	-	0.14	2.23	9.54	nr	**11.77**
110 mm pipes; fixing with pipe or socket brackets; plugged and screwed	6.53	0.33	5.25	11.25	m	**16.50**
Extra for						
shoe	7.64	0.22	3.50	9.50	nr	**13.01**
bend	11.34	0.33	5.25	13.58	nr	**18.83**
single branch	16.77	0.44	7.00	19.57	nr	**26.58**
two bends to form offset 229 mm projection	22.67	0.33	5.25	25.05	nr	**30.30**
loose drain connector; cement and sand (1:2) joint	-	0.32	5.09	7.90	nr	**13.00**
65 mm square pipes; fixing with pipe or socket brackets; plugged and screwed	3.14	0.31	4.93	5.41	m	**10.34**
Extra for						
shoe	2.39	0.20	3.18	3.55	nr	**6.73**
bend	3.66	0.31	4.93	4.94	nr	**9.88**
single branch	7.36	0.41	6.53	9.03	nr	**15.56**
two bends to form offset 229 mm projection	7.32	0.31	4.93	8.55	nr	**13.49**
drain connector; square to round; cement and sand (1:2) joint	-	0.32	5.09	4.07	nr	**9.16**
Rainwater head; rectangular; for pipes						
50 mm diameter	13.02	0.42	6.69	15.69	nr	**22.38**
68 mm diameter	10.51	0.43	6.84	13.49	nr	**20.33**
110 mm diameter	21.93	0.51	8.12	26.41	nr	**34.53**
65 mm square	10.51	0.43	6.84	13.49	nr	**20.33**
uPVC gutters and fittings; BS 4576						
76 mm half round gutters; on brackets screwed to timber	3.07	0.28	4.88	5.05	m	**9.93**
Extra for						
stop end	1.10	0.12	2.09	1.59	nr	**3.68**
running outlet	3.09	0.23	4.01	3.14	nr	**7.14**
stop end outlet	3.08	0.12	2.09	3.50	nr	**5.59**
angle	3.09	0.23	4.01	3.85	nr	**7.85**
112 mm half round gutters; on brackets screwed to timber	3.09	0.31	5.40	6.49	m	**11.89**
Extra for						
stop end	1.72	0.12	2.09	2.66	nr	**4.76**
running outlet	3.37	0.26	4.53	3.44	nr	**7.97**
stop end outlet	3.37	0.12	2.09	4.21	nr	**6.30**
angle	3.77	0.26	4.53	5.42	nr	**9.95**

R DISPOSAL SYSTEMS

Item	PC £	Labour hours	Labour £	Material £	Unit	Total rate £
R10 RAINWATER PIPEWORK/GUTTERS - cont'd						
uPVC gutters and fittings; BS 4576 - cont'd						
170 mm half round gutters; on brackets; screwed to timber	6.46	0.31	5.40	11.41	m	16.81
Extra for						
stop end	2.91	0.15	2.61	4.34	nr	6.95
running outlet	6.47	0.29	5.05	6.56	nr	11.61
stop end outlet	6.16	0.15	2.61	7.34	nr	9.96
angle	8.44	0.29	5.05	10.98	nr	16.04
114 mm rectangular gutters; on brackets; screwed to timber	3.17	0.31	5.40	6.45	m	11.85
Extra for						
stop end	1.72	0.12	2.09	2.49	nr	4.58
running outlet	3.37	0.29	5.05	3.43	nr	8.49
stop end outlet	3.37	0.12	2.09	4.03	nr	6.12
angle	3.77	0.26	4.53	5.06	nr	9.59
R11 FOUL DRAINAGE ABOVE GROUND						
Cast iron "Timesaver" pipes and fittings or other equal and approved; BS 416						
50 mm pipes; primed; 3 m lengths; fixing with expanding bolts; to masonry	11.45	0.51	8.12	20.87	m	28.99
Extra for						
fittings with two ends	-	0.51	8.13	16.12	nr	24.25
fittings with three ends	-	0.69	10.98	27.31	nr	38.29
bends; short radius	10.44	0.51	8.12	16.12	nr	24.23
access bends; short radius	25.73	0.51	8.12	32.98	nr	41.10
boss; 38 BSP	21.62	0.51	8.12	28.13	nr	36.25
single branch	15.71	0.69	10.98	27.89	nr	38.87
isolated "Timesaver" coupling joint	5.93	0.28	4.46	6.54	nr	11.00
connection to clay pipes; cement and sand (1:2) joint	-	0.12	1.91	0.10	nr	2.01
75 mm pipes; primed; 3 m lengths; fixing with standard brackets; plugged and screwed to masonry	12.81	0.51	8.12	22.79	m	30.90
Extra for						
bends; short radius	10.44	0.55	8.75	16.57	nr	25.32
access bends; short radius	25.73	0.51	8.12	33.43	nr	41.55
boss; 38 BSP	21.62	0.55	8.75	28.90	nr	37.66
single branch	15.71	0.79	12.57	28.80	nr	41.38
double branch	26.41	1.02	16.24	47.82	nr	64.06
offset 115 mm projection	15.41	0.55	8.75	20.38	nr	29.13
offset 150 mm projection	14.70	0.55	8.75	19.17	nr	27.93
access pipe	25.12	0.55	8.75	30.88	nr	39.63
isolated "Timesaver" coupling joint	6.54	0.32	5.09	7.22	nr	12.31
connection to clay pipes; cement and sand (1:2) joint	-	0.14	2.23	0.10	nr	2.32
100 mm pipes; primed; 3 m lengths; fixing with standard brackets; plugged and screwed to masonry	15.48	0.55	8.75	31.91	m	40.67
Extra for						
WC bent connector; 450 mm long tail	23.14	0.55	8.75	28.75	nr	37.50
bends; short radius	14.46	0.62	9.87	22.75	nr	32.62
access bends; short radius	30.58	0.62	9.87	40.53	nr	50.40
boss; 38 BSP	25.82	0.62	9.87	35.29	nr	45.16
single branch	22.34	0.93	14.80	39.38	nr	54.18
double branch	27.63	1.20	19.10	54.65	nr	73.75

R DISPOSAL SYSTEMS

Item	PC £	Labour hours	Labour £	Material £	Unit	Total rate £
offset 225 mm projection	21.76	0.62	9.87	28.53	nr	**38.40**
offset 300 mm projection	23.42	0.62	9.87	29.83	nr	**39.70**
access pipe	26.41	0.62	9.87	33.31	nr	**43.18**
roof connector; for asphalt	24.96	0.62	9.87	33.72	nr	**43.59**
isolated "Timesaver" coupling joint	8.54	0.39	6.21	9.43	nr	**15.63**
transitional clayware socket; cement and sand (1:2) joint	17.00	0.37	5.89	28.27	nr	**34.16**
150 mm pipes; primed; 3 m lengths; fixing with standard brackets; plugged and screwed to masonry	32.35	0.69	10.98	64.58	m	**75.56**
Extra for						
bends; short radius	25.82	0.77	12.26	41.84	nr	**54.09**
access bends; short radius	43.42	0.77	12.26	61.24	nr	**73.50**
boss; 38 BSP	42.14	0.77	12.26	58.92	nr	**71.17**
single branch	55.39	1.11	17.67	88.90	nr	**106.57**
double branch	77.83	1.48	23.56	130.85	nr	**154.41**
access pipe	43.93	0.77	12.26	54.35	nr	**66.61**
isolated "Timesaver" coupling joint	-	0.46	7.32	18.83	nr	**26.16**
transitional clayware socket; cement and sand (1:2) joint	29.77	0.48	7.64	51.77	nr	**59.41**
Cast iron "Ensign" lightweight pipes and fittings or other equal and approved; EN 877						
50 mm pipes; primed; 3 m lengths; fixing with standard brackets; plugged and screwed to masonry	-	0.31	5.01	13.38	m	**18.39**
Extra for						
bends; short radius	-	0.27	4.37	11.15	nr	**15.52**
single branch	-	0.33	5.32	19.49	nr	**24.82**
access pipe	-	0.27	4.23	22.89	nr	**27.12**
70 mm pipes; primed; 3 m lengths; fixing with standard brackets; plugged and screwed to masonry	-	0.34	5.51	14.94	m	**20.44**
Extra for						
bends; short radius	-	0.30	4.82	12.43	nr	**17.26**
single branch	-	0.37	5.96	20.93	nr	**26.89**
access pipe	-	0.30	4.82	24.39	nr	**29.21**
100 mm pipes; primed; 3 m lengths; fixing with standard brackets; plugged and screwed to masonry	-	0.37	5.96	17.63	m	**23.59**
Extra for						
bends; short radius	-	0.32	5.19	15.27	nr	**20.45**
single branch	-	0.39	6.28	28.10	nr	**34.38**
double branch	-	0.46	7.42	66.62	nr	**74.04**
access pipe	-	0.32	5.19	27.73	nr	**32.92**
connector	-	0.21	3.37	25.77	nr	**29.14**
reducer	-	0.32	5.19	18.62	nr	**23.81**

R DISPOSAL SYSTEMS

Item	PC £	Labour hours	Labour £	Material £	Unit	Total rate £
R11 FOUL DRAINAGE ABOVE GROUND - cont'd						
Polypropylene (PP) waste pipes and fittings; BS 5254; push fit "O" - ring joints						
32 mm pipes; fixing with pipe clips; plugged and screwed	1.24	0.20	3.18	2.14	m	**5.32**
Extra for						
fittings with one end	-	0.15	2.39	1.16	nr	**3.55**
fittings with two ends	-	0.20	3.18	1.21	nr	**4.40**
fittings with three ends	-	0.28	4.46	2.04	nr	**6.50**
access plug	1.00	0.15	2.39	1.16	nr	**3.55**
double socket	0.79	0.14	2.23	0.91	nr	**3.14**
male iron to PP coupling	1.86	0.26	4.14	2.15	nr	**6.29**
sweep bend	0.98	0.20	3.18	1.14	nr	**4.32**
spigot bend	1.32	0.23	3.66	1.53	nr	**5.19**
40 mm pipes; fixing with pipe clips; plugged and screwed	1.53	0.20	3.18	2.51	m	**5.69**
Extra for						
fittings with one end	-	0.18	2.87	1.24	nr	**4.11**
fittings with two ends	-	0.28	4.46	1.43	nr	**5.89**
fittings with three ends	-	0.37	5.89	2.21	nr	**8.10**
access plug	1.07	0.18	2.87	1.24	nr	**4.11**
double socket	0.81	0.19	3.02	0.93	nr	**3.96**
universal connector	2.11	0.23	3.66	2.44	nr	**6.10**
sweep bend	1.10	0.28	4.46	1.28	nr	**5.74**
spigot bend	1.38	0.28	4.46	1.60	nr	**6.06**
reducer 40 mm - 32 mm	0.97	0.28	4.46	1.13	nr	**5.59**
50 mm pipes; fixing with pipe clips; plugged and screwed	1.80	0.32	5.09	3.39	m	**8.48**
Extra for						
fittings with one end	-	0.19	3.02	2.04	nr	**5.06**
fittings with two ends	-	0.32	5.09	2.33	nr	**7.42**
fittings with three ends	-	0.43	6.84	3.21	nr	**10.06**
access plug	1.76	0.19	3.02	2.04	nr	**5.06**
double socket	1.48	0.21	3.34	1.72	nr	**5.06**
sweep bend	1.94	0.32	5.09	2.24	nr	**7.34**
spigot bend	2.80	0.32	5.09	3.25	nr	**8.34**
reducer 50 mm - 40 mm	1.27	0.32	5.09	1.47	nr	**6.56**
muPVC waste pipes and fittings; BS 5255; solvent welded joints						
32 mm pipes; fixing with pipe clips; plugged and screwed	1.47	0.23	3.66	2.50	m	**6.17**
Extra for						
fittings with one end	-	0.16	2.55	1.28	nr	**3.83**
fittings with two ends	-	0.23	3.66	1.37	nr	**5.03**
fittings with three ends	-	0.31	4.93	1.82	nr	**6.75**
access plug	0.90	0.16	2.55	1.28	nr	**3.83**
straight coupling	0.97	0.16	2.55	1.36	nr	**3.90**
expansion coupling	1.70	0.23	3.66	2.16	nr	**5.82**
male iron to muPVC coupling	1.72	0.35	5.57	2.04	nr	**7.61**
sweep bend	0.98	0.23	3.66	1.37	nr	**5.03**
spigot/socket bend	-	0.23	3.66	2.06	nr	**5.72**
sweep tee	1.32	0.31	4.93	1.82	nr	**6.75**

R DISPOSAL SYSTEMS

Item	PC £	Labour hours	Labour £	Material £	Unit	Total rate £
40 mm pipes; fixing with pipe clips; plugged and screwed	1.82	0.28	4.46	2.95	m	7.41
Extra for						
fittings with one end	-	0.18	2.87	1.28	nr	4.14
fittings with two ends	-	0.28	4.46	1.49	nr	5.95
fittings with three ends	-	0.37	5.89	2.20	nr	8.09
fittings with four ends	4.06	0.49	7.80	4.98	nr	12.78
access plug	0.90	0.18	2.87	1.28	nr	4.14
straight coupling	0.96	0.19	3.02	1.35	nr	4.37
expansion coupling	2.05	0.28	4.46	2.55	nr	7.00
male iron to muPVC coupling	1.72	0.35	5.57	2.04	nr	7.61
level invert taper	1.20	0.28	4.46	1.62	nr	6.07
sweep bend	1.09	0.28	4.46	1.49	nr	5.95
spigot/socket bend	1.85	0.28	4.46	2.33	nr	6.78
sweep tee	1.67	0.37	5.89	2.20	nr	8.09
sweep cross	4.06	0.49	7.80	4.98	nr	12.78
50 mm pipes; fixing with pipe clips; plugged and screwed	2.75	0.32	5.09	4.76	m	9.85
Extra for						
fittings with one end	-	0.19	3.02	1.71	nr	4.73
fittings with two ends	-	0.32	5.09	2.41	nr	7.51
fittings with three ends	-	0.43	6.84	3.95	nr	10.80
fittings with four ends	-	0.57	9.07	5.20	nr	14.27
access plug	1.29	0.19	3.02	1.71	nr	4.73
straight coupling	1.76	0.21	3.34	2.23	nr	5.57
expansion coupling	2.78	0.32	5.09	3.35	nr	8.44
male iron to muPVC coupling	2.48	0.42	6.69	2.88	nr	9.56
level invert taper	1.50	0.32	5.09	1.94	nr	7.03
sweep bend	1.92	0.32	5.09	2.41	nr	7.51
spigot/socket bend	2.62	0.32	5.09	3.18	nr	8.27
sweep tee	1.67	0.37	5.89	2.20	nr	8.09
sweep cross	4.25	0.57	9.07	5.20	nr	14.27
uPVC overflow pipes and fittings; solvent welded joints						
19 mm pipes; fixing with pipe clips; plugged and screwed	0.87	0.20	3.18	1.64	m	4.82
Extra for						
splay cut end	-	0.01	0.16	-	nr	0.16
fittings with one end	-	0.16	2.55	1.14	nr	3.68
fittings with two ends	-	0.16	2.55	1.32	nr	3.87
fittings with three ends	-	0.20	3.18	1.50	nr	4.68
straight connector	0.92	0.16	2.55	1.14	nr	3.68
female iron to uPVC coupling	-	0.19	3.02	1.78	nr	4.80
bend	1.09	0.16	2.55	1.32	nr	3.87
bent tank connector	1.71	0.19	3.02	1.91	nr	4.94
uPVC pipes and fittings; BS 4514; with solvent welded joints (unless otherwise described)						
82 mm pipes; fixing with holderbats; plugged and screwed	6.26	0.37	5.89	10.68	m	16.57
Extra for						
socket plug	4.73	0.19	3.02	5.95	nr	8.98
slip coupling; push fit	10.32	0.34	5.41	11.38	nr	16.79
expansion coupling	4.97	0.37	5.89	6.22	nr	12.11
sweep bend	8.33	0.37	5.89	9.93	nr	15.82
boss connector	4.55	0.25	3.98	5.76	nr	9.74
single branch	11.65	0.49	7.80	14.03	nr	21.83
access door	11.09	0.56	8.91	12.60	nr	21.52

R DISPOSAL SYSTEMS

Item	PC £	Labour hours	Labour £	Material £	Unit	Total rate £
R11 FOUL DRAINAGE ABOVE GROUND - cont'd						
uPVC pipes and fittings; BS 4514 – cont'd						
110 mm pipes; fixing with holderbats; plugged and screwed	6.37	0.41	6.53	11.04	m	17.56
Extra for						
socket plug	5.73	0.20	3.18	7.28	nr	10.46
slip coupling; push fit	12.92	0.37	5.89	14.25	nr	20.14
expansion coupling	5.07	0.41	6.53	6.55	nr	13.08
W.C. connector	9.22	0.27	4.30	10.69	nr	14.99
sweep bend	9.75	0.41	6.53	11.72	nr	18.24
W.C. connecting bend	15.13	0.27	4.30	17.21	nr	21.51
access bend	27.05	0.43	6.84	30.80	nr	37.64
boss connector	4.55	0.27	4.30	5.98	nr	10.28
single branch	12.90	0.54	8.60	15.71	nr	24.30
single branch with access	22.08	0.56	8.91	25.84	nr	34.75
double branch	29.38	0.68	10.82	34.40	nr	45.23
W.C. manifold	12.66	0.27	4.30	15.45	nr	19.75
access door	-	0.56	8.91	12.60	nr	21.52
access pipe connector	20.40	0.46	7.32	23.46	nr	30.78
connection to clay pipes; caulking ring and cement and sand (1:2) joint	-	0.39	6.21	9.20	nr	15.41
160 mm pipes; fixing with holderbats; plugged and screwed	16.53	0.46	7.32	26.60	m	33.92
Extra for						
socket plug	10.52	0.23	3.66	13.75	nr	17.42
slip coupling; push fit	33.07	0.42	6.69	36.48	nr	43.16
expansion coupling	15.28	0.46	7.32	19.00	nr	26.33
sweep bend	24.28	0.46	7.32	28.93	nr	36.26
boss connector	6.45	0.31	4.93	9.27	nr	14.20
single branch	27.38	0.61	9.71	33.39	nr	43.10
double branch	57.59	0.77	12.26	67.75	nr	80.00
access door	19.81	0.56	8.91	22.23	nr	31.14
access pipe connector	20.40	0.46	7.32	23.46	nr	30.78
Weathering apron; for pipe						
82 mm diameter	2.35	0.31	4.93	2.97	nr	7.90
110 mm diameter	2.70	0.35	5.57	3.49	nr	9.06
160 mm diameter	8.11	0.39	6.21	9.98	nr	16.19
Weathering slate; for pipe						
110 mm diameter	28.63	0.83	13.21	32.10	nr	45.32
Vent cowl; for pipe						
82 mm diameter	2.35	0.31	4.93	2.97	nr	7.90
110 mm diameter	2.37	0.31	4.93	3.13	nr	8.07
160 mm diameter	6.21	0.31	4.93	7.89	nr	12.83
Polypropylene ancillaries; screwed joint to waste fitting						
Tubular "S" trap; bath; shallow seal						
40 mm diameter	5.85	0.51	8.12	6.45	nr	14.57
Trap; "P"; two piece; 76 mm seal						
32 mm diameter	3.95	0.35	5.57	4.35	nr	9.92
40 mm diameter	4.56	0.42	6.69	5.03	nr	11.71
Trap; "S"; two piece; 76 mm seal						
32 mm diameter	5.00	0.35	5.57	5.52	nr	11.09
40 mm diameter	5.85	0.42	6.69	6.45	nr	13.14
Bottle trap; "P"; 76 mm seal						
32 diameter	4.40	0.35	5.57	4.85	nr	10.43
40 diameter	5.25	0.42	6.69	5.79	nr	12.47

R DISPOSAL SYSTEMS

Item	PC £	Labour hours	Labour £	Material /Plant £	Unit	Total rate £
R12 DRAINAGE BELOW GROUND						
NOTE: Prices for drain trenches are for excavation in "firm" soil and it has been assumed that earthwork support will only be required for trenches 1.00 m or more in depth.						
Excavating trenches; by machine; grading bottoms; earthwork support; filling with excavated material and compacting; disposal of surplus soil; spreading on site average 50 m						
Pipes not exceeding 200 mm nominal size						
average depth of trench 0.50 m	-	0.28	3.06	1.66	m	4.71
average depth of trench 0.75 m	-	0.37	4.04	2.45	m	6.49
average depth of trench 1.00 m	-	0.79	8.62	4.67	m	13.29
average depth of trench 1.25 m	-	1.16	12.66	5.29	m	17.95
average depth of trench 1.50 m	-	1.48	16.15	6.01	m	22.16
average depth of trench 1.75 m	-	1.85	20.19	6.63	m	26.82
average depth of trench 2.00 m	-	2.13	23.25	7.54	m	30.78
average depth of trench 2.25 m	-	2.64	28.81	9.46	m	38.27
average depth of trench 2.50 m	-	3.10	33.83	11.02	m	44.86
average depth of trench 2.75 m	-	3.42	37.32	12.32	m	49.64
average depth of trench 3.00 m	-	3.75	40.92	13.56	m	54.48
average depth of trench 3.25 m	-	4.07	44.42	14.43	m	58.84
average depth of trench 3.50 m	-	4.35	47.47	15.23	m	62.70
Pipes exceeding 200 mm nominal size; 225 mm nominal size						
average depth of trench 0.50 m	-	0.28	3.06	1.66	m	4.71
average depth of trench 0.75 m	-	0.37	4.04	2.45	m	6.49
average depth of trench 1.00 m	-	0.79	8.62	4.67	m	13.29
average depth of trench 1.25 m	-	1.16	12.66	5.29	m	17.95
average depth of trench 1.50 m	-	1.48	16.15	6.01	m	22.16
average depth of trench 1.75 m	-	1.85	20.19	6.63	m	26.82
average depth of trench 2.00 m	-	2.13	23.25	7.54	m	30.78
average depth of trench 2.25 m	-	2.64	28.81	9.46	m	38.27
average depth of trench 2.50 m	-	3.10	33.83	11.02	m	44.86
average depth of trench 2.75 m	-	3.42	37.32	12.32	m	49.64
average depth of trench 3.00 m	-	3.75	40.92	13.56	m	54.48
average depth of trench 3.25 m	-	4.07	44.42	14.43	m	58.84
average depth of trench 3.50 m	-	4.35	47.47	15.23	m	62.70
Pipes exceeding 200 mm nominal size; 300 mm nominal size						
average depth of trencg 0.75 m	-	0.44	4.80	3.07	m	7.87
average depth of trench 1.00 m	-	0.93	10.15	4.67	m	14.82
average depth of trench 1.25 m	-	1.25	13.64	5.47	m	19.11
average depth of trench 1.50 m	-	1.62	17.68	6.19	m	23.87
average depth of trench 1.75 m	-	1.85	20.19	6.82	m	27.01
average depth of trench 2.00 m	-	2.13	23.25	8.15	m	31.40
average depth of trench 2.25 m	-	2.64	28.81	9.83	m	38.64
average depth of trench 2.50 m	-	3.10	33.83	11.27	m	45.10
average depth of trench 2.75 m	-	3.42	37.32	12.51	m	49.83
average depth of trench 3.00 m	-	3.75	40.92	13.74	m	54.67
average depth of trench 3.25 m	-	4.07	44.42	15.04	m	59.46
average depth of trench 3.50 m	-	4.35	47.47	15.66	m	63.13

R DISPOSAL SYSTEMS

Item	PC £	Labour hours	Labour £	Material /Plant £	Unit	Total rate £
R12 DRAINAGE BELOW GROUND - cont'd						
Excavating trenches; by machine - cont'd						
Pipes exceeding 200 mm nominal size; 375 mm nominal size						
average depth of trench 0.75 m	-	0.46	5.02	3.68	m	8.70
average depth of trench 1.00 m	-	0.97	10.59	5.28	m	15.87
average depth of trench 1.25 m	-	1.34	14.62	6.52	m	21.14
average depth of trench 1.50 m	-	1.71	18.66	6.99	m	25.65
average depth of trench 1.75 m	-	1.99	21.72	7.86	m	29.58
average depth of trench 2.00 m	-	2.27	24.77	8.34	m	33.11
average depth of trench 2.25 m	-	2.82	30.78	10.44	m	41.21
average depth of trench 2.50 m	-	3.38	36.89	12.07	m	48.95
average depth of trench 2.75 m	-	3.70	40.38	13.12	m	53.50
average depth of trench 3.00 m	-	4.02	43.87	14.17	m	58.04
average depth of trench 3.25 m	-	4.35	47.47	15.41	m	62.88
average depth of trench 3.50 m	-	4.67	50.96	16.46	m	67.42
Pipes exceeding 200 mm nominal size; 450 mm nominal size						
average depth of trench 0.75 m	-	0.51	5.57	3.68	m	9.25
average depth of trench 1.00 m	-	1.02	11.13	5.65	m	16.78
average depth of trench 1.25 m	-	1.48	16.15	6.94	m	23.10
average depth of trench 1.50 m	-	1.85	20.19	7.61	m	27.79
average depth of trench 1.75 m	-	2.13	23.25	8.29	m	31.53
average depth of trench 2.00 m	-	2.45	26.74	8.95	m	35.69
average depth of trench 2.25 m	-	3.05	33.29	10.87	m	44.15
average depth of trench 2.50 m	-	3.61	39.40	12.68	m	52.08
average depth of trench 2.75 m	-	3.98	43.43	13.92	m	57.35
average depth of trench 3.00 m	-	4.26	46.49	15.21	m	61.70
average depth of trench 3.25 m	-	4.63	50.53	16.63	m	67.16
average depth of trench 3.50 m	-	5.00	54.57	18.12	m	72.68
Pipes exceeding 200 mm nominal size; 600 mm nominal size						
average depth of trench 1.00 m	-	1.11	12.11	6.08	m	18.19
average depth of trench 1.25 m	-	1.57	17.13	7.31	m	24.45
average depth of trench 1.50 m	-	2.04	22.26	8.46	m	30.73
average depth of trench 1.75 m	-	2.31	25.21	8.90	m	34.11
average depth of trench 2.00 m	-	2.73	29.79	9.81	m	39.60
average depth of trench 2.25 m	-	3.28	35.80	12.10	m	47.89
average depth of trench 2.50 m	-	3.89	42.45	14.09	m	56.54
average depth of trench 2.75 m	-	4.30	46.93	15.76	m	62.68
average depth of trench 3.00 m	-	4.72	51.51	17.24	m	68.75
average depth of trench 3.25 m	-	5.09	55.55	18.47	m	74.02
average depth of trench 3.50 m	-	5.46	59.59	19.53	m	79.11
Pipes exceeding 200 mm nominal size; 900 mm nominal size						
average depth of trench 1.25 m	-	1.90	20.74	8.54	m	29.27
average depth of trench 1.50 m	-	2.41	26.30	9.69	m	35.99
average depth of trench 1.75 m	-	2.78	30.34	10.31	m	40.65
average depth of trench 2.00 m	-	3.10	33.83	11.83	m	45.66
average depth of trench 2.25 m	-	3.84	41.91	14.37	m	56.27
average depth of trench 2.50 m	-	4.53	49.44	16.55	m	65.98
average depth of trench 2.75 m	-	5.00	54.57	18.21	m	72.78
average depth of trench 3.00 m	-	5.46	59.59	19.88	m	79.46
average depth of trench 3.25 m	-	5.92	64.61	21.54	m	86.15
average depth of trench 3.50 m	-	6.38	69.63	23.02	m	92.65

R DISPOSAL SYSTEMS

Item	PC £	Labour hours	Labour £	Material /Plant £	Unit	Total rate £
Pipes exceeding 200 mm nominal size; 1200 mm nominal size						
average depth of trench 1.50 m	-	2.73	29.79	10.30	m	**40.10**
average depth of trench 1.75 m	-	3.19	34.81	11.97	m	**46.78**
average depth of trench 2.00 m	-	3.56	38.85	13.67	m	**52.52**
average depth of trench 2.25 m	-	4.35	47.47	16.57	m	**64.05**
average depth of trench 2.50 m	-	5.18	56.53	19.00	m	**75.53**
average depth of trench 2.75 m	-	5.69	62.10	21.09	m	**83.19**
average depth of trench 3.00 m	-	6.20	67.66	22.94	m	**90.61**
average depth of trench 3.25 m	-	6.75	73.66	24.85	m	**98.52**
average depth of trench 3.50 m	-	7.26	79.23	26.70	m	**105.93**
Extra over excavating trenches; irrespective of depth; breaking out existing materials						
brick	-	1.80	19.64	7.82	m³	**27.46**
concrete	-	2.54	27.72	10.77	m³	**38.49**
reinforced concrete	-	3.61	39.40	15.57	m³	**54.96**
Extra over excavating trenches; irrespective of depth; breaking out existing hard pavings; 75 mm thick						
tarmacadam	-	0.19	2.07	0.82	m²	**2.89**
Extra over excavating trenches; irrsepective of depth; breaking out existing hard pavings; 150 mm thick						
concrete	-	0.37	4.04	1.78	m²	**5.82**
tarmacadam and hardcore	-	0.28	3.06	0.91	m²	**3.97**
Excavating trenches; by hand; grading bottoms; earthwork support; filling with excavated material and compacting; disposal of surplus soil on site; spreading on site average 50 m						
Pipes not exceeding 200 mm nominal size						
average depth of trench 0.50 m	-	0.93	10.15	-	m	**10.15**
average depth of trench 0.75 m	-	1.39	15.17	-	m	**15.17**
average depth of trench 1.00 m	-	2.04	22.26	1.17	m	**23.43**
average depth of trench 1.25 m	-	2.87	31.32	1.61	m	**32.93**
average depth of trench 1.50 m	-	3.93	42.89	1.96	m	**44.85**
average depth of trench 1.75 m	-	5.18	56.53	2.34	m	**58.87**
average depth of trench 2.00 m	-	5.92	64.61	2.63	m	**67.24**
average depth of trench 2.25 m	-	7.40	80.76	3.51	m	**84.27**
average depth of trench 2.50 m	-	8.88	96.91	4.09	m	**101.00**
average depth of trench 2.75 m	-	9.76	106.51	4.53	m	**111.04**
average depth of trench 3.00 m	-	10.64	116.12	4.97	m	**121.09**
average depth of trench 3.25 m	-	11.52	125.72	5.41	m	**131.13**
average depth of trench 3.50 m	-	12.40	135.32	5.85	m	**141.17**
Pipes exceeding 200 mm nominal size; 225 mm nominal size						
average depth of trench 0.50 m	-	0.93	10.15	-	m	**10.15**
average depth of trench 0.75 m	-	1.39	15.17	-	m	**15.17**
average depth of trench 1.00 m	-	2.04	22.26	1.17	m	**23.43**
average depth of trench 1.25 m	-	2.87	31.32	1.61	m	**32.93**
average depth of trench 1.50 m	-	3.93	42.89	1.96	m	**44.85**
average depth of trench 1.75 m	-	5.18	56.53	2.34	m	**58.87**
average depth of trench 2.00 m	-	5.92	64.61	2.63	m	**67.24**
average depth of trench 2.25 m	-	7.40	80.76	3.51	m	**84.27**
average depth of trench 2.50 m	-	8.88	96.91	4.09	m	**101.00**
average depth of trench 2.75 m	-	9.76	106.51	4.53	m	**111.04**
average depth of trench 3.00 m	-	10.64	116.12	4.97	m	**121.09**
average depth of trench 3.25 m	-	11.52	125.72	5.41	m	**131.13**
average depth of trench 3.50 m	-	12.40	135.32	5.85	m	**141.17**

R DISPOSAL SYSTEMS

Item	PC £	Labour hours	Labour £	Material £	Unit	Total rate £
R12 DRAINAGE BELOW GROUND - cont'd						
Excavating trenches; by hand - cont'd						
Pipes exceeding 200 mm nominal size; 300 mm nominal size						
average depth of trench 0.75 m	-	1.62	17.68	-	m	17.68
average depth of trench 1.00 m	-	2.36	25.76	1.17	m	26.92
average depth of trench 1.25 m	-	3.33	36.34	1.61	m	37.95
average depth of trench 1.50 m	-	4.44	48.45	1.96	m	50.41
average depth of trench 1.75 m	-	5.18	56.53	2.34	m	58.87
average depth of trench 2.00 m	-	5.92	64.61	2.63	m	67.24
average depth of trench 2.25 m	-	7.40	80.76	3.51	m	84.27
average depth of trench 2.50 m	-	8.88	96.91	4.09	m	101.00
average depth of trench 2.75 m	-	9.76	106.51	4.53	m	111.04
average depth of trench 3.00 m	-	10.64	116.12	4.97	m	121.09
average depth of trench 3.25 m	-	11.52	125.72	5.41	m	131.13
average depth of trench 3.50 m	-	12.40	135.32	5.85	m	141.17
Pipes exceeding 200 mm nominal size; 375 mm nominal size						
average depth of trench 0.75 m	-	1.80	19.64	-	m	19.64
average depth of trench 1.00 m	-	2.64	28.81	1.17	m	29.98
average depth of trench 1.25 m	-	3.70	40.38	1.61	m	41.99
average depth of trench 1.50 m	-	4.93	53.80	1.96	m	55.76
average depth of trench 1.75 m	-	5.74	62.64	2.34	m	64.98
average depth of trench 2.00 m	-	6.57	71.70	2.63	m	74.33
average depth of trench 2.25 m	-	8.23	89.82	3.51	m	93.32
average depth of trench 2.50 m	-	9.90	108.04	4.09	m	112.13
average depth of trench 2.75 m	-	10.87	118.63	4.53	m	123.16
average depth of trench 3.00 m	-	11.84	129.21	4.97	m	134.18
average depth of trench 3.25 m	-	12.86	140.34	5.41	m	145.75
average depth of trench 3.50 m	-	13.88	151.48	5.85	m	157.32
Pipes exceeding 200 mm nominal size; 450 mm nominal size						
average depth of trench 0.75 m	-	2.04	22.26	-	m	22.26
average depth of trench 1.00 m	-	2.94	32.08	1.17	m	33.25
average depth of trench 1.25 m	-	4.13	45.07	1.61	m	46.68
average depth of trench 1.50 m	-	5.41	59.04	1.96	m	61.00
average depth of trench 1.75 m	-	6.31	68.86	2.34	m	71.20
average depth of trench 2.00 m	-	7.22	78.79	2.63	m	81.42
average depth of trench 2.25 m	-	9.05	98.76	3.51	m	102.27
average depth of trench 2.50 m	-	10.87	118.63	4.09	m	122.72
average depth of trench 2.75 m	-	11.96	130.52	4.53	m	135.05
average depth of trench 3.00 m	-	13.04	142.31	4.97	m	147.28
average depth of trench 3.25 m	-	14.11	153.99	5.41	m	159.39
average depth of trench 3.50 m	-	15.17	165.55	5.85	m	171.40
Pipes exceeding 200 mm nominal size; 600 mm nominal size						
average depth of trench 1.00 m	-	3.24	35.36	1.17	m	36.53
average depth of trench 1.25 m	-	4.63	50.53	1.61	m	52.14
average depth of trench 1.50 m	-	6.20	67.66	1.96	m	69.62
average depth of trench 1.75 m	-	7.17	78.25	2.34	m	80.59
average depth of trench 2.00 m	-	8.19	89.38	2.63	m	92.01
average depth of trench 2.25 m	-	9.20	100.40	3.51	m	103.91
average depth of trench 2.50 m	-	11.56	126.16	4.09	m	130.25
average depth of trench 2.75 m	-	12.35	134.78	4.53	m	139.31
average depth of trench 3.00 m	-	14.80	161.52	4.97	m	166.48
average depth of trench 3.25 m	-	16.03	174.94	5.41	m	180.35
average depth of trench 3.50 m	-	17.25	188.25	5.85	m	194.10

R DISPOSAL SYSTEMS

Item	PC £	Labour hours	Labour £	Material £	Unit	Total rate £
Pipes exceeding 200 mm nominal size; 900 mm nominal size						
average depth of trench 1.25 m	-	5.78	63.08	1.61	m	64.69
average depth of trench 1.50 m	-	7.63	83.27	1.96	m	85.23
average depth of trench 1.75 m	-	8.88	96.91	2.34	m	99.25
average depth of trench 2.00 m	-	10.13	110.55	2.63	m	113.18
average depth of trench 2.25 m	-	12.72	138.82	3.51	m	142.32
average depth of trench 2.50 m	-	15.31	167.08	4.09	m	171.17
average depth of trench 2.75 m	-	16.84	183.78	4.53	m	188.31
average depth of trench 3.00 m	-	18.32	199.93	4.97	m	204.90
average depth of trench 3.25 m	-	19.84	216.52	5.41	m	221.93
average depth of trench 3.50 m	-	21.37	233.22	5.85	m	239.06
Pipes exceeding 200 mm nominal size; 1200 mm nominal size						
average depth of trench 1.50 m	-	9.11	99.42	1.96	m	101.38
average depth of trench 1.75 m	-	10.59	115.57	2.34	m	117.91
average depth of trench 2.00 m	-	12.12	132.27	2.63	m	134.90
average depth of trench 2.25 m	·	15.20	165.88	3.51	m	169.39
average depth of trench 2.50 m	-	18.27	199.38	4.09	m	203.48
average depth of trench 2.75 m	-	20.07	219.03	4.53	m	223.56
average depth of trench 3.00 m	-	21.88	238.78	4.97	m	243.75
average depth of trench 3.25 m	-	23.66	258.21	5.41	m	263.61
average depth of trench 3.50 m	-	25.44	277.63	5.85	m	283.48
Extra over excavating trenches irrespective of depth; breaking out existing materials						
brick	-	2.78	30.34	5.92	m³	36.26
concrete	-	4.16	45.40	9.86	m³	55.26
reinforced concrete	-	5.55	60.57	13.82	m³	74.38
concrete; 150 mm thick	-	0.65	7.09	1.39	m²	8.48
tarmacadam and hardcore; 150 mm thick	-	0.46	5.02	0.98	m²	6.00
Extra over excavating trenches irrespective of depth; breaking out existing hard pavings, 75 mm thick						
tarmacadam	-	0.37	4.04	0.79	m²	4.83
Extra over excavating trenches irrespective of depth; breaking out existing hard pavings, 150 mm thick						
concrete	-	0.65	7.09	1.39	m²	8.48
tarmacadam and hardcore	-	0.46	5.02	0.98	m²	6.00
Sand filling						
Beds; to receive pitch fibre pipes						
600 mm x 50 mm thick	⸴	0.07	0.76	0.94	m	1.70
700 mm x 50 mm thick	-	0.09	0.98	1.09	m	2.08
800 mm x 50 mm thick	-	0.11	1.20	1.25	m	2.45
Granular (shingle) filling						
Beds; 100 mm thick; to pipes						
100 mm nominal size	-	0.09	0.98	1.23	m	2.22
150 mm nominal size	-	0.09	0.98	1.44	m	2.42
225 mm nominal size	-	0.11	1.20	1.65	m	2.85
300 mm nominal size	-	0.13	1.42	1.85	m	3.27
375 mm nominal size	-	0.15	1.64	2.06	m	3.69
450 mm nominal size	-	0.17	1.86	2.26	m	4.12
600 mm nominal size	-	0.19	2.07	2.47	m	4.54

R DISPOSAL SYSTEMS

Item	PC £	Labour hours	Labour £	Material £	Unit	Total rate £
R12 DRAINAGE BELOW GROUND - cont'd						
Granular (shingle) filling - cont'd						
Beds; 150 mm thick; to pipes						
100 mm nominal size	-	0.13	1.42	1.85	m	**3.27**
150 mm nominal size	-	0.15	1.64	2.06	m	**3.69**
225 mm nominal size	-	0.17	1.86	2.26	m	**4.12**
300 mm nominal size	-	0.19	2.07	2.47	m	**4.54**
375 mm nominal size	-	0.22	2.40	3.08	m	**5.48**
450 mm nominal size	-	0.24	2.62	3.29	m	**5.91**
600 mm nominal size	-	0.28	3.06	3.91	m	**6.96**
Beds and benchings; beds 100 mm thick; to pipes						
100 nominal size	-	0.21	2.29	2.26	m	**4.55**
150 nominal size	-	0.23	2.51	2.26	m	**4.77**
225 nominal size	-	0.28	3.06	3.08	m	**6.14**
300 nominal size	-	0.32	3.49	3.49	m	**6.99**
375 nominal size	-	0.42	4.58	4.73	m	**9.31**
450 nominal size	-	0.48	5.24	5.34	m	**10.58**
600 nominal size	-	0.62	6.77	6.99	m	**13.76**
Beds and benchings; beds 150 mm thick; to pipes						
100 nominal size	-	0.23	2.51	2.47	m	**4.98**
150 nominal size	-	0.26	2.84	2.67	m	**5.51**
225 nominal size	-	0.32	3.49	3.70	m	**7.19**
300 nominal size	-	0.42	4.58	4.52	m	**9.11**
375 nominal size	-	0.48	5.24	5.34	m	**10.58**
450 nominal size	-	0.57	6.22	6.37	m	**12.59**
600 nominal size	-	0.68	7.42	8.22	m	**15.64**
Beds and coverings; 100 mm thick; to pipes						
100 nominal size	-	0.33	3.60	3.08	m	**6.68**
150 nominal size	-	0.42	4.58	3.70	m	**8.28**
225 nominal size	-	0.56	6.11	5.14	m	**11.25**
300 nominal size	-	0.67	7.31	6.17	m	**13.48**
375 nominal size	-	0.80	8.73	7.40	m	**16.13**
450 nominal size	-	0.94	10.26	8.84	m	**19.10**
600 nominal size	-	1.22	13.31	11.31	m	**24.62**
Beds and coverings; 150 mm thick; to pipes						
100 nominal size	-	0.50	5.46	4.52	m	**9.98**
150 nominal size	-	0.56	6.11	5.14	m	**11.25**
225 nominal size	-	0.72	7.86	6.58	m	**14.44**
300 nominal size	-	0.86	9.39	7.81	m	**17.20**
375 nominal size	-	1.00	10.91	9.25	m	**20.16**
450 nominal size	-	1.19	12.99	11.10	m	**24.09**
600 nominal size	-	1.44	15.71	13.36	m	**29.08**
Plain in situ ready mixed designated concrete; C10 - 40 mm aggregate						
Beds; 100 mm thick; to pipes						
100 mm nominal size	-	0.17	2.17	3.66	m	**5.83**
150 mm nominal size	-	0.17	2.17	3.66	m	**5.83**
225 mm nominal size	-	0.20	2.55	4.39	m	**6.94**
300 mm nominal size	-	0.23	2.93	5.13	m	**8.06**
375 mm nominal size	-	0.27	3.44	5.86	m	**9.30**
450 mm nominal size	-	0.30	3.83	6.59	m	**10.42**
600 mm nominal size	-	0.33	4.21	7.32	m	**11.53**
900 mm nominal size	-	0.40	5.10	8.78	m	**13.89**
1200 mm nominal size	-	0.54	6.89	11.71	m	**18.60**

R DISPOSAL SYSTEMS

Item	PC £	Labour hours	Labour £	Material £	Unit	Total rate £
Beds; 150 mm thick; to pipes						
100 mm nominal size	-	0.23	2.93	5.13	m	8.06
150 mm nominal size	-	0.27	3.44	5.86	m	9.30
225 mm nominal size	-	0.30	3.83	6.59	m	10.42
300 mm nominal size	-	0.33	4.21	7.32	m	11.53
375 mm nominal size	-	0.40	5.10	8.78	m	13.89
450 mm nominal size	-	0.43	5.48	9.52	m	15.00
600 mm nominal size	-	0.50	6.38	10.98	m	17.36
900 mm nominal size	-	0.63	8.03	13.91	m	21.95
1200 mm nominal size	-	0.77	9.82	16.84	m	26.66
Beds and benchings; beds 100 mm thick; to pipes						
100 mm nominal size	-	0.33	4.21	6.59	m	10.80
150 mm nominal size	-	0.38	4.85	7.32	m	12.17
225 mm nominal size	-	0.45	5.74	8.78	m	14.52
300 mm nominal size	-	0.53	6.76	10.25	m	17.01
375 mm nominal size	-	0.68	8.67	13.18	m	21.85
450 mm nominal size	-	0.80	10.20	15.37	m	25.57
600 mm nominal size	-	1.02	13.01	19.77	m	32.78
900 mm nominal size	-	1.65	21.04	32.21	m	53.25
1200 mm nominal size	-	2.44	31.12	47.58	m	78.70
Beds and benchings; beds 150 mm thick; to pipes						
100 mm nominal size	-	0.38	4.85	7.32	m	12.17
150 mm nominal size	-	0.42	5.36	8.05	m	13.41
225 mm nominal size	-	0.53	6.76	10.25	m	17.01
300 mm nominal size	-	0.68	8.67	13.18	m	21.85
375 mm nominal size	-	0.80	10.20	15.37	m	25.57
450 mm nominal size	-	0.94	11.99	18.30	m	30.29
600 mm nominal size	-	1.20	15.30	23.42	m	38.73
900 mm nominal size	-	1.91	24.36	37.34	m	61.70
1200 mm nominal size	-	2.70	34.43	52.70	m	87.14
Beds and coverings; 100 mm thick; to pipes						
100 mm nominal size	-	0.50	6.38	8.78	m	15.16
150 mm nominal size	-	0.58	7.40	10.25	m	17.65
225 mm nominal size	-	0.83	10.59	14.64	m	25.23
300 mm nominal size	-	1.00	12.75	17.57	m	30.32
375 mm nominal size	-	1.21	15.43	21.23	m	36.66
450 mm nominal size	-	1.42	18.11	24.89	m	43.00
600 mm nominal size	-	1.83	23.34	32.21	m	55.55
900 mm nominal size	-	2.79	35.58	49.05	m	84.63
1200 mm nominal size	-	3.83	48.85	67.35	m	116.19
Beds and coverings; 150 mm thick; to pipes						
100 mm nominal size	-	0.75	9.57	13.18	m	22.74
150 mm nominal size	-	0.83	10.59	14.64	m	25.23
225 mm nominal size	-	1.08	13.77	19.03	m	32.81
300 mm nominal size	-	1.30	16.58	22.69	m	39.27
375 mm nominal size	-	1.50	19.13	26.35	m	45.48
450 mm nominal size	-	1.79	22.83	31.47	m	54.30
600 mm nominal size	-	2.16	27.55	38.06	m	65.61
900 mm nominal size	-	3.54	45.15	62.22	m	107.37
1200 mm nominal size	-	5.00	63.77	87.84	m	151.61

R DISPOSAL SYSTEMS

Item	PC £	Labour hours	Labour £	Material £	Unit	Total rate £
R12 DRAINAGE BELOW GROUND - cont'd						
Plain in situ ready mixed designated concrete; C20 - 40 mm aggregate						
Beds; 100 mm thick; to pipes						
100 mm nominal size	-	0.17	2.17	3.77	m	**5.94**
150 mm nominal size	-	0.17	2.17	3.77	m	**5.94**
225 mm nominal size	-	0.20	2.55	4.52	m	**7.07**
300 mm nominal size	-	0.23	2.93	5.28	m	**8.21**
375 mm nominal size	-	0.27	3.44	6.02	m	**9.47**
450 mm nominal size	-	0.30	3.83	6.78	m	**10.61**
600 mm nominal size	-	0.33	4.21	7.53	m	**11.74**
900 mm nominal size	-	0.40	5.10	9.04	m	**14.14**
1200 mm nominal size	-	0.54	6.89	12.05	m	**18.94**
Beds; 150 mm thick; to pipes						
100 mm nominal size	-	0.23	2.93	5.28	m	**8.21**
150 mm nominal size	-	0.27	3.44	6.02	m	**9.47**
225 mm nominal size	-	0.30	3.83	6.78	m	**10.61**
300 mm nominal size	-	0.33	4.21	7.53	m	**11.74**
375 mm nominal size	-	0.40	5.10	9.04	m	**14.14**
450 mm nominal size	-	0.43	5.48	9.79	m	**15.28**
600 mm nominal size	-	0.50	6.38	11.30	m	**17.68**
900 mm nominal size	-	0.63	8.03	14.31	m	**22.35**
1200 mm nominal size	-	0.77	9.82	17.32	m	**27.14**
Beds and benchings; beds 100 mm thick; to pipes						
100 mm nominal size	-	0.33	4.21	6.78	m	**10.99**
150 mm nominal size	-	0.38	4.85	7.53	m	**12.38**
225 mm nominal size	-	0.45	5.74	9.04	m	**14.78**
300 mm nominal size	-	0.53	6.76	10.54	m	**17.30**
375 mm nominal size	-	0.68	8.67	13.56	m	**22.23**
450 mm nominal size	-	0.80	10.20	15.81	m	**26.01**
600 mm nominal size	-	1.02	13.01	20.34	m	**33.35**
900 mm nominal size	-	1.65	21.04	33.14	m	**54.18**
1200 mm nominal size	-	2.44	31.12	48.95	m	**80.06**
Beds and benchings; beds 150 mm thick; to pipes						
100 mm nominal size	-	0.38	4.85	7.53	m	**12.38**
150 mm nominal size	-	0.42	5.36	8.28	m	**13.64**
225 mm nominal size	-	0.53	6.76	10.54	m	**17.30**
300 mm nominal size	-	0.68	8.67	13.56	m	**22.23**
375 mm nominal size	-	0.80	10.20	15.81	m	**26.01**
450 mm nominal size	-	0.94	11.99	18.82	m	**30.81**
600 mm nominal size	-	1.20	15.30	24.10	m	**39.40**
900 mm nominal size	-	1.91	24.36	38.41	m	**62.77**
1200 mm nominal size	-	2.70	34.43	54.22	m	**88.66**
Beds and coverings; 100 mm thick; to pipes						
100 mm nominal size	-	0.50	6.38	9.04	m	**15.41**
150 mm nominal size	-	0.58	7.40	10.54	m	**17.94**
225 mm nominal size	-	0.83	10.59	15.06	m	**25.65**
300 mm nominal size	-	1.00	12.75	18.07	m	**30.83**
375 mm nominal size	-	1.21	15.43	21.84	m	**37.27**
450 mm nominal size	-	1.42	18.11	25.60	m	**43.71**
600 mm nominal size	-	1.83	23.34	33.14	m	**56.47**
900 mm nominal size	-	2.79	35.58	50.46	m	**86.04**
1200 mm nominal size	-	3.83	48.85	69.28	m	**118.13**

R DISPOSAL SYSTEMS

Item	PC £	Labour hours	Labour £	Material £	Unit	Total rate £
Beds and coverings; 150 mm thick; to pipes						
100 mm nominal size	-	0.75	9.57	13.56	m	23.12
150 mm nominal size	-	0.83	10.59	15.06	m	25.65
225 mm nominal size	-	1.08	13.77	19.58	m	33.35
300 mm nominal size	-	1.30	16.58	23.34	m	39.92
375 mm nominal size	-	1.50	19.13	27.11	m	46.24
450 mm nominal size	-	1.79	22.83	32.38	m	55.21
600 mm nominal size	-	2.16	27.55	39.16	m	66.71
900 mm nominal size	-	3.54	45:15	64.01	m	109.16
1200 mm nominal size	-	5.00	63.77	90.37	m	154.14
NOTE: The following items unless otherwise described include for all appropriate joints/ couplings in the running length. The prices for gullies and rainwater shoes, etc. include for appropriate joints to pipes and for setting on and surrounding accessory with site mixed in situ concrete 10.00 N/mm2 - 40 mm aggregate (1:3:6).						
Cast iron "Timesaver" drain pipes and fittings or other equal and approved; BS 437; coated; with mechanical coupling joints						
100 mm pipes; laid straight	20.55	0.46	4.97	28.17	m	33.14
100 mm pipes; in runs not exceeding 3 m long	20.55	0.63	6.81	43.96	m	50.77
Extra for						
bend; medium radius	24.64	0.56	6.05	38.23	nr	44.28
bend; medium radius with access	68.45	0.56	6.05	86.56	nr	92.61
bend; long radius	40.71	0.56	6.05	54.80	nr	60.85
rest bend	28.26	0.56	6.05	41.06	nr	47.11
single branch	32.69	0.69	7.46	59.44	nr	66.90
single branch; with access	75.39	0.79	8.54	106.55	nr	115.09
double branch	55.57	0.88	9.51	97.36	nr	106.86
isolated "Timesaver" joint	13.18	0.32	3.46	14.54	nr	17.99
transitional pipe; for WC	19.29	0.46	4.97	35.81	nr	40.78
150 mm pipes; laid straight	38.05	0.56	6.05	48.98	m	55.03
150 mm pipes; in runs not exceeding 3 m long	-	0.76	8.21	72.06	m	80.27
Extra for						
bend; medium radius	56.68	0.65	7.02	73.67	nr	80.70
bend; medium radius with access	120.21	0.65	7.02	143.76	nr	150.78
bend; long radius	75.91	0.65	7.02	92.74	nr	99.76
diminishing pipe	32.11	0.65	7.02	44.42	nr	51.45
single branch	70.58	0.79	8.54	79.55	nr	88.09
isolated "Timesaver" joint	15.95	0.39	4.21	17.60	nr	21.81
Accessories in "Timesaver" cast iron or other equal and approved; with mechanical coupling joints						
Gully fittings; comprising low invert gully trap and round hopper						
75 mm outlet	16.50	0.83	8.97	32.54	nr	41.51
100 mm outlet	26.18	0.88	9.51	47.19	nr	56.70
150 mm outlet	65.13	1.20	12.97	93.96	nr	106.93
Add to above for bellmouth 300 mm high; circular plain grating						
100 mm nominal size; 200 mm grating	27.26	0.42	4.54	48.00	nr	52.54
100 mm nominal size; 100 mm horizontal inlet; 200 mm grating	33.33	0.42	4.54	54.70	nr	59.24
100 mm nominal size; 100 mm horizontal inlet; 200 mm grating	34.18	0.42	4.54	55.63	nr	60.17

R DISPOSAL SYSTEMS

Item	PC £	Labour hours	Labour £	Material £	Unit	Total rate £
R12 DRAINAGE BELOW GROUND - cont'd						
Accessories in "Timesaver" cast iron - cont'd						
Yard gully (Deans); trapped; galvanized sediment pan; 267 mm round heavy grating						
100 mm outlet	176.90	2.68	28.96	228.29	nr	257.25
Yard gully (garage); trapless; galvanized sediment pan; 267 mm round heavy grating						
100 mm outlet	172.78	2.50	27.01	209.66	nr	236.68
Yard gully (garage); trapped; with rodding eye, galvanised perforated sediment pan; stopper; 267 mm round heavy grating						
100 mm outlet	335.58	2.50	27.01	425.18	nr	452.20
Grease trap; internal access; galvanized perforated bucket; lid and frame						
100 mm outlet; 20 gallon capacity	307.45	3.70	39.98	379.54	nr	419.52
Cast iron "Ensign" lightweight drain pipes and fittings or other equal and approved; EN 877; ductile iron couplings						
100 mm pipes; laid straight	-	0.19	3.05	18.91	m	21.96
Extra for						
bend; long radius	-	0.19	3.05	33.90	nr	36.95
single branch	-	0.23	3.73	34.24	nr	37.97
150 mm pipes; laid straight	-	0.22	3.55	37.82	m	41.37
Extra for						
bend; medium radius	-	0.22	3.55	93.75	nr	97.29
single branch	-	0.28	4.50	75.38	nr	79.88
Extra strength vitrified clay pipes and fittings; Hepworth "Supersleve" or other equal and approved; plain ends with push fit polypropylene flexible couplings						
100 mm pipes; laid straight	4.76	0.19	2.05	5.38	m	7.44
Extra for						
bend	4.40	0.19	2.05	9.30	nr	11.36
access bend	28.97	0.19	2.05	37.07	nr	39.12
rest bend	7.79	0.19	2.05	13.14	nr	15.19
access pipe	25.17	0.19	2.05	32.41	nr	34.46
socket adaptor	4.67	0.16	1.73	7.62	nr	9.35
adaptor to "HepSeal" pipe	3.80	0.16	1.73	6.64	nr	8.37
saddle	9.33	0.69	7.46	13.27	nr	20.72
single junction	9.51	0.23	2.49	17.42	nr	19.91
single access junction	33.50	0.23	2.49	44.54	nr	47.02
150 mm pipes; laid straight	9.10	0.23	2.49	10.28	m	12.77
Extra for						
bend	9.07	0.22	2.38	17.90	nr	20.27
access bend	4.81	0.22	2.38	46.43	nr	48.81
rest bend	11.65	0.22	2.38	20.82	nr	23.20
taper pipe	13.42	0.22	2.38	20.59	nr	22.96
access pipe	32.69	0.22	2.38	43.84	nr	46.22
socket adaptor	8.79	0.19	2.05	14.14	nr	16.19
adaptor to "HepSeal" pipe	6.24	0.19	2.05	11.25	nr	13.30
saddle	13.28	0.83	8.97	19.95	nr	28.92
single junction	12.14	0.28	3.03	25.56	nr	28.59
single access junction	47.59	0.28	3.03	65.63	nr	68.66

R DISPOSAL SYSTEMS

Item	PC £	Labour hours	Labour £	Material £	Unit	Total rate £
Extra strength vitrified clay pipes and fittings; Hepworth "SuperSeal" or equivalent; socketted; with push-fit flexible joints						
150 mm pipes; laid straight	11.30	0.30	3.24	12.77	m	16.02
Extra for						
bend	20.75	0.23	2.49	19.62	nr	22.11
rest bend	11.65	0.20	2.16	9.34	nr	11.50
stopper	6.55	0.15	1.62	7.40	nr	9.02
taper reducer	11.24	0.23	2.49	8.87	nr	11.35
saddle	13.28	0.75	8.10	15.01	nr	23.11
single junction	-4.52	0.30	3.24	25.54	nr	28.78
225 mm pipes; laid straight	22.37	0.38	4.11	25.28	m	29.39
Extra for						
bend	46.41	0.30	3.24	44.86	nr	48.10
rest bend	56.70	0.30	3.24	56.49	nr	59.73
stopper	9.86	0.19	2.05	11.14	nr	13.20
taper reducer	33.49	0.30	3.24	30.26	nr	33.50
saddle	13.28	1.00	10.81	15.01	nr	25.81
single junction	82.44	0.38	4.11	83.05	nr	87.15
300 mm pipes; laid straight	34.31	0.50	5.40	38.78	m	44.18
Extra for						
bend	88.15	0.40	4.32	87.98	nr	92.30
rest bend	125.61	0.40	4.32	130.31	nr	134.63
stopper	20.60	0.25	2.70	23.28	nr	25.98
taper reducer	90.41	0.40	4.32	90.53	nr	94.86
saddle	13.28	1.33	14.37	15.01	nr	29.38
single junction	172.61	0.50	5.40	179.55	nr	184.96
400 mm pipes; laid straight	71.88	0.67	7.24	81.23	m	88.47
Extra for						
bend	270.09	0.54	5.83	280.85	nr	286.68
single unequal junction	253.06	0.67	7.24	253.49	nr	260.73
450 mm pipes; laid straight	93.36	0.83	8.97	105.50	m	114.47
Extra for						
bend	336.15	0.67	7.24	348.22	nr	355.46
single unequal junction	302.74	0.83	8.97	299.91	nr	308.88
British Standard quality vitrified clay pipes and fittings; socketted; cement and sand (1:2) joints						
100 mm pipes; laid straight	6.10	0.37	4.00	6.99	m	10.98
Extra for						
bend (short/medium/knuckle)	4.27	0.30	3.24	4.92	nr	8.16
bend (long/rest/elbow)	10.02	0.30	3.24	9.35	nr	12.59
single junction	11.19	0.37	4.00	10.01	nr	14.01
double collar	7.35	0.25	2.70	8.40	nr	11.10
150 mm pipes; laid straight	9.37	0.42	4.54	10.69	m	15.23
Extra for						
bend (short/medium/knuckle)	9.37	0.33	3.57	7.51	nr	11.08
bend (long/rest/elbow)	16.93	0.33	3.57	16.05	nr	19.62
taper	22.13	0.33	3.57	21.61	nr	25.18
single junction	18.52	0.42	4.54	16.82	nr	21.35
double collar	12.24	0.28	3.03	13.93	nr	16.95
225 mm pipes; laid straight	18.58	0.51	5.51	21.23	m	26.74
Extra for						
bend (short/medium/knuckle)	29.37	0.41	4.43	27.00	nr	31.44
double collar	28.65	0.33	3.57	32.47	nr	36.03
300 mm pipes; laid straight	31.14	0.69	7.46	35.42	m	42.88

R DISPOSAL SYSTEMS

Item	PC £	Labour hours	Labour £	Material £	Unit	Total rate £
R12 DRAINAGE BELOW GROUND - cont'd						
Accessories in vitrified clay; set in concrete; with polypropylene coupling joints to pipes						
Rodding point; with oval aluminium plate						
100 mm nominal size	23.59	0.46	4.97	30.85	nr	35.82
Gully fittings; comprising low back trap and square hopper; 150 mm x 150 mm square gully grid						
100 mm nominal size	21.79	0.79	8.54	31.53	nr	40.07
Access gully; trapped with rodding eye and integral vertical back inlet; stopper; 150 mm x 150 mm square gully grid						
100 mm nominal size	39.76	0.60	6.48	49.11	nr	55.60
Inspection chamber; comprising base; 300 mm or 450 mm raising piece; integral alloy cover and frame; 100 mm inlets						
straight through; 2 nr inlets	121.98	1.85	19.99	143.35	nr	163.34
Accessories in polypropylene; cover set in concrete; with coupling joints to pipes						
Inspection chamber; 5 nr 100 mm inlets; cast iron cover and frame						
475 mm diameter x 585 mm deep	146.84	2.13	23.02	172.53	nr	195.55
475 mm diameter x 930 mm deep	179.67	2.31	24.96	209.63	nr	234.59
Accessories in vitrified clay; set in concrete; with cement and sand (1:2) joints to pipes						
Gully fittings; comprising low back trap and square hopper; square gully grid						
100 mm outlet; 150 mm x 150 mm grid	32.99	0.93	10.05	37.65	nr	47.69
Yard gully (mud); trapped with rodding eye; galvanized square bucket; stopper; square hinged grate and frame						
100 mm outlet; 225 mm x 225 mm grid	106.04	2.78	30.04	120.27	nr	150.31
150 mm outlet; 300 mm x 300 mm grid	163.08	3.70	39.98	185.10	nr	225.08
Yard gully (garage); trapped with rodding eye; galvanized perforated round bucket; stopper; round hinged grate and frame						
100 mm outlet; 273 mm grid	118.08	2.78	30.04	133.88	nr	163.92
150 mm outlet; 368 mm grid	162.44	3.70	39.98	184.00	nr	223.98
Road gully; trapped with rodding eye and stopper (grate not included)						
300 mm x 600 mm x 100 mm outlet	57.69	3.05	32.96	82.13	nr	115.08
300 mm x 600 mm x 150 mm outlet	59.07	3.05	32.96	83.69	nr	116.65
400 mm x 750 mm x 150 mm outlet	68.51	3.70	39.98	103.13	nr	143.11
450 mm x 900 mm x 150 mm outlet	92.70	4.65	50.25	135.59	nr	185.84
Grease trap; with internal access; galvanized perforated bucket; lid and frame						
450 mm x 300 mm x 525 mm deep; 100 mm outlet	336.03	3.24	35.01	398.32	nr	433.33
600 mm x 450 mm x 600 mm deep; 100 mm outlet	517.52	3.89	42.03	610.09	nr	652.12
Interceptor; trapped with inspection arm; lever locking stopper; chain and staple; cement and sand (1:2) joints to pipes; building in, and cutting and fitting brickwork around						
100 mm outlet; 100 mm inlet	74.33	3.70	39.98	84.41	nr	124.39
150 mm outlet; 150 mm inlet	105.48	4.16	44.95	119.61	nr	164.56
225 mm outlet; 225 mm inlet	287.11	4.63	50.03	324.90	nr	374.93

R DISPOSAL SYSTEMS

Item	PC £	Labour hours	Labour £	Material £	Unit	Total rate £
Accessories; grates and covers						
Aluminium alloy gully grids; set in position						
120 mm x 120 mm	2.36	0.09	0.97	2.67	nr	3.64
150 mm x 150 mm	2.36	0.09	0.97	2.67	nr	3.64
225 mm x 225 mm	7.02	0.09	0.97	7.93	nr	8.91
100 mm diameter	2.36	0.09	0.97	2.67	nr	3.64
150 mm diameter	3.60	0.09	0.97	4.07	nr	5.04
225 mm diameter	7.85	0.09	0.97	8.87	nr	9.85
Aluminium alloy sealing plates and frames; set in cement and sand (1:3)						
150 mm x 150 mm	9.06	0.23	2.49	10.33	nr	12.81
225 mm x 225 mm	16.58	0.23	2.49	18.83	nr	21.31
140 mm diameter (for 100 mm)	7.38	0.23	2.49	8.43	nr	10.92
197 mm diameter (for 150 mm)	10.62	0.23	2.49	12.09	nr	14.58
273 mm diameter (for 225 mm)	17.00	0.23	2.49	19.31	nr	21.79
Coated cast iron heavy duty road gratings and frame; BS 497 Tables 6 and 7; bedding and pointing in cement and sand (1:3); one course half brick thick wall in semi-engineering bricks in cement mortar (1:3)						
440 mm x 400 mm road grating and frame; ref D/TRI D400	29.00	2.31	24.96	34.64	nr	59.60
440 mm x 400 mm hinged road grating and frame; ref D400	29.00	2.31	24.96	34.64	nr	59.60
500 mm x 350 mm hinged road grating and frame; ref D400	39.00	2.31	24.96	45.67	nr	70.63
Vibrated concrete pipes and fittings; with flexible joints; BS 5911 Part 1						
300 mm pipes Class M; laid straight	11.40	0.65	7.02	12.88	m	19.90
Extra for						
bend; 22.5 degree	-	0.65	7.02	48.30	nr	55.32
bend; 45 degree	-	0.65	7.02	80.50	nr	87.52
junction; 300 mm x 100 mm	23.49	0.46	4.97	25.28	nr	30.25
450 mm pipes Class H; laid straight	24.56	1.02	11.02	27.75	m	38.77
Extra for						
bend; 22.5 degree	-	1.02	11.02	104.07	nr	115.09
bend; 45 degree	-	1.02	11.02	173.45	nr	184.48
junction; 450 mm x 150 mm	25.94	0.65	7.02	27.92	nr	34.94
600 mm pipes Class H; laid straight	33.16	1.48	15.99	37.47	m	53.46
Extra for						
bend; 22.5 degree	-	1.48	15.99	140.51	nr	156.50
bend; 45 degree	-	1.48	15.99	234.18	nr	250.17
junction; 600 mm x 150 mm	26.56	0.83	8.97	28.58	nr	37.55
900 mm pipes Class H; laid straight	84.43	2.59	27.99	95.41	m	123.39
Extra for						
bend; 22.5 degree	-	2.59	27.99	357.78	nr	385.76
bend; 45 degree	-	2.59	27.99	596.29	nr	624.28
junction; 900 mm x 225 mm	45.28	1.02	11.02	48.74	nr	59.76
1200 mm pipes Class H; laid straight	107.45	3.70	39.98	121.43	m	161.41
Extra for						
bend; 22.5 degree	-	3.70	39.98	455.34	nr	495.33
bend; 45 degree	-	3.70	39.98	758.91	nr	798.89
junction; 300 mm x 100 mm	55.26	1.48	15.99	59.47	nr	75.46

R DISPOSAL SYSTEMS

Item	PC £	Labour hours	Labour £	Material £	Unit	Total rate £
R12 DRAINAGE BELOW GROUND - cont'd						
Accessories in precast concrete; top set in with rodding eye and stopper; cement and sand (1:2) joint to pipe						
Concrete road gully; BS 5911; trapped with rodding eye and stopper; cement and sand (1:2) joint to pipe						
450 mm diameter x 1050 mm deep; 100 mm or 150 mm outlet	26.09	4.39	47.44	47.59	nr	95.03
"Osmadrain" uPVC pipes and fittings or other equal and approved; BS 4660; with ring seal joints						
82 mm pipes; laid straight	6.94	0.15	1.62	7.84	m	9.47
Extra for						
bend; short radius	12.12	0.13	1.40	13.37	nr	14.78
spigot/socket bend	10.19	0.13	1.40	11.24	nr	12.65
adaptor	5.32	0.07	0.76	5.87	nr	6.62
single junction	15.77	0.18	1.95	17.40	nr	19.34
slip coupler	7.51	0.07	0.76	8.28	nr	9.04
100 mm pipes; laid straight	5.33	0.17	1.84	6.83	m	8.67
Extra for						
bend; short radius	14.09	0.15	1.62	15.18	nr	16.81
bend; long radius	22.82	0.15	1.62	23.37	nr	24.99
spigot/socket bend	11.91	0.15	1.62	16.95	nr	18.57
socket plug	5.71	0.04	0.43	6.30	nr	6.73
adjustable double socket bend	15.59	0.15	1.62	20.86	nr	22.49
adaptor to clay	13.98	0.09	0.97	15.16	nr	16.13
single junction	16.82	0.21	2.27	16.74	nr	19.01
sealed access junction	35.35	0.19	2.05	37.19	nr	39.24
slip coupler	7.51	0.09	0.97	8.28	nr	9.25
160 mm pipes; laid straight	12.04	0.21	2.27	15.09	m	17.36
Extra for						
bend; short radius	31.00	0.18	1.95	33.38	nr	35.32
spigot/socket bend	28.11	0.18	1.95	38.09	nr	40.04
socket plug	11.65	0.07	0.76	12.86	nr	13.61
adaptor to clay	28.08	0.12	1.30	30.26	nr	31.55
level invert taper	16.25	0.18	1.95	24.20	nr	26.14
single junction	50.76	0.24	2.59	55.99	nr	58.59
slip coupler	18.32	0.11	1.19	20.21	nr	21.40
uPVC Osma "Ultra-Rib" ribbed pipes and fittings or other equal and approved; WIS approval; with sealed ring push-fit joints						
150 mm pipes; laid straight	-	0.19	2.05	6.21	m	8.27
Extra for						
bend; short radius	16.87	0.17	1.84	18.24	nr	20.08
adaptor to 160 mm diameter upvc	20.98	0.10	1.08	22.39	nr	23.47
adaptor to clay	4.06	0.10	1.08	4.10	nr	5.18
level invert taper	7.36	0.18	1.95	7.00	nr	8.94
single junction	30.34	0.22	2.38	31.60	nr	33.98
225 mm pipes; laid straight	12.73	0.22	2.38	14.39	m	16.77
Extra for						
bend; short radius	64.57	0.20	2.16	70.37	nr	72.53
adaptor to clay	53.64	0.13	1.40	57.45	nr	58.86
level invert taper	11.23	0.20	2.16	9.80	nr	11.96
single junction	95.20	0.27	2.92	100.70	nr	103.62

R DISPOSAL SYSTEMS

Item	PC £	Labour hours	Labour £	Material £	Unit	Total rate £
300 mm pipes; laid straight	18.91	0.32	3.46	21.38	m	**24.83**
Extra for						
bend; short radius	101.70	0.29	3.13	110.91	nr	**114.04**
adaptor to clay	141.11	0.14	1.51	153.10	nr	**154.61**
level invert taper	33.67	0.29	3.13	33.30	nr	**36.43**
single junction	204.44	0.37	4.00	219.11	nr	**223.11**
Interconnecting drainage channel 100 wide; ACO Polymer Products Ltd or other equal and approved; reinforced slotted galvanised steel grating ref 423/4; bedding and haunching in in situ concrete (not included)						
100 mm wide						
laid level or to falls	-	0.46	4.97	33.00	m	**37.97**
extra for sump unit	-	1.39	15.02	49.36	nr	**64.38**
extra for end caps	-	0.09	0.97	3.25	nr	**4.22**
Interconnecting drainage channel; "Birco-lite" ref 8012 or other equal and approved; Marshalls Plc; galvanised steel grating ref 8041; bedding and haunching in in situ concrete (not included)						
100 mm wide						
laid level or to falls	-	0.46	4.97	34.93	m	**39.90**
extra for 100 mm diameter trapped outlet unit	-	1.39	15.02	60.36	nr	**75.38**
extra for end caps	-	0.09	0.97	4.36	nr	**5.33**
Accessories in uPVC; with ring seal joints to pipes (unless otherwise described)						
Cast iron access point						
110 mm diameter	23.29	0.75	8.10	25.69	nr	**33.80**
Rodding eye						
110 mm diameter	28.81	0.43	4.65	35.45	nr	**40.10**
Universal gulley fitting; comprising gulley trap, plain hopper						
150 mm x 150 mm grate	25.08	0.93	10.05	32.80	nr	**42.85**
Bottle gulley; comprising gulley with bosses closed; sealed access covers						
217 mm x 217 mm grate	45.36	0.78	8.43	55.16	nr	**63.59**
Shallow access pipe; light duty screw down access door assembly						
110 mm diameter	57.53	0.78	8.43	68.59	nr	**77.02**
Shallow access inspection junction; 3 nr 110 mm inlets; light duty screw down access door assembly						
110 mm diameter	89.13	1.11	11.99	100.52	nr	**112.52**
Shallow inspection chamber; 250 mm diameter; 600 mm deep; sealed cover and frame						
4 nr 110 mm outlets/inlets	90.45	1.28	13.83	118.08	nr	**131.91**
Universal inspection chamber; 450 mm diameter; single seal cast iron cover and frame; 4 nr 110 mmoutlets/inlets						
500 mm deep	171.66	1.35	14.59	207.66	nr	**222.25**
730 mm deep	192.93	1.60	17.29	234.79	nr	**252.08**
960 mm deep	214.19	1.85	19.99	261.91	nr	**281.90**

R DISPOSAL SYSTEMS

Item	PC £	Labour hours	Labour £	Material £	Unit	Total rate £
R12 DRAINAGE BELOW GROUND - cont'd						
Accessories in uPVC - cont'd						
Equal manhole base; 750 mm diameter						
6 nr 160 mm outlets/inlets	210.97	1.21	13.07	243.72	nr	**256.79**
Unequal manhole base; 750 mm diameter						
2 nr 160 mm, 4nr 110 mm outlets/inlets	171.07	1.21	13.07	199.70	nr	**212.78**
Kerb to gullies; class B engineering bricks on edge to three sides in cement mortar (1:3) rendering in cement mortar (1:3) to top and two sides and skirting to brickwork 230 mm high; dishing in cement mortar (1:3) to gully; steel trowelled						
230 mm x 230 mm internally	-	1.39	15.02	1.20	nr	**16.22**
Excavating; by machine						
Manholes						
maximum depth not exceeding 1.00 m	-	0.19	2.07	4.29	m³	**6.37**
maximum depth not exceeding 2.00 m	-	0.21	2.29	4.72	m³	**7.02**
maximum depth not exceeding 4.00 m	-	0.25	2.73	5.52	m³	**8.25**
Excavating; by hand						
Manholes						
maximum depth not exceeding 1.00 m	-	3.05	33.29	-	m³	**33.29**
maximum depth not exceeding 2.00 m	-	3.61	39.40	-	m³	**39.40**
maximum depth not exceeding 4.00 m	-	4.63	50.53	-	m³	**50.53**
Earthwork support (average "risk" prices)						
Maximum depth not exceeding 1.00 m						
distance between opposing faces not exceeding 2.00 m	-	0.14	1.53	2.06	m²	**3.58**
Maximum depth not exceeding 2.00 m						
distance between opposing faces not exceeding 2.00 m	-	0.18	1.96	3.82	m²	**5.78**
Maximum depth not exceeding 4.00 m						
distance between opposing faces not exceeding 2.00 m	-	0.22	2.40	5.58	m²	**7.98**
Disposal; by machine						
Excavated material						
off site; to tip not exceeding 13 km (using lorries) including Landfill Tax based on inactive waste	-	-	-	16.36	m³	**16.36**
on site; depositing on site in spoil heaps; average 50 m distance	-	0.14	1.53	2.88	m³	**4.41**
Disposal; by hand						
Excavated material						
off site; to tip not exceeding 13 km (using lorries) including Landfill Tax based on inactive waste	-	0.74	8.08	22.28	m³	**30.35**
on site; depositing on site in spoil heaps; average 50 m distance	-	1.20	13.10	-	m³	**13.10**
Filling to excavations; by machine						
Average thickness not exceeding 0.25 m						
arising excavations	-	0.14	1.53	2.02	m³	**3.55**
Filling to excavations; by hand						
Average thickness not exceeding 0.25 m						
arising from excavations	-	0.93	10.15	-	m³	**10.15**

R DISPOSAL SYSTEMS

Item	PC £	Labour hours	Labour £	Material £	Unit	Total rate £
Plain in situ ready mixed designated concrete; C10 - 40 mm aggregate						
Beds						
thickness not exceeding 150 mm	66.43	2.78	35.45	76.86	m³	112.32
thickness 150 mm - 450 mm	66.43	2.08	26.53	76.86	m³	103.39
thickness exceeding 450 mm	66.43	1.76	22.45	76.86	m³	99.31
Plain in situ ready mixed designated concrete; C20 - 20 mm aggregate						
Beds						
thickness not exceeding 150 mm	68.34	2.78	35.45	79.08	m³	114.53
thickness 150 mm - 450 mm	68.34	2.08	26.53	79.08	m³	105.60
thickness exceeding 450 mm	68.34	1.76	22.45	79.08	m³	101.52
Plain in situ ready mixed designated concrete; C25 - 20 mm aggregate; (small quantities)						
Benching in bottoms						
150 mm - 450 mm average thickness	65.50	8.33	124.25	75.78	m³	200.04
Reinforced in situ ready mixed designated concrete; C20 - 20 mm aggregate; (small quantities)						
Isolated cover slabs						
thickness not exceeding 150 mm	65.09	6.48	82.64	75.31	m³	157.95
Reinforcement; fabric to BS 4483; lapped; in beds or suspended slabs						
Ref A98 (1.54 kg/m²)						
400 mm minimum laps	0.95	0.11	1.66	1.12	m²	2.78
Ref A142 (2.22 kg/m²)						
400 mm minimum laps	0.98	0.11	1.66	1.16	m²	2.82
Ref A193 (3.02 kg/m²)						
400 mm minimum laps	1.34	0.11	1.66	1.59	m²	3.24
Formwork; basic finish						
Soffits of isolated cover slabs						
horizontal	-	2.64	41.80	4.52	m²	46.32
Edges of isolated cover slabs						
height not exceeding 250 mm	-	0.78	12.35	1.41	m	13.76
Precast concrete rectangular access and inspection chambers; "Hepworth" chambers or other equal and approved; comprising cover frame to receive manhole cover (not included) intermediate wall sections and base section with cut outs; bedding; jointing and pointing in cement mortar (1:3) on prepared bed						
Drainage chamber; size 600 mm x 450 mm internally; depth to invert						
600 mm deep	-	4.16	44.95	81.78	nr	126.73
900 mm deep	-	5.55	59.97	102.78	nr	162.75
Drainage chamber; 1200 mm x 750 mm reducing to 600 mm x 600 mm; no base unit; depth of invert						
1050 mm deep	-	6.94	74.99	153.21	nr	228.20
1650 mm deep	-	8.33	90.01	259.11	nr	349.12
2250 mm deep	-	10.18	110.00	364.34	nr	474.34

R DISPOSAL SYSTEMS

Item	PC £	Labour hours	Labour £	Material £	Unit	Total rate £
R12 DRAINAGE BELOW GROUND - cont'd						
Precast concrete circular manhole rings; BS5911 Part 1; bedding, jointing and pointing in cement mortar (1:3) on prepared bed						
Chamber or shaft rings; plain						
900 mm diameter	42.66	5.09	55.00	46.58	m	101.58
1050 mm diameter	46.92	6.01	64.94	51.83	m	116.77
1200 mm diameter	59.71	6.94	74.99	66.27	m	141.26
Chamber or shaft rings; reinforced						
1350 mm diameter	85.31	7.86	84.93	94.48	m	179.42
1500 mm diameter	102.37	8.79	94.98	114.18	m	209.16
1800 mm diameter	127.97	11.10	119.94	143.74	m	263.68
2100 mm diameter	179.15	13.88	149.98	200.83	m	350.81
extra for step irons built in	3.41	0.14	1.51	3.67	nr	5.19
Reducing slabs						
1200 mm diameter	68.25	5.55	59.97	74.79	nr	134.76
1350 mm diameter	89.58	8.79	94.98	99.08	nr	194.06
1500 mm diameter	110.90	10.18	110.00	122.69	nr	232.69
1800 mm diameter	153.55	12.95	139.93	170.61	nr	310.54
Heavy duty cover slabs; to suit rings						
900 mm diameter	38.39	2.78	30.04	41.99	nr	72.03
1050 mm diameter	46.92	3.24	35.01	51.30	nr	86.31
1200 mm diameter	59.71	3.70	39.98	65.60	nr	105.58
1350 mm diameter	85.31	4.16	44.95	93.82	nr	138.77
1500 mm diameter	102.37	4.63	50.03	112.85	nr	162.88
1800 mm diameter	140.76	5.55	59.97	155.20	nr	215.17
2100 mm diameter	285.78	6.48	70.02	312.58	nr	382.60
Common bricks; in cement mortar (1:3)						
Walls to manholes						
one brick thick	28.80	2.22	48.31	37.34	m²	85.65
one and a half brick thick	43.20	3.24	70.51	56.00	m²	126.51
Projections of footings						
two brick thick	57.60	4.53	98.58	74.67	m²	173.25
Class A engineering bricks; in cement mortar (1:3)						
Walls to manholes						
one brick thick	49.62	2.50	54.40	61.42	m²	115.83
one and a half brick thick	49.62	3.61	78.56	63.43	m²	141.99
Projections of footings						
two brick thick	99.25	5.09	110.77	122.85	m²	233.61
Class B engineering bricks; in cement mortar (1:3)						
Walls to manholes						
one brick thick	35.45	2.50	54.40	45.01	m²	99.42
one and a half brick thick	53.17	3.61	78.56	67.52	m²	146.08
Projections of footings						
two brick thick	70.89	5.09	110.77	90.03	m²	200.80
Brickwork sundries						
Extra over for fair face; flush smooth pointing						
manhole walls	-	0.19	4.13	-	m²	4.13
Building ends of pipes into brickwork; making good fair face or rendering						
not exceeding 55 mm nominal size	-	0.09	1.96	-	nr	1.96
55 mm - 110 mm nominal size	-	0.14	3.05	-	nr	3.05
over 110 mm nominal size	-	0.19	4.13	-	nr	4.13

R DISPOSAL SYSTEMS

Item	PC £	Labour hours	Labour £	Material £	Unit	Total rate £
Step irons; BS 1247; malleable; galvanized; building into joints						
general purpose pattern	-	0.14	3.05	4.10	nr	**7.15**
Cement and sand (1:3) in situ finishings; steel trowelled						
13 mm work to manhole walls; one coat; to brickwork base over 300 wide	-	0.65	14.15	1.34	m²	**15.48**
Cast iron inspection chambers; with bolted flat covers; BS 437; bedded in cement mortar (1:3); with mechanical coupling joints						
100 mm x 100 mm						
one branch	97.94	0.97	10.48	108.72	nr	**119.20**
one branch either side	131.75	1.43	15.45	146.01	nr	**161.47**
150 mm x 100 mm						
one branch	136.54	1.16	12.53	151.29	nr	**163.82**
one branch either side	161.79	1.67	18.05	179.82	nr	**197.86**
150 mm x 150 mm						
one branch	169.41	1.25	13.51	188.22	nr	**201.73**
one branch either side	199.49	1.76	19.02	221.41	nr	**240.42**
Cast iron access covers and frames; unless otherwise described; Manhole Covers Ltd or other equal and approved; coated; bedding frame in cement and sand (1:3); cover in grease and sand						
Grade A; light duty; rectangular single seal solid top						
450 mm x 450 mm; ref A15	28.00	1.39	15.02	32.29	nr	**47.31**
600 mm x 450 mm; ref A15	32.00	1.39	15.02	36.83	nr	**51.85**
600 mm x 600 mm; ref A15	38.00	1.39	15.02	43.57	nr	**58.59**
Grade A; light duty; rectangular single seal recessed						
600 mm x 450 mm; ref E15B	55.00	1.39	15.02	62.20	nr	**77.22**
600 mm x 600 mm; ref E15C	58.00	1.39	15.02	65.63	nr	**80.65**
Grade A; light duty; rectangular double seal solid top						
450 mm x 450 mm; galvanized steel; ref 7123	48.00	1.39	15.02	54.36	nr	**69.38**
600 mm x 450 mm; ref E11B	59.00	1.39	15.02	66.61	nr	**81.63**
600 mm x 600 mm; ref E11C	66.00	1.39	15.02	74.46	nr	**89.48**
Grade A; light duty; rectangular double seal recessed						
450 mm x 450 mm; galvanized steel; ref 7123	40.00	1.39	15.02	45.53	nr	**60.55**
600 mm x 450 mm; ref E16B	60.00	1.39	15.02	67.72	nr	**82.74**
600 mm x 600 mm; ref E16C	68.00	1.39	15.02	76.66	nr	**91.68**
Grade B; medium duty; rectangular single seal solid top						
600 mm x 450 mm; ref B125	29.00	1.85	19.99	33.52	nr	**53.51**
600 mm x 600 mm; ref B125	34.00	1.85	19.99	39.16	nr	**59.15**
Grade B; medium duty; rectangular singular seal recessed						
600 mm x 450 mm; ref D400	192.00	1.85	19.99	213.33	nr	**233.32**
600 mm x 600 mm; ref D400	226.00	1.85	19.99	250.96	nr	**270.95**
Grade C; heavy duty solid top						
600 mm diameter; ductile iron; circular single seal; ref D400	89.50	1.85	19.99	100.12	nr	**120.11**
600 mm x 600 mm; ductile iron; double triangular; ref D400	44.00	2.78	30.04	50.19	nr	**80.23**

R DISPOSAL SYSTEMS

Item	PC £	Labour hours	Labour £	Material £	Unit	Total rate £
R12 DRAINAGE BELOW GROUND - cont'd						
British Standard best quality vitrified clay channels; bedding and jointing in cement and sand (1:2)						
Half section straight						
100 mm diameter x 1 m long	3.61	0.74	8.00	4.08	nr	12.07
150 mm diameter x 1 m long	6.01	0.93	10.05	6.79	nr	16.84
225 mm diameter x 1 m long	13.51	1.20	12.97	15.26	nr	28.23
300 mm diameter x 1 m long	27.72	1.48	15.99	31.33	nr	47.32
Half section bend						
100 mm diameter	7.94	0.56	6.05	8.98	nr	15.03
150 mm diameter	13.29	0.69	7.46	15.01	nr	22.47
225 mm diameter	43.29	0.93	10.05	48.92	nr	58.97
300 mm diameter	43.63	1.11	11.99	49.31	nr	61.30
Half section taper straight						
150 mm - 100 mm diameter	16.17	0.65	7.02	18.27	nr	25.29
225 mm - 150 mm diameter	36.09	0.83	8.97	40.79	nr	49.76
300 mm - 225 mm diameter	143.15	1.02	11.02	161.77	nr	172.79
Half section taper bend						
150 mm - 100 mm diameter	24.62	0.83	8.97	27.82	nr	36.79
225 mm - 150 mm diameter	70.53	1.06	11.45	79.70	nr	91.16
300 mm - 225 mm diameter	143.15	1.30	14.05	161.77	nr	175.82
Three quarter section branch bend						
100 mm diameter	8.76	0.46	4.97	9.90	nr	14.87
150 mm diameter	14.71	0.69	7.46	16.62	nr	24.08
225 mm diameter	53.68	0.93	10.05	60.67	nr	70.71
uPVC channels; with solvent weld or lip seal coupling joints; bedding in cement and sand						
Half section cut away straight; with coupling either end						
110 mm diameter	30.68	0.28	3.03	44.40	nr	47.42
160 mm diameter	57.62	0.37	4.00	82.97	nr	86.97
Half section cut away long radius bend; with coupling either end						
110 mm diameter	50.30	0.28	3.03	66.57	nr	69.60
160 mm diameter	108.75	0.37	4.00	140.76	nr	144.76
Channel adaptor to clay; with one coupling						
110 mm diameter	13.39	0.23	2.49	19.99	nr	22.48
160 mm diameter	29.91	0.31	3.35	42.73	nr	46.08
Half section bend						
110 mm diameter	19.42	0.31	3.35	22.39	nr	25.74
160 mm diameter	33.36	0.46	4.97	38.73	nr	43.70
Half section channel connector						
110 mm diameter	5.44	0.07	0.76	7.04	nr	7.79
Half section channel junction						
110 mm diameter	15.07	0.46	4.97	17.47	nr	22.44
Polypropylene slipper bend						
110 mm diameter	14.16	0.37	4.00	16.44	nr	20.44
Glass fibre septic tank; "Klargester" or other equal and approved; fixing lockable manhole cover and frame; placing in position						
3750 litre capacity; 2000 mm diameter; depth to invert						
1000 mm deep; standard grade	732.79	2.27	24.53	870.08	nr	894.61
1500 mm deep; heavy duty grade	921.90	2.54	27.45	1073.61	nr	1101.05

R DISPOSAL SYSTEMS

Item	PC £	Labour hours	Labour £	Material £	Unit	Total rate £
6000 litre capacity; 2300 mm diameter; depth to invert						
1000 mm deep; standard grade	1181.92	2.45	26.47	1373.81	nr	**1400.28**
1500 mm deep; heavy duty grade	1560.14	2.73	29.50	1780.87	nr	**1810.36**
9000 litre capacity; 2660 mm diameter; depth to invert						
1000 mm deep; standard grade	1796.53	2.64	28.53	2035.27	nr	**2063.80**
1500 mm deep; heavy duty grade	2363.85	2.91	31.44	2645.86	nr	**2677.30**
Glass fibre petrol interceptors; "Klargester" or other equal and approved; placing in position						
2000 litre capacity; 2370 mm x 1300 mm diameter; depth to invert						
1000 mm deep	827.35	2.50	27.01	890.43	nr	**917.45**
4000 litre capacity; 4370 mm x 1300 mm diameter; depth to invert						
1000 mm deep	1418.31	2.68	28.96	1526.46	nr	**1555.42**
R13 LAND DRAINAGE						
Excavating; by hand; grading bottoms; earthwork support; filling to within 150 mm of surface with gravel rejects; remainder filled with excavated material and compacting; disposal of surplus soil on site; spreading on site average 50 m						
Pipes not exceeding 200 nominal size						
average depth of trench 0.75 m	-	1.57	17.13	7.04	m	**24.18**
average depth of trench 1.00 m	-	2.08	22.70	11.14	m	**33.84**
average depth of trench 1.25 m	-	2.91	31.76	13.98	m	**45.73**
average depth of trench 1.50 m	-	5.00	54.57	17.02	m	**71.59**
average depth of trench 1.75 m	-	5.92	64.61	19.85	m	**84.45**
average depth of trench 2.00 m	-	6.85	74.76	22.89	m	**97.65**
Disposal; by machine						
Excavated material						
off site; to tip not exceeding 13 km (using lorries) including Landfill Tax based on inactive waste	-	-	-	16.36	m³	**16.36**
hand loaded	-	-	-	22.28	m³	**22.28**
Disposal; by hand						
Excavated material						
off site; to tip not exceeding 13 km (using lorries) including Landfill Tax based on inactive waste	-	0.74	8.08	22.28	m³	**30.35**
Vitrified clay perforated sub-soil pipes; BS 65; Hepworth "Hepline" or other equal and approved						
Pipes; laid straight						
100 mm diameter	5.47	0.20	2.16	6.18	m	**8.35**
150 mm diameter	9.95	0.25	2.70	11.24	m	**13.94**
225 mm diameter	18.28	0.33	3.57	20.66	m	**24.23**

S PIPED SUPPLY SYSTEMS

Item	PC £	Labour hours	Labour £	Material £	Unit	Total rate £
S10/S11 HOT AND COLD WATER						
Copper pipes; EN1057:1996; capillary fittings						
15 mm pipes; fixing with pipe clips and screwed	0.81	0.34	5.41	1.00	m	**6.41**
Extra for						
made bend	-	0.14	2.23	-	nr	**2.23**
stop end	0.82	0.10	1.59	0.91	nr	**2.50**
straight coupling	0.14	0.16	2.55	0.15	nr	**2.70**
union coupling	4.48	0.16	2.55	4.94	nr	**7.48**
reducing coupling	1.53	0.16	2.55	1.69	nr	**4.23**
copper to lead connector	3.49	0.20	3.18	3.85	nr	**7.04**
imperial to metric adaptor	1.79	0.20	3.18	1.98	nr	**5.16**
elbow	0.25	0.16	2.55	0.28	nr	**2.82**
backplate elbow	3.37	0.32	5.09	3.71	nr	**8.81**
return bend	5.04	0.16	2.55	5.56	nr	**8.11**
tee; equal	0.46	0.23	3.66	0.51	nr	**4.17**
tee; reducing	3.67	0.23	3.66	4.05	nr	**7.71**
straight tap connector	1.19	0.47	7.48	1.32	nr	**8.80**
bent tap connector	1.28	0.63	10.03	1.41	nr	**11.44**
tank connector	4.01	0.23	3.66	4.42	nr	**8.08**
22 mm pipes; fixing with pipe clips and screwed	1.63	0.40	6.37	1.92	m	**8.28**
Extra for						
made bend	-	0.19	3.02	-	nr	**3.02**
stop end	1.55	0.12	1.91	1.71	nr	**3.62**
straight coupling	0.36	0.20	3.18	0.40	nr	**3.58**
union coupling	7.18	0.20	3.18	7.92	nr	**11.10**
reducing coupling	0.62	0.20	3.18	0.68	nr	**3.87**
copper to lead connector	4.76	0.29	4.62	5.26	nr	**9.87**
elbow	0.64	0.20	3.18	0.70	nr	**3.89**
backplate elbow	7.22	0.41	6.53	7.97	nr	**14.50**
return bend	9.91	0.20	3.18	10.93	nr	**14.11**
tee; equal	1.48	0.31	4.93	1.63	nr	**6.56**
tee; reducing	1.18	0.31	4.93	1.30	nr	**6.23**
straight tap connector	1.28	0.16	2.55	1.42	nr	**3.96**
28 mm pipes; fixing with pipe clips and screwed	2.10	0.43	6.84	2.45	m	**9.30**
Extra for						
made bend	-	0.23	3.66	-	nr	**3.66**
stop end	2.76	0.14	2.23	3.04	nr	**5.27**
straight coupling	0.77	0.26	4.14	0.85	nr	**4.99**
reducing coupling	2.09	0.26	4.14	2.31	nr	**6.45**
union coupling	7.18	0.26	4.14	7.92	nr	**12.05**
copper to lead connector	8.96	0.36	5.73	9.89	nr	**15.62**
imperial to metric adaptor	4.61	0.36	5.73	5.09	nr	**10.82**
elbow	1.23	0.26	4.14	1.36	nr	**5.50**
return bend	12.65	0.26	4.14	13.96	nr	**18.10**
tee; equal	3.40	0.38	6.05	3.75	nr	**9.80**
tank connector	8.03	0.38	6.05	8.86	nr	**14.90**
35 mm pipes; fixing with pipe clips and screwed	4.58	0.50	7.96	5.25	m	**13.21**
Extra for						
made bend	-	0.28	4.46	-	nr	**4.46**
stop end	6.09	0.16	2.55	6.72	nr	**9.27**
straight coupling	2.48	0.31	4.93	2.74	nr	**7.67**
reducing coupling	4.94	0.31	4.93	5.45	nr	**10.38**
union coupling	13.72	0.31	4.93	15.14	nr	**20.07**
flanged connector	37.85	0.41	6.53	41.75	nr	**48.28**
elbow	5.33	0.31	4.93	5.88	nr	**10.82**
obtuse elbow	8.05	0.31	4.93	8.88	nr	**13.81**
tee; equal	8.68	0.43	6.84	9.58	nr	**16.42**
tank connector	10.29	0.43	6.84	11.35	nr	**18.20**

S PIPED SUPPLY SYSTEMS

Item	PC £	Labour hours	Labour £	Material £	Unit	Total rate £
42 mm pipes; fixing with pipe clips; plugged and screwed	5.61	0.56	8.91	6.41	m	15.33
Extra for						
made bend	-	0.37	5.89	-	nr	5.89
stop end	10.49	0.18	2.87	11.57	nr	14.44
straight coupling	4.15	0.36	5.73	4.58	nr	10.31
reducing coupling	8.26	0.36	5.73	9.11	nr	14.84
union coupling	20.06	0.36	5.73	22.13	nr	27.86
flanged connector	45.24	0.46	7.32	49.91	nr	57.23
elbow	8.81	0.36	5.73	9.72	nr	15.45
obtuse elbow	14.32	0.36	5.73	15.80	nr	21.53
tee; equal	13.93	0.48	7.64	15.37	nr	23.01
tank connector	13.49	0.48	7.64	14.88	nr	22.52
54 mm pipes; fixing with pipe clips; plugged and screwed	7.19	0.62	9.87	8.20	m	18.07
Extra for						
made bend	-	0.51	8.12	-	nr	8.12
stop end	14.64	0.19	3.02	16.15	nr	19.17
straight coupling	7.66	0.41	6.53	8.45	nr	14.97
reducing coupling	13.86	0.41	6.53	15.29	nr	21.82
union coupling	38.16	0.41	6.53	42.10	nr	48.62
flanged connector	68.38	0.46	7.32	75.44	nr	82.76
elbow	18.20	0.41	6.53	20.08	nr	26.60
obtuse elbow	25.91	0.41	6.53	28.58	nr	35.11
tee; equal	28.09	0.53	8.44	30.98	nr	39.42
tank connector	20.61	0.53	8.44	22.74	nr	31.17
Copper pipes; EN1057:1996; compression fittings						
15 mm pipes; fixing with pipe clips; plugged and screwed	0.81	0.39	6.21	1.00	m	7.20
Extra for						
made bend	-	0.14	2.23	-	nr	2.23
stop end	1.57	0.09	1.43	1.73	nr	3.17
straight coupling	1.26	0.14	2.23	1.39	nr	3.62
reducing set	1.35	0.16	2.55	1.49	nr	4.04
male coupling	1.12	0.19	3.02	1.24	nr	4.26
female coupling	1.36	0.19	3.02	1.50	nr	4.52
90 degree bend	1.52	0.14	2.23	1.68	nr	3.91
90 degree backplate bend	4.00	0.28	4.46	4.41	nr	8.87
tee; equal	2.13	0.20	3.18	2.35	nr	5.53
tee; backplate	5.34	0.20	3.18	5.89	nr	9.07
tank coupling	3.21	0.20	3.18	3.54	nr	6.72
22 mm pipes; fixing with pipe clips; plugged and screwed	1.63	0.44	7.00	1.92	m	8.92
Extra for						
made bend	-	0.19	3.02	-	nr	3.02
stop end	2.28	0.11	1.75	2.52	nr	4.27
straight coupling	2.06	0.19	3.02	2.28	nr	5.30
reducing set	1.46	0.05	0.80	1.61	nr	2.40
male coupling	1.71	0.26	4.14	1.89	nr	6.03
female coupling	1.98	0.26	4.14	2.18	nr	6.32
90 degree bend	2.42	0.19	3.02	2.67	nr	5.70
tee; equal	3.53	0.28	4.46	3.90	nr	8.36
tee; reducing	5.48	0.28	4.46	6.04	nr	10.50
tank coupling	3.56	0.28	4.46	3.92	nr	8.38

S PIPED SUPPLY SYSTEMS

Item	PC £	Labour hours	Labour £	Material £	Unit	Total rate £
S10/S11 HOT AND COLD WATER - cont'd						
Copper pipes; EN1057:1996; compression Fittings - cont'd						
28 mm pipes; fixing with pipe clips; plugged and screwed	2.10	0.48	7.64	2.45	m	10.10
Extra for						
made bend	-	0.23	3.66	-	nr	3.66
stop end	4.75	0.13	2.07	5.24	nr	7.30
straight coupling	4.54	0.23	3.66	5.00	nr	8.66
male coupling	3.22	0.32	5.09	3.55	nr	8.64
female coupling	4.16	0.32	5.09	4.59	nr	9.69
90 degree bend	5.86	0.23	3.66	6.47	nr	10.13
tee; equal	9.34	0.34	5.41	10.31	nr	15.72
tee; reducing	9.02	0.34	5.41	9.95	nr	15.37
tank coupling	7.25	0.34	5.41	8.00	nr	13.41
35 mm pipes; fixing with pipe clips; plugged and screwed	4.58	0.55	8.75	5.25	m	14.01
Extra for						
made bend	-	0.28	4.46	-	nr	4.46
stop end	7.31	0.15	2.39	8.06	nr	10.45
straight coupling	9.43	0.28	4.46	10.40	nr	14.86
male coupling	7.16	0.37	5.89	7.90	nr	13.79
female coupling	8.60	0.37	5.89	9.49	nr	15.38
tee; equal	16.56	0.39	6.21	18.27	nr	24.48
tee; reducing	16.18	0.39	6.21	17.85	nr	24.06
tank coupling	8.62	0.39	6.21	9.51	nr	15.72
42 mm pipes; fixing with pipe clips; plugged and screwed	5.61	0.61	9.71	6.41	m	16.12
Extra for						
made bend	-	0.37	5.89	-	nr	5.89
stop end	12.16	0.17	2.71	13.42	nr	16.12
straight coupling	12.40	0.32	5.09	13.67	nr	18.77
male coupling	10.75	0.42	6.69	11.85	nr	18.54
female coupling	11.57	0.42	6.69	12.77	nr	19.45
tee; equal	26.03	0.43	6.84	28.71	nr	35.56
tee; reducing	25.01	0.43	6.84	27.59	nr	34.43
54 mm pipes; fixing with pipe clips; plugged and screwed	7.19	0.67	10.66	8.20	m	18.87
Extra for						
made bend	-	0.51	8.12	-	nr	8.12
straight coupling	18.54	0.37	5.89	20.45	nr	26.34
male coupling	15.88	0.46	7.32	17.51	nr	24.84
female coupling	16.97	0.46	7.32	18.73	nr	26.05
tee; equal	41.81	0.48	7.64	46.12	nr	53.76
tee; reducing	41.81	0.48	7.64	46.12	nr	53.76
Copper, brass and gunmetal ancillaries; screwed joints to fittings						
Stopcock; brass/gunmetal capillary joints to copper						
15 mm nominal size	3.49	0.19	3.02	3.85	nr	6.87
22 mm nominal size	6.51	0.25	3.98	7.18	nr	11.16
28 mm nominal size	18.50	0.31	4.93	20.41	nr	25.35
Stopcock; brass/gunmetal compression joints to copper						
15 mm nominal size	4.78	0.17	2.71	5.28	nr	7.98
22 mm nominal size	8.41	0.22	3.50	9.27	nr	12.78
28 mm nominal size	21.93	0.28	4.46	24.19	nr	28.65

S PIPED SUPPLY SYSTEMS

Item	PC £	Labour hours	Labour £	Material £	Unit	Total rate £
Stopcock; brass/gunmetal compression joints to polyethylene						
15 mm nominal size	11.97	0.24	3.82	13.20	nr	17.02
22 mm nominal size	20.81	0.31	4.93	22.95	nr	27.89
28 mm nominal size	22.19	0.37	5.89	24.48	nr	30.37
Gunmetal "Fullway" gate valve; capillary joints to copper						
15 mm nominal size	10.91	0.19	3.02	12.04	nr	15.06
22 mm nominal size	12.64	0.25	3.98	13.95	nr	17.93
28 mm nominal size	17.60	0.31	4.93	19.42	nr	24.35
35 mm nominal size	39.28	0.38	6.05	43.33	nr	49.38
42 mm nominal size	49.10	0.43	6.84	54.16	nr	61.01
54 mm nominal size	71.23	0.49	7.80	78.57	nr	86.37
Brass gate valve; compression joints to copper						
15 mm nominal size	7.81	0.28	4.46	8.61	nr	13.07
22 mm nominal size	9.10	0.37	5.89	10.04	nr	15.93
28 mm nominal size	15.89	0.46	7.32	17.53	nr	24.85
Chromium plated; lockshield radiator valve; union outlet						
15 mm nominal size	4.06	0.20	3.18	4.47	nr	7.66
Water tanks/cisterns						
Polyethylene cold water feed and expansion cistern; BS 4213; with covers						
ref SC15; 68 litres	33.42	1.16	18.46	35.97	nr	54.43
ref SC25; 114 litres	39.33	1.34	21.33	42.33	nr	63.66
ref SC40; 182 litres	46.19	1.34	21.33	49.72	nr	71.05
ref SC50; 227 litres	63.71	1.80	28.65	68.56	nr	97.21
GRP cold water storage cistern; with covers						
ref 899.10; 30 litres	78.97	1.02	16.24	84.99	nr	101.23
ref 899.25; 68 litres	99.67	1.16	18.46	107.27	nr	125.73
ref 899.40; 114 litres	123.92	1.34	21.33	133.37	nr	154.70
ref 899.70; 227 litres	155.39	1.80	28.65	167.23	nr	195.89
Storage cylinders/calorifiers						
Copper cylinders; single feed coil indirect; BS 1566 Part 2; grade 3						
ref 2; 96 litres	160.50	1.85	29.45	172.74	nr	202.19
ref 3; 114 litres	102.12	2.08	33.11	109.91	nr	143.02
ref 7; 117 litres	100.78	2.31	36.77	108.46	nr	145.23
ref 8; 140 litres	114.09	2.78	44.25	122.79	nr	167.04
ref 9; 162 litres	145.73	3.24	51.57	156.84	nr	208.41
Combination copper hot water storage units; coil direct; BS 3198; (hot/cold)						
400 mm x 900 mm; 65/20 litres	118.61	2.59	41.23	127.65	nr	168.88
450 mm x 900 mm; 85/25 litres	122.15	3.61	57.46	131.46	nr	188.92
450 mm x 1075 mm; 115/25 litres	134.36	4.53	72.11	144.61	nr	216.71
450 mm x 1200 mm; 115/45 litres	143.04	5.09	81.02	153.95	nr	234.97
Combination copper hot water storage						
450 mm x 900 mm; 85/25 litres	153.18	4.07	64.78	164.86	nr	229.65
450 mm x 1200 mm; 115/45 litres	175.16	5.55	88.34	188.52	nr	276.86

S PIPED SUPPLY SYSTEMS

Item	PC £	Labour hours	Labour £	Material £	Unit	Total rate £
S10/S11 HOT AND COLD WATER - cont'd						
Thermal insulation						
19 mm thick rigid mineral glass fibre sectional pipe lagging; plain finish; fixed with aluminium bands to steel or copper pipework; including working over pipe fittings						
around 15/15 pipes	4.91	0.06	0.96	5.54	m	**6.50**
around 20/22 pipes	5.28	0.09	1.43	5.96	m	**7.39**
around 25/28 pipes	5.71	0.10	1.59	6.46	m	**8.05**
around 32/35 pipes	6.30	0.11	1.75	7.12	m	**8.87**
around 40/42 pipes	6.71	0.12	1.91	7.59	m	**9.50**
around 50/54 pipes	7.74	0.14	2.23	8.75	m	**10.98**
19 mm thick rigid mineral glass fibre sectional pipe lagging; canvas or class O lacquered aluminium finish; fixed with aluminium bands to steel or copper pipework; including working over pipe fittings						
around 15/15 pipes	6.68	0.06	0.96	7.55	m	**8.51**
around 20/22 pipes	7.28	0.09	1.43	8.23	m	**9.66**
around 25/28 pipes	7.99	0.10	1.59	9.03	m	**10.62**
around 32/35 pipes	8.70	0.11	1.75	9.83	m	**11.58**
around 40/42 pipes	9.35	0.12	1.91	10.57	m	**12.48**
around 50/54 pipes	10.84	0.14	2.23	12.25	m	**14.48**
60 mm thick glass-fibre filled polyethylene insulating jackets for GRP or polyethylene cold water cisterns; complete with fixing bands; for cisterns size (supply not included)						
450 mm x 300 mm x 300 mm (45 litres)	-	0.37	5.89	-	nr	**5.89**
650 mm x 500 mm x 400 mm (91 litres)	-	0.56	8.91	-	nr	**8.91**
675 mm x 525 mm x 500 mm (136 litres)	-	0.65	10.35	-	nr	**10.35**
675 mm x 575 mm x 525 mm (182 litres)	-	0.74	11.78	-	nr	**11.78**
1000 mm x 625 mm x 525 mm (273 litres)	-	0.79	12.57	-	nr	**12.57**
1125 mm x 650 mm x 575 mm (341 litres)	-	0.79	12.57	-	nr	**12.57**
80 mm thick glass-fibre filled insulating jackets in flame retardant PVC to BS 1763; type 1B; segmental type for hot water cylinders; complete with fixing bands; for cylinders size (supply not included)						
400 mm x 900 mm; ref 2	-	0.31	4.93	-	nr	**4.93**
450 mm x 900 mm; ref 7	-	0.31	4.93	-	nr	**4.93**
450 mm x 1050 mm; ref 8	-	0.37	5.89	-	nr	**5.89**
450 mm x 1200 mm	-	0.46	7.32	-	nr	**7.32**
S13 PRESSURISED WATER						
Blue MDPE pipes; BS 6572; mains pipework; no joints in the running length; laid in trenches						
Pipes						
20 mm nominal size	0.55	0.10	1.59	0.61	m	**2.21**
25 mm nominal size	0.63	0.11	1.75	0.70	m	**2.45**
32 mm nominal size	1.08	0.12	1.91	1.20	m	**3.11**
50 mm nominal size	2.57	0.14	2.23	2.85	m	**5.08**
63 mm nominal size	4.07	0.15	2.39	4.51	m	**6.90**

S PIPED SUPPLY SYSTEMS

Item	PC £	Labour hours	Labour £	Material £	Unit	Total rate £
Ductile iron bitumen coated pipes and fittings; BS 4772; class K9; Stanton's "Tyton" water main pipes or other equal and approved; flexible joints						
100 mm pipes; laid straight	19.12	0.56	6.05	28.21	m	**34.26**
Extra for						
bend; 45 degrees	40.50	0.56	6.05	58.97	nr	**65.02**
branch; 45 degrees; socketed	295.06	0.83	8.97	353.24	nr	**362.21**
tee	63.94	0.83	8.97	92.05	nr	**101.02**
flanged spigot	40.55	0.56	6.05	52.43	nr	**58.48**
flanged socket	38.58	0.56	6.05	50.19	nr	**56.24**
150 mm pipes; laid straight	24.58	0.65	7.02	34.88	m	**41.91**
Extra for						
bend; 45 degrees	63.40	0.65	7.02	85.86	nr	**92.88**
branch; 45 degrees; socketed	376.58	0.97	10.48	446.88	nr	**457.36**
tee	132.81	0.97	10.48	171.40	nr	**181.88**
flanged spigot	47.03	0.65	7.02	60.25	nr	**67.28**
flanged socket	61.30	0.65	7.02	76.38	nr	**83.41**
200 mm pipes; laid straight	33.70	0.93	10.05	48.36	m	**58.41**
Extra for						
bend; 45 degrees	114.42	0.93	10.05	149.85	nr	**159.90**
branch; 45 degrees; socketed	427.71	1.39	15.02	514.15	nr	**529.17**
tee	182.50	1.39	15.02	237.04	nr	**252.06**
flanged spigot	102.42	0.93	10.05	126.02	nr	**136.06**
flanged socket	97.12	0.93	10.05	120.02	nr	**130.07**

T MECHANICAL HEATING/COOLING SYSTEMS ETC

Item	PC £	Labour hours	Labour £	Material £	Unit	Total rate £
T10 GAS/OIL FIRED BOILERS						
Boilers						
Gas fired floor standing domestic boilers; cream or white; enamelled casing; 32 mm diameter BSPT female flow and return tappings; 102 mm diameter flue socket 13 mm diameter BSPT male draw-off outlet						
13.19 kW output (45,000 Btu/Hr)	-	4.63	84.61	485.79	nr	**570.40**
23.45 kW output (80,000 Btu/Hr)	-	4.63	84.61	621.11	nr	**705.72**
T31 LOW TEMPERATURE HOT WATER HEATING						
NOTE: The reader is referred to section "S10/S11 Hot and Cold Water" for rates for copper pipework which will equally apply to this section of work. For further and more detailed information the reader is advised to consult "Spon's Mechanical and Electrical Services Price Book".						
Radiators; Hudevad Heat Emitters or other equal and approved						
"Plan" single panel type; steel; 700 mm high; wheelhead and lockshield valves						
567 mm long	57.68	1.85	33.81	71.18	nr	**104.99**
1200 mm long	105.56	2.08	38.01	122.71	nr	**160.72**
2200 mm long	181.16	2.31	42.21	204.08	nr	**246.29**
3000 mm long	241.64	2.54	46.42	269.25	nr	**315.66**

V ELECTRICAL SYSTEMS

Item	PC £	Labour hours	Labour £	Material £	Unit	Total rate £
V21/V22 GENERAL LIGHTING AND LV POWER						
NOTE: The following items indicate approximate prices for wiring of lighting and power points complete, including accessories and socket outlets, but excluding lighting fittings. Consumer control units are shown separately. For a more detailed breakdown of these costs and specialist costs for a complete range of electrical items, reference should be made to "Spon's Mechanical and Electrical Services Price Book".						
Consumer control units						
8-way 60 amp SP&N surface mounted insulated consumer control units fitted with miniature circuit breakers including 2.00 m long 32 mm screwed welded conduit with three runs of 16 mm2 PVC cables ready for final connections	-	-	-	-	nr	176.14
extra for current operated ELCB of 30 mA tripping current	-	-	-	-	nr	71.56
As above but 100 amp metal cased consumer unit and 25 mm2 PVC cables	-	-	-	-	nr	192.65
extra for current operated ELCB of 30 mA tripping current	-	-	-	-	nr	165.13
Final circuits						
Lighting points						
wired in PVC insulated and PVC sheathed cable in flats and houses; insulated in cavities and roof space; protected where buried by heavy gauge PVC conduit	-	-	-	-	nr	44.03
as above but in commercial property	-	-	-	-	nr	55.04
wired in PVC insulated cable in screwed welded conduit in commercial property	-	-	-	-	nr	170.63
as above but in industrial property	-	-	-	-	nr	187.14
wired in MICC cable in commercial property	-	-	-	-	nr	143.11
as above but in industrial property with PVC sheathed cable	-	-	-	-	nr	159.62
Single 13 amp switched socket outlet points						
wired in PVC insulated and PVC sheathed cable in flats and houses on a ring main circuit; protected where buried by heavy gauge PVC conduit	-	-	-	-	nr	66.05
as above but in commercial property	-	-	-	-	nr	77.06
wired in PVC insulated cable in screwed welded conduit in commercial property	-	-	-	-	nr	176.14
as above but in industrial property	-	-	-	-	nr	192.65
wired in MICC cable on a ring main ciircuit in commercial property	-	-	-	-	nr	181.64
as above but in industrial property with PVC sheathed cable	-	-	-	-	nr	198.15
Cooker control units						
45 amp circuit including unit wired in PVC insulated and PVC sheathed cable; protected where buried by heavy gauge PVC conduit	-	-	-	-	nr	93.57
as above but wired in PVC insulated cable in screwed welded conduit	-	-	-	-	nr	209.16
as above but wired in MICC cable	-	-	-	-	nr	231.18

W SECURITY SYSTEMS

Item	PC £	Labour hours	Labour £	Material £	Unit	Total rate £
W20 LIGHTNING PROTECTION						
Lightning protection equipment						
Copper strip roof or down conductors fixed with bracket or saddle clips						
20 mm x 3 mm flat section	-	-	-	-	m	17.45
25 mm x 3 mm flat section	-	-	-	-	m	20.35
Aluminium strip roof or down conductors fixed with bracket or saddle clips						
20 mm x 3 mm flat section	-	-	-	-	m	12.80
25 mm x 3 mm flat section	-	-	-	-	m	13.96
Joints in tapes	-	-	-	-	nr	9.90
Bonding connections to roof and structural metalwork	-	-	-	-	nr	58.17
Testing points	-	-	-	-	nr	29.09
Earth electrodes						
16 mm diameter driven copper electrodes in 1220 mm long sectional lengths (minimum 2440 mm long overall)	-	-	-	-	nr	151.22
first 2440 mm length driven and tested 25 mm x 3 mm copper strip electrode in 457 mm deep prepared trench	-	-	-	-	m	11.64

PRICES FOR MEASURED WORKS - MINOR WORKS

INTRODUCTION

The "Prices for Measured Works - Minor Works" are intended to apply to a small project in the outer London area costing about £100,000 (including Preliminaries).

The format of this section follows that of the "Major Works" section with minor variations because of the different nature of the work, and reference should be made to the "Introduction" to that section on page 81.

It has been assumed that reasonable quantities of work are involved, equivalent to quantities for two houses, although clearly this would not apply to all trades and descriptions of work in a project of this value. Where smaller quantities of work are involved it will be necessary to adjust the prices accordingly.

For section "C Demolition/Alteration/Renovation" even smaller quantities have been assumed as can be seen from the stated "PC" of the materials involved.

Where work in an existing building is concerned it has been assumed that the building is vacated and that in all cases there is reasonable access and adequate storage space. Should this not be the case, and if any abnormal circumstances have to be taken into account, an allowance can be made either by a lump sum addition or by suitably modifying the percentage factor for overheads and profit. Built-up prices include an allowance of 7½% for overheads and 5% for profit, whereas non-analysed sub-contractor prices only include mark-up of 2½% for profit.

Labour rates are based upon typical gang costs divided by the number of primary working operatives for the trade concerned; and for general building work include an allowance for trade supervision, overheads and profit. The "Labour hours" column gives the total hours allocated to a particular item and the "Labour £" the consolidated cost of such labour. "Labour hours" have not always been given for "spot" items because of the inclusion of Sub-Contractor's labour.

The "Material Plant £" column includes the cost of removal of debris by skips or lorries. Alternative materials prices tables can be found in the appropriate "Prices for Measured Works - Major Works" section. As stated earlier, these prices are "list" prices before deduction of quantity discounts, and therefore require 'discount' adjustment before they can be substituted in place of "PC" figures given for Measured Work items. The reader should bear in mind that although large orders are delivered free of charge, smaller orders generally attract a delivery or part load charge and this should be added to the alternative material price prior to substitution in a rate.

No allowance has been made for any Value Added Tax which will probably be payable on the majority of work of this nature.

A PRELIMINARIES/CONTRACT CONDITIONS FOR MINOR WORKS

When pricing Preliminaries all factors affecting the execution of the works must be considered; some of the more obvious have already been mentioned above.

As mentioned in "A Preliminaries" in the "Prices for Measured Work - Major Works" section (page 101), the current trend is for Preliminaries to be priced at approximately 12%, but for alterations and additions work in particular, care must be exercised in ensuring that all adverse factors are covered. The reader is advised to identify systematically and separately price all preliminary items with cost/time implications in order to reflect as accurately as possible preliminary costs likely to stem from any particular scheme.

Where the Standard Form of Contract applies two clauses which will affect the pricing of Preliminaries should be noted.

(a)   Insurance of the works against Clause 22 Perils
        Clause 22C will apply whereby the Employer and not the Contractor effects the insurance.
(b)   Fluctuations
        An allowance for any shortfall in recovery of increased costs under whichever clause is contained in the Contract may be covered by the inclusion of a lump sum in the Preliminaries or by increasing the prices by a suitable percentage

ADDITIONS AND NEW WORKS WITHIN EXISTING BUILDINGS

Depending upon the contract size either the prices in "Prices for Measured Work - Major Works" or those prices in "Prices for Measured Work - Minor Works" will best apply.

It is likely, however, that conditions affecting the excavations for foundations might preclude the use of mechanical plant, and that it will be necessary to restrict prices to those applicable to hand excavation.

If, in any circumstances, less than what might be termed "normal quantities" are likely to be involved it is stressed that actual quotations should be invited from specialist Sub-contractors for these works.

JOBBING WORK

Jobbing work is outside the scope of this section and no attempt has been made to include prices for such work.

B NEW ITEMS

Item	PC £	Labour hours	Labour £	Material £	Unit	Total rate £
NEW ITEMS are also included in their appropriate Work section						
E05 IN SITU CONCRETE CONSTRUCTION						
Grouting with "Conbextra HF" flowable cementitious grout						
Stanchion bases						
10 mm thick	-	1.33	17.79	1.77	nr	**19.56**
25 mm thick	-	1.60	21.40	4.53	nr	**25.93**
E30 REINFORCEMENT FOR IN SITU CONCRETE						
Bar; BS 6744; stainless steel bars; grade 316						
32 mm diameter nominal size						
straight	3712.50	18.00	284.04	4249.83	tonne	**4533.87**
bent	3822.50	18.00	284.04	4373.99	tonne	**4658.03**
25 mm diameter nominal size						
straight	3712.50	20.00	315.60	4246.80	tonne	**4562.39**
bent	3822.50	20.00	315.60	4370.96	tonne	**4686.56**
20 mm diameter nominal size						
straight	3795.00	22.00	347.16	4344.01	tonne	**4691.17**
bent	3905.00	22.00	347.16	4468.17	tonne	**4815.33**
16 mm diameter nominal size						
straight	3932.50	24.00	378.72	4506.77	tonne	**4885.48**
bent	4042.50	24.00	378.72	4630.93	tonne	**5009.65**
12 mm diameter nominal size						
straight	4042.50	26.00	410.28	4638.48	tonne	**5048.76**
bent	4152.50	26.00	410.28	4762.64	tonne	**5172.92**
10 mm diameter nominal size						
straight	4158.00	28.00	441.84	4777.46	tonne	**5219.30**
bent	4268.00	28.00	441.84	4901.62	tonne	**5343.46**
8 mm diameter nominal size						
straight	4042.50	30.00	470.99	4654.64	tonne	**5125.63**
bent	4152.50	30.00	470.99	4778.80	tonne	**5249.80**
E40 DESIGNED JOINTS IN IN SITU CONCRETE						
Hydrophilic strip water stop; lapped joints; cast into concrete						
5 x 20 mm "Servistrip AH 205"	-	0.35	4.68	6.84	m	**11.52**
50 x 20 mm "Adcor 500S"	-	0.35	4.68	9.03	m	**13.71**
F11 GLASS BLOCK WALLING						
Hollow glass block walling; Pittsburgh Corning sealed "Thinline" or other equal and approved; in cement mortar joints; reinforced with 6 mm diameter stainless steel rods; pointed both sides with mastic or other equal and approved						
Walls; facework both sides						
115 mm x 115 mm x 80 mm flemish blocks	-	-	-	-	m²	**585.27**
190 mm x 190 mm x 80 mm flemish blocks; cross reeded or clear blocks	-	-	-	-	m²	**252.15**
240 mm x 240 mm x 80 mm flemish blocks; cross reeded or clear blocks	-	-	-	-	m²	**243.95**
240 mm x 115 mm x 80 mm flemish blocks; cross reeded or clear blocks	-	-	-	-	m²	**293.15**

B NEW ITEMS

Item	PC £	Labour hours	Labour £	Material £	Unit	Total rate £
F30 ACCESSORIES/SUNDRY ITEMS FOR BRICK/STONE WALLING						
Joint reinforcement						
"Brickforce" galvanised steel joint reinforcement or other equal and approved						
width 60 mm; ref GBF40W60	-	0.06	1.37	0.58	m	**1.95**
width 100 mm; ref GBF40W100	-	0.08	1.83	0.68	m	**2.51**
width 150 mm; ref GBF40W150	-	0.10	2.28	0.84	m	**3.12**
width 175 mm; ref GBF40W175	-	0.11	2.51	1.00	m	**3.51**
"Brickforce" stainless steel joint reinforcement or other equal and approved						
width 60 mm; ref SBF40W60	-	0.06	1.37	1.57	m	**2.94**
width 100 mm; ref SBF40W100	-	0.08	1.83	1.61	m	**3.43**
width 150 mm; ref SBF40W150	-	0.10	2.28	1.64	m	**3.92**
width 175 mm; ref SBF40W175	-	0.11	2.51	1.77	m	**4.28**
"Wallforce" stainless steel joint reinforcement or other equal and approved						
width 240 mm; ref SWF40W240	-	0.13	2.97	4.89	m	**7.86**
width 260 mm; ref SWF40W260	-	0.14	3.20	5.11	m	**8.30**
width 275 mm; ref SWF40W275	-	0.15	3.42	5.29	m	**8.71**
G10 STUCTURAL STEEL FRAMING						
Surface treatment						
At works						
intumescent paint fire protection (30 minutes); spray applied	-	-	-	-	m^2	**10.93**
intumescent paint fire protection (60 minutes); spray applied	-	-	-	-	m^2	**16.39**
Extra over for separate decorative sealer top coat	-	-	-	-	m^2	**3.28**
On site						
intumescent paint fire protection (30 minutes) to universal beams etc.; spray applied	-	-	-	-	m^2	**8.20**
intumescent paint fire protection (30 minutes) to circular columns etc.; spray applied	-	-	-	-	m^2	**13.73**
intumescent paint fire protection (60 minutes) to universal beams etc.; spray applied	-	-	-	-	m^2	**10.38**
intumescent paint fire protection (60 minutes) to circular columns etc.; spray applied	-	-	-	-	m^2	**17.43**
Extra over for separate decorative sealer top coat	-	-	-	-	m^2	**2.73**
H31 METAL PROFILED/FLAT SHEET CLADDING/COVERING/SIDING						
Galvanised steel strip troughed sheets; Corus products or other equal and approved						
Roof cladding or decking; sloping not exceeding 50 degrees; fixing to steel purlins with plastic headed self-tapping screws						
0.7 mm thick; 46 profile	-	-	-	-	m^2	**12.43**
0.7 mm thick; 60 profile	-	-	-	-	m^2	**13.61**
0.7 mm thick; 100 profile	-	-	-	-	m^2	**14.80**

B NEW ITEMS

Item	PC £	Labour hours	Labour £	Material £	Unit	Total rate £
Galvanised steel strip troughed sheets; PMF Strip Mills Products or other equal and approved						
Roof cladding; sloping not exceeding 50 degrees; fixing to steel purlins with plastic headed self-tapping screws						
0.7 mm thick type HPS200 13.5/3 corrugated	-	-	-	-	m²	14.03
0.7 mm thick type HPS200 R32/1000	-	-	-	-	m²	13.37
0.7 mm thick type Acline 40; plasticol finished	-	-	-	-	m²	18.72
Extra over last for aluminium roof cladding or decking	-	-	-	-	m²	7.10
Accessories for roof cladding						
HPS200 Drip flashing; 250 mm girth	-	-	-	-	m	4.35
HPS200 Ridge flashing; 375 mm girth	-	-	-	-	m	5.70
HPS200 Gable flashing; 500 mm girth	-	-	-	-	m	8.03
HPS200 Internal angle; 625 mm girth	-	-	-	-	m	8.35
Extra over steel roofing for						
roof penetration; 150 mm dia. opening; with top hat flashing and collar 150 mm high; and silicone joint to roofsheet	-	-	-	-	nr	58.63
roof penetration; 250 mm dia. opening; with top hat flashing and collar 150 mm high; and silicone joint to roofsheet	-	-	-	-	nr	83.44
H72 ALUMINIUM SHEET COVERINGS/ FLASHINGS						
Aluminium Alumasc "Skyline" coping system; polyester powder coated						
Coping; fixing straps plugged and screwed to brickwork						
362 mm wide; for parapet wall						
271 - 300 mm wide	-	0.58	11.12	24.47	m	35.58
Extra for						
90 degree bend	-	0.28	5.37	58.30	nr	63.66
90 degree tee junction	-	0.40	7.67	62.55	nr	70.21
stop end	-	0.17	3.26	34.47	nr	37.73
stop end upstand	-	0.23	4.41	37.40	nr	41.81
J40 FLEXIBLE SHEET/TANKING/ DAMP PROOF MEMBRANES						
Tanking and damp proofing						
Visqueen self-adhesive damp proof membrane						
over 300 mm wide; horizontal	-	-	-	-	m²	7.10
not exceeding 300 mm wide; horizontal	-	-	-	-	m	2.73
Tanking primer for self-adhesive dpm						
over 300 mm wide; horizontal	-	-	-	-	m²	4.91
not exceeding 300 mm wide; horizontal	-	-	-	-	m	2.25
Ruberoid "Plasprufe 2000SA" self-adhesive damp proof membrane						
over 300 mm wide; horizontal	-	-	-	-	m²	13.53
not exceeding 300 mm wide; horizontal	-	-	-	-	m	5.19
Extra for 50 mm thick sand blinding	-	-	-	-	m²	2.37

B NEW ITEMS

Item	PC £	Labour hours	Labour £	Material £	Unit	Total rate £
K10 PLASTERBOARD DRY LINING/ PARTITIONS/CEILINGS						
Gypsum cladding; Glasroc "Firecase s" board or other equal and approved; fixed with adhesive; joints pointed in adhesive 25 mm thick column linings, faces - 4; 2 hour fire protection rating						
not exceeding 600 mm girth	-	0.33	6.03	17.16	m	**23.19**
600 mm - 1200 mm girth	-	0.50	9.14	26.11	m	**35.25**
1200 mm - 1800 mm girth	-	0.66	12.06	35.07	m	**47.13**
30 mm thick beam linings, faces - 3; 2 hour fire protection rating						
not exceeding 600 mm girth	-	0.65	11.88	16.56	m	**28.44**
600 mm - 1200 mm girth	-	1.00	18.27	26.67	m	**44.95**
1200 mm - 1800 mm girth	-	1.30	23.76	36.78	m	**60.54**
K30 DEMOUNTABLE PARTITIONS						
Insulated panel and two-hour fire wall system for warehouses etc., comprising white polyester coated galvanised steel frame and 0.55 mm galvanised steel panels either side of rockwool infill						
100 mm thick wall; 31 Rw dB acoustic rating	-	-	-	-	m^2	**45.10**
150 mm thick wall; 31 Rw dB acoustic rating	-	-	-	-	m^2	**48.48**
intumescent mastic sealant; bedding frames at perimeters of metal fire walls	-	-	-	-	m	**3.95**
Getalit laminated both sides top hung movable acoustic panel wall with concealed uPVC vertical edge profiles, 9 nr 1106 mm x 3000 mm panels and type K two point panel support system						
105 mm thick wall; 47 Rw dB acoustic rating	-	-	-	-	m^2	**417.18**
105 mm thick wall; 47 Rw dB acoustic rating	-	-	-	-	m^2	**451.00**
105 mm thick wall; 47 Rw dB acoustic rating	-	-	-	-	m^2	**484.82**
K40 DEMOUNTABLE SUSPENDED CEILINGS						
Suspended ceilings; Gyproc M/F suspended ceiling system or other equal and approved; hangers plugged and screwed to concrete soffit, 900 mm x 1800 mm x 12.5 mm tapered edge wallboard infill; joints filled with joint filler and taped to receive direct decoration Lining to ceilings; hangers average 400 mm long						
over 300 mm wide	-	1.43	26.61	12.09	m^2	**38.69**
not exceeding 300 mm wide in isolated strips	-	0.57	10.60	6.15	m	**16.75**
300 mm - 600 mm wide in isolated strips	-	0.90	16.73	7.00	m	**23.73**
Edge treatments						
20 x 20 mm SAS perimeter shadow gap; screwed to plasterboard	-	-	-	-	m	**6.20**
20 x 20 mm SAS shadow gap around 450 mm dia. column; including 15 x 44 mm batten plugged and screwed to concrete	-	-	-	-	m	**31.01**
Vertical bulkhead; including additional hangers						
over 300 mm wide	-	1.65	30.73	12.78	m^2	**43.51**
not exceeding 300 mm wide in isolated strips	-	0.65	12.09	6.84	m	**18.94**
300 mm - 600 mm wide in isolated strips	-	1.03	19.15	7.69	m	**26.85**

B NEW ITEMS

Item	PC £	Labour hours	Labour £	Material £	Unit	Total rate £
M10 SAND CEMENT SCREEDS						
Early drying floor screed; RMC Mortars "Readyscreed"; or other equal and approved; steel trowelled Work to floors; one coat; level; to concrete base; over 300 mm wide						
100 mm thick	-	-	-	-	m²	22.55
Extra over last for galvanised chicken wire anticrack reinforcement	-	-	-	-	m²	1.07
Extra over last for isolation joint to perimeter	-	-	-	-	m	1.40
M60 PAINTING/CLEAR FINISHING - INTERNALLY						
Two coats of epoxy anti-slip floor paint; on screeded concrete surfaces General surfaces						
over 300 mm girth	-	0.28	3.93	13.94	m²	17.87
M60 PAINTING/CLEAR FINISHING - EXTERNALLY						
One coat sealer and two coats of anti-graffiti paint (spray applied) Brick or block walls						
over 300 mm girth	-	0.26	3.65	3.11	m²	6.76
Cement render or concrete walls						
over 300 mm girth	-	0.30	4.21	4.61	m²	8.83
2.5 mm of "Vandalene" anti-climb paint (spray applied) General surfaces						
over 300 mm girth	-	0.35	4.91	4.39	m²	9.31
P10 SUNDRY INSULATION/ PROOFING WORK/FIRE STOPS						
Expanded polystyrene board standard grade SD/N or other equal and approved; fixed with adhesive						
20 mm thick	-	0.15	2.74	3.97	m²	6.71
30 mm thick	-	0.16	2.92	5.44	m²	8.37
60 mm thick	-	0.19	3.47	9.87	m²	13.35
75 mm thick	-	0.20	3.65	12.11	m²	15.76
Corofil C144 fire barrier to edge of slab; fixed with non-flammable contact adhesive						
to suit void 30 mm wide x 100 mm deep; one hour	-	-	-	-	m	13.81

B NEW ITEMS

Item	PC £	Labour hours	Labour £	Material £	Unit	Total rate £
P31 HOLES/CHASES/COVERS/ SUPPORTS FOR SERVICES						
Builder's work for other services						
Cutting or forming holes for pipes or the like; not exceeding 55 mm nominal size; making good						
reinforced concrete; not exceeding 100 mm deep	-	0.82	10.97	0.81	nr	11.78
reinforced concrete; 100 mm - 200 mm deep	-	1.25	16.72	1.19	nr	17.91
reinforced concrete; 200 mm - 300 mm deep	-	1.65	22.07	1.64	nr	23.71
plasterboard partition or suspended ceiling	-	0.38	5.08	-	nr	5.08
Cutting or forming holes for pipes or the like; 55 mm - 110 mm nominal size; making good						
reinforced concrete; not exceeding 100 mm deep	-	1.05	14.04	1.05	nr	15.09
reinforced concrete; 100 mm - 200 mm deep	-	1.60	21.40	1.59	nr	22.99
reinforced concrete; 200 mm - 300 mm deep	-	2.10	28.09	2.09	nr	30.17
plasterboard partition or suspended ceiling	-	0.44	5.89	-	nr	5.89
Cutting or forming holes for pipes or the like; over 110 mm nominal size; making good						
reinforced concrete; not exceeding 100 mm deep	-	1.25	16.72	1.24	nr	17.96
reinforced concrete; 100 mm - 200 mm deep	-	1.90	25.41	1.89	nr	27.30
reinforced concrete; 200 mm - 300 mm deep	-	2.45	32.77	2.43	nr	35.21
plasterboard partition or suspended ceiling	-	0.49	6.55	-	nr	6.55
Add for supplying and fixing one-hour intumescent sleeve						
for pipe; small	-	0.28	3.75	10.65	nr	14.40
for pipe; large	-	0.31	4.15	13.66	nr	17.80
for pipe; extra large	-	0.34	4.55	18.00	nr	22.55
Cutting or forming holes for ducts; girth not exceeding 1.00 m; making good						
plasterboard partition or suspended ceiling	-	0.75	10.03	-	nr	10.03
Cutting or forming holes for ducts; girth 1.00 m - 2.00 m; making good						
plasterboard partition or suspended ceiling	-	0.85	11.37	-	nr	11.37
Cutting or forming holes for ducts; girth 2.00 m - 3.00 m; making good						
plasterboard partition or suspended ceiling	-	1.10	14.71	-	nr	14.71
Cutting or forming holes for ducts; girth 3.00 m - 4.00 m; making good						
plasterboard partition or suspended ceiling	-	1.35	18.06	-	nr	18.06
NOTE: The following rates for cutting holes and mortices in brickwork or blockwork etc. allow for diamond drilling.						
Cutting holes and mortices in brickwork; per 25 mm depth						
25 mm diameter	-	-	-	-	nr	1.18
32 mm diameter	-	-	-	-	nr	1.18
52 mm diameter	-	-	-	-	nr	1.41
76 mm diameter	-	-	-	-	nr	1.58
107 mm diameter	-	-	-	-	nr	1.69
127 mm diameter	-	-	-	-	nr	2.03
152 mm diameter	-	-	-	-	nr	2.37
200 mm diameter	-	-	-	-	nr	3.16
250 mm diameter	-	-	-	-	nr	4.74
300 mm diameter	-	-	-	-	nr	6.31

B NEW ITEMS

Item	PC £	Labour hours	Labour £	Material £	Unit	Total rate £
Diamond chasing; per 25 x 25 mm section						
in facing or common brickwork	-	-	-	-	m	3.10
in semi-engineering brickwork	-	-	-	-	m	6.48
in engineering brickwork	-	-	-	-	m	9.02
in lightweight blockwork	-	-	-	-	m	2.54
in heavtweight blockwork	-	-	-	-	m	5.07
in render/screed	-	-	-	-	m	9.87
Forming boxes; per 25 mm depth (per m of perimeter)						
in facing or common brickwork	-	-	-	-	m	3.10
in semi-engineering brickwork	-	-	-	-	m	6.48
in engineering brickwork	-	-	-	-	m	9.02
in lightweight blockwork	-	-	-	-	m	2.54
in heavtweight blockwork	-	-	-	-	m	5.07
in render/screed	-	-	-	-	m	9.87
Other items						
track mounter or ring sawing in brickwork	-	-	-	-	m	4.79
floor sawing in apshalte	-	-	-	-	m	1.01
stitch drilling 107 mm diameter hole in brickwork	-	-	-	-	nr	1.24

C DEMOLITION/ALTERATION/RENOVATION

Item	PC £	Labour hours	Labour £	Material £	Unit	Total rate £
C20 DEMOLITION						
NOTE: Demolition rates vary considerably from one scheme to another, depending upon access, the type of construction, the method of demolition, whether there are any redundant materials etc. Therefore, it is advisable to obtain specific quotations for each scheme under consideration, however, the following rates (excluding scaffolding costs) for simple demolitions may be of some assistance for comparative purposes.						
Demolishing all structures						
Demolishing to ground level; single storey brick out-building; timber flat roofs; volume						
50 m^3	-	-	-	-	m^3	10.05
200 m^3	-	-	-	-	m^3	7.39
500 m^3	-	-	-	-	m^3	3.76
Demolishing to ground level; two storey brick out-building; timber joisted suspended floor and timber flat roofs; volume						
200 m^3	-	-	-	-	m^3	5.65
Demolishing parts of structures						
Breaking up concrete bed						
100 mm thick	-	0.50	6.69	2.83	m^2	9.52
150 mm thick	-	0.74	9.90	5.43	m^2	15.33
200 mm thick	-	1.00	13.38	5.66	m^2	19.04
300 mm thick	-	1.48	19.80	8.30	m^2	28.10
Breaking up reinforced concrete bed						
100 mm thick	-	0.56	7.49	3.24	m^2	10.73
150 mm thick	-	0.83	11.10	4.77	m^2	15.87
200 mm thick	-	1.11	14.85	6.47	m^2	21.32
300 mm thick	-	1.67	22.34	9.71	m^2	32.05
Demolishing reinforced concrete column or cutting away casing to steel column	-	11.10	148.47	41.52	m^3	189.99
Demolishing reinforced concrete beam or cutting away casing to steel beam	-	12.75	170.54	44.74	m^3	215.28
Demolishing reinforced concrete wall						
100 mm thick	-	1.11	14.85	4.11	m^2	18.95
150 mm thick	-	1.67	22.34	6.11	m^2	28.45
225 mm thick	-	2.50	33.44	9.21	m^2	42.64
300 mm thick	-	3.33	44.54	12.37	m^2	56.91
Demolishing reinforced concrete suspended slabs						
100 mm thick	-	0.93	12.44	3.85	m^2	16.29
150 mm thick	-	1.39	18.59	5.64	m^2	24.24
225 mm thick	-	2.08	27.82	8.46	m^2	36.28
300 mm thick	-	2.78	37.18	11.45	m^2	48.63
Breaking up concrete plinth; making good structures	-	4.26	56.98	26.32	m^3	83.30
Breaking up precast concrete kerb	-	0.46	6.15	1.00	m	7.15
Removing precast concrete window sill; materials for re-use	-	1.48	19.80	-	m	19.80
Breaking up concrete hearth	-	1.67	22.34	1.66	nr	24.00

C DEMOLITION/ALTERATION/RENOVATION

Item	PC £	Labour hours	Labour £	Material £	Unit	Total rate £
Demolishing external brick walls; in gauged mortar						
half brick thick	-	0.65	8.69	2.49	m^2	11.19
two half brick thick skins	-	1.11	14.85	5.32	m^2	20.16
one brick thick	-	1.11	14.85	5.32	m^2	20.16
one and a half brick thick	-	1.57	21.00	8.30	m^2	29.30
two brick thick	-	2.04	27.29	10.63	m^2	37.92
add for plaster, render or pebbledash per side	-	0.09	1.20	0.50	m^2	1.70
Demolishing external brick walls; in cement mortar						
half brick thick	-	0.97	12.97	2.49	m^2	15.47
two half brick thick skins	-	1.62	21.67	5.32	m^2	26.98
one brick thick	-	1.67	22.34	5.32	m^2	27.65
one and a half brick thick	-	2.27	30.36	8.30	m^2	38.67
two brick thick	-	2.91	38.92	10.63	m^2	49.55
add for plaster, render or pebbledash per side	-	0.09	1.20	0.50	m^2	1.70
Demolishing internal partitions; gauged mortar						
half brick thick	-	0.97	12.97	2.49	m^2	15.47
one brick thick	-	1.67	22.34	5.32	m^2	27.65
one and a half brick thick	-	2.36	31.57	8.30	m^2	39.87
75 mm blockwork	-	0.65	8.69	1.83	m^2	10.52
90 mm blockwork	-	0.69	9.23	2.16	m^2	11.39
100 mm blockwork	-	0.74	9.90	2.49	m^2	12.39
115 mm blockwork	-	0.79	10.57	2.49	m^2	13.06
125 mm blockwork	-	0.83	11.10	2.66	m^2	13.76
140 mm blockwork	-	0.88	11.77	2.82	m^2	14.59
150 mm blockwork	-	0.93	12.44	3.16	m^2	15.59
190 mm blockwork	-	1.09	14.58	3.99	m^2	18.57
215 mm blockwork	-	1.20	16.05	4.32	m^2	20.37
255 mm blockwork	-	1.39	18.59	5.15	m^2	23.74
add for plaster per side	-	0.09	1.20	0.50	m^2	1.70
Demolishing internal partitions; cement mortar						
half brick thick	-	1.48	19.80	2.49	m^2	22.29
one brick thick	-	2.45	32.77	5.32	m^2	38.09
one and a half brick thick	-	3.42	45.74	8.30	m^2	54.05
add for plaster per side	-	0.09	1.20	0.50	m^2	1.70
Breaking up brick plinths	-	3.70	49.49	16.61	m^3	66.10
Demolishing bund walls or piers in cement mortar						
one brick thick	-	1.30	17.39	5.32	m^2	22.70
Demolishing walls to roof ventilator housing						
one brick thick	-	1.48	19.80	5.32	m^2	25.11
Demolishing brick chimney to 300 mm below roof level; sealing off flues with slates						
680 mm x 680 mm x 900 mm high above roof	-	11.56	161.71	25.50	nr	187.21
add for each additional 300 height	-	2.31	32.31	4.86	nr	37.18
680 mm x 1030 mm x 900 mm high above roof	-	17.40	243.41	37.47	nr	280.88
add for each additional 300 height	-	3.46	48.36	7.65	nr	56.01
1030 mm x 1030 mm x 900 mm high above roof	-	26.69	373.53	57.90	nr	431.43
add for each additional 300 height	-	5.23	73.26	12.04	nr	85.30

C DEMOLITION/ALTERATION/RENOVATION

Item	PC £	Labour hours	Labour £	Material £	Unit	Total rate £
C20 DEMOLITION – cont'd						
Demolishing parts of structures – cont'd						
Demolishing brick chimneys to 300 mm below						
roof level; sealing off flues with slates; piecing in						
"treated" sawn softwood rafters and making						
good roof coverings over to match existing						
(scaffolding excluded)						
680 mm x 680 mm x 900 mm high above roof	-	-	-	-	nr	200.22
add for each additional 300 mm height	-	-	-	-	nr	33.15
680 mm x 1030 mm x 900 mm high above roof	-	-	-	-	nr	294.06
add for each additional 300 mm height	-	-	-	-	nr	59.45
1030 mm x 1030 mm x 900 mm high above roof	-	-	-	-	nr	437.98
add for each additional 300 mm height	-	-	-	-	nr	143.90
Removing existing chimney pots; materials for						
re-use; demolishing defective chimney stack to						
roof level; re-building using 25% new facing						
bricks to match existing; providing new lead						
flashings; parge and core flues, resetting chimney						
pots including flaunching in cement:mortar						
(scaffolding excluded)						
680 mm x 680 mm x 900 mm high above roof	-	-	-	-	nr	450.49
add for each additional 300 mm height	-	-	-	-	nr	75.08
680 mm x 1030 mm x 900 mm high above roof	-	-	-	-	nr	681.99
add for each additional 300 mm height	-	-	-	-	nr	100.11
1030 mm x 1030 mm x 900 mm high above roof	-	-	-	-	nr	1001.09
add for each additional 300 mm height	-	-	-	-	nr	150.16
Removing fireplace surround and hearth						
interior tiled	-	1.71	22.87	3.82	nr	26.69
cast iron; materials for re-use	-	2.87	38.39	-	nr	38.39
stone iron; materials for re-use	-	7.49	100.18	-	nr	100.18
Removing fireplace; filling in opening; plastering						
and extending skirtings; fixing air brick; breaking						
up hearth and re-screeding						
tiled	-	-	-	-	nr	168.93
cast iron; set aside	-	-	-	-	nr	156.43
stone; set aside	-	-	-	-	nr	256.53
Removing brick-on-edge coping; prepare walls						
for raising						
one brick thick	-	0.42	9.59	0.33	m	9.92
one and a half brick thick	-	0.56	12.78	0.50	m	13.28
Demolishing external stone walls in lime mortar						
300 mm thick	-	1.11	14.85	4.98	m²	19.83
400 mm thick	-	1.48	19.80	6.64	m²	26.44
600 mm thick	-	2.22	29.69	9.97	m²	39.66
Demolishing stone walls in lime mortar; clean off;						
set aside for re-use						
300 mm thick	-	1.67	22.34	1.66	m²	24.00
400 mm thick	-	2.22	29.69	2.16	m²	31.85
600 mm thick	-	3.33	44.54	3.32	m²	47.86
Demolishing metal partitions						
corrugated metal partition	-	0.32	4.28	0.50	m²	4.78
lightweight steel mesh security screen	-	0.46	6.15	0.83	m²	6.98
solid steel demountable partition	-	0.69	9.23	1.16	m²	10.39
glazed sheet demountable partition; including						
removal of glass	-	0.93	12.44	1.66	m²	14.10
Removing metal shutter door and track						
6.20 m x 4.60 m (12.60 m long track)	-	11.10	148.47	24.91	nr	173.38
12.40 m x 4.60 m (16.40 m long track)	-	13.88	185.65	49.83	nr	235.48

C DEMOLITION/ALTERATION/RENOVATION

Item	PC £	Labour hours	Labour £	Material £	Unit	Total rate £
Removing roof timbers complete; including rafters, purlins, ceiling joists, plates, etc., (measured flat on plan)	-	0.31	4.54	1.83	m²	6.37
Removing softwood floor construction						
100 mm deep joists at ground level	-	0.23	3.08	0.33	m²	3.41
175 mm deep joists at first floor level	-	0.46	6.15	0.66	m²	6.82
125 mm deep joists at roof level	-	0.65	8.69	0.50	m²	9.19
Removing individual floor or roof members	-	0.25	3.69	0.33	m	4.02
Removing infected or decayed floor plates	-	0.34	5.04	0.33	m	5.37
Removing boarding; withdrawing nails						
25 mm thick softwood flooring; at ground floor level	-	0.34	4.89	0.50	m²	5.39
25 mm thick softwood flooring; at first floor level	-	0.58	8.49	0.50	m²	8.99
25 mm thick softwood roof boarding	-	0.68	9.98	0.50	m²	10.48
25 mm thick softwood gutter boarding	-	0.74	10.88	0.50	m²	11.38
22 mm thick chipboard flooring; at first floor level	-	0.34	4.89	0.50	m²	5.39
Removing tilting fillet or roll	-	0.14	2.07	0.17	m	2.23
Removing fascia or barge boards	-	0.56	8.23	0.17	m	8.39
Demolishing softwood stud partitions; including finishings both sides etc						
solid	-	0.42	5.62	1.66	m²	7.28
glazed; including removal of glass	-	0.56	7.49	1.66	m²	9.15
Removing windows and doors; and set aside or clear away						
single door	-	0.37	9.39	0.50	nr	9.89
single door and frame or lining	-	0.74	18.78	0.83	nr	19.61
pair of doors	-	0.65	16.49	1.00	nr	17.49
pair of doors and frame or lining	-	1.11	28.17	1.66	nr	29.83
extra for taking out floor spring box	-	0.70	17.76	0.33	nr	18.09
casement window and frame	-	1.11	28.17	0.83	nr	29.00
double hung sash window and frame	-	1.57	39.84	1.66	nr	41.50
pair of french windows and frame	-	3.70	93.88	2.49	nr	96.38
Removing double hung sash window and frame; remove and store for re-use elsewhere	-	2.22	56.33	-	nr	56.33
Demolishing staircase; including balustrades						
single straight flight	-	3.24	82.21	16.61	m	98.82
dogleg flight	-	4.63	117.48	24.91	m	142.40

C30 SHORING/FACADE RETENTION

NOTE: The requirements for shoring and strutting for the formation of large openings are dependant upon a number of factors, for example, the weight of the superimposed structure to be supported, the number (if any) of windows above, the number of floors and the type of roof to be strutted, whether raking shores are required, the depth to a load-bearing surface, and the duration the support is to be in place. Prices, would therefore, be best built-up by assessing the use and waste of materials and the labour involved, including getting timber from and returning to a yard, cutting away and making good, overhead and profit.

C DEMOLITION/ALTERATION/RENOVATION

Item	PC £	Labour hours	Labour £	Material £	Unit	Total rate £
C30 SHORING/FACADE RETENTION – cont'd						
This method is considered a more practical way of pricing than endeavouring to price the work on a cubic metre basis of timber used, and has been adopted in preparing the prices of the examples which follow.						
Support of structures not to be demolished						
Strutting to window openings over proposed new openings	-	0.56	10.23	5.39	nr	**15.62**
Plates, struts, braces and hardwood wedges in supports to floors and roof of opening	-	1.11	20.28	15.65	nr	**35.94**
Dead shore and needle using die square timber with sole plates, braces, hardwood wedges and steel dogs	-	27.75	507.12	68.40	nr	**575.52**
Set of two raking shores using die square timber with 50 mm thick wall piece; hardwood wedges and steel dogs; including forming holes for needles and making good	-	33.30	608.54	69.31	nr	**677.85**
Cut holes through one brick wall for die square needle and make good; including facings externally and plaster internally	-	5.56	127.41	1.26	nr	**128.67**
C41 REPAIRING/RENOVATING/CONSERVING MASONRY						
Repairing/renovating plain/reinforced concrete work						
Reinstating plain concrete bed with site mixed in situ concrete; mix 20.00 N/mm^2 - 20 mm aggregate (1:2:4), where opening no longer required						
100 mm thick	-	0.44	6.47	9.63	m^2	**16.10**
150 mm thick	-	0.72	10.21	14.45	m^2	**24.66**
Reinstating reinforced concrete bed with site mixed in situ concrete; mix 20.00 N/mm^2 - 20 mm aggregate (1:2:4); including mesh reinforcement; where opening no longer required						
100 mm thick	-	0.66	9.41	12.52	m^2	**21.92**
150 mm thick	-	0.91	12.75	17.33	m^2	**30.08**
Reinstating reinforced concrete suspended floor with site mixed in situ concrete; mix 25.00 N/mm^2 - 20 mm aggregate (1:1.5:3); including mesh reinforcement and formwork; where opening no longer required						
150 mm thick	-	2.96	43.14	20.96	m^2	**64.10**
225 mm thick	-	3.47	46.41	28.25	m^2	**74.67**
300 mm thick	-	3.84	51.36	36.59	m^2	**87.95**
Reinstating 150 mm x 150 mm x 150 mm perforation through concrete suspended slab; with site mixed in situ concrete; mix 20.00 N/mm^2 - 20 mm aggregate (1:2:4); including formwork; where opening no longer required	-	0.85	11.37	0.14	nr	**11.51**
Cleaning surfaces of concrete to receive new damp proof membrane	-	0.14	1.87	-	m^2	**1.87**

C DEMOLITION/ALTERATION/RENOVATION

Item	PC £	Labour hours	Labour £	Material £	Unit	Total rate £
Cleaning out existing minor crack and fill in with cement mortar mixed with bonding agent	-	0.31	4.15	0.73	m	4.88
Cleaning out existing crack to form 20 mm x 20 mm groove and fill in with fine cement mixed with bonding agent	-	0.61	8.16	3.92	m	12.07
Making good hole where existing pipe removed; 150 mm deep						
50 mm diameter	-	0.39	5.22	0.44	nr	5.66
100 mm diameter	-	0.51	6.82	0.54	nr	7.36
150 mm diameter	-	0.65	8.69	0.71	nr	9.41
Add for each additional 25 mm thick up to 300 mm thick						
50 mm diameter	-	0.08	1.07	0.08	nr	1.15
100 mm diameter	-	0.11	1.47	0.12	nr	1.59
150 mm diameter	-	0.14	1.87	0.16	nr	2.03
Repairing/renovating brick/blockwork						
Cutting out decayed, defective or cracked work and replacing with new common bricks PC £220.00/1000; in gauged mortar (1:1:6)						
half brick thick	-	4.56	104.07	20.25	m^2	124.33
one brick thick	26.40	8.88	202.67	41.91	m^2	244.59
one and a half brick thick	39.60	12.58	287.12	63.58	m^2	350.70
two brick thick	52.80	16.10	367.46	85.24	m^2	452.70
individual bricks; half brick thick	-	0.28	6.39	0.34	nr	6.73
Cutting out decayed, defective or cracked work and replacing with new facing brickwork in gauged mortar (1:1:6); half brick thick; facing and pointing one side						
small areas; machine made facings PC £310.00/1000	19.53	6.75	154.06	27.93	m^2	181.99
small areas; hand made facings PC £500.00/1000	31.50	6.75	154.06	42.46	m^2	196.52
individual bricks; machine made facings PC £310.00/1000	0.31	0.42	9.59	0.45	nr	10.03
individual bricks; hand made facings PC £500.00/1000	0.50	0.42	9.59	0.68	nr	10.26
ADD or DEDUCT for variation of £10.00/1000 in PC of facing bricks; in flemish bond						
half brick thick	-	-	-	0.73	m^2	0.73
Cutting out decayed, defective or cracked soldier arch and replacing with new; repointing to match existing						
machine made facings PC £310.00/1000	4.96	1.80	41.08	6.61	m	47.69
hand made facings PC £500.00/1000	8.00	1.80	41.08	10.30	m	51.38
Cutting out decayed, defective or cracked work in uncoursed stonework; replacing with cement:mortar to match existing						
small areas; 300 mm thick wall	-	5.18	118.22	13.40	m^2	131.62
small areas; 400 mm thick wall	-	6.48	147.90	18.13	m^2	166.02
small areas; 600 mm thick wall	-	9.25	211.12	27.59	m^2	238.70
Cutting out staggered cracks and repointing to match existing along brick joints	-	0.37	8.44	-	m	8.44
Cutting out raking cracks in brickwork; stitching in new common bricks and repointing to match existing						
half brick thick	5.94	2.96	67.56	9.32	m^2	76.88
one brick thick	11.88	5.41	123.47	19.27	m^2	142.74
one and a half brick thick	17.82	8.09	184.64	28.59	m^2	213.23

C DEMOLITION/ALTERATION/RENOVATION

Item	PC £	Labour hours	Labour £	Material £	Unit	Total rate £
C41 REPAIRING/RENOVATING/CONSERVING MASONRY – cont'd						
Repairing/renovating brick/Blockwork – cont'd						
Cutting out raking cracks in brickwork; stitching in new facing bricks; half brick thick; facing and pointing one side to match existing						
machine made facings PC £310.00/1000	8.37	4.44	101.34	12.19	m²	**113.53**
hand made facings PC £500.00/1000	13.50	4.44	101.34	18.42	m²	**119.75**
Cutting out raking cracks in cavity brickwork; stitching in new common bricks PC £200.00/1000 one side; facing bricks the other side; both skins half brick thick; facing and pointing one side to match existing						
machine made facings PC £310.00/1000	8.37	7.59	173.23	21.44	m²	**194.67**
hand made facings PC £500.00/1000	13.50	7.59	173.23	27.66	m²	**200.89**
Cutting away and replacing with new cement mortar (1:3); angle fillets; 50 mm face width	-	0.23	5.25	2.12	m	**7.37**
Cutting out ends of joists and plates from walls; making good in common bricks PC £220.00/1000; in cement mortar (1:3)						
175 mm deep joists; 400 mm centres	-	0.60	13.69	6.66	m	**20.35**
225 mm deep joists; 400 mm centres	-	0.74	16.89	7.73	m	**24.62**
Cutting and pinning to existing brickwork ends of joists	-	0.37	8.44	-	nr	**8.44**
Making good adjacent work; where intersecting wall removed						
half brick thick	-	0.28	6.39	0.71	m	**7.10**
one brick thick	-	0.37	8.44	1.41	m	**9.86**
100 blockwork	-	0.23	5.25	0.71	m	**5.96**
150 blockwork	-	0.27	6.16	0.71	m	**6.87**
215 blockwork	-	0.32	7.30	1.41	m	**8.72**
255 blockwork	-	0.36	8.22	1.41	m	**9.63**
Removing defective parapet wall; 600 mm high; with two courses of tiles and brick coping over; re-building in new facing bricks, tiles and coping stones						
one brick thick	-	6.16	140.59	50.91	m	**191.50**
Removing defective capping stones and haunching; replacing stones and re-haunching in cement:mortar to match existing						
300 mm thick wall	-	1.25	28.53	3.94	m²	**32.47**
400 mm thick wall	-	1.39	31.72	4.73	m²	**36.45**
600 mm thick wall	-	1.62	36.97	7.09	m²	**44.07**
Cleaning surfaces; moss and lichen from walls	-	0.28	3.75	-	m²	**3.75**
Cleaning surfaces; lime mortar off brickwork; sort and stack for re-use	-	9.25	123.73	-	t	**123.73**
Repointing in cement mortar (1:1:6); to match existing						
raking out existing decayed joints in brickwork walls	-	0.69	15.75	0.71	m²	**16.45**
raking out existing decayed joints in chimney stacks	-	1.11	25.33	0.71	m²	**26.04**
raking out existing decayed joints in brickwork; re-wedging horizontal flashing	-	0.23	5.25	0.35	m	**5.60**
raking out existing decayed joints in brickwork; re-wedging stepped flashing	-	0.34	7.76	0.35	m	**8.11**

C DEMOLITION/ALTERATION/RENOVATION

Item	PC £	Labour hours	Labour £	Material £	Unit	Total rate £
Repointing in cement:mortar (1:3); to match existing						
raking out existing decayed joints in uncoursed stonework	-	1.11	25.33	0.79	m²	**26.12**
Making good hole where small pipe removed						
102 mm brickwork	-	0.19	2.54	0.08	nr	**2.62**
215 mm brickwork	-	0.19	2.54	0.08	nr	**2.62**
327 mm brickwork	-	0.19	2.54	0.08	nr	**2.62**
440 mm brickwork	-	0.19	2.54	0.08	nr	**2.62**
100 mm blockwork	-	0.19	2.54	0.08	nr	**2.62**
150 mm blockwork	-	0.19	2.54	0.08	nr	**2.62**
215 mm blockwork	-	0.19	2.54	0.08	nr	**2.62**
255 mm blockwork	-	0.19	2.54	0.08	nr	**2.62**
Making good hole and facings one side where small pipe removed						
102 mm brickwork	-	0.19	4.34	0.79	nr	**5.12**
215 mm brickwork	-	0.19	4.34	0.79	nr	**5.12**
327 mm brickwork	-	0.19	4.34	0.79	nr	**5.12**
440 mm brickwork	-	0.19	4.34	0.79	nr	**5.12**
Making good hole where large pipe removed						
102 mm brickwork	-	0.28	3.75	0.08	nr	**3.82**
215 mm brickwork	-	0.42	5.62	0.28	nr	**5.89**
327 mm brickwork	-	0.56	7.49	0.47	nr	**7.96**
440 mm brickwork	-	0.69	9.23	0.59	nr	**9.82**
100 mm blockwork	-	0.28	3.75	0.08	nr	**3.82**
150 mm blockwork	-	0.32	4.28	0.16	nr	**4.44**
215 mm blockwork	-	0.37	4.95	0.20	nr	**5.15**
255 mm blockwork	-	0.42	5.62	0.28	nr	**5.89**
Making good hole and facings one side where large pipe removed						
half brick thick	-	0.25	5.71	0.79	nr	**6.49**
one brick thick	-	0.33	7.53	0.87	nr	**8.40**
one and a half brick thick	-	0.42	9.59	0.95	nr	**10.53**
two brick thick	-	0.50	11.41	1.26	nr	**12.67**
Making good hole where extra large pipe removed						
half brick thick	-	0.37	4.95	0.32	nr	**5.26**
one brick thick	-	0.56	7.49	0.67	nr	**8.16**
one and a half brick thick	-	0.74	9.90	1.18	nr	**11.08**
two brick thick	-	0.93	12.44	1.42	nr	**13.86**
100 mm blockwork	-	0.37	4.95	0.32	nr	**5.26**
150 mm blockwork	-	0.43	5.75	0.47	nr	**6.22**
215 mm blockwork	-	0.46	6.15	0.67	nr	**6.82**
255 mm blockwork	-	0.51	6.82	0.82	nr	**7.64**
Making good hole and facings one side where extra large pipe removed						
half brick thick	-	0.33	7.53	1.22	nr	**8.75**
one brick thick	-	0.44	10.04	1.50	nr	**11.54**
one and a half brick thick	-	0.56	12.78	1.89	nr	**14.67**
two brick thick	-	0.67	15.29	2.56	nr	**17.85**
C50 REPAIRING/RENOVATING/CONSERVING METAL						
Repairing metal						
Overhauling and repairing metal casement windows; adjusting and oiling ironmongery; bringing forward affected parts for redecoration	-	1.39	18.59	4.49	nr	**23.08**

C DEMOLITION/ALTERATION/RENOVATION

Item	PC £	Labour hours	Labour £	Material £	Unit	Total rate £
C51 REPAIRING/RENOVATING/CONSERVING TIMBER						
Repairing timber						
Removing or punching in projecting nails; re-fixing softwood or hardwood flooring						
loose boards	-	0.14	2.56	-	m^2	2.56
floorboards previously set aside	-	0.74	13.52	0.51	m^2	14.04
Removing damaged softwood flooring; providing and fixing new 25 mm thick plain edge softwood boarding						
small areas	-	1.06	19.37	16.51	m^2	35.88
individual boards 150 mm wide	-	0.28	5.12	1.63	m	6.75
Sanding down and resurfacing existing flooring; preparing, bodying in with shellac and wax polish						
softwood	-	-	-	-	m^2	11.92
hardwood	-	-	-	-	m^2	11.21
Fitting existing softwood skirting to new frames or architraves						
75 mm high	-	0.09	1.64	-	m	1.64
150 mm high	-	0.12	2.19	-	m	2.19
225 mm high	-	0.15	2.74	-	m	2.74
Piecing in new 25 mm x 150 mm moulded softwood skirtings to match existing where old removed; bringing forward for redecoration	-	0.35	5.68	5.98	m	11.66
Piecing in new 25 mm x 150 mm moulded softwood skirtings to match existing where socket outlet removed; bringing forward for redecoration	-	0.20	3.23	3.43	nr	6.66
Easing and adjusting softwood doors, oiling ironmongery; bringing forward affected parts for redecoration	-	0.71	12.47	1.22	nr	13.69
Removing softwood doors, easing and adjusting; re-hanging; oiling ironmongery; bringing forward affected parts for redecoration	-	1.11	19.65	1.63	nr	21.28
Removing mortice lock, piecing in softwood doors; bringing forward affected parts for redecoration	-	1.02	18.22	0.91	nr	19.13
Fixing only salvaged softwood door	-	1.42	25.95	-	nr	25.95
Removing softwood doors; planing 12 mm from bottom edge; re-hanging	-	1.11	20.28	-	nr	20.28
Removing softwood doors; altering ironmongery; piecing in and rebating frame and door; re-hanging on opposite stile; bringing forward affected parts for redecoration	-	2.45	43.71	1.83	nr	45.54
Removing softwood doors to prepare for fire upgrading; removing ironmongery; replacing existing beads with 25 mm x 38 mm hardwood screwed beads; repairing minor damaged areas; re-hanging on wider butt hinges; adjusting all ironmongery; sealing around frame in cement mortar; bringing forward affected parts for redecoration (replacing glass panes not included)	-	4.85	87.15	16.12	nr	103.27
Upgrading and facing up one side of flush doors with 9 mm thick "Supalux"; screwing	-	1.16	21.20	35.16	nr	56.36
Upgrading and facing up one side of softwood panelled doors with 9 mm thick "Supalux"; screwing; plasterboard infilling to recesses	-	2.50	45.69	36.81	nr	82.49

C DEMOLITION/ALTERATION/RENOVATION

Item	PC £	Labour hours	Labour £	Material £	Unit	Total rate £
Taking off existing softwood doorstops; providing and screwing on new 25 mm x 38 mm doorstop; bringing forward for redecoration	-	0.20	3.23	2.55	nr	5.78
Cutting away defective 75 mm x 100 mm softwood external door frames; providing and splicing in new piece 300 mm long; bedding in cement mortar (1:3); pointing one side; bringing forward for redecoration	-	1.30	22.91	7.91	nr	30.82
Sealing roof trap flush with ceiling	-	0.56	10.23	2.51	nr	12.75
Forming opening 762 mm x 762 mm in existing ceiling for new standard roof trap comprising softwood linings, architraves and 6 mm thick plywood trap doors; trimming ceiling joists (making good to ceiling plaster not included)	-	2.50	45.69	69.82	nr	115.50
Easing and adjusting softwood casement windows, oiling ironmongery; bringing forward affected parts for redecoration	-	0.48	8.26	0.81	nr	9.08
Removing softwood casement windows; easing and adjusting; re-hanging; oiling ironmongery; bringing forward affected parts for redecoration	-	0.71	12.47	0.81	nr	13.28
Renewing solid mullion jambs or transoms of softwood casement windows to match existing; bringing forward affected parts for redecoration (taking off and re-hanging adjoining casements not included)	-	2.59	46.06	19.57	nr	65.63
Temporary linings 6 mm thick plywood infill to window while casement under repair	-	0.74	13.52	3.93	nr	17.45
Overhauling softwood double hung sash windows; easing, adjusting and oiling pulley wheels; re-hanging sashes on new hemp sash lines; re-assembling; bringing forward affected parts for redecoration	-	2.45	44.14	5.54	nr	49.68
Cutting away defective parts of softwood window sills; providing and splicing in new 75 mm x 100 mm weathered and throated pieces 300 mm long; bringing forward affected parts for redecoration	-	1.90	34.09	12.15	nr	46.24
Renewing broken stair nosings to treads or landings	-	1.67	30.52	2.91	nr	33.43
Cutting out infected or decayed structural members; shoring up adjacent work; providing and fixing new "treated" sawn softwood members pieced in						
Floors or flat roofs						
50 mm x 125 mm	-	0.37	6.76	2.08	m	8.84
50 mm x 150 mm	-	0.41	7.49	2.50	m	9.99
50 mm x 175 mm	-	0.44	8.04	2.99	m	11.04
Pitched roofs						
38 mm x 100 mm	-	0.33	6.03	1.29	m	7.32
50 mm x 100 mm	-	0.42	7.68	1.54	m	9.21
50 mm x 125 mm	-	0.46	8.41	2.00	m	10.41
50 mm x 150 mm	-	0.51	9.32	2.37	m	11.69
Kerbs bearers and the like						
50 mm x 75 mm	-	0.42	7.68	1.21	m	8.89
50 mm x 100 mm	-	0.52	9.50	1.54	m	11.04
75 mm x 100 mm	-	0.63	11.51	2.39	m	13.90
Scarfed joint; new to existing; over 450 mm2	-	0.93	17.00	-	nr	17.00
Scarfed and bolted joint; new to existing; including bolt let in flush; over 450 mm2	-	1.34	24.49	1.73	nr	26.21

C DEMOLITION/ALTERATION/RENOVATION

Item	PC £	Labour hours	Labour £	Material £	Unit	Total rate £
C52 FUNGUS/BEETLE ERADICATION						
Treating existing timber						
Removing cobwebs, dust and roof insulation; de-frass; treat exposed joists/rafters with two coats of proprietary insecticide and fungicide; by spray application	-	-	-	-	m²	9.70
Treating boarding with two coats of proprietary insecticide and fungicide; by spray application	-	-	-	-	m²	4.23
Treating individual timbers with two coats proprietary insecticide and fungicide; by brush application						
boarding	-	-	-	-	m²	4.68
structural members	-	-	-	-	m²	4.68
skirtings	-	-	-	-	m	4.68
Lifting necessary floorboards; treating floors with two coats proprietary insecticide and fungicide; by spray application; re-fixing boards	-	-	-	-	m²	7.75
Treating surfaces of adjoining concrete or brickwork with two coats of dry rot fluid; by spray application	-	-	-	-	m²	4.09
C90 ALTERATIONS - SPOT ITEMS						
Composite "spot" items						
NOTE: Few exactly similar composite items of alteration works are encountered on different schemes; for this reason it is considered more accurate for the reader to build up the value of such items from individual prices in the following section.						
However, for estimating purposes, the following "spot" items have been prepared.						
Prices include for removal of debris from site but do not include for shoring, scaffolding or re-decoration, except where stated.						
Removing fittings and fixtures						
Removing shelves, window boards and the like	-	0.31	4.15	0.17	m	4.31
Removing handrails and balustrades						
tubular handrailing and brackets	-	0.28	3.75	0.17	m	3.91
metal balustrades	-	0.46	6.15	0.50	m	6.65
Removing handrails and brackets	-	0.09	2.28	0.50	m	2.78
Removing sloping timber ramps in corridors; at changes of levels	-	1.85	46.94	2.49	nr	49.43
Removing bath panels and bearers	-	0.37	9.39	0.83	nr	10.22
Removing kitchen fittings						
wall units	-	0.42	10.66	2.49	nr	13.15
floor units	-	0.28	7.10	3.65	nr	10.76
larder units	-	0.37	9.39	8.30	nr	17.69
built-in cupboards	-	1.39	35.27	16.61	nr	51.88

C DEMOLITION/ALTERATION/RENOVATION

Item	PC £	Labour hours	Labour £	Material £	Unit	Total rate £
Removing bathroom fittings; making good works disturbed						
toilet roll holder or soap dispenser	-	0.28	3.75	-	nr	3.75
towel holder	-	0.56	7.49	-	nr	7.49
mirror	-	0.60	8.03	-	nr	8.03
Removing pipe casings	-	0.28	7.10	0.66	m	7.77
Removing ironmongery; in preparation for re-decoration; and subsequently re-fixing; including providing any new screws necessary	-	0.23	5.84	0.17	nr	6.00
Removing, withdrawing nails, etc; making good holes						
carpet fixing strip from floors	-	0.04	0.54	-	m	0.54
curtain track from head of window	-	0.23	3.08	-	m	3.08
nameplates or numerals from face of door	-	0.46	6.15	-	nr	6.15
fly screen and frame from window	-	0.83	11.10	-	nr	11.10
small notice board and frame from walls	-	0.82	10.97	-	nr	10.97
fire extinguisher and bracket from walls	-	1.16	15.52	-	nr	15.52
Removing plumbing and engineering installations						
Removing sanitary fittings and supports; temporarily capping off services; to receive new (not included)						
sink or lavatory basin	-	0.93	14.10	9.97	nr	24.06
bath	-	1.85	28.06	14.95	nr	43.01
WC suite	-	1.39	21.08	9.97	nr	31.05
Removing sanitary fittings and supports, complete with associated services, overflows and waste pipes; making good all holes and other works disturbed; bringing forward all surfaces ready for re-decoration						
sink or lavatory basin	-	3.70	56.13	13.80	nr	69.93
range of three lavatory basins	-	7.40	112.25	25.67	nr	137.93
bath	-	5.55	84.19	18.62	nr	102.81
WC suite	-	7.40	112.25	29.13	nr	141.39
2 stall urinal	-	14.80	224.51	27.59	nr	252.10
3 stall urinal	-	22.20	336.76	57.37	nr	394.13
4 stall urinal	-	29.60	449.02	85.05	nr	534.07
Removing taps	-	0.09	1.50	-	nr	1.50
Clearing blocked wastes without dismantling						
sinks	-	0.46	8.82	-	nr	8.82
WC traps	-	0.56	10.73	-	nr	10.73
Removing gutterwork and supports						
uPVC or asbestos	-	0.28	3.75	0.17	m	3.91
cast iron	-	0.32	4.28	0.33	m	4.61
Overhauling sections of rainwater gutterings; cutting out existing joints; adjusting brackets to correct falls; re-making joints						
100 mm diameter uPVC	-	0.23	4.20	0.03	m	4.23
100 mm diameter cast iron including bolt	-	0.83	15.17	0.11	m	15.28
Removing rainwater heads and supports						
uPVC or asbestos	-	0.27	3.61	0.17	nr	3.78
cast iron	-	0.37	4.95	0.33	nr	5.28
Removing pipework and supports						
uPVC or asbestos rainwater stack	-	0.28	3.75	0.17	m	3.91
cast iron rainwater stack	-	0.32	4.28	0.33	m	4.61
cast iron jointed soil stack	-	0.56	7.49	0.33	m	7.82
copper or steel water or gas pipework	-	0.14	1.87	0.17	m	2.04
cast iron rainwater shoe	-	0.07	0.94	0.17	m	1.10

C DEMOLITION/ALTERATION/RENOVATION

Item	PC £	Labour hours	Labour £	Material £	Unit	Total rate £
C90 ALTERATIONS - SPOT ITEMS – cont'd						
Removing plumbing and engineering Installations – cont'd						
Overhauling and re-making leaking joints in pipework						
100 mm diameter upvc	-	0.19	2.54	0.06	nr	**2.60**
100 mm diameter cast iron including bolt	-	0.74	9.90	0.23	nr	**10.12**
Cleaning out existing rainwater installations						
rainwater gutters	-	0.07	0.94	-	m	**0.94**
rainwater gully	-	0.19	2.54	-	nr	**2.54**
rainwater stack; including head, swan-neck and shoe (not exceeding 10 m long)	-	0.69	9.23	-	nr	**9.23**
Removing the following equipment and ancillaries; capping off services; making good works disturbed (excluding any draining down of system)						
expansion tank; 900 mm x 450 mm x 900 mm	-	1.67	25.32	6.64	nr	**31.97**
hot water cylinder; 450 mm diameter x 1050 mm high	-	1.11	16.84	2.82	nr	**19.66**
cold water tank; 1540 mm x 900 mm x 900 mm	-	2.22	33.68	20.43	nr	**54.11**
cast iron radiator	-	1.85	28.06	5.32	nr	**33.38**
gas water heater	-	3.70	56.13	3.32	nr	**59.45**
gas fire	-	1.85	28.06	4.32	nr	**32.38**
Removing cold water tanks and housing on roof; stripping out and capping off all associated piping; making good works disturbed and roof finishings						
1540 mm x 900 mm x 900 mm	-	11.10	168.38	25.41	nr	**193.79**
Turning off supplies; dismantling the following fittings; replacing washers; re-assembling and testing						
15 mm diameter tap	-	0.23	4.41	-	nr	**4.41**
15 mm diameter ball valve	-	0.32	6.13	-	nr	**6.13**
Turning off supplies; removing the following fittings; testing and replacing						
15 mm diameter ball valve	-	0.46	8.82	7.13	nr	**15.94**
Removing lagging from pipes						
up to 42 mm diameter	-	0.09	1.20	0.17	nr	**1.37**
Removing finishings						
Removing plasterboard wall finishings	-	0.37	4.95	-	m²	**4.95**
Removing wall finishings; cutting out and making good cracks						
plasterboard wall finishing	-	0.37	4.95	-	m²	**4.95**
decorative wallpaper and lining	-	0.19	2.54	1.40	m²	**3.94**
heavy wallpaper and lining	-	0.32	4.28	1.40	m²	**5.68**
Hacking off wall finishings						
plaster	-	0.19	2.54	0.83	m²	**3.37**
cement rendering or pebbledash	-	0.37	4.95	0.83	m²	**5.78**
wall tiling and screed	-	0.46	6.15	1.33	m²	**7.48**
Removing wall linings; including battening behind						
plain sheeting	-	0.28	3.75	0.66	m²	**4.41**
matchboarding	-	0.37	4.95	1.00	m²	**5.95**
Removing oak dado wall panel finishings; cleaning off and setting aside for re-use	-	0.60	15.22	-	m²	**15.22**

C DEMOLITION/ALTERATION/RENOVATION

Item	PC £	Labour hours	Labour £	Material £	Unit	Total rate £
Removing defective or damaged plaster wall finishings; re-plastering walls with two coats of gypsum plaster; including dubbing out; jointing new to existing						
small areas	-	1.48	29.17	5.53	m²	34.70
isolated areas not exceeding 0.50 m2	-	1.06	20.89	2.78	nr	23.67
Making good plaster wall finishings with two coats of gypsum plaster where wall or partition removed; dubbing out; trimming back existing and fair jointing to new work						
150 mm wide	-	0.60	11.82	0.83	m	12.66
225 mm wide	-	0.74	14.58	1.24	m	15.83
300 mm wide	-	0.88	17.34	1.67	m	19.01
Removing defective or damaged damp plaster wall finishings, investigating and treating wall; re-plastering walls with two coats of "Thistle Renovating" plaster; including dubbing out; fair jointing to existing work						
small areas	-	1.53	30.15	2.74	m²	32.90
isolated areas not exceeding 0.50 m2	-	1.13	22.27	1.38	m²	23.65
Dubbing out in cement and sand; average 13 mm thick						
over 300 mm wide	-	0.46	9.07	1.02	m²	10.09
Making good plaster wall finishings with plasterboard and skim where wall or partition removed; trimming back existing and fair joint to new work						
150 mm wide	-	0.69	13.60	1.60	m	15.20
225 mm wide	-	0.83	16.36	1.81	m	18.17
300 mm wide	-	0.93	18.33	2.02	m	20.35
Cutting out; making good cracks in plaster wall finishings						
walls	-	0.23	4.53	1.40	m	5.93
ceilings	-	0.31	6.11	1.40	m	7.50
Making good plaster wall finishings where items removed or holes left						
small pipe or conduit	-	0.06	1.18	0.70	nr	1.88
large pipe	-	0.09	1.77	1.40	nr	3.17
extra large pipe	-	0.14	2.76	0.88	nr	3.64
small recess; eg. electrical switch point	-	0.07	1.38	0.17	nr	1.55
Making good plasterboard and skim wall finishings where items removed or holes left						
small pipe or conduit	-	0.06	1.18	0.70	nr	1.88
large pipe	-	0.21	4.14	0.52	nr	4.65
extra large pipe	-	0.28	5.52	0.65	nr	6.17
Removing floor finishings						
carpet and underfelt	-	0.11	1.47	-	m²	1.47
linoleum sheet flooring	-	0.09	1.20	-	m²	1.20
carpet gripper	-	0.02	0.27	-	m	0.27
Removing floor finishings; preparing screed to receive new						
carpet and underfelt	-	0.61	8.16	-	m²	8.16
vinyl or thermoplastic tiles	-	0.79	10.57	-	m²	10.57
Removing woodblock floor finishings; cleaning off and setting aside for re-use	-	0.69	9.23	-	m²	9.23
Breaking up floor finishings						
floor screed	-	0.60	8.03	-	m²	8.03
granolithic flooring and screed	-	0.79	10.57	-	m²	10.57
terrazzo or ceramic floor tiles and screed	-	0.97	12.97	-	m²	12.97

C DEMOLITION/ALTERATION/RENOVATION

Item	PC £	Labour hours	Labour £	Material £	Unit	Total rate £
C90 ALTERATIONS - SPOT ITEMS – cont'd						
Removing finishings – cont'd						
Levelling and repairing floor finishings screed; 5 mm thick						
screed; 5 mm thick; in small areas	-	0.46	9.07	10.15	m^2	**19.21**
screed; 5 mm thick; in isolated areas not exceeding 0.50 m^2	-	0.32	6.31	5.07	m^2	**11.38**
Removing softwood skirtings, picture rails, dado rails, architraves and the like	-	0.09	1.20	-	m	**1.20**
Removing softwood skirtings; cleaning off and setting aside for re-use in making good	-	0.23	3.08	-	m	**3.08**
Breaking up paving						
asphalt	-	0.56	7.49	-	m^2	**7.49**
Removing ceiling finishings						
plasterboard and skim; withdrawing nails	-	0.28	3.75	0.50	m^2	**4.24**
wood lath and plaster; withdrawing nails	-	0.46	6.15	0.83	m^2	**6.98**
suspended ceilings	-	0.69	9.23	0.83	m^2	**10.06**
plaster moulded cornice; 25 mm girth	-	0.14	1.87	0.17	m	**2.04**
Removing part of plasterboard ceiling finishings to facilitate insertion of new steel beam	-	1.02	13.64	1.00	m	**14.64**
Removing ceiling linings; including battening behind						
plain sheeting	-	0.42	5.62	0.66	m^2	**6.28**
matchboarding	-	0.56	7.49	1.00	m^2	**8.49**
Removing defective or damaged ceiling plaster finishings; removing laths or cutting back boarding; preparing and fixing new plasterboard; applying one skim coat of gypsum plaster; fair jointing new to existing						
small areas	-	1.57	30.94	4.29	m^2	**35.23**
isolated areas not exceeding 0.50m^2	-	1.13	22.27	2.42	m^2	**24.69**
Removing coverings						
Removing roof coverings						
slates	-	0.46	6.15	0.33	m^2	**6.49**
slates; set aside for re-use	-	0.56	7.49	-	m^2	**7.49**
nibbed tiles	-	0.37	4.95	0.33	m^2	**5.28**
nibbed tiles; set aside for re-use	-	0.46	6.15	-	m^2	**6.15**
corrugated asbestos sheeting	-	0.37	4.95	0.33	m^2	**5.28**
corrugated metal sheeting	-	0.37	4.95	0.33	m^2	**5.28**
underfelt and nails	-	0.04	0.54	0.17	m^2	**0.70**
three layer felt roofing; cleaning base off for new coverings	-	0.23	3.08	0.33	m^2	**3.41**
sheet metal coverings	-	0.46	6.15	0.33	m^2	**6.49**
Removing roof coverings; selecting and re-fixing; including providing 25% new; including nails, etc.						
asbestos-free artificial blue/black slates; 500 mm x 250 mm	-	1.02	28.09	6.81	m^2	**34.90**
asbestos-free artificial blue/black slates; 600 mm x 300 mm	-	0.93	25.61	5.36	m^2	**30.97**
natural slates; Welsh blue 510 mm x 255 mm	-	1.11	30.57	13.83	m^2	**44.40**
natural slates; Welsh blue 600 mm x 300 mm	-	0.97	26.72	17.72	m^2	**44.44**
clay plain tiles "Dreadnought" machine made; 265 mm x 165 mm; PC £315.00/1000	-	1.02	28.09	7.04	m^2	**35.13**

C DEMOLITION/ALTERATION/RENOVATION

Item	PC £	Labour hours	Labour £	Material £	Unit	Total rate £
concrete interlocking tiles; Marley "Ludlow Major" or other equal and approved; 413 mm x 330 mm; PC £699.00/1000	-	0.65	17.90	2.64	m²	**20.54**
concrete interlocking tiles; Redland "Renown" or other equal and approved; 417 mm x 330 mm; PC £750.00/1000	-	0.65	17.90	2.87	m²	**20.77**
Removing damaged roof coverings in area less than 10 m²; providing and fixing new; including nails, etc.						
asbestos-free artificial blue/black slates; 500 mm x 250 mm	-	1.25	34.43	18.66	m²	**53.09**
asbestos-free artificial blue/black slates; 600 mm x 300 mm	-	1.16	31.95	15.31	m²	**47.26**
natural slates; Welsh blue 510 mm x 255 mm	-	1.34	36.91	50.11	m²	**87.02**
natural slates; Welsh blue 600 mm x 300 mm	-	1.20	33.05	66.95	m²	**100.00**
clay plain tiles "Dreadnought" machine made or other equal and approved; 265 mm x 165 mm; PC £315.00/1000	-	1.25	34.43	22.94	m²	**57.37**
concrete interlocking tiles; Marley "Ludlow Major" or other equal and approved; 413 mm x 330 mm; PC £699.00/1000	-	0.83	22.86	8.47	m²	**31.33**
concrete interlocking tiles; Redland "Renown" or other equal and approved; 417 mm x 330 mm; PC £750.00/1000	-	0.83	22.86	9.44	m²	**32.30**
Removing individual damaged roof coverings; providing and fixing new; including nails, etc.						
asbestos-free artificial blue/black slates; 500 mm x 250 mm	-	0.23	6.33	1.35	nr	**7.68**
asbestos-free artificial blue/black slates; 600 mm x 300 mm	-	0.23	6.33	1.11	nr	**7.44**
natural slates; Welsh blue 510 mm x 255 mm	-	0.28	7.71	2.76	nr	**10.47**
natural slates; Welsh blue 600 mm x 300 mm	-	0.28	7.71	5.40	nr	**13.11**
clay plain tiles "Dreadnought" machine made or other equal and approved; 265 mm x 165 mm; PC £315.00/1000	-	0.14	3.86	0.38	nr	**4.23**
concrete interlocking tiles; Marley "Ludlow Major" or other equal and approved; 413 mm x 330 mm; PC £699.00/1000	-	0.19	5.23	0.83	nr	**6.06**
concrete interlocking tiles; Redland "Renown" or other equal and approved; 417 mm x 330 mm; PC £725.00/1000	-	0.19	5.23	0.92	nr	**6.15**
Breaking up roof coverings						
asphalt	-	0.93	12.44	-	m²	**12.44**
Removing half round ridge or hip tile 300 mm long; providing and fixing new	-	0.46	12.67	3.56	nr	**16.22**
Removing defective metal flashings						
horizontal	-	0.19	2.54	0.33	m	**2.87**
stepped	-	0.23	3.08	0.17	m	**3.24**
Turning back bitumen felt and later dressing up face of new brickwork as skirtings; not exceeding 150 mm girth	-	0.93	18.53	0.11	m	**18.65**
Cutting out crack in asphalt roof coverings; making good to match existing						
20 mm thick two coat	-	1.53	21.48	-	m	**21.48**

C DEMOLITION/ALTERATION/RENOVATION

Item	PC £	Labour hours	Labour £	Material £	Unit	Total rate £
C90 ALTERATIONS - SPOT ITEMS – cont'd						
Removing coverings – cont'd						
Removing bitumen felt roof coverings and boarding to allow access for work to top of walls or beams beneath	-	0.74	9.90	-	m	**9.90**
Removing tiling battens; withdrawing nails	-	0.07	0.94	0.17	m²	**1.10**
Examining roof battens; re-nailing where loose; providing and fixing 25% new						
25 mm x 50 mm slating battens at 262 mm centres	-	0.07	1.93	0.70	m²	**2.63**
25 mm x 38 mm tiling battens at 100 mm centres	-	0.19	5.23	1.55	m²	**6.78**
Removing roof battens and nails; providing and fixing new "treated" softwood battens throughout						
25 mm x 50 mm slating battens at 262 mm centres	-	0.11	3.03	2.37	m²	**5.40**
25 mm x 38 mm tiling battens at 100 mm centres	-	0.23	6.33	4.12	m²	**10.45**
Removing underfelt and nails; providing and fixing new						
unreinforced felt	0.61	0.09	2.48	0.96	m²	**3.44**
reinforced felt	1.15	0.09	2.48	1.59	m²	**4.07**
Cutting openings or recesses						
Cutting openings or recesses through reinforced concrete walls						
150 mm thick	-	5.18	76.71	10.86	m²	**87.57**
225 mm thick	-	7.08	103.74	16.23	m²	**119.97**
300 mm thick	-	9.02	131.14	21.88	m²	**153.02**
Cutting openings or recesses through reinforced concrete suspended slabs						
150 mm thick	-	3.93	57.41	16.95	m²	**74.36**
225 mm thick	-	5.83	85.24	16.34	m²	**101.58**
300 mm thick	-	7.26	105.34	20.66	m²	**126.00**
Cutting openings or recesses through slated, boarded and timbered roof; 700 mm x 1100 mm; for new rooflight; including cutting structure and finishings; trimming timbers in rafters and making good roof coverings (kerb and rooflight not included)	-	-	-	-	nr	**375.41**
Cutting openings or recesses through brick or block walls or partitions; for lintels or beams above openings; in gauged mortar						
half brick thick	-	2.45	55.92	2.82	m²	**58.74**
one brick thick	-	4.07	92.89	5.65	m²	**98.54**
one and a half brick thick	-	5.69	129.86	8.47	m²	**138.34**
two brick thick	-	7.31	166.84	11.29	m²	**178.13**
75 mm blockwork	-	1.48	33.78	1.83	m²	**35.61**
90 mm blockwork	-	1.67	38.11	2.16	m²	**40.27**
100 mm blockwork	-	1.80	41.08	2.49	m²	**43.57**
115 mm blockwork	-	1.84	41.99	2.82	m²	**44.82**
125 mm blockwork	-	2.04	46.56	3.16	m²	**49.72**
140 mm blockwork	-	2.17	49.53	3.49	m²	**53.01**
150 mm blockwork	-	2.27	51.81	3.82	m²	**55.63**
190 mm blockwork	-	2.53	57.74	4.82	m²	**62.56**
215 mm blockwork	-	2.68	61.17	5.32	m²	**66.48**
255 mm blockwork	-	2.94	67.10	6.31	m²	**73.41**

C DEMOLITION/ALTERATION/RENOVATION

Item	PC £	Labour hours	Labour £	Material £	Unit	Total rate £
Cutting openings or recesses through brick walls or partitions; for lintels or beams above openings; in cement mortar						
half brick thick	-	3.52	80.34	2.82	m²	83.16
one brick thick	-	5.83	133.06	5.65	m²	138.71
one and a half brick thick	-	8.14	185.78	8.47	m²	194.25
two brick thick	-	10.45	238.50	11.29	m²	249.80
Cutting openings or recesses through brick or block walls or partitions; for door or window openings; in gauged mortar						
half brick thick	-	1.25	28.53	2.82	m²	31.35
one brick thick	-	2.04	46.56	5.65	m²	52.21
one and a half brick thick	-	2.82	64.36	8.47	m²	72.83
two brick thick	-	3.65	83.31	11.29	m²	94.60
75 mm blockwork	-	0.74	16.89	1.83	m²	18.72
90 mm blockwork	-	0.85	19.40	2.16	m²	21.56
100 mm blockwork	-	0.93	21.23	2.49	m²	23.72
115 mm blockwork	-	0.98	22.37	2.82	m²	25.19
125 mm blockwork	-	1.02	23.28	3.16	m²	26.44
140 mm blockwork	-	1.07	24.42	3.49	m²	27.91
150 mm blockwork	-	1.11	25.33	3.82	m²	29.15
190 mm blockwork	-	1.22	27.84	4.82	m²	32.66
215 mm blockwork	-	1.34	30.58	5.32	m²	35.90
255 mm blockwork	-	1.48	33.78	6.31	m²	40.09
Cutting openings or recesses through brick or block walls or partitions; for door or window openings; in cement mortar						
half brick thick	-	1.76	40.17	2.82	m²	42.99
one brick thick	-	2.91	66.42	5.65	m²	72.06
one and a half brick thick	-	4.02	91.75	8.47	m²	100.22
two brick thick	-	5.23	119.37	11.29	m²	130.66
Cutting openings or recesses through faced wall 1200 mm x 1200 mm (1.44 m²) for new window; including cutting structure, quoining up jambs, cutting and pinning in suitable precast concrete boot lintel with galvanised steel angle bolted on to support, outer brick soldier course in facing bricks to match existing (new window and frame not included)						
one brick thick wall or two half brick thick skins	-	-	-	-	nr	506.81
one and a half brick thick wall	-	-	-	-	nr	531.84
two brick thick wall	-	-	-	-	nr	575.63
Cutting openings or recesses through 100 mm thick softwood stud partition including framing studwork around, making good boarding and any plaster either side and extending floor finish through opening (new door and frame not included)						
single door and frame	-	-	-	-	nr	262.79
pair of doors and frame	-	-	-	-	nr	344.14

C DEMOLITION/ALTERATION/RENOVATION

Item	PC £	Labour hours	Labour £	Material £	Unit	Total rate £
C90 ALTERATIONS - SPOT ITEMS – cont'd						
Cutting openings or recesses – cont'd						
Cutting openings or recesses through internal plastered wall for single door and frame; including cutting structure, quoining or making good jambs, cutting and pinning in suitable precast concrete plate lintel(s), making good plasterwork up to new frame both sides and extending floor finish through new opening (new door and frame not included)						
150 mm reinforced concrete wall	-	-	-	-	nr	300.33
225 mm reinforced concrete wall	-	-	-	-	nr	412.95
half brick thick wall	-	-	-	-	nr	281.56
one brick thick wall or two half brick thick skins	-	-	-	-	nr	369.14
one and a half brick thick wall	-	-	-	-	nr	450.49
two brick thick wall	-	-	-	-	nr	544.33
100 mm block wall	-	-	-	-	nr	262.79
215 mm block wall	-	-	-	-	nr	344.14
Cutting openings or recesses through internal plastered wall for pair of doors and frame; including cutting structure, quoining or making good jambs, cutting and pinning in suitable precast concrete plate lintel(s), making good plasterwork up to new frame both sides and extending floor finish through new opening (new door and frame not included)						
150 mm reinforced concrete wall	-	-	-	-	nr	431.72
225 mm reinforced concrete wall	-	-	-	-	nr	550.60
half brick thick wall	-	-	-	-	nr	331.62
one brick thick wall or two half brick thick skins	-	-	-	-	nr	456.76
one and a half brick thick wall	-	-	-	-	nr	588.15
two brick thick wall	-	-	-	-	nr	700.76
100 mm block wall	-	-	-	-	nr	312.85
215 mm block wall	-	-	-	-	nr	425.46
Cutting back projections						
Cutting back brick projections flush with adjacent wall						
225 mm x 112 mm	-	0.28	6.39	0.17	m	6.56
225 mm x 225 mm	-	0.46	10.50	0.33	m	10.83
337 mm x 112 mm	-	0.65	14.84	0.50	m	15.33
450 mm x 225 mm	-	0.83	18.94	0.66	m	19.61
Cutting back chimney breasts flush with adjacent wall						
half brick thick	-	1.62	36.97	5.32	m²	42.29
one brick thick	-	2.17	49.53	8.30	m²	57.83
Filling in openings						
Removing doors and frames; making good plaster and skirtings across reveals and heads; leaving as blank openings						
single doors	-	-	-	-	nr	112.63
pair of doors	-	-	-	-	nr	131.39
Removing doors and frames in 100 mm thick softwood partitions; filling in openings with timber covered on both sides with boarding or lining to match existing; extending skirtings both sides						
single doors	-	-	-	-	nr	175.19
pair of doors	-	-	-	-	nr	231.50

C DEMOLITION/ALTERATION/RENOVATION

Item	PC £	Labour hours	Labour £	Material £	Unit	Total rate £
Removing single doors and frames in internal walls; filling in openings with brickwork or blockwork; plastering walls and extending skirtings both sides						
half brick thick	-	-	-	-	nr	193.95
one brick thick	-	-	-	-	nr	269.06
one and a half brick thick	-	-	-	-	nr	337.87
two brick thick	-	-	-	-	nr	425.46
100 mm blockwork	-	-	-	-	nr	156.43
215 mm blockwork	-	-	-	-	nr	231.50
Removing pairs of doors and frames in internal walls; filling in openings with brickwork or blockwork; plastering walls and extend skirtings both sides						
half brick thick	-	-	-	-	nr	312.85
one brick thick	-	-	-	-	nr	437.98
one and a half brick thick	-	-	-	-	nr	563.12
two brick thick	-	-	-	-	nr	681.99
100 mm blockwork	-	-	-	-	nr	269.06
215 mm blockwork	-	-	-	-	nr	356.64
Removing 825 mm x 1046 mm (1.16 m^2) sliding sash windows and frames in external faced walls; filling in openings with facing brickwork on outside to match existing and common brickwork on inside; plastering internally						
one brick thick or two half brick thick skins	-	-	-	-	nr	256.53
one and a half brick thick	-	-	-	-	nr	287.82
two brick thick	-	-	-	-	nr	331.62
Removing 825 mm x 1406 mm (1.16 m^2) curved headed sliding sashed windows in external stuccoed walls; filling in openings with common bricks; stucco on outside and plastering internally						
one brick thick or two half brick thick skins	-	-	-	-	nr	287.82
one and a half brick thick	-	-	-	-	nr	331.62
two brick thick	-	-	-	-	nr	412.95
Removing 825 mm x 1406 mm (1.16 m^2) curved headed sliding sash windows in external masonry faced brick walls; filling in openings with facing brickwork on outside and common brickwork on inside; plastering internally						
350 mm wall	-	-	-	-	nr	750.82
500 mm wall	-	-	-	-	nr	819.66
600 mm wall	-	-	-	-	nr	900.98
Quoining up jambs in common bricks; PC £220.00/1000; in gauged mortar (1:1:6); as the work proceeds						
half brick thick or skin of hollow wall	-	0.93	21.23	4.44	m	25.67
one brick thick	-	1.39	31.72	8.89	m	40.61
one and a half brick thick	-	1.80	41.08	13.33	m	54.41
two brick thick	-	2.22	50.67	16.36	m	67.03
75 mm blockwork	-	0.58	13.24	3.79	m	17.03
90 mm blockwork	-	0.62	14.15	5.08	m	19.23
100 mm blockwork	-	0.65	14.84	5.65	m	20.49
115 mm blockwork	-	0.70	15.98	6.40	m	22.38
125 mm blockwork	-	0.74	16.89	7.25	m	24.14
140 mm blockwork	-	0.80	18.26	8.35	m	26.60
150 mm blockwork	-	0.83	18.94	9.20	m	28.14
190 mm blockwork	-	0.93	21.23	11.17	m	32.40
215 mm blockwork	-	1.00	22.82	12.41	m	35.24
225 mm blockwork	-	1.10	25.11	15.24	m	40.35

Prices for Measured Works – Minor Works

C DEMOLITION/ALTERATION/RENOVATION

Item	PC £	Labour hours	Labour £	Material £	Unit	Total rate £
C90 ALTERATIONS - SPOT ITEMS – cont'd						
Filling in openings – cont'd						
Closing at jambs with common brickwork half brick thick						
50 mm cavity; including lead-lined hessian based vertical damp proof course	-	0.37	8.44	7.94	m	16.38
Quoining up jambs in machine made facings; PC £310.00/1000; in gauged mortar (1:1:6); facing and pointing one side to match existing						
half brick thick or skin of hollow wall	-	1.16	26.48	7.77	m	34.25
one brick thick	-	1.39	31.72	14.12	m	45.85
one and a half brick thick	-	2.13	48.61	20.98	m	69.59
two brick thick	-	2.59	59.11	27.69	m	86.81
Quoining up jambs in hand made facings; PC £500.00/1000; in gauged mortar (1:1:6); facing and pointing one side to match existing						
half brick thick or skin of hollow wall	-	1.16	26.48	11.23	m	37.71
one brick thick	-	1.39	31.72	21.04	m	52.76
one and a half brick thick	-	2.13	48.61	31.36	m	79.97
two brick thick	-	2.59	59.11	41.53	m	100.64
Filling existing openings with common brickwork or blockwork in gauged mortar (1:1:6) (cutting and bonding not included)						
half brick thick	-	1.71	39.03	17.43	m^2	56.46
one brick thick	-	2.82	64.36	36.27	m^2	100.63
one and a half brick thick	-	3.89	88.78	54.40	m^2	143.18
two brick thick	-	4.86	110.92	72.54	m^2	183.46
75 mm blockwork	5.45	0.85	19.40	8.11	m^2	27.51
90 mm blockwork	7.46	0.93	21.23	10.60	m^2	31.83
100 mm blockwork	8.37	0.97	22.14	11.74	m^2	33.88
115 mm blockwork	9.63	1.05	23.96	13.30	m^2	37.27
125 mm blockwork	10.47	1.09	24.88	14.34	m^2	39.21
140 mm blockwork	11.73	1.16	26.48	15.90	m^2	42.38
150 mm blockwork	12.57	1.20	27.39	16.94	m^2	44.33
190 mm blockwork	15.91	1.37	31.27	21.80	m^2	53.07
215 mm blockwork	18.01	1.48	33.78	24.41	m^2	58.19
255 mm blockwork	22.19	1.65	37.66	29.60	m^2	67.26
Cutting and bonding ends to existing						
half brick thick	-	0.37	8.44	1.42	m	9.87
one brick thick	-	0.54	12.32	2.77	m	15.10
one and a half brick thick	-	0.80	18.26	3.38	m	21.63
two brick thick	-	1.16	26.48	5.15	m	31.62
75 mm blockwork	-	0.16	3.65	0.59	m	4.24
90 mm blockwork	-	0.19	4.34	0.81	m	5.15
100 mm blockwork	-	0.21	4.79	0.90	m	5.69
115 mm blockwork	-	0.23	5.25	1.05	m	6.30
125 mm blockwork	-	0.24	5.48	1.12	m	6.60
140 mm blockwork	-	0.26	5.93	1.24	m	7.18
150 mm blockwork	0.96	0.27	6.16	1.32	m	7.49
190 mm blockwork	1.21	0.33	7.53	1.75	m	9.28
215 mm blockwork	1.37	0.38	8.67	1.95	m	10.62
255 mm blockwork	1.69	0.44	10.04	2.35	m	12.39
half brick thick in facings; to match existing	2.17	0.56	12.78	3.48	m^2	16.26
Extra over common brickwork for fair face; flush pointing						
walls and the like	-	0.19	4.34	-	m^2	4.34

C DEMOLITION/ALTERATION/RENOVATION

Item	PC £	Labour hours	Labour £	Material £	Unit	Total rate £
Extra over common bricks; PC £220.00/1000 for facing bricks in flemish bond; facing and pointing one side						
machine made facings; PC £310.00/1000	23.25	0.97	22.14	8.19	m²	**30.33**
hand made facings; PC £500.00/1000	37.50	0.97	22.14	25.49	m²	**47.62**
ADD or DEDUCT for variation of £10.00/1000 in PC for facing bricks; in flemish bond						
half brick thick	-	-	-	0.73	m²	**0.73**
Filling in openings to hollow walls with inner skin of common bricks PC £220.00/1000; 50 mm cavity and galvanised steel butterfly ties; outer skin of facings; all in gauged mortar (1:1:6); facing and pointing one side						
two half brick thick skins; outer skin sand faced facings	-	4.26	97.23	39.27	m²	**136.50**
two half brick thick skins; outer skin machine made facings	-	4.26	97.23	44.23	m²	**141.45**
two half brick thick skins; outer skin hand made facings	-	4.26	97.23	58.75	m²	**155.98**
Temporary screens						
Providing and erecting; maintaining; temporary dust proof screens; with 50 mm x 75 mm sawn softwood framing; covering one side with 12 mm thick plywood						
over 300 mm wide	-	0.74	13.52	9.09	m²	**22.61**
Providing and erecting; maintaining; temporary screen; with 50 mm x 100 mm sawn softwood framing; covering one side with 13 mm thick insulating board and other side with single layer of polythene sheet						
over 300 mm wide	-	0.93	17.00	23.57	m²	**40.57**
Providing and erecting; maintaining; temporary screen; with 50 mm x 100 mm sawn softwood framing; covering one side with 19 mm thick exterior quality plywood; softwood cappings; including three coats of gloss paint; clearing away						
over 300 mm wide	-	1.85	30.21	16.41	m²	**46.62**

D GROUNDWORKS

Item	PC £	Labour hours	Labour £	Material /Plant £	Unit	Total rate £
D20 EXCAVATING AND FILLING						
NOTE: Prices are applicable to excavation in firm soil. Multiplying factors for other soils are as follows:						
Mechanical **Hand**						
Clay x 2.00 x 1.20						
Compact gravel x 3.00 x 1.50						
Soft chalk x 4.00 x 2.00						
Hard rock x 5.00 x 6.00						
Running sand or silt x 6.00 x 2.00						
Site preparation						
Removing trees						
girth 600 mm - 1.50 m	-	20.35	232.92	-	nr	**232.92**
girth 1.50 - 3.00 m	-	35.61	407.57	-	nr	**407.57**
girth exceeding 3.00 m	-	50.88	582.35	-	nr	**582.35**
Removing tree stumps						
girth 600 mm - 1.50 m	-	1.02	11.67	40.57	nr	**52.24**
girth 1.50 m - 3.00 m	-	1.02	11.67	59.32	nr	**70.99**
girth exceeding 3.00 m	-	1.02	11.67	81.23	nr	**92.91**
Clearing site vegetation						
bushes, scrub, undergrowth, hedges and trees						
and tree stumps not exceeding 600 mm girth	-	0.03	0.34	-	m²	**0.34**
Lifting turf for preservation						
stacking	-	0.36	4.12	-	m²	**4.12**
Excavating; by machine						
Topsoil for preservation						
average depth 150 mm	-	0.02	0.23	1.13	m²	**1.36**
add or deduct for each 25 mm variation in						
average depth	-	0.01	0.11	0.26	m²	**0.38**
To reduce levels						
maximum depth not exceeding 0.25 m	-	0.06	0.69	1.48	m³	**2.16**
maximum depth not exceeding 1.00 m	-	0.04	0.46	1.04	m³	**1.50**
maximum depth not exceeding 2.00 m	-	0.06	0.69	1.48	m³	**2.16**
maximum depth not exceeding 4.00 m	-	0.08	0.92	1.83	m³	**2.74**
Basements and the like; commencing level						
exceeding 0.25 m below exitsing ground level						
maximum depth not exceeding 1.00 m	-	0.09	1.03	1.21	m³	**2.24**
maximum depth not exceeding 2.00 m	-	0.06	0.69	0.93	m³	**1.62**
maximum depth not exceeding 4.00 m	-	0.09	1.03	1.21	m³	**2.24**
maximum depth not exceeding 6.00 m	-	0.10	1.14	1.58	m³	**2.73**
maximum depth not exceeding 8.00 m	-	0.13	1.49	1.86	m³	**3.35**
Pits						
maximum depth not exceeding 0.25 m	-	0.36	4.12	4.94	m³	**9.06**
maximum depth not exceeding 1.00 m	-	0.38	4.35	4.38	m³	**8.73**
maximum depth not exceeding 2.00 m	-	0.44	5.04	4.94	m³	**9.97**
maximum depth not exceeding 4.00 m	-	0.53	6.07	5.59	m³	**11.65**
maximum depth not exceeding 6.00 m	-	0.55	6.29	5.87	m³	**12.16**
Extra over pit excavating for commencing level						
exceeding 0.25 m below existing ground level						
1.00 m below	-	0.03	0.34	0.65	m³	**1.00**
2.00 m below	-	0.06	0.69	0.93	m³	**1.62**
3.00 m below	-	0.07	0.80	1.21	m³	**2.01**
4.00 m below	-	0.10	1.14	1.58	m³	**2.73**

D GROUNDWORKS

Item	PC £	Labour hours	Labour £	Material /Plant £	Unit	Total rate £
Trenches, width not exceeding 0.30 m						
maximum depth not exceeding 0.25 m	-	0.30	3.43	4.00	m³	7.44
maximum depth not exceeding 1.00 m	-	0.32	3.66	3.45	m³	7.11
maximum depth not exceeding 2.00 m	-	0.37	4.23	4.00	m³	8.24
maximum depth not exceeding 4.00 m	-	0.45	5.15	4.94	m³	10.09
maximum depth not exceeding 6.00 m	-	0.52	5.95	5.87	m³	11.82
Trenches, width exceeding 0.30 m						
maximum depth 0.25 m	-	0.27	3.09	3.72	m³	6.82
maximum depth 1.00 m	-	0.28	3.20	3.07	m³	6.28
maximum depth 2.00 m	-	0.34	3.89	3.72	m³	7.62
maximum depth 4.00 m	-	0.40	4.58	4.38	m³	8.95
maximum depth 6.00 m	-	0.49	5.61	5.59	m³	11.20
Extra over trench excavating for commencing level exceeding 0.25 m below existing ground level						
1.00 m below	-	0.03	0.34	0.65	m³	1.00
2.00 m below	-	0.06	0.69	0.93	m³	1.62
3.00 m below	-	0.07	0.80	1.21	m³	2.01
4.00 m below	-	0.10	1.14	1.58	m³	2.73
For pile caps and ground beams between piles						
maximum depth not exceeding 0.25 m	-	0.45	5.15	6.52	m³	11.67
maximum depth not exceeding 1.00 m	-	0.40	4.58	5.87	m³	10.44
maximum depth not exceeding 2.00 m	-	0.45	5.15	6.52	m³	11.67
To bench sloping ground to receive filling						
maximum depth not exceeding 0.25 m	-	0.10	1.14	1.58	m³	2.73
maximum depth not exceeding 1.00 m	-	0.07	0.80	1.86	m³	2.66
maximum depth not exceeding 2.00 m	-	0.10	1.14	1.58	m³	2.73
Extra over any types of excavating irrespective of depth						
excavating below ground water level	-	0.16	1.83	2.14	m³	3.97
next existing services	-	2.90	33.19	1.21	m³	34.40
around existing services crossing excavation	-	6.70	76.68	3.45	m³	80.13
Extra over any types of excavating irrespective of depth for breaking out existing materials						
rock	-	3.42	39.14	15.14	m³	54.28
concrete	-	2.90	33.19	11.04	m³	44.23
reinforced concrete	-	4.17	47.73	16.37	m³	64.10
brickwork; blockwork or stonework	-	2.08	23.81	8.32	m³	32.13
Extra over any types of excavating irrespective of depth for breaking out existing hard pavings, 75 mm thick						
coated macadam or asphalt	-	0.22	2.52	0.58	m²	3.10
Extra over any types of excavating irrespective of depth for breaking out existing hard pavings; 150 mm thick						
concrete	-	0.45	5.15	1.75	m²	6.90
reinforced concrete	-	0.68	7.78	2.35	m²	10.13
coated macadam or asphalt and hardcore	-	0.30	3.43	0.63	m²	4.07
Working space allowance to excavations						
reduce levels; basements and the like	-	0.09	1.03	1.21	m²	2.24
pits	-	0.22	2.52	3.45	m²	5.96
trenches	-	0.20	2.29	3.07	m²	5.36
pile caps and ground beams between piles	-	0.23	2.63	3.45	m²	6.08
Extra over excavating for working space for backfilling with special materials						
hardcore	-	0.16	1.83	22.57	m²	24.40
sand	-	0.16	1.83	22.21	m²	24.04
40 mm - 20 mm gravel	-	0.16	1.83	23.40	m²	25.23
plain in situ ready mixed designated concrete C7.5 - 40 mm aggregate	-	1.07	14.31	52.39	m²	66.70

D GROUNDWORKS

Item	PC £	Labour hours	Labour £	Material /Plant £	Unit	Total rate £
D20 EXCAVATING AND FILLING – cont'd						
Excavating; by hand						
Topsoil for preservation						
average depth 150 mm	-	0.26	2.98	-	m^2	2.98
add or deduct for each 25 mm variation in						
average depth	-	0.03	0.34	-	m^2	0.34
To reduce levels						
maximum depth not exceeding 0.25 m	-	1.59	18.20	-	m^3	18.20
maximum depth not exceeding 1.00 m	-	1.80	20.60	-	m^3	20.60
maximum depth not exceeding 2.00 m	-	1.99	22.78	-	m^3	22.78
maximum depth not exceeding 4.00 m	-	2.19	25.07	-	m^3	25.07
Basements and the like; commencing level						
exceeding 0.25 m below existing ground level						
maximum depth not exceeding 1.00 m	-	2.09	23.92	-	m^3	23.92
maximum depth not exceeding 2.00 m	-	2.24	25.64	-	m^3	25.64
maximum depth not exceeding 4.00 m	-	3.01	34.45	-	m^3	34.45
maximum depth not exceeding 6.00 m	-	3.66	41.89	-	m^3	41.89
maximum depth not exceeding 8.00 m	-	4.35	49.79	-	m^3	49.79
Pits						
maximum depth not exceeding 0.25 m	-	2.34	26.78	-	m^3	26.78
maximum depth not exceeding 1.00 m	-	2.90	33.19	-	m^3	33.19
maximum depth not exceeding 2.00 m	-	3.60	41.20	-	m^3	41.20
maximum depth not exceeding 4.00 m	-	4.56	52.19	-	m^3	52.19
maximum depth not exceeding 6.00 m	-	5.64	64.55	-	m^3	64.55
Extra over pit excavating for commencing level						
exceeding 0.25 m below existing ground level						
1.00 m below	-	0.45	5.15	-	m^3	5.15
2.00 m below	-	0.97	11.10	-	m^3	11.10
3.00 m below	-	1.43	16.37	-	m^3	16.37
4.00 m below	-	1.88	21.52	-	m^3	21.52
Trenches, width not exceeding 0.30 m						
maximum depth not exceeding 0.25 m	-	2.03	23.23	-	m^3	23.23
maximum depth not exceeding 1.00 m	-	2.99	34.22	-	m^3	34.22
maximum depth not exceeding 2.00 m	-	3.51	40.17	-	m^3	40.17
maximum depth not exceeding 4.00 m	-	4.29	49.10	-	m^3	49.10
maximum depth not exceeding 6.00 m	-	5.53	63.29	-	m^3	63.29
Trenches, width exceeding 0.30 m						
maximum depth not exceeding 0.25 m	-	1.99	22.78	-	m^3	22.78
maximum depth not exceeding 1.00 m	-	2.67	30.56	-	m^3	30.56
maximum depth not exceeding 2.00 m	-	3.12	35.71	-	m^3	35.71
maximum depth not exceeding 4.00 m	-	3.97	45.44	-	m^3	45.44
maximum depth not exceeding 6.00 m	-	5.07	58.03	-	m^3	58.03
Extra over trench excavating for commencing						
level exceeding 0.25 m below existing ground						
level						
1.00 m below	-	0.45	5.15	-	m^3	5.15
2.00 m below	-	0.97	11.10	-	m^3	11.10
3.00 m below	-	1.46	16.71	-	m^3	16.71
4.00 m below	-	1.88	21.52	-	m^3	21.52
For pile caps and ground beams between piles						
maximum depth not exceeding 0.25 m	-	3.05	34.91	-	m^3	34.91
maximum depth not exceeding 1.00 m	-	3.26	37.31	-	m^3	37.31
maximum depth not exceeding 2.00 m	-	3.87	44.29	-	m^3	44.29
To bench sloping ground to receive filling						
maximum depth not exceeding 0.25 m	-	1.43	16.37	-	m^3	16.37
maximum depth not exceeding 1.00 m	-	1.63	18.66	-	m^3	18.66
maximum depth not exceeding 2.00 m	-	1.83	20.95	-	m^3	20.95

D GROUNDWORKS

Item	PC £	Labour hours	Labour £	Material /Plant £	Unit	Total rate £
Extra over any types of excavating irrespective of depth						
excavating below ground water level	-	0.36	4.12	-	m³	4.12
next existing services	-	1.02	11.67	-	m³	11.67
around existing services crossing excavation	-	2.04	23.35	-	m³	23.35
Extra over any types of excavating irrespective of depth for breaking out existing materials						
rock	-	5.09	58.26	7.45	m³	65.71
concrete	-	4.58	52.42	6.21	m³	58.63
reinforced concrete	-	6.11	69.93	8.69	m³	78.63
brickwork; blockwork or stonework	-	3.05	34.91	3.72	m³	38.63
Extra over any types of excavating irrespective of depth for breaking out existing hard pavings, 60 mm thick						
precast concrete paving slabs	-	0.31	3.55	-	m²	3.55
Extra over any types of excavating irrespective of depth for breaking out existing hard pavings, 75 mm thick						
coated macadam or asphalt	-	0.44	5.04	1.02	m²	6.06
Extra over any types of excavating irrespective of depth for breaking out existing hard pavings, 150 mm thick						
concrete	-	0.71	8.13	0.87	m²	9.00
reinforced concrete	-	0.92	10.53	1.24	m²	11.77
coated macadam or asphalt and hardcore	-	0.51	5.84	0.62	m²	6.46
Working space allowance to excavations						
reduce levels; basements and the like	-	2.34	26.78	-	m²	26.78
pits	-	2.44	27.93	-	m²	27.93
trenches	-	2.14	24.49	-	m²	24.49
pile caps and ground beams between piles	-	2.54	29.07	-	m²	29.07
Extra over excavation for working space for backfilling with special materials						
hardcore	-	0.81	9.27	20.57	m²	29.84
sand	-	0.81	9.27	20.21	m²	29.48
40 mm - 20 mm gravel	-	0.81	9.27	21.40	m²	30.67
plain in situ ready mixed designated concrete; C7.5 - 40 mm aggregate	-	1.12	14.98	50.39	m²	65.37
Excavating; by hand; inside existing buildings						
Basements and the like; commencing level exceeding 0.25 m below existing ground level						
maximum depth not exceeding 1.00 m	-	3.14	35.94	-	m³	35.94
maximum depth not exceeding 2.00 m	-	3.36	38.46	-	m³	38.46
maximum depth not exceeding 4.00 m	-	4.51	51.62	-	m³	51.62
maximum depth not exceeding 6.00m	-	5.50	62.95	-	m³	62.95
maximum depth not exceeding 8.00 m	-	6.65	76.11	-	m³	76.11
Pits						
maximum depth not exceeding 0.25 m	-	3.51	40.17	-	m³	40.17
maximum depth not exceeding 1.00 m	-	3.82	43.72	-	m³	43.72
maximum depth not exceeding 2.00 m	-	4.58	52.42	-	m³	52.42
maximum depth not exceeding 4.00 m	-	5.80	66.38	-	m³	66.38
maximum depth not exceeding 6.00 m	-	7.17	82.06	-	m³	82.06
Extra over pit excavating for commencing level exceeding 0.25 m below existing ground level						
1.00 m below	-	0.68	7.78	-	m³	7.78
2.00 m below	-	1.45	16.60	-	m³	16.60
3.00 m below	-	2.14	24.49	-	m³	24.49
4.00 m below	-	2.81	32.16	-	m³	32.16

D GROUNDWORKS

Item	PC £	Labour hours	Labour £	Material /Plant £	Unit	Total rate £
D20 EXCAVATING AND FILLING – cont'd						
Excavating; by hand; inside existing Buildings – cont'd						
Trenches, width not exceeding 0.30 m						
maximum depth not exceeding 0.25 m	-	3.05	34.91	-	m^3	**34.91**
maximum depth not exceeding 1.00 m	-	3.51	40.17	-	m^3	**40.17**
maximum depth not exceeding 2.00 m	-	4.13	47.27	-	m^3	**47.27**
maximum depth not exceeding 4.00 m	-	5.04	57.69	-	m^3	**57.69**
maximum depth not exceeding 6.00 m	-	6.49	74.28	-	m^3	**74.28**
Trenches, width exceeding 0.30 m						
maximum depth not exceeding 0.25 m	-	2.99	34.22	-	m^3	**34.22**
maximum depth not exceeding 1.00 m	-	3.14	35.94	-	m^3	**35.94**
maximum depth not exceeding 2.00 m	-	3.66	41.89	-	m^3	**41.89**
maximum depth not exceeding 4.00 m	-	4.66	53.34	-	m^3	**53.34**
maximum depth not exceeding 6.00 m	-	5.96	68.22	-	m^3	**68.22**
Extra over trench excavating for commencing level exceeding 0.25 m below existing ground level						
1.00 m below	-	0.68	7.78	-	m^3	**7.78**
2.00 m below	-	1.45	16.60	-	m^3	**16.60**
3.00 m below	-	2.14	24.49	-	m^3	**24.49**
4.00 m below	-	2.81	32.16	-	m^3	**32.16**
Extra over any types of excavating irrespective of depth						
excavating below ground water level	-	0.55	6.29	-	m^3	**6.29**
Extra over any types of excavating irrespective of depth for breaking out existing materials						
concrete	-	6.86	78.52	6.21	m^3	**84.72**
reinforced concrete	-	9.16	104.84	8.69	m^3	**113.53**
brickwork; blockwork or stonework	-	4.58	52.42	3.72	m^3	**56.15**
Extra over any types of excavating irrespective of depth for breaking out existing hard pavings, 150 mm thick						
concrete	-	1.07	12.25	0.87	m^2	**13.12**
reinforced concrete	-	1.38	15.79	1.24	m^2	**17.04**
Working space allowance to excavations						
pits	-	3.60	41.20	-	m^2	**41.20**
trenches	-	3.21	36.74	-	m^2	**36.74**
Earthwork support (average "risk" prices)						
Maximum depth not exceeding 1.00 m						
distance between opposing faces not exceeding 2.00 m	-	0.11	1.26	0.46	m^2	**1.72**
distance between opposing faces 2.00 - 4.00 m	-	0.12	1.37	0.54	m^2	**1.91**
distance between opposing faces exceeding 4.00 m	-	0.13	1.49	0.68	m^2	**2.17**
Maximum depth not exceeding 2.00 m						
distance between opposing faces not exceeding 2.00 m	-	0.13	1.49	0.54	m^2	**2.02**
distance between opposing faces 2.00 - 4.00 m	-	0.14	1.60	0.68	m^2	**2.28**
distance between opposing faces exceeding 4.00 m	-	0.16	1.83	0.85	m^2	**2.68**
Maximum depth not exceeding 4.00 m						
distance between opposing faces not exceeding 2.00 m	-	0.16	1.83	0.68	m^2	**2.51**
distance between opposing faces 2.00 - 4.00 m	-	0.18	2.06	0.85	m^2	**2.91**
distance between opposing faces exceeding 4.00 m	-	0.19	2.17	1.07	m^2	**3.25**

D GROUNDWORKS

Item	PC £	Labour hours	Labour £	Material /Plant £	Unit	Total rate £
Maximum depth not exceeding 6.00 m						
distance between opposing faces not exceeding						
2.00 m	-	0.19	2.17	0.81	m²	**2.98**
distance between opposing faces 2.00 - 4.00 m	-	0.21	2.40	1.07	m²	**3.48**
distance between opposing faces exceeding						
4.00 m	-	0.24	2.75	1.34	m²	**4.09**
Maximum depth not exceeding 8.00 m						
distance between opposing faces not exceeding						
2.00 m	-	0.26	2.98	1.07	m²	**4.05**
distance between opposing faces 2.00 - 4.00 m	-	0.31	3.55	1.34	m²	**4.89**
distance between opposing faces exceeding						
4.00 m	-	0.37	4.23	1.61	m²	**5.85**
Earthwork support (open boarded)						
Maximum depth not exceeding 1.00 m						
distance between opposing faces not exceeding						
2.00 m	-	0.31	3.55	0.95	m²	**4.50**
distance between opposing faces 2.00 - 4.00 m	-	0.34	3.89	1.07	m²	**4.97**
distance between opposing faces exceeding						
4.00 m	-	0.39	4.46	1.34	m²	**5.81**
Maximum depth not exceeding 2.00 m						
distance between opposing faces not exceeding						
2.00 m	-	0.39	4.46	1.07	m²	**5.54**
distance between opposing faces 2.00 - 4.00 m	-	0.43	4.92	1.29	m²	**6.22**
distance between opposing faces exceeding						
4.00 m	-	0.49	5.61	1.61	m²	**7.22**
Maximum depth not exceeding 4.00 m						
distance between opposing faces not exceeding						
2.00 m	-	0.49	5.61	1.22	m²	**6.82**
distance between opposing faces 2.00 - 4.00 m	-	0.55	6.29	1.50	m²	**7.80**
distance between opposing faces exceeding						
4.00 m	-	0.61	6.98	1.88	m²	**8.86**
Maximum depth not exceeding 6.00 m						
distance between opposing faces not exceeding						
2.00 m	-	0.61	6.98	1.34	m²	**8.32**
distance between opposing faces 2.00 - 4.00 m	-	0.68	7.78	1.69	m²	**9.47**
distance between opposing faces exceeding						
4.00 m	-	0.78	8.93	2.15	m²	**11.08**
Maximum depth not exceeding 8.00 m						
distance between opposing faces not exceeding						
2.00 m	-	0.81	9.27	1.75	m²	**11.02**
distance between opposing faces 2.00 - 4.00 m	-	0.92	10.53	2.02	m²	**12.55**
distance between opposing faces exceeding						
4.00 m	-	1.06	12.13	2.68	m²	**14.82**
Earthwork support (close boarded)						
Maximum depth not exceeding 1.00 m						
distance between opposing faces not exceeding						
2.00 m	-	0.81	9.27	1.88	m²	**11.15**
distance between opposing faces 2.00 - 4.00 m	-	0.90	10.30	2.15	m²	**12.45**
distance between opposing faces exceeding						
4.00 m	-	0.99	11.33	2.68	m²	**14.02**
Maximum depth not exceeding 2.00 m						
distance between opposing faces not exceeding						
2.00 m	-	1.02	11.67	2.15	m²	**13.82**
distance between opposing faces 2.00 - 4.00 m	-	1.12	12.82	2.57	m²	**15.39**
distance between opposing faces exceeding						
4.00 m	-	1.22	13.96	3.22	m²	**17.19**

D GROUNDWORKS

Item	PC £	Labour hours	Labour £	Material /Plant £	Unit	Total rate £
D20 EXCAVATING AND FILLING – cont'd						
Earthwork support (close boarded) – cont'd						
Maximum depth not exceeding 4.00 m						
distance between opposing faces not exceeding						
2.00 m	-	1.28	14.65	2.42	m²	**17.07**
distance between opposing faces 2.00 - 4.00 m	-	1.43	16.37	3.00	m²	**19.37**
distance between opposing faces exceeding						
4.00 m	-	1.58	18.08	3.76	m²	**21.84**
Maximum depth not exceeding 6.00 m						
distance between opposing faces not exceeding						
2.00 m	-	1.59	18.20	2.68	m²	**20.88**
distance between opposing faces 2.00 - 4.00 m	-	1.73	19.80	3.38	m²	**23.18**
distance between opposing faces exceeding						
4.00 m	-	1.93	22.09	4.30	m²	**26.39**
Maximum depth not exceeding 8.00 m						
distance between opposing faces not exceeding						
2.00 m	-	1.93	22.09	3.49	m²	**25.58**
distance between opposing faces 2.00 - 4.00 m	-	2.14	24.49	4.03	m²	**28.52**
distance between opposing faces exceeding						
4.00 m	-	2.44	27.93	4.83	m²	**32.76**
Extra over earthwork support for						
Curved	-	0.02	0.23	0.46	m²	**0.69**
Below ground water level	-	0.31	3.55	0.41	m²	**3.96**
Unstable ground	-	0.51	5.84	0.81	m²	**6.64**
Next to roadways	-	0.41	4.69	0.68	m²	**5.37**
Left in	-	0.67	7.67	18.79	m²	**26.46**
Earthwork support (average "risk" prices						
- inside existing existing buildings)						
Maximum depth not exceeding 1.00 m						
distance between opposing faces not exceeding						
2.00 m	-	0.19	2.17	0.68	m²	**2.85**
distance between opposing faces 2.00 - 4.00 m	-	0.21	2.40	0.77	m²	**3.18**
distance between opposing faces exceeding						
4.00 m	-	0.24	2.75	0.95	m²	**3.69**
Maximum depth not exceeding 2.00 m						
distance between opposing faces not exceeding						
2.00 m	-	0.24	2.75	0.77	m²	**3.52**
distance between opposing faces 2.00 - 4.00 m	-	0.27	3.09	1.03	m²	**4.12**
distance between opposing faces exceeding						
4.00 m	-	0.32	3.66	1.17	m²	**4.83**
Maximum depth not exceeding 4.00 m						
distance between opposing faces not exceeding						
2.00 m	-	0.31	3.55	1.03	m²	**4.57**
distance between opposing faces 2.00 - 4.00 m	-	0.34	3.89	1.22	m²	**5.11**
distance between opposing faces exceeding						
4.00 m	-	0.38	4.35	1.42	m²	**5.77**
Maximum depth not exceeding 6.00 m						
distance between opposing faces not exceeding						
2.00 m	-	0.38	4.35	1.15	m²	**5.50**
distance between opposing faces 2.00 - 4.00 m	-	0.42	4.81	1.42	m²	**6.23**
distance between opposing faces exceeding						
6.00 m	-	0.48	5.49	1.69	m²	**7.18**
Disposal; by machine						
Excavated material						
off site; to tip not exceeding 13 km (using lorries)						
including Landfill Tax based on inactive waste	-	-	-	18.87	m³	**18.87**

D GROUNDWORKS

Item	PC £	Labour hours	Labour £	Material /Plant £	Unit	Total rate £
on site; depositing in spoil heaps; average 25 m distance	-	-	-	0.87	m³	0.87
on site; spreading; average 25 m distance	-	0.23	2.63	0.61	m³	3.24
on site; depositing in spoil heaps; average 50 m distance	-	-	-	1.48	m³	1.48
on site; spreading; average 50 m distance	-	0.23	2.63	1.13	m³	3.76
on site; depositing in spoil heaps; average 100 m distance	-	-	-	2.61	m³	2.61
on site; spreading; average 100 m distance	-	0.23	2.63	1.74	m³	4.37
on site; depositing in spoil heaps; average 200 m distance	-	-	-	3.74	m³	3.74
on site; spreading; average 200 m distance	-	0.23	2.63	2.35	m³	4.98
Disposal; by hand						
Excavated material						
off site; to tip not exceeding 13 km (using lorries) including Landfill Tax based on inactive waste	-	0.81	9.27	25.70	m³	34.97
on site; depositing in spoil heaps; average 25 m distance	-	1.12	12.82	-	m³	12.82
on site; spreading; average 25 m distance	-	1.48	16.94	-	m³	16.94
on site; depositing in spoil heaps; average 50 m distance	-	1.48	16.94	-	m³	16.94
on site; spreading; average 50 m distance	-	1.79	20.49	-	m³	20.49
on site; depositing in spoil heaps; average 100 m distance	-	2.14	24.49	-	m³	24.49
on site; spreading; average 100 m distance	-	2.44	27.93	-	m³	27.93
on site; depositing in spoil heaps; average 200 m distance	-	3.15	36.05	-	m³	36.05
on site; spreading; average 200 m distance	-	3.46	39.60	-	m³	39.60
Filling to excavations; by machine						
Average thickness not exceeding 0.25 m						
arising from the excavations	-	0.19	2.17	2.35	m³	4.52
obtained off site; hardcore	33.76	0.21	2.40	43.31	m³	45.71
obtained off site; granular fill type one	28.43	0.21	2.40	38.84	m³	41.25
obtained off site; granular fill type two	26.79	0.21	2.40	36.86	m³	39.26
Average thickness exceeding 0.25 m						
arising from the excavations	-	0.16	1.83	1.74	m³	3.57
obtained off site; hardcore	28.94	0.18	2.06	36.85	m³	38.91
obtained off site; granular fill type one	28.43	0.18	2.06	37.97	m³	40.03
obtained off site; granular fill type two	26.79	0.18	2.06	35.99	m³	38.05
Filling to make up levels; by machine						
Average thickness not exceeding 0.25 m						
arising from the excavations	-	0.27	3.09	2.70	m³	5.79
obtained off site; imported topsoil	10.95	0.27	3.09	15.67	m³	18.76
obtained off site; hardcore	33.76	0.31	3.55	43.53	m³	47.08
obatined off site; granular fill type one	28.43	0.31	3.55	39.07	m³	42.61
obtained off site; granular fill type two	26.79	0.31	3.55	37.08	m³	40.63
obtained off site; sand	28.84	0.31	3.55	39.56	m³	43.11
Average thickness exceeding 0.25 m						
arising from the excavations	-	0.22	2.52	1.92	m³	4.44
obtained off site; imported topsoil	10.95	0.22	2.52	14.89	m³	17.41
obtained off site; hardcore	28.94	0.27	3.09	36.94	m³	40.03
obatined off site; granular fill type one	28.43	0.27	3.09	38.07	m³	41.16
obtained off site; granular fill type two	26.79	0.27	3.09	36.08	m³	39.17
obtained off site; sand	28.84	0.27	3.09	38.56	m³	41.65

D GROUNDWORKS

Item	PC £	Labour hours	Labour £	Material /Plant £	Unit	Total rate £
D20 EXCAVATING AND FILLING – cont'd						
Filling to excavations; by hand						
Average thickness not exceeding 0.25 m						
arising from the excavations	-	1.25	14.31	-	m³	**14.31**
obtained off site; hardcore	33.76	1.35	15.45	40.96	m³	**56.41**
obtained off site; granular fill type one	28.43	1.60	18.31	34.50	m³	**52.81**
obtained off site; granular fill; type two	26.79	1.60	18.31	32.51	m³	**50.82**
obtained off site; sand	28.84	1.60	18.31	34.99	m³	**53.31**
Average thickness exceeding 0.25 m						
arising from the excavations	-	1.02	11.67	-	m³	**11.67**
obtained off site; hardcore	28.94	1.19	13.62	35.11	m³	**48.73**
obtained off site; granular fill type one	28.43	1.32	15.11	34.50	m³	**49.61**
obtained off site; granular fill; type two	26.79	1.32	15.11	32.51	m³	**47.62**
obtained off site; sand	28.84	1.32	15.11	34.99	m³	**50.10**
Filling to make up levels; by hand						
Average thickness not exceeding 0.25 m						
arising from the excavations	-	1.38	15.79	4.94	m³	**20.73**
obtained off site; imported soil	10.95	1.38	15.79	17.30	m³	**33.09**
obtained off site; hardcore	33.76	1.71	19.57	47.09	m³	**66.66**
obtained off site; granular fill type one	28.43	1.82	20.83	41.02	m³	**61.85**
obtained off site; granular fill type two	26.79	1.82	20.83	39.04	m³	**59.87**
obtained off site; sand	28.84	1.82	20.83	41.52	m³	**62.35**
Average thickness exceeding 0.25 m						
arising from the excavations	-	1.19	13.62	4.00	m³	**17.62**
arising from on site spoil heaps; average 25 m distance; multiple handling	-	2.44	27.93	8.74	m³	**36.67**
obtained off site; imported soil	10.95	1.19	13.62	16.36	m³	**29.98**
obtained off site; hardcore	28.94	1.57	17.97	40.74	m³	**58.71**
obtained off site; granular fill type one	28.43	1.68	19.23	40.53	m³	**59.76**
obtained off site; granular fill type two	26.79	1.68	19.23	38.54	m³	**57.77**
obtained off site; sand	28.84	1.68	19.23	41.02	m³	**60.25**
Surface packing to filling						
To vertical or battered faces	-	0.19	2.17	0.11	m²	**2.28**
Surface treatments						
Compacting						
filling; blinding with sand	-	0.05	0.57	1.90	m²	**2.48**
bottoms of excavations	-	0.05	0.57	0.02	m²	**0.59**
Trimming						
sloping surfaces	-	0.19	2.17	-	m²	**2.17**
sloping surfaces; in rock	-	1.02	10.72	1.74	m²	**12.45**
Filter membrane; one layer; laid on earth to receive granular material						
"Terram 500" filter membrane; one layer; laid on earth	-	0.05	0.57	0.52	m²	**1.09**
"Terram 700" filter membrane; one layer; laid on earth	-	0.05	0.57	0.55	m²	**1.12**
"Terram 1000" filter membrane; one layer; laid on earth	-	0.05	0.57	0.58	m²	**1.15**
"Terram 2000" filter membrane; one layer; laid on earth	-	0.05	0.57	1.23	m²	**1.80**

D GROUNDWORKS

Item	PC £	Labour hours	Labour £	Material £	Unit	Total rate £
D50 UNDERPINNING						
Excavating; by machine						
Preliminary trenches						
maximum depth not exceeding 1.00 m	-	0.23	2.63	6.70	m³	9.33
maximum depth not exceeding 2.00 m	-	0.28	3.20	8.07	m³	11.28
maximum depth not exceeding 4.00 m	-	0.32	3.66	9.44	m³	13.11
Extra over preliminary trench excavating for						
breaking out existing 150 mm thick concrete paving	-	0.65	7.44	0.87	m²	8.31
Excavating; by hand						
Preliminary trenches						
maximum depth not exceeding 1.00 m	-	2.68	30.67	-	m³	30.67
maximum depth not exceeding 2.00 m	-	3.05	34.91	-	m³	34.91
maximum depth not exceeding 4.00 m	-	3.93	44.98	-	m³	44.98
Extra over preliminary trench excavating for						
breaking out existing 150 mm thick concrete paving	-	0.28	3.20	1.99	m²	5.20
Underpinning pits; commencing from 1.00 m						
below existing ground level						
maximum depth not exceeding 0.25 m	-	4.07	46.58	-	m³	46.58
maximum depth not exceeding 1.00 m	-	4.44	50.82	-	m³	50.82
maximum depth not exceeding 2.00 m	-	5.32	60.89	-	m³	60.89
Underpinning pits; commencing from 2.00 m						
below existing ground level						
maximum depth not exceeding 0.25 m	-	5.00	57.23	-	m³	57.23
maximum depth not exceeding 1.00 m	-	5.37	61.46	-	m³	61.46
maximum depth not exceeding 2.00 m	-	6.24	71.42	-	m³	71.42
Underpinning pits; commencing from 4.00 m						
below existing ground level						
maximum depth not exceeding 0.25 m	-	5.92	67.76	-	m³	67.76
maximum depth not exceeding 1.00 m	-	6.29	71.99	-	m³	71.99
maximum depth not exceeding 2.00 m	-	7.17	82.06	-	m³	82.06
Extra over any types of excavating irrespective of depth						
excavating below ground water level	-	0.32	3.66	-	m³	3.66
Earthwork support to preliminary trenches (open boarded - in 3.00 m lengths)						
Maximum depth not exceeding 1.00 m						
distance between opposing faces not exceeding 2.00 m	-	0.37	4.23	1.75	m²	5.99
Maximum depth not exceeding 2.00 m						
distance between opposing faces not exceeding 2.00 m	-	0.46	5.26	2.15	m²	7.41
Maximum depth not exceeding 4.00 m						
distance between opposing faces not exceeding 2.00 m	-	0.59	6.75	2.68	m²	9.44
Earthwork support to underpinning pits (open boarded - in 3.00 m lengths)						
Maximum depth not exceeding 1.00 m						
distance between opposing faces not exceeding 2.00 m	-	0.41	4.69	1.88	m²	6.57
Maximum depth not exceeding 2.00 m						
distance between opposing faces not exceeding 2.00 m	-	0.51	5.84	2.42	m²	8.25
Maximum depth not exceeding 4.00 m						
distance between opposing faces not exceeding 2.00 m	-	0.65	7.44	2.95	m²	10.39

D GROUNDWORKS

Item	PC £	Labour hours	Labour £	Material £	Unit	Total rate £
D50 UNDERPINNING – cont'd						
Earthwork support to preliminary trenches (closed boarded - in 3.00 m lengths)						
Maximum depth not exceeding 1.00 m						
distance between opposing faces not exceeding 2.00 m	-	0.93	10.64	2.95	m²	**13.60**
Maximum depth not exceeding 2.00 m						
distance between opposing faces not exceeding 2.00 m	-	1.16	13.28	3.76	m²	**17.04**
Maximum depth not exceeding 4.00 m						
distance between opposing faces not exceeding 2.00 m	-	1.43	16.37	4.56	m²	**20.93**
Earthwork support to underpinning pits (closed boarded - in 3.00 m lengths)						
Maximum depth not exceeding 1.00 m						
distance between opposing faces not exceeding 2.00 m	-	1.02	11.67	3.22	m²	**14.90**
Maximum depth not exceeding 2.00 m						
distance between opposing faces not exceeding 2.00 m	-	1.28	14.65	4.03	m²	**18.68**
Maximum depth not exceeding 4.00 m						
distance between opposing faces not exceeding 2.00 m	-	1.57	17.97	5.10	m²	**23.07**
Extra over earthwork support for						
Left in	-	0.69	7.90	18.79	m²	**26.69**
Cutting away existing projecting foundations						
Concrete						
maximum width 150; maximum depth 150 mm	-	0.15	1.72	0.16	m	**1.88**
maximum width 150; maximum depth 225 mm	-	0.22	2.52	0.25	m	**2.77**
maximum width 150; maximum depth 300 mm	-	0.30	3.43	0.33	m	**3.77**
maximum width 300; maximum depth 300 mm	-	0.58	6.64	0.65	m	**7.29**
Masonry						
maximum width one brick thick; maximum depth one course high	-	0.04	0.46	0.05	m	**0.51**
maximum width one brick thick; maximum depth two courses high	-	0.13	1.49	0.15	m	**1.63**
maximum wodth one brick thick; maximum depth three courses high	-	0.25	2.86	0.28	m	**3.14**
maximum width one brick thick; maximum depth four courses high	-	0.42	4.81	0.47	m	**5.27**
Preparing the underside of the existing work to receive the pinning up of the new work						
Width of existing work						
380 mm	-	0.56	6.41	-	m	**6.41**
600 mm	-	0.74	8.47	-	m	**8.47**
900 mm	-	0.93	10.64	-	m	**10.64**
1200 mm	-	1.11	12.70	-	m	**12.70**
Disposal; by hand						
Excavated material						
off site; to tip not exceeding 13 km (using lorries) including Landfill Tax based on inactive waste	-	0.74	8.47	32.13	m³	**40.60**

D GROUNDWORKS

Item	PC £	Labour hours	Labour £	Material £	Unit	Total rate £
Filling to excavations; by hand						
Average thickness exceeding 0.25 m						
arising from the excavations	-	0.93	10.64	-	m³	10.64
Surface treatments						
Compacting						
bottoms of excavations	-	0.05	0.57	0.02	m²	0.59
Plain in situ ready mixed designated concrete C10 - 40 mm aggregate; poured against faces of excavation						
Underpinning						
thickness not exceeding 150 mm	-	3.42	45.74	92.89	m³	138.64
thickness 150 - 450 mm	-	2.87	38.39	92.89	m³	131.28
thickness exceeding 450 mm	-	2.50	33.44	92.89	m³	126.33
Plain in situ ready mixed designated concrete C20 - 20 mm aggregate; poured against faces of excavation						
Underpinning						
thickness not exceeding 150 mm	-	3.42	45.74	95.57	m³	141.31
thickness 150 - 450 mm	-	2.87	38.39	95.57	m³	133.95
thickness exceeding 450 mm	-	2.50	33.44	95.57	m³	129.01
Extra for working around reinforcement	-	0.28	3.75	-	m³	3.75
Sawn formwork; sides of foundations in underpinning						
Plain vertical						
height exceeding 1.00 m	-	1.48	24.57	6.71	m²	31.29
height not exceeding 250 mm	-	0.51	8.47	1.93	m²	10.39
height 250 - 500 mm	-	0.79	13.12	3.58	m²	16.70
height 500 mm - 1.00 m	-	1.20	19.92	6.71	m²	26.64
Reinforcement bar; BS4449; hot rolled plain round mild steel bars						
20 mm diameter nominal size						
bent	378.40	27.00	418.84	470.96	tonne	889.80
16 mm diameter nominal size						
bent	378.40	29.00	450.40	473.77	tonne	924.17
12 mm diameter nominal size						
bent	380.60	31.00	481.96	479.19	tonne	961.15
10 mm diameter nominal size						
bent	383.90	33.00	513.52	486.97	tonne	1000.49
8 mm diameter nominal size						
bent	383.90	35.00	542.68	489.78	tonne	1032.46
Reinforcement bar; BS4461; cold worked deformed high yield steel bars						
20 mm diameter nominal size						
bent	378.40	27.00	418.84	470.96	tonne	889.80
16 mm diameter nominal size						
bent	378.40	29.00	450.40	473.77	tonne	924.17
12 mm diameter nominal size						
bent	380.60	31.00	481.96	479.19	tonne	961.15
10 mm diameter nominal size						
bent	383.90	33.00	513.52	486.97	tonne	1000.49
8 mm diameter nominal size						
bent	383.90	35.00	542.68	489.78	tonne	1032.46

D GROUNDWORKS

Item	PC £	Labour hours	Labour £	Material £	Unit	Total rate £
D50 UNDERPINNING – cont'd						
Common bricks; PC £220.00/1000; in cement mortar (1:3)						
Walls in underpinning						
one brick thick	-	2.22	50.67	36.13	m^2	**86.80**
one and a half brick thick	-	3.05	69.61	53.80	m^2	**123.41**
two brick thick	-	3.79	86.50	74.71	m^2	**161.21**
Class A engineering bricks; PC £383.00/1000; in cement mortar (1:3)						
Walls in underpinning						
one brick thick	-	2.22	50.67	58.56	m^2	**109.22**
one and a half brick thick	-	3.05	69.61	87.44	m^2	**157.05**
two brick thick	-	3.79	86.50	119.56	m^2	**206.06**
Class B engineering bricks; PC £275.00/1000; in cement mortar (1:3)						
Walls in underpinning						
one brick thick	-	2.22	50.67	42.99	m^2	**93.66**
one and a half brick thick	-	3.05	69.61	64.10	m^2	**133.71**
two brick thick	-	3.79	86.50	88.44	m^2	**174.94**
Add or deduct for variation of £10.00/1000 in PC of bricks						
one brick thick	-	-	-	1.46	m^2	**1.46**
one and a half brick thick	-	-	-	2.19	m^2	**2.19**
two brick thick	-	-	-	2.92	m^2	**2.92**
"Pluvex" (hessian based) damp proof course; 200 mm laps; in cement mortar (1:3)						
Horizontal						
width exceeding 225 mm	7.92	0.23	5.25	9.61	m^2	**14.86**
width not exceeding 225 mm	8.10	0.45	10.27	9.83	m^2	**20.10**
"Hyload" (pitch polymer) damp proof course; 150 mm laps; in cement mortar (1:3)						
Horizontal						
width exceeding 225 mm	6.98	0.23	5.25	8.47	m^2	**13.72**
width not exceeding 225 mm	7.14	0.46	10.50	8.67	m^2	**19.17**
"Ledkore" grade A (bitumen based lead cored) damp proof course; 200 mm laps; in cement mortar (1:3)						
Horizontal						
width exceeding 225 mm	21.88	0.31	7.08	26.55	m^2	**33.62**
width not exceeding 225 mm	22.39	0.61	13.92	27.16	m^2	**41.09**
Two courses of slates in cement mortar (1:3)						
Horizontal						
width exceeding 225 mm	-	1.39	31.72	28.87	m^2	**60.59**
width not exceeding 225 mm	-	2.31	52.72	29.52	m^2	**82.24**
Wedging and pinning						
To underside of existing construction with slates in cement mortar (1:3)						
width of wall - half brick thick	-	1.02	23.28	6.78	m	**30.05**
width of wall - one brick thick	-	1.20	27.39	13.55	m	**40.94**
width of wall - one and a half brick thick	-	1.39	31.72	20.33	m	**52.05**

E IN SITU CONCRETE/LARGE PRECAST CONCRETE

Item	PC £	Labour hours	Labour £	Material £	Unit	Total rate £
E05 IN SITU CONCRETE CONSTRUCTION						
Plain in situ ready mixed designated concrete; C7.5 - 40 mm aggregate						
Foundations	69.21	1.39	18.59	86.08	m³	**104.68**
Isolated foundations	-	1.62	21.67	86.08	m³	**107.75**
Beds						
thickness not exceeding 150 mm	-	1.90	25.41	86.08	m³	**111.50**
thickness 150 - 450 mm	-	1.30	17.39	86.08	m³	**103.47**
thickness exceeding 450 mm	-	1.06	14.18	86.08	m³	**100.26**
Screeded beds; protection to compressible formwork						
50 mm thick	-	0.12	1.61	4.20	m²	**5.81**
75 mm thick	-	0.17	2.27	6.30	m²	**8.57**
100 mm thick	-	0.23	3.08	8.40	m²	**11.47**
Filling hollow walls						
thickness not exceeding 150 mm	-	3.61	48.29	86.08	m³	**134.37**
Column casings						
stub columns beneath suspended ground slabs	-	5.20	69.55	86.08	m³	**155.64**
Plain in situ ready mixed designated concrete; C10 - 40 mm aggregate						
Foundations	69.60	1.39	18.59	86.56	m³	**105.15**
Isolated foundations	-	1.62	21.67	86.56	m³	**108.23**
Beds						
thickness not exceeding 150 mm	-	1.90	25.41	86.56	m³	**111.98**
thickness 150 - 450 mm	-	1.30	17.39	86.56	m³	**103.95**
thickness exceeding 450 mm	-	1.06	14.18	86.56	m³	**100.74**
Filling hollow walls						
thickness not exceeding 150 mm	-	3.61	48.29	86.56	m³	**134.85**
Plain in situ ready mixed designated concrete; C10 - 40 mm aggregate; poured on or against earth or unblinded hardcore						
Foundations	69.60	1.43	19.13	88.68	m³	**107.80**
Isolated foundations	-	1.71	22.87	88.68	m³	**111.55**
Beds						
thickness not exceeding 150 mm	-	1.99	26.62	88.68	m³	**115.29**
thickness 150 - 450 mm	-	1.43	19.13	88.68	m³	**107.80**
thickness exceeding 450 mm	-	1.11	14.85	88.68	m³	**103.52**
Plain in situ ready mixed designated concrete; C20 - 20 mm aggregate						
Foundations	71.60	1.39	18.59	89.05	m³	**107.64**
Isolated foundations	-	1.62	21.67	89.05	m³	**110.72**
Beds						
thickness not exceeding 150 mm	-	2.04	27.29	89.05	m³	**116.34**
thickness 150 - 450 mm	-	1.39	18.59	89.05	m³	**107.64**
thickness exceeding 450 mm	-	1.06	14.18	89.05	m³	**103.23**
Filling hollow walls						
thickness not exceeding 150 mm	-	3.61	48.29	89.05	m³	**137.34**

E IN SITU CONCRETE/LARGE PRECAST CONCRETE

Item	PC £	Labour hours	Labour £	Material £	Unit	Total rate £
E05 IN SITU CONCRETE CONSTRUCTION – cont'd						
Plain in situ ready mixed concrete; C20 - 20 mm aggregate; poured on or against earth or unblinded hardcore						
Foundations	71.60	1.43	19.13	91.23	m³	110.35
Isolated foundations	-	1.71	22.87	91.23	m³	114.10
Beds						
thickness not exceeding 150 mm	-	2.13	28.49	91.23	m³	119.72
thickness 150 - 450 mm	-	1.48	19.80	91.23	m³	111.02
thickness exceeding 450 mm	-	1.11	14.85	91.23	m³	106.07
Reinforced in situ ready mixed designated concrete; C25 - 20 mm aggregate						
Foundations	72.05	1.48	19.80	89.61	m³	109.41
Ground beams	-	2.96	39.59	89.61	m³	129.21
Isolated foundations	-	1.80	24.08	89.61	m³	113.69
Beds						
thickness not exceeding 150 mm	-	2.36	31.57	89.61	m³	121.18
thickness 150 - 450 mm	-	1.71	22.87	89.61	m³	112.49
thickness exceeding 450 mm	-	1.39	18.59	89.61	m³	108.21
Slabs						
thickness not exceeding 150 mm	-	3.75	50.16	89.61	m³	139.77
thickness 150 - 450 mm	-	2.96	39.59	89.61	m³	129.21
thickness exceeding 450 mm	-	2.68	35.85	89.61	m³	125.46
Coffered and troughed slabs						
thickness 150 - 450 mm	-	3.42	45.74	89.61	m³	135.36
thickness exceeding 450 mm	-	2.96	39.59	89.61	m³	129.21
Extra over for sloping						
not exceeding 15 degrees	-	0.28	3.75	-	m³	3.75
over 15 degrees	-	0.56	7.49	-	m³	7.49
Walls						
thickness not exceeding 150 mm	-	3.93	52.57	89.61	m³	142.18
thickness 150 - 450 mm	-	3.15	42.13	89.61	m³	131.75
thickness exceeding 450 mm	-	2.75	36.78	89.61	m³	126.40
Beams						
isolated	-	4.26	56.98	89.61	m³	146.59
isolated deep	-	4.67	62.46	89.61	m³	152.08
attached deep	-	4.26	56.98	89.61	m³	146.59
Beam casings						
isolated	-	4.67	62.46	89.61	m³	152.08
isolated deep	-	5.09	68.08	89.61	m³	157.70
attached deep	-	4.67	62.46	89.61	m³	152.08
Columns	-	5.09	68.08	89.61	m³	157.70
Column casings	-	5.64	75.44	89.61	m³	165.05
Staircases	-	6.38	85.34	89.61	m³	174.95
Upstands	-	4.12	55.11	89.61	m³	144.72
Reinforced in situ ready mixed designated concrete; C35 - 20 mm aggregate						
Foundations	76.90	1.48	19.80	95.65	m³	115.44
Ground beams	-	2.96	39.59	95.65	m³	135.24
Isolated foundations	-	1.80	24.08	95.65	m³	119.72
Beds						
thickness not exceeding 150 mm	-	2.36	31.57	95.65	m³	127.21
thickness 150 - 450 mm	-	1.71	22.87	95.65	m³	118.52
thickness exceeding 450 mm	-	1.39	18.59	95.65	m³	114.24
Slabs						
thickness not exceeding 150 mm	-	3.75	50.16	95.65	m³	145.81

E IN SITU CONCRETE/LARGE PRECAST CONCRETE

Item	PC £	Labour hours	Labour £	Material £	Unit	Total rate £
thickness 150 - 450 mm	-	2.96	39.59	95.65	m³	135.24
thickness exceeding 450 mm	-	2.68	35.85	95.65	m³	131.49
Coffered and troughed slabs						
thickness 150 - 450 mm	-	3.42	45.74	95.65	m³	141.39
thickness exceeding 450 mm	-	2.96	39.59	95.65	m³	135.24
Extra over for sloping						
not exceeding 15 degrees	-	0.28	3.75	-	m³	3.75
over 15 degrees	-	0.56	7.49	-	m³	7.49
Walls						
thickness not exceeding 150 mm	-	3.93	52.57	95.65	m³	148.21
thickness 150 - 450 mm	-	3.15	42.13	95.65	m³	137.78
thickness exceeding 450 mm	-	2.75	36.78	95.65	m³	132.43
Beams						
isolated	-	4.26	56.98	95.65	m³	152.63
isolated deep	-	4.67	62.46	95.65	m³	158.11
attached deep	-	4.26	56.98	95.65	m³	152.63
Beam casings						
isolated	-	4.67	62.46	95.65	m³	158.11
isolated deep	-	5.09	68.08	95.65	m³	163.73
attached deep	-	4.67	62.46	95.65	m³	158.11
Columns	-	5.09	68.08	95.65	m³	163.73
Column casings	-	5.64	75.44	95.65	m³	171.09
Staircases	-	6.38	85.34	95.65	m³	180.98
Upstands	-	4.12	55.11	95.65	m³	150.75
Reinforced in situ ready mixed designated concrete; C40 - 20 mm aggregate						
Foundations	77.21	1.48	19.80	96.03	m³	115.83
Ground beams	-	2.96	39.59	96.03	m³	135.62
Isolated foundations	-	1.80	24.08	96.03	m³	120.11
Beds						
thickness not exceeding 150 mm	-	2.36	31.57	96.03	m³	127.60
thickness 150 - 450 mm	-	1.71	22.87	96.03	m³	118.90
thickness exceeding 450 mm	-	1.39	18.59	96.03	m³	114.62
Slabs						
thickness not exceeding 150 mm	-	3.75	50.16	96.03	m³	146.19
thickness 150 - 450 mm	-	2.96	39.59	96.03	m³	135.62
thickness exceeding 450 mm	-	2.68	35.85	96.03	m³	131.88
Coffered and troughed slabs						
thickness 150 - 450 mm	-	3.42	45.74	96.03	m³	141.78
thickness exceeding 450 mm	-	2.96	39.59	96.03	m³	135.62
Extra over for sloping						
not exceeding 15 degrees	-	0.28	3.75	-	m³	3.75
over 15 degrees	-	0.56	7.49	-	m³	7.49
Walls						
thickness not exceeding 150 mm	-	3.93	52.57	96.03	m³	148.60
thickness 150 - 450 mm	-	3.15	42.13	96.03	m³	138.16
thickness exceeding 450 mm	-	2.78	37.18	96.03	m³	133.21
Beams						
isolated	-	4.26	56.98	96.03	m³	153.01
isolated deep	-	4.67	62.46	96.03	m³	158.49
attached deep	-	4.26	56.98	96.03	m³	153.01
Beam casings						
isolated	-	4.67	62.46	96.03	m³	158.49
isolated deep	-	5.09	68.08	96.03	m³	164.11
attached deep	-	4.67	62.46	96.03	m³	158.49
Columns	-	5.09	68.08	96.03	m³	164.11
Column casings	-	5.64	75.44	96.03	m³	171.47
Staircases	-	6.38	85.34	96.03	m³	181.37
Upstands	-	4.12	55.11	96.03	m³	151.14

E IN SITU CONCRETE/LARGE PRECAST CONCRETE

Item	PC £	Labour hours	Labour £	Material £	Unit	Total rate £
E05 IN SITU CONCRETE CONSTRUCTION – cont'd						
Extra over vibrated concrete for						
Reinforcement content over 5%	-	0.58	7.76	-	m^3	**7.76**
Grouting with cement mortar (1:1)						
Stanchion bases						
10 mm thick	-	1.06	14.18	0.15	nr	**14.33**
25 mm thick	-	1.33	17.79	0.39	nr	**18.18**
Grouting with epoxy resin						
Stanchion bases						
10 mm thick	-	1.33	17.79	10.47	nr	**28.26**
25 mm thick	-	1.60	21.40	26.76	nr	**48.16**
Grouting with "Conbextra GP" cementitious grout						
Stanchion bases						
10 mm thick	-	1.33	17.79	1.44	nr	**19.23**
25 mm thick	-	1.60	21.40	3.67	nr	**25.07**
Grouting with "Conbextra HF" flowable cementitious grout						
Stanchion bases						
10 mm thick	-	1.33	17.79	1.77	nr	**19.56**
25 mm thick	-	1.60	21.40	4.53	nr	**25.93**
Filling; plain ready mixed designated concrete; C20 - 20 mm aggregate						
Mortices	-	0.11	1.47	0.56	nr	**2.03**
Holes	-	0.27	3.61	116.30	m^3	**119.91**
Chases exceeding 0.01 m^2	-	0.21	2.81	116.30	m^3	**119.11**
Chases not exceeding 0.01 m^2	-	0.16	2.14	1.17	m	**3.31**
Sheeting to prevent moisture loss						
Building paper; lapped joints						
subsoil grade; horizontal on foundations	-	0.02	0.27	0.56	m^2	**0.83**
standard grade; horizontal on slabs	-	0.05	0.67	0.94	m^2	**1.61**
Polythene sheeting; lapped joints; horiz. on slabs						
250 microns; 0.25 mm thick	-	0.05	0.67	0.55	m^2	**1.22**
"Visqueen" sheeting or other equal and approved; lapped joints; horizontal on slabs						
250 microns; 0.25 mm thick	-	0.05	0.67	0.46	m^2	**1.12**
300 microns; 0.30 mm thick	-	0.06	0.80	0.56	m^2	**1.36**
E20 FORMWORK FOR IN SITU CONCRETE						
NOTE: Generally all formwork based on four uses unless otherwise stated.						
Sides of foundations; basic finish						
Plain vertical						
height exceeding 1.00 m	-	1.70	28.23	6.88	m^2	**35.10**
height exceeding 1.00 m; left in	-	1.49	24.74	16.93	m^2	**41.67**
height not exceeding 250 mm	-	0.48	7.97	2.86	m	**10.83**
height not exceeding 250 mm; left in	-	0.48	7.97	4.99	m	**12.96**
height 250 - 500 mm	-	0.91	15.11	5.77	m	**20.88**
height 250 - 500 mm; left in	-	0.80	13.28	11.61	m	**24.90**
height 500 mm - 1.00 m	-	1.28	21.25	6.88	m	**28.13**
height 500 mm - 1.00 m ; left in	-	1.22	20.26	16.93	m	**37.19**

E IN SITU CONCRETE/LARGE PRECAST CONCRETE

Item	PC £	Labour hours	Labour £	Material £	Unit	Total rate £
Sides of foundations; polystyrene sheet formwork; Cordek "Claymaster" or other equal and approved; 50 mm thick						
Plain vertical						
height exceeding 1.00 m; left in	-	0.34	5.65	8.33	m^2	13.97
height not exceeding 250 mm; left in	-	0.11	1.83	2.08	m	3.91
height 250 - 500 mm; left in	-	0.19	3.15	4.16	m	7.32
height 500 mm - 1.00 m; left in	-	0.28	4.65	8.33	m	12.98
Sides of foundations; polystyrene sheet formwork; Cordek "Claymaster" or other equal and approved; 75 mm thick						
Plain vertical						
height exceeding 1.00 m; left in	-	0.34	5.65	12.48	m^2	18.12
height not exceeding 250 mm; left in	-	0.11	1.83	3.12	m	4.95
height 250 - 500 mm; left in	-	0.19	3.15	6.24	m	9.39
height 500 mm - 1.00 m; left in	-	0.28	4.65	12.48	m	17.13
Sides of foundation; polystyrene sheet formwork; Cordek "Claymaster" or other equal and approved; 100 mm thick						
Plain vertical						
height exceeding 1.00 m; left in	-	0.37	6.14	16.62	m^2	22.76
height not exceeding 250 mm; left in	-	0.12	1.99	4.16	m	6.15
height 250 - 500 mm; left in	-	0.20	3.32	8.31	m	11.63
height 500 mm - 1.00 m; left in	-	0.31	5.15	16.62	m	21.77
Combined heave pressure relief insultaion and compressible board substructure formawork; Cordeck "Cellcore CP" or other equal and approved; butt joints; securely fixed in place						
Plain horizontal						
200 mm thick; beneath slabs; left in	-	0.70	11.62	21.91	m^2	33.53
250 mm thick; beneath slabs; left in	-	0.75	12.45	24.17	m^2	36.62
300 mm thick; beneath slabs; left in	-	0.80	13.28	26.28	m^2	39.56
Sides of ground beams and edges of beds; basic finish						
Plain vertical						
height exceeding 1.00 m	-	1.76	29.22	6.83	m^2	36.05
height not exceeding 250 mm	-	0.53	8.80	2.81	m	11.61
height 250 - 500 mm	-	0.95	15.77	5.72	m	21.49
height 500 mm - 1.00 m	-	1.33	22.08	6.83	m	28.91
Edges of suspended slabs; basic finish						
Plain vertical						
height not exceeding 250 mm	-	0.80	13.28	2.91	m	16.19
height 250 - 500 mm	-	1.17	19.43	4.64	m	24.07
height 500 mm - 1.00 m	-	1.86	30.88	6.93	m	37.81
Sides of upstands; basic finish						
Plain vertical						
height exceeding 1.00 m	-	2.13	35.37	8.60	m^2	43.97
height not exceeding 250 mm	-	0.67	11.12	3.01	m	14.14
height 250 - 500 mm	-	1.06	17.60	5.92	m	23.52
height 500 mm - 1.00 m	-	1.86	30.88	8.60	m	39.49

E IN SITU CONCRETE/LARGE PRECAST CONCRETE

Item	PC £	Labour hours	Labour £	Material £	Unit	Total rate £
E20 FORMWORK FOR IN SITU CONCRETE – cont'd						
Steps in top surfaces; basic finish						
Plain vertical						
height not exceeding 250 mm	-	0.53	8.80	3.06	m	**11.86**
height 250 - 500 mm	-	0.85	14.11	5.97	m	**20.09**
Steps in soffits; basic finish						
Plain vertical						
height not exceeding 250 mm	-	0.58	9.63	2.35	m	**11.98**
height 250 - 500 mm	-	0.93	15.44	4.20	m	**19.64**
Machine bases and plinths; basic finish						
Plain vertical						
height exceeding 1.00 m	-	1.70	28.23	6.83	m^2	**35.05**
height not exceeding 250 mm	-	0.53	8.80	2.81	m	**11.61**
height 250 - 500 mm	-	0.91	15.11	5.72	m	**20.83**
height 500 mm - 1.00 m	-	1.33	22.08	6.83	m	**28.91**
Soffits of slabs; basic finish						
Slab thickness not exceeding 200 mm						
horizontal; height to soffit not exceeding 1.50 m	-	1.92	31.88	6.27	m^2	**38.15**
horizontal; height to soffit 1.50 - 3.00 m	-	1.86	30.88	6.37	m^2	**37.25**
horizontal; height to soffit 1.50 - 3.00 m (5 uses)	-	1.76	29.22	5.30	m^2	**34.52**
horizontal; height to soffit 1.50 - 3.00 m (6 uses)	-	1.70	28.23	4.58	m^2	**32.81**
horizontal; height to soffit 3.00 - 4.50 m	-	1.81	30.05	6.62	m^2	**36.68**
horizontal; height to soffit 4.50 - 6.00 m	-	1.92	31.88	6.88	m^2	**38.76**
Slab thickness 200 - 300 mm						
horizontal; height to soffit 1.50 - 3.00 m	-	1.92	31.88	8.45	m^2	**40.33**
Slab thickness 300 - 400 mm						
horizontal; height to soffit 1.50 - 3.00 m	-	1.97	32.71	9.49	m^2	**42.20**
Slab thickness 400 - 500 mm						
horizontal; height to soffit 1.50 - 3.00 m	-	2.07	34.37	10.53	m^2	**44.90**
Slab thickness 500 - 600 mm						
horizontal; height to soffit 1.50 - 3.00 m	-	2.23	37.03	10.53	m^2	**47.56**
Extra over soffits of slabs for						
sloping not exceeding 15 degrees	-	0.21	3.49	-	m^2	**3.49**
sloping exceeding 15 degrees	-	0.43	7.14	-	m^2	**7.14**
Soffits of slabs; Expamet "Hy-rib" permanent shuttering and reinforcement; ref. 2411						
Slab thickness not exceeding 200 mm						
horizontal; height to soffit 1.50 - 3.00 m	-	1.60	26.57	35.33	m^2	**61.89**
Soffits of landings; basic finish						
Slab thickness not exceeding 200 mm						
horizontal; height to soffit 1.50 - 3.00 m	-	1.92	31.88	6.79	m^2	**38.67**
Slab thickness 200 - 300 mm						
horizontal; height to soffit 1.50 - 3.00 m	-	2.02	33.54	9.11	m^2	**42.65**
Slab thickness 300 - 400 mm						
horizontal; height to soffit 1.50 - 3.00 m	-	2.07	34.37	10.22	m^2	**44.59**
Slab thickness 400 - 500 mm						
horizontal; height to soffit 1.50 - 3.00 m	-	2.18	36.20	11.36	m^2	**47.56**
Slab thickness 500 - 600 mm						
horizontal; height to soffit 1.50 - 3.00 m	-	2.34	38.85	11.36	m^2	**50.22**
Extra over soffits of landings for						
sloping not exceeding 15 degrees	-	0.21	3.49	-	m^2	**3.49**
sloping exceeding 15 degrees	-	0.43	7.14	-	m^2	**7.14**

E IN SITU CONCRETE/LARGE PRECAST CONCRETE

Item	PC £	Labour hours	Labour £	Material £	Unit	Total rate £
Soffits of coffered or troughed slabs; basic finish Cordek "Correx" trough mould or other equal and approved; 300 mm deep; ribs of mould at 600 mm centres and cross ribs at centres of bay; slab thickness 300 - 400 mm						
horizontal; height to soffit 1.50 - 3.00 m	-	2.66	44.17	11.00	m²	55.16
horizontal; height to soffit 3.00 - 4.50 m	-	2.77	45.99	11.25	m²	57.24
horizontal; height to soffit 4.50 - 6.00 m	-	2.88	47.82	11.40	m²	59.22
Top formwork; basic finish Sloping exceeding 15 degrees	-	1.60	26.57	4.95	m²	31.52
Walls; basic finish Vertical	-	1.92	31.88	8.86	m²	40.74
Vertical; height exceeding 3.00 m above floor level	-	2.34	38.85	9.11	m²	47.97
Vertical; interrupted	-	2.23	37.03	9.11	m²	46.14
Vertical; to one side only	-	3.73	61.93	11.45	m²	73.38
Vertical; exceeding 3.00 m high; inside stairwell	-	2.34	38.85	9.11	m²	47.97
Battered	-	2.98	49.48	9.57	m²	59.05
Beams; basic finish Attached to slabs						
regular shaped; square or rectangular; height to soffit 1.50 - 3.00 m	-	2.34	38.85	8.15	m²	47.00
regular shaped; square or rectangular; height to soffit 3.00 - 4.50 m	-	2.44	40.51	8.45	m²	48.96
regular shaped; spaure or rectangular; height to soffit 4.50 - 6.00 m	-	2.55	42.34	8.70	m²	51.04
Attached to walls						
regular shaped; square or rectangular; height to soffit 1.50 - 3.00 m	-	2.44	40.51	8.15	m²	48.66
Isolated						
regular shaped; square or rectangular; height to soffit 1.50 - 3.00 m	-	2.55	42.34	8.15	m²	50.49
regular shaped; square or rectangular; height to soffit 3.00 - 4.50 m	-	2.66	44.17	8.45	m²	52.62
regular shaped; square or rectangular; height to soffit 4.50 - 6.00 m	-	2.77	45.99	8.70	m²	54.70
Extra over beams for						
regular shaped; sloping not exceeding 15 degrees	-	0.32	5.31	0.99	m²	6.30
regular shaped; sloping exceeding 15 degrees	-	0.64	10.63	1.98	m²	12.61
Beam casings; basic finish Attached to slabs						
regular shaped; square or rectangular; height to soffit 1.50 - 3.00 m	-	2.44	40.51	8.15	m²	48.66
regular shaped; square or rectangular; height to soffit 3.00 - 4.50 m	-	2.55	42.34	8.45	m²	50.79
Attached to walls						
regular shaped; square or rectangular; height to soffit 1.50 - 3.00 m	-	2.55	42.34	8.15	m²	50.49
Isolated						
regular shaped; square or rectangular; height to soffit 1.50 - 3.00 m	-	2.66	44.17	8.15	m²	52.31
regular shaped; square or rectangular; height to soffit 3.00 - 4.50 m	-	2.77	45.99	8.45	m²	54.44

E IN SITU CONCRETE/LARGE PRECAST CONCRETE

Item	PC £	Labour hours	Labour £	Material £	Unit	Total rate £
E20 FORMWORK FOR IN SITU CONCRETE – cont'd						
Beam casings; basic finish cont'd						
Extra over beam casings for						
regular shaped; sloping not exceeding 15 degrees	-	0.32	5.31	0.99	m²	6.30
regular shaped; sloping exceeding 15 degrees	-	0.64	10.63	1.98	m²	12.61
Columns; basic finish						
Attached to walls						
regular shaped; square or rectangular; height to soffit 1.50 - 3.00 m	-	2.34	38.85	6.88	m²	45.73
Isolated						
regular shaped; square or rectangular; height to soffit 1.50 - 3.00 m	-	2.44	40.51	6.88	m²	47.39
regular shaped; circular; not exceeding 300 mm diameter; height to soffit 1.50 - 3.00 m	-	4.26	70.73	12.10	m²	82.84
regular shaped; circular; 300 - 600 mm diameter; height to soffit 1.50 - 3.00 m	-	3.99	66.25	10.53	m²	76.78
regular shaped; circular; 600 - 900 mm diameter; height to soffit 1.50 - 3.00 m	-	3.73	61.93	10.28	m²	72.21
Column casings; basic finish						
Attached to walls						
regular shaped; square or rectangular; height to soffit; 1.50 - 3.00 m	-	2.44	40.51	6.88	m²	47.39
Isolated						
regular shaped; square or rectangular; height to soffit 1.50 - 3.00 m	-	2.55	42.34	6.88	m²	49.22
Recesses or rebates						
12 x 12 mm	-	0.07	1.16	0.09	m	1.25
25 x 25 mm	-	0.07	1.16	0.11	m	1.27
25 x 50 mm	-	0.07	1.16	0.15	m	1.31
50 x 50 mm	-	0.07	1.16	0.25	m	1.41
Nibs						
50 x 50 mm	-	0.58	9.63	0.92	m	10.55
100 x 100 mm	-	0.83	13.78	1.15	m	14.93
100 x 200 mm	-	1.11	18.43	2.58	m	21.01
Extra over a basic finish for fine formed finishes						
Slabs	-	0.35	5.81	-	m²	5.81
Walls	-	0.35	5.81	-	m²	5.81
Beams	-	0.35	5.81	-	m²	5.81
Columns	-	0.35	5.81	-	m²	5.81
Add to prices for basic formwork for						
Curved radius 6.00 m - 50%						50%
Curved radius 2.00 m - 100%						100%
Coating with retardant agent	-	0.01	0.17	0.33	m²	0.50
Wall kickers; basic finish						
Height 150 mm	-	0.53	8.80	2.08	m	10.88
Height 225 mm	-	0.69	11.46	2.47	m	13.93
Suspended wall kickers; basic finish						
Height 150 mm	-	0.67	11.12	1.83	m	12.95

E IN SITU CONCRETE/LARGE PRECAST CONCRETE

Item	PC £	Labour hours	Labour £	Material £	Unit	Total rate £
Wall ends, soffits and steps in walls; basic finish						
Plain						
width exceeding 1.00 m	-	2.02	33.54	8.45	m^2	41.99
width not exceeding 250 mm	-	0.64	10.63	2.10	m	12.73
width 250 - 500 mm	-	1.01	16.77	4.73	m	21.50
width 500 mm - 1.00 m	-	1.60	26.57	8.45	m	35.02
Openings in walls						
Plain						
width exceeding 1.00 m	-	2.23	37.03	8.45	m^2	45.48
width not exceeding 250 mm	-	0.69	11.46	2.10	m	13.56
width 250 - 500 mm	-	1.17	19.43	4.73	m	24.16
width 500 mm - 1.00 m	-	1.81	30.05	8.45	m	38.50
Stairflights						
Width 1.00 m; 150 mm waist; 150 mm undercut risers						
string, width 300 mm	-	5.32	88.33	17.94	m	106.27
Width 2.00 m; 300 mm waist; 150 mm undercut risers						
string, width 350 mm	-	9.57	158.90	31.55	m	190.45
Mortices						
Girth not exceeding 500 mm						
depth not exceeding 250 mm; circular	-	0.16	2.66	0.53	nr	3.18
Holes						
Girth not exceeding 500 mm						
depth not exceeding 250 mm; circular	-	0.21	3.49	0.79	nr	4.27
depth 250 - 500 mm; circular	-	0.33	5.48	2.24	nr	7.72
Girth 500 mm - 1.00 m						
depth not exceeding 250 mm; circular	-	0.27	4.48	1.23	nr	5.71
depth 250 - 500 mm; circular	-	0.41	6.81	3.91	nr	10.71
Girth 1.00 - 2.00 m						
depth not exceeding 250 mm; circular	-	0.48	7.97	3.91	nr	11.88
depth 250 - 500 mm; circular	-	0.71	11.79	8.35	nr	20.14
Girth 2.00 - 3.00 m						
depth not exceeding 250 mm; circular	-	0.64	10.63	7.79	nr	18.41
depth 250 - 500 mm; circular	-	0.95	15.77	16.27	nr	32.05
E30 REINFORCEMENT FOR IN SITU CONCRETE						
Bar; BS 4449; hot rolled deformed high steel bars grade 460						
40 mm diameter nominal size						
straight	383.90	17.00	268.26	474.67	tonne	742.92
bent	427.90	17.00	268.26	526.81	tonne	795.07
32 mm diameter nominal size						
straight	380.60	18.00	284.04	472.50	tonne	756.54
bent	424.60	18.00	284.04	524.65	tonne	808.69
25 mm diameter nominal size						
straight	378.40	20.00	315.60	469.23	tonne	784.83
bent	422.40	20.00	315.60	521.38	tonne	836.98
20 mm diameter nominal size						
straight	378.40	22.00	347.16	470.96	tonne	818.12
bent	422.40	22.00	347.16	523.11	tonne	870.26

E IN SITU CONCRETE/LARGE PRECAST CONCRETE

Item	PC £	Labour hours	Labour £	Material £	Unit	Total rate £
E30 REINFORCEMENT FOR IN SITU CONCRETE – cont'd						
Bar; BS 4449; hot rolled deformed high steel bars grade 460 – cont'd						
16 mm diameter nominal size						
straight	378.40	24.00	378.72	473.77	tonne	**852.49**
bent	422.40	24.00	378.72	525.92	tonne	**904.63**
12 mm diameter nominal size						
straight	380.60	26.00	410.28	479.19	tonne	**889.46**
bent	424.60	26.00	410.28	531.33	tonne	**941.61**
10 mm diameter nominal size						
straight	383.90	28.00	441.84	486.97	tonne	**928.81**
bent	427.90	28.00	441.84	539.12	tonne	**980.95**
8 mm diameter nominal size						
straight	392.70	30.00	470.99	500.21	tonne	**971.20**
links	392.70	33.00	518.33	503.71	tonne	**1022.04**
bent	414.70	30.00	470.99	526.28	tonne	**997.28**
6 mm diameter nominal size						
straight	403.70	35.00	549.89	513.25	tonne	**1063.14**
links	448.80	39.00	613.01	566.70	tonne	**1179.71**
bent	448.80	35.00	549.89	566.70	tonne	**1116.59**
Bar; BS 6744; stainless steel bars; grade 304						
32 mm diameter nominal size						
straight	2475.00	18.00	284.04	2853.00	tonne	**3137.04**
bent	2585.00	18.00	284.04	2977.16	tonne	**3261.20**
25 mm diameter nominal size						
straight	2475.00	20.00	315.60	2849.97	tonne	**3165.57**
bent	2585.00	20.00	315.60	2974.13	tonne	**3289.73**
20 mm diameter nominal size						
straight	2530.00	22.00	347.16	2916.14	tonne	**3263.30**
bent	2640.00	22.00	347.16	3040.31	tonne	**3387.46**
16 mm diameter nominal size						
straight	2629.00	24.00	378.72	3035.44	tonne	**3414.16**
bent	2739.00	24.00	378.72	3159.60	tonne	**3538.32**
12 mm diameter nominal size						
straight	2695.00	26.00	410.28	3117.49	tonne	**3527.77**
bent	2805.00	26.00	410.28	3241.65	tonne	**3651.93**
10 mm diameter nominal size						
straight	2772.00	28.00	441.84	3213.01	tonne	**3654.85**
bent	2882.00	28.00	441.84	3337.18	tonne	**3779.01**
8 mm diameter nominal size						
straight	2695.00	30.00	470.99	3133.65	tonne	**3604.64**
bent	2805.00	30.00	470.99	3257.81	tonne	**3728.81**
Bar; BS 6744; stainless steel bars; grade 316						
32 mm diameter nominal size						
straight	3712.50	18.00	284.04	4249.83	tonne	**4533.87**
bent	3822.50	18.00	284.04	4373.99	tonne	**4658.03**
25 mm diameter nominal size						
straight	3712.50	20.00	315.60	4246.80	tonne	**4562.39**
bent	3822.50	20.00	315.60	4370.96	tonne	**4686.56**
20 mm diameter nominal size						
straight	3795.00	22.00	347.16	4344.01	tonne	**4691.17**
bent	3905.00	22.00	347.16	4468.17	tonne	**4815.33**
16 mm diameter nominal size						
straight	3932.50	24.00	378.72	4506.77	tonne	**4885.48**
bent	4042.50	24.00	378.72	4630.93	tonne	**5009.65**

E IN SITU CONCRETE/LARGE PRECAST CONCRETE

Item	PC £	Labour hours	Labour £	Material £	Unit	Total rate £
12 mm diameter nominal size						
straight	4042.50	26.00	410.28	4638.48	tonne	5048.76
bent	4152.50	26.00	410.28	4762.64	tonne	5172.92
10 mm diameter nominal size						
straight	4158.00	28.00	441.84	4777.46	tonne	5219.30
bent	4268.00	28.00	441.84	4901.62	tonne	5343.46
8 mm diameter nominal size						
straight	4042.50	30.00	470.99	4654.64	tonne	5125.63
bent	4152.50	30.00	470.99	4778.80	tonne	5249.80
Fabric; BS 4483						
Ref A98 (1.54 kg/ m^2)						
400 mm minimum laps	1.04	0.13	2.05	1.30	m^2	3.35
strips in one width; 600 mm width	1.04	0.16	2.52	1.30	m^2	3.82
strips in one width; 900 mm width	1.04	0.15	2.37	1.30	m^2	3.66
strips in one width; 1200 mm width	1.04	0.14	2.21	1.30	m^2	3.51
Ref A142 (2.22 kg/m^2)						
400 mm minimum laps	1.08	0.13	2.05	1.34	m^2	3.39
strips in one width; 600 mm width	1.08	0.16	2.52	1.34	m^2	3.86
strips in one width; 900 mm width	1.08	0.15	2.37	1.34	m^2	3.71
strips in one width; 1200 mm width	1.08	0.14	2.21	1.34	m^2	3.55
Ref A193 (3.02 kg/m^2)						
400 mm minimum laps	1.47	0.13	2.05	1.83	m^2	3.88
strips in one width; 600 mm width	1.47	0.16	2.52	1.83	m^2	4.36
strips in one width; 900 mm width	1.47	0.15	2.37	1.83	m^2	4.20
strips in one width; 1200 mm width	1.47	0.14	2.21	1.83	m^2	4.04
Ref A252 (3.95 kg/m^2)						
400 mm minimum laps	1.91	0.14	2.21	2.38	m^2	4.59
strips in one width; 600 mm width	1.91	0.17	2.68	2.38	m^2	5.06
strips in one width; 900 mm width	1.91	0.16	2.52	2.38	m^2	4.90
strips in one width; 1200 mm width	1.91	0.15	2.37	2.38	m^2	4.74
Ref A393 (6.16 kg/m^2)						
400 mm minimum laps	2.99	0.16	2.52	3.71	m^2	6.24
strips in one width; 600 mm width	2.99	0.19	3.00	3.71	m^2	6.71
strips in one width; 900 mm width	2.99	0.18	2.84	3.71	m^2	6.56
strips in one width; 1200 mm width	2.99	0.17	2.68	3.71	m^2	6.40
Ref B196 (3.05 kg/m^2)						
400 mm minimum laps	1.49	0.13	2.05	1.84	m^2	3.90
strips in one width; 600 mm width	1.49	0.16	2.52	1.84	m^2	4.37
strips in one width; 900 mm width	1.49	0.15	2.37	1.84	m^2	4.21
strips in one width; 1200 mm width	1.49	0.14	2.21	1.84	m^2	4.05
Ref B283 (3.73 kg/m^2)						
400 mm minimum laps	1.83	0.13	2.05	2.27	m^2	4.32
strips in one width; 600 mm width	1.83	0.16	2.52	2.27	m^2	4.79
strips in one width; 900 mm width	1.83	0.15	2.37	2.27	m^2	4.63
strips in one width; 1200 mm width	1.83	0.14	2.21	2.27	m^2	4.48
Ref B385 (4.53 kg/m^2)						
400 mm minimum laps	2.20	0.14	2.21	2.73	m^2	4.94
strips in one width; 600 mm width	2.20	0.17	2.68	2.73	m^2	5.41
strips in one width; 900 mm width	2.20	0.16	2.52	2.73	m^2	5.26
strips in one width; 1200 mm width	2.20	0.15	2.37	2.73	m^2	5.10
Ref B503 (5.93 kg/m^2)						
400 mm minimum laps	2.89	0.16	2.52	3.59	m^2	6.12
strips in one width; 600 mm width	2.89	0.19	3.00	3.59	m^2	6.59
strips in one width; 900 mm width	2.89	0.18	2.84	3.59	m^2	6.43
strips in one width; 1200 mm width	2.89	0.17	2.68	3.59	m^2	6.27

E IN SITU CONCRETE/LARGE PRECAST CONCRETE

Item	PC £	Labour hours	Labour £	Material £	Unit	Total rate £
E30 REINFORCEMENT FOR IN SITU CONCRETE – cont'd						
Fabric; BS 4483 – cont'd						
Ref B785 (8.14 kg/m^2)						
400 mm minimum laps	3.96	0.19	3.00	4.92	m^2	7.92
strips in one width; 600 mm width	3.96	0.22	3.47	4.92	m^2	8.39
strips in one width; 900 mm width	3.96	0.21	3.31	4.92	m^2	8.23
strips in one width; 1200 mm width	3.96	0.20	3.16	4.92	m^2	8.07
Ref B1131 (10.90 kg/m^2)						
400 mm minimum laps	5.30	0.20	3.16	6.58	m^2	9.74
strips in one width; 600 mm width	5.30	0.26	4.10	6.58	m^2	10.69
strips in one width; 900 mm width	5.30	0.24	3.79	6.58	m^2	10.37
strips in one width; 1200 mm width	5.30	0.22	3.47	6.58	m^2	10.05
Ref C385 (3.41 kg/m^2)						
400 mm minimum laps	1.66	0.13	2.05	2.06	m^2	4.11
strips in one width; 600 mm width	1.66	0.16	2.52	2.06	m^2	4.59
strips in one width; 900 mm width	1.66	0.15	2.37	2.06	m^2	4.43
strips in one width; 1200 mm width	1.66	0.14	2.21	2.06	m^2	4.27
Ref C503 (4.34 kg/m^2)						
400 mm minimum laps	2.11	0.14	2.21	2.62	m^2	4.83
strips in one width; 600 mm width	2.11	0.17	2.68	2.62	m^2	5.30
strips in one width; 900 mm width	2.11	0.16	2.52	2.62	m^2	5.15
strips in one width; 1200 mm width	2.11	0.15	2.37	2.62	m^2	4.99
Ref C636 (5.55 kg/m^2)						
400 mm minimum laps	2.71	0.15	2.37	3.36	m^2	5.73
strips in one width; 600 mm width	2.71	0.18	2.84	3.36	m^2	6.20
strips in one width; 900 mm width	2.71	0.17	2.68	3.36	m^2	6.04
strips in one width; 1200 mm width	2.71	0.16	2.52	3.36	m^2	5.88
Ref C785 (6.72 kg/m^2)						
400 mm minimum laps	3.26	0.15	2.37	4.04	m^2	6.41
strips in one width; 600 mm width	3.26	0.18	2.84	4.04	m^2	6.88
strips in one width; 900 mm width	3.26	0.17	2.68	4.04	m^2	6.73
strips in one width; 1200 mm width	3.26	0.16	2.52	4.04	m^2	6.57
Ref D49 (0.77 kg/m^2)						
100 mm minimum laps; bent	1.14	0.26	4.10	1.42	m^2	5.52
Ref D98 (1.54 kg/m^2)						
200 mm minimum laps; bent	1.28	0.26	4.10	1.58	m^2	5.69
E40 DESIGNED JOINTS IN IN SITU CONCRETE						
Formed; Fosroc impregnated fibreboard joint filler or other equal and approved						
Width not exceeding 150 mm						
12.50 mm thick	-	0.16	2.66	1.47	m	4.12
20 mm thick	-	0.20	3.32	2.24	m	5.56
25 mm thick	-	0.25	4.15	2.33	m	6.48
Width 150 - 300 mm						
12.50 mm thick	-	0.26	4.32	2.31	m	6.62
20 mm thick	-	0.26	4.32	3.59	m	7.91
25 mm thick	-	0.26	4.32	4.25	m	8.57
Width 300 - 450 mm						
12.50 mm thick	-	0.31	5.15	3.23	m	8.38
20 mm thick	-	0.31	5.15	5.00	m	10.15
25 mm thick	-	0.31	5.15	5.91	m	11.06

E IN SITU CONCRETE/LARGE PRECAST CONCRETE

Item	PC £	Labour hours	Labour £	Material £	Unit	Total rate £
Formed; Grace Servicised "Kork-pak" waterproof bonded cork joint filler board or other equal and approved						
Width not exceeding 150 mm						
10 mm thick	-	0.16	2.66	3.66	m	6.32
13 mm thick	-	0.16	2.66	3.72	m	6.38
19 mm thick	-	0.16	2.66	4.91	m	7.57
25 mm thick	-	0.16	2.66	5.65	m	8.31
Width 150 - 300 mm						
10 mm thick	-	0.20	3.32	6.83	m	10.15
13 mm thick	-	0.20	3.32	6.95	m	10.27
19 mm thick	-	0.20	3.32	9.33	m	12.65
25 mm thick	-	0.20	3.32	10.81	m	14.13
Width 300 - 450 mm						
10 mm thick	-	0.26	4.32	10.39	m	14.71
13 mm thick	-	0.26	4.32	10.58	m	14.89
19 mm thick	-	0.26	4.32	14.15	m	18.47
25 mm thick	-	0.26	4.32	16.37	m	20.68
Sealants; Fosroc "Pliastic 77" hot poured rubberized bituminous compound or other equal and approved						
Width 10 mm						
25 mm depth	-	0.19	3.15	1.03	m	4.19
Width 12.50 mm						
25 mm depth	-	0.20	3.32	1.27	m	4.59
Width 20 mm						
25 mm depth	-	0.21	3.49	2.07	m	5.56
Width 25 mm						
25 mm depth	-	0.22	3.65	2.54	m	6.19
Sealants; Fosroc "Thioflex 600" gun grade two part polysulphide or other equal and approved						
Width 10 mm						
25 mm depth	-	0.06	1.00	3.93	m	4.93
Width 12.50 mm						
25 mm depth	-	0.07	1.16	4.92	m	6.08
Width 20 mm						
25 mm depth	-	0.08	1.33	7.87	m	9.19
Width 25 mm						
25 mm depth	-	0.09	1.49	9.83	m	11.33
Sealants; Grace Servicised "Paraseal" polysulphide compound or other equal and approved; priming with Grace Servicised "Servicised P" or other equal and approved						
Width 10 mm						
25 mm depth	-	0.20	2.68	3.62	m	6.30
Width 13 mm						
25 mm depth	-	0.20	2.68	4.64	m	7.32
Width 19 mm						
25 mm depth	-	0.26	3.48	6.69	m	10.16
Width 25 mm						
25 mm depth	-	0.26	3.48	8.73	m	12.21

E IN SITU CONCRETE/LARGE PRECAST CONCRETE

Item	PC £	Labour hours	Labour £	Material £	Unit	Total rate £
E40 DESIGNED JOINTS IN IN SITU CONCRETE – cont'd						
Waterstops; Grace Servicised or other equal and approved						
Hydrophilic strip water stop; lapped joints; cast in						
5 x 20 mm "Servistrip AH 205"	-	0.35	4.68	6.84	m	11.52
50 x 20 mm "Adcor 500S"	-	0.35	4.68	9.03	m	13.71
"Servitite" internal 10 mm thick pvc water stop; flat dumbbell type; heat welded joints; cast in						
Servitite 150; 150 mm wide	3.37	0.26	4.10	4.17	m	8.28
flat angle	13.40	0.31	4.89	17.19	nr	22.08
vertical angle	13.31	0.31	4.89	17.09	nr	21.98
flat three way intersection	19.32	0.41	6.47	24.89	nr	31.36
vertical three way intersection	22.38	0.41	6.47	28.43	nr	34.90
four way intersection	23.68	0.51	8.05	30.77	nr	38.82
Servitite 230; 230 mm wide	3.17	0.26	4.10	3.93	m	8.03
flat angle	15.89	0.31	4.89	19.98	nr	24.87
vertical angle	19.44	0.31	4.89	24.08	nr	28.97
flat three way intersection	23.04	0.41	6.47	29.04	nr	35.51
vertical three way intersection	43.95	0.41	6.47	53.24	nr	59.71
four way intersection	2.53	0.51	8.05	29.68	nr	37.72
Servitite AT200; 200 mm wide	12.61	0.26	4.10	15.12	m	19.22
flat angle	21.04	0.31	4.89	30.41	nr	35.30
vertical angle	23.24	0.31	4.89	32.95	nr	37.84
flat three way intersection	37.66	0.41	6.47	52.67	nr	59.14
vertical three way intersection	27.88	0.41	6.47	41.36	nr	47.83
four way intersection	43.56	0.51	8.05	62.53	nr	70.58
Servitite K305; 305 mm wide	5.45	0.31	4.89	6.64	m	11.53
flat angle	25.98	0.36	5.68	33.37	nr	39.05
vertical angle	28.59	0.36	5.68	36.40	nr	42.08
flat three way intersection	36.55	0.45	7.10	47.27	nr	54.37
vertical three way intersection	44.63	0.45	7.10	56.62	nr	63.72
four way intersection	49.74	0.56	8.84	64.19	nr	73.02
"Serviseal" external pvc water stop; centre bulb type; heat welded joints; cast into concrete						
Serviseal 195; 195 mm wide	3.30	0.26	4.10	4.09	m	8.19
flat angle	9.59	0.31	4.89	12.75	nr	17.64
vertical angle	17.23	0.31	4.89	21.59	nr	26.48
flat three way intersection	16.46	0.41	6.47	21.53	nr	28.00
vertical three way intersection	9.19	0.41	6.47	13.12	nr	19.59
four way intersection	24.82	0.51	8.05	32.02	nr	40.07
Serviseal 240; 240 mm wide	3.03	0.26	4.10	3.76	m	7.86
flat angle	10.91	0.31	4.89	14.14	nr	19.03
vertical angle	18.02	0.31	4.89	22.37	nr	27.26
flat three way intersection	18.45	0.41	6.47	23.63	nr	30.10
vertical three way intersection	9.28	0.41	6.47	13.03	nr	19.50
four way intersection	27.45	0.51	8.05	34.81	nr	42.86
Serviseal AT240; 240 mm wide	19.85	0.26	4.10	23.70	m	27.80
flat angle	19.60	0.31	4.89	32.17	nr	37.07
vertical angle	18.48	0.31	4.89	30.88	nr	35.77
flat three way intersection	30.19	0.41	6.47	49.19	nr	55.66
vertical three way intersection	8.30	0.41	6.47	23.85	nr	30.32
four way intersection	45.46	0.51	8.05	71.59	nr	79.64
Serviseal K320; 320 mm wide	6.35	0.31	4.89	7.70	m	12.59
flat angle	24.57	0.36	5.68	32.27	nr	37.95
vertical angle	20.91	0.36	5.68	28.04	nr	33.72
flat three way intersection	35.97	0.45	7.10	47.40	nr	54.50
vertical three way intersection	7.85	0.45	7.10	14.87	nr	21.97
four way intersection	44.80	0.56	8.84	59.53	nr	68.36

E IN SITU CONCRETE/LARGE PRECAST CONCRETE

Item	PC £	Labour hours	Labour £	Material £	Unit	Total rate £
E41 WORKED FINISHES/CUTTING TO IN SITU CONCRETE						
Worked finishes						
Tamping by mechanical means	-	0.02	0.27	0.04	m^2	0.31
Power floating	-	0.18	2.41	0.14	m^2	2.55
Trowelling	-	0.33	4.41	-	m^2	4.41
Hacking						
by mechanical means	-	0.33	4.41	0.34	m^2	4.76
by hand	-	0.71	9.50	-	m^2	9.50
Lightly shot blasting surface of concrete	-	0.41	5.48	-	m^2	5.48
Blasting surface of concrete						
to produce textured finish	-	0.71	9.50	0.72	m^2	10.22
Wood float finish	-	0.13	1.74	-	m^2	1.74
Tamped finish						
level or to falls	-	0.07	0.94	-	m^2	0.94
to falls	-	0.10	1.34	-	m^2	1.34
Spade finish	-	0.16	2.14	-	m^2	2.14
Cutting chases						
Depth not exceeding 50 mm						
width 10 mm	-	0.33	4.41	0.55	m	4.97
width 50 mm	-	0.51	6.82	0.73	m	7.55
width 75 mm	-	0.68	9.10	0.89	m	9.99
Depth 50 - 100 mm						
width 75 mm	-	0.92	12.31	1.40	m	13.71
width 100 mm	-	1.02	13.64	1.50	m	15.15
width 100 mm; in reinforced concrete	-	1.53	20.46	2.37	m	22.84
Depth 100 - 150 mm						
width 100 mm	-	1.32	17.66	1.76	m	19.41
width 100 mm; in reinforced concrete	-	2.04	27.29	3.05	m	30.33
width 150 mm	-	1.63	21.80	2.07	m	23.87
width 150 mm; in reinforced concrete	-	2.44	32.64	3.43	m	36.06
Cutting rebates						
Depth not exceeding 50 mm						
width 50 mm	-	0.51	6.82	0.73	m	7.55
Depth 50 - 100 mm						
width 100 mm	-	1.02	13.64	1.50	m	15.15
NOTE: The following rates for cutting holes and mortices in concrete allow for diamond drilling.						
Cutting holes and mortices in concrete; per 25 mm depth						
25 mm diameter	-	-	-	-	nr	1.43
32 mm diameter	-	-	-	-	nr	1.43
52 mm diameter	-	-	-	-	nr	1.76
76 mm diameter	-	-	-	-	nr	2.04
107 mm diameter	-	-	-	-	nr	2.20
127 mm diameter	-	-	-	-	nr	2.37
152 mm diameter	-	-	-	-	nr	2.86
200 mm diameter	-	-	-	-	nr	3.79
250 mm diameter	-	-	-	-	nr	5.67
300 mm diameter	-	-	-	-	nr	7.48

E IN SITU CONCRETE/LARGE PRECAST CONCRETE

Item	PC £	Labour hours	Labour £	Material £	Unit	Total rate £
E41 WORKED FINISHES/CUTTING TO IN SITU CONCRETE - cont'd						
Cutting holes and mortices in reinforced concrete; per 25 mm depth						
25 mm diameter	-	-	-	-	nr	2.09
32 mm diameter	-	-	-	-	nr	2.09
52 mm diameter	-	-	-	-	nr	2.04
76 mm diameter	-	-	-	-	nr	2.15
107 mm diameter	-	-	-	-	nr	2.48
127 mm diameter	-	-	-	-	nr	2.86
152 mm diameter	-	-	-	-	nr	3.41
200 mm diameter	-	-	-	-	nr	4.84
250 mm diameter	-	-	-	-	nr	7.42
300 mm diameter	-	-	-	-	nr	9.57
Other items in reinforced concrete						
Diamond chasing; per 25 x 25 mm section	-	-	-	-	m	12.54
Forming box; per 25 mm depth (per m of perimeter)	-	-	-	-	m	12.65
Diamond floor sawing; per 25 mm depth	-	-	-	-	m	3.63
Diamond track mount or ring sawing; per 25 mm depth	-	-	-	-	m	8.25
Stitch drilling 107 mm diameter hole; per 25 mm depth	-	-	-	-	nr	2.20
E42 ACCESSORIES CAST INTO IN SITU CONCRETE						
Foundation bolt boxes						
Temporary plywood; for group of 4 nr bolts						
75 x 75 x 150 mm	-	0.45	7.47	0.96	nr	8.43
75 x 75 x 250 mm	-	0.45	7.47	1.21	nr	8.68
Expanded metal; Expamet Building Products Ltd or other equal and approved						
75 mm diameter x 150 mm long	-	0.31	5.15	1.55	nr	6.70
75 mm diameter x 300 mm long	-	0.31	5.15	2.25	nr	7.40
100 mm diameter x 450 mm long	-	0.31	5.15	2.70	nr	7.85
Foundation bolts and nuts						
Black hexagon						
10 mm diameter x 100 mm long	-	0.26	4.32	0.74	nr	5.05
12 mm diameter x 120 mm long	-	0.26	4.32	1.12	nr	5.44
16 mm diameter x 160 mm long	-	0.31	5.15	3.11	nr	8.26
20 mm diameter x 180 mm long	-	0.31	5.15	3.63	nr	8.78
Masonry slots						
Galvanised steel; dovetail slots; 1.20 mm thick; 18G						
75 mm long	-	0.08	1.33	0.26	nr	1.59
100 mm long	-	0.08	1.33	0.29	nr	1.61
150 mm long	-	0.09	1.49	0.35	nr	1.85
225 mm long	-	0.10	1.66	0.50	nr	2.16
Galvanised steel; metal insert slots; Halfen Ltd or other equal and approved; 2.50 mm thick; end caps and foam filling						
41 mm x 41 mm; ref P3270	-	0.41	6.81	7.14	m	13.95
41 mm x 41 mm x 75 mm; ref P3249	-	0.10	1.66	0.89	nr	2.55
41 mm x 41 mm x 100 mm; ref P3250	-	0.10	1.66	0.98	nr	2.64
41mm x 41 mm x 150 mm; ref P3251	-	0.10	1.66	1.25	nr	2.91

E IN SITU CONCRETE/LARGE PRECAST CONCRETE

Item	PC £	Labour hours	Labour £	Material £	Unit	Total rate £
Cramps Mild steel; once bent; one end shot fired into concrete; other end flanged and built into brickwork joint						
200 mm girth	-	0.16	2.92	0.69	nr	3.61
Column guards White nylon coated steel; "Rigifix"; Huntley and Sparks Ltd or other equal and approved; plugging; screwing to concrete; 1.50 mm thick						
75 x 75 x 1000 mm	-	0.81	13.45	21.94	nr	35.39
Galvanised steel; "Rigifix"; Huntley and Sparks Ltd or other equal and approved; 3 mm thick						
75 x 75 x 1000 mm	-	0.61	10.13	15.62	nr	25.74
Galvanised steel; "Rigifix"; Huntley and Sparks Ltd or other equal and approved; 4.50 mm thick						
75 x 75 x 1000 mm	-	0.61	10.13	20.99	nr	31.12
Stainless steel; "HKW"; Halfen Ltd or other equal and approved; 5 mm thick						
50 x 50 x 1200 mm	-	1.02	16.94	66.21	nr	83.14
50 x 50 x 2000 mm	-	1.22	20.26	88.27	nr	108.53
E60 PRECAST/COMPOSITE CONCRETE DECKING						
Prestressed precast flooring planks; Bison "Drycast" or other equal and approved; cement:sand (1:3) grout between planks and on prepared bearings 100 mm thick suspended slabs; horizontal						
600 mm wide planks	-	-	-	-	m²	39.70
1200 mm wide planks	-	-	-	-	m²	37.66
150 mm thick suspended slabs; horizontal						
1200 mm wide planks	-	-	-	-	m²	39.26

F MASONRY

Item	PC £	Labour hours	Labour £	Material £	Unit	Total rate £
F10 BRICK/BLOCK WALLING						
Common bricks; PC £220.00/1000; in gauged mortar (1:1:6)						
Walls						
half brick thick	-	1.06	24.19	18.13	m²	42.33
half brick thick; building against other work; concrete	-	1.16	26.48	19.55	m²	46.02
half brick thick; building overhand	-	1.34	30.58	18.13	m²	48.72
half brick thick; curved; 6.00 m radii	-	1.39	31.72	18.13	m²	49.86
half brick thick; curved; 1.50 m radii	-	1.80	41.08	20.80	m²	61.88
one brick thick	-	1.80	41.08	36.27	m²	77.35
one brick thick; curved; 6.00 m radii	-	2.36	53.86	38.94	m²	92.80
one brick thick; curved; 1.50 m radii	-	2.91	66.42	39.64	m²	106.06
one and a half brick thick	-	2.45	55.92	54.40	m²	110.32
one and a half brick thick; battering	-	2.82	64.36	54.40	m²	118.76
two brick thick	-	2.96	67.56	72.54	m²	140.09
two brick thick; battering	-	3.52	80.34	72.54	m²	152.87
337 mm average thick; tapering, one side	-	3.10	70.75	54.40	m²	125.15
450 mm average thick; tapering, one side	-	3.98	90.84	72.54	m²	163.37
337 mm average thick; tapering both sides	-	3.56	81.25	54.40	m²	135.65
450 mm average thick; tapering both sides	-	4.49	102.48	73.24	m²	175.72
facework one side, half brick thick	-	1.16	26.48	18.13	m²	44.61
facework one side, one brick thick	-	1.90	43.36	36.27	m²	79.63
facework one side, one and a half brick thick	-	2.54	57.97	54.40	m²	112.37
facework one side, two brick thick	-	3.10	70.75	72.54	m²	143.29
facework both sides, half brick thick	-	1.30	29.67	18.13	m²	47.80
facework both sides, one brick thick	-	2.04	46.56	36.27	m²	82.83
facework both sides, one and a half brick thick	-	2.68	61.17	54.40	m²	115.57
facework both sides, two brick thick	-	3.19	72.81	72.54	m²	145.34
Isolated piers						
one brick thick	-	2.73	62.31	36.27	m²	98.58
two brick thick	-	4.26	97.23	73.24	m²	170.47
three brick thick	-	5.37	122.56	110.21	m²	232.78
Isolated casings						
half brick thick	-	1.39	31.72	18.13	m²	49.86
one brick thick	-	2.36	53.86	36.27	m²	90.13
Chimney stacks						
one brick thick	-	2.73	62.31	36.27	m²	98.58
two brick thick	-	4.26	97.23	73.24	m²	170.47
three brick thick	-	5.37	122.56	110.21	m²	232.78
Projections						
225 mm width; 112 mm depth; vertical	-	0.32	7.30	3.81	m	11.11
225 mm width; 225 mm depth; vertical	-	0.65	14.84	7.61	m	22.45
337 mm width; 225 mm depth; vertical	-	0.97	22.14	11.42	m	33.56
440 mm width; 225 mm depth; vertical	-	1.06	24.19	15.22	m	39.42
Closing cavities						
with of 50 mm, closing with common brickwork half brick thick; vertical	-	0.32	7.30	0.92	m	8.22
with of 50 mm, closing with common brickwork half brick thick; horizontal	-	0.32	7.30	2.82	m	10.12
with of 50 mm, closing with common brickwork half brick thick; including damp proof course; vertical	-	0.43	9.81	1.90	m	11.72
with of 50 mm, closing with common brickwork half brick thick; including damp proof course; horizontal	-	0.37	8.44	3.53	m	11.98

F MASONRY

Item	PC £	Labour hours	Labour £	Material £	Unit	Total rate £
Common bricks; PC £220.00/1000; – cont'd						
Closing cavities – cont'd						
with of 75 mm, closing with common brickwork half brick thick; vertical	-	0.32	7.30	1.35	m	8.65
with of 75 mm, closing with common brickwork half brick thick; horizontal	-	0.32	7.30	4.15	m	11.46
with of 75 mm, closing with common brickwork half brick thick; including damp proof course; vertical	-	0.43	9.81	2.33	m	12.15
with of 50 mm, closing with common brickwork half brick thick; including damp proof course; horizontal	-	0.37	8.44	4.87	m	13.31
Bonding to existing						
half brick thick	-	0.32	7.30	1.00	m	8.30
one brick thick	-	0.46	10.50	1.99	m	12.49
one and a half brick thick	-	0.74	16.89	2.99	m	19.88
two brick thick	-	1.02	23.28	3.98	m	27.26
Arches						
height on face 102 mm, width of exposed soffit 102 mm, shape of arch - segmental, one ring	-	1.80	33.18	6.39	m	39.57
height on face 102 mm, width of exposed soffit 215 mm, shape of arch - segmental, segmental, one ring	-	2.36	46.31	8.45	m	54.76
height on face 102 mm, width of exposed soffit 102 mm, shape of arch - semi-circular, one ring	-	2.31	45.17	6.39	m	51.56
height on face 102 mm, width of exposed soffit 215 mm, shape of arch - semi-circular, one ring	-	2.87	58.30	8.45	m	66.75
height on face 215 mm, width of exposed soffit 102 mm, shape of arch - segmental, two ring	-	2.31	45.17	8.31	m	53.48
height on face 215 mm, width of exposed soffit 215 mm, shape of arch - segmental, two ring	-	2.82	57.16	12.29	m	69.45
height on face 215 mm, width of exposed soffit 102 mm, shape of arch semi-circular, two ring	-	3.10	63.73	8.31	m	72.04
height on face 215 mm, width of exposed soffit 215 mm, shape of arch - semi-circular, two ring	-	3.52	73.58	12.29	m	85.87
ADD or DEDUCT to walls for variation of £10.00/1000 in PC of common bricks						
half brick thick	-	-	-	0.73	m²	0.73
one brick thick	-	-	-	1.46	m²	1.46
one and a half brick thick	-	-	-	2.19	m²	2.19
two brick thick	-	-	-	2.92	m²	2.92
Class B engineering bricks; PC £275.00/1000; in cement mortar (1:3)						
Walls						
half brick thick	-	1.16	26.48	21.81	m²	48.29
one brick thick	-	1.90	43.36	43.63	m²	86.99
one brick thick; building against other work	-	2.27	51.81	45.99	m²	97.80
one brick thick; curved; 6.00 m radii	-	2.54	57.97	43.63	m²	101.60
one and a half brick thick	-	2.54	57.97	65.44	m²	123.41
one and a half brick thick; building against other work	-	3.10	70.75	65.44	m²	136.19
two brick thick	-	3.27	74.63	87.25	m²	161.88
337 mm average thick; tapering, one side	-	3.28	74.86	65.44	m²	140.30
450 mm average thick; tapering, one side	-	4.26	97.23	87.25	m²	184.48
337 mm average thick; tapering, both sides	-	3.84	87.64	65.44	m²	153.08
450 mm average thick; tapering, both sides	-	4.86	110.92	88.04	m²	198.96

F MASONRY

Item	PC £	Labour hours	Labour £	Material £	Unit	Total rate £
F10 BRICK/BLOCK WALLING – cont'd						
Class B engineering bricks; PC						
£275.00/1000 – cont'd						
Walls – cont'd						
facework one side, half brick thick	-	1.30	29.67	21.81	m²	51.48
facework one side, one brick thick	-	2.04	46.56	43.63	m²	90.18
facework one side, one and a half brick thick	-	2.68	61.17	65.44	m²	126.60
facework one side, two brick thick	-	3.28	74.86	87.25	m²	162.11
facework both sides, half brick thick	-	1.39	31.72	21.81	m²	53.54
facework both sides, one brick thick	-	2.13	48.61	43.63	m²	92.24
facework both sides, one and a half brick thick	-	2.78	63.45	65.44	m²	128.89
facework both sides, two brick thick	-	3.42	78.06	87.25	m²	165.31
Isolated piers						
one brick thick	-	2.96	67.56	43.63	m²	111.18
two brick thick	-	4.67	106.58	88.04	m²	194.62
three brick thick	-	5.74	131.01	132.45	m²	263.46
Isolated casings						
half brick thick	-	1.48	33.78	21.81	m²	55.59
one brick thick	-	2.54	57.97	43.63	m²	101.60
Projections						
225 mm width; 112 mm depth; vertical	-	0.37	8.44	4.60	m	13.04
225 mm width; 225 mm depth; vertical	-	0.69	15.75	9.20	m	24.94
337 mm width; 225 mm depth; vertical	-	1.02	23.28	13.79	m	37.07
440 mm width; 225 mm depth; vertical	-	1.16	26.48	18.39	m	44.87
Bonding to existing						
half brick thick	-	0.37	8.44	1.20	m	9.64
one brick thick	-	0.56	12.78	2.40	m	15.18
one and a half brick thick	-	0.74	16.89	3.60	m	20.49
two brick thick	-	1.11	25.33	4.79	m	30.13
ADD or DEDUCT to walls for variation of						
£10.00/1000 in PC of bricks						
half brick thick	-	-	-	0.73	m²	0.73
one brick thick	-	-	-	1.46	m²	1.46
one and a half brick thick	-	-	-	2.19	m²	2.19
two brick thick	-	-	-	2.92	m²	2.92
Facing bricks; machine made facings;						
PC £310.00/1000 (unless otherwise						
stated); in gauged mortar (1:1:6)						
Walls						
facework one side, half brick thick; stretcher bond	-	1.39	31.72	24.69	m²	56.41
facework one side, half brick thick, flemish bond with snapped headers	-	1.62	36.97	24.69	m²	61.66
facework one side, half brick thick; stretcher bond; building against other work; concrete	-	1.48	33.78	26.10	m²	59.88
facework one side, half brick thick; flemish bond with snapped headers; building against other work; concrete	-	1.71	39.03	26.10	m²	65.13
facework one side, half brick thick, stretcher bond; building overhand	-	1.71	39.03	24.69	m²	63.71
facework one side, half brick thick; flemish bond with snapped headers; building overhand	-	1.90	43.36	24.69	m²	68.05
facework one side, half brick thick; stretcher bond; curved; 6.00 m radii	-	2.04	46.56	24.69	m²	71.25
facework one side, half brick thick; flemish bond with snapped headers; curved; 6.00 m radii	-	2.27	51.81	24.69	m²	76.50
facework one side, half brick thick; stretcher bond; curved; 1.50 m radii	-	2.54	57.97	28.45	m²	86.42

F MASONRY

Item	PC £	Labour hours	Labour £	Material £	Unit	Total rate £
facework one side; half brick thick; stretcher bond; curved; 1.50 m radii	-	2.96	67.56	28.45	m²	**96.01**
facework both sides, one brick thick; two stretcher skins tied together	-	2.41	55.00	51.13	m²	**106.13**
facework both sides, one brick thick; flemish bond	-	3.28	74.86	49.37	m²	**124.23**
facework both sides, one brick thick; two stretcher skins tied together; curved; 6.00 m radii	-	3.42	78.06	54.89	m²	**132.95**
facework both sides, one brick thick; flemish bond; curved; 6.00 m radii	-	3.42	78.06	53.14	m²	**131.19**
facework both sides, one brick thick; two stretcher skins tied together; curved; 1.50 m radii	-	4.12	94.03	59.36	m²	**153.39**
facework both sides, one brick thick; flemish bond; curved; 1.50 m radii	-	2.26	51.58	57.60	m²	**109.18**
Isolated piers						
facework both sides, one brick thick; two stretcher skins tied together	-	2.82	64.36	52.13	m²	**116.49**
facework both sides, one brick thick; flemish bond	-	2.87	65.50	52.13	m²	**117.63**
Isolated casings						
facework one side, half brick thick; stretcher bond	-	2.13	48.61	24.69	m²	**73.30**
facework one side, half brick thick; flemish bond with snapped headers	-	2.36	53.86	24.69	m²	**78.55**
Projections						
225 mm width; 112 mm depth; stretcher bond; vertical	-	0.32	7.30	5.26	m	**12.57**
225 mm width; 112 mm depth; flemish bond with snapped headers; vertical	-	0.42	9.59	5.26	m	**14.85**
225 mm width; 225 mm depth; flemish bond; vertical	-	0.69	15.75	10.52	m	**26.27**
328 mm width; 112 mm depth; stretcher bond; vertical	-	0.65	14.84	7.90	m	**22.73**
328 mm width; 112 mm depth; flemish bond with snapped headers; vertical	-	0.74	16.89	7.90	m	**24.79**
328 mm width; 225 mm depth; flemish bond; vertical	-	1.30	29.67	15.75	m	**45.42**
440 mm width; 112 mm depth; stretcher bond; vertical	-	0.97	22.14	10.52	m	**32.66**
440 mm width; 112 mm depth; flemish bond with snapped headers; vertical	-	1.02	23.28	10.52	m	**33.80**
440 mm width; 225 mm depth; flemish bond; vertical	-	1.85	42.22	21.05	m	**63.27**
Arches						
height on face 215 mm, width of exposed soffit 102 mm, shape of arch - flat	-	1.06	21.03	7.01	m	**28.05**
height on face 215 mm, width of exposed soffit 215 mm, shape of arch - flat	-	1.57	33.02	12.47	m	**45.50**
height on face 215 mm, width of exposed soffit 102 mm, shape of arch - segmental, one ring	-	2.04	37.87	9.77	m	**47.63**
height on face 215 mm, width of exposed soffit 215 mm, shape of arch - segmental, one ring	-	2.45	47.57	14.92	m	**62.50**
height on face 215 mm, width of exposed soffit 102 mm, shape of arch - semi-circular, one ring	-	3.10	62.85	9.77	m	**72.62**
height on face 215 mm, width of exposed soffit 215 mm, shape of arch - semi-circular, one ring	-	4.16	87.83	14.92	m	**102.75**
height on face 215 mm, width of exposed soffit 102 mm, shape of arch - segmental, two ring height on face 215 mm, width of exposed soffit	-	2.50	48.72	9.77	m	**58.48**

F MASONRY

Item	PC £	Labour hours	Labour £	Material £	Unit	Total rate £
F10 BRICK/BLOCK WALLING – cont'd						
Facing bricks; machine made facings;						
PC £310.00/1000 – cont'd						
Arches – cont'd						
215 mm, shape of arch - segmental, two ring	-	3.24	66.13	14.92	m	81.05
height on face 215 mm, width of exposed soffit						
102 mm, shape of arch - semi-circular, two ring	-	4.16	87.83	9.77	m	97.60
height on face 215 mm, width of exposed soffit						
215 mm, shape of arch - semi-circular, two ring	-	5.74	124.95	14.92	m	139.87
Arches; cut voussoirs; PC £3200.00/1000						
height on face 215 mm, width of exposed soffit						
102 mm, shape of arch - segmental, one ring	-	2.08	38.87	56.53	m	95.39
height on face 215 mm, width of exposed soffit						
215 mm, shape of arch - segmental, one ring	-	2.49	49.45	108.44	m	157.89
height on face 215 mm, width of exposed soffit						
102 mm, shape of arch - semi-circular, one ring	-	2.36	45.43	56.53	m	101.96
height on face 215 mm, width of exposed soffit						
215 mm, shape of arch - semi-circular, one ring	-	2.96	59.57	108.44	m	168.00
height on face 320 mm, width of exposed soffit						
102 mm, shape of arch - segmental, one and a half ring	-	2.78	55.28	108.44	m	163.72
height on face 320 mm, width of exposed soffit						
215 mm, shape of arch - segmental, one and a half ring	-	3.61	74.84	220.17	m	295.01
Arches; bullnosed specials; PC £1800.00/1000						
height on face 215 mm, width of exposed soffit						
102 mm, shape of arch - flat	-	1.11	22.17	31.12	m	53.29
height on face 215 mm, width of exposed soffit						
215 mm, shape of arch - flat	-	1.62	34.16	61.29	m	95.45
Bullseye windows; 600 mm diameter						
height on face 215 mm, width of exposed soffit						
102 mm, two rings	-	5.32	115.10	12.89	nr	127.99
height on face 215 mm, width of exposed soffit						
215 mm, two rings	-	7.55	166.61	24.23	nr	190.83
Bullseye windows; 600 mm diameter; cut voussoirs; PC £3200.00/1000						
height on face 215 mm, width of exposed soffit						
102 mm, one ring	-	4.49	95.54	138.26	nr	233.80
height on face 215 mm, width of exposed soffit,						
215 mm, one ring	-	6.15	134.66	274.97	nr	409.62
Bullseye windows; 1200 mm diameter						
height on face 215 mm, width of exposed soffit						
102 mm, two rings	-	8.28	184.76	28.07	nr	212.83
height on face 215 mm, width of exposed soffit						
215 mm, two rings	-	11.93	270.70	51.39	nr	322.09
Bullseye windows; 1200 mm diameter; cut voussoirs; PC £3200.00/1000						
height on face 215 mm, width of exposed soffit						
102 mm, one ring	-	7.03	155.35	240.69	nr	396.04
height on face 215 mm, width of exposed soffit						
215 mm, one ring	-	9.99	225.02	475.21	nr	700.23
ADD or DEDUCT for variation of £10.00/1000 in PC of facing bricks in 102 mm high arches with 215 mm soffit	-	-	-	0.32	m	0.32

F MASONRY

Item	PC £	Labour hours	Labour £	Material £	Unit	Total rate £
Facework sills						
150 mm x 102 mm; headers on edge; pointing top and one side; set weathering; horizontal	-	0.60	13.69	5.26	m	18.96
150 mm x 102 mm; cant headers on edge; PC £1800.00/1000; pointing top and one side; set weathering; horizontal	-	0.65	14.84	29.37	m	44.20
150 mm x 102 mm; bullnosed specials; PC £1800.00/1000; headers on flat; pointing top and one side; horizontal	-	0.56	12.78	29.37	m	42.15
Facework copings						
215 mm x 102 mm; headers on edge; pointing top and both sides; horizontal	-	0.46	10.50	5.37	m	15.87
260 mm x 102 mm; headers on edge; pointing top and both sides; horizontal	-	0.74	16.89	7.97	m	24.86
215 mm x 102 mm; double bullnose specials; PC £1800.00/1000; headers on edge; pointing top and both sides; horizontal	-	0.56	12.78	29.48	m	42.26
260 mm x 102 mm; single bullnose specials; PC £1800.00/1000; headers on edge; pointing top and both sides; horizontal	-	0.74	16.89	63.79	m	80.68
ADD or DEDUCT for variation of £10.00/1000 in PC of facing bricks in copings 215 mm wide, 102 mm high	-	-	-	0.16	m	0.16
Extra over facing bricks for; facework ornamental bands and the like, plain bands; PC £340.00/1000						
flush; horizontal; 225 mm width; entirely of stretchers	0.40	0.23	5.25	0.49	m	5.74
Extra over facing bricks for; facework quoins; PC £340.00/1000						
flush; mean girth 320 mm	-	0.32	7.30	0.49	m	7.79
Bonding to existing						
facework one side, half brick thick; stretcher bond	-	0.56	12.78	1.36	m	14.14
facework one side, half brick thick; flemish bond with snapped headers	-	0.56	12.78	1.36	m	14.14
facework both sides, one brick thick; two stretcher skins tied together	-	0.74	16.89	2.72	m	19.61
facework both sides, one brick thick; flemish bond	-	0.74	16.89	2.72	m	19.61
ADD or DEDUCT for variation of £10.00/1000 in PC of facing bricks; in walls built entirely of facings; in stretcher or flemish bond						
half brick thick	-	-	-	0.73	m²	0.73
one brick thick	-	-	-	1.46	m²	1.46
Facing bricks; hand made; PC £500.00/1000 (unless otherwise stated); in gauged mortar (1:1:6)						
Walls						
facework one side, half brick thick; stretcher bond	-	1.39	31.72	38.52	m²	70.25
facework one side, half brick thick; flemish bond with snapped headers	-	1.62	36.97	38.52	m²	75.50
facework one side, half brick thick; stretcher bond; building against other work; concrete	-	1.48	33.78	39.93	m²	73.71
facework one side, half brick thick; flemish bond with snapped headers; building against other work; concrete	-	1.71	39.03	39.93	m²	78.96

F MASONRY

Item	PC £	Labour hours	Labour £	Material £	Unit	Total rate £
F10 BRICK/BLOCK WALLING – cont'd						
Facing bricks; hand made; PC						
£500.00/1000 – cont'd						
Walls – cont'd						
facework one side, half brick thick; stretcher bond; building overhand	-	1.71	39.03	38.52	m²	77.55
facework one side, half brick thick; flemish bond with snapped headers; building overhand	-	1.90	43.36	38.52	m²	81.89
facework one side, half brick thick; stretcher bond; curved; 6.00 m radii	-	2.04	46.56	38.52	m²	85.08
facework one side, half brick thick; flemish bond with snapped headers; curved; 6.00 m radii	-	2.27	51.81	43.07	m²	94.88
facework one side; half brick thick; stretcher bond; curved; 1.50 m radii	-	2.54	57.97	38.52	m²	96.49
facework one side; half brick thick; flemish bond with snapped headers; curved; 1.50 m radii	-	2.96	67.56	46.11	m²	113.66
facework both sides, one brick thick; two stretcher skins tied together	-	2.41	55.00	78.80	m²	133.80
facework both sides; one brick thick; flemish bond	-	2.45	55.92	77.04	m²	132.96
facework both sides; one brick thick; two stretcher skins tied together; curved; 6.00 m radii	-	3.28	74.86	84.87	m²	159.73
facework both sides; one brick thick; flemish bond; curved; 6.00 m radii	-	3.42	78.06	83.11	m²	161.17
facework both sides; one brick thick; two stretcher skins tied together; curved; 1.50 m radii	-	4.12	94.03	91.64	m²	185.67
facework both sides; one brick thick; flemish bond; curved; 1.50 m radii	-	4.26	97.23	89.89	m²	187.11
Isolated piers						
facework both sides, one brick thick; two stretcher skins tied together	-	2.82	64.36	79.80	m²	144.16
facework both sides, one brick thick; flemish bond	-	2.87	65.50	79.80	m²	145.30
Isolated casings						
facework one side, half brick thick; stretcher bond	-	2.13	48.61	38.52	m²	87.14
facework one side, half brick thick; flemish bond with snapped headers	-	2.36	53.86	38.52	m²	92.39
Projections						
225 mm width; 112 mm depth; stretcher bond; vertical	-	0.32	7.30	8.34	m	15.64
225 mm width; 112 mm depth; flemish bond with snapped headers; vertical	-	0.42	9.59	8.34	m	17.92
225 mm width; 225 mm depth; flemish bond; vertical	-	0.69	15.75	16.67	m	32.42
328 mm width; 112 mm depth; stretcher bond; vertical	-	0.65	14.84	12.52	m	27.35
328 mm width; 112 mm depth; flemish bond with snapped headers; vertical	-	0.74	16.89	12.52	m	29.41
328 mm width; 225 mm depth; flemish bond; vertical	-	1.30	29.67	24.98	m	54.65
440 mm width; 112 mm depth; stretcher bond; vertical	-	0.97	22.14	16.67	m	38.81
440 mm width; 112 mm depth; flemish bond with snapped headers; vertical	-	1.02	23.28	16.67	m	39.95
440 mm width; 225 mm depth; flemish bond; vertical	-	1.85	42.22	33.35	m	75.57

F MASONRY

Item	PC £	Labour hours	Labour £	Material £	Unit	Total rate £
Arches						
height on face 215 mm, width of exposed soffit 102 mm, shape of arch - flat	-	1.06	21.03	10.09	m	31.12
height on face 215 mm, width of exposed soffit 215 mm, shape of arch - flat	-	1.57	33.02	18.70	m	51.72
height on face 215 mm, width of exposed soffit 102 mm, shape of arch - segmental, one ring	-	2.04	37.87	12.84	m	50.71
height on face 215 mm, width of exposed soffit 215 mm, shape of arch - segmental, one ring	-	2.45	47.57	21.07	m	68.65
height on face 215 mm, width of exposed soffit 102 mm, shape of arch - semi-circular, one ring	-	2.50	48.72	12.84	m	61.56
height on face 215 mm, width of exposed soffit 215 mm, shape of arch - semi-circular, one ring	-	3.24	66.13	21.07	m	87.20
height on face 215 mm, width of exposed soffit 102 mm, shape of arch - segmental, two ring	-	2.50	48.72	12.84	m	61.56
height on face 215 mm, width of exposed soffit 215 mm, shape of arch - segmental, two ring	-	3.24	66.13	21.07	m	87.20
height on face 215 mm, width of exposed soffit 102 mm, shape of arch - semi-circular, two ring	-	4.16	87.83	12.84	m	100.67
height on face 215 mm, width of exposed soffit 215 mm, shape of arch - semi-circular, two ring	-	5.74	124.95	21.07	m	146.02
Arches; cut voussoirs; PC £3200.00/1000						
height on face 215 mm, width of exposed soffit 102 mm, shape of arch - segmental, one ring	42.67	2.08	38.87	56.53	m	95.39
height on face 215 mm, width of exposed soffit 215 mm, shape of arch - segmental, one ring	-	2.59	50.86	108.44	m	159.29
height on face 215 mm, width of exposed soffit 102 mm, shape of arch - semi-circular, one ring	-	2.36	45.43	56.53	m	101.96
height on face 215 mm, width of exposed soffit 215 mm, shape of arch - semi-circular, one ring	-	2.96	59.57	108.44	m	168.00
height on face 320 mm, width of exposed soffit 102 mm, shape of arch - segmental, one and a half ring	-	2.78	55.28	108.44	m	163.72
height on face 320 mm, width of exposed soffit 215 mm, shape of arch - segmental, one and a half ring	-	3.61	74.84	220.17	m	295.01
Arches; bullnosed specials; PC £1800.00/1000						
height on face 215 mm, width of exposed soffit 102 mm, shape of arch - flat	-	1.11	22.17	31.12	m	53.29
height on face 215 mm, width of exposed soffit 215 mm, shape of arch - flat	-	1.62	34.16	61.29	m	95.45
Bullseye windows; 600 mm diameter						
height on face 215 mm, width of exposed soffit 102 mm, two ring	-	5.32	115.10	19.35	nr	134.44
height on face 215 mm, width of exposed soffit 215 mm, two ring	-	7.45	165.20	49.85	nr	215.05
Bullseye windows; 1200 mm diameter						
height on face 215 mm, width of exposed soffit 102 mm, two ring	-	8.28	184.76	40.98	nr	225.75
height on face 215 mm, width of exposed soffit 215 mm, two ring	-	11.93	270.70	77.22	nr	347.92
Bullseye windows; 600 mm diameter; cut voussoirs; PC £3200.00/1000						
height on face 215 mm, width of exposed soffit 102 mm, one ring	-	4.49	95.54	138.26	nr	233.80
height on face 215 mm, width of exposed soffit 215 mm, one ring	-	6.15	134.66	274.97	nr	409.62

F MASONRY

Item	PC £	Labour hours	Labour £	Material £	Unit	Total rate £
F10 BRICK/BLOCK WALLING – cont'd						
Facing bricks; hand made; PC £500.00/1000 – cont'd						
Bullseye windows; 1200 mm diameter; cut voussoirs; PC £3200.00/1000						
height on face 215 mm, width of exposed soffit 102 mm, one ring	-	7.03	155.35	240.69	nr	**396.04**
height on face 215 mm, width of exposed soffit 215 mm, one ring	-	9.99	225.02	475.21	nr	**700.23**
ADD or DEDUCT for variation of £10.00/1000 in PC of facing bricks in 102 high arches with 215 mm soffit	-	-	-	0.32	m	**0.32**
Facework sills						
150 mm x 102 mm; headers on edge; pointing top and one side; set weathering; horizontal	-	0.60	13.69	8.34	m	**22.03**
150 mm x 102 mm; cant headers on edge; PC £1800.00/1000; pointing top and one side; set weathering; horizontal	-	0.65	14.84	29.37	m	**44.20**
150 mm x 102 mm; bullnosed specials; PC £1800.00/1000; headers on flat; pointing top and one side; horizontal	-	0.56	12.78	29.37	m	**42.15**
Facework copings						
215 mm x 102 mm; headers on edge; pointing top and both sides; horizontal	-	0.46	10.50	8.44	m	**18.94**
260 mm x 102 mm; headers on edge; pointing top and both sides; horizontal	-	0.74	16.89	12.58	m	**29.47**
215 mm x 102 mm; double bullnose specials; PC £1800.00/1000; headers on edge; pointing top and both sides	-	0.56	12.78	29.48	m	**42.26**
260 mm x 102 mm; single bullnose specials; PC £1800.00/1000; headers on edge; pointing top and both sides	-	0.74	16.89	58.69	m	**75.58**
ADD or DEDUCT for variation of £10.00/1000 in PC of facing bricks in copings 215 mm wide, 102 mm high	-	-	-	0.16	m	**0.16**
Extra over facing bricks for; facework ornamental bands and the like, plain bands; PC £530.00/1000						
flush; horizontal; 225 mm width; entirely of stretchers	-	0.23	5.25	0.49	m	**5.74**
Extra over facing bricks for; facework quoins; PC £530.00/1000						
flush; mean girth 320 mm	-	0.32	7.30	0.49	m	**7.79**
Bonding ends to existing						
facework one side, half brick thick; stretcher bond	-	0.56	12.78	2.13	m	**14.91**
facework one side, half brick thick; flemish bond with snapped headers	-	0.56	12.78	2.13	m	**14.91**
facework both sides, one brick thick; two stretcher skins tied together	-	0.74	16.89	4.26	m	**21.15**
facework both sides, one brick thick; flemish bond	-	0.74	16.89	4.26	m	**21.15**
ADD or DEDUCT for variation of £10.00/1000 in PC of facing bricks; in walls built entirely of facings; in stretcher or flemish bond						
half brick thick	-	-	-	0.73	m²	**0.73**
one brick thick	-	-	-	1.46	m²	**1.46**

F MASONRY

Item	PC £	Labour hours	Labour £	Material £	Unit	Total rate £
Facing bricks slips 50 mm thick; PC £1,200.00/100; in gauged mortar (1:1:6) built up against concrete including flushing up at back (ties not included)						
Walls	-	2.13	48.61	89.48	m²	**138.10**
Edges of suspended slabs; 200 mm wide	-	0.65	14.84	17.90	m	**32.73**
Columns; 400 mm wide	-	1.30	29.67	35.79	m	**65.46**
Engineering bricks; PC £383.00/1000; and specials at PC £1800.00/100; in cement mortar (1:3)						
Facework steps						
215 mm x 102 mm; all headers-on-edge; edges set with bullnosed specials; pointing top and one						
side; set weathering; horizontal	-	0.60	13.69	29.40	m	**43.09**
returned ends pointed	-	0.14	3.20	5.62	nr	**8.82**
430 mm x 102 mm; all headers-on-edge; edges set with bullnosed specials; pointing top and one						
side; set weathering; horizontal	-	0.83	18.94	35.72	m	**54.67**
returned ends pointed	-	0.23	5.25	7.13	nr	**12.38**
Lightweight aerated concrete blocks; Thermalite "Turbo" blocks or other equal and approved; in gauged mortar (1:2:9)						
Walls						
100 mm thick	7.98	0.56	12.78	10.36	m²	**23.14**
115 mm thick	9.18	0.56	12.78	11.91	m²	**24.69**
125 mm thick	9.97	0.56	12.78	12.94	m²	**25.72**
130 mm thick	10.37	0.56	12.78	13.46	m²	**26.24**
140 mm thick	11.17	0.60	13.69	14.50	m²	**28.20**
150 mm thick	11.97	0.60	13.69	15.54	m²	**29.24**
190 mm thick	15.15	0.65	14.84	19.67	m²	**34.51**
200 mm thick	15.95	0.65	14.84	20.72	m²	**35.55**
215 mm thick	17.15	0.65	14.84	22.27	m²	**37.11**
Isolated piers or chimney stacks						
190 mm thick	-	0.97	22.14	19.67	m²	**41.81**
215 mm thick	-	0.97	22.14	22.27	m²	**44.41**
Isolated casings						
100 mm thick	-	0.60	13.69	10.36	m²	**24.06**
115 mm thick	-	0.60	13.69	11.91	m²	**25.61**
125 mm thick	-	0.60	13.69	12.94	m²	**26.64**
140 mm thick	-	0.65	14.84	14.50	m²	**29.34**
Extra over for fair face; flush pointing						
walls; one side	-	0.04	0.91	-	m²	**0.91**
walls; both sides	-	0.09	2.05	-	m²	**2.05**
Closing cavities						
width of cavity 50 mm, closing with lightweight blockwork 100 mm; thick	-	0.27	6.16	0.58	m	**6.74**
width of cavity 50 mm, closing with lightweight blockwork 100 mm; thick; including damp proof course; vertical	-	0.32	7.30	1.56	m	**8.86**
width of cavity 75 mm, closing with lightweight blockwork 100 mm; thick	-	0.27	6.16	0.83	m	**6.99**
width of cavity 75 mm, closing with lightweight blockwork 100 mm; thick; including damp proof course; vertical	-	0.32	7.30	1.81	m	**9.12**

F MASONRY

Item	PC £	Labour hours	Labour £	Material £	Unit	Total rate £
F10 BRICK/BLOCK WALLING – cont'd						
Lightweight aerated concrete blocks;						
Thermalite "Turbo" blocks – cont'd						
Bonding ends to common brickwork						
100 mm thick	-	0.14	3.20	1.19	m	**4.38**
115 mm thick	-	0.14	3.20	1.37	m	**4.56**
125 mm thick	-	0.28	6.39	1.49	m	**7.88**
130 mm thick	-	0.28	6.39	1.55	m	**7.94**
140 mm thick	-	0.28	6.39	1.68	m	**8.07**
150 mm thick	-	0.28	6.39	1.79	m	**8.18**
190 mm thick	-	0.32	7.30	2.26	m	**9.56**
200 mm thick	-	0.32	7.30	2.38	m	**9.69**
215 mm thick	-	0.37	8.44	2.57	m	**11.02**
Lightweight aerated concrete blocks;						
Thermalite "Shield" blocks or other						
equal and approved; in gauged mortar						
(1:2:9)						
Walls						
75 mm thick	5.19	0.46	10.50	6.79	m²	**17.29**
90 mm thick	7.10	0.46	10.50	9.23	m²	**19.73**
100 mm thick	7.90	0.56	12.78	9.37	m²	**22.15**
140 mm thick	11.06	0.60	13.69	13.12	m²	**26.81**
150 mm thick	11.85	0.60	13.69	14.06	m²	**27.75**
190 mm thick	15.00	0.60	13.69	17.79	m²	**31.49**
200 mm thick	15.79	0.65	14.84	18.73	m²	**33.57**
Isolated piers or chimney stacks						
190 mm thick	-	0.97	22.14	17.79	m²	**39.93**
Isolated casings						
75 mm thick	-	0.60	13.69	6.79	m²	**20.48**
90 mm thick	-	0.60	13.69	9.23	m²	**22.92**
100 mm thick	-	0.60	13.69	9.37	m²	**23.06**
140 mm thick	-	0.65	14.84	13.12	m²	**27.95**
Extra over for fair face; flush pointing						
walls; one side	-	0.04	0.91	-	m²	**0.91**
walls; both sides	-	0.09	2.05	-	m²	**2.05**
Closing cavities						
width of cavity 50 mm, closing with lightweight						
blockwork 100 mm; thick	-	0.27	6.16	0.53	m	**6.69**
width of cavity 50 mm, closing with lightweight						
blockwork 100 mm; thick; including damp proof						
course; vertical	-	0.32	7.30	1.51	m	**8.81**
width of cavity 75 mm, closing with lightweight						
blockwork 100 mm; thick	-	0.27	6.16	0.76	m	**6.92**
width of cavity 75 mm, closing with lightweight						
blockwork 100 mm; thick; including damp proof						
course; vertical	-	0.32	7.30	1.74	m	**9.04**
Bonding ends to common brickwork						
75 mm thick	-	0.09	2.05	0.78	m	**2.84**
90 mm thick	-	0.09	2.05	1.06	m	**3.12**
100 mm thick	-	0.14	3.20	1.08	m	**4.27**
140 mm thick	-	0.28	6.39	1.52	m	**7.91**
150 mm thick	-	0.28	6.39	1.62	m	**8.01**
190 mm thick	-	0.32	7.30	2.05	m	**9.36**
200 mm thick	-	0.32	7.30	2.16	m	**9.47**

F MASONRY

Item	PC £	Labour hours	Labour £	Material £	Unit	Total rate £
Lightweight smooth face aerated concrete blocks; Thermalite "Smooth Face" blocks or other equal and approved; in gauged mortar (1:2:9); flush pointing one side						
Walls						
100 mm thick	12.53	0.65	14.84	16.01	m²	30.85
140 mm thick	17.54	0.74	16.89	22.41	m²	39.30
150 mm thick	18.79	0.74	16.89	24.02	m²	40.91
190 mm thick	23.80	0.83	18.94	30.41	m²	49.36
200 mm thick	25.06	0.83	18.94	32.02	m²	50.96
215 mm thick	26.94	0.83	18.94	34.42	m²	53.37
Isolated piers or chimney stacks						
190 mm thick	-	1.06	24.19	30.41	m²	54.60
200 mm thick	-	1.06	24.19	32.02	m²	56.21
215 mm thick	-	1.06	24.19	34.42	m²	58.61
Isolated casings						
100 mm thick	-	0.79	18.03	16.01	m²	34.04
140 mm thick	-	0.83	18.94	22.41	m²	41.35
Extra over for flush pointing						
walls; both sides	-	0.04	0.91	-	m²	0.91
Bonding ends to common brickwork						
100 mm thick	-	0.28	6.39	1.82	m	8.21
140 mm thick	-	0.28	6.39	2.56	m	8.95
150 mm thick	-	0.32	7.30	2.73	m	10.03
190 mm thick	-	0.37	8.44	3.45	m	11.90
200 mm thick	-	0.37	8.44	3.64	m	12.09
215 mm thick	-	0.37	8.44	3.92	m	12.36
Lightweight smooth face aerated concrete blocks; Thermalite "Party Wall" blocks or other equal and approved; in gauged mortar (1:2:9); flush pointing one side						
Walls						
100 mm thick	7.90	0.65	14.84	9.37	m²	24.21
215 mm thick	16.98	0.83	18.94	20.14	m²	39.08
Isolated piers or chimney stacks						
215 mm thick	-	1.06	24.19	20.14	m²	44.33
Isolated casings						
100 mm thick	-	0.79	18.03	9.37	m²	27.40
Extra over for flush pointing						
walls; both sides	-	0.04	0.91	-	m²	0.91
Bonding ends to common brickwork						
100 mm thick	-	0.28	6.39	1.08	m	7.47
215 mm thick	-	0.37	8.44	2.33	m	10.78
Lightweight aerated high strength concrete blocks (7.00 N/mm2); Thermalite "High Strength" blocks or other equal and approved; in cement mortar (1:3)						
Walls						
100 mm thick	8.40	0.56	12.78	10.96	m²	23.74
140 mm thick	13.07	0.60	13.69	16.96	m²	30.66
150 mm thick	14.01	0.60	13.69	18.18	m²	31.87
190 mm thick	17.74	0.65	14.84	23.01	m²	37.85
200 mm thick	18.67	0.65	14.84	24.23	m²	39.07
215 mm thick	20.07	0.65	14.84	26.05	m²	40.88

F MASONRY

Item	PC £	Labour hours	Labour £	Material £	Unit	Total rate £
F10 BRICK/BLOCK WALLING – cont'd						
Lightweight Thermalite "High Strength" concrete blocks (7.00 N/mm2) – cont'd						
Isolated piers or chimney stacks						
190 mm thick	-	0.97	22.14	23.01	m^2	45.15
200 mm thick	-	0.97	22.14	24.23	m^2	46.37
215 mm thick	-	0.97	22.14	26.05	m^2	48.19
Isolated casings						
100 mm thick	-	0.60	13.69	10.96	m^2	24.65
140 mm thick	-	0.65	14.84	16.96	m^2	31.80
150 mm thick	-	0.65	14.84	18.18	m^2	33.02
190 mm thick	-	0.79	18.03	23.01	m^2	41.05
200 mm thick	-	0.79	18.03	24.23	m^2	42.26
215 mm thick	-	0.79	18.03	26.05	m^2	44.08
Extra over for flush pointing						
walls; one side	-	0.04	0.91	-	m^2	0.91
walls; both sides	-	0.09	2.05	-	m^2	2.05
Bonding ends to common brickwork						
100 mm thick	-	0.28	6.39	1.26	m	7.65
140 mm thick	-	0.28	6.39	1.96	m	8.35
150 mm thick	-	0.32	7.30	2.09	m	9.39
190 mm thick	-	0.37	8.44	2.64	m	11.09
200 mm thick	-	0.37	8.44	2.79	m	11.23
215 mm thick	-	0.37	8.44	3.01	m	11.45
Lightweight aerated high strength concrete blocks; Thermalite "Trenchblock" blocks; in cement mortar (1:4)						
Walls						
255 mm thick	20.74	0.83	18.94	24.44	m^2	43.38
275 mm thick	22.38	0.88	20.08	26.56	m^2	46.64
305 mm thick	24.41	0.93	21.23	28.99	m^2	50.22
355 mm thick	28.88	1.02	23.28	34.23	m^2	57.51
Lightweight smooth face medium dense concrete blocks; Lignacite common grey 3.50N/mm2 blocks or other equal and approved; in gauged mortar (1:2:9); flush pointing one side						
Walls						
100 mm thick	7.78	0.71	16.20	10.12	m^2	26.32
140 mm thick	10.70	0.83	18.94	13.92	m^2	32.86
150 mm thick	11.86	0.85	19.40	15.41	m^2	34.81
190 mm thick	14.33	1.00	22.82	18.66	m^2	41.48
215 mm thick	17.07	1.10	25.11	22.18	m^2	47.28
Isolated piers or chimney stacks						
190 mm thick	-	1.33	30.36	18.66	m^2	49.01
215 mm thick	-	1.46	33.32	22.18	m^2	55.50
Isolated casings						
100 mm thick	-	0.88	20.08	10.12	m^2	30.20
140 mm thick	-	1.04	23.74	13.92	m^2	37.66
Extra over for flush pointing						
walls; both sides	-	0.04	0.91	-	m^2	0.91
Bonding ends to common brickwork						
100 mm thick	-	0.28	6.39	1.16	m	7.55
140 mm thick	-	0.28	6.39	1.61	m	8.00
150 mm thick	-	0.32	7.30	1.77	m	9.08
190 mm thick	-	0.37	8.44	2.15	m	10.59
215 mm thick	-	0.37	8.44	2.56	m	11.00

F MASONRY

Item	PC £	Labour hours	Labour £	Material £	Unit	Total rate £
Lightweight smooth face medium dense concrete blocks; Lignacite common grey 7.00N/mm2 blocks or other equal and approved; in gauged mortar (1:2:9); flush pointing one side						
Walls						
100 mm thick	8.01	0.71	16.20	10.40	m²	26.60
140 mm thick	11.72	0.83	18.94	15.18	m²	34.12
150 mm thick	12.90	0.85	19.40	16.70	m²	36.10
190 mm thick	16.51	1.00	22.82	21.36	m²	44.18
215 mm thick	18.02	1.10	25.11	23.36	m²	48.46
Isolated piers or chimney stacks						
190 mm thick	-	1.33	30.36	21.36	m²	51.71
215 mm thick	-	1.46	33.32	23.36	m²	56.68
Isolated casings						
100 mm thick	-	0.88	20.08	10.40	m²	30.48
140 mm thick	-	1.03	23.51	15.18	m²	38.69
Dense aggregate concrete blocks; "ARC Conbloc" or other equal and approved; in gauged mortar (1:2:9)						
Walls						
75 mm thick; solid	5.72	0.65	17.04	7.44	m²	24.49
100 mm thick; solid	6.33	0.79	20.71	8.31	m²	29.03
140 mm thick; solid	12.44	0.97	25.43	16.08	m²	41.51
140 mm thick; hollow	11.94	0.83	21.76	15.46	m²	37.23
190 mm thick; hollow	14.09	1.06	27.79	18.35	m²	46.15
215 mm thick; hollow	14.69	1.16	30.42	19.22	m²	49.64
Isolated piers or chimney stacks						
140 mm thick; hollow	-	1.16	30.42	15.46	m²	45.88
190 mm thick; hollow	-	1.53	40.12	18.35	m²	58.47
215 mm thick; hollow	-	1.76	46.15	19.22	m²	65.37
Isolated casings						
75 mm thick; solid	-	0.79	20.71	7.44	m²	28.16
100 mm thick; solid	-	0.83	21.76	8.31	m²	30.08
140 mm thick; solid	-	1.06	27.79	16.08	m²	43.87
Extra over for fair face; flush pointing						
walls; one side	-	0.09	2.36	-	m²	2.36
walls; both sides	-	0.14	3.67	-	m²	3.67
Bonding ends to common brickwork						
75 mm thick solid	-	0.14	3.67	0.86	m	4.53
100 mm thick solid	-	0.28	7.34	0.96	m	8.30
140 mm thick solid	-	0.32	8.39	1.85	m	10.24
140 mm thick hollow	-	0.32	8.39	1.78	m	10.17
190 mm thick hollow	-	0.37	9.70	2.11	m	11.82
215 mm thick hollow	-	0.42	11.01	2.23	m	13.24
Dense aggregate concrete blocks; (7.00 N/mm2) Forticrete "Shepton Mallet Common" blocks; in cement mortar (1:3)						
Walls						
75 mm thick; solid	6.73	0.65	17.04	8.74	m²	25.79
100 mm thick; hollow	7.84	0.79	20.71	10.27	m²	30.98
100 mm thick; solid	5.07	0.79	20.71	6.82	m²	27.53
140 mm thick; hollow	10.84	0.83	21.76	14.20	m²	35.96
140 mm thick; solid	7.77	0.97	25.43	10.38	m²	35.81
190 mm thick; hollow	14.39	1.06	27.79	18.86	m²	46.65
190 mm thick; solid	10.61	1.16	30.42	14.17	m²	44.59
215 mm thick; hollow	11.44	1.16	30.42	15.33	m²	45.75
215 mm thick; solid	11.32	1.34	35.14	15.18	m²	50.31

F MASONRY

Item	PC £	Labour hours	Labour £	Material £	Unit	Total rate £
F10 BRICK/BLOCK WALLING – cont'd						
Forticrete "Shepton Mallet Common" blocks – cont'd						
Dwarf support wall						
140 mm thick; solid	-	1.34	35.14	10.38	m^2	45.52
190 mm thick; solid	-	1.53	40.12	14.17	m^2	54.29
215 mm thick; solid	-	1.76	46.15	15.18	m^2	61.33
Isolated piers or chimney stacks						
140 mm thick; hollow	-	1.16	30.42	14.20	m^2	44.61
190 mm thick; hollow	-	1.53	40.12	18.86	m^2	58.98
215 mm thick; hollow	-	1.76	46.15	15.33	m^2	61.48
Isolated casings						
75 mm thick; solid	-	0.79	20.71	8.74	m^2	29.46
100 mm thick; solid	-	0.83	21.76	6.82	m^2	28.58
140 mm thick; solid	-	1.06	27.79	10.38	m^2	38.17
Extra over for fair face; flush pointing						
walls; one side	-	0.09	2.36	-	m^2	2.36
walls; both sides	-	0.14	3.67	-	m^2	3.67
Bonding ends to common brickwork						
75 mm thick solid	-	0.14	3.67	1.00	m	4.67
100 mm thick solid	-	0.28	7.34	0.79	m	8.13
140 mm thick solid	-	0.32	8.39	1.21	m	9.60
190 mm thick solid	-	0.37	9.70	1.64	m	11.34
215 mm thick solid	-	0.42	11.01	1.77	m	12.78
Dense aggregate coloured concrete blocks; Forticrete "Shepton Mallet Bathstone" or other equal and approved; in coloured gauged mortar (1:1:6); flush pointing one side						
Walls						
100 mm thick hollow	17.52	0.83	21.76	21.35	m^2	43.12
100 mm thick solid	21.23	0.83	21.76	25.75	m^2	47.51
140 mm thick hollow	23.06	0.97	25.43	28.15	m^2	53.58
140 mm thick solid	30.92	1.06	27.79	37.47	m^2	65.26
190 mm thick hollow	29.31	1.16	30.42	35.84	m^2	66.26
190 mm thick solid	42.46	1.34	35.14	51.43	m^2	86.56
215 mm thick hollow	30.93	1.34	35.14	37.92	m^2	73.05
215 mm thick solid	45.00	1.39	36.45	54.59	m^2	91.04
Isolated piers or chimney stacks						
140 mm thick solid	-	1.43	37.50	37.47	m^2	74.96
190 mm thick solid	-	1.62	42.48	51.43	m^2	93.90
215 mm thick solid	-	1.80	47.20	54.59	m^2	101.79
Extra over blocks for						
100 mm thick half lintel blocks ref D14	-	0.28	7.34	19.77	m	27.11
140 mm thick half lintel blocks ref H14	-	0.32	8.39	25.17	m	33.56
140 mm thick quoin blocks ref H16	-	0.37	9.70	28.62	m	38.32
140 mm thick cavity closer blocks ref H17	-	0.37	9.70	34.33	m	44.03
140 mm thick cill blocks ref H21	-	0.32	8.39	20.38	m	28.77
190 mm thick half lintel blocks ref A14	-	0.37	9.70	28.91	m	38.61
190 mm thick cill blocks ref A21	-	0.37	9.70	21.23	m	30.93

F MASONRY

Item	PC £	Labour hours	Labour £	Material £	Unit	Total rate £
Astra-Glaze satin-gloss glazed finish blocks or other equal and approved; Aldwick Design Ltd; standard colours; in gauged mortar (1:1:6); joints raked out; gun applied latex grout to joints						
Walls						
100 mm thick; glazed one side	83.16	1.06	27.79	99.03	m²	**126.83**
extra; glazed square end return	53.74	0.42	11.01	33.31	m	**44.33**
150 mm thick; glazed one side	95.04	1.16	30.42	113.35	m²	**143.76**
extra; glazed square end return	85.97	0.56	14.68	67.28	m	**81.96**
200 mm thick; glazed one side	106.92	1.34	35.14	127.66	m²	**162.80**
extra; glazed square end return	-	0.60	15.73	94.99	m	**110.72**
100 mm thick; glazed both sides	118.80	1.30	34.09	141.27	m²	**175.36**
150 mm thick; glazed both sides	130.68	1.39	36.45	155.59	m²	**192.03**
100 mm thick lintel 200 mm high; glazed one side	-	0.97	19.10	27.21	m	**46.31**
150 mm thick lintel 200 mm high; glazed one side	-	1.11	22.89	32.95	m	**55.84**
200 mm thick lintel 200 mm high; glazed one side	-	1.42	28.46	30.15	m	**58.61**
F11 GLASS BLOCK WALLING						
NOTE: The following specialist prices for glass block walling; supplied by Roger Wilde Ltd; assume standard blocks in panels of 50 m2; no fire rating; work in straight walls at ground level; and all necessary ancillary fixing; strengthening; easy access; pointing and expansion materials etc.						
Hollow glass block walling; Pittsburgh Corning sealed "Thinline" or other equal and approved; in cement mortar joints; reinforced with 6 mm diameter stainless steel rods; pointed both sides with mastic or other equal and approved						
Walls; facework both sides						
115 mm x 115 mm x 80 mm flemish blocks	-	-	-	-	m²	**585.27**
190 mm x 190 mm x 80 mm flemish blocks; cross reeded or clear blocks	-	-	-	-	m²	**252.15**
240 mm x 240 mm x 80 mm flemish blocks; cross reeded or clear blocks	-	-	-	-	m²	**243.95**
240 mm x 115 mm x 80 mm flemish blocks; cross reeded or clear blocks	-	-	-	-	m²	**293.15**
F20 NATURAL STONE RUBBLE WALLING						
Cotswold Guiting limestone or other equal and approved; laid dry						
Uncoursed random rubble walling						
275 mm thick	-	2.36	56.16	40.62	m²	**96.79**
350 mm thick	-	2.82	66.52	51.70	m²	**118.22**
425 mm thick	-	3.24	75.73	62.78	m²	**138.52**
500 mm thick	-	3.61	84.28	73.86	m²	**158.14**

F MASONRY

Item	PC £	Labour hours	Labour £	Material £	Unit	Total rate £
F20 NATURAL STONE RUBBLE WALLING – cont'd						
Cotswold Guiting limestone or other equal and approved; bedded; jointed and pointed in cement; lime mortar (1:2:9)						
Uncoursed random rubble walling; faced and pointed; both sides						
275 mm thick	-	2.27	53.76	44.76	m²	**98.52**
350 mm thick	-	2.50	58.04	56.97	m²	**115.00**
425 mm thick	-	2.78	63.58	69.17	m²	**132.75**
500 mm thick	-	2.96	67.19	81.38	m²	**148.57**
Coursed random rubble walling; rough dressed; faced and pointed one side						
114 mm thick	-	1.71	38.93	58.01	m²	**96.95**
150 mm thick	-	2.16	52.89	58.55	m²	**111.44**
Fair returns on walling						
114 mm wide	-	0.02	0.46	-	m	**0.46**
150 mm wide	-	0.04	0.91	-	m	**0.91**
275 mm wide	-	0.07	1.60	-	m	**1.60**
350 mm wide	-	0.09	2.05	-	m	**2.05**
425 mm wide	-	0.12	2.74	-	m	**2.74**
500 mm wide	-	0.14	3.20	-	m	**3.20**
Fair raking cutting on walling						
114 mm wide	-	0.23	5.30	8.44	m	**13.74**
150 mm wide	-	0.29	6.70	8.44	m	**15.14**
Level uncoursed rubble walling for damp proof courses and the like						
275 mm wide	-	0.22	5.58	2.90	m	**8.48**
350 mm wide	-	0.23	5.84	3.63	m	**9.46**
425 mm wide	-	0.24	6.09	4.43	m	**10.52**
500 mm wide	-	0.26	6.60	5.22	m	**11.81**
Copings formed of rough stones; faced and pointed all round						
275 mm x 200 mm (average) high	-	0.64	15.64	10.49	m	**26.13**
350 mm x 250 mm (average) high	-	0.86	20.74	14.60	m	**35.34**
425 mm x 300 mm (average) high	-	1.12	26.74	20.19	m	**46.93**
500 mm x 300 mm (average) high	-	1.42	33.51	27.28	m	**60.79**
F22 CAST STONE ASHLAR WALLING DRESSINGS						
Reconstructed limestone walling; "Bradstone 100 bed Weathered Cotswold" or "North Cerney" masonry blocks or other equal and approved; laid to pattern or course recommended; bedded; jointed and pointed in approved coloured cement:lime mortar (1:2:9)						
Walls; facing and pointing one side						
masonry blocks; random uncoursed	-	1.19	27.16	42.13	m²	**69.28**
extra; returned ends	-	0.43	9.81	23.31	m	**33.12**
extra; plain L shaped quoins	-	0.14	3.20	-9.69	m	**-6.49**
traditional walling; coursed squared	-	1.49	34.01	42.13	m²	**76.13**
squared random rubble	-	1.49	34.01	43.19	m²	**77.19**
squared coursed rubble (large module)	-	1.38	31.50	43.01	m²	**74.51**
squared coursed rubble (small module)	-	1.43	32.64	43.37	m²	**76.00**
squared and pitched rock faced walling; coursed	-	1.54	35.15	43.19	m²	**78.34**
rough hewn rock faced walling; random	-	1.60	36.52	43.01	m²	**79.53**
extra; returned ends	-	0.17	3.88	-	m	**3.88**

F MASONRY

Item	PC £	Labour hours	Labour £	Material £	Unit	Total rate £
Isolated piers or chimney stacks; facing and pointing one side						
masonry blocks; random uncoursed	-	1.65	37.66	42.13	m^2	79.78
traditional walling; coursed squared	-	2.07	47.24	42.13	m^2	89.37
squared random rubble	-	2.07	47.24	43.19	m^2	90.43
squared coursed rubble (large module)	-	1.91	43.59	43.01	m^2	86.60
squared coursed rubble (small module)	-	2.02	46.10	43.37	m^2	89.47
squared and pitched rock faced walling; coursed	-	2.18	49.75	43.19	m^2	92.94
rough hewn rock faced walling; random	-	2.23	50.90	43.01	m^2	93.91
Isolated casings; facing and pointing one side						
masonry blocks; random uncoursed	-	1.43	32.64	42.13	m^2	74.76
traditional walling; coursed squared	-	1.81	41.31	42.13	m^2	83.44
squared random rubble	-	1.81	41.31	43.19	m^2	84.50
squared coursed rubble (large module)	-	1.65	37.66	43.01	m^2	80.67
squared coursed rubble (small module)	-	1.76	40.17	43.37	m^2	83.53
squared and pitched rock faced walling; coursed	-	1.86	42.45	43.19	m^2	85.64
rough hewn rock faced walling; random	-	1.91	43.59	43.01	m^2	86.60
Fair returns 100 mm wide						
masonry blocks; random uncoursed	-	0.13	2.97	-	m^2	2.97
traditional walling; coursed squared	-	0.16	3.65	-	m^2	3.65
squared random rubble	-	0.16	3.65	-	m^2	3.65
squared coursed rubble (large module)	-	0.15	3.42	-	m^2	3.42
squared coursed rubble (small module)	-	0.15	3.42	-	m^2	3.42
squared and pitched rock faced walling; coursed	-	0.16	3.65	-	m^2	3.65
rough hewn rock faced walling; random	-	0.17	3.88	-	m^2	3.88
Fair raking cutting on masonry blocks						
100 mm wide	-	0.19	4.34	-	m	4.34
Reconstructed limestone dressings; "Bradstone Architectural" dressings in weathered "Cotswold" or "North Cerney" shades or other equal and approved; bedded, jointed and pointed in approved coloured cement:lime mortar (1:2:9)						
Copings; twice weathered and throated						
152 mm x 76 mm; type A	-	0.35	7.99	14.46	m	22.45
178 mm x 64 mm; type B	-	0.35	7.99	14.03	m	22.02
305 mm x 76 mm; type A	-	0.43	9.81	27.42	m	37.23
Extra for						
fair end	-	-	-	5.97	nr	5.97
returned mitred fair end	-	-	-	5.97	nr	5.97
Copings; once weathered and throated						
191 mm x 76 mm	-	0.35	7.99	15.59	m	23.58
305 mm x 76 mm	-	0.43	9.81	26.99	m	36.81
365 mm x 76 mm	-	0.43	9.81	28.89	m	38.70
Extra for						
fair end	-	-	-	5.97	nr	5.97
returned mitred fair end	-	-	-	5.97	nr	5.97
Chimney caps; four times weathered and throated; once holed						
553 mm x 553 mm x 76 mm	-	0.43	9.81	33.67	nr	43.48
686 mm x 686 mm x 76 mm	-	0.43	9.81	55.18	nr	64.99
Pier caps; four times weathered and throated						
305 mm x 305 mm	-	0.27	6.16	12.13	nr	18.29
381 mm x 381 mm	-	0.27	6.16	16.80	nr	22.97
457 mm x 457 mm	-	0.32	7.30	22.77	nr	30.08
533 mm x 533 mm	-	0.32	7.30	32.17	nr	39.48
Splayed corbels						
479 mm x 100 mm x 215 mm	-	0.16	3.65	15.57	nr	19.22
665 mm x 100 mm x 215 mm	-	0.21	4.79	25.04	nr	29.83

F MASONRY

Item	PC £	Labour hours	Labour £	Material £	Unit	Total rate £
F22 CAST STONE ASHLAR WALLING DRESSINGS – cont'd						
Reconstructed limestone dressings; "Bradstone Architectural"– cont'd						
Air bricks						
300 mm x 140 mm x 76 mm	-	0.08	1.83	8.87	nr	10.70
100 mm x 140 mm lintels; rectangular; reinforced with mild steel bars						
not exceeding 1.22 m long	-	0.26	5.93	24.62	m	30.56
1.37 m - 1.67 m long	-	0.28	6.39	24.62	m	31.02
1.83 m - 1.98 m long	-	0.30	6.85	24.62	m	31.47
100 mm x 215 mm lintels; rectangular; reinforced with mild steel bars						
not exceeding 1.67 m long	-	0.28	6.39	33.14	m	39.53
1.83 m - 1.98 m long	-	0.30	6.85	33.14	m	39.99
2.13 m - 2.44 m long	-	0.32	7.30	33.14	m	40.44
2.59 m - 2.90 m long	-	0.34	7.76	33.14	m	40.90
197 mm x 67 mm sills to suit standard softwood windows; stooled at ends						
not exceeding 2.54 m long	-	0.32	7.30	38.57	m	45.88
Window surround; traditional with label moulding; for single light; sill 146 mm x 133 mm; jambs 146 mm x 146 mm; head 146 mm x 105 mm; including all dowels and anchors						
overall size 508 mm x 1479 mm	172.37	0.95	21.68	196.33	nr	218.02
Window surround; traditional with label moulding; three light; for windows 508 mm x 1219 mm; sill 146 mm x 133 mm; jambs 146 mm x 146 mm; head 146 mm x 103 mm; mullions 146 mm x 108 mm; including all dowels and anchors						
overall size 1975 mm x 1479 mm	368.52	2.50	57.06	420.40	nr	477.46
Door surround; moulded continuous jambs and head with label moulding; including all dowels and anchors						
door 839 mm x 1981 mm in 102 mm x 64 mm frame	315.02	1.76	40.17	356.46	nr	396.63
F30 ACCESSORIES/SUNDRY ITEMS FOR BRICK/BLOCK/STONE WALLING						
Forming cavities						
In hollow walls						
width of cavity 50 mm; galvanised steel butterfly wall ties; three wall ties per m^2	-	0.06	1.37	0.23	m^2	1.60
width of cavity 50 mm; galvanised steel twisted wall ties; three wall ties per m^2	-	0.06	1.37	0.46	m^2	1.83
width of cavity 50 mm; stainless steel butterfly wall ties; three wall ties per m^2	-	0.06	1.37	0.48	m^2	1.85
width of cavity 50 mm; stainless steel twisted wall ties; three wall ties per m^2	-	0.06	1.37	0.94	m^2	2.31
width of cavity 75 mm; galvanised steel butterfly wall ties; three wall ties per m^2	-	0.06	1.37	0.29	m^2	1.66
width of cavity 75 mm; galvanised steel twisted wall ties; three wall ties per m^2	-	0.06	1.37	0.51	m^2	1.88
width of cavity 75 mm; stainless steel butterfly wall ties; three wall ties per m^2	-	0.06	1.37	0.68	m^2	2.05
width of cavity 75 mm; stainless steel twisted wall ties; three wall ties per m^2	-	0.06	1.37	1.03	m^2	2.40

F MASONRY

Item	PC £	Labour hours	Labour £	Material £	Unit	Total rate £
Damp proof courses etc.						
"Pluvex No 1" (hessian based) damp proof course or other equal and approved; 200 mm laps; in gauged mortar (1:1:6)						
width exceeding 225 mm; horizontal	7.36	0.27	6.16	8.94	m²	15.10
width exceeding 225 mm; forming cavity gutters in hollow walls	-	0.43	9.81	8.94	m²	18.75
width not exceeding 225 mm; horizontal	-	0.53	12.10	8.94	m²	21.03
width not exceeding 225 mm; horizontal	-	0.80	18.26	8.94	m²	27.20
"Pluvex No 2" (fibre based) damp proof course or other equal and approved; 200 mm laps; in gauged mortar (1:1:6)						
width exceeding 225 mm; horizontal	4.94	0.27	6.16	6.00	m²	12.16
width exceeding 225 mm; forming cavity gutters in hollow walls	-	0.43	9.81	6.00	m²	15.81
width not exceeding 225 mm; horizontal	-	0.53	12.10	6.00	m²	18.09
width not exceeding 225 mm; vertical	-	0.80	18.26	6.00	m²	24.26
"Rubberthene" polythylene damp proof course or other equal and approved; 200 mm laps; in gauged mortar (1:1:6)						
width exceeding 225 mm; horizontal	1.15	0.27	6.16	1.39	m²	7.55
width exceeding 225 mm; forming cavity gutters in hollow walls	-	0.43	9.81	1.39	m²	11.21
width not exceeding 225 mm; horizontal	-	0.53	12.10	1.39	m²	13.49
width not exceeding 225 mm; vertical	-	0.80	18.26	1.39	m²	19.65
"Permabit" bitumen polymer damp proof course or other equal and approved; 150 mm laps; in gauged mortar (1:1:6)						
width exceeding over 225 mm	6.49	0.27	6.16	7.88	m²	14.04
width exceeding 225 mm; forming cavity gutters in hollow walls	-	0.43	9.81	7.88	m²	17.69
width not exceeding 225 mm; horizontal	-	0.53	12.10	7.88	m²	19.98
width not exceeding 225 mm; vertical	-	0.80	18.26	7.88	m²	26.14
"Hyload" (pitch polymer) damp proof course or other equal and approved; 150 mm laps; in gauged mortar (1:1:6)						
width exceeding 225 mm; horizontal	6.49	0.27	6.16	7.88	m²	14.04
width exceeding 225 mm; forming cavity gutters in hollow walls	-	0.43	9.81	7.88	m²	17.69
width not exceeding 225 mm; horizontal	-	0.53	12.10	7.88	m²	19.98
width not exceeding 225 mm; vertical	-	0.80	18.26	7.88	m²	26.14
"Ledkore" grade A (bitumen based lead cored) damp proof course or other equal and approved; 200 mm laps; in gauged mortar (1:1:6)						
width exceeding 225 mm; horizontal	20.35	0.35	7.99	24.69	m²	32.68
width exceeding 225 mm wide; forming cavity gutters in hollow walls; horizontal	-	0.56	12.78	24.69	m²	37.48
width not exceeding 225 mm; horizontal	-	0.68	15.52	24.69	m²	40.21
width not exceeding 225 mm; vertical	-	0.80	18.26	24.69	m²	42.95
Milled lead damp proof course; BVS 1178; 1.80 mm thick (code 4), 175 mm laps, in cement:lime mortar (1:2:9)						
width exceeding 225 mm; horizontal	-	2.13	48.61	20.42	m²	69.03
width not exceeding 225 mm; horizontal	-	3.19	72.81	20.42	m²	93.22
Two courses slates in cement mortar (1:3)						
width exceeding 225 mm; horizontal	-	1.60	36.52	12.76	m²	49.28
width exceeding 225 mm; vertical	-	2.40	54.78	12.76	m²	67.54

F MASONRY

Item	PC £	Labour hours	Labour £	Material £	Unit	Total rate £
F30 ACCESSORIES/SUNDRY ITEMS FOR BRICK/BLOCK/STONE WALLING – cont'd						
Damp proof courses etc. – cont'd						
"Peter Cox" chemical transfusion damp proof course system or other equal and approved						
half brick thick; horizontal	-	-	-	-	m	17.84
one brick thick; horizontal	-	-	-	-	m	35.53
one and a half brick thick; horizontal	-	-	-	-	m	53.30
Silicone injection damp-proofing; 450 mm centres; making good brickwork						
half brick thick; horizontal	-	-	-	-	m	9.41
one brick thick; horizontal	-	-	-	-	m	17.41
one and a half brick thick; horizontal	-	-	-	-	m	22.30
"Synthprufe" damp proof membrane or other equal and approved; PC £52.15/25 litres; three coats brushed on						
width not exceeding 150 mm; vertical	-	0.36	3.78	7.84	m^2	11.62
width 150 mm - 225 mm; vertical	-	0.34	3.57	7.84	m^2	11.41
width 225 mm - 300 mm; vertical	-	0.32	3.36	7.84	m^2	11.20
width exceeding 300 mm; vertical	-	0.30	3.15	7.84	m^2	10.99
Joint reinforcement						
"Brickforce" galvanised steel joint reinforcement or other equal and approved						
width 60 mm; ref GBF40W60	-	0.06	1.37	0.58	m	1.95
width 100 mm; ref GBF40W100	-	0.08	1.83	0.68	m	2.51
width 150 mm; ref GBF40W150	-	0.10	2.28	0.84	m	3.12
width 175 mm; ref GBF40W175	-	0.11	2.51	1.00	m	3.51
"Brickforce" stainless steel joint reinforcement or other equal and approved						
width 60 mm; ref SBF35W60	-	0.06	1.37	1.21	m	2.58
width 100 mm; ref SBF35W100	-	0.08	1.83	1.24	m	3.06
width 150 mm; ref SBF35W150	-	0.10	2.28	1.36	m	3.64
width 175 mm; ref SBF35W175	-	0.11	2.51	1.36	m	3.87
width 60 mm; ref SBF40W60	-	0.06	1.37	1.57	m	2.94
width 100 mm; ref SBF40W100	-	0.08	1.83	1.61	m	3.43
width 150 mm; ref SBF40W150	-	0.10	2.28	1.64	m	3.92
width 175 mm; ref SBF40W175	-	0.11	2.51	1.77	m	4.28
"Wallforce" stainless steel joint reinforcement or other equal and approved						
width 240 mm; ref SWF35W240	-	0.13	2.97	3.49	m	6.45
width 260 mm; ref SWF35W260	-	0.14	3.20	3.65	m	6.85
width 275 mm; ref SWF35W275	-	0.15	3.42	-	m	3.42
width 240 mm; ref SWF40W240	-	0.13	2.97	4.89	m	7.86
width 260 mm; ref SWF40W260	-	0.14	3.20	5.11	m	8.30
width 275 mm; ref SWF40W275	-	0.15	3.42	5.29	m	8.71
Weather fillets						
Weather fillets in cement mortar (1:3)						
50 mm face width	-	0.13	2.97	0.05	m	3.01
100 mm face width	-	0.21	4.79	0.20	m	4.99
Bedding wall plates or similar in cement mortar (1:3)						
100 mm wide	-	0.06	1.37	0.08	m	1.45
Bedding wood frames in cement mortar (1:3) and point						
one side	-	0.08	1.83	0.08	m	1.90
both sides	-	0.11	2.51	0.10	m	2.61
one side in mortar; other side in mastic	-	0.22	4.14	0.65	m	4.79

F MASONRY

Item	PC £	Labour hours	Labour £	Material £	Unit	Total rate £
Angle fillets						
Angle fillets in cement mortar (1:3)						
50 mm face width	-	0.13	2.97	0.05	m	3.01
100 mm face width	-	0.21	4.79	0.20	m	4.99
Pointing in						
Pointing with mastic						
wood frames or sills	-	0.11	1.54	0.57	m	2.12
Pointing with polysulphide sealant						
wood frames or sills	-	0.11	1.54	1.81	m	3.35
Wedging and pinning						
To underside of existing construction with slates in cement mortar (1:3)						
width of wall - one brick thick	-	0.85	19.40	2.76	m	22.16
width of wall - one and a half brick thick	-	1.06	24.19	5.51	m	29.71
width of wall - two brick thick	-	1.28	29.21	8.27	m	37.48
Joints						
Hacking joints and faces of brickwork or blockwork						
to form key for plaster	-	0.28	2.94	-	m²	2.94
Raking out joint in brickwork or blockwork for turned-in edge of flashing						
horizontal	-	0.16	3.65	-	m	3.65
stepped	-	0.21	4.79	-	m	4.79
Raking out and enlarging joint in brickwork or blockwork for nib of asphalt						
horizontal	-	0.21	4.79	-	m	4.79
Cutting grooves in brickwork or blockwork						
for water bars and the like	-	0.27	2.84	0.34	m	3.18
for nib of asphalt; horizontal	-	0.27	2.84	0.34	m	3.18
Preparing to receive new walls						
top existing 215 mm wall	-	0.21	4.79	-	m	4.79
Cleaning and priming both faces; filling with pre-formed closed cell joint filler and pointing one side with polysulphide sealant; 12 mm deep						
expansion joints; 12 mm wide	-	0.27	5.28	3.60	m	8.89
expansion joints; 20 mm wide	-	0.31	5.85	5.27	m	11.12
expansion joints; 25 mm wide	-	0.37	6.69	6.36	m	13.05
Fire resisting horizontal expansion joints; filling with joint filler; fixed with high temperature slip adhesive; between top of wall and soffit						
wall not exceeding 215 mm wide; 10 mm wide joint with 30 mm deep filler (one hour fire seal)	-	0.27	6.16	7.37	m	13.53
wall not exceeding 215 mm wide; 10 mm wide joint with 30 mm deep filler (two hour fire seal)	-	0.27	6.16	7.37	m	13.53
wall not exceeding 215 mm wide; 20 mm wide joint with 45 mm deep filler (two hour fire seal)	-	0.32	7.30	11.06	m	18.36
wall not exceeding 215 mm wide; 30 mm wide joint with 75 mm deep filler (three hour fire seal)	-	0.37	8.44	27.53	m	35.98
Fire resisting vertical expansion joints; filling with joint filler; fixed with high temperature slip adhesive; with polysulphide sealant one side; between end of wall of wall and concrete						
wall not exceeding 215 mm wide; 20 mm wide joint with 45 mm deep filler (two hour fire seal)	-	0.43	9.11	14.68	m	23.79

F MASONRY

Item	PC £	Labour hours	Labour £	Material £	Unit	Total rate £
F30 ACCESSORIES/SUNDRY ITEMS FOR BRICK/BLOCK/STONE WALLING – cont'd						
Slates and tile sills						
Sills; two courses of machine made plain roofing tiles						
set weathering; bedded and pointed	-	0.64	14.61	5.23	m	19.83
Sundries						
Weep holes						
Perpend units; plastic	-	0.02	0.46	0.17	nr	0.63
Chimney pots; red terracotta; plain or cannon-head; setting and flaunching in cement mortar (1:3)						
185 mm diameter x 300 mm long	13.14	1.91	43.59	16.41	nr	60.00
185 mm diameter x 600 mm long	23.31	2.13	48.61	27.89	nr	76.50
185 mm diameter x 900 mm long	42.48	2.13	48.61	49.53	nr	98.14
Air bricks						
Air bricks; red terracotta; building into prepared openings						
215 mm x 65 mm	-	0.08	1.83	1.46	nr	3.28
215 mm x 140 mm	-	0.08	1.83	2.03	nr	3.85
215 mm x 215 mm	-	0.08	1.83	5.51	nr	7.34
Gas flue blocks						
Gas flue system; Marflex "HP" or other equal and approved; concrete blocks built in; in flue joint mortar mix; cutting brickwork or Blockwork around						
recess; ref HP1	-	0.11	2.51	2.01	nr	4.52
cover; ref HP2	-	0.11	2.51	4.48	nr	6.99
222 mm standard block with nib; ref HP3	-	0.11	2.51	3.16	nr	5.67
112 mm standard block with nib; ref HP3112	-	0.11	2.51	2.48	nr	4.99
72 mm standard block with nib; ref HP372	-	0.11	2.51	2.48	nr	4.99
vent block; ref HP3BH	-	0.11	2.51	2.43	nr	4.94
222 mm standard block without nib; ref HP4	-	0.11	2.51	3.10	nr	5.61
112 mm standard block without nib; ref HP4112	-	0.11	2.51	2.48	nr	4.99
72 mm standard block without nib; ref HP472	-	0.11	2.51	2.48	nr	4.99
120 mm side offset block; ref HP5	-	0.11	2.51	3.33	nr	5.84
70 mm back offset block; ref HP6	-	0.11	2.51	9.77	nr	12.28
vertical exit block; ref HP7	-	0.11	2.51	6.41	nr	8.92
angled entry/exit block; ref HP8	-	0.11	2.51	6.41	nr	8.92
reverse rebate block; ref HP9	-	0.11	2.51	4.60	nr	7.11
corbel block; ref HP10	-	0.11	2.51	6.16	nr	8.67
lintel unit; ref HP11	-	0.11	2.51	5.80	nr	8.31
Flue linings						
Flue linings; Marflex "ML 200" square refractory concrete flue linings or other equal and approved; rebated joints in flue joint mortar mix						
linings; ref. MLS1U	-	0.32	7.30	12.17	m	19.47
bottom swivel unit; ref MLS2U	-	0.11	2.51	10.01	nr	12.52
45 degree bend; ref MLS4U	-	0.11	2.51	7.31	nr	9.82
90 mm offset liner; ref MLS5U	-	0.11	2.51	4.84	nr	7.35
70 mm offset liner; ref MLS6U	-	0.11	2.51	4.36	nr	6.87
57 mm offset liner; ref MLS7U	-	0.11	2.51	10.61	nr	13.12
pot; ref MLSP83R	-	0.11	2.51	18.84	nr	21.35
single cap unit; ref MLS10U	-	0.27	6.16	23.98	nr	30.14
double cap unit; ref MLS11U	-	0.32	7.30	22.05	nr	29.35
combined gather lintel; ref MLSLUL4	-	0.32	7.30	22.42	nr	29.72

F MASONRY

Item	PC £	Labour hours	Labour £	Material £	Unit	Total rate £
Proprietary items						
External door and window cavity closers; "Thermabate" or equivalent; inclusive of flange clips; jointing strips; wall fixing ties and adhesive tape						
closing cavities; width of cavity 50 mm	-	0.16	3.65	3.64	m	**7.29**
closing cavities; width of cavity 75 mm	-	0.16	3.65	3.88	m	**7.53**
closing cavities; width of cavity 100 mm	-	0.16	3.65	4.37	m	**8.03**
"Westbrick" cavity closers or other equal and approved; Manthorpe Building Products Ltd						
closing cavities; width of cavity 50 mm	-	0.16	3.65	6.05	m	**9.70**
"Type H cavicloser" or other equal and approved; uPVC universal cavity closer, insulator and damp-proof course by Cavity Trays Ltd; built into cavity wall as work proceeds, complete with face closer and ties						
closing cavities; width of cavity 50 mm - 100 mm	-	0.08	1.83	6.12	m	**7.95**
"Type L" durropolythelene lintel stop ends or other equal and approved; Cavity Trays Ltd; fixing to lintel with butyl anchoring strip; building in as the work proceeds						
adjusted to lintel as required	-	0.05	1.14	0.61	nr	**1.76**
"Type W" polypropylene weeps/vents or other equal and approved; Cavity Trays Ltd; built into cavity wall as work proceeds						
100 mm/115 mm x 65 mm x 10 mm including lock fit wedges	-	0.05	1.14	0.47	nr	**1.61**
extra; extension duct 200 mm/225 mm x 65 mm x 10 mm	-	0.08	1.83	0.79	nr	**2.62**
"Type X" polypropylene abutment cavity tray or other equal and approved; Cavity Trays; built into facing brickwork as the work proceeds; complete with Code 4 lead flashing; intermediate/catchment tray with short leads (requiring soakers); to suit roof of						
17 - 20 degree pitch	-	0.06	1.37	5.20	nr	**6.57**
21 - 25 degree pitch	-	0.06	1.37	4.82	nr	**6.19**
26 - 45 degree pitch	-	0.06	1.37	4.61	nr	**5.98**
"Type X" polypropylene abutment cavity tray or other equal and approved; Cavity Trays; built into facing brickwork as the work proceeds; complete with Code 4 lead flashing; intermediate/catchment tray with long leads (suitable only for corrugated roof tiles); to suit roof of						
17 - 20 degree pitch	-	0.06	1.37	7.01	nr	**8.38**
21 - 25 degree pitch	-	0.06	1.37	6.45	nr	**7.81**
26 - 45 degree pitch	-	0.06	1.37	5.95	nr	**7.31**
"Type X" polypropylene abutment cavity tray or other equal and approved; Cavity Trays; built into facing brickwork as the work proceeds; complete with Code 4 lead flashing; ridge tray with short/long leads; to suit roof of						
17 - 20 degree pitch	-	0.06	1.37	11.80	nr	**13.17**
21 - 25 degree pitch	-	0.06	1.37	10.94	nr	**12.31**
26 - 45 degree pitch	-	0.06	1.37	9.74	nr	**11.11**

F MASONRY

Item	PC £	Labour hours	Labour £	Material £	Unit	Total rate £
F30 ACCESSORIES/SUNDRY ITEMS FOR BRICK/BLOCK/STONE WALLING – cont'd						
Proprietary items – cont'd						
Servicised "Bit-uthene" self-adhesive cavity flashing or other equal and approved; type "CA"; well lapped at joints; in gauged mortar (1:1:6)						
width exceeding 225 mm; horizontal	-	0.91	20.77	22.25	m²	**43.02**
"Expamet" stainless steel wall starters or other equal and approved; plugged and screwed						
to suit walls 60 mm - 75 mm thick	-	0.27	2.84	7.22	m	**10.06**
to suit walls 100 mm - 115 mm thick	-	0.27	2.84	7.94	m	**10.77**
to suit walls 125 mm - 180 mm thick	-	0.43	4.52	10.64	m	**15.15**
to suit walls 190 mm - 260 mm thick	-	0.53	5.57	13.58	m	**19.15**
Stainless steel posts, channels and ties						
Windposts; 130 x 70 x 6 mm; including one piece through ties						
1200 mm long	-	-	-	-	nr	**135.53**
3000 mm long	-	-	-	-	nr	**203.30**
4800 mm long	-	-	-	-	nr	**298.17**
Wall restraint channel ties; vertical channels; welded to steel work; with lateral restraint ties						
channel reference 28/15; tie reference HTS-B9; 200 mm long; one end of tie secured to channel; other end and debonding sleeve built into						
horizontal joint of masonry at 250 mm centres	-	0.14	3.20	10.91	m	**14.11**
Head restraints; sliding brick anchors reference SBA/L at 900 mm horizontal centres; 450 mm deep; tying into two courses of blockwork; fixed to steelwork						
ties built into horizontal joint of masonry	-	0.06	1.37	7.97	nr	**9.34**
Wall restraint; individually fixed ties; fixed to steelwork						
ties reference HTS-B9; 200 mm long; one end of tie secured to channel; other end and debonding sleeve built into horizontal joint of masonry at 250 mm centres	-	0.02	0.46	0.64	nr	**1.10**
Ties in walls; 200 mm long butterfly type; building into joints of brickwork or blockwork						
galvanised steel or polypropylene	-	0.02	0.46	0.10	nr	**0.55**
stainless steel	-	0.02	0.46	0.20	nr	**0.65**
Ties in walls; 20 mm x 3 mm x 200 mm long twisted wall type; building into joints of brickwork or blockwork						
galvanised steel	-	0.02	0.46	0.19	nr	**0.64**
stainless steel	-	0.02	0.46	0.38	nr	**0.84**
Anchors in walls; 25 mm x 3 mm x 100 mm long; one end dovetailed; other end building into joints of brickwork or blockwork						
galvanised steel	-	0.06	1.37	0.26	nr	**1.62**
stainless steel	-	0.06	1.37	0.40	nr	**1.77**
Fixing cramp 25 mm x 3 mm x 250 mm long; once bent; fixed to back of frame; other end building into joints of brickwork or blockwork						
galvanised steel	-	0.06	1.37	0.20	nr	**1.57**

F MASONRY

Item	PC £	Labour hours	Labour £	Material £	Unit	Total rate £
Lintels						
Galvanised steel lintels; "Catnic" or other equal and approved; built into brickwork or blockwork; "CN7" combined lintel; 143 mm high; for standard cavity walls						
750 mm long	29.92	0.27	6.16	33.81	nr	39.97
900 mm long	36.22	0.32	7.30	40.93	nr	48.23
1200 mm long	46.95	0.37	8.44	53.04	nr	61.49
1500 mm long	56.70	0.43	9.81	64.04	nr	73.86
1800 mm long	73.95	0.48	10.96	83.51	nr	94.46
2100 mm long	87.37	0.53	12.10	98.66	nr	110.75
Galvanised steel lintels; "Catnic" or other equal and approved; built into brickwork or blockwork; "CN8" combined lintel; 219 mm high; for standard cavity walls						
2400 mm long	110.17	0.64	14.61	124.39	nr	139.00
2700 mm long	155.29	0.74	16.89	175.33	nr	192.22
3000 mm long	166.84	0.85	19.40	188.37	nr	207.77
3300 mm long	186.22	0.95	21.68	210.24	nr	231.92
3600 mm long	204.36	1.06	24.19	230.72	nr	254.91
3900 mm long	248.37	1.17	26.70	280.39	nr	307.09
4200 mm long	248.50	0.53	12.10	280.54	nr	292.63
Galvanised steel lintels; "Catnic" or other equal and approved; built into brickwork or blockwork; "CN92" single lintel; for 75 mm internal walls						
900 mm long	4.45	0.32	7.30	5.05	nr	12.35
1050 mm long	5.39	0.32	7.30	6.10	nr	13.41
1200 mm long	6.10	0.37	8.44	6.91	nr	15.36
Galvanised steel lintels; "Catnic" or other equal and approved; builtin to brickwork or blockwork; "CN102" single lintel; for 100 mm internal walls						
900 mm long	5.69	0.32	7.30	6.44	nr	13.74
1050 mm long	6.82	0.32	7.30	7.72	nr	15.02
1200 mm long	7.53	0.37	8.44	8.53	nr	16.97
F31 PRECAST CONCRETE SILLS/LINTELS/ COPINGS/FEATURES						
Mix 20.00 N/mm^2 - 20 mm aggregate (1:2:4)						
Lintels; plate; prestressed bedded						
100 mm x 70 mm x 750 mm long	3.21	0.43	9.81	3.65	nr	13.46
100 mm x 70 mm x 900 mm long	3.80	0.43	9.81	4.31	nr	14.13
100 mm x 70 mm x 1050 mm long	4.51	0.43	9.81	5.12	nr	14.93
100 mm x 70 mm x 1200 mm long	5.11	0.43	9.81	5.80	nr	15.61
150 mm x 70 mm x 900 mm long	5.22	0.53	12.10	5.93	nr	18.03
150 mm x 70 mm x 1050 mm long	6.09	0.53	12.10	6.92	nr	19.01
150 mm x 70 mm x 1200 mm long	6.96	0.53	12.10	7.89	nr	19.99
220 mm x 70 mm x 900 mm long	8.05	0.64	14.61	9.14	nr	23.75
220 mm x 70 mm x 1200 mm long	10.70	0.64	14.61	12.13	nr	26.74
220 mm x 70 mm x 1500 mm long	13.42	0.74	16.89	15.20	nr	32.09
265 mm x 70 mm x 900 mm long	8.59	0.64	14.61	9.76	nr	24.37
265 mm x 70 mm x 1200 mm long	11.47	0.64	14.61	13.01	nr	27.62
265 mm x 70 mm x 1500 mm long	14.29	0.74	16.89	16.20	nr	33.09
265 mm x 70 mm x 1800 mm long	17.12	0.85	19.40	19.38	nr	38.78

F MASONRY

Item	PC £	Labour hours	Labour £	Material £	Unit	Total rate £
F31 PRECAST CONCRETE SILLS/LINTELS/ COPINGS/FEATURES – cont'd						
Mix 20.00 N/mm² - 20 mm aggregate (1:2:4) – cont'd						
Lintels; rectangular; reinforced with mild steel bars; bedded						
100 mm x 145 mm x 900 mm long	7.77	0.64	14.61	8.80	nr	**23.41**
100 mm x 145 mm x 1050 mm long	9.13	0.64	14.61	10.33	nr	**24.94**
100 mm x 145 mm x 1200 mm long	9.95	0.64	14.61	11.26	nr	**25.86**
225 mm x 145 mm x 1200 mm long	13.11	0.85	19.40	14.85	nr	**34.25**
225 mm x 225 mm x 1800 mm long	25.39	1.60	36.52	28.72	nr	**65.24**
Lintels; boot; reinforced with mild steel bars; bedded						
250 mm x 225 mm x 1200 mm long	21.04	1.28	29.21	23.81	nr	**53.02**
275 mm x 225 mm x 1800 mm long	28.21	1.91	43.59	31.89	nr	**75.49**
Padstones						
300 mm x 100 mm x 75 mm	4.30	0.32	7.30	4.87	nr	**12.18**
225 mm x 225 mm x 150 mm	6.52	0.43	9.81	7.40	nr	**17.21**
450 mm x 450 mm x 150 mm	17.23	0.64	14.61	19.61	nr	**34.21**
Mix 30.00 N/mm² - 20 mm aggregate (1:1:2)						
Copings; once weathered; once throated; bedded and pointed						
152 mm x 76 mm	5.22	0.74	16.89	6.26	m	**23.15**
178 mm x 64 mm	5.76	0.74	16.89	6.90	m	**23.79**
305 mm x 76 mm	9.72	0.85	19.40	11.70	m	**31.10**
extra for fair ends	-	-	-	5.03	nr	**5.03**
extra for angles	-	-	-	5.71	nr	**5.71**
Copings; twice weathered; twice throated; bedded and pointed						
152 mm x 76 mm	5.22	0.74	16.89	6.26	m	**23.15**
178 mm x 64 mm	5.71	0.74	16.89	6.85	m	**23.74**
305 mm x 76 mm	9.72	0.85	19.40	11.70	m	**31.10**
extra for fair ends	-	-	-	5.03	nr	**5.03**
extra for angles	-	-	-	5.71	nr	**5.71**

G STRUCTURAL/CARCASSING METAL/TIMBER

Item	PC £	Labour hours	Labour £	Material £	Unit	Total rate £
G10 STRUCTURAL STEEL FRAMING						
Framing, fabrication; weldable steel; BS EN 10025: 1993 Grade S275; hot rolled structural steel sections; welded fabrication						
Columns						
weight not exceeding 40 kg/m	-	-	-	-	tonne	1423.72
weight not exceeding 40 kg/m; castellated	-	-	-	-	tonne	1685.10
weight not exceeding 40 kg/m; curved	-	-	-	-	tonne	1894.20
weight not exceeding 40 kg/m; square hollow section	-	-	-	-	tonne	1703.55
weight not exceeding 40 kg/m; circular hollow section	-	-	-	-	tonne	1800.92
weight 40 - 100 kg/m	-	-	-	-	tonne	1232.05
weight 40 - 100 kg/m; castellated	-	-	-	-	tonne	1441.15
weight 40 - 100 kg/m; curved	-	-	-	-	tonne	1597.97
weight 40 - 100 kg/m; square hollow section	-	-	-	-	tonne	1541.60
weight 40 - 100 kg/m; circular hollow section	-	-	-	-	tonne	1629.75
weight exceeding 100 kg/m	-	-	-	-	tonne	1107.00
weight exceeding 100 kg/m; castellated	-	-	-	-	tonne	1263.83
weight exceeding 100 kg/m; curved	-	-	-	-	tonne	1420.65
weight exceeding 100 kg/m; square hollow section	-	-	-	-	tonne	1483.17
weight exceeding 100 kg/m; circular hollow section	-	-	-	-	tonne	1587.72
Beams						
weight not exceeding 40 kg/m	-	-	-	-	tonne	1483.17
weight not exceeding 40 kg/m; castellated	-	-	-	-	tonne	1744.55
weight not exceeding 40 kg/m; curved	-	-	-	-	tonne	1953.65
weight not exceeding 40 kg/m; square hollow section	-	-	-	-	tonne	1997.72
weight not exceeding 40 kg/m; circular hollow section	-	-	-	-	tonne	2371.85
weight 40 - 100 kg/m	-	-	-	-	tonne	1180.80
weight 40 - 100 kg/m; castellated	-	-	-	-	tonne	1389.90
weight 40 - 100 kg/m; curved	-	-	-	-	tonne	1546.72
weight 40 - 100 kg/m; square hollow section	-	-	-	-	tonne	1870.63
weight 40 - 100 kg/m; circular hollow section	-	-	-	-	tonne	2194.53
weight exceeding 100 kg/m	-	-	-	-	tonne	1123.40
weight exceeding 100 kg/m; castellated	-	-	-	-	tonne	1280.22
weight exceeding 100 kg/m; curved	-	-	-	-	tonne	1437.05
weight exceeding 100 kg/m; square hollow section	-	-	-	-	tonne	1813.22
weight exceeding 100 kg/m; circular hollow section	-	-	-	-	tonne	2074.60
Bracings						
weight not exceeding 40 kg/m	-	-	-	-	tonne	1734.30
weight not exceeding 40 kg/m; square hollow section	-	-	-	-	tonne	1995.67
weight not exceeding 40 kg/m; circular hollow section	-	-	-	-	tonne	1995.67
weight 40 - 100 kg/m	-	-	-	-	tonne	1609.25
weight 40 - 100 kg/m; square hollow section	-	-	-	-	tonne	1870.63
weight 40 - 100 kg/m; circular hollow section	-	-	-	-	tonne	1870.63
weight exceeding 100 kg/m	-	-	-	-	tonne	1520.08
weight exceeding 100 kg/m; square hollow section	-	-	-	-	tonne	1781.45
weight exceeding 100 kg/m; circular hollow section	-	-	-	-	tonne	1781.45

G STRUCTURAL/CARCASSING METAL/TIMBER

Item	PC £	Labour hours	Labour £	Material £	Unit	Total rate £
G10 STRUCTURAL STEEL FRAMING – cont'd						
Framing, fabrication; weldable steel; BS EN 10025: 1993 Grade S275 – cont'd						
Purlins and cladding rails						
weight not exceeding 40 kg/m	-	-	-	-	tonne	1326.35
weight not exceeding 40 kg/m; square hollow section	-	-	-	-	tonne	2226.30
weight not exceeding 40 kg/m; circular hollow section	-	-	-	-	tonne	2226.30
weight 40 - 100 kg/m	-	-	-	-	tonne	1175.67
weight 40 - 100 kg/m; square hollow section	-	-	-	-	tonne	1995.67
weight 40 - 100 kg/m; circular hollow section	-	-	-	-	tonne	1995.67
weight exceeding 100 kg/m	-	-	-	-	tonne	1081.38
weight exceeding 100 kg/m; square hollow section	-	-	-	-	tonne	1928.03
weight exceeding 100 kg/m; circular hollow section	-	-	-	-	tonne	1928.03
Grillages						
weight not exceeding 40 kg/m	-	-	-	-	tonne	1483.17
weight 40 - 100 kg/m	-	-	-	-	tonne	1180.80
weight exceeding 100 kg/m	-	-	-	-	tonne	1123.40
Trestles, towers and built up columns						
straight	-	-	-	-	tonne	1062.92
Trusses and built up girders						
straight	-	-	-	-	tonne	1985.42
curved	-	-	-	-	tonne	2455.90
Fittings	-	-	-	-	tonne	1985.42
Add to the above forementioned prices for:						
grade 355 steelwork	-	-	-	-	%	8.92
Framing, erection						
Trial erection	-	-	-	-	tonne	307.50
Permanent erection on site	-	-	-	-	tonne	307.50
Surface preparation						
At works						
blast cleaning	-	-	-	-	m²	2.56
Surface treatment						
At works						
galvanising	-	-	-	-	m²	11.31
shotblasting and priming to SA 2.5	-	-	-	-	m²	6.84
touch up primer and one coat of two pack epoxy zinc phosphate primer	-	-	-	-	m²	4.70
intumescent paint fire protection (30 minutes); spray applied	-	-	-	-	m²	10.93
intumescent paint fire protection (60 minutes); spray applied	-	-	-	-	m²	16.39
Extra for separate decorative sealer top coat	-	-	-	-	m²	3.28
On site						
intumescent paint fire protection (30 minutes) to universal beams etc.; spray applied	-	-	-	-	m²	8.20
intumescent paint fire protection (30 minutes) to circular columns etc.; spray applied	-	-	-	-	m²	13.73
intumescent paint fire protection (60 minutes) to universal beams etc.; spray applied	-	-	-	-	m²	10.38
intumescent paint fire protection (60 minutes) to circular columns etc.; spray applied	-	-	-	-	m²	17.43
Extra for separate decorative sealer top coat	-	-	-	-	m²	2.73

G STRUCTURAL/CARCASSING METAL/TIMBER

Item	PC £	Labour hours	Labour £	Material £	Unit	Total rate £
Cold formed galvanised steel; Kingspan "Multibeam" or other equal and approved						
Cold rolled purlins and cladding rails						
175 x 60 x 1.4 mm gauge purlins or rails; fixed to steelwork	-	0.05	0.83	10.48	m	**11.31**
175 x 60 x 1.65 mm gauge purlins or rails; fixed to steelwork	-	0.05	0.83	11.42	m	**12.25**
175 x 60 x 2.0 mm gauge purlins or rails; fixed to steelwork	-	0.05	0.83	13.87	m	**14.70**
205 x 60 x 1.45 mm gauge purlins or rails; fixed to steelwork	-	0.05	0.83	12.05	m	**12.88**
205 x 60 x 1.65 mm gauge purlins or rails; fixed to steelwork	-	0.05	0.83	13.37	m	**14.20**
205 x 60 x 2.0 mm gauge purlins or rails; fixed to steelwork	-	0.05	0.83	14.81	m	**15.64**
Heavy duty Zed section spacers						
vertically; across cladding rails; fixed to steelwork	-	0.06	1.00	9.58	m	**10.57**
Cleats						
weld-on for 175 mm purlin or rail	-	0.12	1.99	3.09	nr	**5.08**
bolt-on for 175 mm purlin or rail; including fixing bolts	-	0.03	0.50	5.98	nr	**6.48**
weld-on for 205 mm purlin or rail	-	0.12	1.99	3.51	nr	**5.51**
bolt-on for 205 mm purlin or rail; including fixing bolts	-	0.03	0.50	6.50	nr	**6.99**
Tubular ties						
150 mm long; bolted diagonally across purlins or cladding rails	-	0.03	0.50	6.46	nr	**6.96**
G12 ISOLATED STRUCTURAL METAL MEMBERS						
Isolated structural member; weldable steel; BS EN 10025: 1993 Grade S275; hot rolled structural steel sections						
Plain member; beams						
weight not exceeding 40 kg/m	-	-	-	-	tonne	**1049.60**
weight 40 - 100 kg/m	-	-	-	-	tonne	**1018.85**
weight exceeding 100 kg/m	-	-	-	-	tonne	**992.20**
Metsec open web steel lattice beams; in single members; raised 3.50 m above ground; ends built in						
Beams; one coat zinc phosphate primer at works						
200 mm deep; to span 5.00 m (7.69 kg/m); ref B22	-	0.20	5.07	45.29	m	**50.36**
200 mm deep; to span 5.00 m (7.64 kg/m); ref B27	-	0.26	6.60	41.10	m	**47.69**
300 mm deep; to span 7.00 m (10.26 kg/m); ref B30	-	0.26	6.60	49.47	m	**56.06**
350 mm deep; to span 8.50 m (10.60 kg/m); ref B35	-	0.26	6.60	53.66	m	**60.26**
350 mm deep; to span 10.00 m (12.76 kg/m); ref D35	-	0.31	7.87	74.59	m	**82.46**
350 mm deep; to span 11.50 m (17.08 kg/m); ref D50	-	0.36	9.13	82.96	m	**92.09**
450 mm deep; to span 13.00 m (25.44 kg/m); ref G50	-	0.51	12.94	119.76	m	**132.70**

G STRUCTURAL/CARCASSING METAL/TIMBER

Item	PC £	Labour hours	Labour £	Material £	Unit	Total rate £
G12 ISOLATED STRUCTURAL METAL MEMBERS – cont'd						
Metsec open web steel lattice beams – cont'd						
Beams; galvanised						
200 mm deep; to span 5.00 m (7.69 kg/m); ref B22	-	0.20	5.07	46.65	m	**51.72**
200 mm deep; to span 5.00 m (7.64 kg/m); ref B27	-	0.26	6.60	42.33	m	**48.92**
300 mm deep; to span 7.00 m (10.26 kg/m); ref B30	-	0.26	6.60	50.97	m	**57.57**
350 mm deep; to span 8.50 m (10.60 kg/m); ref B35	-	0.26	6.60	55.29	m	**61.89**
350 mm deep; to span 10.00 m (12.76 kg/m); ref D35	-	0.31	7.87	76.91	m	**84.77**
350 mm deep; to span 11.50 m (17.08 kg/m); ref D50	-	0.36	9.13	85.55	m	**94.68**
450 mm deep; to span 13.00 m (25.44 kg/m); ref G50	-	0.51	12.94	123.55	m	**136.49**
G20 CARPENTRY/TIMBER FRAMING/FIRST FIXING						
Sawn softwood; untreated						
Floor members						
38 mm x 100 mm	-	0.12	2.19	1.06	m	**3.25**
38 mm x 150 mm	-	0.14	2.56	1.58	m	**4.14**
50 mm x 75 mm	-	0.12	2.19	0.98	m	**3.18**
50 mm x 100 mm	-	0.14	2.56	1.21	m	**3.77**
50 mm x 125 mm	-	0.14	2.56	1.58	m	**4.14**
50 mm x 150 mm	-	0.16	2.92	1.86	m	**4.78**
50 mm x 175 mm	-	0.16	2.92	2.26	m	**5.18**
50 mm x 200 mm	-	0.17	3.11	2.44	m	**5.55**
50 mm x 225 mm	-	0.17	3.11	2.77	m	**5.87**
50 mm x 250 mm	-	0.18	3.29	3.07	m	**6.36**
75 mm x 125 mm	-	0.17	3.11	2.64	m	**5.75**
75 mm x 150 mm	-	0.17	3.11	3.16	m	**6.27**
75 mm x 175 mm	-	0.17	3.11	3.60	m	**6.70**
75 mm x 200 mm	-	0.18	3.29	4.16	m	**7.45**
75 mm x 225 mm	-	0.18	3.29	4.63	m	**7.92**
75 mm x 250 mm	-	0.19	3.47	5.14	m	**8.61**
100 mm x 150 mm	-	0.22	4.02	4.22	m	**8.24**
100 mm x 200 mm	-	0.23	4.20	5.63	m	**9.83**
100 mm x 250 mm	-	0.26	4.75	6.98	m	**11.73**
100 mm x 300 mm	-	0.28	5.12	2.31	m	**7.42**
Wall or partition members						
25 mm x 25 mm	-	0.07	1.28	0.30	m	**1.58**
25 mm x 38 mm	-	0.07	1.28	0.34	m	**1.62**
25 mm x 75 mm	-	0.09	1.64	0.58	m	**2.23**
38 mm x 38 mm	-	0.09	1.64	0.51	m	**2.15**
38 mm x 50 mm	-	0.09	1.64	0.58	m	**2.23**
38 mm x 75 mm	-	0.12	2.19	0.86	m	**3.05**
38 mm x 100 mm	-	0.16	2.92	1.06	m	**3.98**
50 mm x 50 mm	-	0.12	2.19	0.73	m	**2.93**
50 mm x 75 mm	-	0.16	2.92	1.01	m	**3.94**
50 mm x 100 mm	-	0.19	3.47	1.24	m	**4.72**
50 mm x 125 mm	-	0.19	3.47	1.61	m	**5.08**
75 mm x 75 mm	-	0.19	3.47	1.61	m	**5.08**
75 mm x 100 mm	-	0.21	3.84	2.12	m	**5.96**
100 mm x 100 mm	-	0.21	3.84	2.91	m	**6.74**

G STRUCTURAL/CARCASSING METAL/TIMBER

Item	PC £	Labour hours	Labour £	Material £	Unit	Total rate £
Roof members; flat						
38 mm x 75 mm	-	0.14	2.56	0.86	m	3.42
38 mm x 100 mm	-	0.14	2.56	1.06	m	3.61
38 mm x 125 mm	-	0.14	2.56	1.38	m	3.94
38 mm x 150 mm	-	0.14	2.56	1.58	m	4.14
50 mm x 100 mm	-	0.14	2.56	1.21	m	3.77
50 mm x 125 mm	-	0.14	2.56	1.58	m	4.14
50 mm x 150 mm	-	0.16	2.92	1.86	m	4.78
50 mm x 175 mm	-	0.16	2.92	2.26	m	5.18
50 mm x 200 mm	-	0.17	3.11	2.44	m	5.55
50 mm x 225 mm	-	0.17	3.11	2.77	m	5.87
50 mm x 250 mm	-	0.18	3.29	3.07	m	6.36
75 mm x 150 mm	-	0.17	3.11	3.16	m	6.27
75 mm x 175 mm	-	0.17	3.11	3.60	m	6.70
75 mm x 200 mm	-	0.18	3.29	4.16	m	7.45
75 mm x 225 mm	-	0.18	3.29	4.63	m	7.92
75 mm x 250 mm	-	0.19	3.47	5.14	m	8.61
Joist strutting; herringbone strutting						
50 mm x 50 mm; depth of joist 150 mm	-	0.51	9.32	1.77	m	11.09
50 mm x 50 mm; depth of joist 175 mm	-	0.51	9.32	1.80	m	11.12
50 mm x 50 mm; depth of joist 200 mm	-	0.51	9.32	1.84	m	11.16
50 mm x 50 mm; depth of joist 225 mm	-	0.51	9.32	1.87	m	11.19
50 mm x 50 mm; depth of joist 250 mm	-	0.51	9.32	1.90	m	11.22
Joist strutting; block						
50 mm x 150 mm; depth of joist 150 mm	-	0.31	5.67	2.25	m	7.91
50 mm x 175 mm; depth of joist 175 mm	-	0.31	5.67	2.65	m	8.31
50 mm x 200 mm; depth of joist 200 mm	-	0.31	5.67	2.83	m	8.50
50 mm x 225 mm; depth of joist 225 mm	-	0.31	5.67	3.16	m	8.82
50 mm x 250 mm; depth of joist 250 mm	-	0.31	5.67	3.46	m	9.13
Cleats						
225 mm x 100 mm x 75 mm	-	0.20	3.65	0.49	nr	4.15
Extra for stress grading to above timbers						
general structural (GS) grade	-	-	-	22.55	m³	22.55
special structural (SS) grade	-	-	-	43.38	m³	43.38
structural (SC3) grade	-	-	-	8.91	%	8.91
structural (SC4) grade	-	-	-	14.84	%	14.84
structural (SC16) grade	-	-	-	26.72	%	26.72
Extra for protecting and flameproofing timber with "Celgard CF" protection						
small sections	-	-	-	142.67	m³	142.67
large sections	-	-	-	136.96	m³	136.96
Wrot surfaces						
plain; 50 mm wide	-	0.02	0.37	-	m	0.37
plain; 100 mm wide	-	0.03	0.55	-	m	0.55
plain; 150 mm wide	-	0.05	0.91	-	m	0.91
Sawn softwood; "Tanalised"						
Floor members						
38 mm x 75 mm	-	0.12	2.19	1.01	m	3.21
38 mm x 100 mm	-	0.12	2.19	1.26	m	3.45
38 mm x 150 mm	-	0.14	2.56	1.87	m	4.43
50 mm x 75 mm	-	0.12	2.19	1.18	m	3.38
50 mm x 100 mm	-	0.14	2.56	1.48	m	4.03
50 mm x 125 mm	-	0.14	2.56	1.91	m	4.47
50 mm x 150 mm	-	0.16	2.92	2.25	m	5.17
50 mm x 175 mm	-	0.16	2.92	2.72	m	5.64
50 mm x 200 mm	-	0.17	3.11	2.96	m	6.07
50 mm x 225 mm	-	0.17	3.11	3.36	m	6.46
50 mm x 250 mm	-	0.18	3.29	3.72	m	7.01

G STRUCTURAL/CARCASSING METAL/TIMBER

Item	PC £	Labour hours	Labour £	Material £	Unit	Total rate £
G20 CARPENTRY/TIMBER FRAMING/FIRST FIXING – cont'd						
Sawn softwood; "Tanalised" – cont'd						
Floor members – cont'd						
75 mm x 125 mm	-	0.17	3.11	3.13	m	6.24
75 mm x 150 mm	-	0.17	3.11	3.75	m	6.86
75 mm x 175 mm	-	0.17	3.11	4.28	m	7.39
75 mm x 200 mm	-	0.18	3.29	4.94	m	8.23
75 mm x 225 mm	-	0.18	3.29	5.52	m	8.81
75 mm x 250 mm	-	0.19	3.47	6.12	m	9.60
100 mm x 150 mm	-	0.22	4.02	5.00	m	9.02
100 mm x 200 mm	-	0.23	4.20	6.68	m	10.88
100 mm x 250 mm	-	0.26	4.75	8.29	m	13.04
100 mm x 300 mm	-	0.28	5.12	3.88	m	9.00
Wall or partition members						
25 mm x 25 mm	-	0.07	1.28	0.33	m	1.61
25 mm x 38 mm	-	0.07	1.28	0.39	m	1.67
25 mm x 75 mm	-	0.09	1.64	0.68	m	2.32
38 mm x 38 mm	-	0.09	1.64	0.58	m	2.23
38 mm x 50 mm	-	0.09	1.64	0.68	m	2.32
38 mm x 75 mm	-	0.12	2.19	1.01	m	3.21
38 mm x 100 mm	-	0.16	2.92	1.26	m	4.18
50 mm x 50 mm	-	0.12	2.19	0.87	m	3.06
50 mm x 75 mm	-	0.16	2.92	1.21	m	4.14
50 mm x 100 mm	-	0.19	3.47	1.51	m	4.98
50 mm x 125 mm	-	0.19	3.47	1.94	m	5.41
75 mm x 75 mm	-	0.19	3.47	1.90	m	5.37
75 mm x 100 mm	-	0.21	3.84	2.52	m	6.36
100 mm x 100 mm	-	0.21	3.84	3.43	m	7.27
Roof members; flat						
38 mm x 75 mm	-	0.14	2.56	1.01	m	3.57
38 mm x 100 mm	-	0.14	2.56	1.26	m	3.81
38 mm x 125 mm	-	0.14	2.56	1.64	m	4.19
38 mm x 150 mm	-	0.14	2.56	1.87	m	4.43
50 mm x 100 mm	-	0.14	2.56	1.48	m	4.03
50 mm x 125 mm	-	0.14	2.56	1.91	m	4.47
50 mm x 150 mm	-	0.16	2.92	2.25	m	5.17
50 mm x 175 mm	-	0.16	2.92	2.72	m	5.64
50 mm x 200 mm	-	0.17	3.11	2.96	m	6.07
50 mm x 225 mm	-	0.17	3.11	3.36	m	6.46
50 mm x 250 mm	-	0.18	3.29	3.72	m	7.01
75 mm x 150 mm	-	0.17	3.11	3.75	m	6.86
75 mm x 175 mm	-	0.17	3.11	4.28	m	7.39
75 mm x 200 mm	-	0.18	3.29	4.94	m	8.23
75 mm x 225 mm	-	0.18	3.29	5.52	m	8.81
75 mm x 250 mm	-	0.19	3.47	6.12	m	9.60
Roof members; pitched						
25 mm x 100 mm	-	0.12	2.19	0.87	m	3.06
25 mm x 125 mm	-	0.12	2.19	1.06	m	3.25
25 mm x 150 mm	-	0.16	2.92	1.26	m	4.18
25 mm x 175 mm	-	0.18	3.29	1.49	m	4.78
25 mm x 200 mm	-	0.19	3.47	1.68	m	5.15
38 mm x 100 mm	-	0.16	2.92	1.26	m	4.18
38 mm x 125 mm	-	0.16	2.92	1.64	m	4.56
38 mm x 150 mm	-	0.16	2.92	1.87	m	4.80
50 mm x 50 mm	-	0.12	2.19	0.84	m	3.03
50 mm x 75 mm	-	0.16	2.92	1.18	m	4.11
50 mm x 100 mm	-	0.19	3.47	1.48	m	4.95
50 mm x 125 mm	-	0.19	3.47	1.91	m	5.38

G STRUCTURAL/CARCASSING METAL/TIMBER

Item	PC £	Labour hours	Labour £	Material £	Unit	Total rate £
50 mm x 150 mm	-	0.21	3.84	2.25	m	6.09
50 mm x 175 mm	-	0.21	3.84	2.72	m	6.56
50 mm x 200 mm	-	0.21	3.84	2.96	m	6.80
50 mm x 225 mm	-	0.21	3.84	3.36	m	7.19
75 mm x 100 mm	-	0.26	4.75	2.46	m	7.21
75 mm x 125 mm	-	0.26	4.75	3.13	m	7.88
75 mm x 150 mm	-	0.26	4.75	3.75	m	8.50
100 mm x 150 mm	-	0.31	5.67	5.03	m	10.70
100 mm x 175 mm	-	0.31	5.67	5.89	m	11.56
100 mm x 200 mm	-	0.31	5.67	6.68	m	12.34
100 mm x 225 mm	-	0.33	6.03	7.49	m	13.52
100 mm x 250 mm	-	0.33	6.03	8.29	m	14.32
Plates						
38 mm x 75 mm	-	0.12	2.19	1.01	m	3.21
38 mm x 100 mm	-	0.16	2.92	1.26	m	4.18
50 mm x 75 mm	-	0.16	2.92	1.21	m	4.14
50 mm x 100 mm	-	0.19	3.47	1.51	m	4.98
75 mm x 100 mm	-	0.21	3.84	2.52	m	6.36
75 mm x 125 mm	-	0.24	4.39	3.10	m	7.49
75 mm x 150 mm	-	0.27	4.93	3.72	m	8.65
Plates; fixing by bolting						
38 mm x 75 mm	-	0.21	3.84	1.01	m	4.85
38 mm x 100 mm	-	0.25	4.57	1.26	m	5.82
50 mm x 75 mm	-	0.25	4.57	1.21	m	5.78
50 mm x 100 mm	-	0.28	5.12	1.51	m	6.62
75 mm x 100 mm	-	0.31	5.67	2.52	m	8.18
75 mm x 125 mm	-	0.33	6.03	3.10	m	9.13
75 mm x 150 mm	-	0.36	6.58	3.72	m	10.30
Joist strutting; herringbone						
50 mm x 50 mm; depth of joist 150 mm	-	0.51	9.32	2.04	m	11.36
50 mm x 50 mm; depth of joist 175 mm	-	0.51	9.32	2.08	m	11.40
50 mm x 50 mm; depth of joist 200 mm	-	0.51	9.32	2.12	m	11.44
50 mm x 50 mm; depth of joist 225 mm	-	0.51	9.32	2.16	m	11.48
50 mm x 50 mm; depth of joist 250 mm	-	0.51	9.32	2.19	m	11.51
Joist strutting; block						
50 mm x 150 mm; depth of joist 150 mm	-	0.31	5.67	2.64	m	8.31
50 mm x 175 mm; depth of joist 175 mm	-	0.31	5.67	3.11	m	8.78
50 mm x 200 mm; depth of joist 200 mm	-	0.31	5.67	3.36	m	9.02
50 mm x 225 mm; depth of joist 225 mm	-	0.31	5.67	3.75	m	9.41
50 mm x 250 mm; depth of joist 250 mm	-	0.31	5.67	4.12	m	9.78
Cleats						
225 mm x 100 mm x 75 mm	-	0.20	3.65	0.58	nr	4.24
Extra for stress grading to above timbers						
general structural (GS) grade	-	-	-	22.55	m³	22.55
special structural (SS) grade	-	-	-	43.38	m³	43.38
Extra for protecting and flameproofing timber with "Celgard CF" protection or other equal or approved						
small sections	-	-	-	142.67	m³	142.67
large sections	-	-	-	136.96	m³	136.96
Wrot surfaces						
plain; 50 mm wide	-	0.02	0.37	-	m	0.37
plain; 100 mm wide	-	0.03	0.55	-	m	0.55
plain; 150 mm wide	-	0.05	0.91	-	m	0.91

G STRUCTURAL/CARCASSING METAL/TIMBER

Item	PC £	Labour hours	Labour £	Material £	Unit	Total rate £
G20 CARPENTRY/TIMBER FRAMING/FIRST FIXING – cont'd						
Trussed rafters, stress graded sawn softwood pressure impregnated; raised through two storeys and fixed in position						
"W" type truss (Fink); 22.50 degree pitch; 450 mm eaves overhang						
5.00 m span	-	1.63	29.79	35.41	nr	65.20
7.60 m span	-	1.79	32.71	44.62	nr	77.33
10.00 m span	-	2.04	37.28	58.08	nr	95.36
"W" type truss (Fink); 30 degree pitch; 450 mm eaves overhang						
5.00 m span	-	1.63	29.79	35.15	nr	64.93
7.60 m span	-	1.79	32.71	45.84	nr	78.56
10.00 m span	-	2.04	37.28	65.71	nr	102.99
"W" type truss (Fink); 45 degree pitch; 450 mm eaves overhang						
4.60 m span	-	1.63	29.79	37.74	nr	67.53
7.00 m span	-	1.79	32.71	50.80	nr	83.51
"Mono" type truss; 17.50 degree pitch; 450 mm eaves overhang						
3.30 m span	-	1.43	26.13	28.58	nr	54.71
5.60 m span	-	1.63	29.79	40.46	nr	70.24
7.00 m span	-	1.88	34.36	50.80	nr	85.15
"Mono" type truss; 30 degree pitch; 450 mm eaves overhang						
3.30 m span	-	1.43	26.13	30.69	nr	56.82
5.60 m span	-	1.63	29.79	43.78	nr	73.57
7.00 m span	-	1.88	34.36	57.67	nr	92.03
"Attic" type truss; 45 degree pitch; 450 mm eaves overhang						
5.00 m span	-	3.21	58.66	76.45	nr	135.11
7.60 m span	-	3.36	61.40	124.01	nr	185.41
9.00 m span	-	3.56	65.06	158.78	nr	223.84
"Moelven Toreboda" glulam timber beams or other equal and approved; Moelven Laminated Timber Structures; LB grade whitewood; pressure impregnated; phenbol resorcinal adhesive; clean planed finish; fixed						
Laminated roof beams						
56 mm x 225 mm	-	0.56	10.23	8.15	m	18.39
66 mm x 315 mm	-	0.71	12.97	13.47	m	26.44
90 mm x 315 mm	-	0.92	16.81	18.36	m	35.18
90 mm x 405 mm	-	1.17	21.38	23.62	m	45.00
115 mm x 405 mm	-	1.48	27.05	30.18	m	57.22
115 mm x 495 mm	-	1.83	33.44	36.88	m	70.33
115 mm x 630 mm	-	2.24	40.93	46.95	m	87.89
"Masterboard" or other equal and approved; 6 mm thick						
Eaves, verge soffit boards, fascia boards and the like						
over 300 mm wide	7.19	0.71	12.97	9.33	m²	22.30
75 mm wide	-	0.21	3.84	0.71	m	4.55
150 mm wide	-	0.24	4.39	1.40	m	5.79
225 mm wide	-	0.29	5.30	2.08	m	7.38
300 mm wide	-	0.31	5.67	2.77	m	8.43

G STRUCTURAL/CARCASSING METAL/TIMBER

Item	PC £	Labour hours	Labour £	Material £	Unit	Total rate £
Plywood; external quality; 12 mm thick						
Eaves, verge soffit boards, fascia boards and the like						
over 300 mm wide	5.36	0.83	15.17	7.10	m²	**22.27**
75 mm wide	-	0.26	4.75	0.55	m	**5.30**
150 mm wide	-	0.30	5.48	1.07	m	**6.55**
225 mm wide	-	0.33	6.03	1.58	m	**7.61**
300 mm wide	-	0.38	6.94	2.10	m	**9.04**
Plywood; external quality; 15 mm thick						
Eaves, verge soffit boards, fascia boards and the like						
over 300 mm wide	6.53	0.83	15.17	8.52	m²	**23.69**
75 mm wide	-	0.26	4.75	0.65	m	**5.41**
150 mm wide	-	0.30	5.48	1.28	m	**6.76**
225 mm wide	-	0.33	6.03	1.90	m	**7.93**
300 mm wide	-	0.38	6.94	2.53	m	**9.47**
Plywood; external quality; 18 mm thick						
Eaves, verge soffit boards, fascia boards and the like						
over 300 mm wide	7.56	0.83	15.17	9.77	m²	**24.94**
75 mm wide	-	0.26	4.75	0.75	m	**5.50**
150 mm wide	-	0.30	5.48	1.47	m	**6.95**
225 mm wide	-	0.33	6.03	2.18	m	**8.21**
300 mm wide	-	0.38	6.94	2.90	m	**9.85**
Plywood; marine quality; 18 mm thick						
Gutter boards; butt joints						
over 300 mm wide	9.92	0.94	17.18	12.64	m²	**29.82**
150 mm wide	-	0.33	6.03	1.90	m	**7.93**
225 mm wide	-	0.38	6.94	2.86	m	**9.80**
300 mm wide	-	0.42	7.68	3.79	m	**11.47**
Eaves, verge soffit boards, fascia boards and the like						
over 300 mm wide	-	0.83	15.17	12.64	m²	**27.81**
75 mm wide	-	0.26	4.75	0.96	m	**5.71**
150 mm wide	-	0.30	5.48	1.90	m	**7.38**
225 mm wide	-	0.33	6.03	2.83	m	**8.86**
300 mm wide	-	0.38	6.94	3.76	m	**10.71**
Plywood; marine quality; 25 mm thick						
Gutter boards; butt joints						
over 300 mm wide	13.78	1.02	18.64	17.32	m²	**35.96**
150 mm wide	-	0.36	6.58	2.60	m	**9.18**
225 mm wide	-	0.41	7.49	3.91	m	**11.41**
300 mm wide	-	0.45	8.22	5.20	m	**13.42**
Eaves, verge soffit boards, fascia boards and the like						
over 300 mm wide	-	0.90	16.45	17.32	m²	**33.77**
75 mm wide	-	0.27	4.93	1.31	m	**6.25**
150 mm wide	-	0.31	5.67	2.60	m	**8.26**
225 mm wide	-	0.31	5.67	3.88	m	**9.55**
300 mm wide	-	0.41	7.49	5.17	m	**12.66**

G STRUCTURAL/CARCASSING METAL/TIMBER

Item	PC £	Labour hours	Labour £	Material £	Unit	Total rate £
G20 CARPENTRY/TIMBER FRAMING/FIRST FIXING – cont'd						
Sawn softwood; untreated						
Gutter boards; butt joints						
19 mm thick; sloping	-	1.28	23.39	7.04	m²	30.44
19 mm thick; 75 mm wide	-	0.36	6.58	0.58	m	7.15
19 mm thick; 150 mm wide	-	0.41	7.49	1.02	m	8.51
19 mm thick; 225 mm wide	-	0.45	8.22	1.52	m	9.75
25 mm thick; sloping	-	1.28	23.39	7.69	m²	31.08
25 mm thick; 75 mm wide	-	0.36	6.58	0.61	m	7.19
25 mm thick; 150 mm wide	-	0.41	7.49	1.12	m	8.61
25 mm thick; 225 mm wide	-	0.45	8.22	1.67	m	9.89
Cesspools with 25 mm thick sides and bottom						
225 mm x 225 mm x 150 mm	-	1.22	22.29	1.43	nr	23.72
300 mm x 300 mm x 150 mm	-	1.42	25.95	1.88	nr	27.83
Individual supports; firrings						
50 mm wide x 36 mm average depth	-	0.16	2.92	0.99	m	3.92
50 mm wide x 50 mm average depth	-	0.16	2.92	1.16	m	4.09
50 mm wide x 75 mm average depth	-	0.16	2.92	1.65	m	4.57
Individual supports; bearers						
25 mm x 50 mm	-	0.10	1.83	0.52	m	2.35
38 mm x 50 mm	-	0.10	1.83	0.64	m	2.47
50 mm x 50 mm	-	0.10	1.83	0.76	m	2.59
50 mm x 75 mm	-	0.10	1.83	1.04	m	2.87
Individual supports; angle fillets						
38 mm x 38 mm	-	0.10	1.83	0.46	m	2.29
50 mm x 50 mm	-	0.10	1.83	0.61	m	2.43
75 mm x 75 mm	-	0.12	2.19	1.26	m	3.45
Individual supports; tilting fillets						
19 mm x 38 mm	-	0.10	1.83	0.46	m	2.29
25 mm x 50 mm	-	0.10	1.83	0.42	m	2.25
38 mm x 75 mm	-	0.10	1.83	0.73	m	2.56
50 mm x 75 mm	-	0.10	1.83	0.64	m	2.47
75 mm x 100 mm	-	0.16	2.92	1.92	m	4.84
Individual supports; grounds or battens						
13 mm x 19 mm	-	0.05	0.91	0.28	m	1.19
13 mm x 32 mm	-	0.05	0.91	0.30	m	1.22
25 mm x 50 mm	-	0.05	0.91	0.46	m	1.37
Individial supports; grounds or battens; plugged and screwed						
13 mm x 19 mm	-	0.16	2.92	0.33	m	3.25
13 mm x 32 mm	-	0.16	2.92	0.35	m	3.28
25 mm x 50 mm	-	0.16	2.92	0.51	m	3.44
Framed supports; open-spaced grounds or battens; at 300 mm centres one way						
25 mm x 50 mm	-	0.16	2.92	1.52	m²	4.44
25 mm x 50 mm; plugged and screwed	-	0.45	8.22	1.70	m²	9.93
Framed supports; at 300 mm centres one way and 600 mm centres the other way						
25 mm x 50 mm	-	0.77	14.07	2.27	m²	16.35
38 mm x 50 mm	-	0.77	14.07	2.88	m²	16.95
50 mm x 50 mm	-	0.77	14.07	3.49	m²	17.56
50 mm x 75 mm	-	0.77	14.07	4.88	m²	18.95
75 mm x 75 mm	-	0.77	14.07	7.86	m²	21.93

G STRUCTURAL/CARCASSING METAL/TIMBER

Item	PC £	Labour hours	Labour £	Material £	Unit	Total rate £
Framed supports; at 300 mm centres one way and 600 mm centres the other way; plugged and screwed						
25 mm x 50 mm	-	1.28	23.39	2.80	m²	26.19
38 mm x 50 mm	-	1.28	23.39	3.41	m²	26.80
50 mm x 50 mm	-	1.28	23.39	4.02	m²	27.41
50 mm x 75 mm	-	1.28	23.39	5.41	m²	28.80
75 mm x 75 mm	-	1.28	23.39	8.38	m²	31.78
Framed supports; at 500 mm centres both ways						
25 mm x 50 mm; to bath panels	-	0.92	16.81	2.97	m²	19.78
Framed supports; as bracketing and cradling around steelwork						
25 mm x 50 mm	-	1.42	25.95	3.23	m²	29.18
50 mm x 50 mm	-	1.53	27.96	4.92	m²	32.88
50 mm x 75 mm	-	1.63	29.79	6.88	m²	36.67
Sawn softwood; "Tanalised"						
Gutter boards; butt joints						
19 mm thick; sloping	-	1.28	23.39	8.04	m²	31.43
19 mm thick; 75 mm wide	-	0.36	6.58	0.65	m	7.23
19 mm thick; 150 mm wide	-	0.41	7.49	1.17	m	8.66
19 mm thick; 225 mm wide	-	0.45	8.22	1.75	m	9.97
25 mm thick; sloping	-	1.28	23.39	9.00	m²	32.39
25 mm thick; 75 mm wide	-	0.36	6.58	0.71	m	7.29
25 mm thick; 150 mm wide	-	0.41	7.49	1.32	m	8.81
25 mm thick; 225 mm wide	-	0.45	8.22	1.96	m	10.18
Cesspools with 25 mm thick sides and bottom						
225 mm x 225 mm x 150 mm	-	1.22	22.29	1.69	nr	23.99
300 mm x 300 mm x 150 mm	-	1.42	25.95	2.24	nr	28.19
Individual supports; firrings						
50 mm wide x 36 mm average depth	-	0.16	2.92	1.09	m	4.02
50 mm wide x 50 mm average depth	-	0.16	2.92	1.30	m	4.22
50 mm wide x 75 mm average depth	-	0.16	2.92	1.85	m	4.77
Individual suports; bearers						
25 mm x 50 mm	-	0.10	1.83	0.59	m	2.42
38 mm x 50 mm	-	0.10	1.83	0.74	m	2.57
50 mm x 50 mm	-	0.10	1.83	0.90	m	2.72
50 mm x 75 mm	-	0.10	1.83	1.24	m	3.07
Individual supports; angle fillets						
38 mm x 38 mm	-	0.10	1.83	0.50	m	2.33
50 mm x 50 mm	-	0.10	1.83	0.67	m	2.50
75 mm x 75 mm	-	0.12	2.19	1.41	m	3.60
Individual supports; tilting fillets						
19 mm x 38 mm	-	0.10	1.83	0.48	m	2.31
25 mm x 50 mm	-	0.10	1.83	0.45	m	2.28
38 mm x 75 mm	-	0.10	1.83	0.80	m	2.63
50 mm x 75 mm	-	0.10	1.83	0.74	m	2.57
75 mm x 100 mm	-	0.16	2.92	2.12	m	5.04
Individual supports; grounds or battens						
13 mm x 19 mm	-	0.05	0.91	0.29	m	1.20
13 mm x 32 mm	-	0.05	0.91	0.32	m	1.24
25 mm x 50 mm	-	0.05	0.91	0.53	m	1.44
Individual supports; grounds or battens; plugged and screwed						
13 mm x 19 mm	-	0.16	2.92	0.34	m	3.26
13 mm x 32 mm	-	0.16	2.92	0.37	m	3.30
25 mm x 50 mm	-	0.16	2.92	0.58	m	3.50

G STRUCTURAL/CARCASSING METAL/TIMBER

Item	PC £	Labour hours	Labour £	Material £	Unit	Total rate £
G20 CARPENTRY/TIMBER FRAMING/FIRST FIXING – cont'd						
Sawn softwood; "Tanalised" – cont'd						
Framed supports; open-spaced grounds or battens; at 300 mm centres one way						
25 mm x 50 mm	-	0.16	2.92	1.74	m²	4.66
25 mm x 50 mm; plugged and screwed	-	0.45	8.22	1.92	m²	10.15
Framed supports; at 300 mm centres one way and 600 mm centres the other way						
25 mm x 50 mm	-	0.77	14.07	2.61	m²	16.68
38 mm x 50 mm	-	0.77	14.07	3.38	m²	17.45
50 mm x 50 mm	-	0.77	14.07	4.14	m²	18.21
50 mm x 75 mm	-	0.77	14.07	5.87	m²	19.94
75 mm x 75 mm	-	0.77	14.07	9.33	m²	23.40
Framed supports; at 300 mm centres one way and 600 mm centres the other way; plugged and screwed						
25 mm x 50 mm	-	1.28	23.39	3.13	m²	26.53
38 mm x 50 mm	-	1.28	23.39	3.91	m²	27.30
50 mm x 50 mm	-	1.28	23.39	4.67	m²	28.06
50 mm x 75 mm	-	1.28	23.39	6.40	m²	29.79
75 mm x 75 mm	-	1.28	23.39	9.86	m²	33.25
Framed supports; at 500 mm centres both ways						
25 mm x 50 mm; to bath panels	-	0.92	16.81	3.39	m²	20.20
Framed supports; as bracketing and cradling around steelwork						
25 mm x 50 mm	-	1.42	25.95	3.69	m²	29.64
50 mm x 50 mm	-	1.53	27.96	5.84	m²	33.80
50 mm x 75 mm	-	1.63	29.79	8.26	m²	38.05
Wrought softwood						
Gutter boards; tongued and grooved joints						
19 mm thick; sloping	-	1.53	27.96	12.64	m²	40.60
19 mm thick; 75 mm wide	-	0.41	7.49	1.22	m	8.72
19 mm thick; 150 mm wide	-	0.45	8.22	1.86	m	10.08
19 mm thick; 225 mm wide	-	0.51	9.32	3.02	m	12.34
25 mm thick; sloping	-	1.53	27.96	15.26	m²	43.22
25 mm thick; 75 mm wide	-	0.41	7.49	1.22	m	8.72
25 mm thick; 150 mm wide	-	0.45	8.22	2.18	m	10.40
25 mm thick; 225 mm wide	-	0.51	9.32	3.31	m	12.63
Eaves, verge soffit boards, fascia boards and the like						
19 mm thick; over 300 mm wide	-	1.26	23.03	11.20	m²	34.22
19 mm thick; 150 mm wide; once grooved	-	0.20	3.65	1.95	m	5.60
25 mm thick; 150 mm wide; once grooved	-	0.20	3.65	1.95	m	5.60
25 mm thick; 175 mm wide; once grooved	-	0.22	4.02	2.25	m	6.27
32 mm thick; 225 mm wide; once grooved	-	0.26	4.75	2.91	m	7.66
Wrought softwood; "Tanalised"						
Gutter boards; tongued and grooved joints						
19 mm thick; sloping	-	1.53	27.96	13.64	m²	41.60
19 mm thick; 75 mm wide	-	0.41	7.49	1.30	m	8.79
19 mm thick; 150 mm wide	-	0.45	8.22	2.01	m	10.23
19 mm thick; 225 mm wide	-	0.51	9.32	3.25	m	12.57
25 mm thick; sloping	-	1.53	27.96	16.57	m²	44.53
25 mm thick; 75 mm wide	-	0.41	7.49	1.32	m	8.81
25 mm thick; 150 mm wide	-	0.45	8.22	2.38	m	10.60
25 mm thick; 225 mm wide	-	0.51	9.32	3.60	m	12.92

G STRUCTURAL/CARCASSING METAL/TIMBER

Item	PC £	Labour hours	Labour £	Material £	Unit	Total rate £
Eaves, verge soffit boards, fascia boards and the like						
19 mm thick; over 300 mm wide	-	1.26	23.03	12.19	m²	**35.22**
19 mm thick; 150 mm wide; once grooved	-	0.20	3.65	2.10	m	**5.76**
25 mm thick; 150 mm wide; once grooved	-	0.20	3.65	2.15	m	**5.80**
25 mm thick; 175 mm wide; once grooved	-	0.22	4.02	2.47	m	**6.49**
32 mm thick; 225 mm wide; once grooved	-	0.26	4.75	3.29	m	**8.04**
Straps; mild steel; galvanised						
Straps; standard twisted vertical restraint; fixing to softwood and brick or blockwork						
30 mm x 2.50 mm x 400 mm girth	-	0.26	4.75	0.96	nr	**5.72**
30 mm x 2.50 mm x 600 mm girth	-	0.27	4.93	1.36	nr	**6.29**
30 mm x 2.50 mm x 800 mm girth	-	0.28	5.12	1.91	nr	**7.02**
30 mm x 2.50 mm x 1000 mm girth	-	0.31	5.67	2.46	nr	**8.12**
30 mm x 2.50 mm x 1200 mm girth	-	0.31	5.67	2.94	nr	**8.61**
Hangers; mild steel; galvanised						
Joist hangers 0.90 mm thick; The Expanded Metal Company Ltd "Speedy" or other equal and approved; for fixing to softwood; joist sizes						
50 mm wide; all sizes to 225 mm deep	1.07	0.12	2.19	1.40	nr	**3.60**
75 mm wide; all sizes to 225 mm deep	1.12	0.16	2.92	1.53	nr	**4.45**
100 mm wide; all sizes to 225 mm deep	1.21	0.19	3.47	1.70	nr	**5.17**
Joist hangers 2.50 mm thick; for building in; joist sizes						
50 mm x 100 mm	2.07	0.08	1.55	2.54	nr	**4.10**
50 mm x 125 mm	2.08	0.08	1.55	2.55	nr	**4.11**
50 mm x 150 mm	1.95	0.10	1.92	2.45	nr	**4.36**
50 mm x 175 mm	2.06	0.10	1.92	2.57	nr	**4.49**
50 mm x 200 mm	2.28	0.12	2.28	2.88	nr	**5.16**
50 mm x 225 mm	2.42	0.12	2.28	3.04	nr	**5.32**
75 mm x 150 mm	3.02	0.10	1.92	3.71	nr	**5.63**
75 mm x 175 mm	2.84	0.10	1.92	3.50	nr	**5.42**
75 mm x 200 mm	3.02	0.12	2.28	3.75	nr	**6.03**
75 mm x 225 mm	3.22	0.12	2.28	4.00	nr	**6.28**
75 mm x 250 mm	3.42	0.14	2.65	4.28	nr	**6.93**
100 mm x 200 mm	3.76	0.12	2.28	4.63	nr	**6.92**
Metal connectors; mild steel; galvanised						
Round toothed plate; for 10 mm or 12 mm diameter bolts						
38 mm diameter; single sided	-	0.02	0.37	0.25	nr	**0.61**
38 mm diameter; double sided	-	0.02	0.37	0.27	nr	**0.64**
50 mm diameter; single sided	-	0.02	0.37	0.36	nr	**0.73**
50 mm diameter; double sided	-	0.02	0.37	0.41	nr	**0.77**
63 mm diameter; single sided	-	0.02	0.37	0.53	nr	**0.90**
63 mm diameter; double sided	-	0.02	0.37	0.59	nr	**0.96**
75 mm diameter; single sided	-	0.02	0.37	0.79	nr	**1.15**
75 mm diameter; double sided	-	0.02	0.37	0.82	nr	**1.18**
framing anchor	-	0.16	2.92	0.54	nr	**3.46**
Bolts; mild steel; galvanised						
Fixing only bolts; 50 mm - 200 mm long						
6 mm diameter	-	0.03	0.55	-	nr	**0.55**
8 mm diameter	-	0.03	0.55	-	nr	**0.55**
10 mm diameter	-	0.05	0.91	-	nr	**0.91**
12 mm diameter	-	0.05	0.91	-	nr	**0.91**
16 mm diameter	-	0.06	1.10	-	nr	**1.10**
20 mm diameter	-	0.06	1.10	-	nr	**1.10**

G STRUCTURAL/CARCASSING METAL/TIMBER

Item	PC £	Labour hours	Labour £	Material £	Unit	Total rate £
G20 CARPENTRY/TIMBER FRAMING/FIRST FIXING – cont'd						
Bolts						
Expanding bolts; "Rawlbolt" projecting type or other equal and approved; The Rawlplug Company; plated; one nut; one washer						
6 mm diameter; ref M6 10P	-	0.10	1.83	0.87	nr	2.70
6 mm diameter; ref M6 25P	-	0.10	1.83	0.97	nr	2.80
6 mm diameter; ref M6 60P	-	0.10	1.83	1.02	nr	2.85
8 mm diameter; ref M8 25P	-	0.10	1.83	1.15	nr	2.98
8 mm diameter; ref M8 60P	-	0.10	1.83	1.23	nr	3.06
10 mm diameter; ref M10 15P	-	0.10	1.83	1.50	nr	3.33
10 mm diameter; ref M10 30P	-	0.10	1.83	1.57	nr	3.40
10 mm diameter; ref M10 60P	-	0.10	1.83	1.64	nr	3.47
12 mm diameter; ref M12 15P	-	0.10	1.83	2.39	nr	4.21
12 mm diameter; ref M12 30P	-	0.10	1.83	2.57	nr	4.39
12 mm diameter; ref M12 75P	-	0.10	1.83	3.20	nr	5.02
16 mm diameter; ref M16 35P	-	0.10	1.83	6.11	nr	7.93
16 mm diameter; ref M16 75P	-	0.10	1.83	6.40	nr	8.23
Expanding bolts; "Rawlbolt" loose bolt type or other equal and approved; The Rawlplug Company; plated; one bolt; one washer						
6 mm diameter; ref M6 10L	-	0.10	1.83	0.87	nr	2.70
6 mm diameter; ref M6 25L	-	0.10	1.83	0.92	nr	2.75
6 mm diameter; ref M6 40L	-	0.10	1.83	0.92	nr	2.75
8 mm diameter; ref M8 25L	-	0.10	1.83	1.13	nr	2.96
8 mm diameter; ref M8 40L	-	0.10	1.83	1.20	nr	3.03
10 mm diameter; ref M10 10L	-	0.10	1.83	1.45	nr	3.28
10 mm diameter; ref M10 25L	-	0.10	1.83	1.49	nr	3.32
10 mm diameter; ref M10 50L	-	0.10	1.83	1.57	nr	3.40
10 mm diameter; ref M10 75L	-	0.10	1.83	1.63	nr	3.46
12 mm diameter; ref M12 10L	-	0.10	1.83	2.16	nr	3.99
12 mm diameter; ref M12 25L	-	0.10	1.83	2.39	nr	4.21
12 mm diameter; ref M12 40L	-	0.10	1.83	2.49	nr	4.32
12 mm diameter; ref M12 60L	-	0.10	1.83	2.62	nr	4.45
16 mm diameter; ref M16 30L	-	0.10	1.83	5.81	nr	7.63
16 mm diameter; ref M16 60L	-	0.10	1.83	6.28	nr	8.11
Truss clips; mild steel galvanised						
Truss clips; fixing to softwood; joist size						
38 mm wide	0.18	0.16	2.92	0.48	nr	3.41
50 mm wide	0.20	0.16	2.92	0.50	nr	3.42
Sole plate angles; mild steel; galvanised						
Sole plate angles; fixing to softwood and concrete						
112 mm x 40 mm x 76 mm	0.48	0.20	3.65	1.75	nr	5.40
Chemical anchors						
"Kemfix" capsules and standard studs or other equal and approved; The Rawlplug Company; with nuts and washers; drilling masonry						
capsule ref 60-408; stud ref 60-448	-	0.28	5.12	1.61	nr	6.73
capsule ref 60-410; stud ref 60-454	-	0.31	5.67	1.81	nr	7.48
capsule ref 60-412; stud ref 60-460	-	0.34	6.21	2.22	nr	8.43
capsule ref 60-416; stud ref 60-472	-	0.38	6.94	3.49	nr	10.44
capsule ref 60-420; stud ref 60-478	-	0.40	7.31	5.69	nr	13.00
capsule ref 60-424; stud ref 60-484	-	0.43	7.86	8.74	nr	16.60

G STRUCTURAL/CARCASSING METAL/TIMBER

Item	PC £	Labour hours	Labour £	Material £	Unit	Total rate £
"Kemfix" capsules and stainless steel studs or other equal and approved; The Rawlplug Company; with nuts and washers; drilling masonry						
capsule ref 60-408; stud ref 60-905	-	0.28	5.12	2.93	nr	8.05
capsule ref 60-410; stud ref 60-910	-	0.31	5.67	3.94	nr	9.61
capsule ref 60-412; stud ref 60-915	-	0.34	6.21	5.44	nr	11.66
capsule ref 60-416; stud ref 60-920	-	0.38	6.94	9.30	nr	16.25
capsule ref 60-420; stud ref 60-925	-	0.40	7.31	14.72	nr	22.03
capsule ref 60-424; stud ref 60-930	-	0.43	7.86	24.07	nr	31.93
"Kemfix" capsules and standard internal threaded sockets or other equal and approved; The Rawlplug Company; drilling masonry						
capsule ref 60-408; socket ref 60-650	-	0.28	5.12	1.59	nr	6.71
capsule ref 60-410; socket ref 60-656	-	0.31	5.67	2.04	nr	7.70
capsule ref 60-412; socket ref 60-662	-	0.34	6.21	2.54	nr	8.76
capsule ref 60-416; socket ref 60-668	-	0.38	6.94	3.47	nr	10.41
capsule ref 60-420; socket ref 60-674	-	0.40	7.31	4.47	nr	11.78
capsule ref 60-424; socket ref 60-676	-	0.43	7.86	7.54	nr	15.40
"Kemfix" capsules and stainless steel internal threaded sockets or other equal and approved; The Rawlplug Company; drilling masonry						
capsule ref 60-408; socket ref 60-943	-	0.28	5.12	3.61	nr	8.72
capsule ref 60-410; socket ref 60-945	-	0.31	5.67	3.69	nr	9.35
capsule ref 60-412; socket ref 60-947	-	0.34	6.21	4.26	nr	10.47
capsule ref 60-416; socket ref 60-949	-	0.38	6.94	6.03	nr	12.98
capsule ref 60-420; socket ref 60-951	-	0.40	7.31	7.57	nr	14.88
capsule ref 60-424; socket ref 60-955	-	0.43	7.86	14.13	nr	21.99
"Kemfix" capsules, perforated sleeves and standard studs or other equal and approved; The Rawlplug Company; in low density material; with nuts and washers; drilling masonry						
capsule ref 60-408; sleeve ref 60-538 stud ref 60-448	-	0.28	5.12	2.41	nr	7.53
capsule ref 60-410; sleeve ref 60-544; stud ref 60-454	-	0.31	5.67	2.65	nr	8.32
capsule ref 60-412; sleeve ref 60-550; stud ref 60-460	-	0.34	6.21	3.18	nr	9.40
capsule ref 60-416; sleeve ref 60-562; stud ref 60-472	-	0.38	6.94	4.68	nr	11.62
"Kemfix" capsules, perforated sleeves and stainless steel studs or other equal and approved; The Rawlplug Company; in low density material; with nuts and washers; drilling masonry						
capsule ref 60-408; sleeve ref 60-538; stud ref 60-905	-	0.28	5.12	3.73	nr	8.85
capsule ref 60-410; sleeve ref 60-544; stud ref 60-910	-	0.31	5.67	4.78	nr	10.45
capsule ref 60-412; sleeve ref 60-550; stud ref 60-915	-	0.34	6.21	6.41	nr	12.62
capsule ref 60-416; sleeve ref 60-562; stud ref 60-920	-	0.38	6.94	10.48	nr	17.43

G STRUCTURAL/CARCASSING METAL/TIMBER

Item	PC £	Labour hours	Labour £	Material £	Unit	Total rate £
G20 CARPENTRY/TIMBER FRAMING/FIRST FIXING – cont'd						
Chemical anchors – cont'd						
"Kemfix" capsules, perforated sleeves and standard internal threaded sockets or other equal and approved; The Rawlplug Company; in low density material; with nuts and washers; drilling masonry						
capsule ref 60-408; sleeve ref 60-538; socket ref 60-650	-	0.28	5.12	2.39	nr	**7.51**
capsule ref 60-410; sleeve ref 60-544; socket ref 60-656	-	0.31	5.67	2.87	nr	**8.54**
capsule ref 60-412; sleeve ref 60-550; socket ref 60-662	-	0.34	6.21	3.51	nr	**9.72**
capsule ref 60-416; sleeve ref 60-562; socket ref 60-668	-	0.38	6.94	4.65	nr	**11.60**
"Kemfix" capsules, perforated sleeves and stainless steel internal threaded sockets or other equal and approved; The Rawlplug Company; in low density material; drilling masonry						
capsule ref 60-408; sleeve ref 60-538; socket ref 60-943	-	0.28	5.12	4.40	nr	**9.52**
capsule ref 60-410; sleeve ref 60-544; socket ref 60-945	-	0.31	5.67	4.52	nr	**10.19**
capsule ref 60-412; sleeve ref 60-550; socket ref 60-947	-	0.34	6.21	5.22	nr	**11.44**
capsule ref 60-416; sleeve ref 60-562; socket ref 60-949	-	0.38	6.94	7.21	nr	**14.16**

H CLADDING/COVERING

Item	PC £	Labour hours	Labour £	Material £	Unit	Total rate £
H10 PATENT GLAZING						
Patent glazing; aluminium alloy bars 2.55 m long at 622 mm centres; fixed to supports						
Roof cladding						
glazing with 7 mm thick Georgian wired cast glass	-	-	-	-	m²	157.00
Associated code 4 lead flashings						
top flashing; 210 mm girth	-	-	-	-	m	54.35
bottom flashing; 240 mm girth	-	-	-	-	m	40.45
end flashing; 300 mm girth	-	-	-	-	m	90.58
Wall cladding						
glazing with 7 mm thick Georgian wired cast glass	-	-	-	-	m²	163.04
glazing with 6 mm thick plate glass	-	-	-	-	m²	150.96
Extra for aluminium alloy members						
38 mm x 38 mm x 3 mm angle jamb	-	-	-	-	m	24.15
pressed cill member	-	-	-	-	m	48.31
pressed channel head and PVC case	-	-	-	-	m	39.26
"Kawneer" window frame system or other equal and approved; polyester powder coated glazing bars; glazed with double hermetically sealed units in toughened safety glass; one 6 mm thick air space; overall 18 mm thick						
Vertical surfaces						
single tier; aluminium glazing bars at 850 mm centres x 890 mm long; timber supports at 890 mm centres	-	-	-	-	m²	227.90
"Kawneer" window frame system or other equal and approved; polyester powder coated glazing bars; glazed with clear toughened safety glass; 10.70 mm thick						
Vertical surfaces						
single tier; aluminium glazing bars at 850 mm centres x 890 mm long; timber supports at 890 mm centres	-	-	-	-	m²	216.51
H20 RIGID SHEET CLADDING						
"Resoplan" sheet or other equal and approved; Eternit UK Ltd; flexible neoprene gasket joints; fixing with stainless steel screws and coloured caps						
6 mm thick cladding to walls						
over 300 mm wide	-	2.23	40.75	66.02	m²	106.78
not exceeding 300 mm wide	-	0.74	13.52	22.76	m	36.29
Eternit 2000 "Glasal" sheet or other equal and approved; Eternit UK Ltd; flexible neoprene gasket joints; fixing with stainless steel screws and coloured caps						
7.50 mm thick cladding to walls						
over 300 mm wide	-	2.23	40.75	54.14	m²	94.89
not exceeding 300 mm wide	-	0.74	13.52	19.20	m	32.72
external angle trim	-	0.11	2.01	9.92	m	11.93

H CLADDING/COVERING

Item	PC £	Labour hours	Labour £	Material £	Unit	Total rate £
H20 RIGID SHEET CLADDING – cont'd						
Eternit 2000 "Glasal" sheet – cont'd						
7.50 mm thick cladding to eaves; verges fascias or the like						
100 mm wide	-	0.53	9.69	9.29	m	**18.98**
200 mm wide	-	0.64	11.70	14.25	m	**25.94**
300 mm wide	-	0.74	13.52	19.20	m	**32.72**
H30 FIBRE CEMENT PROFILED SHEET CLADDING						
Asbestos-free corrugated sheets; Eternit "2000" or other equal and approved						
Roof cladding; sloping not exceeding 50 degrees; fixing to timber purlins with drive screws						
"Profile 3"; natural grey	14.52	0.21	5.78	19.42	m²	**25.21**
"Profile 3"; coloured	17.42	0.21	5.78	22.70	m²	**28.49**
"Profile 6"; natural grey	11.17	0.27	7.44	15.56	m²	**23.00**
"Profile 6"; coloured	13.66	0.27	7.44	18.36	m²	**25.80**
"Profile 6"; natural grey; insulated 60 mm glass fibre infill; lining panel	-	0.48	13.22	38.17	m²	**51.39**
Roof cladding; sloping not exceeding 50 degrees; fixing to steel purlins with hook bolts						
"Profile 3"; natural grey	-	0.27	7.44	21.19	m²	**28.62**
"Profile 3"; coloured	-	0.27	7.44	24.46	m²	**31.90**
"Profile 6"; natural grey	-	0.32	8.81	17.32	m²	**26.14**
"Profile 6"; coloured	-	0.32	8.81	20.13	m²	**28.94**
"Profile 6"; natural grey; insulated 60 mm glass fibre infill; lining panel	-	0.53	14.60	34.88	m²	**49.48**
Wall cladding; vertical; fixing to steel rails with hook bolts						
"Profile 3"; natural grey	-	0.32	8.81	21.19	m²	**30.00**
"Profile 3"; coloured	-	0.32	8.81	24.46	m²	**33.28**
"Profile 6"; natural grey	-	0.37	10.19	17.32	m²	**27.51**
"Profile 6"; coloured	-	0.37	10.19	20.13	m²	**30.32**
"Profile 6"; natural grey; insulated 60 mm glass fibre infill; lining panel	-	0.58	15.97	34.88	m²	**50.86**
raking cutting	-	0.16	4.41	-	m	**4.41**
holes for pipes and the like	-	0.16	4.41	-	nr	**4.41**
Accessories; to "Profile 3" cladding; natural grey						
eaves filler	-	0.11	3.03	14.08	m	**17.11**
vertical corrugation closer	-	0.13	3.58	14.08	m	**17.66**
apron flashing	-	0.13	3.58	14.08	m	**17.66**
plain wing or close fitting two piece adjustable capping to ridge	-	0.19	5.23	13.21	m	**18.44**
ventilating two piece adjustable capping to ridge	-	0.19	5.23	19.81	m	**25.04**
Accessories; to "Profile 3" cladding; coloured						
eaves filler	-	0.11	3.03	17.21	m	**20.24**
vertical corrugation closer	-	0.13	3.58	17.21	m	**20.79**
apron flashing	-	0.13	3.58	17.21	m	**20.79**
plain wing or close fitting two piece adjustable capping to ridge	-	0.19	5.23	15.75	m	**20.98**
ventilating two piece adjustable capping to ridge	-	0.19	5.23	24.38	m	**29.61**
Accessories; to "Profile 6" cladding; natural grey						
eaves filler	-	0.11	3.03	9.14	m	**12.17**
vertical corrugation closer	-	0.13	3.58	9.14	m	**12.72**
apron flashing	-	0.13	3.58	10.16	m	**13.74**
underglazing flashing	-	0.13	3.58	9.14	m	**12.72**
plain cranked crown to ridge	-	0.19	5.23	20.11	m	**25.35**

H CLADDING/COVERING

Item	PC £	Labour hours	Labour £	Material £	Unit	Total rate £
plain wing or close fitting two piece adjustable capping to ridge	-	0.19	5.23	18.29	m	23.52
ventilating two piece adjustable capping to ridge	-	0.19	5.23	23.37	m	28.60
Accessories; to "Profile 6" cladding; coloured						
eaves filler	-	0.11	3.03	11.68	m	14.71
vertical corrugation closer	-	0.13	3.58	11.68	m	15.26
apron flashing	-	0.13	3.58	12.70	m	16.28
underglazing flashing	-	0.13	3.58	11.17	m	14.75
plain cranked crown to ridge	-	0.19	5.23	24.58	m	29.82
plain wing or close fitting two piece adjustable capping to ridge	-	0.19	5.23	22.35	m	27.58
ventilating two piece adjustable capping to ridge	-	0.19	5.23	29.46	m	34.69
H31 METAL PROFILED/FLAT SHEET CLADDING/COVERING/SIDING						
Lightweight galvanised steel roof tiles; Decra Roof Systems (UK) Ltd or other equal and approved; coated finish						
Roof coverings	-	0.26	7.16	16.68	m²	23.84
Accessories for roof cladding						
pitched "D" ridge	-	0.10	2.75	8.99	m	11.74
barge cover (handed)	-	0.10	2.75	96.31	m	99.06
in line air vent	-	0.10	2.75	41.72	nr	44.48
in line soil vent	-	0.10	2.75	65.20	nr	67.96
gas flue terminal	-	0.20	5.51	90.87	nr	96.38
Galvanised steel strip troughed sheets; Corus products or other equal and approved						
Roof cladding or decking; sloping not exceeding 50 degrees; fixing to steel purlins with plastic headed self-tapping screws						
0.7 mm thick; 46 profile	-	-	-	-	m²	12.43
0.7 mm thick; 60 profile	-	-	-	-	m²	13.61
0.7 mm thick; 100 profile	-	-	-	-	m²	14.80
Galvanised steel strip troughed sheets; PMF Strip Mills Products or other equal and approved						
Roof cladding; sloping not exceeding 50 degrees; fixing to steel purlins with plastic headed self-tapping screws						
0.7 mm thick type HPS200 13.5/3 corrugated	-	-	-	-	m²	14.03
0.7 mm thick type HPS200 R32/1000	-	-	-	-	m²	13.37
0.7 mm thick type Acline 40; plasticol finished	-	-	-	-	m²	18.72
Extra over last for aluminium roof cladding or decking	-	-	-	-	m²	7.10
Accessories for roof cladding						
HPS200 Drip flashing; 250 mm girth	-	-	-	-	m	4.35
HPS200 Ridge flashing; 375 mm girth	-	-	-	-	m	5.70
HPS200 Gable flashing; 500 mm girth	-	-	-	-	m	8.03
HPS200 Internal angle; 625 mm girth	-	-	-	-	m	8.35
Extra over steel roofing for						
roof penetration; 150 mm dia. opening; with top hat flashing and collar 150 mm high; and silicone joint to roofsheet	-	-	-	-	nr	58.63
roof penetration; 250 mm dia. opening; with top hat flashing and collar 150 mm high; and silicone joint to roofsheet	-	-	-	-	nr	83.44

H CLADDING/COVERING

Item	PC £	Labour hours	Labour £	Material £	Unit	Total rate £
H31 METAL PROFILED/FLAT SHEET CLADDING/COVERING/SIDING – cont'd						
Zalutite coated flat steel composite panel cladding; Kingspan or other equal and approved; outer panel 0.7 mm gauge HPS200 colourcoated; HCFC free LPCB FM/FW core and 0.4 mm stucco embossed lining panel with bright white polyester paint finish						
Roof cladding; horizontal fixing to steel purlins (measured elsewhere)						
KS1000RW 80 mm roof panel	-	-	-	-	m²	37.29
Wall cladding; vertical fixing to steel cladding rails (measured elsewhere)						
KS1000RW 60 mm wall panel	-	-	-	-	m²	35.87
KS1000RW 70 mm wall panel	-	-	-	-	m²	36.70
KS1000RW 80 mm wall panel	-	-	-	-	m²	37.53
KS1000MR 70 mm wall panel	-	-	-	-	m²	51.38
KS1000MR 80 mm wall panel	-	-	-	-	m²	52.21
KS900MR 70 mm wall panel	-	-	-	-	m²	54.70
KS900MR 80 mm wall panel	-	-	-	-	m²	55.52
KS600MR 70 mm wall panel	-	-	-	-	m²	75.53
KS600MR 80 mm wall panel	-	-	-	-	m²	76.24
Extra over for						
raking cutting on 60 mm KS1000RW roof panel; including waste	-	-	-	-	m	18.94
raking cutting on 70 mm KS1000RW roof panel; including waste	-	-	-	-	m	19.33
raking cutting on 80 mm KS1000RW roof panel; including waste	-	-	-	-	m	19.74
raking cutting on 70 mm KS1000MR wall panel; including waste	-	-	-	-	m	26.87
raking cutting on 80 mm KS1000MR wall panel; including waste	-	-	-	-	m	27.23
raking cutting on 70 mm KS900MR wall panel; including waste	-	-	-	-	m	28.41
raking cutting on 80 mm KS900MR wall panel; including waste	-	-	-	-	m	28.80
raking cutting on 70 mm KS600MR wall panel; including waste	-	-	-	-	m	37.88
raking cutting on 80 mm KS600MR wall panel; including waste	-	-	-	-	m	38.27
panel bearers at 1500 mm centres	-	-	-	-	m	6.55
vertical tophat joint in HPS200	-	-	-	-	m	11.21
vertical tophat joint with cap in HPS200	-	-	-	-	m	14.56
cranked panel KS1000MR	-	-	-	-	m	108.94
cranked panel KS900MR	-	-	-	-	m	121.04
cranked panel KS600MR	-	-	-	-	m	181.57
GRP Transluscent rooflights; factory assembled						
Rooflight; vertical fixing to steel purlins (measued elsewhere)						
double skin; class 3 over 1	-	-	-	-	m²	55.89
triple skin; class 3 over 1	-	-	-	-	m²	58.60

H CLADDING/COVERING

Item	PC £	Labour hours	Labour £	Material £	Unit	Total rate £
H32 PLASTICS PROFILED SHEET CLADDING/COVERING/SIDING						
Extended, hard skinned, foamed PVC-UE profiled sections; Swish Celuka or other equal and approved; Class 1 fire rated to BS 476; Part 7; 1987; in white finish						
Wall cladding; vertical; fixing to timber						
100 mm shiplap profiles Code 001	-	0.39	7.13	20.74	m²	**27.87**
150 mm shiplap profiles Code 002	-	0.36	6.58	27.26	m²	**33.84**
125 mm feather-edged profiles Code C208	-	0.38	6.94	24.84	m²	**31.78**
Vertical angles	-	0.20	3.65	4.32	m	**7.97**
Raking cutting	-	0.16	2.92	-	m	**2.92**
Holes for pipes and the like	-	0.03	0.55	-	nr	**0.55**
H41 GLASS REINFORCED PLASTICS CLADDING/FEATURES						
Glass fibre translucent sheeting grade AB class 3						
Roof cladding; sloping not exceeding 50 degrees; fixing to timber purlins with drive screws; to suit						
"Profile 3" or other equal and approved	14.11	0.21	5.78	18.99	m²	**24.77**
"Profile 6" or other equal and approved	13.23	0.27	7.44	17.94	m²	**25.38**
Roof cladding; sloping not exceeding 50 degrees; fixing to timber purlins with hook bolts; to suit						
"Profile 3" or other equal and approved	14.11	0.27	7.44	20.75	m²	**28.18**
Profile 6" or other equal and approved	13.23	0.32	8.81	19.70	m²	**28.52**
"Longrib 1000" or other equal and approved	13.00	0.32	8.81	19.44	m²	**28.25**
H60 PLAIN ROOF TILING						
NOTE: The following items of tile roofing unless otherwise described, include for conventional fixing assuming normal exposure with appropriate nails and/or rivets or clips to pressure impregnated softwood battens fixed with galvanised nails; prices also include for all bedding and pointing at verges, beneath ridge tiles etc.						
Clay interlocking pantiles; Sandtoft "20/20" red sand faced or other equal and approved; PC £867.00/1000; 370 mm x 223 mm; to 75 mm lap; on 25 mm x 38 mm battens and type 1F reinforced underlay						
Roof coverings	-	0.48	13.22	11.91	m²	**25.13**
Extra over coverings for						
fixing every tile	-	0.03	0.83	1.95	m²	**2.78**
double course at eaves	-	0.32	8.81	11.60	m	**20.41**
verges	-	0.32	8.81	4.43	m	**13.24**
open valleys; cutting both sides	-	0.19	5.23	3.49	m	**8.73**
dry ridge tiles	-	0.64	17.63	12.07	m	**29.70**
dry hips; cutting both sides	-	0.80	22.03	16.91	m	**38.95**
holes for pipes and the like	-	0.21	5.78	-	nr	**5.78**

H CLADDING/COVERING

Item	PC £	Labour hours	Labour £	Material £	Unit	Total rate £
H60 PLAIN ROOF TILING – cont'd						
Clay pantiles; Sandtoft Goxhill "Old English"; red sand faced or other equal and approved; PC £967.00/1000; 342 mm x 241 mm; to 75 mm lap; on 25 mm x 38 mm battens and type 1F reinforced underlay						
Roof coverings	-	0.48	13.22	20.10	m^2	**33.32**
Extra over coverings for						
fixing every tile	-	0.02	0.55	4.88	m^2	**5.43**
other colours	-	-	-	0.56	m^2	**0.56**
double course at eaves	-	0.35	9.64	5.52	m	**15.16**
verges; extra single undercloak course of plain tiles	-	0.32	8.81	10.88	m	**19.69**
open valleys; cutting both sides	-	0.19	5.23	3.90	m	**9.13**
ridge tiles; tile slips	-	0.64	17.63	27.04	m	**44.67**
hips; cutting both sides	-	0.80	22.03	30.94	m	**52.97**
holes for pipes and the like	-	0.21	5.78	-	nr	**5.78**
Clay pantiles; William Blyth's "Lincoln" natural or other equal and approved; 343 mm x 280 mm; to 75 mm lap; PC £1,135.00/1000; on 19 mm x 38 mm battens and type 1F reinforced underlay						
Roof coverings	-	0.48	13.22	24.05	m^2	**37.26**
Extra over coverings for						
fixing every tile	-	0.02	0.55	4.88	m^2	**5.43**
other colours	-	-	-	1.72	m^2	**1.72**
double course at eaves	-	0.35	9.64	6.67	m	**16.31**
verges; extra single undercloak course of plain tiles	-	0.32	8.81	14.24	m	**23.06**
open valleys; cutting both sides	-	0.19	5.23	5.04	m	**10.27**
ridge tiles; tile slips	-	0.64	17.63	25.15	m	**42.78**
hips; cutting both sides	-	0.80	22.03	30.19	m	**52.23**
holes for pipes and the like	-	0.21	5.78	-	nr	**5.78**
Clay plain tiles; Hinton, Perry and Davenhill "Dreadnought" smooth red machine-made or other equal and approved; PC £315.00/1000; 265 mm x 165 mm; on 19 mm x 38 mm battens and type 1F reinforced underlay						
Roof coverings; to 64 mm lap	-	1.12	30.85	28.09	m^2	**58.93**
Wall coverings; to 38 mm lap	-	1.33	36.63	23.79	m^2	**60.42**
Extra over coverings for						
other colours	-	-	-	2.45	m^2	**2.45**
ornamental tiles	-	-	-	16.72	m^2	**16.72**
double course at eaves	-	0.27	7.44	3.42	m	**10.86**
verges	-	0.32	8.81	1.19	m	**10.00**
swept valleys; cutting both sides	-	0.69	19.00	37.63	m	**56.64**
bonnet hips; cutting both sides	-	0.85	23.41	37.63	m	**61.04**
external vertical angle tiles; supplementary nail fixings	-	0.43	11.84	42.81	m	**54.66**
half round ridge tiles	-	0.64	17.63	12.03	m	**29.66**
holes for pipes and the like	-	0.21	5.78	-	nr	**5.78**

H CLADDING/COVERING

Item	PC £	Labour hours	Labour £	Material £	Unit	Total rate £
Concrete interlocking tiles; Marley "Bold Roll" granule finish tiles or other equal and aqpproved; PC £715.00/1000; 420 mm x 330 mm; to 75 mm lap; on 25 mm x 38 mm battens and type 1F reinforced underlay						
Roof coverings	-	0.37	10.19	10.94	m^2	21.13
Extra over coverings for						
fixing every tile	-	0.02	0.55	0.81	m^2	1.36
eaves; eaves filler	-	0.05	1.38	1.24	m	2.61
verges; 150 mm wide asbestos free strip undercloak	-	0.24	6.61	1.47	m	8.08
valley trough tiles; cutting both sides	-	0.58	15.97	21.82	m	37.80
segmental ridge tiles; tile slips	-	0.58	15.97	12.32	m	28.29
segmental hip tiles; tile slips; cutting both sides	-	0.74	20.38	14.78	m	35.16
dry ridge tiles; segmental including batten sections; unions and filler pieces	-	0.32	8.81	17.26	m	26.07
segmental mono-ridge tiles	-	0.58	15.97	17.21	m	33.18
gas ridge terminal	-	0.53	14.60	67.54	nr	82.14
holes for pipes and the like	-	0.21	5.78	-	nr	5.78
Concrete interlocking tiles; Marley "Ludlow Major" granule finish tiles or other equal and approved; PC £699.00/1000; 420 mm x 330 mm; to 75 mm lap; on 25 mm x 38 mm battens and type 1F reinforced underlay						
Roof coverings	-	0.37	10.19	10.84	m^2	21.03
Extra over coverings for						
fixing every tile	-	0.02	0.55	0.81	m^2	1.36
eaves; eaves filler	-	0.05	1.38	0.58	m	1.96
verges; 150 mm wide asbestos free strip undercloak	-	0.24	6.61	1.47	m	8.08
dry verge system; extruded white pvc	-	0.16	4.41	8.57	m	12.98
segmental ridge cap to dry verge	-	0.02	0.55	3.13	m	3.68
valley trough tiles; cutting both sides	-	0.58	15.97	21.79	m	37.76
segmental ridge tiles	-	0.53	14.60	8.46	m	23.06
segmental hip tiles; cutting both sides	-	0.69	19.00	10.87	m	29.87
dry ridge tiles; segmental including batten sections; unions and filler pieces	-	0.32	8.81	17.26	m	26.07
segmental mono-ridge tiles	-	0.53	14.60	14.96	m	29.56
gas ridge terminal	-	0.53	14.60	67.54	nr	82.14
holes for pipes and the like	-	0.21	5.78	-	nr	5.78
Concrete interlocking tiles; Marley "Mendip" granule finish double pantiles or other equal and approved; PC £715.00/1000; 420 mm x 330 mm; to 75 mm lap; on 22 mm x 38 mm battens and type 1F reinforced underlay						
Roof coverings	-	0.37	10.19	10.94	m^2	21.13
Extra over coverings for						
fixing every tile	-	0.02	0.55	0.81	m^2	1.36
eaves; eaves filler	-	0.02	0.55	0.75	m	1.30
verges; 150 mm wide asbestos free strip undercloak	-	0.24	6.61	1.47	m	8.08
dry verge system; extruded white pvc	-	0.16	4.41	8.57	m	12.98
segmental ridge cap to dry verge	-	0.02	0.55	3.13	m	3.68
valley trough tiles; cutting both sides	-	0.58	15.97	21.82	m	37.80

H CLADDING/COVERING

Item	PC £	Labour hours	Labour £	Material £	Unit	Total rate £
H60 PLAIN ROOF TILING – cont'd						
Concrete interlocking tiles; Marley "Mendip" – cont'd						
Extra over coverings for – cont'd						
segmental ridge tiles	-	0.58	15.97	12.32	m	28.29
segmental hip tiles; cutting both sides	-	0.74	20.38	14.78	m	35.16
dry ridge tiles; segmental including batten sections; unions and filler pieces	-	0.32	8.81	17.26	m	26.07
segmental mono-ridge tiles	-	0.53	14.60	16.89	m	31.48
gas ridge terminal	-	0.53	14.60	67.54	nr	82.14
holes for pipes and the like	-	0.21	5.78	-	nr	5.78
Concrete interlocking tiles; Marley "Modern" smooth finish tiles or other equal and approved; PC £735.00/1000; 420 mm x 220 mm; to 75 mm lap; on 25 mm x 38 mm battens and type 1F reinforced underlay						
Roof coverings	-	0.37	10.19	11.41	m²	21.60
Extra over coverings for						
fixing every tile	-	0.02	0.55	0.81	m²	1.36
verges; 150 mm wide asbestos free strip undercloak	-	0.24	6.61	1.47	m	8.08
dry verge system; extruded white pvc	-	0.21	5.78	8.57	m	14.36
"Modern" ridge cap to dry verge	-	0.02	0.55	3.13	m	3.68
valley trough tiles; cutting both sides	-	0.58	15.97	21.87	m	37.84
"Modern" ridge tiles	-	0.53	14.60	8.85	m	23.44
"Modern" hip tiles; cutting both sides	-	0.69	19.00	11.37	m	30.38
dry ridge tiles; "Modern"; including batten sections; unions and filler pieces	-	0.32	8.81	17.64	m	26.46
"Modern" mono-ridge tiles	-	0.53	14.60	14.96	m	29.56
gas ridge terminal	-	0.53	14.60	67.54	nr	82.14
holes for pipes and the like	-	0.21	5.78	-	nr	5.78
Concrete interlocking tiles; Marley "Wessex" smooth finish tiles or other equal and approved; PC £1,202.00/1000; 413 mm x 330 mm; to 75 mm lap; on 25 mm x 38 mm battens and type 1F reinforced underlay						
Roof coverings	-	0.37	10.19	16.72	m²	26.91
Extra over coverings for						
fixing every tile	-	0.02	0.55	0.81	m²	1.36
verges; 150 mm wide asbestos free strip undercloak	-	0.24	6.61	1.47	m	8.08
dry verge system; extruded white pvc	-	0.21	5.78	8.57	m	14.36
"Modern" ridge cap to dry verge	-	0.02	0.55	3.13	m	3.68
valley trough tiles; cutting both sides	-	0.58	15.97	22.94	m	38.91
"Modern" ridge tiles	-	0.53	14.60	8.85	m	23.44
"Modern" hip tiles; cutting both sides	-	0.69	19.00	12.98	m	31.98
dry ridge tiles; "Modern"; including batten sections; unions and filler pieces	-	0.32	8.81	17.64	m	26.46
"Modern" mono-ridge tiles	-	0.53	14.60	14.96	m	29.56
gas ridge terminal	-	0.53	14.60	67.54	nr	82.14
holes for pipes and the like	-	0.21	5.78	-	nr	5.78

H CLADDING/COVERING

Item	PC £	Labour hours	Labour £	Material £	Unit	Total rate £
Concrete interlocking slates; Redland "Richmond" smooth finish tiles; PC £980.00/ 1000; 430 mm x 380 mm; to 75 mm lap; on 25 mm x 38 mm battens and type 1F reinforced underlay						
Roof coverings	-	0.37	10.19	12.45	m²	**22.64**
Extra over coverings for						
fixing every tile	-	0.02	0.55	0.81	m²	**1.36**
eaves; eaves filler	-	0.02	0.55	5.95	m	**6.50**
verges; extra single undercloak course of plain tiles	-	0.27	7.44	3.86	m	**11.29**
ambi-dry verge system	-	0.21	5.78	11.31	m	**17.09**
ambi-dry verge eave/ridge end piece	-	0.02	0.55	4.03	m	**4.58**
valley trough tiles; cutting both sides	-	0.64	17.63	35.17	m	**52.79**
"Richmond" ridge tiles	-	0.53	14.60	12.18	m	**26.78**
"Richmond" hip tiles; cutting both sides	-	0.69	19.00	15.67	m	**34.67**
"Richmond" mono-ridge tiles	-	0.53	14.60	23.66	m	**38.26**
gas ridge terminal	-	0.53	14.60	72.30	nr	**86.89**
ridge vent with 110 mm diameter flexible adaptor	-	0.53	14.60	86.16	nr	**100.76**
holes for pipes and the like	-	0.21	5.78	-	nr	**5.78**
Concrete interlocking tiles; Redland "Norfolk" smooth finish pantiles; PC £548.00/1000; 381 mm x 229 mm; to 75 mm lap; on 25 mm x 38 mm battens and type 1F reinforced underlay						
Roof coverings	-	0.48	13.22	14.90	m²	**28.12**
Extra over coverings for						
fixing every tile	-	0.05	1.38	0.36	m²	**1.73**
eaves; eaves filler	-	0.05	1.38	1.27	m	**2.64**
verges; extra single undercloak course of plain tiles	-	0.32	8.81	6.76	m	**15.57**
valley trough tiles; cutting both sides	-	0.64	17.63	33.77	m	**51.39**
universal ridge tiles	-	0.53	14.60	12.90	m	**27.50**
universal hip tiles; cutting both sides	-	0.69	19.00	16.15	m	**35.15**
universal gas flue ridge tile	-	0.53	14.60	73.34	nr	**87.94**
universal ridge vent tile with 110 mm diameter adaptor	-	0.53	14.60	87.21	nr	**101.81**
holes for pipes and the like	-	0.21	5.78	-	nr	**5.78**
Concrete interlocking tiles; Redland "Regent" granule finish bold roll tiles; PC £774.00/1000; 418 mm x 332 mm; to 75 mm lap; on 25 mm x 38 mm battens and type 1F reinforced underlay						
Roof coverings	-	0.37	10.19	12.09	m²	**22.28**
Extra over coverings for						
fixing every tile	-	0.04	1.10	0.79	m²	**1.90**
eaves; eaves filler	-	0.05	1.38	0.96	m	**2.33**
verges; extra single undercloak course of plain tiles	-	0.27	7.44	3.19	m	**10.63**
cloaked verge system	-	0.16	4.41	7.62	m	**12.03**
valley trough tiles; cutting both sides	-	0.58	15.97	33.27	m	**49.25**
universal ridge tiles	-	0.53	14.60	12.90	m	**27.50**
universal hip tiles; cutting both sides	-	0.69	19.00	15.65	m	**34.66**
dry ridge system; universal ridge tiles	-	0.27	7.44	42.90	m	**50.34**
universal half round mono-pitch ridge tiles	-	0.58	15.97	27.04	m	**43.02**
universal gas flue ridge tile	-	0.53	14.60	73.34	nr	**87.94**
universal ridge vent tile with 110 mm diameter adaptor	-	0.53	14.60	87.21	nr	**101.81**
holes for pipes and the like	-	0.21	5.78	-	nr	**5.78**

H CLADDING/COVERING

Item	PC £	Labour hours	Labour £	Material £	Unit	Total rate £
H60 PLAIN ROOF TILING – cont'd						
Concrete interlocking tiles; Redland "Renown" granule finish tiles; PC £750.00/1000; 418 mm x 330 mm; to 75 mm lap; on 25 mm x 38 mm battens and type 1F reinforced underlay						
Roof coverings	-	0.37	10.19	11.81	m^2	22.00
Extra over coverings for						
fixing every tile	-	0.02	0.55	0.43	m^2	0.98
verges; extra single undercloak course of plain tiles	-	0.27	7.44	3.86	m	11.29
cloaked verge system	-	0.16	4.41	7.70	m	12.11
valley trough tiles; cutting both sides	-	0.58	15.97	33.19	m	49.16
universal ridge tiles	-	0.53	14.60	12.90	m	27.50
universal hip tiles; cutting both sides	-	0.69	19.00	15.57	m	34.57
dry ridge system; universal ridge tiles	-	0.27	7.44	42.90	m	50.34
universal half round mono-pitch ridge tiles	-	0.58	15.97	27.04	m	43.02
universal gas flue ridge tile	-	0.53	14.60	73.34	nr	87.94
universal ridge vent tile with 110 mm diameter adaptor	-	0.53	14.60	87.21	nr	101.81
holes for pipes and the like	-	0.21	5.78	-	nr	5.78
Concrete interlocking tiles; Redland "Stonewold II" smooth finish tiles; PC £1,470.00/ 1000; 430 mm x 380 mm; to 75 mm lap; on 25 x 38 mm battens and type 1F reinforced underlay						
Roof coverings	-	0.37	10.19	20.35	m^2	30.54
Extra over coverings for						
fixing every tile	-	0.02	0.55	1.45	m^2	2.00
verges; extra single undercloak course of plain tiles	-	0.31	8.54	3.86	m	12.40
ambi-dry verge system	-	0.21	5.78	11.31	m	17.09
ambi-dry verge eave/ridge end piece	-	0.02	0.55	4.03	m	4.58
valley trough tiles; cutting both sides	-	0.58	15.97	35.75	m	51.72
universal angle ridge tiles	-	0.53	14.60	9.58	m	24.18
universal hip tiles; cutting both sides	-	0.69	19.00	14.81	m	33.81
dry ridge system; universal angle ridge tiles	-	0.27	7.44	26.06	m	33.49
universal monopitch angle ridge tiles	-	0.58	15.97	18.38	m	34.35
universal gas flue angle ridge tile	-	0.53	14.60	88.28	nr	102.88
universal angle ridge vent tile with 110 mm diameter adaptor	-	0.53	14.60	86.26	nr	100.86
holes for pipes and the like	-	0.21	5.78	-	nr	5.78
Concrete plain tiles; EN 490 and 491 group A; PC £315.00/1000; 267 mm x 165 mm; on 25 x 38 mm battens and type 1F reinforced underlay						
Roof coverings; to 64 mm lap	-	1.12	30.85	29.51	m^2	60.35
Wall coverings; to 38 mm lap	-	1.33	36.63	25.04	m^2	61.67
Extra over coverings for						
ornamental tiles	-	-	-	18.48	m^2	18.48
double course at eaves	-	0.27	7.44	3.56	m	11.00
verges	-	0.35	9.64	1.42	m	11.06
swept valleys; cutting both sides	-	0.69	19.00	32.58	m	51.58
bonnet hips; cutting both sides	-	0.85	23.41	32.58	m	55.99
external vertical angle tiles; supplementary nail fixings	-	0.43	11.84	23.16	m	35.00
half round ridge tiles	-	0.53	14.60	7.90	m	22.50
third round hip tiles; cutting both sides	-	0.53	14.60	10.14	m	24.74
holes for pipes and the like	-	0.21	5.78	-	nr	5.78

H CLADDING/COVERING

Item	PC £	Labour hours	Labour £	Material £	Unit	Total rate £
Sundries						
Hip irons						
galvanised mild steel; fixing with screws	-	0.11	3.03	3.46	nr	**6.49**
"Rytons Clip strip" or other equal and approved; continuous soffit ventilator						
51 mm wide; plastic; code CS351	-	0.32	8.81	1.13	m	**9.95**
"Rytons over fascia ventilator" or other equal and approved; continuous eaves ventilator						
40 mm wide; plastic; code OFV890	-	0.11	3.03	1.90	m	**4.93**
"Rytons roof ventilator" or other equal and approved; to suit rafters at 600 centres						
250 mm deep x 43 mm high; plastic; code TV600	-	0.11	3.03	1.93	m	**4.95**
"Rytons push and lock ventilators" or other equal and approved; circular						
83 mm diameter; plastic; code PL235	-	0.05	0.91	0.32	nr	**1.23**
Fixing only						
lead soakers (supply cost given elsewhere)	-	0.08	1.53	-	nr	**1.53**
Pressure impregnated softwood counter battens; 25 x 50						
450 mm centres	-	0.07	1.93	1.28	m²	**3.21**
600 mm centres	-	0.05	1.38	0.97	m²	**2.35**
Underlay; BS 747 type 1B; bitumen felt weighing 14kg/10m2; 75 mm laps						
To sloping or vertical surfaces	0.61	0.03	0.83	1.44	m²	**2.27**
Underlay; BS 747 type 1F; reinforced bitumen felt weighing 22.5kg/10 m2; 75 mm laps						
To sloping or vertical surfaces	1.15	0.03	0.83	2.07	m²	**2.90**
Underlay; Visqueen "Tilene 200P" or other equal and approved; micro-perforated sheet; 75 mm laps						
To sloping or vertical surfaces	0.60	0.03	0.83	1.46	m²	**2.28**
Underlay; "Powerlon 250 BM" or other equal and approved; reinforced breather membrane; 75 mm laps						
To sloping or vertical surfaces	0.64	0.03	0.83	1.51	m²	**2.34**
Underlay; "Anticon" sarking membrane or other equal and approved; Euroroof Ltd; polyethylene; 75 mm laps						
To sloping or vertical surfaces	1.08	0.03	0.83	1.99	m²	**2.82**
H61 FIBRE CEMENT SLATING						
Asbestos-free artificial slates; Eternit "Garsdale/E2000T" or other equal and approved; to 75 mm lap; on 19 mm x 50 mm battens and type 1F reinforced underlay						
Coverings; 400 mm x 200 mm slates						
roof coverings	-	0.85	23.41	33.31	m²	**56.72**
wall coverings	-	1.12	30.85	33.31	m²	**64.15**
Coverings; 500 mm x 250 mm slates						
roof coverings	-	0.69	19.00	22.26	m²	**41.26**
wall coverings	-	0.85	23.41	22.26	m²	**45.67**

H CLADDING/COVERING

Item	PC £	Labour hours	Labour £	Material £	Unit	Total rate £
H61 FIBRE CEMENT SLATING – cont'd						
Asbestos-free artificial slates; Eternit						
"Garsdale/E2000T" – cont'd						
Coverings; 600 mm x 300 mm slates						
roof coverings	-	0.53	14.60	18.47	m²	33.06
wall coverings	-	0.69	19.00	18.47	m²	37.47
Extra over slate coverings for						
double course at eaves	-	0.27	7.44	4.49	m	11.93
verges; extra single undercloak course	-	0.35	9.64	0.98	m	10.62
open valleys; cutting both sides	-	0.21	5.78	3.92	m	9.70
valley gutters; cutting both sides	-	0.58	15.97	24.04	m	40.01
half round ridge tiles	-	0.53	14.60	26.42	m	41.02
stop end	-	0.11	3.03	9.38	nr	12.41
roll top ridge tiles	-	0.64	17.63	59.66	m	77.28
stop end	-	0.11	3.03	12.04	nr	15.07
mono-pitch ridge tiles	-	0.53	14.60	33.43	m	48.02
stop end	-	0.11	3.03	36.30	nr	39.33
duo-pitch ridge tiles	-	0.53	14.60	27.06	m	41.66
stop end	-	0.11	3.03	26.62	nr	29.65
mitred hips; cutting both sides	-	0.21	5.78	3.92	m	9.70
half round hip tiles; cutting both sides	-	0.21	5.78	30.33	m	36.12
holes for pipes and the like	-	0.21	5.78	-	nr	5.78
H62 NATURAL SLATING						
NOTE: The following items of slate roofing unless otherwise described, include for conventional fixing assuming "normal exposure" with appropriate nails and/or rivets or clips to pressure impregnated softwood battens fixed with galvanised nails; prices also include for all bedding and pointing at verges, beneath verge tiles etc.						
Natural slates; BS 680 Part 2; Welsh blue;						
uniform size; to 75 mm lap; on 25 mm x 50 mm						
battens and type 1F reinforced underlay						
Coverings; 400 mm x 250 mm slates						
roof coverings	-	0.95	26.16	40.23	m²	66.39
wall coverings	-	1.22	33.60	40.23	m²	73.83
Coverings; 500 mm x 300 mm slates						
roof coverings	-	0.80	22.03	53.91	m²	75.94
wall coverings	-	0.95	26.16	53.91	m²	80.08
Coverings; 600 mm x 300 mm slates						
roof coverings	-	0.64	17.63	70.59	m²	88.21
wall coverings	-	0.80	22.03	70.59	m²	92.62
Extra over coverings for						
double course at eaves	-	0.32	8.81	18.56	m	27.37
verges; extra single undercloak course	-	0.44	12.12	10.86	m	22.98
open valleys; cutting both sides	-	0.23	6.33	42.80	m	49.14
blue/black glazed ware 152 mm half round ridge tiles	-	0.53	14.60	21.89	m	36.49
blue/black glazed ware 125 mm x 125 mm plain angle ridge tiles	-	0.53	14.60	17.50	m	32.09
mitred hips; cutting both sides	-	0.23	6.33	42.80	m	49.14
blue/black glazed ware 152 mm half round hip tiles; cutting both sides	-	0.74	20.38	64.69	m	85.07
blue/black glazed ware 125 mm x 125 mm plain angle hip tiles; cutting both sides	-	0.74	20.38	60.30	m	80.68
holes for pipes and the like	-	0.21	5.78	-	nr	5.78

H CLADDING/COVERING

Item	PC £	Labour hours	Labour £	Material £	Unit	Total rate £
Natural slates; Westmoreland green; PC £2,331.00/tonne; random lengths; 457 mm - 229 mm proportionate widths to 75 mm lap; in diminishing courses; on 25 mm x 50 mm battens and type 1F underlay						
Roof coverings	-	1.22	33.60	155.67	m²	189.28
Wall coverings	-	1.54	42.41	155.67	m²	198.09
Extra over coverings for						
double course at eaves	-	0.70	19.28	28.76	m	48.04
verges; extra single undercloak course slates						
152 mm wide	-	0.80	22.03	25.00	m	47.03
holes for pipes and the like	-	0.32	8.81	-	nr	8.81
H63 RECONSTRUCTED STONE SLATING/ TILING						
Reconstructed stone slates; "Hardrow Slates" or other equal and approved; standard colours; or similar; PC £1,029.00/1000 75 lap; on 25 mm x 50 mm battens and type 1F reinforced underlay						
Coverings; 457 mm x 305 mm slates						
roof coverings	-	0.85	23.41	26.38	m²	49.79
wall coverings	-	1.06	29.19	26.38	m²	55.57
Coverings; 457 mm x 457 mm slates						
roof coverings	-	0.69	19.00	25.91	m²	44.92
wall coverings	-	0.91	25.06	25.91	m²	50.98
Extra over 457 mm x 305 mm coverings for						
double course at eaves	-	0.32	8.81	4.77	m	13.59
verges; pointed	-	0.44	12.12	0.07	m	12.19
open valleys; cutting both sides	-	0.23	6.33	11.47	m	17.80
ridge tiles	-	0.53	14.60	29.08	m	43.68
hip tiles; cutting both sides	-	0.74	20.38	24.55	m	44.93
holes for pipes and the like	-	0.21	5.78	-	nr	5.78
Reconstructed stone slates; "Hardrow Slates" green/oldstone colours or other equal and approved; PC £1,029.00/1000 75 mm lap; on 25 mm x 50 mm battens and type 1F reinforced underlay						
Coverings; 457 mm x 305 mm slates						
roof coverings	-	0.85	23.41	26.38	m²	49.79
wall coverings	-	1.06	29.19	26.38	m²	55.57
Coverings; 457 mm x 457 mm slates						
roof coverings	-	0.69	19.00	25.91	m²	44.92
wall coverings	-	0.91	25.06	25.91	m²	50.98
Extra over 457 mm x 305 mm coverings for						
double course at eaves	-	0.32	8.81	4.77	m	13.59
verges; pointed	-	0.44	12.12	0.07	m	12.19
open valleys; cutting both sides	-	0.23	6.33	11.47	m	17.80
ridge tiles	-	0.53	14.60	29.08	m	43.68
hip tiles; cutting both sides	-	0.74	20.38	24.55	m	44.93
holes for pipes and the like	-	0.21	5.78	-	nr	5.78

H CLADDING/COVERING

Item	PC £	Labour hours	Labour £	Material £	Unit	Total rate £
H63 RECONSTRUCTED STONE SLATING/ TILING – cont'd						
Reconstructed stone slates; Bradstone "Cotswold" style or other equal and approved; random lengths 550 mm - 300 mm; proportional widths; to 80 mm lap; in diminishing courses; on 25 mm x 50 mm battens and type 1F reinforced underlay						
Roof coverings (all-in rate inclusive of eaves and verges)	27.13	1.12	30.85	38.80	m²	69.65
Extra over coverings for						
open valleys/mitred hips; cutting both sides	-	0.48	13.22	14.47	m²	27.69
ridge tiles	-	0.70	19.28	19.24	m	38.52
hip tiles; cutting both sides	-	1.12	30.85	32.70	m	63.55
holes for pipes and the like	-	0.32	8.81	-	nr	8.81
Reconstructed stone slates; Bradstone "Moordale" style or other equal and approved; random lengths 550 mm - 450 mm; proportional widths; to 80 lap; in diminishing course; on 25 mm x 50 mm battens and type 1F reinforced underlay						
Roof coverings (all-in rate inclusive of eaves and verges)	25.53	1.12	30.85	36.90	m²	67.75
Extra over coverings for						
open valleys/mitred hips; cutting both sides	-	0.48	13.22	13.62	m²	26.84
ridge tiles	-	0.70	19.28	19.24	m	38.52
holes for pipes and the like	-	0.32	8.81	-	nr	8.81
H64 TIMBER SHINGLING						
Red cedar sawn shingles preservative treated; PC £36.92/bundle; uniform length 400 mm; to 125 mm gauge; on 25 mm x 38 mm battens and type 1F reinforced underlay						
Roof coverings; 125 mm gauge, 2.28 m2/bundle	-	1.12	30.85	23.05	m²	53.90
Wall coverings; 190 mm gauge, 3.47 m2/bundle	-	0.85	23.41	15.70	m²	39.11
Extra over coverings for						
double course at eaves	1.83	0.21	5.78	2.28	m	8.06
open valleys; cutting both sides	3.66	0.21	5.78	4.24	m	10.02
pre-formed ridge capping	-	0.32	8.81	7.60	m	16.41
pre-formed hip capping; cutting both sides	-	0.53	14.60	11.84	m	26.43
double starter course to cappings	-	0.11	3.03	0.80	m	3.83
holes for pipes and the like	-	0.16	4.41	-	nr	4.41
H71 LEAD SHEET COVERINGS/FLASHINGS						
Milled lead; BS 1178; PC £850.00/t						
1.32 mm thick (code 3) roof coverings						
flat	-	2.88	55.20	14.97	m²	70.17
sloping 10 - 50 degrees	-	3.19	61.14	14.97	m²	76.11
vertical or sloping over 50 degrees	-	3.51	67.27	14.97	m²	82.24
1.80 mm thick (code 4) roof coverings						
flat	-	3.08	59.03	20.42	m²	79.45
sloping 10 - 50 degrees	-	3.40	65.17	20.42	m²	85.58
vertical or sloping over 50 degrees	-	3.73	71.49	20.42	m²	91.91

H CLADDING/COVERING

Item	PC £	Labour hours	Labour £	Material £	Unit	Total rate £
1.80 mm thick (code 4) dormer coverings						
flat	-	3.62	69.38	20.42	m²	89.80
sloping 10 - 50 degrees	-	4.15	79.54	20.42	m²	99.96
vertical or sloping over 50 degrees	-	4.47	85.67	20.42	m²	106.09
2.24 mm thick (code 5) roof coverings						
flat	-	3.29	63.06	27.22	m²	90.28
sloping 10 - 50 degrees	-	3.62	69.38	27.22	m²	96.60
vertical or sloping over 50 degrees	-	3.93	75.32	27.22	m²	102.55
2.24 mm thick (code 5) dormer coverings						
flat	-	3.93	75.32	27.22	m²	102.55
sloping 10 - 50 degrees	-	4.36	83.56	27.22	m²	110.79
vertical or sloping over 50 degrees	-	4.78	91.61	27.22	m²	118.84
2.65 mm thick (code 6) roof coverings						
flat	-	3.51	67.27	30.06	m²	97.33
sloping 10 - 50 degrees	-	3.83	73.41	30.06	m²	103.47
vertical or sloping over 50 degrees	-	4.15	79.54	30.06	m²	109.60
2.65 mm thick (code 6) dormer coverings						
flat	-	4.26	81.65	30.06	m²	111.71
sloping 10 - 50 degrees	-	4.57	87.59	30.06	m²	117.65
vertical or sloping over 50 degrees	-	5.00	95.83	30.06	m²	125.89
3.15 mm thick (code 7) roof coverings						
flat	-	3.73	71.49	35.73	m²	107.22
sloping 10 - 50 degrees	-	4.04	77.43	35.73	m²	113.16
vertical or sloping over 50 degrees	-	4.36	83.56	35.73	m²	119.30
3.15 mm thick (code 7) dormer coverings						
flat	-	4.47	85.67	35.73	m²	121.40
sloping 10 - 50 degrees	-	4.78	91.61	35.73	m²	127.34
vertical or sloping over 50 degrees	-	5.22	100.05	35.73	m²	135.78
3.55 mm thick (code 8) roof coverings						
flat	-	3.93	75.32	40.27	m²	115.59
sloping 10 - 50 degrees	-	4.26	81.65	40.27	m²	121.92
vertical or sloping over 50 degrees	-	4.57	87.59	40.27	m²	127.86
3.55 mm thick (code 8) dormer coverings						
flat	-	4.78	91.61	40.27	m²	131.88
sloping 10 - 50 degrees	-	5.11	97.94	40.27	m²	138.21
vertical or sloping over 50 degrees	-	5.53	105.99	40.27	m²	146.26
Dressing over glazing bars and glass	-	0.35	6.71	-	m	6.71
Soldered dot	-	0.16	3.07	-	nr	3.07
Copper nailing 75 mm centres	-	0.21	4.02	0.49	m	4.51
1.80 mm thick (code 4) lead flashings, etc.						
Flashings; wedging into grooves						
150 mm girth	-	0.85	16.29	4.49	m	20.78
240 mm girth	-	0.95	18.21	7.16	m	25.37
Stepped flashings; wedging into grooves						
180 mm girth	-	0.95	18.21	5.34	m	23.55
270 mm girth	-	1.06	20.32	8.01	m	28.32
Linings to sloping gutters						
390 mm girth	-	1.28	24.53	11.65	m	36.18
450 mm girth	-	1.38	26.45	13.35	m	39.80
750 mm girth	-	1.28	24.53	15.31	m	39.85
Cappings to hips or ridges						
450 mm girth	-	1.60	30.67	13.35	m	44.01
600 mm girth	-	1.70	32.58	17.84	m	50.42
Soakers						
200 mm x 200 mm	-	0.16	3.07	0.82	nr	3.88
300 mm x 300 mm	-	0.21	4.02	1.84	nr	5.86

H CLADDING/COVERING

Item	PC £	Labour hours	Labour £	Material £	Unit	Total rate £
H71 LEAD SHEET COVERINGS/FLASHINGS – cont'd						
1.80 mm thick (code 4) lead flashings, etc. – cont'd						
Saddle flashings; at intersections of hips and ridges; dressing and bossing						
450 mm x 600 mm	-	1.91	36.61	8.01	nr	**44.62**
Slates; with 150 mm high collar						
450 mm x 450 mm; to suit 50 mm diameter pipe	-	1.81	34.69	6.90	nr	**41.60**
450 mm x 450 mm; to suit 100 mm diameter pipe	-	2.13	40.82	7.58	nr	**48.40**
2.24 mm (code 5) lead flashings, etc.						
Flashings; wedging into grooves						
150 mm girth	-	0.85	16.29	5.58	m	**21.87**
240 mm girth	-	0.95	18.21	8.86	m	**27.07**
Stepped flashings; wedging into grooves						
180 mm girth	-	0.95	18.21	6.67	m	**24.88**
270 mm girth	-	1.06	20.32	9.95	m	**30.27**
Linings to sloping gutters						
390 mm girth	-	1.28	24.53	14.44	m	**38.97**
450 mm girth	-	1.38	26.45	16.62	m	**43.07**
Cappings to hips or ridges						
450 mm girth	-	1.60	30.67	16.62	m	**47.29**
600 mm girth	-	1.70	32.58	22.21	m	**54.79**
Soakers						
200 mm x 200 mm	-	0.16	3.07	1.09	nr	**4.16**
300 mm x 300 mm	-	0.21	4.02	2.45	nr	**6.47**
Saddle flashings; at intersections of hips and ridges; dressing and bossing						
450 mm x 600 mm	-	1.91	36.61	9.97	nr	**46.58**
Slates; with 150 mm high collar						
450 mm x 450 mm; to suit 50 mm diameter pipe	-	1.81	34.69	8.60	nr	**43.29**
450 mm x 450 mm; to suit 100 mm diameter pipe	-	2.13	40.82	9.43	nr	**50.26**
H72 ALUMINIUM SHEET COVERINGS/ FLASHINGS						
Aluminium roofing; commercial grade						
0.90 mm thick roof coverings						
flat	-	3.19	61.14	7.75	m²	**68.89**
sloping 10 - 50 degrees	-	3.52	67.47	7.75	m²	**75.22**
vertical or sloping over 50 degrees	-	3.84	73.60	7.75	m²	**81.35**
0.90 mm thick dormer coverings						
flat	-	3.84	73.60	7.75	m²	**81.35**
sloping 10 - 50 degrees	-	4.26	81.65	7.75	m²	**89.40**
vertical or sloping over 50 degrees	-	4.67	89.51	7.75	m²	**97.26**
Aluminium nailing; 75 mm spacing	-	0.21	4.02	0.36	m	**4.38**
0.90 mm commercial grade aluminium flashings, etc.						
Flashings; wedging into grooves						
150 mm girth	-	0.85	16.29	1.21	m	**17.50**
240 mm girth	-	0.97	18.59	1.96	m	**20.55**
300 mm girth	-	1.11	21.27	2.39	m	**23.66**
Stepped flashings; wedging into grooves						
180 mm girth	-	0.97	18.59	1.42	m	**20.02**
270 mm girth	-	1.06	20.32	2.23	m	**22.54**

H CLADDING/COVERING

Item	PC £	Labour hours	Labour £	Material £	Unit	Total rate £
1.20 mm commercial grade aluminium flashings; polyester powder coated						
Flashings; fixed with self tapping screws						
170 mm girth	-	0.97	18.59	1.66	m	**20.25**
200 mm girth	-	1.02	19.55	2.20	m	**21.75**
280 mm girth	-	1.16	22.23	2.88	m	**25.12**
Aluminium Alumasc "Skyline" coping system; polyester powder coated						
Coping; fixing straps plugged and screwed to brickwork						
362 mm wide; for parapet wall						
271 - 300 mm wide	-	0.58	11.12	24.47	m	**35.58**
Extra for						
90 degree bend	-	0.28	5.37	58.30	nr	**63.66**
90 degree tee junction	-	0.40	7.67	62.55	nr	**70.21**
stop end	-	0.17	3.26	34.47	nr	**37.73**
stop end upstand	-	0.23	4.41	37.40	nr	**41.81**
H73 COPPER STRIP/SHEET COVERINGS/ FLASHINGS						
Copper roofing; BS 2870						
0.56 mm thick (24 swg) roof coverings						
flat	23.02	3.42	65.55	27.28	m²	**92.83**
sloping 10 - 50 degrees	-	3.75	71.87	27.28	m²	**99.16**
vertical or sloping over 50 degrees	-	4.02	77.05	27.28	m²	**104.33**
0.56 mm thick (24 swg) dormer coverings						
flat	23.02	4.02	77.05	27.28	m²	**104.33**
sloping 10 - 50 degrees	-	4.49	86.06	27.28	m²	**113.34**
vertical or sloping over 50 degrees	-	4.90	93.91	27.28	m²	**121.20**
0.61 mm thick (23 swg) roof coverings						
flat	-	3.42	65.55	29.83	m²	**95.37**
sloping 10 - 50 degrees	-	3.75	71.87	29.83	m²	**101.70**
vertical or sloping over 50 degrees	-	4.02	77.05	29.83	m²	**106.87**
0.61 mm thick (23 swg) dormer coverings						
flat	-	4.02	77.05	29.83	m²	**106.87**
sloping 10 - 50 degrees	-	4.49	86.06	29.83	m²	**115.88**
vertical or sloping over 50 degrees	-	4.90	93.91	29.83	m²	**123.74**
Copper nailing; 75 mm spacing	-	0.21	4.02	0.49	m	**4.51**
0.56 mm thick copper flashings, etc.						
Flashings; wedging into grooves						
150 mm girth	-	0.85	16.29	4.28	m	**20.57**
240 mm girth	-	0.97	18.59	6.88	m	**25.47**
300 mm girth	-	1.11	21.27	8.63	m	**29.91**
Stepped flashings; wedging into grooves						
180 mm girth	-	0.97	18.59	5.19	m	**23.78**
270 mm girth	-	1.06	20.32	7.75	m	**28.06**
0.61 mm thick copper flashings, etc.						
Flashings; wedging into grooves						
150 mm girth	-	0.85	16.29	4.66	m	**20.95**
240 mm girth	-	0.97	18.59	7.50	m	**26.10**
300 mm girth	-	1.11	21.27	9.38	m	**30.65**
Stepped flashings; wedging into grooves						
180 mm girth	-	0.97	18.59	5.63	m	**24.22**
270 mm girth	-	1.06	20.32	8.43	m	**28.74**

H CLADDING/COVERING

Item	PC £	Labour hours	Labour £	Material £	Unit	Total rate £
H74 ZINC STRIP/SHEET COVERINGS/ FLASHINGS						
Zinc; BS 849						
0.80 mm roof coverings						
flat	-	3.42	65.55	17.93	m²	83.47
sloping 10 - 50 degrees	-	3.75	71.87	17.93	m²	89.80
vertical or sloping over 50 degrees	-	4.02	77.05	17.93	m²	94.97
0.61 mm thick (23 swg) dormer coverings						
flat	-	4.02	77.05	17.93	m²	94.97
sloping 10 - 50 degrees	-	4.49	86.06	17.93	m²	103.98
vertical or sloping over 50 degrees	-	4.90	93.91	17.93	m²	111.84
0.80 mm thick zinc flashings, etc.						
Flashings; wedging into grooves						
150 mm girth	-	0.85	16.29	2.78	m	19.07
240 mm girth	-	0.97	18.59	4.50	m	23.09
300 mm girth	-	1.11	21.27	5.67	m	26.94
Stepped flashings; wedging into grooves						
180 mm girth	-	0.97	18.59	3.40	m	21.99
270 mm girth	-	1.06	20.32	5.07	m	25.39
H76 FIBRE BITUMEN THERMOPLASTIC SHEET COVERINGS/FLASHINGS						
Glass fibre reinforced bitumen strip slates; "Ruberglas 105" or other equal and approved; 1000 mm x 336 mm mineral finish; to external quality plywood boarding (boarding not included)						
Roof coverings	-	0.27	7.44	15.03	m²	22.46
Wall coverings	-	0.43	11.84	15.03	m²	26.87
Extra over coverings for						
double course at eaves; felt soaker	-	0.21	5.78	10.09	m	15.88
verges; felt soaker	-	0.16	4.41	8.37	m	12.77
valley slate; cut to shape; felt soaker and cutting						
both sides	-	0.48	13.22	13.26	m	26.48
ridge slate; cut to shape	-	0.32	8.81	8.37	m	17.18
hip slate; cut to shape; felt soaker andcutting						
both sides	-	0.48	13.22	13.12	m	26.34
holes for pipes and the like	-	0.56	15.42	-	nr	15.42
Evode "Flashband Original" sealing strips and flashings or other equal and approved; special grey finish						
Flashings; wedging at top if required; pressure bonded; flashband primer before application; to walls						
75 mm girth	-	0.18	3.45	1.18	m	4.63
100 mm girth	-	0.27	5.17	1.61	m	6.79
150 mm girth	-	0.35	6.71	2.41	m	9.12
225 mm girth	-	0.43	8.24	3.77	m	12.01
300 mm girth	-	0.48	9.20	4.74	m	13.94

J WATERPROOFING

Item	PC £	Labour hours	Labour £	Material £	Unit	Total rate £
J10 SPECIALIST WATERPROOF RENDERING						
"Sika" waterproof rendering or other						
equal and approved; steel trowelled						
20 mm work to walls; three coat; to concrete base						
over 300 mm wide	-	-	-	-	m^2	46.73
not exceeding 300 mm wide	-	-	-	-	m^2	72.98
25 mm work to walls; three coat; to concrete base						
over 300 mm wide	-	-	-	-	m^2	53.13
not exceeding 300 mm wide	-	-	-	-	m^2	83.22
40 mm work to walls; four coat; to concrete base						
over 300 mm wide	-	-	-	-	m^2	79.38
not exceeding 300 mm wide	-	-	-	-	m^2	128.02
J20 MASTIC ASPHALT TANKING/DAMP PROOF MEMBRANES						
Mastic asphalt to BS 6925 Type T 1097						
13 mm thick one coat coverings to concrete base; flat; subsequently covered						
over 300 mm wide	-	-	-	-	m^2	9.89
225 mm - 300 mm wide	-	-	-	-	m^2	23.48
150 mm - 225 mm wide	-	-	-	-	m^2	25.82
not exceeding 150 mm wide	-	-	-	-	m^2	32.21
20 mm thick two coat coverings to concrete base; flat; subsequently covered						
over 300 mm wide	-	-	-	-	m^2	14.30
225 mm - 300 mm wide	-	-	-	-	m^2	26.13
150 mm - 225 mm wide	-	-	-	-	m^2	28.53
not exceeding 150 mm wide	-	-	-	-	m^2	34.87
30 mm thick three coat coverings to concrete base; flat; subsequently covered						
over 300 mm wide	-	-	-	-	m^2	20.45
225 mm - 300 mm wide	-	-	-	-	m^2	29.69
150 mm - 225 mm wide	-	-	-	-	m^2	32.21
not exceeding 150 mm wide	-	-	-	-	m^2	38.42
13 mm thick two coat coverings to brickwork base; vertical; subsequently covered						
over 300 mm wide	-	-	-	-	m^2	39.72
225 mm - 300 mm wide	-	-	-	-	m^2	48.46
150 mm - 225 mm wide	-	-	-	-	m^2	57.25
not exceeding 150 mm wide	-	-	-	-	m^2	74.20
20 mm thick three coat coverings to brickwork base; vertical; subsequently covered						
over 300 mm wide	-	-	-	-	m^2	62.17
225 mm - 300 mm wide	-	-	-	-	m^2	66.89
150 mm - 225 mm wide	-	-	-	-	m^2	71.04
not exceeding 150 mm wide	-	-	-	-	m^2	91.86
Turning into groove 20 mm deep	-	-	-	-	m	0.78
Internal angle fillets; subsequently covered	-	-	-	-	m	4.59

J WATERPROOFING

Item	PC £	Labour hours	Labour £	Material £	Unit	Total rate £
J21 MASTIC ASPHALT ROOFING/ INSULATION/FINISHES						
Mastic asphalt to BS 6925 Type R 988						
20 mm thick two coat coverings; felt isolating membrane; to concrete (or timber) base; flat or to falls or slopes not exceeding 10 degrees from horizontal						
over 300 mm wide	-	-	-	-	m^2	14.10
225 mm - 300 mm wide	-	-	-	-	m^2	25.88
150 mm - 225 mm wide	-	-	-	-	m^2	28.66
not exceeding 150 mm wide	-	-	-	-	m^2	34.61
Add to the above for covering with:						
10 mm thick limestone chippings in hot bitumen	-	-	-	-	m^2	2.78
coverings with solar reflective paint	-	-	-	-	m^2	2.52
300 mm x 300 mm x 8 mm g.r.p. tiles in hot bitumen	-	-	-	-	m^2	36.95
Cutting to line; jointing to old asphalt	-	-	-	-	m	6.21
13 mm thick two coat skirtings to brickwork base						
not exceeding 150 mm girth	-	-	-	-	m	11.07
150 mm - 225 mm girth	-	-	-	-	m	12.75
225 mm - 300 mm girth	-	-	-	-	m	14.30
13 mm thick three coat skirtings; expanded metal lathing reinforcement nailed to timber base						
not exceeding 150 mm girth	-	-	-	-	m	17.53
150 mm - 225 mm girth	-	-	-	-	m	20.70
225 mm - 300 mm girth	-	-	-	-	m	24.14
13 mm thick two coat fascias to concrete base						
not exceeding 150 mm girth	-	-	-	-	m	11.07
150 mm - 225 mm girth	-	-	-	-	m	12.75
20 mm thick two coat linings to channels to concrete base						
not exceeding 150 mm girth	-	-	-	-	m	27.04
150 mm - 225 mm girth	-	-	-	-	m	28.66
225 mm - 300 mm girth	-	-	-	-	m	32.36
20 mm thick two coat lining to cesspools						
250 mm x 150 mm x 150 mm deep	-	-	-	-	nr	26.26
Collars around pipes, standards and like members	-	-	-	-	nr	12.75
Accessories						
Eaves trim; extruded aluminium alloy; working asphalt into trim						
"Alutrim"; type A roof edging or other equal and approved	-	-	-	-	m	12.29
extra; angle	-	-	-	-	nr	6.86
Roof screed ventilator - aluminium alloy						
"Extr-aqua-vent" or other equal and approved; set on screed over and including dished sinking; working collar around ventilator	-	-	-	-	nr	23.81
J30 LIQUID APPLIED TANKING/DAMP PROOF MEMBRANES						
Tanking and damp proofing						
"Synthaprufe"or other equal and approved; blinding with sand; horizontal on slabs						
two coats	-	0.20	2.68	3.62	m^2	6.29
three coats	-	0.29	3.88	5.36	m^2	9.24

J WATERPROOFING

Item	PC £	Labour hours	Labour £	Material £	Unit	Total rate £
"Tretolastex 202T" or other equal and approved; on vertical surfaces of concrete						
two coats	-	0.20	2.68	0.67	m²	3.34
three coats	-	0.29	3.88	1.00	m²	4.88
One coat Vandex "Super" 0.75 kg/m² slurry or other equal and approved; one consolidating coat of Vandex "Premix" 1 kg/m2 slurry or simiar; horizontal on beds						
over 225 mm wide	-	0.36	4.82	3.21	m²	8.02
J40 FLEXIBLE SHEET TANKING/DAMP PROOF MEMBRANES						
Tanking and damp proofing						
Visqueen self-adhesive damp proof membrane						
over 300 mm wide; horizontal	-	-	-	-	m²	7.10
not exceeding 300 mm wide; horizontal	-	-	-	-	m	2.73
Tanking primer for self-adhesive dpm						
over 300 mm wide; horizontal	-	-	-	-	m²	4.91
not exceeding 300 mm wide; horizontal	-	-	-	-	m	2.25
"Bituthene" sheeting or other equal and approved; lapped joints; horizontal on slabs						
3000 grade	-	0.10	1.34	5.97	m²	7.31
8000 grade	-	0.11	1.47	8.29	m²	9.76
500HD heavy duty grade	-	0.13	1.74	7.89	m²	9.63
"Bituthene" sheeting or other equal and approved; lapped joints; dressed up vertical face of concrete						
8000 grade	-	0.19	2.54	8.29	m²	10.83
RIW "Structureseal" tanking and damp proof membrane; or other equal and approved						
over 300 mm wide; horizontal	-	-	-	-	m²	8.84
"Structureseal" Fillet						
40 mm x 40mm	-	-	-	-	m	6.48
Ruberoid "Plasprufe 2000SA" self-adhesive damp proof membrane						
over 300 mm wide; horizontal	-	-	-	-	m²	13.53
not exceeding 300 mm wide; horizontal	-	-	-	-	m	5.19
Extra for 50 mm thick sand blinding	-	-	-	-	m²	2.37
"Servi-pak" protection board or other equal and approved; butt jointed; taped joints; to horizontal surfaces;						
3 mm thick	-	0.16	2.14	6.33	m²	8.47
6 mm thick	-	0.16	2.14	9.47	m²	11.61
12 mm thick	-	0.20	2.68	16.73	m²	19.41
"Servi-pak" protection board or other equal and approved; butt jointed; taped joints; to vertical surfaces						
3 mm thick	-	0.20	2.68	6.33	m²	9.00
6 mm thick	-	0.20	2.68	9.47	m²	12.15
12 mm thick	-	0.26	3.48	16.73	m²	20.21
"Bituthene" reinforcing strip or other equal and approved; 300 mm wide						
Bitutape 4000	-	0.10	1.34	2.49	m	3.82
Expandite "Famflex" hot bitumen bonded waterproof tanking or other equal and approved; 150 mm laps						
horizontal; over 300 mm wide	-	0.41	5.48	15.41	m²	20.90
vertical; over 300 mm wide	-	0.67	8.96	15.41	m²	24.38

J WATERPROOFING

Item	PC £	Labour hours	Labour £	Material £	Unit	Total rate £
J41 BUILT UP FELT ROOF COVERINGS						
NOTE: The following items of felt roofing, unless otherwise described, include for conventional lapping, laying and bonding between layers and to base; and laying flat or to falls, to crossfalls or to slopes not exceeding 10 degrees - but exclude any insulation etc.						
Felt roofing; BS 747; suitable for flat roofs						
Three layer coverings first layer type 3G; subsequent layers type 3B bitumen glass fibre based felt	-	-	-	-	m^2	9.79
Extra over felt for covering with and bedding in hot bitumen						
13 mm thick stone chippings	-	-	-	-	m^2	3.22
300 mm x 300 mm x 8 mm g.r.p. tiles	-	-	-	-	m^2	54.13
working into outlet pipes and the like	-	-	-	-	m^2	13.33
Skirtings; three layer; top layer mineral surfaced; dressed over tilting fillet; turned into groove						
not exceeding 200 mm girth	-	-	-	-	m	9.86
200 mm - 400 mm girth	-	-	-	-	m	11.81
Coverings to kerbs; three layer						
400 mm - 600 mm girth	-	-	-	-	m	24.88
Linings to gutters; three layer						
400 mm - 600 mm girth	-	-	-	-	m	16.86
Collars around pipes and the like; three layer mineral surface; 150 mm high						
not exceeding 55 mm nominal size	-	-	-	-	nr	11.24
55 mm - 110 mm nominal size	-	-	-	-	nr	11.24
Three layer coverings; two base layers type 5U bitumen polyester based felt; top layer type 5B polyester based mineral surfaced felt; 10 mm stone chipping covering; bitumen bonded	-	-	-	-	m^2	20.72
Coverings to kerbs						
not exceeding 200 mm girth	-	-	-	-	m	13.01
200 mm - 400 mm girth	-	-	-	-	m	16.35
Outlets and dishing to gullies						
300 mm diameter	-	-	-	-	nr	13.33
"Andersons" high performance polyester-based roofing system or other equal and approved						
Two layer coverings; first layer HT 125 underlay; second layer HT 350; fully bonded to wood; fibre or cork base	-	-	-	-	m^2	14.77
Extra over for						
top layer mineral surfaced	-	-	-	-	m^2	2.85
13 mm thick stone chippings	-	-	-	-	m^2	3.22
third layer of type 3B as underlay for concrete or screeded base	-	-	-	-	m^2	2.85
working into outlet pipes and the like	-	-	-	-	nr	13.33
Skirtings; two layer; top layer mineral surfaced; dressed over tilting fillet; turned into groove						
not exceeding 200 mm girth	-	-	-	-	m	10.48
200 mm - 400 mm girth	-	-	-	-	m	12.63
Coverings to kerbs; two layer						
400 mm - 600 mm girth	-	-	-	-	m	29.36

J WATERPROOFING

Item	PC £	Labour hours	Labour £	Material £	Unit	Total rate £
Linings to gutters; three layer						
400 mm - 600 mm girth	-	-	-	-	m	21.54
Collars around pipes and the like; two layer; 150 high						
not exceeding 55 mm nominal size	-	-	-	-	nr	11.24
55 mm - 110 mm nominal size	-	-	-	-	nr	11.24
"Ruberglas 120 GP" high performance roofing or other equal and approved						
Two layer coverings; first and second layers "Ruberglas 120 GP"; fully bonded to wood, fibre or cork base	-	-	-	-	m²	9.15
Extra over for						
top layer mineral surfaced	-	-	-	-	m²	2.85
13 mm thick stone chippings	-	-	-	-	m²	3.22
third layer of "Rubervent 3G" as underlay for concrete or screeded base	-	-	-	-	m²	2.85
working into outlet pipes and the like	-	-	-	-	nr	13.33
Skirtings; two layer; top layer mineral surfaced; dressed over tilting fillet; turned into groove						
not exceeding 200 mm girth	-	-	-	-	m	9.15
200 mm - 400 mm girth	-	-	-	-	m	10.62
Coverings to kerbs; two layer						
400 mm - 600 mm girth	-	-	-	-	m	18.30
Linings to gutters; three layer						
400 mm - 600 mm girth	-	-	-	-	m	15.15
Collars around pipes and the like; two layer, 150 mm high						
not exceeding 55 mm nominal size	-	-	-	-	nr	11.24
55 mm - 110 mm nominal size	-	-	-	-	nr	11.24
"Ruberfort HP 350" high performance roofing or other equal and approved						
Two layer coverings; first layer "Ruberfort HP 180"; second layer "Ruberfort HP 350"; fully bonded; to wood; fibre or cork base	-	-	-	-	m²	14.15
Extra over for						
top layer mineral surfaced	-	-	-	-	m²	2.85
13 mm thick stone chippings	-	-	-	-	m²	3.22
third layer of "Rubervent 3G"; as underlay for concrete or screeded base	-	-	-	-	m²	2.97
working into outlet pipes and the like	-	-	-	-	nr	13.33
Skirtings; two layer; top layer mineral surface; dressed over tilting fillet; turned into groove						
not exceeding 200 mm girth	-	-	-	-	m	10.10
200 mm - 400 mm girth	-	-	-	-	m	11.93
Coverings to kerbs; two layer						
400 mm - 600 mm girth	-	-	-	-	m	28.36
Linings to gutters; three layer						
400 mm - 600 mm girth	-	-	-	-	m	20.39
Collars around pipes and the like; two layer; 150 mm high						
not exceeding 55 mm nominal size	-	-	-	-	nr	11.24
55 mm - 110 mm nominal size	-	-	-	-	nr	11.24

J WATERPROOFING

Item	PC £	Labour hours	Labour £	Material £	Unit	Total rate £
J41 BUILT UP FELT ROOF COVERINGS – cont'd						
"Polybit 350" elastomeric roofing or other equal or applied						
Two layer coverings; first layer "Polybit 180"; second layer "Polybit 350"; fully bonded to wood; fibre or cork base	-	-	-	-	m²	14.46
Extra over for						
top layer mineral surfaced	-	-	-	-	m²	2.85
13 mm thick stone chippings	-	-	-	-	m²	3.22
third layer of "Rubervent 3G" as underlay for concrete or screeded base	-	-	-	-	m²	2.85
working into outlet pipes and the like	-	-	-	-	nr	13.33
Skirtings; two layer; top layer mineral surfaced; dressed over tilting fillet; turned into groove						
not exceeding 200 mm girth	-	-	-	-	m	10.35
200 mm - 400 mm girth	-	-	-	-	m	12.38
Coverings to kerbs; two layer						
400 mm - 600 mm girth	-	-	-	-	m	28.97
Linings to gutters; three layer						
400 mm - 600 mm girth	-	-	-	-	m	21.03
Collars around pipes and the like; two layer; 150 mm high						
not exceeding 55 mm nominal size	-	-	-	-	nr	11.24
55 mm - 110 mm nominal size	-	-	-	-	nr	11.24
"Hyload 150 E" elastomeric roofing or other equal and approved						
Two layer coverings; first layer "Ruberglas 120 GHP"; second layer "Hyload 150 E" fully bonded to wood; fibre or cork base	-	-	-	-	m²	29.56
Extra over for						
13 mm thick stone chippings	-	-	-	-	m²	3.22
third layer of "Rubervent 3G" as underlay for concrete or screeded base	-	-	-	-	m²	2.85
working into outlet pipes and the like	-	-	-	-	nr	13.26
Skirtings; two layer; dressed over tilting fillet; turned into groove						
not exceeding 200 mm girth	-	-	-	-	m	16.60
200 mm - 400 mm girth	-	-	-	-	m	27.03
Coverings to kerbs; two layer						
400 mm - 600 mm girth	-	-	-	-	m	55.13
Linings to gutters; three layer						
400 mm - 600 mm girth	-	-	-	-	m	36.56
Collars around pipes and the like; two layer; 150 high						
not exceeding 55 mm nominal size	-	-	-	-	nr	11.24
55 mm - 110 mm nominal size	-	-	-	-	nr	11.24
Accessories						
Eaves trim; extruded aluminium alloy; working felt into trim						
"Alutrim"; type F roof edging or other equal and approved	-	-	-	-	m	9.25
extra over for external angle	-	-	-	-	nr	12.53
Roof screed ventilator - aluminium alloy						
"Extr-aqua-vent" or other equal and approved - set on screed over and including dished sinking and collar	-	-	-	-	nr	27.62

J WATERPROOFING

Item	PC £	Labour hours	Labour £	Material £	Unit	Total rate £
Insulation board underlays						
Vapour barrier						
reinforced; metal lined	-	-	-	-	m²	13.33
Cork boards; density 112 - 125 kg/ m³						
60 mm thick	-	-	-	-	m²	17.46
Rockwool; slab RW4 or other equal and approved						
60 mm thick	-	-	-	-	m²	21.16
Perlite boards or other equal and approved; density 170 - 180 kg/ m³						
60 mm thick	-	-	-	-	m²	27.62
Polyurethane boards; density 32 kg/ m³						
30 mm thick	-	-	-	-	m²	10.95
35 mm thick	-	-	-	-	m²	11.46
50 mm thick	-	-	-	-	m²	12.82
Wood fibre boards; impregnated; density 220 - 350 kg/ m³						
12.70 mm thick	-	-	-	-	m²	4.82
Insulation board overlays						
Dow "Roofmate SL" extruded polystyrene foam boards or other equal and approved						
50 mm thick	-	0.32	8.81	16.17	m²	24.98
75 mm thick	-	0.32	8.81	22.12	m²	30.93
Dow "Roofmate LG" extruded polystyrene foam boards or other equal and approved						
60 mm thick	-	0.32	8.81	29.01	m²	37.82
90 mm thick	-	0.32	8.81	32.92	m²	41.73
110 mm thick	-	0.32	8.81	36.39	m²	45.20
Dow "Roofmate PR" extruded polystyrene foam boards or other equal and approved						
90 mm thick	-	0.32	8.81	24.91	m²	33.72
120 mm thick	-	0.32	8.81	33.19	m²	42.00
J42 SINGLE LAYER PLASTICS ROOF COVERINGS						
"Trocal S" PVC roofing or other equal and approved						
Coverings	-	-	-	-	m²	18.44
Skirtings; dressed over metal upstands						
not exceeding 200 mm girth	-	-	-	-	m	14.33
200 mm - 400 mm girth	-	-	-	-	m	17.61
Coverings to kerbs						
400 mm - 600 mm girth	-	-	-	-	m	32.23
Collars around pipes and the like; 150 mm high						
not exceeding 55 mm nominal size	-	-	-	-	nr	9.85
55 mm - 110 mm nominal size	-	-	-	-	nr	9.85
"Trocal" metal upstands or other equal and approved						
not exceeding 200 mm girth	-	-	-	-	m	10.44
200 mm - 400 mm girth	-	-	-	-	m	13.55

J WATERPROOFING

Item	PC £	Labour hours	Labour £	Material £	Unit	Total rate £
J42 SINGLE LAYER PLASTICS ROOF COVERINGS – cont'd						
Sarnafil G410 - 12LEF light grey polyester reinforced fleece lined single layer roofing material fully adhered to and including SarnaTherm 90 mm insulation board on Sarnavap 1000 gauge polythene vapour control layer						
Roof coverings; to concrete base						
1.2 mm gauge	-	-	-	-	m^2	34.26
1.5 mm gauge	-	-	-	-	m^2	37.88
1.8 mm gauge	-	-	-	-	m^2	41.12
Extra over for						
welded pvc cord to perimeters	-	-	-	-	m	1.07
Sarnabars for direct fixing to trapezoidal metal decking centrally at 3.2m spacings one way and at 1.61 m spacings at perimeters	-	-	-	-	m	6.54
movement joint	-	-	-	-	m	27.70
Sarnatred walkway tiles	-	-	-	-	m	46.05
Standard details						
hip or valley	-	-	-	-	m	10.18
gutter edge	-	-	-	-	m	36.57
parapet	-	-	-	-	m	36.89

K LININGS/SHEATHING/DRY PARTITIONING

Item	PC £	Labour hours	Labour £	Material £	Unit	Total rate £
K10 PLASTERBOARD DRY LINING/ PARTITIONS/CEILINGS						
Linings; "Gyproc GypLyner" metal framed wall lining system; floor and ceiling channels plugged and screwed to concrete						
Tapered edge panels; joints filled with joint filler and joint tape to receive direct decoration; one layer of 12.5 mm thick Gyproc Wallboard; or other equal and approved						
height 2.10 m - 2.40 m	-	1.15	21.49	15.96	m	**37.45**
height 2.40 m - 2.70 m	-	1.26	23.57	17.53	m	**41.10**
height 2.70 m - 3.00 m	-	1.41	26.43	19.50	m	**45.93**
height 3.00 m - 3.30 m	-	1.60	30.03	21.16	m	**51.19**
height 3.30 m - 3.60 m	-	1.79	33.63	20.86	m	**54.49**
height 3.60 m - 3.90 m	-	2.07	38.90	24.49	m	**63.40**
height 3.90 m - 4.20 m	-	2.34	43.97	26.15	m	**70.12**
Linings; "Gyproc GypLyner IWL" independent walling system; comprising 48 mm wide metal I stud frame; 50 mmm wide metal C stud floor and ceiling channels; plugged and screwed to concrete						
62.5 mm partition; outer skin of 12.50 mm thick tapered edge wallboard one side; joints filled with joint filler and joint tape to receive direct decoration						
height 2.10 m - 2.40 m	-	3.40	63.42	10.90	m	**74.32**
height 2.40 m - 2.70 m	-	3.95	74.12	13.21	m	**87.33**
height 2.70 m - 3.00 m	-	4.35	81.72	14.46	m	**96.17**
height 3.00 m - 3.30 m	-	5.05	94.79	15.75	m	**110.55**
height 3.30 m - 3.60 m	-	5.45	102.46	17.06	m	**119.52**
height 3.60 m - 3.90 m	-	6.00	112.51	18.42	m	**130.94**
height 3.90 m - 4.20 m	-	6.80	127.71	19.76	m	**147.47**
62.5 mm partition; outer skin of 12.50 mm thick tapered edge wallboard one side; filling cavity with "Isowool high performance slab (2405); wallboard joints filled with joint filler and joint tape to receive direct decoration						
height 2.10 m - 2.40 m	-	3.40	63.42	18.92	m	**82.34**
height 2.40 m - 2.70 m	-	3.95	74.12	22.23	m	**96.35**
height 2.70 m - 3.00 m	-	4.35	81.72	24.48	m	**106.20**
height 3.00 m - 3.30 m	-	5.05	94.79	26.78	m	**121.57**
height 3.30 m - 3.60 m	-	5.45	102.46	29.09	m	**131.55**
height 3.60 m - 3.90 m	-	6.00	112.51	31.45	m	**143.97**
height 3.90 m - 4.20 m	-	6.80	127.71	33.80	m	**161.50**
"Gyproc" laminated proprietary partitions; two skins of gypsum plasterboard bonded to a centre core of plasterboard square edge plank 19 mm thick; fixing with nails to softwood perimeter battens (excluded); joints filled with filler and joint tape; to receive direct decoration						
50 mm partition; two outer skins of 12.50 mm thick tapered edge wallboard						
height 2.10 m - 2.40 m	-	2.04	38.57	18.69	m	**57.26**
height 2.40 m - 2.70 m	-	2.64	50.11	21.72	m	**71.83**
height 2.70 m - 3.00 m	-	2.96	56.31	23.71	m	**80.02**
height 3.00 m - 3.30 m	-	3.24	61.72	25.70	m	**87.42**
height 3.30 m - 3.60 m	-	3.56	67.92	27.81	m	**95.73**

K LININGS/SHEATHING/DRY PARTITIONING

Item	PC £	Labour hours	Labour £	Material £	Unit	Total rate £
K10 PLASTERBOARD DRY LINING/ PARTITIONS/CEILINGS – cont'd						
"Gyproc" laminated proprietary partitions – cont'd						
65 mm partition; two outer skins of 19 mm thick tapered edge planks						
height 2.10 m - 2.40 m	-	2.27	42.77	26.41	m	69.18
height 2.40 m - 2.70 m	-	2.82	53.40	29.92	m	83.32
height 2.70 m - 3.00 m	-	3.15	59.79	32.39	m	92.18
height 3.00 m - 3.30 m	-	3.52	66.83	34.87	m	101.71
height 3.30 m - 3.60 m	-	3.84	73.04	37.46	m	110.50
Labours and associated additional wrought softwood studwork						
Floor, wall or ceiling battens						
25 mm x 38 mm	-	0.12	2.19	0.31	m	2.50
Forming openings in 2400 mm high partition; 25 mm x 38 mm softwood framing						
900 mm x 2100 mm	-	0.51	9.32	1.68	nr	11.00
fair ends	-	0.20	3.81	0.50	m	4.32
angle	-	0.31	5.98	0.97	m	6.95
Cutting and fitting around steel joists, angles, trunking, ducting, ventilators, pipes, tubes, etc.						
over 2.00 m girth	-	0.09	1.64	-	nr	1.64
not exceeding 0.30 m girth	-	0.05	0.91	-	nr	0.91
0.30 m - 1.00 m girth	-	0.07	1.28	-	nr	1.28
1.00 m - 2.00 m girth	-	0.11	2.01	-	nr	2.01
"Gyprwall Rapid/db Plus" metal stud housing partitioning system or other equal and approved; floor and ceiling channels plugged and screwed to concrete						
75 mm partition; 43/44 mm studs and channels; one layer of 15 mm thick Gyproc SoundBloc each side; joints filled with joint filler and joint tape to receive direct decoration						
height 2.10 m - 2.40 m; studs at 900 mm centres	-	2.97	56.17	25.72	m	81.88
height 2.10 m - 2.40 m; studs at 900 mm centres with 25 mm Isowool 1200 insulation within the stud cavity	-	2.97	56.17	27.51	m	83.67
height 2.10 m - 2.40 m; studs at 450 mm centres	-	4.07	76.27	27.93	m	104.20
height 2.10 m - 2.40 m; studs at 450 mm centres with 25 mm Isowool 1200 insulation within the stud cavity	-	4.07	76.27	29.72	m	105.99
height 2.40 m - 2.70 m; studs at 450 mm centres	-	4.48	83.95	31.10	m	115.05
height 2.40 m - 2.70 m; studs at 450 mm centres with 25 mm Isowool 1200 insulation within the stud cavity	-	4.48	83.95	32.89	m	116.84
102 mm partition; 70/72 mm studs and channels; one layer of 15 mm thick Gyproc SoundBloc each side; joints filled with joint filler and joint tape to receive direct decoration						
height 2.10 m - 2.40 m; studs at 900 mm centres	-	3.50	65.85	28.19	m	94.05
height 2.10 m - 2.40 m; studs at 900 mm centres with 25 mm Isowool 1200 insulation within the stud cavity	-	3.50	65.85	29.98	m	95.84
height 2.10 m - 2.40 m; studs at 450 mm centres	-	4.42	82.67	31.83	m	114.50

K LININGS/SHEATHING/DRY PARTITIONING

Item	PC £	Labour hours	Labour £	Material £	Unit	Total rate £
height 2.10 m - 2.40 m; studs at 450 mm centres with 25 mm Isowool 1200 insulation within the stud cavity	-	4.42	82.67	33.62	m	**116.29**
height 2.40 m - 2.70 m; studs at 900 mm centres	-	3.65	68.78	31.11	m	**99.89**
height 2.40 m - 2.70 m; studs at 900 mm centres with 25 mm Isowool 1200 insulation within the stud cavity	-	3.65	68.78	32.90	m	**101.68**
height 2.40 m - 2.70 m; studs at 450 mm centres	-	4.75	88.88	35.41	m	**124.29**
height 2.40 m - 2.70 m; studs at 450 mm centres with 25 mm Isowool 1200 insulation within the stud cavity	-	4.75	88.88	37.20	m	**126.08**
"Gyproc" metal stud proprietary partitions; comprising 48 mm wide metal stud frame; 50 mm wide floor channel plugged and screwed to concrete through 38 mm x 48 mm tanalised softwood sole plate						
Tapered edge panels; joints filled with joint filler and joint tape to receive direct decoration; 80 mm thick partition; one hour; one layer of 15 mm thick "Fireline" board each side						
height 2.10 m - 2.40 m	-	4.30	79.87	21.24	m	**101.11**
height 2.40 m - 2.70 m	-	4.90	91.41	24.76	m	**116.17**
height 2.70 m - 3.00 m	-	5.50	102.73	27.23	m	**129.96**
height 3.00 m - 3.30 m	-	6.34	118.37	29.95	m	**148.32**
height 3.30 m - 3.60 m	-	6.98	130.42	32.29	m	**162.72**
height 3.60 m - 3.90 m	-	8.33	155.38	34.84	m	**190.22**
height 3.90 m - 4.20 m	-	8.93	166.63	37.40	m	**204.03**
angles	-	0.20	3.81	1.41	m	**5.22**
T-junctions	-	0.10	1.83	-	m	**1.83**
fair ends	-	0.20	3.81	0.55	m	**4.37**
Tapered edge panels; joints filled with joint filler and joint tape to receive direct decoration; 100 mm thick partition; two hour; two layers of 12.50 mm thick "Fireline" board both sides						
height 2.10 m - 2.40 m	-	5.32	98.51	29.01	m	**127.52**
height 2.40 m - 2.70 m	-	6.06	112.61	33.52	m	**146.13**
height 2.70 m - 3.00 m	-	6.80	126.49	36.95	m	**163.44**
height 3.00 m - 3.30 m	-	6.75	125.86	40.65	m	**166.51**
height 3.30 m - 3.60 m	-	8.51	158.38	43.95	m	**202.34**
height 3.60 m - 3.90 m	-	8.33	155.38	47.63	m	**203.01**
height 3.90 m - 4.20 m	-	10.73	199.53	50.99	m	**250.52**
angles	-	0.31	5.82	1.51	m	**7.33**
T-junctions	-	0.10	1.83	-	m	**1.83**
fair ends	-	0.31	5.82	0.65	m	**6.47**
Gypsum plasterboard; BS 1230; plain grade tapered edge wallboard; fixing with nails; joints left open to receive "Artex" finish or other equal and approved; to softwood base						
9.50 mm board to ceilings						
over 300 mm wide	-	0.26	4.75	1.65	m²	**6.40**
9.50 mm board to beams						
girth not exceeding 600 mm	-	0.31	5.67	1.01	m²	**6.68**
girth 600 mm - 1200 mm	-	0.41	7.49	2.00	m²	**9.49**
12.50 mm board to ceilings						
over 300 mm wide	-	0.33	6.03	1.85	m²	**7.88**
12.50 mm board to beams						
girth not exceeding 600 mm	-	0.31	5.67	1.15	m²	**6.81**
girth 600 mm - 1200 mm	-	0.41	7.49	2.22	m²	**9.71**

K LININGS/SHEATHING/DRY PARTITIONING

Item	PC £	Labour hours	Labour £	Material £	Unit	Total rate £
K10 PLASTERBOARD DRY LINING/ PARTITIONS/CEILINGS – cont'd						
Gypsum plasterboard to BS 1230; fixing with nails; joints filled with joint filler and joint tape to receive direct decoration; to softwood base						
Plain grade tapered edge wallboard						
9.50 mm board to walls						
wall height 2.40 m - 2.70 m	-	1.02	19.57	5.95	m	**25.52**
wall height 2.70 m - 3.00 m	-	1.16	22.27	6.62	m	**28.90**
wall height 3.00 m - 3.30 m	-	1.34	25.78	7.29	m	**33.07**
wall height 3.30 m - 3.60 m	-	1.53	29.39	8.01	m	**37.40**
9.50 mm board to reveals and soffits of openings and recesses						
not exceeding 300 mm wide	-	0.20	3.81	1.36	m	**5.17**
300 mm - 600 mm wide	-	0.41	7.81	1.84	m	**9.65**
9.50 mm board to faces of columns - 4 nr						
not exceeding 600 mm total girth	-	0.52	9.90	2.77	m	**12.67**
600 mm - 1200 mm total girth	-	1.02	19.51	3.73	m	**23.25**
1200 mm - 1800 mm total girth	-	1.32	25.38	4.70	m	**30.08**
9.50 mm board to ceilings						
over 300 mm wide	-	0.43	8.17	2.21	m²	**10.38**
9.50 mm board to faces of beams - 3 nr						
not exceeding 600 mm total girth	-	0.61	11.62	2.72	m	**14.34**
600 mm - 1200 mm total girth	-	1.12	21.41	3.69	m	**25.10**
1200 mm - 1800 mm total girth	-	1.43	27.48	4.65	m	**32.13**
12.50 mm board to walls						
wall height 2.40 m - 2.70 m	-	1.20	23.00	6.41	m	**29.42**
wall height 2.70 m - 3.00 m	-	1.34	25.71	7.13	m	**32.83**
wall height 3.00 m - 3.30 m	-	1.48	28.41	7.85	m	**36.26**
wall height 3.30 m - 3.60 m	-	1.76	33.74	8.61	m	**42.35**
12.50 mm board to reveals and soffits of openings and recesses						
not exceeding 300 mm wide	-	0.20	3.81	1.44	m	**5.25**
300 mm - 600 mm wide	-	0.41	7.81	1.96	m	**9.76**
12.50 mm board to faces of columns - 4 nr						
not exceeding 600 mm total girth	-	0.52	9.90	2.93	m	**12.83**
600 mm - 1200 mm total girth	-	1.02	19.51	3.98	m	**23.49**
1200 mm - 1800 mm total girth	-	1.32	25.38	5.03	m	**30.42**
12.50 mm board to ceilings						
over 300 mm wide	-	0.44	8.36	2.38	m²	**10.73**
12.50 mm board to faces of beams - 3 nr						
not exceeding 600 mm total girth	-	0.61	11.62	2.86	m	**14.48**
600 mm - 1200 mm total girth	-	1.12	21.41	3.91	m	**25.32**
1200 mm - 1800 mm total girth	-	1.43	27.48	4.96	m	**32.44**
external angle; with joint tape bedded and covered with "Jointex" or other equal and approved	-	0.12	2.37	0.42	m	**2.78**
Tapered edge wallboard TEN						
12.50 mm board to walls						
wall height 2.40 m - 2.70 m	-	1.20	23.00	7.36	m	**30.37**
wall height 2.70 m - 3.00 m	-	1.34	25.71	8.19	m	**33.89**
wall height 3.00 m - 3.30 m	-	1.48	28.41	9.01	m	**37.42**
wall height 3.30 m - 3.60 m	-	1.76	33.74	9.88	m	**43.62**

K LININGS/SHEATHING/DRY PARTITIONING

Item	PC £	Labour hours	Labour £	Material £	Unit	Total rate £
12.50 mm board to reveals and soffits of openings and recesses						
not exceeding 300 mm wide	-	0.20	3.81	1.55	m	**5.36**
300 mm - 600 mm wide	-	0.41	7.81	2.17	m	**9.97**
12.50 mm board to faces of columns - 4 nr						
not exceeding 600 mm total girth	-	0.52	9.90	3.14	m	**13.04**
600 mm - 1200 mm total girth	-	1.02	19.51	4.40	m	**23.92**
1200 mm - 1800 mm total girth	-	1.32	25.38	5.67	m	**31.05**
12.50 mm board to ceilings						
over 300 mm wide	-	0.44	8.36	2.73	m²	**11.08**
12.50 mm board to faces of beams - 3 nr						
not exceeding 600 mm total girth	-	0.61	11.62	3.07	m	**14.69**
600 mm - 1200 mm total girth	-	1.12	21.41	4.33	m	**25.75**
1200 mm - 1800 mm total girth	-	1.43	27.48	5.60	m	**33.08**
external angle; with joint tape bedded and covered with "Jointex" or other equal and approved	-	0.12	2.37	0.42	m	**2.78**
Tapered edge plank						
19 mm plank to walls						
wall height 2.40 m - 2.70 m	-	1.11	21.22	10.76	m	**31.98**
wall height 2.70 m - 3.00 m	-	1.30	24.83	11.96	m	**36.80**
wall height 3.00 m - 3.30 m	-	1.43	27.42	13.17	m	**40.59**
wall height 3.30 m - 3.60 m	-	1.71	32.68	14.41	m	**47.10**
19 mm plank to reveals and soffits of openings and recesses						
not exceeding 300 mm wide	-	0.22	4.18	1.92	m	**6.10**
300 mm - 600 mm wide	-	0.46	8.72	2.92	m	**11.64**
19 mm plank to faces of columns - 4 nr						
not exceeding 600 mm total girth	-	0.56	10.64	3.89	m	**14.53**
600 mm - 1200 mm total girth	-	1.07	20.43	5.91	m	**26.34**
1200 mm - 1800 mm total girth	-	1.38	26.48	7.93	m	**34.41**
19 mm plank to ceilings						
over 300 mm wide	-	0.47	8.90	3.99	m²	**12.89**
19 mm plank to faces of beams - 3 nr						
not exceeding 600 mm total girth	-	0.67	12.72	3.82	m	**16.54**
600 mm - 1200 mm total girth	-	1.17	22.33	5.84	m	**28.17**
1200 mm - 1800 mm total girth	-	1.48	28.39	7.87	m	**36.26**
Thermal Board						
27 mm board to walls						
wall height 2.40 m - 2.70 m	-	1.16	22.13	17.94	m	**40.07**
wall height 2.70 m - 3.00 m	-	1.34	25.56	19.94	m	**45.51**
wall height 3.00 m - 3.30 m	-	1.48	28.26	21.94	m	**50.21**
wall height 3.30 m - 3.60 m	-	1.80	34.33	23.99	m	**58.32**
27 mm board to reveals and soffits of openings and recesses						
not exceeding 300 mm wide	-	0.23	4.36	2.72	m	**7.08**
300 mm - 600 mm wide	-	0.47	8.90	4.52	m	**13.42**
27 mm board to faces of columns - 4 nr						
not exceeding 600 mm total girth	-	0.57	10.82	5.49	m	**16.31**
600 mm - 1200 mm total girth	-	1.13	21.52	9.11	m	**30.63**
1200 mm - 1800 mm total girth	-	1.42	27.21	12.72	m	**39.93**
27 mm board to ceilings						
over 300 mm wide	-	0.51	9.64	6.65	m²	**16.28**
27 mm board to faces of beams - 3 nr						
not exceeding 600 mm total girth	-	0.62	11.73	5.42	m	**17.15**
600 mm - 1200 mm total girth	-	1.17	22.26	9.04	m	**31.29**
1200 mm - 1800 mm total girth	-	1.58	30.22	12.65	m	**42.87**

K LININGS/SHEATHING/DRY PARTITIONING

Item	PC £	Labour hours	Labour £	Material £	Unit	Total rate £
K10 PLASTERBOARD DRY LINING/ PARTITIONS/CEILINGS – cont'd						
Thermal Board – cont'd						
50 mm board to walls						
wall height 2.40 m - 2.70 m	-	1.16	22.13	19.06	m	**41.19**
wall height 2.70 m - 3.00 m	-	1.39	26.48	21.20	m	**47.68**
wall height 3.00 m - 3.30 m	-	1.62	30.82	23.32	m	**54.15**
wall height 3.30 m - 3.60 m	-	1.90	36.16	25.50	m	**61.66**
50 mm board to reveals and soffits of openings and recesses						
not exceeding 300 mm wide	-	0.26	4.91	2.85	m	**7.76**
300 mm - 600 mm wide	-	0.51	9.64	4.78	m	**14.42**
50 mm board to faces of columns - 4 nr						
not exceeding 600 mm total girth	-	0.62	11.73	5.80	m	**17.53**
600 mm - 1200 mm total girth	-	1.23	23.35	9.65	m	**33.01**
1200 mm - 1800 mm total girth	-	1.58	30.14	13.51	m	**43.65**
50 mm board to ceilings						
over 300 mm wide	-	0.54	10.18	7.07	m^2	**17.25**
50 mm board to faces of beams - 3 nr						
not exceeding 600 mm total girth	-	0.65	12.28	5.84	m	**18.12**
600 mm - 1200 mm total girth	-	1.30	24.63	9.75	m	**34.38**
1200 mm - 1800 mm total girth	-	1.74	33.15	13.65	m	**46.79**
White plastic faced gypsum plasterboard to BS 1230; industrial grade square edge wallboard; fixing with screws; butt joints; to softwood base						
9.50 mm board to walls						
wall height 2.40 m - 2.70 m	-	0.69	12.61	11.25	m	**23.86**
wall height 2.70 m - 3.00 m	-	0.88	16.08	12.49	m	**28.58**
wall height 3.00 m - 3.30 m	-	1.02	18.64	13.74	m	**32.38**
wall height 3.30 m - 3.60 m	-	1.16	21.20	14.98	m	**36.18**
9.50 mm board to reveals and soffits of openings and recesses						
not exceeding 300 mm wide	-	0.16	2.92	1.26	m	**4.19**
300 mm - 600 mm wide	-	0.31	5.67	2.50	m	**8.17**
9.50 mm board to faces of columns - 4 nr						
not exceeding 600 mm total girth	-	0.41	7.49	2.58	m	**10.07**
600 mm - 1200 mm total girth	-	0.81	14.80	5.11	m	**19.91**
1200 mm - 1800 mm total girth	-	1.06	19.37	7.61	m	**26.98**
12.50 mm board to walls						
wall height 2.40 m - 2.70 m	-	0.79	14.44	12.90	m	**27.33**
wall height 2.70 m - 3.00 m	-	0.93	17.00	14.32	m	**31.32**
wall height 3.00 m - 3.30 m	-	1.06	19.37	15.75	m	**35.12**
wall height 3.30 m - 3.60 m	-	1.20	21.93	17.17	m	**39.10**
12.50 mm board to reveals and soffits of openings and recesses						
not exceeding 300 mm wide	-	0.17	3.11	1.45	m	**4.56**
300 mm - 600 mm wide	-	0.32	5.85	2.87	m	**8.71**
12.50 mm board to faces of columns - 4 nr						
not exceeding 600 mm total girth	-	0.43	7.86	2.98	m	**10.84**
600 mm - 1200 mm total girth	-	0.85	15.53	5.89	m	**21.43**
1200 mm - 1800 mm total girth	-	1.12	20.47	8.76	m	**29.23**
Plasterboard jointing system; filling joint with jointing compounds						
To ceilings						
to suit 9.50 mm or 12.50 mm thick boards	-	0.10	1.83	2.25	m	**4.08**

K LININGS/SHEATHING/DRY PARTITIONING

Item	PC £	Labour hours	Labour £	Material £	Unit	Total rate £
Angle trim; plasterboard edge support system						
To ceilings						
to suit 9.50 mm or 12.50 mm thick boards	-	0.10	1.83	2.10	m	**3.93**
Gypsum SoundBloc plasterboard with higher density core; fixing with nails; joints filled with joint filler and joint tape to receive direct decoration; to softwood base						
Tapered edge board						
12.50 mm board to walls						
wall height 2.40 m - 2.70 m	-	1.06	20.32	9.59	m	**29.91**
wall height 2.70 m - 3.00 m	-	1.22	23.40	10.67	m	**34.06**
wall height 3.00 m - 3.30 m	-	1.36	26.11	11.73	m	**37.85**
wall height 3.30 m - 3.60 m	-	1.57	30.11	12.81	m	**42.92**
12.50 mm board to ceilings						
over 300 mm wide	-	0.45	8.54	3.56	m²	**12.09**
15.00 mm board to walls						
wall height 2.40 m - 2.70 m	-	1.10	21.05	10.38	m	**31.42**
wall height 2.70 m - 3.00 m	-	1.25	23.95	11.54	m	**35.49**
wall height 3.00 m - 3.30 m	-	1.40	26.85	12.70	m	**39.54**
wall height 3.30 m - 3.60 m	-	1.61	30.84	13.86	m	**44.71**
15.00 mm board to reveals and soffits of openings and recesses						
not exceeding 300 mm wide	-	0.22	4.18	1.40	m	**5.57**
300 mm - 600 mm wide	-	0.42	7.99	2.21	m	**10.20**
15.00 mm board to ceilings						
over 300 mm wide	-	0.47	8.90	3.90	m²	**12.81**
Two layers of gypsum plasterboard to BS 1230; plain grade square and tapered edge wallboard; fixing with nails; joints filled with joint filler and joint tape; top layer to receive direct decoration; to softwood base						
19 mm two layer board to walls						
wall height 2.40 m - 2.70 m	-	1.43	27.06	10.54	m	**37.61**
wall height 2.70 m - 3.00 m	-	1.62	30.68	11.73	m	**42.41**
wall height 3.00 m - 3.30 m	-	1.85	35.10	12.91	m	**48.01**
wall height 3.30 m - 3.60 m	-	2.13	40.36	14.14	m	**54.50**
19 mm two layer board to reveals and soffits of openings and recesses						
not exceeding 300 mm wide	-	0.31	5.82	1.93	m	**7.76**
300 mm - 600 mm wide	-	0.61	11.46	2.90	m	**14.36**
19 mm two layer board to faces of columns - 4 nr						
not exceeding 600 mm total girth	-	0.77	14.47	3.96	m	**18.43**
600 mm - 1200 mm total girth	-	1.38	26.09	5.91	m	**32.01**
1200 mm - 1800 mm total girth	-	1.83	34.70	7.86	m	**42.57**
25 mm two layer board to walls						
wall height 2.40 m - 2.70 m	-	1.53	28.89	11.30	m	**40.19**
wall height 2.70 m - 3.00 m	-	1.71	32.32	12.57	m	**44.89**
wall height 3.00 m - 3.30 m	-	1.94	36.74	13.84	m	**50.58**
wall height 3.30 m - 3.60 m	-	2.27	42.92	15.14	m	**58.06**
25 mm two layer board to reveals and soffits of openings and recesses						
not exceeding 300 mm wide	-	0.31	5.82	2.05	m	**7.87**
300 mm - 600 mm wide	-	0.61	11.46	3.08	m	**14.54**
25 mm two layer board to faces of columns - 4 nr						
not exceeding 600 mm total girth	-	0.77	14.47	4.19	m	**18.66**
600 mm - 1200 mm total girth	-	1.38	26.09	6.29	m	**32.39**
1200 mm - 1800 mm total girth	-	1.83	34.70	8.40	m	**43.11**

K LININGS/SHEATHING/DRY PARTITIONING

Item	PC £	Labour hours	Labour £	Material £	Unit	Total rate £
K10 PLASTERBOARD DRY LINING/ PARTITIONS/CEILINGS – cont'd						
Gyproc Dri-Wall dry lining system or other equal and approved; plain grade tapered edge wallboard; fixed to walls with adhesive; joints filled with joint filler and joint tape; to receive direct decoration						
9.50 mm board to walls						
wall height 2.40 m - 2.70 m	-	1.20	22.86	7.80	m	**30.66**
wall height 2.70 m - 3.00 m	-	1.39	26.48	8.65	m	**35.12**
wall height 3.00 m - 3.30 m	-	1.62	30.89	9.50	m	**40.39**
wall height 3.30 m - 3.60 m	-	1.85	35.24	10.41	m	**45.65**
9.50 mm board to reveals and soffits of openings and recesses						
not exceeding 300 mm wide	-	0.26	4.91	1.52	m	**6.42**
300 mm - 600 mm wide	-	0.51	9.64	2.20	m	**11.83**
9.50 mm board to faces of columns - 4 nr						
not exceeding 600 mm total girth	-	0.65	12.28	3.03	m	**15.31**
600 mm - 1200 mm total girth	-	1.26	23.90	4.54	m	**28.44**
1200 mm - 1800 mm total girth	-	1.58	30.14	5.76	m	**35.89**
Angle; with joint tape bedded and covered with "Jointex" or other equal and approved						
internal	-	0.06	1.18	0.42	m	**1.60**
external	-	0.12	2.37	0.42	m	**2.78**
Gyproc Dri-Wall M/F dry lining system or other equal and approved; mild steel furrings fixed to walls with adhesive; tapered edge wallboard screwed to furrings; joints filled with joint filler and joint tape						
12.50 mm board to walls						
wall height 2.40 m - 2.70 m	-	1.62	30.54	11.74	m	**42.27**
wall height 2.70 m - 3.00 m	-	1.85	34.88	13.03	m	**47.91**
wall height 3.00 m - 3.30 m	-	2.13	40.21	14.34	m	**54.55**
wall height 3.30 m - 3.60 m	-	2.45	46.21	15.70	m	**61.90**
12.50 mm board to reveals and soffits of openings and recesses						
not exceeding 300 mm wide	-	0.26	4.91	1.35	m	**6.26**
300 mm - 600 mm wide	-	0.51	9.64	1.86	m	**11.50**
add for one coat of "Dry-Wall" top coat or other equal and approved	-	0.05	0.99	0.91	m²	**1.90**
Gypsum cladding; Glasroc "Firecase s" board or other equal and approved; fixed with adhesive; joints pointed in adhesive						
25 mm thick column linings, faces - 4; 2 hour fire protection rating						
not exceeding 600 mm girth	-	0.33	6.03	17.16	m	**23.19**
600 mm - 1200 mm girth	-	0.50	9.14	26.11	m	**35.25**
1200 mm - 1800 mm girth	-	0.66	12.06	35.07	m	**47.13**
30 mm thick beam linings, faces - 3; 2 hour fire protection rating						
not exceeding 600 mm girth	-	0.65	11.88	16.56	m	**28.44**
600 mm - 1200 mm girth	-	1.00	18.27	26.67	m	**44.95**
1200 mm - 1800 mm girth	-	1.30	23.76	36.78	m	**60.54**

K LININGS/SHEATHING/DRY PARTITIONING

Item	PC £	Labour hours	Labour £	Material £	Unit	Total rate £
Vermiculite gypsum cladding; "Vermiculux" board or other equal and approved; fixed with adhesive; joints pointed in adhesive						
25 mm thick column linings, faces - 4; 2 hour fire protection rating						
not exceeding 600 mm girth	-	0.33	6.03	17.13	m	**23.17**
600 mm - 1200 mm girth	-	0.50	9.14	33.97	m	**43.10**
1200 mm - 1800 mm girth	-	0.66	12.06	50.80	m	**62.86**
30 mm thick beam linings, faces - 3; 2 hour fire protection rating						
not exceeding 600 mm girth	-	0.65	11.88	22.52	m	**34.40**
600 mm - 1200 mm girth	-	1.00	18.27	44.73	m	**63.01**
1200 mm - 1800 mm girth	-	1.30	23.76	66.95	m	**90.70**
55 mm thick column linings, faces - 4 ; 4 hour fire protection rating						
not exceeding 600 mm girth	-	0.92	16.81	47.89	m	**64.71**
600 mm - 1200 mm girth	-	1.12	20.47	95.48	m	**115.95**
1200 mm - 1800 mm girth	-	1.53	27.96	143.08	m	**171.04**
60 mm thick beam linings, faces - 3; 4 hour fire protection rating						
not exceeding 600 mm girth	-	0.77	14.07	51.75	m	**65.82**
600 mm - 1200 mm girth	-	0.92	16.81	103.20	m	**120.02**
1200 mm - 1800 mm girth	-	1.12	20.47	154.65	m	**175.12**
Add to the above for						
plus 3% for work 3.50 m - 5.00 m high						**3%**
plus 6% for work 5.00 m - 6.50 m high						**6%**
plus 12% for work 6.50 m - 8.00m high						**12%**
plus 18% for work over 8.00 m high						**18%**
Cutting and fitting around steel joints, angles, trunking, ducting, ventilators, pipes, tubes, etc.						
over 2.00 m girth	-	0.45	8.22	-	m	**8.22**
not exceeding 0.30 m girth	-	0.31	5.67	-	nr	**5.67**
0.30 m - 1.00 m girth	-	0.41	7.49	-	nr	**7.49**
1.00 m - 2.00 m girth	-	0.56	10.23	-	nr	**10.23**
K11 RIGID SHEET FLOORING/SHEATHING/ LININGS/CASINGS						
Blockboard (Birch faced)						
Lining to walls 12 mm thick						
over 300 mm wide	5.32	0.48	8.77	6.69	m²	**15.46**
not exceeding 300 mm wide	-	0.31	5.67	2.03	m	**7.69**
holes for pipes and the like	-	0.03	0.55	-	nr	**0.55**
Two-sided 12 mm thick pipe casing; to softwood framing (not included)						
300 mm girth	-	0.79	14.44	2.12	m	**16.55**
600 mm girth	-	0.93	17.00	4.05	m	**21.05**
Three-sided 12 mm thick pipe casing; to softwood framing (not included)						
450 mm girth	-	1.02	18.64	3.18	m	**21.82**
900 mm girth	-	1.20	21.93	6.11	m	**28.04**
Extra for 400 x 400 removable access panel; brass cups and screws; additional framing	-	1.02	18.64	0.94	nr	**19.58**
Lining to walls 18 mm thick						
over 300 mm wide	6.19	0.51	9.32	7.75	m²	**17.07**
not exceeding 300 mm wide	-	0.32	5.85	2.34	m	**8.19**
Lining to walls 25 mm thick						
over 300 mm wide	10.26	0.55	10.05	12.75	m²	**22.81**
not exceeding 300 mm wide	-	0.36	6.58	3.83	m	**10.41**
holes for pipes and the like	-	0.06	1.10	-	nr	**1.10**

K LININGS/SHEATHING/DRY PARTITIONING

Item	PC £	Labour hours	Labour £	Material £	Unit	Total rate £
K11 RIGID SHEET FLOORING/SHEATHING/ LININGS/CASINGS – cont'd						
Chipboard (plain)						
Lining to walls 12 mm thick						
over 300 mm wide	1.13	0.39	7.13	1.62	m²	8.74
not exceeding 300 mm wide	-	0.22	4.02	0.50	m	4.52
holes for pipes and the like	-	0.02	0.37	-	nr	0.37
Lining to walls 15 mm thick						
over 300 mm wide	1.42	0.41	7.49	1.96	m²	9.45
not exceeding 300 mm wide	-	0.24	4.39	0.61	m	4.99
holes for pipes and the like	-	0.03	0.55	-	nr	0.55
Two-sided 15 mm thick pipe casing; to softwood framing (not included)						
300 mm girth	-	0.60	10.96	0.70	m	11.66
600 mm girth	-	0.69	12.61	1.21	m	13.82
Three-sided 15 mm thick pipe casing; to softwood framing (not included)						
450 mm girth	-	1.30	23.76	1.05	m	24.80
900 mm girth	-	1.53	27.96	1.85	m	29.81
Extra for 400 x 400 removable access panel; brass cups and screws; additional framing	-	1.02	18.64	0.94	nr	19.58
Lining to walls 18 mm thick						
over 300 mm wide	1.70	0.43	7.86	2.37	m²	10.22
not exceeding 300 mm wide	-	0.28	5.12	0.71	m	5.83
holes for pipes and the like	-	0.05	0.91	-	nr	0.91
Fire-retardant chipboard; Antivlam or other equal and approved; Class 1 spread of flame						
Lining to walls 12 mm thick						
over 300 mm wide	-	0.39	7.13	9.23	m²	16.36
not exceeding 300 mm wide	-	0.22	4.02	2.79	m	6.81
holes for pipes and the like	-	0.02	0.37	-	nr	0.37
Lining to walls 18 mm thick						
over 300 mm wide	-	0.43	7.86	12.17	m²	20.02
not exceeding 300 mm wide	-	0.28	5.12	3.67	m	8.78
holes for pipes and the like	-	0.05	0.91	-	nr	0.91
Lining to walls 22 mm thick						
over 300 mm wide	-	0.44	8.04	15.43	m²	23.47
not exceeding 300 mm wide	-	0.31	5.67	4.65	m	10.31
holes for pipes and the like	-	0.06	1.10	-	nr	1.10
Chipboard Melamine faced; white matt finish; laminated masking strips						
Lining to walls 15 mm thick						
over 300 mm wide	2.51	1.06	19.37	3.58	m²	22.95
not exceeding 300 mm wide	-	0.69	12.61	1.20	m	13.81
holes for pipes and the like	-	0.07	1.28	-	nr	1.28
Chipboard boarding and flooring						
Boarding to floors; butt joints						
18 mm thick	2.35	0.31	5.67	3.16	m²	8.82
22 mm thick	3.06	0.33	6.03	4.01	m²	10.04
Boarding to floors; tongued and grooved joints						
18 mm thick	2.33	0.32	5.85	3.13	m²	8.97
22 mm thick	2.89	0.36	6.58	3.81	m²	10.39
Boarding to roofs; butt joints						
18 mm thick	2.65	0.33	6.03	3.51	m²	9.54

K LININGS/SHEATHING/DRY PARTITIONING

Item	PC £	Labour hours	Labour £	Material £	Unit	Total rate £
Durabella "Westbourne" flooring system or other equal and approved; comprising 19 mm thick tongued and grooved chipboard panels secret nailed to softwood MK 10X-profiled foam backed battens at 600 mm centres; on concrete floor						
Flooring tongued and grooved joints						
63 mm thick overall; 44 mm x 54 mm nominal size battens	-	-	-	-	m²	23.87
75 mm thick overall; 56 mm x 54 mm nominal size battens	-	-	-	-	m²	25.82
Plywood flooring						
Boarding to floors; tongued and grooved joints						
15 mm thick	17.68	0.41	7.49	21.76	m²	29.25
18 mm thick	22.73	0.44	8.04	27.88	m²	35.92
Plywood; external quality; 18 mm thick						
Boarding to roofs; butt joints						
flat to falls	7.56	0.41	7.49	9.47	m²	16.96
sloping	7.56	0.43	7.86	9.47	m²	17.33
vertical	7.56	0.58	10.60	9.47	m²	20.07
Plywood; external quality; 12 mm thick						
Boarding to roofs; butt joints						
flat to falls	5.36	0.41	7.49	6.80	m²	14.29
sloping	5.36	0.43	7.86	6.80	m²	14.66
vertical	5.36	0.58	10.60	6.80	m²	17.40
Glazed hardboard to BS 1142; on and including 38 mm x 38 mm sawn softwood framing						
3.20 mm thick panel						
to side of bath	-	1.82	33.26	4.60	nr	37.86
to end of bath	-	0.71	12.97	1.32	nr	14.29
Insulation board to BS 1142						
Lining to walls 12 mm thick						
over 300 mm wide	1.71	0.24	4.39	2.31	m²	6.70
not exceeding 300 mm wide	-	0.14	2.56	0.71	m	3.27
holes for pipes and the like	-	0.01	0.18	-	nr	0.18
Lining to walls 18 mm thick						
over 300 mm wide	2.68	0.27	4.93	3.49	m²	8.43
not exceeding 300 mm wide	-	0.17	3.11	1.07	m	4.17
holes for pipes and the like	-	0.01	0.18	-	nr	0.18
Non-asbestos board; "Masterboard" or other equal and approved; sanded finish						
Lining to walls 6 mm thick						
over 300 mm wide	7.19	0.33	6.03	8.91	m²	14.94
not exceeding 300 mm wide	-	0.20	3.65	2.68	m	6.33

K LININGS/SHEATHING/DRY PARTITIONING

Item	PC £	Labour hours	Labour £	Material £	Unit	Total rate £
K11 RIGID SHEET FLOORING/SHEATHING/ LININGS/CASINGS – cont'd						
Non-asbestos board; "Masterboard – cont'd						
Lining to ceilings 6 mm thick						
over 300 mm wide	7.19	0.44	8.04	8.91	m²	**16.95**
not exceeding 300 mm wide	-	0.28	5.12	2.68	m	**7.79**
holes for pipes and the like	-	0.02	0.37	-	nr	**0.37**
Lining to walls 9 mm thick						
over 300 mm wide	15.18	0.37	6.76	18.60	m²	**25.36**
not exceeding 300 mm wide	-	0.20	3.65	5.59	m	**9.24**
Lining to ceilings 9 mm thick						
over 300 mm wide	15.18	0.45	8.22	18.60	m²	**26.83**
not exceeding 300 mm wide	-	0.30	5.48	5.59	m	**11.07**
holes for pipes and the like	-	0.03	0.55	-	nr	**0.55**
Non-asbestos board; "Supalux" or other equal and approved; sanded finish						
Lining to walls 6 mm thick						
over 300 mm wide	11.39	0.33	6.03	14.00	m²	**20.03**
not exceeding 300 mm wide	-	0.20	3.65	4.21	m	**7.86**
Lining to ceilings 6 mm thick						
over 300 mm wide	11.39	0.44	8.04	14.00	m²	**22.04**
not exceeding 300 mm wide	-	0.28	5.12	4.21	m	**9.32**
holes for pipes and the like	-	0.02	0.37	-	nr	**0.37**
Lining to walls 9 mm thick						
over 300 mm wide	16.94	0.37	6.76	20.73	m²	**27.49**
not exceeding 300 mm wide	-	0.20	3.65	6.23	m	**9.88**
Lining to ceilings 9 mm thick						
over 300 mm wide	16.94	0.45	8.22	20.73	m²	**28.96**
not exceeding 300 mm wide	-	0.30	5.48	6.23	m	**11.71**
holes for pipes and the like	-	0.03	0.55	-	nr	**0.55**
Lining to walls 12 mm thick						
over 300 mm wide	5.04	0.41	7.49	6.30	m²	**13.79**
not exceeding 300 mm wide	-	0.24	4.39	1.90	m	**6.28**
Lining to ceilings 12 mm thick						
over 300 mm wide	5.04	0.54	9.87	6.30	m²	**16.17**
not exceeding 300 mm wide	-	0.32	5.85	1.90	m	**7.74**
holes for pipes and the like	-	0.05	0.91	-	nr	**0.91**
Non-asbestos board; "Monolux 40" or other equal and approved; 6 mm x 50 mm "Supalux" cover fillets or other equal and approved one side						
Lining to walls 19 mm thick						
over 300 mm wide	43.33	0.71	12.97	55.02	m²	**68.00**
not exceeding 300 mm wide	-	0.51	9.32	18.66	m	**27.98**
Lining to walls 25 mm thick						
over 300 mm wide	51.95	0.77	14.07	65.48	m²	**79.55**
not exceeding 300 mm wide	-	0.54	9.87	21.80	m	**31.66**
Plywood (Far Eastern); internal quality						
Lining to walls 4 mm thick						
over 300 mm wide	1.90	0.38	6.94	2.55	m²	**9.50**
not exceeding 300 mm wide	-	0.24	4.39	0.78	m	**5.17**
Lining to ceilings 4 mm thick						
over 300 mm wide	1.90	0.51	9.32	2.55	m²	**11.87**
not exceeding 300 mm wide	-	0.32	5.85	0.78	m	**6.63**
holes for pipes and the like	-	0.02	0.37	-	nr	**0.37**

K LININGS/SHEATHING/DRY PARTITIONING

Item	PC £	Labour hours	Labour £	Material £	Unit	Total rate £
Lining to walls 6 mm thick						
over 300 mm wide	2.64	0.41	7.49	3.45	m²	10.94
not exceeding 300 mm wide	-	0.27	4.93	1.05	m	5.99
Lining to ceilings 6 mm thick						
over 300 mm wide	2.64	0.54	9.87	3.45	m²	13.32
not exceeding 300 mm wide	-	0.36	6.58	1.05	m	7.63
holes for pipes and the like	-	0.02	0.37	-	nr	0.37
Two-sided 6 mm thick pipe casings; to softwood framing (not included)						
300 mm girth	-	0.83	15.17	1.14	m	16.31
600 mm girth	-	1.02	18.64	2.10	m	20.74
Three-sided 6 mm thick pipe casing; to softwood framing (not included)						
450 mm girth	-	1.16	21.20	1.71	m	22.91
900 mm girth	-	1.39	25.40	3.19	m	28.59
Lining to walls 9 mm thick						
over 300 mm wide	3.57	0.43	7.86	4.57	m²	12.43
not exceeding 300 mm wide	-	0.29	5.30	1.39	m	6.69
Lining to ceilings 9 mm thick						
over 300 mm wide	3.57	0.58	10.60	4.57	m²	15.17
not exceeding 300 mm wide	-	0.38	6.94	1.39	m	8.33
holes for pipes and the like	-	0.03	0.55	-	nr	0.55
Lining to walls 12 mm thick						
over 300 mm wide	4.49	0.47	8.59	5.69	m²	14.28
not exceeding 300 mm wide	-	0.31	5.67	1.73	m	7.39
Lining to ceilings 12 mm thick						
over 300 mm wide	4.49	0.62	11.33	5.69	m²	17.02
not exceeding 300 mm wide	-	0.41	7.49	1.73	m	9.22
holes for pipes and the like	-	0.03	0.55	-	nr	0.55
Plywood (Far Eastern); external quality						
Lining to walls 4 mm thick						
over 300 mm wide	2.22	0.38	6.94	2.94	m²	9.88
not exceeding 300 mm wide	-	0.24	4.39	0.90	m	5.29
Lining to ceilings 4 mm thick						
over 300 mm wide	2.22	0.51	9.32	2.94	m²	12.26
not exceeding 300 mm wide	-	0.32	5.85	0.90	m	6.75
holes for pipes and the like	-	0.02	0.37	-	nr	0.37
Lining to walls 6 mm thick						
over 300 mm wide	2.86	0.41	7.49	3.71	m²	11.21
not exceeding 300 mm wide	-	0.27	4.93	1.13	m	6.07
Lining to ceilings 6 mm thick						
over 300 mm wide	2.86	0.54	9.87	3.71	m²	13.58
not exceeding 300 mm wide	-	0.36	6.58	1.13	m	7.71
holes for pipes and the like	-	0.02	0.37	-	nr	0.37
Two-sided 6 mm thick pipe casings; to softwood framing (not included)						
300 mm girth	-	0.83	15.17	1.22	m	16.39
600 mm girth	-	1.02	18.64	2.26	m	20.91
Three-sided 6 mm thick pipe casing; to softwood framing (not included)						
450 mm girth	-	1.16	21.20	1.83	m	23.03
900 mm girth	-	1.39	25.40	3.43	m	28.83
Lining to walls 9 mm thick						
over 300 mm wide	4.11	0.43	7.86	5.23	m²	13.09
not exceeding 300 mm wide	-	0.29	5.30	1.59	m	6.89
Lining to ceilings 9 mm thick						
over 300 mm wide	4.11	0.58	10.60	5.23	m²	15.83
not exceeding 300 mm wide	-	0.38	6.94	1.59	m	8.53
holes for pipes and the like	-	0.03	0.55	-	nr	0.55

K LININGS/SHEATHING/DRY PARTITIONING

Item	PC £	Labour hours	Labour £	Material £	Unit	Total rate £
K11 RIGID SHEET FLOORING/SHEATHING/ LININGS/CASINGS – cont'd						
Plywood (Far Eastern); external quality – cont'd						
Lining to walls 12 mm thick						
over 300 mm wide	5.33	0.47	8.59	6.71	m²	**15.30**
not exceeding 300 mm wide	-	0.31	5.67	2.03	m	**7.70**
Lining to ceilings 12 mm thick						
over 300 mm wide	5.33	0.62	11.33	6.71	m²	**18.04**
not exceeding 300 mm wide	-	0.41	7.49	2.03	m	**9.52**
holes for pipes and the like	-	0.03	0.55	-	nr	**0.55**
Extra over wall linings fixed with nails for screwing	-	-	-	-	m²	**1.80**
Preformed white melamine faced plywood casings; Pendock Profiles Ltd or other equal and approved; to softwood battens (not included)						
Skirting trunking profile; plain butt joints in the running length						
45 mm x 150 mm; ref TK150	-	0.12	2.19	11.49	m	**13.68**
extra for stop end	-	0.05	0.91	9.58	nr	**10.50**
extra for external corner	-	0.10	1.83	11.79	nr	**13.62**
extra for internal corner	-	0.10	1.83	8.82	nr	**10.65**
Casing profiles						
150 mm x 150 mm ref MX150/150; 5 mm thick	-	0.12	2.19	18.38	m	**20.57**
extra for stop end	-	0.05	0.91	7.49	nr	**8.40**
extra for external corner	-	0.10	1.83	27.82	nr	**29.65**
extra for internal corner	-	0.10	1.83	8.82	nr	**10.65**
Internal quality American Cherry veneered plywood; 6 mm thick						
Lining to walls						
over 300 mm wide	5.23	0.44	8.04	6.52	m²	**14.56**
not exceeding 300 mm wide	-	0.30	5.48	1.99	m	**7.48**
"Tacboard" or other equal and approved; Eternit UK Ltd; fire resisting boards; butt joints; to softwood base						
Lining to walls; 6 mm thick						
over 300 mm wide	-	0.33	6.03	10.79	m²	**16.82**
not exceeding 300 mm wide	-	0.20	3.65	3.27	m	**6.93**
Lining to walls; 9 mm thick						
over 300 mm wide	-	0.37	6.76	19.74	m²	**26.50**
not exceeding 300 mm wide	-	0.22	4.02	5.96	m	**9.98**
Lining to walls; 12 mm thick						
over 300 mm wide	-	0.41	7.49	25.64	m²	**33.14**
not exceeding 300 mm wide	-	0.24	4.39	7.73	m	**12.12**
"Tacfire" or other equal and approved; Eternit UK Ltd; fire resisting boards						
Lining to walls; 6 mm thick						
over 300 mm wide	-	0.33	6.03	14.44	m²	**20.47**
not exceeding 300 mm wide	-	0.20	3.65	4.37	m	**8.02**
Lining to walls; 9 mm thick						
over 300 mm wide	-	0.37	6.76	22.02	m²	**28.78**
not exceeding 300 mm wide	-	0.22	4.02	6.64	m	**10.66**
Lining to walls; 12 mm thick						
over 300 mm wide	-	0.41	7.49	28.99	m²	**36.49**
not exceeding 300 mm wide	-	0.24	4.39	8.73	m	**13.12**

K LININGS/SHEATHING/DRY PARTITIONING

Item	PC £	Labour hours	Labour £	Material £	Unit	Total rate £
K14 GLASS REINFORCED GYPSUM LININGS/ PANELLING/CASINGS/MOULDINGS						
Glass reinforced gypsum Glasroc Multi-board or other equal and approved; fixing with nails; joints filled with joint filler and joint tape; finishing with "Jointex" or other equal and approved to receive decoration; to softwood base						
10 mm board to walls						
wall height 2.40 m - 2.70 m	-	1.02	19.57	41.53	m	61.10
wall height 2.70 m - 3.00 m	-	1.16	22.27	46.15	m	68.43
wall height 3.00 m - 3.30 m	-	1.34	25.78	50.77	m	76.55
wall height 3.30 m - 3.60 m	-	1.53	29.39	55.44	m	84.84
12.50 mm board to walls						
wall height 2.40 m - 2.70 m	-	1.06	20.30	54.20	m	74.50
wall height 2.70 m - 3.00 m	-	1.20	23.00	60.23	m	83.23
wall height 3.00 m - 3.30 m	-	1.39	26.69	66.26	m	92.95
wall height 3.30 m - 3.60 m	-	1.57	30.12	72.33	m	102.46
K20 TIMBER BOARD FLOORING/SHEATHING/ LININGS/CASINGS						
Sawn softwood; untreated						
Boarding to roofs; 150 mm wide boards; butt joints						
19 mm thick; flat; over 300 mm wide	4.93	0.45	8.22	6.59	m²	14.81
19 mm thick; flat; not exceeding 300 mm wide	-	0.31	5.67	2.01	m	7.67
19 mm thick; sloping; over 300 mm wide	-	0.51	9.32	6.59	m²	15.91
19 mm thick; sloping; not exceeding 300 mm wide	-	0.33	6.03	2.01	m	8.04
19 mm thick; sloping; laid diagonally; over 300 mm wide	-	0.64	11.70	6.59	m²	18.29
19 mm thick; sloping; laid diagonally; not exceeding 300 mm wide	-	0.41	7.49	2.01	m	9.50
25 mm thick; flat; over 300 mm wide	-	0.45	8.22	7.24	m²	15.46
25 mm thick; flat; not exceeding 300 mm wide	-	0.31	5.67	2.20	m	7.87
25 mm thick; sloping; over 300 mm wide	-	0.51	9.32	7.24	m²	16.56
25 mm thick; sloping; not exceeding 300 mm wide	-	0.33	6.03	2.20	m	8.23
25 mm thick; sloping; laid diagonally; over 300 mm wide	-	0.64	11.70	7.24	m²	18.93
25 mm thick; sloping; laid diagonally; not exceeding 300 mm wide	-	0.41	7.49	2.20	m	9.69
Boarding to tops or cheeks of dormers; 150 mm wide boards; butt joints						
19 mm thick; laid diagonally; over 300 mm wide	PC	0.81	14.80	6.59	m²	21.39
19 mm thick; laid diagonally; not exceeding 300 mm wide	-	0.51	9.32	2.01	m	11.33
19 mm thick; laid diagonally; area not exceeding 1.00 m2 irrespective of width	-	1.02	18.64	6.20	nr	24.84
Sawn softwood; "Tanalised"						
Boarding to roofs; 150 mm wide boards; butt joints						
19 mm thick; flat; over 300 mm wide	-	0.45	8.22	7.58	m²	15.81
19 mm thick; flat; not exceeding 300 mm wide	-	0.31	5.67	2.30	m	7.97
19 mm thick; sloping; over 300 mm wide	-	0.51	9.32	7.58	m²	16.91
19 mm thick; sloping; not exceeding 300 mm wide	-	0.33	6.03	2.30	m	8.34

K LININGS/SHEATHING/DRY PARTITIONING

Item	PC £	Labour hours	Labour £	Material £	Unit	Total rate £
K20 TIMBER BOARD FLOORING/SHEATHING/ LININGS/CASINGS – cont'd						
Sawn softwood; "Tanalised" – cont'd						
19 mm thick; sloping; laid diagonally; over 300 mm wide	-	0.64	11.70	7.58	m²	19.28
19 mm thick; sloping; laid diagonally; not exceeding 300 mm wide	-	0.41	7.49	2.30	m	9.80
25 mm thick; flat; over 300 mm wide	-	0.45	8.22	8.55	m²	16.77
25 mm thick; flat; not exceeding 300 mm wide	-	0.31	5.67	2.60	m	8.26
25 mm thick; sloping; over 300 mm wide	-	0.51	9.32	8.55	m²	17.87
25 mm thick; sloping; not exceeding 300 mm wide	-	0.33	6.03	2.60	m	8.63
25 mm thick; sloping; laid diagonally; over 300 mm wide	-	0.64	11.70	8.55	m²	20.24
25 mm thick; sloping; laid diagonally; not exceeding 300 mm wide	-	0.41	7.49	2.60	m	10.09
Boarding to tops or cheeks of dormers; 150 mm wide boards; butt joints						
19 mm thick; laid diagonally; over 300 mm wide	-	0.81	14.80	7.58	m²	22.39
19 mm thick; laid diagonally; not exceeding 300 mm wide	-	0.51	9.32	2.30	m	11.62
19 mm thick; laid diagonally; area not exceeding 1.00 m² irrespective of width	-	1.02	18.64	7.19	nr	25.83
Wrought softwood						
Boarding to floors; butt joints						
19 mm x 75 mm boards	-	0.61	11.15	8.75	m²	19.90
19 mm x 125 mm boards	-	0.56	10.23	9.61	m²	19.85
22 mm x 150 mm boards	-	0.52	9.50	10.28	m²	19.78
25 mm x 100 mm boards	-	0.56	10.23	11.10	m²	21.33
25 mm x 150 mm boards	-	0.52	9.50	11.91	m²	21.41
25 mm boarding and bearers to floors; butt joints; In making good where partitions removed or openings formed (boards running in same direction)						
150 mm wide	-	0.28	5.12	1.79	m	6.90
225 mm wide	-	0.42	7.68	2.93	m	10.60
300 mm wide	-	0.56	10.23	3.51	m	13.75
25 mm boarding and bearers to floors; butt joints; in making good where partitions removed or openings formed (boards running at right angles)						
150 mm wide	-	0.42	7.68	3.96	m	11.64
225 mm wide	-	0.65	11.88	5.38	m	17.26
300 mm wide	-	0.83	15.17	6.16	m	21.33
450 mm wide	-	1.25	22.84	8.19	m	31.03
Boarding to floors; tongued and grooved joints						
19 mm x 75 mm boards	-	0.71	12.97	9.56	m²	22.53
19 mm x 125 mm boards	-	0.67	12.24	10.40	m²	22.65
22 mm x 150 mm boards	-	0.62	11.33	11.10	m²	22.43
25 mm x 100 mm boards	-	0.67	12.24	11.91	m²	24.15
25 mm x 150 mm boards	-	0.62	11.33	12.71	m²	24.04
Boarding to internal walls; tongued and grooved and V-jointed						
12 mm x 100 mm boards	-	0.81	14.80	9.03	m²	23.83
16 mm x 100 mm boards	-	0.81	14.80	12.10	m²	26.91
19 mm x 100 mm boards	-	0.81	14.80	13.58	m²	28.38
19 mm x 125 mm boards	-	0.77	14.07	14.28	m²	28.36
19 mm x 125 mm boards; chevron pattern	-	1.22	22.29	14.28	m²	36.58
25 mm x 125 mm boards	-	0.77	14.07	18.41	m²	32.48
12 mm x 100 mm boards; knotty pine	-	0.81	14.80	8.40	m²	23.20

K LININGS/SHEATHING/DRY PARTITIONING

Item	PC £	Labour hours	Labour £	Material £	Unit	Total rate £
Boarding to internal ceilings						
12 mm x 100 mm boards	-	1.02	18.64	9.03	m^2	**27.67**
16 mm x 100 mm boards	-	1.02	18.64	12.10	m^2	**30.74**
19 mm x 100 mm boards	-	1.02	18.64	13.58	m^2	**32.22**
19 mm x 125 mm boards	-	0.97	17.73	14.28	m^2	**32.01**
19 mm x 125 mm boards; chevron pattern	-	1.42	25.95	14.28	m^2	**40.23**
25 mm x 125 mm boards	-	0.97	17.73	18.41	m^2	**36.14**
12 mm x 100 mm boards; knotty pine	-	1.02	18.64	8.40	m^2	**27.04**
Boarding to roofs; tongued and grooved joints						
19 mm thick; flat to falls	-	0.56	10.23	12.19	m^2	**22.43**
19 mm thick; sloping	-	0.61	11.15	12.19	m^2	**23.34**
19 mm thick; sloping; laid diagonally	-	0.79	14.44	12.19	m^2	**26.63**
25 mm thick; flat to falls	-	0.56	10.23	14.51	m^2	**24.74**
25 mm thick; sloping	-	0.61	11.15	14.51	m^2	**25.66**
Boarding to tops or cheeks of dormers; tongued and grooved joints						
19 mm thick; laid diagonally	-	1.02	18.64	12.19	m^2	**30.83**
Wrought softwood; "Tanalised"						
Boarding to roofs; tongued and grooved joints						
19 mm thick; flat to falls	-	0.56	10.23	13.19	m^2	**23.42**
19 mm thick; sloping	-	0.61	11.15	13.19	m^2	**24.33**
19 mm thick; sloping; laid diagonally	-	0.79	14.44	13.19	m^2	**27.62**
25 mm thick; flat to falls	-	0.56	10.23	15.82	m^2	**26.05**
25 mm thick; sloping	-	0.61	11.15	15.82	m^2	**26.97**
Boarding to tops or cheeks of dormers; tongued and grooved joints						
19 mm thick; laid diagonally	-	1.02	18.64	13.19	m^2	**31.83**
Wood strip; 22 mm thick; "Junckers" **pre-treated or other and approved;** **tongued and grooved joints; pre-finished** **boards; level fixing to cement and sand** **base**						
Strip flooring; over 300 mm wide						
Sylvasport Premium on 57 mm deep BluBat battens	-	-	-	-	m^2	**53.81**
unsealed Sylvasport Premium on 57 mm deep BluBat battens	-	-	-	-	m^2	**59.19**
beech Classic on battens	-	-	-	-	m^2	**64.58**
oak Harmony on battens	-	-	-	-	m^2	**64.58**
oak Harmony on polylay and clips	-	-	-	-	m^2	**68.88**
Wrought hardwood						
Strip flooring to floors; 25 mm thick x 75 mm wide; tongue and grooved joints; secret fixing; surface sanded after laying						
american oak	-	-	-	-	m^2	**59.13**
canadian maple	-	-	-	-	m^2	**62.83**
gurjun	-	-	-	-	m^2	**55.44**
iroko	-	-	-	-	m^2	**51.74**

K LININGS/SHEATHING/DRY PARTITIONING

Item	PC £	Labour hours	Labour £	Material £	Unit	Total rate £
K30 DEMOUNTABLE PARTITIONS						
Insulated panel and two-hour fire wall system for warehouses etc., comprising white polyester coated galvanised steel frame and 0.55 mm galvanised steel panels either side of rockwool infill						
100 mm thick wall; 31 Rw dB acoustic rating	-	-	-	-	m²	45.10
150 mm thick wall; 31 Rw dB acoustic rating	-	-	-	-	m²	48.48
intumescent mastic sealant; bedding frames at perimeters of metal fire walls	-	-	-	-	m	3.95
Getalit laminated both sides top hung movable acoustic panel wall with concealed uPVC vertical edge profiles, 9 nr 1106 mm x 3000 mm panels and type K two point panel support system						
105 mm thick wall; 47 Rw dB acoustic rating	-	-	-	-	m²	417.18
105 mm thick wall; 47 Rw dB acoustic rating	-	-	-	-	m²	451.00
105 mm thick wall; 47 Rw dB acoustic rating	-	-	-	-	m²	484.82
K40 DEMOUNTABLE SUSPENDED CEILINGS						
Suspended ceilings; Gyproc M/F suspended ceiling system or other equal and approved; hangers plugged and screwed to concrete soffit, 900 mm x 1800 mm x 12.5 mm tapered edge wallboard infill; joints filled with joint filler and taped to receive direct decoration						
Lining to ceilings; hangers average 400 mm long						
over 300 mm wide	-	1.43	26.61	12.09	m²	38.69
not exceeding 300 mm wide in isolated strips	-	0.57	10.60	6.15	m	16.75
300 mm - 600 mm wide in isolated strips	-	0.90	16.73	7.00	m	23.73
Edge treatments						
20 x 20 mm SAS perimeter shadow gap; screwed to plasterboard	-	-	-	-	m	6.20
20 x 20 mm SAS shadow gap around 450 mm dia. column; including 15 x 44 mm batten plugged and screwed to concrete	-	-	-	-	m	31.01
Vertical bulkhead; including additional hangers						
over 300 mm wide	-	1.65	30.73	12.78	m²	43.51
not exceeding 300 mm wide in isolated strips	-	0.65	12.09	6.84	m	18.94
300 mm - 600 mm wide in isolated strips	-	1.03	19.15	7.69	m	26.85

L WINDOWS/DOORS/STAIRS

Item	PC £	Labour hours	Labour £	Material £	Unit	Total rate £
L10 WINDOWS/ROOFLIGHTS/SCREENS/ LOUVRES						
Standard windows; "treated" wrought softwood; Jeld-Wen or other equal and approved						
Side hung casement windows without glazing bars; factory glazed with low E 24 mm double glazing; with 140 mm wide softwood sills; opening casements and ventilators hung on rustproof hinges; fitted with aluminized lacquered finish casement stays and fasteners						
500 mm x 750 mm; ref N07V	124.04	0.69	12.61	140.32	nr	**152.93**
500 mm x 900 mm; ref N09V	126.12	0.83	15.17	142.67	nr	**157.84**
600 mm x 750 mm; ref 107V	137.46	0.83	15.17	155.47	nr	**170.64**
600 mm x 750 mm; ref 107C	112.09	0.83	15.17	126.84	nr	**142.00**
600 mm x 900 mm; ref 109V	142.43	0.93	17.00	161.08	nr	**178.08**
600 mm x 900 mm; ref 109C	120.87	0.83	15.17	136.75	nr	**151.91**
600 mm x 1050 mm; ref 109V	149.02	0.83	15.17	168.63	nr	**183.80**
600 mm x 1050 mm; ref 110V	125.29	1.02	18.64	141.84	nr	**160.48**
915 mm x 900 mm; ref 2NO9W	171.35	1.11	20.28	193.72	nr	**214.01**
915 mm x 1050 mm; ref 2N1OW	180.01	1.16	21.20	203.61	nr	**224.81**
915 mm x 1200 mm; ref 2N12W	194.79	1.20	21.93	220.29	nr	**242.22**
915 mm x 1350 mm; ref 2N13W	204.21	1.39	25.40	230.92	nr	**256.32**
915 mm x 1500 mm; ref 2N15W	231.71	1.43	26.13	262.07	nr	**288.20**
1200 mm x 750 mm; ref 2O7C	176.12	1.16	21.20	199.21	nr	**220.41**
1200 mm x 750 mm; ref 2O7CV	222.75	1.16	21.20	251.84	nr	**273.04**
1200 mm x 900 mm; ref 2O9C	187.35	1.20	21.93	211.90	nr	**233.83**
1200 mm x 900 mm; ref 2O9W	197.16	1.20	21.93	222.96	nr	**244.89**
1200 mm x 900 mm; ref 2O9CV	232.76	1.20	21.93	263.14	nr	**285.07**
1200 mm x 1050 mm; ref 210C	198.33	1.39	25.40	224.39	nr	**249.79**
1200 mm x 1050 mm; ref 210W	208.99	1.39	25.40	236.42	nr	**261.82**
1200 mm x 1050 mm; ref 210T	246.57	1.39	25.40	278.85	nr	**304.25**
1200 mm x 1050 mm; ref 210CV	241.82	1.39	25.40	273.48	nr	**298.88**
1200 mm x 1200 mm; ref 212C	207.09	1.48	27.05	234.38	nr	**261.43**
1200 mm x 1200 mm; ref 212W	221.03	1.48	27.05	250.12	nr	**277.17**
1200 mm x 1200 mm; ref 212TX	287.25	1.48	27.05	324.86	nr	**351.90**
1200 mm x 1200 mm; ref 212CV	254.72	1.48	27.05	288.15	nr	**315.19**
1200 mm x 1350 mm; ref 213W	237.29	1.57	28.69	268.47	nr	**297.16**
1200 mm x 1350 mm; ref 213CV	281.74	1.57	28.69	318.64	nr	**347.33**
1200 mm x 1500 mm; ref 215W	275.18	1.71	31.25	311.34	nr	**342.59**
1770 mm x 750 mm; ref 307CC	258.66	1.43	26.13	292.59	nr	**318.72**
1770 mm x 900 mm; ref 309CC	275.20	1.71	31.25	311.27	nr	**342.52**
1770 mm x 1050 mm; ref 310C	260.82	1.80	32.89	295.03	nr	**327.92**
1770 mm x 1050 mm; ref 310T	343.80	1.71	31.25	388.69	nr	**419.94**
1770 mm x 1050 mm; ref 310CC	288.79	1.43	26.13	326.59	nr	**352.73**
1770 mm x 1050 mm; ref 310WW	304.11	1.43	26.13	343.89	nr	**370.02**
1770 mm x 1200 mm; ref 312C	278.54	1.85	33.81	315.13	nr	**348.94**
1770 mm x 1200 mm; ref 312T	333.93	1.85	33.81	377.65	nr	**411.46**
1770 mm x 1200 mm; ref 312CC	311.24	1.85	33.81	352.05	nr	**385.85**
1770 mm x 1200 mm; ref 312WW	322.36	1.85	33.81	364.60	nr	**398.41**
1770 mm x 1200 mm; ref 312CVC	363.15	1.85	33.81	410.64	nr	**444.45**
1770 mm x 1350 mm; ref 313CC	352.44	1.94	35.45	398.55	nr	**434.01**
1770 mm x 1350 mm; ref 313WW	351.02	1.94	35.45	396.95	nr	**432.40**
1770 mm x 1350 mm; ref 313CVC	395.39	1.94	35.45	447.04	nr	**482.49**
1770 mm x 1500 mm; ref 315T	419.33	2.04	37.28	474.06	nr	**511.34**
2340 mm x 1050 mm; ref 410CWC	401.14	1.99	36.37	453.52	nr	**489.89**
2340 mm x 1200 mm; ref 412CWC	426.14	2.08	38.01	481.84	nr	**519.85**
2340 mm x 1350 mm; ref 413CWC	468.57	2.22	40.57	529.85	nr	**570.41**

L WINDOWS/DOORS/STAIRS

Item	PC £	Labour hours	Labour £	Material £	Unit	Total rate £
L10 WINDOWS/ROOFLIGHTS/SCREENS/ LOUVRES – cont'd						
Standard windows; "treated" wrought Softwood – cont'd						
Top hung casement windows; factory glazed with low E 24 mm double glazing; with 140 mm wide softwood sills; opening casements and ventilators hung on rustproof hinges; fitted with aluminized lacquered finish casement stays						
600 mm x 750 mm; ref 107A	120.84	0.83	15.17	136.71	nr	151.88
600 mm x 900 mm; ref 109A	127.54	0.93	17.00	144.28	nr	161.27
600 mm x 1050 mm; ref 110A	135.11	1.02	18.64	152.93	nr	171.57
915 mm x 750 mm; ref 2N07A	146.75	1.06	19.37	165.96	nr	185.33
915 mm x 900 mm; ref 2N09A	164.65	1.11	20.28	186.17	nr	206.45
915 mm x 1050 mm; ref 2N10A	175.17	1.16	21.20	198.14	nr	219.34
915 mm x 1350 mm; ref 2N13AS	221.67	1.39	25.40	250.73	nr	276.13
1200 mm x 750 mm; ref 207A	172.67	1.16	21.20	195.32	nr	216.52
1200 mm x 900 mm; ref 209A	188.45	1.20	21.93	213.14	nr	235.07
1200 mm x 1050 mm; ref 210A	201.47	1.39	25.40	227.94	nr	253.34
1200 mm x 1200 mm; ref 212A	218.36	1.48	27.05	247.00	nr	274.04
1200 mm x 1350 mm; ref 213AS	254.97	1.57	28.69	288.42	nr	317.11
1200 mm x 1500 mm; ref 215AS	278.23	1.71	31.25	314.68	nr	345.93
1770 mm x 1050 mm; ref 310AE	278.95	1.71	31.25	315.49	nr	346.74
1770 mm x 1200 mm; ref 312A	297.27	1.85	33.81	336.17	nr	369.98
High performance single light with canopy sash windows; factory glazed with low E 24 mm double glazing; ventilators; weather stripping; opening sashes and fanlights hung on rustproof hinges; fitted with aluminized lacquered espagnolette bolts						
600 mm x 900 mm; ref AL0609	187.56	0.93	17.00	212.03	nr	229.02
900 mm x 900 mm; ref AL0909	194.58	1.11	20.28	219.95	nr	240.24
900 mm x 1050 mm; ref AL0910	195.62	1.16	21.20	221.12	nr	242.32
900 mm x 1200 mm; ref AL0912	199.50	1.30	23.76	225.61	nr	249.36
900 mm x 1500 mm; ref AL0915	210.21	1.43	26.13	237.69	nr	263.83
1200 mm x 1050 mm; ref AL1210	226.73	1.39	25.40	256.34	nr	281.74
1200 mm x 1200 mm; ref AL1212	228.17	1.48	27.05	258.07	nr	285.12
1200 mm x 1500 mm; ref AL1215	257.60	1.71	31.25	291.40	nr	322.65
1500 mm x 1050 mm; ref AL1510	227.11	1.71	31.25	256.87	nr	288.12
1500 mm x 1200 mm; ref AL1512	238.49	1.71	31.25	269.71	nr	300.96
1500 mm x 1500 mm; ref AL1515	256.83	1.85	33.81	290.63	nr	324.44
1500 mm x 1650 mm; ref AL1516	265.09	1.94	35.45	299.84	nr	335.30
High performance double hung sash windows with glazing bars; factory glazed with low E 24 mm double glazing; solid frames; 63 mm x 175 mm softwood sills; standard flush external linings; spiral spring balances and sash catch						
635 mm x 1050 mm; ref VS0610B	337.34	2.04	37.28	381.20	nr	418.48
635 mm x 1350 mm; ref VS0613B	349.97	2.22	40.57	395.55	nr	436.12
635 mm x 1650 mm; ref VS0616B	373.02	2.50	45.69	421.68	nr	467.36
860 mm x 1050 mm; ref VS0810B	354.10	2.36	43.13	400.11	nr	443.24
860 mm x 1350 mm; ref VS0813B	373.33	2.64	48.24	421.92	nr	470.17
860 mm x 1650 mm; ref VS0816B	411.31	3.05	55.74	464.89	nr	520.63
1085 mm x 1050 mm; ref VS1010B	379.47	2.64	48.24	428.75	nr	476.99
1085 mm x 1350 mm; ref VS1013B	410.08	3.05	55.74	463.40	nr	519.14
1085 mm x 1650 mm; ref VS1016B	445.85	3.75	68.53	503.88	nr	572.41
1725 mm x 1050 mm; ref VS1710B	616.22	3.75	68.53	696.09	nr	764.62
1725 mm x 1350 mm; ref VS1713B	656.14	4.67	85.34	741.24	nr	826.59
1725 mm x 1650 mm; ref VS1716B	731.26	4.76	86.99	826.15	nr	913.13

L WINDOWS/DOORS/STAIRS

Item	PC £	Labour hours	Labour £	Material £	Unit	Total rate £
Standard windows; Jeld-Wen Hardwood or other equal and approved; factory applied preservative stain base coat						
Side hung casement windows; factory glazed with low E 24 mm double glazing; 45 mm x 140 mm hardwood sills; weather stripping; opening sashes on canopy hinges; fitted with fasteners; brown finish ironmongery						
630 mm x 750 mm; ref LEW107CH	220.25	0.97	17.73	248.93	nr	**266.65**
630 mm x 900 mm; ref LEW109CH	232.90	1.20	21.93	263.20	nr	**285.13**
630 mm x 900 mm; ref LEW109VH	266.43	0.97	17.73	301.05	nr	**318.78**
630 mm x 1050 mm; ref LEW110VH	327.26	1.34	24.49	369.71	nr	**394.19**
915 mm x 900 mm; ref LEW2N09WH	314.82	1.53	27.96	355.77	nr	**383.73**
915 mm x 1050 mm; ref LEW2N10WH	327.26	1.62	29.60	369.92	nr	**399.52**
915 mm x 1200 mm; ref LEW2N12WH	341.68	1.71	31.25	386.19	nr	**417.44**
915 mm x 1350 mm; ref LEW2N13WH	355.77	1.85	33.81	402.10	nr	**435.90**
915 mm x 1550 mm; ref LEW2N15WH	392.25	1.94	35.45	443.38	nr	**478.83**
1200 mm x 900 mm; ref LEW209CH	343.02	1.71	31.25	387.50	nr	**418.75**
1200 mm x 900 mm; ref LEW209CVH	432.04	1.71	31.25	487.98	nr	**519.23**
1200 mm x 1050 mm; ref LEW210CH	354.24	1.85	33.81	400.16	nr	**433.97**
1200 mm x 1050 mm; ref LEW210CVH	452.26	1.85	33.81	510.81	nr	**544.61**
1200 mm x 1200 mm; ref LEW212CH	388.95	1.99	36.37	439.45	nr	**475.82**
1200 mm x 1200 mm; ref LEW212CVH	474.14	1.99	36.37	535.60	nr	**571.97**
1200 mm x 1350 mm; ref LEW213CVH	506.70	2.13	38.92	572.36	nr	**611.28**
1200 mm x 1550 mm; ref LEW215CVH	542.77	2.22	40.57	613.07	nr	**653.64**
1770 mm x 1050 mm; ref LEW310TH	541.13	2.31	42.21	611.32	nr	**653.54**
1770 mm x 1050 mm; ref LEW310CCH	541.13	2.31	42.21	611.32	nr	**653.54**
1770 mm x 1200 mm; ref LEW312CH	576.30	2.45	44.77	651.02	nr	**695.79**
1770 mm x 1200 mm; ref LEW312CCH	576.30	2.45	44.77	651.02	nr	**695.79**
2339 mm x 1200 mm; ref LEW412CMCH	744.46	2.64	48.24	840.93	nr	**889.18**
Top hung casement windows; factory glazed with low E 24 mm double glazing; 45 mm x 140 mm hardwood sills; weather stripping; opening sashes on canopy hinges; fitted with fasteners; brown finish ironmongery						
630 mm x 900 mm; ref LEW109AH	244.65	0.97	17.73	276.46	nr	**294.19**
630 mm x 1050 mm; ref LEW110AH	256.65	1.34	24.49	290.11	nr	**314.60**
915 mm x 900 mm; ref LEW2N09AH	316.23	1.53	27.96	357.25	nr	**385.21**
915 mm x 1050 mm; ref LEW2N10AH	334.02	1.62	29.60	377.44	nr	**407.05**
915 mm x 1350 mm; ref LEW2N13ASH	384.85	1.85	33.81	434.93	nr	**468.73**
1200 mm x 1050 mm; ref LEW210AH	381.07	1.71	31.25	430.55	nr	**461.80**
1200 mm x 1350 mm; ref LEW212ASH	405.85	1.85	33.81	458.53	nr	**492.33**
1770 mm x 1050 mm; ref LEW310AEH	513.21	1.94	35.45	579.80	nr	**615.26**
Purpose made window casements; "treated" wrought softwood						
Casements; rebated; moulded - supply only						
44 mm thick	-	-	-	57.93	m²	**57.93**
57 mm thick	-	-	-	60.84	m²	**60.84**
Casements; rebated; moulded; in medium panes - supply only						
44 mm thick	-	-	-	92.60	m²	**92.60**
57 mm thick	-	-	-	96.49	m²	**96.49**
Casements; rebated; moulded; with semi-circular head - supply only						
44 mm thick	-	-	-	121.08	m²	**121.08**
57 mm thick	-	-	-	124.87	m²	**124.87**

L WINDOWS/DOORS/STAIRS

Item	PC £	Labour hours	Labour £	Material £	Unit	Total rate £
L10 WINDOWS/ROOFLIGHTS/SCREENS/ LOUVRES – cont'd						
Purpose made window casements; "treated" wrought softwood – cont'd						
Casements; rebated; moulded; to bullseye window - supply only						
44 mm thick; 600 mm diameter	-	-	-	191.92	nr	**191.92**
44 mm thick; 900 mm diameter	-	-	-	228.64	nr	**228.64**
57 mm thick; 600 mm diameter	-	-	-	200.96	nr	**200.96**
57 mm thick; 900 mm diameter	-	-	-	27.65	nr	**27.65**
Fitting and hanging casements						
square or rectangular	-	-	-	13.54	nr	**13.54**
semi-circular	-	-	-	22.01	nr	**22.01**
bullseye	-	-	-	27.65	nr	**27.65**
Purpose made window casements; selected Sapele						
Casements; rebated; moulded - supply only						
44 mm thick	-	-	-	65.85	m^2	**65.85**
57 mm thick	-	-	-	72.15	m^2	**72.15**
Casements; rebated; moulded; in medium panes - supply only						
44 mm thick	-	-	-	106.63	m^2	**106.63**
57 mm thick	-	-	-	115.05	m^2	**115.05**
Casements; rebated; moulded with semi-circular head - supply only						
44 mm thick	-	-	-	134.33	m^2	**134.33**
57 mm thick	-	-	-	142.55	m^2	**142.55**
Casements; rebated; moulded; to bullseye window - supply only						
44 mm thick; 600 mm diameter	-	-	-	237.41	nr	**237.41**
44 mm thick; 900 mm diameter	-	-	-	285.71	nr	**285.71**
57 mm thick; 600 mm diameter	-	-	-	256.99	nr	**256.99**
57 mm thick; 900 mm diameter	-	-	-	310.65	nr	**310.65**
Fitting and hanging casements						
square or rectangular	-	-	-	14.67	nr	**14.67**
semi-circular	-	-	-	24.27	nr	**24.27**
bullseye	-	-	-	31.04	nr	**31.04**
Purpose made window frames; "treated" wrought softwood; prices indicated are for supply only as part of a complete window frame; the reader is referred to the previous pages for fixing costs for frames based on the overall window size						
Frames; rounded; rebated check grooved						
44 mm x 69 mm	-	-	-	15.00	m	**15.00**
44 mm x 94 mm	-	-	-	15.72	m	**15.72**
44 mm x 119 mm	-	-	-	16.43	m	**16.43**
57 mm x 94 mm	-	-	-	16.47	m	**16.47**
69 mm x 144 mm	-	-	-	21.72	m	**21.72**
90 mm x 140 mm	-	-	-	30.81	m	**30.81**
Mullions and transoms; twice rounded, rebated and check grooved						
57 mm x 69 mm	-	-	-	17.46	m	**17.46**
57 mm x 94 mm	-	-	-	18.35	m	**18.35**
69 mm x 94 mm	-	-	-	20.76	m	**20.76**
69 mm x 144 mm	-	-	-	30.48	m	**30.48**

L WINDOWS/DOORS/STAIRS

Item	PC £	Labour hours	Labour £	Material £	Unit	Total rate £
Sill; sunk weathered, rebated and grooved						
69 mm x 94 mm	-	-	-	36.44	m	36.44
69 mm x 144 mm	-	-	-	38.57	m	38.57
Add 5% to the above material prices for "selected" softwood for staining						
Purpose made window frames; selected Sapele; prices given are for supply only as part of a complete window frame; the reader is referred to the previous pages for fixing costs for frames based on the overall window size						
Frames; rounded; rebated check grooved						
44 mm x 69 mm	-	-	-	19.14	m	19.14
44 mm x 94 mm	-	-	-	20.60	m	20.60
44 mm x 119 mm	-	-	-	22.04	m	22.04
57 mm x 94 mm	-	-	-	24.11	m	24.11
69 mm x 144 mm	-	-	-	34.54	m	34.54
90 mm x 140 mm	-	-	-	49.07	m	49.07
Mullions and transoms; twice rounded, rebated and check grooved						
57 mm x 69 mm	-	-	-	21.76	m	21.76
57 mm x 94 mm	-	-	-	25.32	m	25.32
69 mm x 94 mm	-	-	-	30.36	m	30.36
69 mm x 144 mm	-	-	-	46.14	m	46.14
Sill; sunk weathered, rebated and grooved						
69 mm x 94 mm	-	-	-	43.01	m	43.01
69 mm x 144 mm	-	-	-	47.67	m	47.67
Purpose made double hung sash windows; "treated" wrought softwood						
Cased frames of 100 mm x 25 mm grooved inner linings; 114 mm x 25 mm grooved outer linings; 125 mm x 44 mm twice rebated head linings; 125 mm x 32 mm twice rebated grooved pulley stiles; 150 mm x 13 mm linings; 50 mm x 19 mm partings slips; 25 mm x 19 mm inside beads; 150 mm x 69 mm Oak twice sunk weathered throated sill; 57 mm thick rebated and moulded sashes; moulded horns						
over 1.25 m² each; both sashes in medium panes; including spiral spring balances	386.34	2.31	42.21	515.30	m²	557.52
As above but with cased mullions	439.13	2.54	46.42	574.89	m²	621.31
Purpose made double hung sash windows; selected Sapele						
Cased frames of 100 mm x 25 mm grooved inner linings; 114 mm x 25 mm grooved outer linings; 125 mm x 38 mm twice reabated head linings; 125 mm x 32 mm twice rebated grooved pulley stiles; 150 mm x 13 mm linings; 50 mm x 19 mm parting slips; 25 mm x 19 mm inside beads; 150 mm x 75 mm Oak twice sunk weathered throated sill; 50 mm thick rebated and moulded sashes; moulded horns						
over 1.25 m² each; both sashes in medium panes; including spiral sash balances	430.03	3.05	55.74	564.62	m²	620.36
As above but with cased mullions	461.43	3.38	61.77	600.06	m²	661.83

L WINDOWS/DOORS/STAIRS

Item	PC £	Labour hours	Labour £	Material £	Unit	Total rate £
L10 WINDOWS/ROOFLIGHTS/SCREENS/ LOUVRES – cont'd						
uPVC windows; Jeld-Wen or other equal and approved; reinforced where appropriate with aluminium alloy; including standard ironmongery; cills and factory glazed with low E 24mm double glazing; fixed in position; including lugs plugged and screwed to brickwork or blockwork						
Casement/fixed light; including e.p.d.m.glazing gaskets and weather seals						
630 mm x 900 mm; ref P109C	100.61	1.53	27.96	113.98	nr	**141.94**
630 mm x 1200 mm; ref P112C	112.27	1.80	32.89	127.25	nr	**160.15**
1200 mm x 1200 mm; ref P212C	147.27	2.04	37.28	166.86	nr	**204.14**
1770 mm x 1200 mm; ref P312CC	239.13	2.04	37.28	270.55	nr	**307.82**
Casement/fixed light; including vents, e.p.d.m.glazing gaskets and weather seals						
630 mm x 900 mm; ref P109C	115.19	1.53	27.96	130.44	nr	**158.40**
630 mm x 1200 mm; ref P112V	126.85	1.80	32.89	143.71	nr	**176.61**
1200 mm x 1200 mm; ref P212W	147.27	2.04	37.28	166.86	nr	**204.14**
1200 mm x 1200 mm; ref P212CV	210.70	2.04	37.28	238.45	nr	**275.73**
1770 mm x 1200 mm; ref P312WW	252.25	2.04	37.28	285.36	nr	**322.64**
1770 mm x 1200 mm; ref P312CV	287.25	2.04	37.28	324.86	nr	**362.14**
Galvanised steel fixed, casement and fanlight windows; Crittall "Homelight" range or other equal and approved; site glazing not included; fixed in position including lugs plugged and screwed to brickwork or blockwork						
Basic fixed lights; including easy-glaze beads						
628 mm x 292 mm; ref ZNG5	26.31	1.20	21.93	29.90	nr	**51.83**
628 mm x 923 mm; ref ZNC5	36.10	1.20	21.93	41.07	nr	**62.99**
628 mm x 1513 mm; ref ZNDV5	51.57	1.20	21.93	58.74	nr	**80.66**
1237 mm x 292 mm; ref ZNG13	41.26	1.20	21.93	46.78	nr	**68.71**
1237 mm x 923 mm; ref ZNC13	51.57	1.80	32.89	58.53	nr	**91.42**
1237 mm x 1218 mm; ref ZND13	61.88	1.80	32.89	70.27	nr	**103.16**
1237 mm x 1513 mm; ref ZNDV13	67.04	1.80	32.89	76.20	nr	**109.09**
1846 mm x 292 mm; ref ZNG14	51.57	1.20	21.93	58.53	nr	**80.45**
1846 mm x 923 mm; ref ZNC14	61.88	1.80	32.89	70.38	nr	**103.27**
1846 mm x 1513 mm; ref ZNDV14	77.35	2.22	40.57	88.05	nr	**128.61**
Basic opening lights; including easy-glaze beads and weatherstripping						
628 mm x 292 mm; ref ZNG1	67.04	1.20	21.93	75.88	nr	**97.81**
1237 mm x 292 mm; ref ZNG13G	97.98	1.20	21.93	110.80	nr	**132.73**
1846 mm x 292 mm; ref ZNG4	165.02	1.20	21.93	186.68	nr	**208.61**
One piece composites; including easy-glaze beads and weatherstripping						
628 mm x 923 mm; ref ZNC5F	92.82	1.20	21.93	105.09	nr	**127.02**
628 mm x 1513 mm; ref ZNDV5F	108.30	1.20	21.93	122.77	nr	**144.70**
1237 mm x 923 mm; ref ZNC2F	175.34	1.80	32.89	198.23	nr	**231.12**
1237 mm x 1218 mm; ref ZND2F	206.28	1.80	32.89	233.25	nr	**266.15**
1237 mm x 1513 mm; ref ZNDV2V	242.38	1.80	32.89	274.11	nr	**307.00**
1846 mm x 923 mm; ref ZNC4F	268.16	1.80	32.89	303.21	nr	**336.10**
1846 mm x 1218 mm; ref ZND10F	257.85	2.22	40.57	291.67	nr	**332.24**

L WINDOWS/DOORS/STAIRS

Item	PC £	Labour hours	Labour £	Material £	Unit	Total rate £
Reversible windows; including easy-glaze beads						
997 mm x 923 mm; ref NC13R	232.06	1.57	28.69	262.25	nr	290.94
997 mm x 1067 mm; ref NCO13R	242.38	1.57	28.69	273.90	nr	302.59
1237 mm x 923 mm; ref ZNC13R	252.69	2.36	43.13	285.54	nr	328.67
1237 mm x 1218 mm; ref ZND13R	273.32	2.36	43.13	308.93	nr	352.05
1237 mm x 1513 mm; ref ZNDV13RS	309.41	2.36	43.13	349.77	nr	392.90
Pressed steel sills; to suit above window widths						
628 mm long	15.99	0.37	6.76	18.05	nr	24.82
997 mm long	20.62	0.46	8.41	23.28	nr	31.69
1237 mm long	26.31	0.56	10.23	29.69	nr	39.93
1846 mm long	36.10	0.79	14.44	40.75	nr	55.19
Factory finished steel fixed light;						
casement and fanlight windows; Crittall						
polyester powder coated "Homelight"						
range or other equal and approved; site						
glazing not included; fixed in position;						
including lugs plugged and screwed to						
brickwork or blockwork						
Basic fixed lights; including easy-glaze beads						
628 mm x 292 mm; ref ZNG5	33.51	1.20	21.93	38.03	nr	59.96
628 mm x 923 mm; ref ZNC5	46.42	1.20	21.93	52.71	nr	74.63
628 mm x 1513 mm; ref ZNDV5	67.04	1.20	21.93	76.20	nr	98.12
1237 mm x 292 mm; ref ZNG13	51.57	1.20	21.93	58.42	nr	80.35
1237 mm x 923 mm; ref ZNC13	67.04	1.80	32.89	75.99	nr	108.88
1237 mm x 1218 mm; ref ZND13	77.35	1.80	32.89	87.73	nr	120.62
1237 mm x 1513 mm; ref ZNDV13	82.51	1.80	32.89	93.66	nr	126.55
1846 mm x 292 mm; ref ZNG14	67.04	1.20	21.93	75.88	nr	97.81
1846 mm x 923 mm; ref ZNC14	82.51	1.80	32.89	93.45	nr	126.34
1846 mm x 1513 mm; ref ZNDV14	97.98	2.22	40.57	111.12	nr	151.69
Basic opening lights; including easy-glaze beads and weatherstripping						
628 mm x 292 mm; ref ZNG1	79.93	1.20	21.93	90.43	nr	112.36
1237 mm x 292 mm; ref ZNG13G	113.46	1.20	21.93	128.27	nr	150.20
1846 mm x 292 mm; ref ZNG4	195.96	1.20	21.93	221.40	nr	243.33
One piece composites; including easy-glaze beads and weatherstripping						
628 mm x 923 mm; ref ZNC5F	108.30	1.20	21.93	122.56	nr	144.49
628 mm x 1513 mm; ref ZNDV5F	134.08	1.20	21.93	151.87	nr	173.80
1237 mm x 923 mm; ref ZNC2F	216.59	1.80	32.89	244.79	nr	277.68
1237 mm x 1218 mm; ref ZND2F	247.54	1.80	32.89	279.72	nr	312.61
1237 mm x 1513 mm; ref ZNDV2V	288.79	1.80	32.89	326.49	nr	359.38
1846 mm x 923 mm; ref ZNC4F	324.89	1.80	32.89	367.03	nr	399.93
1846 mm x 1218 mm; ref ZND10F	309.41	2.22	40.57	349.77	nr	390.34
Reversible windows; including easy-glaze beads						
997 mm x 923 mm; ref NC13R	299.10	1.57	28.69	337.92	nr	366.61
997 mm x 1218 mm; ref NCO13R	314.58	1.57	28.69	355.39	nr	384.08
1237 mm x 923 mm; ref ZNC13R	324.89	2.36	43.13	367.03	nr	410.16
1237 mm x 1218 mm; ref ZND13R	355.82	2.36	43.13	402.06	nr	445.18
1237 mm x 1513 mm; ref ZNDV13RS	397.08	2.36	43.13	448.73	nr	491.86
Pressed steel sills; to suit above window widths						
628 mm long	20.62	0.37	6.76	23.28	nr	30.04
997 mm long	27.85	0.46	8.41	31.43	nr	39.84
1237 mm long	33.00	0.56	10.23	37.25	nr	47.49
1846 mm long	46.42	0.79	14.44	52.39	nr	66.83

L WINDOWS/DOORS/STAIRS

Item	PC £	Labour hours	Labour £	Material £	Unit	Total rate £
L10 WINDOWS/ROOFLIGHTS/SCREENS/ LOUVRES – cont'd						
Rooflights, skylights, roof windows and frames; pre-glazed; "treated" Nordic Red Pine and aluminium trimmed "Velux" windows or other equal and approved; type U flashings and soakers (for tiles and pantiles), and sealed double glazing unit (trimming opening not included)						
Roof windows						
550 mm x 780 mm; ref GGL-3000-C02	135.87	2.05	37.46	153.72	nr	**191.18**
550 mm x 980 mm; ref GGL-3000-C04	149.69	2.31	42.21	169.31	nr	**211.52**
660 mm x 1180 mm; ref GGL-3000-F06	177.35	2.54	46.42	200.61	nr	**247.02**
780 mm x 980 mm; ref GGL-3000-M04	169.18	2.54	46.42	191.38	nr	**237.80**
780 mm x 1180 mm; ref GGL-3000-M06	189.67	3.05	55.74	214.71	nr	**270.45**
780 mm x 1400 mm; ref GGL-3000-M08	204.44	2.54	46.42	231.31	nr	**277.73**
940 mm x 1600 mm; ref GGL-3000-P10	244.72	3.05	55.74	276.85	nr	**332.59**
1140 mm x 1180 mm; ref GGL-3000-S06	225.77	3.05	55.74	255.47	nr	**311.21**
1340 mm x 980 mm; ref GGL-3000-U04	233.18	3.05	55.74	263.83	nr	**319.57**
Rooflights, skylights, roof windows and frames; uPVC; plugged and screwed to concrete; or screwed to timber						
Rooflight; Cox "Suntube" range or other equal and approved; double skin polycarbonate dome						
230 mm dia.; for flat roof using felt or membrane	259.00	3.10	56.65	293.06	nr	**349.71**
230 mm dia.; for up to 30 degrees pitch roof with standard tiles	259.00	3.75	68.53	292.93	nr	**361.46**
230 mm dia.; for up to 30 degrees pitch roof with bold roll tiles	329.00	3.75	68.53	372.01	nr	**440.54**
Rooflight; Cox "Galaxy" range or other equal and approved; double skin polycarbonate dome						
600 mm x 600 mm	111.00	1.90	34.72	125.29	nr	**160.01**
900 mm x 900 mm	205.00	2.20	40.20	231.39	nr	**271.60**
1200 mm x 1200 mm	314.00	2.50	45.69	354.43	nr	**400.11**
Rooflight; Cox " Trade" range or other equal and approved; double skin polycarbonate dome on 150mm PVCU upstand						
600 mm x 600 mm	244.00	2.50	45.69	275.42	nr	**321.10**
900 mm x 900 mm	386.00	2.80	51.17	435.70	nr	**486.87**
1200 mm x 1200 mm	546.00	3.10	56.65	616.30	nr	**672.95**
Rooflight; Cox "2000" range or other equal and approved; double skin polycarbonate dome on 235mm PVCU upstand						
900 mm x 900 mm	972.00	3.10	56.65	1097.60	nr	**1154.25**
1200 mm x 1200 mm	1335.00	3.75	68.53	1507.40	nr	**1575.93**
Louvres and frames; polyester powder coated aluminium; fixing in position including brackets						
Louvre; Gil Airvac "Plusaire 75SP" weatherlip or other equal and approved						
1250 mm x 675 mm	-	-	-	-	nr	**579.45**
2000 mm x 530 mm	-	-	-	-	nr	**579.45**

L WINDOWS/DOORS/STAIRS

Item	PC £	Labour hours	Labour £	Material £	Unit	Total rate £
L20 DOORS/SHUTTERS/HATCHES						
Doors; standard matchboarded; wrought softwood						
Matchboarded, ledged and braced doors; 25 mm thick ledges and braces; 19 mm thick tongued, grooved and V-jointed boarding; one side vertical boarding						
762 mm x 1981 mm	67.05	1.53	27.96	75.68	nr	103.64
838 mm x 1981 mm	67.05	1.53	27.96	75.68	nr	103.64
Matchboarded, framed, ledged and braced doors; 44 mm thick overall; 19 mm thick tongued, grooved and V-jointed boarding; one side vertical boarding						
762 mm x 1981 mm	82.94	1.85	33.81	93.61	nr	127.42
838 mm x 1981 mm	82.94	1.85	33.81	93.61	nr	127.42
Doors; standard flush; softwood composition						
Flush door; internal quality; skeleton or cellular core; hardboard faced both sides; Jeld-Wen "Carrwood" or other equal and approved						
457 mm x 1981 mm x 35 mm	20.72	1.30	23.76	23.39	nr	47.14
533 mm x 1981 mm x 35 mm	20.72	1.30	23.76	23.39	nr	47.14
610 mm x 1981 mm x 35 mm	20.72	1.30	23.76	23.39	nr	47.14
686 mm x 1981 mm x 35 mm	21.12	1.30	23.76	23.84	nr	47.59
762 mm x 1981 mm x 35 mm	21.42	1.30	23.76	24.18	nr	47.93
838 mm x 1981 mm x 35 mm	22.55	1.30	23.76	25.46	nr	49.21
626 mm x 2040 mm x 40 mm	22.38	1.30	23.76	25.26	nr	49.02
726 mm x 2040 mm x 40 mm	22.81	1.30	23.76	25.75	nr	49.51
Flush door; internal quality; skeleton or cellular core; chipboard veneered; faced both sides; lipped on two long edges; Jeld-Wen "Paint grade veneered" or other equal and approved						
457 mm x 1981 mm x 35 mm	28.04	1.30	23.76	31.64	nr	55.40
533 mm x 1981 mm x 35 mm	28.04	1.30	23.76	31.64	nr	55.40
610 mm x 1981 mm x 35 mm	28.04	1.30	23.76	31.64	nr	55.40
686 mm x 1981 mm x 35 mm	28.04	1.30	23.76	31.64	nr	55.40
762 mm x 1981 mm x 35 mm	28.74	1.30	23.76	32.44	nr	56.20
838 mm x 1981 mm x 35 mm	30.04	1.30	23.76	33.91	nr	57.67
526 mm x 2040 mm x 40 mm	29.86	1.30	23.76	33.71	nr	57.46
626 mm x 2040 mm x 40 mm	29.86	1.30	23.76	33.71	nr	57.46
726 mm x 2040 mm x 40 mm	30.51	1.30	23.76	34.44	nr	58.20
826 mm x 2040 mm x 40 mm	31.52	1.30	23.76	35.58	nr	59.34
Flush door; internal quality; skeleton or cellular core; veneer faced both sides; lipped on two long edges; Jeld-Wen "Sapele veneered" or other equal and approved						
457 mm x 1981 mm x 35 mm	36.67	1.39	25.40	41.39	nr	66.79
533 mm x 1981 mm x 35 mm	36.67	1.39	25.40	41.39	nr	66.79
610 mm x 1981 mm x 35 mm	36.67	1.39	25.40	41.39	nr	66.79
686 mm x 1981 mm x 35 mm	36.85	1.39	25.40	41.59	nr	66.99
762 mm x 1981 mm x 35 mm	37.04	1.39	25.40	41.81	nr	67.22
838 mm x 1981 mm x 35 mm	38.46	1.39	25.40	43.41	nr	68.81
526 mm x 2040 mm x 40 mm	37.76	1.39	25.40	42.62	nr	68.02
626 mm x 2040 mm x 40 mm	38.46	1.39	25.40	43.41	nr	68.81
726 mm x 2040 mm x 40 mm	38.68	1.39	25.40	43.66	nr	69.06
826 mm x 2040 mm x 40 mm	39.87	1.39	25.40	45.00	nr	70.40

L WINDOWS/DOORS/STAIRS

Item	PC £	Labour hours	Labour £	Material £	Unit	Total rate £
L20 DOORS/SHUTTERS/HATCHES – cont'd						
Doors; standard flush; softwood composition – cont'd						
Flush door; half-hour fire resisting (FD30); hardboard faced both sides; Jeld-Wen "Silverwood" or other equal and approved						
762 mm x 1981 mm x 44 mm	47.47	1.80	32.89	53.58	nr	**86.47**
838 mm x 1981 mm x 44 mm	49.57	1.80	32.89	55.95	nr	**88.84**
726 mm x 2040 mm x 44 mm	48.42	1.80	32.89	54.65	nr	**87.55**
826 mm x 2040 mm x 44 mm	50.71	1.80	32.89	57.24	nr	**90.13**
Flush door; half-hour fire resisting (FD30); chipboard veneered; faced both sides; lipped on two long edges; Jeld-Wen "Paint grade veneered" or other equal and approved						
610 mm x 1981 mm x 44 mm	47.47	1.80	32.89	53.58	nr	**86.47**
686 mm x 1981 mm x 44 mm	47.47	1.80	32.89	53.58	nr	**86.47**
762 mm x 1981 mm x 44 mm	47.47	1.80	32.89	53.58	nr	**86.47**
838 mm x 1981 mm x 44 mm	49.41	1.80	32.89	55.77	nr	**88.66**
526 mm x 2040 mm x 44 mm	49.81	1.80	32.89	56.23	nr	**89.12**
626 mm x 2040 mm x 44 mm	49.81	1.80	32.89	56.23	nr	**89.12**
726 mm x 2040 mm x 44 mm	49.81	1.80	32.89	56.23	nr	**89.12**
826 mm x 2040 mm x 44 mm	51.95	1.80	32.89	58.64	nr	**91.53**
Flush door; half-hour fire resisting (FD30); veneer faced both sides; lipped on two long edges; Jeld-Wen "Sapele veneered" or other equal and approved						
610 mm x 1981 mm x 44 mm	75.52	1.90	34.72	85.25	nr	**119.97**
686 mm x 1981 mm x 44 mm	75.52	1.90	34.72	85.25	nr	**119.97**
762 mm x 1981 mm x 44 mm	75.52	1.90	34.72	85.25	nr	**119.97**
838 mm x 1981 mm x 44 mm	78.22	1.90	34.72	88.29	nr	**123.01**
726 mm x 2040 mm x 44 mm	76.55	1.90	34.72	86.40	nr	**121.12**
826 mm x 2040 mm x 44 mm	79.19	1.90	34.72	89.39	nr	**124.11**
Flush door; half hour fire resisting; chipboard for painting; hardwood lipping two long edges; "Leaderflush" type B30 or other equal and approved						
526 mm x 2040 mm x 44 mm	92.48	1.90	34.72	104.39	nr	**139.11**
626 mm x 2040 mm x 44 mm	94.55	1.90	34.72	106.72	nr	**141.44**
726 mm x 2040 mm x 44 mm	96.06	1.90	34.72	108.43	nr	**143.15**
826 mm x 2040 mm x 44 mm	102.73	1.90	34.72	115.96	nr	**150.68**
Flush door; half hour fire resisting; American light oak veneer; hardwood lipping all edges; "Leaderflush" type B30 or other equal and approved						
526 mm x 2040 mm x 44 mm	124.62	1.90	34.72	140.66	nr	**175.39**
626 mm x 2040 mm x 44 mm	128.40	1.90	34.72	144.93	nr	**179.65**
726 mm x 2040 mm x 44 mm	130.80	1.90	34.72	147.64	nr	**182.36**
826 mm x 2040 mm x 44 mm	139.12	1.90	34.72	157.03	nr	**191.75**
Flush door; one hour fire resisting (FD60); plywood faced both sides; lipped on two long edges; Jeld-Wen "Paint grade veneered" or other equal and approved						
762 mm x 1981 mm x 54 mm	168.75	2.04	37.28	190.48	nr	**227.76**
838 mm x 1981 mm x 54 mm	179.38	2.04	37.28	202.47	nr	**239.75**
726 mm x 2040 mm x 54 mm	177.18	2.04	37.28	199.99	nr	**237.27**
826 mm x 2040 mm x 54 mm	188.64	2.04	37.28	212.93	nr	**250.21**

L WINDOWS/DOORS/STAIRS

Item	PC £	Labour hours	Labour £	Material £	Unit	Total rate £
Flush door; one hour fire resisting (FD60); veneer faced both sides; lipped on two long edges; Jeld-Wen "Sapele veneered" or other equal and approved						
762 mm x 1981 mm x 54 mm	113.74	2.13	38.92	128.39	nr	**167.31**
838 mm x 1981 mm x 54 mm	118.28	2.13	38.92	133.51	nr	**172.43**
Flush door; one hour fire resisting; Iroko veneer; hardwood lipping all edges; "Leaderflush" type B60 or other equal and approved; including groove and "Leaderseal" intumescent strip						
457 mm x 1981 mm x 54 mm	151.62	2.13	38.92	171.14	nr	**210.07**
533 mm x 1981 mm x 54 mm	153.30	2.13	38.92	173.04	nr	**211.96**
610 mm x 1981 mm x 54 mm	158.07	2.13	38.92	178.42	nr	**217.35**
686 mm x 1981 mm x 54 mm	159.25	2.13	38.92	179.75	nr	**218.68**
762 mm x 1981 mm x 54 mm	170.46	2.13	38.92	192.41	nr	**231.33**
838 mm x 1981 mm x 54 mm	171.88	2.13	38.92	194.01	nr	**232.93**
526 mm x 2040 mm x 54 mm	153.49	2.13	38.92	173.25	nr	**212.18**
626 mm x 2040 mm x 54 mm	158.85	2.13	38.92	179.30	nr	**218.23**
726 mm x 2040 mm x 54 mm	160.62	2.13	38.92	181.30	nr	**220.22**
826 mm x 2040 mm x 54 mm	172.42	2.13	38.92	194.62	nr	**233.54**
Flush door; external quality; skeleton or cellular core; plywood faced both sides; lipped on all four edges						
762 mm x 1981 mm x 54 mm	53.64	1.80	32.89	60.55	nr	**93.44**
838 mm x 1981 mm x 54 mm	55.57	1.80	32.89	62.72	nr	**95.62**
Flush door; external quality with standard glass opening; skeleton or cellular core; plywood faced both sides; lipped on all four edges; including glazing beads						
762 mm x 1981 mm x 54 mm	67.40	1.80	32.89	76.08	nr	**108.97**
838 mm x 1981 mm x 54 mm	69.17	1.80	32.89	78.07	nr	**110.97**
Doors; purpose made panelled; wrought softwood						
Panelled doors; one open panel for glass; including glazing beads						
686 mm x 1981 mm x 44 mm	93.60	1.80	32.89	105.65	nr	**138.55**
762 mm x 1981 mm x 44 mm	94.38	1.80	32.89	106.53	nr	**139.43**
838 mm x 1981 mm x 44 mm	95.16	1.80	32.89	107.41	nr	**140.31**
Panelled doors; two open panel for glass; including glazing beads						
686 mm x 1981 mm x 44 mm	130.87	1.80	32.89	147.72	nr	**180.61**
762 mm x 1981 mm x 44 mm	132.00	1.80	32.89	149.00	nr	**181.89**
838 mm x 1981 mm x 44 mm	133.13	1.80	32.89	150.27	nr	**183.16**
Panelled doors; four 19 mm thick plywood panels; mouldings worked on solid both sides						
686 mm x 1981 mm x 44 mm	198.73	1.80	32.89	224.32	nr	**257.21**
762 mm x 1981 mm x 44 mm	201.30	1.80	32.89	227.22	nr	**260.11**
838 mm x 1981 mm x 44 mm	203.87	1.80	32.89	230.12	nr	**263.01**
Panelled doors; six 25 mm thick panels raised and fielded; mouldings worked on solid both sides						
686 mm x 1981 mm x 44 mm	365.67	2.13	38.92	412.75	nr	**451.67**
762 mm x 1981 mm x 44 mm	369.32	2.13	38.92	416.87	nr	**455.79**
838 mm x 1981 mm x 44 mm	372.97	2.13	38.92	420.99	nr	**459.91**
rebated edges beaded	-	-	-	2.48	m	**2.48**
rounded edges or heels	-	-	-	0.56	m	**0.56**
weatherboard fixed to bottom rail	-	0.28	5.12	8.82	m	**13.93**
stopped groove for weatherboard	-	-	-	2.82	m	**2.82**

L WINDOWS/DOORS/STAIRS

Item	PC £	Labour hours	Labour £	Material £	Unit	Total rate £
L20 DOORS/SHUTTERS/HATCHES – cont'd						
Doors; purpose made panelled; selected Sapele						
Panelled doors; one open panel for glass; including glazing beads						
686 mm x 1981 mm x 44 mm	126.72	2.54	46.42	143.04	nr	**189.45**
762 mm x 1981 mm x 44 mm	128.43	2.54	46.42	144.97	nr	**191.38**
838 mm x 1981 mm x 44 mm	130.15	2.54	46.42	146.91	nr	**193.32**
686 mm x 1981 mm x 57 mm	135.45	2.82	51.53	152.89	nr	**204.42**
762 mm x 1981 mm x 57 mm	137.49	2.82	51.53	155.19	nr	**206.73**
838 mm x 1981 mm x 57 mm	139.52	2.82	51.53	157.48	nr	**209.02**
Panelled doors; 250 mm wide cross tongued intermediate rail; two open panels for glass; mouldings worked on the solid one side; 19 mm x 13 mm beads one side; fixing with brass cups and screws						
686 mm x 1981 mm x 44 mm	193.74	2.54	46.42	218.68	nr	**265.10**
762 mm x 1981 mm x 44 mm	197.00	2.54	46.42	222.36	nr	**268.78**
838 mm x 1981 mm x 44 mm	206.57	2.54	46.42	233.17	nr	**279.58**
686 mm x 1981 mm x 57 mm	206.57	2.82	51.53	233.17	nr	**284.70**
762 mm x 1981 mm x 57 mm	210.45	2.82	51.53	237.55	nr	**289.08**
838 mm x 1981 mm x 57 mm	214.41	2.82	51.53	242.02	nr	**293.55**
Panelled doors; four panels; (19 mm thick for 44 mm doors, 25 mm thick for 57 mm doors); mouldings worked on solid both sides						
686 mm x 1981 mm x 44 mm	272.23	2.54	46.42	307.28	nr	**353.70**
762 mm x 1981 mm x 44 mm	293.45	2.54	46.42	331.23	nr	**377.65**
838 mm x 1981 mm x 44 mm	307.95	2.54	46.42	347.60	nr	**394.02**
686 mm x 1981 mm x 57 mm	277.73	2.82	51.53	313.49	nr	**365.02**
762 mm x 1981 mm x 57 mm	300.70	2.82	51.53	339.42	nr	**390.95**
838 mm x 1981 mm x 57 mm	283.24	2.82	51.53	319.71	nr	**371.24**
Panelled doors; 150 mm wide stiles in one width; 430 mm wide cross tongued bottom rail; six panels raised and fielded one side; (19 mm thick for 44 mm doors, 25 mm thick for 57 mm doors); mouldings worked on solid both sides						
686 mm x 1981 mm x 44 mm	464.71	2.54	46.42	524.54	nr	**570.96**
762 mm x 1981 mm x 44 mm	512.83	2.54	46.42	578.86	nr	**625.27**
838 mm x 1981 mm x 44 mm	522.57	2.54	46.42	589.85	nr	**636.27**
686 mm x 1981 mm x 57 mm	494.85	2.82	51.53	558.56	nr	**610.10**
762 mm x 1981 mm x 57 mm	545.64	2.82	51.53	615.89	nr	**667.43**
838 mm x 1981 mm x 57 mm	588.06	2.82	51.53	663.77	nr	**715.31**
rebated edges beaded	-	-	-	3.16	m	**3.16**
rounded edges or heels	-	-	-	0.85	m	**0.85**
weatherboard fixed to bottom rail	-	0.32	5.85	11.92	m	**17.77**
stopped groove for weatherboard	-	-	-	2.93	m	**2.93**
Doors; galvanised steel "up and over" type garage doors; Catnic "Horizon 90" or other equal and approved; spring counterbalanced; fixed to timber frame (not included)						
Garage door						
2135 mm x 1980 mm	217.78	4.07	74.38	246.24	nr	**320.61**
2135 mm x 2135 mm	249.65	4.07	74.38	282.21	nr	**356.59**
2400 mm x 2135 mm	305.42	4.07	74.38	345.23	nr	**419.61**
3965 mm x 2135 mm	754.25	6.11	111.66	852.34	nr	**964.00**

L WINDOWS/DOORS/STAIRS

Item	PC £	Labour hours	Labour £	Material £	Unit	Total rate £
Doorsets; galvanised steel IG "Weatherbeater Original" door and frame units or other equal and approved; treated softwood frame, primed hardwood sill; fixing in position; plugged and screwed to brickwork or blockwork						
Door and frame						
762 mm x 1981 mm; ref IGD1	174.11	3.05	55.74	196.95	nr	252.68
Doorsets; steel door and frame units; Jandor Architectural Ltd or other equal and approved; polyester powder coated; ironmongery						
Single action door set; "Metset MD01" doors and "Metset MF" frames						
900 mm x 2100 mm	-	-	-	-	nr	2237.98
pair 1800 mm x 2100 mm	-	-	-	-	nr	3091.50
Rolling shutters and collapsible gates; steel counter shutters; Bolton Brady Ltd or other equal and approved; push-up, self-coiling; polyester power coated; fixing by bolting						
Shutters						
3000 mm x 1000 mm	-	-	-	-	nr	1347.25
4000 mm x 1000 mm; in two panels	-	-	-	-	nr	2339.95
Rolling shutters and collapsible gates; galvanised steel; Bolton Brady Type 474 or other equal and approved; one hour fibre resisting; self-coiling; activated by fusible link; fixing with bolts						
Rolling shutters and collapsible gates						
1000 mm x 2750 mm	-	-	-	-	nr	1630.88
1500 mm x 2750 mm	-	-	-	-	nr	1715.97
2400 mm x 2750 mm	-	-	-	-	nr	1985.41
Sliding/folding partitions; aluminium double glazed sliding patio doors; Crittall "Luminaire" or other equal and approved; white acrylic finish; with and including 18 thick annealed double glazing; fixed in position; including lugs plugged and screwed to brickwork or blockwork						
Patio doors						
1800 mm x 2100 mm; ref PF1821	1374.78	2.54	46.42	1553.04	nr	1599.46
2400 mm x 2100 mm; ref PF2421	1649.74	3.05	55.74	1863.40	nr	1919.14
2700 mm x 2100 mm; ref PF2721	1833.05	3.56	65.06	2070.31	nr	2135.37
Grilles; "Galaxy" nylon rolling counter grille or other equal and approved; Bolton Brady Ltd; colour, off-white; self-coiling; fixing by bolting						
Grilles						
3000 mm x 1000 mm	-	-	-	-	nr	1056.22
4000 mm x 1000 mm	-	-	-	-	nr	1615.40

L WINDOWS/DOORS/STAIRS

Item	PC £	Labour hours	Labour £	Material £	Unit	Total rate £
L20 DOORS/SHUTTERS/HATCHES – cont'd						
External softwood door frame composite standard joinery sets						
External door frame composite set; 56 mm x 78mm wide (finished); for external doors						
686 mm x 1981 mm x 44 mm	41.93	0.83	15.17	47.75	nr	**62.92**
762 mm x 1981 mm x 44 mm	42.58	0.83	15.17	48.49	nr	**63.65**
838 mm x 1981 mm x 44 mm	44.53	0.83	15.17	50.68	nr	**65.85**
External door frame composite set; 56 mm x 78mm wide (finished); with 45 mm x 140 mm (finished) hardwood cill; for external doors						
686 mm x 1981 mm x 44 mm	69.11	1.10	20.10	78.43	nr	**98.53**
762 mm x 1981 mm x 44 mm	71.27	1.10	20.10	80.87	nr	**100.97**
838 mm x 1981 mm x 44 mm	74.13	1.10	20.10	84.09	nr	**104.19**
826 mm x 2040 mm x 44 mm	76.38	1.10	20.10	86.64	nr	**106.74**
Internal white foiled moisture-resistant MDF door lining composite standard joinery set						
22 mm x 77mm wide (finished) set; with loose stops; for internal doors						
610 mm x 1981 mm x 35 mm	18.51	0.78	14.25	21.31	nr	**35.57**
686 mm x 1981 mm x 35 mm	18.49	0.78	14.25	21.29	nr	**35.54**
762 mm x 1981 mm x 35 mm	18.49	0.78	14.25	21.29	nr	**35.54**
838 mm x 1981 mm x 35 mm	19.36	0.78	14.25	22.27	nr	**36.53**
864 mm x 1981 mm x 35 mm	19.36	0.78	14.25	22.27	nr	**36.53**
22 mm x 150mm wide (finished) set; with loose stops; for internal doors						
610 mm x 1981 mm x 35 mm	23.98	0.78	14.25	27.48	nr	**41.74**
686 mm x 1981 mm x 35 mm	23.76	0.78	14.25	27.24	nr	**41.49**
762 mm x 1981 mm x 35 mm	23.98	0.78	14.25	27.48	nr	**41.74**
838 mm x 1981 mm x 35 mm	25.14	0.78	14.25	28.79	nr	**43.05**
864 mm x 1981 mm x 35 mm	25.14	0.78	14.25	28.79	nr	**43.05**
Mitred architrave set; 22 mm x 59mm wide (finished); ogee or torus; to one side of internal door						
610 mm x 1981 mm x 35 mm	7.97	0.34	6.21	9.27	nr	**15.49**
686 mm x 1981 mm x 35 mm	7.97	0.34	6.21	9.27	nr	**15.49**
762 mm x 1981 mm x 35 mm	7.97	0.34	6.21	9.27	nr	**15.49**
838 mm x 1981 mm x 35 mm	8.28	0.34	6.21	9.63	nr	**15.84**
864 mm x 1981 mm x 35 mm	8.28	0.34	6.21	9.63	nr	**15.84**
Mitred architrave sets; 22 mm x 69 mm wide (finished); ogee or torus; to one side of internal door						
610 mm x 1981 mm x 35 mm	8.37	0.34	6.21	9.72	nr	**15.94**
686 mm x 1981 mm x 35 mm	8.37	0.34	6.21	9.72	nr	**15.94**
762 mm x 1981 mm x 35 mm	8.37	0.34	6.21	9.72	nr	**15.94**
838 mm x 1981 mm x 35 mm	8.74	0.34	6.21	10.14	nr	**16.35**
864 mm x 1981 mm x 35 mm	8.74	0.34	6.21	10.14	nr	**16.35**
Door frames and door linings, sets; purpose made; wrought softwood						
Jambs and heads; as linings						
32 mm x 63 mm	-	0.19	3.47	6.13	m	**9.60**
32 mm x 100 mm	-	0.19	3.47	6.90	m	**10.37**
32 mm x 140 mm	-	0.19	3.47	7.40	m	**10.87**

L WINDOWS/DOORS/STAIRS

Item	PC £	Labour hours	Labour £	Material £	Unit	Total rate £
Jambs and heads; as frames; rebated, rounded and grooved						
44 mm x 75 mm	-	0.19	3.47	9.83	m	**13.31**
44 mm x 100 mm	-	0.19	3.47	10.58	m	**14.05**
44 mm x 115 mm	-	0.19	3.47	10.68	m	**14.16**
44 mm x 140 mm	-	0.19	3.47	11.19	m	**14.66**
57 mm x 100 mm	-	0.19	3.47	11.35	m	**14.82**
57 mm x 125 mm	-	0.19	3.47	11.98	m	**15.45**
69 mm x 88 mm	-	0.19	3.47	11.51	m	**14.98**
69 mm x 100 mm	-	0.19	3.47	12.26	m	**15.73**
69 mm x 125 mm	-	0.19	3.47	13.12	m	**16.59**
69 mm x 100 mm	-	0.19	3.47	12.37	m	**15.84**
69 mm x 125 mm	-	0.23	4.20	13.12	m	**17.33**
69 mm x 150 mm	-	0.23	4.20	13.89	m	**18.09**
94 mm x 100 mm	-	0.28	5.12	18.70	m	**23.82**
94 mm x 150 mm	-	0.28	5.12	21.78	m	**26.90**
Mullions and transoms; in linings						
32 mm x 63 mm	-	0.14	2.56	8.10	m	**10.66**
32 mm x 100 mm	-	0.14	2.56	8.87	m	**11.43**
32 mm x 140 mm	-	0.14	2.56	9.26	m	**11.81**
Mullions and transoms; in frames; twice rebated, rounded and grooved						
44 mm x 75 mm	-	0.14	2.56	12.28	m	**14.84**
44 mm x 100 mm	-	0.14	2.56	12.79	m	**15.35**
44 mm x 115 mm	-	0.14	2.56	12.79	m	**15.35**
44 mm x 140 mm	-	0.14	2.56	13.30	m	**15.86**
57 mm x 100 mm	-	0.14	2.56	13.45	m	**16.01**
57 mm x 125 mm	-	0.14	2.56	14.09	m	**16.65**
69 mm x 88 mm	-	0.14	2.56	13.30	m	**15.86**
69 mm x 100 mm	-	0.14	2.56	14.06	m	**16.62**
69 mm x 100 mm	-	0.14	2.56	16.08	m	**18.64**
Add 5% to the above material prices for selected softwood for staining						
Door frames and door linings, sets; purpose made; selected Sapele						
Jambs and heads; as linings						
32 mm x 63 mm	6.32	0.23	4.20	7.24	m	**11.44**
32 mm x 100 mm	10.28	0.23	4.20	11.71	m	**15.91**
32 mm x 140 mm	11.25	0.23	4.20	12.91	m	**17.11**
Jambs and heads; as frames; rebated, rounded and grooved						
44 mm x 75 mm	13.63	0.23	4.20	15.49	m	**19.69**
44 mm x 100 mm	15.53	0.23	4.20	17.63	m	**21.84**
44 mm x 115 mm	16.05	0.23	4.20	18.33	m	**22.53**
44 mm x 140 mm	16.82	0.28	5.12	19.20	m	**24.31**
57 mm x 100 mm	17.20	0.28	5.12	19.62	m	**24.74**
57 mm x 125 mm	18.82	0.28	5.12	21.45	m	**26.57**
69 mm x 88 mm	17.18	0.28	5.12	19.50	m	**24.61**
69 mm x 100 mm	19.11	0.28	5.12	21.68	m	**26.79**
69 mm x 125 mm	21.04	0.28	5.12	23.96	m	**29.08**
69 mm x 100 mm	19.11	0.28	5.12	21.78	m	**26.90**
69 mm x 125 mm	21.04	0.32	5.85	23.96	m	**29.81**
69 mm x 150 mm	22.97	0.32	5.85	26.14	m	**31.98**
94 mm x 100 mm	26.83	0.32	5.85	30.49	m	**36.34**
94 mm x 150 mm	32.91	0.32	5.85	37.36	m	**43.20**
Mullions and transoms; in linings						
32 mm x 63 mm	10.44	0.19	3.47	11.78	m	**15.26**
32 mm x 100 mm	12.39	0.19	3.47	13.99	m	**17.46**
32 mm x 140 mm	13.37	0.19	3.47	15.09	m	**18.56**

L WINDOWS/DOORS/STAIRS

Item	PC £	Labour hours	Labour £	Material £	Unit	Total rate £
L20 DOORS/SHUTTERS/HATCHES – cont'd						
Door frames and door linings, sets;						
purpose made; selected Sapele – cont'd						
Mullions and transoms; in frames; twice rebated,						
rounded and grooved						
44 mm x 75 mm	16.78	0.19	3.47	18.94	m	**22.41**
44 mm x 100 mm	18.06	0.19	3.47	20.39	m	**23.86**
44 mm x 115 mm	18.58	0.19	3.47	20.97	m	**24.44**
44 mm x 140 mm	19.35	0.19	3.47	21.84	m	**25.31**
57 mm x 100 mm	19.74	0.19	3.47	22.28	m	**25.75**
57 mm x 125 mm	21.36	0.19	3.47	24.11	m	**27.58**
69 mm x 88 mm	19.35	0.19	3.47	21.84	m	**25.31**
69 mm x 100 mm	21.78	0.19	3.47	24.58	m	**28.06**
69 mm x 100 mm	27.12	0.19	3.47	30.61	m	**34.08**
Sills; once sunk weathered; once rebated, three						
times grooved						
57 mm x 175 mm	48.21	0.32	5.85	54.42	m	**60.26**
69 mm x 125 mm	46.43	0.32	5.85	52.41	m	**58.26**
69 mm x 150 mm	48.62	0.32	5.85	54.88	m	**60.73**
Door frames and door linings, sets;						
European Oak						
Sills; once sunk weathered; once rebated, three						
times grooved						
57 mm x 175 mm	79.24	0.32	5.85	89.44	m	**95.29**
69 mm x 125 mm	78.23	0.32	5.85	88.30	m	**94.15**
69 mm x 150 mm	85.53	0.32	5.85	96.54	m	**102.39**
Bedding and pointing frames						
Pointing wood frames or sills with mastic						
one side	-	0.09	1.26	0.57	m	**1.83**
both sides	-	0.19	2.67	1.14	m	**3.81**
Pointing wood frames or sills with polysulphide						
sealant						
one side	-	0.09	1.26	1.81	m	**3.07**
both sides	-	0.19	2.67	3.62	m	**6.29**
Bedding wood frames in cement mortar (1:3) and						
point						
one side	-	0.09	2.05	0.08	m	**2.13**
both sides	-	0.09	2.05	0.10	m	**2.16**
one side in mortar; other side in mastic	-	0.19	3.55	0.65	m	**4.20**
L30 STAIRS/WALKWAYS/BALUSTRADES						
Standard staircases; wrought softwood						
(parana pine)						
Stairs; 25 mm thick treads with rounded nosings;						
9 mm thick plywood risers; 32 mm thick strings;						
bullnose bottom tread; 50 mm x 75 mm hardwood						
handrail; 32 mm square plain balusters; 100 mm						
square plain newel posts						
straight flight; 838 mm wide; 2676 mm going;						
2600 mm rise; with two newel posts	-	7.12	130.11	485.48	nr	**615.59**
straight flight with turn; 838 wide; 2676 going;						
2600 rise; with two newel posts; three top treads						
winding	-	7.12	130.11	614.13	nr	**744.24**
dogleg staircase; 838 mm wide; 2676 mm going;						
2600 mm rise; with two newel posts; quarter						
space landing third riser from top	-	7.12	130.11	516.11	nr	**646.22**

L WINDOWS/DOORS/STAIRS

Item	PC £	Labour hours	Labour £	Material £	Unit	Total rate £
dogleg staircase; 838 mm wide; 2676 mm going; 2600 mm rise; with two newel posts; half space landing third riser from top	-	8.14	148.75	546.74	nr	**695.49**
Standard balustrades; wrought softwood Landing balustrade; 50 mm x 75 mm hardwood handrail; three 32 mm x 140 mm balustrade kneerails; two 32 mm x 50 mm stiffeners; one end of handrail jointed to newel post; other end built into wall; (newel post and mortices both not included)						
3.00 m long	-	2.82	51.53	165.41	nr	**216.94**
Landing balustrade; 50 mm x 75 mm hardwood handrail; 32 mm square plain balusters; one end of handrail jointed to newel post; other end built into wall; balusters housed in at bottom (newel post and mortices both not included)						
3.00 m long	-	4.07	74.38	104.14	nr	**178.52**
Hardwood staircases; purpose made; assembled at works Fixing only complete staircase including landings, balustrades, etc.						
plugging and screwing to brickwork or blockwork	-	15.26	278.87	2.56	nr	**281.43**
The following are supply only prices for purpose made staircase components in selected Sapele supplied as part of an assembled staircase and may be used to arrive at a guide price for a complete hardwood staircase Board landings; cross-tongued joints; 100 mm x 50 mm sawn softwood bearers						
25 mm thick	-	-	-	106.96	m²	**106.96**
32 mm thick	-	-	-	120.25	m²	**120.25**
Treads; cross-tongued joints and risers; rounded nosings; tongued, grooved, glued and blocked together; one 175 mm x 50 mm sawn softwood carriage						
25 mm treads; 19 mm risers	-	-	-	214.96	m²	**214.96**
ends; quadrant	-	-	-	65.49	nr	**65.49**
ends; housed to hardwood	-	-	-	1.21	nr	**1.21**
32 mm treads; 25 mm risers	-	-	-	222.71	m²	**222.71**
ends; quadrant	-	-	-	84.17	nr	**84.17**
ends; housed to hardwood	-	-	-	1.21	nr	**1.21**
Winders; cross-tongued joints and risers in one width; rounded nosings; tongued, grooved glued and blocked together; one 175 mm x 50 mm sawn softwood carriage						
25 mm treads; 19 mm risers	-	-	-	298.84	m²	**298.84**
32 mm treads; 25 mm risers	-	-	-	305.86	m²	**305.86**
wide ends; housed to hardwood	-	-	-	2.42	nr	**2.42**
narrow ends; housed to hardwood	-	-	-	1.82	nr	**1.82**
Closed strings; in one width; 230 mm wide; rounded twice						
32 mm thick	-	-	-	39.36	m	**39.36**
44 mm thick	-	-	-	42.86	m	**42.86**
57 mm thick	-	-	-	47.73	m	**47.73**

L WINDOWS/DOORS/STAIRS

Item	PC £	Labour hours	Labour £	Material £	Unit	Total rate £
L30 STAIRS/WALKWAYS/BALUSTRADES – cont'd						
Purpose made staircase components in selected Sapele – cont'd						
Closed strings; cross-tongued joints; 280 mm wide; once rounded						
32 mm thick	-	-	-	51.09	m	**51.09**
extra for short ramp	-	-	-	26.24	nr	**26.24**
44 mm thick	-	-	-	55.73	m	**55.73**
extra for short ramp	-	-	-	29.83	nr	**29.83**
57 mm thick	-	-	-	62.19	m	**62.19**
extra for short ramp	-	-	-	36.94	nr	**36.94**
Closed strings; ramped; crossed tongued joints 280 mm wide; once rounded						
32 mm thick	-	-	-	51.09	m	**51.09**
44 mm thick	-	-	-	55.73	m	**55.73**
57 mm thick	-	-	-	62.19	m	**62.19**
Apron linings; in one width 230 mm wide						
19 mm thick	-	-	-	13.59	m	**13.59**
25 mm thick	-	-	-	16.01	m	**16.01**
Handrails; rounded						
40 mm x 50 mm	-	-	-	14.75	m	**14.75**
50 mm x 75 mm	-	-	-	17.79	m	**17.79**
57 mm x 87 mm	-	-	-	20.87	m	**20.87**
69 mm x 100 mm	-	-	-	25.94	m	**25.94**
Handrails; moulded						
40 mm x 50 mm	-	-	-	16.41	m	**16.41**
50 mm x 75 mm	-	-	-	19.45	m	**19.45**
57 mm x 87 mm	-	-	-	22.54	m	**22.54**
69 mm x 100 mm	-	-	-	27.60	m	**27.60**
Add to above for						
grooved once	-	-	-	0.73	m	**0.73**
ends; framed	-	-	-	6.91	nr	**6.91**
ends; framed on rake	-	-	-	8.47	nr	**8.47**
Heading joints to handrail; mitred or raked						
overall size not exceeding 50 mm x 75 mm	-	-	-	33.86	nr	**33.86**
overall size not exceeding 69 mm x 100 mm	-	-	-	42.33	nr	**42.33**
Knee piece to handrail; mitred or raked						
overall size not exceeding 69 mm x 100 mm	-	-	-	90.30	nr	**90.30**
Balusters; stiffeners						
25 mm x 25 mm	-	-	-	3.77	m	**3.77**
32 mm x 32 mm	-	-	-	4.30	m	**4.30**
44 mm x 44 mm	-	-	-	5.64	m	**5.64**
ends; housed	-	-	-	1.69	nr	**1.69**
Sub rails						
32 mm x 63 mm	-	-	-	8.70	m	**8.70**
ends; framed joint to newel	-	-	-	7.34	nr	**7.34**
Knee rails						
32 mm x 140 mm	-	-	-	14.44	m	**14.44**
ends; framed joint to newel	-	-	-	7.34	nr	**7.34**
Newel posts						
44 mm x 94 mm; half newel	-	-	-	10.01	m	**10.01**
69 mm x 69 mm	-	-	-	10.87	m	**10.87**
94 mm x 94 mm	-	-	-	22.23	m	**22.23**
Newel caps; splayed on four sides						
62.50 mm x 125 mm x 50 mm	-	-	-	10.60	nr	**10.60**
100 mm x 100 mm x 50 mm	-	-	-	10.82	nr	**10.82**
125 mm x 125 mm x 50 mm	-	-	-	11.37	nr	**11.37**

L WINDOWS/DOORS/STAIRS

Item	PC £	Labour hours	Labour £	Material £	Unit	Total rate £
The following are supply only prices for purpose made staircase components in selected American Oak; supplied as part of an assembled staircase						
Board landings; cross-tongued joints; 100 mm x 50 mm sawn softwood bearers						
25 mm thick	-	-	-	157.80	m²	157.80
32 mm thick	-	-	-	190.56	m²	190.56
Treads; cross-tongued joints and risers; rounded nosings; tongued, grooved, glued and blocked together; one 175 mm x 50 mm softwood carriage						
25 mm treads; 19 mm risers	-	-	-	261.96	m²	261.96
ends; quadrant	-	-	-	130.86	nr	130.86
ends; housed to hardwood	-	-	-	1.60	nr	1.60
32 mm treads; 25 mm risers	-	-	-	300.17	m²	300.17
ends; quadrant	-	-	-	161.08	nr	161.08
ends; housed to hardwood	-	-	-	1.60	nr	1.60
Winders; cross-tongued joints and risers in one width; rounded nosings; tongued, grooved glued and blocked together; one 175 mm x 50 mm sawn softwood carriage						
25 mm treads; 19 mm risers	-	-	-	332.07	m²	332.07
32 mm treads; 25 mm risers	-	-	-	362.32	m²	362.32
wide ends; housed to hardwood	-	-	-	3.23	nr	3.23
narrow ends; housed to hardwood	-	-	-	2.42	nr	2.42
Closed strings; in one width; 230 mm wide; rounded twice						
32 mm thick	-	-	-	61.89	m	61.89
44 mm thick	-	-	-	71.43	m	71.43
57 mm thick	-	-	-	98.07	m	98.07
Closed strings; cross-tongued joints; 280 mm wide; once rounded						
32 mm thick	-	-	-	78.63	m	78.63
extra for short ramp	-	-	-	44.96	nr	44.96
44 mm thick	-	-	-	91.14	m	91.14
extra for short ramp	-	-	-	51.21	nr	51.21
57 mm thick	-	-	-	124.94	m	124.94
extra for short ramp	-	-	-	68.12	nr	68.12
Closed strings; ramped; crossed tongued joints 280 mm wide; once rounded						
32 mm thick	-	-	-	90.42	m	90.42
44 mm thick	-	-	-	104.80	m	104.80
57 mm thick	-	-	-	143.68	m	143.68
Apron linings; in one width 230 mm wide						
19 mm thick	-	-	-	21.07	m	21.07
25 mm thick	-	-	-	25.83	m	25.83
Handrails; rounded						
40 mm x 50 mm	-	-	-	17.08	m	17.08
50 mm x 75 mm	-	-	-	21.89	m	21.89
57 mm x 87 mm	-	-	-	32.85	m	32.85
69 mm x 100 mm	-	-	-	44.22	m	44.22
Handrails; moulded						
40 mm x 50 mm	-	-	-	18.74	m	18.74
50 mm x 75 mm	-	-	-	23.55	m	23.55
57 mm x 87 mm	-	-	-	34.51	m	34.51
69 mm x 100 mm	-	-	-	45.88	m	45.88
Add to above for						
grooved once	-	-	-	0.85	m	0.85
ends; framed	-	-	-	8.47	nr	8.47
ends; framed on rake	-	-	-	10.72	nr	10.72

L WINDOWS/DOORS/STAIRS

Item	PC £	Labour hours	Labour £	Material £	Unit	Total rate £
L30 STAIRS/WALKWAYS/BALUSTRADES – cont'd						
Purpose made staircase components in selected American Oak – cont'd						
Heading joints to handrail; mitred or raked						
overall size not exceeding 50 mm x 75 mm	-	-	-	45.15	nr	45.15
overall size not exceeding 69 mm x 100 mm	-	-	-	53.62	nr	53.62
Knee piece to handrail; mitred or raked						
overall size not exceeding 69 mm x 100 mm	-	-	-	95.94	nr	95.94
Balusters; stiffeners						
25 mm x 25 mm	-	-	-	3.88	m	3.88
32 mm x 32 mm	-	-	-	4.91	m	4.91
44 mm x 44 mm	-	-	-	7.75	m	7.75
ends; housed	-	-	-	1.98	nr	1.98
Sub rails						
32 mm x 63 mm	-	-	-	10.51	m	10.51
ends; framed joint to newel	-	-	-	8.47	nr	8.47
Knee rails						
32 mm x 140 mm	-	-	-	18.26	m	18.26
ends; framed joint to newel	-	-	-	8.47	nr	8.47
Newel posts						
44 mm x 94 mm; half newel	-	-	-	13.70	m	13.70
69 mm x 69 mm	-	-	-	23.34	m	23.34
94 mm x 94 mm	-	-	-	58.27	m	58.27
Newel caps; splayed on four sides						
62.50 mm x 125 mm x 50 mm	-	-	-	11.75	nr	11.75
100 mm x 100 mm x 50 mm	-	-	-	12.42	nr	12.42
125 mm x 125 mm x 50 mm	-	-	-	13.66	nr	13.66
Aluminium alloy folding loft ladders; "Zig Zag" stairways, model B or other equal and approved; Light Alloy Ltd; on and including plywood backboard; fixing with screws to timber lining (not included)						
Loft ladders						
ceiling height not exceeding 2500 mm; model 888801	-	1.02	18.64	569.15	nr	587.79
ceiling height not exceeding 2800 mm; model 888802	-	1.02	18.64	624.06	nr	642.70
ceiling height not exceeding 3100 mm; model 888803	-	1.02	18.64	696.49	nr	715.13
Flooring, balustrades and handrails; mild steel						
Chequer plate flooring; over 300 mm wide; bolted to steel supports						
6 mm thick	-	-	-	158.03	m²	158.03
8 mm thick	-	-	-	191.89	m²	191.89
Open grid steel flooring; Eurogrid Ltd; "Safeway" type D38 diamond pattern flooring or other equal and approved; to steel supports at 1200 mm centres; galvanised; to BS 729 part 1						
30 mm x 5 mm sections; in one mat; fixing to 10 mm thick channels with type F5 clamps	-	-	-	146.85	m²	146.85

L WINDOWS/DOORS/STAIRS

Item	PC £	Labour hours	Labour £	Material £	Unit	Total rate £
Balustrades; welded construction; 1070 mm high; galvanized; 50 mm x 50 mm x 3.20 mm rhs top rail; 38 mm x 13 mm bottom rail, 50 mm x 50 mm x 3.20 mm rhs standards at 1830 mm centres with base plate drilled and bolted to concrete; 13 mm x 13 mm balusters at 102 mm centres	-	-	-	304.76	m	304.76
Balusters; isolated; one end ragged and cemented in; one 76 mm x 25 mm x 6 mm flange plate welded on; ground to a smooth finish; countersunk drilled and tap screwed to underside of handrail						
19 mm square 914 mm long bar	-	-	-	27.09	nr	27.09
Core-rails; joints prepared, welded and ground to a smooth finish; fixing on brackets (not included)						
38 mm x 10 mm flat bar	-	-	-	27.09	m	27.09
50 mm x 8 mm flat bar	-	-	-	30.48	m	30.48
Handrails; joints prepared, welded and ground to a smooth finish; fixing on brackets (not included)						
38 mm x 12 mm half oval bar	-	-	-	29.35	m	29.35
44 mm x 13 mm half oval bar	-	-	-	33.86	m	33.86
Handrail bracket; comprising 40 mm x 5 mm plate with mitred and welded angle; one end welded to 100 mm diameter x 5 mm backplate; three times holed and plugged and screwed to brickwork; other end scribed and welded to underside of handrail						
140 mm girth	-	-	-	72.24	nr	72.24
Holes						
Holes; countersunk; for screws or bolts						
6 mm diameter; 3 mm thick	-	-	-	0.79	nr	0.79
6 mm diameter; 6 mm thick	-	-	-	1.07	nr	1.07
8 mm diameter; 6 mm thick	-	-	-	1.07	nr	1.07
10 mm diameter; 6 mm thick	-	-	-	1.33	nr	1.33
12 mm diameter; 8 mm thick	-	-	-	1.58	nr	1.58
L40 GENERAL GLAZING						
Standard plain glass; BS 952; clear float; panes area 0.15 m² - 4.00 m²						
3 mm thick; glazed with						
screwed beads	-	-	-	-	m²	26.00
4 mm thick; glazed with						
screwed beads	-	-	-	-	m²	27.57
5 mm thick; glazed with						
screwed beads	-	-	-	-	m²	33.58
6 mm thick; glazed with						
screwed beads	-	-	-	-	m²	36.79
Standard plain glass; BS 952; obscure patterned; panes area 0.15 m² - 4.00 m²						
4 mm thick; glazed with						
screwed beads	-	-	-	-	m²	38.99
6 mm thick; glazed with						
screwed beads	-	-	-	-	m²	42.92
Standard plain glass; BS 952; rough cast; panes area 0.15 m² - 4.00 m²						
6 mm thick; glazed with						
screwed beads	-	-	-	-	m²	31.17

L WINDOWS/DOORS/STAIRS

Item	PC £	Labour hours	Labour £	Material £	Unit	Total rate £
L40 GENERAL GLAZING – cont'd						
Standard plain glass; BS 952; Georgian wired cast; panes area 0.15 m^2 - 4.00 m^2						
7 mm thick; glazed with						
screwed beads	-	-	-	-	m^2	31.71
Extra for lining up wired glass	-	-	-	-	m^2	3.17
Standard plain glass; BS 952; Georgian wired polished; panes area 0.15 m^2 - 4.00 m^2						
6 mm thick; glazed with						
screwed beads	-	-	-	-	m^2	49.20
Extra for lining up wired glass	-	-	-	-	m^2	3.17
Special glass; BS 952; toughened clear float; panes area 0.15 m^2 - 4.00 m^2						
4 mm thick; glazed with						
screwed beads	-	-	-	-	m^2	27.65
5 mm thick; glazed with						
screwed beads	-	-	-	-	m^2	36.73
6 mm thick; glazed with						
screwed beads	-	-	-	-	m^2	40.40
10 mm thick; glazed with						
screwed beads	-	-	-	-	m^2	67.03
Special glass; BS 952; clear laminated safety glass; panes area 0.15 m^2 - 4.00 m^2						
4.40 mm thick; glazed with						
screwed beads	-	-	-	-	m^2	44.30
6.40 mm thick; glazed with						
screwed beads	-	-	-	-	m^2	52.99
Special glass; BS 952; "Pyran" half-hour fire resisting glass or other equal and approved						
6.50 mm thick rectangular panes; glazed with screwed hardwood beads and Sealmaster "Fireglaze" intumescent compound or other equal and approved to rebated frame						
300 mm x 400 mm pane	-	0.42	11.57	38.48	nr	50.04
400 mm x 800 mm pane	-	0.51	14.05	95.45	nr	109.50
500 mm x 1400 mm pane	-	0.83	22.86	201.50	nr	224.36
600 mm x 1800 mm pane	-	1.02	28.09	339.27	nr	367.36
Special glass; BS 952; "Pyrostop" one-hour fire resisting glass or other equal and approved						
15 mm thick regular panes; glazed with screwed hardwood beads and Sealmaster "Fireglaze" intumescent liner and compound or other equal and approved both sides						
300 mm x 400 mm pane	-	1.20	33.05	86.37	nr	119.41
400 mm x 800 mm pane	-	1.53	42.14	168.33	nr	210.47
500 mm x 1400 mm pane	-	2.04	56.18	331.69	nr	387.87
600 mm x 1800 mm pane	-	2.54	69.96	483.11	nr	553.07

L WINDOWS/DOORS/STAIRS

Item	PC £	Labour hours	Labour £	Material £	Unit	Total rate £
Special glass; BS 952; clear laminated security glass 7.50 mm thick regular panes; glazed with screwed hardwood beads and "Intergens" intumescent strip or other equal and approved						
300 mm x 400 mm pane	-	0.42	11.57	23.83	nr	35.40
400 mm x 800 mm pane	-	0.51	14.05	56.95	nr	71.00
500 mm x 1400 mm pane	-	0.83	22.86	117.45	nr	140.31
600 mm x 1800 mm pane	-	1.02	28.09	208.45	nr	236.54
Mirror panels; BS 952; silvered; insulation backing 4 mm thick float; fixing with adhesive						
1000 mm x 1000 mm	-	-	-	-	nr	31.05
1000 mm x 2000 mm	-	-	-	-	nr	62.15
1000 mm x 4000 mm	-	-	-	-	nr	226.50
Glass louvres; BS 952; with long edges ground or smooth 6 mm thick float						
150 mm wide	-	-	-	-	m	13.69
7 mm thick Georgian wired cast						
150 mm wide	-	-	-	-	m	19.00
6 mm thick Georgian wire polished						
150 mm wide	-	-	-	-	m	27.10
Factory made double hermetically sealed units; to wood or metal with screwed or clipped beads Two panes; BS 952; clear float glass; 4 mm thick; 6 mm air space						
0.35 m^2 - 2.00 m^2	-	-	-	-	m^2	69.72
Two panes; BS 952; clear float glass; 6 mm thick; 6 mm air space						
0.35 m^2 - 2.00 m^2	-	-	-	-	m^2	81.19
2.00 m^2 - 4.00 m^2	-	-	-	-	m^2	122.08

M SURFACE FINISHES

Item	PC £	Labour hours	Labour £	Material £	Unit	Total rate £
M10 CEMENT:SAND/CONCRETE SCREEDS/ TOPPING						
Cement:sand (1:3) screeds ; steel trowelled						
Work to floors; one coat; level and to falls not exceeding 15 degrees from horizontal; to concrete base; over 300 mm wide						
25 mm thick	-	0.39	7.69	2.07	m^2	9.76
32 mm thick	-	0.40	7.88	2.65	m^2	10.53
40 mm thick	-	0.41	8.08	3.31	m^2	11.39
48 mm thick	-	0.42	8.28	3.97	m^2	12.25
50 mm thick	-	0.43	8.47	4.14	m^2	12.61
60 mm thick	-	0.44	8.67	4.97	m^2	13.64
65 mm thick	-	0.45	8.87	5.38	m^2	14.25
70 mm thick	-	0.47	9.26	5.79	m^2	15.06
75 mm thick	-	0.50	9.85	6.21	m^2	16.06
100 mm thick	-	0.55	10.84	8.28	m^2	19.12
Add to the above for work to falls and crossfalls and to slopes						
not exceeding 15 degrees from horizontal	-	0.02	0.39	-	m^2	0.39
over 15 degrees from horizontal	-	0.10	1.97	-	m^2	1.97
water repellent additive incorporated in the mix	-	0.02	0.39	5.59	m^2	5.99
oil repellent additive incorporated in the mix	-	0.08	1.58	4.85	m^2	6.43
Fine concrete (1:4-5) levelling screed; steel trowelled						
Work to floors; one coat; level; to concrete base; over 300 mm wide						
50 mm thick	-	-	-	-	m^2	12.58
75 mm thick	-	-	-	-	m^2	16.65
Extra over last for isolation joint to perimeter	-	-	-	-	m	1.40
Early drying floor screed; RMC Mortars "Readyscreed"; or other equal and approved; steel trowelled						
Work to floors; one coat; level; to concrete base; over 300 mm wide						
100 mm thick	-	-	-	-	m^2	22.55
Extra over last for galvanised chicken wire anticrack reinforcement	-	-	-	-	m^2	1.07
Granolithic paving; cement and granite chippings 5 mm to dust (1:1:2); steel trowelled						
Work to floors; one coat; level; laid on concrete while green; bonded; over 300 mm wide						
25 mm thick	-	-	-	-	m^2	28.63
38 mm thick	-	-	-	-	m^2	31.87
Work to floors; two coat; laid on hacked concrete with slurry; over 300 mm wide						
50 mm thick	-	-	-	-	m^2	35.24
75 mm thick	-	-	-	-	m^2	43.38
Work to landings; one coat; level; laid on concrete while green; bonded; over 300 mm wide						
25 mm thick	-	-	-	-	m^2	42.84
38 mm thick	-	-	-	-	m^2	47.80
Work to landings; two coat; laid on hacked concrete with slurry; over 300 mm wide						
50 mm thick	-	-	-	-	m^2	52.87
75 mm thick	-	-	-	-	m^2	65.07

M SURFACE FINISHES

Item	PC £	Labour hours	Labour £	Material £	Unit	Total rate £
Add to the above over 300 mm wide for						
liquid hardening additive incorporated in the mix	-	0.05	0.99	0.64	m²	1.63
oil-repellent additive incorporated in the mix	-	0.08	1.58	4.85	m²	6.43
25 mm work to treads; one coat; to concrete base						
225 mm wide	-	0.92	23.34	10.39	m	33.74
275 mm wide	-	0.92	23.34	11.64	m	34.98
returned end	-	0.19	4.82	-	nr	4.82
13 mm skirtings; rounded top edge and coved bottom junction; to brickwork or blockwork base						
75 mm wide on face	-	0.56	14.21	0.50	m	14.71
150 mm wide on face	-	0.77	19.54	9.15	m	28.68
ends; fair	-	0.05	1.27	-	nr	1.27
angles	-	0.07	1.78	-	nr	1.78
13 mm outer margin to stairs; to follow profile of and with rounded nosing to treads and risers; fair edge and arris at bottom, to concrete base						
75 mm wide	-	0.92	23.34	4.99	m	28.33
angles	-	0.07	1.78	-	nr	1.78
13 mm wall string to stairs; fair edge and arris on top; coved bottom junction with treads and risers; to brickwork or blockwork base						
275 mm (extreme) wide	-	0.81	20.55	8.73	m	29.28
ends	-	0.05	1.27	-	nr	1.27
angles	-	0.07	1.78	-	nr	1.78
ramps	-	0.08	2.03	-	nr	2.03
ramped and wreathed corners	-	0.10	2.54	-	nr	2.54
13 mm outer string to stairs; rounded nosing on top at junction with treads and risers; fair edge and arris at bottom; to concrete base						
300 mm (extreme) wide	-	0.81	20.55	10.81	m	31.36
ends	-	0.05	1.27	-	nr	1.27
angles	-	0.07	1.78	-	nr	1.78
ramps	-	0.08	2.03	-	nr	2.03
ramps and wreathed corners	-	0.10	2.54	-	nr	2.54
19 mm thick skirtings; rounded top edge and coved bottom junction; to brickwork or blockwork base						
75 mm wide on face	-	0.56	14.21	9.15	m	23.35
150 mm wide on face	-	0.77	19.54	14.13	m	33.67
ends; fair	-	0.05	0.99	-	nr	0.99
angles	-	0.07	1.78	-	nr	1.78
19 mm risers; one rounded nosing; to concrete base						
150 mm high; plain	-	0.92	23.34	7.90	m	31.24
150 mm high; undercut	-	0.92	23.34	7.90	m	31.24
180 mm high; plain	-	0.92	23.34	10.81	m	34.15
180 mm high; undercut	-	0.92	23.34	10.81	m	34.15
M11 MASTIC ASPHALT FLOORING/ FLOOR UNDERLAYS						
Mastic asphalt flooring to BS 6925 Type F 1076; black						
20 mm thick; one coat coverings; felt isolating membrane; to concrete base; flat						
over 300 mm wide	-	-	-	-	m²	16.88
225 mm - 300 mm wide	-	-	-	-	m²	31.36
150 mm - 225 mm wide	-	-	-	-	m²	34.45
not exceeding 150 mm wide	-	-	-	-	m²	42.17

M SURFACE FINISHES

Item	PC £	Labour hours	Labour £	Material £	Unit	Total rate £
M11 MASTIC ASPHALT FLOORING/ FLOOR UNDERLAYS – cont'd						
Mastic asphalt flooring to BS 6925 Type F 1076; black – cont'd						
25 mm thick; one coat coverings; felt isolating membrane; to concrete base; flat						
over 300 mm wide	-	-	-	-	m²	19.60
225 mm - 300 mm wide	-	-	-	-	m²	33.46
150 mm - 225 mm wide	-	-	-	-	m²	36.47
not exceeding 150 mm wide	-	-	-	-	m²	44.21
20 mm thick; three coat skirtings to brickwork base						
not exceeding 150 mm girth	-	-	-	-	m	17.25
150 mm - 225 mm girth	-	-	-	-	m	21.08
225 mm - 300 mm girth	-	-	-	-	m	24.92
Mastic asphalt flooring; acid-resisting; black						
20 mm thick; one coat coverings; felt isolating membrane; to concrete base flat						
over 300 mm wide	-	-	-	-	m²	19.78
225 mm - 300 mm wide	-	-	-	-	m²	36.17
150 mm - 225 mm wide	-	-	-	-	m²	37.35
not exceeding 150 mm wide	-	-	-	-	m²	45.06
25 mm thick; one coat coverings; felt isolating membrane; to concrete base; flat						
over 300 mm wide	-	-	-	-	m²	23.36
225 mm - 300 mm wide	-	-	-	-	m²	37.18
150 mm - 225 mm wide	-	-	-	-	m²	40.23
not exceeding 150 mm wide	-	-	-	-	m²	47.97
20 mm thick; three coat skirtings to brickwork base						
not exceeding 150 mm girth	-	-	-	-	m	17.43
150 mm - 225 mm girth	-	-	-	-	m	20.30
225 mm - 300 mm girth	-	-	-	-	m	23.04
Mastic asphalt flooring to BS 6925 Type F 1451; red						
20 mm thick; one coat coverings; felt isolating membrane; to concrete base; flat						
over 300 mm wide	-	-	-	-	m²	27.66
225 mm - 300 mm wide	-	-	-	-	m²	45.70
150 mm - 225 mm wide	-	-	-	-	m²	49.37
not exceeding 150 mm wide	-	-	-	-	m²	59.05
20 mm thick; three coat skirtings to brickwork base						
not exceeding 150 mm girth	-	-	-	-	m	21.72
150 mm - 225 mm girth	-	-	-	-	m	27.66
M12 TROWELLED BITUMEN/RESIN/RUBBER LATEX FLOORING						
Latex cement floor screeds; steel trowelled						
Work to floors; level; to concrete base; over 300 mm wide						
3 mm thick; one coat	-	-	-	-	m²	4.69
5 mm thick; two coats	-	-	-	-	m²	6.57

M SURFACE FINISHES

Item	PC £	Labour hours	Labour £	Material £	Unit	Total rate £
Isocrete K screeds or other equal and approved; steel trowelled Work to floors; level; to concrete base; over 300 mm wide						
35 mm thick; plus polymer bonder coat	-	-	-	-	m²	15.51
40 mm thick	-	-	-	-	m²	14.31
45 mm thick	-	-	-	-	m²	15.13
50 mm thick	-	-	-	-	m²	15.94
Work to floors; to falls or crossfalls; to concrete base; over 300 mm wide						
55 mm (average) thick	-	-	-	-	m²	16.75
60 mm (average) thick	-	-	-	-	m²	17.57
65 mm (average) thick	-	-	-	-	m²	18.38
75 mm (average) thick	-	-	-	-	m²	20.01
90 mm (average) thick	-	-	-	-	m²	22.45
Bituminous lightweight insulating roof screeds "Bit-Ag" or similar roof screed or other equal and approved; to falls or crossfalls; bitumen felt vapour barrier; over 300 mm wide						
75 mm (average) thick	-	-	-	-	m²	44.37
100 mm (average) thick	-	-	-	-	m²	56.24
M20 PLASTERED/RENDERED/ROUGHCAST COATINGS						
Prepare and brush down 2 coats of "Unibond" bonding agent or other equal and approved Brick or block walls						
over 300 mm wide	-	0.16	3.15	1.04	m²	4.19
Concrete walls or ceilings						
over 300 mm wide	-	0.12	2.37	0.83	m²	3.20
Cement:sand (1:3) beds and backings 10 mm thick work to walls; one coat; to brickwork or blockwork base						
over 300 mm wide	-	-	-	-	m²	14.90
not exceeding 300 mm wide	-	-	-	-	m	7.46
13 mm thick; work to walls; two coats; to brickwork or blockwork base						
over 300 mm wide	-	-	-	-	m²	17.92
not exceeding 300 mm wide	-	-	-	-	m	8.97
15 mm thick work to walls; two coats; to brickwork or blockwork base						
over 300 mm wide	-	-	-	-	m²	19.32
not exceeding 300 mm wide	-	-	-	-	m	9.67
Cement:sand (1:3); steel trowelled 13 mm thick work to walls; two coats; to brickwork or blockwork base						
over 300 mm wide	-	-	-	-	m²	15.60
not exceeding 300 mm wide	-	-	-	-	m	7.80
16 mm thick work to walls; two coats; to brickwork or blockwork base						
over 300 mm wide	-	-	-	-	m²	17.47
not exceeding 300 mm wide	-	-	-	-	m	8.76

M SURFACE FINISHES

Item	PC £	Labour hours	Labour £	Material £	Unit	Total rate £
M20 PLASTERED/RENDERED/ROUGHCAST COATINGS – cont'd						
Cement:sand (1:3); steel trowelled – cont'd						
19 mm thick work to walls; two coats; to						
brickwork or blockwork base						
over 300 mm wide	-	-	-	-	m²	20.21
not exceeding 300 mm wide	-	-	-	-	m	10.11
ADD to above						
over 300 mm wide in water repellant cement	-	-	-	-	m²	4.14
finishing coat in colour cement	-	-	-	-	m²	8.82
Cement:lime:sand (1:2:9); steel trowelled						
19 mm thick work to walls; two coats; to						
brickwork or blockwork base						
over 300 mm wide	-	-	-	-	m²	19.60
not exceeding 300 mm wide	-	-	-	-	m	9.80
Cement:lime:sand (1:1:6); steel trowelled						
13 mm thick work to walls; two coats; to						
brickwork or blockwork base						
over 300 mm wide	-	-	-	-	m²	16.03
not exceeding 300 mm wide	-	-	-	-	m	7.90
Add to the above over 300 wide for						
waterproof additive	-	-	-	-	m²	2.70
19 mm thick work to ceilings; three coats; to						
metal lathing base						
over 300 mm wide	-	-	-	-	m²	18.85
not exceeding 300 mm wide	-	-	-	-	m	11.02
Plaster; first 11 mm coat of "Thistle Hardwall" plaster; second 2 mm finishing coat of "Thistle Multi Finish" plaster; steel trowelled						
13 mm thick work to walls; two coats; to						
brickwork or blockwork base						
over 300 mm wide	-	-	-	-	m²	12.37
over 300 mm wide; in staircase areas or plant rooms	-	-	-	-	m²	14.85
not exceeding 300 mm wide	-	-	-	-	m	6.58
13 mm thick work to isolated brickwork or						
blockwork columns; two coats						
over 300 mm wide	-	-	-	-	m²	23.30
not exceeding 300 mm wide	-	-	-	-	m	11.65
Plaster; first 11 mm coat of "Thistle Browning" plaster; second 2 mm finishing coat of "Thistle Multi Finish" plaster; steel trowelled						
13 mm thick; work to walls; two coats; to						
brickwork or blockwork base						
over 300 mm wide	-	-	-	-	m²	12.37
over 300 mm wide; in staircase areas or plant rooms	-	-	-	-	m²	14.85
not exceeding 300 mm wide	-	-	-	-	m	6.58
13 mm thick work to isolated columns; two coats						
over 300 mm wide	-	-	-	-	m²	23.31
not exceeding 300 mm wide	-	-	-	-	m	10.33

M SURFACE FINISHES

Item	PC £	Labour hours	Labour £	Material £	Unit	Total rate £
Plaster; first 8 mm or 11 mm coat of "Thistle Bonding" plaster; second 2 mm finishing coat of "Thistle Multi Finish" plaster; steel trowelled						
13 mm thick work to walls; two coats; to concrete base						
over 300 mm wide	-	-	-	-	m^2	13.85
over 300 mm wide; in staircase areas or plant rooms	-	-	-	-	m^2	16.40
not exceeding 300 mm wide	-	-	-	-	m	6.34
13 mm thick work to isolated piers or columns; two coats; to concrete base						
over 300 mm wide	-	-	-	-	m^2	24.74
not exceeding 300 mm wide	-	-	-	-	m	11.59
10 mm thick work to ceilings; two coats; to concrete base						
over 300 mm wide	-	-	-	-	m^2	11.85
over 300 mm wide; 3.50 m - 5.00 m high	-	-	-	-	m^2	14.22
over 300 mm wide; in staircase areas or plant rooms	-	-	-	-	m^2	15.73
not exceeding 300 mm wide	-	-	-	-	m	6.62
10 mm thick work to isolated beams; two coats; to concrete base						
over 300 mm wide	-	-	-	-	m^2	23.70
over 300 mm wide; 3.50 m - 5.00 m high	-	-	-	-	m^2	25.27
not exceeding 300 mm wide	-	-	-	-	m	11.40
Plaster; one coat "Snowplast" plaster or other equal and approved; steel trowelled						
13 mm thick work to walls; one coat; to brickwork or blockwork base						
over 300 mm wide	-	-	-	-	m^2	13.68
over 300 mm wide; in staircase areas or plant rooms	-	-	-	-	m^2	16.25
not exceeding 300 mm wide	-	-	-	-	m	6.86
13 mm thick work to isolated columns; one coat						
over 300 mm wide	-	-	-	-	m^2	16.55
not exceeding 300 mm wide	-	-	-	-	m	8.30
Plaster; first coat of "Limelite" renovating plaster; finishing coat of "Limelite" finishing plaster; or other equal and approved; steel trowelled						
13 mm thick work to walls; two coats; to brickwork or blockwork base						
over 300 mm wide	-	-	-	-	m^2	18.97
over 300 mm wide; in staircase areas or plant rooms	-	-	-	-	m^2	20.82
not exceeding 300 mm wide	-	-	-	-	m	9.48
Dubbing out existing walls with undercoat plaster; average 6 mm thick						
over 300 mm wide	-	-	-	-	m^2	5.69
not exceeding 300 mm wide	-	-	-	-	m	2.88
Dubbing out existing walls with undercoat plaster; average 12 mm thick						
over 300 mm wide	-	-	-	-	m^2	11.38
not exceeding 300 mm wide	-	-	-	-	m	5.69

M SURFACE FINISHES

Item	PC £	Labour hours	Labour £	Material £	Unit	Total rate £
M20 PLASTERED/RENDERED/ROUGHCAST COATINGS – cont'd						
Plaster; first coat of "Thistle X-ray" plaster or other equal and approved; finishing coat of "Thistle X-ray" finishing plaster or other equal and approved; steel trowelled						
17 mm thick work to walls; two coats; to brickwork or blockwork base						
over 300 mm wide	-	-	-	-	m^2	61.55
over 300 mm wide; in staircase areas or plant rooms	-	-	-	-	m^2	66.13
not exceeding 300 mm wide	-	-	-	-	m	24.61
17 mm thick work to isolated columns; two coats						
over 300 mm wide	-	-	-	-	m^2	12.72
not exceeding 300 mm wide	-	-	-	-	m	39.90
Plaster, one coat "Thistle" projection plaster or other equal and approved; steel trowelled						
13 mm thick work to walls; one coat; to brickwork or blockwork base						
over 300 mm wide	-	-	-	-	m^2	13.20
over 300 mm wide; in staircase areas or plant rooms	-	-	-	-	m^2	15.09
not exceeding 300 mm wide	-	-	-	-	m	6.59
10 mm thick work to isolated columns; one coat						
over 300 mm wide	-	-	-	-	m^2	16.06
not exceeding 300 mm wide	-	-	-	-	m	8.02
Plaster; first 11 mm coat of "Thistle Bonding" plaster; second 2 mm finishing coat of "Thistle Multi Finish" plaster; steel trowelled						
13 mm thick work to ceilings; three coats to metal lathing base						
over 300 mm wide	-	-	-	-	m^2	14.38
over 300 mm wide; in staircase areas or plant rooms	-	-	-	-	m^2	17.25
not exceeding 300 mm wide	-	-	-	-	m	7.75
13 mm thick work to swept soffit of metal lathing arch former						
not exceeding 300 mm wide	-	-	-	-	m	10.35
300 mm - 400 mm wide	-	-	-	-	m	13.84
13 mm thick work to vertical face of metal lathing arch former						
not exceeding 0.50 m^2 per side	-	-	-	-	nr	14.70
0.50 m^2 - 1.00 m^2 per side	-	-	-	-	nr	22.04
"Tyrolean" decorative rendering or other equal and approved; 13 mm thick first coat of cement:lime:sand (1:1:6); finishing three coats of "Cullamix" or other equal and approved applied with approved hand operated machine external						
To walls; four coats; to brickwork or blockwork base						
over 300 mm wide	-	-	-	-	m^2	31.54
not exceeding 300 mm wide	-	-	-	-	m	15.75

M SURFACE FINISHES

Item	PC £	Labour hours	Labour £	Material £	Unit	Total rate £
Drydash (pebbledash) finish of Derbyshire Spar chippings or other equal and approved on and including cement:lime:sand (1:2:9) backing						
18 mm thick work to walls; two coats; to brickwork or blockwork base						
over 300 mm wide	-	-	-	-	m²	27.34
not exceeding 300 mm wide	-	-	-	-	m	13.68
Plaster; one coat "Thistle" board finish or other equal and approved; steel trowelled (prices included within plasterboard rates)						
3 mm thick work to walls or ceilings; one coat; to plasterboard base						
over 300 mm wide	-	-	-	-	m²	5.58
over 300 mm wide; in staircase areas or plant rooms	-	-	-	-	m²	6.69
not exceeding 300 mm wide	-	-	-	-	m	2.23
Plaster; one coat "Thistle" board finish or other equal and approved; steel trowelled 3 mm work to walls or ceilings; one coat on and including gypsum plasterboard; BS 1230; fixing with nails; 3 mm joints filled with plaster and jute scrim cloth; to softwood base; plain grade baseboard or lath with rounded edges						
9.50 mm thick boards to walls						
over 300 mm wide	-	1.07	14.04	2.93	m²	16.97
not exceeding 300 mm wide	-	0.42	5.90	2.14	m	8.04
9.50 mm thick boards to walls; in staircase areas or plant rooms						
over 300 mm wide	-	1.17	15.44	2.93	m²	18.37
not exceeding 300 mm wide	-	0.52	7.30	2.14	m	9.45
9.50 mm thick boards to isolated columns						
over 300 mm wide	-	1.17	15.44	2.93	m²	18.37
not exceeding 300 mm wide	-	0.62	8.71	2.14	m	10.85
9.50 mm thick boards to ceilings						
over 300 mm wide	-	0.99	12.91	2.93	m²	15.84
over 300 mm wide; 3.50 m - 5.00 m high	-	1.14	15.02	2.93	m²	17.95
not exceeding 300 mm wide	-	0.47	6.60	2.14	m	8.74
9.50 mm thick boards to ceilings; in staircase areas or plant rooms						
over 300 mm wide	-	1.09	14.32	2.93	m²	17.25
not exceeding 300 mm wide	-	0.52	7.30	2.14	m	9.45
9.50 mm thick boards to isolated beams						
over 300 mm wide	-	1.16	15.30	2.93	m²	18.23
not exceeding 300 mm wide	-	0.56	7.86	2.14	m	10.01
12.50 mm thick boards to walls; in staircase areas or plant rooms						
over 300 mm wide	-	1.12	14.74	3.04	m²	17.78
not exceeding 300 mm wide	-	0.53	7.44	2.18	m	9.62
12.50 mm thick boards to isolated columns						
over 300 mm wide	-	1.16	15.30	3.04	m²	18.34
not exceeding 300 mm wide	-	0.56	7.86	2.18	m	10.04

M SURFACE FINISHES

Item	PC £	Labour hours	Labour £	Material £	Unit	Total rate £
M20 PLASTERED/RENDERED/ROUGHCAST COATINGS – cont'd						
Plaster; one coat "Thistle" board finish on and including gypsum plasterboard – cont'd						
12.50 mm thick boards to ceilings						
over 300 mm wide	-	1.05	13.75	3.04	m²	**16.80**
over 300 mm wide; 3.50 m - 5.00 m high	-	1.17	15.44	3.04	m²	**18.48**
not exceeding 300 mm wide	-	0.50	7.02	2.18	m	**9.20**
12.50 mm thick boards to ceilings; in staircase areas or plant rooms						
over 300 mm wide	-	1.17	15.44	3.04	m²	**18.48**
not exceeding 300 mm wide	-	0.56	7.86	2.18	m	**10.04**
12.50 mm thick boards to isolated beams						
over 300 wide	-	1.27	16.84	3.04	m²	**19.89**
not exceeding 300 mm wide	-	0.62	8.71	2.18	m	**10.88**
Accessories						
"Expamet" render beads or other equal and approved; white PVC nosings; to brickwork or blockwork base						
external stop bead; ref 573	-	0.08	1.12	1.68	m	**2.80**
"Expamet" render beads or other equal and approved; stainless steel; to brickwork or blockwork base						
stop bead; ref 546	-	0.08	1.12	2.96	m	**4.08**
stop bead; ref 547	-	0.08	1.12	2.96	m	**4.08**
"Expamet" plaster beads or other equal and approved; galvanised steel; to brickwork or blockwork base						
angle bead; ref 550	-	0.09	1.26	0.71	m	**1.98**
architrave bead; ref 579	-	0.11	1.54	1.91	m	**3.45**
stop bead; ref 562	-	0.08	1.12	0.88	m	**2.00**
stop beads; ref 563	-	0.08	1.12	0.88	m	**2.00**
movement bead; ref 588	-	0.10	1.40	6.83	m	**8.23**
"Expamet" plaster beads or other equal and approved; stainless steel; to brickwork or blockwork base						
angle bead; ref 545	-	0.09	1.26	3.32	m	**4.59**
stop bead; ref 534	-	0.08	1.12	2.96	m	**4.08**
stop bead; ref 533	-	0.08	1.12	2.96	m	**4.08**
"Expamet" thin coat plaster beads or other equal and approved; galvanised steel; to timber base						
angle bead; ref 553	-	0.08	1.12	0.67	m	**1.79**
angle bead; ref 554	-	0.08	1.12	0.56	m	**1.68**
stop bead; ref 560	-	0.07	0.98	1.01	m	**2.00**
stop bead; ref 561	-	0.07	0.98	1.01	m	**2.00**
M22 SPRAYED MINERAL FIBRE COATINGS						
Prepare and apply by spray "Mandolite CP2" fire protection or other equal and approved on structural steel/metalwork						
16 mm thick (one hour) fire protection						
to walls and columns	-	-	-	-	m²	**10.97**
to ceilings and beams	-	-	-	-	m²	**12.19**
to isolated metalwork	-	-	-	-	m²	**24.02**

M SURFACE FINISHES

Item	PC £	Labour hours	Labour £	Material £	Unit	Total rate £
22 mm thick (one and a half hour) fire protection						
to walls and columns	-	-	-	-	m²	12.63
to ceilings and beams	-	-	-	-	m²	14.01
to isolated metalwork	-	-	-	-	m²	28.18
28 mm thick (two hour) fire protection						
to walls and columns	-	-	-	-	m²	14.82
to ceilings and beams	-	-	-	-	m²	16.47
to isolated metalwork	-	-	-	-	m²	32.30
52 mm thick (four hour) fire protection						
to walls and columns	-	-	-	-	m²	22.69
to ceilings and beams	-	-	-	-	m²	25.00
to isolated metalwork	-	-	-	-	m²	49.99
Prepare and apply by spray; cementitious "Pyrok WF26" render or other equal and approved; on expanded metal lathing (not included)						
15 mm thick						
to ceilings and beams	-	-	-	-	m²	34.63
M30 METAL MESH LATHING/ANCHORED REINFORCEMENT FOR PLASTERED COATING						
Accessories						
Pre-formed galvanised expanded steel arch-frames; "Simpson Strong-Tie" or other equal and approved; semi-circular; to suit walls up to 230 mm thick						
375 mm radius; for 800 mm opening; ref SC 750	30.65	0.52	6.31	35.46	nr	41.77
425 mm radius; for 850 mm opening; ref SC 850	29.27	0.52	6.31	33.86	nr	40.17
450 mm radius; for 900 mm opening; ref SC 900	30.27	0.52	6.31	35.02	nr	41.33
600 mm radius; for 1200 mm opening; ref SC 1200	35.02	0.52	6.31	40.51	nr	46.83
"Newlath" damp free lathing or other equal and approved; plugging and screwing to background at 250 mm centres each way						
Linings to walls						
over 300 mm wide	-	1.28	23.39	11.18	m²	34.57
not exceeding 300 mm wide	-	0.41	7.49	3.47	m²	10.96
Lathing; Expamet "BB" expanded metal lathing or other and approved; BS 1369; 50 mm laps						
6 mm thick mesh linings to ceilings; fixing with staples; to softwood base; over 300 mm wide						
ref BB263; 0.500 mm thick	4.51	0.61	7.40	5.35	m²	12.75
ref BB264; 0.675 mm thick	6.31	0.61	7.40	7.48	m²	14.88
6 mm thick mesh linings to ceilings; fixing with wire; to steelwork; over 300 mm wide						
ref BB263; 0.500 mm thick	-	0.65	7.89	5.35	m²	13.24
ref BB264; 0.675 mm thick	-	0.65	7.89	7.48	m²	15.37
6 mm thick mesh linings to ceilings; fixing with wire; to steelwork; not exceeding 300 mm wide						
ref BB263; 0.500 mm thick	-	0.41	4.98	5.35	m²	10.33
ref BB264; 0.675 mm thick	-	0.41	4.98	7.48	m²	12.46
raking cutting	-	0.20	2.81	-	m	2.81
cutting and fitting around pipes; not exceeding 0.30 m girth	-	0.31	4.35	-	nr	4.35

M SURFACE FINISHES

Item	PC £	Labour hours	Labour £	Material £	Unit	Total rate £
M30 METAL MESH LATHING/ANCHORED REINFORCEMENT FOR PLASTERED COATING – cont'd						
Lathing; Expamet "Riblath" or "Spraylath" stiffened expanded metal lathing or other equal and approved; 50 mm laps						
10 mm thick mesh lining to walls; fixing with nails; to softwood base; over 300 mm wide						
"Riblath" ref 269; 0.30 mm thick	6.39	0.52	6.31	7.71	m²	**14.02**
"Riblath" ref 271; 0.50 mm thick	7.36	0.52	6.31	8.86	m²	**15.17**
"Spraylath" ref 273; 0.50 mm thick	-	0.52	6.31	7.83	m²	**14.14**
10 mm thick mesh lining to walls; fixing with nails; to softwood base; not exceeding 300 mm wide						
"Riblath" ref 269; 0.30 mm thick	-	0.31	3.75	2.36	m²	**6.11**
"Riblath" ref 271; 0.50 mm thick	-	0.31	3.75	2.71	m²	**6.46**
"Spraylath" ref 273; 0.50 mm thick	-	0.31	3.75	2.44	m²	**6.19**
10 mm thick mesh lining to walls; fixing to brick or blockwork; over 300 mm wide						
"Red-rib" ref 274; 0.50 mm thick	8.13	0.41	4.98	10.50	m²	**15.48**
stainless steel "Riblath" ref 267; 0.30 mm thick	17.18	0.41	4.98	21.22	m²	**26.20**
10 mm thick mesh lining to ceilings; fixing with wire; to steelwork; over 300 mm wide						
"Riblath" ref 269; 0.30 mm thick	-	0.65	7.89	8.32	m²	**16.21**
"Riblath" ref 271; 0.50 mm thick	-	0.65	7.89	9.46	m²	**17.35**
"Spraylath" ref 273; 0.50 mm thick	-	0.65	7.89	8.43	m²	**16.32**
M31 FIBROUS PLASTER						
Fibrous plaster; fixing with screws; plugging; countersinking; stopping; filling and pointing joints with plaster						
16 mm thick plain slab coverings to ceilings						
over 300 mm wide	-	-	-	-	m²	**131.26**
not exceeding 300 mm wide	-	-	-	-	m	**44.15**
Coves; not exceeding 150 mm girth						
per 25 mm girth	-	-	-	-	m	**6.33**
Coves; 150 mm - 300 mm girth						
per 25 mm girth	-	-	-	-	m	**7.76**
Cornices						
per 25 mm girth	-	-	-	-	m	**7.87**
Cornice enrichments						
per 25 mm girth; depending on degree of enrichments	-	-	-	-	m	**9.30**
Fibrous plaster; fixing with plaster wadding filling and pointing joints with plaster; to steel base						
16 mm thick plain slab coverings to ceilings						
over 300 mm wide	-	-	-	-	m²	**131.26**
not exceeding 300 mm wide	-	-	-	-	m	**44.15**
16 mm thick plain casings to stanchions						
per 25 mm girth	-	-	-	-	m	**3.94**
16 mm thick plain casings to beams						
per 25 mm girth	-	-	-	-	m	**3.94**

M SURFACE FINISHES

Item	PC £	Labour hours	Labour £	Material £	Unit	Total rate £
Gyproc cove or other equal and approved; fixing with adhesive; filling and pointing joints with plaster						
Coves						
125 mm girth	-	0.20	2.81	1.03	m	3.84
angles	-	0.03	0.42	0.65	nr	1.07
M40 STONE/CONCRETE/QUARRY/CERAMIC TILING/MOSAIC						
Clay floor quarries; BS 6431; class 1; Daniel Platt "Crown" tiles or other equal and approved; level bedding 10 mm thick and jointing in cement and sand (1:3); butt joints; straight both ways; flush pointing with grout; to cement and sand base						
Work to floors; over 300 mm wide						
150 mm x 150 mm x 12.50 mm thick; red	-	0.81	15.96	22.69	m²	38.65
150 mm x 150 mm x 12.50 mm thick; brown	-	0.81	15.96	27.74	m²	43.70
200 mm x 200 mm x 19 mm thick; brown	-	0.67	13.20	39.19	m²	52.39
Works to floors; in staircase areas or plant rooms						
150 mm x 150 mm x 12.50 mm thick; red	-	0.92	18.13	22.69	m²	40.82
150 mm x 150 mm x 12.50 mm thick; brown	-	0.92	18.13	27.74	m²	45.87
200 mm x 200 mm x 19 mm thick; brown	-	0.77	15.18	39.19	m²	54.37
Work to floors; not exceeding 300 mm wide						
150 mm x 150 mm x 12.50 mm thick; red	-	0.41	8.08	5.23	m²	13.31
150 mm x 150 mm x 12.50 mm thick; brown	-	0.41	8.08	6.75	m²	14.83
200 mm x 200 mm x 19 mm thick; brown	-	0.33	6.50	10.18	m²	16.68
fair square cutting against flush edges of existing finishes	-	0.12	1.58	1.18	m	2.76
raking cutting	-	0.21	2.81	1.33	m	4.14
cutting around pipes; not exceeding 0.30 m girth	-	0.16	2.25	-	nr	2.25
extra for cutting and fitting into recessed manhole cover 600 mm x 600 mm	-	1.02	14.32	-	nr	14.32
Work to sills; 150 mm wide; rounded edge tiles						
150 mm x 150 mm x 12.50 mm thick; red	-	0.33	6.50	4.68	m	11.18
150 mm x 150 mm x 12.50 mm thick; brown	-	0.33	6.50	6.19	m	12.70
fitted end	-	0.16	2.25	-	m	2.25
Coved skirtings; 138 mm high; rounded top edge						
150 mm x 138 mm x 12.50 mm thick; red	-	0.26	5.12	5.54	m	10.66
150 mm x 138 mm x 12.50 mm thick; brown	-	0.26	5.12	6.08	m	11.21
ends	-	0.05	0.70	-	nr	0.70
angles	-	0.16	2.25	2.18	nr	4.42
Glazed ceramic wall tiles; BS 6431; fixing with adhesive; butt joints; straight both ways; flush pointing with white grout; to plaster base						
Work to walls; over 300 mm wide						
152 mm x 152 mm x 5.50 mm thick; white	12.25	0.61	15.48	20.60	m²	36.07
152 mm x 152 mm x 5.50 mm thick; light colours	14.95	0.61	15.48	23.79	m²	39.27
152 mm x 152 mm x 5.50 mm thick; dark colours	16.34	0.61	15.48	25.44	m²	40.92
extra for RE or REX tile	-	-	-	7.45	m²	7.45
200 mm x 100 mm x 6.50 mm thick; white and light colours	12.25	0.61	15.48	20.60	m²	36.07
250 mm x 200 mm x 7 mm thick; white and light colours	13.27	0.61	15.48	21.80	m²	37.28

M SURFACE FINISHES

Item	PC £	Labour hours	Labour £	Material £	Unit	Total rate £
M40 STONE/CONCRETE/QUARRY/CERAMIC TILING/MOSAIC – cont'd						
Glazed ceramic wall tiles; BS 6431 – cont'd						
Work to walls; in staircase areas or plant rooms						
152 mm x 152 mm x 5.50 mm thick; white	-	0.68	17.25	20.60	m²	37.85
Work to walls; not exceeding 300 mm wide						
152 mm x 152 mm x 5.50 mm thick; white	-	0.31	7.87	6.11	m	13.97
152 mm x 152 mm x 5.50 mm thick; light colours	-	0.31	7.87	9.96	m	17.83
152 mm x 152 mm x 5.50 mm thick; dark colours	-	0.31	7.87	10.45	m	18.32
200 mm x 100 mm x 6.50 mm thick; white and light colours	-	0.31	7.87	6.11	m	13.97
250 mm x 200 mm x 7 mm thick; white and light colours	-	0.26	6.60	6.47	m	13.07
cutting around pipes; not exceeding 0.30 m girth	-	0.10	1.40	-	nr	1.40
Work to sills; 150 mm wide; rounded edge tiles						
152 mm x 152 mm x 5.50 mm thick; white	-	0.26	6.60	3.05	m	9.65
fitted end	-	0.10	1.40	-	nr	1.40
198 mm x 64.50 mm x 6 mm thick wall tiles; fixing with adhesive; butt joints; straight both ways; flush pointing with white grout; to plaster base						
Work to walls						
over 300 mm wide	25.94	1.83	46.44	36.81	m²	83.25
not exceeding 300 mm wide	-	0.71	18.02	10.97	m	28.99
20 mm x 20 mm x 5.50 mm thick glazed mosaic wall tiles; fixing with adhesive; butt joints; straight both ways; flush pointing with white grout; to plaster base						
Work to walls						
over 300 mm wide	31.83	1.93	48.97	44.87	m²	93.84
not exceeding 300 mm wide	-	0.77	19.54	16.14	m	35.68
50 mm x 50 mm x 5 mm thick slip resistant mosaic floor tiles, Series 2 or other equal and approved; fixing with adhesive; butt joints; straight both ways; flush pointing with white grout; to cement:sand base						
Work to floors						
over 300 mm wide	33.13	1.93	38.04	47.65	m²	85.69
not exceeding 300 mm wide	-	0.77	15.18	16.60	m	31.78
Riven Welsh slate floor tiles; level; bedding 10 mm thick and jointing in cement and sand (1:3); butt joints; straight both ways; flush pointing with coloured mortar; to cement:sand base						
Work to floors; over 300 mm wide						
250 mm x 250 mm x 12 mm - 15 mm thick	-	0.61	15.48	45.63	m²	61.11
Work to floors; not exceeding 300 mm wide						
250 mm x 250 mm x 12 mm - 15 mm thick	-	0.31	7.87	13.78	m	21.64

M SURFACE FINISHES

Item	PC £	Labour hours	Labour £	Material £	Unit	Total rate £
M41 TERRAZZO TILING/ IN SITU TERRAZZO						
Terrazzo tiles BS 4131; aggregate size random ground grouted and polished to 80's grit finish; standard colour range; 3 mm jonts symmetrical layout; bedding in 42 mm cement semi-dry mix (1:4); grouting with neat matching cement 300 mm x 300 mm x 28 mm (nominal) Terrazzo tile units; hydraulically pressed, mechanically vibrated, steam cured; to floors on concrete base (not included); sealed with penetrating case hardener or other equal and approved; 2 coats applied immediately after final polishing						
plain; laid level	-	-	-	-	m²	38.68
plain; to slopes exceeding 15 degrees from horizontal	-	-	-	-	m²	44.17
to small areas/toilets	-	-	-	-	m²	91.22
Accessories						
plastic division strips 6 mm x 38 mm; set into floor tiling above crack inducing joints; to the nearest full tile module	-	-	-	-	m	2.83
M42 WOOD BLOCK/COMPOSITION BLOCK/ PARQUET FLOORING						
Wood block; Vigers, Stevens & Adams "Vigerflex" or other equal and approved; 7.50 mm thick; level; fixing with adhesive; to cement:sand base Work to floors; over 300 mm wide						
"Maple 7"	-	0.51	10.05	20.31	m²	30.36
Wood blocks 25 mm thick; tongued and grooved joints; herringbone pattern; level; fixing with adhesive; to cement:sand base Work to floors; over 300 mm wide						
iroko	-	-	-	-	m²	54.70
"Maple 7" or other equal and approved	-	-	-	-	m²	59.13
french oak	-	-	-	-	m²	81.30
american oak	-	-	-	-	m²	73.91
fair square cutting against flush edges of existing finishings	-	-	-	-	m	7.03
extra for cutting and fitting into recessed duct covers 450 mm wide; lining up with adjoining work	-	-	-	-	m	18.03
cutting around pipes; not exceeding 0.30 m girth	-	-	-	-	nr	2.96
extra for cutting and fitting into recessed manhole covers 600 mm x 600 mm; lining up with adjoining work	-	-	-	-	nr	13.30
Add to wood block flooring over 300 mm wide for						
sanding; one coat sealer; one coat wax polish	-	-	-	-	m²	5.91
sanding; two coats sealer; buffing with steel wool	-	-	-	-	m²	5.76
sanding; three coats polyurethane lacquer; buffing down between coats	-	-	-	-	m²	8.87

M SURFACE FINISHES

Item	PC £	Labour hours	Labour £	Material £	Unit	Total rate £
M50 RUBBER/PLASTICS/CORK/LINO/ CARPET TILING/SHEETING						
Linoleum sheet; Forbo-Nairn "Marmoleum Real" or other equal and approved; level; fixing with adhesive; butt joints; to cement:sand base						
Work to floors; over 300 mm wide						
2.50 mm thick; plain	-	0.41	8.08	12.52	m²	**20.60**
3.20 mm thick; marbled	-	0.41	8.08	15.54	m²	**23.62**
Linoleum sheet; Forbo-Nairn "Walton" or other equal and approved; level; with welded seams; fixing with adhesive; to cement:sand base						
Work to floors; over 300 mm wide						
2.50 mm thick	-	0.51	10.05	14.38	m²	**24.43**
Vinyl sheet; Altro "Safety" range or other equal and approved; with welded seams; level; fixing with adhesive; to cement:sand base						
Work to floors; over 300 mm wide						
2.00 mm thick; "Marine T20"	-	0.61	12.02	17.45	m²	**29.47**
2.50 mm thick; "Classic D25"	-	0.71	13.99	19.77	m²	**33.76**
3.50 mm thick; "Stronghold"	-	0.81	15.96	25.95	m²	**41.91**
Slip resistant vinyl sheet; Forbo-Nairn "Surestep" or other equal and approved; level with welded seams; fixing with adhesive; to cement:sand base						
Work to floors; over 300 mm wide						
2.00 mm thick	-	0.51	10.05	15.42	m²	**25.47**
Vinyl sheet; heavy duty; Marley "HD" or other equal and approved; level; with welded seams; fixing with adhesive; level; to cement:sand base						
Work to floors; over 300 mm wide						
2.00 mm thick	-	0.45	8.87	9.43	m²	**18.30**
2.50 mm thick	-	0.51	10.05	8.99	m²	**19.04**
2.00 mm thick skirtings						
100 high	-	0.12	2.37	1.85	m	**4.21**
Vinyl sheet; Marley "Sport" or other equal and approved; level; with welded seams; fixing with adhesive; level; to cement:sand base						
Work to floors; over 300 mm wide						
6.70 mm thick	-	1.00	19.71	25.95	m²	**45.66**
8.00 mm thick	-	1.10	21.68	30.22	m²	**51.90**
Vinyl sheet; "Gerflex" standard sheet; "Classic" range or other equal and approved; level; with welded seams; fixing with adhesive; to cement:sand base						
Work to floors; over 300 mm wide						
2.00 mm thick	-	0.51	10.05	8.28	m²	**18.33**

M SURFACE FINISHES

Item	PC £	Labour hours	Labour £	Material £	Unit	Total rate £
Vinyl sheet; "Armstrong Rhino Contract" or other equal and approved; level; with welded seams; fixing with adhesive; to cement:sand base Work to floors; over 300 mm wide						
2.50 mm thick	-	0.51	10.05	9.70	m^2	**19.75**
Vinyl tiles; "Accoflex" or other equal and approved; level; fixing with adhesive; butt joints; straight both ways; to cement:sand base Work to floors; over 300 mm wide						
300 mm x 300 mm x 2.00 mm thick	-	0.26	5.12	5.89	m^2	**11.01**
Vinyl semi-flexible tiles; "Arlon" or other equal and approved; level; fixing with adhesive; butt joints; straight both ways; to cement:sand base Work to floors; over 300 mm wide						
250 mm x 250 mm x 2.00 mm thick	-	0.26	5.12	5.99	m^2	**11.11**
Vinyl semi-flexible tiles; Marley "Marleyflex" or other equal and approved; level; fixing with adhesive; butt joints; straight both ways; to cement:sand base Work to floors; over 300 mm wide						
300 mm x 300 mm x 2.00 mm thick	-	0.26	5.12	6.68	m^2	**11.80**
300 mm x 300 mm x 2.50 mm thick	-	0.26	5.12	8.05	m^2	**13.18**
Vinyl semi-flexible tiles; "Vylon" or other equal and approved; level; fixing with adhesive; butt joints; straight both ways; to cement:sand base Work to floors; over 300 mm wide						
250 mm x 250 mm x 2.00 mm thick	-	0.29	5.72	6.35	m^2	**12.06**
Vinyl tiles; anti-static; level; fixing with adhesive; butt joints; straight both ways; to cement:sand base Work to floors; over 300 mm wide						
457 mm x 457 mm x 2.00 mm thick	-	0.45	8.87	12.74	m^2	**21.61**
Vinyl tiles; "Polyflex" or other equal and approved; level; fixing with adhesive; butt joints; straight both ways; to cement:sand base Work to floors; over 300 mm wide						
300 mm x 300 mm x 1.50 mm thick	-	0.26	5.12	5.50	m^2	**10.63**
300 mm x 300 mm x 2.00 mm thick	-	0.26	5.12	6.08	m^2	**11.21**
Vinyl tiles; "Polyflor XL" or other equal and approved; level; fixing with adhesive; butt joints; straight both ways; to cement:sand base Work to floors; over 300 mm wide						
300 mm x 300 mm x 2.00 mm thick	-	0.36	7.09	7.50	m^2	**14.60**

M SURFACE FINISHES

Item	PC £	Labour hours	Labour £	Material £	Unit	Total rate £
M50 RUBBER/PLASTICS/CORK/LINO/ CARPET TILING/SHEETING – cont'd						
Vinyl tiles; Marley "HD" or other equal and approved; level; fixing with adhesive; butt joints; straight both ways; to cement:sand base Work to floors; over 300 mm wide						
300 mm x 300 mm x 2.00 mm thick	-	0.36	7.09	9.43	m²	**16.53**
Thermoplastic tiles; Marley "Marleyflex" or other equal and approved; level; fixing with adhesive; butt joints; straight both ways; to cement:sand base Work to floors; over 300 mm wide						
300 mm x 300 mm x 2.00 mm thick; series 2	-	0.23	4.53	5.89	m²	**10.42**
300 mm x 300 mm x 2.00 mm thick; series 4	-	0.23	4.53	6.33	m²	**10.86**
Linoleum tiles; BS 6826; Forbo-Nairn Floors or other equal and approved; level; fixing with adhesive; butt joints; straight both ways; to cement:sand base Work to floors; over 300 mm wide						
2.50 mm thick (marble pattern)	-	0.31	6.11	14.05	m²	**20.16**
Cork tiles Wicanders "Cork-Master" or other equal and approved; level; fixing with adhesive; butt joints; straight both ways; to cement:sand base Work to floors; over 300 mm wide						
300 mm x 300 mm x 4.00 mm thick	-	0.41	8.08	26.76	m²	**34.84**
Rubber studded tiles; Altro "Mondopave" or other equal and approved; level; fixing with adhesive; butt joints; straight to cement:sand base Work to floors; over 300 mm wide						
500 mm x 500 mm x 2.50 mm thick; type MRB; black	-	0.61	12.02	28.63	m²	**40.65**
500 mm x 500 mm x 4.00 mm thick; type MRB; black	-	0.61	12.02	27.35	m²	**39.37**
Work to landings; over 300 mm wide						
500 mm x 500 mm x 4.00 mm thick; type MRB; black	-	0.81	15.96	27.35	m²	**43.32**
4.00 mm thick to treads						
275 mm wide	-	0.51	10.05	8.14	m	**18.19**
4.00 mm thick to risers						
180 mm wide	-	0.61	12.02	5.75	m	**17.77**
Sundry floor sheeting underlays For floor finishings; over 300 mm wide						
building paper to BS 1521; class A; 75 mm lap (laying only)	-	0.06	0.63	-	m²	**0.63**
3.20 mm thick hardboard	-	0.20	5.07	1.53	m²	**6.60**
6.00 mm thick plywood	-	0.31	7.87	5.05	m²	**12.91**
Skirtings; plastic; Gradus or equivalent Set-in skirtings; type P						
100 mm high; ref SI 100 2.5P	-	0.12	2.37	2.24	m	**4.60**
150 mm high; ref SI 150 2P	-	0.24	4.73	3.37	m	**8.10**

M SURFACE FINISHES

Item	PC £	Labour hours	Labour £	Material £	Unit	Total rate £
Set-on skirtings; type P						
100 mm high; ref SO 100 P	-	0.24	4.73	1.41	m	**6.14**
Stair nosings						
Light duty hard aluminium alloy stair tread						
nosings; plugged and screwed in concrete						
57 mm x 32 mm	7.53	0.26	3.65	8.87	m	**12.52**
84 mm x 32 mm	10.42	0.31	4.35	12.22	m	**16.57**
Heavy duty aluminium alloy stair tread nosings;						
plugged and screwed to concrete						
60 mm x 32 mm	8.96	0.31	4.35	10.52	m	**14.87**
92 mm x 32 mm	12.27	0.36	5.05	14.36	m	**19.41**
Heavy duty carpet tiles; Heuga "580						
Olympic" or other and approved; to						
cement:sand base						
Work to floors						
over 300 mm wide	20.72	0.31	6.11	24.56	m²	**30.67**
M51 EDGE FIXED CARPETING						
Fitted carpeting; Wilton wool/nylon or						
other equal and approved; 80/20 velvet						
pile; heavy domestic plain						
Work to floors						
over 300 mm wide	38.52	0.42	5.62	47.83	m²	**53.44**
Work to treads and risers						
over 300 mm wide	-	0.83	11.10	47.83	m²	**58.93**
Underlay to carpeting						
Work to floors						
over 300 mm wide	3.76	0.08	1.07	4.46	m²	**5.53**
Sundries						
Carpet gripper fixed to floor; standard edging						
22 mm wide	-	0.05	0.53	0.27	m	**0.80**
M52 DECORATIVE PAPERS/FABRICS						
Lining paper; PC £2.16/roll; and hanging						
Plaster walls or columns						
over 300 mm girth	-	0.20	2.81	0.53	m²	**3.33**
Plaster ceilings or beams						
over 300 mm girth	-	0.24	3.37	0.53	m²	**3.90**
Decorative vinyl wallpaper; PC						
£10.80/roll; and hanging						
Plaster walls or columns						
over 300 mm girth	-	0.26	3.65	2.39	m²	**6.04**

M SURFACE FINISHES

Item	PC £	Labour hours	Labour £	Material £	Unit	Total rate £
M60 PAINTING/CLEAR FINISHING - INTERNALLY						
PREPARATION OF EXISTING SURFACES – INTERNALLY						
NOTE: The prices for preparation given hereunder assume that existing surfaces are in fair condition and should be increased for badly dilapidated surfaces.						
Wash down walls; cut out and make good cracks						
Emulsion painted surfaces; including bringing forward bare patches	-	0.07	0.98	-	m^2	0.98
Gloss painted surfaces	-	0.05	0.70	-	m^2	0.70
Wash down ceilings; cut out and make good cracks						
Distempered surfaces	-	0.09	1.26	-	m^2	1.26
Emulsion painted surfaces; including bringing forward bare patches	-	0.10	1.40	-	m^2	1.40
Gloss painted surfaces	-	0.09	1.26	-	m^2	1.26
Wash down plaster cornices; cut out and make good cracks						
Distempered surfaces	-	0.13	1.83	-	m^2	1.83
Emulsion painted surfaces; including bringing forward bare patches	-	0.16	2.25	-	m^2	2.25
Wash and rub down iron and steel surfaces; bringing forward						
General surfaces						
over 300 mm girth	-	0.12	1.69	-	m^2	1.69
isolated surfaces not exceeding 300 mm girth	-	0.05	0.70	-	m^2	0.70
isolated areas not exceeding 0.50 m^2 irrespective of girth	-	0.09	1.26	-	nr	1.26
Glazed windows and screens						
panes; area not exceeding 0.10 m^2	-	0.20	2.81	-	m^2	2.81
panes; area 0.10 - 0.50 m^2	-	0.16	2.25	-	m^2	2.25
panes; area 0.50 - 1.00 m^2	-	0.13	1.83	-	m^2	1.83
panes; area over 1.00 m^2	-	0.12	1.69	-	m^2	1.69
Wash and rub down wood surfaces; prime bare patches; bringing forward						
General surfaces						
over 300 mm girth	-	0.19	2.67	-	m^2	2.67
isolated surfaces not exceeding 300 mm girth	-	0.07	0.98	-	m^2	0.98
isolated areas not exceeding 0.50 m^2 irrespective of girth	-	0.14	1.97	-	nr	1.97
Glazed windows and screens						
panes; area not exceeding 0.10 m^2	-	0.31	4.35	-	m^2	4.35
panes; area 0.10 - 0.50 m^2	-	0.24	3.37	-	m^2	3.37
panes; area 0.50 - 1.00 m^2	-	0.20	2.81	-	m^2	2.81
panes; area over 1.00 m^2	-	0.19	2.67	-	m^2	2.67

M SURFACE FINISHES

Item	PC £	Labour hours	Labour £	Material £	Unit	Total rate £
Wash down and remove paint with chemical stripper from iron, steel or wood surfaces						
General surfaces						
over 300 mm girth	-	0.56	7.86	-	m²	**7.86**
isolated surfaces not exceeding 300 mm girth	-	0.24	3.37	-	m²	**3.37**
isolated areas not exceeding 0.50 m²						
irrespective of girth	-	0.42	5.90	-	nr	**5.90**
Glazed windows and screens						
panes; area not exceeding 0.10 m²	-	1.18	16.57	-	m²	**16.57**
panes; area 0.10 - 0.50 m²	-	0.94	13.20	-	m²	**13.20**
panes; area 0.50 - 1.00 m²	-	0.81	11.37	-	m²	**11.37**
panes; area over 1.00 m²	-	0.71	9.97	-	m²	**9.97**
Burn off and rub down to remove paint from iron, steel or wood surfaces						
General surfaces						
over 300 mm girth	-	0.68	9.55	-	m²	**9.55**
isolated surfaces not exceeding 300 mm girth	-	0.31	4.35	-	m²	**4.35**
isolated areas not exceeding 0.50 m²						
irrespective of girth	-	0.52	7.30	-	nr	**7.30**
Glazed windows and screens						
panes; area not exceeding 0.10 m²	-	1.48	20.78	-	m²	**20.78**
panes; area 0.10 - 0.50 m²	-	1.18	16.57	-	m²	**16.57**
panes; area 0.50 - 1.00 m²	-	1.02	14.32	-	m²	**14.32**
panes; area over 1.00 m²	-	0.89	12.50	-	m²	**12.50**
NOTE: The following prices include for preparing surfaces. Painting woodwork also includes for knotting prior to applying the priming coat and for the stopping of all nail holes etc.						
One coat primer; on wood surfaces before fixing						
General surfaces						
over 300 mm girth	-	0.10	1.40	0.96	m²	**2.36**
isolated surfaces not exceeding 300 mm girth	-	0.03	0.42	0.34	m	**0.76**
isolated areas not exceeding 0.50 m²						
irrespective of girth	-	0.07	0.98	0.38	nr	**1.37**
One coat polyurethane sealer; on wood surfaces before fixing						
General surfaces						
over 300 mm girth	-	0.12	1.69	0.96	m²	**2.64**
isolated surfaces not exceeding 300 mm girth	-	0.04	0.56	0.34	m	**0.90**
isolated areas not exceeding 0.50 m²						
irrespective of girth	-	0.09	1.26	0.46	nr	**1.73**
One coat of Sikkens "Cetol HLS" stain or other equal and approved; on wood surfaces before fixing						
General surfaces						
over 300 mm girth	-	0.13	1.83	1.03	m²	**2.86**
isolated surfaces not exceeding 300 mm girth	-	0.04	0.56	0.40	m	**0.96**
isolated areas not exceeding 0.50 m²						
irrespective of girth	-	0.09	1.26	0.50	nr	**1.76**

M SURFACE FINISHES

Item	PC £	Labour hours	Labour £	Material £	Unit	Total rate £
M60 PAINTING/CLEAR FINISHING - INTERNALLY – cont'd						
One coat of Sikkens "Cetol TS" interior stain or other equal and approved; on wood surfaces before fixing						
General surfaces						
over 300 mm girth	-	0.13	1.83	1.45	m²	3.28
isolated surfaces not exceeding 300 mm girth	-	0.04	0.56	0.56	m	1.12
isolated areas not exceeding 0.50 m²						
irrespective of girth	-	0.09	1.26	0.71	nr	1.97
One coat Cuprinol clear wood preservative or other equal and approved; on wood surfaces before fixing						
General surfaces						
over 300 mm girth	-	0.09	1.26	0.56	m²	1.82
isolated surfaces not exceeding 300 mm girth	-	0.03	0.42	0.20	m	0.62
isolated areas not exceeding 0.50 m²						
irrespective of girth	-	0.06	0.84	0.26	nr	1.10
One coat HCC Protective Coatings Ltd "Permacor" urethane alkyd gloss finishing coat or other equal and approved; on previously primed steelwork						
Members of roof trusses						
over 300 mm girth	-	0.08	1.12	1.90	m²	3.03
Two coats emulsion paint						
Brick or block walls						
over 300 mm girth	-	0.25	3.51	0.88	m²	4.39
Cement render or concrete						
over 300 mm girth	-	0.24	3.37	0.85	m²	4.22
isolated surfaces not exceeding 300 mm girth	-	0.12	1.69	0.27	m	1.95
Plaster walls or plaster/plasterboard ceilings						
over 300 mm girth	-	0.22	3.09	0.82	m²	3.90
over 300 mm girth; in multi colours	-	0.30	4.21	0.99	m²	5.20
over 300 mm girth; in staircase areas	-	0.25	3.51	0.94	m²	4.45
cutting in edges on flush surfaces	-	0.09	1.26	-	m	1.26
Plaster/plasterboard ceilings						
over 300 mm girth; 3.50 m - 5.00 m high	-	0.25	3.51	0.82	m²	4.34
One mist and two coats emulsion paint						
Brick or block walls						
over 300 mm girth	-	0.23	3.23	1.25	m²	4.48
Cement render or concrete						
over 300 mm girth	-	0.23	3.23	1.15	m²	4.38
Plaster walls or plaster/plasterboard ceilings						
over 300 mm girth	-	0.22	3.09	1.15	m²	4.24
over 300 mm girth; in multi colours	-	0.31	4.35	1.17	m²	5.52
over 300 mm girth; in staircase areas	-	0.25	3.51	1.15	m²	4.66
cutting in edges on flush surfaces	-	0.10	1.40	-	m	1.40
Plaster/plasterboard ceilings						
over 300 mm girth; 3.50 m - 5.00 m high	-	0.21	2.95	1.15	m²	4.10

M SURFACE FINISHES

Item	PC £	Labour hours	Labour £	Material £	Unit	Total rate £
One mist Supermatt; one full Supermatt and one full coat of quick drying Acrylic Eggshell						
Brick or block walls						
over 300 mm girth	-	0.23	3.23	2.15	m^2	5.38
Cement render or concrete						
over 300 mm girth	-	0.23	3.23	1.98	m^2	5.21
Plaster walls or plaster/plasterboard ceilings						
over 300 mm girth	-	0.22	3.09	1.98	m^2	5.07
over 300 mm girth; in multi colours	-	0.31	4.35	1.98	m^2	6.33
over 300 mm girth; in staircase areas	-	0.25	3.51	1.98	m^2	5.49
cutting in edges on flush surfaces	-	0.10	1.40	-	m	1.40
Plaster/plasterboard ceilings						
over 300 mm girth; 3.50 m - 5.00 m high	-	0.21	2.95	1.98	m^2	4.93
One coat "Tretol No 10" sealer or other equal and approved; two coats Tretol sprayed "Supercover Spraytone" emulsion paint or other equal and approved						
Plaster walls or plaster/plasterboard ceilings						
over 300 mm girth	-	-	-	-	m^2	5.46
Textured plastic; "Artex" finish or other equal and approved						
Plasterboard ceilings						
over 300 mm girth	-	0.23	3.23	2.10	m^2	5.33
Concrete walls or ceilings						
over 300 mm girth	-	0.25	3.51	1.95	m^2	5.46
Touch up primer; one undercoat and one finishing coat of gloss oil paint; on wood surfaces						
General surfaces						
over 300 mm girth	-	0.27	3.79	2.15	m^2	5.94
isolated surfaces not exceeding 300 mm girth	-	0.11	1.54	0.72	m	2.27
isolated areas not exceeding 0.50 m^2						
irrespective of girth	-	0.20	2.81	1.11	nr	3.92
Glazed windows and screens						
panes; area not exceeding 0.10 m^2	-	0.44	6.18	1.72	m^2	7.89
panes; area 0.10 - 0.50 m^2	-	0.36	5.05	1.28	m^2	6.33
panes; area 0.50 - 1.00 m^2	-	0.31	4.35	1.04	m^2	5.40
panes; area over 1.00 m^2	-	0.27	3.79	0.89	m^2	4.68
Knot; one coat primer; stop; one undercoat and one finishing coat of gloss oil paint; on wood surfaces						
General surfaces						
over 300 mm girth	-	0.39	5.48	2.18	m^2	7.65
isolated surfaces not exceeding 300 mm girth	-	0.16	2.25	0.72	m	2.97
isolated areas not exceeding 0.50 m^2						
irrespective of girth	-	0.30	4.21	1.44	nr	5.65
Glazed windows and screens						
panes; area not exceeding 0.10 m^2	-	0.67	9.41	2.18	m^2	11.58
panes; area 0.10 - 0.50 m^2	-	0.54	7.58	1.81	m^2	9.39
panes; area 0.50 - 1.00 m^2	-	0.46	6.46	1.81	m^2	8.27
panes; area over 1.00 m^2	-	0.39	5.48	1.34	m^2	6.82

M SURFACE FINISHES

Item	PC £	Labour hours	Labour £	Material £	Unit	Total rate £
M60 PAINTING/CLEAR FINISHING - INTERNALLY – cont'd						
One coat primer; one undercoat and one finishing coat of gloss oil paint						
Plaster surfaces						
over 300 mm girth	-	0.35	4.91	2.76	m^2	**7.67**
One coat primer; two undercoats and one finishing coat of gloss oil paint						
Plaster surfaces						
over 300 mm girth	-	0.46	6.46	3.75	m^2	**10.20**
One coat primer; two undercoats and one finishing coat of eggshell paint						
Plaster surfaces						
over 300 mm girth	-	0.46	6.46	4.11	m^2	**10.57**
Touch up primer; one undercoat and one finishing coat of gloss paint; on iron or steel surfaces						
General surfaces						
over 300 mm girth	-	0.27	3.79	1.67	m^2	**5.46**
isolated surfaces not exceeding 300 mm girth	-	0.11	1.54	0.56	m	**2.11**
isolated areas not exceeding 0.50 m^2						
irrespective of girth	-	0.20	2.81	0.89	nr	**3.70**
Glazed windows and screens						
panes; area not exceeding 0.10 m^2	-	0.44	6.18	1.70	m^2	**7.88**
panes; area 0.10 - 0.50 m^2	-	0.36	5.05	1.29	m^2	**6.34**
panes; area 0.50 - 1.00 m^2	-	0.31	4.35	1.02	m^2	**5.37**
panes; area over 1.00 m^2	-	0.27	3.79	0.86	m^2	**4.66**
Structural steelwork						
over 300 mm girth	-	0.30	4.21	1.72	m^2	**5.93**
Members of roof trusses						
over 300 mm girth	-	0.40	5.62	1.96	m^2	**7.58**
Ornamental railings and the like; each side measured overall						
over 300 mm girth	-	0.46	6.46	2.13	m^2	**8.59**
Iron or steel radiators						
over 300 mm girth	-	0.27	3.79	1.80	m^2	**5.59**
Pipes or conduits						
over 300 mm girth	-	0.40	5.62	1.86	m^2	**7.48**
not exceeding 300 mm girth	-	0.16	2.25	0.62	m	**2.86**
One coat primer; one undercoat and one finishing coat of gloss oil paint; on iron or steel surfaces						
General surfaces						
over 300 mm girth	-	0.27	3.79	1.67	m^2	**5.46**
isolated surfaces not exceeding 300 mm girth	-	0.14	1.97	0.98	m	**2.94**
isolated areas not exceeding 0.50 m^2						
irrespective of girth	-	0.27	3.79	1.61	nr	**5.40**
Glazed windows and screens						
panes; area not exceeding 0.10 m^2	-	0.58	8.14	2.64	m^2	**10.78**
panes; area 0.10 - 0.50 m^2	-	0.46	6.46	2.10	m^2	**8.56**
panes; area 0.50 - 1.00 m^2	-	0.40	5.62	1.81	m^2	**7.43**
panes; area over 1.00 m^2	-	0.35	4.91	1.61	m^2	**6.52**
Structural steelwork						
over 300 mm girth	-	0.39	5.48	2.58	m^2	**8.06**

M SURFACE FINISHES

Item	PC £	Labour hours	Labour £	Material £	Unit	Total rate £
Members of roof trusses						
over 300 mm girth	-	0.53	7.44	2.70	m^2	**10.14**
Ornamental railings and the like; each side measured overall						
over 300 mm girth	-	0.60	8.43	3.21	m^2	**11.64**
Iron or steel radiators						
over 300 mm girth	-	0.35	4.91	2.70	m^2	**7.61**
Pipes or conduits						
over 300 mm girth	-	0.53	7.44	2.70	m^2	**10.14**
not exceeding 300 mm girth	-	0.20	2.81	0.89	m	**3.69**
Two coats of bituminous paint; on iron or steel surfaces						
General surfaces						
over 300 mm girth	-	0.27	3.79	0.67	m^2	**4.46**
Inside of galvanized steel cistern						
over 300 mm girth	-	0.40	5.62	0.80	m^2	**6.42**
Two coats bituminous paint; first coat blinded with clean sand prior to second coat; on concrete surfaces						
General surfaces						
over 300 mm girth	-	0.93	13.06	1.76	m^2	**14.82**
Mordant solution; one coat HCC Protective Coatings Ltd "Permacor alkyd MIO" or other equal and approved; one coat "Permacor Epoxy Gloss" finishing coat or other equal and approved on galvanised steelwork						
Structural steelwork						
over 300 mm girth	-	0.52	7.30	3.16	m^2	**10.46**
One coat HCC Protective Coatings Ltd "Permacor Epoxy Zinc Primer" or other equal and approved; two coats "Permacor alkyd MIO" or other equal and approved; one coat "Permatex Epoxy Gloss" finishing coat or other equal and approved on steelwork						
Structural steelwork						
over 300 mm girth	-	0.74	10.39	5.76	m^2	**16.15**
Steel protection; HCC Protective Coatings Ltd "Unitherm" or other equal and approved; two coats to steelwork						
Structural steelwork						
over 300 mm girth	-	1.16	16.29	1.97	m^2	**18.26**
Two coats of epoxy anti-slip floor paint; on screeded concrete surfaces						
General surfaces						
over 300 mm girth	-	0.28	3.93	13.94	m^2	**17.87**
"Nitoflor Lithurin" floor hardener and dust proofer or other equal and approved; Fosroc Expandite Ltd; two coats; on concrete surfaces						
General surfaces						
over 300 mm girth	-	0.28	2.94	0.57	m^2	**3.51**

M SURFACE FINISHES

Item	PC £	Labour hours	Labour £	Material £	Unit	Total rate £
M60 PAINTING/CLEAR FINISHING - INTERNALLY – cont'd						
Two coats of boiled linseed oil; on hardwood surfaces						
General surfaces						
over 300 mm girth	-	0.20	2.81	1.60	m²	**4.41**
isolated surfaces not exceeding 300 mm girth	-	0.08	1.12	0.52	m	**1.64**
isolated areas not exceeding 0.50 m²						
irrespective of girth	-	0.16	2.25	0.93	nr	**3.17**
Two coats polyurethane varnish; on wood surfaces						
General surfaces						
over 300 mm girth	-	0.20	2.81	1.69	m²	**4.50**
isolated surfaces not exceeding 300 mm girth	-	·0.08	1.12	0.62	m	**1.75**
isolated areas not exceeding 0.50 m²						
irrespective of girth	-	0.16	2.25	0.20	nr	**2.44**
Three coats polyurethane varnish; on wood surfaces						
General surfaces						
over 300 mm girth	-	0.31	4.35	2.59	m²	**6.94**
isolated surfaces not exceeding 300 mm girth	-	0.12	1.69	0.79	m	**2.47**
isolated areas not exceeding 0.50 m²						
irrespective of girth	-	0.23	3.23	1.44	nr	**4.67**
One undercoat; and one finishing coat; of "Albi" clear flame retardant surface coating or other equal and approved; on wood surfaces						
General surfaces						
over 300 mm girth	-	0.40	5.62	3.79	m²	**9.41**
isolated surfaces not exceeding 300 mm girth	-	0.17	2.39	1.31	m	**3.70**
isolated areas not exceeding 0.50 m²						
irrespective of girth	-	0.23	3.23	2.88	nr	**6.11**
Two undercoats; and one finishing coat; of "Albi" clear flame retardant surface coating or other equal and approved; on wood surfaces						
General surfaces						
over 300 mm girth	-	0.47	6.60	5.56	m²	**12.16**
isolated surfaces not exceeding 300 mm girth	-	0.24	3.37	1.92	m	**5.29**
isolated areas not exceeding 0.50 m²						
irrespective of girth	-	0.39	5.48	3.08	nr	**8.56**
Seal and wax polish; dull gloss finish on wood surfaces						
General surfaces						
over 300 mm girth	-	-	-	-	m²	**10.36**
isolated surfaces not exceeding 300 mm girth	-	-	-	-	m	**4.69**
isolated areas not exceeding 0.50 m²						
irrespective of girth	-	-	-	-	nr	**7.23**

M SURFACE FINISHES

Item	PC £	Labour hours	Labour £	Material £	Unit	Total rate £
One coat of "Sadolin Extra" or other equal and approved; clear or pigmented; one further coat of "Holdex" clear interior silk matt lacquer or other equal and approved						
General surfaces						
over 300 mm girth	-	0.30	4.21	5.62	m^2	9.84
isolated surfaces not exceeding 300 mm girth	-	0.12	1.69	2.63	m	4.31
isolated areas not exceeding 0.50 m^2						
irrespective of girth	-	0.22	3.09	2.73	nr	5.82
Glazed windows and screens						
panes; area not exceeding 0.10 m^2	-	0.49	6.88	3.21	m^2	10.10
panes; area 0.10 - 0.50 m^2	-	0.39	5.48	2.99	m^2	8.47
panes; area 0.50 - 1.00 m^2	-	0.34	4.77	2.77	m^2	7.55
panes; area over 1.00 m^2	-	0.30	4.21	2.63	m^2	6.84
Two coats of "Sadolins Extra" or other equal and approved; clear or pigmented; two further coats of "Holdex" clear interior silk matt lacquer or other equal and approved						
General surfaces						
over 300 mm girth	-	0.46	6.46	10.39	m^2	16.85
isolated surfaces not exceeding 300 mm girth	-	0.19	2.67	5.20	m	7.86
isolated areas not exceeding 0.50 m^2						
irrespective of girth	-	0.35	4.91	5.93	nr	10.84
Glazed windows and screens						
panes; area not exceeding 0.10 m^2	-	0.77	10.81	6.37	m^2	17.18
panes; area 0.10 - 0.50 m^2	-	0.61	8.57	5.93	m^2	14.49
panes; area 0.50 - 1.00 m^2	-	0.54	7.58	5.49	m^2	13.07
panes; area over 1.00 m^2	-	0.46	6.46	5.20	m^2	11.65
Two coats of Sikkens "Cetol TS" interior stain or other equal and approved; on wood surfaces						
General surfaces						
over 300 mm girth	-	0.21	2.95	2.62	m^2	5.57
isolated surfaces not exceeding 300 mm girth	-	0.09	1.26	0.92	m	2.18
isolated areas not exceeding 0.50 m^2						
irrespective of girth	-	0.16	2.25	1.43	nr	3.67
Body in and wax polish; dull gloss finish; on hardwood surfaces						
General surfaces						
over 300 mm girth	-	-	-	-	m^2	11.92
isolated surfaces not exceeding 300 mm girth	-	-	-	-	m	5.41
isolated areas not exceeding 0.50 m^2						
irrespective of girth	-	-	-	-	nr	8.33
Stain; body in and wax polish; dull gloss finish; on hardwood surfaces						
General surfaces						
over 300 mm girth	-	-	-	-	m^2	16.49
isolated surfaces not exceeding 300 mm girth	-	-	-	-	m	7.43
isolated areas not exceeding 0.50 m^2						
irrespective of girth	-	-	-	-	nr	11.60

M SURFACE FINISHES

Item	PC £	Labour hours	Labour £	Material £	Unit	Total rate £
M60 PAINTING/CLEAR FINISHING - INTERNALLY – cont'd						
Seal; two coats of synthetic resin lacquer; decorative flatted finish; wire down, wax and burnish; on wood surfaces						
General surfaces						
over 300 mm girth	-	-	-	-	m^2	19.81
isolated surfaces not exceeding 300 mm girth	-	-	-	-	m	8.92
isolated areas not exceeding 0.50 m^2						
irrespective of girth	-	-	-	-	nr	13.88
Stain; body in and fully French polish; full gloss finish; on hardwood surfaces						
General surfaces						
over 300 mm girth	-	-	-	-	m^2	22.80
isolated surfaces not exceeding 300 mm girth	-	-	-	-	m	10.29
isolated areas not exceeding 0.50 m^2						
irrespective of area	-	-	-	-	nr	15.96
Stain; fill grain and fully French polish; full gloss finish; on hardwood surfaces						
General surfaces						
over 300 mm girth	-	-	-	-	m^2	31.28
isolated surfaces not exceeding 300 mm girth	-	-	-	-	m	14.07
isolated areas not exceeding 0.50 m^2						
irrespective of girth	-	-	-	-	nr	21.90
Stain black; body in and fully French polish; ebonized finish; on hardwood surfaces						
General surfaces						
over 300 mm girth	-	-	-	-	m^2	39.09
isolated surfaces not exceeding 300 mm girth	-	-	-	-	m	16.29
isolated areas not exceeding 0.50 m^2						
irrespective of girth	-	-	-	-	nr	27.37
M60 PAINTING/CLEAR FINISHING - EXTERNALLY						
PREPARATION OF EXISTING SURFACES – EXTERNALLY						
Wash and rub down iron and steel surfaces; bringing forward						
General surfaces						
over 300 mm girth	-	0.15	2.11	-	m^2	2.11
isolated surfaces not exceeding 300 mm girth	-	0.05	0.70	-	m	0.70
isolated areas not exceeding 0.50 m^2						
irrespective of girth	-	0.11	1.54	-	nr	1.54
Glazed windows and screens						
panes; area not exceeding 0.10 m^2	-	0.24	3.37	-	m^2	3.37
panes; area 0.10 - 0.50 m^2	-	0.20	2.81	-	m^2	2.81
panes; area 0.50 - 1.00 m^2	-	0.17	2.39	-	m^2	2.39
panes; area over 1.00 m^2	-	0.15	2.11	-	m^2	2.11

M SURFACE FINISHES

Item	PC £	Labour hours	Labour £	Material £	Unit	Total rate £
Wash and rub down wood surfaces; prime bare patches; bringing forward						
General surfaces						
over 300 mm girth	-	0.24	3.37	-	m^2	**3.37**
isolated surfaces not exceeding 300 mm girth	-	0.09	1.26	-	m	**1.26**
isolated areas not exceeding 0.50 m^2						
irrespective of girth	-	0.18	2.53	-	nr	**2.53**
Glazed windows and screens						
panes; area not exceeding 0.10 m^2	-	0.41	5.76	-	m^2	**5.76**
panes; area 0.10 - 0.50 m^2	-	0.32	4.49	-	m^2	**4.49**
panes; area 0.50 - 1.00 m^2	-	0.28	3.93	-	m^2	**3.93**
panes; area over 1.00 m^2	-	0.24	3.37	-	m^2	**3.37**
Wash down and remove paint with chemical stripper from iron, steel or wood surfaces						
General surfaces						
over 300 mm girth	-	0.74	10.39	-	m^2	**10.39**
isolated surfaces not exceeding 300 mm girth	-	0.33	4.63	-	m	**4.63**
isolated areas not exceeding 0.50 m^2						
irrespective of girth	-	0.56	7.86	-	nr	**7.86**
Glazed windows and screens						
panes; area not exceeding 0.10 m^2	-	1.58	22.19	-	m^2	**22.19**
panes; area 0.10 - 0.50 m^2	-	1.26	17.69	-	m^2	**17.69**
panes; area 0.50 - 1.00 m^2	-	1.09	15.31	-	m^2	**15.31**
panes; area over 1.00 m^2	-	0.94	13.20	-	m^2	**13.20**
Burn off and rub down to remove paint from iron, steel or wood surfaces						
General surfaces						
over 300 mm girth	-	0.91	12.78	-	m^2	**12.78**
isolated surfaces not exceeding 300 mm girth	-	0.42	5.90	-	m	**5.90**
isolated surfaces not exceeding 0.50 m^2	-	0.68	9.55	-	nr	**9.55**
Glazed windows and screens						
panes over 1m^2	-	1.18	16.57	-	m^2	**16.57**
panes 0.50 - 1.00m^2	-	1.35	18.96	-	m^2	**18.96**
panes 0.10 - 0.50m^2	-	1.57	22.05	-	m^2	**22.05**
panes not exceeding 0.10m^2	-	1.97	27.66	-	m^2	**27.66**
Two coats of cement paint, "Sandtex Matt" or other equal and approved						
Brick or block walls						
over 300 mm girth	-	0.31	4.35	1.69	m^2	**6.04**
Cement render or concrete walls						
over 300 mm girth	-	0.27	3.79	1.12	m^2	**4.91**
Roughcast walls						
over 300 mm girth	-	0.46	6.46	1.12	m^2	**7.58**
One coat sealer and two coats of external grade emulsion paint, Dulux "Weathershield" or other equal and approved						
Brick or block walls						
over 300 mm girth	-	0.50	7.02	7.71	m^2	**14.73**
Cement render or concrete walls						
over 300 mm girth	-	0.39	5.48	5.14	m^2	**10.62**
Concrete soffits						
over 300 mm girth	-	0.46	6.46	5.14	m^2	**11.60**

M SURFACE FINISHES

Item	PC £	Labour hours	Labour £	Material £	Unit	Total rate £
M60 PAINTING/CLEAR FINISHING **- EXTERNALLY** – cont'd						
One coat sealer (applied by brush) and two coats of external grade emulsion paint, Dulux "Weathershield" or other equal and approved (spray applied)						
Roughcast						
over 300 mm girth	-	0.33	4.63	10.40	m^2	15.03
One coat sealer and two coats of anti-graffiti paint (spray applied)						
Brick or block walls						
over 300 mm girth	-	0.26	3.65	3.11	m^2	6.76
Cement render or concrete walls						
over 300 mm girth	-	0.30	4.21	4.61	m^2	8.83
2.5 mm of "Vandalene" anti-climb paint (spray applied)						
General surfaces						
over 300 mm girth	-	0.35	4.91	4.39	m^2	9.31
Two coats solar reflective aluminium paint; on bituminous roofing						
General surfaces						
over 300 mm girth	-	0.52	7.30	13.86	m^2	21.17
Touch up primer; two undercoats and one finishing coat of gloss oil paint; on wood surfaces						
General surfaces						
over 300 mm girth	-	0.42	5.90	2.18	m^2	8.08
isolated surfaces not exceeding 300 mm girth	-	0.17	2.39	0.58	m	2.96
isolated areas not exceeding 0.50 m^2						
irrespective of girth	-	0.31	4.35	1.15	nr	5.51
Glazed windows and screens						
panes; area not exceeding 0.10 m^2	-	0.69	9.69	1.93	m^2	11.61
panes; area 0.10 - 0.50 m^2	-	0.69	9.69	1.62	m^2	11.31
panes; area 0.50 - 1.00 m^2	-	0.56	7.86	1.41	m^2	9.27
panes; area over 1.00 m^2	-	0.42	5.90	1.15	m^2	7.05
Glazed windows and screens; multi- coloured work						
panes; area not exceeding 0.10 m^2	-	0.80	11.23	1.93	m^2	13.16
panes; area 0.10 - 0.50 m^2	-	0.64	8.99	1.67	m^2	10.66
panes; area 0.50 - 1.00 m^2	-	0.56	7.86	1.41	m^2	9.27
panes; area over 1.00 m^2	-	0.48	6.74	1.15	m^2	7.89
Knot; one coat primer; two undercoats and one finishing coat of gloss oil paint; on wood surfaces						
General surfaces						
over 300 mm girth	-	0.55	7.72	2.27	m^2	9.99
isolated surfaces not exceeding 300 mm girth	-	0.22	3.09	0.81	m	3.90
isolated areas not exceeding 0.50 m^2						
irrespective of girth	-	0.42	5.90	1.58	nr	7.48
Glazed windows and screens						
panes; area not exceeding 0.10 m^2	-	0.92	12.92	2.53	m^2	15.45
panes; area 0.10 - 0.50 m^2	-	0.73	10.25	2.25	m^2	12.51
panes; area 0.50 - 1.00 m^2	-	0.64	8.99	1.72	m^2	10.71
panes; area over 1.00 m^2	-	0.55	7.72	1.19	m^2	8.91

M SURFACE FINISHES

Item	PC £	Labour hours	Labour £	Material £	Unit	Total rate £
Glazed windows and screens; multi-coloured work						
panes; area not exceeding 0.10 m²	-	1.05	14.74	2.53	m²	**17.28**
panes; area 0.10 - 0.50 m²	-	0.85	11.94	2.27	m²	**14.20**
panes; area 0.50 - 1.00 m²	-	0.75	10.53	1.72	m²	**12.25**
panes; area over 1.00 m²	-	0.63	8.85	1.19	m²	**10.03**
Touch up primer; two undercoats and one finishing coat of gloss oil paint; on iron or steel surfaces						
General surfaces						
over 300 mm girth	-	0.42	5.90	1.64	m²	**7.53**
isolated surfaces not exceeding 300 mm girth	-	0.17	2.39	0.44	m	**2.83**
isolated areas not exceeding 0.50 m² irrespective of girth	-	0.31	4.35	0.92	nr	**5.27**
Glazed windows and screens						
panes; area not exceeding 0.10 m²	-	0.69	9.69	1.67	m²	**11.36**
panes; area 0.10 - 0.50 m²	-	0.56	7.86	1.44	m²	**9.30**
panes; area 0.50 - 1.00 m²	-	0.48	6.74	1.21	m²	**7.95**
panes; area over 1.00 m²	-	0.42	5.90	0.98	m²	**6.87**
Structural steelwork						
over 300 mm girth	-	0.47	6.60	1.70	m²	**8.30**
Members of roof trusses						
over 300 mm girth	-	0.63	8.85	1.93	m²	**10.77**
Ornamental railings and the like; each side measured overall						
over 300 mm girth	-	0.71	9.97	1.99	m²	**11.96**
Eaves gutters						
over 300 mm girth	-	0.75	10.53	2.19	m²	**12.72**
not exceeding 300 mm girth	-	0.30	4.21	0.91	m	**5.13**
Pipes or conduits						
over 300 mm girth	-	0.63	8.85	2.19	m²	**11.04**
not exceeding 300 mm girth	-	0.25	3.51	0.75	m	**4.26**
One coat primer; two undercoats and one finishing coat of gloss oil paint; on iron or steel surfaces						
General surfaces						
over 300 mm girth	-	0.50	7.02	1.90	m²	**8.92**
isolated surfaces not exceeding 300 mm girth	-	0.20	2.81	0.49	m	**3.30**
isolated areas not exceeding 0.50 m² irrespective of girth	-	0.38	5.34	0.98	nr	**6.32**
Glazed windows and screens						
panes; area not exceeding 0.10 m²	-	0.83	11.65	1.73	m²	**13.39**
panes; area 0.10 - 0.50 m²	-	0.67	9.41	1.50	m²	**10.91**
panes; area 0.50 - 1.00 m²	-	0.58	8.14	1.27	m²	**9.42**
panes; area over 1.00 m²	-	0.50	7.02	0.98	m²	**8.00**
Structural steelwork						
over 300 mm girth	-	0.56	7.86	1.96	m²	**9.83**
Members of roof trusses						
over 300 mm girth	-	0.75	10.53	2.19	m²	**12.72**
Ornamental railings and the like; each side measured overall						
over 300 mm girth	-	0.85	11.94	2.19	m²	**14.13**
Eaves gutters						
over 300 mm girth	-	0.90	12.64	2.49	m²	**15.13**
not exceeding 300 mm girth	-	0.36	5.05	0.85	m	**5.91**
Pipes or conduits						
over 300 mm girth	-	0.75	10.53	2.49	m²	**13.02**
not exceeding 300 mm girth	-	0.30	4.21	0.83	m	**5.04**

M SURFACE FINISHES

Item	PC £	Labour hours	Labour £	Material £	Unit	Total rate £
M60 PAINTING/CLEAR FINISHING - EXTERNALLY – cont'd						
One coat of Andrews "Hammerite" paint or other equal and approved; on iron or steel surfaces						
General surfaces						
over 300 mm girth	-	0.18	2.53	1.50	m^2	**4.02**
isolated surfaces not exceeding 300 mm girth	-	0.09	1.26	0.46	m	**1.72**
isolated areas not exceeding 0.50 m^2						
irrespective of girth	-	0.13	1.83	0.86	nr	**2.69**
Glazed windows and screens						
panes; area not exceeding 0.10 m^2	-	0.30	4.21	1.14	m^2	**5.35**
panes; area 0.10 - 0.50 m^2	-	0.23	3.23	1.25	m^2	**4.48**
panes; area 0.50 - 1.00 m^2	-	0.21	2.95	1.12	m^2	**4.07**
panes; area over 1.00 m^2	-	0.18	2.53	1.12	m^2	**3.65**
Structural steelwork						
over 300 mm girth	-	0.20	2.81	1.37	m^2	**4.18**
Members of roof trusses						
over 300 mm girth	-	0.27	3.79	1.50	m^2	**5.29**
Ornamental railings and the like; each side measured overall						
over 300 mm girth	-	0.30	4.21	1.50	m^2	**5.71**
Eaves gutters						
over 300 mm girth	-	0.31	4.35	1.62	m^2	**5.97**
not exceeding 300 mm girth	-	0.10	1.40	0.75	m	**2.15**
Pipes or conduits						
over 300 mm girth	-	0.30	4.21	1.37	m^2	**5.58**
not exceeding 300 mm girth	-	0.10	1.40	0.62	m	**2.03**
Two coats of creosote; on wood surfaces						
General surfaces						
over 300 mm girth	-	0.19	2.67	0.38	m^2	**3.05**
isolated surfaces not exceeding 300 mm girth	-	0.06	0.84	0.23	m	**1.07**
Two coats of "Solignum" wood preservative or other equal and approved; on wood surfaces						
General surfaces						
over 300 mm girth	-	0.17	2.39	1.62	m^2	**4.00**
isolated surfaces not exceeding 300 mm girth	-	0.06	0.84	0.48	m	**1.33**
Three coats of polyurethane; on wood surfaces						
General surfaces						
over 300 mm girth	-	0.33	4.63	2.87	m^2	**7.50**
isolated surfaces not exceeding 300 mm girth	-	0.13	1.83	1.41	m	**3.23**
isolated areas not exceeding 0.50 m^2						
irrespective of girth	-	0.25	3.51	1.63	nr	**5.14**
Two coats of "New Base" primer or other and approved; and two coats of "Extra"; Sadolin Ltd or other equal and approved; pigmented; on wood surfaces						
General surfaces						
over 300 mm girth	-	0.50	7.02	5.38	m^2	**12.40**
isolated surfaces not exceeding 300 mm girth	-	0.31	4.35	1.83	m	**6.19**

M SURFACE FINISHES

Item	PC £	Labour hours	Labour £	Material £	Unit	Total rate £
Glazed windows and screens						
panes; area not exceeding 0.10 m^2	-	0.84	11.79	3.83	m^2	**15.63**
panes; area 0.10 - 0.50 m^2	-	0.68	9.55	3.61	m^2	**13.16**
panes; area 0.50 - 1.00 m^2	-	0.58	8.14	3.39	m^2	**11.53**
panes; area over 1.00 m^2	-	0.50	7.02	2.72	m^2	**9.74**
Two coats Sikkens "Cetol Filter 7" exterior stain or other equal and approved; on wood surfaces						
General surfaces						
over 300 mm girth	-	0.21	2.95	4.40	m^2	**7.34**
isolated surfaces not exceeding 300 mm girth	-	0.09	1.26	1.51	m	**2.77**
isolated areas not exceeding 0.50 m^2						
irrespective of girth	-	0.16	2.25	2.23	nr	**4.47**

N FURNITURE/EQUIPMENT

Item	PC £	Labour hours	Labour £	Material £	Unit	Total rate £
N10/11 GENERAL FIXTURES/ KITCHEN FITTINGS						
SUPPLY ONLY PRICES						
NOTE: The fixing of general fixtures will vary considerably depending upon the size of the fixture and the method of fixing employed. Prices for fixing like sized kitchen fittings may be suitable for certain fixtures, although adjustment to those rates will almost invariably be necessary and the reader is directed to section "G20" for information on bolts, plugging brickwork and blockwork etc. which should prove useful in building up a suitable rate.						
The following supply only prices are for purpose made fittings components in various materials supplied as part of an assembled fitting and therefore may be used to arrive at a guide price for a complete fitting.						
Fitting components; medium density fibreboard						
Backs, fronts, sides or divisions; over 300 mm wide						
12 mm thick	-	-	-	26.14	m^2	**26.14**
18 mm thick	-	-	-	27.71	m^2	**27.71**
25 mm thick	-	-	-	30.84	m^2	**30.84**
Shelves or worktops; over 300 mm wide						
18 mm thick	-	-	-	27.71	m^2	**27.71**
25 mm thick	-	-	-	30.84	m^2	**30.84**
Flush doors; lipped on four edges						
450 mm x 750 mm x 18 mm	-	-	-	40.13	nr	**40.13**
450 mm x 750 mm x 25 mm	-	-	-	40.89	nr	**40.89**
600 mm x 900 mm x 18 mm	-	-	-	47.35	nr	**47.35**
600 mm x 900 mm x 25 mm	-	-	-	48.60	nr	**48.60**
Fitting components; moisture-resistant medium density fibreboard						
Backs, fronts, sides or divisions; over 300 mm wide						
12 mm thick	-	-	-	29.27	m^2	**29.27**
18 mm thick	-	-	-	32.40	m^2	**32.40**
25 mm thick	-	-	-	35.52	m^2	**35.52**
Shelves or worktops; over 300 mm wide						
18 mm thick	-	-	-	32.40	m^2	**32.40**
25 mm thick	-	-	-	35.52	m^2	**35.52**
Flush doors; lipped on four edges						
450 mm x 750 mm x 18 mm	-	-	-	40.89	nr	**40.89**
450 mm x 750 mm x 25 mm	-	-	-	42.05	nr	**42.05**
600 mm x 900 mm x 18 mm	-	-	-	48.60	nr	**48.60**
600 mm x 900 mm x 25 mm	-	-	-	50.50	nr	**50.50**

N FURNITURE/EQUIPMENT

Item	PC £	Labour hours	Labour £	Material £	Unit	Total rate £
Fitting components; medium density board; melamine faced both sides						
Backs, fronts, sides or divisions; over 300 mm wide						
12 mm thick	-	-	-	34.49	m²	34.49
18 mm thick	-	-	-	38.41	m²	38.41
Shelves or worktops; over 300 mm wide						
18 mm thick	-	-	-	38.41	m²	38.41
Flush doors; lipped on four edges						
450 mm x 750 mm x 18 mm	-	-	-	28.70	nr	28.70
600 mm x 900 mm x 25 mm	-	-	-	36.41	nr	36.41
Fitting components; medium density board; formica faced both sides						
Backs, fronts, sides or divisions; over 300 mm wide						
12 mm thick	-	-	-	105.04	m²	105.04
18 mm thick	-	-	-	109.22	m²	109.22
Shelves or worktops; over 300 mm wide						
18 mm thick	-	-	-	109.22	m²	109.22
Flush doors; lipped on four edges						
450 mm x 750 mm x 18 mm	-	-	-	57.84	nr	57.84
600 mm x 900 mm x 25 mm	-	-	-	59.09	nr	59.09
Fitting components; wrought softwood						
Backs, fronts, sides or divisions; cross-tongued joints; over 300 mm wide						
25 mm thick	-	-	-	50.20	m²	50.20
Shelves or worktops; cross-tongued joints; over 300 mm wide						
25 mm thick	-	-	-	50.20	m²	50.20
Bearers						
19 mm x 38 mm	-	-	-	2.63	m	2.63
25 mm x 50 mm	-	-	-	2.91	m	2.91
44 mm x 44 mm	-	-	-	3.10	m	3.10
44 mm x 69 mm	-	-	-	3.59	m	3.59
Bearers; framed; to backs, fronts or sides						
19 mm x 38 mm	-	-	-	6.00	m	6.00
25 mm x 50 mm	-	-	-	6.50	m	6.50
44 mm x 44 mm	-	-	-	8.40	m	8.40
44 mm x 69 mm	-	-	-	9.64	m	9.64
Add 5% for selected softwood for staining						5%
Fitting components; selected Sapele						
Backs, fronts, sides or divisions; cross-tongued joints; over 300 mm wide						
25 mm thick	-	-	-	79.01	m²	79.01
Shelves or worktops; cross-tongued joints; over 300 mm wide						
25 mm thick	-	-	-	79.01	m²	79.01
Bearers						
19 mm x 38 mm	-	-	-	3.96	m	3.96
25 mm x 50 mm	-	-	-	4.93	m	4.93
50 mm x 50 mm	-	-	-	5.54	m	5.54
50 mm x 75 mm	-	-	-	7.21	m	7.21
Bearers; framed; to backs, fronts or sides						
19 mm x 38 mm	-	-	-	7.65	m	7.65
25 mm x 50 mm	-	-	-	8.49	m	8.49
50 mm x 50 mm	-	-	-	11.38	m	11.38
50 mm x 75 mm	-	-	-	14.27	m	14.27

N FURNITURE/EQUIPMENT

Item	PC £	Labour hours	Labour £	Material £	Unit	Total rate £
N10/11 GENERAL FIXTURES/ KITCHEN FITTINGS – cont'd						
Fitting components; Iroko						
Backs, fronts, sides or divisions; cross-tongued joints; over 300 mm wide						
25 mm thick	-	-	-	87.09	m²	87.09
Shelves or worktops; cross-tongued joints; over 300 mm wide						
25 mm thick	-	-	-	87.09	m²	87.09
Draining boards; cross-tongued joints; over 300 mm wide						
25 mm thick	-	-	-	109.13	m²	109.13
stopped flutes	-	-	-	5.64	m	5.64
grooves; cross-grain	-	-	-	0.85	m	0.85
Bearers						
19 mm x 38 mm	-	-	-	4.33	m	4.33
25 mm x 50 mm	-	-	-	5.53	m	5.53
50 mm x 50 mm	-	-	-	6.29	m	6.29
50 mm x 75 mm	-	-	-	8.29	m	8.29
Bearers; framed; to backs, fronts or sides						
19 mm x 38 mm	-	-	-	7.91	m	7.91
25 mm x 50 mm	-	-	-	8.82	m	8.82
50 mm x 50 mm	-	-	-	11.90	m	11.90
50 mm x 75 mm	-	-	-	15.45	m	15.45
SUPPLY AND FIX PRICES						
NOTE: Kitchen fittings prices vary considerably. PC supply prices for reasonable quantities for a moderately priced range of kitchen fittings have been shown.						
Supplying and fixing to backgrounds requiring plugging; including any pre-assembly						
Wall units						
300 mm x 300 mm x 720 mm	70.01	1.20	16.85	79.30	nr	96.15
500 mm x 300 mm x 720 mm	82.50	1.30	18.25	93.40	nr	111.65
600 mm x 300 mm x 720 mm	92.46	1.43	20.08	104.64	nr	124.72
800 mm x 300 mm x 720 mm	140.68	1.62	22.75	159.07	nr	181.82
Floor units with drawers						
500 mm x 600 mm x 870 mm	122.86	1.30	18.25	138.97	nr	157.22
600 mm x 600 mm x 870 mm	135.36	1.43	20.08	153.07	nr	173.15
1000 mm x 600 mm x 870 mm	210.78	1.71	24.01	238.21	nr	262.22
Sink units (excluding sink top)						
1000 mm x 600 mm x 870 mm	214.00	1.62	22.75	241.83	nr	264.58
Larder units						
500 mm x 600 mm x 870 mm	122.86	1.50	21.06	139.25	nr	160.31
Laminated plastics worktops; single rolled edge; prices include for fixing						
38 mm thick; 600 mm wide	33.27	0.41	5.76	39.57	m	45.33
extra for forming hole for inset sink	-	0.77	10.81	-	nr	10.81
extra for jointing strip at corner intersection of worktops	-	0.16	2.25	8.23	nr	10.48
extra for butt and scribe joint at corner intersection of worktops	-	4.58	64.31	-	nr	64.31

N FURNITURE/EQUIPMENT

Item	PC £	Labour hours	Labour £	Material £	Unit	Total rate £
Lockers; Welconstruct Distribution or other equal and approved						
Standard clothes lockers; steel body and door within reinforced 19G frame, powder coated finish, cam locks						
1 compartment; placing in position	-	-	-	-	-	-
300 mm x 300 mm x 1800 mm	-	0.25	2.63	59.73	nr	62.36
380 mm x 380 mm x 1800 mm	-	0.25	2.63	72.38	nr	75.01
450 mm x 450 mm x 1800 mm	-	0.30	3.15	85.03	nr	88.19
610 mm x 450 mm x 1800 mm	-	0.30	3.15	116.13	nr	119.28
Compartment lockers; steel body and door with reinforced 19G frame, powder coated finish, cam locks						
2 compartments; placing in position	-	-	-	-	-	-
300 mm x 300 mm x 1800 mm	-	0.25	2.63	84.93	nr	87.55
380 mm x 380 mm x 1800 mm	-	0.25	2.63	87.29	nr	89.91
450 mm x 450 mm x 1800 mm	-	0.30	3.15	107.98	nr	111.13
4 compartments; placing in position	-	-	-	-	-	-
300 mm x 300 mm x 1800 mm	-	0.25	2.63	90.72	nr	93.34
380 mm x 380 mm x 1800 mm	-	0.25	2.63	102.19	nr	104.82
450 mm x 450 mm x 1800 mm	-	0.30	3.15	125.14	nr	128.29
Wet area lockers; stainless steel; cam locks						
1 compartment; placing in position	-	-	-	-	-	-
305 mm x 305 mm x 1780 mm	-	0.25	2.63	379.60	nr	382.23
2 compartments; placing in position	-	-	-	-	-	-
305 mm x 305 mm x 1780 mm	-	0.25	2.63	461.09	nr	463.72
305 mm x 460 mm x 1780 mm	-	0.25	2.63	527.58	nr	530.21
4 compartments; placing in position	-	-	-	-	-	-
305 mm x 305 mm x 1780 mm	-	0.25	2.63	549.02	nr	551.65
305 mm x 460 mm x 1780 mm	-	0.25	2.63	629.45	nr	632.07
Extra for	-	-	-	-	-	-
coin operated lock; coin returned	-	-	-	54.90	nr	54.90
coin operated lock; coin retained	-	-	-	85.25	nr	85.25
Timber clothes lockers; veneered MDF finish, routed door, cam locks						
1 compartment; placing in position	-	-	-	-	-	-
380 mm x 380 mm x 1830 mm	-	0.30	3.15	205.35	nr	208.50
4 compartments; placing in position	-	-	-	-	-	-
380 mm x 380 mm x 1830 mm	-	0.30	3.15	381.74	nr	384.90
Shelving support systems; Welconstruct Distribution or other equal and approved						
Shelving support systems; steel body; stove enamelled finish; assembling						
open initial bay; 5 shelves; placing in position	-	-	-	-	-	-
915 mm x 305 mm x 1905 mm	-	0.75	10.03	130.29	nr	140.32
915 mm x 460 mm x 1905 mm	-	0.75	10.03	179.08	nr	189.11
open extension bay; 5 shelves; placing in position	-	-	-	-	-	-
915 mm x 305 mm x 1905 mm	-	0.90	12.04	95.76	nr	107.80
915 mm x 460 mm x 1905 mm	-	0.90	12.04	119.88	nr	131.92
closed initial bay; 5 shelves; placing in position	-	-	-	-	-	-
915 mm x 305 mm x 1905 mm	-	0.75	10.03	164.60	nr	174.63
915 mm x 460 mm x 1905 mm	-	0.75	10.03	213.39	nr	223.42
closed extension bay; 5 shelves; placing in position	-	-	-	-	-	-
915 mm x 305 mm x 1905 mm	-	0.90	12.04	136.29	nr	148.33
915 mm x 460 mm x 1905 mm	-	0.90	12.04	168.89	nr	180.93
extra for pair of doors; fixing in position	-	-	-	-	-	-
1000 mm x 1850 mm	-	0.81	10.83	156.39	nr	167.22

N FURNITURE/EQUIPMENT

Item	PC £	Labour hours	Labour £	Material £	Unit	Total rate £
N10/11 GENERAL FIXTURES/ KITCHEN FITTINGS – cont'd						
6 mm thick rectangular glass mirrors; silver backed; fixed with chromium plated domed headed screws; to background requiring plugging						
Mirror with polished edges						
365 mm x 254 mm	6.04	0.81	11.37	7.09	nr	**18.47**
400 mm x 300 mm	-	0.81	11.37	9.17	nr	**20.55**
560 mm x 380 mm	13.65	0.92	12.92	15.68	nr	**28.60**
640 mm x 460 mm	17.85	1.02	14.32	20.43	nr	**34.75**
Mirror with bevelled edges						
365 mm x 254 mm	10.76	0.81	11.37	12.42	nr	**23.80**
400 mm x 300 mm	12.60	0.81	11.37	14.50	nr	**25.87**
560 mm x 380 mm	21.00	0.92	12.92	23.98	nr	**36.90**
640 mm x 460 mm	26.25	1.02	14.32	29.91	nr	**44.23**
Door mats						
Entrance mats; "Tuftiguard type C" or other equal and approved; laying in position; 12 mm thick						
900 mm x 550 mm	95.63	0.51	5.36	107.94	nr	**113.30**
1200 mm x 750 mm	172.13	0.51	5.36	194.29	nr	**199.65**
2400 mm x 1200 mm	550.80	1.02	10.72	621.72	nr	**632.43**
Matwells						
Polished aluminium matwell; comprising 34 mm x 26 mm x 6 mm angle rim; with brazed angles and lugs brazed on; to suit mat size						
914 mm x 560 mm	11.02	1.02	10.72	12.44	nr	**23.16**
1067 mm x 610 mm	12.10	1.02	10.72	13.66	nr	**24.38**
1219 mm x 762 mm	14.30	1.02	10.72	16.14	nr	**26.86**
Internal blinds; Luxaflex Ltd or other equal and approved						
Roller blinds; Luxaflex "Safeweave RB"; fire resisting material; 1200 mm drop; fixing with screws						
1000 mm wide	48.77	1.02	10.72	55.05	nr	**65.77**
2000 mm wide	68.07	1.60	16.81	76.84	nr	**93.65**
3000 mm wide	84.33	2.16	22.70	95.19	nr	**117.88**
Roller blinds; Luxaflex "Plain RB"; plain type material; 1200 mm drop; fixing with screws						
1000 mm wide	48.77	1.02	10.72	55.05	nr	**65.77**
2000 mm wide	68.07	1.60	16.81	76.84	nr	**93.65**
3000 mm wide	84.33	2.16	22.70	95.19	nr	**117.88**
Roller blinds; Luxaflex "Dimout plain RB"; blackout material; 1200 mm drop; fixing with screws						
1000 mm wide	56.90	1.02	10.72	64.22	nr	**74.94**
2000 mm wide	86.36	1.60	16.81	97.48	nr	**114.29**
3000 mm wide	112.78	2.16	22.70	127.30	nr	**149.99**
Roller blinds; Luxaflex "Lite-master Crank Op"; 100% blackout; 1200 mm drop; fixing with screws						
1000 mm wide	233.68	2.15	22.59	263.77	nr	**286.36**
2000 mm wide	289.56	3.02	31.74	326.84	nr	**358.58**
3000 mm wide	386.08	3.89	40.88	435.79	nr	**476.67**

N FURNITURE/EQUIPMENT

Item	PC £	Labour hours	Labour £	Material £	Unit	Total rate £
Vertical louvre blinds; 89 mm wide louvres; Luxaflex "Finessa 3430" Group 0 ; 1200 mm drop; fixing with screws						
1000 mm wide	68.07	0.91	9.56	76.84	nr	86.40
2000 mm wide	88.39	1.42	14.92	99.77	nr	114.69
3000 mm wide	119.89	1.94	20.39	135.32	nr	155.71
Vertical louvre blinds; 127 mm wide louvres; "Finessa 3420" Group 0; 1200 mm drop; fixing with screws						
1000 mm wide	54.86	0.97	10.19	61.93	nr	72.12
2000 mm wide	78.23	1.50	15.76	88.30	nr	104.07
3000 mm wide	103.63	2.00	21.02	116.97	nr	137.99

N13 SANITARY APPLIANCES/FITTINGS

NOTE: Sanitary fittings are largely a matter of selection material prices vary considerably; the PC values given below are for "average quality".

Item	PC £	Labour hours	Labour £	Material £	Unit	Total rate £
Sanitary fittings						
Sink; white glazed fireclay; BS 1206; cast iron cantilever brackets						
455 mm x 380 mm x 205 mm	111.40	3.60	69.00	231.34	nr	300.34
610 mm x 455 mm x 255 mm	150.78	3.60	69.00	275.79	nr	344.79
760 mm x 455 mm x 255 mm	238.61	3.60	69.00	374.93	nr	443.92
Sink; stainless steel combined bowl and draining board; chain and self colour plug; to BS 3380						
1050 mm x 500 mm with bowl 420 mm x 350 mm x 175 mm	128.74	2.10	40.25	145.31	nr	185.56
Sink; stainless steel combined bowl and double draining board; chain and self colour plug to BS 3380						
1550 mm x 500 mm with bowl 420 mm x 350 mm x 200 mm	154.48	2.10	40.25	174.37	nr	214.62
Lavatory basin; vitreous china; BS 1188; 32 mm diameter chromium plated waste; chain, stay and plug; pair 13 mm diameter chromium plated easy clean pillar taps to BS 1010; painted cantilever brackets; plugged and screwed						
500 mm x 400 mm	130.36	2.75	52.71	188.49	nr	241.20
500 mm x 400 mm; coloured	155.25	2.75	52.71	216.58	nr	269.29
600 mm x 450 mm	172.44	2.75	52.71	235.99	nr	288.69
600 mm x 450 mm; coloured	160.50	2.75	52.71	222.51	nr	275.22
Lavatory basin and pedestal; vitreous china; BS 1188; 32 mm diameter chromium plated waste; chain, stay and plug; pair 13 mm diameter chromium plated easy clean pillar taps to BS 1010; pedestal; wall brackets; plugged and screwed						
560 mm x 455 mm	141.25	3.00	57.50	177.94	nr	235.43
560 mm x 455 mm; coloured	152.50	3.00	57.50	190.63	nr	248.13
610 mm x 470 mm	149.24	3.00	57.50	186.95	nr	244.45
610 mm x 470 mm; coloured	210.50	3.00	57.50	256.10	nr	313.60
Lavatory basin range; overlap joints; white glazed fireclay; 32 mm diameter chromium plated waste, chain, stay and plug; pair 13 mm diameter chromium plated easy clean pillar taps to BS 1010; painted cast iron cantilever brackets						
range of four; 500 mm x 400 mm	565.00	10.55	202.20	803.13	nr	1005.33
add for each additional basin in range	141.25	2.40	46.00	200.78	nr	246.78

N FURNITURE/EQUIPMENT

Item	PC £	Labour hours	Labour £	Material £	Unit	Total rate £
N13 SANITARY APPLIANCES/FITTINGS – cont'd						
Drinking fountain; white glazed fireclay; 19 mm diameter chromium plated waste; self-closing non-concussive tap; regulating valve; plugged and screwed with chromium plated screws						
drinking fountain	175.08	3.00	57.50	197.62	nr	**255.12**
Bath; reinforced acrylic rectangular pattern; chromium plated overflow chain and plug; 40 mm diameter chromium plated waste; cast brass "P" trap with plain outlet and overflow connection; pair 20 mm diameter chromium easy clean pillar taps to BS 1010						
1700 mm long; white	210.91	4.20	80.50	238.06	nr	**318.56**
1700 mm long; coloured	221.42	4.20	80.50	249.93	nr	**330.43**
Bath; enamelled steel; medium gauge rectangular pattern; 40 mm diameter chromium plated overflow chain and plug; 40 mm diameter chromium plated waste; cast brass "P" trap with plain outlet and overflow connection; pair 20 mm diameter chromium plated easy clean pillar taps to BS 1010						
1700 mm long; white	308.97	4.20	80.50	348.75	nr	**429.25**
1700 mm long; coloured	329.57	4.20	80.50	372.00	nr	**452.50**
Shower tray; glazed fireclay with outlet and grated waste; chain and plug; bedding and pointing in waterproof cement mortar						
760 mm x 760 mm x 180 mm; white	139.04	3.60	69.00	156.94	nr	**225.94**
760 mm x 760 mm x 180 mm; coloured	195.68	3.60	69.00	220.87	nr	**289.87**
Shower fitting; riser pipe with mixing valve and shower rose; chromium plated; plugging and screwing mixing valve and pipe bracket						
15 mm diameter riser pipe; 127 mm diameter shower rose	247.17	6.00	115.00	279.00	nr	**393.99**
WC suite; high level; vitreous china pan; black plastic seat; 9 litre white vitreous china cistern and brackets; low pressure ball valve; galvanized steel flush pipe and clip; plugged and screwed; mastic joint to drain						
WC suite; white	238.74	3.95	75.71	277.51	nr	**353.22**
WC suite; coloured	276.54	3.95	75.71	320.18	nr	**395.89**
WC suite; low level; vitreous china pan; black plastic seat; 9 litre white vitreous china cistern and brackets; low pressure ball valve and plastic flush pipe; plugged and screwed; mastic joint to drain						
WC suite; white	179.82	3.60	69.00	211.01	nr	**280.01**
WC suite; coloured	200.50	3.60	69.00	234.35	nr	**303.35**
Bidet; vitreous china; chromium plated waste; mixer tap with hand wheels						
600 mm x 400 mm x 400 mm; white	200.83	4.20	80.50	226.69	nr	**307.18**
Slop sink; white glazed fireclay with hardwood pad; aluminium bucket grating; vitreous china cistern and porcelain enamelled brackets; galvanized steel flush pipe and clip; plugged and screwed; mastic joint to drain						
slop sink	617.94	4.20	80.50	697.50	nr	**778.00**

N FURNITURE/EQUIPMENT

Item	PC £	Labour hours	Labour £	Material £	Unit	Total rate £
Bowl type wall urinal; white galzed vitreous china; white vitreous china automatic flushing cistern and brackets; 38 diameter chromium plated waste; chromium plated flush pipes and spreaders; cistern brackets and flush pipe plugged and screwed with chromium plated screws						
single; 400 mm	236.29	4.80	92.00	266.71	nr	**358.71**
range of two	391.44	9.00	172.50	441.84	nr	**614.33**
range of three	524.72	13.20	252.99	592.28	nr	**845.27**
add for each additional urinal	260.17	3.85	73.79	293.67	nr	**367.46**
add for divisions between urinals	64.92	0.90	17.25	73.28	nr	**90.53**
Bath screen; clear glass; chrome frame; plugged and screwed						
690 mm x 1340 mm	293.53	1.80	34.50	331.32	nr	**365.82**
N15 SIGNS/NOTICES						
Plain script; in gloss oil paint; on painted or varnished surfaces						
Capital letters; lower case letters or numerals						
per coat; per 25 mm high	-	0.10	1.40	-	nr	**1.40**
Stops						
per coat	-	0.02	0.28	-	nr	**0.28**

P BUILDING FABRIC SUNDRIES

Item	PC £	Labour hours	Labour £	Material £	Unit	Total rate £
P10 SUNDRY INSULATION/PROOFING WORK/ FIRESTOPS						
"Sisalkraft" building papers/vapour barriers or other equal and approved						
Building paper; 150 mm laps; fixed to softwood						
"Moistop" grade 728 (class A1F)	-	0.09	1.20	1.32	m²	**2.53**
Vapour barrier/reflective insulation 150 mm laps; fixed to softwood						
"Insulex" grade 714; single sided	-	0.09	1.20	1.42	m²	**2.62**
"Insulex" grade 714; double sided	-	0.09	1.20	2.35	m²	**3.56**
Mat or quilt insulation						
Glass fibre quilt; Isowool "Modular roll" or other equal and approved; laid loose between members at 600 mm centres						
60 mm thick	2.20	0.10	1.34	2.48	m²	**3.82**
80 mm thick	2.90	0.11	1.47	3.27	m²	**4.74**
100 mm thick	3.46	0.12	1.61	3.90	m²	**5.50**
150 mm thick	5.28	0.13	1.74	5.95	m²	**7.69**
Mineral fibre quilt; Isowool "APR 1200" or other equal and approved; pinned vertically to softwood						
25 mm thick	1.51	0.09	1.20	1.70	m²	**2.91**
50 mm thick	2.41	0.10	1.34	2.72	m²	**4.06**
Glass fibre building roll; pinned vertically to softwood						
60 mm thick	1.46	0.10	1.34	1.73	m²	**3.07**
80 mm thick	1.92	0.11	1.47	2.27	m²	**3.74**
100 mm thick	2.29	0.12	1.61	2.71	m²	**4.32**
"Crown Dritherm" glass fibre semi-rigid or rigid batt or other equal and approved; as full or partial cavity fill; including retaining discs						
50 mm thick	2.80	0.13	1.74	3.56	m²	**5.29**
75 mm thick	3.72	0.14	1.87	4.64	m²	**6.52**
100 mm thick	4.94	0.15	2.01	6.09	m²	**8.10**
"Crown Frametherm" glass fibre semi-rigid or rigid batt or other equal and approved; pinned vertically in timber frame construction						
80 mm thick	3.47	0.14	1.87	4.12	m²	**5.99**
100 mm thick	4.18	0.15	2.01	4.95	m²	**6.96**
150 mm thick	6.35	0.16	2.14	7.52	m²	**9.66**
Glass fibre flanged building roll; paper faces; pinned vertically or to slope between timber framing						
60 mm thick	3.23	0.19	3.47	3.82	m²	**7.30**
80 mm thick	4.02	0.20	3.65	4.76	m²	**8.42**
100 mm thick	4.70	0.21	3.84	5.57	m²	**9.40**
Glass fibre aluminium foil faced roll; pinned to softwood						
80 mm thick	-	0.19	3.47	4.02	m²	**7.50**
Board or slab insulation						
"Kingspan Thermawall TW50" zero ODP rigid urethene insulation board or other equal and approved; as full or partial cavity fill; including retaining discs and cutting around ties						
50 mm thick	6.10	0.19	3.47	7.47	m²	**10.94**
75 mm thick	9.01	0.20	3.65	10.91	m²	**14.57**
100 mm thick	11.71	0.21	3.84	14.11	m²	**17.95**

P BUILDING FABRIC SUNDRIES

Item	PC £	Labour hours	Labour £	Material £	Unit	Total rate £
Expanded polystyrene board standard grade SD/N or other equal and approved; fixed with adhesive						
20 mm thick	-	0.15	2.74	3.97	m²	6.71
25 mm thick	-	0.15	2.74	4.70	m²	7.45
30 mm thick	-	0.16	2.92	5.44	m²	8.37
40 mm thick	-	0.45	8.22	6.26	m²	14.48
50 mm thick	-	0.18	3.29	8.40	m²	11.69
60 mm thick	-	0.19	3.47	9.87	m²	13.35
75 mm thick	-	0.20	3.65	12.11	m²	15.76
100 mm thick	-	0.21	3.84	15.80	m²	19.63
"Styrofoam Floormate 350" extruded polystyrene foam or other equal and approved						
50 mm thick	-	0.51	9.32	25.42	m²	34.74
75 mm thick	-	0.51	9.32	38.12	m²	47.44
100 mm thick	-	0.51	9.32	50.82	m²	60.14
Fire stops						
Cape "Firecheck" channel or other equal and approved; intumescent coatings on cut mitres; fixing with brass cups and screws						
19 mm x 44 mm or 19 mm x 50 mm	11.28	0.61	11.15	13.88	m	25.03
"Sealmaster" intumescent fire and smoke seals or other equal and approved; pinned into groove in timber						
type N30; for single leaf half hour door	6.44	0.31	5.67	7.63	m	13.29
type N60; for single leaf one hour door	9.80	0.33	6.03	11.61	m	17.64
type IMN or IMP; for meeting or pivot stiles of pair of one hour doors; per stile	9.80	0.33	6.03	11.61	m	17.64
intumescent plugs in timber; including boring	-	0.10	1.83	0.02	nr	1.85
Rockwool fire stops or other equal and approved; between top of brick/block wall and concrete soffit						
25 mm deep x 100 mm wide	-	0.08	1.46	2.66	m	4.12
25 mm deep x 150 mm wide	-	0.10	1.83	3.55	m	5.37
25 mm deep x 200 mm wide	-	0.12	2.19	4.43	m	6.62
50 mm deep x 100 mm wide	-	0.09	1.64	2.66	m	4.30
50 mm deep x 150 mm wide	-	0.10	1.83	6.67	m	8.50
50 mm deep x 200 mm wide	-	0.12	2.19	8.34	m	10.53
90 mm deep x 100 mm wide	-	0.11	2.01	8.75	m	10.76
90 mm deep x 150 mm wide	-	0.13	2.38	11.66	m	14.04
90 mm deep x 200 mm wide	-	0.15	2.74	14.58	m	17.32
Fire protection compound						
Quelfire "QF4", fire protection compound or other equal and approved; filling around pipes, ducts and the like; including all necessary formwork						
300 mm x 300 mm x 250 mm; pipes - 2	-	1.25	18.98	40.67	nr	59.65
Fire barriers						
Corofil C144 fire barrier to edge of slab; fixed with non-flammable contact adhesive						
to suit void 30 mm wide x 100 mm deep; one hour	-	-	-	-	m	13.81
Rockwool fire barrier or other and approved between top of suspended ceiling and concrete soffit						
one 50 mm layer x 900 mm wide; half hour	-	0.61	11.15	7.09	m²	18.24
two 50 mm layers x 900 mm wide; one hour	-	0.92	16.81	13.89	m²	30.70

P BUILDING FABRIC SUNDRIES

Item	PC £	Labour hours	Labour £	Material £	Unit	Total rate £
P10 SUNDRY INSULATION/PROOFING WORK/ FIRESTOPS – cont'd						
Fire barriers – cont'd						
Lamatherm fire barrier or other equal and approved; to void below raised access floors						
75 mm thick x 300 mm wide; half hour	-	0.17	3.11	15.71	m	**18.82**
75 mm thick x 600 mm wide; half hour	-	0.17	3.11	35.60	m	**38.71**
90 mm thick x 300 mm wide; half hour	-	0.17	3.11	18.84	m	**21.94**
90 mm thick x 600 mm wide; half hour	-	0.17	3.11	44.02	m	**47.13**
Dow Chemicals "Styrofoam 1B" or other equal and approved; cold bridging insulation fixed with adhesive to brick, block or concrete base						
Insulation to walls						
25 mm thick	-	0.34	6.21	7.11	m²	**13.33**
50 mm thick	-	0.37	6.76	13.07	m²	**19.84**
75 mm thick	-.	0.39	7.13	19.49	m²	**26.61**
Insulation to isolated columns						
25 mm thick	-	0.42	7.68	7.11	m²	**14.79**
50 mm thick	-	0.44	8.04	13.07	m²	**21.11**
75 mm thick	-	0.48	8.77	19.49	m²	**28.26**
Insulation to ceilings						
25 mm thick	-	0.37	6.76	7.11	m²	**13.87**
50 mm thick	-	0.40	7.31	13.07	m²	**20.38**
75 mm thick	-	0.43	7.86	19.49	m²	**27.35**
Insulation to isolated beams						
25 mm thick	-	0.44	8.04	7.11	m²	**15.15**
50 mm thick	-	0.48	8.77	13.07	m²	**21.85**
75 mm thick	-	0.51	9.32	19.49	m²	**28.81**
P11 FOAMED/FIBRE/BEAD CAVITY WALL INSULATION						
Injected insulation						
Cavity wall insulation; injecting 65 mm cavity with						
blown EPS granules	-	-	-	-	m²	**3.27**
blown mineral wool	-	-	-	-	m²	**3.39**
P20 UNFRAMED ISOLATED TRIMS/ SKIRTINGS/SUNDRY ITEMS						
Medium density fibreboard primed profiles; Balcas Kildare Ltd or other equal and approved						
Window boards; rounded and rebated						
25 mm x 220 mm	-	0.31	5.67	4.70	m	**10.36**
25 mm x 245 mm	-	0.31	5.67	5.11	m	**10.77**
Skirtings						
14.50 mm x 45 mm; rounded	-	0.10	1.83	0.91	m	**2.74**
14.50 mm x 70 mm; rounded	-	0.10	1.83	1.24	m	**3.07**
14.50 mm x 95 mm; rounded	-	0.10	1.83	1.46	m	**3.29**
14.50 mm x 95 mm; moulded	-	0.10	1.83	1.46	m	**3.29**
14.50 mm x 120 mm; moulded	-	0.10	1.83	1.69	m	**3.52**
18 mm x 70 mm; moulded	-	0.10	1.83	1.36	m	**3.19**
18 mm x 145 mm; moulded	-	0.10	1.83	2.19	m	**4.02**
Dado rail						
18 mm x 58 mm; moulded	-	0.10	1.83	1.37	m	**3.20**

P BUILDING FABRIC SUNDRIES

Item	PC £	Labour hours	Labour £	Material £	Unit	Total rate £
Medium density fibreboard (Sapele veneered one side); 18 mm thick						
Window boards and the like; rebated; hardwood lipped on one edge						
18 mm x 200 mm	-	0.28	5.12	17.16	m	22.28
18 mm x 250 mm	-	0.31	5.67	18.06	m	23.73
18 mm x 300 mm	-	0.33	6.03	18.51	m	24.54
18 mm x 350 mm	-	0.37	6.76	19.86	m	26.62
returned and fitted ends	-	0.22	4.02	3.18	nr	7.20
Medium density fibreboard (American White Ash veneered one side); 18 mm thick						
Window boards and the like; rebated; hardwood lipped on one edge						
18 mm x 200 mm	-	0.28	5.12	17.84	m	22.95
18 mm x 250 mm	-	0.31	5.67	18.96	m	24.63
18 mm x 300 mm	-	0.33	6.03	19.52	m	25.55
18 mm x 350 mm	-	0.37	6.76	21.20	m	27.96
returned and fitted ends	-	0.22	4.02	3.18	nr	7.20
Wrought softwood						
Skirtings, picture rails, dado rails and the like; splayed or moulded						
19 mm x 44 mm; splayed	-	0.10	1.83	3.31	m	5.14
19 mm x 44 mm; moulded	-	0.10	1.83	3.31	m	5.14
19 mm x 69 mm; splayed	-	0.10	1.83	3.59	m	5.42
19 mm x 69 mm; moulded	-	0.10	1.83	3.59	m	5.42
19 mm x 94 mm; splayed	-	0.10	1.83	4.03	m	5.86
19 mm x 94 mm; moulded	-	0.10	1.83	4.03	m	5.86
19 mm x 144 mm; moulded	-	0.12	2.19	4.74	m	6.94
19 mm x 169 mm; moulded	-	0.12	2.19	5.02	m	7.21
25 mm x 50 mm; moulded	-	0.10	1.83	3.61	m	5.43
25 mm x 69 mm; splayed	-	0.10	1.83	3.84	m	5.67
25 mm x 94 mm; splayed	-	0.10	1.83	4.30	m	6.13
25 mm x 144 mm; splayed	-	0.12	2.19	5.23	m	7.42
25 mm x 144 mm; moulded	-	0.12	2.19	5.23	m	7.42
25 mm x 169 mm; moulded	-	0.12	2.19	5.81	m	8.00
25 mm x 219 mm; moulded	-	0.14	2.56	7.56	m	10.12
returned ends	-	0.16	2.92	-	nr	2.92
mitres	-	0.10	1.83	-	nr	1.83
Architraves, cover fillets and the like; half round; splayed or moulded						
13 mm x 25 mm; half round	-	0.12	2.19	3.00	m	5.19
13 mm x 50 mm; moulded	-	0.12	2.19	3.46	m	5.66
16 mm x 32 mm; half round	-	0.12	2.19	3.18	m	5.37
16 mm x 38 mm; moulded	-	0.12	2.19	3.31	m	5.50
16 mm x 50 mm; moulded	-	0.12	2.19	3.46	m	5.66
19 mm x 50 mm; splayed	-	0.12	2.19	3.46	m	5.66
19 mm x 63 mm; splayed	-	0.11	2.01	3.59	m	5.60
19 mm x 69 mm; splayed	-	0.12	2.19	3.82	m	6.01
25 mm x 44 mm; splayed	-	0.12	2.19	3.43	m	5.62
25 mm x 50 mm; moulded	-	0.12	2.19	3.61	m	5.80
25 mm x 63 mm; splayed	-	0.12	2.19	3.76	m	5.95
25 mm x 69 mm; splayed	-	0.12	2.19	4.28	m	6.47
32 mm x 88 mm; moulded	-	0.12	2.19	4.30	m	6.50
38 mm x 38 mm; moulded	-	0.12	2.19	3.81	m	6.00
50 mm x 50 mm; moulded	-	0.12	2.19	4.43	m	6.63
returned ends	-	0.16	2.92	-	nr	2.92
mitres	-	0.10	1.83	-	nr	1.83

P BUILDING FABRIC SUNDRIES

Item	PC £	Labour hours	Labour £	Material £	Unit	Total rate £
P20 UNFRAMED ISOLATED TRIMS/ SKIRTINGS/SUNDRY ITEMS – cont'd						
Wrought softwood – cont'd						
Stops; screwed on						
16 mm x 38 mm	-	0.10	1.83	1.57	m	3.39
16 mm x 50 mm	-	0.10	1.83	1.70	m	3.52
19 mm x 38 mm	-	0.10	1.83	1.57	m	3.39
25 mm x 38 mm	-	0.10	1.83	1.71	m	3.54
25 mm x 50 mm	-	0.10	1.83	1.76	m	3.58
Glazing beads and the like						
13 mm x 16 mm	-	0.05	0.91	1.90	m	2.81
13 mm x 19 mm	-	0.05	0.91	1.90	m	2.81
13 mm x 25 mm	-	0.05	0.91	1.94	m	2.86
13 mm x 25 mm; screwed	-	0.05	0.91	2.04	m	2.95
13 mm x 25 mm; fixing with brass cups and						
screws	-	0.05	0.91	1.94	m	2.86
16 mm x 25 mm; screwed	-	0.05	0.91	3.26	m	4.18
16 mm quadrant	-	0.05	0.91	2.89	m	3.81
19 mm quadrant or scotia	-	0.05	0.91	2.89	m	3.81
19 mm x 36 mm; screwed	-	0.05	0.91	3.30	m	4.21
25 mm x 38 mm; screwed	-	0.05	0.91	3.44	m	4.35
25 mm quadrant or scotia	-	0.05	0.91	3.06	m	3.97
38 mm scotia	-	0.05	0.91	3.69	m	4.60
50 mm scotia	-	0.05	0.91	4.31	m	5.23
Isolated shelves, worktops, seats and the like						
19 mm x 150 mm	-	0.17	3.11	4.02	m	7.12
19 mm x 200 mm	-	0.22	4.02	5.55	m	9.57
25 mm x 150 mm	-	0.17	3.11	4.59	m	7.69
25 mm x 200 mm	-	0.22	4.02	6.51	m	10.53
32 mm x 150 mm	-	0.17	3.11	5.36	m	8.46
32 mm x 200 mm	-	0.22	4.02	7.32	m	11.34
Isolated shelves, worktops, seats and the like; cross-tongued joints						
19 mm x 300 mm	-	0.29	5.30	16.52	m	21.82
19 mm x 450 mm	-	0.34	6.21	24.91	m	31.13
19 mm x 600 mm	-	0.41	7.49	32.23	m	39.72
25 mm x 300 mm	-	0.29	5.30	17.73	m	23.03
25 mm x 450 mm	-	0.34	6.21	26.87	m	33.08
25 mm x 600 mm	-	0.41	7.49	34.93	m	42.42
32 mm x 300 mm	-	0.29	5.30	18.77	m	24.07
32 mm x 450 mm	-	0.34	6.21	28.55	m	34.76
32 mm x 600 mm	-	0.41	7.49	37.25	m	44.74
Isolated shelves, worktops, seats and the like; slatted with 50 mm wide slats at 75 mm centres						
19 mm thick	-	0.66	12.06	39.35	m	51.41
25 mm thick	-	0.66	12.06	40.23	m	52.29
32 mm thick	-	0.66	12.06	40.99	m	53.05
Window boards, nosings, bed moulds and the like; rebated and rounded						
19 mm x 75 mm	-	0.19	3.47	4.89	m	8.37
19 mm x 150 mm	-	0.20	3.65	6.07	m	9.72
19 mm x 219 mm; in one width	-	0.27	4.93	7.55	m	12.48
19 mm x 300 mm; cross-tongued joints	-	0.31	5.67	17.52	m	23.18
25 mm x 75 mm	-	0.19	3.47	5.19	m	8.66
25 mm x 150 mm	-	0.20	3.65	6.70	m	10.35
25 mm x 219 mm; in one width	-	0.27	4.93	8.47	m	13.41
25 mm x 300 mm; cross-tongued joints	-	0.31	5.67	18.94	m	24.60

P BUILDING FABRIC SUNDRIES

Item	PC £	Labour hours	Labour £	Material £	Unit	Total rate £
32 mm x 75 mm	-	0.19	3.47	5.45	m	8.92
32 mm x 150 mm	-	0.20	3.65	7.23	m	10.88
32 mm x 219 mm; in one width	-	0.27	4.93	9.27	m	14.20
32 mm x 300 mm; cross-tongued joints	-	0.31	5.67	20.16	m	25.82
38 mm x 75 mm	-	0.19	3.47	5.97	m	9.45
38 mm x 150 mm	-	0.20	3.65	8.31	m	11.96
38 mm x 219 mm; in one width	-	0.27	4.93	10.84	m	15.78
38 mm x 300 mm; cross-tongued joints	-	0.31	5.67	22.59	m	28.25
returned and fitted ends	-	0.16	2.92	-	nr	2.92
Handrails; mopstick						
50 mm diameter	-	0.26	4.75	11.26	m	16.01
Handrails; rounded						
44 mm x 50 mm	-	0.26	4.75	10.90	m	15.66
50 mm x 75 mm	-	0.28	5.12	11.92	m	17.04
57 mm x 87 mm	-	0.31	5.67	13.21	m	18.88
69 mm x 100 mm	-	0.36	6.58	16.20	m	22.78
Handrails; moulded						
44 mm x 50 mm	-	0.23	4.20	10.90	m	15.11
50 mm x 75 mm	-	0.25	4.57	11.92	m	16.49
57 mm x 87 mm	-	0.28	5.12	13.21	m	18.33
69 mm x 100 mm	-	0.32	5.85	16.20	m	22.05
Add 5% to the above material prices for selected softwood for staining						5%
Medium Density Fibreboard						
Skirtings, picture rails, dado rails and the like; splayed or moulded						
18 mm x 50 mm; splayed	9.00	0.14	2.56	10.79	m	13.35
18 mm x 50 mm; moulded	2.66	0.14	2.56	3.27	m	5.83
18 mm x 75 mm; splayed	2.77	0.14	2.56	3.40	m	5.96
18 mm x 75 mm; moulded	2.77	0.14	2.56	3.40	m	5.96
18 mm x 100 mm; splayed	2.89	0.14	2.56	3.55	m	6.10
18 mm x 100 mm; moulded	2.89	0.14	2.56	3.55	m	6.10
18 mm x 150 mm; moulded	3.16	0.17	3.11	3.87	m	6.97
18 mm x 175 mm; moulded	3.28	0.17	3.11	4.01	m	7.12
22 mm x 100 mm; splayed	3.05	0.14	2.56	3.74	m	6.29
25 mm x 50 mm; moulded	2.79	0.14	2.56	3.43	m	5.99
25 mm x 75 mm; splayed	2.96	0.14	2.56	3.63	m	6.19
25 mm x 100 mm; splayed	3.15	0.14	2.56	3.85	m	6.41
25 mm x 150 mm; splayed	3.56	0.17	3.11	4.34	m	7.45
25 mm x 150 mm; moulded	3.56	0.17	3.11	4.34	m	7.45
25 mm x 175 mm; moulded	3.75	0.17	3.11	4.57	m	7.67
25 mm x 225 mm; moulded	4.02	0.19	3.47	4.89	m	8.36
returned ends	-	0.22	4.02	-	nr	4.02
mitres	-	0.16	2.92	-	nr	2.92
Architraves, cover fillets and the like; half round; splayed or moulded						
12 mm x 25 mm; half round	2.53	0.17	3.11	3.12	m	6.23
12 mm x 50 mm; moulded	2.61	0.17	3.11	3.21	m	6.32
15 mm x 32 mm; half round	2.55	0.17	3.11	3.14	m	6.25
15 mm x 38 mm; moulded	2.57	0.17	3.11	3.17	m	6.27
15 mm x 50 mm; moulded	2.61	0.17	3.11	3.21	m	6.32
15 mm x 50 mm; splayed	2.61	0.17	3.11	3.21	m	6.32
15 mm x 63 mm; splayed	2.73	0.17	3.11	3.36	m	6.46
15 mm x 75 mm; splayed	2.79	0.17	3.11	3.43	m	6.53
25 mm x 44 mm; splayed	2.79	0.17	3.11	3.43	m	6.53
25 mm x 50 mm; moulded	2.79	0.17	3.11	3.43	m	6.53
25 mm x 63 mm; splayed	2.89	0.17	3.11	3.55	m	6.65
25 mm x 75 mm; splayed	2.99	0.17	3.11	3.66	m	6.77

P BUILDING FABRIC SUNDRIES

Item	PC £	Labour hours	Labour £	Material £	Unit	Total rate £
P20 UNFRAMED ISOLATED TRIMS/ SKIRTINGS/SUNDRY ITEMS – cont'd						
Medium Density Fibreboard – cont'd						
Architraves – cont'd						
30 mm x 88 mm; moulded	3.91	0.17	3.11	4.75	m	**7.86**
38 mm x 88 mm; moulded	3.33	0.17	3.11	4.07	m	**7.17**
50 mm x 50 mm; moulded	3.50	0.17	3.11	4.27	m	**7.38**
returned ends	-	0.22	4.02	-	nr	**4.02**
mitres	-	0.16	2.92	-	nr	**2.92**
Stops; screwed on						
15 mm x 38 mm	1.44	0.16	2.92	1.71	m	**4.63**
15 mm x 50 mm	1.49	0.16	2.92	1.77	m	**4.69**
18 mm x 38 mm	1.48	0.16	2.92	1.75	m	**4.68**
25 mm x 38 mm	1.56	0.16	2.92	1.85	m	**4.77**
25 mm x 50 mm	1.64	0.16	2.92	1.94	m	**4.87**
Glazing beads and the like						
12 mm x 16 mm	1.73	0.05	0.91	2.05	m	**2.96**
12 mm x 19 mm	1.74	0.05	0.91	2.06	m	**2.98**
12 mm x 25 mm	5.35	0.05	0.91	6.34	m	**7.25**
12 mm x 25 mm; screwed	5.35	0.08	1.46	6.55	m	**8.02**
12 mm x 25 mm; fixing with brass cups and screws	5.35	0.16	2.92	6.34	m	**9.26**
15 mm x 25 mm; screwed	2.53	0.08	1.46	3.21	m	**4.67**
15 mm quadrant	2.49	0.07	1.28	2.95	m	**4.23**
18 mm quadrant or scotia	2.50	0.07	1.28	2.96	m	**4.24**
18 mm x 36 mm; screwed	2.58	0.07	1.28	3.27	m	**4.55**
25 mm x 38 mm; screwed	2.70	0.07	1.28	3.41	m	**4.69**
25 mm quadrant or scotia	2.61	0.07	1.28	3.09	m	**4.37**
38 mm scotia	2.48	0.07	1.28	2.94	m	**4.22**
50 mm scotia	2.88	0.07	1.28	3.41	m	**4.69**
Isolated shelves, worktops, seats and the like						
18 mm x 150 mm	3.27	0.22	4.02	3.88	m	**7.90**
18 mm x 200 mm	3.44	0.31	5.67	4.08	m	**9.74**
25 mm x 150 mm	3.75	0.22	4.02	4.44	m	**8.46**
25 mm x 200 mm	4.01	0.31	5.67	4.75	m	**10.42**
30 mm x 150 mm	5.26	0.22	4.02	6.23	m	**10.25**
30 mm x 200 mm	5.83	0.31	5.67	6.91	m	**12.57**
Isolated shelves, worktops, seats and the like; cross-tongued joints						
18 mm x 300 mm	10.65	0.39	7.13	12.62	m	**19.75**
18 mm x 450 mm	12.18	0.45	8.22	14.44	m	**22.66**
18 mm x 600 mm	20.30	0.56	10.23	24.06	m	**34.29**
25 mm x 300 mm	11.22	0.39	7.13	13.30	m	**20.42**
25 mm x 450 mm	13.73	0.45	8.22	16.27	m	**24.50**
25 mm x 600 mm	19.82	0.56	10.23	23.49	m	**33.72**
30 mm x 300 mm	12.95	0.39	7.13	15.35	m	**22.48**
30 mm x 450 mm	15.42	0.45	8.22	18.28	m	**26.50**
30 mm x 600 mm	22.44	0.56	10.23	26.60	m	**36.83**
Isolated shelves, worktops, seats and the like; slatted with 50 mm wide slats at 75 mm centres						
18 mm thick	32.20	0.66	12.06	38.62	m²	**50.68**
25 mm thick	34.19	0.66	12.06	40.97	m²	**53.04**
30 mm thick	36.01	0.66	12.06	43.13	m²	**55.19**
Window boards, nosings, bed moulds and the like; rebated and rounded						
18 mm x 75 mm	2.83	0.24	4.39	3.63	m	**8.01**
18 mm x 150 mm	3.23	0.28	5.12	4.10	m	**9.22**
18 mm x 225 mm	3.56	0.37	6.76	4.49	m	**11.25**
18 mm x 300 mm	10.30	0.41	7.49	12.47	m	**19.97**

P BUILDING FABRIC SUNDRIES

Item	PC £	Labour hours	Labour £	Material £	Unit	Total rate £
25 mm x 75 mm	2.99	0.24	4.39	3.82	m	8.20
25 mm x 150 mm	3.56	0.28	5.12	4.49	m	9.61
25 mm x 225 mm	4.01	0.37	6.76	5.02	m	11.79
25 mm x 300 mm	4.54	0.41	7.49	5.65	m	13.15
30 mm x 75 mm	4.18	0.24	4.39	5.23	m	9.61
30 mm x 150 mm	5.20	0.28	5.12	6.44	m	11.55
30 mm x 225 mm	-	0.37	6.76	7.40	m	14.16
30 mm x 300 mm	6.96	0.41	7.49	8.52	m	16.01
38 mm x 75 mm	4.76	0.24	4.39	5.91	m	10.30
38 mm x 150 mm	5.98	0.28	5.12	7.36	m	12.48
38 mm x 225 mm	6.95	0.37	6.76	8.51	m	15.27
38 mm x 300 mm	8.09	0.41	7.49	9.86	m	17.35
returned and fitted ends	-	0.23	4.20	-	nr	4.20
Selected Sapele						
Skirtings, picture rails, dado rails and the like; splayed or moulded						
19 mm x 44 mm; splayed	4.19	0.14	2.56	5.09	m	7.65
19 mm x 44 mm; moulded	4.19	0.14	2.56	5.09	m	7.65
19 mm x 69 mm; splayed	4.87	0.14	2.56	5.89	m	8.45
19 mm x 69 mm; moulded	4.87	0.14	2.56	5.89	m	8.45
19 mm x 94 mm; splayed	5.69	0.14	2.56	6.86	m	9.42
19 mm x 94 mm; moulded	5.69	0.14	2.56	6.86	m	9.42
19 mm x 144 mm; moulded	7.56	0.17	3.11	9.08	m	12.19
19 mm x 169 mm; moulded	8.37	0.17	3.11	10.04	m	13.15
25 mm x 44 mm; moulded	4.71	0.14	2.56	5.70	m	8.26
25 mm x 75 mm; splayed	5.61	0.14	2.56	6.77	m	9.33
25 mm x 94 mm; splayed	6.87	0.14	2.56	8.26	m	10.82
25 mm x 144 mm; splayed	9.03	0.17	3.11	10.82	m	13.93
25 mm x 144 mm; moulded	9.03	0.17	3.11	10.82	m	13.93
25 mm x 169 mm; moulded	10.11	0.17	3.11	12.10	m	15.21
25 mm x 219 mm; moulded	11.55	0.19	3.47	13.81	m	17.28
returned end	-	0.22	4.02	-	nr	4.02
mitres	-	0.16	2.92	-	nr	2.92
Architraves, cover fillets and the like; half round; splayed or moulded						
13 mm x 25 mm; half round	2.54	0.17	3.11	3.13	m	6.24
13 mm x 50 mm; moulded	4.07	0.17	3.11	4.94	m	8.05
16 mm x 32 mm; half round	3.70	0.17	3.11	4.51	m	7.61
16 mm x 38 mm; moulded	3.92	0.17	3.11	4.77	m	7.87
16 mm x 50 mm; moulded	4.19	0.17	3.11	5.09	m	8.19
19 mm x 50 mm; splayed	4.19	0.17	3.11	5.09	m	8.19
19 mm x 63 mm; splayed	4.55	0.17	3.11	5.51	m	8.62
19 mm x 69 mm; splayed	4.87	0.17	3.11	5.89	m	9.00
25 mm x 44 mm; splayed	4.53	0.17	3.11	5.49	m	8.60
25 mm x 50 mm; moulded	4.71	0.17	3.11	5.70	m	8.81
25 mm x 63 mm; splayed	5.25	0.17	3.11	6.34	m	9.45
25 mm x 69 mm; splayed	5.61	0.17	3.11	6.77	m	9.88
32 mm x 88 mm; moulded	6.83	0.17	3.11	8.22	m	11.32
38 mm x 88 mm; moulded	5.37	0.17	3.11	6.49	m	9.59
50 mm x 50 mm; moulded	7.02	0.17	3.11	8.44	m	11.55
returned end	-	0.22	4.02	-	nr	4.02
mitres	-	0.16	2.92	-	nr	2.92
Stops; screwed on						
16 mm x 38 mm	1.73	0.16	2.92	2.05	m	4.97
16 mm x 50 mm	1.86	0.16	2.92	2.20	m	5.13
19 mm x 38 mm	1.73	0.16	2.92	2.05	m	4.97
25 mm x 38 mm	2.18	0.16	2.92	2.58	m	5.51
25 mm x 50 mm	2.53	0.16	2.92	3.00	m	5.92

P BUILDING FABRIC SUNDRIES

Item	PC £	Labour hours	Labour £	Material £	Unit	Total rate £
P20 UNFRAMED ISOLATED TRIMS/ SKIRTINGS/SUNDRY ITEMS – cont'd						
Selected Sapele – cont'd						
Glazing beads and the like						
13 mm x 16 mm	2.26	0.07	1.28	2.68	m	3.96
13 mm x 19 mm	2.26	0.07	1.28	2.68	m	3.96
13 mm x 25 mm	5.97	0.07	1.28	7.08	m	8.35
13 mm x 25 mm; screwed	2.26	0.07	1.28	2.89	m	4.17
13 mm x 25 mm; with brass cups and screws	5.97	0.07	1.28	7.08	m	8.35
16 mm x 25 mm; screwed	3.29	0.08	1.46	4.11	m	5.57
16 mm quadrant	3.17	0.07	1.28	3.76	m	5.04
19 mm quadrant or scotia	31.70	0.07	1.28	37.57	m	38.85
19 mm x 36 mm; screwed	4.05	0.07	1.28	5.01	m	6.29
25 mm x 38 mm; screwed	4.42	0.07	1.28	5.45	m	6.73
25 mm quadrant or scotia	3.62	0.07	1.28	4.29	m	5.57
38 mm scotia	5.37	0.07	1.28	6.36	m	7.64
50 mm scotia	7.02	0.07	1.28	8.32	m	9.60
Isolated shelves; worktops, seats and the like						
19 mm x 150 mm	7.70	0.22	4.02	9.13	m	13.15
19 mm x 200 mm	9.10	0.31	5.67	10.79	m	16.45
25 mm x 150 mm	9.03	0.22	4.02	10.70	m	14.72
25 mm x 200 mm	10.83	0.31	5.67	12.84	m	18.50
32 mm x 150 mm	10.18	0.22	4.02	12.07	m	16.09
32 mm x 200 mm	12.31	0.31	5.67	14.59	m	20.25
Isolated shelves, worktops, seats and the like; cross-tongued joints						
19 mm x 300 mm	20.82	0.39	7.13	24.68	m	31.80
19 mm x 450 mm	32.60	0.45	8.22	38.64	m	46.86
19 mm x 600 mm	43.31	0.56	10.23	51.33	m	61.56
25 mm x 300 mm	23.38	0.39	7.13	27.71	m	34.84
25 mm x 450 mm	36.73	0.45	8.22	43.53	m	51.76
25 mm x 600 mm	48.82	0.56	10.23	57.86	m	68.09
32 mm x 300 mm	25.57	0.39	7.13	30.31	m	37.43
32 mm x 450 mm	40.27	0.45	8.22	47.73	m	55.95
32 mm x 600 mm	53.54	0.56	10.23	63.45	m	73.69
Isolated shelves, worktops, seats and the like; slatted with 50 mm wide slats at 75 mm centres						
19 mm thick	58.60	0.88	16.08	69.91	m²	85.99
25 mm thick	62.74	0.88	16.08	74.81	m²	90.89
32 mm thick	66.28	0.88	16.08	79.01	m²	95.09
Window boards, nosings, bed moulds and the like; rebated and rounded						
19 mm x 75 mm	5.94	0.24	4.39	7.31	m	11.70
19 mm x 150 mm	8.61	0.28	5.12	10.48	m	15.59
19 mm x 219 mm; in one width	10.58	0.37	6.76	12.81	m	19.57
19 mm x 300 mm; cross-tongued joints	21.53	0.41	7.49	25.79	m	33.28
25 mm x 75 mm	6.53	0.24	4.39	8.01	m	12.40
25 mm x 150 mm	9.59	0.28	5.12	11.64	m	16.75
25 mm x 219 mm; in one width	12.59	0.37	6.76	15.19	m	21.96
25 mm x 300 mm; cross-tongued joints	25.02	0.41	7.49	29.93	m	37.42
32 mm x 75 mm	7.10	0.24	4.39	8.69	m	13.07
32 mm x 150 mm	10.67	0.28	5.12	12.92	m	18.03
32 mm x 219 mm; in one width	14.23	0.37	6.76	17.14	m	23.90
32 mm x 300 mm; cross-tongued joints	27.52	0.41	7.49	32.89	m	40.38
38 mm x 75 mm	6.55	0.24	4.39	8.04	m	12.42
38 mm x 150 mm	10.65	0.28	5.12	12.89	m	18.01
38 mm x 219 mm; in one width	14.76	0.37	6.76	17.77	m	24.53
38 mm x 300 mm; cross-tongued joints	29.20	0.41	7.49	34.88	m	42.37
returned and fitted ends	-	0.23	4.20	-	nr	4.20

P BUILDING FABRIC SUNDRIES

Item	PC £	Labour hours	Labour £	Material £	Unit	Total rate £
Handrails; rounded						
44 mm x 50 mm	9.02	0.33	6.03	10.69	m	16.72
50 mm x 75 mm	15.76	0.37	6.76	18.68	m	25.44
57 mm x 87 mm	18.49	0.41	7.49	21.91	m	29.41
69 mm x 100 mm	22.98	0.45	8.22	27.24	m	35.46
Handrails; moulded						
44 mm x 50 mm	14.54	0.33	6.03	17.23	m	23.26
50 mm x 75 mm	17.23	0.37	6.76	20.42	m	27.18
57 mm x 87 mm	19.97	0.41	7.49	23.67	m	31.16
69 mm x 100 mm	24.45	0.45	8.22	28.98	m	37.20
Pin-boards; medium board						
Sundeala "A" pin-board or other equal and approved; fixed with adhesive to backing (not included); over 300 mm wide						
6.40 mm thick	-	0.61	11.15	21.64	m²	32.79
Sundries on softwood/hardwood						
Extra over fixing with nails for						
gluing and pinning	-	0.02	0.37	0.08	m	0.44
masonry nails	-	-	-	-	m	0.31
steel screws	-	-	-	-	m	0.29
self-tapping screws	-	-	-	-	m	0.30
steel screws; gluing	-	-	-	-	m	0.51
steel screws; sinking; filling heads	-	-	-	-	m	0.65
steel screws; sinking; pellating over	-	-	-	-	m	1.41
brass cups and screws	-	-	-	-	m	1.73
Extra over for						
countersinking	-	-	-	-	m	0.26
pellating	-	-	-	-	m	1.22
Head or nut in softwood						
let in flush	-	-	-	-	nr	0.65
Head or nut; in hardwood						
let in flush	-	-	-	-	nr	0.96
let in over; pellated	-	-	-	-	nr	2.24
Metalwork; mild steel						
Angle section bearers; for building in						
90 mm x 90 mm x 6 mm	-	0.33	6.50	6.46	m	12.96
120 mm x 120 mm x 8 mm	-	0.36	7.09	9.78	m	16.87
200 mm x 150 mm x 12 mm	-	0.41	8.08	26.19	m	34.27
Metalwork; mild steel; galvanized						
Water bars; groove in timber						
6 mm x 30 mm	-	0.51	9.32	8.00	m	17.32
6 mm x 40 mm	-	0.51	9.32	9.36	m	18.68
6 mm x 50 mm	-	0.51	9.32	12.52	m	21.84
Angle section bearers; for building in						
90 mm x 90 mm x 6 mm	-	0.33	6.50	8.59	m	15.10
120 mm x 120 mm x 8 mm	-	0.36	7.09	13.04	m	20.13
200 mm x 150 mm x 12 mm	-	0.41	8.08	34.90	m	42.98
Dowels; mortice in timber						
8 mm diameter x 100 mm long	-	0.05	0.91	0.36	nr	1.27
10 mm diameter x 50 mm long	-	0.05	0.91	0.83	nr	1.74
Cramps						
25 mm x 3 mm x 230 mm girth; one end bent, holed and screwed to softwood; other end fishtailed for building in	-	0.07	1.28	0.83	nr	2.11

P BUILDING FABRIC SUNDRIES

Item	PC £	Labour hours	Labour £	Material £	Unit	Total rate £
P20 UNFRAMED ISOLATED TRIMS/ SKIRTINGS/SUNDRY ITEMS – cont'd						
Metalwork; stainless steel						
Angle section bearers; for building in						
90 mm x 90 mm x 6 mm	-	0.33	6.50	33.93	m	**40.44**
120 mm x 120 mm x 8 mm	-	0.36	7.09	50.16	m	**57.25**
200 mm x 150 mm x 12 mm	-	0.41	8.08	130.37	m	**138.45**
P21 IRONMONGERY						
NOTE: Ironmongery is largely a matter of selection and prices vary considerably, indicative prices for reasonable quantities of "good quality" ironmongery are given below.						
Ironmongery; Allgood or other equal and approved; to softwood						
Bolts						
75 x 35 mm Modric anodised aluminium straight barrel bolt	-	0.33	6.03	7.22	nr	**13.25**
150 x 35 mm Modric anodised aluminium straight barrel bolt	-	0.33	6.03	10.78	nr	**16.81**
75 x 35 mm Modric anodised aluminium necked barrel bolt	-	0.33	6.03	9.59	nr	**15.63**
150 x 35 mm Modric anodised aluminium necked barrel bolt	-	0.33	6.03	12.59	nr	**18.62**
11 mm Easiclean socket	-	0.11	2.01	3.10	nr	**5.11**
Security hinge bolt chubb WS12	-	0.55	10.05	14.22	nr	**24.27**
203 x 19 x 11 mm Complete bolt set, with floor socket and intumescent pack for FD30 and FD60 fire doors	-	0.66	12.06	35.39	nr	**47.45**
203/457 x 19 mm Complete bolt set, with floor socket and intumescent pack for FD30 and FD60 fire doors	-	0.66	12.06	71.39	nr	**83.45**
203/609 x 19 mm Complete bolt set, with floor socket and intumescent pack for FD30 and FD60 fire doors	-	0.66	12.06	83.25	nr	**95.31**
11 mm Dust excluding socket, satin nickel plated	-	0.11	2.01	9.31	nr	**11.32**
Stainless steel indicating bolt complete with outside indicator and emergency release	-	0.66	12.06	67.61	nr	**79.67**
Catches						
Magnetic catch	-	0.22	4.02	1.02	nr	**5.04**
Door closers and furniture						
13 mm Satin chrome rebate component for 7204/08/78/79/86	-	0.66	12.06	20.99	nr	**33.06**
90 x 90 mm Modric anodised aluminium electrically powered hold open wall magnet. CE marked to BS EN1155:1997 & A1:2002 3-5-6/3-1-1-3	-	0.44	8.04	11.51	nr	**19.55**
Modric anodised aluminium bathroom configuration with quadaxial assembly, turn, release and optional indicator	-	0.88	16.08	76.75	nr	**92.84**
Concealed overhead door restraining stay with stainless steel arm and aluminium channel & bracket and adjustable friction slide block, spring buffer to curtail door opening; not for use with concealed door closing devices	-	1.10	20.10	26.53	nr	**46.63**

P BUILDING FABRIC SUNDRIES

Item	PC £	Labour hours	Labour £	Material £	Unit	Total rate £
213 x 48 x 48 mm Overhead door closers complete with fixings for fig 1 and fig 6 applications. Certifire listed. CE Marked to BS EN1154 4-8-3-1-1-3	-	1.10	20.10	57.62	nr	**77.72**
Concealed jamb door closer check action	-	1.10	20.10	90.36	nr	**110.46**
75 x 57 x 170 mm Modric anodised aluminium door co-ordinator for pairs of rebated leaves, CE Marked to BS EN1158 3-5-3/5-1-1-0	-	0.88	16.08	30.87	nr	**46.95**
263 x 50 x 48 mm Modric anodised aluminium overhead door closer Fig 1 available power 1-4 with adjustable backcheck, intumescent protected bracket. Certifire listed and CE Marked to BS EN1154 4-8-4-1-1-3	-	1.10	20.10	65.52	nr	**85.63**
290 x 48 x 50 mm Modric anodised aluminium rectangular overhead door closer with adjustable power and adjustable backcheck intumescent protected arm heavy duty U.L. & certifire listed & CE Marked to BS EN1154 4-8-2/4-1-1-3 and Kitemarked.	-	1.10	20.10	82.91	nr	**103.01**
Stainless steel overhead door closer Fig 1. Projecting armset, Power EN 2-5, CE marked , c/w Backcheck, Latch action and Speed control. Max door width 1100 mm, Max door weight 100kg	-	1.10	20.10	82.17	nr	**102.28**
Stainless steel finished track and arm to suit 9124 fully concealed door closer	-	0.88	16.08	56.27	nr	**72.35**
92 x 45 mm Stainless steel heavy duty floor pivot set with thrust roller bearing 400kg load capacity. Complete with forged steel intumescent protected double action strap with 10 mm height adjustment, new low profile top centre, and matching cover plate	-	2.50	45.69	176.88	nr	**222.56**
92 x 45 mm Stainless steel heavy duty floor pivot set with thrust roller bearing 400kg load capacity, with stainless steel intumescent protected S/A 25 mm offset strap & top centre, matching plate	-	2.50	45.69	220.22	nr	**265.91**
Double action pivot set for door maximum width 1100 mm and maximum weight 80kg	-	2.50	45.69	85.11	nr	**130.79**
305 x 80 x 50 mm Stainless steel 'Cavalier' floor spring, intumescent protected forged steel D/A strap with 10 mm height adjustment & low profile top centre, matching covers & box. CE Marked to BS EN1154 4-8-*-1-1-3. Adjustable power 2/4	-	2.50	45.69	252.95	nr	**298.64**
305 x 80 x 50 mm Stainless steel 'Cavalier' floor spring adjustable power 2/4 stainless steel intumsecent protected S/A 16 mm offset strap & top centre, matching covers & box. Certifire listed and CE marked to BSEN1154 4-8-2/4-1-1-3	-	2.50	45.69	296.30	nr	**341.98**
Surface vertical rod push bar panic bolt, reversible, tp suit doors 2500x1100 mm maximum, silver finish, CE marked to EN1125 class 3-7-5-1-1-3-2-2-A	-	1.65	30.15	123.26	nr	**153.41**
Rim push bar panic latch, reversible, to suit doors 1100 mm wide maximum, silver finish, CE marked to EN1125 class 3-7-5-1-1-3-2-2-A	-	1.43	26.13	85.67	nr	**111.80**
76 x 51 x 13 mm Adjustable heavy roller catch satin chrome	-	0.66	12.06	6.83	nr	**18.89**

P BUILDING FABRIC SUNDRIES

Item	PC £	Labour hours	Labour £	Material £	Unit	Total rate £
P21 IRONMONGERY – cont'd						
Ironmongery; Allgood; to softwood – cont'd						
Door closers and furniture – cont'd						
External access device for use with XX10280/2 panic hardware to suit door thickness 45-55 mm, complete with SS3006N lever, SS755 rose, SS796 profile escutcheon and spindle.For use with MA7420A51 or MA7420A55 profile cylinders	-	1.43	26.13	29.46	nr	55.59
142 x 22 mm Ø Concealed jamb door closer light duty	-	0.88	16.08	11.01	nr	27.09
112 x 42 mm Emergency release door stop for toilet doors	-	1.10	20.10	84.77	nr	104.87
Modric anodised aluminium quadaxial lever assembly tested to BS EN1906 4/7/-/1/1/4/0/U	-	0.88	16.08	30.14	pair	46.22
Modric anodised aluminium quadaxial lever assembly Tested to BS EN1906 4/7/-/1/1/4/0/U	-	0.88	16.08	31.04	pair	47.12
Modric anodised aluminium quadaxial lever assembly Tested to BS EN1906 4/7/-/1/1/4/0/U with Biocote® anti-bacterial protection	-	0.88	16.08	37.25	pair	53.33
Modric stainless steel quadaxial lever assembly Tested to BS EN1906 4/7/-/1/1/4/0/U	-	0.88	16.08	66.14	pair	82.23
152 x 38 x 13 mm Modric anodised aluminium security door chain leather covered	-	0.44	8.04	51.02	nr	59.06
50 Ø x 3 mm Circular covered rose for profile cylinder	-	0.11	2.01	3.61	nr	5.62
50 Ø x 3 mm Modric anodised aluminium circular covered rose with indicator and emergency release	-	0.15	2.74	9.31	nr	12.05
50 Ø x 3 mm Modric anodised aluminium circular covered rose with heavy turn, 5-8 mm spindle	-	0.15	2.74	14.50	nr	17.25
Budget lock escutcheon - satin stainless steel 316	-	0.11	2.01	5.02	nr	7.03
50 Ø x 3 mm Stainless steel circular covered rose for profile cylinder	-	0.11	2.01	6.55	nr	8.56
50 Ø x 3 mm Stainless steel circular covered rose with indicator and emergency release	-	0.17	3.11	15.97	nr	19.08
50 Ø x 3 mm Stainless steel circular covered rose with heavy turn, 5-8 mm spindle	-	0.17	3.11	22.86	nr	25.96
330 x 76 x 1.6 mm Modric anodised aluminium push plate	-	0.17	3.11	3.61	nr	6.72
330 x 76 x 1.6 mm Stainless steel push plate	-	0.17	3.11	7.00	nr	10.10
800 x 150 x 1.5 mm Modric anodised aluminium kicking plate, drilled and countersunk with screws.	-	0.28	5.12	8.24	nr	13.36
900 x 150 x 1.5 mm Modric anodised aluminium kicking plate, drilled and countersunk with screws.	-	0.28	5.12	9.20	nr	14.32
1000 x 150 x 1.5 mm Modric anodised aluminium kicking plate, drilled & countersunk with screws.	-	0.28	5.12	10.16	nr	15.28
800 x 150 x 1.5 mm Stainless steel kicking plate, drilled and countersunk with screws.	-	0.28	5.12	18.29	nr	23.40
900 x 150 x 1.5 mm Stainless steel kicking plate, drilled and countersunk with screws.	-	0.28	5.12	20.60	nr	25.72
1000 x 150 x 1.5 mm Stainless steel kicking plate, drilled & countersunk with screws.	-	0.28	5.12	22.80	nr	27.92

P BUILDING FABRIC SUNDRIES

Item	PC £	Labour hours	Labour £	Material £	Unit	Total rate £
305 x 80 x 3 mm Stainless steel letter plate with spring loaded flap opening 250 x 45 mm only for doors up to 60 mm 316 stainless steel	-	1.38	25.22	59.09	nr	84.31
19 mm Ø Stainless steel straight pull handle with M8 threaded holes, fixing centres 300 mm, satin stainless steel 316	-	0.36	6.58	35.44	nr	42.02
610 x 70 x 19 mm Ø Modric anodised aluminium grab handle bolt through fixing	-	0.44	8.04	36.52	nr	44.56
457 x 457 x 25 mm Ø Modric anodised aluminium heavy duty grab handle 3 point fixing 70 mm projection	-	0.44	8.04	117.50	nr	125.54
Hinges						
100 x 75 x 2.5 mm Stainless steel triple knuckle button tipped butt hinges satin chrome plated on steel, jig drilled CE Marked to EN1935	-	0.28	5.12	9.93	pair	15.05
100 x 75 x 2.5 mm Stainless steel triple knuckle concealed twin Newton bearings, button tipped hinges, satin chrome plated steel, jig drilled, CE marked to EN1935 4-7-7-1-1-4-0-14	-	0.28	5.12	13.54	pair	18.66
100 x 75 x 3 mm Stainless steel triple knuckle concealed twin Newton bearings, button tipped hinges, jig drilled, stainless steel 316 CE marked to EN1935 4-7-7-1-1-4-0-14	-	0.28	5.12	16.82	pair	21.94
90 x 90 x 3 mm Stainless steel triple knuckle concealed twin Newton bearings, button tipped hinges, template drilled to ANSI 156.7 and BS7352 satin stainless steel 316 CE marked to EN1935 4-7-6-1-1-4-0-13	-	0.28	5.12	24.38	pair	29.50
100 x 75 x 3 mm Stainless steel triple knuckle concealed twin Newtonbearings, button tipped butt hinges, jig drilled for metal doors/frames, complete with M6x12MT 'undercut' machine screws, stainless steel 316 CE marked to EN1935 4-7-7-1-1-4-0-14	-	0.28	5.12	25.06	pair	30.18
100 x 100 x 3 mm Stainless steel triple knuckle concealed twin Newton bearings, button tipped hinges, jig drilled, stainless steel grade 316 CE marked to EN1935 4-7-7-1-1-4-0-14	-	0.28	5.12	25.85	pair	30.97
Latches						
Modric anodised aluminium 'Advanced' round cylinder for rim night latch or locking attachment, anti-pick paracentric keyway with exclusive 'TG' pins, hardened driver and body insert, 2 keyed	-	0.44	8.04	15.18	nr	23.22
93 x 75 mm Cylinder rim non-deadlocking night latch case only 60 mm backset	-	0.44	8.04	17.04	nr	25.08
92 x 60 mm b/s Stainless steel 'HL' series mortice latch, case only, Stainless Steel low friction latchbolt, unique Griptight follower, heavy spring for levers, squared ended forend and strike, CE marked to BSEN 12209 3/X/8/1/0/F/1/3/0/3/0	-	0.88	16.08	18.62	nr	34.71
Satin chrome 'Advanced' round cylinder for rim night latch or locking attachment, anti-pick paracentric keyway with exclusive 'TG' pins. hardened driver and body insert, 2 keyed under Master Key	-	0.88	16.08	21.28	nr	37.36
Modric anodised aluminium latch configuration with quadaxial assembly	-	0.88	16.08	47.01	nr	63.09
Modric anodised aluminium nightlatch configuration with quadaxial assembly and single cylinder	-	0.88	16.08	91.49	nr	107.57

P BUILDING FABRIC SUNDRIES

Item	PC £	Labour hours	Labour £	Material £	Unit	Total rate £
P21 IRONMONGERY – cont'd						
Ironmongery; Allgood; to softwood – cont'd						
Locks						
44 mm case Bright zinc plated steel mortice budget lock with slotted strike plate 33 mm backset	-	0.88	16.08	10.50	nr	**26.58**
76 x 58 mm b/s Stainless steel cubicle mortice deadlock with 8 mm follower	-	0.88	16.08	12.70	nr	**28.78**
Advanced' profile single cylinder, anti-pick paracentric keyway with exclusive "TG" pins, hardened drivers and body insert, 2 keyed, Satin Nickel finish.	-	0.88	16.08	15.92	nr	**32.00**
Advanced' profile single cylinder, anti-pick paracentric keyway with exclusive "TG" pins, hardened drivers and body insert, 2 keyed under Master Key, Satin Nickel finish.	-	0.88	16.08	22.29	nr	**38.37**
65 mm 'Advanced' profile cylinder with Allgood inside turn anti-pick paracentric keyway with exclusive "TG" pins, hardened driver and body inserts. 2 keyed. satin nickel finish.	-	0.88	16.08	25.62	nr	**41.70**
65 mm 'Advanced' profile cylinder with Allgood inside turn anti-pick paracentric keyway with exclusive "TG" pins, hardened driver and body insert. 2 keyed. Under master key Satin nickel finish.	-	0.88	16.08	32.40	nr	**48.48**
Advanced' profile double cylinder, anti-pick paracentric keyway with exclusive "TG" pins, hardened drivers and body insert, 2 keyd under Master key, Satin Nickel finish	-	0.88	16.08	35.67	nr	**51.75**
55 mm 'Advanced' cylinder hardened steel padlock, anti-pick paracentric keyway with exclusive 'TG' pins, hardened driver and body insert, 2 keyed under Master Key.	-	0.88	16.08	68.63	nr	**84.71**
92 x 60 mm b/s Stainless steel 'HL' series profile cylinder mortice deadlock, case only, single throw 20 mm stainless steel deadbolt, square forend and plain flat strike CE Marked to BS EN12209 3/X/8/1/0/F/1/K/A/0/0	-	0.88	16.08	18.62	nr	**34.71**
92 x 60 mm b/s Stainless steel 'HL' series bathroom lock, case only, Stainless Steel low friction latchbolt, unique Griptight follower, heavy spring for levers, twin 8 mm followers at 78 mm centres, square ended forend and strike	-	0.88	16.08	19.75	nr	**35.83**
92 x 60 mm b/s Stainless steel ' HL' series profile cyl mort lock, case only, s/steel low friction l/bolt, unique Griptight follower, hvy spring for lvrs, 20 mm throw d/bolt, cyl can w/draw both bolts sq f/end & strike. CE marked to BSEN 12209 3/X/8/1/0/F/1/K/A/3/0	-	0.88	16.08	19.75	nr	**35.83**
92 x 60 mm b/s Stainless steel 'HL' series profile cylinder split follower entrance door lockcase with safety re-entry function. Stainless steel latch & single throw 20 mm throw deadbolt. Inside lever withdraws both bolts and unlocks outside lever.	-	0.88	16.08	65.81	nr	**81.89**
Modric anodised aluminium lock configuration with quadaxial assembly and cylinder with turn	-	0.88	16.08	86.01	nr	**102.09**

P BUILDING FABRIC SUNDRIES

Item	PC £	Labour hours	Labour £	Material £	Unit	Total rate £
Sundries						
76 mm Ø Modric anodised aluminium circular sex symbol male	-	0.09	1.64	5.87	nr	**7.51**
76 mm Ø Modric anodised aluminium circular symbol fire door keep locked	-	0.09	1.64	5.87	nr	**7.51**
76 mm Ø Modric anodised aluminium circular symbol fire door keep shut	-	0.11	2.01	5.87	nr	**7.88**
38 x 47 mm Ø Modric anodised aluminium heavy circular floor door stop with cover	-	0.11	2.01	8.52	nr	**10.53**
38 x 47 mm Ø Stainless steel heavy circular floor door stop with cover	-	0.10	1.83	9.26	nr	**11.08**
102 x 25 mm Ø Modric anodised aluminium circular heavy duty skirting buffer with thief resistant insert	-	0.11	2.01	11.12	nr	**13.13**
102 x 25 mm Ø Stainless steel circular heavy duty skirting buffer with thief resistant insert	-	0.11	2.01	16.48	nr	**18.49**
152 mm Cabin hook satin chrome on brass	-	0.17	3.11	15.97	nr	**19.08**
Stainless steel toilet roll holder, length 145 mm, colour white, satin stainless steel 316	-	0.17	3.11	39.56	nr	**42.67**
Stainless steel towel rail with bushes, fixing centres 450 mm, satin stainless steel 316	-	0.28	5.12	58.19	nr	**63.30**
Stainless steel toilet brush holder with toilet brush with bushes, satin stainless steel 316	-	0.22	4.02	84.15	nr	**88.17**
Set of stainless steel rails, one lift-up, 3 straight, and one backrest for use in toilets for the disabled, to meet the requirements of Part M of the Building Regulations	-	1.65	30.15	402.74	nr	**432.89**
Ironmongery; Allgood or other equal and approved; to hardwood						
Bolts						
75 x 35 mm Modric anodised aluminium straight barrel bolt	-	0.45	8.22	7.22	nr	**15.45**
150 x 35 mm Modric anodised aluminium straight barrel bolt	-	0.45	8.22	10.78	nr	**19.00**
75 x 35 mm Modric anodised aluminium necked barrel bolt	-	0.45	8.22	9.59	nr	**17.82**
150 x 35 mm Modric anodised aluminium necked barrel bolt	-	0.45	8.22	12.59	nr	**20.81**
11 mm Easiclean socket	-	0.15	2.74	3.10	nr	**5.85**
Security hinge bolt chubb WS12	-	0.75	13.71	14.22	nr	**27.93**
203 x 19 x 11 mm Complete bolt set, with floor socket and intumescent pack for FD30 and FD60 fire doors	-	0.90	16.45	35.39	nr	**51.83**
203/457 x 19 mm Complete bolt set, with floor socket and intumescent pack for FD30 and FD60 fire doors	-	0.90	16.45	71.39	nr	**87.84**
203/609 x 19 mm Complete bolt set, with floor socket and intumescent pack for FD30 and FD60 fire doors	-	0.90	16.45	83.25	nr	**99.69**
11 mm Dust excluding socket, satin nickel plated	-	0.15	2.74	9.31	nr	**12.05**
Stainless steel indicating bolt complete with outside indicator and emergency release	-	0.90	16.45	67.61	nr	**84.06**
Catches						
Magnetic catch	-	0.30	5.48	1.02	nr	**6.50**

P BUILDING FABRIC SUNDRIES

Item	PC £	Labour hours	Labour £	Material £	Unit	Total rate £
P21 IRONMONGERY – cont'd						
Ironmongery; Allgood; to hardwood – cont'd						
Door closers and furniture						
13 mm Satin chrome rebate component for 7204/08/78/79/86	-	0.90	16.45	20.99	nr	37.44
90 x 90 mm Modric anodised aluminium electrically powered hold open wall magnet. CE marked to BS EN1155:1997 & A1:2002 3-5-6/3-1-1-3	-	0.60	10.96	11.51	nr	22.48
Modric anodised aluminium bathroom configuration with quadaxial assembly, turn, release and optional indicator	-	1.15	21.02	76.75	nr	97.77
Concealed overhead door restraining stay with stainless steel arm and aluminium channel & bracket and adjustable friction slide block, spring buffer to curtail door opening; not for use with concealed door closing devices	-	1.45	26.50	26.53	nr	53.02
213 x 48 x 48 mm Overhead door closers complete with fixings for fig 1 and fig 6 applications. Certifire listed. CE Marked to BS EN1154 4-8-3-1-1-3	-	1.45	26.50	57.62	nr	84.12
Concealed jamb door closer check action	-	1.45	26.50	90.36	nr	116.85
75 x 57 x 170 mm Modric anodised aluminium door co-ordinator for pairs of rebated leaves, CE Marked to BS EN1158 3-5-3/5-1-1-0	-	1.15	21.02	30.87	nr	51.89
263 x 50 x 48 mm Modric anodised aluminium overhead door closer Fig 1 available power 1-4 with adjustable backcheck, intumescent protected bracket. Certifire listed and CE Marked to BS EN1154 4-8-4-1-1-3	-	1.45	26.50	65.52	nr	92.02
290 x 48 x 50 mm Modric anodised aluminium rectangular overhead door closer with adjustable power and adjustable backcheck intumescent protected arm heavy duty U.L. & certifire listed & CE Marked to BS EN1154 4-8-2/4-1-1-3 and Kitemarked.	-	1.45	26.50	82.91	nr	109.40
Stainless steel overhead door closer Fig 1. Projecting armset, Power EN 2-5, CE marked , c/w Backcheck, Latch action and Speed control. Max door width 1100 mm, Max door weight 100kg	-	1.45	26.50	82.17	nr	108.67
Stainless steel finished track and arm to suit 9124 fully concealed door closer	-	1.15	21.02	56.27	nr	77.28
92 x 45 mm Stainless steel heavy duty floor pivot set with thrust roller bearing 400kg load capacity. Complete with forged steel intumescent protected double action strap with 10 mm height adjustment, new low profile top centre, and matching cover plate	-	3.30	60.31	176.88	nr	237.18
92 x 45 mm Stainless steel heavy duty floor pivot set with thrust roller bearing 400kg load capacity, with stainless steel intumescent protected S/A 25 mm offset strap & top centre, matching plate	-	3.30	60.31	220.22	nr	280.52
Double action pivot set for door maximum width 1100 mm and maximum weight 80kg	-	3.30	60.31	85.11	nr	145.41

P BUILDING FABRIC SUNDRIES

Item	PC £	Labour hours	Labour £	Material £	Unit	Total rate £
305 x 80 x 50 mm Stainless steel 'Cavalier' floor spring, intumescent protected forged steel D/A strap with 10 mm height adjustment & low profile top centre, matching covers & box. CE Marked to BS EN1154 4-8-*-1-1-3. Adjustable power 2/4	-	3.30	60.31	252.95	nr	313.26
305 x 80 x 50 mm Stainless steel 'Cavalier' floor spring adjustable power 2/4 stainless steel intumsecent protected S/A 16 mm offset strap & top centre, matching covers & box. Certifire listed and CE marked to BSEN1154 4-8-2/4-1-1-3	-	3.30	60.31	296.30	nr	356.60
Surface vertical rod push bar panic bolt, reversible, tp suit doors 2500x1100 mm maximum, silver finish, CE marked to EN1125 class 3-7-5-1-1-3-2-2-A	-	2.20	40.20	123.26	nr	163.46
Rim push bar panic latch, reversible, to suit doors 1100 mm wide maximum, silver finish, CE marked to EN1125 class 3-7-5-1-1-3-2-2-A	-	1.90	34.72	85.67	nr	120.39
76 x 51 x 13 mm Adjustable heavy roller catch satin chrome	-	0.90	16.45	6.83	nr	23.28
External access device for use with XX10280/2 panic hardware to suit door thickness 45-55 mm, complete with SS3006N lever, SS755 rose, SS796 profile escutcheon and spindle.For use with MA7420A51 or MA7420A55 profile cylinders	-	1.90	34.72	29.46	nr	64.18
142 x 22 mm Ø Concealed jamb door closer light duty	-	1.15	21.02	11.01	nr	32.02
112 x 42 mm Emergency release door stop for toilet doors	-	1.45	26.50	84.77	nr	111.27
Modric anodised aluminium quadaxial lever assembly tested to BS EN1906 4/7/-/1/1/4/0/U	-	1.15	21.02	30.14	pair	51.15
Modric anodised aluminium quadaxial lever assembly Tested to BS EN1906 4/7/-/1/1/4/0/U	-	1.15	21.02	31.04	pair	52.06
Modric anodised aluminium quadaxial lever assembly Tested to BS EN1906 4/7/-/1/1/4/0/U with Biocote® anti-bacterial protection	-	1.15	21.02	37.25	pair	58.26
Modric stainless steel quadaxial lever assembly Tested to BS EN1906 4/7/-/1/1/4/0/U	-	1.15	21.02	66.14	pair	87.16
152 x 38 x 13 mm Modric anodised aluminium security door chain leather covered	-	0.60	10.96	51.02	nr	61.98
50 Ø x 3 mm Circular covered rose for profile cylinder	-	0.15	2.74	3.61	nr	6.35
50 Ø x 3 mm Modric anodised aluminium circular covered rose with indicator and emergency release	-	0.20	3.65	9.31	nr	12.97
50 Ø x 3 mm Modric anodised aluminium circular covered rose with heavy turn, 5-8 mm spindle	-	0.20	3.65	14.50	nr	18.16
Budget lock escutcheon - satin stainless steel 316	-	0.15	2.74	5.02	nr	7.76
50 Ø x 3 mm Stainless steel circular covered rose for profile cylinder	-	0.15	2.74	6.55	nr	9.29
50 Ø x 3 mm Stainless steel circular covered rose with indicator and emergency release	-	0.25	4.57	15.97	nr	20.54
50 Ø x 3 mm Stainless steel circular covered rose with heavy turn, 5-8 mm spindle	-	0.25	4.57	22.86	nr	27.43
330 x 76 x 1.6 mm Modric anodised aluminium push plate	-	0.25	4.57	3.61	nr	8.18
330 x 76 x 1.6 mm Stainless steel push plate	-	0.25	4.57	7.00	nr	11.57

P BUILDING FABRIC SUNDRIES

Item	PC £	Labour hours	Labour £	Material £	Unit	Total rate £
P21 IRONMONGERY – cont'd						
Ironmongery; Allgood; to hardwood – cont'd						
Door closers and furniture – cont'd						
800 x 150 x 1.5 mm Modric anodised aluminium kicking plate, drilled and countersunk with screws.	-	0.35	6.40	8.24	nr	**14.64**
900 x 150 x 1.5 mm Modric anodised aluminium kicking plate, drilled and countersunk with screws.	-	0.35	6.40	9.20	nr	**15.60**
1000 x 150 x 1.5 mm Modric anodised aluminium kicking plate, drilled & countersunk with screws.	-	0.35	6.40	10.16	nr	**16.55**
800 x 150 x 1.5 mm Stainless steel kicking plate, drilled and countersunk with screws.	-	0.35	6.40	18.29	nr	**24.68**
900 x 150 x 1.5 mm Stainless steel kicking plate, drilled and countersunk with screws.	-	0.35	6.40	20.60	nr	**27.00**
1000 x 150 x 1.5 mm Stainless steel kicking plate, drilled & countersunk with screws.	-	0.35	6.40	22.80	nr	**29.20**
305 x 80 x 3 mm Stainless steel letter plate with spring loaded flap opening 250 x 45 mm only for doors up to 60 mm 316 stainless steel	-	1.85	33.81	59.09	nr	**92.90**
19 mm Ø Stainless steel straight pull handle with M8 threaded holes, fixing centres 300 mm, satin stainless steel 316	-	0.50	9.14	35.44	nr	**44.58**
610 x 70 x 19 mm Ø Modric anodised aluminium grab handle bolt through fixing	-	0.60	10.96	36.52	nr	**47.48**
457 x 457 x 25 mm Ø Modric anodised aluminium heavy duty grab handle 3 point fixing 70 mm projection	-	0.60	10.96	117.50	nr	**128.47**
Hinges						
100 x 75 x 2.5 mm Stainless steel triple knuckle button tipped butt hinges satin chrome plated on steel, jig drilled CE Marked to EN1935	-	0.35	6.40	9.93	pair	**16.33**
100 x 75 x 2.5 mm Stainless steel triple knuckle concealed twin Newton bearings, button tipped hinges, satin chrome plated steel, jig drilled, CE marked to EN1935 4-7-7-1-1-4-0-14	-	0.35	6.40	13.54	pair	**19.94**
100 x 75 x 3 mm Stainless steel triple knuckle concealed twin Newton bearings, button tipped hinges, jig drilled, stainless steel 316 CE marked to EN1935 4-7-7-1-1-4-0-14	-	0.35	6.40	16.82	pair	**23.21**
90 x 90 x 3 mm Stainless steel triple knuckle concealed twin Newton bearings, button tipped hinges, template drilled to ANSI 156.7 and BS7352 satin stainless steel 316 CE marked to EN1935 4-7-6-1-1-4-0-13	-	0.35	6.40	24.38	pair	**30.78**
100 x 75 x 3 mm Stainless steel triple knuckle concealed twin Newtonbearings, button tipped butt hinges, jig drilled for metal doors/frames, complete with M6x12MT 'undercut' machine screws, stainless steel 316 CE marked to EN1935 4-7-7-1-1-4-0-14	-	0.35	6.40	25.06	pair	**31.45**
100 x 100 x 3 mm Stainless steel triple knuckle concealed twin Newton bearings, button tipped hinges, jig drilled, stainless steel grade 316 CE marked to EN1935 4-7-7-1-1-4-0-14	-	0.35	6.40	25.85	pair	**32.24**

P BUILDING FABRIC SUNDRIES

Item	PC £	Labour hours	Labour £	Material £	Unit	Total rate £
Latches						
Modric anodised aluminium 'Advanced' round cylinder for rim night latch or locking attachment, anti-pick paracentric keyway with exclusive 'TG' pins, hardened driver and body insert, 2 keyed	-	0.60	10.96	15.18	nr	26.15
93 x 75 mm Cylinder rim non-deadlocking night latch case only 60 mm backset	-	0.60	10.96	17.04	nr	28.01
92 x 60 mm b/s Stainless steel 'HL' series mortice latch, case only, Stainless Steel low friction latchbolt, unique Griptight follower, heavy spring for levers, squared ended forend and strike, CE marked to BSEN 12209 3/X/8/1/0/F/1/3/0/3/0	-	1.15	21.02	18.62	nr	39.64
Satin chrome 'Advanced' round cylinder for rim night latch or locking attachment, anti-pick paracentric keyway with exclusive 'TG' pins. hardened driver and body insert, 2 keyed under Master Key	-	1.15	21.02	21.28	nr	42.29
Modric anodised aluminium latch configuration with quadaxial assembly	-	1.15	21.02	47.01	nr	68.03
Modric anodised aluminium nightlatch configuration with quadaxial assembly and single cylinder	-	1.15	21.02	91.49	nr	112.50
Locks						
44 mm case Bright zinc plated steel mortice budget lock with slotted strike plate 33 mm backset	-	1.15	21.02	10.50	nr	31.51
76 x 58 mm b/s Stainless steel cubicle mortice deadlock with 8 mm follower	-	1.15	21.02	12.70	nr	33.71
Advanced' profile single cylinder, anti-pick paracentric keyway with exclusive "TG" pins, hardened drivers and body insert, 2 keyed, Satin Nickel finish.	-	1.15	21.02	15.92	nr	36.93
Advanced' profile single cylinder, anti-pick paracentric keyway with exclusive "TG" pins, hardened drivers and body insert, 2 keyed under Master Key, Satin Nickel finish.	-	1.15	21.02	22.29	nr	43.31
65 mm 'Advanced' profile cylinder with Allgood inside turn anti-pick paracentric keyway with exclusive "TG" pins, hardened driver and body inserts. 2 keyed. satin nickel finish.	-	1.15	21.02	25.62	nr	46.64
65 mm 'Advanced' profile cylinder with Allgood inside turn anti-pick paracentric keyway with exclusive "TG" pins, hardened driver and body insert. 2 keyed. Under master key Satin nickel finish.	-	1.15	21.02	32.40	nr	53.41
Advanced' profile double cylinder, anti-pick paracentric keyway with exclusive "TG" pins, hardened drivers and body insert, 2 keyd under Master key, Satin Nickel finish	-	1.15	21.02	35.67	nr	56.68
55 mm 'Advanced' cylinder hardened steel padlock, anti-pick paracentric keyway with exclusive 'TG' pins, hardened driver and body insert, 2 keyed under Master Key.	-	1.15	21.02	68.63	nr	89.64
92 x 60 mm b/s Stainless steel 'HL' series profile cylinder mortice deadlock, case only, single throw 20 mm stainless steel deadbolt, square forend and plain flat strike CE Marked to BS EN12209 3/X/8/1/0/F/1/K/A/0/0	-	1.15	21.02	18.62	nr	39.64

P BUILDING FABRIC SUNDRIES

Item	PC £	Labour hours	Labour £	Material £	Unit	Total rate £
P21 IRONMONGERY – cont'd						
Iromongery; Allgood; to hardwood – cont'd						
Locks – cont'd						
92 x 60 mm b/s Stainless steel 'HL' series bathroom lock, case only, Stainless Steel low friction latchbolt, unique Griptight follower, heavy spring for levers, twin 8 mm followers at 78 mm centres, square ended forend and strike	-	1.15	21.02	19.75	nr	40.77
92 x 60 mm b/s Stainless steel ' HL' series profile cyl mort lock, case only, s/steel low friction l/bolt, unique Griptight follower, hvy spring for lvrs, 20 mm throw d/bolt, cyl can w/draw both bolts sq f/end & strike. CE marked to BSEN 12209 3/X/8/1/0/F/1/K/A/3/0	-	1.15	21.02	19.75	nr	40.77
92 x 60 mm b/s Stainless steel 'HL' series profile cylinder split follower entrance door lockcase with safety re-entry function. Stainless steel latch & single throw 20 mm throw deadbolt. Inside lever withdraws both bolts and unlocks outside lever.	-	1.15	21.02	65.81	nr	86.82
Modric anodised aluminium lock configuration with quadaxial assembly and cylinder with turn	-	1.15	21.02	86.01	nr	107.03
Sundries						
76 mm Ø Modric anodised aluminium circular sex symbol male	-	0.10	1.83	5.87	nr	7.70
76 mm Ø Modric anodised aluminium circular symbol fire door keep locked	-	0.10	1.83	5.87	nr	7.70
76 mm Ø Modric anodised aluminium circular symbol fire door keep shut	-	0.15	2.74	5.87	nr	8.61
38 x 47 mm Ø Modric anodised aluminium heavy circular floor door stop with cover	-	0.15	2.74	8.52	nr	11.26
38 x 47 mm Ø Stainless steel heavy circular floor door stop with cover	-	0.15	2.74	9.26	nr	12.00
102 x 25 mm Ø Modric anodised aluminium circular heavy duty skirting buffer with thief resistant insert	-	0.15	2.74	11.12	nr	13.86
102 x 25 mm Ø Stainless steel circular heavy duty skirting buffer with thief resistant insert	-	0.15	2.74	16.48	nr	19.22
152 mm Cabin hook satin chrome on brass	-	0.25	4.57	15.97	nr	20.54
Stainless steel toilet roll holder, length 145 mm, colour white, satin stainless steel 316	-	0.25	4.57	39.56	nr	44.13
Stainless steel towel rail with bushes, fixing centres 450 mm, satin stainless steel 316	-	0.35	6.40	58.19	nr	64.58
Stainless steel toilet brush holder with toilet brush with bushes, satin stainless steel 316	-	0.30	5.48	84.15	nr	89.63
Set of stainless steel rails, one lift-up, 3 straight, and one backrest for use in toilets for the disabled, as Part M of the Building Regulations	-	2.20	40.20	402.74	nr	442.94
Sliding door gear; Hillaldam Coburn Ltd; Commercial/Light industrial; for top hung timber/metal doors, weight less than 365 kg						
Sliding door gear						
bottom guide; fixed to concrete in groove	9.88	0.46	8.41	11.15	m	19.56
top track	26.33	0.23	4.20	29.72	m	33.93
detachable locking bar and padlock	42.58	0.31	5.67	48.06	nr	53.73
hangers; timber doors	49.18	0.46	8.41	55.51	nr	63.91
hangers; metal doors	35.06	0.46	8.41	39.58	nr	47.98
head brackets; side fixing; bolting to masonry	6.68	0.46	8.41	11.20	nr	19.61
head brackets; soffit fixing; screwing to timber	6.43	0.32	5.85	7.33	nr	13.18

P BUILDING FABRIC SUNDRIES

Item	PC £	Labour hours	Labour £	Material £	Unit	Total rate £
door guide to timber door	16.24	0.23	4.20	18.33	nr	22.53
door stop; rubber buffers; to masonry	27.10	0.69	12.61	30.59	nr	43.20
drop bolt; screwing to timber	21.44	0.46	8.41	24.20	nr	32.60
bow handle; to timber	10.92	0.23	4.20	12.32	nr	16.53
Sundries						
rubber door stop; plugged and screwed to concrete	5.71	0.09	1.64	6.44	nr	8.09
P30 TRENCHES/PIPEWAYS/PITS FOR BURIED ENGINEERING SERVICES						
Excavating trenches; by machine; grading bottoms; earthwork support; filling with excavated material and compacting; disposal of surplus soil; spreading on site average 50 m						
Services not exceeding 200 mm nominal size						
average depth of run 0.50 m	-	0.30	3.43	1.42	m	4.85
average depth of run 0.75 m	-	0.45	5.15	2.34	m	7.49
average depth of run 1.00 m	-	0.90	10.30	4.32	m	14.62
average depth of run 1.25 m	-	1.33	15.22	5.93	m	21.15
average depth of run 1.50 m	-	1.71	19.57	7.76	m	27.33
average depth of run 1.75 m	-	2.08	23.81	9.91	m	33.71
average depth of run 2.00 m	-	2.46	28.16	11.37	m	39.52
Excavating trenches; by hand; grading bottoms; earthwork support; filling with excavated material and compacting; disposal; of surplus soil; spreading on site average 50 m						
Services not exceeding 200 mm nominal size						
average depth of run 0.50 m	-	1.06	12.13	-	m	12.13
average depth of run 0.75 m	-	1.60	18.31	-	m	18.31
average depth of run 1.00 m	-	2.34	26.78	1.38	m	28.16
average depth of run 1.25 m	-	3.29	37.66	1.90	m	39.55
average depth of run1.50 m	-	4.52	51.73	2.31	m	54.04
average depth of run 1.75 m	-	5.96	68.22	2.79	m	71.01
average depth of run 2.00 m	-	6.81	77.94	3.07	m	81.01
Stop cock pits, valves chambers and the like; excavating; half brick thick walls in common bricks in cement mortar (1:3); on in situ concrete designated C20 - 20 mm aggregate bed; 100 mm thick						
Pits						
100 mm x 100 mm x 750 mm deep; internal holes for one small pipe; polypropylene hinged box cover; bedding in cement mortar (1:3)	-	4.49	102.48	31.72	nr	134.20

P BUILDING FABRIC SUNDRIES

Item	PC £	Labour hours	Labour £	Material £	Unit	Total rate £
P31 HOLES/CHASES/COVERS/SUPPORTS FOR SERVICES						
Builders' work for electrical installations; cutting away for and making good after electrician; including cutting or leaving all holes, notches, mortices, sinkings and chases, in both the structure and its coverings, for the following electrical points						
Exposed installation						
lighting points	-	0.32	4.47	-	nr	**4.47**
socket outlet points	-	0.54	7.79	-	nr	**7.79**
fitting outlet points	-	0.54	7.79	-	nr	**7.79**
equipment points or control gear points	-	0.75	11.10	-	nr	**11.10**
Concealed installation						
lighting points	-	0.43	6.08	-	nr	**6.08**
socket outlet points	-	0.75	11.10	-	nr	**11.10**
fitting outlet points	-	0.75	11.10	-	nr	**11.10**
equipment points or control gear points	-	1.06	15.37	-	nr	**15.37**
Builders' work for other services installations						
Cutting chases in brickwork						
for one pipe; not exceeding 55 mm nominal size; vertical	-	0.43	4.52	-	m	**4.52**
for one pipe; 55 mm - 110 mm nominal size; vertical	-	0.74	7.78	-	m	**7.78**
Cutting and pinning to brickwork or blockwork; ends of supports						
for pipes not exceeding 55 mm nominal size	-	0.21	4.79	-	nr	**4.79**
for cast iron pipes 55 mm - 110 mm nominal size	-	0.35	7.99	-	nr	**7.99**
Cutting or forming holes for pipes or the like; not exceeding 55 mm nominal size; making good						
reinforced concrete; not exceeding 100 mm deep	-	0.82	10.97	0.81	nr	**11.78**
reinforced concrete; 100 mm - 200 mm deep	-	1.25	16.72	1.19	nr	**17.91**
reinforced concrete; 200 mm - 300 mm deep	-	1.65	22.07	1.64	nr	**23.71**
half brick thick	-	0.35	4.68	-	nr	**4.68**
one brick thick	-	0.58	7.76	-	nr	**7.76**
one and a half brick thick	-	0.95	12.71	-	nr	**12.71**
100 mm blockwork	-	0.32	4.28	-	nr	**4.28**
140 mm blockwork	-	0.43	5.75	-	nr	**5.75**
215 mm blockwork	-	0.53	7.09	-	nr	**7.09**
plasterboard partition or suspended ceiling	-	0.38	5.08	-	nr	**5.08**
Cutting or forming holes for pipes or the like; 55 mm - 110 mm nominal size; making good						
reinforced concrete; not exceeding 100 mm deep	-	1.05	14.04	1.05	nr	**15.09**
reinforced concrete; 100 mm - 200 mm deep	-	1.60	21.40	1.59	nr	**22.99**
reinforced concrete; 200 mm - 300 mm deep	-	2.10	28.09	2.09	nr	**30.17**
half brick thick	-	0.43	5.75	-	nr	**5.75**
one brick thick	-	0.74	9.90	-	nr	**9.90**
one and a half brick thick	-	1.17	15.65	-	nr	**15.65**
100 mm blockwork	-	0.37	4.95	-	nr	**4.95**
140 mm blockwork	-	0.53	7.09	-	nr	**7.09**
215 mm blockwork	-	0.64	8.56	-	nr	**8.56**
plasterboard partition or suspended ceiling	-	0.44	5.89	-	nr	**5.89**

P BUILDING FABRIC SUNDRIES

Item	PC £	Labour hours	Labour £	Material £	Unit	Total rate £
Cutting or forming holes for pipes or the like; over 110 mm nominal size; making good						
reinforced concrete; not exceeding 100 mm deep	-	1.25	16.72	1.24	nr	17.96
reinforced concrete; 100 mm - 200 mm deep	-	1.90	25.41	1.89	nr	27.30
reinforced concrete; 200 mm - 300 mm deep	-	2.45	32.77	2.43	nr	35.21
half brick thick	-	0.53	7.09	-	nr	7.09
one brick thick	-	0.91	12.17	-	nr	12.17
one and a half brick thick	-	1.43	19.13	-	nr	19.13
100 mm blockwork	-	0.48	6.42	-	nr	6.42
140 mm blockwork	-	0.64	8.56	-	nr	8.56
215 mm blockwork	-	0.80	10.70	-	nr	10.70
plasterboard partition or suspended ceiling	-	0.49	6.55	-	nr	6.55
Add for making good fair face or facings one side						
pipe; not exceeding 55 mm nominal size	-	0.08	1.83	-	nr	1.83
pipe; 55 mm - 110 mm nominal size	-	0.11	2.51	-	nr	2.51
pipe; over 110 mm nominal size	-	0.13	2.97	-	nr	2.97
Add for fixing sleeve (supply not included)						
for pipe; small	-	0.16	3.65	-	nr	3.65
for pipe; large	-	0.21	4.79	-	nr	4.79
for pipe; extra large	-	0.32	7.30	-	nr	7.30
Add for supplying and fixing one-hour intumescent sleeve						
for pipe; small	-	0.28	3.75	10.65	nr	14.40
for pipe; large	-	0.31	4.15	13.66	nr	17.80
for pipe; extra large	-	0.34	4.55	18.00	nr	22.55
Cutting or forming holes for ducts; girth not exceeding 1.00 m; making good						
half brick thick	-	0.64	8.56	-	nr	8.56
one brick thick	-	1.06	14.18	-	nr	14.18
one and a half brick thick	-	1.70	22.74	-	nr	22.74
100 mm blockwork	-	0.53	7.09	-	nr	7.09
140 mm blockwork	-	0.74	9.90	-	nr	9.90
215 mm blockwork	-	0.95	12.71	-	nr	12.71
plasterboard partition or suspended ceiling	-	0.75	10.03	-	nr	10.03
Cutting or forming holes for ducts; girth 1.00 m - 2.00 m; making good						
half brick thick	-	0.74	9.90	-	nr	9.90
one brick thick	-	1.28	17.12	-	nr	17.12
one and a half brick thick	-	2.02	27.02	-	nr	27.02
100 mm blockwork	-	0.64	8.56	-	nr	8.56
140 mm blockwork	-	0.85	11.37	-	nr	11.37
215 mm blockwork	-	1.06	14.18	-	nr	14.18
plasterboard partition or suspended ceiling	-	0.85	11.37	-	nr	11.37
Cutting or forming holes for ducts; girth 2.00 m - 3.00 m; making good						
half brick thick	-	1.17	15.65	-	nr	15.65
one brick thick	-	2.02	27.02	-	nr	27.02
one and a half brick thick	-	3.19	42.67	-	nr	42.67
100 mm blockwork	-	1.01	13.51	-	nr	13.51
140 mm blockwork	-	1.38	18.46	-	nr	18.46
215 mm blockwork	-	1.76	23.54	-	nr	23.54
plasterboard partition or suspended ceiling	-	1.10	14.71	-	nr	14.71

P BUILDING FABRIC SUNDRIES

Item	PC £	Labour hours	Labour £	Material £	Unit	Total rate £
P31 HOLES/CHASES/COVERS/SUPPORTS FOR SERVICES – cont'd						
Builders' work for other services						
Installations – cont'd						
Cutting or forming holes for ducts; girth 3.00 m - 4.00 m; making good						
half brick thick	-	1.60	21.40	-	nr	21.40
one brick thick	-	2.66	35.58	-	nr	35.58
one and a half brick thick	-	4.26	56.98	-	nr	56.98
100 mm blockwork	-	1.17	15.65	-	nr	15.65
140 mm blockwork	-	1.60	21.40	-	nr	21.40
215 mm blockwork	-	2.02	27.02	-	nr	27.02
plasterboard partition or suspended ceiling	-	1.35	18.06	-	nr	18.06
Mortices in brickwork						
for expansion bolt	-	0.21	2.81	-	nr	2.81
for 20 mm diameter bolt; 75 mm deep	-	0.16	2.14	-	nr	2.14
for 20 mm diameter bolt; 150 mm deep	-	0.27	3.61	-	nr	3.61
Mortices in brickwork; grouting with cement mortar (1:1)						
75 mm x 75 mm x 200 mm deep	-	0.32	4.28	-	nr	4.28
75 mm x 75 mm x 300 mm deep	-	0.43	5.75	-	nr	5.75
Holes in softwood for pipes, bars, cables and the like						
12 mm thick	-	0.04	0.73	-	nr	0.73
25 mm thick	-	0.06	1.10	-	nr	1.10
50 mm thick	-	0.11	2.01	-	nr	2.01
100 mm thick	-	0.16	2.92	-	nr	2.92
Holes in hardwood for pipes, bars, cables and the like						
12 mm thick	-	0.06	1.10	-	nr	1.10
25 mm thick	-	0.09	1.64	-	nr	1.64
50 mm thick	-	0.16	2.92	-	nr	2.92
100 mm thick	-	0.23	4.20	-	nr	4.20
NOTE: The following rates for cutting holes and mortices in brickwork or blockwork etc. allow for diamond drilling.						
Cutting holes and mortices in brickwork; per 25 mm depth						
25 mm diameter	-	-	-	-	nr	1.18
32 mm diameter	-	-	-	-	nr	1.18
52 mm diameter	-	-	-	-	nr	1.41
76 mm diameter	-	-	-	-	nr	1.58
107 mm diameter	-	-	-	-	nr	1.69
127 mm diameter	-	-	-	-	nr	2.03
152 mm diameter	-	-	-	-	nr	2.37
200 mm diameter	-	-	-	-	nr	3.16
250 mm diameter	-	-	-	-	nr	4.74
300 mm diameter	-	-	-	-	nr	6.31
Diamond chasing; per 25 x 25 mm section						
in facing or common brickwork	-	-	-	-	m	3.10
in semi-engineering brickwork	-	-	-	-	m	6.48
in engineering brickwork	-	-	-	-	m	9.02
in lightweight blockwork	-	-	-	-	m	2.54
in heavtweight blockwork	-	-	-	-	m	5.07
in render/screed	-	-	-	-	m	9.87

P BUILDING FABRIC SUNDRIES

Item	PC £	Labour hours	Labour £	Material £	Unit	Total rate £
Forming boxes; per 25 mm depth (per m of perimeter)						
in facing or common brickwork	-	-	-	-	m	3.10
in semi-engineering brickwork	-	-	-	-	m	6.48
in engineering brickwork	-	-	-	-	m	9.02
in lightweight blockwork	-	-	-	-	m	2.54
in heavtweight blockwork	-	-	-	-	m	5.07
in render/screed	-	-	-	-	m	9.87
Other items						
track mounter or ring sawing in brickwork	-	-	-	-	m	4.79
floor sawing in apshalte	-	-	-	-	m	1.01
stitch drilling 107 mm diameter hole in brickwork	-	-	-	-	nr	1.24
"XDT Screeduct" or other equal and approved; MDT Ducting Ltd; laid within floor screed; galvanised mild steel						
Floor ducting						
100 mm wide x 50 mm deep	4.32	0.21	3.84	5.12	m	8.96
Extra for						
bend	4.28	0.11	2.01	5.07	nr	7.08
tee section	4.28	0.11	2.01	5.07	nr	7.08
connector / stop end	0.57	0.11	2.01	0.68	nr	2.69
ply cover 15 mm/16 mm thick WBP exterior grade	1.43	0.11	2.01	1.69	m	3.70
200 mm wide x 75 mm deep	7.13	0.21	3.84	8.44	m	12.28
Extra for						
bend	6.89	0.11	2.01	8.16	nr	10.17
tee section	6.89	0.11	2.01	8.16	nr	10.17
connector / stop end	7.60	0.12	2.19	9.01	nr	11.20
ply cover 15 mm/16 mm thick WBP exterior grade	2.38	0.11	2.01	2.81	m	4.83
"SFD Screeduct" or other equal and approved; MDT Ducting Ltd; with side flanges; laid within floor screed; galvanised mild steel						
Floor ducting						
100 mm wide x 50 mm deep	7.13	0.21	3.84	8.44	m	12.28
Extra for						
bend	5.46	0.11	2.01	6.47	nr	8.48
tee section	5.46	0.11	2.01	6.47	nr	8.48
connector / stop end	0.57	0.11	2.01	0.68	nr	2.69
ply cover 15 mm/16 mm thick WBP exterior grade	1.43	0.11	2.01	1.69	m	3.70
200 mm wide x 75 mm deep	9.03	0.21	3.84	10.70	m	14.53
Extra for						
bend	7.13	0.11	2.01	8.44	nr	10.45
tee section	7.13	0.11	2.01	8.44	nr	10.45
connector / stop end	0.76	0.12	2.19	0.90	nr	3.10
ply cover 15 mm/16 mm thick WBP exterior grade	2.38	0.11	2.01	2.81	m	4.83

Q PAVING/PLANTING/FENCING/SITE FURNITURE

Item	PC £	Labour hours	Labour £	Material £	Unit	Total rate £
Q10 KERBS/EDGINGS/CHANNELS/ PAVING ACCESSORIES						
Excavating; by machine						
Excavating trenches; to receive kerb foundations; average size						
300 mm x 100 mm	-	0.02	0.23	0.35	m	**0.58**
450 mm x 150 mm	-	0.02	0.23	0.71	m	**0.94**
600 mm x 200 mm	-	0.04	0.46	0.99	m	**1.45**
Excavating curved trenches; to receive kerb foundations; average size						
300 mm x 100 mm	-	0.01	0.11	0.57	m	**0.68**
450 mm x 150 mm	-	0.03	0.34	0.85	m	**1.19**
600 mm x 200 mm	-	0.05	0.57	1.06	m	**1.63**
Excavating; by hand						
Excavating trenches; to receive kerb foundations; average size						
150 mm x 50 mm	-	0.02	0.23	-	m	**0.23**
200 mm x 75 mm	-	0.07	0.80	-	m	**0.80**
250 mm x 100 mm	-	0.12	1.37	-	m	**1.37**
300 mm x 100 mm	-	0.15	1.72	-	m	**1.72**
Excavating curved trenches; to receive kerb foundations; average size						
150 mm x 50 mm	-	0.04	0.46	-	m	**0.46**
200 mm x 75 mm	-	0.08	0.92	-	m	**0.92**
250 mm x 100 mm	-	0.13	1.49	-	m	**1.49**
300 mm x 100 mm	-	0.16	1.83	-	m	**1.83**
Plain in situ ready mixed designated concrete; C7.5 - 40 mm aggregate; poured on or against earth or unblinded hardcore						
Foundations	72.67	1.33	17.79	88.19	m^3	**105.97**
Blinding beds						
not exceeding 150 mm thick	72.67	1.97	26.35	88.19	m^3	**114.54**
Plain in situ ready mixed designated concrete; C10 - 40 mm aggregate; poured on or against earth or unblinded hardcore						
Foundations	73.08	1.33	17.79	88.68	m^3	**106.47**
Blinding beds						
not exceeding 150 mm thick	73.08	1.97	26.35	88.68	m^3	**115.03**
Plain in situ ready mixed designated concrete; C20 - 20 mm aggregate; poured on or against earth or unblinded hardcore						
Foundations	75.18	1.33	17.79	91.23	m^3	**109.02**
Blinding beds						
not exceeding 150 mm thick	75.18	1.97	26.35	91.23	m^3	**117.58**
Precast concrete kerbs, channels, edgings, etc.; BS 340; bedded, jointed and pointed in cement mortar (1:3); including haunching up one side with in situ ready mixed designated concrete C10 - 40 mm aggregate; to concrete base						
Edgings; straight; square edge, fig 12						
50 mm x 150 mm	-	0.27	5.32	3.43	m	**8.75**
50 mm x 200 mm	-	0.27	5.32	4.08	m	**9.40**
50 mm x 255 mm	-	0.27	5.32	4.38	m	**9.70**

Q PAVING/PLANTING/FENCING/SITE FURNITURE

Item	PC £	Labour hours	Labour £	Material £	Unit	Total rate £
Kerbs; straight						
125 mm x 255 mm; fig 7	-	0.35	6.90	6.41	m	**13.31**
150 mm x 305 mm; fig 6	-	0.35	6.90	9.25	m	**16.15**
Kerbs; curved						
125 mm x 255 mm; fig 7	-	0.53	10.45	8.31	m	**18.75**
150 mm x 305 mm; fig 6	-	0.53	10.45	15.08	m	**25.52**
Channels; 255 mm x 125 mm; fig 8						
straight	-	0.35	6.90	5.81	m	**12.71**
curved	-	0.53	10.45	7.67	m	**18.11**
Quadrants; fig 14						
305 mm x 305 mm x 150 mm	-	0.37	7.29	9.24	nr	**16.53**
305 mm x 305 mm x 255 mm	-	0.37	7.29	9.93	nr	**17.22**
457 mm x 457 mm x 150 mm	-	0.43	8.47	10.90	nr	**19.37**
457 mm x 457 mm x 255 mm	-	0.43	8.47	11.60	nr	**20.08**
Q20 HARDCORE/GRANULAR/CEMENT BOUND BASES/SUB-BASES TO ROADS/PAVINGS						
Filling to make up levels; by machine						
Average thickness not exceeding 0.25 m						
obtained off site; hardcore	-	0.32	3.66	42.51	m³	**46.17**
obtained off site; granular fill type one	-	0.32	3.66	36.04	m³	**39.71**
obtained off site; granular fill type two	-	0.32	3.66	34.06	m³	**37.72**
Average thickness exceeding 0.25 m						
obtained off site; hardcore	-	0.28	3.20	36.39	m³	**39.59**
obtained off site; granular fill type one	-	0.28	3.20	35.78	m³	**38.98**
obtained off site; granular fill type two	-	0.28	3.20	33.79	m³	**37.00**
Filling to make up levels; by hand						
Average thickness not exceeding 0.25 m						
obtained off site; hardcore	-	0.70	8.01	43.15	m³	**51.16**
obtained off site; sand	-	0.82	9.39	37.55	m³	**46.93**
Average thickness exceeding 0.25 m						
obtained off site; hardcore	-	0.58	6.64	36.93	m³	**43.57**
obtained off site; sand	-	0.69	7.90	37.15	m³	**45.05**
Surface treatments						
Compacting						
filling; blinding with sand	-	0.05	0.57	1.90	m²	**2.48**
Q21 IN SITU CONCRETE ROADS/PAVINGS						
Reinforced in situ ready mixed designated concrete; C10 - 40 mm aggregate						
Roads; to hardcore base						
thickness not exceeding 150 mm	69.60	2.17	29.03	84.45	m³	**113.47**
thickness 150 mm - 450 mm	69.60	1.53	20.46	84.45	m³	**104.91**
Reinforced in situ ready mixed designated concrete; C20 - 20 mm aggregate						
Roads; to hardcore base						
thickness not exceeding 150 mm	71.60	2.17	29.03	86.88	m³	**115.90**
thicness 150 mm - 450 mm	71.60	1.53	20.46	86.88	m³	**107.34**
Reinforced in situ ready mixed designated concrete; C25 - 20 mm aggregate						
Roads; to hardcore base						
thickness not exceeding 150 mm	72.05	2.17	29.03	87.43	m³	**116.45**
thickness 150 mm - 450 mm	72.05	1.53	20.46	87.43	m³	**107.89**

Q PAVING/PLANTING/FENCING/SITE FURNITURE

Item	PC £	Labour hours	Labour £	Material £	Unit	Total rate £
Q21 IN SITU CONCRETE ROADS/PAVINGS – cont'd						
Formwork; sides of foundations; basic finish						
Plain vertical						
height not exceeding 250 mm	-	0.44	7.31	1.51	m	**8.81**
height 250 mm - 500 mm	-	0.66	10.96	2.51	m	**13.47**
height 500 mm - 1.00 m	-	0.95	15.77	4.56	m	**20.34**
add to above for curved radius 6.00 m	-	0.04	0.66	0.20	m	**0.87**
Reinforcement; fabric; BS 4483; lapped; in roads, footpaths or pavings						
Ref A142 (2.22 kg/ m^2)						
400 mm minimum laps	1.08	0.16	2.52	1.34	m^2	**3.86**
Ref A193 (3.02 kg/ m^2)						
400 mm minimum laps	-	0.16	2.52	1.83	m^2	**4.36**
Formed joints; Fosroc Expoandite "Flexcell" impregnated joint filler or other equal and approved						
Width not exceeding 150 mm						
12.50 mm thick	-	0.16	2.66	1.83	m	**4.48**
25 mm thick	-	0.21	3.49	2.76	m	**6.25**
Width 150 - 300 mm						
12.50 mm thick	-	0.21	3.49	2.88	m	**6.36**
25 mm thick	-	0.21	3.49	4.66	m	**8.15**
Width 300 - 450 mm						
12.50 mm thick	-	0.27	4.48	4.31	m	**8.80**
25 mm thick	-	0.27	4.48	6.99	m	**11.47**
Sealants; Fosroc Expandite "Pliastic N2" hot poured rubberized bituminous compound or other equal and approved						
Width 25 mm						
25 mm depth	-	0.22	3.65	1.90	m	**5.55**
Concrete sundries						
Treating surfaces of unset concrete; grading to cambers; tamping with a 75 mm thick steel shod tamper	-	0.27	3.61	-	m^2	**3.61**
Q22 COATED MACADAM/ASPHALT ROADS/ PAVINGS						
NOTE: The prices for all bitumen macadam and hot rolled asphalt materials are for individual courses to roads and footpaths and need combining to arrive at complete specifications and costs for full construction. Intermediate course thicknesses can be interpolated so long as BS 594 and BS 4987 allow the material type to be compacted to the required thickness. Costs include for work to falls, crossfalls or slopes not exceeding 15 degrees from horizontal; for laying on prepared bases (prices not included) and for rolling with an appropriate roller.						

Q PAVING/PLANTING/FENCING/SITE FURNITURE

Item	PC £	Labour hours	Labour £	Material £	Unit	Total rate £
The following rates are based on black bitumen macadam. Red bitumen macadam rates are approximately 50% dearer. PSV is Polished Stone Value.						
Dense BItumen macadam base course; BS 4987 - 1:2003; bitumen penetration 100/125						
Carriageway, hardshoulder and hardstop						
100 mm thick; one coat; with 0/32 mm aggregate size; to clause 5.2	-	-	-	-	m^2	11.20
200 mm thick; one coat; with 0/32 mm aggregate size; to clause 5.2	-	-	-	-	m^2	20.18
Extra over above items for increase / reduction in 10 mm increments	-	-	-	-	m^2	1.00
Hot rolled asphalt base course; BS 594 - 1:2003						
Carriageway, hardshoulder and hardstop						
150 mm thick; one coat; 60% 0/32 mm aggregate size; to column 2/5	-	-	-	-	m^2	17.57
200 mm thick; one coat; 60% 0/32 mm aggregate size; to column 2/5	-	-	-	-	m^2	21.31
Extra over above items for increase / reduction in 10 mm increments	-	-	-	-	m^2	1.00
Dense BItumen macadam binder course; BS 4987 - 1:2003; bitumen penetration 100/125						
Carriageway, hardshoulder and hardstop						
60 mm thick; one coat; with 0/32 mm aggregate size; to clause 6.4	-	-	-	-	m^2	7.67
60 mm thick; one coat; with 0/32 mm aggregate size; to clause 6.5	-	-	-	-	m^2	7.74
Extra over above items for increase / reduction in 10 mm increments	-	-	-	-	m^2	0.86
Hot rolled asphalt binder course; BS 594 - 1:2003						
Carriageway, hardshoulder and hardstop						
40 mm thick; one coat; 50% 0/14 aggregate size; to column 2/2; 55 PSV	-	-	-	-	m^2	7.93
60 mm thick; one coat; 50% 0/14 aggregate size; to column 2/2	-	-	-	-	m^2	8.46
60 mm thick; one coat; 50% 0/20 aggregate size; to column 2/2	-	-	-	-	m^2	8.30
60 mm thick; one coat; 60% 0/32 aggregate size; to column 2/2	-	-	-	-	m^2	7.87
100 mm thick; one coat; 60% 0/32 aggregate size; to column 2/2	-	-	-	-	m^2	12.14
Extra over above items for increase / reduction in 10 mm increments	-	-	-	-	m^2	1.37

Q PAVING/PLANTING/FENCING/SITE FURNITURE

Item	PC £	Labour hours	Labour £	Material £	Unit	Total rate £
Q22 COATED MACADAM/ASPHALT ROADS/ PAVINGS – cont'd						
Macadam surface course; BS 4987 - 1:2003; bitumen penetration 100/125						
Carriageway, hardshoulder and hardstop						
30 mm thick; one coat; medium graded with 0/6 mm nominal aggregate binder; to clause 7.6	-	-	-	-	m^2	5.59
40 mm thick; one coat; close graded with 0/14 mm nominal aggregate binder; to clause 7.3	-	-	-	-	m^2	6.49
40 mm thick; one coat; close graded with 0/10 mm nominal aggregate binder; to clause 7.4	-	-	-	-	m^2	6.49
Extra over above items for increase / reduction in 10 mm increments	-	-	-	-	m^2	1.02
Extra over above items for coarse aggregate 60-64 PSV	-	-	-	-	m^2	1.08
Extra over above items for coarse aggregate 65-67 PSV	-	-	-	-	m^2	1.19
Extra over above for coarse aggregate 68 PSV	-	-	-	-	m^2	1.47
Hot rolled asphalt surface course; BS 594 - 1:2003; bitumen penetration 40/60						
Carriageway, hardshoulder and hardstop						
40 mm thick; one coat; 30% mix 0/10 aggregate size; to column 3/2; with 20 mm pre-coated chippings 60-64 PSV	-	-	-	-	m^2	8.06
40 mm thick; one coat; 30% mix 0/10 aggregate size; to column 3/2; with 14 mm pre-coated chippings 60-64 PSV	-	-	-	-	m^2	8.10
Extra over above items for increase / reduction in 10 mm increments	-	-	-	-	m^2	1.08
Extra over above items for coarse aggregate 65-67 PSV	-	-	-	-	m^2	0.05
Extra over above items for coarse aggregate 68 PSV	-	-	-	-	m^2	0.11
Extra over above items for 6-10KN High Traffic Flows	-	-	-	-	m^2	0.50
Stone mastic asphalt surface course; BS 594 - 1:2003;						
Carriageway, hardshoulder and hardstop						
35 mm thick; one coat; with 0/14 mm nominal aggregate size; 55 PSV	-	-	-	-	m^2	7.08
35 mm thick; one coat; with 0/10 mm nominal aggregate size; 55 PSV	-	-	-	-	m^2	7.08
Extra over above items for increase / reduction in 10 mm increments	-	-	-	-	m^2	1.37
Thin surface course with 60 PSV						
Carriageway, hardshoulder and hardstop						
35 mm thick; one coat; with 0/10 mm nominal aggregate size	-	-	-	-	m^2	7.08
Extra over above items for increase / reduction in 10 mm increments	-	-	-	-	m^2	0.68
Extra over above items for coarse aggregate 60-64 PSV	-	-	-	-	m^2	0.17
Extra over above items for coarse aggregate 65-67 PSV	-	-	-	-	m^2	0.17
Extra over above for coarse aggregate 68 PSV	-	-	-	-	m^2	0.35

Q PAVING/PLANTING/FENCING/SITE FURNITURE

Item	PC £	Labour hours	Labour £	Material £	Unit	Total rate £
Regulating courses						
Carriageway, hardshoulder and hardstop						
Dense Bitumen Macadam; bitumen penetration						
100/125; with 0/20 mm nominal aggregate						
regulating course (BS 4987 - clause 6.5)	-	-	-	-	tonne	64.03
Hot rolled asphalte; 50% 0/20 aggregate size						
(BS 594 - 1:2003 column 2/3)	-	-	-	-	tonne	69.38
Stone mastic asphalte; 0/6 mm aggregate	-	-	-	-	tonne	90.18
Bitumen Emulsion tack coats						
Carriageway, hardshoulder and hardstop						
K1-40; applied 0.35-0.45l/m2	-	-	-	-	m²	0.11
K1-70; applied 0.35-0.45l/m2	-	-	-	-	m²	0.19
Q23 GRAVEL/HOGGIN/WOODCHIP ROADS/ PAVINGS						
Two coat gravel paving; level and to falls; first layer course clinker aggregate and wearing layer fine gravel aggregate						
Pavings; over 300 mm wide						
50 mm thick	-	0.08	1.58	1.92	m²	3.50
63 mm thick	-	0.10	1.97	2.52	m²	4.49
Q25 SLAB/BRICK/BLOCK/SETT/ COBBLE PAVINGS						
Artificial stone paving; Redland Aggregates "Texitone" or other equal and approved; to falls or crossfalls; bedding 25 mm thick in cement mortar (1:3); staggered joints; jointing in coloured cement mortar (1:3), brushed in; to sand base						
Pavings; over 300 mm wide						
450 mm x 600 mm x 50 mm thick; grey or coloured	14.00	0.48	9.46	19.84	m²	29.30
600 mm x 600 mm x 50 mm thick; grey or coloured	12.18	0.44	8.67	17.69	m²	26.36
750 mm x 600 mm x 50 mm thick; grey or coloured	11.36	0.42	8.28	16.72	m²	24.99
900 mm x 600 mm x 50 mm thick; grey or coloured	10.82	0.38	7.49	16.07	m²	23.56
Brick paviors; 215 mm x 103 mm x 65 mm rough stock bricks; PC £340.00/1000; to falls or crossfalls; bedding 10 mm thick in cement mortar (1:3); jointing in cement mortar (1:3); as work proceeds; to concrete base						
Pavings; over 300 mm wide; straight joints both ways						
bricks laid flat	-	0.85	19.40	18.87	m²	38.27
bricks laid on edge	-	1.19	27.16	27.91	m²	55.07
Pavings; over 300 mm wide; laid to herringbone pattern						
bricks laid flat	-	1.06	24.19	18.87	m²	43.06
bricks laid on edge	-	1.49	34.01	27.91	m²	61.91
Add or deduct for variation of £10.00/1000 in PC of brick paviours						
bricks laid flat	-	-	-	0.51	m²	0.51
bricks laid on edge	-	-	-	0.77	m²	0.77

Q PAVING/PLANTING/FENCING/SITE FURNITURE

Item	PC £	Labour hours	Labour £	Material £	Unit	Total rate £
Q25 SLAB/BRICK/BLOCK/SETT/ **COBBLE PAVINGS** – cont'd						
River washed cobble paving; 50 mm - 75 mm; **PC £116.00/tonne; to falls or crossfalls;** **bedding 13 mm thick in cement mortar (1:3);** **jointing to a height of two thirds of cobbles in** **dry mortar (1:3); tightly butted, washed and** **brushed; to concrete**						
Pavings; over 300 mm wide						
regular	-	4.26	83.96	28.93	m²	**112.89**
laid to pattern	-	5.32	104.85	28.93	m²	**133.78**
Concrete paving flags; BS 7263; to falls **or crossfalls; bedding 25 mm thick in** **cement and sand mortar (1:4); butt joints** **straight both ways; jointing in cement** **and sand (1:3); brushed in; to sand base**						
Pavings; over 300 mm wide						
450 mm x 600 mm x 50 mm thick; grey	7.34	0.48	9.46	10.28	m²	**19.74**
450 mm x 600 mm x 60 mm thick; coloured	8.46	0.48	9.46	11.60	m²	**21.06**
600 mm x 600 mm x 50 mm thick; grey	6.29	0.44	8.67	9.03	m²	**17.70**
600 mm x 600 mm x 50 mm thick; coloured	7.27	0.44	8.67	10.20	m²	**18.87**
750 mm x 600 mm x 50 mm thick; grey	5.91	0.42	8.28	8.58	m²	**16.86**
750 mm x 600 mm x 50 mm thick; coloured	6.81	0.42	8.28	9.65	m²	**17.93**
900 mm x 600 mm x 50 mm thick; grey	5.45	0.38	7.49	8.03	m²	**15.52**
900 mm x 600 mm x 50 mm thick; coloured	6.37	0.38	7.49	9.13	m²	**16.62**
Concrete rectangular paving blocks; to **falls or crossfalls; bedding 50 mm thick** **in dry sharp sand; filling joints with sharp** **sand brushed in; on earth base**						
Pavings; "Keyblock" or other equal and approved; over 300 mm wide; straight joints both ways						
200 mm x 100 mm x 65 mm thick; grey	8.69	0.80	15.77	13.97	m²	**29.74**
200 mm x 100 mm x 65 mm thick; coloured	9.52	0.80	15.77	14.96	m²	**30.72**
200 mm x 100 mm x 80 mm thick; grey	9.48	0.85	16.75	15.22	m²	**31.97**
200 mm x 100 mm x 80 mm thick; coloured	11.03	0.85	16.75	17.05	m²	**33.80**
Pavings; "Keyblock" or other equal and approved; over 300 mm wide; laid to herringbone pattern						
200 mm x 100 mm x 60 mm thick; grey	-	1.00	19.71	13.97	m²	**33.68**
200 mm x 100 mm x 60 mm thick; coloured	-	1.00	19.71	14.96	m²	**34.66**
200 mm x 100 mm x 80 mm thick; grey	-	1.06	20.89	15.22	m²	**36.11**
200 mm x 100 mm x 80 mm thick; coloured	-	1.06	20.89	17.05	m²	**37.94**
Extra for two row boundary edging to herringbone paved areas; 200 wide; including a 150 mm high ready mixed designated concrete C10 - 40 mm aggregate haunching to one side; blocks laid breaking joint						
200 mm x 100 mm x 65 mm; coloured	-	0.32	6.31	2.48	m	**8.79**
200 mm x 100 mm x 80 mm; coloured	-	0.32	6.31	2.60	m	**8.91**
Pavings; "Mount Sorrel" or other equal and approved; over 300 mm wide; straight joints both ways						
200 mm x 100 mm x 60 mm thick; grey	7.87	0.80	15.77	13.00	m²	**28.77**
200 mm x 100 mm x 60 mm thick; coloured	9.06	0.80	15.77	14.42	m²	**30.18**
200 mm x 100 mm x 80 mm thick; grey	9.36	0.85	16.75	15.08	m²	**31.83**
200 mm x 100 mm x 80 mm thick; coloured	10.76	0.85	16.75	16.73	m²	**33.48**

Q PAVING/PLANTING/FENCING/SITE FURNITURE

Item	PC £	Labour hours	Labour £	Material £	Unit	Total rate £
Pavings; "Pedesta" or other equal and approved; over 300 mm wide; straight joints both ways						
200 mm x 100 mm x 60 mm thick; grey	10.80	0.80	15.77	16.47	m²	**32.24**
200 mm x 100 mm x 60 mm thick; coloured	10.80	0.80	15.77	16.47	m²	**32.24**
200 mm x 100 mm x 80 mm thick; grey	13.77	0.85	16.75	20.30	m²	**37.05**
200 mm x 100 mm x 80 mm thick; coloured	13.77	0.85	16.75	20.30	m²	**37.05**
Pavings; "Intersett" or other equal and approved; over 300 mm wide; straight joints both ways						
200 mm x 100 mm x 60 mm thick; grey	10.54	0.80	15.77	16.16	m²	**31.93**
200 mm x 100 mm x 60 mm thick; coloured	11.70	0.80	15.77	17.54	m²	**33.31**
200 mm x 100 mm x 80 mm thick; grey	12.61	0.85	16.75	18.92	m²	**35.67**
200 mm x 100 mm x 80 mm thick; coloured	14.00	0.85	16.75	20.57	m²	**37.32**
Concrete rectangular paving blocks; to falls or crossfalls; 6 mm wide joints; symmetrical layout; bedding in 15 mm semi-dry cement mortar (1:4); jointing and pointing in cement:sand (1:4); on concrete base						
Pavings; "Trafica" or other equal and approved; over 300 mm wide						
400 mm x 400 mm x 65 mm; Standard; natural	10.10	0.51	10.05	13.40	m²	**23.45**
400 mm x 400 mm x 65 mm; Standard; buff	14.55	0.51	10.05	18.67	m²	**28.72**
400 mm x 400 mm x 65 mm; Saxon textured; natural	19.87	0.51	10.05	24.98	m²	**35.03**
400 mm x 400 mm x 65 mm; Saxon textured; buff	23.51	0.51	10.05	29.29	m²	**39.34**
400 mm x 400 mm x 65 mm; Perfecta; natural	23.78	0.51	10.05	29.61	m²	**39.66**
400 mm x 400 mm x 65 mm; Perfecta; buff	28.22	0.51	10.05	34.88	m²	**44.93**
450 mm x 450 mm x 70 mm; Standard; natural	11.62	0.49	9.66	15.20	m²	**24.86**
450 mm x 450 mm x 70 mm; Standard; buff	15.46	0.49	9.66	19.75	m²	**29.41**
450 mm x 450 mm x 70 mm; Saxon textured; natural	19.51	0.49	9.66	24.55	m²	**34.21**
450 mm x 450 mm x 70 mm; Saxon textured; buff	23.14	0.49	9.66	28.85	m²	**38.51**
450 mm x 450 mm x 70 mm; Perfecta; natural	23.35	0.49	9.66	29.10	m²	**38.76**
450 mm x 450 mm x 70 mm; Perfecta; buff	27.51	0.49	9.66	34.03	m²	**43.69**
450 mm x 450 mm x 100 mm; Standard; natural	31.03	0.51	10.05	38.20	m²	**48.25**
450 mm x 450 mm x 100 mm; Standard; buff	38.38	0.51	10.05	46.92	m²	**56.97**
450 mm x 450 mm x 100 mm; Saxon textured; natural	34.97	0.51	10.05	42.87	m²	**52.93**
450 mm x 450 mm x 100 mm; Saxon textured; buff	41.32	0.51	10.05	50.39	m²	**60.44**
450 mm x 450 mm x 100 mm; Perfecta; natural	37.53	0.51	10.05	45.91	m²	**55.96**
450 mm x 450 mm x 100 mm; Perfecta; buff	43.87	0.51	10.05	53.43	m²	**63.48**
York stone slab pavings; to falls or crossfalls; bedding 25 mm thick in cement and sand mortar (1:4); 5 wide joints; jointing in coloured cement mortar (1:3); brushed in; to sand base						
Pavings; over 300 mm wide						
50 mm thick; random rectangular pattern	95.67	0.80	18.26	112.60	m²	**130.86**
600 mm x 600 mm x 50 mm thick	109.01	0.44	10.04	128.03	m²	**138.08**
600 mm x 900 mm x 50 mm thick	115.96	0.38	8.67	136.08	m²	**144.76**

Q PAVING/PLANTING/FENCING/SITE FURNITURE

Item	PC £	Labour hours	Labour £	Material £	Unit	Total rate £
Q25 SLAB/BRICK/BLOCK/SETT/ COBBLE PAVINGS – cont'd						
Granite setts; BS 435; 200 mm x 100 mm x 100 mm; PC £209.00/t; standard "C" dressing; tightly butted to falls or crossfalls; bedding 25 mm thick in cement mortar (1:3); filling joints with dry mortar (1:6); washed and brushed; on concrete base						
Pavings; over 300 mm wide						
straight joints	-	1.70	33.50	68.66	m²	102.16
laid to pattern	-	2.13	41.98	68.66	m²	110.64
Two rows of granite setts as boundary edging; 200 mm wide; including a 150 mm high in situ concrete mix 10.00 N/mm2 - 40 mm aggregate (1:3.6); haunching to one side; blocks laid						
breaking joint	-	0.74	14.58	15.36	m	29.95
Q26 SPECIAL SURFACINGS/PAVINGS FOR SPORT/GENERAL AMENITY						
Sundries						
Line marking						
width not exceeding 300 mm	-	0.05	0.70	0.15	m	0.86
Q30 SEEDING/TURFING						
Vegetable soil						
Selected from spoil heaps; grading; prepared for turfing or seeding; to general surfaces						
average 75 mm thick	-	0.23	2.63	-	m²	2.63
average 100 mm thick	-	0.25	2.86	-	m²	2.86
average 125 mm thick	-	0.27	3.09	-	m²	3.09
average 150 mm thick	-	0.29	3.32	-	m²	3.32
average 175 mm thick	-	0.30	3.43	-	m²	3.43
average 200 mm thick	-	0.31	3.55	-	m²	3.55
Ditto; to cuttings or embankments						
average 75 mm thick	-	0.27	3.09	-	m²	3.09
average 100 mm thick	-	0.29	3.32	-	m²	3.32
average 125 mm thick	-	0.30	3.43	-	m²	3.43
average 150 mm thick	-	0.31	3.55	-	m²	3.55
average 175 mm thick	-	0.33	3.78	-	m²	3.78
average 200 mm thick	-	0.36	4.12	-	m²	4.12
Imported vegetable soil						
Grading; prepared for turfing or seeding; to general surfaces						
average 75 mm thick	-	0.21	2.40	0.98	m²	3.39
average 100 mm thick	-	0.23	2.63	1.28	m²	3.91
average 125 mm thick	-	0.24	2.75	1.87	m²	4.61
average 150 mm thick	-	0.26	2.98	2.46	m²	5.43
average 175 mm thick	-	0.27	3.09	2.75	m²	5.84
average 200 mm thick	-	0.29	3.32	3.05	m²	6.37
Ditto; to cuttings or embankments						
average 75 mm thick	-	0.23	2.63	0.98	m²	3.61
average 100 mm thick	-	0.26	2.98	1.28	m²	4.25
average 125 mm thick	-	0.27	3.09	1.87	m²	4.96
average 150 mm thick	-	0.29	3.32	2.46	m²	5.78
average 175 mm thick	-	0.30	3.43	2.75	m²	6.18
average 200 mm thick	-	0.31	3.55	3.05	m²	6.59

Q PAVING/PLANTING/FENCING/SITE FURNITURE

Item	PC £	Labour hours	Labour £	Material £	Unit	Total rate £
Fertilizer; PC £9.56/25kg						
Fertilizer 0.07 kg/m2; raking in						
general surfaces	-	0.03	0.34	0.03	m^2	0.37
Selected grass seed; PC £84.26/25 kg						
Grass seed; sowing at a rate of 0.042 kg/m2 two applications; raking in						
general surfaces	-	0.07	0.80	0.32	m^2	1.12
cuttings or embankments	-	0.08	0.92	0.32	m^2	1.24
Preserved turf from stack on site						
Turfing						
general surfaces	-	0.20	2.29	-	m^2	2.29
cuttings or embankments; shallow	-	0.22	2.52	-	m^2	2.52
cuttings or embankments; steep; pegged	-	0.31	3.55	-	m^2	3.55
Imported turf; selected meadow turf						
Turfing						
general surfaces	1.75	0.20	2.29	1.97	m^2	4.26
cuttings or embankments; shallow	1.75	0.22	2.52	1.97	m^2	4.49
cuttings or embankments; steep; pegged	1.75	0.31	3.55	1.97	m^2	5.52
Q31 PLANTING						
Planting only						
Hedge plants						
height not exceeding 750 mm	-	0.26	2.98	-	nr	2.98
height 750 mm - 1.50 m	-	0.61	6.98	-	nr	6.98
Saplings						
height not exceeding 3.00 m	-	1.73	19.80	-	nr	19.80
Q40 FENCING						
NOTE: The prices for all fencing include for setting posts in position, to a depth of 0.60 m for fences not exceeding 1.40 m high and of 0.76 m for fences over 1.40 m high. The prices allow for excavating post holes; filling to within 150 mm of ground level with concrete and all necessary backfilling.						
Strained wire fences; BS 1722 Part 3; 4 mm diameter galvanized mild steel plain wire threaded through posts and strained with eye bolts						
Fencing; height 900 mm; three line; concrete posts at 2750 mm centres	-	-	-	-	m	17.85
Extra for						
end concrete straining post; one strut	-	-	-	-	nr	43.40
angle concrete straining post; two struts	-	-	-	-	nr	50.41
Fencing; height 1.07 m; six line; concrete posts at 2750 mm centres	-	-	-	-	m	18.57
Extra for						
end concrete straining post; one strut	-	-	-	-	nr	48.81
angle concrete straining post; two struts	-	-	-	-	nr	55.81

Q PAVING/PLANTING/FENCING/SITE FURNITURE

Item	PC £	Labour hours	Labour £	Material £	Unit	Total rate £
Q40 FENCING – cont'd						
Strained wire fencing; BS 1722 Part 3 – cont'd						
Fencing; height 1.20 m; six line; concrete posts at 2750 mm centres	-	-	-	-	m	18.68
Extra for						
end concrete straining post; one strut	-	-	-	-	nr	50.18
angle concrete straining post; two struts	-	-	-	-	nr	57.17
Fencing; height 1.40 m; eight line; concrete posts at 2750 mm centres	-	-	-	-	m	19.20
Extra for						
end concrete straining post; one strut	-	-	-	-	nr	51.27
angle concrete straining post; two struts	-	-	-	-	nr	58.26
Chain link fencing; BS 1722 Part 1; 3 mm diameter galvanized mild steel wire; 50 mm mesh; galvanized mild steel tying and line wire; three line wires threaded through posts and strained with eye bolts and winding brackets						
Fencing; height 900 mm; galvanized mild steel angle posts at 3.00 m centres	-	-	-	-	m	25.10
Extra for						
end steel straining post; one strut	-	-	-	-	nr	72.35
angle steel straining post; two struts	-	-	-	-	nr	83.45
Fencing; height 900 mm; concrete posts at 3.00 m centres	-	-	-	-	m	18.19
Extra for						
end concrete straining post; one strut	-	-	-	-	nr	38.87
angle concrete straining post; two struts	-	-	-	-	nr	45.87
Fencing; height 1.20 m; galvanized mild steel angle posts at 3.00 m centres	-	-	-	-	m	18.51
Extra for						
end steel straining post; one strut	-	-	-	-	nr	77.20
angle steel straining post; two struts	-	-	-	-	nr	98.87
Fencing; height 1.20 m; concrete posts at 3.00 m centres	-	-	-	-	m	17.74
Extra for						
end concrete straining post; one strut	-	-	-	-	nr	44.48
angle concrete straining post; two struts	-	-	-	-	nr	52.55
Fencing; height 1.80 m; galvanized mild steel angle posts at 3.00 m centres	-	-	-	-	m	20.82
Extra for						
end steel straining post; one strut	-	-	-	-	nr	78.53
angle steel straining post; two struts	-	-	-	-	nr	97.68
Fencing; height 1.80 m; concrete posts at 3.00 m centres	-	-	-	-	m	24.04
Extra for						
end concrete straining post; one strut	-	-	-	-	nr	62.21
angle concrete straining post; two struts	-	-	-	-	nr	73.39
Pair of gates and gate posts; gates to match galvanized chain link fencing, with angle framing, braces, etc., complete with hinges, locking bar, lock and bolts; two 100 mm x 100 mm angle section gate posts; each with one strut						
2.44 m x 0.90 m	-	-	-	-	nr	610.12
2.44 m x 1.20 m	-	-	-	-	nr	629.66
2.44 m x 1.80 m	-	-	-	-	nr	679.23

Q PAVING/PLANTING/FENCING/SITE FURNITURE

Item	PC £	Labour hours	Labour £	Material £	Unit	Total rate £
Chain link fencing; BS 1722 Part 1; 3 mm diameter plastic coated mild steel wire; 50 mm mesh; plastic coated mild steel tying and line wire; three line wires threaded through posts and strained with eye bolts and winding brackets						
Fencing; height 900 mm; galvanized mild steel angle posts at 3.00 m centres	-	-	-	-	m	23.02
Extra for						
end steel straining post; one strut	-	-	-	-	nr	63.80
angle steel straining post; two struts	-	-	-	-	nr	71.02
Fencing; height 900 mm; concrete posts at 3.00 m centres	-	-	-	-	m	17.17
Extra for						
end concrete straining post; one strut	-	-	-	-	nr	38.87
angle concrete straining post; two struts	-	-	-	-	nr	45.87
Fencing; height 1.20 m; galvanized mild steel angle posts at 3.00 m centres	-	-	-	-	m	17.00
Extra for						
end steel straining post; one strut	-	-	-	-	nr	66.92
angle steel straining post; two struts	-	-	-	-	nr	71.49
Fencing; height 1.20 m; concrete posts at 3.00 m centres	-	-	-	-	m	17.40
Extra for						
end concrete straining post; one strut	-	-	-	-	nr	44.48
angle concrete straining post; two struts	-	-	-	-	nr	52.55
Fencing; height 1.80 m; galvanized mild steel angle posts at 3.00 m centres	-	-	-	-	m	19.28
Extra for						
end steel straining post; one strut	-	-	-	-	nr	66.24
angle steel straining post; two struts	-	-	-	-	nr	79.11
Fencing; height 1.80 m; concrete posts at 3.00 m centres	-	-	-	-	m	22.17
Extra for						
end concrete straining post; one strut	-	-	-	-	nr	62.21
angle concrete straining post; two struts	-	-	-	-	nr	73.39
Pair of gates and gate posts; gates to match plastic chain link fencing; with angle framing, braces, etc. complete with hinges, locking bar, lock and bolts; two 100 mm x 100 mm angle section gate posts; each with one strut						
2.44 m x 0.90 m	-	-	-	-	nr	533.49
2.44 m x 1.20 m	-	-	-	-	nr	547.40
2.44 m x 1.80 m	-	-	-	-	nr	589.57
Chain link fencing for tennis courts; BS 1722 Part 13; 2.50 mm diameter galvanised mild wire; 45 mm mesh; line and tying wires threaded through 45 mm x 45 mm x 5 mm galvanised mild steel angle standards, posts and struts; 60 mm x 60 mm x 6 mm straining posts and gate posts; straining posts and struts strained with eye bolts and winding brackets						
Fencing to tennis court 36.00 m x 18.00 m; including gate 1.07 mm x 1.98 m complete with hinges, locking bar, lock and bolts						
height 2745 mm; standards at 3.00 m centres	-	-	-	-	nr	2627.94
height 3660 mm; standards at 2.50 m centres	-	-	-	-	nr	3555.77

Q PAVING/PLANTING/FENCING/SITE FURNITURE

Item	PC £	Labour hours	Labour £	Material £	Unit	Total rate £
Q40 FENCING – cont'd						
Cleft chestnut pale fencing; BS 1722						
Part 4; pales spaced 51 mm apart; on two						
lines of galvanized wire; 64 mm diameter						
posts; 76 mm x 51 mm struts						
Fencing; height 900 mm; posts at 2.50 m centres	-	-	-	-	m	10.35
Extra for						
straining post; one strut	-	-	-	-	nr	27.59
corner straining post; two struts	-	-	-	-	nr	27.59
Fencing; height 1.05 m; posts at 2.50 m centres	-	-	-	-	m	11.73
Extra for						
straining post; one strut	-	-	-	-	nr	27.96
corner straining post; two struts	-	-	-	-	nr	27.96
Close boarded fencing; BS 1722 Part 5;						
76 mm x 38 mm softwood rails; 89 mm x						
19 mm softwood pales lapped 13 mm;						
152 mm x 25 mm softwood gravel						
boards; all softwood "treated"; posts at						
3.00 m centres						
Fencing; two rail; concrete posts						
1.00 m	-	-	-	-	m	31.84
1.20 m	-	-	-	-	m	32.13
Fencing; three rail; concrete posts						
1.40 m	-	-	-	-	m	35.34
1.60 m	-	-	-	-	m	35.42
1.80 m	-	-	-	-	m	36.78
Precast concrete slab fencing; 305 mm x						
38 mm x 1753 mm slabs; fitted into twice						
grooved concrete posts at 1830 mm						
centres						
Fencing						
height 1.50 m	-	-	-	-	m	62.40
height 1.80 m	-	-	-	-	m	69.11
Mild steel unclimbable fencing; in						
rivetted panels 2440 mm long; 44 mm x						
13 mm flat section top and bottom rails;						
two 44 mm x 19 mm flat section						
standards; one with foot plate, and 38						
mm x 13 mm raking stay with foot plate;						
20 mm diameter pointed verticals at 120						
mm centres; two 44 mm x 19 mm						
supports 760 mm long with ragged ends						
to bottom rail; the whole bolted together;						
coated with red oxide primer; setting						
standards and stays in ground at 2440						
mm centres and supports at 815 mm						
centres						
Fencing						
height 1.67 m	-	-	-	-	m	139.29
height 2.13 m	-	-	-	-	m	159.19

Q PAVING/PLANTING/FENCING/SITE FURNITURE

Item	PC £	Labour hours	Labour £	Material £	Unit	Total rate £
Pair of gates and gate posts, to match mild steel unclimbable fencing; with flat section framing, braces, etc., complete with locking bar, lock, handles, drop bolt, gate stop and holding back catches; two 102 mm x 102 mm hollow section gate posts with cap and foot plates						
2.44 m x 1.67 m	-	-	-	-	nr	1225.50
2.44 m x 2.13 m	-	-	-	-	nr	1433.97
4.88 m x 1.67 m	-	-	-	-	nr	1895.11
4.88 m x 2.13 m	-	-	-	-	nr	2400.47
PVC coated, galvanised mild steel high security fencing; "Sentinel Sterling fencing" or other equal and approved; Twil Wire Products Ltd; 50 mm x 50 mm mesh; 3 mm/3.50 mm gauge wire; barbed edge - 1; "Sentinal Bi-steel" colour coated posts at 2440 mm centres						
Fencing						
height 1.80 m	-	1.02	11.67	38.44	m	**50.12**
height 2.10 m	-	1.02	11.67	42.46	m	**54.13**

R DISPOSAL SYSTEMS

Item	PC £	Labour hours	Labour £	Material £	Unit	Total rate £
R10 RAINWATER PIPEWORK/GUTTERS						
Aluminium pipes and fittings; BS 2997; ears cast on; polyester powder coated finish						
63 mm diameter pipes; plugged and screwed	11.65	0.41	6.84	14.60	m	21.44
Extra for						
fittings with one end	-	0.24	4.01	7.57	nr	11.57
fittings with two ends	-	0.46	7.68	7.82	nr	15.50
fittings with three ends	-	0.67	11.19	10.36	nr	21.55
shoe	7.13	0.24	4.01	7.57	nr	11.57
bend	7.61	0.46	7.68	7.82	nr	15.50
single branch	9.92	0.67	11.19	10.36	nr	21.55
offset 228 mm projection	17.54	0.46	8.41	18.37	nr	26.78
offset 304 mm projection	19.57	0.46	7.68	20.71	nr	28.39
access pipe	21.67	-	-	21.68	nr	21.68
connection to clay pipes; cement and sand (1:2) joint	-	0.17	2.84	0.12	nr	2.96
76.50 mm diameter pipes; plugged and screwed	13.57	0.44	7.35	16.88	m	24.23
Extra for						
shoe	9.79	0.28	4.67	10.47	nr	15.15
bend	9.61	0.50	8.35	9.98	nr	18.33
single branch	11.95	0.72	12.02	12.48	nr	24.50
offset 228 mm projection	19.40	0.50	8.35	20.14	nr	28.49
offset 304 mm projection	21.58	0.50	8.35	22.67	nr	31.01
access pipe	23.68	-	-	23.45	nr	23.45
connection to clay pipes; cement and sand (1:2) joint	-	0.19	3.17	0.12	nr	3.29
100 mm diameter pipes; plugged and screwed	23.17	0.50	8.35	28.28	m	36.62
Extra for						
shoe	11.79	0.32	5.34	11.91	nr	17.25
bend	13.39	0.56	9.35	13.49	nr	22.84
single branch	16.00	0.83	13.86	15.88	nr	29.73
offset 228 mm projection	22.44	0.56	9.35	21.40	nr	30.75
offset 304 mm projection	24.91	0.56	9.35	24.26	nr	33.61
access pipe	28.07	-	-	25.71	nr	25.71
connection to clay pipes; cement and sand (1:2) joint	-	0.22	3.67	0.12	nr	3.79
Roof outlets; circular aluminium; with flat or domed grating; joint to pipe						
50 mm diameter	64.67	0.67	18.45	73.00	nr	91.45
75 mm diameter	84.76	0.72	19.83	95.67	nr	115.50
100 mm diameter	110.37	0.78	21.48	124.58	nr	146.06
150 mm diameter	141.40	0.83	22.86	159.61	nr	182.47
Roof outlets; d-shaped; balcony; with flat or domed grating; joint to pipe						
50 mm diameter	76.59	0.67	18.45	86.45	nr	104.90
75 mm diameter	88.05	0.72	19.83	99.39	nr	119.22
100 mm diameter	108.15	0.78	21.48	122.07	nr	143.56
Galvanized wire balloon grating; BS 416 for pipes or outlets						
50 mm diameter	1.84	0.07	1.93	2.07	nr	4.00
63 mm diameter	1.86	0.07	1.93	2.10	nr	4.03
75 mm diameter	1.98	0.07	1.93	2.23	nr	4.16
100 mm diameter	2.19	0.09	2.48	2.47	nr	4.95

R DISPOSAL SYSTEMS

Item	PC £	Labour hours	Labour £	Material £	Unit	Total rate £
Aluminium gutters and fittings; BS 2997; polyester powder coated finish						
100 mm half round gutters; on brackets; screwed to timber	10.69	0.39	7.13	15.95	m	**23.08**
Extra for						
stop end	2.90	0.18	3.29	6.46	nr	**9.75**
running outlet	6.42	0.37	6.76	7.37	nr	**14.13**
stop end outlet	5.71	0.18	3.29	8.70	nr	**11.99**
angle	5.93	0.37	6.76	5.71	nr	**12.47**
113 mm half round gutters; on brackets; screwed to timber	11.20	0.39	7.13	16.58	m	**23.71**
Extra for						
stop end	3.04	0.18	3.29	6.65	nr	**9.94**
running outlet	7.00	0.37	6.76	7.99	nr	**14.76**
stop end outlet	6.55	0.18	3.29	9.63	nr	**12.92**
angle	6.69	0.37	6.76	6.44	nr	**13.20**
125 mm half round gutters; on brackets; screwed to timber	12.58	0.44	8.04	19.89	m	**27.94**
Extra for						
stop end	3.71	0.20	3.65	8.95	nr	**12.60**
running outlet	7.57	0.39	7.13	8.53	nr	**15.66**
stop end outlet	6.96	0.20	3.65	11.51	nr	**15.16**
angle	7.42	0.39	7.13	8.50	nr	**15.63**
100 mm ogee gutters; on brackets; screwed to timber	13.33	0.41	7.49	20.40	m	**27.89**
Extra for						
stop end	3.06	0.19	3.47	4.24	nr	**7.72**
running outlet	7.53	0.39	7.13	7.80	nr	**14.93**
stop end outlet	5.84	0.19	3.47	9.73	nr	**13.21**
angle	6.34	0.39	7.13	5.05	nr	**12.18**
112 mm ogee gutters; on brackets; screwed to timber	14.83	0.46	8.41	22.46	m	**30.86**
Extra for						
stop end	3.27	0.19	3.47	4.50	nr	**7.97**
running outlet	7.62	0.39	7.13	7.76	nr	**14.89**
stop end outlet	6.54	0.19	3.47	10.65	nr	**14.12**
angle	7.56	0.39	7.13	6.17	nr	**13.29**
125 mm ogee gutters; on brackets; screwed to timber	16.38	0.46	8.41	24.68	m	**33.09**
Extra for						
stop end	3.58	0.21	3.84	4.86	nr	**8.70**
running outlet	8.33	0.41	7.49	8.45	nr	**15.94**
stop end outlet	7.42	0.21	3.84	11.89	nr	**15.72**
angle	8.82	0.41	7.49	7.33	nr	**14.82**
Cast iron pipes and fittings; EN 1462; ears cast on; joints						
65 mm pipes; primed; nailed to masonry	19.54	0.57	9.52	23.57	m	**33.09**
Extra for						
shoe	17.14	0.35	5.84	18.34	nr	**24.18**
bend	10.49	0.63	10.52	10.65	nr	**21.17**
single branch	20.63	0.80	13.36	21.66	nr	**35.01**
offset 225 mm projection	18.70	0.63	10.52	18.76	nr	**29.28**
offset 305 mm projection	21.90	0.63	10.52	21.99	nr	**32.51**
connection to clay pipes; cement and sand (1:2) joint	-	0.17	2.84	0.13	nr	**2.97**

R DISPOSAL SYSTEMS

Item	PC £	Labour hours	Labour £	Material £	Unit	Total rate £
R10 RAINWATER PIPEWORK/GUTTERS						
– cont'd						
Cast iron pipes and fittings; EN 1462;						
ears cast on; joints – cont'd						
75 mm pipes; primed; nailed to masonry	19.54	0.61	10.18	23.81	m	33.99
Extra for						
shoe	17.14	0.39	6.51	18.42	nr	24.93
bend	12.73	1.33	23.17	13.33	nr	36.49
single branch	22.31	0.83	13.86	23.76	nr	37.62
offset 225 mm projection	18.70	0.67	11.19	18.84	nr	30.03
offset 305 mm projection	22.99	0.67	11.19	23.33	nr	34.52
connection to clay pipes; cement and sand (1:2)						
joint	-	0.19	3.17	0.13	nr	3.31
100 mm pipes; primed; nailed to masonry	26.23	0.67	11.19	32.01	m	43.20
Extra for						
shoe	22.76	0.44	7.35	24.45	nr	31.79
bend	17.99	0.72	12.02	18.93	nr	30.95
single branch	26.50	0.89	14.86	27.97	nr	42.83
offset 225 mm projection	36.70	0.72	12.02	38.71	nr	50.73
offset 305 mm projection	37.41	0.72	12.02	38.91	nr	50.93
connection to clay pipes; cement and sand (1:2)						
joint	-	0.22	3.67	0.12	nr	3.79
100 mm x 75 mm rectangular pipes; primed;						
nailing to masonry	75.78	0.67	11.19	90.75	m	101.93
Extra for						
shoe	64.21	0.44	7.35	67.70	nr	75.04
bend	61.13	0.72	12.02	64.14	nr	76.16
offset 225 mm projection	86.09	0.44	7.35	87.63	nr	94.98
offset 305 mm projection	92.02	0.44	7.35	92.69	nr	100.03
connection to clay pipes; cement and sand (1:2)						
joint	-	0.22	3.67	0.12	nr	3.79
Rainwater head; rectangular; for pipes						
65 mm diameter	27.79	0.63	10.52	32.52	nr	43.04
75 mm diameter	27.79	0.67	11.19	32.60	nr	43.78
100 mm diameter	38.38	0.72	12.02	45.00	nr	57.02
Rainwater head; octagonal; for pipes						
65 mm diameter	15.88	0.63	10.52	18.74	nr	29.26
75 mm diameter	18.05	0.67	11.19	21.33	nr	32.52
100 mm diameter	40.00	0.72	12.02	46.87	nr	58.89
Copper wire balloon grating; BS 416 for pipes or						
outlets						
50 mm diameter	2.24	0.07	1.17	2.53	nr	3.69
63 mm diameter	2.26	0.07	1.17	2.55	nr	3.72
75 mm diameter	2.55	0.07	1.17	2.88	nr	4.05
100 mm diameter	2.90	0.09	1.50	3.27	nr	4.78
Cast iron gutters and fittings; EN 1462						
100 mm half round gutters; primed; on brackets;						
screwed to timber	10.04	0.44	8.04	15.19	m	23.23
Extra for						
stop end	2.53	0.19	3.47	4.45	nr	7.92
running outlet	7.33	0.39	7.13	7.52	nr	14.64
angle	7.52	0.39	7.13	9.31	nr	16.44
115 mm half round gutters; primed; on brackets;						
screwed to timber	10.46	0.44	8.04	15.73	m	23.77
Extra for						
stop end	3.28	0.19	3.47	5.29	nr	8.76
running outlet	7.99	0.39	7.13	8.23	nr	15.36
angle	7.75	0.39	7.13	9.49	nr	16.61

R DISPOSAL SYSTEMS

Item	PC £	Labour hours	Labour £	Material £	Unit	Total rate £
125 mm half round gutters; primed; on brackets; screwed to timber	12.24	0.50	9.14	17.84	m	26.98
Extra for						
stop end	3.28	0.22	4.02	5.30	nr	9.32
running outlet	9.13	0.44	8.04	9.36	nr	17.40
angle	9.13	0.44	8.04	10.70	nr	18.74
150 mm half round gutters; primed; on brackets; screwed to timber	20.91	0.56	10.23	27.71	m	37.95
Extra for						
stop end	4.54	0.24	4.39	8.66	nr	13.04
running outlet	15.81	0.50	9.14	16.17	nr	25.31
angle	16.69	0.50	9.14	18.35	nr	27.49
100 mm ogee gutters; primed; on brackets; screwed to timber	11.19	0.46	8.41	16.77	m	25.18
Extra for						
stop end	2.58	0.20	3.65	5.98	nr	9.64
running outlet	8.00	0.41	7.49	8.18	nr	15.67
angle	7.86	0.41	7.49	9.68	nr	17.17
115 mm ogee gutters; primed; on brackets; screwed to timber	12.31	0.46	8.41	18.13	m	26.54
Extra for						
stop end	3.35	0.20	3.65	6.85	nr	10.50
running outlet	8.51	0.41	7.49	8.65	nr	16.14
angle	8.51	0.41	7.49	10.20	nr	17.69
125 mm ogee gutters; primed; on brackets; screwed to timber	12.91	0.52	9.50	19.24	m	28.75
Extra for						
stop end	3.35	0.23	4.20	7.21	nr	11.42
running outlet	9.30	0.46	8.41	9.48	nr	17.89
angle	9.30	0.46	8.41	11.33	nr	19.73
3 mm thick galvanised heavy pressed steel gutters and fittings; joggle joints; BS 1091						
200 mm x 100 mm (400 mm girth) box gutter; screwed to timber	-	0.72	12.02	24.15	m	36.17
Extra for						
stop end	-	0.39	6.51	13.43	nr	19.94
running outlet	-	0.78	13.02	22.26	nr	35.28
stop end outlet	-	0.39	6.51	31.12	nr	37.63
angle	-	0.78	13.02	24.71	nr	37.73
381 mm boundary wall gutters; 900 mm girth; screwed to timber	-	0.72	12.02	39.69	m	51.71
Extra for						
stop end	-	0.44	7.35	22.88	nr	30.23
running outlet	-	0.78	13.02	30.63	nr	43.65
stop end outlet	-	0.39	6.51	43.13	nr	49.64
angle	-	0.78	13.02	35.84	nr	48.86
457 mm boundary wall gutters; 1200 mm girth; screwed to timber	-	0.83	13.86	52.95	m	66.80
Extra for						
stop end	-	0.44	7.35	29.37	nr	36.71
running outlet	-	0.89	14.86	44.28	nr	59.14
stop end outlet	-	0.44	7.35	47.10	nr	54.44
angle	-	0.89	14.86	48.44	nr	63.30

R DISPOSAL SYSTEMS

Item	PC £	Labour hours	Labour £	Material £	Unit	Total rate £
R10 RAINWATER PIPEWORK/GUTTERS – cont'd						
uPVC external rainwater pipes and fittings; BS 4576; slip-in joints						
50 mm pipes; fixing with pipe or socket brackets; plugged and screwed	4.98	0.33	5.51	7.93	m	13.44
Extra for						
shoe	2.94	0.22	3.67	4.22	nr	7.89
bend	3.44	0.33	5.51	4.79	nr	10.30
two bends to form offset 229 mm projection	6.88	0.33	5.51	7.77	nr	13.28
connection to clay pipes; cement and sand (1:2) joint	-	0.15	2.50	0.14	nr	2.64
68 mm pipes; fixing with pipe or socket brackets; plugged and screwed	3.85	0.37	6.18	6.96	m	13.14
Extra for						
shoe	2.94	0.24	4.01	4.58	nr	8.59
bend	4.50	0.37	6.18	6.38	nr	12.56
single branch	9.06	0.49	8.18	11.66	nr	19.84
two bends to form offset 229 mm projection	9.01	0.37	6.18	10.82	nr	17.00
loose drain connector; cement and sand joint	-	0.17	2.84	12.31	nr	15.15
110 mm pipes; fixing with pipe or socket brackets; plugged and screwed	8.03	0.40	6.68	14.52	m	21.20
Extra for						
shoe	9.41	0.27	4.51	12.27	nr	16.78
bend	13.95	0.40	6.68	17.53	nr	24.20
single branch	20.64	0.54	9.01	25.26	nr	34.28
two bends to form offset 229 mm projection	27.90	0.40	6.68	32.34	nr	39.01
loose drain connector; cement and sand (1:2) joint	-	0.39	6.51	10.20	nr	16.71
65 mm square pipes; fixing with pipe or socket brackets; plugged and screwed	3.87	0.37	6.18	6.98	m	13.16
Extra for						
shoe	2.94	0.24	4.01	4.58	nr	8.59
bend	4.50	0.37	6.18	6.38	nr	12.56
single branch	9.06	0.49	8.18	11.66	nr	19.84
two bends to form offset 229 mm projection	9.01	0.37	6.18	11.04	nr	17.22
drain connector; square to round; cement and sand (1:2) joint	-	0.39	6.51	5.25	nr	11.76
Rainwater head; rectangular; for pipes						
50 mm diameter	16.02	0.50	8.35	20.27	nr	28.61
68 mm diameter	12.94	0.52	8.68	17.42	nr	26.10
110 mm diameter	26.99	0.61	10.18	34.10	nr	44.29
65 mm square	12.94	0.52	8.68	17.42	nr	26.10
uPVC gutters and fittings; BS 4576						
76 mm half round gutters; on brackets screwed to timber	3.78	0.33	6.03	6.53	m	12.56
Extra for						
stop end	1.35	0.15	2.74	2.06	nr	4.80
running outlet	3.81	0.28	5.12	4.05	nr	9.16
stop end outlet	3.79	0.15	2.74	4.52	nr	7.27
angle	3.81	0.28	5.12	4.97	nr	10.09
112 mm half round gutters; on brackets screwed to timber	3.80	0.37	6.76	8.38	m	15.14
Extra for						
stop end	2.11	0.15	2.74	3.44	nr	6.18
running outlet	4.15	0.32	5.85	4.44	nr	10.29
stop end outlet	4.15	0.15	2.74	5.44	nr	8.18
angle	4.64	0.32	5.85	7.00	nr	12.85

R DISPOSAL SYSTEMS

Item	PC £	Labour hours	Labour £	Material £	Unit	Total rate £
170 mm half round gutters; on brackets; screwed to timber	7.95	0.37	6.76	14.73	m	21.49
Extra for						
stop end	3.58	0.18	3.29	5.60	nr	8.89
running outlet	7.97	0.34	6.21	8.46	nr	14.68
stop end outlet	7.57	0.18	3.29	9.46	nr	12.75
angle	10.38	0.34	6.21	14.18	nr	20.39
114 mm rectangular gutters; on brackets; screwed to timber	3.90	0.37	6.76	8.21	m	14.98
Extra for						
stop end	2.11	0.15	2.74	3.21	nr	5.96
running outlet	4.15	0.34	6.21	4.44	nr	10.66
stop end outlet	4.15	0.15	2.74	5.21	nr	7.95
angle	4.64	0.32	5.85	6.55	nr	12.40
R11 FOUL DRAINAGE ABOVE GROUND						
Cast iron "Timesaver" pipes and fittings or other equal and approved; BS 416						
50 mm pipes; primed; 2.00 m lengths; fixing with expanding bolts; to masonry	12.88	0.61	10.18	24.90	m	35.09
Extra for						
fittings with two ends	-	0.61	10.18	19.01	nr	29.20
fittings with three ends	-	0.83	13.86	32.22	nr	46.08
bends; short radius	11.74	0.61	10.18	19.01	nr	29.20
access bends; short radius	28.94	0.61	10.18	38.91	nr	49.10
boss; 38 BSP	24.33	0.66	11.02	33.19	nr	44.21
single branch	17.68	0.83	13.86	32.91	nr	46.76
access pipe	26.78	0.61	10.18	34.74	nr	44.92
roof connector; for asphalt	29.08	0.61	10.18	39.30	nr	49.48
isolated "Timesaver" coupling joint	6.67	0.33	5.51	7.72	nr	13.22
connection to clay pipes; cement and sand (1:2) joint	-	0.15	2.50	0.12	nr	2.62
75 mm pipes; primed; 3.00 m lengths; fixing with standard brackets; plugged and screwed to masonry	14.41	0.61	10.18	26.90	m	37.08
Extra for						
bends; short radius	11.74	0.67	11.19	19.54	nr	30.73
access bends; short radius	28.94	0.61	10.18	39.44	nr	49.63
boss; 38 BSP	24.33	0.67	11.19	34.10	nr	45.29
single branch	17.68	0.94	15.69	33.98	nr	49.68
double branch	29.71	1.22	20.37	56.42	nr	76.79
offset 115 mm projection	17.33	0.67	11.19	24.05	nr	35.23
offset 150 mm projection	16.54	0.67	11.19	22.62	nr	33.80
access pipe	28.26	0.67	11.19	36.43	nr	47.62
roof connector; for asphalt	33.10	0.67	11.19	44.08	nr	55.27
isolated "Timesaver" coupling joint	7.36	0.39	6.51	8.52	nr	15.03
connection to clay pipes; cement and sand (1:2) joint	-	0.17	2.84	0.12	nr	2.96
100 mm pipes; primed; 3.00 m lengths; fixing with standard brackets; plugged and screwed to masonry	17.41	0.67	11.19	37.67	m	48.85
Extra for						
WC bent connector; 450 mm long tail	26.04	0.67	11.19	33.92	nr	45.10
bends; short radius	16.26	0.74	12.35	26.84	nr	39.19
access bends; short radius	34.40	0.74	12.35	47.82	nr	60.18
boss; 38 BSP	29.05	0.74	12.35	41.64	nr	53.99
single branch	25.13	1.11	18.53	46.46	nr	64.99
double branch	31.09	1.44	24.04	64.48	nr	88.52

R DISPOSAL SYSTEMS

Item	PC £	Labour hours	Labour £	Material £	Unit	Total rate £
R11 FOUL DRAINAGE ABOVE GROUND – cont'd						
100 mm cast iron "Timesaver" pipes – cont'd						
Extra for						
offset 225 mm projection	24.48	0.74	12.35	33.66	nr	46.02
offset 300 mm projection	26.34	0.74	12.35	35.20	nr	47.55
access pipe	29.71	0.74	12.35	39.30	nr	51.65
roof connector; for asphalt	28.08	0.74	12.35	39.79	nr	52.14
roof connector; for roofing felt	77.61	0.74	12.35	97.09	nr	109.44
isolated "Timesaver" coupling joint	9.61	0.46	7.68	11.12	nr	18.80
transitional clayware socket; cement and sand (1:2) joint	19.13	0.44	7.35	33.37	nr	40.71
150 mm pipes; primed; 3.00 m lengths; fixing with standard brackets; plugged and screwed to masonry	36.36	0.83	13.86	76.18	m	90.03
Extra for						
bends; short radius	29.05	0.93	15.53	49.37	nr	64.89
access bends; short radius	48.84	0.93	15.53	72.27	nr	87.79
boss; 38 BSP	47.40	0.93	15.53	69.52	nr	85.05
single branch	62.32	1.33	22.20	104.90	nr	127.11
double branch	87.56	1.78	29.72	154.40	nr	184.11
access pipe	49.42	0.93	15.53	64.14	nr	79.67
roof connector; for asphalt	62.09	0.93	15.53	84.15	nr	99.67
isolated "Timesaver" coupling joint	-	0.56	9.35	22.22	nr	31.57
transitional clayware socket; cement and sand (1:2) joint	33.49	0.57	9.52	61.09	nr	70.60
Cast iron "Ensign" lightweight pipes and fittings or other equal and approved; EN 877						
50 mm pipes; primed 3.00 m lengths; fixing with standard brackets; plugged and screwed to masonry	-	0.31	5.25	15.79	m	21.04
Extra for						
bends; short radius	-	0.27	4.58	13.16	nr	17.74
single branch	-	0.33	5.58	23.00	nr	28.58
access pipe	-	0.27	4.58	27.01	nr	31.59
70 mm pipes; primed 3.00 m lengths; fixing with standard brackets; plugged and screwed to masonry	-	0.34	5.73	17.63	m	23.35
Extra for						
bends; short radius	-	0.30	5.06	14.67	nr	19.73
single branch	-	0.37	6.25	24.70	nr	30.95
access pipe	-	0.30	5.06	28.78	nr	33.84
100 mm pipes; primed 3.00 m lengths; fixing with standard brackets; plugged and screwed to masonry	-	0.37	6.25	20.80	m	27.05
Extra for						
bends; short radius	-	0.32	5.44	18.01	nr	23.45
single branch	-	0.39	6.58	33.16	nr	39.74
double branch	-	0.46	7.78	46.58	nr	54.36
access pipe	-	0.32	5.44	32.72	nr	38.16
connector	-	0.21	3.53	30.41	nr	33.94
reducer	-	0.32	5.44	21.97	nr	27.41

R DISPOSAL SYSTEMS

Item	PC £	Labour hours	Labour £	Material £	Unit	Total rate £
Polypropylene (PP) waste pipes and fittings; BS 5254; push fit "O" - ring joints						
32 mm pipes; fixing with pipe clips; plugged and screwed	1.52	0.24	4.01	2.64	m	6.64
Extra for						
fittings with one end	-	0.18	3.00	1.43	nr	4.43
fittings with two ends	-	0.24	4.01	1.49	nr	5.50
fittings with three ends	-	0.33	5.51	2.51	nr	8.02
access plug	1.23	0.18	3.00	1.43	nr	4.43
double socket	0.97	0.17	2.84	1.12	nr	3.96
sweep bend	1.21	0.24	4.01	1.40	nr	5.40
spigot bend	1.62	0.28	4.67	1.88	nr	6.55
40 mm pipes; fixing with pipe clips; plugged and screwed	1.88	0.24	4.01	3.09	m	7.10
Extra for						
fittings with one end	-	0.21	3.51	1.53	nr	5.03
fittings with two ends	-	0.33	5.51	1.76	nr	7.27
fittings with three ends	-	0.44	7.35	2.72	nr	10.07
access plug	1.32	0.21	3.51	1.53	nr	5.03
double socket	0.99	0.22	3.67	1.15	nr	4.82
universal connector	2.59	0.28	4.67	3.00	nr	7.67
sweep bend	1.36	0.33	5.51	1.57	nr	7.08
spigot bend	1.70	0.33	5.51	1.97	nr	7.48
reducer 40 mm - 32 mm	1.20	0.33	5.51	1.39	nr	6.90
50 mm pipes; fixing with pipe clips; plugged and screwed	2.22	0.39	6.51	4.17	m	10.68
Extra for						
fittings with one end	-	0.23	3.84	2.51	nr	6.35
fittings with two ends	-	0.39	6.51	2.86	nr	9.37
fittings with three ends	-	0.52	8.68	3.95	nr	12.63
access plug	2.17	0.23	3.84	2.51	nr	6.35
double socket	1.82	0.26	4.34	2.11	nr	6.45
sweep bend	2.38	0.39	6.51	2.76	nr	9.27
spigot bend	3.45	0.39	6.51	3.99	nr	10.50
reducer 50 mm - 40 mm	1.56	0.39	6.51	1.80	nr	8.32
muPVC waste pipes and fittings; BS 5255; solvent welded joints						
32 mm pipes; fixing with pipe clips; plugged and screwed	1.81	0.28	4.67	3.24	m	7.91
Extra for						
fittings with one end	-	0.19	3.17	1.65	nr	4.82
fittings with two ends	-	0.28	4.67	1.77	nr	6.44
fittings with three ends	-	0.37	6.18	2.35	nr	8.52
access plug	1.10	0.19	3.17	1.65	nr	4.82
straight coupling	1.19	0.19	3.17	1.75	nr	4.92
expansion coupling	2.09	0.28	4.67	2.79	nr	7.46
male iron to muPVC coupling	2.11	0.43	7.18	2.63	nr	9.81
sweep bend	1.21	0.28	4.67	1.77	nr	6.44
spigot/socket bend	-	0.28	4.67	2.66	nr	7.33
sweep tee	1.62	0.37	6.18	2.35	nr	8.52

R DISPOSAL SYSTEMS

Item	PC £	Labour hours	Labour £	Material £	Unit	Total rate £
R11 FOUL DRAINAGE ABOVE GROUND – cont'd						
muPVC waste pipes and fittings – cont'd 40 mm pipes; fixing with pipe clips; plugged and screwed	2.24	0.33	5.51	3.81	m	**9.32**
Extra for						
fittings with one end	-	0.21	3.51	1.65	nr	**5.16**
fittings with two ends	-	0.33	5.51	1.93	nr	**7.44**
fittings with three ends	-	0.44	7.35	2.85	nr	**10.19**
fittings with four ends	4.99	0.59	9.85	6.43	nr	**16.28**
access plug	1.10	0.21	3.51	1.65	nr	**5.16**
straight coupling	1.18	0.22	3.67	1.74	nr	**5.42**
expansion coupling	2.52	0.33	5.51	3.29	nr	**8.80**
male iron to muPVC coupling	2.11	0.43	7.18	2.63	nr	**9.81**
level invert taper	1.48	0.33	5.51	2.09	nr	**7.59**
sweep bend	1.34	0.33	5.51	1.93	nr	**7.44**
spigot/socket bend	2.27	0.33	5.51	3.00	nr	**8.51**
sweep tee	2.06	0.44	7.35	2.85	nr	**10.19**
sweep cross	4.99	0.59	9.85	6.43	nr	**16.28**
50 mm pipes; fixing with pipe clips; plugged and screwed	3.38	0.39	6.51	6.15	m	**12.66**
Extra for						
fittings with one end	-	0.23	3.84	2.21	nr	**6.05**
fittings with two ends	-	0.39	6.51	3.11	nr	**9.62**
fittings with three ends	-	0.52	8.68	5.10	nr	**13.78**
fittings with four ends	-	0.69	11.52	6.71	nr	**18.23**
access plug	1.58	0.23	3.84	2.21	nr	**6.05**
straight coupling	2.17	0.26	4.34	2.88	nr	**7.22**
expansion coupling	3.42	0.39	6.51	4.33	nr	**10.84**
male iron to muPVC coupling	3.05	0.50	8.35	3.71	nr	**12.06**
level invert taper	1.84	0.39	6.51	2.50	nr	**9.01**
sweep bend	2.37	0.39	6.51	3.11	nr	**9.62**
spigot/socket bend	3.22	0.39	6.51	4.10	nr	**10.61**
sweep tee	2.06	0.44	7.35	2.85	nr	**10.19**
sweep cross	5.23	0.69	11.52	6.71	nr	**18.23**
uPVC overflow pipes and fittings; solvent welded joints 19 mm pipes; fixing with pipe clips; plugged and screwed	1.07	0.24	4.01	2.13	m	**6.14**
Extra for						
splay cut end	-	0.02	0.33	-	nr	**0.33**
fittings with one end	-	0.19	3.17	1.50	nr	**4.67**
fittings with two ends	-	0.19	3.17	1.74	nr	**4.91**
fittings with three ends	-	0.24	4.01	1.97	nr	**5.98**
straight connector	1.14	0.19	3.17	1.50	nr	**4.67**
female iron to uPVC coupling	-	0.22	3.67	2.35	nr	**6.02**
bend	1.34	0.19	3.17	1.74	nr	**4.91**
bent tank connector	2.10	0.22	3.67	2.53	nr	**6.20**

R DISPOSAL SYSTEMS

Item	PC £	Labour hours	Labour £	Material £	Unit	Total rate £
uPVC pipes and fittings; BS 4514; with solvent welded joints (unless otherwise described)						
82 mm pipes; fixing with holderbats; plugged and screwed	7.70	0.44	7.35	13.79	m	21.13
Extra for						
socket plug	5.82	0.22	3.67	7.66	nr	11.33
slip coupling; push fit	12.70	0.41	6.84	14.69	nr	21.53
expansion coupling	6.11	0.44	7.35	8.00	nr	15.35
sweep bend	10.26	0.44	7.35	12.80	nr	20.14
boss connector	5.60	0.30	5.01	7.41	nr	12.42
single branch	14.34	0.59	9.85	18.08	nr	27.93
access door	13.65	0.67	11.19	16.26	nr	27.44
110 mm pipes; fixing with holderbats; plugged and screwed	7.84	0.49	8.18	14.25	m	22.43
Extra for						
socket plug	7.05	0.24	4.01	9.37	nr	13.37
slip coupling; push fit	15.90	0.44	7.35	18.39	nr	25.74
expansion coupling	6.24	0.49	8.18	8.43	nr	16.61
W.C. connector	11.35	0.32	5.34	13.79	nr	19.13
sweep bend	12.00	0.49	8.18	15.10	nr	23.28
W.C. connecting bend	18.62	0.32	5.34	22.20	nr	27.54
access bend	33.29	0.51	8.51	39.73	nr	48.24
boss connector	5.60	0.32	5.34	7.69	nr	13.03
single branch	15.87	0.65	10.85	20.23	nr	31.08
single branch with access	27.18	0.67	11.19	33.31	nr	44.49
double branch	36.16	0.81	13.52	44.35	nr	57.88
W.C. manifold	15.58	0.32	5.34	19.89	nr	25.24
access door	-	0.67	11.19	16.26	nr	27.44
access pipe connector	25.10	0.56	9.35	30.26	nr	39.61
connection to clay pipes; caulking ring and cement and sand (1:2) joint	-	0.46	7.68	11.86	nr	19.54
160 mm pipes; fixing with holderbats; plugged and screwed	20.34	0.56	9.35	34.34	m	43.69
Extra for						
socket plug	12.95	0.28	4.67	17.69	nr	22.36
slip coupling; push fit	40.70	0.50	8.35	47.08	nr	55.43
expansion coupling	18.81	0.56	9.35	24.46	nr	33.81
sweep bend	29.89	0.56	9.35	37.28	nr	46.63
boss connector	7.94	0.37	6.18	11.89	nr	18.07
single branch	33.70	0.79	13.19	42.44	nr	55.63
double branch	70.88	0.93	15.53	87.32	nr	102.84
access door	24.38	0.67	11.19	28.68	nr	39.86
access pipe connector	25.10	0.56	9.35	30.26	nr	39.61
Weathering apron; for pipe						
82 mmm diameter	2.90	0.38	6.34	3.82	nr	10.16
110 mm diameter	3.32	0.43	7.18	4.49	nr	11.67
160 mm diameter	9.98	0.46	7.68	12.85	nr	20.53
Weathering slate; for pipe						
110 mm diameter	35.24	1.00	16.69	41.42	nr	58.12
Vent cowl; for pipe						
82 mm diameter	2.90	0.37	6.18	3.82	nr	9.99
110 mm diameter	2.92	0.37	6.18	4.03	nr	10.21
160 mm diameter	7.65	0.37	6.18	10.15	nr	16.33

R DISPOSAL SYSTEMS

Item	PC £	Labour hours	Labour £	Material /Plant £	Unit	Total rate £
R11 FOUL DRAINAGE ABOVE GROUND – cont'd						
Polypropylene ancillaries; screwed joint to waste fitting						
Tubular "S" trap; bath; shallow seal						
40 mm diameter	7.20	0.61	10.18	8.33	nr	**18.51**
Trap; "P"; two piece; 76 mm seal						
32 mm diameter	4.86	0.43	7.18	5.62	nr	**12.80**
40 mm diameter	5.61	0.50	8.35	6.49	nr	**14.84**
Trap; "S"; two piece; 76 mm seal						
32 mm diameter	6.16	0.43	7.18	7.13	nr	**14.31**
40 mm diameter	7.20	0.50	8.35	8.33	nr	**16.68**
Bottle trap; "P"; 76 mm seal						
32 mm diameter	5.42	0.43	7.18	6.27	nr	**13.44**
40 mm diameter	6.46	0.45	7.51	7.47	nr	**14.98**
R12 DRAINAGE BELOW GROUND						
NOTE: Prices for drain trenches are for excavation in "firm" soil and it has been assumed that earthwork support will only be required for trenches 1.00 m or more in depth.						
Excavating trenches; by machine; grading bottoms; earthwork support; filling with excav. material and compacting; disposal of surplus soil on site; spreading on site average 50 m						
Pipes not exceeding 200 mm nominal size						
average depth of trench 0.50 m	-	0.30	3.43	1.91	m	**5.34**
average depth of trench 0.75 m	-	0.45	5.15	2.83	m	**7.98**
average depth of trench 1.00 m	-	0.89	10.19	5.41	m	**15.60**
average depth of trench 1.25 m	-	1.33	15.22	6.14	m	**21.37**
average depth of trench 1.50 m	-	1.71	19.57	6.98	m	**26.56**
average depth of trench 1.75 m	-	2.08	23.81	7.71	m	**31.52**
average depth of trench 2.00 m	-	2.46	28.16	8.77	m	**36.92**
average depth of trench 2.25 m	-	3.02	34.57	11.00	m	**45.57**
average depth of trench 2.50 m	-	3.57	40.86	12.83	m	**53.69**
average depth of trench 2.75 m	-	3.95	45.21	14.33	m	**59.54**
average depth of trench 3.00 m	-	4.31	49.33	15.77	m	**65.10**
average depth of trench 3.25 m	-	4.66	53.34	16.78	m	**70.12**
average depth of trench 3.50 m	-	4.99	57.11	17.73	m	**74.84**
Pipes exceeding 200 mm nominal size; 225 mm nominal size						
average depth of trench 0.50 m	-	0.30	3.43	1.91	m	**5.34**
average depth of trench 0.75 m	-	0.45	5.15	2.83	m	**7.98**
average depth of trench 1.00 m	-	0.89	10.19	5.41	m	**15.60**
average depth of trench 1.25 m	-	1.33	15.22	6.14	m	**21.37**
average depth of trench 1.50 m	-	1.71	19.57	6.98	m	**26.56**
average depth of trench 1.75 m	-	2.08	23.81	7.71	m	**31.52**
average depth of trench 2.00 m	-	2.46	28.16	8.77	m	**36.92**
average depth of trench 2.25 m	-	3.02	34.57	11.00	m	**45.57**
average depth of trench 2.50 m	-	3.57	40.86	12.83	m	**53.69**
average depth of trench 2.75 m	-	3.95	45.21	14.33	m	**59.54**
average depth of trench 3.00 m	-	4.31	49.33	15.77	m	**65.10**
average depth of trench 3.25 m	-	4.66	53.34	16.78	m	**70.12**
average depth of trench 3.50 m	-	4.99	57.11	17.73	m	**74.84**

R DISPOSAL SYSTEMS

Item	PC £	Labour hours	Labour £	Material /Plant £	Unit	Total rate £
Pipes exceeding 200 mm nominal size; 300 mm nominal size						
average depth of trench 0.75 m	-	0.51	5.84	3.54	m	9.38
average depth of trench 1.00 m	-	1.04	11.90	5.41	m	17.32
average depth of trench 1.25 m	-	1.42	16.25	6.36	m	22.61
average depth of trench 1.50 m	-	1.86	21.29	7.20	m	28.48
average depth of trench 1.75 m	-	2.16	24.72	7.93	m	32.65
average depth of trench 2.00 m	-	2.46	28.16	9.47	m	37.63
average depth of trench 2.25 m	-	3.02	34.57	11.43	m	45.99
average depth of trench 2.50 m	-	3.57	40.86	13.11	m	53.97
average depth of trench 2.75 m	-	3.95	45.21	14.55	m	59.76
average depth of trench 3.00 m	-	4.31	49.33	15.98	m	65.31
average depth of trench 3.25 m	-	4.66	53.34	17.49	m	70.83
average depth of trench 3.50 m	-	4.99	57.11	18.22	m	75.33
Extra over excavating trenches; irrespective of depth; breaking out materials						
brick	-	2.08	23.81	9.02	m³	32.83
concrete	-	2.91	33.31	12.42	m³	45.73
reinforced concrete	-	4.17	47.73	17.96	m³	65.69
Extra over excavating trenches; irrespective of depth; breaking out existing hard pavings; 75 mm thick						
tarmacadam	-	0.22	2.52	0.95	m²	3.46
Extra over excavating trenches; irrespective of depth; breaking out existing hard pavings; 150 mm thick						
concrete	-	0.45	5.15	2.05	m²	7.20
tarmacadam and hardcore	-	0.30	3.43	1.06	m²	4.49
Excavating trenches; by hand; grading bottoms; earthwork support; filling with excavated material and compacting; disposal of surplus soil on site; spreading on site average 50 m						
Pipes not exceeding 200 mm nominal size; average depth						
average depth of trench 0.50 m	-	1.02	11.67	-	m	11.67
average depth of trench 0.75 m	-	1.53	17.51	-	m	17.51
average depth of trench 1.00 m	-	2.24	25.64	1.38	m	27.02
average depth of trench 1.25 m	-	3.15	36.05	1.90	m	37.95
average depth of trench 1.50 m	-	4.33	49.56	2.31	m	51.87
average depth of trench 1.75 m	-	5.70	65.24	2.76	m	68.00
average depth of trench 2.00 m	-	6.51	74.51	3.10	m	77.61
average depth of trench 2.25 m	-	8.14	93.17	4.14	m	97.31
average depth of trench 2.50 m	-	9.77	111.82	4.83	m	116.65
average depth of trench 2.75 m	-	10.74	122.92	5.35	m	128.27
average depth of trench 3.00 m	-	11.70	133.91	5.86	m	139.78
average depth of trench 3.25 m	-	12.67	145.01	6.38	m	151.40
average depth of trench 3.50 m	-	13.64	156.12	6.90	m	163.01
Pipes exceeding 200 mm nominal size; 225 mm nominal size						
average depth of trench 0.50 m	-	1.02	11.67	-	m	11.67
average depth of trench 0.75 m	-	1.53	17.51	-	m	17.51
average depth of trench 1.00 m	-	2.24	25.64	1.38	m	27.02
average depth of trench 1.25 m	-	3.15	36.05	1.90	m	37.95
average depth of trench 1.50 m	-	4.33	49.56	2.31	m	51.87
average depth of trench 1.75 m	-	5.70	65.24	2.76	m	68.00
average depth of trench 2.00 m	-	6.51	74.51	3.10	m	77.61
average depth of trench 2.25 m	-	8.14	93.17	4.14	m	97.31
average depth of trench 2.50 m	-	9.77	111.82	4.83	m	116.65

R DISPOSAL SYSTEMS

Item	PC £	Labour hours	Labour £	Material £	Unit	Total rate £
R12 DRAINAGE BELOW GROUND – cont'd						
Excavating trenches; by hand – cont'd						
Pipes exceeding 200 mm nominal size; 225 mm nominal size – cont'd						
average depth of trench 2.75 m	-	10.74	122.92	5.35	m	128.27
average depth of trench 3.00 m	-	11.70	133.91	5.86	m	139.78
average depth of trench 3.25 m	-	12.67	145.01	6.38	m	151.40
average depth of trench 3.50 m	-	13.64	156.12	6.90	m	163.01
Pipes exceeding 200 mm nominal size; 300 mm nominal size						
average depth of trench 0.75 m	-	1.79	20.49	-	m	20.49
average depth of trench 1.00 m	-	2.60	29.76	1.38	m	31.14
average depth of trench 1.25 m	-	3.66	41.89	1.90	m	43.79
average depth of trench 1.50 m	-	4.88	55.85	2.31	m	58.16
average depth of trench 1.75 m	-	5.70	65.24	2.76	m	68.00
average depth of trench 2.00 m	-	6.51	74.51	3.10	m	77.61
average depth of trench 2.25 m	-	8.14	93.17	4.14	m	97.31
average depth of trench 2.50 m	-	9.77	111.82	4.83	m	116.65
average depth of trench 2.75 m	-	10.74	122.92	5.35	m	128.27
average depth of trench 3.00 m	-	11.74	134.37	5.86	m	140.23
average depth of trench 3.25 m	-	12.67	145.01	6.38	m	151.40
average depth of trench 3.50 m	-	13.64	156.12	6.90	m	163.01
Extra over excavating trenches; irrespective of depth; breaking out existing materials						
brick	-	3.05	34.91	6.83	m³	41.74
concrete	-	4.58	52.42	11.38	m³	63.80
reinforced concrete	-	6.11	69.93	15.94	m³	85.87
Extra over excavating trenches; irrespective of depth; breaking out existing hard pavings; 75 mm thick						
tarmacadam	-	0.41	4.69	0.92	m²	5.61
Extra over excavating trenches; irrespective of depth; breaking out existing hard pavings; 150 mm thick						
concrete	-	0.71	8.13	1.60	m²	9.72
tarmacadam and hardcore	-	0.51	5.84	1.13	m²	6.97
Extra for taking up						
precast concrete paving slabs	-	0.33	3.78	-	m²	3.78
Sand filling						
Beds; to receive pitch fibre pipes						
600 mm x 50 mm thick	-	0.08	0.92	1.15	m	2.06
700 mm x 50 mm thick	-	0.10	1.14	1.34	m	2.48
800 mm x 50 mm thick	-	0.12	1.37	1.53	m	2.90
Granular (shingle) filling						
Beds; 100 mm thick; to pipes						
100 mm nominal size	-	0.10	1.14	1.66	m	2.81
150 mm nominal size	-	0.10	1.14	1.94	m	3.09
225 mm nominal size	-	0.12	1.37	2.22	m	3.59
300 mm nominal size	-	0.14	1.60	2.49	m	4.10
Beds; 150 mm thick; to pipes						
100 mm nominal size	-	0.14	1.60	2.49	m	4.10
150 mm nominal size	-	0.17	1.95	2.77	m	4.72
225 mm nominal size	-	0.19	2.17	3.05	m	5.22
300 mm nominal size	-	0.20	2.29	3.33	m	5.62

R DISPOSAL SYSTEMS

Item	PC £	Labour hours	Labour £	Material £	Unit	Total rate £
Beds and benchings; beds 100 mm thick; to pipes						
100 mm nominal size	-	0.23	2.63	3.05	m	5.68
150 mm nominal size	-	26.00	297.58	3.05	m	300.63
225 mm nominal size	-	0.31	3.55	4.16	m	7.71
300 mm nominal size	-	0.36	4.12	4.71	m	8.83
Beds and benchings; beds 150 mm thick; to pipes						
100 mm nominal size	-	0.26	2.98	3.33	m	6.30
150 mm nominal size	-	0.29	3.32	3.60	m	6.92
225 mm nominal size	-	0.36	4.12	4.99	m	9.11
300 mm nominal size	-	0.45	5.15	6.10	m	11.25
Beds and coverings; 100 mm thick; to pipes						
100 mm nominal size	-	0.37	4.23	4.16	m	8.39
150 mm nominal size	-	0.45	5.15	4.99	m	10.14
225 mm nominal size	-	0.61	6.98	6.93	m	13.91
300 mm nominal size	-	0.73	8.36	8.32	m	16.67
Beds and coverings; 150 mm thick; to pipes						
100 mm nominal size	-	0.55	6.29	6.10	m	12.39
150 mm nominal size	-	0.61	6.98	6.93	m	13.91
225 mm nominal size	-	0.80	9.16	8.87	m	18.03
300 mm nominal size	-	0.94	10.76	10.53	m	21.29
Plain in situ ready mixed designated concrete; C10 - 40 mm aggregate						
Beds; 100 mm thick; to pipes						
100 mm nominal size	-	0.21	2.81	4.23	m	7.04
150 mm nominal size	-	0.21	2.81	4.23	m	7.04
225 mm nominal size	-	0.26	3.48	5.07	m	8.54
300 mm nominal size	-	0.29	3.88	5.92	m	9.79
Beds; 150 mm thick; to pipes						
100 mm nominal size	-	0.29	3.88	5.92	m	9.79
150 mm nominal size	-	0.33	4.41	6.76	m	11.17
225 mm nominal size	-	0.37	4.95	7.60	m	12.55
300 mm nominal size	-	0.42	5.62	8.44	m	14.06
Beds and benchings; beds 100 mm thick; to pipes						
100 mm nominal size	-	0.42	5.62	7.60	m	13.22
150 mm nominal size	-	0.47	6.29	8.44	m	14.73
225 mm nominal size	-	0.56	7.49	10.13	m	17.62
300 mm nominal size	-	0.66	8.83	11.82	m	20.65
Beds and benchings; beds 150 mm thick; to pipes						
100 mm nominal size	-	0.47	6.29	8.44	m	14.73
150 mm nominal size	-	0.52	6.96	9.29	m	16.24
225 mm nominal size	-	0.66	8.83	11.82	m	20.65
300 mm nominal size	-	0.84	11.24	15.20	m	26.44
Beds and coverings; 100 mm thick; to pipes						
100 mm nominal size	-	0.63	8.43	10.13	m	18.56
150 mm nominal size	-	0.73	9.76	11.82	m	21.59
225 mm nominal size	-	1.05	14.04	16.89	m	30.93
300 mm nominal size	-	1.25	16.72	20.27	m	36.99
Beds and coverings; 150 mm thick; to pipes						
100 mm nominal size	-	0.93	12.44	15.20	m	27.64
150 mm nominal size	-	1.05	14.04	16.89	m	30.93
225 mm nominal size	-	1.35	18.06	21.96	m	40.01
300 mm nominal size	-	1.62	21.67	26.18	m	47.84

R DISPOSAL SYSTEMS

Item	PC £	Labour hours	Labour £	Material £	Unit	Total rate £
R12 DRAINAGE BELOW GROUND – cont'd						
Plain in situ ready mixed designated concrete; C20 - 40 mm aggregate						
Beds 100 mm thick; to pipes						
100 mm nominal size	-	0.21	2.81	4.35	m	**7.16**
150 mm nominal size	-	0.21	2.81	4.35	m	**7.16**
225 mm nominal size	-	0.26	3.48	5.21	m	**8.69**
300 mm nominal size	-	0.29	3.88	6.09	m	**9.96**
Beds; 150 mm thick; to pipes						
100 mm nominal size	-	0.29	3.88	6.09	m	**9.96**
150 mm nominal size	-	0.33	4.41	6.95	m	**11.36**
225 mm nominal size	-	0.37	4.95	7.82	m	**12.77**
300 mm nominal size	-	0.42	5.62	8.69	m	**14.31**
Beds and benchings; beds 100 mm thick; to pipes						
100 mm nominal size	-	0.42	5.62	7.82	m	**13.44**
150 mm nominal size	-	0.47	6.29	8.69	m	**14.97**
225 mm nominal size	-	0.56	7.49	10.43	m	**17.92**
300 mm nominal size	-	0.66	8.83	12.16	m	**20.99**
Beds and benchings; beds 150 mm thick; to pipes						
100 mm nominal size	-	0.47	6.29	8.69	m	**14.97**
150 mm nominal size	-	0.52	6.96	9.55	m	**16.51**
225 mm nominal size	-	0.66	8.83	12.16	m	**20.99**
300 mm nominal size	-	0.84	11.24	15.64	m	**26.87**
Beds and coverings; 100 mm thick; to pipes						
100 mm nominal size	-	0.63	8.43	10.43	m	**18.85**
150 mm nominal size	-	0.73	9.76	12.16	m	**21.93**
225 mm nominal size	-	1.05	14.04	17.38	m	**31.42**
300 mm nominal size	-	1.25	16.72	20.85	m	**37.57**
Beds and coverings; 150 mm thick; to pipes						
100 mm nominal size	-	0.93	12.44	15.64	m	**28.08**
150 mm nominal size	-	1.05	14.04	17.38	m	**31.42**
225 mm nominal size	-	1.35	18.06	22.59	m	**40.65**
300 mm nominal size	-	1.62	21.67	26.93	m	**48.60**
NOTE: The following items unless otherwise described include for all appropriate joints/couplings in the running length. The prices for gullies and rainwater shoes, etc. include for appropriate joints to pipes and for setting on and surrounding accessory with site mixed in situ concrete 10.00 N/mm2 - 40 mm aggregate (1:3:6)						
Cast iron "Timesaver" drain pipes and fittings or other equal and approved; BS 437; coated; with mechanical coupling joints						
75 mm pipes; laid straight	19.18	0.48	5.44	26.98	m	**32.42**
75 mm pipes; in runs not exceeding 3.00 m long	18.63	0.64	7.25	34.55	m	**41.81**
Extra for						
bend; medium radius	19.39	0.53	6.01	31.50	nr	**37.51**
single branch	26.89	0.74	8.39	50.38	nr	**58.76**
isolated "Timesaver" joint	10.78	0.32	3.63	12.47	nr	**16.10**

R DISPOSAL SYSTEMS

Item	PC £	Labour hours	Labour £	Material £	Unit	Total rate £
100 mm pipes; laid straight	23.12	0.53	6.01	33.24	m	39.24
100 mm pipes; in runs not exceeding 3.00 m long	22.03	0.72	8.16	43.26	m	51.42
Extra for						
bend; medium radius	27.72	0.64	7.25	45.11	nr	52.36
bend; medium radius with access	77.00	0.64	7.25	102.13	nr	109.38
bend; long radius	45.80	0.64	7.25	64.66	nr	71.91
rest bend	31.79	0.64	7.25	48.45	nr	55.70
diminishing pipe	22.45	0.64	7.25	37.64	nr	44.89
single branch	36.77	0.80	9.07	70.13	nr	79.20
single branch; with access	84.82	0.91	10.31	125.72	nr	136.03
double branch	62.51	1.01	11.45	114.87	nr	126.31
double branch; with access	97.14	1.01	11.45	154.93	nr	166.37
isolated "Timesaver" joint	14.82	0.37	4.19	17.15	nr	21.34
transitional pipe; for WC	21.70	0.53	6.01	42.25	nr	48.26
150 mm pipes; laid straight	42.80	0.64	7.25	57.79	m	65.04
150 mm pipes; in runs not exceeding 3.00 m long	40.77	0.87	9.86	69.08	m	78.94
Extra for						
bend; medium radius	63.77	0.74	8.39	86.93	nr	95.31
bend; medium radius with access	135.23	0.74	8.39	169.61	nr	178.00
bend; long radius	85.40	0.74	8.39	109.42	nr	117.81
diminishing pipe	36.13	0.74	8.39	52.41	nr	60.80
single branch	79.41	0.91	10.31	93.86	nr	104.18
isolated "Timesaver" joint	17.95	0.44	4.99	20.76	nr	25.75
Accessories in "Timesaver" cast iron or other equal and approved; with mechanical coupling joints						
Gully fittings; comprising low invert gully trap and round hopper						
75 mm outlet	20.36	0.95	10.77	40.38	nr	51.15
100 mm outlet	33.14	1.01	11.45	59.84	nr	71.29
150 mm outlet	40.00	1.38	15.64	72.25	nr	87.89
Add to above for; bellmouth 300 mm high; circular plain grating						
100 mm nominal size; 200 mm grating	33.63	0.48	5.44	60.45	nr	65.89
100 mm nominal size; 100 mm horizontal inlet; 200 mm grating	41.12	0.48	5.44	69.11	nr	74.55
100 mm nominal size; 100 mm horizontal inlet; 200 mm grating	42.16	0.48	5.44	70.32	nr	75.76
Yard gully (Deans); trapped; galvanized sediment pan; 267 mm round heavy grating						
100 mm outlet	218.25	3.08	34.90	316.54	nr	351.45
Yard gully (garage); trapless; galvanized sediment pan; 267 mm round heavy grating						
100 mm outlet	222.63	2.88	32.64	279.94	nr	312.58
Yard gully (garage); trapped; with rodding eye, galvanised perforated sediment pan; stopper; 267 mm round heavy grating						
100 mm outlet	414.01	2.88	32.64	547.86	nr	580.49
Grease trap; internal access; galvanized perforated bucket; lid and frame						
100 mm outlet; 20 gallon capacity	379.30	4.26	48.28	486.17	nr	534.45
Cast iron "Ensign" lightweight pipes and fittings or other equal and approved; EN 877; ductile iron couplings						
100 mm pipes; laid straight	-	0.19	3.15	22.32	m	25.46
Extra for						
bend; long radius	-	0.19	3.15	40.00	nr	43.14
single branch	-	0.23	3.82	40.40	nr	44.22

R DISPOSAL SYSTEMS

Item	PC £	Labour hours	Labour £	Material £	Unit	Total rate £
R12 DRAINAGE BELOW GROUND – cont'd						
Cast iron "Ensign" lightweight pipes – cont'd						
150 mm pipes; laid straight	-	0.22	3.62	44.86	m	48.48
Extra for						
bend; long radius	-	0.22	3.62	110.61	nr	114.23
single branch	-	0.28	4.62	88.94	nr	93.56
Extra strength vitrified clay pipes and fittings; Hepworth "Supersleve" or other equal and approved; plain ends with push fit polypropylene flexible couplings						
100 mm pipes; laid straight	5.86	0.21	2.38	6.95	m	9.33
Extra for						
bend	5.42	0.21	2.38	12.01	nr	14.39
access bend	35.66	0.21	2.38	47.85	nr	50.23
rest bend	9.59	0.21	2.38	16.96	nr	19.34
access pipe	30.98	0.21	2.38	41.83	nr	44.21
socket adaptor	5.74	0.19	2.15	9.84	nr	11.99
adaptor to "HepSeal" pipe	4.67	0.19	2.15	8.57	nr	10.72
saddle	11.49	0.80	9.07	17.12	nr	26.19
single junction	11.70	0.27	3.06	22.49	nr	25.55
single access junction	41.23	0.27	3.06	57.49	nr	60.55
150 mm pipes; laid straight	11.20	0.27	3.06	13.27	m	16.33
Extra for						
bend	11.16	0.26	2.95	23.10	nr	26.05
access bend	5.92	0.26	2.95	59.94	nr	62.88
rest bend	14.34	0.26	2.95	26.88	nr	29.82
taper pipe	16.51	0.26	2.95	26.57	nr	29.52
access pipe	40.23	0.26	2.95	56.60	nr	59.54
socket adaptor	10.82	0.21	2.38	18.25	nr	20.63
adaptor to "HepSeal" pipe	7.68	0.21	2.38	14.52	nr	16.90
saddle	16.34	0.95	10.77	25.75	nr	36.52
single junction	14.94	0.32	3.63	33.00	nr	36.62
single access junction	58.58	0.32	3.63	84.72	nr	88.34
Extra strength vitrified clay pipes and fittings; Hepworth "SuperSeal" or other equal and approved; socketted; with push-fit flexible joints						
150 mm pipes; laid straight	13.91	0.34	3.85	16.49	m	20.34
Extra for						
bend	25.54	0.27	3.06	25.33	nr	28.39
rest bend	14.34	0.23	2.61	12.05	nr	14.66
stopper	8.06	0.17	1.93	9.55	nr	11.47
taper reducer	13.83	0.27	3.06	11.45	nr	14.51
saddle	16.34	0.86	9.75	19.37	nr	29.12
single junction	33.38	0.34	3.85	32.97	nr	36.82
225 mm pipes; laid straight	27.54	0.44	4.99	32.64	m	37.62
Extra for						
bend	57.12	0.34	3.85	57.91	nr	61.76
rest bend	69.78	0.34	3.85	72.92	nr	76.77
stopper	12.14	0.22	2.49	14.38	nr	16.88
taper reducer	41.22	0.34	3.85	39.06	nr	42.91
saddle	16.34	1.15	13.03	19.37	nr	32.40
single junction	101.46	0.44	4.99	107.20	nr	112.19

R DISPOSAL SYSTEMS

Item	PC £	Labour hours	Labour £	Material £	Unit	Total rate £
300 mm pipes; laid straight	42.23	0.57	6.46	50.05	m	**56.51**
Extra for						
bend	108.49	0.45	5.10	113.56	nr	**118.66**
rest bend	154.59	0.45	5.10	168.20	nr	**173.30**
stopper	25.35	0.29	3.29	30.05	nr	**33.33**
taper reducer	111.27	0.45	5.10	116.86	nr	**121.96**
saddle	16.34	1.54	17.45	19.37	nr	**36.82**
single junction	212.45	0.57	6.46	231.77	nr	**238.23**
400 mm pipes; laid straight	88.46	0.77	8.73	104.85	m	**113.57**
Extra for						
bend	332.42	0.62	7.03	362.52	nr	**369.55**
single unequal junction	311.46	0.77	8.73	327.20	nr	**335.93**
450 mm pipes; laid straight	114.90	0.95	10.77	136.18	m	**146.95**
Extra for						
bend	437.73	0.77	8.73	477.94	nr	**486.66**
single unequal junction	372.60	0.95	10.77	387.13	nr	**397.89**
British Standard quality vitrified clay pipes and fittings; socketted; cement:sand (1:2) joints						
100 mm pipes; laid straight	7.50	0.43	4.87	9.01	m	**13.89**
Extra for						
bend (short/medium/knuckle)	5.25	0.34	3.85	6.35	nr	**10.20**
bend (long/rest/elbow)	12.33	0.34	3.85	12.06	nr	**15.92**
single junction	13.78	0.43	4.87	12.92	nr	**17.79**
double collar	9.05	0.29	3.29	10.84	nr	**14.13**
150 mm pipes; laid straight	11.54	0.48	5.44	13.79	m	**19.23**
Extra for						
bend (short/medium/knuckle)	11.54	0.38	4.31	9.69	nr	**14.00**
bend (long/rest/elbow)	20.84	0.38	4.31	20.72	nr	**25.02**
taper	27.24	0.38	4.31	27.89	nr	**32.20**
single junction	22.80	0.48	5.44	21.70	nr	**27.14**
double collar	15.06	0.32	3.63	17.97	nr	**21.60**
225 mm pipes; laid straight	22.87	0.58	6.57	27.39	m	**33.97**
Extra for						
bend (short/medium/knuckle)	36.14	0.47	5.33	34.85	nr	**40.18**
double collar	35.26	0.38	4.31	41.91	nr	**46.21**
300 mm pipes; laid straight	38.33	0.80	9.07	45.71	m	**54.78**
Accessories in vitrified clay; set in concrete; with polypropylene coupling joints to pipes						
Rodding point; with oval aluminium plate						
100 mm nominal size	29.04	0.53	6.01	39.62	nr	**45.62**
Gully fittings; comprising low back trap and square hopper; 150 mm x 150 mm square gully grid						
100 mm nominal size	26.82	0.91	10.31	40.50	nr	**50.81**
Access gully; trapped with rodding eye and integral vertical back inlet; stopper; 150 mm x 150 mm square gully grid						
100 mm nominal size	48.94	0.69	7.82	63.20	nr	**71.02**
Inspection chamber; comprising base; 300 mm or 450 mm raising piece; integral alloy cover and frame; 100 mm inlets						
straight through; 2 nr inlets	150.13	2.13	24.14	185.03	nr	**209.17**

R DISPOSAL SYSTEMS

Item	PC £	Labour hours	Labour £	Material £	Unit	Total rate £
R12 DRAINAGE BELOW GROUND – cont'd						
Accessories in polypropylene; cover set in concrete; with coupling joints to pipes						
Inspection chamber; 5 nr 100 mm inlets; cast iron cover and frame						
475 mm diameter x 585 mm deep	180.73	2.44	27.65	221.80	nr	**249.45**
475 mm diameter x 930 mm deep	221.13	2.66	30.14	269.68	nr	**299.83**
Accessories in vitrified clay; set in concrete; with cement:sand (1:2) joints to pipes						
Gully fittings; comprising low back trap and square hopper; square gully grid						
100 mm outlet; 150 mm x 150 mm grid	38.56	1.06	12.01	46.13	nr	**58.14**
Yard gully; combined filter and slit bucket; square hinged grate and frame (up to one tonne)						
100 mm outlet; 300 mm x 300 mm grid	109.32	3.19	36.15	130.08	nr	**166.23**
100 mm outlet; 100 mm back inlet; 300 mm x 300 mm grid	141.66	4.26	48.28	168.84	nr	**217.12**
150 mm outlet; 300 mm x 300 mm grid	109.32	3.19	36.15	130.08	nr	**166.23**
150 mm outlet; 150 mm back inlet; 300 m x 300 mm grid	144.50	4.26	48.28	171.78	nr	**220.06**
Road gully; trapped with rodding eye and stopper (grate not included)						
300 mm x 600 mm x 100 mm outlet	71.00	3.51	39.78	103.70	nr	**143.47**
300 mm x 600 mm x 150 mm outlet	72.70	3.51	39.78	105.72	nr	**145.49**
400 mm x 750 mm x 150 mm outlet	84.32	4.26	48.28	129.61	nr	**177.89**
450 mm x 900 mm x 150 mm outlet	114.09	5.32	60.29	170.80	nr	**231.09**
Grease trap; with internal access; galvanized perforated bucket; lid and frame						
600 mm x 450 mm x 600 mm deep; 100 mm outlet	636.94	4.47	50.66	784.08	nr	**834.74**
Interceptor; trapped with inspection arm; lever locking stopper; chain and staple; cement and sand (1:2) joints to pipes; building in, and cutting and fitting brickwork around						
100 mm outlet; 100 mm inlet	91.49	4.26	48.28	108.95	nr	**157.22**
150 mm outlet; 150 mm inlet	129.82	4.78	54.17	154.38	nr	**208.55**
225 mm outlet; 225 mm inlet	353.36	5.32	60.29	419.37	nr	**479.66**
Accessories; grates and covers						
Aluminium alloy gully grids; set in position						
120 mm x 120 mm	2.90	0.11	1.25	3.44	nr	**4.69**
150 mm x 150 mm	2.90	0.11	1.25	3.44	nr	**4.69**
225 mm x 225 mm	8.64	0.11	1.25	10.24	nr	**11.49**
100 mm diameter	2.90	0.11	1.25	3.44	nr	**4.69**
150 mm diameter	4.43	0.11	1.25	5.25	nr	**6.50**
225 mm diameter	9.66	0.11	1.25	11.45	nr	**12.70**
Aluminium alloy sealing plates and frames; set in cement and sand (1:3)						
150 x 150	11.15	0.27	3.06	13.32	nr	**16.38**
225 x 225	20.41	0.27	3.06	24.29	nr	**27.35**
300 x 150	20.13	0.27	3.06	23.96	nr	**27.02**
140 diameter (for 100 mm)	9.09	0.27	3.06	10.88	nr	**13.94**
197 diameter (for 150 mm)	13.07	0.27	3.06	15.60	nr	**18.66**
273 diameter (for 225 mm)	20.93	0.27	3.06	24.91	nr	**27.97**

R DISPOSAL SYSTEMS

Item	PC £	Labour hours	Labour £	Material £	Unit	Total rate £
Coated cast iron heavy duty road gratings and frame; BS 497 Tables 6 and 7; bedding and pointing in cement and sand (1:3); one course half brick thick wall in semi-engineering bricks in cement mortar (1:3)						
440 mm x 400 mm grating and frame; ref D/TRI D400	38.00	2.66	30.14	46.89	nr	77.03
440 mm x 400 mm hinged grating and frame; ref D400	38.00	2.66	30.14	46.89	nr	77.03
500 mm x 350 mm hinged grating and frame; ref D400	54.00	2.66	30.14	65.40	nr	95.54
Accessories in precast concrete; top set in with rodding eye and stopper; cement and sand (1:2) joint to pipe Concrete road gully; BS 5911; trapped with rodding eye and stopper; cement and sand (1:2) joint to pipe						
450 mm diameter x 1050 mm deep; 100 mm or 150 mm outlet	32.11	5.05	57.23	58.81	nr	116.04
"Osmadrain" uPVC pipes and fittings or other equal and approved; BS 4660; with ring seal joints						
82 mm pipes; laid straight	8.54	0.17	1.93	10.13	m	12.05
Extra for						
bend; short radius	14.92	0.14	1.59	17.26	nr	18.85
spigot/socket bend	12.54	0.14	1.59	14.51	nr	16.10
adaptor	6.54	0.08	0.91	7.57	nr	8.48
single junction	19.41	0.19	2.15	22.45	nr	24.61
slip coupler	9.24	0.08	0.91	10.69	nr	11.60
100 mm pipes; laid straight	6.56	0.19	2.15	8.82	m	10.97
Extra for						
bend; short radius	17.34	0.17	1.93	19.60	nr	21.53
bend; long radius	28.09	0.17	1.93	30.16	nr	32.09
spigot/socket bend	14.66	0.17	1.93	21.88	nr	23.80
socket plug	7.02	0.05	0.57	8.13	nr	8.69
adjustable double socket bend	19.19	0.17	1.93	26.93	nr	28.86
adaptor to clay	17.21	0.10	1.13	19.56	nr	20.70
single junction	20.70	0.23	2.61	21.61	nr	24.22
sealed access junction	43.50	0.20	2.27	48.00	nr	50.27
slip coupler	9.24	0.10	1.13	10.69	nr	11.82
160 mm pipes; laid straight	14.82	0.23	2.61	19.47	m	22.08
Extra for						
bend; short radius	38.15	0.19	2.15	43.09	nr	45.24
spigot/socket bend	34.59	0.19	2.15	49.17	nr	51.32
socket plug	14.34	0.08	0.91	16.60	nr	17.50
adaptor to clay	34.56	0.13	1.47	39.05	nr	40.52
level invert taper	20.00	0.19	2.15	31.23	nr	33.39
single junction	62.47	0.27	3.06	72.28	nr	75.34
sealed access junction	69.61	0.24	2.72	80.53	nr	83.25
slip coupler	22.54	0.12	1.36	26.08	nr	27.44

R DISPOSAL SYSTEMS

Item	PC £	Labour hours	Labour £	Material £	Unit	Total rate £
R12 DRAINAGE BELOW GROUND – cont'd						
uPVC Osma "Ultra-Rib" ribbed pipes and fittings or other equal and approved; WIS approval; with sealed ring push-fit joints						
150 mm pipes; laid straight	-	0.21	2.38	8.02	m	10.40
Extra for						
bend; short radius	20.77	0.19	2.15	23.55	nr	25.70
adaptor to 160 diameter upvc	25.82	0.11	1.25	28.91	nr	30.15
adaptor to clay	52.99	0.11	1.25	60.83	nr	62.08
level invert taper	9.06	0.19	2.15	9.03	nr	11.19
single junction	37.34	0.24	2.72	40.79	nr	43.51
225 mm pipes; laid straight	15.67	0.24	2.72	18.57	m	21.29
Extra for						
bend; short radius	79.47	0.22	2.49	90.83	nr	93.33
adaptor to clay	66.02	0.14	1.59	74.16	nr	75.75
level invert taper	13.82	0.22	2.49	12.65	nr	15.14
single junction	117.97	0.30	3.40	130.91	nr	134.31
300 mm pipes; laid straight	23.28	0.36	4.08	27.59	m	31.67
Extra for						
bend; short radius	125.17	0.32	3.63	143.16	nr	146.79
adaptor to clay	173.67	0.16	1.81	197.62	nr	199.44
level invert taper	41.44	0.32	3.63	42.98	nr	46.60
single junction	251.62	0.41	4.65	282.83	nr	287.48
Interconnecting drainage channel; ref N100; ACO Polymer Products Ltd or other equal and approved; reinforced slotted galvanised steel grating ref 423/4; bedding and haunching in in situ concrete (not included)						
100 mm wide						
laid level or to falls	-	0.51	5.78	86.52	m	92.30
extra for sump unit	-	1.53	17.34	135.43	nr	152.77
extra for end caps	-	0.10	1.13	8.10	nr	9.24
Interconnecting drainage channel; "Birco-lite" ref 8012 or other equal and approved; Marshalls Plc; galvanised steel grating ref 8041; bedding and haunching in in situ concrete (not included)						
100 mm wide						
laid level or to falls	-	0.51	5.78	47.10	m	52.88
extra for 100 mm diameter trapped outlet unit	-	1.53	17.34	81.39	nr	98.73
extra for end caps	-	0.10	1.13	5.88	nr	7.01
Accessories in uPVC; with ring seal joints to pipes (unless otherwise described)						
Cast iron access point						
110 mm diameter	32.00	0.82	9.29	37.02	nr	46.32
Rodding eye						
110 mm diameter	35.46	0.47	5.33	45.26	nr	50.58
Universal gulley fitting; comprising gulley trap, plain hopper						
150 mm x 150 mm grate	30.87	1.02	11.56	41.63	nr	53.19

R DISPOSAL SYSTEMS

Item	PC £	Labour hours	Labour £	Material £	Unit	Total rate £
Bottle gulley; comprising gulley with bosses closed; sealed access covers						
217 mm x 217 mm grate	55.82	0.85	9.63	70.50	nr	80.13
Shallow access pipe; light duty screw down access door assembly						
110 mm diameter	70.80	0.85	9.63	87.83	nr	97.46
Shallow access junction; 3 nr 110 mm inlets; light duty screw down access door assembly						
110 mm diameter	109.70	1.22	13.83	129.45	nr	143.28
Shallow inspection chamber; 250 mm diameter; 600 mm deep; sealed cover and frame						
4 nr 110 mm outlets/inlets	111.33	1.41	15.98	149.91	nr	165.89
Universal inspection chamber; 450 mm diameter; single seal cast iron cover and frame; 4 nr 110 mm outlets/inlets						
500 mm deep	211.78	1.49	16.89	266.13	nr	283.01
730 mm deep	237.95	1.76	19.95	300.64	nr	320.58
960 mm deep	264.13	2.04	23.12	335.14	nr	358.26
Equal manhole base; 750 mm diameter						
6 nr 160 mm outlets/inlets	259.66	1.33	15.07	313.09	nr	328.16
Unequal manhole base; 750 mm diameter						
2 nr 160 mm, 4 nr 110 mm outlets/inlets	210.55	1.33	15.07	256.27	nr	271.35
Kerb to gullies; class B engineering bricks on edge to three sides in cement mortar (1:3) rendering in cement mortar (1:3) to top and two sides and skirting to brickwork 230 mm high; dishing in cement mortar (1:3) to gully; steel trowelled						
230 mm x 230 mm internally	-	1.53	17.34	1.42	nr	18.76
Excavating; by machine						
Manholes						
maximum depth not exceeding 1.00 m	-	0.22	2.52	4.95	m³	7.47
maximum depth not exceeding 2.00 m	-	0.24	2.75	5.45	m³	8.20
maximum depth not exceeding 4.00 m	-	0.29	3.32	6.37	m³	9.69
Excavating; by hand						
Manholes						
maximum depth not exceeding 1.00 m	-	3.52	40.29	-	m³	40.29
maximum depth not exceeding 2.00 m	-	4.16	47.61	-	m³	47.61
maximum depth not exceeding 4.00 m	-	5.32	60.89	-	m³	60.89
Earthwork support (average "risk" prices)						
Maximum depth not exceeding 1.00 m						
distance between opposing faces not exceeding 2.00 m	-	0.16	1.83	2.43	m²	4.26
Maximum depth not exceeding 2.00 m						
distance between opposing faces not exceeding 2.00 m	-	0.19	2.17	4.51	m²	6.68
Maximum depth not exceeding 4.00 m						
distance between opposing faces not exceeding 2.00 m	-	0.24	2.75	6.59	m²	9.33
Disposal; by machine						
Excavated material						
off site; to tip not exceeding 13 km (using lorries) including Landfill Tax based on inactive waste	-	-	-	18.87	m³	18.87
on site depositing; in spoil heaps; average 50 m distance	-	0.16	1.83	3.33	m³	5.16

R DISPOSAL SYSTEMS

Item	PC £	Labour hours	Labour £	Material £	Unit	Total rate £
R12 DRAINAGE BELOW GROUND – cont'd						
Disposal; by hand						
Excavated material						
off site; to tip not exceeding 13 km (using lorries) including Landfill Tax based on inactive waste	-	0.81	9.27	25.70	m³	34.97
on site depositing; in spoil heaps; average 50 m distance	-	1.32	15.11	-	m³	15.11
Filling to excavations; by machine						
Average thickness not exceeding 0.25 m						
arising from the exacavations	-	0.16	1.83	2.34	m³	4.17
Filling to excavations; by hand						
Average thickness not exceeding 0.25 m						
arising from the exacavations	-	1.02	11.67	-	m³	11.67
Plain in situ ready mixed designated concrete; C10 - 40 mm aggregate						
Beds						
thickness not exceeding 150 mm	73.08	3.20	42.80	88.68	m³	131.48
thickness 150 mm - 450 mm	73.08	2.40	32.10	88.68	m³	120.78
thickness exceeding 450 mm	73.08	2.02	27.02	88.68	m³	115.69
Plain in situ ready mixed designated concrete; C20 - 20 mm aggregate						
Beds						
thickness not exceeding 150 mm	75.18	3.20	42.80	91.23	m³	134.03
thickness 150 mm - 450 mm	75.18	2.40	32.10	91.23	m³	123.33
thickness exceeding 450 mm	75.18	2.02	27.02	91.23	m³	118.25
Plain in situ ready mixed designated concrete; C25 - 20 mm aggregate; (small quantities)						
Benching in bottoms						
150 mm - 450 mm average thickness	72.05	9.57	149.73	87.43	m³	237.16
Reinforced in situ ready mixed designated concrete; C20 - 20 mm aggregate; (small quantities)						
Isolated cover slabs						
thickness not exceeding 150 mm	71.60	7.45	99.65	86.88	m³	186.53
Reinforcement; fabric to BS 4483; lapped; in beds or suspended slabs						
Ref A98 (1.54 kg/m²)						
400 mm minimum laps	1.04	0.13	2.05	1.30	m²	3.35
Ref A142 (2.22 kg/m²)						
400 mm minimum laps	1.08	0.13	2.05	1.34	m²	3.39
Ref A193 (3.02 kg/m²)						
400 mm minimum laps	1.47	0.13	2.05	1.83	m²	3.88
Formwork; basic finish						
Soffits of isolated cover slabs						
horizontal	-	3.03	50.31	5.36	m²	55.67
Edges of isolated cover slabs						
height not exceeding 250 mm	-	0.90	14.94	1.71	m	16.65

R DISPOSAL SYSTEMS

Item	PC £	Labour hours	Labour £	Material £	Unit	Total rate £
Precast concrete rectangular access and inspection chambers; "Hepworth" chambers or other equal and approved; comprising cover frame to receive manhole cover (not included) intermediate wall sections and base section with cut outs; bedding; jointing and pointing in cement mortar (1:3) on prepared bed						
Drainage chamber; size 600 mm x 450 mm internally; depth to invert						
600 mm deep	-	4.78	54.17	105.34	nr	**159.51**
900 mm deep	-	6.38	72.30	132.37	nr	**204.67**
Drainage chamber; 1200 mm x 750 mm reducing to 600 mm x 600 mm; no base unit; depth of invert						
1050 mm deep	-	7.98	90.43	197.39	nr	**287.83**
1650 mm deep	-	9.57	108.45	333.86	nr	**442.32**
2250 mm deep	-	11.70	132.59	469.55	nr	**602.14**
Common bricks; in cement mortar (1:3)						
Walls to manholes						
one brick thick	31.68	2.55	58.20	43.17	m²	**101.37**
one and a half brick thick	47.52	3.73	85.13	64.75	m²	**149.88**
Projections of footings						
two brick thick	63.36	5.22	119.14	86.33	m²	**205.47**
Class A engineering bricks; in cement mortar (1:3)						
Walls to manholes						
one brick thick	55.14	2.88	65.73	70.08	m²	**135.81**
one and a half brick thick	55.14	4.15	94.72	72.44	m²	**167.16**
Projections of footings						
two brick thick	110.28	5.85	133.52	140.16	m²	**273.67**
Class B engineering bricks; in cement mortar (1:3)						
Walls to manholes						
one brick thick	39.38	2.88	65.73	51.40	m²	**117.14**
one and a half brick thick	59.08	4.15	94.72	77.11	m²	**171.82**
Projections of footings						
two brick thick	78.77	5.85	133.52	102.81	m²	**236.33**
Brickwork sundries						
Extra over for fair face; flush smooth pointing						
manhole walls	-	0.21	4.79	-	m²	**4.79**
Building ends of pipes into brickwork; making good fair face or rendering						
not exceeding 55 mm nominal size	-	0.11	2.51	-	nr	**2.51**
55 mm - 110 mm nominal size	-	0.16	3.65	-	nr	**3.65**
over 110 mm nominal size	-	0.21	4.79	-	nr	**4.79**
Step irons; BS 1247; malleable; galvanized; building into joints						
general purpose pattern	-	0.16	3.65	5.16	nr	**8.81**
Cement:sand (1:3) in situ finishings; steel trowelled						
13 mm work to manhole walls; one coat; to brickwork base over 300 mm wide	-	0.74	16.89	1.58	m²	**18.47**

R DISPOSAL SYSTEMS

Item	PC £	Labour hours	Labour £	Material £	Unit	Total rate £
R12 DRAINAGE BELOW GROUND – cont'd						
Cast iron inspection chambers; with bolted flat covers; BS 437; bedded in cement mortar (1:3); with mechanical coupling joints						
100 mm x 100 mm						
one branch	117.97	1.11	12.58	137.28	nr	**149.86**
one branch either side	158.25	1.67	18.93	183.88	nr	**202.81**
150 mm x 100 mm						
one branch	165.29	1.34	15.19	192.02	nr	**207.21**
one branch either side	195.01	1.90	21.53	227.20	nr	**248.73**
150 mm x 150 mm						
one branch	205.54	1.43	16.21	239.38	nr	**255.59**
one branch either side	240.91	2.04	23.12	280.30	nr	**303.42**
Cast iron access covers and frames; unless otherwise described; Manhole Covers Ltd or other equal and approved; coated; bedding frame in cement and sand (1:3); cover in grease and sand						
Grade A; light duty; rectangular single seal solid top						
450 mm x 450 mm; ref A15	38.00	1.62	18.36	45.68	nr	**64.04**
600 mm x 450 mm; ref A15	40.00	1.62	18.36	48.15	nr	**66.51**
600 mm x 600 mm; ref A15	48.00	1.62	18.36	57.56	nr	**75.92**
Grade A; light duty; rectangular single seal recessed						
600 mm x 450 mm; ref E15B	70.00	1.62	18.36	82.86	nr	**101.22**
600 mm x 600 mm; ref E15C	70.00	1.62	18.36	83.01	nr	**101.37**
Grade A; light duty; rectangular double seal solid top						
450 mm x 450 mm; galvanized steel; ref 7123	64.00	1.62	18.36	75.76	nr	**94.12**
600 mm x 450 mm; ref E11B	75.00	1.62	18.36	88.64	nr	**107.00**
600 mm x 600 mm; ref E11C	82.00	1.62	18.36	96.90	nr	**115.25**
Grade A; light duty; rectangular double seal recessed						
450 mm x 450 mm; galvanized steel; ref 7123	70.00	1.62	18.36	82.70	nr	**101.06**
600 mm x 450 mm; ref E16B	78.00	1.62	18.36	92.11	nr	**110.47**
600 mm x 600 mm; ref E16C	88.00	1.62	18.36	103.84	nr	**122.20**
Grade B; medium duty; rectangular single seal solid top						
600 mm x 450 mm; ref B125	44.00	2.13	24.14	52.78	nr	**76.91**
600 mm x 600 mm; ref B125	52.00	2.13	24.14	62.19	nr	**86.33**
Grade B; medium duty; rectangular singular seal recessed						
600 mm x 450 mm; ref D400	210.00	2.13	24.14	244.83	nr	**268.97**
600 mm x 600 mm; ref D400	240.00	2.13	24.14	279.70	nr	**303.84**
Grade C; heavy duty solid top						
600 mm diameter; ductile iron; circular single seal; ref D400	110.00	2.13	24.14	128.96	nr	**153.09**
600 mm x 600 mm; uctile iron; double triangular; ref D400	68.00	3.19	36.15	80.70	nr	**116.85**

R DISPOSAL SYSTEMS

Item	PC £	Labour hours	Labour £	Material £	Unit	Total rate £
British Standard best quality vitrified clay channels; bedding and jointing in cement:sand (1:2)						
Half section straight						
100 mm diameter x 1.00 m long	4.44	0.85	9.63	5.26	nr	14.89
150 mm diameter x 1.00 m long	7.40	1.06	12.01	8.77	nr	20.78
225 mm diameter x 1.00 m long	16.62	1.38	15.64	19.70	nr	35.34
300 mm diameter x 1.00 m long	34.12	1.70	19.27	40.44	nr	59.70
Half section bend						
100 mm diameter	9.78	0.64	7.25	11.59	nr	18.84
150 mm diameter	16.35	0.80	9.07	19.38	nr	28.45
225 mm diameter	53.28	1.06	12.01	63.15	nr	75.16
300 mm diameter	53.70	1.28	14.51	63.65	nr	78.16
Half section taper straight						
150 mm - 100 mm diameter	19.90	0.74	8.39	23.58	nr	31.97
225 mm - 150 mm diameter	44.42	0.95	10.77	52.65	nr	63.42
300 mm - 225 mm diameter	176.18	1.17	13.26	208.81	nr	222.07
Half section taper bend						
150 mm - 100 mm diameter	30.30	0.95	10.77	35.91	nr	46.67
225 mm - 150 mm diameter	86.81	1.22	13.83	102.88	nr	116.71
300 mm - 225 mm diameter	176.18	1.49	16.89	208.81	nr	225.70
Three quarter section branch bend						
100 mm diameter	10.78	0.53	6.01	12.78	nr	18.79
150 mm diameter	18.10	0.80	9.07	21.46	nr	30.52
225 mm diameter	66.07	1.06	12.01	78.31	nr	90.32
300 mm diameter	120.11	1.42	16.09	142.36	nr	158.45
uPVC channels; with solvent weld or lip seal coupling joints; bedding in cement:sand						
Half section cut away straight; with coupling either end						
110 mm diameter	37.76	0.32	3.63	57.31	nr	60.93
160 mm diameter	70.91	0.43	4.87	107.10	nr	111.98
Half section cut away long radius bend; with coupling either end						
110 mm diameter	61.91	0.32	3.63	85.93	nr	89.56
160 mm diameter	133.85	0.43	4.87	181.69	nr	186.57
Channel adaptor to clay; with one coupling						
110 mm diameter	16.48	0.27	3.06	25.81	nr	28.87
160 mm diameter	36.81	0.35	3.97	55.15	nr	59.12
Half section bend						
110 mm diameter	23.90	0.35	3.97	28.89	nr	32.86
160 mm diameter	41.06	0.53	6.01	49.96	nr	55.97
Half section channel connector						
110 mm diameter	6.70	0.08	0.91	9.05	nr	9.96
160 mm diameter	14.28	0.11	1.25	19.53	nr	20.78
Half section channel junction						
110 mm diameter	18.54	0.53	6.01	22.54	nr	28.54
160 mm diameter	47.92	0.65	7.37	58.10	nr	65.47
Polypropylene slipper bend						
110 mm diameter	17.42	0.43	4.87	21.21	nr	26.08

R DISPOSAL SYSTEMS

Item	PC £	Labour hours	Labour £	Material £	Unit	Total rate £
R12 DRAINAGE BELOW GROUND – cont'd						
Glass fibre septic tank; "Klargester" or other equal and approved; fixing lockable manhole cover and frame; placing in position						
3750 litre capacity; 2000 mm diameter; depth to invert						
1000 mm deep; standard grade	814.22	2.50	28.33	1013.91	nr	**1042.25**
1500 mm deep; heavy duty grade	1024.34	2.82	31.96	1251.09	nr	**1283.05**
6000 litre capacity; 2300 mm diameter; depth to invert						
1000 mm deep; standard grade	1313.25	2.68	30.37	1600.92	nr	**1631.29**
1500 mm deep; heavy duty grade	1733.49	3.01	34.11	2075.26	nr	**2109.37**
9000 litre capacity; 2660 mm diameter; depth to invert						
1000 mm deep; standard grade	1996.14	2.91	32.98	2371.73	nr	**2404.71**
1500 mm deep; heavy duty grade	2626.50	3.19	36.15	3083.25	nr	**3119.40**
Glass fibre petrol interceptors; "Klargester" or other equal and approved; placing in position						
2000 litre capacity; 2370 mm x 1300 mm diameter; depth to invert						
1000 mm deep	919.27	2.73	30.94	1037.63	nr	**1068.57**
4000 litre capacity; 4370 mm x 1300 mm diameter; depth to invert						
1000 mm deep	1575.90	2.96	33.54	1778.80	nr	**1812.34**
R13 LAND DRAINAGE						
Excavating; by hand; grading bottoms; earthwork support; filling to within 150 mm of surface with gravel rejects; remainder filled with excavated material and compacting; disposal of surplus soil on site; spreading on site average 50 m						
Pipes not exceeding 200 mm nominal size						
average depth of trench 0.75 m	-	1.71	19.57	9.20	m	**28.77**
average depth of trench 1.00 m	-	2.31	26.44	14.68	m	**41.12**
average depth of trench 1.25 m	-	3.19	36.51	18.45	m	**54.96**
average depth of trench 1.50 m	-	5.50	62.95	22.51	m	**85.46**
average depth of trench 1.75 m	-	6.52	74.62	26.27	m	**100.90**
average depth of trench 2.00 m	-	7.54	86.30	30.33	m	**116.62**
Disposal; by machine						
Excavated material						
off site; to tip not exceeding 13 km (using lorries) including Landfill Tax based on inactive waste	-	-	-	18.87	m³	**18.87**
Disposal; by hand						
Excavated material						
off site; to tip not exceeding 13 km (using lorries) including Landfill Tax based on inactive waste	-	0.88	10.07	25.70	m³	**35.77**
Vitrified clay perforated sub-soil pipes; BS 65; Hepworth "Hepline" or other equal and approved						
Pipes; laid straight						
100 mm diameter	6.74	0.23	2.61	7.98	m	**10.59**
150 mm diameter	12.24	0.29	3.29	14.51	m	**17.79**
225 mm diameter	22.50	0.38	4.31	26.67	m	**30.98**

S PIPED SUPPLY SYSTEMS

Item	PC £	Labour hours	Labour £	Material £	Unit	Total rate £
S12 HOT AND COLD WATER (SMALL SCALE)						
Copper pipes; EN1057:1996; capillary fittings						
15 mm pipes; fixing with pipe clips and screwed	1.39	0.37	6.18	1.75	m	**7.93**
Extra for						
made bend	-	0.17	2.84	-	nr	**2.84**
stop end	1.10	0.12	2.00	1.27	nr	**3.27**
straight coupling	0.18	0.19	3.17	0.21	nr	**3.38**
union coupling	5.97	0.19	3.17	6.90	nr	**10.08**
reducing coupling	2.04	0.19	3.17	2.36	nr	**5.53**
copper to lead connector	4.66	0.24	4.01	5.39	nr	**9.39**
imperial to metric adaptor	2.39	0.24	4.01	2.77	nr	**6.77**
elbow	0.34	0.19	3.17	0.39	nr	**3.56**
backplate elbow	4.49	0.39	6.51	5.19	nr	**11.70**
return bend	6.72	0.19	3.17	7.77	nr	**10.95**
tee; equal	0.62	0.28	4.67	0.71	nr	**5.39**
tee; reducing	4.90	0.28	4.67	5.66	nr	**10.34**
straight tap connector	1.59	0.56	9.35	1.84	nr	**11.19**
bent tap connector	1.70	0.76	12.69	1.97	nr	**14.66**
tank connector	5.34	0.28	4.67	6.18	nr	**10.86**
overflow bend	9.02	0.24	4.01	10.44	nr	**14.45**
22 mm pipes; fixing with pipe clips and screwed	2.79	0.43	7.18	3.41	m	**10.59**
Extra for						
made bend	-	0.22	3.67	-	nr	**3.67**
stop end	2.06	0.15	2.50	2.39	nr	**4.89**
straight coupling	0.48	0.24	4.01	0.56	nr	**4.56**
union coupling	9.57	0.24	4.01	11.07	nr	**15.08**
reducing coupling	0.82	0.24	4.01	0.95	nr	**4.96**
copper to lead connector	6.35	0.34	5.68	7.35	nr	**13.03**
elbow	0.85	0.24	4.01	0.98	nr	**4.99**
backplate elbow	9.63	0.49	8.18	11.14	nr	**19.32**
return bend	13.21	0.24	4.01	15.28	nr	**19.29**
tee; equal	1.97	0.37	6.18	2.28	nr	**8.45**
tee; reducing	1.57	0.37	6.18	1.81	nr	**7.99**
straight tap connector	1.71	0.19	3.17	1.98	nr	**5.15**
tank connector	2.79	0.37	6.18	3.31	nr	**9.48**
28 mm pipes; fixing with pipe clips and screwed	3.61	0.46	7.68	4.38	m	**12.06**
Extra for						
made bend	-	0.28	4.67	-	nr	**4.67**
stop end	3.68	0.17	2.84	4.26	nr	**7.10**
straight coupling	1.02	0.31	5.18	1.18	nr	**6.36**
reducing coupling	2.79	0.31	5.18	3.23	nr	**8.41**
union coupling	9.57	0.31	5.18	11.07	nr	**16.25**
copper to lead connector	11.95	0.43	7.18	13.83	nr	**21.01**
imperial to metric adaptor	6.15	0.43	7.18	7.12	nr	**14.30**
elbow	1.64	0.31	5.18	1.90	nr	**7.07**
return bend	16.87	0.31	5.18	19.52	nr	**24.70**
tee; equal	4.54	0.45	7.51	5.25	nr	**12.76**
tank connector	3.61	0.45	7.51	4.27	nr	**11.79**
35 mm pipes; fixing with pipe clips and screwed	7.85	0.53	8.85	9.41	m	**18.25**
Extra for						
made bend	-	0.33	5.51	-	nr	**5.51**
stop end	8.12	0.19	3.17	9.39	nr	**12.57**
straight coupling	3.31	0.37	6.18	3.83	nr	**10.01**
reducing coupling	6.58	0.37	6.18	7.62	nr	**13.79**
union coupling	18.30	0.37	6.18	21.17	nr	**27.34**
flanged connector	50.46	0.49	8.18	58.39	nr	**66.57**
elbow	7.11	0.37	6.18	8.23	nr	**14.41**
tee; equal	11.58	0.51	8.51	13.39	nr	**21.91**
tank connector	13.72	0.51	8.51	15.87	nr	**24.39**

S PIPED SUPPLY SYSTEMS

Item	PC £	Labour hours	Labour £	Material £	Unit	Total rate £
S12 HOT AND COLD WATER (SMALL SCALE) – cont'd						
Copper pipes; capillary fittings – cont'd						
42 mm pipes; fixing with pipe clips; plugged and screwed	9.61	0.59	9.85	11.50	m	**21.35**
Extra for						
made bend	-	0.44	7.35	-	nr	**7.35**
stop end	13.98	0.21	3.51	16.18	nr	**19.68**
straight coupling	5.54	0.43	7.18	6.41	nr	**13.58**
reducing coupling	11.01	0.43	7.18	12.74	nr	**19.91**
union coupling	26.74	0.43	7.18	30.94	nr	**38.12**
flanged connector	60.32	0.56	9.35	69.79	nr	**79.14**
elbow	11.75	0.43	7.18	13.60	nr	**20.78**
obtuse elbow	19.10	0.43	7.18	22.09	nr	**29.27**
tee; equal	18.58	0.57	9.52	21.49	nr	**31.01**
tank connector	17.98	0.57	9.52	20.81	nr	**30.32**
54 mm pipes; fixing with pipe clips; plugged and screwed	12.32	0.65	10.85	14.71	m	**25.56**
Extra for						
made bend	-	0.61	10.18	-	nr	**10.18**
stop end	19.52	0.23	3.84	22.58	nr	**26.42**
straight coupling	10.21	0.49	8.18	11.81	nr	**19.99**
reducing coupling	18.48	0.49	8.18	21.38	nr	**29.56**
union coupling	50.88	0.49	8.18	58.87	nr	**67.05**
flanged connector	91.18	0.56	9.35	105.49	nr	**114.84**
elbow	24.26	0.49	8.18	28.07	nr	**36.25**
obtuse elbow	34.54	0.49	8.18	39.97	nr	**48.15**
tee; equal	37.45	0.63	10.52	43.33	nr	**53.84**
tank connector	27.48	0.63	10.52	31.79	nr	**42.31**
Copper pipes; EN1057:1996; compression fittings						
15 mm pipes; fixing with pipe clips; plugged and screwed	1.39	0.42	7.01	1.75	m	**8.77**
Extra for						
made bend	-	0.17	2.84	-	nr	**2.84**
stop end	2.10	0.11	1.84	2.42	nr	**4.26**
straight coupling	1.68	0.17	2.84	1.94	nr	**4.78**
reducing set	1.80	0.19	3.17	2.08	nr	**5.25**
male coupling	1.50	0.22	3.67	1.73	nr	**5.40**
female coupling	1.81	0.22	3.67	2.09	nr	**5.76**
90 degree bend	2.03	0.17	2.84	2.35	nr	**5.19**
90 degree backplate bend	5.33	0.33	5.51	6.16	nr	**11.67**
tee; equal	2.84	0.24	4.01	3.29	nr	**7.29**
tee; backplate	7.12	0.24	4.01	8.24	nr	**12.24**
tank coupling	4.28	0.24	4.01	4.95	nr	**8.96**
22 mm pipes; fixing with pipe clips; plugged and screwed	2.79	0.47	7.85	3.41	m	**11.26**
Extra for						
made bend	-	0.22	3.67	-	nr	**3.67**
stop end	3.04	0.13	2.17	3.52	nr	**5.69**
straight coupling	2.75	0.22	3.67	3.18	nr	**6.86**
reducing set	1.94	0.06	1.00	2.25	nr	**3.25**
male coupling	2.28	0.31	5.18	2.64	nr	**7.81**
female coupling	2.64	0.31	5.18	3.05	nr	**8.23**
90 degree bend	3.23	0.22	3.67	3.74	nr	**7.41**
tee; equal	4.71	0.33	5.51	5.45	nr	**10.96**
tee; reducing	7.30	0.33	5.51	8.45	nr	**13.96**
tank coupling	4.74	0.33	5.51	5.49	nr	**11.00**

S PIPED SUPPLY SYSTEMS

Item	PC £	Labour hours	Labour £	Material £	Unit	Total rate £
28 mm pipes; fixing with pipe clips; plugged and screwed	3.61	0.51	8.51	4.38	m	12.89
Extra for						
made bend	-	0.28	4.67	-	nr	4.67
stop end	6.33	0.16	2.67	7.32	nr	9.99
straight coupling	6.05	0.28	4.67	7.00	nr	11.67
male coupling	4.29	0.39	6.51	4.96	nr	11.47
female coupling	5.55	0.39	6.51	6.42	nr	12.93
90 degree bend	7.82	0.28	4.67	9.04	nr	13.72
tee; equal	12.46	0.41	6.84	14.41	nr	21.26
tee; reducing	12.03	0.41	6.84	13.92	nr	20.77
tank coupling	9.66	0.41	6.84	11.18	nr	18.03
35 mm pipes; fixing with pipe clips; plugged and screwed	7.85	0.57	9.52	9.41	m	18.92
Extra for						
made bend	-	0.33	5.51	-	nr	5.51
stop end	9.74	0.18	3.00	11.27	nr	14.28
straight coupling	12.57	0.33	5.51	14.54	nr	20.05
male coupling	9.55	0.44	7.35	11.05	nr	18.40
female coupling	11.47	0.44	7.35	13.27	nr	20.62
tee; equal	22.08	0.46	7.68	25.55	nr	33.23
tee; reducing	21.58	0.46	7.68	24.96	nr	32.64
tank coupling	11.50	0.46	7.68	13.30	nr	20.98
42 mm pipes; fixing with pipe clips; plugged and screwed	9.61	0.64	10.68	11.50	m	22.18
Extra for						
made bend	-	0.44	7.35	-	nr	7.35
stop end	16.22	0.20	3.34	18.76	nr	22.10
straight coupling	16.05	0.39	6.51	18.57	nr	25.08
male coupling	14.33	0.50	8.35	16.58	nr	24.92
female coupling	15.43	0.50	8.35	17.85	nr	26.20
tee; equal	34.70	0.52	8.68	40.15	nr	48.83
tee; reducing	33.34	0.52	8.68	38.58	nr	47.26
54 mm pipes; fixing with pipe clips; plugged and screwed	12.32	0.69	11.52	14.71	m	26.23
Extra for						
made bend	-	0.61	10.18	-	nr	10.18
straight coupling	24.72	0.44	7.35	28.60	nr	35.95
male coupling	21.17	0.56	9.35	24.49	nr	33.84
female coupling	22.63	0.56	9.35	26.18	nr	35.53
tee; equal	55.74	0.57	9.52	64.49	nr	74.01
tee; reducing	55.74	0.57	9.52	64.49	nr	74.01
Copper, brass and gunmetal ancillaries; screwed joints to fittings						
Stopcock; brass/gunmetal capillary joints to copper						
15 mm nominal size	4.65	0.22	3.67	5.38	nr	9.05
22 mm nominal size	8.68	0.30	5.01	10.04	nr	15.05
28 mm nominal size	24.67	0.38	6.34	28.54	nr	34.89
Stopcock; brass/gunmetal compression joints to copper						
15 mm nominal size	6.38	0.20	3.34	7.38	nr	10.72
22 mm nominal size	11.21	0.27	4.51	12.97	nr	17.47
28 mm nominal size	29.24	0.33	5.51	33.83	nr	39.34
Stopcock; brass/gunmetal compression joints to polyethylene						
15 mm nominal size	15.96	0.29	4.84	18.47	nr	23.31
22 mm nominal size	27.74	0.37	6.18	32.10	nr	38.28
28 mm nominal size	29.58	0.44	7.35	34.23	nr	41.57

S PIPED SUPPLY SYSTEMS

Item	PC £	Labour hours	Labour £	Material £	Unit	Total rate £
S12 HOT AND COLD WATER (SMALL SCALE) – cont'd						
Copper, brass and gunmetal ancillaries – cont'd Gunmetal "Fullway" gate valve; capillary joints to copper						
15 mm nominal size	14.55	0.22	3.67	16.84	nr	20.51
22 mm nominal size	16.86	0.30	5.01	19.50	nr	24.51
28 mm nominal size	23.47	0.38	6.34	27.16	nr	33.50
35 mm nominal size	52.37	0.45	7.51	60.59	nr	68.10
42 mm nominal size	65.46	0.52	8.68	75.74	nr	84.42
54 mm nominal size	94.97	0.59	9.85	109.88	nr	119.72
Brass gate valve; compression joints to copper						
15 mm nominal size	10.41	0.33	5.51	12.04	nr	17.55
22 mm nominal size	12.14	0.44	7.35	14.04	nr	21.39
28 mm nominal size	21.17	0.56	9.35	24.49	nr	33.84
Chromium plated; lockshield radiator valve; union outlet						
15 mm nominal size	5.41	0.24	4.01	6.26	nr	10.26
Water tanks/cisterns						
Polyethylene cold water feed and expansion cistern; BS 4213; with covers						
ref SC15; 68 litres	53.47	1.39	23.20	60.36	nr	83.56
ref SC25; 114 litres	62.93	1.61	26.88	71.03	nr	97.91
ref SC40; 182 litres	73.91	1.61	26.88	83.43	nr	110.30
ref SC50; 227 litres	101.93	2.16	36.06	115.05	nr	151.11
GRP cold water storage cistern; with covers						
ref 899.10; 30 litres	126.35	1.22	20.37	142.62	nr	162.99
ref 899.25; 68 litres	159.47	1.39	23.20	180.00	nr	203.21
ref 899.40; 114 litres	198.27	1.61	26.88	223.80	nr	250.67
ref 899.70; 227 litres	248.62	2.16	36.06	280.63	nr	316.69
Storage cylinders/calorifiers						
Copper cylinders; single feed coil indirect; BS 1566 Part 2; grade 3						
ref 2; 96 litres	-	2.22	37.06	203.82	nr	240.88
ref 3; 114 litres	114.89	2.50	41.74	129.68	nr	171.41
ref 7; 117 litres	113.37	2.78	46.41	127.97	nr	174.38
ref 8; 140 litres	128.35	3.33	55.59	144.88	nr	200.47
ref 9; 162 litres	163.94	3.89	64.94	185.05	nr	249.99
Combination copper hot water storage units; coil direct; BS 3198; (hot/cold)						
400 mm x 900 mm; 65/20 litres	133.43	3.11	51.92	150.61	nr	202.53
450 mm x 900 mm; 85/25 litres	137.41	4.33	72.29	155.11	nr	227.39
450 mm x 1075 mm; 115/25 litres	151.16	5.44	90.82	170.62	nr	261.44
450 mm x 1200 mm; 115/45 litres	160.92	6.11	102.00	181.64	nr	283.64
Combination copper hot water storage						
450 mm x 900 mm; 85/25 litres	172.33	4.88	81.47	194.51	nr	275.98
450 mm x 1200 mm; 115/45 litres	197.06	6.66	111.18	222.43	nr	333.61

S PIPED SUPPLY SYSTEMS

Item	PC £	Labour hours	Labour £	Material £	Unit	Total rate £
Thermal insulation						
19 mm thick rigid mineral glass fibre sectional pipe lagging; plain finish; fixed with aluminium bands to steel or copper pipework; including working over pipe fittings						
around 15/15 pipes	6.87	0.07	1.17	8.14	m	9.31
around 20/22 pipes	7.39	0.11	1.84	8.75	m	10.59
around 25/28 pipes	8.00	0.12	2.00	9.48	m	11.48
around 32/35 pipes	8.82	0.13	2.17	10.45	m	12.62
around 40/42 pipes	9.40	0.15	2.50	11.14	m	13.64
around 50/54 pipes	10.84	0.17	2.84	12.85	m	15.68
19 mm thick rigid mineral glass fibre sectional pipe lagging; canvas or class O lacquered aluminium finish; fixed with aluminium bands to steel or copper pipework; including working over pipe fittings						
around 15/15 pipes	9.36	0.07	1.17	11.09	m	12.26
around 20/22 pipes	10.19	0.11	1.84	12.08	m	13.92
around 25/28 pipes	11.18	0.12	2.00	13.25	m	15.26
around 32/35 pipes	12.18	0.13	2.17	14.43	m	16.60
around 40/42 pipes	13.09	0.15	2.50	15.52	m	18.02
around 50/54 pipes	15.18	0.17	2.84	17.99	m	20.83
60 mm thick glass-fibre filled polyethylene insulating jackets for GRP or polyethylene cold water cisterns; complete with fixing bands; for cisterns size						
450 mm x 300 mm x 300 mm (45 litres)	-	0.44	7.35	-	nr	7.35
650 mm x 500 mm x 400 mm (91 litres)	-	0.67	11.19	-	nr	11.19
675 mm x 525 mm x 500 mm (136 litres)	-	0.78	13.02	-	nr	13.02
675 mm x 575 mm x 525 mm (182 litres)	-	0.89	14.86	-	nr	14.86
1000 mm x 625 mm x 525 mm (273 litres)	-	0.94	15.69	-	nr	15.69
1125 mm x 650 mm x 575 mm (341 litres)	-	0.94	15.69	-	nr	15.69
80 mm thick glass-fibre filled insulating jackets in flame retardant PVC to BS 1763; type 1B; segmental type for hot water cylinders; complete with fixing bands; for cylinders size						
400 mm x 900 mm; ref 2	-	0.37	6.18	-	nr	6.18
450 mm x 900 mm; ref 7	-	0.37	6.18	-	nr	6.18
450 mm x 1050 mm; ref 8	-	0.44	7.35	-	nr	7.35
450 mm x 1200 mm	-	0.56	9.35	-	nr	9.35
S13 PRESSURISED WATER						
Blue MDPE pipes; BS 6572; mains pipework; no joints in the running length; laid in trenches						
Pipes						
20 mm nominal size	0.66	0.12	2.00	0.77	m	2.77
25 mm nominal size	0.75	0.13	2.17	0.87	m	3.04
32 mm nominal size	1.29	0.15	2.50	1.50	m	4.00
50 mm nominal size	3.06	0.17	2.84	3.55	m	6.39
63 mm nominal size	4.83	0.18	3.00	5.62	m	8.62

S PIPED SUPPLY SYSTEMS

Item	PC £	Labour hours	Labour £	Material £	Unit	Total rate £
S13 PRESSURISED WATER – cont'd						
Ductile iron bitumen coated pipes and fittings; EN598; class K9; Stanton's "Tyton" water main pipes or other equal and approved; flexible joints						
100 mm pipes; laid straight	21.51	0.67	7.59	33.29	m	40.88
Extra for						
bend; 45 degrees	45.57	0.67	7.59	69.58	nr	77.17
branch; 45 degrees; socketted	331.95	1.00	11.33	416.78	nr	428.11
tee	71.93	1.00	11.33	108.61	nr	119.94
flanged spigot	45.62	0.67	7.59	61.86	nr	69.45
flanged socket	43.40	0.67	7.59	59.22	nr	66.81
150 mm pipes; laid straight	27.65	0.78	8.84	41.16	m	50.00
Extra for						
bend; 45 degrees	71.33	0.78	8.84	101.30	nr	110.14
branch; 45 degrees; socketted	423.66	1.17	13.26	527.26	nr	540.52
tee	149.41	1.17	13.26	202.23	nr	215.49
flanged spigot	52.91	0.78	8.84	71.09	nr	79.93
flanged socket	69.06	0.78	8.84	90.23	nr	99.07
200 mm pipes; laid straight	37.92	1.11	12.58	57.06	m	69.64
Extra for						
bend; 45 degrees	128.73	1.11	12.58	176.80	nr	189.38
branch; 45 degrees; socketted	481.18	1.67	18.93	606.64	nr	625.56
tee	205.31	1.67	18.93	279.68	nr	298.61
flanged spigot	115.23	1.11	12.58	148.68	nr	161.26
flanged socket	109.26	1.11	12.58	141.61	nr	154.19

T MECHANICAL HEATING/COOLING SYSTEMS ETC.

Item	PC £	Labour hours	Labour £	Material £	Unit	Total rate £
T10 GAS/OIL FIRED BOILERS						
Boilers						
Gas fired floor standing domestic boilers; cream or white; enamelled casing; 32 mm diameter BSPT female flow and return tappings; 102 mm diameter flue socket 13 mm diameter BSPT male draw-off outlet						
13.19 kW output (45,000 Btu/Hr)	-	5.55	106.37	767.20	nr	**873.57**
23.45 kW output (80,000 Btu/Hr)	-	5.55	106.37	980.92	nr	**1087.29**
T31 LOW TEMPERATURE HOT WATER HEATING						
NOTE: The reader is referred to section "S12 Hot and Cold Water (Small Scale)" for rates for copper pipework which will equally apply to this section of work. For further and more detailed information the reader is advised to consult "Spon's Mechanical and Electrical Services Price Book".						
Radiators; Hudevad Heat Emitters or other equal and approved						
"Plan"; single panel type; steel 700 mm high; wheelhead and lockshield valves						
567 mm long	83.36	2.22	42.55	106.82	nr	**149.37**
1200 mm long	147.32	2.50	47.92	179.02	nr	**226.93**
2200 mm long	232.61	2.78	53.28	275.28	nr	**328.56**
3000 mm long	339.21	3.05	58.46	395.71	nr	**454.17**

V ELECTRICAL SYSTEMS

Item	PC £	Labour hours	Labour £	Material £	Unit	Total rate £
V21/V22 GENERAL LIGHTING AND LV POWER						
NOTE: The following items indicate approximate prices for wiring of lighting and power points complete, including accessories and socket outlets but excluding lighting fittings. Consumer control units are shown separately. For a more detailed breakdown of these costs and specialist costs for a complete range of electrical items, reference should be made to "Spon's Mechanical and Electrical Services Price Book".						
Consumer control units 8-way 60 amp SP&N surface mounted insulated consumer control units fitted with miniature circuit breakers including 2 m long 32 mm screwed welded conduit with three runs of 16 mm2 PVC cables ready for final connections	-	-	-	-	nr	193.75
extra for current operated ELCB of 30 mA tripping current	-	-	-	-	nr	78.71
As above but 100 amp metal cased consumer unit and 25 mm2 PVC cables	-	-	-	-	nr	211.91
extra for current operated ELCB of 30 mA tripping current	-	-	-	-	nr	181.64
Final circuits Lighting points						
wired in PVC insulated and PVC sheathed cable in flats and houses; insulated in cavities and roof space; protected where buried by heavy gauge PVC conduit	-	-	-	-	nr	48.44
as above but in commercial property	-	-	-	-	nr	60.55
wired in PVC insulated cable in screwed welded conduit in commercial property	-	-	-	-	nr	187.69
as above but in industrial property	-	-	-	-	nr	205.86
wired in MICC cable in commercial property	-	-	-	-	nr	157.42
as above but in industrial property with PVC sheathed cable	-	-	-	-	nr	175.59
Single 13 amp switched socket outlet points						
wired in PVC insulated and PVC sheathed cable in flats and houses on a ring main circuit; protected where buried by heavy gauge PVC conduit	-	-	-	-	nr	72.66
as above but in commercial property	-	-	-	-	nr	84.77
wired in PVC insulated cable in screwed welded conduit throughout on a ring main in commercial property	-	-	-	-	nr	193.75
as above but in industrial property	-	-	-	-	nr	205.86
wired in MICC cable on a ring main circuit in commercial property	-	-	-	-	nr	199.80
as above but in industrial property with PVC sheathed cable	-	-	-	-	nr	217.97
Cooker control units						
45 amp circuit including unit wired in PVC insulated and PVC sheathed cable; protected where buried by heavy gauge PVC conduit	-	-	-	-	nr	102.93
as above but wired in PVC insulated cable in screwed welded conduit	-	-	-	-	nr	230.08
as above but wired in MICC cable	-	-	-	-	nr	254.30

W SECURITY SYSTEMS

Item	PC £	Labour hours	Labour £	Material £	Unit	Total rate £
W20 LIGHTNING PROTECTION						
Lightning protection equipment						
Copper strip roof or down conductors fixed with bracket or saddle clips						
20 mm x 3 mm flat section	-	-	-	-	m	**20.35**
25 mm x 3 mm flat section	-	-	-	-	m	**23.27**
Aluminium strip roof or down conductors fixed with bracket or saddle clips						
20 mm x 3 mm flat section	-	-	-	-	m	**15.84**
25 mm x 3 mm flat section	-	-	-	-	m	**16.80**
Joints in tapes	-	-	-	-	nr	**12.41**
Bonding connections to roof and structural metalwork	-	-	-	-	nr	**71.09**
Testing points	-	-	-	-	nr	**34.90**
Earth electrodes						
16 mm diameter driven copper electrodes in 1220 mm long sectional lengths (minimum 2440 mm long overall)	-	-	-	-	nr	**187.42**
first 2440 mm length driven and tested 25 mm x 3 mm copper strip electrode in 457 mm deep prepared trench	-	-	-	-	m	**14.22**

The Presentation and Settlement of Contractors' Claims
Second Edition

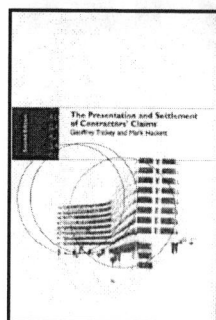

Geoffrey Trickey and Mark Hackett

Contractual disputes, often involving large sums of money, occur with increasing frequency in the construction industry. This book presents - in non-legal language - sound professional advice from a recognized expert in the field on the practical aspects of claims. This edition has been brought right up to date by taking into account legal decisions promulgated over the last 17 years, as well as reflecting the effect of current inflation on claims.

This new, fully updated edition of this practical guide is based on the 1998 JCT contract. The title contains numerous worked examples to support the advice offered, relating it to practitioners' experiences.

Contents: General. Introduction. 1998 edition of the Joint Contracts Tribunal standard form of building contract. Extensions of time. Variations and disruption. Ascertaining the loss or expense. Nominated sub-contractors and suppliers. Determination of the employment of the contractor. Comparison between the various editions of the JCT standard form of building contract. The JCT family of forms. The control of claims. A worked example of the ascertainment of direct loss and/or expense. Index.

November 2000: 234x156 mm: 512 pp.
5 line illustrations
HB: 0-419-20500-4: £85.00

To Order: Tel: +44 (0) 1264 343071 Fax: +44 (0) 1264 343005, or
Post: Taylor and Francis Customer Services, Thomson Publishing Services, Cheriton House, Andover, Hants, SP10 5BE, UK Email: book.orders@tandf.co.uk

For a complete listing of all our titles visit:
www.sponpress.com

Taylor & Francis
Taylor & Francis Group plc

The Contractor of Choice

Tindale Cresent
Bishop Auckland
Co Durham
DL14 9TL

Tel:-   01388 605636
Fax:-   01388 608841

www.hathaway-roofing.co.uk

Formed in 1967, Hathaway Roofing is the UK's leading Roofing and cladding contractor undertaking individual contracts from a value of approx. £400,000 up to our largest contract to date, Terminal 5 at Heathrow, which is worth in excess of £30 million.

From our head office and fabrication facilities in the North East Hathaway are involved in the construction of many major projects throughout the UK. We can undertake the most complex of building designs, producing construction solutions quickly and efficiently.

We actively seek early involvement in the contract where our in depth experience of a wide range of specifications and materials ensures the most suitable and cost effective solution for any individual project.

Whatever your project, visit our website for contact information and details of projects we have completed to date.

Operating Sectors

- Retail
- Distribution
- Manufacturing
- Leisure
- Commercial

Hathaway – The Complete Envelope Solution

Approximate Estimating

This part of the book contains the following sections:

Building Costs and Tender Prices

The tables which follow show the changes in building costs and tender prices since 1985. To avoid confusion it is essential that the terms "building costs" and "tender prices" are clearly defined and understood. "Building costs" are the costs incurred by the builder in the course of his business, the principal ones being those for labour and materials. "Tender Price" is the price for which a builder offers to erect a building.

Building costs
This table reflects the fluctuations since 1985 in wages and materials costs to the builder. In compiling the table, the proportion of labour to material has been assumed to be 40:60. The wages element has been assessed from a contract wages sheet revalued for each variation in labour costs, whilst the changes in the costs of materials have been based upon the indices prepared by the Department of Trade and Industry. No allowance has been made for changes in productivity, plus rates or hours worked which may occur in particular conditions and localities.

1976 = 100 (commencing from 1985)

Year	First quarter	Second Quarter	Third quarter	Fourth quarter	Annual Average
1985	243	245	252	254	248
1986	256	258	266	267	262
1987	270	272	281	282	276
1988	284	286	299	302	293
1989	305	307	322	323	314
1990	326	329	346	347	337
1991	350	350	360	360	355
1992	361	362	367	368	365
1993	370	371	373	374	372
1994	376	379	385	388	382
1995	392	397	407	407	401
1996	407	408	414	414	411
1997	416	417	423	429	421
1998	430	431	448	447	439
1999	446	443	473	478	460
2000	480	482	497	498	489
2001	498	499	516	515	507
2002	516	522	553	554	536
2003	555	560	578	577	568
2004	579	586	617	618	600
2005	621 (P)	624 (F)	664 (F)	666 (F)	644 (F)
2006	668 (F)	670 (F)	689 (F)	690 (F)	679 (F)
2007	692 (F)	696 (F)	716 (F)	717(F)	705 (F)
2008	720 (F)	723 (F)	739 (F)	742 (F)	731 (F)

Note: P = Provisional   F = Forecast

Tender Prices

Tender prices are similar to "building costs" but also takes into account market considerations such as the availability of labour and materials, and prevailing economic situation. This means that in "boom" periods, when there is a surfeit of building work to be done, "tender prices" may increase at a greater rate than "building costs", whilst in a period when work is scarce, "tender prices" may actually fall when "building costs" are rising.

This table reflects the changes in tender prices since 1985. It indicates the level of pricing contained in the lowest competitive tenders for new work in the Greater London area (over £2,500,000 in value).

1976 = 100 (commencing from 1985)

Year	First quarter	Second Quarter	Third quarter	Fourth quarter	Annual average
1985	215	219	219	220	218
1986	221	226	234	234	229
1987	242	249	265	279	258
1988	289	299	321	328	309
1989	341	335	340	345	340
1990	320	315	312	290	309
1991	272	262	261	254	262
1992	250	248	241	233	243
1993	227	242	233	239	235
1994	239	247	266	256	252
1995	258	265	266	270	265
1996	265	262	270	270	267
1997	275	287	284	287	283
1998	305	312	318	318	313
1999	325	332	330	342	332
2000	348	353	362	375	359
2001	375	383	388	392	384
2002	398	405	423	421	412
2003	425	424	432	434	429
2004	434	436	442	454	442
2005	461(P)	466(F)	473(F)	477(F)	469(F)
2006	481(F)	488(F)	495(F)	500(F)	491(F)
2007	505(F)	514(F)	522(F)	528(F)	517(F)
2008	534(F)	540(F)	548(F)	553(F)	544(F)

Note: P = Provisional   F = Forecast

Tender prices for the Greater London area during 2004 rose by approximately 6% to the first quarter of 2005. Although construction activity in London has slowed, and there are growing concerns about a static housing market at what is normally a buoyant time of year, there is still a certain amount of optimism regarding construction activity and investment for 2005/6. Our current prediction is that most regions will see tender inflation of between 4% and 5% over the year ahead.

Tender Prices – cont'd

Readers will be kept abreast of tender price movements in the free *Spon's Updates* and also in the *Tender Price Forecast* and *Cost Update* articles, published quarterly in *Building* magazine.

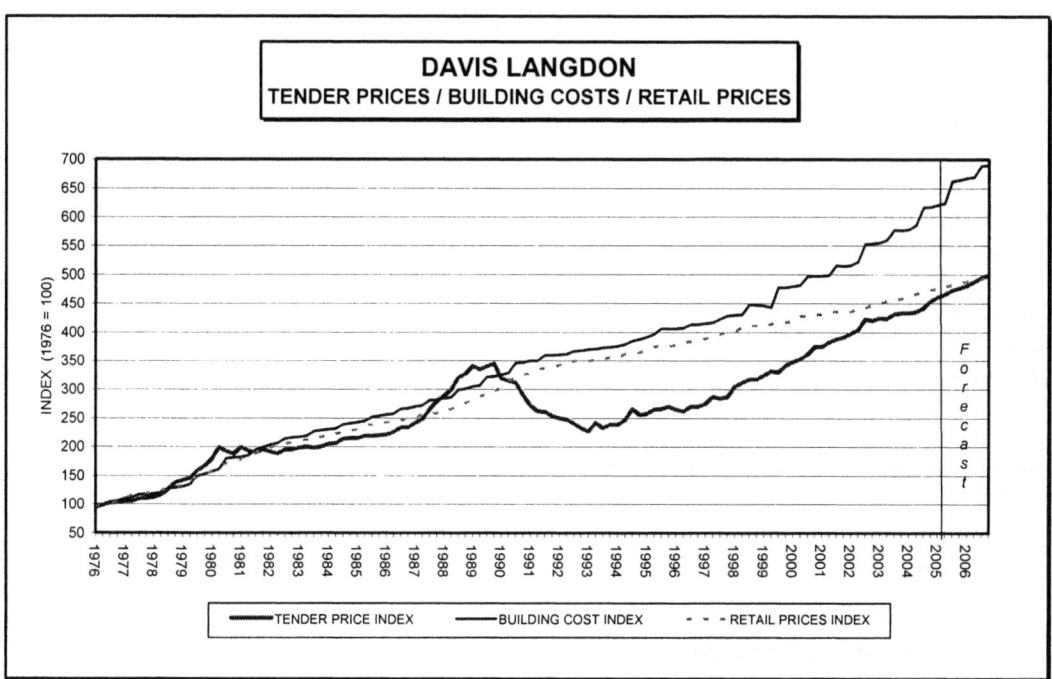

Regional Variations

As well as being aware of inflationary trends when preparing an estimate, it is also important to establish the appropriate price level for the project location.

Prices throughout this book reflect price levels for between the first quarter of 2006 in Outer London. Regional variations for certain inner London boroughs can be up to 14% higher while prices in the North and Yorkshire and Humberside can be as much as 16% lower. Broad regional adjustment factors to assist with the preparation of initial estimates are shown in the table on the next page.

Over time, price differentials can change depending on regional workloads and local "hot spots". Workloads and prices are expected to rise faster in most of the regions than Greater London and South East. In the year to the first quarter 2004 prices in Greater London rose by about 6%, but in other regions prices rose by up to 9%. The effect of this will be a convergence of rates and regional variations. *Spon's Updates* and the *Tender Price Forecast* and *Cost Update* featured in *Building* magazine will keep readers informed of the latest regional developments and changes as they occur.

The regional variations shown in the table on the next page are based on our forecast of price differentials in each of the economic planning regions in the first quarter 2006. The table shows the forecast first quarter 2006 tender price index for each region plus the recommended percentage adjustments required to the Major Works section of the Prices for Measured Work. (Prices in the book are at a Tender Price Index level of 480 for Outer London).

Region	Forecast first quarter 2006 tender price index	Percentage adjustment to *Major Works* section
Outer London	481	-
Inner London	519	+8
East Anglia	447	-7
East Midlands	414	-14
Northern	409	-15
Northern Ireland	313	-35
North West	443	-8
Scotland	409	-15
South East	467	-3
South West	443	-8
Wales	418	-13
West Midlands	418	-13
Yorkshire and Humberside	404	-16

Special further adjustment to the above percentages may be necessary when considering city centre or very isolated locations.

The following example illustrates the adjustment of an estimate prepared using *Spon's A&B 2006*, to a price level that reflects the forecast Outer London market conditions for competitive tenders in the first quarter 2006:

			£
A	Value of items priced using Spon's A&B 2006 i.e. Tender Price Index 480		1,565,000
B	Adjustment to reduce value of A to forecast price level for first quarter 2006 i.e. Forecast Tender Price Index 481 $\frac{(480-481)}{481} \times 100 =$ say 0% say		-
			1,565,000
C	Value of items priced using competitive quotations that reflect the market conditions in the first quarter 2006		800,000
			2,365,000
D	Allowance for preliminaries +12% say		285,000
E	Total value of estimate at first quarter 2006 price levels	£	2,650,000

Alternatively, for a similar estimate in Scotland:

			£
A	Value of items priced using Spon's A&B 2006 i.e. Tender Price Index 480		1,565,000
B	Adjustment to reduce value of A to forecast price level for first quarter 2006 for Scotland (from regional variation table) i.e. Tender Price Index 361 $\frac{(409 - 481)}{481} \times 100 = -15\%$ deduct 15% say		-235,000
			1,330,000
C	Value of items priced using competitive quotations that reflect the market conditions in the first quarter 2006		800,000
			2,130,000
D	Allowance for preliminaries +12% say		255,000
E	Total value of estimate at first quarter 2006 price levels	£	2,385,000

Scotland 409

Spons Architects` and
Builders` Price Book
2006 Edition
(Tender Index 480)

Map Base Index 481

Northern
Ireland 313

Northern 409

Yorkshire &
Humberside
404

North
West
443

East
Midlands
414

East Anglia
447

West
Midlands
418

Wales
418

Southeast
467
(excl Lond)

Southwest 443

Inner London 519
Outer London 481

Building Prices per Functional Unit

Prices given under this heading are average prices, on a *fluctuating basis*, for typical buildings based on a tender price level index of 480(1976 = 100). Prices includes for Preliminaries at 12% and overheads and profit. Unless otherwise stated, prices do not allow for external works, furniture, loose or special equipment and are, of course, exclusive of fees for professional services.

On certain types of buildings there exists a close relationship between its cost and the number of functional units that it accommodates. During the early stages of a project therefore an approximate estimate can be derived by multiplying the proposed unit of accommodation (i.e. hotel bedrooms, car parking spaces etc.) by an appropriate cost.

The following indicative unit areas and costs have been derived from historic data. It is emphasized that the prices must be treated with reserve, as they represent the average of prices from our records and cannot provide more than a rough guide to the cost of a building. There are limitations when using this method of estimating, for example, the functional areas and costs of football stadia are strongly influenced by the extent of front and back of house facilities housed within it, and these areas can vary considerably from scheme to scheme.

The areas may also be used as a "rule of thumb" in order to check on economy of designs. Where we have chosen not to show indicative areas, this is because either ranges are extensive or such figures may be misleading.

Costs have been expressed within a range, although this is not to suggest that figures outside this range will not be encountered, but simply that the calibre of such a type of building can itself vary significantly.

For assistance with the compilation of a closer estimate, or of a Cost Plan, the reader is directed to the *"Building Prices per Square Metre"* and *"Approximate Estimates"* sections. As elsewhere in this edition, prices do not include V.A.T., which is generally applied at the current rate to all non-domestic building (except those with charitable status).

Function:		Indicative functional unit area:	Indicative functional cost:
Utilities, civil engineering facilities (CI/SfB 1)			
Car Parking	- surface level	20 – 22 m²/car	£900 - £1,500/car
	- ground level (under buildings)	22 – 24 m²/car	£2,000 - £4,000/car
	- multi storey	23 – 27 m²/car	£4,000 - £10,000/car
	- semi basement	27 – 30 m²/car	£10,000 - £15,000/car
	- basement	28 – 37 m²/car	£20,000 - £30,000/car
Administrative, commercial protective service facilities (CI/SfB 3)			
Office – air conditioned	- low density cellular	15 m²/person	£10,000 - £20,000/person
	- high density open plan	20 m²/person	£14,000 - £28,000/person
Health and welfare facilities (CI/SfB 4)			
Hospitals	- district general	65 – 85 m²/bed	£82,500 - £123,000/bed
	- teaching	120 + m²/bed	£110,000 - £150,000/bed
	- private	75 – 100 m²/bed	£120,000 - £185,000/bed
Nursing Homes	- residential home	-	£24,600 - £47,600/bed
	- nursing homes	-	£34,000 - £95,800/bed

Building Prices per Functional Unit

Function:		Indicative functional unit area:	Indicative functional cost:
Recreational facilities (Cl/SfB 5)			
Football	- basic stand	0.50 – 0.85 m²/seat	£650 - £950/seat
Stadia	- stand plus basic	0.85 – 1.28 m²/seat	£950 - £1,570/seat
facilities			
	- stand plus extensive facilities	1.00 – 1.30 m²/seat	£1,400 - £1,950/seat
	- national stadia plus extensive facilities	1.20 – 1.80 m²/seat	£2,670 - £4,000/seat
Theatres	- theatre refurbishment	-	£9,100 - £13,100/seat
	- workshop (fewer than 500 seats)	-	£4,500 - £12,000/seat
	- more than 500 seats	-	£20,000 - £30,000/seat
Educational, scientific, information facilities (Cl/SfB 7)			
Schools	- nursery	3 – 5 m²/child	£4,000 - £9,500/child
	- secondary	6 – 10 m²/child	£8,000 - £16,000/child
	- boarding	10 – 12 m²/child	£10,000 - £18,000/child
	- special	18 – 20 m²/child	£25,000 - £38,000/child
Residential facilities (Cl/SfB 8)			
Housing (private	- terraced; two bedroom	55 – 65 m²/gifa	£40,000 - £47,500/house
developer)	- semi-detached; three bedroom	70 – 90 m²/gifa	£61,500 - £67,500 house
	- detached; four bedroom	90 – 100 m²/gifa	£82,450 - £122,500/house
	- low rise flats; two bedroom	55 – 65 m²/gifa	£45,000 - £65,000/flat
	- medium rise flat; two room	55 – 65 m²/gifa	£55,000 - £75,000/flat
Hotels	- budget roadside hotel		
	- two-three storey lodge, excluding dining facilities	28 – 35 m²/bedroom	£34,000 - £45,000/bedroom
	- budget city-centre hotel (office conversation) four-six storeys, excluding dining facilities	32 – 38 m²/bedroom	£30,750 - £61,000/bedroom
	- mid-range provincial hotel two-three storeys, bedroom extension	33 – 40 m²/bedroom	£46,000 - £66,000/bedroom

Function: **Residential facilities (CI/SfB 8)** **Hotels** – cont'd		**Indicative functional unit area:**	**Indicative Functional cost:**
	- budget city-centre hotel (new build) four-six storeys, dining bar and facilities	35 – 45 m²/bedroom	£38,500 - £61,500/bedroom
	- city centre apart hotel 4 to seven storeys, apartments with self-catering facilities	50 – 60 m²/bedroom	£61,500 - £95,500/bedroom
	- mid range provincial hotel two to three storeys, conference and leisure facilities	50 – 60 m²/bedroom	£75,000 -£118,000/bedroom
	- business town centre provincial hotel four to six storeys, conference and wet leisure facilities	70 – 100m²/bedroom	£130,000 - £185,000/bedroom
	- luxury city-centre hotel – multi-storey conference and wet leisure facilities	70 – 130 m²/bedroom	£185,000 - £275,000/bedroom
Hotel furniture, fittings and equipment	- budget hotel - mid-range hotel - luxury hotel	- - -	£3,750 - £7,750/bedroom £13,000 - £20,000/bedroom £32,000 - £78,000/bedroom
Students Residences	- large turnkey budget schemes (200 + units), simple design, open site; en suite accommodation	18 – 20 m²/bedroom	£14,000 - £30,000/bedroom
	- smaller schemes (40 – 100 units) with mid range specifications, some with en suite bathroom and kitchen facilities	19 – 24 m²/bedroom	£25,000 - £50,000/bedroom
	- smaller high quality courtyard schemes of collegiate style in restricted city centre sites	24 – 28 m²/bedroom	£40,000 - £66,000/bedroom

2nd Edition
Spon's Irish Construction Price Book

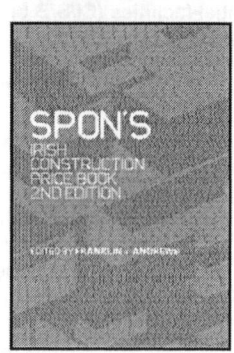

Franklin + Andrews

This new edition of *Spon's Irish Construction Price Book*, edited by Franklin + Andrews, is the only complete and up-to-date source of cost data for this important market.

• All the materials costs, labour rates, labour constants and cost per square metre are based on current conditions in Ireland

• Structured according to the new Agreed Rules of Measurement (second edition)

• 30 pages of Approximate Estimating Rates for quick pricing

This price book is an essential aid to profitable contracting for all those operating in Ireland's booming construction industry.

Franklin + Andrews, Construction Economists, have offices in 100 countries and in-depth experience and expertise in all sectors of the construction industry.

April 2004: 246x174 mm: 448 pages
HB: 0-415-34409-3: £125.00

To Order: Tel: +44 (0) 1264 343071 Fax: +44 (0) 1264 343005, or
Post: Taylor and Francis Customer Services, Thomson Publishing Services, Cheriton House, Andover, Hants, SP10 5BE, UK Email: book.orders@tandf.co.uk

For a complete listing of all our titles visit:
www.sponpress.com

Taylor & Francis
Taylor & Francis Group plc

Building Prices per Square Metre

Prices given under this heading are average prices, on a *fluctuating basis*, for typical buildings based on a tender price level index of 480 (1976 = 100). Prices allow for Preliminaries at 12% and overheads and profit. Unless otherwise stated, prices do not allow for external works, furniture, loose or special equipment and are, of course, exclusive of fees for professional services.

Prices are based upon the total floor area of all storeys, measured between external walls and without deduction for internal walls, columns, stairwells, lift wells and the like.

As in previous editions it is emphasized that the prices must be treated with reserve, as they represent the average of prices from our records and cannot provide more than a rough guide to the cost of a building.

In many instances normal commercial pressures together with a limited range of available specifications ensure that a single rate is sufficient to indicate the prevailing average price. However, where such restrictions do not apply a range has been given; this is not to suggest that figures outside this range will not be encountered, but simply that the calibre of such a type of building can itself vary significantly.

For assistance with the compilation of a closer estimate, or of a Cost Plan, the reader is directed to the *"Approximate Estimates"* sections. As elsewhere in this edition, prices do not include V.A.T., which is generally applied at the current rate to all non-domestic building (except those with charitable status).

Utilities, civil engineering facilities (CI/SfB 1)	Square metre excluding VAT £		
Surface car parking	45	to	70
Surface car parking; landscaped	65	to	110
Multi storey car parks			
grade & upper level	180	to	250
flat slab	300	to	500
Underground car parks			
partially underground under buildings; naturally ventilated	400	to	480
completely underground under buildings	700	to	850
completely underground with landscaped roof	860	to	1,020
Railway stations	1,500	to	2,500
Bus and coach stations	700	to	1,500
Bus garages	820	to	890
Petrol stations	1,100	to	2,150
Garage showrooms	630	to	1,000
Garages, domestic	450	to	900
Airport facilities (excluding aprons)			
airport terminals	1,540	to	3,370
airport piers/satellites	1,880	to	4,200
Airport campus facilities			
cargo handling bases	560	to	910
distribution centres	280	to	560
hangars (type C and D aircraft)	1,180	to	1,390

	Square metre excluding VAT £		
Utilities, civil engineering facilities (CI/SfB 1) - cont'd			
TV, radio and video studios	1,070	to	2,100
Telephone exchanges	850	to	1,300
Telephone engineering centres	710	to	800
Branch Post Offices	890	to	1,210
Postal Delivery Offices/Sorting Offices	905	to	1,240
Mortuaries	1,620	to	2,260
Substations	1,210	to	1,820
Bi Light industrial/offices buildings			
economical shell, and core with heating only	490	to	850
medium shell and core with heating and ventilation	760	to	1,120
high quality shell and core with air-conditioning	1,000	to	1,820
developers Category A fit out	400	to	690
tenants Category B fit out	180	to	540
Industrial facilities (CI/SfB 2)			
Agricultural storage buildings	430	to	730
Factories			
for letting (incoming services only)	300	to	430
for letting (including lighting, power and heating)	400	to	550
nursery units (including lighting, power and heating)	490	to	730
workshops	460	to	900
maintenance/motor transport workshops	560	to	960
owner occupation for light industrial use	565	to	730
owner occupation for heavy industrial use	950	to	1,100
Factory/office buildings high technology production			
for letting (shell and core only)	540	to	730
for owner occupation (controlled environment, fully finished)	1,160	to	1,530
Laboratory workshops and offices	1,040	to	1,310
High technology laboratory workshop centres, air conditioned	2,420	to	3,100
Warehouse and Distribution centres			
high bay (10-15 m high) for owner occupation (no heating) up to 10,000m^2	270	to	350
high bay (10-15 m high) for owner occupation (no heating) 10,000m^2 to 20,000m^2	200	to	270
high bay (16-24 m high) for owner occupation (no heating) over 10,000 to 20,000m^2	290	to	380
high bay (16-24 m high) for owner occupation (no heating) over 20,000m^2	220	to	350
Fit out cold stores, refrigerated stores	425	to	790

Industrial facilities (CI/SfB 2) – cont'd

Square metre
excluding VAT
£

Industrial Buildings

Shell with heating to office areas only

500 - 1000 m²	295	to	700
1000 - 2000 m²	235	to	620
greater than 2000 m²	300	to	620

Unit including services to production area

500 - 1000 m²	535	to	835
1000 - 2000 m²	480	to	770
greater than 2000 m²	480	to	770

Administrative, commercial protective service facilities (CI/SfB 3)

Embassies	1,680	to	2,420
County Courts	1,490	to	1,850
Magistrates Courts	1,130	to	1,430
Civic offices			
non air conditioned	1,130	to	1,430
fully air conditioned	1,430	to	1,680
Probation/Registrar Offices	830	to	1,180
Offices for letting			
low rise, air conditioned, high quality speculative	1,150	to	1,450
medium rise, air conditioned, high quality speculative, 8-20 storeys	1,400	to	1,900
medium rise, air conditioned, city fringe, deep plan speculative office towers	1,700	to	2,000
Offices for owner occupation			
low rise, air conditioned	1,150	to	1,450
medium rise, air conditioned	1,700	to	2,000
high rise, air conditioned	1,900	to	2,400
Offices, prestige			
high rise, air conditioned, iconic speculative towers	1,900	to	2,400
Business park offices			
Functional non air conditioned less than 2000m²	700	to	900
Functional non air conditioned more than 2000m²	600	to	850
Medium quality non air conditioned less than 2000m²	800	to	1,000
Medium quality non air conditioned more than 2000m²	750	to	950
Medium quality air conditioned less than 2000m²	900	to	1,050
Medium quality air conditioned more than 2000m²	850	to	1,050
Good quality - naturally ventilated to meet BCO specification (exposed soffits, solar shading) less than 2000m²	950	to	1,050
Good quality - naturally ventilated to meet BCO specification (exposed soffits, solar shading) more than 2000m²	900	to	1,050
High quality air conditioned less than 2000m²	950	to	1,250
High quality air conditioned more than 2000m²	900	to	1,300

Administrative, commercial protective service facilities (CI/SfB 3)
- cont'd

	Square metre excluding VAT £		
Large trading floors in medium rise offices	2,650	to	3,160
Two storey ancillary office accommodation to warehouses/factories	850	to	1,140
Fitting out offices			
basic fitting out including carpets, decorations, partitions and services, good quality fitting out including carpets, decorations, partitions, ceilings - City/West End (nia)	325	to	450
basic fitting out including carpets, decorations, partitions and services, good quality fitting out including carpets, decorations, partitions, ceilings - Out-of-town (nia South East)	250	to	325
General office space - open plan City/West End (nia)	425	to	550
General office space - open plan - Out-of-town (nia South East)	275	to	400
General office space - part cellular City/West End (nia)	525	to	800
General office space - part cellular Out-of-town (nia South East)	350	to	550
furniture and services	520	to	620
high quality fitting out including raised floors and carpets, decorations, partitions, ceilings, furniture, air conditioning and electrical services - City/West End (nia)	600	to	900
high quality fitting out including raised floors and carpets, decorations, partitions, ceilings, furniture, air conditioning and electrical services - Out-of-town (nia South East)	550	to	900
Meeting areas	650	to	900
Conference suites Out-of-town (nia South East)	1,100	to	1,500
Conference suites Out-of-town (nia South East)	1,000	to	1,500
Reception area	950	to	1,200
Sub equipment room - City/West End (nia)	1,500	to	1,900
Sub equipment room - Out-of-town (nia South East)	1,200	to	1,700
Back of house / storage - City/West End (nia)	530	to	650
Back of house / storage - Out-of-town (nia South East)	280	to	400
Kitchen - City/West End (nia)	2,100	to	2,600
Kitchen Out-of-town (nia South East)	2,000	to	2,600
Restaurants City/West End (nia)	1,150	to	1,950
Restaurants Out-of-town (nia South East)	1,100	to	1,950
Office refurbishment (including developers finish - gifa; central London)			
minor refurbishment	200	to	720
medium refurbishment	700	to	1,100
major refurbishment	1,100	to	1,600
Banks			
local	1,320	to	1,650
city centre/head office	1,890	to	2,440
Building Society Branch Offices	1,200	to	1,560
refurbishment	670	to	1,170
Shop shells			
small	570	to	730
large including department stores and supermarkets	490	to	690

Administrative, commercial protective service facilities (CI/SfB 3)
- cont'd

	Square metre excluding VAT £

Fitting out shell for small shop (including shop fittings)			
simple store	560	to	670
fashion store	1,060	to	1,300
Fitting out shell for department store or supermarket	1,000	to	2,200
Retail Warehouses			
shell	360	to	530
fitting out	250	to	290
Supermarkets			
shell	250	to	500
supermarket fit-out	750	to	1,050
hypermarket fit-out	650	to	850
Shopping centres			
malls including fitting out			
comfort cooled	2,700	to	4,150
air conditioned	3,500	to	5,130
food court	3,500	to	5,040
factory outlet centre mall - enclosed	2,350	to	3,800
factory outlet centre mall - open	430	to	800
Anchor tenants, capped off services	650	to	950
Medium/small store units, capped off services	600	to	850
Centre management	1,700	to	2,100
Enclosed surface level service yard	1,300	to	1,600
Landlords back of house and service corridors	1,300	to	1,600
Refurbishment			
mall; limited scope	875	to	1,350
mall; comprehensive	1,250	to	1,900
*Ambulance stations	760	to	1,130
Ambulance controls centre	1,060	to	1,950
Fire stations	1,140	to	1,590
Police stations	1,150	to	1,650
Prisons	1,300	to	1,900

Health and welfare facilities (CI/SfB 4)

District hospitals	1,210	to	1,650
Refurbishment	560	to	1,140
Hospice	1,280	to	1,570
Private hospitals	1,180	to	1,800
Pharmacies	1,200	to	1,500
Hospital laboratories	1,500	to	2,190
Ward blocks	1,140	to	1,430
Refurbishment	530	to	850

Health and welfare facilities (Cl/SfB 4) – cont'd

Square metre
excluding VAT
£

Geriatric units	1,160	to	1,570
Psychiatric units	1,160	to	1,450
Psycho-geriatric units	1,100	to	1,610
Maternity units	1,160	to	1,570
Operating theatres	1,240	to	1,930
Outpatients/casualty units	1,270	to	1,680
Hospital teaching centres	950	to	1,350
Health centres	1,150	to	1,200
Welfare centres	1,210	to	1,440
Day centres	1,050	to	1,440
Group practice surgeries	930	to	1,170
Homes for the physically handicapped - houses	1,190	to	1,250
Homes for the mentally handicapped	960	to	1,330
Geriatric day hospital	1,050	to	1,350
Accommodation for the elderly			
residential homes	740	to	1,180
nursing homes	1,030	to	1,400
Children's homes	860	to	1,350
Homes for the aged	890	to	1,190
Refurbishment	350	to	840
Observation and assessment units	710	to	1,360
Primary Health Care			
Doctors surgery - basic	910	to	1,230
Doctors surgery / medical centre	1,180	to	1,500
Hospitals			
Diagnostic and treatment centres	1,850	to	2,300
Acute services hospitals	1,700	to	2,250
Radiotherapy and oncology units	1,650	to	2,500
Community hospitals	1,250	to	1,650
Trauma unit	1,650	to	2,000

Recreational facilities (Cl/SfB 5)

Public houses	1,020	to	1,400
Dining blocks and canteens in shop and factory	1,000	to	1,400
Restaurants	1,180	to	1,680
Community centres	840	to	1,200
General purpose halls	840	to	1,300
Visitors' centres	1,130	to	1,950
Youth clubs	790	to	1,170
Arts and drama centres	1,170	to	1,320

Recreational facilities (CI/SfB 5) – cont'd

	Square metre excluding VAT £		
Galleries			
refurbishment of historic building to create international standard gallery	3,220	to	5,310
international-standard art gallery	2,670	to	3,660
national-standard art gallery	2,160	to	2,670
independent commercial art gallery	1,160	to	1,500
Arts and drama centres	1,140	to	1,320
Theatres, including seating and stage equipment			
large over 500 seats	3,000	to	4,000
studio/workshop less than 500 seats	2,200	to	3,000
refurbishment	1,400	to	2,400
Concert halls, including seating and stage equipment	2,100	to	3,430
Cinema			
shell	660	to	860
multiplex; shell only	1,200	to	2,200
fitting out including all equipment, air-conditioned	720	to	1,320
Exhibition centres	1,310	to	1,750
Swimming pools			
international standard	2,500	to	3,100
local authority standard	1,400	to	2,250
school standard	1,060	to	1,180
leisure pools, including wave making equipment	2,520	to	3,220
Ice rinks	1,170	to	1,380
Rifle ranges	920	to	1,160
Leisure centres			
Dry	1,000	to	1,500
extension to hotels (shell and fit-out - including pool)	1,750	to	2,450
wet and dry	1,650	to	2,300
Sports halls including changing	660	to	1,170
School gymnasiums	790	to	930
Squash courts	790	to	1,110
Indoor bowls halls	490	to	940
Bowls pavilions	790	to	960
Health and fitness clubs			
out-of-town (shell and fit-out - including pool)	1,100	to	1,800
town centre (fit-out - excluding pool)			
Sports pavilions	825	to	1,270
changing only	1,000	to	1,350
social and changing	840	to	1,450
Grandstands			
simple stands	640	to	750
first class stands with ancillary accommodation	1,130	to	1,430

Recreational facilities (Cl/SfB 5) – cont'd

Square metre
excluding VAT
£

Football Stadia

basic stand	490	to	980
medium quality including basic facilities	850	to	1,200
high quality including extensive facilities	1,200	to	2,000
national stadium including extensive facilities	2,000	to	3,000
Indoor arena with permanent ice pad and demountable running track with 50% retractable seating (rate per seat)	4,500 seat	to	5,500 seat
Clubhouses	840	to	1,140
Golf clubhouses	800	to	1,400

Religious facilities (Cl/SfB 6)

Temples, mosques, synagogues	1,220	to	1,450
Churches	1,020	to	1,460
Mission halls, meeting houses	1,190	to	1,570
Convents	1,110	to	1,720
Crematoria	1,490	to	1,830

Educational, scientific, information facilities (Cl/SfB 7)

Nursery Schools	1,020	to	1,500
Primary/junior school	1,200	to	1,600
Secondary/middle schools	1,400	to	1,800
*Secondary school and further education college buildings			
classrooms	900	to	1,150
laboratories	920	to	1,390
craft design and technology	910	to	1,390
music	850	to	1,750
*Extensions to schools			
classrooms	1,000	to	1,400
laboratories	1,270	to	1,380
Sixth form colleges	950	to	1,300
*Special schools	840	to	1,200
*Training colleges	815	to	1,220
Management training centres	1,130	to	1,530
*Universities			
arts buildings	1,020	to	1,270
science buildings	1,130	to	1,600
College/University Libraries	950	to	1,350
Laboratories and offices, low level servicing	1,100	to	1,800
Laboratories (specialist, controlled environment)	1,570	to	2,930
Computer buildings	1,340	to	2,010

Educational, scientific, information facilities (CI/SfB 7) – cont'd	Square metre excluding VAT £		
Museums and art galleries			
national-standard museum	2,500	to	3,500
national-standard independent specialist museum (excluding fit-out)	1,820	to	2,250
regional, including full air conditioning	2,000	to	3,000
local, air conditioned	1,500	to	2,200
conversion of existing warehouse to regional standard	1,100	to	1,680
conversion of existing warehouse to local standard	950	to	1,430
Learning resource centre			
economical	910	to	1,390
high quality	1,230	to	1,700
Libraries			
branch	950	to	1,280
city centre	1,400	to	1,875
collegiate; including fittings	2,200	to	2,800

Residential facilities (CI/SfB 8)

*Local authority and housing association schemes			
Bungalows			
semi detached	750	to	890
terraced	640	to	810
Two storey housing			
detached	700	to	850
semi detached	650	to	800
terraced	540	to	750
Three storey housing			
semi detached	660	to	910
terraced	580	to	860
Flats			
low rise excluding lifts	750	to	950
medium rise excluding lifts	820	to	1,050
Sheltered housing with wardens' accommodation	750	to	1,080
Terraced blocks of garages	490	to	570
Private developments			
Single detached houses	850	to	1,320
Houses two or three storey	750	to	1,850
High-quality apartments in residential tower - Inner London	2,200	to	2,400
High-quality multi-storey apartments - Inner London	1,700	to	1,950
Mid market apartments in residential tower - Outer London	1,700	to	2,050
Affordable apartments in mixed tenure development - Inner London			
three-to-four storey villa - Inner London	1,180	to	1,400
multi-storey	1,350	to	1,500

Residential facilities (CI/SfB 8) – cont'd

	Square metre excluding VAT £		
Prestige-quality apartments multi-storey - Inner London	2,200	to	2,400
Flats			
standard	730	to	950
Warehouse conversions to apartments	850	to	1,270
Rehabilitation			
Housing	320	to	540
Flats	490	to	790
Hotels (including fittings, furniture and equipment)			
luxury city-centre hotel - multi-storey conference and wet leisure facilities	1,900	to	2,600
business town centre/provincial hotel - 4-to-6 storeys, conference and wet leisure facilities	1,400	to	2,100
mid range provincial hotel - 2-to-3 storeys, conference and leisure facilities	1,350	to	1,750
mid-range provincial hotel - 2-to-3 storeys, bedroom extension	1,100	to	1,600
city centre apart hotel - 4-to-7 storeys, apartments with self-catering facilities	1,000	to	1,400
budget city-centre hotel - 4-to-6 storeys, dining and bar facilities	1,100	to	1,300
budget city-centre hotel (office conversion) - 4-to-6 storeys, excluding dining facilities	800	to	1,250
budget roadside hotel - 2-to-3 storey lodge, excluding dining facilities	900	to	1,250
Hotel accommodation facilities (excluding fittings, furniture and equipment)			
bedroom areas	760	to	1,090
front of house and reception	1,010	to	1.330
restaurant areas	1,120	to	1,680
bar areas	980	to	1,540
function rooms/conference facilities	840	to	1,540
Students' residences			
large budget schemes with en-suite accommodation	950	to	1,450
smaller schemes (40 - 100 units) with mid-range specifications, some with en-suite bathroom and kitchen facilities	1,240	to	1,620
smaller high-quality courtyard schemes, college style	1,620	to	2,360
Hostels	920	to	1,150

Common facilities, other facilities (CI/SfB 9)

Conference centres	1,590	to	2,170
Public conveniences	1,760	to	2,510

Approximate Estimates

(incorporating Comparative Prices)

Estimating by means of priced approximate quantities is always more accurate than by using overall prices per square metre. Prices given in this section, which is arranged in elemental order, are derived from "Prices for Measured Works - Major Works" section, but also include for all incidental items and labours which are normally measured separately in Bills of Quantities. As in other sections, they have been established with a tender price index level of 480 (1976 = 100). They include overheads and profit but do not include for preliminaries, details of which are given in Part II and which in the current tendering climate currently amount to 12% of the value of measured work or fees for professional services.

Whilst every effort has been made to ensure the accuracy of these figures, they have been prepared for approximate estimating purposes and on no account should be used for the preparation of tenders.

Unless otherwise described, units denoted as m^2 refer to appropriate area unit (rather than gross floor) areas.

As elsewhere in this edition, prices do not include Value Added Tax, which should be applied at the current rate to all non-domestic building.

Item nr SPECIFICATIONS

1.00. SUBSTRUCTURE

ground floor plan area (unless otherwise described)

comprising:

Trench fill foundations
Strip foundations
Column bases
Pile caps
Strip or base foundations
Raft foundations
Piled foundations
Underpinning
Other foundations/Extras
Basements

Trench fill foundations
Machine excavation, disposal, plain in situ concrete 20.00M/mm²

		Unit	450 x 760 mm £
	- 20 mm aggregate (1:2:4) trench fill, 300 mm high brickwork in cement mortar (1:3), pitch polymer damp proof course		
	With common bricks PC £200.00/1000 in		
1.0.1	half brick wall	m	46.00
1.0.2	one brick wall	m	54.00
1.0.3	cavity wall	m	55.00
	With engineering bricks PC £246.00/1000 in		
1.0.4	one brick wall	m	61.00
1.0.5	cavity wall	m	63.00
	With facing bricks PC £275.000 in		
1.0.6	one brick wall	m	63.00
1.0.7	cavity wall	m	64.00
	With facing bricks PC £450.00/1000 in		
1.0.8	one brick wall	m	77.00
1.0.9	cavity wall	m	78.00

Strip foundations
Excavate trench, partial backfill, partial disposal, earthwork support (risk item), compact base of trench, plain insitu concrete 20.00 N/mm² - 20 mm aggregate (1:2:4) 250 mm thick, brickwork in cement mortar (1:3), pitch polymer damp proof course

	A = Wall thickness	A	Half brick
	B = Concrete footing width	B	350 mm wide
	C = Brick bonding	C	Stretcher
			£
	Hand excavation, depth of wall		
1.0.10	600 mm deep	m	53.00
1.0.11	900 mm deep	m	62.00
1.0.12	1200 mm deep	m	81.00
1.0.13	1500 mm deep	m	96.00
	Machine excavation, depth of wall		
1.0.14	600 mm deep	m	48.00
1.0.15	900 mm deep	m	57.00
1.0.16	1200 mm deep	m	71.00
1.0.17	1500 mm deep	m	81.00
	Extra over for three courses of facing bricks		
1.0.18	PC £275.00/1000	m	-
1.0.19	PC £350.00/1000	m	-
1.0.20	PC £450.00/1000	m	-

450 x 1000 mm £	600 x 760 mm £	600 x 1200 mm £	750 x 1200 mm £	750 x 1500 mm £	Item nr
55.00	55.00	81.00	101.00	125.00	1.0.1
65.00	65.00	92.00	110.00	135.00	1.0.2
67.00	67.00	94.00	110.00	135.00	1.0.3
71.00	71.00	96.00	115.00	135.00	1.0.4
73.00	73.00	101.00	115.00	144.00	1.0.5
72.00	72.00	99.00	118.00	137.00	1.0.6
74.00	78.00	104.00	118.00	146.00	1.0.7
88.00	88.00	113.00	132.00	156.00	1.0.8
90.00	90.00	118.00	132.00	156.00	1.0.9

COMMON BRICKS PC £200.00/1000	ENGINEERING BRICKS PC £246.00/1000	FACING BRICKS PC £275.00/1000

One brick 600 mm wide English £	Cavity wall 750 mm wide Stretcher £	One brick 600 mm wide English £	Cavity wall 750 mm wide Stretcher £	One brick 600 mm wide English £	Cavity wall 750 mm wide Stretcher £	
82.00	86.00	91.00	96.00	98.00	92.00	1.0.10
101.00	121.00	115.00	135.00	114.00	146.00	1.0.11
130.00	153.00	153.00	173.00	154.00	162.00	1.0.12
153.00	183.00	183.00	211.00	183.00	203.00	1.0.13
71.00	82.00	82.00	96.00	93.00	94.00	1.0.14
96.00	105.00	113.00	125.00	116.00	116.00	1.0.15
115.00	135.00	135.00	153.00	145.00	156.00	1.0.16
135.00	158.00	163.00	183.00	166.00	172.00	1.0.17
0.18	0.29	-	-	-	-	1.0.18
0.90	1.70	-	-	-	-	1.0.19
2.80	5.70	1.70	3.30	-	-	1.0.20

Item nr	SPECIFICATIONS		
		Unit	900 mm deep
1.00	**SUBSTRUCTURE - cont'd**		

ground floor plan area (unless otherwise described)

Column bases
Excavate pit in firm ground, partial backfill, partial disposal, earthwork support, compact base of pit, plain insitu concrete 20.00 N/mm² - 20 mm aggregate (1:2:4), formwork
Hand excavation, base size

1.0.21	600 mm x 600 mm x 300 mm	nr	58.00
1.0.22	900 mm x 900 mm x 450 mm	nr	107.00
1.0.23	1200 mm x 1200 mm x 450 mm	nr	177.00
1.0.24	1500 mm x 1500 mm x 600 mm	nr	313.00

Machine excavation, base size

1.0.25	600 mm x 600 mm x 300 mm	nr	49.00
1.0.26	900 mm x 900 mm x 450 mm	nr	98.00
1.0.27	1200 mm x 1200 mm x 450 mm	nr	148.00
1.0.28	1500 mm x 1500 mm x 600 mm	nr	275.00

Excavate pit in firm ground by machine, partial backfill, partial disposal, earthwork support, compact base of pit, reinforced in siti concrete 20.00 N/mm² - 20 mm aggregate (1:2:4), formwork
Reinforcement at 50 kg/m³ concrete, base size

1.0.29	1750 mm x 1750 mm x 500 mm	nr	313.00
1.0.30	2000 mm x 2000 mm x 500 mm	nr	392.00
1.0.31	2200 mm x 2200 mm x 600 mm	nr	588.00
1.0.32	2400 mm x 2400 mm x 600 mm	nr	666.00

Reinforcement at 75 kg/m³ concrete, base size

1.0.33	1750 mm x 1750 mm x 500 mm	nr	334.00
1.0.34	2000 mm x 2000 mm x 500 mm	nr	412.00
1.0.35	2200 mm x 2200 mm x 600 mm	nr	607.00
1.0.36	2400 mm x 2400 mm x 600 mm	nr	706.00

Pile caps
Excavate pit in firm ground by machine, partial backfill partial disposal, earthwork support, compact base of pit, cut off top of pile and prepare reinforcement, reinforced insitu concrete 25.00 N/mm² - 20 mm aggregate (1:2:4), formwork
Reinforcement at 50 kg/m³ concrete, cap size

1.0.37	900 mm x 900 mm x 1400 mm; one pile	nr	-
1.0.38	2700 mm x 900 mm x 1400 mm; two piles	nr	-
1.0.39	2700 mm x 1475 mm x 1400 mm; three piles*	nr	-
1.0.40	2700 mm x 2700 mm x 1400 mm; four piles	nr	-
1.0.41	3700 mm x 2700 mm x 1400 mm; six piles	nr	-

Reinforcement at 75 kg/m³ concrete, cap size

1.0.42	900 mm x 900 mm x 1400 mm; one pile	nr	-
1.0.43	2700 mm x 900 mm x 1400 mm; two piles	nr	-
1.0.44	2700 mm x 1475 mm x 1400 mm; three piles*	nr	-
1.0.45	2700 mm x 2700 mm x 1400 mm; four piles	nr	-
1.0.46	3700 mm x 2700 mm x 1400 mm; six piles	nr	-

* = triangular on plan, overall dimensions given

1.0.47	Additional cost of alternative strength concrete	m³	-

1200 mm deep £	1500 mm deep £	DEPTH OF PIT 1800 mm deep £	2100 mm deep £	2500 mm deep £	Item nr
62.00	68.00	79.00	89.00	98.00	1.0.21
127.00	137.00	148.00	177.00	196.00	1.0.22
196.00	215.00	246.00	284.00	313.00	1.0.23
353.00	391.00	411.00	489.00	539.00	1.0.24
49.00	58.00	61.00	68.00	73.00	1.0.25
107.00	107.00	117.00	127.00	137.00	1.0.26
157.00	167.00	177.00	196.00	205.00	1.0.27
294.00	313.00	320.00	353.00	363.00	1.0.28
332.00	353.00	372.00	401.00	430.00	1.0.29
412.00	442.00	462.00	498.00	538.00	1.0.30
607.00	637.00	666.00	706.00	745.00	1.0.31
706.00	734.00	765.00	822.00	883.00	1.0.32
353.00	372.00	392.00	412.00	442.00	1.0.33
442.00	471.00	489.00	529.00	550.00	1.0.34
637.00	666.00	685.00	745.00	783.00	1.0.35
745.00	783.00	803.00	862.00	901.00	1.0.36

1500 mm deep £	1800 mm deep	2100 mm deep	2400 mm deep		
312	316	332	342	-	1.0.37
783	778	803	822	-	1.0.38
1422	1427	1469	1517	-	1.0.39
1812	1862	1875	1958	-	1.0.40
2449	2496	2591	2640	-	1.0.41
312	320	332	351	-	1.0.42
783	796	831	860	-	1.0.43
1440	1489	1565	1613	-	1.0.44
1958	1995	1980	2055	-	1.0.45
2591	2649	2745	2784	-	1.0.46

30.00 N/mm² 20 mm aggregate		40.00 N/mm² 20 mm aggregate			
1.40	-	3.30	-	-	1.0.47

Item nr	SPECIFICATIONS	Unit	RESIDENTIAL £ range £	
1.00	**SUBSTRUCTURE - cont'd**			
	ground floor plan area (unless otherwise described)			
	Strip or base foundations			
	Foundations in good ground; reinforced concrete bed: for one storey development			
1.0.48	shallow foundations	m²	-	-
1.0.49	deep foundations	m²	-	-
	Foundations in good ground; reinforced concrete bed: for two storey development			
1.0.50	shallow foundations	m²	-	-
1.0.51	deep foundations	m²	-	-
	Extra for			
1.0.52	each additional storey	m²	-	-
	Raft foundations			
	Raft on poor ground for development			
1.0.53	one storey high	m²	-	-
1.0.54	two storey high	m²	-	-
	Extra for			
1.0.55	each additional storey	m²	-	-
	Piled foundations			
	Foundations in poor ground; reinforced concrete slab and ground beams; for two storey residential development			
1.0.56	short bore piled	m²	168.00 -	224.00
1.0.57	fully piled	m²	205.00 -	256.00
	Foundations in poor ground; hollow ground floor; timber and boarding; for two storey residential			
1.0.58	short bore piled	m²	195.00 -	233.00
	Foundation in poor ground; reinforced concrete slab; for one storey commercial development			
1.0.59	short bore piles to columns only	m²	-	-
1.0.60	short bore piles	m²	-	-
1.0.61	fully piled	m²	-	-
	Foundations in poor ground; reinforced concrete slab and ground beams; for two storey commercial development			
1.0.62	short bore piles	m²	-	-
1.0.63	fully piled	m²	-	-
	Extra for			
1.0.64	each additional storey	m²	-	-
	Foundations in bad ground; inner city redevelopment; reinforced concrete slab and ground beams; for two storey commercial development			
1.0.65	fully piled	m²	-	-
	Underpinning			
	In stages not exceeding 1500 mm long from one side of existing wall and foundation, excavate preliminary trench by machine and underpinning pit by hand, partial backfill, partial disposal, earthwork support (open boarded), cutting away projecting foundations, prepare underside of existing, compact base of pit, plain in situ concrete 20.00 N/mm² - 20 mm aggregate (1:2:4), formwork, brickwork in cement mortar (1:3), pitch polymer damp proof course, wedge and pin to underside of existing with slates			
	With common bricks PC £200.00/1000, depth of underpinning			
1.0.66	900 mm high, one brick wall	m²	-	
1.0.67	900 mm high, two brick wall	m²	-	
1.0.68	1200 mm high, one brick wall	m²	-	
1.0.69	1200 mm high, two brick wall	m²	-	
1.0.70	1500 mm high, one brick wall	m²	-	
1.0.71	1500 mm high, two brick wall	m²	-	
1.0.72	1800 mm high, one brick wall	m²	-	
1.0.73	1800 mm high, two brick wall	m²	-	

INDUSTRIAL £ range £			RETAILING £ range £			LEISURE £ range £			OFFICES £ range £			HOTELS £ range £			Item nr
58.00	-	79.00	68.00	-	98.00	68.00	-	98.00	-		-	-		-	1.0.48
98.00	-	117.00	107.00	-	137.00	98.00	-	117.00	-		-	-		-	1.0.49
68.00	-	107.00	79.00	-	117.00	69.00	-	117.00	79.00	-	117.00	79.00	-	117.00	1.0.50
107.00	-	167.00	117.00	-	167.00	117.00	-	167.00	117.00	-	167.00	117.00	-	167.00	1.0.51
23.00	-	27.00	20.00	-	25.00	20.00	-	25.00	20.00	-	25.00	20.00	-	25.00	1.0.52
79.00	-	137.00	89.00	-	137.00	98.00	-	155.00	-		-	-		-	1.0.53
127.00	-	186.00	146.00	-	206.00	146.00	-	206.00	146.00	-	201.00	146.00	-	201.00	1.0.54
23.00	-	27.00	20.00	-	25.00	20.00	-	25.00	20.00	-	25.00	20.00	-	25.00	1.0.55
-		-	-		-	-		-	-		-	-		-	1.0.56
-		-	-		-	-		-	-		-	-		-	1.0.57
-		-	-		-	-		-	-		-	-		-	1.0.58
98.00	-	148.00	107.00	-	148.00	98.00	-	148.00	-		-	-		-	1.0.59
127.00	-	167.00	127.00	-	177.00	127.00	-	177.00	127.00	-	177.00	127.00	-	177.00	1.0.60
167.00	-	234.00	186.00	-	255.00	186.00	-	255.00	186.00	-	255.00	186.00	-	255.00	1.0.61
-		-	148.00	-	186.00	148.00	-	186.00	148.00	-	186.00	148.00	-	186.00	1.0.62
-		-	234.00	-	322.00	234.00	-	322.00	234.00	-	322.00	234.00	-	321.00	1.0.63
23.00	-	27.00	14.00	-	16.00	14.00	-	16.00	14.00	-	16.00	14.00	-	16.00	1.0.64
-		-	274.00	-	401.00	-	-	-	274.00	-	471.00	274.00	-	401.00	1.0.65

EXCAVATION COMMENCING AT

1.00 m below ground level	2.00 m below ground level	3.00 m below ground level	4.00 m below ground level		
289.00	338.00	399.00	435.00	-	1.0.66
342.00	393.00	455.00	489.00	-	1.0.67
359.00	416.00	481.00	515.00	-	1.0.68
433.00	489.00	555.00	589.00	-	1.0.69
412.00	476.00	546.00	580.00	-	1.0.70
501.00	563.00	632.00	666.00	-	1.0.71
467.00	531.00	610.00	645.00	-	1.0.72
570.00	639.00	712.00	748.00	-	1.0.73

Item nr	SPECIFICATIONS	Unit	

1.00   SUBSTRUCTURE - cont'd

ground floor plan area (unless otherwise described)

Underpinning - cont'd
With engineering bricks PC £210/1000, depth of underpinning

Item nr	Description	Unit	
1.0.74	900 mm high; one brick wall	m	-
1.0.75	900 mm high; two brick wall	m	-
1.0.76	1200 mm high, one brick wall	m	-
1.0.77	1200 mm high, two brick wall	m	-
1.0.78	1500 mm high; one brick wall	m	-
1.0.79	1500 mm high; two brick wall	m	-
1.0.80	1800 mm high; one brick wall	m	-
1.0.81	1800 mm high; two brick wall	m	-

Ground slabs
Mechanical excavation to reduce levels, disposal, level and compact, hardcore bed blinded with sand, 1200 gauge polythene damp proof membrane concrete 20.00 N/mm² - 20 mm aggregate (1:2:4) ground slab, tamped finish

150 mm thick £

Plain insitu concrete ground slab, thickness of hardcore bed

Item nr	Description	Unit	£
1.0.82	150 mm thick	m²	47.00
1.0.83	175 mm thick	m²	47.00
1.0.84	200 mm thick	m²	49.00

Add to the foregoing prices for
Fabric reinforcement B.S. 4483, lapped

Item nr	Description	Unit	£
1.0.85	A142 (2.22kg/m²) 1 layer	m²	3.90
1.0.86	2 layers	m²	5.80
1.0.87	A193 (3.02kg/m²) 1 layer	m²	3.90
1.0.88	2 layers	m²	6.80
1.0.89	A252 (3.95kg/m²) 1 layer	m²	3.90
1.0.90	2 layers	m²	7.90
1.0.91	A393 (6.16kg/m²) 1 layer	m²	5.80
1.0.92	2 layers	m²	11.70

High yield steel bar reinforcement B.S. 4449 straight or bent, at a rate of

Item nr	Description	Unit	£
1.0.93	25kg/m³	m²	3.90
1.0.94	50 kg/m³	m²	6.80
1.0.95	75 kg/m³	m²	9.80
1.0.96	100 kg/m³	m²	12.90

Alternative concrete mixes in lieu of 20.00 N/mm² 20 mm aggregate (1:2:4)

Item nr	Description	Unit	£
1.0.97	25.00 N/mm²	m²	0.38
1.0.98	30.00 N/mm²	m²	0.52
1.0.99	40.00 N/mm²	m²	0.90

RESIDENTIAL
£ range £

Other foundations/alternative slabs/extras

Item nr	Description	Unit	£ range £	
1.0.100	Cantilevered foundations in good ground; reinforced concrete slab for two storey commercial development	m²	-	-
1.0.101	Underpinning foundations of existing buildings abutting site	m	-	-
	Extra to substructure rates for			
1.0.102	watertight pool construction	m²	-	-
1.0.103	ice pad	m²	-	-
	Reinforced concrete bed including excavation and hardcore under			
1.0.104	150 mm thick	m²	25.00 - 35.00	
1.0.105	200 mm thick	m²	35.00 - 45.00	
1.0.106	300 mm thick	m²	-	-

EXCAVATION COMMENCING AT

1.00 m below ground level	2.00 m below ground level	3.00 m below ground level	4.00 m below ground level		Item nr
302.00	354.00	414.00	450.00	-	1.0.74
371.00	422.00	481.00	515.00	-	1.0.75
378.00	437.00	501.00	536.00	-	1.0.76
467.00	523.00	591.00	627.00	-	1.0.77
438.00	497.00	568.00	602.00	-	1.0.78
546.00	626.00	678.00	712.00	-	1.0.79
494.00	563.00	639.00	671.00	-	1.0.80
626.00	691.00	766.00	800.00	-	1.0.81

THICKNESS OF CONCRETE SLAB

200 mm thick £	250 mm thick £	300 mm thick £	375 mm thick £	450 mm thick £	
49.00	55.00	57.00	64.00	71.00	1.0.82
51.00	55.00	59.00	66.00	73.00	1.0.83
51.00	57.00	59.00	68.00	73.00	1.0.84
3.90	3.90	3.90	3.90	3.90	1.0.85
5.80	5.80	6.80	6.80	6.80	1.0.86
3.90	3.90	3.90	3.90	4.90	1.0.87
6.80	7.90	7.90	8.00	7.90	1.0.88
4.90	4.90	4.90	6.00	5.80	1.0.89
7.90	8.80	8.80	8.80	9.80	1.0.90
5.80	5.80	5.80	6.80	6.80	1.0.91
11.70	11.70	11.70	11.70	11.70	1.0.92
4.90	5.80	7.90	10.00	10.80	1.0.93
8.80	11.70	13.80	18.00	20.50	1.0.94
13.80	16.80	19.80	25.00	29.20	1.0.95
17.70	21.60	25.40	33.00	39.30	1.0.96
0.49	0.62	0.73	0.94	1.11	1.0.97
0.70	0.87	1.04	1.30	1.55	1.0.98
1.22	1.51	1.81	2.26	2.71	1.0.99

INDUSTRIAL £ range £		RETAILING £ range £		LEISURE £ range £		OFFICES £ range £		HOTELS £ range £		
-	-	332.00	- 433.00	332.00	- 433.00	332.00	- 433.00	332.00	- 433.00	1.0.100
-	-	783.00	- 1,075	783.00	- 1,075	783.00	- 1,075	783.00	- 1,075	1.0.101
-	-	-	-	126.00	- 186.00	-	-	-	-	1.0.102
-	-	-	-	148.00	- 224.00	-	-	-	-	1.0.103
35.00	- 45.00	35.00	- 45.00	35.00	- 45.00	35.00	- 45.00	35.00	- 45.00	1.0.104
47.00	- 61.00	43.00	- 57.00	43.00	- 53.00	43.00	- 53.00	43.00	- 53.00	1.0.105
58.00	- 82.00	53.00	- 74.00	53.00	- 67.00	53.00	- 67.00	53.00	- 67.00	1.0.106

Item nr	SPECIFICATIONS	Unit	RESIDENTIAL
			£ range £

1.00   SUBSTRUCTURE - cont'd

ground floor plan area (unless otherwise described)

Other foundations/alternative slabs/extras - cont'd
Hollow ground floor with timber and boarding, including excavation,
concrete and hardcore under

1.0.107	300 mm deep	m²	42.00	-	54.00
	Extra for				
1.0.108	sound reducing quilt in screed	m²	3.80	-	5.10
1.0.109	50 mm insulation under slab and at edges	m²	3.80	-	6.60
1.0.110	75 mm insulation under slab and at edges	m²	-		-
1.0.111	suspended precast concrete slabs in lieu of in situ slab	m²	6.60	-	9.80

Basement (excluding bulk excavation costs)
basement floor/wall area (as appropriate)
Reinforced concrete basement floors

1.0.112	non-waterproofed	m²	-		-
1.0.113	waterproofed	m²	-		-
	Reinforced concrete basement walls				
1.0.114	non-waterproofed	m²	-		-
1.0.115	waterproofed	m²	-		-
1.0.116	sheet piled	m²	-		-
1.0.117	diaphragm walling	m²	-		-
	Extra for				
1.0.118	each additional basement level	%	-		-

2.0.   SUPERSTRUCTURE

2.1   FRAME & UPPER FLOORS
Upper floor area (unless otherwise described)

comprising:

Reinforced concrete frame
Steel frame
Other frames/extras

Reinforced Concrete Frame   20N/mm² - 200mm
Reinforced insitu concrete column, bar reinforcement, formwork (assumed   Formwork
four uses)   Basic
Reinforcement rate 180 kg/m³, column size   £

2.1.1	225 mm x 225 mm	m	45.00
2.1.2	300 mm x 300 mm	m	63.00
2.1.3	300 mm x 450 mm	m	88.00
2.1.4	300 mm x 600 mm	m	109.00
2.1.5	450 mm x 450 mm	m	113.00
2.1.6	450 mm x 600mm	m	140.00
2.1.7	450 mm x 900 mm	m	194.00
	Reinforcement rate 200 kg/m³, column size		
2.1.8	225 mm x 225 mm	m	47.00
2.1.9	300 mm x 300 mm	m	66.00
2.1.10	300 mm x 450 mm	m	88.00
2.1.11	300 mm x 600 mm	m	111.00
2.1.12	450 mm x 450 mm	m	115.00
2.1.13	450 mm x 600mm	m	142.00
2.1.14	450 mm x 900 mm	m	198.00

INDUSTRIAL £ range £		RETAILING £ range £		LEISURE £ range £		OFFICES £ range £		HOTELS £ range £		Item nr
-	-	-	-	-	-	-	-	-	-	1.0.107
3.80	- 6.60	3.80	- 6.60	3.80	- 6.60	3.80	- 6.60	3.80	- 6.60	1.0.108
6.20	- 8.90	6.20	- 8.90	6.20	- 8.90	6.20	- 8.90	6.20	- 8.90	1.0.109
7.50	- 11.30	7.50	- 11.30	7.50	- 11.30	7.50	- 11.30	7.50	- 11.30	1.0.110
16.00	- 20.00	13.10	- 16.00	13.10	- 16.00	13.10	- 16.00	13.10	- 16.00	1.0.111
-	-	62.00	- 83.00	62.00	- 83.00	62.00	- 83.00	62.00	- 83.00	1.0.112
-	-	83.00	- 113.00	83.00	- 113.00	83.00	- 113.00	83.00	- 113.00	1.0.113
-	-	185.00	- 235.00	185.00	- 235.00	185.00	- 235.00	185.00	- 235.00	1.0.114
-	-	215.00	- 268.00	215.00	- 268.00	215.00	- 268.00	215.00	- 268.00	1.0.115
-	-	380.00	- 463.00	380.00	- 463.00	380.00	- 463.00	380.00	- 463.00	1.0.116
-	-	420.00	- 493.00	420.00	- 493.00	420.00	- 493.00	420.00	- 493.00	1.0.117
-	-	+ 20%		+ 20%		+ 20%		+ 20%		1.0.118

ALTERNATIVE MIXES AND FINISHES

aggregate (1:2:4) finish Smooth £	30.00 N/mm² - 20 mm aggregate (1:1:2), Formwork finish Basic £	Smooth £	40.00 N/mm² - 20 mm aggregate Formwork finish Basic £	Smooth £	
49.00	45.00	49.00	47.00	51.00	2.1.1
70.00	66.00	70.00	68.00	75.00	2.1.2
94.00	88.00	94.00	92.00	98.00	2.1.3
115.00	109.00	115.00	115.00	122.00	2.1.4
118.00	115.00	122.00	117.00	125.00	2.1.5
148.00	140.00	150.00	148.00	155.00	2.1.6
205.00	195.00	207.00	205.00	215.00	2.1.7
51.00	47.00	51.00	47.00	51.00	2.1.8
72.00	66.00	72.00	68.00	75.00	2.1.9
96.00	88.00	96.00	92.00	98.00	2.1.10
117.00	111.00	117.00	115.00	123.00	2.1.11
122.00	115.00	123.00	118.00	127.00	2.1.12
152.00	144.00	152.00	150.00	159.00	2.1.13
209.00	199.00	211.00	209.00	219.00	2.1.14

Item nr	SPECIFICATIONS	Unit	20N/mm²-20mm Formwork Basic £
2.10	**FRAME & UPPER FLOORS - cont'd**		
	upper floor area (unless otherwise described)		
	Reinforced Concrete Frame - cont'd		
	Reinforcement rate 220 kg/m³, column size		
2.1.15	225 mm x 225 mm	m	47.00
2.1.16	300 mm x 300 mm	m	66.00
2.1.17	300 mm x 450 mm	m	90.00
2.1.18	300 mm x 600 mm	m	111.00
2.1.19	450 mm x 450 mm	m	115.00
2.1.20	450 mm x 600 mm	m	144.00
2.1.21	450 mm x 900 mm	m	202.00
	Reinforcement rate 240 kg/m³, column size		
2.1.22	225 mm x 225 mm	m	47.00
2.1.23	300 mm x 300 mm	m	68.00
2.1.24	300 mm x 450 mm	m	92.00
2.1.25	300 mm x 600 mm	m	115.00
2.1.26	450 mm x 450 mm	m	117.00
2.1.27	450 mm x 600 mm	m	148.00
2.1.28	450 mm x 900 mm	m	205.00
	In situ concrete casing to steel column, formwork (assumed four uses), column size		
2.1.29	225 mm x 225 mm	m	43.00
2.1.30	300 mm x 300 mm	m	59.00
2.1.31	300 mm x 450 mm	m	79.00
2.1.32	300 mm x 600 mm	m	94.00
2.1.33	450 mm x 450 mm	m	98.00
2.1.34	450 mm x 600 mm	m	118.00
2.1.35	450 mm x 900 mm	m	165.00
	Reinforced in situ concrete isolated beams, bar reinforcement, formwork (assumed four uses)		
	Reinforcement rate 200 kg/m³, beam size		
2.1.36	225 mm x 450 mm	m	79.00
2.1.37	225 mm x 600 mm	m	100.00
2.1.38	300 mm x 600 mm	m	115.00
2.1.39	300 mm x 900 mm	m	159.00
2.1.40	300 mm x 1200 mm	m	205.00
2.1.41	450 mm x 600 mm	m	148.00
2.1.42	450 mm x 900 mm	m	203.00
2.1.43	450 mm x 1200 mm	m	257.00
2.1.44	600 mm x 600 mm	m	181.00
2.1.45	600 mm x 900 mm	m	244.00
2.1.46	600 mm x 1200 mm	m	311.00
	Reinforcement rate 220 kg/m³, beam size		
2.1.47	225 mm x 450 mm	m	81.00
2.1.48	225 mm x 600 mm	m	100.00
2.1.49	300 mm x 600 mm	m	115.00
2.1.50	300 mm x 900 mm	m	163.00
2.1.51	300 mm x 1200 mm	m	207.00
2.1.52	450 mm x 600 mm	m	150.00
2.1.53	450 mm x 900 mm	m	207.00
2.1.54	450 mm x 1200 mm	m	262.00
2.1.55	600 mm x 600 mm	m	182.00
2.1.56	600 mm x 900 mm	m	248.00
2.1.57	600 mm x 1200 mm	m	317.00
	Reinforcement rate 240 kg/m³, beam size		
2.1.58	225 mm x 450 mm	m	83.00
2.1.59	225 mm x 600 mm	m	104.00
2.1.60	300 mm x 600 mm	m	117.00
2.1.61	300 mm x 900 mm	m	165.00
2.1.62	300 mm x 1200 mm	m	211.00
2.1.63	450 mm x 600 mm	m	152.00
2.1.64	450 mm x 900 mm	m	211.00
2.1.65	450 mm x 1200 mm	m	268.00

aggregate (1:2:4) finish	30.00 N/mm² - 20 mm aggregate (1:2:2), Formwork finish		40.00 N/mm² - 20 mm aggregate Formwork finish		Item nr
Smooth £	Basic	Smooth	Basic	Smooth	
51.00	47.00	51.00	49.00	54.00	2.1.15
72.00	68.00	72.00	70.00	75.00	2.1.16
96.00	90.00	96.00	94.00	100.00	2.1.17
118.00	113.00	118.00	117.00	125.00	2.1.18
125.00	117.00	125.00	122.00	129.00	2.1.19
153.00	146.00	155.00	153.00	163.00	2.1.20
212.00	203.00	215.00	212.00	226.00	2.1.21
51.00	47.00	51.00	49.00	54.00	2.1.22
75.00	68.00	75.00	70.00	76.00	2.1.23
98.00	92.00	98.00	96.00	104.00	2.1.24
122.00	115.00	122.00	118.00	125.00	2.1.25
125.00	118.00	127.00	125.00	135.00	2.1.26
155.00	148.00	157.00	155.00	165.00	2.1.27
215.00	209.00	218.00	215.00	231.00	2.1.28
47.00	43.00	47.00	45.00	49.00	2.1.29
63.00	62.00	63.00	63.00	68.00	2.1.30
87.00	81.00	87.00	83.00	88.00	2.1.31
104.00	96.00	105.00	100.00	109.00	2.1.32
108.00	98.00	108.00	105.00	113.00	2.1.33
130.00	122.00	129.00	127.00	138.00	2.1.34
174.00	165.00	177.00	174.00	186.00	2.1.35
85.00	81.00	87.00	83.00	88.00	2.1.36
108.00	100.00	109.00	105.00	113.00	2.1.37
122.00	115.00	123.00	118.00	127.00	2.1.38
169.00	163.00	172.00	167.00	177.00	2.1.39
215.00	207.00	218.00	215.00	228.00	2.1.40
155.00	148.00	157.00	155.00	165.00	2.1.41
215.00	205.00	215.00	215.00	227.00	2.1.42
271.00	261.00	273.00	271.00	289.00	2.1.43
191.00	182.00	191.00	191.00	199.00	2.1.44
260.00	245.00	261.00	261.00	273.00	2.1.45
325.00	315.00	328.00	330.00	346.00	2.1.46
87.00	81.00	87.00	83.00	88.00	2.1.47
109.00	104.00	111.00	108.00	113.00	2.1.48
122.00	117.00	125.00	121.00	129.00	2.1.49
173.00	165.00	174.00	169.00	181.00	2.1.50
222.00	209.00	222.00	216.00	230.00	2.1.51
159.00	152.00	160.00	159.00	165.00	2.1.52
216.00	209.00	220.00	216.00	230.00	2.1.53
275.00	265.00	281.00	278.00	291.00	2.1.54
194.00	186.00	195.00	194.00	203.00	2.1.55
264.00	254.00	268.00	268.00	277.00	2.1.56
332.00	320.00	337.00	341.00	351.00	2.1.57
88.00	83.00	88.00	85.00	88.00	2.1.58
111.00	105.00	111.00	108.00	115.00	2.1.59
125.00	118.00	126.00	122.00	130.00	2.1.60
174.00	168.00	177.00	173.00	182.00	2.1.61
224.00	212.00	226.00	222.00	233.00	2.1.62
164.00	153.00	165.00	160.00	169.00	2.1.63
222.00	212.00	224.00	222.00	233.00	2.1.64
282.00	269.00	286.00	285.00	295.00	2.1.65

Item nr	SPECIFICATIONS	Unit	

2.10	**FRAME & UPPER FLOORS - cont'd**		20N/mm² - 20 mm
	upper floor area (unless otherwise described)		Formwork
			Basic
	Reinforced Concrete Frame - cont'd		£
	Reinforcement rate 240 kg/m³, beam size - cont'd		
2.1.66	600 mm x 600 mm	m	186.00
2.1.67	600 mm x 900 mm	m	258.00
2.1.68	600 mm x 1200 mm	m	324.00
	In situ concrete casing to steel attached beams, formwork (assumed four uses), beam size		
2.1.69	225 mm x 450 mm	m	73.00
2.1.70	225 mm x 600 mm	m	92.00
2.1.71	300 mm x 600 mm	m	105.00
2.1.72	300 mm x 900 mm	m	143.00
2.1.73	300 mm x 1200 mm	m	181.00
2.1.74	450 mm x 600 mm	m	129.00
2.1.75	450 mm x 900 mm	m	174.00
2.1.76	450 mm x 1200 mm	m	218.00
2.1.77	600 mm x 600 mm	m	156.00
2.1.78	600 mm x 900 mm	m	205.00
2.1.79	600 mm x 1200 mm	m	258.00

	Steel		
	Fabricated steelwork grade S275 erected on site with bolted connections		
2.1.80	universal beams	tonne	-
2.1.81	rectangular section beams	tonne	-
2.1.82	composite beams	tonne	-
2.1.83	lattice beams	tonne	-
2.1.84	rectangular section columns	tonne	-
2.1.85	composite columns	tonne	-
2.1.86	roof trusses	tonne	-
2.1.87	smaller sections	tonne	-
2.1.88	hollow section circular, square, rectangular	tonne	-

			RESIDENTIAL	
	Other frames/extras		£ range £	
	Space deck on steel frame			
2.1.89	unprotected	m²	-	-
2.1.90	Exposed steel frame for tent/mast structures	m²	-	-
	Columns and beams to 18.00 m high bay warehouse			
2.1.91	unprotected	m²	-	-
	Columns and beams to mansard			
2.1.92	protected	m²	-	-
	Feature columns and beams to glazed atrium roof			
2.1.93	unprotected	m²	-	-

aggregate (1:2:4) finish	30.00 N/mm² - 20 mm aggregate (1:1:2) Formwork finish		40.00 N/mm² - 20 mm aggregate Formwork finish		
Smooth £	Basic £	Smooth £	Basic £	Smooth £	
198.00	189.00	199.00	198.00	207.00	2.1.66
268.00	260.00	271.00	271.00	285.00	2.1.67
341.00	325.00	345.00	345.00	359.00	2.1.68
79.00	73.00	81.00	77.00	83.00	2.1.69
98.00	92.00	100.00	96.00	105.00	2.1.70
113.00	105.00	113.00	109.00	117.00	2.1.71
155.00	146.00	155.00	151.00	164.00	2.1.72
194.00	182.00	195.00	191.00	203.00	2.1.73
138.00	129.00	139.00	138.00	147.00	2.1.74
186.00	177.00	189.00	186.00	199.00	2.1.75
232.00	222.00	235.00	233.00	248.00	2.1.76
168.00	159.00	169.00	168.00	174.00	2.1.77
218.00	209.00	222.00	222.00	233.00	2.1.78
271.00	262.00	275.00	277.00	294.00	2.1.79

STEEL FRAME

£	With galvanising £				
1,270	1,510	-	-	-	2.1.80
1,650	1,920	-	-	-	2.1.81
1,570	1,840	-	-	-	2.1.82
1,480	1,760	-	-	-	2.1.83
1,690	1,970	-	-	-	2.1.84
1,530	1,820	-	-	-	2.1.85
1,530	1,820	-	-	-	2.1.86
1,260	1,540	-	-	-	2.1.87
1,840	2,070	-	-	-	2.1.88

INDUSTRIAL £ range £		RETAILING £ range £		LEISURE £ range £		OFFICES £ range £		HOTELS £ range £		
147.00 -	294.00	159.00 -	294.00	159.00 -	294.00	159.00 -	294.00	-	-	2.1.89
252.00 -	376.00	252.00 -	376.00	252.00 -	376.00	-	-	-	-	2.1.90
159.00 -	218.00	-	-	-	-	-	-	-	-	2.1.91
-	-	105.00 -	146.00	105.00 -	159.00	109.00 -	159.00	109.00 -	159.00	2.1.92
-	-	-	-	-	-	121.00 -	189.00	-	-	2.1.93

Item nr	SPECIFICATIONS	Unit	RESIDENTIAL £ range £	
2.2.	**FRAME & UPPER FLOORS - cont'd** **upper floor area** (unless otherwise described)			
	comprising:			
	Softwood floors; no frame			
	Softwood floors; steel frame			
	Reinforced concrete floors; no frame			
	Reinforced concrete floors and frame			
	Reinforced concrete floors; steel frame			
	Precast concrete floors; no frame			
	Precast concrete floors and frame			
	Precast concrete floors; steel frame			
	Other floor and frame constructions/extras			
	Softwood floors; no frame Joisted floor; supported on layers; 22 mm thick chipboard t&g flooring; herringbone strutting; no coverings or finishes			
2.2.1	150 mm x 50 mm thick joists	m²	28.00 -	33.00
2.2.2	175 mm x 50 mm thick joists	m²	31.00 -	37.00
2.2.3	200 mm x 50 mm thick joists	m²	33.00 -	37.00
2.2.4	225 mm x 50 mm thick joists	m²	34.00 -	38.00
2.2.5	250 mm x 50 mm thick joists	m²	37.00 -	41.00
2.2.6	275 mm x 50 mm thick joists	m²	41.00 -	46.00
2.2.7	Joisted floor; average depth; plasterboard; skim; emulsion; vinyl flooring and painted softwood skirtings	m²	64.00 -	83.00
	Softwood construction; steel frame			
2.2.8	Joisted floor; average depth; plasterboard; skim; emulsion; vinyl flooring and painted softwood skirtings	m²	-	-
	Reinforced concrete floors; no frame Suspended slab; no coverings or finishes			
2.2.9	3.65 m span; 300 kN/m² loading	m²	55.00 -	58.00
2.2.10	4.25 m span; 300 kN/m² loading	m²	63.00 -	68.00
2.2.11	2.75 m span; 800 kN/m² loading	m²	-	-
2.2.12	3.35 m span; 800 kN/m² loading	m²	-	-
2.2.13	4.25 m span; 800 kN/m² loading	m²	-	-
	Suspended slab; no coverings or finishes			
2.2.14	150 mm thick	m²	63.00 -	81.00
2.2.15	225 mm thick	m²	94.00 -	113.00
	Reinforced concrete floors and frame Suspended slab; no coverings or finishes			
2.2.16	up to six storeys	m²	-	-
2.2.17	seven to twelve storeys	m²	-	-
2.2.18	thirteen to eighteen storeys	m²	-	-
	Extra for			
2.2.19	section 20 fire regulations	m²	-	-
	Wide span suspended slab			
2.2.20	up to six storeys	m²	-	-
	Reinforced concrete floors; steel frame Suspended slab; average depth; "Holorib" permanent steel shuttering; protected steel frame; no coverings or finishes			
2.2.21	up to six storeys	m²	-	-
	Extra for			
2.2.22	spans 7.50 m to 15.00 m	m²	-	-
2.2.23	seven to twelve storeys	m²	-	-
	Extra for			
2.2.24	section 20 fire regulations	m²	-	-

INDUSTRIAL £ range £		RETAILING £ range £		LEISURE £ range £		OFFICES £ range £		HOTELS £ range £		Item nr
-	-	-	-	-	-	-	-	-	-	2.2.1
-	-	-	-	-	-	-	-	-	-	2.2.2
-	-	-	-	-	-	-	-	-	-	2.2.3
-	-	-	-	-	-	-	-	-	-	2.2.4
-	-	-	-	-	-	-	-	-	-	2.2.5
-	-	-	-	-	-	-	-	-	-	2.2.6
-	-	-	-	-	-	-	-	-	-	2.2.7
104.00	- 113.00	113.00	- 155.00	113.00	- 155.00	113.00	- 155.00	113.00	- 155.00	2.2.8
-	-	-	-	54.00	- 63.00	54.00	- 63.00	54.00	- 63.00	2.2.9
-	-	-	-	63.00	- 67.00	63.00	- 77.00	63.00	- 77.00	2.2.10
54.00	- 63.00	54.00	- 63.00	54.00	- 63.00	54.00	- 63.00	54.00	- 63.00	2.2.11
62.00	- 72.00	62.00	- 72.00	62.00	- 72.00	62.00	- 72.00	62.00	- 72.00	2.2.12
79.00	- 88.00	79.00	- 88.00	79.00	- 88.00	79.00	- 92.00	79.00	- 92.00	2.2.13
72.00	- 104.00	62.00	- 104.00	62.00	- 94.00	62.00	- 90.00	62.00	- 104.00	2.2.14
113.00	- 129.00	94.00	- 129.00	94.00	- 118.00	94.00	- 118.00	94.00	- 129.00	2.2.15
138.00	- 185.00	113.00	- 165.00	118.00	- 174.00	113.00	- 146.00	113.00	- 155.00	2.2.16
-	-	-	-	-	-	146.00	- 226.00	-	-	2.2.17
-	-	-	-	-	-	226.00	- 289.00	-	-	2.2.18
-	-	-	-	-	-	10.50	- 14.40	-	-	2.2.19
155.00	- 190.00	122.00	- 181.00	138.00	- 185.00	122.00	- 165.00	122.00	- 174.00	2.2.20
185.00	- 226.00	155.00	- 215.00	155.00	- 205.00	155.00	- 190.00	155.00	- 199.00	2.2.21
22.00	- 56.00	28.00	- 63.00	22.00	- 56.00	22.00	- 56.00	22.00	- 56.00	2.2.22
-	-	-	-	-	-	174.00	- 268.00	-	-	2.2.23
-	-	-	-	-	-	22.00	- 26.00	-	-	2.2.24

Item nr.	SPECIFICATIONS	Unit	RESIDENTIAL £ range £		
2.2.	**FRAME & UPPER FLOORS - cont'd**				
	upper floor area (unless otherwise described)				
	Reinforced concrete floors; steel frame - cont'd				
	Suspended slab; average depth; protected steel frame; no coverings or finishes				
2.2.25	up to six storeys	m²	-		-
2.2.26	seven to twelve storeys	m²	-		-
	Extra for				
2.2.27	section 20 fire regulations	m²	-		-
	Precast concrete floors; no frame				
	Suspended slab; 75 mm thick screed; no coverings or finishes				
2.2.28	3.00 m span; 5.00 kN/m² loading	m²	46.00	-	56.00
2.2.29	6.00 m span; 5.00 kN/m² loading	m²	46.00	-	59.00
2.2.30	7.50 m span; 5.00 kN/m² loading	m²	49.00	-	62.00
2.2.31	3.00 m span; 8.50 kN/m² loading	m²	-		-
2.2.32	6.00 m span; 8.50 kN/m² loading	m²	-		-
2.2.33	7.50 m span; 8.50 kN/m² loading	m²	-		-
2.2.34	3.00 m span; 12.50 kN/m² loading	m²	-		-
2.2.35	6.00 m span; 12.50 kN/m² loading	m²	-		-
2.2.36	Suspended slab; average depth; no coverings or finishes	m²	42.00	-	67.00
	Precast concrete floors; reinforced concrete frame				
2.2.37	Suspended slab;average depth; no coverings or finishes	m²	-		-
	Precast concrete floors and frame				
2.2.38	Suspended slab;average depth; no coverings or finishes	m²	-		-
	Precast concrete floors; steel frame				
	Suspended slabs; average depth; unprotected steel frame; no coverings or finishes				
2.2.39	up to three storeys	m²	-		-
	Suspended slabs; average depth; protected steel frame; no coverings or finishes				
2.2.40	up to six storeys	m²	-		-
2.2.41	seven to twelve storeys	m²	-		-
	Other floor and frame construction/extras				
2.2.42	Reinforced concrete cantilevered balcony	nr	1,929	-	2,589
2.2.43	Reinforced concrete cantilevered walkways	m²	-		-
2.2.44	Reinforced concrete walkways and supporting frame	m²	-		-
	Reinforced concrete core with steel umbrella framer				
2.2.45	twelve to twenty four storeys	m²	-		-
	Extra for				
2.2.46	wrought formwork	m²	3.80	-	4.90
2.2.47	sound reducing quilt in screed	m²	4.30	-	5.60
2.2.48	insulation to avoid cold bridging	m²	4.30	-	7.20

INDUSTRIAL £ range £		RETAILING £ range £		LEISURE £ range £		OFFICES £ range £		HOTELS £ range £		Item nr
174.00	- 235.00	155.00	- 226.00	174.00	- 226.00	155.00	- 205.00	155.00	- 205.00	2.2.25
-	-	-	-	-	-	174.00	- 289.00	-	-	2.2.26
-	-	-	-	-	-	22.00	- 26.00			2.2.27
-	-	55.00	- 63.00	55.00	- 63.00	55.00	- 63.00	55.00	- 63.00	2.2.28
-	-	55.00	- 66.00	55.00	- 66.00	55.00	- 63.00	62.00	- 66.00	2.2.29
-	-	58.00	- 72.00	58.00	- 72.00	58.00	- 63.00	66.00	- 72.00	2.2.30
58.00	- 66.00	-	-	-	-	-	-	-	-	2.2.31
62.00	- 70.00	-	-	-	-	-	-	-	-	2.2.32
63.00	- 72.00	-	-	-	-	-	-	-	-	2.2.33
62.00	- 68.00	-	-	-	-	-	-	-	-	2.2.34
68.00	- 75.00	-	-	-	-	-	-	-	-	2.2.35
55.00	- 81.00	-	-	-	-	-	-	-	-	2.2.36
90.00	- 118.00	81.00	- 129.00	81.00	- 118.00	81.00	- 115.00	81.00	- 129.00	2.2.37
90.00	- 172.00	81.00	- 174.00	81.00	- 172.00	81.00	- 172.00	81.00	- 195.00	2.2.38
100.00	- 181.00	94.00	- 164.00	94.00	- 152.00	81.00	- 152.00	94.00	- 164.00	2.2.39
164.00	- 209.00	138.00	- 195.00	152.00	- 195.00	138.00	- 185.00	138.00	- 185.00	2.2.40
-	-	-	-	-	-	174.00	- 268.00	-	-	2.2.41
-	-	-	-	-	-	-	-	-	-	2.2.42
-	-	142.00	- 174.00	-	-	-	-	-	-	2.2.43
-	-	160.00	- 195.00	-	-	-	-	-	-	2.2.44
-	-	-	-	-	-	-	-	-	-	
-	-	-	-	-	-	328.00	- 442.00	-	-	2.2.45
3.80	- 5.00	3.80	- 8.00	3.80	- 8.00	3.80	- 8.00	3.80	- 10.00	2.2.46
4.20	- 7.00	4.20	- 7.00	4.20	- 7.00	4.20	- 7.00	4.20	- 7.00	2.2.47
7.20	- 10.00	7.20	- 10.00	7.20	- 10.00	7.20	- 10.00	7.20	- 10.00	2.2.48

Item nr	SPECIFICATIONS	Unit	RESIDENTIAL £ range £

2.3   ROOF

roof plan area (Unless otherwise described)

comprising:

Softwood flat roofs
Softwood trussed pitched roofs
Steel trussed pitch roofs
Concrete flat roofs
Flat roof decking and finishes
Roof claddings
Rooflights/patent glazing and glazed roofs
Comparative over/underlays
Comparative tiling and slating finishes/perimeter treatments
Comparative cladding finishes/perimeter treatments
Comparative waterproofing finishes/perimeter treatments

Softwood flat roofs
Structure only comprising roof joists; 100 mm x 50 mm wall plates;
herringbone strutting; 50 mm woodwool slabs; no coverings or finishes

Item nr	SPECIFICATIONS	Unit	£ low		£ high
2.3.1	150 mm x 50 mm joists	m²	36.00	-	42.00
2.3.2	200 mm x 50 mm joists	m²	41.00	-	45.00
2.3.3	250 mm x 50 mm joists	m²	45.00	-	50.00

Structure only comprising roof joists; 100 mm x 50 mm wall plates;
herringbone strutting; 25 mm softwood boarding; no coverings or finishes

2.3.4	150 mm x 50 mm joists	m²	39.00	-	45.00
2.3.5	200 mm x 50 mm joists	m²	45.00	-	49.00
2.3.6	250 mm x 50 mm joists	m²	49.00	-	54.00

Roof joists; average depth; 25 mm softwood boarding; PVC rainwater
goods; plasterboard; skim and emulsion

2.3.7	three layer felt and chippings	m²	87.00	-	109.00
2.3.8	two coat asphalt and chippings	m²	83.00	-	121.00

Softwood trussed pitched roofs
Structure only comprising 75 mm x 50 mm Fink roof trusses at 600 mm
centres (measured on plan)

2.3.9	22.50° pitch	m²	24.00	-	28.00

Structure only comprising 100 mm x 38 mm Fink roof trusses at 600 mm
centres (measured on plan)

2.3.10	30° pitch	m²	25.00	-	30.00
2.3.11	35° pitch	m²	26.00	-	30.00
2.3.12	40° pitch	m²	29.00	-	34.00

Structure only comprising 100 mm x 50 mm Fink roof trusses at 375 mm
centres (measured on plan)

2.3.13	30° pitch	m²	39.00	-	45.00
2.3.14	35° pitch	m²	39.00	-	45.00
2.3.15	40° pitch	m²	42.00	-	49.00

Extra for

2.3.16	forming dormers	nr	481.00	-	674.00

Structure only for "Mansard" roof comprising 100 mm x 50 mm roof trusses
at 600 mm centres

2.3.17	70° pitch	m²	25.00	-	33.00

Fink roof trusses; narrow span; 100 mm thick insulation; uPVC rainwater
goods; plasterboard; skim and emulsion

2.3.18	concrete interlocking tile coverings	m²	81.00	-	108.00
2.3.19	clay pantile coverings	m²	90.00	-	115.00
2.3.20	composition slate coverings	m²	94.00	-	118.00
2.3.21	plain clay tile coverings	m²	115.00	-	131.00
2.3.22	natural slate coverings	m²	115.00	-	152.00
2.3.23	reconstructed stone coverings	m²	96.00	-	161.00

INDUSTRIAL £ range £		RETAILING £ range £			LEISURE £ range £		OFFICES £ range £			HOTELS £ range £			Item nr
-	-	35.00	-	42.00	-	-	35.00	-	42.00	35.00	-	42.00	2.3.1
		42.00	-	45.00	-	-	42.00	-	45.00	42.00	-	45.00	2.3.2
		45.00	-	50.00	-	-	45.00	-	50.00	45.00	-	50.00	2.3.3
-	-	39.00	-	45.00	-	-	39.00	-	45.00	39.00	-	45.00	2.3.4
		45.00	-	49.00	-	-	45.00	-	49.00	45.00	-	49.00	2.3.5
		46.00	-	71.00	-	-	46.00	-	71.00	46.00	-	54.00	2.3.6
-	-	87.00	-	109.00	-	-	87.00	-	109.00	87.00	-	109.00	2.3.7
		85.00	-	121.00	-	-	85.00	-	121.00	85.00	-	121.00	2.3.8
-	-	25.00	-	30.00	-	-	25.00	-	30.00	25.00	-	30.00	2.3.9
-	-	28.00	-	31.00	-	-	28.00	-	31.00	28.00	-	31.00	2.3.10
-	-	29.00	-	31.00	-	-	29.00	-	31.00	29.00	-	31.00	2.3.11
-	-	30.00	-	35.00	-	-	30.00	-	35.00	30.00	-	35.00	2.3.12
-	-	39.00	-	45.00	-	-	39.00	-	45.00	39.00	-	45.00	2.3.13
-	-	42.00	-	46.00	-	-	42.00	-	46.00	42.00	-	46.00	2.3.14
-	-	42.00	-	50.00	-	-	42.00	-	50.00	42.00	-	50.00	2.3.15
-	-	484.00	-	674.00	-	-	484.00	-	674.00	484.00	-	674.00	2.3.16
-	-	25.00	-	35.00	-	-	25.00	-	35.00	25.00	-	35.00	2.3.17
-	-	88.00	-	121.00	-	-	88.00	-	129.00	98.00	-	134.00	2.3.18
-	-	96.00	-	129.00	-	-	96.00	-	134.00	104.00	-	142.00	2.3.19
-	-	102.00	-	131.00	-	-	102.00	-	139.00	109.00	-	148.00	2.3.20
-	-	121.00	-	152.00	-	-	121.00	-	160.00	129.00	-	168.00	2.3.21
-	-	129.00	-	160.00	-	-	129.00	-	165.00	134.00	-	174.00	2.3.22
-	-	104.00	-	165.00	-	-	104.00	-	173.00	111.00	-	181.00	2.3.23

Item nr	SPECIFICATIONS	Unit	RESIDENTIAL £ range £		

2.3   **ROOF - cont'd**
             roof plan area (unless otherwise described)

Softwood trussed pitched roofs - cont'd
Monopitch roof trusses; 100 mm thick insulation; PVC rainwater goods;
plasterboard; skim and emulsion

2.3.24	concrete interlocking tile coverings	m²	90.00	-	111.00
2.3.25	clay pantile coverings	m²	96.00	-	118.00
2.3.26	composition slate coverings	m²	102.00	-	125.00
2.3.27	plain clay tile coverings	m²	118.00	-	142.00
2.3.28	natural slate coverings	m²	129.00	-	152.00
2.3.29	reconstructed stone coverings	m²	102.00	-	165.00

Dormer roof trusses; 100 mm thick insulation; PVC rainwater goods;
plasterboard; skim and emulsion

2.3.30	concrete interlocking tile coverings	m²	121.00	-	152.00
2.3.31	clay pantile coverings	m²	129.00	-	161.00
2.3.32	composition slate coverings	m²	131.00	-	182.00
2.3.33	plain clay tile coverings	m²	151.00	-	182.00
2.3.34	natural slate coverings	m²	160.00	-	186.00
2.3.35	reconstructed stone coverings	m²	131.00	-	203.00

Extra for

2.3.36	end of terrace semi/detached configuration	m²	33.00	-	35.00
2.3.37	hipped roof configuration	m²	33.00	-	42.00

Steel trussed pitched roofs
Fink roof trusses; wide span; 100 mm thick insulation

2.3.38	concrete interlocking tile coverings	m²	-		-
2.3.39	clay pantile coverings	m²	-		-
2.3.40	composition slate coverings	m²	-		-
2.3.41	plain clay tile coverings	m²	-		-
2.3.42	natural slate coverings	m²	-		-
2.3.43	reconstructed stone coverings	m²	-		-

Steel roof trusses and beams; thermal and acoustic insulation

2.3.44	aluminium profiled composite cladding	m²	-		-
2.3.45	copper roofing or boarding	m²	-		-

Steel roof and glulam beams; thermal and acoustic insulation

2.3.46	aluminium profiled composite cladding	m²	-		-

Concrete flat roofs
Structure only comprising reinforced concrete suspended slab; no
coverings or finishes

2.3.47	3.65 m span; 3.00 kN/m² loading	m²	58.00	-	59.00
2.3.48	4.25 m span; 3.00 kN/m² loading	m²	68.00	-	72.00
2.3.49	3.65 m span; 8.00 kN/m² loading	m²	-		-
2.3.50	4.25 m span; 8.00 kN/m² loading	m²	-		-

Precast concrete suspended slab; average depth; 100 mm thick insulation;
uPVC rainwater goods

2.3.51	two coat asphalt coverings and chippings	m²	-		-
2.3.52	polyester roofing	m²	-		-

Reinforced concrete or waffle suspended slabs; average depth; 100 mm
thick insulation; uPVC rainwater goods

2.3.53	two coat asphalt coverings and chippings	m²	-		-
2.3.54	two coat asphalt coverings and paving slabs	m²	-		-

Reinforced concrete slabs; on "Holorib" permanent steel shuttering;
average depth; 100 mm thick insulation; uPVC rainwater goods

2.3.55	two coat asphalt coverings and chippings	m²	-		-

INDUSTRIAL £ range £		RETAILING £ range £		LEISURE £ range £		OFFICES £ range £		HOTELS £ range £		Item nr
-	-	96.00	- 129.00	-	-	96.00	- 131.00	105.00	- 142.00	2.3.24
-	-	105.00	- 131.00	-	-	105.00	- 142.00	111.00	- 152.00	2.3.25
-	-	111.00	- 142.00	-	-	111.00	- 152.00	115.00	- 160.00	2.3.26
-	-	129.00	- 161.00	-	-	129.00	- 165.00	131.00	- 173.00	2.3.27
-	-	131.00	- 165.00	-	-	131.00	- 173.00	142.00	- 182.00	2.3.28
-	-	109.00	- 173.00	-	-	109.00	- 182.00	118.00	- 186.00	2.3.29
-	-	129.00	- 165.00	-	-	129.00	- 173.00	131.00	- 182.00	2.3.30
-	-	131.00	- 173.00	-	-	131.00	- 182.00	142.00	- 186.00	2.3.31
-	-	135.00	- 182.00	-	-	135.00	- 186.00	147.00	- 195.00	2.3.32
-	-	160.00	- 195.00	-	-	160.00	- 203.00	165.00	- 209.00	2.3.33
-	-	165.00	- 203.00	-	-	165.00	- 209.00	173.00	- 218.00	2.3.34
-	-	142.00	- 209.00	-	-	142.00	- 218.00	151.00	- 226.00	2.3.35
-	-	-	-	-	-	-	-	-	-	2.3.36
-	-	-	-	-	-	-	-	-	-	2.3.37
-	-	151.00	- 195.00	147.00	- 186.00	151.00	- 205.00	161.00	- 211.00	2.3.38
-	-	161.00	- 205.00	151.00	- 195.00	161.00	- 211.00	169.00	- 222.00	2.3.39
-	-	147.00	- 209.00	161.00	- 205.00	165.00	- 215.00	177.00	- 226.00	2.3.40
-	-	186.00	- 230.00	181.00	- 218.00	185.00	- 235.00	194.00	- 248.00	2.3.41
-	-	194.00	- 235.00	186.00	- 230.00	194.00	- 248.00	205.00	- 256.00	2.3.42
-	-	181.00	- 256.00	172.00	- 248.00	181.00	- 265.00	186.00	- 273.00	2.3.43
230.00	- 273.00	209.00	- 256.00	205.00	- 248.00	209.00	- 233.00	-	-	2.3.44
-	-	230.00	- 282.00	233.00	- 282.00	247.00	- 273.00	-	-	2.3.45
-	-	230.00	- 306.00	218.00	- 298.00	230.00	- 294.00	-	-	2.3.46
-	-	-	-	55.00	- 66.00	55.00	- 66.00	55.00	- 66.00	2.3.47
-	-	-	-	63.00	- 68.00	63.00	- 76.00	63.00	- 76.00	2.3.48
62.00	- 72.00	62.00	- 72.00	62.00	- 72.00	62.00	- 72.00	62.00	- 72.00	2.3.49
77.00	- 88.00	77.00	- 88.00	75.00	- 88.00	75.00	- 88.00	75.00	- 88.00	2.3.50
104.00	- 146.00	94.00	- 156.00	94.00	- 148.00	94.00	- 146.00	94.00	- 156.00	2.3.51
109.00	- 129.00	105.00	- 146.00	105.00	- 138.00	105.00	- 126.00	105.00	- 142.00	2.3.52
113.00	- 148.00	105.00	- 164.00	105.00	- 156.00	105.00	- 146.00	105.00	- 164.00	2.3.53
156.00	- 195.00	148.00	- 209.00	148.00	- 199.00	148.00	- 195.00	148.00	- 212.00	2.3.54
105.00	- 126.00	94.00	- 142.00	94.00	- 138.00	94.00	- 126.00	75.00	- 142.00	2.3.55

Item nr	SPECIFICATIONS	Unit	RESIDENTIAL	
			£ range £	

2.3   **ROOF - cont'd**

 roof plan area (unless otherwise described)

Flat roof decking and finishes

Woodwool roof decking

| 2.3.56 | 50 mm thick; two coat asphalt coverings to BS 5925 and chippings | m² | - | - |

Galvanised steel roof decking; 100 mm thick insulation; three layer felt
roofing and chippings

2.3.57	0.70 mm thick; 2.38 m span	m²	-	-
2.3.58	0.70 mm thick; 2.96 m span	m²	-	-
2.3.59	0.70 mm thick; 3.74 m span	m²	-	-
2.3.60	0.70 mm thick; 5.13 m span	m²	-	-

Aluminium roof decking; 100 mm thick insulation; three layer felt roofing and
chippings

| 2.3.61 | 0.90 mm thick; 1.79 m span | m² | - | - |
| 2.3.62 | 0.90 mm thick; 2.34 m span | m² | - | - |

Metal decking; 100 mm thick insulation; on wool/steel open lattice beams

2.3.63	three layer felt roofing and chippings	m²	-	-
2.3.64	two layer high performance felt roofing and chippings	m²	-	-
2.3.65	two coats asphalt coverings and chippings	m²	-	-

Metal decking to "Mansard"; excluding frame; 50 mm thick insulation; two
coat asphalt coverings and chippings on decking

| 2.3.66 | natural slate covering to "Mansard" faces | m² | - | - |

Roof claddings

Non-asbestos profiled cladding

2.3.67	"Profile 3"; natural	m²	-	-
2.3.68	"Profile 3"; coloured	m²	-	-
2.3.69	"Profile 6"; natural	m²	-	-
2.3.70	"Profile 6"; coloured	m²	-	-
2.3.71	"Profile 6"; natural; insulated; inner lining panel	m²	-	-

Non-asbestos profiled cladding on steel purlins

2.3.72	insulated	m²	-	-
2.3.73	insulated; with 10% translucent sheets	m²	-	-
2.3.74	insulated; plasterboard inner lining of metal tees	m²	-	-

Asbestos cement profiled cladding on steel purlins

2.3.75	insulated	m²	-	-
2.3.76	insulated; with 10% translucent sheets	m²	-	-
2.3.77	insulated; plasterboard inner lining of metal tees	m²	-	-
2.3.78	insulated; steel sheet liner on metal tees	m²	-	-

PVF2 coated galvanised steel profiled cladding

2.3.79	0.72 mm thick; "profile 20 B"	m²	-	-
2.3.80	0.72 mm thick; "profile TOP 40"	m²	-	-
2.3.81	0.72 mm thick; "profile 45"	m²	-	-

Extra for

| 2.3.82 | 80 mm thick insulation and 0.40 mm thick coated inner lining sheet | m² | - | - |

PVF2 coated galvanised steel profiled cladding on steel purlins

2.3.83	insulated	m²	-	-
2.3.84	insulated; plasterboard inner lining of metal tees	m²	-	-
2.3.85	insulated; plasterboard inner lining of metal tees; with 1% fire vents	m²	-	-
2.3.86	insulated; plasterboard inner lining of metal tees; with 2.50% fire vents	m²	-	-
2.3.87	insulated; coloured inner lining panel	m²	-	-
2.3.88	insulated; coloured inner lining panel; with 1% fire vents	m²	-	-
2.3.89	insulated; coloured inner lining panel; with 2.50% fire vents	m²	-	-
2.3.90	insulated; sandwich panel	m²	-	-

INDUSTRIAL £ range £		RETAILING £ range £		LEISURE £ range £		OFFICES £ range £		HOTELS £ range £		Item nr
43.00	- 60.00	47.00 -	59.00	50.00 -	62.00	43.00 -	62.00	50.00 -	62.00	2.3.56
49.00	- 62.00	49.00 -	62.00	49.00 -	62.00	49.00 -	62.00	49.00 -	62.00	2.3.57
50.00	- 64.00	50.00 -	64.00	50.00 -	64.00	50.00 -	64.00	50.00 -	64.00	2.3.58
51.00	- 66.00	51.00 -	66.00	51.00 -	66.00	51.00 -	66.00	51.00 -	66.00	2.3.59
54.00	- 67.00	54.00 -	67.00	54.00 -	67.00	54.00 -	67.00	54.00 -	67.00	2.3.60
58.00	- 71.00	58.00 -	71.00	58.00 -	71.00	58.00 -	71.00	58.00 -	71.00	2.3.61
60.00	- 75.00	60.00 -	75.00	60.00 -	75.00	60.00 -	75.00	60.00 -	75.00	2.3.62
90.00	- 111.00	96.00 -	113.00	96.00 -	113.00	96.00 -	113.00	96.00 -	117.00	2.3.63
94.00	- 113.00	96.00 -	113.00	96.00 -	121.00	96.00 -	121.00	96.00 -	121.00	2.3.64
90.00	- 118.00	90.00 -	121.00	90.00 -	121.00	90.00 -	121.00	96.00 -	130.00	2.3.65
-	-	165.00 -	269.00	151.00 -	248.00	151.00 -	248.00	164.00 -	289.00	2.3.66
15.00	- 19.00	-	-	-	-	-	-	-	-	2.3.67
17.00	- 21.00	-	-	-	-	-	-	-	-	2.3.68
17.00	- 21.00	-	-	-	-	-	-	-	-	2.3.69
19.00	- 21.00	-	-	-	-	-	-	-	-	2.3.70
31.00	- 41.00	-	-	-	-	-	-	-	-	2.3.71
31.00	- 39.00	-	-	-	-	-	-	-	-	2.3.72
34.00	- 41.00	-	-	-	-	-	-	-	-	2.3.73
50.00	- 58.00	-	-	-	-	-	-	-	-	2.3.74
31.00	- 37.00	-	-	-	-	-	-	-	-	2.3.75
34.00	- 41.00	-	-	-	-	-	-	-	-	2.3.76
48.00	- 58.00	-	-	-	-	-	-	-	-	2.3.77
47.00	- 58.00	-	-	-	-	-	-	-	-	2.3.78
21.00	- 28.00	29.00 -	39.00	29.00 -	39.00	-	-	-	-	2.3.79
21.00	- 26.00	28.00 -	36.00	28.00 -	36.00	-	-	-	-	2.3.80
23.00	- 31.00	31.00 -	41.00	31.00 -	41.00	-	-	-	-	2.3.81
14.00	- 15.00	14.00 -	15.00	14.00 -	15.00	-	-	-	-	2.3.82
37.00	- 50.00	42.00 -	55.00	42.00 -	55.00	-	-	-	-	2.3.83
55.00	- 72.00	60.00 -	79.00	60.00 -	79.00	-	-	-	-	2.3.84
65.00	- 90.00	73.00 -	98.00	73.00 -	98.00	-	-	-	-	2.3.85
81.00	- 105.00	90.00 -	113.00	90.00 -	113.00	-	-	-	-	2.3.86
57.00	- 74.00	65.00 -	81.00	65.00 -	81.00	-	-	-	-	2.3.87
65.00	- 81.00	73.00 -	90.00	73.00 -	90.00	-	-	-	-	2.3.88
81.00	- 105.00	89.00 -	105.00	89.00 -	105.00	-	-	-	-	2.3.89
121.00	- 186.00	154.00 -	211.00	154.00 -	211.00	-	-	-	-	2.3.90

Item nr	SPECIFICATIONS	Unit	RESIDENTIAL £ range £		
2.3	**ROOF** - cont'd				
	roof plan area (unless otherwise described)				
	Roof claddings - cont'd				
	Pre-painted "Rigidal" aluminium profiled cladding				
2.3.91	0.70 mm thick; type WA6	m²	-		-
2.3.92	0.90 mm thick; type A7	m²	-		-
	PVF2 coated aluminium profiled cladding on steel purlins				
2.3.93	insulated; plasterboard inner lining on metal tees	m²	-		-
2.3.94	insulated; coloured inner lining panel	m²	-		-
	Rooflights/patent glazing and glazed roofs				
	Rooflights				
2.3.95	standard PVC	m²	-		-
2.3.96	feature/ventilating	m²	-		-
	Patent glazing; including flashings				
	standard aluminium georgian wired				
2.3.97	single glazed	m²	-		-
2.3.98	double glazed	m²	-		-
	purpose made polyester powder coated aluminium;				
2.3.99	double glazed low emissivity glass	m²	-		-
2.3.100	feature; to covered walkways	m²	-		-
	Glazed roofing on framing; to covered walkways				
2.3.101	feature; single glazed	m²	-		-
2.3.102	feature; double glazed barrel vault	m²	-		-
2.3.103	feature; very expensive	m²	-		-
	Comparative over/underlays				
	Roofing felt; unreinforced				
2.3.104	sloping (measured on face)	m²	1.50	-	1.90
	Roofing felt; reinforced				
2.3.105	sloping (measured on face)	m²	1.90	-	2.20
	Sloping (measured on plan)				
2.3.106	20° pitch	m²	2.20	-	2.80
2.3.107	30° pitch	m²	2.40	-	3.10
2.3.108	35° pitch	m²	3.10	-	3.40
2.3.109	40° pitch	m²	3.10	-	3.50
2.3.110	Building paper	m²	1.30	-	2.80
2.3.111	Vapour barrier	m²	2.00	-	6.00
	Insulation quilt; laid over ceiling joists				
2.3.112	80 mm thick	m²	3.80	-	4.10
2.3.113	100 mm thick	m²	4.50	-	4.80
2.3.114	150 mm thick	m²	6.20	-	6.90
2.3.115	200 mm thick	m²	8.30	-	9.00
	Wood fibre insulation boards; impregnated; density 220 - 350 kg/m³				
2.3.116	12.70 mm thick	m²	-		-
	Polystyrene insulation boards; fixed vertically with adhesive				
2.3.117	12 mm thick	m²	-		-
2.3.118	25 mm thick	m²	-		-
2.3.119	50 mm thick	m²	-		-
2.3.120	Limestone ballast	m²	-		-
	Polyurethane insulation boards; density 32k/m³				
2.3.121	30 mm thick	m²	-		-
2.3.122	35 mm thick	m²	-		-
2.3.123	50 mm thick	m²	-		-
	Cork insulation boards; density 112 - 125 kg/m³				
2.3.124	60 mm thick	m²	-		-
	Glass fibre insulation boards; density 120 - 130 kg/m²				
2.3.125	60 mm thick	m²	-		-
	Extruded polystyrene foam boards				
2.3.126	50 mm thick	m²	-		-
2.3.127	50 mm thick; with cement topping	m²	-		-
2.3.128	75 mm thick	m²	-		-

INDUSTRIAL £ range £			RETAILING £ range £			LEISURE £ range £			OFFICES £ range £			HOTELS £ range £			Item nr
29.00	-	37.00	37.00	-	45.00	37.00	-	45.00	-		-	-		-	2.3.91
33.00	-	41.00	41.00	-	50.00	41.00	-	50.00	-		-	-		-	2.3.92
-		-	-		-	-		-							
58.00	-	73.00	66.00	-	81.00	66.00	-	81.00	-		-	-		-	2.3.93
60.00	-	75.00	70.00	-	85.00	70.00	-	85.00	-		-	-		-	2.3.94
135.00	-	241.00	135.00	-	241.00	135.00	-	241.00	135.00	-	241.00	135.00	-	241.00	2.3.95
-		-	241.00	-	442.00	241.00	-	442.00	241.00	-	442.00	241.00	-	442.00	2.3.96
173.00	-	241.00	182.00	-	241.00	182.00	-	241.00	182.00	-	241.00	191.00	-	269.00	2.3.97
202.00	-	260.00	220.00	-	278.00	220.00	-	278.00	220.00	-	278.00	241.00	-	307.00	2.3.98
241.00	-	289.00	260.00	-	307.00	260.00	-	307.00	260.00	-	307.00	269.00	-	337.00	2.3.99
-		-	269.00	-	480.00	269.00	-	480.00	269.00	-	480.00	269.00	-	529.00	2.3.100
-		-	375.00	-	557.00	375.00	-	557.00	375.00	-	557.00	412.00	-	614.00	2.3.101
-		-	557.00	-	829.00	557.00	-	829.00	557.00	-	829.00	557.00	-	904.00	2.3.102
-		-	829.00	-	1,035	829.00	-	1,035	829.00	-	1,035	829.00	-	1,102	2.3.103
-		-	1.50	-	2.00	-		-	1.50	-	2.00	1.50	-	2.00	2.3.104
-		-	2.00	-	2.20	-		-	2.00	-	2.20	2.00	-	2.20	2.3.105
-		-	2.20	-	2.80	-		-	2.20	-	2.80	2.20	-	2.80	2.3.106
-		-	2.40	-	3.10	-		-	2.40	-	3.10	2.40	-	3.10	2.3.107
-		-	3.10	-	3.40	-		-	3.10	-	3.40	3.10	-	3.40	2.3.108
-		-	3.10	-	3.40	-		-	3.10	-	3.40	3.10	-	3.40	2.3.109
-		-	1.50	-	2.80	-		-	1.50	-	2.80	1.50	-	2.80	2.3.110
-		-	2.00	-	6.00	-		-	2.00	-	6.00	2.00	-	6.00	2.3.111
-		-	3.80	-	4.10	-		-	3.80	-	4.10	3.80	-	4.10	2.3.112
-		-	4.50	-	4.80	-		-	4.50	-	4.80	1.50	-	4.80	2.3.113
-		-	6.00	-	7.00	-		-	6.00	-	7.00	1.50	-	7.00	2.3.114
-		-	8.30	-	9.00	-		-	8.30	-	9.00	1.50	-	9.00	2.3.115
-		-	5.50	-	7.70	-		-	-		-	-		-	2.3.116
6.00	-	7.50	6.00	-	7.50	6.00	-	7.50	6.00	-	7.50	6.00	-	7.50	2.3.117
7.50	-	8.70	7.50	-	8.70	7.50	-	8.70	7.50	-	8.70	7.50	-	8.70	2.3.118
8.70	-	10.40	8.70	-	10.40	8.70	-	10.40	8.70	-	10.40	8.70	-	10.40	2.3.119
6.00	-	10.40	6.00	-	10.40	6.00	-	10.40	6.00	-	10.40	6.00	-	10.40	2.3.120
8.70	-	10.40	8.70	-	10.40	8.70	-	10.40	8.70	-	10.40	8.70	-	10.40	2.3.121
10.40	-	10.90	10.40	-	10.90	10.40	-	10.90	10.40	-	10.90	10.40	-	10.90	2.3.122
12.10	-	13.80	12.10	-	13.80	12.10	-	13.80	12.10	-	13.80	12.10	-	13.80	2.3.123
10.90	-	15.20	10.90	-	15.20	10.90	-	15.20	10.90	-	15.20	10.90	-	15.20	2.3.124
16.00	-	19.00	16.00	-	19.00	16.00	-	19.00	16.00	-	19.00	16.00	-	19.00	2.3.125
15.00	-	17.00	15.00	-	17.00	15.00	-	17.00	15.00	-	17.00	15.00	-	17.00	2.3.126
25.00	-	28.00	25.00	-	28.00	25.00	-	28.00	25.00	-	28.00	25.00	-	28.00	2.3.127
20.00	-	22.00	20.00	-	22.00	20.00	-	22.00	20.00	-	22.00	20.00	-	22.00	2.3.128

Item nr	SPECIFICATIONS	Unit	RESIDENTIAL £ range £		
2.3	**ROOF - cont'd**				
	roof plan area (unless otherwise described)				
	Comparative over/underlays - cont'd				
	"Perlite" insulation board; density 170 - 180 kg/m³				
2.3.129	60 mm thick	m²	-		-
	Foam glass insulation board; density 125 - 135 kg/m³				
2.3.130	60 mm thick	m²	-		-
	Screeds to receive roof coverings				
2.3.131	50 mm thick cement and sand screed	m²	10.00	-	11.30
2.3.132	60 mm thick (average) "Isocrete K" screed; density 500 kg/m³	m²	10.80	-	11.70
2.3.133	75 mm thick lightweight bituminous screed and vapour barrier	m²	17.00	-	19.00
2.3.134	100 mm thick lightweight bituminous screed and vapour barrier	m²	21.00	-	23.00
	50 mm thick woodwool slabs; unreinforced				
2.3.135	sloping (measured on face)	m²	10.80	-	13.80
	sloping (measured on plan)				
2.3.136	20° pitch	m²	12.00	-	15.00
2.3.137	30° pitch	m²	15.00	-	18.00
2.3.138	35° pitch	m²	17.00	-	20.00
2.3.139	40° pitch	m²	17.00	-	20.00
2.3.140	50 mm thick woodwool slabs; unreinforced; on and including steel purlins at 600 mm thick centres	m²	19.00	-	23.00
2.3.141	sloping (measure on face)	m²	12.00	-	15.00
	sloping (measured on plan)				
2.3.142	20° pitch	m²	14.00	-	16.00
2.3.143	30° pitch	m²	16.00	-	19.00
2.3.144	35° pitch	m²	19.00	-	22.00
2.3.145	40° pitch	m²	19.00	-	22.00
	25 mm thick "Tanalised" softwood boarding				
2.3.146	sloping (measured on face)	m²	15.00	-	17.00
	sloping (measured on plan)				
2.3.147	20° pitch	m²	16.00	-	18.00
2.3.148	30° pitch	m²	19.00	-	22.00
2.3.149	35° pitch	m²	21.00	-	24.00
2.3.150	40° pitch	m²	23.00	-	25.00
	18 mm thick external quality plywood boarding				
2.3.151	sloping (measured on face)	m²	19.00	-	23.00
	sloping (measured on plan)				
2.3.152	20° pitch	m²	21.00	-	24.00
2.3.153	30° pitch	m²	25.00	-	30.00
2.3.154	35° pitch	m²	29.00	-	33.00
2.3.155	40° pitch	m²	30.00	-	33.00
	Comparative tiling and slating finishes/perimeter treatments				
	(including underfelt, battening, eaves courses and ridges)				
	Concrete troughed interlocking tiles; 413 mm x 300 mm; 75 mm lap				
2.3.156	sloping (measured on face)	m²	18.00	-	22.00
	sloping (measured on plan)				
2.3.157	30° pitch	m²	23.00	-	27.00
2.3.158	35° pitch	m²	26.00	-	29.00
2.3.159	40° pitch	m²	28.00	-	30.00
	Concrete interlocking slates; 430 mm x 330 mm; 75 mm lap				
2.3.160	sloping (measured on face)	m²	19.00	-	23.00
	sloping (measured on plan)				
2.3.161	30° pitch	m²	20.00	-	28.00
2.3.162	35° pitch	m²	27.00	-	31.00
2.3.163	40° pitch	m²	28.00	-	31.00

INDUSTRIAL £ rate £		RETAILING £ rate £		LEISURE £ rate £		OFFICES £ rate £		HOTELS £ rate £		Item nr.
16.00	- 18.00	16.00	- 18.00	16.00	- 18.00	16.00	- 18.00	16.00	- 18.00	2.3.129
21.00	- 24.00	21.00	- 24.00	21.00	- 24.00	21.00	- 24.00	21.00	- 24.00	2.3.130
-	-	10.00	- 11.30	-	-	10.00	- 11.30	10.00	- 11.30	2.3.131
-	-	10.80	- 11.80	-	-	10.80	- 11.70	10.80	- 11.80	2.3.132
-	-	17.00	- 19.00	-	-	17.00	- 19.00	17.00	- 19.00	2.3.133
-	-	20.00	- 23.00	-	-	20.00	- 23.00	20.00	- 23.00	2.3.134
10.80	- 13.80	-	-	-	-	10.80	- 13.80	-	-	2.3.135
12.20	- 15.20	-	-	-	-	12.20	- 15.20	-	-	2.3.136
15.00	- 18.00	-	-	-	-	15.00	- 18.00	-	-	2.3.137
17.00	- 20.00	-	-	-	-	17.00	- 20.00	-	-	2.3.138
17.00	- 20.00	-	-	-	-	17.00	- 20.00	-	-	2.3.139
19.00	- 23.00	-	-	-	-	19.00	- 23.00	-	-	2.3.140
-	-	12.20	- 15.20	-	-	12.20	- 15.20	12.20	- 15.20	2.3.141
-	-	13.80	- 17.00	-	-	13.80	- 17.00	13.80	- 17.00	2.3.142
-	-	17.00	- 19.00	-	-	17.00	- 19.00	17.00	- 19.00	2.3.143
-	-	19.00	- 21.00	-	-	19.00	- 21.00	19.00	- 21.00	2.3.144
-	-	19.00	- 22.00	-	-	19.00	- 22.00	19.00	- 22.00	2.3.145
-	-	14.30	- 17.00	-	-	14.30	- 17.00	14.30	- 17.00	2.3.146
-	-	15.00	- 18.00	-	-	15.00	- 18.00	15.00	- 18.00	2.3.147
-	-	19.00	- 22.00	-	-	19.00	- 22.00	19.00	- 22.00	2.3.148
-	-	22.00	- 24.00			22.00	- 24.00	22.00	- 24.00	2.3.149
-	-	23.00	- 25.00	-	-	23.00	- 25.00	23.00	- 25.00	2.3.150
-	-	19.00	- 23.00	-	-	19.00	- 23.00	19.00	- 23.00	2.3.151
-	-	21.00	- 24.00	-	-	21.00	- 24.00	21.00	- 24.00	2.3.152
-	-	25.00	- 29.00	-	-	25.00	- 29.00	25.00	- 29.00	2.3.153
-	-	29.00	- 33.00	-	-	29.00	- 33.00	29.00	- 33.00	2.3.154
-	-	29.00	- 33.00	-	-	29.00	- 33.00	29.00	- 33.00	2.3.155
-	-	18.00	- 22.00	-	-	17.80	- 22.20	17.80	- 22.20	2.3.156
-	-	23.00	- 28.00	-	-	23.10	- 27.80	23.10	- 27.80	2.3.157
-	-	26.00	- 30.00	-	-	25.80	- 29.60	25.80	- 29.60	2.3.158
-	-	28.00	- 31.00	-	-	27.80	- 30.60	27.80	- 30.60	2.3.159
-	-	19.00	- 22.00	-	-	18.80	- 22.20	18.80	- 22.20	2.3.160
-	-	24.00	- 28.00	-	-	24.00	- 27.80	24.00	- 27.80	2.3.161
-	-	27.00	- 31.00	-	-	26.90	- 30.60	26.90	- 30.60	2.3.162
-	-	28.00	- 31.00	-	-	27.80	- 30.60	27.80	- 30.60	2.3.163

Item nr.	SPECIFICATIONS	Unit	RESIDENTIAL £ range £		
2.3	**ROOF - cont'd**				
	roof floor area (unless otherwise described)				
	Comparative tiling and slating finishes/perimeter treatments - cont'd				
	Glass fibre reinforced bitumen slates; 900 mm x 300 mm thick; fixed to boarding (not included)				
2.3.164	sloping (measured on face)	m²	17.00	-	21.00
	sloping (measured on plan)				
2.3.165	30° pitch	m²	22.00	-	25.00
2.3.166	35° pitch	m²	24.00	-	29.00
2.3.167	40° pitch	m²	26.00	-	31.00
	Concrete bold roll interlocking tiles; 418 mm x 332 mm; 75 mm lap				
2.3.168	sloping (measured on face)	m²	18.00	-	22.00
	sloping (measured on plan)				
2.3.169	30° pitch	m²	23.00	-	28.00
2.3.170	35° pitch	m²	26.00	-	30.00
2.3.171	40° pitch	m²	26.00	-	30.00
	Tudor clay pantiles; 470 mm x 285 mm; 100 mm lap				
2.3.172	sloping (measured on face)	m²	25.00	-	30.00
	sloping (measured on plan)				
2.3.173	30° pitch	m²	31.00	-	39.00
2.3.174	35° pitch	m²	35.00	-	43.00
2.3.175	40° pitch	m²	37.00	-	45.00
	Natural red pantiles; 337 mm x 241 mm; 76 mm head and 38 mm side laps				
2.3.176	sloping (measured on face)	m²	30.00	-	36.00
	sloping (measured on plan)				
2.3.177	30° pitch	m²	39.00	-	45.00
2.3.178	35° pitch	m²	42.00	-	48.00
2.3.179	40° pitch	m²	44.00	-	50.00
	Blue composition (non-asbestos) slates; 600 mm x 300 mm; 75 mm lap				
2.3.180	sloping (measured on face)	m²	31.00	-	38.00
2.3.181	sloping to mansard (measured on face)	m²	43.00	-	50.00
	sloping (measured on plan)				
2.3.182	30° pitch	m²	41.00	-	47.00
2.3.183	35° pitch	m²	45.00	-	51.00
2.3.184	40° pitch	m²	46.00	-	52.00
2.3.185	vertical to "Mansard"; including 18 mm thick blockboard (measured on face)	m²	62.00	-	74.00
2.3.186	sloping (measured on face)	m²	41.00	-	50.00
	sloping (measured on plan)				
2.3.187	30° pitch	m²	51.00	-	62.00
2.3.188	35° pitch	m²	57.00	-	69.00
2.3.189	40° pitch	m²	62.00	-	74.00
	Machine maid clay plain tiles; 267 mm x 165 mm; 64 mm lap				
2.3.190	sloping (measured on face)	m²	47.00	-	55.00
	sloping (measured on plan)				
2.3.191	30° pitch	m²	58.00	-	69.00
2.3.192	35° pitch	m²	65.00	-	77.00
2.3.193	40° pitch	m²	70.00	-	83.00
	Black "Sterreberg" glazed interlocking pantiles; 335 mm x 240 mm; 76 mm head and 38 mm side laps				
2.3.194	sloping (measured on face)	m²	41.00	-	52.00
	sloping (measured on plan)				
2.3.195	30° pitch	m²	52.00	-	64.00
2.3.196	35° pitch	m²	58.00	-	73.00
2.3.197	40° pitch	m²	64.00	-	78.00

INDUSTRIAL £ range £		RETAILING £ range £			LEISURE £ range £		OFFICES £ range £			HOTELS £ range £			Item nr
-	-	17.00	-	21.00	-	-	17.00	-	21.00	17.00	-	21.00	2.3.164
-	-	22.00	-	25.00	-	-	22.00	-	25.00	22.00	-	25.00	2.3.165
-	-	24.00	-	29.00	-	-	24.00	-	29.00	24.00	-	29.00	2.3.166
-	-	26.00	-	31.00	-	-	26.00	-	31.00	26.00	-	31.00	2.3.167
-	-	18.00	-	22.00	-	-	18.00	-	22.00	18.00	-	22.00	2.3.168
-	-	23.00	-	28.00	-	-	23.00	-	28.00	23.00	-	28.00	2.3.169
-	-	26.00	-	30.00	-	-	26.00	-	30.00	26.00	-	30.00	2.3.170
-	-	26.00	-	30.00	-	-	26.00	-	30.00	26.00	-	30.00	2.3.171
-	-	25.00	-	30.00	-	-	25.00	-	30.00	25.00	-	30.00	2.3.172
-	-	31.00	-	39.00	-	-	31.00	-	39.00	31.00	-	39.00	2.3.173
-	-	35.00	-	43.00	-	-	35.00	-	43.00	35.00	-	43.00	2.3.174
-	-	37.00	-	45.00	-	-	37.00	-	45.00	37.00	-	45.00	2.3.175
-	-	30.00	-	36.00	-	-	30.00	-	36.00	30.00	-	36.00	2.3.176
-	-	39.00	-	45.00	-	-	39.00	-	45.00	39.00	-	45.00	2.3.177
-	-	42.00	-	48.00	-	-	42.00	-	48.00	42.00	-	48.00	2.3.178
-	-	44.00	-	50.00	-	-	44.00	-	50.00	44.00	-	50.00	2.3.179
-	-	31.00	-	38.00	-	-	31.00	-	38.00	31.00	-	38.00	2.3.180
-	-	43.00	-	50.00	-	-	43.00	-	50.00	43.00	-	50.00	2.3.181
-	-	41.00	-	47.00	-	-	41.00	-	47.00	41.00	-	47.00	2.3.182
-	-	45.00	-	51.00	-	-	45.00	-	51.00	45.00	-	51.00	2.3.183
-	-	46.00	-	52.00	-	-	46.00	-	52.00	46.00	-	52.00	2.3.184
-	-	62.00	-	74.00	-	-	62.00	-	74.00	62.00	-	74.00	2.3.185
-	-	41.00	-	50.00	-	-	41.00	-	50.00	41.00	-	50.00	2.3.186
-	-	51.00	-	62.00	-	-	51.00	-	62.00	51.00	-	62.00	2.3.187
-	-	57.00	-	69.00	-	-	57.00	-	69.00	57.00	-	69.00	2.3.188
-	-	62.00	-	74.00	-	-	62.00	-	74.00	62.00	-	74.00	2.3.189
-	-	47.00	-	55.00	-	-	47.00	-	55.00	47.00	-	55.00	2.3.190
-	-	58.00	-	69.00	-	-	58.00	-	69.00	58.00	-	69.00	2.3.191
-	-	65.00	-	77.00	-	-	65.00	-	77.00	65.00	-	77.00	2.3.192
-	-	70.00	-	83.00	-	-	70.00	-	83.00	70.00	-	83.00	2.3.193
-	-	41.00	-	52.00	-	-	41.00	-	52.00	41.00	-	52.00	2.3.194
-	-	52.00	-	64.00	-	-	52.00	-	64.00	52.00	-	64.00	2.3.195
-	-	58.00	-	73.00	-	-	58.00	-	73.00	58.00	-	73.00	2.3.196
-	-	64.00	-	78.00	-	-	64.00	-	78.00	64.00	-	78.00	2.3.197

Item nr	SPECIFICATIONS	Unit	RESIDENTIAL £ range £		

2.3   ROOF - cont'd
  roof plan area (Unless otherwise described)

Comparative tiling and slating finishes/perimeter treatments
Red cedar sawn shingles; 450 mm long; 125 mm lap

2.3.198	sloping (measured on face)	m²	48.00	-	59.00
	sloping (measured on plan)				
2.3.199	30° pitch	m²	60.00	-	73.00
2.3.200	35° pitch	m²	67.00	-	81.00
2.3.201	40° pitch	m²	75.00	-	87.00

Welsh natural slates; 510 mm x 255 mm; 76 mm lap

2.3.202	sloping (measured on face)	m²	52.00	-	61.00
	sloping (measured on plan)				
2.3.203	30° pitch	m²	67.00	-	81.00
2.3.204	35° pitch	m²	76.00	-	85.00
2.3.205	40° pitch	m²	79.00	-	87.00

Welsh slates; 610 mm x 305 mm; 76 mm lap

2.3.206	sloping (measured on face)	m²	54.00	-	61.00
	sloping (measured on plan)			-	
2.3.207	30° pitch	m²	67.00	-	79.00
2.3.208	35° pitch	m²	79.00	-	87.00
2.3.209	40° pitch	m²	79.00	-	89.00

Reconstructed stone slates; random slates; 80 mm lap

2.3.210	sloping (measured on face)	m²	33.00	-	61.00
	sloping (measured on plan)				
2.3.211	30° pitch	m²	41.00	-	79.00
2.3.212	35° pitch	m²	42.00	-	87.00
2.3.213	40° pitch	m²	48.00	-	90.00

Handmade sandfaced plain tiles; 267 mm x 165 mm; 64 mm lap

2.3.214	sloping (measured on face)	m²	67.00	-	83.00
	sloping (measured on plan)				
2.3.215	30° pitch	m²	87.00	-	103.00
2.3.216	35° pitch	m²	94.00	-	115.00
2.3.217	40° pitch	m²	103.00	-	122.00

Westmoreland green slates; random sizes; 76 mm lap

2.3.218	sloping (measured on face)	m²	137.00	-	160.00
	sloping (measured on plan)				
2.3.219	30° pitch	m²	164.00	-	199.00
2.3.220	35° pitch	m²	199.00	-	217.00
2.3.221	40° pitch	m²	199.00	-	233.00

Verges to sloping roofs; 250 mm x 25 mm
painted softwood bargeboard

2.3.222	6 mm thick "Masterboard" soffit lining 150 mm wide	m	17.00	-	20.00
2.3.223	19 mm x 150 mm painted soffit softwood	m	20.00	-	23.00

Eaves to sloping roofs; 200 mm x 25 mm painted softwood fascia; 6 mm
thick "Masterboard" soffit lining 225 mm wide

2.3.224	100 mm uPVC gutter	m	23.00	-	31.00
2.3.225	150 mm uPVC gutter	m	29.00	-	38.00
2.3.226	100 mm cast iron gutter; decorated	m	37.00	-	44.00
2.3.227	150 mm cast iron gutter; decorated	m	45.00	-	52.00

Eaves to sloping roofs; 200 mm x 25 mm painted softwood fascia; 19 mm x
225 mm painted softwood

2.3.228	100 mm uPVC gutter	m	28.00	-	34.00
2.3.229	150 mm uPVC gutter	m	34.00	-	41.00
2.3.230	100 mm cast iron gutter; decorated	m	41.00	-	47.00
2.3.231	150 mm cast iron gutter; decorated	m	49.00	-	55.00

INDUSTRIAL £ range £		RETAILING £ range £			LEISURE £ range £		OFFICES £ range £			HOTELS £ range £			Item nr
-	-	48.00	-	59.00	-	-	48.00	-	59.00	48.00	-	59.00	2.3.198
-	-	59.00	-	73.00	-	-	59.00	-	73.00	59.00	-	73.00	2.3.199
-	-	67.00	-	81.00	-	-	67.00	-	81.00	67.00	-	81.00	2.3.200
-	-	73.00	-	89.00	-	-	73.00	-	89.00	73.00	-	89.00	2.3.201
-	-	52.00	-	61.00	-	-	52.00	-	61.00	52.00	-	61.00	2.3.202
-	-	67.00	-	81.00	-	-	67.00	-	81.00	67.00	-	81.00	2.3.203
-	-	77.00	-	85.00	-	-	77.00	-	85.00	77.00	-	85.00	2.3.204
-	-	79.00	-	87.00	-	-	79.00	-	87.00	79.00	-	87.00	2.3.205
-	-	54.00	-	61.00	-	-	54.00	-	61.00	54.00	-	61.00	2.3.206
-	-	67.00	-	79.00	-	-	67.00	-	79.00	67.00	-	79.00	2.3.207
-	-	77.00	-	87.00	-	-	77.00	-	87.00	77.00	-	87.00	2.3.208
-	-	79.00	-	89.00	-	-	79.00	-	89.00	79.00	-	89.00	2.3.209
-	-	33.00	-	61.00	-	-	33.00	-	61.00	33.00	-	61.00	2.3.210
-	-	41.00	-	79.00	-	-	41.00	-	79.00	41.00	-	79.00	2.3.211
-	-	42.00	-	87.00	-	-	42.00	-	87.00	42.00	-	87.00	2.3.212
-	-	48.00	-	90.00	-	-	48.00	-	90.00	48.00	-	90.00	2.3.213
-	-	67.00	-	83.00	-	-	67.00	-	83.00	67.00	-	83.00	2.3.214
-	-	85.00	-	105.00	-	-	85.00	-	105.00	85.00	-	105.00	2.3.215
-	-	96.00	-	117.00	-	-	96.00	-	117.00	96.00	-	117.00	2.3.216
-	-	102.00	-	121.00	-	-	102.00	-	121.00	102.00	-	121.00	2.3.217
-	-	137.00	-	160.00	-	-	137.00	-	160.00	137.00	-	160.00	2.3.218
-	-	164.00	-	199.00	-	-	164.00	-	199.00	164.00	-	199.00	2.3.219
-	-	199.00	-	217.00	-	-	199.00	-	217.00	199.00	-	217.00	2.3.220
-	-	207.00	-	233.00	-	-	207.00	-	233.00	207.00	-	233.00	2.3.221
-	-	16.00	-	20.00	-	-	16.00	-	20.00	16.00	-	20.00	2.3.222
-	-	20.00	-	23.00	-	-	20.00	-	23.00	20.00	-	23.00	2.3.223
-	-	23.00	-	31.00	-	-	23.00	-	31.00	23.00	-	31.00	2.3.224
-	-	29.00	-	38.00	-	-	29.00	-	38.00	29.00	-	38.00	2.3.225
-	-	37.00	-	44.00	-	-	37.00	-	44.00	37.00	-	44.00	2.3.226
-	-	45.00	-	52.00	-	-	45.00	-	52.00	45.00	-	52.00	2.3.227
-	-	28.00	-	35.00	-	-	28.00	-	35.00	28.00	-	35.00	2.3.228
-	-	34.00	-	41.00	-	-	34.00	-	41.00	34.00	-	41.00	2.3.229
-	-	41.00	-	47.00	-	-	41.00	-	47.00	41.00	-	47.00	2.3.230
-	-	49.00	-	56.00	-	-	49.00	-	56.00	49.00	-	56.00	2.3.231

Item nr	SPECIFICATIONS	Unit	RESIDENTIAL £ range £	

2.3   **ROOF - cont'd**
                 roof plan area (unless otherwise described)

Comparative tiling and slating finishes/perimeter treatments
Rainwater pipes; fixed to backgrounds; including
offsets and shoe

Item nr	SPECIFICATIONS	Unit	£		£
2.3.232	68 mm diameter uPVC	m	8.10	-	11.00
2.3.233	110 mm diameter uPVC	m	12.20	-	15.00
2.3.234	75 mm diameter cast iron; decorated	m	29.00	-	34.00
2.3.235	100 mm diameter cast iron; decorated	m	34.00	-	41.00
	Ridges				
2.3.236	concrete half round tiles	m	16.00	-	20.00
2.3.237	machine-made clay half round tiles	m	20.00	-	24.00
2.3.238	hand-made clay half round tiles	m	20.00	-	33.00
	Hips; including cutting roof tiles				
2.3.239	concrete half round tiles	m	21.00	-	28.00
2.3.240	machine-made clay half round tiles	m	30.00	-	33.00
2.3.241	hand-made clay half round tiles	m	30.00	-	35.00
2.3.242	hand-made clay bonnet hip tiles	m	49.00	-	55.00

Comparative cladding finishes (including underfelt, labourers, etc.)
0.91 mm thick aluminium roofing; commercial grade

Item nr	SPECIFICATIONS	Unit			
2.3.243	flat	m²	-		-
	0.91 mm thick aluminium roofing; commercial grade; fixed to boarding				
2.3.244	sloping (measured on face)	m²	-		-
	sloping (measured on plan)				
2.3.245	20° pitch	m²	-		-
2.3.246	30° pitch	m²	-		-
2.3.247	35° pitch	m²	-		-
2.3.248	40° pitch	m²	-		-
	0.81 mm thick zinc roofing				
2.3.249	flat	m²	-		-
	0.81 mm thick zinc roofing; fixed to boarding (included)				
2.3.250	sloping (measured on face)	m²	-		-
	sloping (measured on plan)				
2.3.251	20° pitch	m²	-		-
2.3.252	30° pitch	m²	-		-
2.3.253	35° pitch	m²	-		-
2.3.254	40° pitch	m²	-		-
	Copper roofing				
2.3.255	0.56 mm thick; flat	m²	-		-
2.3.256	0.61 mm thick; flat	m²	-		-
	Copper roofing; fixed to boarding (included)				
2.3.257	0.56 mm thick; sloping (measured on face)	m²	-		-
	0.56 mm thick; sloping (measured on plan)				
2.3.258	20° pitch	m²	-		-
2.3.259	30° pitch	m²	-		-
2.3.260	35° pitch	m²	-		-
2.3.261	40° pitch	m²	-		-
2.3.262	0.61 mm thick; sloping (measured on face)	m²	-		-
	0.61 mm thick; sloping (measured on plan)				
2.3.263	20° pitch	m²	-		-
2.3.264	30° pitch	m²	-		-
2.3.265	35° pitch	m²	-		-
2.3.266	40° pitch	m²	-		-
	Stainless steel sheeting				
2.3.267	0.40 mm thick; sloping (measured on face)	m²	-		-
2.3.268	0.40 mm thick; sloping (measured on plan)	m²	-		-
2.3.269	20° pitch	m²	-		-
2.3.270	30° pitch	m²	-		-
2.3.271	35° pitch	m²	-		-
2.3.272	40° pitch	m²	-		-

INDUSTRIAL £ range £		RETAILING £ range £			LEISURE £ range £			OFFICES £ range £			HOTELS £ range £			Item nr
-	-	8.10	-	11.50	-		-	8.10	-	11.50	8.10	-	11.50	2.3.232
-	-	12.10	-	15.00	-		-	12.10	-	15.00	12.10	-	15.00	2.3.233
-	-	29.00	-	35.00	-		-	29.00	-	35.00	29.00	-	35.00	2.3.234
-	-	35.00	-	41.00	-		-	35.00	-	41.00	35.00	-	41.00	2.3.235
-	-	16.00	-	20.00	-		-	16.00	-	20.00	16.00	-	20.00	2.3.236
-	-	21.00	-	24.00	-		-	21.00	-	24.00	21.00	-	24.00	2.3.237
-	-	20.00	-	33.00	-		-	20.00	-	33.00	20.00	-	33.00	2.3.238
-	-	21.00	-	28.00	-		-	21.00	-	28.00	21.00	-	28.00	2.3.239
-	-	30.00	-	34.00	-		-	30.00	-	34.00	30.00	-	34.00	2.3.240
-	-	30.00	-	35.00	-		-	30.00	-	35.00	30.00	-	35.00	2.3.241
-	-	49.00	-	55.00	-		-	49.00	-	55.00	49.00	-	55.00	2.3.242
-	-	66.00	-	94.00	66.00	-	94.00	66.00	-	94.00	66.00	-	94.00	2.3.243
-	-	70.00	-	100.00	70.00	-	100.00	70.00	-	100.00	70.00	-	100.00	2.3.244
-	-	77.00	-	110.00	77.00	-	110.00	77.00	-	110.00	77.00	-	110.00	2.3.245
-	-	91.00	-	130.00	91.00	-	130.00	91.00	-	130.00	91.00	-	130.00	2.3.246
-	-	105.00	-	150.00	105.00	-	150.00	105.00	-	150.00	105.00	-	150.00	2.3.247
-	-	112.00	-	160.00	112.00	-	160.00	112.00	-	160.00	112.00	-	160.00	2.3.248
-	-	72.00	-	98.00	72.00	-	98.00	72.00	-	98.00	72.00	-	98.00	2.3.249
-	-	81.00	-	105.00	81.00	-	105.00	81.00	-	105.00	81.00	-	105.00	2.3.250
-	-	89.00	-	116.00	89.00	-	116.00	89.00	-	116.00	89.00	-	116.00	2.3.251
-	-	105.00	-	137.00	105.00	-	137.00	105.00	-	137.00	105.00	-	137.00	2.3.252
-	-	122.00	-	158.00	122.00	-	158.00	122.00	-	158.00	122.00	-	158.00	2.3.253
-	-	130.00	-	168.00	130.00	-	168.00	130.00	-	168.00	130.00	-	168.00	2.3.254
-	-	79.00	-	108.00	79.00	-	108.00	79.00	-	108.00	79.00	-	108.00	2.3.255
-	-	85.00	-	111.00	85.00	-	111.00	85.00	-	111.00	85.00	-	111.00	2.3.256
-	-	85.00	-	114.00	85.00	-	114.00	85.00	-	114.00	85.00	-	114.00	2.3.257
-	-	94.00	-	125.00	94.00	-	125.00	94.00	-	125.00	94.00	-	125.00	2.3.258
-	-	111.00	-	148.00	111.00	-	148.00	111.00	-	148.00	111.00	-	148.00	2.3.259
-	-	128.00	-	171.00	128.00	-	171.00	128.00	-	171.00	128.00	-	171.00	2.3.260
-	-	136.00	-	182.00	136.00	-	182.00	136.00	-	182.00	136.00	-	182.00	2.3.261
-	-	92.00	-	118.00	92.00	-	118.00	92.00	-	118.00	92.00	-	118.00	2.3.262
-	-	101.00	-	130.00	101.00	-	130.00	101.00	-	130.00	101.00	-	130.00	2.3.263
-	-	120.00	-	153.00	120.00	-	153.00	120.00	-	153.00	120.00	-	153.00	2.3.264
-	-	138.00	-	177.00	138.00	-	177.00	138.00	-	177.00	138.00	-	177.00	2.3.265
-	-	147.00	-	189.00	147.00	-	189.00	147.00	-	189.00	147.00	-	189.00	2.3.266
-	-	93.00	-	111.00	93.00	-	111.00	93.00	-	111.00	93.00	-	111.00	2.3.267
-	-	100.00	-	118.00	100.00	-	118.00	100.00	-	118.00	100.00	-	118.00	2.3.268
-	-	110.00	-	130.00	110.00	-	130.00	110.00	-	130.00	110.00	-	130.00	2.3.269
-	-	130.00		153.00	130.00		153.00	130.00		153.00	130.00		153.00	2.3.270
-	-	150.00		177.00	150.00		177.00	150.00		177.00	150.00		177.00	2.3.271
-	-	160.00		189.00	160.00		189.00	160.00		189.00	160.00		189.00	2.3.272

Item nr	SPECIFICATIONS	Unit	RESIDENTIAL
			£ range £

2.3   **ROOF - cont'd**

roof plan area (unless otherwise described)

Comparative cladding finishes (including underfelt, labours, etc.) cont'd

Lead roofing

2.3.273	code 4 sheeting; flat	m²	-	-
2.3.274	code 5 sheeting; flat	m²	-	-
2.3.275	code 6 sheeting; flat	m²	-	-
2.3.276	code 5 sheeting; sloping (measured on face)	m²	-	-
	code 5 sheeting; sloping (measured on plan)			
2.3.277	20° pitch	m²	-	-
2.3.278	30° pitch	m²	-	-
2.3.279	35° pitch	m²	-	-
2.3.280	40° pitch	m²	-	-
	code 5 sheeting; vertical to mansard; including			
2.3.281	insulation (measured on face)	m²	-	-

Comparative waterproof finishes/perimeter treatments

Liquid applied coatings

2.3.282	spray applied bitumen	m²	-	-
2.3.283	spray applied co-polymer	m²	-	-
2.3.284	spray applied polyurethane	m²	-	-
	20 mm two coat asphalt roofing; laid flat; on felt underlay			
2.3.285	to BS 6925	m²	-	-
2.3.286	to BS 6577	m²	-	-
	Extra for			
2.3.287	solar reflective paint	m²	-	-
2.3.288	limestone chipping finish	m²	-	-
2.3.289	grip tiles in hot bitumen	m²	-	-
	20 mm two coat reinforced asphaltic compound; laid flat on felt underlay			
2.3.290	to BS 6577	m²	-	-
	Built-up bitumen felt roofing; laid flat			
2.3.291	three layer glass fibre roofing	m²	35.00	55.00
2.3.292	three layer asbestos based roofing	m²	35.00	55.00
	Extra for			
2.3.293	granite chipping finish	m²	2.90	7.00
	Built-up self finished asbestos based bitumen felt roofing; laid sloping			
2.3.294	two layer roofing (measured on face)	m²	45.00 -	60.00
2.3.295	35° pitch	m²	60.00 -	80.00
2.3.296	40° pitch	m²	62.00 -	85.00
2.3.297	three layer roofing (measured on face)	m²	50.00 -	65.00
	three layer roofing (measured on plan)			
2.3.298	20° pitch	m²	55.00 -	70.00
2.3.299	30° pitch	m²	58.00 -	75.00
	High performance roofing system; including insulation and vapour barrier; laid to falls			
2.3.300	Bitumen felt roofing system	m²	-	-
2.3.301	Polymer modified bitmen membrane	m²	-	-
2.3.302	Single layer polymer roofing system	m²	-	-

INDUSTRIAL £ range £		RETAILING £ range £		LEISURE £ range £		OFFICES £ range £		HOTELS £ range £		Item nr
-	-	77.00 - 85.00		77.00 - 85.00		77.00 - 85.00		77.00 - 85.00		2.3.273
-	-	90.00 - 98.00		90.00 - 98.00		90.00 - 98.00		90.00 - 98.00		2.3.274
-	-	96.00 - 105.00		96.00 - 105.00		96.00 - 105.00		96.00 - 105.00		2.3.275
-	-	96.00 - 105.00		96.00 - 105.00		96.00 - 105.00		96.00 - 105.00		2.3.276
-	-	106.00 - 116.00		106.00 - 116.00		106.00 - 116.00		106.00 - 116.00		2.3.277
-	-	125.00 - 137.00		125.00 - 137.00		125.00 - 137.00		125.00 - 137.00		2.3.278
-	-	144.00 - 158.00		144.00 - 158.00		144.00 - 158.00		144.00 - 158.00		2.3.279
-	-	154.00 - 168.00		154.00 - 168.00		154.00 - 168.00		154.00 - 168.00		2.3.280
-	-	138.00 - 199.00		138.00 - 199.00		138.00 - 199.00		138.00 - 199.00		2.3.281
-	-	6.80 - 11.30		6.80 - 11.30		6.80 - 11.30		6.80 - 11.30		2.3.282
-	-	8.10 - 12.50		8.10 - 12.50		8.10 - 12.50		8.10 - 12.50		2.3.283
-	-	13.50 - 18.00		15.20 - 18.00		15.20 - 18.00		15.20 - 18.00		2.3.284
-	-	14.40 - 19.00		14.40 - 19.00		14.40 - 19.00		14.40 - 19.00		2.3.285
-	-	20.00 - 25.00		20.00 - 25.00		20.00 - 25.00		20.00 - 25.00		2.3.286
-	-	2.40 - 3.30		2.40 - 3.30		2.40 - 3.30		2.40 - 3.30		2.3.287
-	-	2.90 - 7.70		2.90 - 7.70		2.90 - 7.70		2.90 - 7.70		2.3.288
-	-	33.00 - 41.00		33.00 - 41.00		33.00 - 41.00		33.00 - 41.00		2.3.289
-	-	47.00 - 79.00		47.00 - 79.00		47.00 - 79.00		47.00 - 79.00		2.3.290
-	-	-	-	-	-	-	-	-	-	2.3.291
-	-	-	-	-	-	-	-	-	-	2.3.292
-	-	-	-	-	-	-	-	-	-	2.3.293
-	-	-	-	-	-	-	-	-	-	2.3.294
-	-	-	-	-	-	-	-	-	-	2.3.295
-	-	-	-	-	-	-	-	-	-	2.3.296
-	-	-	-	-	-	-	-	-	-	2.3.297
-	-	-	-	-	-	-	-	-	-	2.3.298
-	-	-	-	-	-	-	-	-	-	2.3.299
70.00 - 79.00		70.00 - 79.00		70.00 - 79.00		70.00 - 79.00		70.00 - 79.00		2.3.300
75.00 - 92.00		75.00 - 92.00		75.00 - 92.00		75.00 - 92.00		75.00 - 92.00		2.3.301
78.70 - 131.10		78.70 - 131.10		78.70 - 131.10		78.70 - 131.10		78.70 - 131.10		2.3.302

Item nr	SPECIFICATIONS	Unit	RESIDENTIAL £ range £		
2.3	**ROOF - cont'd**				
	roof plan area (unless otherwise described)				
	Comparative waterproof finishes/perimeter treatments - cont'd				
	Thermoplastic single ply roofing; laid flat				
	uPVC membrane				
2.3.303	laid loose	m²	-		-
2.3.304	mechanically fixed	m²	-		-
2.3.305	fully adhered	m²	-		-
2.3.306	"CPE" membrane; laid loose	m²	-		-
2.3.307	"CPSG" membrane; fully adhered	m²	-		-
2.3.308	"PIB" membrane; laid loose	m²	-		-
	Extra for				
2.3.309	ballast	m²	-		-
	High performance built-up felt roofing; laid flat				
	three layer "Ruberglass 120 GP" felt roofing				
2.3.310	granite chipping finish	m²	-		-
	"Andersons" three layer self-finished polyester				
2.3.311	based bitumen felt roofing	m²	-		-
	Three layer polyester based modified bitumen felt roofing				
2.3.312	roofing	m²	-		-
	"Andersons" three layer polyester based bitumen				
2.3.313	felt roofing;granite chipping finish	m²	-		-
	Three layer metal faced glass cloth reinforced				
2.3.314	bitumen roofing	m²	-		-
	Three layer "Ruberfort" HP 350" felt roofing; granite				
2.3.315	chipping finish	m²	-		-
	Three layer "Hyload 150E" elastomeric roofing; granite				
2.3.316	chipping finish	m²	-		-
	Three layer "Polybit 350" elastomeric roofing; granite				
2.3.317	chipping finish	m²	-		-
	Torch on roofing; laid flat				
2.3.318	three layer polyester based modified bitumen roofing	m²	-		-
2.3.319	two layer polymeric isotropic roofing	m²	-		-
	Extra for				
2.3.320	granite chipping finish	m²	-		-
	Edges to felt flat roofs; softwood splayed fillet;				
	280 mm x 25 mm painted softwood fascia; no gutter				
2.3.321	aluminium edge trim	m	33.00	-	35.00
	Edges to flat roofs; code 4 lead drip dresses into gutter; 230 mm x 25 mm				
	painted softwood fascia				
2.3.322	100 mm uPVC gutter	m²	31.00	-	41.00
2.3.323	150 mm uPVC gutter	m²	39.00	-	46.00
2.3.324	100 mm cast iron gutter; decorated	m²	46.00	-	57.00
2.3.325	150 mm cast iron gutter; decorated	m²	57.00	-	69.00
	Landscaped roofs				
	Vapour barrier, polyester based elastomeric bitumen waterproofing and				
	vapour equalisation layer, copper lined bitumen membrane root barrier and				
	waterproofing layer, separation and slip layers, protection layer, 50 mm				
2.3.326	thick drainage board, filter fleece, insulation, top soil and seed	m²	157.00	-	191.00

INDUSTRIAL £ range £		RETAILING £ range £		LEISURE £ range £		OFFICES £ range £		HOTELS £ range £		Item nr
22.00	- 26.00	22.00	- 26.00	22.00	- 26.00	22.00	- 26.00	22.00	- 26.00	2.3.303
28.00	- 33.00	28.00	- 33.00	28.00	- 33.00	28.00	- 33.00	28.00	- 33.00	2.3.304
31.00	- 35.00	31.00	- 35.00	31.00	- 35.00	31.00	- 35.00	31.00	- 35.00	2.3.305
25.00	- 31.00	25.00	- 31.00	25.00	- 31.00	25.00	- 31.00	25.00	- 31.00	2.3.306
25.00	- 31.00	25.00	- 31.00	25.00	- 31.00	25.00	- 31.00	25.00	- 31.00	2.3.307
29.00	- 35.00	29.00	- 35.00	29.00	- 35.00	29.00	- 35.00	29.00	- 35.00	2.3.308
6.80	- 11.30	6.80	- 11.30	6.80	- 11.30	6.80	- 11.30	6.80	- 11.30	2.3.309
31.00	- 33.00	31.00	- 33.00	31.00	- 33.00	31.00	- 33.00	31.00	- 33.00	2.3.310
31.00	- 35.00	31.00	- 35.00	31.00	- 35.00	31.00	- 35.00	31.00	- 35.00	2.3.311
31.00	- 35.00	31.00	- 35.00	31.00	- 35.00	31.00	- 35.00	31.00	- 35.00	2.3.312
35.00	- 39.00	35.00	- 39.00	35.00	- 39.00	35.00	- 39.00	35.00	- 39.00	2.3.313
39.00	- 43.00	39.00	- 43.00	39.00	- 43.00	39.00	- 43.00	39.00	- 43.00	2.3.314
39.00	- 43.00	39.00	- 43.00	39.00	- 43.00	39.00	- 43.00	39.00	- 43.00	2.3.315
41.00	- 45.00	41.00	- 45.00	41.00	- 45.00	41.00	- 45.00	41.00	- 45.00	2.3.316
43.00	- 48.00	43.00	- 48.00	43.00	- 48.00	43.00	- 48.00	43.00	- 48.00	2.3.317
-	-	28.00	- 33.00	28.00	- 33.00	28.00	- 33.00	28.00	- 33.00	2.3.318
-	-	28.00	- 33.00	28.00	- 33.00	28.00	- 33.00	28.00	- 33.00	2.3.319
-	-	2.60	- 7.00	2.60	- 7.00	2.60	- 7.00	2.60	- 7.00	2.3.320
-	-	33.00	- 35.00	33.00	- 35.00	33.00	- 35.00	33.00	- 35.00	2.3.321
-	-	31.00	- 41.00	-	-	31.00	- 41.00	31.00	- 41.00	2.3.322
-	-	39.00	- 47.00	-	-	39.00	- 47.00	39.00	- 47.00	2.3.323
-	-	46.00	- 57.00	-	-	46.00	- 57.00	46.00	- 57.00	2.3.324
-	-	57.00	- 73.00	-	-	57.00	- 73.00	57.00	- 73.00	2.3.325
-	-	-	-	157.00	- 191.00	-	-	-	-	2.3.326

Item nr	SPECIFICATIONS	Unit	RESIDENTIAL £ range £		
2.4	**STAIRS**				
	storey (unless otherwise described)				
	comprising				
	Timber construction				
	Reinforced concrete construction				
	Metal construction				
	Comparative finishes/balustrading				
	Timber construction				
	Softwood staircase; softwood balustrades and hardwood handrail; plasterboard; skim and emulsion to soffit				
2.4.1	2.60 m rise; standard; straight flight	nr	691.00	-	1,047
2.4.2	2.60 m rise; standard; top three treads winding	nr	845.00	-	1,162
2.4.3	2.60 m rise; standard; dogleg	nr	969.00	-	1,229
	Oak staircase; balustrades and handrails; plasterboard; skim and emulsion to soffit				
2.4.4	2.60 m rise; purpose made; dogleg	nr	-		-
	plus or minus for				
2.4.5	each 300 mm variation in storey height	nr	-		-
	Reinforced concrete construction				
	Escape staircase; granolithic finish; mild steel balustrades and handrails				
2.4.6	3.00 m rise; dogleg	nr	3,605	-	4,611
	plus or minus for				
2.4.7	each 300 mm variation in storey height	nr	350.00		451.00
	Staircase; terrazzo finish; mild steel balustrades and handrails; plastered soffit; balustrades and staircase soffit decorated				
2.4.8	3.00 m rise; dogleg	nr	-		-
	plus or minus for				
2.4.9	each 300 mm variation in storey height	nr	-		-
	Staircase; terrazzo finish; stainless steel balustrades and handrails; plastered and decorated soffit				
2.4.10	3.00 m rise; dogleg	nr	-		-
	plus or minus for				
2.4.11	each 300 mm variation in storey height	nr	-		-
	Staircase; high quality finishes; stainless steel and glass balustrades; plastered and decorated soffit				
2.4.12	3.00 m rise; dogleg	nr	-		-
	plus or minus for				
2.4.13	each 300 mm variation in storey height	nr	-		-
	Metal construction				
	Steel access/fire ladder				
2.4.14	3.00 m high	nr	-		-
2.4.15	4.00 m high; epoxide finished	nr	-		-
	Light duty metal staircase; galvanised finish; perforated treads; no risers; balustrades and handrails; decorated				
2.4.16	3.00 m rise; spiral; 1548 mm diameter	nr	-		-
	plus or minus for				
2.4.17	each 300 mm variation in storey height	nr	-		-
2.4.18	3.00 m rise; spiral; 1936 mm diameter	nr	-		-
	plus or minus for				
2.4.19	each 300 mm variation in storey height	nr	-		-
2.4.20	3.00 m rise; spiral; 2072 mm diameter	nr	-		-
	plus or minus for				
2.4.21	each 300 mm variation in storey height	nr	-		-

INDUSTRIAL £ rate £			RETAILING £ rate £			LEISURE £ rate £			OFFICES £ rate £			HOTELS £ rate £			Item nr.
-		-	-		-	-		-	-		-	-		-	2.4.1
-		-	-		-	-		-	-		-	-		-	2.4.2
-		-	-		-	-		-	-		-	-		-	2.4.3
-		-	-		-	-		-	-		-	6,240	-	8,498	2.4.4
-		-	-		-	-		-	-		-	1,007	-	1,102	2.4.5
5,138	-	6,382	3,605	-	6,382	4,942	-	5,760	4,942	-	5,760	3,605	-	7,200	2.4.6
518.00	-	649.00	346.00	-	649.00	480.00	-	574.00	480.00	-	574.00	346.00	-	725.00	2.4.7
7,200	-	9,026	7,200	-	9,647	6,767	-	9,026	6,767	-	9,262	5,562	-	10,466	2.4.8
725.00	-	904.00	725.00	-	969.00	687.00	-	904.00	687.00	-	922.00	555.00	-	1,045	2.4.9
-		-	7,200	-	11,718	8,207	-	10,795	8,207	-	11,811	7,200	-	12,527	2.4.10
-			725.00	-	1,176	818.00	-	1,073	818.00	-	1,176	725.00	-	1,233	2.4.11
14,400	-	15,639	15,935	-	16,833	14,400	-	15,639	13,920	-	14,820	16,942	-	18,020	2.4.12
1,440	-	2,005	1,591	-	2,165	1,440	-	2,005	1,393	-	1,902	1,694	-	2,315	2.4.13
546.00	-	762.00	-		-	555.00	-	574.00	-		-	-		-	2.4.14
-		-	-		-	762.00	-	1,309	-		-	-		-	2.4.15
2,682	-	3,266	-		-	-		-	-		-	-		-	2.4.16
269.00	-	329.00	-		-	-		-	-		-	-		-	2.4.17
3,078	-	3,840	-		-	-		-	-		-	-		-	2.4.18
307.00	-	386.00	-		-	-		-	-		-	-		-	2.4.19
3,266	-	3,840	-		-	-		-	-		-	-		-	2.4.20
325.00	-	384.00	-		-	-		-	-		-	-		-	2.4.21

Item nr.	SPECIFICATIONS	Unit	RESIDENTIAL £ range £	

2.4   **STAIRS - cont'd**

                 storey (unless otherwise described)

Metal construction - cont'd

Light duty metal staircase; galvanised finish; perforated treads; no risers; balustrades and handrails; decorated - cont'd

Item nr.	SPECIFICATIONS	Unit	RESIDENTIAL £ range £	
2.4.22	3.00 m rise; straight; 760 mm wide	nr	-	-
	plus or minus for			
2.4.23	each 300 mm variation in storey height	nr	-	-
2.4.24	3.00 m rise; straight; 900 mm wide	nr	-	-
	plus or minus for			
2.4.25	each 300 mm variation in storey height	nr	-	-
2.4.26	3.00 m rise; straight; 1070 mm wide	nr	-	-
	plus or minus for			
2.4.27	each 300 mm variation in storey height	nr	-	-

Heavy duty cast iron staircase; perforated treads; no risers; balustrades and hand rails; decorated

2.4.28	3.00 m rise; spiral; 1548 mm diameter	nr	-	-
	plus or minus for			
2.4.29	each 300 mm variation in storey height	nr	-	-
2.4.30	3.00 m rise; straight	nr	-	-
	plus or minus for			
2.4.31	each 300 mm variation in storey height	nr	-	-

Feature metal staircase; galvanised finish perforated treads; no risers; decorated

2.4.32	3.00 m rise; spiral balustrades and handrails	nr	-	-
	plus or minus for			
2.4.33	each 300 mm variation in storey height	nr	-	-
2.4.34	3.00 m rise; dogleg; hardwood balustrades and handrails	nr	-	-
	3.00 m rise; dogleg; stainless steel balustrades			
2.4.35	and handrails	nr	-	-

Feature metal staircase; galvanised finish; concrete treads; balustrades and handrails; decorated

2.4.36	3.00 m rise; dogleg	nr	-	-

Feature metal staircase to water chute; steel springers; stainless steel treads in-filled with tiling; landings every one metre rise

2.4.37	9.00 m rise; spiral	nr	-	-

Galvanised steel catwalk; nylon coated balustrading

2.4.38	450 mm wide	m	-	-

Comparative finishes/balustrading

Finishes to treads and risers; inlcuding nosings etc.

2.4.39	vinyl or rubber	m	-	-
2.4.40	carpet	m	-	-

Wall handrails

2.4.41	timber handrails and brackets	m	-	-
2.4.42	mild steel handrails and brackets	m	-	-
2.4.43	stainless steel handrail and brackets	m	-	-

Balustrading and handrails

2.4.44				
2.4.45	mild steel balustrades and steel or timber handrails	m	-	-
2.4.46	balustrades and handrails with metal infill panels	m	-	-
2.4.47	balustrades and handrails with glass infil panels	m	-	-
2.4.48	stainless steel balustrades and handrails	m	-	-
2.4.49	stainless steel and glass balustrades	m	-	-

INDUSTRIAL £ range £		RETAILING £ range £		LEISURE £ range £		OFFICES £ range £		HOTELS £ range £		Item nr
3,840	- 6,051	-	-	-	-	-	-	-	-	2.4.22
307.00	- 384.00	-	-	-	-	-	-	-	-	2.4.23
3,266	- 4,131	-	-	-	-	-	-	-	-	2.4.24
346.00	- 414.00	-	-	-	-	-	-	-	-	2.4.25
3,454	- 4,131	-	-	-	-	-	-	-	-	2.4.26
346.00	- 412.00	-	-	-	-	-	-	-	-	2.4.27
4,226	- 5,571	-	-	-	-	-	-	-	-	2.4.28
422.00	- 555.00	-	-	-	-	-	-	-	-	2.4.29
4,611	- 6,240	-	-	-	-	-	-	-	-	2.4.30
462.00	- 622.00	-	-	-	-	-	-	-	-	2.4.31
-	-	-	-	6,051	- 6,531	-	-	-	-	2.4.32
-	-	-	-	605.00	- 653.00	-	-	-	-	2.4.33
-	-	-	-	6,240	- 8,640	-	-	-	-	2.4.34
-	-	-	-	7,106	- 11,524	-	-	-	-	2.4.35
-	-	-	-	10,655	- 14,400	-	-	-	-	2.4.36
-	-	-	-	34,560	- 42,240	-	-	-	-	2.4.37
298.00	- 375.00	-	-	316.00	- 405.00	-	-	-	-	2.4.38
-	-	10.00	- 20.00	10.00	- 20.00	10.00	- 20.00	10	- 20.00	2.4.39
-	-	26.00	- 39.00	26.00	- 39.00	26.00	- 39.00	26.00	- 39.00	2.4.40
-	-	52.00	- 79.00	52.00	- 79.00	52.00	- 79.00	52.00	- 79.00	2.4.41
-	-	131.00	- 151.00	131.00	- 151.00	131.00	- 151.00	131.00	- 151.00	2.4.42
-	-	125.00	- 164.00	125.00	- 164.00	125.00	- 164.00	125.00	- 164.00	2.4.43
		197.00	- 282.00	197.00	- 282.00	197.00	- 282.00	197.00	- 282.00	2.4.44
-	-	236.00	- 302.00	236.00	- 302.00	236.00	- 302.00	236.00	- 302.00	2.4.45
-	-	289.00	- 393.00	289.00	- 393.00	289.00	- 393.00	289.00	- 393.00	2.4.46
-	-	328.00	- 420.00	328.00	- 420.00	328.00	- 420.00	328.00	- 420.00	2.4.47
-	-	393.40	- 570.50	393.40	- 570.50	393.40	- 570.50	393.40	- 570.50	2.4.48
-	-	603.00	- 754.00	603.00	- 754.00	603.00	- 754.00	603.00	- 754.00	2.4.49

Item nr	SPECIFICATIONS	UNIT	RESIDENTIAL £ range £

2.5   EXTERNAL WALLS

external wall area (unless otherwise described)

comprising:

Timber framed walling
Brick/block walling
Reinforced concrete walling
Panelled walling
Wall claddings
Curtain/glazed walling
Comparative external finishes

Timber framed walling

Structure only comprising softwood studs at 400 mm x 600 mm centres;
head and sole plates

Item	Description	Unit	Low		High
2.5.1	125 mm x 50 mm	m²	18.00	-	22.00
2.5.2	125 mm x 50 mm; one layer of double sided building paper	m²	21.00	-	26.00
	Softwood stud wall; vapour barrier and plasterboard inner lining; decorated				
2.5.3	uPVC weatherboard outer lining	m²	74.00	-	96.00
2.5.4	tile hanging on battens outer lining	m²	89.00	-	105.00

Brick/block walling
Autoclaved aerated lightweight block walls

Item	Description	Unit	Low		High
2.5.5	100 mm thick	m²	22.00	-	31.00
2.5.6	140 mm thick	m²	29.00	-	41.00
2.5.7	190 mm thick	m²	42.00	-	55.00
	Dense aggregate block walls				
2.5.8	100 mm thick	m²	20.00	-	29.00
2.5.9	140 mm thick	m²	33.00	-	40.00
	Coloured dense aggregate masonry block walls				
2.5.10	100 mm thick; hollow	m²	38.00	-	41.00
2.5.11	100 m thick; solid	m²	41.00	-	45.00
2.5.12	140 mm thick; hollow	m²	43.00	-	50.00
2.5.13	140 m thick; solid	m²	57.00	-	61.00
	Common brick solid walls; bricks PC £180.00/1000				
2.5.14	half brick thick	m²	33.00	-	36.00
2.5.15	one brick brick	m²	57.00	-	61.00
2.5.16	one and a half brick thick	m²	81.00	-	89.00
	Add or deduct for				
	each variation of £10.00/1000 in PC value				
2.5.17	half brick thick	m²	0.90	-	1.30
2.5.18	one brick brick	m²	1.70	-	2.10
2.5.19	one and a half brick thick	m²	2.60	-	3.10
	Extra for				
2.5.20	fair face one side	m²	1.70	-	2.40
	Engineering brick walls; class B; bricks PC £275.00/1000				
2.5.21	half brick thick	m²	41.00	-	47.00
2.5.22	one brick thick	m²	78.00	-	86.00
	Facing brick walls; sand faced facings; bricks PC £270.00/1000				
2.5.23	half brick thick; pointed one side	m²	41.00	-	47.00
2.5.24	one brick thick; pointed both sides	m²	78.00	-	86.00
	Facing brick walls; machine made facings; bricks PC £350.00/1000				
2.5.25	half brick thick; pointed one side	m²	57.00	-	61.00
2.5.26	half brick thick; built against concrete	m²	59.00	-	65.00
2.5.27	one brick thick; pointed both sides	m²	109.00	-	122.00
	Facing bricks solid walls; hand made facings; bricks PC £450.00/1000				
2.5.28	half brick thick; pointed one side	m²	75.00	-	85.00
2.5.29	one brick thick; pointed both sides	m²	148.00	-	167.00

INDUSTRIAL £ range £		RETAILING £ range £		LEISURE £ range £		OFFICES £ range £		HOTELS £ range £		Item nr
-	-	-	-	-	-	-	-	-	-	2.5.1
-	-	-	-	-	-	-	-	-	-	2.5.2
-	-	-	-	-	-	-	-	-	-	2.5.3
-	-	-	-	-	-	-	-	-	-	2.5.4
22.00 -	31.00	22.00 -	31.00	22.00 -	31.00	22.00 -	31.00	22.00 -	31.00	2.5.5
29.00 -	41.00	29.00 -	41.00	29.00 -	41.00	29.00 -	41.00	29.00 -	41.00	2.5.6
42.00 -	55.00	42.00 -	55.00	42.00 -	55.00	42.00 -	55.00	42.00 -	55.00	2.5.7
20.00 -	29.00	20.00 -	29.00	20.00 -	29.00	20.00 -	29.00	20.00 -	29.00	2.5.8
33.00 -	40.00	33.00 -	40.00	33.00 -	40.00	33.00 -	40.00	33.00 -	40.00	2.5.9
35.00 -	39.00	35.00 -	39.00	35.00 -	39.00	35.00 -	39.00	39.00 -	43.00	2.5.10
39.00 -	43.00	39.00 -	43.00	39.00 -	43.00	39.00 -	43.00	43.00 -	47.00	2.5.11
44.00 -	48.00	44.00 -	48.00	44.00 -	48.00	44.00 -	48.00	48.00 -	52.00	2.5.12
52.00 -	59.00	52.00 -	59.00	52.00 -	59.00	52.00 -	59.00	57.00 -	65.00	2.5.13
30.00 -	33.00	30.00 -	33.00	30.00 -	33.00	30.00 -	33.00	34.00 -	37.00	2.5.14
54.00 -	59.00	54.00 -	59.00	54.00 -	59.00	54.00 -	59.00	57.00 -	65.00	2.5.15
77.00 -	87.00	77.00 -	87.00	77.00 -	87.00	77.00 -	87.00	83.00 -	90.00	2.5.16
0.90 -	1.20	0.90 -	1.20	0.90 -	1.20	0.90 -	1.20	0.90 -	1.20	2.5.17
1.70 -	2.00	1.70 -	2.00	1.70 -	2.00	1.70 -	2.00	1.70 -	2.00	2.5.18
2.60 -	3.10	2.60 -	3.10	2.60 -	3.10	2.60 -	3.10	2.60 -	3.10	2.5.19
2.00 -	2.50	2.00 -	2.50	2.00 -	2.50	2.00 -	2.50	2.00 -	2.50	2.5.20
40.00 -	45.00	41.00 -	47.00	41.00 -	47.00	41.00 -	47.00	44.00 -	49.00	2.5.21
76.00 -	82.00	78.00 -	86.00	78.00 -	86.00	78.00 -	86.00	80.00 -	88.00	2.5.22
40.00 -	45.00	41.00 -	47.00	41.00 -	47.00	41.00 -	47.00	44.00 -	49.00	2.5.23
76.00 -	82.00	78.00 -	86.00	78.00 -	86.00	78.00 -	86.00	80.00 -	88.00	2.5.24
54.00 -	61.00	54.00 -	61.00	54.00 -	61.00	54.00 -	61.00	57.00 -	65.00	2.5.25
57.00 -	63.00	59.00 -	65.00	59.00 -	65.00	59.00 -	65.00	61.00 -	69.00	2.5.26
105.00 -	122.00	105.00 -	122.00	105.00 -	122.00	105.00 -	122.00	111.00 -	124.00	2.5.27
73.00 -	81.00	75.00 -	83.00	75.00 -	83.00	75.00 -	83.00	79.00 -	90.00	2.5.28
141.00 -	158.00	147.00 -	160.00	147.00 -	160.00	147.00 -	160.00	154.00 -	167.00	2.5.29

Item nr	SPECIFICATIONS	Unit	RESIDENTIAL £ range £		

2.5 EXTERNAL WALLS - cont'd

external wall area (unless otherwise described)

Brick/block walling - cont'd

Add or deduct for

each variation of £10.00/100 in PC value

Item nr	SPECIFICATIONS	Unit			
2.5.30	half brick thick	m²	0.90	-	1.30
2.5.31	one brick thick	m²	1.70	-	2.00

Composite solid walls; facing brick on outside; bricks
PC £350.00/1000 and common brick on inside; bricks
PC £200.00/1000

2.5.32	one brick thick; pointed one side	m²	87.00	-	96.00

Extra for

2.5.33	one and a half brick thick; pointed one side	m²	4.70	-	7.50
2.5.34	weather pointing as a separate operation	m²	113.00	-	29.00

Composite cavity wall; block outer skin; 50 mm thick insulation; lightweight
block inner skin

2.5.35	outer block rendered	m²	62.00	-	79.00

outer block rendered; no insulation; inner skin

2.5.36	insulating	m²	1.20	-	2.40
2.5.37	outer block roughcast	m²	0.50	-	2.40
2.5.38	coloured masonry outer block	m²	1.20	-	2.40

Extra for

2.5.39	heavyweight block inner skin	m²	2.40	-	3.80
2.5.40	fair face one side	m²	12.20	-	15.00
2.5.41	75 mm thick cavity insulation	m²	1.00	-	3.60
2.5.42	100 mm thick cavity insulation	m²	7.50	-	8.90
2.5.43	plaster and emulsion to inner skin	m²	12.80	-	15.00

Composite cavity wall; facing brick outer skin; 50 mm thick insulation;
plasterboard on stud inner skin; emulsion

2.5.44	sand faced facings; PC £275.00/1000	m²	73.00	-	87.00
2.5.45	machine made facings; PC £350.00/1000	m²	90.00	-	102.00
2.5.46	hand made facings; PC £450.00/1000	m²	108.00	-	121.00

As above but with plaster on lightweight block inner skin; emulsion

2.5.47	sand faced facings; PC £275.00/1000	m²	69.00	-	86.00
2.5.48	machine made facings; PC £350.00/1000	m²	88.00	-	101.00
2.5.49	hand made facings; PC £450.00/1000	m²	100.00	-	118.00

Add or deduct for

2.5.50	each variation of £10.00/1000 in PC value	m²	0.90	-	1.20

Extra for

2.5.51	heavyweight block inner skin	m²	1.20	-	2.40
2.5.52	insulating block inner skin	m²	2.40	-	6.20
2.5.53	30 mm thick cavity wall slab	m²	2.80	-	6.80
2.5.54	50 mm thick cavity insulation	m²	3.40	-	4.20
2.5.55	75 mm thick cavity insulation	m²	4.90	-	5.50
2.5.56	100 mm thick cavity insulation	m²	6.20	-	6.80
2.5.57	weather pointing as a separate operation	m²	4.90	-	7.70
2.5.58	purpose made feature course to windows	m²	6.20	-	12.30

Composite cavity wall; facing brick outer skin; 50 mm thick insulation
common brick inner skin; fair face on inside

2.5.59	sand faced facings; PC £275.00/1000	m²	74.00	-	91.00
2.5.60	machine made facings; PC £350.00/1000	m²	92.00	-	106.00
2.5.61	hand made facings; PC £450.00/1000	m²	109.00	-	125.00

Composite cavity wall; facing brick outer skin; 50 mm thick insulation
common brick inner skin; plaster and emulsion

2.5.62	sand faced facings; PC £275.00/1000	m²	84.00	-	99.00
2.5.63	machine made facings; PC £350.00/1000	m²	103.00	-	116.00
2.5.64	hand made facings; PC £450.00/1000	m²	118.00	-	138.00
2.5.65	Composite cavity wall; coloured masonry block; outer and inner skins; fair faced both sides	m²	113.00	-	152.00

INDUSTRIAL £ range £	RETAILING £ range £	LEISURE £ range £	OFFICES £ range £	HOTELS £ range £	Item nr
0.90 - 1.30	0.90 - 1.30	0.90 - 1.30	0.90 - 1.30	0.90 - 1.30	2.5.30
1.70 - 2.00	1.70 - 2.00	1.70 - 2.00	1.70 - 2.00	1.70 - 2.00	2.5.31
85.00 - 94.00	88.00 - 96.00	88.00 - 96.00	88.00 - 96.00	88.00 - 96.00	2.5.32
4.60 - 7.50	4.60 - 7.50	4.60 - 7.50	4.60 - 7.50	4.60 - 7.50	2.5.33
20.00 - 24.00	25.00 - 29.00	25.00 - 29.00	25.00 - 29.00	30.00 - 35.00	2.5.34
59.00 - 75.00	62.00 - 79.00	62.00 - 79.00	62.00 - 79.00	66.00 - 83.00	2.5.35
1.20 - 2.40	1.20 - 2.40	1.20 - 2.40	1.20 - 2.40	1.20 - 2.40	2.5.36
0.50 - 2.40	0.50 - 2.40	0.50 - 2.40	0.50 - 2.40	0.50 - 2.40	2.5.37
1.20 - 2.40	1.20 - 2.40	1.20 - 2.40	1.20 - 2.40	1.20 - 2.40	2.5.38
2.40 - 3.80	2.40 - 3.80	2.40 - 3.80	2.40 - 3.80	2.40 - 3.80	2.5.39
11.10 - 16.00	11.10 - 16.00	11.10 - 16.00	11.10 - 16.00	13.00 - 17.00	2.5.40
1.30 - 6.30	1.00 - 3.60	1.00 - 3.60	1.00 - 3.60	0.90 - 3.60	2.5.41
6.60 - 11.60	7.50 - 8.90	7.50 - 8.90	7.50 - 8.90	4.80 - 7.50	2.5.42
13.10 - 15.00	12.80 - 15.00	12.80 - 15.00	12.80 - 15.00	12.70 - 15.00	2.5.43
71.00 - 85.00	73.00 - 87.00	73.00 - 87.00	73.00 - 87.00	75.00 - 88.00	2.5.44
88.00 - 100.00	92.00 - 102.00	92.00 - 102.00	92.00 - 102.00	94.00 - 105.00	2.5.45
102.00 - 115.00	108.00 - 121.00	108.00 - 121.00	108.00 - 121.00	111.00 - 125.00	2.5.46
66.00 - 82.00	69.00 - 86.00	69.00 - 86.00	69.00 - 86.00	84.00 - 90.00	2.5.47
82.00 - 97.00	88.00 - 101.00	88.00 - 101.00	88.00 - 101.00	92.00 - 105.00	2.5.48
96.00 - 118.00	100.00 - 118.00	100.00 - 118.00	100.00 - 118.00	104.00 - 125.00	2.5.49
0.90 - 1.20	0.90 - 1.20	0.90 - 1.20	0.90 - 1.20	0.90 - 1.20	2.5.50
1.20 - 2.40	1.20 - 2.40	1.20 - 2.40	1.20 - 2.40	1.20 - 2.40	2.5.51
2.40 - 6.20	2.40 - 6.20	2.40 - 6.20	2.40 - 6.20	2.40 - 6.20	2.5.52
2.80 - 6.80	2.80 - 6.80	2.80 - 6.80	2.80 - 6.80	2.80 - 6.80	2.5.53
3.80 - 4.50	3.80 - 4.50	3.80 - 4.50	3.80 - 4.50	3.80 - 4.50	2.5.54
4.90 - 5.50	4.90 - 5.50	4.90 - 5.50	4.90 - 5.50	4.90 - 5.50	2.5.55
6.20 - 6.80	6.20 - 6.80	6.20 - 6.80	6.20 - 6.80	6.20 - 6.80	2.5.56
4.90 - 7.70	4.90 - 7.70	4.90 - 7.70	4.90 - 7.70	4.90 - 7.70	2.5.57
6.20 - 12.50	6.20 - 12.50	6.20 - 12.50	6.20 - 12.50	6.20 - 12.50	2.5.58
70.00 - 90.00	74.00 - 91.00	74.00 - 91.00	74.00 - 91.00	77.00 - 94.00	2.5.59
89.00 - 103.00	92.00 - 106.00	92.00 - 106.00	92.00 - 106.00	95.00 - 110.00	2.5.60
104.00 - 118.00	109.00 - 125.00	109.00 - 125.00	109.00 - 125.00	113.00 - 131.00	2.5.61
82.00 - 97.00	84.00 - 99.00	84.00 - 99.00	84.00 - 99.00	88.00 - 107.00	2.5.62
99.00 - 114.00	103.00 - 116.00	103.00 - 116.00	103.00 - 116.00	108.00 - 119.00	2.5.63
113.00 - 130.00	118.00 - 138.00	118.00 - 138.00	118.00 - 138.00	125.00 - 146.00	2.5.64
108.00 - 146.00	113.00 - 152.00	113.00 - 152.00	113.00 - 152.00	117.00 - 156.00	2.5.65

Item nr	SPECIFICATIONS	Unit	RESIDENTIAL £ range £		
2.5	**EXTERNAL WALLS - cont'd**				
	external wall area (unless otherwise described)				
	Reinforced concrete walling				
	In situ reinforced concrete 25.00 N/mm²; 13 kg/m² reinforcement; formwork both sides				
2.5.66	150 mm thick	m²	121.00	-	168.00
2.5.67	225 mm thick	m²	142.00	-	181.00
	Panelled walling				
	Precast concrete panels; including insulation; lining and fixings				
2.5.68	standard panels	m²	-		-
2.5.69	standard panels; exposed aggregate finish	m²	-		-
2.5.70	brick clad panels	m²	-		-
2.5.71	reconstructed stone faced panels	m²	-		-
2.5.72	natural stone faced panels	m²	-		-
2.5.73	marble or granite faced panels	m²	-		-
	GRP/laminate panels; including battens; back up walls; plaster and emulsion				
2.5.74	melamine finished solid laminate panels	m²	-		-
2.5.75	single skin panels	m²	-		-
2.5.76	double skin panels				
2.5.77	insulated sandwich panels	m²	-		-
	Wall claddings				
	Non-asbestos profiled cladding				
2.5.78	"Profile 3"; natural	m²	-		-
2.5.79	"Profile 3"; coloured	m²	-		-
2.5.80	"Profile 6"; natural	m²	-		-
2.5.81	"Profile 6"; coloured	m²	-		-
2.5.82	insulated; inner lining of plasterboard	m²	-		-
2.5.83	"Profile 6"; natural; insulated; inner lining panel	m²	-		-
2.5.84	insulated; with 2.80 m high block inner skin; emulsion	m²	-		-
	insulated; with 2.80 m high block inner skin				
2.5.85	plasterboard lining on metal tees; emulsion	m²	-		-
	Asbestos cement profiled cladding on steel rails				
2.5.86	insulated; with 2.80 m high block inner skin; emulsion	m²	-		-
	insulated; with 2.80 m high block inner skin				
2.5.87	plasterboard lining on metal tees; emulsion	m²	-		-
	PVF2 coated galvanised steel profiled cladding				
2.5.88	0.60 mm thick; "profile 20B"; corrugations vertical	m²	-		-
2.5.89	0.60 mm thick; "profile 30"; corrugations vertical	m²	-		-
2.5.90	0.60 mm thick; "profile TOP 40"; corrugations vertical	m²	-		-
2.5.91	0.60 mm thick; "profile 60B"; corrugations vertical	m²	-		-
2.5.92	0.60 mm thick; "profile 30"; corrugations horizontal	m²	-		-
2.5.93	0.60 mm thick; "profile 60B"; corrugations horizontal	m²	-		-
	Extra for				
2.5.94	80 mm thick insulation and 0.40 mm thick coated inner lining	m²	-		-
	PVF2 coated galvanised steel profiled cladding on steel rails				
2.5.95	insulated	m²	-		-
2.5.96	2.80 m high insulating block inner skin; emulsion	m²	-		-
	2.80 m high insulating block inner skin; plastered				
2.5.97	lining on metal tees; emulsion	m²	-		-
2.5.98	insulated; coloured inner lining panel	m²	-		-
	insulated; full height insulating block inner skin;				
2.5.99	plaster and emulsion	m²	-		-
2.5.100	insulated; metal sandwich panel system	m²	-		-

INDUSTRIAL £ range £		RETAILING £ range £		LEISURE £ range £		OFFICES £ range £		HOTELS £ range £		Item nr
121.00	- 168.00	121.00	- 168.00	121.00	- 168.00	121.00	- 168.00	121.00	- 168.00	2.5.66
142.00	- 181.00	142.00	- 181.00	142.00	- 181.00	142.00	- 181.00	142.00	- 181.00	2.5.67
122.00	- 185.00	126.00	- 185.00	126.00	- 185.00	126.00	- 185.00	126.00	- 199.00	2.5.68
185.00	- 260.00	202.00	- 260.00	202.00	- 260.00	202.00	- 260.00	202.00	- 278.00	2.5.69
241.00	- 307.00	260.00	- 307.00	260.00	- 307.00	260.00	- 307.00	260.00	- 325.00	2.5.70
-	-	249.00	- 450.00	249.00	- 450.00	249.00	- 450.00	249.00	- 450.00	2.5.71
-	-	400.00	- 600.00	400.00	- 600.00	400.00	- 600.00	400.00	- 600.00	2.5.72
-	-	450.00	- 750.00	450.00	- 750.00	450.00	- 750.00	450.00	- 750.00	2.5.73
155.00	- 202.00	155.00	- 202.00	155.00	- 202.00	-	-	-	-	2.5.74
173.00	- 220.00	182.00	- 220.00	182.00	- 220.00	146.00	- 182.00	-	-	2.5.75
						220.00	- 278.00	-	-	2.5.76
-	-	289.00	- 367.00	289.00	- 367.00	278.00	- 349.00	278.00	- 349.00	2.5.77
20.00	- 23.00	-	-	-	-	-	-	-	-	2.5.78
22.00	- 25.00	-	-	-	-	-	-	-	-	2.5.79
22.00	- 25.00	-	-	-	-	-	-	-	-	2.5.80
23.00	- 26.00	-	-	-	-	-	-	-	-	2.5.81
39.00	- 50.00	-	-	-	-	-	-	-	-	2.5.82
39.00	- 50.00	-	-	-	-	-	-	-	-	2.5.83
34.00	- 39.00	-	-	-	-	-	-	-	-	2.5.84
47.00	- 55.00	-	-	-	-	-	-	-	-	2.5.85
34.00	- 39.00	-	-	-	-	-	-	-	-	2.5.86
45.00	- 54.00	-	-	-	-	-	-	-	-	2.5.87
28.00	- 34.00	34.00	- 43.00	34.00	- 43.00	-	-	-	-	2.5.88
28.00	- 34.00	34.00	- 43.00	34.00	- 43.00	-	-	-	-	2.5.89
26.00	- 33.00	33.00	- 41.00	33.00	- 41.00	-	-	-	-	2.5.90
33.00	- 41.00	41.00	- 47.00	41.00	- 47.00	-	-	-	-	2.5.91
29.00	- 37.00	37.00	- 45.00	37.00	- 45.00	-	-	-	-	2.5.92
33.00	- 41.00	41.00	- 50.00	41.00	- 50.00	-	-	-	-	2.5.93
15.00	- 16.00	15.00	- 16.00	15.00	- 16.00	-	-	-	-	2.5.94
45.00	- 58.00	-	-	-	-	-	-	-	-	2.5.95
58.00	- 70.00	-	-	-	-	-	-	-	-	2.5.96
64.00	- 83.00	-	-	-	-	-	-	-	-	2.5.97
64.00	- 83.00	73.00	- 96.00	73.00	- 96.00	-	-	-	-	2.5.98
81.00	- 109.00	90.00	- 117.00	90.00	- 117.00	90.00	- 117.00	-	-	2.5.99
164.00	- 250.00	191.00	- 260.00	182.00	- 250.00	211.00	- 250.00	-	-	2.5.100

Item nr	SPECIFICATIONS	Unit	RESIDENTIAL
			£ range £

2.5   EXTERNAL WALLS - cont'd

external wall area (unless otherwise described)

Wall cladding - cont'd

PVF2 coated aluminium profiled cladding on steel rails

2.5.101	insulated	m²	-	-
2.5.102	insulated; plasterboard lining on metal tees; emulsion	m²	-	-
2.5.103	insulated; coloured inner lining panel	m²	-	-
2.5.104	insulated; full height insulating block inner skin; plaster and emulsion	m²	-	-
	Extra for			
2.5.105	heavyweight block inner skin	m²	-	-
2.5.106	insulated; aluminium sandwich panel system	m²	-	-
	insulated; aluminium sandwich panel system; on framing;			
2.5.107	on block inner skin; fair face one side	m²	-	-
	Other cladding systems			
	vitreous enamelled insulated steel sandwich panel system; with non-			
2.5.108	asbestos fibre insulating board on inner face	m²	-	-
2.5.109	Formalux sandwich panel system; with coloured lining tray; on steel cladding rails	m²	-	-
2.5.110	aluminium over cladding system rain screen	m²	-	-
2.5.111	natural stone cladding on full height insulating block inner skin; plaster and emulsion	m²	-	-

Curtain/glazed walling

12 mm Toughened glass single glazed polyester powder coated aluminium site constructed 'stick' standard curtain walling system to

2.5.112	internal trim	m²	-	-
	Extra for			
2.5.113	single door; including hardware	m²	-	-
2.5.114	half hour fire resistant glazing	m²	-	-
2.5.115	6 mm Toughened glass single glazed polyester powder coated aluminium site constructed 'stick' standard curtain walling system to internal trim	m²	-	-
2.5.116	6 mm Clear float glass double glazed polyester powder coated aluminium site constructed 'stick' economical quality standard curtain walling system	m²	-	-
	Extra for			
2.5.117	tinted glass	m²	-	-
2.5.118	high performance glass	m²	-	-
2.5.119	low E glass	m²	-	-
2.5.120	laminated clear float glass	m²	-	-
2.5.121	clear solar control glass	m²	-	-
2.5.122	translucent thermal insulating glass	m²	-	-
2.5.123	screen printing (fritting)	m²	-	-
2.5.124	sand blasting opaque glass	m²	-	-
2.5.125	acid etched opaque glass	m²	-	-
2.5.126	'look-a-like' steel faced insulating spandrel panels	m²	-	-
2.5.127	'look-a-like' aluminium insulating spandrel panels	m²	-	-
2.5.128	'look-a-like' laminate opaque insulating spandrel panels	m²	-	-
2.5.129	block back up wall including plaster and emulsion	m²	-	-
2.5.130	opening lights; manual (actual area)	m²	-	-
2.5.131	opening lights; mechanically operated (actual area)	m²	-	-
2.5.132	single door; including hardware	nr	-	-
2.5.133	6 mm Clear float glass double glazed polyester powder coated aluminium site constructed 'stick' medium quality standard curtain walling system including opaque insulated spandrel panels	m²	-	-
2.5.134	6 mm Clear float glass double glazed polyester powder coated aluminium site constructed 'stick' medium quality standard curtain walling system including opaque insulated spandrel panels	m²	-	-

INDUSTRIAL £ range £		RETAILING £ range £		LEISURE £ range £		OFFICES £ range £		HOTELS £ range £		Item nr
51.00	- 66.00	-	-	-	-	-	-	-	-	2.5.101
70.00	- 81.00	-	-	-	-	-	-	-	-	2.5.102
73.00	- 90.00	81.00	- 102.00	81.00	- 102.00	-	-	-	-	2.5.103
96.00	- 121.00	102.00	- 130.00	102.00	- 130.00	102.00	- 138.00	-	-	2.5.104
1.30	- 2.60	1.30	- 2.80	1.30	- 2.80	1.30	- 2.80	-	-	2.5.105
137.00	- 183.00	183.00	- 230.00	183.00	- 250.00	192.00	- 250.00	-	-	2.5.106
-	-	211.00	- 355.00	-	-	-	-	-	-	2.5.107
156.00	- 191.00	-	-	-	-	-	-	-	-	2.5.108
182.00	- 220.00	202.00	- 230.00	202.00	- 230.00	202.00	- 230.00	-	-	2.5.109
230.00	- 260.00	-	-	-	-	-	-	-	-	2.5.110
-	-	-	-	-	-	414.00	- 593.00	433.00	- 611.00	2.5.111
-	-	256.00	- 328.00	256.00	- 328.00	256.00	- 328.00	256.00	- 328.00	2.5.112
-	-	1,154	- 1,443	1,154	- 1,443	1,154	- 1,443	1,154	- 1,443	2.5.113
-	-	203.00	- 289.00	203.00	- 289.00	203.00	- 289.00	203.00	- 289.00	2.5.114
-	-	328.00	- 400.00	328.00	- 400.00	328.00	- 400.00	328.00	- 400.00	2.5.115
-	-	361.00	- 433.00	361.00	- 433.00	361.00	- 433.00	361.00	- 433.00	2.5.116
-	-	11.80	- 14.40	11.80	- 14.40	11.80	- 14.40	11.80	- 14.40	2.5.117
-	-	29.00	- 43.00	29.00	- 43.00	29.00	- 43.00	29.00	- 43.00	2.5.118
-	-	37.00	- 43.00	37.00	- 43.00	37.00	- 43.00	37.00	- 43.00	2.5.119
-	-	29.00	- 43.00	29.00	- 43.00	29.00	- 43.00	29.00	- 43.00	2.5.120
-	-	72.00	- 87.00	72.00	- 87.00	72.00	- 87.00	72.00	- 87.00	2.5.121
-	-	115.00	- 144.00	115.00	- 144.00	115.00	- 144.00	115.00	- 144.00	2.5.122
-	-	43.00	- 52.00	43.00	- 52.00	43.00	- 52.00	43.00	- 52.00	2.5.123
-	-	22.00	- 29.00	22.00	- 29.00	22.00	- 29.00	22.00	- 29.00	2.5.124
-	-	72.00	- 101.00	72.00	- 101.00	72.00	- 101.00	72.00	- 101.00	2.5.125
-	-	43.00	- 58.00	43.00	- 58.00	43.00	- 58.00	43.00	- 58.00	2.5.126
-	-	29.00	- 43.00	29.00	- 43.00	29.00	- 43.00	29.00	- 43.00	2.5.127
-	-	87.00	- 101.00	87.00	- 101.00	87.00	- 101.00	87.00	- 101.00	2.5.128
-	-	43.00	- 58.00	43.00	- 58.00	43.00	- 58.00	43.00	- 58.00	2.5.129
-	-	216.00	- 361.00	216.00	- 361.00	216.00	- 361.00	216.00	- 361.00	2.5.130
-	-	577.00	- 793.00	577.00	- 793.00	577.00	- 793.00	577.00	- 793.00	2.5.131
-	-	1,154	- 1,443	1,154	- 1,443	1,154	- 1,443	1,154	- 1,443	2.5.132
-	-	433.00	- 721.00	433.00	- 721.00	433.00	- 721.00	433.00	- 721.00	2.5.133
-	-	505.00	- 721.00	505.00	- 721.00	505.00	- 721.00	505.00	- 721.00	2.5.134

Item nr	SPECIFICATIONS	Unit	RESIDENTIAL £ range £	

2.5   EXTERNAL WALLS - cont'd

external wall area (unless otherwise described)

Curtain/glazed walling - cont'd

Item nr	SPECIFICATIONS	Unit		
2.5.135	6 mm Laminate glass double glazed polyester powder coated aluminium site constructed 'stick' high quality bespoke curtain walling system, including opaque insulated spandrel panels	m²	-	-
2.5.136	Extra over for triple glazing	m²	-	-
2.5.137	6 mm Laminate glass double glazed polyester powder coated aluminium factory produced 'unitised/panelled' high quality standard curtain walling system, including opaque insulated spandrel panels	m²	-	-
	Extra over for			
2.5.138	opening lights; manual	m²	-	-
2.5.139	opening lights; mechanically opened	m²	-	-
2.5.140	10 mm Laminate glass double glazed polyester powder coated aluminium factory produced 'unitised/panelled' medium quality bespoke curtain walling system, including opaque insulated spandrel panels	m²	-	-
	Extra over for			
2.5.141	stainless steel clad curtain walling	m²	-	-
2.5.142	PVF2 finished curtain walling	m²	-	-
2.5.143	brise soleil	m	-	-
2.5.144	stone spandrel panels (actual area)	m²	-	-
2.5.145	triple glazing	m²	-	-
2.5.146	triple glazing with wide cavity	m²	-	-
2.5.147	interstitial blind	m²	-	-
2.5.148	bomb proof glazing	m²	-	-
2.5.149	one hour fire protection	m²	-	-
2.5.150	facetted glazing	%	-	-
2.5.151	curved glazing	%	-	-
2.5.152	15 mm Clear and laminate triple glazed polyester powder coated aluminium factory produced modular 'unitised/panelled' prestigious quality bespoke curtain walling system, including opaque insulated spandrel panels	m²	-	-
2.5.153	15 mm Clear and laminate triple glazed bronze finished aluminium factory produced large span 'unitised/panelled' prestigious quality bespoke curtain walling system, including stone faced spandrel panels	m²	-	-
2.5.154	10 mm and 6 mm Clear and laminate structural silliconed double glazed standard 'stick and panel' assembly, with aluminium spacer bar and carrier frame, site constructed curtain walling system	m²	-	-
2.5.155	10 mm and 6 mm Clear and laminate structural silliconed double glazed standard 'unitised/panelled' assembly on aluminium frame, factory produced curtain walling system	m²	-	-
2.5.156	10 mm and 6 mm Clear and laminate structural silliconed double glazed bespoke 'unitised/panelled' assembly on aluminium frame, factory produced curtain walling system	m²	-	-
	Extra over for			
2.5.157	triple glazing with wide cavity	m²	-	-
2.5.158	12 mm Toughened structural silliconed single glazed standard 'unitised/panelled'; assembly factory produced curtain walling system excluding support	m²	-	-
2.5.159	10 mm and 6 mm Clear and laminate structural silliconed double glazed standard 'unitised/panelled' assembly factory produced curtain walling system excluding support	m²	-	-
	Extra over for			
2.5.160	secondary steel supports	m²	-	-
2.5.161	supporting structure for glass vertical fins	m²	-	-
2.5.162	10 mm Clear and laminate structural silliconed inverted suspended double glazed standard 'unitised/panelled' assembly factory produced curtain walling system	m²	-	-
2.5.163	Fixed Brise Soleil including unistrut supports	m	-	-
2.5.164	Retractable Brise Soleil including unistrut supports	m	-	-

INDUSTRIAL £ rate £		RETAILING £ rate £			LEISURE £ rate £			OFFICES £ rate £			HOTELS £ rate £			Item nr.
-	-	649.00	-	866.00	649.00	-	866.00	649.00	-	866.00	649.00	-	866.00	2.5.135
-	-	115.00	-	173.00	115.00	-	173.00	115.00	-	173.00	115.00	-	173.00	2.5.136
-	-	649.00	-	793.00	649.00	-	793.00	649.00	-	793.00	649.00	-	793.00	2.5.137
-	-	216.00	-	361.00	216.00	-	361.00	216.00	-	361.00	216.00	-	361.00	2.5.138
-	-	577.00	-	793.00	577.00	-	793.00	577.00	-	793.00	577.00	-	793.00	2.5.139
-	-	793.00	-	1,010	793.00	-	1,010	793.00	-	1,010	793.00	-	1,010	2.5.140
-	-	87.00	-	131.00	87.00	-	131.00	87.00	-	131.00	87.00	-	131.00	2.5.141
-	-	115.00	-	144.00	115.00	-	144.00	115.00	-	144.00	115.00	-	144.00	2.5.142
-	-	317.00	-	361.00	317.00	-	361.00	317.00	-	361.00	317.00	-	361.00	2.5.143
-	-	289.00	-	433.00	289.00	-	433.00	289.00	-	433.00	289.00	-	433.00	2.5.144
-	-	115.00	-	144.00	115.00	-	144.00	115.00	-	144.00	115.00	-	144.00	2.5.145
-	-	144.00	-	203.00	144.00	-	203.00	144.00	-	203.00	144.00	-	203.00	2.5.146
-	-	72.00	-	216.00	72.00	-	216.00	72.00	-	216.00	72.00	-	216.00	2.5.147
-	-	131.00	-	173.00	131.00	-	173.00	131.00	-	173.00	131.00	-	173.00	2.5.148
-	-	577.00	-	866.00	577.00	-	866.00	577.00	-	866.00	577.00	-	866.00	2.5.149
-	-	22.00	-	72.00	22.00	-	72.00	22.00	-	72.00	22.00	-	72.00	2.5.150
-	-	144.00	-	164.00	144.00	-	164.00	144.00	-	164.00	144.00	-	164.00	2.5.151
-	-	1,154	-	1,443	1,154	-	1,443	1,154	-	1,443	1,154	-	1,443	2.5.152
-	-	1,731	-	2,164	1,731	-	2,164	1,731	-	2,164	1,731	-	2,164	2.5.153
-	-	505.00	-	649.00	505.00	-	649.00	505.00	-	649.00	505.00	-	649.00	2.5.154
-	-	649.00	-	793.00	649.00	-	793.00	649.00	-	793.00	649.00	-	793.00	2.5.155
-	-	866.00	-	1,010	866.00	-	1,010	866.00	-	1,010	866.00	-	1,010	2.5.156
-	-	144.00	-	203.00	144.00	-	203.00	144.00	-	203.00	144.00	-	203.00	2.5.157
-	-	433.00	-	721.00	433.00	-	721.00	433.00	-	721.00	433.00	-	721.00	2.5.158
-	-	649.00	-	938.00	649.00	-	938.00	649.00	-	938.00	649.00	-	938.00	2.5.159
-	-	144.00	-	289.00	144.00	-	289.00	144.00	-	289.00	144.00	-	289.00	2.5.160
-	-	108.00	-	216.00	108.00	-	216.00	108.00	-	216.00	108.00	-	216.00	2.5.161
-	-	1,010	-	1,154	1,010	-	1,154	1,010	-	1,154	1,010	-	1,154	2.5.162
-	-	200.00	-	300.00	200.00	-	300.00	200.00	-	300.00	200.00	-	300.00	2.5.163
-	-	700.00	-	900.00	700.00	-	900.00	700.00	-	900.00	700.00	-	900.00	2.5.164

Item nr.	SPECIFICATIONS	Unit	RESIDENTIAL £ range £	
2.5	**EXTERNAL WALLS** - cont'd			
	external wall area (unless otherwise described)			
	Curtain/glazed walling - cont'd			
2.5.165	Lift surround of double glazed or laminated glass with aluminium or stainless steel framing	m²	-	-
2.5.166	Patent glazing systems; excluding opening lights and lead flashings etc, 7 mm Georgian wired cast glass, aluminium glazing bars spanning up to 3m at 600 - 626 mm spacing	m²	-	-
2.5.167	Patent glazing systems; excluding opening lights and lead flashings etc, 6.4 mm Laminate glass, aluminium glazing bars spanning up to 3m at 600 - 626 mm spacing	m²	-	-
	Comparative external finishes			
	Comparative concrete wall finishes			
2.5.168	wrought formwork one side including rubbing down	m²	-	-
2.5.169	shotblasting to expose aggregate	m²	-	-
2.5.170	bush hammering to expose aggregate	m²	-	-
	Comparative insitu finishes			
2.5.171	two coats "Sandtex Matt" cement paint	m²	-	-
2.5.172	cement and sand plain face rendering	m²	-	-
2.5.173	three coat "Tyroclean" rendering; including backing	m²	-	-
2.5.174	"Mineralite" decorative rendering; including backing	m²	-	-
	Comparative cladding			
	25 mm thick tongued and grooved "Tanalised" softwood			
2.5.175	boarding; including battens	m²	-	-
	25 mm thick tongued and grooved western red cedar boarding including			
2.5.176	battens	m²	-	-
2.5.177	machine made tiles; including battens	m²	-	-
2.5.178	best hand made sand faced tiles; including battens	m²	-	-
	20 mm x 20 mm thick mosaic glass or ceramic; in common colours;			
2.5.179	fixed on prepared surface	m²	-	-
2.5.180	75 mm thick Portland stone facing slabs and fixing; including clamps	m²	-	-
2.5.181	75 mm thick Ancaster stone facing slabs and fixing; including clamps	m²	-	-
	Comparative curtain wall finishes			
	Extra over aluminium mill finish for			
2.5.182	natural anodising	m²	-	-
2.5.183	polyester powder coating	m²	-	-
2.5.184	brinze anodising	m²	-	-
2.6	**WINDOWS AND EXTERNAL DOORS**			
	window and external door area (unless otherwise described)			
	comprising:			
	Softwood windows and external doors			
	Steel windows and external doors			
	Steel roller shutters			
	Hardwood windows and external doors			
	uPVC windows and external doors			
	Aluminium windows, entrance screen and doors			
	Stainless steel entrance screens and doors			
	Shop fronts, shutters and grilles			
	Softwood windows and external doors			
	Standard windows; painted			
2.6.1	single glazed	m²	220.00 -	289.00
2.6.2	double glazed	m²	289.00 -	346.00
	Purpose made windows; painted			
2.6.3	single glazed	m²	289.00 -	367.00
2.6.4	double glazed	m²	367.00 -	462.00

INDUSTRIAL £ range £		RETAILING £ range £		LEISURE £ range £		OFFICES £ range £		HOTELS £ range £		Item nr
-	-	649.00 - 1,082		649.00 - 1,082		649.00 - 1,082		649.00 - 1,082		2.5.165
-	-	131.00 - 157.00		131.00 - 157.00		131.00 - 157.00		131.00 - 157.00		2.5.166
-	-	393.00 - 479.00		393.00 - 479.00		393.00 - 479.00		393.00 - 479.00		2.5.167
-	-	3.30 - 6.60		3.30 - 6.60		3.30 - 6.60		3.30 - 6.60		2.5.168
-	-	4.20 - 8.10		4.20 - 8.10		4.20 - 8.10		4.20 - 8.10		2.5.169
-	-	13.10 - 18.00		13.10 - 18.00		13.10 - 18.00		13.10 - 18.00		2.5.170
-	-	7.70 - 10.80		7.70 - 10.80		7.70 - 10.80		7.70 - 10.80		2.5.171
-	-	13.50 - 20.00		13.50 - 20.00		13.50 - 20.00		13.50 - 20.00		2.5.172
-	-	33.00 - 39.00		33.00 - 39.00		33.00 - 39.00		33.00 - 44.00		2.5.173
-	-	65.00 - 75.00		65.00 - 75.00		65.00 - 75.00		69.00 - 85.00		2.5.174
-	-	31.00 - 39.00		31.00 - 39.00		31.00 - 39.00		31.00 - 39.00		2.5.175
-	-	36.00 - 46.00		36.00 - 46.00		36.00 - 46.00		36.00 - 46.00		2.5.176
-	-	39.00 - 45.00		39.00 - 45.00		39.00 - 45.00		39.00 - 45.00		2.5.177
-	-	47.00 - 52.00		47.00 - 52.00		47.00 - 52.00		47.00 - 52.00		2.5.178
-	-	99.70 - 116.70		99.70 - 116.70		99.70 - 116.70		99.70 - 116.70		2.5.179
-	-	-	-	-	-	385.60 - 480.00		405.20 - 527.20		2.5.180
-	-	-	-	-	-	423.60 - 527.20		-	-	2.5.181
-	-	18.00 - 24.00		18.00 - 24.00		18.00 - 24.00		18.00 - 24.00		2.5.182
-	-	24.00 - 41.00		24.00 - 41.00		24.00 - 41.00		24.00 - 39.00		2.5.183
-	-	33.00 - 50.00		33.00 - 50.00		33.00 - 50.00		33.00 - 50.00		2.5.184
211.00 - 269.00		202.00 - 278.00		220.00 - 289.00		220.00 - 289.00		220.00 - 307.00		2.6.1
260.00 - 337.00		278.00 - 337.00		288.00 - 367.00		289.00 - 367.00		289.00 - 367.00		2.6.2
289.00 - 367.00		289.00 - 289.00		307.00 - 376.00		298.00 - 376.00		298.00 - 395.00		2.6.3
358.00 - 424.00		358.00 - 424.00		323.00 - 414.00		358.00 - 414.00		376.00 - 442.00		2.6.4

Item nr	SPECIFICATIONS	UNIT	RESIDENTIAL £ range £
2.6	**WINDOWS AND EXTERNAL DOORS - cont'd**		
	window and external door area (unless otherwise described)		
	Softwood windows and external doors - cont'd		
	Standard external softwood doors and hardwood frames; doors painted; including ironmongery		
2.6.5	two panelled door; plywood panels	nr	376.00 - 451.00
2.6.6	solid flush door	nr	424.00 - 489.00
2.6.7	two panelled door; glazed panels	nr	800.00 - 894.00
	heavy duty solid flush door		
2.6.8	single leaf	nr	- -
2.6.9	double leaf	nr	- -
	Extra for		
2.6.10	emergency fire exit door	nr	- -
	Steel windows and external doors		
	Standard windows		
2.6.11	single glazed; galvanised; painted	m²	230.00 - 298.00
2.6.12	single glazed; powder coated	m²	241.00 - 307.00
2.6.13	double glazed; galvanised; painted	m²	298.00 - 355.00
2.6.14	double glazed; powder coated	m²	307.00 - 376.00
	Purpose made windows		
2.6.15	double glazed; powder coated	m²	- -
	Steel roller shutters		
	Shutters; galvanised		
2.6.16	manual	m²	- -
2.6.17	electric	m²	- -
2.6.18	manual; insulated	m²	- -
2.6.19	electric; insulated	m²	- -
2.6.20	electric; insulated; fire resistant	m²	- -
	Hardwood windows and external doors		
	Standard windows; stained or uPVC coated		
2.6.21	single glazed	m²	307.00 - 433.00
2.6.22	double glazed	m²	395.00 - 498.00
	Purpose made windows; stained or uPVC coated		
2.6.23	single glazed	m²	355.00 - 480.00
2.6.24	double glazed	m²	433.00 - 555.00
	uPVC windows and external doors		
	Purpose made windows		
2.6.25	double glazed	m²	622.00 - 771.00
	Extra for		
2.6.26	tinted glass	m²	- -
	Aluminium windows, entrance screens and doors		
	Standard windows; anodised finish		
2.6.27	single glazed; horizontal sliding sash	m²	- -
2.6.28	single glazed; vertical sliding sash	m²	- -
2.6.29	single glazed; casement; in hardwood sub-frame	m²	325.00 - 433.00
2.6.30	double glazed; vertical sliding slash	m²	- -
2.6.31	double glazed; casement; in hardwood sub-frame	m²	395.00 - 527.00
	Purpose made windows		
2.6.32	single glazed	m²	- -
2.6.33	double glazed	m²	- -
2.6.34	double glazed; feature; with precast concrete surrounds m²	m²	- -
	Purpose made entrance screens and doors		
2.6.35	double glazed	m²	- -
	Purpose made revolving door		
2.6.36	2000 mm diameter; double glazed	nr	- -

INDUSTRIAL £ range £		RETAILING £ range £		LEISURE £ range £		OFFICES £ range £		HOTELS £ range £		Item nr
-	-	-	-	-	-	-	-	-	-	2.6.5
555.00	- 978.00	442.00	- 498.00	442.00	- 498.00	442.00	- 498.00	451.00	- 518.00	2.6.6
-	-	-	-	-	-	-	-	-	-	2.6.7
640.00	- 978.00	725.00	- 904.00	725.00	- 885.00	-	-	-	-	2.6.8
1,129	- 1,609	1,374	- 1,534	1,374	- 1,534	-	-	-	-	2.6.9
-	-	241.00	- 376.00	241.00	- 376.00	-	-	-	-	2.6.10
211.00	- 278.00	211.00	- 289.00	230.00	- 289.00	289.00	- 289.00	230.00	- 316.00	2.6.11
220.00	- 289.00	220.00	- 289.00	241.00	- 307.00	241.00	- 307.00	241.00	- 325.00	2.6.12
278.00	- 346.00	278.00	- 346.00	289.00	- 365.00	365.00	- 365.00	298.00	- 386.00	2.6.13
278.00	- 346.00	278.00	- 365.00	298.00	- 376.00	298.00	- 376.00	307.00	- 395.00	2.6.14
-	-	395.00	- 498.00	395.00	- 498.00	395.00	- 498.00	302.00	- 527.00	2.6.15
230.00	- 298.00	211.00	- 278.00	211.00	- 289.00	-	-	-	-	2.6.16
278.00	- 395.00	260.00	- 386.00	260.00	- 386.00	-	-	-	-	2.6.17
386.00	- 451.00	355.00	- 433.00	355.00	- 433.00	-	-	-	-	2.6.18
433.00	- 546.00	414.00	- 527.00	414.00	- 527.00	-	-	-	-	2.6.19
1,045	- 1,251	1,007	- 1,251	1,007	- 1,251	-	-	-	-	2.6.20
395.00	- 480.00	395.00	- 480.00	395.00	- 480.00	395.00	- 480.00	414.00	- 498.00	2.6.21
498.00	- 602.00	498.00	- 602.00	498.00	- 602.00	498.00	- 602.00	498.00	- 518.00	2.6.22
480.00	- 555.00	480.00	- 555.00	480.00	- 555.00	480.00	- 555.00	480.00	- 602.00	2.6.23
555.00	- 678.00	555.00	- 678.00	555.00	- 678.00	555.00	- 678.00	555.00	- 706.00	2.6.24
574.00	- 640.00	574.00	- 640.00	574.00	- 640.00	574.00	- 640.00	574.00	- 640.00	2.6.25
29.00	- 39.30	29.00	- 39.30	29.00	- 39.30	29.00	- 39.30	29.00	- 39.30	2.6.26
278.00	- 337.00	278.00	- 337.00	278.00	- 337.00	278.00	- 337.00	278.00	- 355.00	2.6.27
433.00	- 518.00	433.00	- 518.00	433.00	- 518.00	433.00	- 518.00	433.00	- 527.00	2.6.28
-	-	-	-	-	-	-	-	-	-	2.6.29
480.00	- 555.00	536.00	- 678.00	536.00	- 678.00	536.00	- 678.00	536.00	- 715.00	2.6.30
-	-	-	-	-	-	-	-	-	-	2.6.31
278.00	- 395.00	278.00	- 395.00	278.00	- 395.00	278.00	- 395.00	278.00	- 395.00	2.6.32
622.00	- 753.00	622.00	- 753.00	622.00	- 753.00	622.00	- 753.00	622.00	- 771.00	2.6.33
-	-	-	-	1,562	- 2,353	-	-	-	-	2.6.34
-	-	771.00	- 1,251	771.00	- 1,251	771.00	- 1,251	-	-	2.6.35
-	-	27,671	- 35,388	27,671	- 35,388	27,238	- 35,388	27,238	- 35,388	2.6.36

Item nr	SPECIFICATIONS	Unit	RESIDENTIAL £ range £	
2.6	**WINDOWS AND EXTERNAL DOORS - cont'd** **window and external door area** (unless otherwise described)			
	Stainless steel entrance screens and doors Purpose made screen; double glazed			
2.6.37	with manual doors	m²	-	-
2.6.38	with automatic doors	m²	-	-
	Purpose made revolving door			
2.6.39	2000 mm diameter; double glazed	nr	-	-
	Shop fronts, shutters and grilles **shop front length**			
2.6.40	Temporary timber shop fronts	m	-	-
2.6.41	Grilles or shutters	m	-	-
2.6.42	Fire shutters; power operated	m	-	-
	Shop front			
2.6.43	flat façade; glass in aluminium framing; manual centre doors only	m	-	-
2.6.44	flat façade; glass in aluminium framing; automatic centre doors only	m	-	-
2.6.45	hardwood and glass; including high enclosed window beds	m	-	-
	high quality; marble or granite plasters and stair risers; window beds			
2.6.46	and backings; illuminated signs	m	-	-
2.7	**INTERNAL WALLS, PARTITIONS AND DOORS** **internal wall area** (unless otherwise described)			
	comprising:			
	Timber or metal stud partitions and doors **Brick/block partitions and doors** **Reinforced concrete walls** **Solid partitioning and doors** **Glazed partitioning and doors** **Special partitioning and doors** **WC/Changing cubicles** **Comparative doors/door linings/frames** **Perimeter treatments**			
	Timber or metal stud partitions and doors Structure only comprising softwood studs at 400 mm x 600 mm centres; head and sole plates			
2.7.1	100 mm x 38 mm	m²	14.00	-	17.00
	Softwood stud and plasterboard partitions			
2.7.2	57 mm thick "Paramount" dry partition	m²	25.00	-	28.00
2.7.3	65 mm thick "Paramount" dry partition	m²	28.00	-	31.00
2.7.4	50 mm thick laminated partition	m²	27.00	-	30.00
2.7.5	65 mm thick laminated partition	m²	31.00	-	34.00
2.7.6	65 mm thick laminated partition; emulsion both sides	m²	39.00	-	42.00
2.7.7	100 mm thick partition; taped joints; emulsion both sides	m²	42.00	-	49.00
2.7.8	100 mm thick partition; skim and emulsion both sides	m²	49.00	-	55.00
2.7.9	150 mm thick partition as party wall; skim and emulsion both sides	m²	58.00	-	69.00
	Metal stud and plasterboard partitions			
2.7.10	170 mm thick partition; one hour; taped joints; emulsion both sides	m²	-	-
2.7.11	200 mm thick partition; one hour; taped joints; emulsion both sides	m²	-	-
2.7.12	325 mm thick two layer partition; cavity insulation	m²	-	-
	Extra for			
2.7.13	curved work	m²	-	-

INDUSTRIAL £ range £		RETAILING £ range £		LEISURE £ range £		OFFICES £ range £		HOTELS £ range £		Item nr
-	-	1,251 - 1,882		-	-	-	-	-	-	2.6.37
-	-	1,553 - 2,211		-	-	-	-	-	-	2.6.38
-	-	38,024 - 47,624		35,849 - 44,900		35,849 - 44,900		35,849 - 44,900		2.6.39
-	-	51.00 - 72.00		-	-	-	-	-	-	2.6.40
-	-	622.00 - 1,251		-	-	-	-	-	-	2.6.41
-	-	1,102 - 1,571		-	-	-	-	-	-	2.6.42
-	-	1,251 - 2,880		-	-	-	-	-	-	2.6.43
-	-	1,562 - 3,502		-	-	-	-	-	-	2.6.44
-	-	4,424 - 5,365		-	-	-	-	-	-	2.6.45
-	-	4,989 - 6,918		-	-	-	-	-	-	2.6.46
-	-	-	-	-	-	-	-	-	-	2.7.1
-	-	-	-	-	-	-	-	-	-	2.7.2
-	-	-	-	-	-	-	-	-	-	2.7.3
-	-	-	-	-	-	-	-	-	-	2.7.4
-	-	-	-	-	-	-	-	-	-	2.7.5
-	-	-	-	-	-	-	-	-	-	2.7.6
-	-	-	-	-	-	-	-	-	-	2.7.7
-	-	-	-	-	-	-	-	-	-	2.7.8
-	-	-	-	-	-	-	-	-	-	2.7.9
49.00 - 60.00		52.00 - 64.00		52.00 - 64.00		52.00 - 64.00		55.00 - 64.00		2.7.10
70.00 - 77.00		73.00 - 79.00		73.00 - 79.00		73.00 - 79.00		75.00 - 81.00		2.7.11
117.00 - 164.00		125.00 - 169.00		125.00 - 169.00		125.00 - 169.00		125.00 - 169.00		2.7.12
+50%		+50%		+50%		+50%		+50%		2.7.13

Item nr	SPECIFICATIONS	Unit	RESIDENTIAL £ range £		

2.7   INTERNAL WALLS, PARTITIONS AND DOORS - cont'd
internal wall area (unless otherwise described)

Timber or metal stud partitions and doors - cont'd
Metal stud and plasterboard partitions; emulsion both sides; softwood doors
and frames; painted

Item nr	SPECIFICATIONS	Unit			
2.7.14	170 mm thick partition	m²	-		-
2.7.15	200 mm thick partition; insulated	m²	-		-
	Stud or plasterboard partitions; softwood doors and frames; painted				
2.7.16	partition; plaster and emulsion both sides	m²	83.00	-	105.00
	Extra for				
2.7.17	vinyl paper in lieu of emulsion	m²	5.50	-	8.10
2.7.18	hardwood doors and frames in lieu of softwood	m²	23.00	-	27.00
2.7.19	partition; plaster and vinyl both sides	m²	98.00	-	118.00
	Stud or plasterboard partitions; hardwood doors and frames				
2.7.20	partition; plaster and emulsion both sides	m²	105.00	-	131.00
2.7.21	partition; plaster and vinyl both sides	m²	121.00	-	148.00
	Brick/block partitions and doors				
	Autoclaved aerated/lightweight block partitions				
2.7.22	75 mm thick	m²	16.00	-	19.00
2.7.23	100 mm thick	m²	21.00	-	25.00
2.7.24	130 mm thick; insulating	m²	26.00	-	29.00
2.7.25	150 mm thick	m²	29.00	-	31.00
2.7.26	190 mm thick	m²	34.00	-	39.00
	Extra for				
2.7.27	fair face both sides	m²	2.80	-	5.50
2.7.28	curved work		+10%	-	+20%
2.7.29	average thickness; fair face both sides	m²	28.00	-	34.00
2.7.30	average thickness; fair face and emulsion both sides	m²	33.00	-	41.00
2.7.31	average thickness; plaster and emulsion both sides	m²	50.00	-	59.00
	Concrete block partitions				
2.7.32	to retail units	m²	-		-
	Dense aggregate block partitions				
2.7.33	average thickness; fair face both sides	m²	33.00	-	39.00
2.7.34	average thickness; fair face and emulsion both sides	m²	38.00	-	45.00
2.7.35	average thickness; plaster and emulsion both sides	m²	55.00	-	63.00
	Coloured dense aggregate masonry block partition				
2.7.36	fair face both sides	m²	-		-
	Common brick partitions; bricks PC £120.00/1000				
2.7.37	half brick thick	m²	30.00	-	33.00
2.7.38	half brick thick; fair face both sides	m²	33.00	-	39.00
2.7.39	half brick thick; fair face and emulsion both sides	m²	38.00	-	45.00
2.7.40	half brick thick; plaster and emulsion both sides	m²	54.00	-	69.00
2.7.41	one brick thick	m²	55.00	-	63.00
2.7.42	one brick thick; fair face and emulsion both sides	m²	59.00	-	69.00
2.7.43	one brick thick; fair face and emulsion both sides	m²	65.00	-	75.00
2.7.44	one brick thick; plaster and emulsion both sides	m²	81.00	-	96.00
2.7.45	Block partitions; softwood doors and frames; painted partition	m²	46.00	-	61.00
2.7.46	partition; fair faced both sides	m²	48.00	-	65.00
2.7.47	partition; fair face and emulsion both sides	m²	55.00	-	71.00
2.7.48	partition; plastered and emulsioned both sides	m²	73.00	-	92.00
	Block partitions; hardwood doors and frames				
2.7.49	partition	m²	70.00	-	88.00
2.7.50	partition; plaster and emulsion both sides	m²	94.00	-	118.00
	Reinforced concrete walls				
	Walls				
2.7.51	150 mm thick	m²	96.00	-	115.00
2.7.52	150 mm thick; plaster and emulsion both sides	m²	128.00	-	154.00

INDUSTRIAL £ range £	RETAILING £ range £	LEISURE £ range £	OFFICES £ range £	HOTELS £ range £	Item nr
66.00 - 88.00	70.00 - 92.00	70.00 - 92.00	70.00 - 92.00	70.00 - 94.00	2.7.14
88.00 - 108.00	90.00 - 111.00	90.00 - 111.00	90.00 - 111.00	90.00 - 118.00	2.7.15
81.00 - 102.00	85.00 - 105.00	85.00 - 105.00	85.00 - 105.00	85.00 - 111.00	2.7.16
-	6.20 - 8.70	6.20 - 8.70	6.20 - 8.70	6.20 - 13.90	2.7.17
24.00 - 27.00	24.00 - 27.00	24.00 - 27.00	24.00 - 27.00	24.00 - 37.00	2.7.18
66.00 - 115.00	96.00 - 118.00	96.00 - 118.00	96.00 - 118.00	105.00 - 139.00	2.7.19
104.00 - 126.00	105.00 - 131.00	105.00 - 131.00	105.00 - 131.00	105.00 - 139.00	2.7.20
140.00 - 138.00	121.00 - 148.00	121.00 - 148.00	121.00 - 148.00	121.00 - 168.00	2.7.21
16.00 - 18.00	16.00 - 19.00	16.00 - 19.00	16.00 - 19.00	16.00 - 19.00	2.7.22
19.00 - 24.00	20.00 - 25.00	20.00 - 25.00	20.00 - 25.00	20.00 - 25.00	2.7.23
24.00 - 28.00	26.00 - 30.00	26.00 - 30.00	26.00 - 30.00	26.00 - 30.00	2.7.24
27.00 - 30.00	28.00 - 31.00	28.00 - 31.00	28.00 - 31.00	28.00 - 31.00	2.7.25
33.00 - 38.00	34.00 - 39.00	34.00 - 39.00	34.00 - 39.00	34.00 - 39.00	2.7.26
2.90 - 6.20	2.90 - 6.20	2.90 - 6.20	2.90 - 6.20	2.90 - 6.20	2.7.27
+10% - +20%	+10% - +20%	+10% - +20%	+10% - +20%	+10% - +20%	2.7.28
28.00 - 33.00	21.00 - 34.00	30.00 - 34.00	30.00 - 34.00	31.00 - 37.00	2.7.29
33.00 - 41.00	33.00 - 41.00	33.00 - 41.00	33.00 - 41.00	35.00 - 43.00	2.7.30
49.00 - 57.00	50.00 - 59.00	50.00 - 59.00	50.00 - 59.00	52.00 - 63.00	2.7.31
-	44.00 - 50.00	-	-	-	2.7.32
33.00 - 38.00	33.00 - 39.00	33.00 - 39.00	33.00 - 39.00	33.00 - 41.00	2.7.33
37.00 - 45.00	38.00 - 45.00	38.00 - 45.00	38.00 - 45.00	39.00 - 47.00	2.7.34
54.00 - 59.00	55.00 - 63.00	55.00 - 63.00	55.00 - 63.00	55.00 - 65.00	2.7.35
-	-	61.00 - 75.00	-	-	2.7.36
28.00 - 31.00	30.00 - 33.00	30.00 - 33.00	30.00 - 33.00	31.00 - 34.00	2.7.37
31.00 - 38.00	33.00 - 39.00	33.00 - 39.00	33.00 - 39.00	33.00 - 41.00	2.7.38
36.00 - 45.00	38.00 - 45.00	38.00 - 45.00	38.00 - 45.00	39.00 - 47.00	2.7.39
52.00 - 67.00	54.00 - 69.00	54.00 - 69.00	54.00 - 69.00	55.00 - 75.00	2.7.40
54.00 - 59.00	55.00 - 63.00	55.00 - 63.00	55.00 - 63.00	59.00 - 65.00	2.7.41
57.00 - 65.00	59.00 - 69.00	59.00 - 69.00	59.00 - 69.00	61.00 - 69.00	2.7.42
61.00 - 71.00	65.00 - 75.00	65.00 - 75.00	65.00 - 75.00	69.00 - 79.00	2.7.43
79.00 - 90.00	81.00 - 94.00	81.00 - 94.00	81.00 - 94.00	87.00 - 100.00	2.7.44
44.00 - 59.00	46.00 - 61.00	46.00 - 61.00	46.00 - 61.00	48.00 - 63.00	2.7.45
46.00 - 61.00	48.00 - 65.00	48.00 - 65.00	48.00 - 65.00	52.00 - 65.00	2.7.46
52.00 - 69.00	55.00 - 71.00	55.00 - 71.00	55.00 - 71.00	57.00 - 71.00	2.7.47
71.00 - 89.00	73.00 - 92.00	73.00 - 92.00	73.00 - 92.00	73.00 - 95.70	2.7.48
67.00 - 85.00	69.00 - 89.00	69.00 - 89.00	69.00 - 89.00	75.00 - 90.00	2.7.49
90.00 - 115.00	94.00 - 118.00	94.00 - 118.00	94.00 - 118.00	85.00 - 108.00	2.7.50
96.00 - 113.00	96.00 - 113.00	95.70 - 112.80	95.70 - 112.80	96.00 - 113.00	2.7.51
129.00 - 155.00	129.00 - 155.00	128.50 - 154.80	128.50 - 154.80	129.00 - 155.00	2.7.52

Item nr	SPECIFICATIONS	Unit	RESIDENTIAL £ range £	
2.7	**INTERNAL WALLS, PARTITION AND DOORS - cont'd**			
	internal wall area (unless otherwise described)			
	Solid partitioning and doors			
	Patent partitioning; softwood doors			
2.7.53	frame and sheet	m²	-	-
2.7.54	frame and panel	m²	-	-
2.7.55	panel to panel	m²	-	-
2.7.56	economical	m²	-	-
	Patent partitioning; hardwood doors			
2.7.57	economical	m²	-	-
	Demountable partitioning; hardwood doors			
2.7.58	medium quality; vinyl faced	m²	-	-
2.7.59	high quality; vinyl faced	m²	-	-
	Glazed partitioning and doors			
	Aluminium internal patent glazing			
2.7.60	single glazed	m²	-	-
2.7.61	double glazed	m²	-	-
	Demountable steel partitioning and doors			
2.7.62	medium quality	m²	-	-
2.7.63	high quality	m²	-	-
	Demountable aluminium/steel partitioning and doors			
2.7.64	high quality	m²	-	-
2.7.65	high quality; sliding	m²	-	-
	Stainless steel glazed manual doors and screens			
2.7.66	high quality; to inner lobby of malls	m²	-	-
	Special partitioning and doors			
	Demountable fire partitions			
2.7.67	enamelled steel; half hour	m²	-	-
2.7.68	stainless steel; half hour	m²	-	-
	Soundproof partitions; hardwood doors			
2.7.69	luxury veneered	m²	-	-
	Folding Screens			
2.7.70	gym divider; electronically operated	m²	-	-
2.7.71	bar divider	m²	-	-
2.7.72	Squash court glass back wall and door	m²	-	-
	WC/Changing cubicles **each** (unless otherwise described)			
2.7.73	WC cubicles	nr	-	-
	Changing cubicles			
2.7.74	aluminium	nr	-	-
2.7.75	aluminium; textured glass and bench seating	nr	-	-
	Comparative doors/door linings/frames			
	Standard softwood doors; excluding ironmongery; linings and frames			
	40 mm thick flush; hollow core; painted			
2.7.76	726 mm x 2040 mm	nr	45.00 -	55.00
2.7.77	826 mm x 2040 mm	nr	45.00 -	55.00
	40 mm thick flush; hollow core; plywood faced; painted			
2.7.78	726 mm x 2040 mm	nr	55.00 -	70.00
2.7.79	826 mm x 2040 mm	nr	55.00 -	70.00
	40 mm thick flush; hollow core; sapele veneered hard board faced			
2.7.80	726 mm x 2040 mm	nr	45.00 -	55.00
2.7.81	826 mm x 2040 mm	nr	45.00 -	55.00
	40 mm thick flush; hollow core; teak veneered hard board faced			
2.7.82	726 mm x 2040 mm	nr	108.00 -	131.00
2.7.83	826 mm x 2040 mm	nr	108.00 -	131.00

INDUSTRIAL £ range £		RETAILING £ range £		LEISURE £ range £		OFFICES £ range £		HOTELS £ range £		Item nr
62.00	- 121.00	70.00	- 125.00	70.00	- 125.00	70.00	- 125.00	70.00	- 152.00	2.7.53
51.00	- 96.00	55.00	- 100.00	55.00	- 100.00	55.00	- 100.00	55.00	- 125.00	2.7.54
76.00	- 164.00	83.00	- 172.00	83.00	- 172.00	83.00	- 172.00	83.00	- 191.00	2.7.55
83.00	- 105.00	88.00	- 113.00	88.00	- 113.00	88.00	- 113.00	88.00	- 139.00	2.7.56
90.00	- 111.00	90.00	- 118.00	90.00	- 118.00	90.00	- 118.00	90.00	- 125.00	2.7.57
118.00	- 155.00	125.00	- 155.00	125.00	- 155.00	125.00	- 155.00	125.00	- 168.00	2.7.58
156.00	- 218.00	156.00	- 218.00	156.00	- 218.00	156.00	- 218.00	164.00	- 237.00	2.7.59
105.00	- 146.00	-	-	-	-	-	-	-	-	2.7.60
178.00	- 222.00	-	-	-	-	-	-	-	-	2.7.61
191.00	- 241.00	-	-	-	-	191.00	- 260.00	-	-	2.7.62
241.00	- 298.00	-	-	-	-	260.00	- 307.00	-	-	2.7.63
-	-	-	-	289.00	- 518.00	-	-	411.80	- 518.00	2.7.64
-	-	-	-	691.00	- 845.00	-	-	-	-	2.7.65
-	-	412.00	- 1,106	-	-	-	-	-	-	2.7.66
431.00	- 653.00	498.00	- 700.00	498.00	- 700.00	498.00	- 700.00	-	-	2.7.67
-	-	873.00	- 1,106	873.00	- 1,106	873.00	- 1,106	-	-	2.7.68
220.00	- 298.00	241.00	- 337.00	241.00	- 337.00	241.00	- 337.00	241.00	- 365.00	2.7.69
-	-	-	-	164.00	- 182.00	-	-	-	-	2.7.70
-	-	-	-	433.00	- 489.00	-	-	-	-	2.7.71
-	-	-	-	289.00	- 341.00	-	-	-	-	2.7.72
307.00	- 480.00	316.00	- 480.00	316.00	- 480.00	307.00	- 682.00	384.00	- 682.00	2.7.73
-	-	-	-	375.00	- 682.00	-	-	-	-	2.7.74
-	-	-	-	623.00	- 817.00	-	-	-	-	2.7.75
45.00	- 55.00	45.00	- 55.00	45.00	- 55.00	45.00	- 55.00	45.00	- 55.00	2.7.76
45.00	- 55.00	45.00	- 55.00	45.00	- 55.00	45.00	- 55.00	45.00	- 55.00	2.7.77
55.00	- 70.00	55.00	- 70.00	55.00	- 70.00	55.00	- 70.00	55.00	- 70.00	2.7.78
55.00	- 70.00	55.00	- 70.00	55.00	- 70.00	55.00	- 70.00	55.00	- 70.00	2.7.79
45.00	- 55.00	45.00	- 55.00	45.00	- 55.00	45.00	- 55.00	31.00	- 55.00	2.7.80
45.00	- 55.00	45.00	- 55.00	45.00	- 55.00	45.00	- 55.00	45.00	- 55.00	2.7.81
108.00	- 130.00	108.00	- 130.00	108.00	- 130.00	108.00	- 130.00	108.00	- 130.00	2.7.82
108.00	- 130.00	108.00	- 130.00	108.00	- 130.00	108.00	- 130.00	108.00	- 130.00	2.7.83

Item nr	SPECIFICATIONS	Unit	RESIDENTIAL £ range £		
2.7	**INTERNAL WALLS, PARTITION AND DOORS - cont'd**				
	each (unless otherwise described)				
	Comparative doors/door linings/frames - cont'd				
	Standard softwood fire doors; excluding ironmongery; lining and frames				
	44 mm thick flush; half hour fire check; plywood faced; painted				
2.7.84	726 mm x 2040 mm	nr	70.00	-	77.00
2.7.85	826 mm x 2040 mm	nr	73.00	-	83.00
	44 mm thick flush; half hour fire check; plywood faced; painted				
2.7.86	726 mm x 2040 mm	nr	90.00	-	100.00
2.7.87	826 mm x 2040 mm	nr	92.00	-	104.00
	54 mm thick flush; one hour fire check; sapele veneered hardboard faced				
2.7.88	726 mm x 2040 mm	nr	278.00	-	307.00
2.7.89	826 mm x 2040 mm	nr	289.00	-	307.00
	54 mm thick flush; one hour fire check; sapele veneered hardboard faced				
2.7.90	726 mm x 2040 mm	nr	298.00	-	337.00
2.7.91	826 mm x 2040 mm	nr	307.00	-	346.00
	Purpose made softwood doors; excluding ironmongery; linings and frames				
	44 mm thick four panel door; painted				
2.7.92	726 mm x 2040 mm	nr	155.00	-	173.00
2.7.93	826 mm x 2040 mm	nr	164.00	-	182.00
	50 mm thick four door panel; wax polished				
2.7.94	726 mm x 2040 mm	nr	298.00	-	337.00
2.7.95	826 mm x 2040 mm	nr	316.00	-	346.00
	Purpose made softwood door frames/linings; painted including grounds				
	32 mm x 100 mm lining				
2.7.96	726 mm x 2040 mm opening	nr	92.00	-	104.00
2.7.97	826 mm x 2040 mm opening	nr	96.00	-	108.00
	32 mm x 140 mm lining				
2.7.98	726 mm x 2040 mm opening	nr	104.00	-	118.00
2.7.99	826 mm x 2040 mm opening	nr	105.00	-	121.00
	32 mm x 250 mm cross tongued lining				
2.7.100	726 mm x 2040 mm opening	nr	135.00	-	156.00
2.7.101	826 mm x 2040 mm opening	nr	138.00	-	159.00
	32 mm x 375 mm cross tongued lining				
2.7.102	726 mm x 2040 mm opening	nr	177.00	-	202.00
2.7.103	826 mm x 2040 mm opening	nr	182.00	-	202.00
	75 mm x 100 mm rebated frame				
2.7.104	726 mm x 2040 mm opening	nr	121.00	-	129.00
2.7.105	826 mm x 2040 mm opening	nr	126.00	-	134.00
	Purpose made mahogany door frames/linings; wax polished including grounds				
	32 mm x 100 mm lining				
2.7.106	726 mm x 2040 mm opening	nr	125.00	-	134.00
2.7.107	826 mm x 2040 mm opening	nr	126.00	-	138.00
	32 mm x 140 mm lining				
2.7.108	726 mm x 2040 mm opening	nr	138.00	-	156.00
2.7.109	826 mm x 2040 mm opening	nr	142.00	-	159.00
	32 mm x 250 mm cross tongued lining				
2.7.110	726 mm x 2040 mm opening	nr	159.00	-	169.00
2.7.111	826 mm x 2040 mm opening	nr	161.00	-	174.00
	32 mm x 375 mm cross tongued lining				
2.7.112	726 mm x 2040 mm opening	nr	241.00	-	260.00
2.7.113	826 mm x 2040 mm opening	nr	241.00	-	269.00
	75 mm x 100 mm rebated frame				
2.7.114	726 mm x 2040 mm opening	nr	173.00	-	182.00
2.7.115	826 mm x 2040 mm opening	nr	173.00	-	182.00

INDUSTRIAL £ rate £		RETAILING £ rate £		LEISURE £ rate £		OFFICES £ rate £		HOTELS £ rate £		Item nr.
70.00 - 77.00		70.00 - 77.00		70.00 - 77.00		70.00 - 77.00		70.00 - 77.00		2.7.84
73.00 - 83.00		73.00 - 83.00		73.00 - 83.00		73.00 - 83.00		73.00 - 83.00		2.7.85
88.00 - 100.00		88.00 - 100.00		88.00 - 100.00		88.00 - 100.00		88.00 - 100.00		2.7.86
92.00 - 104.00		92.00 - 104.00		92.00 - 104.00		92.00 - 104.00		92.00 - 104.00		2.7.87
278.00 - 307.00		278.00 - 307.00		278.00 - 307.00		278.00 - 307.00		278.00 - 307.00		2.7.88
289.00 - 307.00		289.00 - 307.00		289.00 - 307.00		289.00 - 307.00		289.00 - 307.00		2.7.89
298.00 - 337.00		298.00 - 337.00		298.00 - 337.00		298.00 - 337.00		298.00 - 337.00		2.7.90
307.00 - 346.00		307.00 - 346.00		307.00 - 346.00		307.00 - 346.00		307.00 - 346.00		2.7.91
155.00 - 173.00		155.00 - 173.00		155.00 - 173.00		155.00 - 173.00		155.00 - 173.00		2.7.92
164.00 - 182.00		164.00 - 182.00		164.00 - 182.00		164.00 - 182.00		164.00 - 182.00		2.7.93
298.00 - 337.00		298.00 - 337.00		298.00 - 337.00		298.00 - 337.00		298.00 - 337.00		2.7.94
316.00 - 346.00		316.00 - 346.00		316.00 - 346.00		316.00 - 346.00		316.00 - 346.00		2.7.95
92.00 - 104.00		92.00 - 104.00		92.00 - 104.00		92.00 - 104.00		92.00 - 104.00		2.7.96
96.00 - 108.00		96.00 - 108.00		96.00 - 108.00		96.00 - 108.00		96.00 - 108.00		2.7.97
102.00 - 118.00		102.00 - 118.00		102.00 - 118.00		102.00 - 118.00		102.00 - 118.00		2.7.98
105.00 - 122.00		105.00 - 122.00		105.00 - 122.00		105.00 - 122.00		105.00 - 122.00		2.7.99
135.00 - 156.00		135.00 - 156.00		135.00 - 156.00		135.00 - 156.00		135.00 - 156.00		2.7.100
138.00 - 159.00		138.00 - 159.00		138.00 - 159.00		138.00 - 159.00		138.00 - 159.00		2.7.101
186.00 - 194.00		186.00 - 194.00		186.00 - 194.00		186.00 - 194.00		186.00 - 194.00		2.7.102
186.00 - 199.00		186.00 - 199.00		186.00 - 199.00		186.00 - 199.00		186.00 - 199.00		2.7.103
121.00 - 129.00		121.00 - 129.00		121.00 - 129.00		121.00 - 129.00		121.00 - 129.00		2.7.104
129.00 - 135.00		129.00 - 135.00		129.00 - 135.00		129.00 - 135.00		129.00 - 135.00		2.7.105
126.00 - 135.00		126.00 - 135.00		126.00 - 135.00		126.00 - 135.00		126.00 - 135.00		2.7.106
129.00 - 138.00		129.00 - 138.00		129.00 - 138.00		129.00 - 138.00		129.00 - 138.00		2.7.107
138.00 - 156.00		138.00 - 156.00		138.00 - 156.00		138.00 - 156.00		138.00 - 156.00		2.7.108
142.00 - 159.00		142.00 - 159.00		142.00 - 159.00		142.00 - 159.00		142.00 - 159.00		2.7.109
156.00 - 169.00		156.00 - 169.00		156.00 - 169.00		156.00 - 169.00		156.00 - 169.00		2.7.110
164.00 - 178.00		164.00 - 178.00		164.00 - 178.00		164.00 - 178.00		164.00 - 178.00		2.7.111
230.00 - 260.00		230.00 - 260.00		230.00 - 260.00		230.00 - 260.00		230.00 - 260.00		2.7.112
241.00 - 269.00		241.00 - 269.00		241.00 - 269.00		241.00 - 269.00		241.00 - 269.00		2.7.113
173.00 - 182.00		173.00 - 182.00		173.00 - 182.00		173.00 - 182.00		173.00 - 182.00		2.7.114
173.00 - 182.00		173.00 - 182.00		173.00 - 182.00		173.00 - 182.00		173.00 - 182.00		2.7.115

Item nr.	SPECIFICATIONS	Unit	RESIDENTIAL £ range £		

2.7   INTERNAL WALLS, PARTITION AND DOORS - cont'd

each (unless otherwise described)

Comparative doors/door linings/frames - cont'd

Standard softwood doors and frames; including ironmongery and painting

2.7.116	flush; hollow core	nr	230.00	-	289.00
2.7.117	flush; hollow core; hardwood faced	nr	230.00	-	307.00
	flush; solid core				
2.7.118	single leaf	nr	269.00	-	346.00
2.7.119	double leaf	nr	393.00	-	529.00
2.7.120	flush; solid core; hardwood faced	nr	278.00	-	365.00
2.7.121	four panel door	nr	393.00	-	480.00

Purpose made softwood doors and hardwood frames;
including ironmongery; painting and polishing flush
    solid core; heavy duty

2.7.122	single leaf	nr	-		-
2.7.123	double leaf	nr	-		-
	flush solid core; heavy duty; plastic laminate faced				
2.7.124	single leaf	nr	-		-
2.7.125	double leaf	nr	-		-

Purpose made softwood fire doors and hardwood frames;including
ironmongery; painting and polishing
    flush; one hour fire resisting

2.7.126	single leaf	nr	-		-
2.7.127	double leaf	nr	-		-
	flush; one hour fire resisting; plastic laminate faced				
2.7.128	single leaf	nr	-		-
2.7.129	double leaf	nr	-		-

Purpose made softwood doors and pressed steel frames;

2.7.130	flush; half hour fire check; plastic laminate faced	nr	-		-

Purpose made mahogany doors and frames; including ironmongery and
polishing

2.7.131	four panel door	nr	-		-

Perimeter treatments

Precast concrete lintels; in block walls

2.7.132	75 mm wide	nr	12.20	-	20.00
2.7.133	100 mm wide	nr	20.00	-	25.00
	Precast concrete lintels; in brick walls				
2.7.134	half brick thick	nr	20.00	-	25.00
2.7.135	one brick thick	nr	32.00	-	41.00

Purpose made softwood architraves; painted; including grounds
    25 mm x 50 mm; to both sides of openings

2.7.136	726 mm x 2040 mm opening	nr	90.00	-	98.00
2.7.137	826 mm x 2040 mm opening	nr	92.00	-	100.00

Purpose made mahogany architraves; wax polished; including grounds
    25 mm x 50 mm; to both sides of openings

2.7.138	726 mm x 2040 mm opening	nr	148.00	-	164.00
2.7.139	826 mm x 2040 mm opening	nr	148.00	-	164.00

INDUSTRIAL £ range £	RETAILING £ range £	LEISURE £ range £	OFFICES £ range £	HOTELS £ range £	Item nr
230.00 - 289.00	230.00 - 289.00	230.00 - 289.00	230.00 - 289.00	230.00 - 289.00	2.7.116
230.00 - 307.00	230.00 - 307.00	230.00 - 307.00	230.00 - 307.00	230.00 - 307.00	2.7.117
269.00 - 346.00	269.00 - 346.00	269.00 - 346.00	269.00 - 346.00	269.00 - 346.00	2.7.118
393.00 - 529.00	393.00 - 529.00	393.00 - 529.00	393.00 - 529.00	393.00 - 529.00	2.7.119
278.00 - 365.00	278.00 - 365.00	278.00 - 365.00	278.00 - 365.00	278.00 - 365.00	2.7.120
393.00 - 480.00	393.00 - 480.00	393.00 - 480.00	393.00 - 480.00	393.00 - 480.00	2.7.121
662.00 - 778.00	662.00 - 778.00	662.00 - 778.00	662.00 - 778.00	662.00 - 778.00	2.7.122
902.00 - 1,151	902.00 - 1,151	902.00 - 1,151	902.00 - 1,151	902.00 - 1,151	2.7.123
805.00 - 913.00	805.00 - 913.00	805.00 - 913.00	805.00 - 913.00	805.00 - 913.00	2.7.124
1,115 - 1,249	1,115 - 1,249	1,115 - 1,249	1,115 - 1,249	1,115 - 1,249	2.7.125
873.00 - 978.00	873.00 - 978.00	873.00 - 978.00	873.00 - 978.00	873.00 - 978.00	2.7.126
1,115 - 1,363	1,115 - 1,363	1,115 - 1,363	1,115 - 1,363	1,115 - 1,363	2.7.127
1,085 - 1,190	1,085 - 1,190	1,085 - 1,190	1,085 - 1,190	1,085 - 1,190	2.7.128
1,393 - 1,506	1,393 - 1,506	1,393 - 1,506	1,393 - 1,506	1,393 - 1,506	2.7.129
1,007 - 1,211	1,007 - 1,211	1,007 - 1,211	1,007 - 1,211	1,007 - 1,211	2.7.130
835.00 - 978.00	835.00 - 978.00	835.00 - 978.00	835.00 - 978.00	835.00 - 978.00	2.7.131
9.20 - 14.60	9.20 - 14.60	9.20 - 14.60	9.20 - 14.60	9.20 - 14.60	2.7.132
11.50 - 16.00	11.50 - 16.00	11.50 - 16.00	11.50 - 16.00	11.50 - 16.00	2.7.133
11.50 - 16.00	11.50 - 16.00	11.50 - 16.00	11.50 - 16.00	11.50 - 16.00	2.7.134
18.00 - 22.00	18.00 - 22.00	18.00 - 22.00	18.00 - 22.00	18.00 - 22.00	2.7.135
90.00 - 98.00	90.00 - 98.00	90.00 - 98.00	90.00 - 98.00	90.00 - 98.00	2.7.136
92.00 - 100.00	91.80 - 100.00	92.00 - 100.00	92.00 - 100.00	92.00 - 90.00	2.7.137
148.00 - 164.00	148.00 - 164.00	148.00 - 164.00	148.00 - 164.00	148.00 - 164.00	2.7.138
151.00 - 164.00	151.00 - 164.00	151.00 - 164.00	151.00 - 164.00	151.00 - 164.00	2.7.139

Item nr	SPECIFICATIONS	Unit	RESIDENTIAL £ range £		
3.1	**WALL FINISHES**				
	wall finish area (unless otherwise described)				
	comprising:				
	Sheet/board finishes				
	In situ wall finishes				
	Rigid tile/panel finishes				
	Sheet/board finishes				
	Dry plasterboard lining; taped joints; for direct decoration				
3.1.1	9.50 mm thick Gyproc Wallboard	m²	12.60	-	16.40
	Extra for				
3.1.2	insulating grade	m²	0.50	-	0.70
3.1.3	insulating grade; plastic faced	m²	2.00	-	2.40
3.1.4	12.50 mm thick Gyproc wallboard (half hour fire resisting)	m²	13.50	-	17.80
	Extra for				
3.1.5	insulating grade	m²	0.70	-	0.90
3.1.6	insulating grade; plastic faced	m²	1.80	-	2.00
3.1.7	two layers of 12.50 mm thick Gyproc wallboard (one hour fire resisting)	m²	21.00	-	26.00
3.1.8	9 mm thick Supalux (half hour fire resisting)	m²	23.00	-	27.00
	Dry plasterboard lining; taped joints; for direct decoration; including metal dabs				
3.1.9	9.50 mm thick Gyproc Wallboard	m²	13.50	-	17.80
	Dry plasterboard lining; taped joints; for direct decoration; including metal tees				
3.1.10	9.50 mm thick Gyproc Wallboard	m²	-		-
3.1.11	12.50 mm thick Gyproc Wallboard	m²	-		-
	Dry lining/steel panelling; including battens; plugged to wall				
3.1.12	6.40 mm thick hardboard	m²	10.50	-	12.50
3.1.13	9.50 mm thick Gyproc wallboard	m²	15.00	-	21.00
3.1.14	6 mm thick birch faced plywood	m²	17.00	-	20.00
3.1.15	6 mm thick WAM plywood	m²	21.00	-	25.00
3.1.16	15 mm thick chipboard	m²	15.00	-	17.00
3.1.17	15 mm thick melamine faced chipboard	m²	28.00	-	34.00
3.1.18	13.20 mm thick "Formica" faced chipboard	m²	37.00	-	55.00
	Timber boarding/panelling; on and including battens; plugged to wall				
3.1.19	12 mm thick softwood boarding	m²	24.00	-	31.00
3.1.20	25 mm thick softwood boarding	m²	34.00	-	39.00
3.1.21	hardwood panelling; t&g & v-jointed	m²	55.00	-	125.00
	In situ wall finishes				
	Extra over common brickwork for				
3.1.22	fair face and pointing both sides	m²	3.40	-	4.90
	Comparative finishes				
3.1.23	one mist and two coats emulsion paint	m²	2.80	-	4.10
3.1.24	multi coloured gloss paint	m²	4.90	-	6.20
3.1.25	two coats of lightweight plaster	m²	9.60	-	12.50
3.1.26	9.50 mm thick Gyproc Wallboard and skim coat	m²	12.10	-	15.50
3.1.27	12.50 mm thick Gyproc Wallboard and skim coat	m²	13.90	-	17.00
3.1.28	two coats of "Thistle" plaster	m²	12.10	-	16.00
3.1.29	plaster and emulsion	m²	12.10	-	19.00
	Extra for				
3.1.30	gloss paint in lieu of emulsion	m²	2.10	-	2.50
3.1.31	two coat render and emulsion	m²	21.00	-	29.00
3.1.32	plaster and vinyl	m²	17.00	-	25.00
3.1.33	plaster and fabric	m²	17.00	-	38.00
3.1.34	squash court plaster "including markings"	m²	-		-
3.1.35	6 mm thick terrazzo wall lining; including backing	m²	-		-
3.1.36	glass reinforced gypsum	m²	-		-

INDUSTRIAL £ range £			RETAILING £ range £			LEISURE £ range £			OFFICES £ range £			HOTELS £ range £			Item nr
12.60	-	16.40	12.60	-	16.40	12.60	-	16.40	12.60	-	16.40	12.60	-	16.40	3.1.1
0.50	-	0.80	0.50	-	0.80	0.50	-	0.80	0.50	-	0.80	0.50	-	0.80	3.1.2
2.00	-	2.40	2.00	-	2.40	2.00	-	2.40	2.00	-	2.40	2.00	-	2.40	3.1.3
13.50	-	17.80	13.50	-	17.80	13.50	-	17.80	13.50	-	17.80	13.50	-	17.80	3.1.4
0.70	-	0.90	0.70	-	0.90	0.70	-	0.90	0.70	-	0.90	0.70	-	0.90	3.1.5
1.70	-	2.00	1.70	-	2.00	1.70	-	2.00	1.70	-	2.00	1.70	-	2.00	3.1.6
21.00	-	26.00	21.00	-	26.00	21.00	-	26.00	21.00	-	26.00	21.00	-	26.00	3.1.7
23.00	-	27.00	23.00	-	27.00	23.00	-	27.00	23.00	-	27.00	23.00	-	27.00	3.1.8
13.50	-	17.80	13.50	-	17.80	13.50	-	17.80	13.50	-	17.80	13.50	-	17.80	3.1.9
21.00	-	25.00	-		-	-		-	-		-	-		-	3.1.10
22.00	-	26.00	-		-	-		-	-		-	-		-	3.1.11
10.50	-	12.50	10.50	-	12.00	10.50	-	12.00	10.50	-	12.00	11.50	-	14.00	3.1.12
15.00	-	20.00	15.00	-	21.00	15.00	-	21.00	15.00	-	21.00	17.00	-	22.00	3.1.13
16.00	-	19.00	17.00	-	20.00	17.00	-	20.00	17.00	-	20.00	18.00	-	22.00	3.1.14
20.00	-	25.00	21.00	-	26.00	21.00	-	26.00	21.00	-	26.00	22.00	-	26.00	3.1.15
15.00	-	17.00	15.00	-	17.00	15.00	-	17.00	15.00	-	17.00	17.00	-	19.00	3.1.16
26.00	-	32.00	28.00	-	34.00	28.00	-	34.00	28.00	-	34.00	29.00	-	35.00	3.1.17
35.00	-	54.00	38.00	-	55.00	38.00	-	55.00	38.00	-	55.00	38.00	-	61.00	3.1.18
24.00	-	31.00	24.00	-	31.00	24.00	-	31.00	24.00	-	31.00	25.80	-	33.00	3.1.19
33.00	-	37.00	34.00	-	39.00	34.00	-	39.00	34.00	-	39.00	35.30	-	41.00	3.1.20
55.00	-	125.00	55.00	-	125.00	55.00	-	125.00	39.00	-	125.00	62.00	-	138.00	3.1.21
3.40	-	4.90	3.40	-	4.90	3.40	-	4.90	3.40	-	4.90	3.40	-	4.90	3.1.22
2.80	-	4.20	2.80	-	4.20	2.80	-	4.20	2.80	-	4.20	2.80	-	4.20	3.1.23
4.90	-	6.20	4.90	-	6.20	4.90	-	6.20	4.90	-	6.20	4.90	-	6.20	3.1.24
8.70	-	12.50	9.60	-	12.50	9.60	-	12.50	9.60	-	12.50	9.60	-	13.90	3.1.25
11.50	-	14.40	12.50	-	14.40	12.50	-	14.40	12.50	-	14.40	13.00	-	16.00	3.1.26
13.00	-	16.00	13.90	-	16.00	13.90	-	16.00	13.90	-	16.00	13.90	-	16.00	3.1.27
12.50	-	16.00	12.50	-	16.00	12.50	-	16.00	12.50	-	16.00	13.00	-	16.00	3.1.28
11.50	-	17.00	12.50	-	19.00	12.50	-	19.00	12.50	-	19.00	13.90	-	22.00	3.1.29
2.10	-	2.40	2.10	-	2.40	2.10	-	2.40	2.10	-	2.40	2.10	-	2.40	3.1.30
20.00	-	28.00	21.00	-	29.00	21.00	-	29.00	21.00	-	29.00	22.00	-	31.00	3.1.31
-		-	17.00	-	25.00	17.00	-	25.00	17.00	-	25.00	19.00	-	26.00	3.1.32
-		-	17.00	-	38.00	17.00	-	38.00	17.00	-	38.00	19.00	-	41.00	3.1.33
-		-	-		-	24.00	-	30.00	-		-	-		-	3.1.34
-		-	173.00	-	220.00	173.00	-	220.00	173.00	-	220.00	182.00	-	241.00	3.1.35
-		-	155.00	-	241.00	155.00	-	241.00	155.00	-	241.00	173.00	-	250.00	3.1.36

Item nr	SPECIFICATIONS	Unit	RESIDENTIAL £ range £		
3.1	**WALL FINISHES - cont'd**				
	wall finish area (unless otherwise described)				
	Rigid tile/panel finishes				
	Ceramic wall times; including backing				
3.1.37	economical	m²	23.00	-	42.00
3.1.38	medium quality	m²	42.00	-	75.00
3.1.39	high quality; to toilet blocks; kitchens and first aid rooms	m²	-		-
3.1.40	high quality; to changing areas; toilets, showers and fitness areas	m²	-		-
	Porcelain mosaic tiling; including backing to swimming pool lining; walls and				
3.1.41	floors	m²	-		-
	"Roman Travertine" marble wall linings; polished				
3.1.42	19 mm thick	m²	-		-
3.1.43	40 mm thick	m²	-		-
3.1.44	Metal mirror cladding panels	m²	-		-
3.2	**FLOOR FINISHES**				
	floor finish area (unless otherwise described)				
	comprising;				
	Sheet/board flooring				
	In situ screed and floor finishes				
	Rigid tile/slab finishes				
	Parquet/Wood block finishes				
	Flexible tiling/sheet finishes				
	Carpet tiles/Carpeting				
	Access floors and finishes				
	Perimeter treatments and sundries				
	Sheet/board flooring				
	Chipboard flooring; t&g joints				
3.2.1	18 mm thick	m²	8.70	-	10.50
3.2.2	22 mm thick	m²	10.50	-	12.50
	Wrought softwood flooring				
3.2.3	25 mm thick; butt joints	m²	19.00	-	21.00
3.2.4	25 mm thick; butt joints; cleaned off and polished	m²	22.00	-	26.00
3.2.5	25 mm thick; t&g joints	m²	20.00	-	25.00
3.2.6	25 mm thick; t&g joints; cleaned off and polished	m²	24.00	-	30.00
3.2.7	Wrought softwood t&g strip flooring; 25 mm thick; polished; including fillets	m²	30.00	-	38.00
3.2.8	maple	m²	-		-
3.2.9	gurjun	m²	-		-
3.2.10	iroko	m²	-		-
3.2.11	American oak	m²	-		-
	Wrought hardwood t&g strip flooring; 25 mm thick; polished; including fillets				
3.2.12	maple	m²	-		-
3.2.13	gurjun	m²	-		-
3.2.14	iroko	m²	-		-
3.2.15	American oak	m²	-		-
	Wrought hardwood t&g strip flooring; 25 mm thick; polished; including rubber pads				
3.2.16	maple	m²	-		-
	In situ screed and floor finishes				
	Extra over concrete floor for				
3.2.17	power floating	m²	-		-
3.2.18	power floating; surface hardener	m²	-		-

INDUSTRIAL £ range £		RETAILING £ range £		LEISURE £ range £		OFFICES £ range £		HOTELS £ range £		Item nr
22.00	- 39.00	24.00	- 42.00	24.00	- 42.00	24.00	- 42.00	28.00	- 50.00	3.1.37
39.00	- 69.00	42.00	- 77.00	42.00	- 77.00	42.00	- 77.00	48.00	- 85.00	3.1.38
-	-	69.00	- 89.00	69.00	- 89.00	69.00	- 89.00	69.00	- 89.00	3.1.39
-	-	-	-	89.00	- 105.00	-	-	-	-	3.1.40
-	-	-	-	55.00	- 75.00	-	-	-	-	3.1.41
-	-	278.00	- 375.00	278.00	- 375.00	278.00	- 375.00	278.00	- 375.00	3.1.42
-	-	384.30	- 489.00	384.30	- 489.00	384.30	- 489.00	384.30	- 489.00	3.1.43
-	-	289.00	- 489.00	278.00	- 471.00	-	-	306.90	- 498.00	3.1.44
-	-	-	-	-	-	-	-	-	-	3.2.1
-	-	-	-	-	-	-	-	-	-	3.2.2
-	-	-	-	-	-	-	-	-	-	3.2.3
-	-	-	-	-	-	-	-	-	-	3.2.4
-	-	-	-	-	-	-	-	-	-	3.2.5
-	-	-	-	-	-	-	-	-	-	3.2.6
-	-	-	-	-	-	-	-	-	-	3.2.7
-	-	-	-	52.00	- 59.00	52.00	- 59.00	52.00	- 61.00	3.2.8
-	-	-	-	-	-	46.00	- 52.00	46.00	- 49.00	3.2.9
-	-	-	-	-	-	52.00	- 57.00	52.00	- 54.00	3.2.10
-	-	-	-	-	-	55.00	- 61.00	55.00	- 63.00	3.2.11
-	-	-	-	57.00	- 65.00	57.00	- 65.00	59.00	- 67.00	3.2.12
-	-	-	-	-	-	52.00	- 57.00	54.00	- 59.00	3.2.13
-	-	-	-	-	-	57.00	- 65.00	59.00	- 65.00	3.2.14
-	-	-	-	-	-	59.00	- 69.00	61.00	- 73.00	3.2.15
-	-	-	-	69.00	- 83.00	-	-	-	-	3.2.16
4.90	- 9.60	3.40	- 9.60	-	-	-	-	-	-	3.2.17
9.60	- 13.90	7.20	- 12.50	-	-	-	-	-	-	3.2.18

Item nr	SPECIFICATIONS	Unit	RESIDENTIAL £ range £	
3.2	**FLOOR FINISHES - cont'd**			
	floor finish area (unless otherwise described)			
	In situ screed and floor finishes - cont'd			
	Latex cement screeds			
3.2.19	3 mm thick; one coat	m²	-	-
3.2.20	5 mm thick; two coats	m²	-	-
3.2.21	Rubber latex non slip solution and epoxy sealant	m²	-	-
	Cement and sand (1:3) screeds			
3.2.22	25 mm thick	m²	9.60 -	10.50
3.2.23	50 mm thick	m²	11.50 -	13.50
3.2.24	75 mm thick	m²	16.00 -	18.00
	Cement and sand (1:3) paving			
3.2.25	paving	m²	8.70 -	11.50
3.2.26	32 mm thick; surface hardener	m²	10.50 -	16.00
3.2.27	screed only (for subsequent finish)	m²	13.50 -	20.00
3.2.28	screed only (for subsequent finish); allowance for skirtings	m²	15.00 -	24.00
	Mastic asphalt paving			
3.2.29	20 mm thick; BS 1076; black	m²	-	-
3.2.30	20 mm thick; BS 1471; red	m²	-	-
	Granolithic			
3.2.31	20 mm thick	m²	-	-
3.2.32	25 mm thick	m²	-	-
3.2.33	25 mm thick; including screed	m²	-	-
3.2.34	38 mm thick; including screed	m²	-	-
	"Synthanite"; on and including building paper			
3.2.35	25 mm thick	m²	-	-
3.2.36	50 mm thick	m²	-	-
3.2.37	75 mm thick	m²	-	-
	Acrylic polymer floor finish			
3.2.38	10 mm thick	m²	-	-
	Epoxy floor finish			
3.2.39	1.50 mm - 2.00 mm thick	m²	-	-
3.2.40	5.00 mm - 6.00 mm thick	m²	-	-
	Polyester resin floor finish			
3.2.41	5.00 mm - 9.00 mm thick	m²	-	-
	Terrazzo paving; divided into squares with ebonite strip; polished			
3.2.42	16 mm thick	m²	-	-
3.2.43	16 mm thick; including screed	m²	-	-
	Rigid Tile/slab finishes			
	Quarry tile flooring			
3.2.44	150 mm x 150 mm x 12.50 mm thick; red	m²	-	-
3.2.45	150 mm x 150 mm x 12.50 mm thick; brown	m²	-	-
3.2.46	200 mm x 200 mm x 19 mm thick; brown	m²	-	-
3.2.47	average tiling	m²	-	-
3.2.48	tiling; including screed	m²	-	-
3.2.49	tiling; including screed and allowance for skirtings	m²	-	-
	Brick paving			
3.2.50	paving	m²	-	-
3.2.51	paving; including screed	m²	-	-
	Glazed ceramic tiled flooring			
3.2.52	100 mm x 100 mm x 9 mm thick; red	m²	-	-
3.2.53	150 mm x 150 mm x 12 mm thick; red	m²	-	-
3.2.54	100 mm x 100 mm x 9 mm thick; black	m²	-	-
3.2.55	150 mm x 150 mm x 12 mm thick; black	m²	-	-
3.2.56	150 mm x 150 mm x 12 mm thick; anti-slip	m²	-	-
3.2.57	fully vitrified	m²	-	-
3.2.58	fully vitrified; including screed	m²	-	-
3.2.59	fully vitrified; including screed and allowance for skirtings	m²	-	-
3.2.60	high quality; to service areas; kitchen and toilet blocks; including screed	m²	-	-

INDUSTRIAL £ range £		RETAILING £ range £		LEISURE £ range £		OFFICES £ range £		HOTELS £ range £		Item nr
4.90	- 5.50	-	-	-	-	4.90	- 5.50	-	-	3.2.19
6.60	- 7.30	-	-	-	-	6.60	- 7.20	-	-	3.2.20
8.10	- 19.30	-	-	-	-	-	-	-	-	3.2.21
9.60	- 10.50	9.60	- 10.50	9.60	- 10.50	9.60	- 10.50	9.60	- 10.50	3.2.22
11.50	- 13.50	11.50	- 13.50	11.50	- 13.50	11.50	- 13.50	11.50	- 13.50	3.2.23
16.00	- 18.00	16.00	- 18.00	16.00	- 18.00	16.00	- 18.00	16.00	- 18.00	3.2.24
8.10	- 10.50	8.70	- 11.50	8.70	- 11.50	8.70	- 11.50	8.70	- 11.50	3.2.25
9.60	- 15.30	11.50	- 16.00	11.50	- 16.00	11.50	- 16.00	11.50	- 16.00	3.2.26
12.50	- 19.00	13.50	- 19.00	13.50	- 19.00	14.00	- 19.00	13.50	- 19.00	3.2.27
15.30	- 22.00	16.00	- 24.00	16.00	- 24.00	16.00	- 24.00	16.00	- 25.00	3.2.28
19.00	- 23.00	20.00	- 24.00	20.00	- 24.00	-	-	-	-	3.2.29
23.00	- 26.00	24.00	- 28.00	24.00	- 28.00	-	-	-	-	3.2.30
10.50	- 16.00	11.50	- 17.00	11.50	- 17.00	11.50	- 17.00	11.50	- 17.00	3.2.31
14.40	- 19.00	15.30	- 19.00	15.00	- 19.00	15.00	- 19.00	15.00	- 21.00	3.2.32
24.00	- 26.00	25.00	- 28.00	25.00	- 28.00	25.00	- 28.00	25.00	- 28.00	3.2.33
34.00	- 39.00	35.00	- 41.00	35.00	- 41.00	35.00	- 41.00	37.00	- 41.00	3.2.34
22.00	- 26.00	22.00	- 28.00	22.00	- 28.00	22.00	- 28.00	-	-	3.2.35
31.00	- 35.00	33.00	- 38.00	33.00	- 38.00	33.00	- 38.00	-	-	3.2.36
38.00	- 44.00	41.00	- 45.00	41.00	- 45.00	41.00	- 45.00	-	-	3.2.37
22.00	- 28.00	23.00	- 30.00	23.00	- 30.00	23.00	- 30.00	-	-	3.2.38
22.00	- 28.00	23.00	- 31.00	23.00	- 31.00	23.00	- 31.00	-	-	3.2.39
45.00	- 52.00	46.00	- 53.00	46.00	- 53.00	46.00	- 53.00	-	-	3.2.40
51.00	- 57.00	52.00	- 59.00	52.00	- 59.00	52.00	- 59.00	-	-	3.2.41
-	-	51.00	- 57.00	51.00	- 57.00	51.00	- 57.00	55.00	- 69.00	3.2.42
-	-	75.00	- 87.00	75.00	- 87.00	75.00	- 87.00	81.00	- 100.00	3.2.43
28.00	- 31.00	29.00	- 31.00	29.00	- 31.00	29.00	- 31.00	29.00	- 33.00	3.2.44
33.00	- 39.00	35.00	- 39.00	35.00	- 39.00	35.00	- 39.00	37.00	- 41.00	3.2.45
41.00	- 46.00	42.00	- 47.00	42.00	- 47.00	42.00	- 47.00	44.00	- 49.00	3.2.46
28.00	- 46.00	29.00	- 47.00	29.00	- 47.00	29.00	- 47.00	29.00	- 49.00	3.2.47
39.00	- 59.00	41.00	- 61.00	41.00	- 61.00	41.00	- 61.00	42.00	- 61.00	3.2.48
53.00	- 73.00	55.00	- 75.00	55.00	- 75.00	55.00	- 75.00	55.00	- 77.00	3.2.49
-	-	29.00	- 59.00	41.00	- 59.00	41.00	- 59.00	41.00	- 59.00	3.2.50
-	-	52.00	- 75.00	52.00	- 75.00	52.00	- 75.00	52.00	- 75.00	3.2.51
-	-	37.00	- 42.00	37.00	- 42.00	37.00	- 42.00	39.00	- 44.00	3.2.52
-	-	33.00	- 37.00	33.00	- 37.00	33.00	- 37.00	33.00	- 39.00	3.2.53
-	-	41.00	- 45.00	41.00	- 45.00	41.00	- 45.00	42.00	- 47.00	3.2.54
-	-	33.00	- 41.00	33.00	- 41.00	33.00	- 41.00	34.00	- 42.00	3.2.55
-	-	41.00	- 43.00	41.00	- 43.00	41.00	- 43.00	41.00	- 45.00	3.2.56
-	-	43.00	- 61.00	43.00	- 61.00	43.00	- 61.00	44.00	- 65.00	3.2.57
-	-	52.00	- 79.00	52.00	- 79.00	52.00	- 79.00	55.00	- 81.00	3.2.58
-	-	59.00	- 94.00	59.00	- 94.00	59.00	- 94.00	59.00	- 100.00	3.2.59
-	-	-	-	82.00	- 96.00	-	-	-	-	3.2.60

Item nr	SPECIFICATIONS	Unit	RESIDENTIAL £ range £	
3.2	**FLOOR FINISHES - cont'd**			
	floor finish area (unless otherwise described)			
	Rigid Tile/slab finishes - cont'd			
	Glazed ceramic tile flooring - cont'd			
3.2.61	high quality; to foyer; fitness and bar areas; including screed	m²	-	-
	high quality; to pool surround, bottoms, steps and changing room;			
3.2.62	including screed	m²	-	-
	Porcelain mosaic paving; including screed to swimming pool lining; walls			
3.2.63	and floors	m²	-	-
	Extra for			
3.2.64	non slip finish to pool lining; beach and changing areas and showers	m²	-	-
	Terrazzo tile flooring			
3.2.65	28 mm thick white "Sicilian" marble aggregate tiling	m²	-	-
3.2.66	tiling; including screed	m²	-	-
	York stone			
3.2.67	50 mm thick paving	m²	-	-
3.2.68	paving; including screed	m²	-	-
	Slate			
3.2.69	200 mm x 400 mm x 10 mm thick; blue - grey	m²	-	-
3.2.70	otta riven	m²	-	-
3.2.71	otta boned (polished)	m²	-	-
	Portland stone			
3.2.72	50 mm thick paving	m²	-	-
	Fined sanded "Roman Travertine" marble			
3.2.73	20 mm thick paving	m²	-	-
3.2.74	paving; including screed	m²	-	-
3.2.75	paving; including screed and allowance for skirtings	m²	-	-
	Granite			
3.2.76	20 mm thick paving	m²	-	-
	Parquet/wood block finishes			
	Parquet flooring; polished			
3.2.77	8 mm thick girjun "Feltwood"	m²	28.00 -	31.00
	Wrought hardwood block floorings; 25 mm thick; polished; t&g joints			
	herringbone pattern			
3.2.78	merbau	m²	-	-
3.2.79	iroko	m²	-	-
3.2.80	iroko, including screed	m²	-	-
3.2.81	oak	m²	-	-
3.2.82	oak; including screed	m²	-	-
	Composition block flooring			
3.2.83	174 mm x 57 mm blocks	m²	-	-
	Flexible tiling			
	Thermoplastic tile flooring			
3.2.84	2 mm thick (series 2)	m²	8.10 -	9.60
3.2.85	2 mm thick (series 4)	m²	8.10 -	9.60
3.2.86	2 mm thick; including screed	m²	18.00 -	21.00
	Cork tile flooring			
3.2.87	3.20 mm thick	m²	14.40 -	18.00
3.2.88	3.20 mm thick; including screed	m²	26.00 -	34.00
3.2.89	6.30 mm thick	m²	-	-
3.2.90	6.30 mm thick; including screed	m²	-	-
	Vinyl floor tiling			
3.2.91	2 mm thick; semi-flexible tiles	m²	8.70 -	12.50
3.2.92	2 mm thick; fully flexible tiles	m²	8.10 -	11.50
3.2.93	2.50 mm thick; semi flexible tiles	m²	10.50 -	13.90
3.2.94	tiling; including screed	m²	22.00 -	28.00
3.2.95	tiling; including screed and allowance for skirtings	m²	24.00 -	33.00
3.2.96	tiling; anti-static	m²	-	-
3.2.97	tiling; anti-static; including screed	m²	-	-

INDUSTRIAL £ range £		RETAILING £ range £		LEISURE £ range £		OFFICES £ range £		HOTELS £ range £		Item nr
-	-	-	-	87.00 - 100.00		-	-	-	-	3.2.61
-	-	-	-	90.00 - 105.00		-	-	-	-	3.2.62
-	-	-	-	55.00 - 75.00		-	-	-	-	3.2.63
-	-	-	-	1.40 - 2.80		-	-	-	-	3.2.64
-	-	81.00 - 90.00		81.00 - 90.00		81.00 - 90.00		83.00 - 96.00		3.2.65
-	-	103.00 - 117.00		104.00 - 117.00		104.00 - 117.00		108.00 - 125.00		3.2.66
-	-	105.00 - 139.00		105.00 - 135.00		105.00 - 135.00		111.00 - 151.00		3.2.67
-	-	115.00 - 152.00		115.00 - 152.00		115.00 - 152.00		122.00 - 169.00		3.2.68
-	-	130.00 - 147.00		130.00 - 147.00		130.00 - 147.00		-	-	3.2.69
-	-	147.00 - 160.00		147.00 - 160.00		147.00 - 160.00		-	-	3.2.70
-	-	160.00 - 173.00		160.00 - 173.00		160.00 - 173.00		-	-	3.2.71
-	-	220.00 - 260.00		220.00 - 260.00		220.00 - 260.00		-	-	3.2.72
-	-	279.00 - 337.00		278.00 - 337.00		278.00 - 337.00		289.00 - 355.00		3.2.73
-	-	288.00 - 355.00		289.00 - 354.00		289.00 - 354.00		298.00 - 365.00		3.2.74
-	-	356.00 - 442.00		355.00 - 442.00		355.00 - 442.00		365.00 - 462.00		3.2.75
-	-	384.00 - 451.00		384.30 - 451.10		384.30 - 451.10		384.00 - 489.00		3.2.76
-	-	-	-	-	-	-	-	-	-	3.2.77
-	-	57.00 - 67.00		57.00 - 67.00		57.00 - 67.00		57.00 - 67.00		3.2.78
-	-	61.00 - 69.00		61.00 - 69.00		61.00 - 69.00		65.00 - 73.00		3.2.79
-	-	73.00 - 89.00		73.00 - 89.00		73.00 - 89.00		73.00 - 89.00		3.2.80
-	-	59.00 - 77.00		59.00 - 77.00		59.00 - 77.00		59.00 - 77.00		3.2.81
-	-	71.00 - 87.00		71.00 - 87.00		71.00 - 87.00		73.00 - 87.00		3.2.82
-	-	69.00 - 77.00		69.00 - 77.00		69.00 - 77.00		69.00 - 81.00		3.2.83
-	-	-	-	-	-	-	-	-	-	3.2.84
-	-	-	-	-	-	-	-	-	-	3.2.85
-	-	-	-	-	-	-	-	-	-	3.2.86
-	-	-	-	-	-	-	-	-	-	3.2.87
-	-	-	-	-	-	-	-	-	-	3.2.88
-	-	26.00 - 30.00		26.00 - 30.00		26.00 - 30.00		28.00 - 31.00		3.2.89
-	-	34.00 - 45.00		34.00 - 45.00		34.00 - 45.00		35.00 - 47.00		3.2.90
-	-	9.60 - 12.50		9.60 - 12.50		9.60 - 12.50		9.60 - 12.50		3.2.91
-	-	8.70 - 11.50		8.70 - 11.50		8.70 - 11.50		8.70 - 11.50		3.2.92
-	-	9.60 - 13.90		9.60 - 13.90		9.60 - 13.90		9.60 - 13.90		3.2.93
-	-	22.00 - 28.00		22.00 - 28.00		22.00 - 28.00		22.00 - 28.00		3.2.94
-	-	24.00 - 33.00		24.00 - 33.00		24.00 - 33.00		24.00 - 33.00		3.2.95
-	-	41.00 - 46.00		41.00 - 46.00		41.00 - 46.00		41.00 - 46.00		3.2.96
-	-	50.00 - 62.00		50.00 - 62.00		50.00 - 62.00		50.00 - 62.00		3.2.97

Item nr	SPECIFICATIONS	Unit	RESIDENTIAL £ range £	
3.2	**FLOOR FINISHES - cont'd**			
	floor finish area (unless otherwise described)			
	Flexible tiling/sheet finishes - cont'd			
	Vinyl sheet flooring; heavy duty			
3.2.98	2 mm thick	m²	-	-
3.2.99	2.50 mm thick	m²	-	-
3.2.100	3 mm thick; needle felt backed	m²	-	-
3.2.101	3 mm thick; foam backed	m²	-	-
	Sheeting; including screed and allowance for skirtings			
3.2.102	Altro "Safety" flooring	m²	-	-
3.2.103	2 mm thick; Altro "Marine T20" flooring	m²	-	-
3.2.104	2.50 mm thick; Altro "Classic D25" flooring	m²	-	-
3.2.105	3.50 thick; Altro "Stronghold" flooring	m²	-	-
3.2.106	flooring	m²	-	-
3.2.107	flooring; including screed	m²	-	-
	Linoleum tile flooring			
3.2.108	3.20 mm thick; coloured	m²	-	-
3.2.109	3.20 mm thick; coloured; including screed	m²	-	-
	Linoleum sheet flooring			
3.2.110	3.20 mm thick; coloured	m²	-	-
3.2.111	3.20 mm thick; marbled; including screed	m²	-	-
	Rubber tile flooring; smooth; ribbed or studded tiles			
3.2.112	2.50 mm thick	m²	-	-
3.2.113	5 mm thick	m²	-	-
3.2.114	5 mm thick; including screed	m²	-	-
	Carpet tiles/Carpeting			
3.2.115	Underlay	m²	4.90 -	6.80
	Carpet tiles			
3.2.116	nylon needlepunch (stick down)	m²	12.50 -	15.00
3.2.117	80% animal hair; 20% wool cord	m²	-	-
3.2.118	100% wool	m²	-	-
3.2.119	80% wool; 20% nylon antistatic economical; including screed and allowance for	m²	-	-
3.2.120	skirtings	m²	-	-
3.2.121	good quality	m²	-	-
3.2.122	good quality; including screed	m²	-	-
3.2.123	good quality; including screed and allowance for skirtings	m²	-	-
	Carpet; including underlay			
3.2.124	nylon needlepunch	m²	-	-
3.2.125	100% acrylic; light duty	m²	16.00 -	20.00
3.2.126	80% animal hair; 20% wool cord	m²	-	-
3.2.127	open weave matting poolside carpet (no underlay)	m²	-	-
3.2.128	80% wool; 20% acrylic; light duty	m²	-	-
3.2.129	100% acrylic; heavy duty	m²	-	-
3.2.130	cord	m²	-	-
3.2.131	100% wool	m²	-	-
3.2.132	good quality; including screed	m²	-	-
	good quality (grade 5); including screed and allowance			
3.2.133	for skirtings	m²	-	-
3.2.134	80% wool; 20% acrylic; heavy duty	m²	-	-
3.2.135	"Wilton"/pile carpet	m²	-	-
3.2.136	high quality; including screed	m²	-	-
3.2.137	high quality; including screed and allowance for skirtings	m²	-	-
	Access floors and finishes			
	Shallow void block and battened floors			
3.2.138	chipboard on softwood battens; partial access	m²	24.00 -	31.00
3.2.139	chipboard on softwood cradles (for uneven floors)	m²	29.00 -	33.00
	chipboard on softwood battens and cross battens;			
3.2.140	full access	m²	-	-

INDUSTRIAL £ rate £		RETAILING £ rate £			LEISURE £ rate £			OFFICES £ rate £			HOTELS £ rate £			Item nr.
-	-	15.00	-	17.00	15.00	-	17.00	15.00	-	17.00	15.00	-	17.00	3.2.98
-	-	15.00	-	19.00	15.00	-	19.00	15.00	-	19.00	15.00	-	19.00	3.2.99
-	-	10.50	-	13.90	10.50	-	13.90	10.50	-	13.90	10.50	-	13.90	3.2.100
-	-	15.00	-	19.00	15.00	-	19.00	15.00	-	19.00	15.00	-	19.00	3.2.101
-	-	29.00	-	35.00	29.00	-	35.00	29.00	-	35.00	29.00	-	35.00	3.2.102
-	-	22.00	-	28.00	22.00	-	28.00	22.00	-	28.00	-		-	3.2.103
-	-	28.00	-	33.00	28.00	-	33.00	28.00	-	33.00	-		-	3.2.104
-	-	35.00	-	41.00	35.00	-	41.00	35.00	-	41.00	-		-	3.2.105
-	-	22.00	-	41.00	22.00	-	41.00	22.00	-	41.00	-		-	3.2.106
-	-	33.00	-	55.00	33.00	-	55.00	33.00	-	55.00	-		-	3.2.107
-	-	17.00	-	20.00	17.00	-	20.00	17.00	-	20.00	-		-	3.2.108
-	-	28.00	-	38.00	28.00	-	38.00	28.00	-	38.00	-		-	3.2.109
-	-	18.00	-	20.00	18.00	-	24.00	18.00	-	24.00	-		-	3.2.110
-	-	29.00	-	38.00	29.00	-	38.00	29.00	-	38.00	-		-	3.2.111
-	-	28.00	-	33.00	28.00	-	33.00	28.00	-	33.00	-		-	3.2.112
-	-	33.00	-	38.00	33.00	-	38.00	33.00	-	38.00	-		-	3.2.113
-	-	44.00	-	55.00	44.00	-	55.00	44.00	-	55.00	-		-	3.2.114
-	-	4.90	-	6.70	4.90	-	6.70	4.90	-	6.70	-		-	3.2.115
-	-	12.50	-	15.00	12.50	-	15.00	12.50	-	15.00	-		-	3.2.116
-	-	22.00	-	25.00	22.00	-	25.00	22.00	-	25.00	-		-	3.2.117
-	-	31.00	-	38.00	31.00	-	38.00	31.00	-	38.00	-		-	3.2.118
-	-	33.00	-	45.00	33.00	-	45.00	33.00	-	45.00	-		-	3.2.119
-	-	33.00	-	38.00	33.00	-	38.00	33.00	-	38.00	-		-	3.2.120
-	-	31.00	-	45.00	31.00	-	45.00	31.00	-	45.00	31.00	-	50.00	3.2.121
-	-	41.00	-	55.00	41.00	-	55.00	41.00	-	55.00	41.00	-	61.00	3.2.122
-	-	46.00	-	61.00	46.00	-	61.00	46.00	-	61.00	46.00	-	69.00	3.2.123
-	-	16.00	-	20.00	16.00	-	20.00	16.00	-	20.00	-		-	3.2.124
-	-	21.00	-	25.00	21.00	-	25.00	21.00	-	25.00	-		-	3.2.125
-	-	26.00	-	33.00	26.00	-	33.00	26.00	-	33.00	-		-	3.2.126
-	-	-		-	22.00	-	28.00	-		-	-		-	3.2.127
-	-	33.00	-	42.00	33.00	-	42.00	33.00	-	42.00	-		-	3.2.128
-	-	33.00	-	41.00	33.00	-	41.00	33.00	-	41.00	-		-	3.2.129
-	-	-		-	41.00	-	45.00	-		-	-		-	3.2.130
-	-	41.00	-	53.00	41.00	-	53.00	41.00	-	53.00	41.00	-	53.00	3.2.131
-	-	50.00	-	69.00	50.00	-	69.00	50.00	-	69.00	50.00	-	69.00	3.2.132
-	-	52.00	-	73.00	52.00	-	73.00	52.00	-	73.00	57.00	-	77.00	3.2.133
-	-	53.00	-	63.00	53.00	-	63.00	53.00	-	63.00	57.00	-	66.00	3.2.134
-	-	57.00	-	63.00	57.00	-	63.00	57.00	-	63.00	59.00	-	66.00	3.2.135
-	-	69.00	-	81.00	69.00	-	81.00	69.00	-	81.00	73.00	-	83.00	3.2.136
-	-	73.00	-	83.00	73.00	-	83.00	73.00	-	83.00	75.00	-	90.00	3.2.137
-	-	-		-	-		-	24.00	-	31.00	-		-	3.2.138
-	-	-		-	-		-	29.00	-	33.00	-		-	3.2.139
-	-	-		-	-		-	36.00	-	39.00	-		-	3.2.140

Item nr.	SPECIFICATIONS	Unit	RESIDENTIAL £ range £		
3.2	**FLOOR FINISHES - cont'd**				
	floor finish area (unless otherwise described)				
	Access floors and finishes - cont'd				
	Shallow void block and battened floors - cont'd				
3.2.141	fibre and particle board; on lightweight concrete pedestal blocks	m²	-		-
	Shallow void block and battened floors; including carpet tile finish				
3.2.142	fibre and particle board; on lightweight concrete pedestal blocks	m²	-		-
	Access floors; excluding finish				
	600 mm x 600 mm chipboard panels faced both sides with galvanised steel sheet; on adjustable steel/aluminium pedestals; cavity 100 mm - 300 mm high				
3.2.143	light grade duty	m²	-		-
3.2.144	medium grade duty	m²	-		-
3.2.145	heavy grade duty	m²	-		-
3.2.146	extra heavy grade duty	m²	-		-
	600 mm x 600 mm chipboard panels faced both sides with galvanised steel sheet; on adjustable steel/aluminium pedestals; cavity 300 mm - 600 mm high				
3.2.147	medium grade duty	m²	-		-
3.2.148	heavy grade duty	m²	-		-
3.2.149	extra heavy grade duty	m²	-		-
	Access floor with medium quality carpeting				
3.2.150	"Durabella" suspended floor	m²	-		-
3.2.151	"Buroplan" partial access raised floor	m²	-		-
3.2.152	"Pedestal" partial access raised floor	m²	-		-
3.2.153	modular floor; 100% access raised floor	m²	-		-
	Access floor with high quality carpeting				
3.2.154	computer loading; 100% access raised floor	m²	-		-
	Common floor coverings bonded to access floor panels				
3.2.155	heavy duty fully flexible vinyl; to BS 3261; type A	m²	-		-
3.2.156	fibre bonded carpet	m²	-		-
3.2.157	high pressure laminate; to BS 2794; class D	m²	-		-
3.2.158	anti static grade fibre bonded carpet	m²	-		-
3.2.159	anti static grade sheet PVC; to BS 3261	m²	-		-
3.2.160	low loop tufted carpet	m²	-		-
	Perimeter treatments and sundries				
	Comparative skirtings				
3.2.161	25 mm x 75 mm softwood skirting; painted; including grounds	m	10.10	-	11.90
3.2.162	25 mm x 100 mm mahogany skirting; polished; including grounds	m	14.20	-	16.00
3.2.163	12.50 mm x 150 mm quarry tile skirting; including backing	m	14.40	-	18.00
3.2.164	13 mm x 75 mm granolithic skirting; including backing	m	20.00	-	24.00
3.2.165	6 mm x 75 mm terrazzo; including backing	m	35.00	-	42.00
3.2.166	Entrance matting in aluminium-framed matwell	m²	-		-

INDUSTRIAL £ range £		RETAILING £ range £		LEISURE £ range £		OFFICES £ range £		HOTELS £ range £		Item nr
-	-	-	-	-	-	33.00 - 41.00		-	-	3.2.141
-	-	-	-	-	-	50.00 - 57.00		-	-	3.2.142
-	-	-	-	-	-	45.00 - 54.00		-	-	3.2.143
-	-	-	-	-	-	52.00 - 60.00		-	-	3.2.144
-	-	-	-	-	-	65.00 - 82.00		-	-	3.2.145
-	-	-	-	-	-	73.00 - 82.00		-	-	3.2.146
-	-	-	-	-	-	59.00 - 67.00		-	-	3.2.147
-	-	-	-	-	-	67.00 - 83.00		-	-	3.2.148
-	-	-	-	-	-	75.00 - 83.00		-	-	3.2.149
-	-	-	-	-	-	66.00 - 71.00		-	-	3.2.150
-	-	-	-	-	-	73.00 - 83.00		-	-	3.2.151
-	-	-	-	-	-	83.00 - 102.00		-	-	3.2.152
-	-	-	-	-	-	108.00 - 136.00		-	-	3.2.153
-	-	-	-	-	-	121.00 - 178.00		-	-	3.2.154
-	-	-	-	-	-	8.10 - 23.00		-	-	3.2.155
-	-	-	-	-	-	8.70 - 16.80		-	-	3.2.156
-	-	-	-	-	-	8.70 - 26.00		-	-	3.2.157
-	-	-	-	-	-	10.50 - 18.00		-	-	3.2.158
-	-	-	-	-	-	14.80 - 23.00		-	-	3.2.159
-	-	-	-	-	-	18.00 - 26.00		-	-	3.2.160
9.20 - 10.90		10.10 - 11.90		10.10 - 11.90		10.10 - 11.90		11.90 - 12.90		3.2.161
13.80 - 15.00		14.20 - 15.90		14.20 - 16.00		14.20 - 16.00		15.10 - 17.00		3.2.162
13.50 - 17.00		14.40 - 18.00		14.40 - 18.00		14.40 - 18.00		14.80 - 18.00		3.2.163
19.00 - 24.00		20.00 - 24.00		20.00 - 24.00		20.00 - 24.00		21.00 - 26.00		3.2.164
-	-	36.00 - 41.00		36.00 - 41.00		36.00 - 41.00		37.60 - 43.00		3.2.165
-	-	337.00 - 480.00		325.00 - 442.00		325.00 - 451.00		325.00 - 451.00		3.2.166

Item nr	SPECIFICATIONS	Unit	RESIDENTIAL £ range £		
3.3	**CEILING FINISHES**				
	ceiling finish area (unless otherwise described)				
	comprising:				
	In situ board finishes				
	Suspended and integrated ceilings				
	In situ/board finishes				
	Decoration only to soffits				
3.3.1	to exposed steelwork	m²	-		-
3.3.2	to concrete soffits	m²	2.80	-	4.20
3.3.3	one mist and two coats emulsion paint; to plaster/plasterboard	m²	2.80	-	4.20
	Plaster to soffits				
3.3.4	lightweight plaster	m²	9.60	-	13.00
3.3.5	plaster and emulsion	m²	13.00	-	19.00
	Extra for				
3.3.6	gloss paint in lieu of emulsion	m²	2.10	-	2.50
	Plasterboard to soffits				
3.3.7	9.50 mm Gyproc lath and skim coat	m²	13.90	-	16.00
3.3.8	9.50 mm Gyproc insulating lath and skim coat	m²	14.40	-	16.00
3.3.9	plasterboard, skim and emulsion	m²	16.00	-	20.00
	Extra for				
3.3.10	gloss paint in lieu of emulsion	m²	2.10	-	2.50
3.3.11	plasterboard and "Artex"	m²	11.50	-	13.90
3.3.12	plasterboard; "Artex" and emulsion	m²	13.90	-	17.00
3.3.13	plaster and emulsion; including metal lathing	m²	22.00	-	31.00
	Other board finishes; with fire-resisting properties; excluding decoration				
3.3.14	12.50 mm thick Gyproc "Fireline"; half hour	m²	-		-
3.3.15	6 mm thick "Supalux"; half hour	m²	-		-
3.3.16	two layers of 12.50 mm thick Gyproc "Wallboard"; half hour	m²	-		-
3.3.17	two layers of 12.50 mm thick Gyproc "Fireline"; one hour	m²	-		-
3.3.18	9 mm thick "Supalux"; one hour; on fillets	m²	-		-
	Specialist plasters; to soffits				
3.3.19	sprayed acoustic plaster; self-finished	m²	-		-
3.3.20	rendering; "Tyrolean" finish	m²	-		-
	Other ceiling finishes				
3.3.21	50 mm thick wood wool slabs as permanent lining	m²	-		-
3.3.22	12 mm thick pine t&g boarding	m²	17.00	-	21.00
3.3.23	16 mm thick softwood t&g boardings	m²	21.00	-	25.00
	Suspended and integrated ceilings				
	Suspended ceiling				
3.3.24	economical; exposed grid	m²	-		-
3.3.25	jointless; plasterboard	m²	-		-
3.3.26	semi-concealed grid	m²	-		-
3.3.27	medium quality; "Minatone"; concealed grid	m²	-		-
3.3.28	high quality; "Travertone"; concealed grid	m²	-		-
	Other suspended ceilings				
3.3.29	metal linear strip; "Dampa"/"Luxalon"	m²	-		-
3.3.30	metal tray	m²	-		-
3.3.31	egg-crate	m²	-		-
3.3.32	open grid; "Formalux"/"Dimension"	m²	-		-
	Integrated ceilings				
3.3.33	coffered; with steel surfaces	m²	-		-
	Acoustic suspended ceilings				
3.3.34	on anti vibration mountings	m²	-		-

INDUSTRIAL £ range £	RETAILING £ range £	LEISURE £ range £	OFFICES £ range £	HOTELS £ range £	Item nr
3.40 - 4.90	2.80 - 4.20	- -	- -	- -	3.3.1
2.80 - 4.20	2.80 - 4.20	2.80 - 4.20	2.80 - 4.20	2.80 - 4.20	3.3.2
2.80 - 4.20	2.80 - 4.20	2.80 - 4.20	2.80 - 4.20	2.80 - 4.20	3.3.3
9.60 - 12.50	9.60 - 12.50	9.60 - 12.50	9.60 - 12.50	9.60 - 12.50	3.3.4
12.50 - 19.00	13.00 - 20.00	13.00 - 20.00	13.00 - 20.00	14.80 - 22.00	3.3.5
2.10 - 2.50	2.10 - 2.50	2.10 - 2.50	2.10 - 2.50	2.10 - 2.50	3.3.6
13.00 - 16.00	13.90 - 16.00	13.90 - 16.00	13.90 - 16.00	14.80 - 16.00	3.3.7
13.90 - 16.00	14.80 - 16.00	14.80 - 16.00	14.80 - 16.00	14.80 - 17.00	3.3.8
14.80 - 20.00	16.00 - 20.00	16.00 - 20.00	16.40 - 20.00	16.00 - 21.00	3.3.9
2.10 - 2.50	2.10 - 2.50	2.10 - 2.50	2.10 - 2.50	2.10 - 2.50	3.3.10
9.60 - 13.00	10.50 - 13.90	10.50 - 13.90	10.50 - 13.90	11.50 - 14.80	3.3.11
13.00 - 16.00	13.90 - 17.00	13.90 - 17.00	13.90 - 17.00	14.80 - 18.00	3.3.12
21.00 - 31.00	22.00 - 31.00	22.00 - 31.00	22.00 - 31.00	22.00 - 31.00	3.3.13
10.50 - 13.90	11.50 - 13.90	11.50 - 13.90	11.50 - 13.90	12.10 - 15.50	3.3.14
13.90 - 15.00	15.00 - 16.40	14.80 - 16.40	14.80 - 16.40	18.20 - 19.30	3.3.15
15.00 - 18.00	16.00 - 18.90	16.40 - 18.90	16.40 - 18.90	16.40 - 19.30	3.3.16
18.00 - 21.00	19.00 - 22.20	18.90 - 22.20	18.90 - 22.20	19.30 - 22.20	3.3.17
20.00 - 25.00	20.00 - 24.90	20.20 - 24.90	20.20 - 24.90	22.20 - 25.80	3.3.18
28.00 - 39.00	- -	- -	- -	- -	3.3.19
- -	- -	28.70 - 41.40	- -	- -	3.3.20
- -	- -	- -	13.00 - 16.00	- -	3.3.21
- -	17.00 - 21.00	17.00 - 21.00	17.00 - 21.00	18.00 - 22.00	3.3.22
- -	22.00 - 25.00	22.00 - 25.00	22.00 - 25.00	22.00 - 25.00	3.3.23
22.00 - 30.00	24.00 - 31.00	24.00 - 31.00	24.00 - 31.00	24.00 - 35.00	3.3.24
28.00 - 35.00	29.00 - 38.00	29.00 - 38.00	29.00 - 38.00	29.00 - 41.00	3.3.25
30.00 - 38.00	33.00 - 41.00	33.00 - 41.00	33.00 - 41.00	33.00 - 44.00	3.3.26
33.00 - 44.00	33.00 - 47.00	33.00 - 47.00	33.00 - 47.00	33.00 - 50.00	3.3.27
46.00 - 74.00	46.00 - 74.00	46.00 - 74.00	46.00 - 74.00	46.00 - 74.00	3.3.28
42.00 - 51.00	45.00 - 55.00	45.00 - 55.00	45.00 - 55.00	- -	3.3.29
42.00 - 55.00	46.00 - 55.00	46.00 - 55.00	46.00 - 55.00	- -	3.3.30
46.00 - 98.00	50.00 - 100.00	50.00 - 100.00	50.00 - 100.00	- -	3.3.31
85.00 - 104.00	87.00 - 108.00	87.00 - 108.00	87.00 - 108.00	- -	3.3.32
96.00 - 160.00	96.00 - 160.00	96.00 - 160.00	96.00 - 160.00	- -	3.3.33
- -	- -	52.00 - 66.00	- -	- -	3.3.34

Item nr	SPECIFICATIONS	Unit	RESIDENTIAL £ range £		

3.4   DECORATIONS
surface area (unless otherwise described)

comprising:

Comparative wall and ceiling finishes
Comparative steel/metalwork finishes
Comparative woodwork finishes

Item nr	SPECIFICATIONS	Unit	£		£
	Comparative wall and ceiling finishes				
	Emulsion				
3.4.1	two coats	m²	2.00	-	2.50
3.4.2	one mist and two coats	m²	2.50	-	3.40
	"Artex" plastic compound				
3.4.3	one coat; textured	m²	3.10	-	4.30
3.4.4	Wall paper	m²	4.30	-	7.10
3.4.5	Hessian wall coverings	m²	-		-
	Gloss				
3.4.6	primer and two coats	m²	3.70	-	5.10
3.4.7	primer and three coats	m²	5.10	-	6.30
	Comparative steel/metalwork finishes				
	Primer				
3.4.8	only	m²	-		-
3.4.9	grit blast and one coat zinc chromate primer	m²	-		-
3.4.10	touch up primer and one coat of two pack epoxy zinc phosphate primer	m²	-		-
	Gloss				
3.4.11	three coats	m²	5.10	-	6.20
	Sprayed mineral fibre				
3.4.12	one hour	m²	-		-
3.4.13	two hour	m²	-		-
	Sprayed vermiculite cement				
3.4.14	one hour	m²	-		-
3.4.15	two hour	m²	-		-
	Intumescent coating with decorative top seal				
3.4.16	half hour	m²	-		-
3.4.17	one hour	m²	-		-
	Comparative woodwork finishes				
	Primer				
3.4.18	only	m²	1.40	-	1.60
	Gloss				
3.4.19	two coats; touch up primer	m²	2.80	-	3.10
3.4.20	three coats; touch up primer	m²	3.70	-	4.70
3.4.21	primer and two coat	m²	4.30	-	5.10
3.4.22	primer and three coat	m²	5.60	-	6.20
	Polyurethane lacquer				
3.4.23	two coats	m²	2.80	-	3.40
3.4.24	three coats	m²	4.30	-	5.10
	Flame-retardant paint				
3.4.25	three coats	m²	6.60	-	8.10
	Polish				
3.4.26	wax polish; seal	m²	7.10	-	9.60
3.4.27	wax polish; stain and body in	m²	11.80	-	13.50
3.4.28	French polish; stain and body in	m²	17.00	-	21.00

INDUSTRIAL £ range £		RETAILING £ range £		LEISURE £ range £		OFFICES £ range £		HOTELS £ range £		Item nr
2.00	2.50	2.00	2.50	2.00	2.50	2.00	2.50	2.00	2.50	3.4.1
2.50	3.40	2.50	3.40	2.50	3.40	2.50	3.40	2.50	3.40	3.4.2
3.30	4.30	3.30	4.30	3.30	4.30	3.30	4.30	3.30	4.30	3.4.3
4.30	7.50	4.30	7.50	4.30	7.50	4.30	7.50	4.50	11.30	3.4.4
-	-	9.60	13.90	9.60	13.90	9.60	13.90	10.90	17.20	3.4.5
3.70	5.10	3.70	5.10	3.70	5.10	3.70	5.10	3.70	5.10	3.4.6
5.10	6.20	5.10	6.20	5.10	6.20	5.10	6.20	5.10	6.20	3.4.7
0.80	1.40	-	-	-	-	-	-	-	-	3.4.8
1.60	2.50	-	-	-	-	-	-	-	-	3.4.9
2.20	2.80	-	-	-	-	-	-	-	-	3.4.10
-	-	-	-	-	-	-	-	-	-	3.4.11
9.60	14.80	-	-	-	-	-	-	-	-	3.4.12
16.10	19.30	-	-	-	-	-	-	-	-	3.4.13
10.90	16.10	-	-	-	-	-	-	-	-	3.4.14
13.10	19.30	-	-	-	-	-	-	-	-	3.4.15
17.40	19.30	17.40	19.30	17.40	19.30	-	-	-	-	3.4.16
28.00	34.00	28.00	34.00	28.00	34.00	-	-	-	-	3.4.17
1.30	1.60	1.30	1.60	1.30	1.60	1.30	1.60	1.30	1.60	3.4.18
2.80	3.10	2.80	3.10	2.80	3.10	2.80	3.10	2.80	3.10	3.4.19
3.70	4.90	3.70	4.90	3.70	4.90	3.70	4.90	3.70	4.90	3.4.20
4.30	5.10	4.30	5.10	4.30	5.10	4.30	5.10	4.30	5.10	3.4.21
5.60	6.20	5.60	6.20	5.60	6.20	5.60	6.20	5.60	6.20	3.4.22
2.80	3.40	2.80	3.40	2.80	3.40	2.80	3.40	2.80	3.40	3.4.23
4.30	5.10	4.30	5.10	4.30	5.10	4.30	5.10	4.30	5.10	3.4.24
6.60	7.90	6.60	7.90	6.60	7.90	6.60	7.90	6.60	7.90	3.4.25
6.60	7.90	6.60	9.60	6.60	9.60	6.60	9.60	6.60	9.60	3.4.26
11.80	13.50	11.80	13.50	11.80	13.50	11.80	13.50	11.80	13.50	3.4.27
17.00	21.00	17.00	21.00	17.00	21.00	17.00	21.00	17.00	21.00	3.4.28

Item nr	SPECIFICATIONS	Unit	RESIDENTIAL £ range £

4.1   FITTINGS AND FURNISHINGS

gross internal area or individual units

comprising:

Residential fittings
Comparative fittings/sundries
Industrial/Office furniture, fittings and equipment
Retail furniture, fittings and equipment
Leisure furniture, fittings and equipment
Hotel furniture, fittings and equipment

Residential fittings
Kitchen fittings for residential units

Item nr	Specification	Unit	Low		High
4.1.1	one person flat/bed-sit	nr	1,250	-	2,500
4.1.2	two person flat/house	nr	1,500	-	4,000
4.1.3	three person flat/house	nr	2,000	-	5,510
4.1.4	four person house	nr	2,100	-	7,500
4.1.5	five person house	nr	2,620	-	10,000

Comparative residential fittings/sundries
Individual kitchen fittings

Item nr	Specification	Unit	Low		High
4.1.6	600 mm x 800 mm x 300 mm wall unit	nr	210.00	-	269.00
4.1.7	1200 mm x 800 mm x 300 mm wall unit	nr	249.00	-	302.00
4.1.8	500 mm x 900 mm x 600 mm floor unit	nr	230.00	-	289.00
4.1.9	600 mm x 500 mm x 195 mm store cupboard	nr	299.00	-	400.00
4.1.10	1200 mm x 900 mm x 600 mm sink unit (excluding top)	nr	350.00	-	400.00

Comparative wrought softwood shelving

Item nr	Specification	Unit	Low		High
4.1.11	25 mm x 225 mm including black japanned brackets	m	11.80	-	13.80
4.1.12	25 mm thick slatted shelving; including bearers	m²	49.00	-	55.00
4.1.13	25 mm thick cross-tongued shelving; including bearers	m²	62.00	-	69.00

Industrial/Office furniture, fittings and equipment
Reception desk, shelves and cupboards for general areas

Item nr	Specification	Unit	Low		High
4.1.14	economical	m²	-		-
4.1.15	medium quality	m²	-		-
4.1.16	high quality	m²	-		-

Extra for

Item nr	Specification	Unit	Low		High
4.1.17	high quality finishes to reception areas	m²	-		-
4.1.18	full kitchen equipment (one cover/20m²)	m²	-		-

Furniture and fittings to general office area

Item nr	Specification	Unit	Low		High
4.1.19	economical	m²	-		-
4.1.20	medium quality	m²	-		-
4.1.21	high quality	m²	-		-

Retail fitting out, furniture, fittings and equipment
Mall furniture, etc.

Item nr	Specification	Unit	Low		High
4.1.22	minimal provision	m²	-		-
4.1.23	good provision	m²	-		-
4.1.24	internal planting	m²	-		-
4.1.25	glazed metal balustrades to voids	m²	-		-
4.1.26	feature pond and fountain	m²	-		-
4.1.27	Fitting out a retail warehouse	m²	-		-

Fitting out shell for small shop (including shop fittings)

Item nr	Specification	Unit	Low		High
4.1.28	simple store	m²	-		-
4.1.29	fashion store	m²	-		-

Fitting out for department store or supermarket

Item nr	Specification	Unit	Low		High
4.1.30	excluding shop fittings	m²	-		-
4.1.31	including shop fittings	m²	-		-

INDUSTRIAL £ range £		RETAILING £ range £		LEISURE £ range £		OFFICES £ range £		HOTELS £ range £		Item nr
-	-	-	-	-	-	-	-	-	-	4.1.1
-	-	-	-	-	-	-	-	-	-	4.1.2
-	-	-	-	-	-	-	-	-	-	4.1.3
-	-	-	-	-	-	-	-	-	-	4.1.4
-	-	-	-	-	-	-	-	-	-	4.1.5
-	-	-	-	-	-	-	-	-	-	4.1.6
-	-	-	-	-	-	-	-	-	-	4.1.7
-	-	-	-	-	-	-	-	-	-	4.1.8
-	-	-	-	-	-	-	-	-	-	4.1.9
-	-	-	-	-	-	-	-	-	-	4.1.10
11.90 - 13.80		11.90 - 13.80		11.90 - 13.80		11.90 - 13.80		11.90 - 13.80		4.1.11
46.00 - 55.00		46.00 - 55.00		46.00 - 55.00		46.00 - 55.00		46.00 - 55.00		4.1.12
62.00 - 69.00		62.00 - 69.00		62.00 - 69.00		62.00 - 69.00		62.00 - 69.00		4.1.13
3.80 - 8.70		-	-	-	-	6.60 - 13.40		-	-	4.1.14
6.80 - 13.80		-	-	-	-	10.10 - 18.20		-	-	4.1.15
11.00 - 21.00		-	-	-	-	15.50 - 25.00		-	-	4.1.16
-	-	-	-	-	-	6.80 - 10.10		-	-	4.1.17
10.10 - 11.90		-	-	-	-	11.00 - 13.80		-	-	4.1.18
-	-	-	-	-	-	8.10 - 11.00		-	-	4.1.19
-	-	-	-	-	-	11.00 - 17.00		-	-	4.1.20
-	-	-	-	-	-	19.00 - 28.00		-	-	4.1.21
-	-	10.10 - 19.00		-	-	-	-	-	-	4.1.22
-	-	42.00 - 50.00		-	-	-	-	-	-	4.1.23
-	-	22.00 - 28.00		-	-	-	-	-	-	4.1.24
-	-	743.00 - 941.00		-	-	-	-	-	-	4.1.25
-	-	41,280 - 63,360		-	-	-	-	-	-	4.1.26
-	-	259.00 - 297.00		-	-	-	-	-	-	4.1.27
-	-	649.00 - 743.00		-	-	-	-	-	-	4.1.28
-	-	979.00 - 1,393		-	-	-	-	-	-	4.1.29
-	-	687.00 - 932.00		-	-	-	-	-	-	4.1.30
-	-	979.00 - 1,393		-	-	-	-	-	-	4.1.31

Item nr	SPECIFICATIONS	Unit	RESIDENTIAL £ range £

4.1   FITTINGS AND FURNISHINGS - cont'd

gross internal or internal units
(unless otherwise described)

**Retail fitting out, furniture, fittings and
equipment - cont'd**
Special fittings/equipment

Item nr	SPECIFICATIONS	Unit		
4.1.32	refrigerated installation for cold stores; display fittings in food stores	m²	-	-
4.1.33	food court furniture; fittings and special finishes (excluding catering display units)	m²	-	-
4.1.34	bakery ovens	nr	-	-
4.1.35	refuse compactors	nr	-	-

Leisure furniture, fittings and equipment
General fittings

Item nr	SPECIFICATIONS	Unit		
4.1.36	internal planting	m²	-	-
4.1.37	signs, notice-boards, shelving, fixed seating, curtains and blinds	m²	-	-
4.1.38	electric hand-dryers, incinerators, mirrors	m²	-	-

Specific fittings

Item nr	SPECIFICATIONS	Unit		
4.1.39	lockers, coin return locks	nr	-	-
4.1.40	kitchen units; excluding equipment	nr	-	-
4.1.41	folding sun bed	nr	-	-
4.1.42	security grille	nr	-	-
4.1.43	entrance balustrading and control turnstile	nr	-	-
4.1.44	sports nets, screens etc in a medium sized sports hall reception counter, fittings and reception counter	nr	-	-
4.1.45	screen	nr	-	-
4.1.46	bar and fittings	nr	-	-
4.1.47	telescopic seating	nr	-	-

Swimming pool fittings

Item nr	SPECIFICATIONS	Unit		
4.1.48	metal balustrades to pool areas	nr	-	-
4.1.49	skimmer grilles to pool edge	nr	-	-
	stainless steel pool access ladder			
4.1.50	1700 mm high	nr	-	-
4.1.51	2500 mm high	nr	-	-
4.1.52	stainless steel tube ladders and fixing sockets to pool	nr	-	-
4.1.53	level deck starting blocks	nr	-	-
4.1.54	turning boards and brackets	nr	-	-
4.1.55	backstroke warning set and infill tubes	nr	-	-
4.1.56	false start equipment set including infill tubes	nr	-	-
4.1.57	set of four 25 m large rope sets; storage trolley and flush deck level adapters	nr	-	-
4.1.58	electrically operated cover to pool	nr	-	-

Leisure pool fittings

Item nr	SPECIFICATIONS	Unit		
4.1.59	stainless steel lighting post	nr	-	-
4.1.60	water cannons	nr	-	-
4.1.61	fountain or water sculpture	nr	-	-
4.1.62	loudspeaker tower	nr	-	-
	grp water chute; 65.00 m - 80.00 m long; steel supports;			
4.1.63	spiral stairs and balustrading	nr		-

Sports halls

Item nr	SPECIFICATIONS	Unit		
4.1.64	administration areas	m²	-	-
4.1.65	aerobic dance studios	m²	-	-
4.1.66	badminton courts	m²	-	-
4.1.67	bowls halls	m²	-	-
4.1.68	café/restaurant areas	seat	-	-
4.1.69	changing rooms/WCs	m²	-	-
4.1.70	circulation areas	m²	-	-
4.1.71	creche areas	m²	-	-
4.1.72	fitness areas	m²	-	-
4.1.73	indoor cricket	m²	-	-
4.1.74	rifle ranges	m²	-	-
4.1.75	reception areas	m²	-	-
4.1.76	school gymnasium (no changing)	m²	-	-

INDUSTRIAL £ range £		RETAILING £ range £		LEISURE £ range £		OFFICES £ range £		HOTELS £ range £		Item nr
-	-	27.00	- 84.00	-	-	-	-	-	-	4.1.32
-	-	885.00	- 960.00	-	-	-	-	-	-	4.1.33
-	-	11,144	- 16,800	-	-	-	-	-	-	4.1.34
-	-	11,906	- 21,882	-	-	-	-	-	-	4.1.35
-	-	-	-	16.50	- 21.00	-	-	-	-	4.1.36
-	-	-	-	11.90	- 13.80	-	-	-	-	4.1.37
-	-	-	-	3.10	- 4.60	-	-	-	-	4.1.38
-	-	-	-	125.00	- 191.00	-	-	-	-	4.1.39
-	-	-	-	2,306	- 3,078	-	-	-	-	4.1.40
-	-	-	-	5,571	- 6,136	-	-	-	-	4.1.41
-	-	-	-	7,680	- 10,955	-	-	-	-	4.1.42
-	-	-	-	14,024	- 15,360	-	-	-	-	4.1.43
-	-	-	-	19,200	- 23,040	-	-	-	-	4.1.44
-	-	-	-	23,040	- 38,400	-	-	-	-	4.1.45
-	-	-	-	38,400	- 46,118	-	-	-	-	4.1.46
-	-	-	-	53,760	- 61,440	-	-	-	-	4.1.47
-	-	-	-	367.00	- 622.00	-	-	-	-	4.1.48
-	-	-	-	307.00	- 393.00	-	-	-	-	4.1.49
-	-	-	-	1,158	- 1,272	-	-	-	-	4.1.50
-	-	-	-	1,262	- 1,448	-	-	-	-	4.1.51
-	-	-	-	514.00	- 582.00	-	-	-	-	4.1.52
-	-	-	-	719.00	- 788.00	-	-	-	-	4.1.53
-	-	-	-	479.00	- 548.00	-	-	-	-	4.1.54
-	-	-	-	548.00	- 615.00	-	-	-	-	4.1.55
-	-	-	-	273.00	- 342.00	-	-	-	-	4.1.56
-	-	-	-	3,428	- 3,840	-	-	-	-	4.1.57
-	-	-	-	8,228	- 13,716	-	-	-	-	4.1.58
-	-	-	-	155.00	- 191.00	-	-	-	-	4.1.59
-	-	-	-	1,054	- 1,393	-	-	-	-	4.1.60
-	-	-	-	4,235	- 21,177	-	-	-	-	4.1.61
-	-	-	-	5,384	- 6,344	-	-	-	-	4.1.62
-	-	-	-	130,895	- 145,380	-	-	-	-	4.1.63
-	-	-	-	159.00	- 316.00	-	-	-	-	4.1.64
-	-	-	-	81.00	- 109.00	-	-	-	-	4.1.65
-	-	-	-	31.00	- 47.00	-	-	-	-	4.1.66
-	-	-	-	17.00	- 31.00	-	-	-	-	4.1.67
-	-	-	-	1,715	- 1,988	-	-	-	-	4.1.68
-	-	-	-	79.00	- 156.00	-	-	-	-	4.1.69
-	-	-	-	7.90	- 17.00	-	-	-	-	4.1.70
-	-	-	-	64.00	- 96.00	-	-	-	-	4.1.71
-	-	-	-	631.00	- 947.00	-	-	-	-	4.1.72
-	-	-	-	17.00	- 31.00	-	-	-	-	4.1.73
-	-	-	-	17.00	- 31.00	-	-	-	-	4.1.74
-	-	-	-	159.00	- 315.00	-	-	-	-	4.1.75
-	-	-	-	64.00	- 79.00	-	-	-	-	4.1.76

Item nr	SPECIFICATIONS	Unit	RESIDENTIAL £ range £	
4.1	**FITTINGS AND FURNISHINGS** - cont'd			
	gross internal or internal units (unless otherwise described)			
	Leisure furniture, fittings and equipment - cont'd			
	Sports hall - cont'd			
4.1.77	sports hall (with changing)	m²	-	-
4.1.78	squash courts	m²	-	-
4.1.79	table tennis	m²	-	-
4.1.80	tennis courts	m²	-	-
4.1.81	viewing areas	m²	-	-
	Football stadia			
4.1.82	facilities to basic stand	m²	-	-
	Theatres			
	Stage engineering equipment to large-scale modern touring theatre			
4.1.83	flying	nr	-	-
4.1.84	safety curtains and fire doors	nr	-	-
4.1.85	lighting access	nr	-	-
4.1.86	stage/pit lifts	nr	-	-
4.1.87	hoists	nr	-	-
4.1.88	curtains and masking	nr	-	-
	Stage engineering equipment to medium-scale modern repertory touring theatre			
4.1.89	flying	nr	-	-
4.1.90	safety curtains and fire doors	nr	-	-
4.1.91	lighting access	nr	-	-
4.1.92	stage/pit lifts	nr	-	-
4.1.93	hoists	nr	-	-
4.1.94	curtains and masking	nr	-	-
	Museums and art galleries	nr	-	-
	Display and retail areas			
4.1.95	display cases and lighting, finishes	m²	-	-
4.1.96	display fittings and power	m²	-	-
4.1.97	interactive display	m²	-	-
4.1.98	ticketing and retail	m²	-	-
4.1.99	display case (to 1.50 m x 1.50 m)	nr	-	-
4.1.100	fibre optic lighting to display case	nr	-	-
4.1.101	interactive "hands on" feature	nr	-	-
4.1.102	interactive video installations			
4.1.103	video wall	nr	-	-
4.1.104	video monitor hardware	nr	-	-
4.1.105	AV installation to cinema	nr	-	-
	Aviation			
	Airport passenger lounges			
4.1.106	international airport	m²	-	-
4.1.107	domestic airport	m²	-	-
4.1.108	allowance for furniture	m²	-	-
4.1.109	baggage handling facilities	m²	-	-
	Education			
	Schools and colleges			
4.1.110	general teaching	m²	-	-
4.1.111	laboratories	m²	-	-
4.1.112	information technology and business studies	m²	-	-
4.1.113	design and technology	m²	-	-
4.1.114	art and design	m²	-	-
4.1.115	library resource centre	m²	-	-
4.1.116	circulation	m²	-	-
4.1.117	laboratory preparation	m²	-	-
4.1.118	staff accommodation	m²	-	-

INDUSTRIAL £ rate £		RETAILING £ rate £		LEISURE £ rate £			OFFICES £ rate £		HOTELS £ rate £		Item nr.
-	-	-	-	31.00	-	64.00	-	-	-	-	4.1.77
-	-	-	-	7.90	-	17.00	-	-	-	-	4.1.78
-	-	-	-	7.90	-	17.00	-	-	-	-	4.1.79
-	-	-	-	7.90	-	17.00	-	-	-	-	4.1.80
-	-	-	-	17.00	-	157.00	-	-	-	-	4.1.81
-	-	-	-	315.00	-	493.00	-	-	-	-	4.1.82
-	-	-	-	534,847	-	623,989	-	-	-	-	4.1.83
-	-	-	-	479,993	-	569,131	-	-	-	-	4.1.84
-	-	-	-	322,279	-	377,136	-	-	-	-	4.1.85
-	-	-	-	356,565	-	445,705	-	-	-	-	4.1.86
-	-	-	-	267,427	-	301,707	-	-	-	-	4.1.87
-	-	-	-	411,421	-	278,043	-	-	-	-	4.1.88
-	-	-	-	233,137	-	271,448	-	-	-	-	4.1.89
-	-	-	-	109,711	-	157,711	-	-	-	-	4.1.90
-	-	-	-	267,427	-	301,707	-	-	-	-	4.1.91
-	-	-	-	123,426	-	178,281	-	-	-	-	4.1.92
-	-	-	-	54,855	-	89,141	-	-	-	-	4.1.93
-	-	-	-	34,287	-	89,141	-	-	-	-	4.1.94
-	-	-	-	3,291	-	6,582	-	-	-	-	4.1.95
-	-	-	-	1,645	-	2,963	-	-	-	-	4.1.96
-	-	-	-	2,468	-	4,113	-	-	-	-	4.1.97
-	-	-	-	1,645	-	2,468	-	-	-	-	4.1.98
-	-	-	-	4,935	-	2,468	-	-	-	-	4.1.99
-	-	-	-	1,152	-	1,647	-	-	-	-	4.1.100
-	-	-	-	11,520	-	16,451	-	-	-	-	4.1.101
											4.1.102
-	-	-	-	411,422	-	575,992	-	-	-	-	4.1.103
-	-	-	-	5,759	-	8,235	-	-	-	-	4.1.104
-	-	-	-	164,568	-	575,992	-	-	-	-	4.1.105
-	-	-	-	1,700	-	1,927	-	-	-	-	4.1.106
-	-	-	-	960.00	-	1,630	-	-	-	-	4.1.107
-	-	-	-	268.00	-	475.00	-	-	-	-	4.1.108
-	-	-	-	2,517	-	3,112	-	-	-	-	4.1.109
-	-	-	-	157.00	-	247.00	-	-	-	-	4.1.110
-	-	-	-	205.00	-	342.00	-	-	-	-	4.1.111
-	-	-	-	446.00	-	631.00	-	-	-	-	4.1.112
-	-	-	-	433.00	-	485.00	-	-	-	-	4.1.113
-	-	-	-	289.00	-	342.00	-	-	-	-	4.1.114
-	-	-	-	485.00	-	546.00	-	-	-	-	4.1.115
-	-	-	-	49.00	-	83.00	-	-	-	-	4.1.116
-	-	-	-	446.00	-	518.00	-	-	-	-	4.1.117
-	-	-	-	519.00	-	546.00	-	-	-	-	4.1.118

Item nr.	SPECIFICATIONS	Unit	RESIDENTIAL £ range £		
5.1	**SANITARY AND DISPOSAL INSTALLATIONS**				
	gross internal area (unless otherwise described)				
	comprising:				
	Comparative sanitary fittings/sundries				
	sanitary and disposal installations				
	Comparative sanitary fittings/sundries				
	Note: Material prices vary considerably, the following composite rates are based on "average" prices for mid priced fittings:				
	Individual sanitary appliances (including fittings)				
	lavatory basins; vitreous china; chromium plated taps; waste; chain and plug; cantilever brackets				
5.1.1	white	nr	211.00	-	240.00
5.1.2	coloured	nr	240.00	-	289.00
	low level WC's; vitreous china pan and cistern; black plastic seat; low pressure ball valve; plastic flush pipe; fixing brackets				
	- on ground floor				
5.1.3	white	nr	182.00	-	211.00
5.1.4	coloured	nr	231.00	-	249.00
	- one of a range; on upper floors				
5.1.5	white	nr	346.00	-	393.00
5.1.6	coloured	nr	393.00	-	433.00
	Extra for				
	bowl type wall urinal; white glazed vitreous china flushing cistern; chromium plated flush pipes and spreaders; fixing brackets				
5.1.7	white	nr	-		-
	shower tray; glazed fireclay; chromium plated waste; chain and plug; riser pipe; rose and mixing valve				
5.1.8	white	nr	-		-
5.1.9	coloured	nr	480.00	-	557.00
	sink; glazed fireclay; chromium plated waste; chain and plug; fixing				
5.1.10	white	nr	538.00	-	595.00
	sink; stainless steel; chromium plated waste; chain and self coloured				
5.1.11	single drainer	nr	-		-
5.1.12	double drainer	nr	231.00	-	289.00
	bath; reinforced acrylic; chromium plated taps; overflow; waste; chain and plug; "P" trap and overflow connections				
5.1.13	white	nr	269.00	-	424.00
5.1.14	coloured	nr	346.00	-	424.00
	bath; enamelled steel; chromium plated taps; overflow; waste; chain and plug; "P" trap and overflow connections				
5.1.15	white	nr	384.00	-	462.00
5.1.16	coloured	nr	424.00	-	498.00
	Soil waste stacks; 3.15 m storey height; branch and connection to drain				
5.1.17	110 mm diameter PVC	nr	307.00	-	346.00
	Extra for				
5.1.18	additional floors	nr	153.00	-	173.00
5.1.19	100 mm diameter cast iron; decorated	nr	-		-
	Extra for				
5.1.20	additional floors	nr	-		-

INDUSTRIAL £ range £		RETAILING £ range £		LEISURE £ range £		OFFICES £ range £		HOTELS £ range £		Item nr
182.00	- 231.00	211.00	- 289.00	211.00	- 289.00	211.00	- 289.00	211.00	- 346.00	5.1.1
-	-	-	-	240.00	- 338.00	240.00	- 338.00	240.00	- 338.00	5.1.2
173.00	- 211.00	182.00	- 211.00	182.00	- 211.00	182.00	- 211.00	182.00	- 249.00	5.1.3
-	-	-	-	231.00	- 289.00	231.00	- 289.00	231.00	- 316.00	5.1.4
337.00	- 395.00	346.00	- 393.00	346.00	- 393.00	346.00	- 393.00	346.00	- 424.00	5.1.5
-	-	-	-	393.00	- 442.00	393.00	- 462.00	393.00	- 489.00	5.1.6
153.00	- 182.00	173.00	- 211.00	173.00	- 211.00	173.00	- 211.00	173.00	- 211.00	5.1.7
451.00	- 509.00	489.00	- 555.00	489.00	- 555.00	489.00	- 555.00	489.00	- 555.00	5.1.8
-	-	-	-	489.00	- 593.00	489.00	- 622.00	489.00	- 913.00	5.1.9
231.00	- 289.00	231.00	- 393.00	-	-	231.00	- 393.00	-	-	5.1.10
-	-	-	-	-	-	-	-	-	-	5.1.11
-	-	-	-	-	-	-	-	-	-	5.1.12
-	-	-	-	-	-	-	-	346.00	- 498.00	5.1.13
-	-	-	-	-	-	-	-	346.00	- 498.00	5.1.14
-	-	-	-	-	-	-	-	384.00	- 536.00	5.1.15
-	-	-	-	-	-	-	-	422.00	- 555.00	5.1.16
307.00	- 346.00	307.00	- 346.00	307.00	- 346.00	307.00	- 346.00	307.00	- 346.00	5.1.17
153.00	- 182.00	153.00	- 182.00	153.00	- 182.00	153.00	- 182.00	155.00	- 182.00	5.1.18
622.00	- 658.00	622.00	- 658.00	622.00	- 658.00	622.00	- 658.00	622.00	- 658.00	5.1.19
307.00	- 346.00	307.00	- 346.00	307.00	- 346.00	307.00	- 346.00	307.00	- 346.00	5.1.20

Item nr	SPECIFICATIONS	Unit	RESIDENTIAL £ range £		

5.1	**SANITARY AND DISPOSAL INSTALLATIONS** - cont'd				
	gross internal area (unless otherwise described)				

	Sanitary and disposal installations				
	Residential units				
5.1.21	range including WC; wash handbasin; bath	nr	1,534	-	2,589
5.1.22	range including WC; wash handbasin; bidet; bath	nr	1,920	-	3,078
5.1.23	and kitchen sink	nr	2,306	-	3,416
	range including two WC's; two wash handbasins; bidet				
5.1.24	bath and kitchen sink	nr	2,879	-	3,987
	Extra for				
5.1.25	rainwater pipe per storey	nr	69.00	-	87.00
5.1.26	soil pipe per storey	nr	153.00	-	173.00
5.1.27	shower over bath	nr	384.00	-	546.00
	Industrial buildings				
	warehouse				
5.1.28	minimum provision	m²	-		-
5.1.29	high provision	m²	-		-
	production unit				
5.1.30	minimum provision	m²	-		-
5.1.31	minimum provision; area less than 1000 m²	m²	-		-
5.1.32	high provision	m²	-		-
	Retailing outlets				
5.1.33	to superstore	m²	-		-
	to shopping centre malls; public conveniences; branch				
5.1.34	connections to shop shells	m²	-		-
5.1.35	fitting out public conveniences in shopping mall block	m²	-		-
5.1.36	Leisure buildings	m²	-		-
	Office and industrial office buildings				
5.1.37	speculative; low rise; area less than 1000 m²	m²	-		-
5.1.38	speculative; low rise	m²	-		-
5.1.39	speculative; medium rise; area less than 1000 m²	m²	-		-
5.1.40	speculative; medium rise	m²	-		-
5.1.41	speculative; high rise	m²	-		-
5.1.42	owner-occupied; low rise; area less than 1000 m²	m²	-		-
5.1.43	owner-occupied; low rise	m²	-		-
5.1.44	owner-occupied; medium rise; area less than 1000 m²	m²	-		-
5.1.45	owner-occupied; medium rise	m²	-		-
5.1.46	owner-occupied; high rise	m²	-		-
	Hotels				
5.1.47	WC; bath; shower; basin to each bedroom; sanitary accommodation to public areas	m²	-		-

5.20	**WATER INSTALLATIONS**	**gross internal area**			

	Hot and cold water installations				
5.2.1	Complete installations	m²	16.00	-	29.00
5.2.2	To mall public conveniences; branch connections to shop shells	m²	-		-

INDUSTRIAL £ range £		RETAILING £ range £		LEISURE £ range £		OFFICES £ range £		HOTELS £ range £		Item nr
-	-	-	-	-	-	-	-	-	-	5.1.21
-	-	-	-	-	-	-	-	-	-	5.1.22
-	-	-	-	-	-	-	-	-	-	5.1.23
-	-	-	-	-	-	-	-	-	-	5.1.24
-	-	-	-	-	-	-	-	-	-	5.1.25
-	-	-	-	-	-	-	-	-	-	5.1.26
-	-	-	-	-	-	-	-	-	-	5.1.27
10.10	- 13.90	-	-	-	-	-	-	-	-	5.1.28
13.90	- 21.00	-	-	-	-	-	-	-	-	5.1.29
13.90	- 21.00	-	-	-	-	-	-	-	-	5.1.30
16.00	- 28.00	-	-	-	-	-	-	-	-	5.1.31
15.00	- 25.00	-	-	-	-	-	-	-	-	5.1.32
-	-	3.50	- 8.70	-	-	-	-	-	-	5.1.33
-	-	7.00	- 11.30	-	-	-	-	-	-	5.1.34
-	-	5,233	- 8,405	-	-	-	-	-	-	5.1.35
-	-	-	-	11.90	- 15.30	-	-	-	-	5.1.36
5.10	- 13.10	-	-	-	-	5.10	- 13.10	-	-	5.1.37
9.60	- 17.00	-	-	-	-	9.20	- 17.00	-	-	5.1.38
-	-	-	-	-	-	10.10	- 18.00	-	-	5.1.39
-	-	-	-	-	-	13.60	- 21.00	-	-	5.1.40
-	-	-	-	-	-	13.60	- 21.00	-	-	5.1.41
-	-	-	-	-	-	8.70	- 17.00	-	-	5.1.42
8.70	- 17.00	-	-	-	-	13.60	- 21.00	-	-	5.1.43
13.60	- 21.00	-	-	-	-	13.60	- 21.00	-	-	5.1.44
-	-	-	-	-	-	16.00	- 24.00	-	-	5.1.45
-	-	-	-	-	-	19.00	- 27.00	-	-	5.1.46
-	-	-	-	-	-	-	-	24.00	- 59.00	5.1.47
										5.20
6.80	- 18.00	-	-	22.00	- 31.00	12.50	- 18.00	35.00	- 42.00	5.2.1
-	-	5.00	- 8.70	-	-	-	-	-	-	5.2.2

Item nr	SPECIFICATIONS	Unit	RESIDENTIAL £ range £	
5.3	**HEATING, AIR-CONDITIONING AND VENTILATING INSTALLATIONS** **gross internal area services** (unless otherwise described)			
	comprising:			
	Solid fuel radiator heating			
	Gas or oil-fired radiator heating			
	Gas or oil-fired convector heating			
	Electric and under floor heating			
	Hot air systems			
	Ventilation systems			
	Heating and ventilation systems			
	Comfort cooling systems			
	Full air-conditioning systems			
	Solid fuel radiator heating			
5.3.1	Chimney stack; hearth and surround to independent residential unit	nr	2,118 -	2,494
	Chimney; hot water service and central heating for			
5.3.2	two radiators	nr	3,078 -	3,642
5.3.3	three radiators	nr	3,642 -	4,050
5.3.4	four radiators	nr	4,047 -	4,462
5.3.5	five radiators	nr	4,462 -	4,894
5.3.6	six radiators	nr	4,894 -	5,327
5.3.7	seven radiators	nr	5,327 -	6,240
	Gas or oil-fired radiator heating			
	Gas-fired hot water service and central heating for			
5.3.8	three radiators	nr	2,306 -	3,266
5.3.9	four radiators	nr	3,266 -	3,558
5.3.10	five radiators	nr	3,558 -	3,793
5.3.11	six radiators	nr	3,793 -	4,047
5.3.12	seven radiators	nr	4,226 -	4,800
	Oil-fired hot water service, tank and central heating for			
5.3.13	seven radiators	nr	3,771 -	4,964
5.3.14	ten radiators	nr	4,203 -	4,118
5.3.15	LPHW radiator system	m²	31.00 -	49.00
5.3.16	speculative; area less than 1000 m²	m²	-	-
5.3.17	speculative	m²	-	-
5.3.18	owner-occupied; area less than 1000 m²	m²	-	-
5.3.19	owner-occupied	m²	-	-
5.3.20	LPHW radiant panel system	m²	-	-
5.3.21	speculative;less than 1000 m²	m²	-	-
5.3.22	speculative	m²	-	-
5.3.23	LPHW fin tube heating	m²	-	-
	Gas or oil-fired convector heating			
5.3.24	LPHW convector system	m²	-	-
5.3.25	speculative; area less than 1000 m²	m²	-	-
5.3.26	speculative	m²	-	-
5.3.27	owner-occupied; area less than 1000 m²	m²	-	-
5.3.28	owner-occupied	m²	-	-
	LPHW sill-line convector system			
5.3.29	owner-occupied	m²	-	-
	Electric and under floor heating			
5.3.30	Panel heaters	m²	-	-
5.3.31	Skirting heaters	m²	-	-
5.3.32	Storage heaters	m²	-	-
5.3.33	Underfloor heating in changing areas	m²	-	-

INDUSTRIAL £ range £		RETAILING £ range £		LEISURE £ range £		OFFICES £ range £		HOTELS £ range £		Item nr
-	-	-	-	-	-	-	-	-	-	5.3.1
-	-	-	-	-	-	-	-	-	-	5.3.2
-	-	-	-	-	-	-	-	-	-	5.3.3
-	-	-	-	-	-	-	-	-	-	5.3.4
-	-	-	-	-	-	-	-	-	-	5.3.5
-	-	-	-	-	-	-	-	-	-	5.3.6
-	-	-	-	-	-	-	-	-	-	5.3.7
-	-	-	-	-	-	-	-	-	-	2.3.8
-	-	-	-	-	-	-	-	-	-	5.3.9
-	-	-	-	-	-	-	-	-	-	5.3.10
-	-	-	-	-	-	-	-	-	-	5.3.11
-	-	-	-	-	-	-	-	-	-	2.3.12
-	-	-	-	-	-	-	-	-	-	5.3.13
-	-	-	-	-	-	-	-	-	-	5.3.14
46.00	- 65.00	46.00	- 65.00	57.00	- 75.00	-	-	69.00	- 96.00	5.3.15
-	-	-	-	-	-	57.00	- 71.00	-	-	5.3.16
-	-	-	-	-	-	61.00	- 85.00	-	-	5.3.17
-	-	-	-	-	-	61.00	- 83.00	-	-	5.3.18
-	-	-	-	-	-	65.00	- 92.00	-	-	5.3.19
-	-	55.00	- 85.00	69.00	- 85.00	-	-	-	-	5.3.20
61.00	- 73.00	-	-	-	-	-	-	-	-	5.3.21
63.00	- 75.00	-	-	-	-	-	-	-	-	5.3.22
81.00	- 119.00	-	-	-	-	-	-	-	-	5.3.23
48.00	- 63.00	47.00	- 89.00	61.00	- 79.00	-	-	81.00	- 102.00	5.3.24
-	-	-	-	-	-	63.00	- 75.00	-	-	5.3.25
-	-	-	-	-	-	65.00	- 89.00	-	-	5.3.26
-	-	-	-	-	-	69.00	- 85.00	-	-	5.3.27
-	-	-	-	-	-	77.00	- 96.00	-	-	5.3.28
-	-	-	-	-	-	100.00	- 139.00	-	-	5.3.29
-	-	-	-	-	-	13.60	- 18.00	-	-	5.3.30
-	-	-	-	-	-	21.00	- 28.00	-	-	5.3.31
-	-	-	-	-	-	25.00	- 33.00	-	-	5.3.32
-	-	-	-	53.00	- 67.00	-	-	-	-	5.3.33

Item nr	SPECIFICATIONS	Unit	RESIDENTIAL £ range £		
5.3	**HEATING, AIR-CONDITIONING AND VENTILATING INSTALLATIONS - cont**				
	gross internal area serviced (unless otherwise described)				
	Hot air systems				
	Hot water service and ducted hot air heating to				
5.3.34	three rooms	nr	2,118	-	2,729
5.3.35	five rooms	nr	2,824	-	3,218
5.3.36	"Elvaco" warm air heating	m²	-		-
5.3.37	Gas-fired hot air space heating	m²	-		-
5.3.38	Warm air curtains; 1.60 m long electrically-operated	nr	-		-
5.3.39	Hot water-operated; including supply pipework	nr	-		-
	Ventilation system				
	Local ventilation to				
5.3.40	WC's	nr	231.00	-	307.00
5.3.41	toilet areas	m²	-		-
5.3.42	bathroom and toilet areas	m²	-		-
5.3.43	Air extract system	m²	-		-
5.3.44	Air supply and extract system	m²	-		-
5.3.45	Service yard vehicle extract system	m²	-		-
	Heating and ventilation systems				
5.3.46	Space heating and ventilation - economical	m²	-		-
5.3.47	Heating and ventilation	m²	-		-
5.3.48	warm air heating and ventilation	m²	-		-
5.3.49	Hot air heating and ventilation to shopping malls; including automatic remote vents in rooflights	m²	-		-
	Extra for				
5.3.50	comfort cooling	m²	-		-
5.3.51	full air-conditioning	m²	-		-
	Comfort cooling systems				
5.3.52	Fan coil/induction systems	m²	-		-
5.3.53	speculative; area less than 1000 m²	m²	-		-
5.3.54	speculative	m²	-		-
5.3.55	owner-occupied; area less than 1000 m²	m²	-		-
5.3.56	owner-occupied	m²	-		-
5.3.57	"VAV" system	m²	-		-
5.3.58	speculative; area less than 1000 m²	m²	-		-
5.3.59	speculative	m²	-		-
5.3.60	owner-occupied; area less than 1000 m²	m²	-		-
5.3.61	owner-occupied	m²	-		-
	Full air-conditioning				
	Stand-alone air-conditioning unit systems				
5.3.62	air supply and extract	m²	-		-
5.3.63	air supply and extract; including heat re-claim	m²	-		-
	Extra for				
5.3.64	automatic control installation	m²	-		-
5.3.65	Full air-conditioning with dust and humidity control	m²	-		-
5.3.66	Fan/coil/induction systems	m²	-		-
5.3.67	speculative; area less than 1000 m²	m²	-		-
5.3.68	speculative	m²	-		-
5.3.69	owner-occupied; area less than 1000 m²	m²	-		-
5.3.70	owner-occupied	m²	-		-
5.3.71	"VAV" system	m²	-		-
5.3.72	speculative; area less than 1000 m²	m²	-		-
5.3.73	speculative	m²	-		-
5.3.74	owner-occupied; area less than 1000 m²	m²	-		-
5.3.75	owner-occupied	m²	-		-

INDUSTRIAL £ range £		RETAILING £ range £		LEISURE £ range £		OFFICES £ range £		HOTELS £ range £		Item nr
-	-	-	-	-	-	-	-	-	-	5.3.34
-	-	-	-	-	-	-	-	-	-	5.3.35
-	-	-	-	-	-	75.00	- 96.00	-	-	5.3.36
28.00	- 55.00	-	-	-	-	-	-	-	-	5.3.37
-	-	2,306	- 3,125	-	-	-	-	-	-	5.3.38
-	-	4,658	- 5,271	-	-	-	-	-	-	5.3.39
-	-	-	-	-	-	-	-	-	-	5.3.40
-	-	-	-	-	-	4.20	- 10.40	-	-	5.3.41
-	-	-	-	-	-	-	-	23.00	- 23.00	5.3.42
-	-	39.00	- 52.00	39.00	- 52.00	39.00	- 52.00	42.00	- 55.00	5.3.43
-	-	-	-	-	-	55.00	- 85.00	-	-	5.3.44
-	-	39.00	- 52.00	-	-	-	-	-	-	5.3.45
23.00	- 54.00	25.00	- 47.00	-	-	-	-	-	-	5.3.46
61.00	- 77.00	-	-	-	-	-	-	-	-	5.3.47
-	-	115.00	- 147.00	115.00	- 147.00	115.00	- 147.00	125.00	- 173.00	5.3.48
-	-	100.00	- 130.00	-	-	-	-	-	-	5.3.49
-	-	87.00	- 125.00	-	-	-	-	-	-	5.3.50
-	-	100.00	- 182.00	-	-	-	-	-	-	5.3.51
-	-	-	-	-	-	-	-	173.00	- 240.00	5.3.52
-	-	-	-	-	-	173.00	- 214.00	173.00	- 240.00	5.3.53
-	-	-	-	-	-	182.00	- 220.00	-	-	5.3.54
-	-	-	-	-	-	182.00	- 231.00	-	-	5.3.55
-	-	-	-	-	-	191.00	- 240.00	-	-	5.3.56
-	-	173.00	- 240.00	-	-	-	-	211.00	- 307.00	5.3.57
-	-	-	-	-	-	191.00	- 289.00	-	-	5.3.58
-	-	-	-	-	-	202.00	- 289.00	-	-	5.3.59
-	-	-	-	-	-	211.00	- 298.00	-	-	5.3.60
-	-	-	-	-	-	211.00	- 307.00	-	-	5.3.61
-	-	-	-	144.00	- 191.00	-	-	-	-	5.3.62
-	-	-	-	164.00	- 211.00	-	-	-	-	5.3.63
-	-	-	-	14.00	- 42.00	-	-	-	-	5.3.64
173.00	- 289.00	-	-	-	-	-	-	-	-	5.3.65
-	-	191.00	- 289.00	-	-	-	-	202.00	- 307.00	5.3.66
-	-	-	-	-	-	182.00	- 231.00	-	-	5.3.67
-	-	-	-	-	-	182.00	- 260.00	-	-	5.3.68
-	-	-	-	-	-	191.00	- 289.00	-	-	5.3.69
-	-	-	-	-	-	202.00	- 307.00	-	-	5.3.70
-	-	-	-	-	-	-	-	231.00	- 346.00	5.3.71
-	-	-	-	-	-	220.00	- 289.00	-	-	5.3.72
-	-	-	-	-	-	231.00	- 307.00	-	-	5.3.73
-	-	-	-	-	-	231.00	- 334.00	-	-	5.3.74
-	-	-	-	-	-	231.00	- 346.00	-	-	5.3.75

Item nr	SPECIFICATIONS	Unit	RESIDENTIAL £ range £		
5.4	**ELECTRICAL INSTALLATIONS** **gross internal area serviced** (unless otherwise described)				
	comprising:				
	Mains and sub-mains switchgear and distribution				
	Lighting installation				
	Lighting and power installation				
	Comparative fittings/rates per point				
	Mains and sub-mains switchgear and distribution				
5.4.1	Mains intake only	m²	-		-
5.4.2	Mains switchgear only	m²	2.80	-	4.60
	Mains and sub-mains distribution				
5.4.3	to floors only	m²	-		-
5.4.4	to floors; including small power and supplies to equipment	m²	-		-
	to floors; including lighting and power to landlords areas and supplies				
5.4.5	to equipment	m²	-		-
5.4.6	to floors; including power, communication and supplies to equipment	m²	-		-
5.4.7	to shop units; including fire alarms and telephone distribution	m²	-		-
	Lighting installation				
	Lighting to				
5.4.8	warehouse area	m²	-		-
5.4.9	production area	m²	-		-
5.4.10	General lighting; including luminaries	m²	-		-
5.4.11	Emergency lighting	m²	-		-
5.4.12	standby generators only	m²	-		-
5.4.13	Underwater lighting	m²	-		-
	Lighting and power installations				
	Lighting and power to residential units				
5.4.14	one person flat/bed-sit	nr	1,054	-	1,638
5.4.15	two person flat/house	nr	1,253	-	2,306
5.4.16	three person flat/house	nr	1,440	-	2,786
5.4.17	four person house	nr	1,733	-	4,226
5.4.18	five/six person house	nr	2,118	-	4,226
	Extra for				
5.4.19	intercom	nr	422.00	-	480.00
	Lighting and power to industrial buildings				
5.4.20	warehouse area	m²	-		-
5.4.21	production area	m²	-		-
5.4.22	production area; high provision	m²	-		-
5.4.23	office area	m²	-		-
5.4.24	office area; high provision	m²	-		-
	Lighting and power to retail outlets				
5.4.25	shopping mall and landlords' areas	m²	-		-
	Lighting and power to offices				
5.4.26	speculative office areas; average standard	m²	-		-
5.4.27	speculative office areas; high standard	m²	-		-
5.4.28	owner-occupied office areas; average standard	m²	-		-
5.4.29	owner-occupied office areas; high standard	m²	-		-
	Comparative fittings/rates per point				
5.4.30	Consumer control unit	nr	173.00	-	192.00
	Fittings; excluding lamps or light fittings				
5.4.31	lighting point; PVC cables	nr	55.00	-	59.00
5.4.32	lighting point; PVC cables in screwed conduits	nr	117.00	-	128.00
5.4.33	lighting point; MICC cables	nr	100.00	-	107.00

INDUSTRIAL £ range £		RETAILING £ range £		LEISURE £ range £		OFFICES £ range £		HOTELS £ range £		Item nr
1.80	- 3.40	-	-	-	-	-	-	-	-	5.4.1
4.60	- 9.20	4.20	- 9.60	-	-	-	-	-	-	5.4.2
5.20	- 10.10	-	-	21.00	- 39.00	15.00	- 27.00	-	-	5.4.3
-	-	-	-	15.00	- 18.00	-	-	-	-	5.4.4
10.10	- 24.00	-	-	-	-	39.00	- 63.00	-	-	5.4.5
-	-	-	-	-	-	-	-	63.00	- 90.00	5.4.6
-	-	6.20	- 15.30	-	-	-	-	-	-	5.4.7
22.00	- 42.00	-	-	-	-	-	-	-	-	5.4.8
27.00	- 47.00	-	-	-	-	-	-	-	-	5.4.9
-	-	-	-	27.00	- 46.00	-	-	24.00	- 39.00	5.4.10
-	-	-	-	10.10	- 15.30	-	-	4.20	- 7.70	5.4.11
2.80	- 11.00	2.80	- 11.00	2.80	- 11.00	2.80	- 11.00	2.80	- 11.00	5.4.12
-	-	-	-	7.00	- 13.60	-	-	-	-	5.4.13
-	-	-	-	-	-	-	-	-	-	5.4.14
-	-	-	-	-	-	-	-	-	-	5.4.15
-	-	-	-	-	-	-	-	-	-	5.4.16
-	-	-	-	-	-	-	-	-	-	5.4.17
-	-	-	-	-	-	-	-	-	-	5.4.18
-	-	-	-	-	-	-	-	-	-	5.4.19
42.00	- 69.00	-	-	-	-	-	-	-	-	5.4.20
48.00	- 77.00	-	-	-	-	-	-	-	-	5.4.21
69.00	- 90.00	-	-	-	-	-	-	-	-	5.4.22
103.00	- 124.00	-	-	-	-	-	-	-	-	5.4.23
138.00	- 166.00	-	-	-	-	-	-	-	-	5.4.24
-	-	69.00	- 118.00	-	-	-	-	-	-	5.4.25
-	-	-	-	-	-	92.00	- 130.00	-	-	5.4.26
-	-	-	-	-	-	117.00	- 138.00	-	-	5.4.27
-	-	-	-	-	-	124.00	- 166.00	-	-	5.4.28
-	-	-	-	-	-	146.00	- 183.00	-	-	5.4.29
-	-	-	-	-	-	-	-	-	-	5.4.30
-	-	61.00	- 69.00	61.00	- 69.00	61.00	- 69.00	61.00	- 69.00	5.4.31
166.00	- 183.00	137.00	- 155.00	137.00	- 155.00	137.00	- 155.00	137.00	- 155.00	5.4.32
137.00	- 155.00	119.00	- 131.00	119.00	- 131.00	119.00	- 131.00	119.00	- 131.00	5.4.33

Item nr	SPECIFICATIONS	Unit	RESIDENTIAL £ range £	
5.4	**ELECTRICAL INSTALLATIONS - cont'd**			
	gross internal area serviced			
	Comparative fittings/rates per point - cont'd			
	Switch socket outlet; PVC cables			
5.4.34	single	nr	58.00 -	66.00
5.4.35	double	nr	70.00 -	79.00
	Switch socket outlet; PVC cables in screwed conduit			
5.4.36	single	nr	90.00 -	96.00
5.4.37	double	nr	94.00 -	105.00
	Switch socket outlet; MICC cables			
5.4.38	single	nr	90.00 -	96.00
5.4.39	double	nr	96.00 -	108.00
5.4.40	Immersion heater point (excluding heater)	nr	85.00 -	96.00
5.4.41	Cooker point; including control unit	nr	119.00 -	191.00
5.5	**GAS INSTALLATION**			
5.5.1	Connection charge	nr	622.00 -	791.00
	Supply to heaters within shopping mall and capped off			
5.5.2	Supply to shop shells	m²	-	-
5.6	**LIFT AND CONVEYOR INSTALLATIONS**			
	lift or escalator (unless otherwise described)			
	comprising:			
	Passenger lifts			
	Escalators			
	Goods lift			
	Dock levellers			
	Electro-hydraulic passenger lifts			
	Eight to twelve person lifts			
5.6.1	8 person; 0.30 m/sec ; 2 - 3 levels	nr	-	-
5.6.2	8 person; 0.63 m/sec ; 3 - 5 levels	nr	-	-
5.6.3	8 person; 1.50 m/sec ; 3 levels	nr	-	-
5.6.4	8 person; 1.60 m/sec ; 6 - 9 levels	nr	-	-
5.6.5	10 person; 0.63 m/sec ; 2 - 4 levels	nr	-	-
5.6.6	10 person; 1.00 m/sec ; 2 levels	nr	-	-
5.6.7	10 person; 1.00 m/sec ; 3 - 6 levels	nr	-	-
5.6.8	10 person; 1.00 m/sec ; 3 - 6 levels	nr	-	-
5.6.9	10 person; 1.60 m/sec ; 4 levels	nr	-	-
5.6.10	10 person; 1.60 m/sec ; 10 levels	nr	-	-
5.6.11	10 person; 1.60 m/sec ; 13 levels	nr	-	-
5.6.12	10 person; 2.50 m/sec ; 18 levels	nr	-	-
5.6.13	12 person; 1.00 m/sec ; 2 - 3 levels	nr	-	-
5.6.14	12 person; 1.00 m/sec ; 3 - 6 levels	nr	-	-
	Thirteen person lifts			
5.6.15	13 person; 0.30 m/sec ; 2 - 3 levels	nr	-	-
5.6.16	13 person; 0.63 m/sec ; 4 levels	nr	-	-
5.6.17	13 person; 1.00 m/sec ; 2 levels	nr	-	-
5.6.18	13 person; 1.00 m/sec ; 2 - 3 levels	nr	-	-
5.6.19	13 person; 1.00 m/sec ; 3 - 6 levels	nr	-	-
5.6.20	13 person; 1.60 m/sec ; 7 - 11 levels	nr	-	-
5.6.21	13 person; 2.50 m/sec ; 7 - 11 levels	nr	-	-
5.6.22	13 person; 2.50 m/sec ; 12 - 15 levels	nr	-	-
	Sixteen person lifts			
5.6.23	16 person; 1.00 m/sec ; 2 levels	nr	-	-
5.6.24	16 person; 1.00 m/sec ; 3 levels	nr	-	-
5.6.25	16 person; 1.00 m/sec ; 3 - 6 levels	nr	-	-
5.6.26	16 person; 1.60 m/sec ; 3 - 6 levels	nr	-	-
5.6.27	16 person; 1.60 m/sec ; 7 - 11 levels	nr	-	-
5.6.28	16 person; 2.50 m/sec ; 7 - 11 levels	nr	-	-
5.6.29	16 person; 2.50 m/sec ; 12 - 15 levels	nr	-	-
5.6.30	16 person; 3.50 m/sec ; 12 - 15 levels	nr	-	-

INDUSTRIAL £ rate £		RETAILING £ rate £		LEISURE £ rate £		OFFICES £ rate £		HOTELS £ rate £		Item nr.
-	-	71.00	- 77.00	71.00	- 77.00	71.00	- 77.00	71.00	- 77.00	5.4.34
131.00	- 150.00	85.00	- 92.00	85.00	- 92.00	85.00	- 92.00	85.00	- 92.00	5.4.35
109.00	- 122.00	100.00	- 104.00	100.00	- 104.00	100.00	- 104.00	100.00	- 104.00	5.4.36
125.00	- 135.00	108.00	- 119.00	108.00	- 119.00	108.00	- 119.00	108.00	- 119.00	5.4.37
117.00	- 122.00	100.00	- 105.00	100.00	- 105.00	100.00	- 105.00	100.00	- 105.00	5.4.38
125.00	- 156.00	108.00	- 121.00	108.00	- 121.00	108.00	- 121.00	108.00	- 121.00	5.4.39
-	-	-	-	-	-	-	-	-	-	5.4.40
-	-	-	-	-	-	-	-	-	-	5.4.41
-	-	-	-	-	-	-	-	-	-	5.5.1
-	-	8.00	- 12.00	-	-	-	-	-	-	5.5.2
-	-	-	-	37,600	- 52,200	35,100	- 52,200	-	-	5.6.1
-	-	-	-	-	-	65,100	- 90,200	-	-	5.6.2
83,600	- 108,300	-	-	-	-	-	-	-	-	5.6.3
-	-	-	-	-	-	116,400	- 139,700	-	-	5.6.4
-	-	-	-	-	-	77,400	- 101,100	-	-	5.6.5
-	-	-	-	-	-	65,100	- 72,200	-	-	5.6.6
-	-	-	-	-	-	88,400	- 112,100	-	-	5.6.7
-	-	-	-	-	-	94,100	- 117,400	-	-	5.6.8
-	-	-	-	-	-	94,100	- 120,500	-	-	5.6.9
-	-	-	-	-	-	130,100	- 148,200	-	-	5.6.10
-	-	-	-	-	-	149,200	- 171,500	-	-	5.6.11
-	-	-	-	-	-	250,300	- 285,700	-	-	5.6.12
87,400	- 107,100	-	-	-	-	-	-	-	-	5.6.13
-	-	-	-	-	-	-	-	103,800	- 123,100	5.6.14
-	-	-	-	-	-	41,400	- 54,200	-	-	5.6.15
-	-	-	-	-	-	88,400	- 110,300	-	-	5.6.16
-	-	103,400	- 116,100	-	-	-	-	-	-	5.6.17
87,400	- 114,200	-	-	-	-	-	-	-	-	5.6.18
-	-	-	-	-	-	88,400	- 117,400	103,800	- 129,200	5.6.19
-	-	-	-	-	-	115,500	- 144,400	124,900	- 143,800	5.6.20
-	-	-	-	-	-	185,700	- 201,300	-	-	5.6.21
-	-	-	-	-	-	201,300	- 221,100	-	-	5.6.22
-	-	98,200	- 124,900	-	-	-	-	-	-	5.6.23
-	-	116,100	- 133,900	-	-	-	-	-	-	5.6.24
-	-	-	-	-	-	101,100	- 130,200	-	-	5.6.25
-	-	-	-	-	-	108,300	- 137,300	-	-	5.6.26
-	-	-	-	-	-	149,200	- 171,600	-	-	5.6.27
-	-	-	-	-	-	194,700	- 213,500	-	-	5.6.28
-	-	-	-	-	-	211,800	- 247,500	-	-	5.6.29
-	-	-	-	-	-	222,000	- 256,100	-	-	5.6.30

Item nr.	SPECIFICATIONS	Unit	RESIDENTIAL £ range £	
5.6	**LIFT AND CONVEYOR INSTALLATIONS - cont'd**			
	lift or escalator (unless otherwise described)			
	Electro-hydraulic passenger lifts - cont'd			
	Twenty one person lifts			
5.6.31	21 person/bed; 040 m/sec ; 3 levels	nr	-	-
5.6.32	21 person; 0.60 m/sec ; 2 levels	nr	-	-
5.6.33	21 person; 1.00 m/sec ; 4 levels	nr	-	-
5.6.34	21 person; 1.60 m/sec ; 4 levels	nr	-	-
5.6.35	21 person; 1.60 m/sec ; 7 - 11 levels	nr	-	-
5.6.36	21 person; 1.60 m/sec ; 10 levels	nr	-	-
5.6.37	21 person; 1.60 m/sec ; 13 levels	nr	-	-
5.6.38	21 person; 2.50 m/sec ; 7 - 11 levels	nr	-	-
5.6.39	21 person; 2.50 m/sec ; 12 - 15 levels	nr	-	-
5.6.40	21 person; 2.50 m/sec ; 18 levels	nr	-	-
5.6.41	21 person; 3.50 m/sec ; 12 - 15 levels	nr	-	-
	Extra for			
5.6.42	enhanced finish to car	nr	-	-
5.6.43	glass backed observation car	nr	-	-
	Ten person wall climber lifts			
5.6.44	10 person; 0.50 m/sec ; 2 levels	nr	-	-
	Escalators			
	30° escalator; 0.50 m/sec; enamelled steel glass balustrades			
5.6.45	3.50 m rise; 600 mm step width	nr	-	-
5.6.46	3.50 m rise; 800 mm step width	nr	-	-
5.6.47	3.50 m rise; 1000 mm step width	nr	-	-
	Extra for			
5.6.48	enhanced finish	nr	-	-
5.6.49	4.40 m rise; 800 mm step width	nr	-	-
5.6.50	4.40 m rise; 1000 mm step width	nr	-	-
5.6.51	5.20 m rise; 800 mm step width	nr	-	-
5.6.52	5.20 m rise; 1000 mm step width	nr	-	-
5.6.53	6.00 m rise; 800 mm step width	nr	-	-
5.6.54	6.00 m rise; 1000 mm step width	nr	-	-
	Extras (per escalator)			
5.6.55	under step lighting	nr	-	-
5.6.56	under handrail lighting	nr	-	-
5.6.57	stainless steel balustrades	nr	-	-
5.6.58	mirror glass cladding to sides and soffits	nr	-	-
5.6.59	heavy duty chairs	nr	-	-
	Good lifts			
5.6.60	Hoist	nr	-	-
	Kitchen service hoist			
5.6.61	50 kg; 2 levels	nr	-	-
	Electric heavy duty goods lifts			
5.6.62	500 kg; 2 levels	nr	-	-
5.6.63	500 kg; 2 - 3 levels	nr	-	-
5.6.64	500 kg; 5 levels	nr	-	-
5.6.65	1000 kg; 2 levels	nr	-	-
5.6.66	1000 kg; 2 - 3 levels	nr	-	-
5.6.67	1000 kg; 5 levels	nr	-	-
5.6.68	1500 kg; 3 levels	nr	-	-
5.6.69	1500 kg; 4 levels	nr	-	-
5.6.70	1500 kg; 7 levels	nr	-	-
5.6.71	2000 kg; 2 levels	nr	-	-
5.6.72	2000 kg; 3 levels	nr	-	-
5.6.73	3000 kg; 2 levels	nr	-	-
5.6.74	3000 kg; 3 levels	nr	-	-
	Oil hydraulic heavy duty goods lifts			
5.6.75	500 kg; 3 levels	nr	-	-
5.6.76	1000 kg; 3 levels	nr	-	-
5.6.77	2000 kg; 3 levels	nr	-	-

INDUSTRIAL £ range £		RETAILING £ range £		LEISURE £ range £		OFFICES £ range £		HOTELS £ range £		Item n
-	-	-	-	-	-	74,000	- 83,100	-	-	5.6.31
-	-	-	-	-	-	106,400	- 130,200	-	-	5.6.32
-	-	-	-	-	-	126,300	- 149,300	-	-	5.6.33
-	-	-	-	-	-	112,000	- 130,200	-	-	5.6.34
-	-	-	-	-	-	149,300	- 184,200	-	-	5.6.35
-	-	-	-	-	-	168,100	- 167,200	-	-	5.6.36
-	-	-	-	-	-	184,200	- 204,000	-	-	5.6.37
-	-	-	-	-	-	212,800	- 252,400	-	-	5.6.38
-	-	-	-	-	-	239,800	- 279,900	-	-	5.6.39
-	-	-	-	-	-	288,700	- 315,700	-	-	5.6.40
-	-	-	-	-	-	270,600	- 297,600	-	-	5.6.41
-	-	-	-	-	-	-	-	14,200	- 15,200	5.6.42
-	-	-	-	-	-	-	-	16,100	- 28,900	5.6.43
-	-	234,700	- 294,300	-	-	234,700	- 297,600	234,700	- 297,600	5.6.44
-	-	-	-	-	-	77,500	- 95,500	-	-	5.6.45
-	-	-	-	-	-	83,100	- 101,100	-	-	5.6.46
-	-	112,100	- 148,100	90,300	- 108,200	90,300	- 108,200	93,100	- 131,100	5.6.47
-	-	33,200	- 47,000	23,300	- 32,200	23,300	- 32,200	33,200	- 50,400	5.6.48
-	-	93,100	- 117,400	-	-	-	-	-	-	5.6.49
-	-	106,400	- 126,200	-	-	-	-	-	-	5.6.50
-	-	99,200	- 122,000	-	-	-	-	-	-	5.6.51
-	-	112,200	- 133,200	-	-	-	-	-	-	5.6.52
-	-	105,200	- 126,200	-	-	-	-	-	-	5.6.53
-	-	117,400	- 139,700	-	-	-	-	-	-	5.6.54
-	-	522.00	- 714.00	-	-	-	-	-	-	5.6.55
-	-	2,100	- 4,100	-	-	-	-	-	-	5.6.56
-	-	2,300	- 4,500	-	-	-	-	-	-	5.6.57
-	-	16,200	- 19,900	-	-	-	-	-	-	5.6.58
-	-	19,900	- 28,000	-	-	-	-	-	-	5.6.59
8,100	- 28,900	-	-	-	-	-	-	-	-	5.6.60
-	-	-	-	9,500	- 10,400	-	-	-	-	5.6.61
-	-	70,300	- 79,800	-	-	68,500	- 79,800	68,500	- 79,800	5.6.62
30,700	- 43,200	-	-	-	-	-	-	-	-	5.6.63
-	-	-	-	-	-	83,100	- 104,500	-	-	5.6.64
-	-	66,500	- 90,300	-	-	74,000	- 90,300	76,000	- 86,400	5.6.65
39,900	- 54,200	-	-	-	-	-	-	-	-	5.6.66
-	-	-	-	-	-	-	-	90,300	- 103,600	5.6.67
83,100	- 99,300	-	-	-	-	94,100	- 112,100	-	-	5.6.68
-	-	-	-	-	-	101,100	- 121,100	-	-	5.6.69
-	-	-	-	-	-	121,100	- 139,100	-	-	5.6.70
-	-	-	-	-	-	94,100	- 112,100	-	-	5.6.71
-	-	-	-	-	-	112,100	- 130,200	-	-	5.6.72
-	-	-	-	-	-	101,100	- 121,100	-	-	5.6.73
-	-	-	-	-	-	126,300	- 149,200	-	-	5.6.74
94,100	- 112,100	-	-	-	-	-	-	-	-	5.6.75
99,300	- 117,400	-	-	-	-	-	-	-	-	5.6.76
115,500	- 133,600	-	-	-	-	-	-	-	-	5.6.77

Item nr	SPECIFICATIONS	Unit	RESIDENTIAL £ range £	

5.6   **LIFT AND CONVEYOR INSTALLATIONS - cont'd**
            lift or escalator (unless otherwise described)

Dock levellers

5.6.78	Dock levellers	nr	-	-
5.6.79	Dock leveller and canopy	nr	-	-

5.7   **PROTECTIVE, COMMUNICATION AND SPECIAL INSTALLATIONS**
            s internal area served (unless otherwise described)

comprising:

Fire fighting/protective installations
Security/communication installations
Special installations

Fire fighting/protective installations
Fire alarms/appliances

5.7.1	loose fire fighting equipment	m²	-	-
5.7.2	smoke detectors; alarms and controls	m²	-	-
5.7.3	hosereels; dry risers and extinguishers	m²	-	-
	Sprinkler installations			
5.7.4	landlords areas; supply to shop shells; including fire alarms; appliances etc.	m²	-	-
5.7.5	single level sprinkler systems; alarms and smoke detectors; low hazard	m²	-	-
	Extra for			
5.7.6	ordinary hazard	m²	-	-
5.7.7	single level sprinkler systems; alarms and smoke detectors; ordinary hazard	m²	-	-
5.7.8	double level sprinkler systems; alarms and smoke detectors; high hazard	m²	-	-
	Smoke vents			
5.7.9	automatic smoke vents over glazed shopping mall	m²	-	-
5.7.10	smoke control ventilation to atria	m²	-	-
5.7.11	Lighting protection	m²	-	-

Security/communication installations

5.7.12	Clock installation	m²	-	-
5.7.13	Security alarm system	m²	-	-
5.7.14	Telephone system	m²	-	-
5.7.15	Public address, television aerial and clocks	m²	-	-
5.7.16	Closed-circuit television	m²	-	-
5.7.17	Public address system	m²	-	-
5.7.18	Closed-circuit television and public address system	m²	-	-

Special installations
Window cleaning equipment

5.7.19	twin track	m	-	-
5.7.20	manual trolley/cradle	nr	-	-
5.7.21	automatic trolley/cradle	nr	-	-
5.7.22	Refrigeration installation for ice rinks	m²	-	-
5.7.23	Pool water treatment installation	m²	-	-
5.7.24	Laundry chute	nr	-	-
5.7.25	Sauna	nr	-	-
5.7.26	Jacuzzi installation	nr	-	-
5.7.27	wave machine; four chamber wave generation equipment	nr	-	-
	Swimming pool; size 13.00 m x 6.00 m			
5.7.28	Extra over cost including structure; finishings, ventilation; heating and filtration	m²	-	-

INDUSTRIAL £ range £	RETAILING £ range £	LEISURE £ range £	OFFICES £ range £	HOTELS £ range £	Item nr
10,024 - 24,000	10,222 - 24,000	- -	- -	10,024 - 24,000	5.6.78
14,400 - 33,129	14,400 - 33,129	- -	- -	- -	5.6.79
- -	- -	0.20 - 0.40	- -	- -	5.7.1
3.50 - 6.90	3.50 - 6.90	6.90 - 8.70	3.50 - 6.90	7.70 - 13.80	5.7.2
5.40 - 12.90	5.40 - 12.90	- -	6.10 - 12.90	5.90 - 11.90	5.7.3
- -	10.10 - 18.00	- -	- -	- -	5.7.4
12.70 - 19.00	13.70 - 19.00	- -	- -	- -	5.7.5
5.40 - 6.90	5.40 - 6.90	- -	- -	- -	5.7.6
18.00 - 25.00	19.00 - 25.00	- -	16.00 - 24.00	14.40 - 23.00	5.7.7
27.00 - 35.00	31.00 - 36.00	- -	27.00 - 35.00	- -	5.7.8
- -	19.00 - 31.00	- -	- -	- -	5.7.9
- -	- -	- -	59.00 - 69.00	59.00 - 75.00	5.7.10
0.70 - 0.90	1.30 - 2.70	0.70 - 0.90	1.00 - 1.80	1.00 - 1.80	5.7.11
- -	- -	0.20 - 1.30	- -	- -	5.7.12
- -	- -	1.90 - 2.80	1.90 - 2.80	- -	5.7.13
- -	- -	1.00 - 2.30	1.00 - 2.30	- -	5.7.14
2.70 - 4.20	- -	3.10 - 4.60	- -	2.70 - 5.80	5.7.15
- -	4.20 - 5.10	4.20 - 5.10	- -	- -	5.7.16
- -	10.90 - 12.90	10.90 - 12.90	- -	- -	5.7.17
- -	25.00 - 50.00	15.30 - 18.00	- -	- -	5.7.18
- -	155.00 - 182.30	- -	136.00 - 164.00	150.00 - 173.00	5.7.19
- -	10,033 - 12,000	- -	10,033 - 12,000	9,600 - 11,520	5.7.20
- -	22,118 - 28,329	- -	23,529 - 28,329	23,058 - 28,329	5.7.21
- -	- -	537.70 - 625.60	- -	- -	5.7.22
- -	- -	537.70 - 583.60	- -	- -	5.7.23
- -	- -	13,695 - 16,800	- -	- -	5.7.24
- -	- -	- -	- -	13,482 - 16,538	5.7.25
- -	- -	15,372 - 20,849	- -	8,077 - 16,538	5.7.26
- -	- -	50,962 - 71,811	- -	- -	5.7.27
- -	- -	- -	- -	1,043 - 1,187	5.7.28

Item nr	SPECIFICATIONS	Unit	RESIDENTIAL £ range £	
5.8	**BUILDERS' WORK IN CONNECTION WITH SERVICES** **gross internal area**			
	General builders work to			
5.8.1	main supplies, lighting and power to landlords areas	m²	-	-
5.8.2	central heating and electrical installation	m²	-	-
5.8.3	space heating and electrical installation	m²	-	-
5.8.4	central heating, electrical and lift installations	m²	-	-
5.8.5	space heating, electrical and ventilation installations	m²	-	-
5.8.6	air-conditioning	m²	-	-
5.8.7	air-conditioning and electrical installation	m²	-	-
5.8.8	air-conditioning, electrical and lift installations	m²	-	-
	General builders work, including allowance for plant rooms; to			
5.8.9	central heating and electrical installation	m²	-	-
5.8.10	central heating, electrical and lift installations	m²	-	-
5.8.11	air-conditioning	m²	-	-
5.8.12	air-conditioning and electrical installation	m²	-	-
5.8.13	air-conditioning, electrical and lift installations	m²	-	-

INDUSTRIAL £ range £		RETAILING £ range £		LEISURE £ range £		OFFICES £ range £		HOTELS £ range £		Item nr
2.00	- 5.50	-	-	-	-	-	-	-	-	5.8.1
3.90	- 13.20	6.60	- 14.80	6.60	- 14.80	9.60	- 14.80	9.60	- 14.80	5.8.2
5.10	- 14.80	8.70	- 15.30	8.70	- 15.30	11.10	- 15.30	11.10	- 15.30	5.8.3
5.80	- 15.30	9.60	- 16.00	9.60	- 16.00	13.00	- 17.00	13.00	- 17.00	5.8.4
8.70	- 20.00	13.00	- 22.00	13.00	- 24.00	18.00	- 24.00	18.00	- 24.00	5.8.5
14.60	- 23.00	17.00	- 24.00	17.00	- 24.00	21.00	- 27.00	21.00	- 27.00	5.8.6
16.00	- 24.00	20.00	- 27.00	20.00	- 27.00	23.00	- 30.00	23.00	- 30.00	5.8.7
18.00	- 27.00	22.00	- 30.00	22.00	- 30.00	26.00	- 32.00	26.00	- 32.00	5.8.8
-	-	26.00	- 33.00	25.80	- 32.70	32.70	- 40.50	33.00	- 41.00	5.8.9
-	-	33.00	- 41.00	32.70	- 40.50	40.50	- 46.20	41.00	- 46.00	5.8.10
-	-	46.00	- 54.00	46.20	- 53.60	59.30	- 64.90	59.00	- 65.00	5.8.11
-	-	59.00	- 65.00	59.30	- 64.90	72.90	- 80.90	73.00	- 81.00	5.8.12
-	-	73.00	- 81.00	72.90	- 80.90	84.70	- 94.20	85.00	- 94.00	5.8.13

Item nr	SPECIFICATIONS	Unit	ALL AREAS £ range £		
6.1	**SITE WORK**				
	surface area (unless otherwise described)				

comprising:

Preparatory excavation	**Roadbridges**
Seeded and planted areas	**Underpasses**
Sports Pitches	**Roundabouts**
Parklands	**Guard rails and parking bollards,**
Paved areas	**etc.**
Car parking alternatives	**Street furniture**
Roads and barriers	**Playground equipment**
Road Crossing	**Fencing and screen walls, ancillary**
Footbridges	**buildings etc.**

Item nr	SPECIFICATIONS	Unit	£ range		£
	Preparatory excavation and sub-bases				
	Excavating				
6.1.1	top soil; average 150 mm deep	m²	1.00	-	1.90
	top soil; 225 mm deep; preserving in spoil heaps				
6.1.2	by machine	m²	1.90	-	2.60
6.1.3	by hand	m²	4.70	-	7.30
	to reduce levels; not exceeding 0.25 m deep				
6.1.4	by machine	m²	3.00	-	3.30
6.1.5	by hand	m²	13.00	-	14.40
6.1.6	to form new foundation levels and contours	m²	3.30	-	15.00
	Filling; imported top soil				
6.1.7	150 mm thick; spread and levelled for planting	m²	6.00	-	7.00
	Comparative sub-bases/beds				
6.1.8	50 mm thick; sand	m²	2.10	-	2.30
6.1.9	75 mm thick; ashes	m²	1.80	-	2.10
6.1.10	75 mm thick; sand	m²	3.00	-	3.30
6.1.11	50 mm thick; blinding concrete (1:8)	m²	3.50	-	3.90
6.1.12	100 mm thick; granular fill	m²	3.50	-	3.90
6.1.13	150 mm thick; granular fill	m²	5.50	-	5.70
6.1.14	75 mm thick; blinding concrete (1:3:6)	m²	5.20	-	5.70
	Seeded and planted areas				
	Plant supply, planting, maintenance and 12 months guarantee				
6.1.15	seeded areas	m²	3.50	-	7.00
6.1.16	turfed areas	m²	4.50	-	9.00
	Planted areas (per m² of surface area)				
6.1.17	herbaceous plants	m²	3.90	-	5.20
6.1.18	climbing plants	m²	5.20	-	9.00
6.1.19	general planting	m²	11.60	-	23.50
6.1.20	woodland	m²	18.00	-	35.00
6.1.21	shrubbed planting	m²	23.00	-	64.00
6.1.22	dense planting	m²	29.00	-	57.00
6.1.23	shrubbed area including allowance for small trees	m²	35.00	-	81.00
	Trees				
6.1.24	advanced nursery stock trees (12 - 20 cm girth)	tree	142.00	-	173.00
	semi-mature trees; 5 - 8 m high				
6.1.25	coniferous	tree	462.00	-	1,162
6.1.26	deciduous	tree	700.00	-	1,920

Item nr	SPECIFICATIONS	Unit	ALL AREAS £ range £
6.1	**SITE WORK - cont'd**		
	surface area (unless otherwise described)		
	Sports pitches		
	Costs include for cultivating ground, bringing to appropriate levels for the specified game, applying fertiliser, weedkiller, seeding and rolling and white line marking with nets, posts, etc. as required		
6.1.27	football pitch (114 m x 72 m)	nr	16,706
6.1.28	cricket outfield (160 m x 142 m)	nr	56,847
6.1.29	cricket square (20 x 20 m) including imported marl or clay loam, bringing to accurate levels, seeding with cricket square type grass	nr	5,176
6.1.30	bowling green (38 m x 38 m) rink including French drain and gravel path on four sides	nr	20,565
6.1.31	grass tennis courts 1 court (35 m x 17 m) including bringing to accurate levels, chain link perimeter fencing and gate; tennis posts and net	nr	20,942
6.1.32	two grass tennis courts (35 m x 32 m) ditto	pair	35,529
6.1.33	artificial surface tennis courts (35 m x 17 m) including chain link fencing gate, posts and net	nr	16,518
6.1.34	two courts (45 m x 32 m) ditto	pair	30,918
6.1.35	artificial football pitch, including sub-base, bitumen macadam open textured base and heavy duty "Astroturf" type carpet	nr	326,400
6.1.36	golf-putting green	hole	1,675
6.1.37	pitch and putt course	hole	5,176 - 7,858
6.1.38	full length golf course, full specifications including watering system	hole	18,312 - 34,694
6.1.39	championship golf course	hole	up to 128,753
	Parklands		
	NOTE: Work on parklands will involve different techniques of earth shifting and cultivation. The following rates include for normal surface excavation, they include for the provision of any land drainage.		
6.1.40	Parklands, including cultivating ground, applying fertiliser, etc and seeding with parks type grass	ha	15,953
6.1.41	General sports field	ha	19,011
	Lakes including excavation average 10 m deep, laying 1.50 mm thick butyl rubber sheet and spreading top soil evenly on top 300 mm deep		
6.1.42	under 1 hectare in area	ha	349,400
6.1.43	between 1 and 5 hectare in area	ha	326,400
6.1.44	Extra for planting aquatic plants in lake top soil	m²	51.00
	Land drainage		
	NOTE: If land drainage is required on a project, the propensity of the land to flood will decide the spacing of the land drains. Costs include for excavation and backfilling of trenches and laying agricultural clay drain pipes with 75 mm diameter lateral runs average 600 mm deep, and 100 mm diameter mains runs average 750 mm deep.		
	land drainage to parkland with laterals at		
6.1.45	30 m centres and main runs at 100 m centres	ha	3,294
	land drainage to parkland with laterals at		
6.1.46	10 m centres and main runs at 33 m centres	ha	9,600

Item nr	SPECIFICATIONS	Unit	ALL AREAS £ range £

6.1 **SITE WORK - cont'd**

surface area (unless otherwise described)

	Paved areas			
	Gravel paving rolled to falls and cambers			
6.1.47	50 mm thick	m²	2.40	- 3.10
6.1.48	paving on sub-base; including excavation	m²	9.00	- 13.00
	Cold bitumen emulsion paving; in three layers			
6.1.49	25 mm thick	m²	4.50	- 5.80
	Tarmacadam paving; two layers; limestone or igneous chipping finish			
6.1.50	65 mm thick	m²	7.00	- 8.70
6.1.51	paving on sub-base; including excavation	m²	17.00	- 24.00
	Precast concrete paving slabs			
6.1.52	50 mm thick	m²	10.10	- 21.00
6.1.53	50 mm thick "Texitone" slabs	m²	14.00	- 20.00
6.1.54	slabs on sub-base; including excavation	m²	23.00	- 33.00
	Precast concrete block paviours			
6.1.55	65 mm thick "Keyblock" grey paving	m²	19.00	- 24.00
6.1.56	65 mm thick "Mount Sorrel" grey paving	m²	19.00	- 23.00
6.1.57	65 mm thick "Intersett" paving	m²	20.00	- 24.00
6.1.58	60 mm thick "Pedesta" paving	m²	15.00	- 24.00
6.1.59	paviours on sub-base; including excavation	m²	28.00	- 39.00
	Brick paviours			
	229 mm x 114 mm x 38 mm paving bricks			
6.1.60	laid flat	m²	31.00	- 39.00
6.1.61	laid to herringbone pattern	m²	52.00	- 57.00
6.1.62	paviours on sub-base; including excavation	m²	59.00	- 69.00
	Granite setts			
6.1.63	200 mm x 100 mm x 100 mm paving bricks	m²	81.00	- 89.00
6.1.64	setts on sub-base; including excavation	m²	98.00	- 105.00
	York stone slab paving			
6.1.65	paving on sub-base; including excavation	m²	105.00	- 125.00
	Cobblestone paving			
6.1.66	50 mm - 75 mm diameter	m²	59.00	- 73.00
6.1.67	cobblestones on sub-base; including excavation	m²	69.00	- 90.00
	Car Parking alternatives			
	Surface level parking; including lighting and drainage			
6.1.68	tarmacadam on sub-base	car	1,098	- 1,510
6.1.69	concrete interlocking blocks	car	1,235	- 1,647
6.1.70	"Grasscrete" precast concrete units filled with top soil and grass seed	car	671.00	- 918.00
6.1.71	at ground level with deck or building over	car	5,630	- 6,515
	Garages etc			
6.1.72	single car park	nr	738.00	- 1,158
6.1.73	single; traditional construction; in a block	nr	2,304	- 3,291
6.1.74	single; traditional construction; pitched roof	nr	2,274	- 6,720
6.1.75	double; traditional construction; pitched roof	nr	7,529	- 9,645
	Multi-storey parking; including lighting and drainage on roof of two storey shopping centre; including			
6.1.76	ramping and strengthening structure	car	4,800	- 7,295
6.1.77	split level/parking ramp	car	6,634	- 7,473
6.1.78	multi-storey flat slab	car	8,030	- 9,645
6.1.79	multi-storey warped slab	car	8,471	- 10,285
	Extra for			
6.1.80	feature cladding and pitched roof	car	1,028	- 1,748
	Underground parking; including lighting and drainage			
6.1.81	partially underground; natural ventilation; no sprinklers	car	10,971	- 15,087
6.1.82	completely underground; mechanical ventilation and sprinklers	car	15,087	- 20,142
	completely underground; mechanical ventilation; sprinklers and			
6.1.83	landscaped roof	car	17,726	- 24,687

Item nr.	SPECIFICATIONS		Unit	ALL AREAS £ range £		
6.1	**SITE WORK - cont'd**					
	surface area (unless otherwise described)					
	Roads and barriers					
	Tarmacadam or reinforced concrete roads, including all earthworks,					
	drainage, pavements, lighting, signs, fencing and safety barriers (where					
	necessary); average cut 1.50 m					
6.1.84	two lane road 7.30 m wide-rural location		m	1,700	-	1,900
6.1.85	two lane road 7.30 m wide-urban location		m	1,900	-	2,300
6.1.86	two lane road 10.00 m wide-rural location		m	1,800	-	2,100
6.1.87	two lane road 10.00 m wide-urban location		m	2,100	-	2,300
	Road crossings					
	NOTE: Costs include road markings, beacons, lights, signs, advance					
	danger signs etc.					
6.1.88	Zebra crossing		nr	4,400	-	5,200
6.1.89	Pelican crossing		nr	18,100	-	19,200
	Footbridges					
	Footbridge of either precast concrete or steel construction 4.00 m wide,					
	6.00 m high including deck, access stairs and ramp, parapets etc.					
6.1.90	15.00 m - 20.00 m span to two lane road		nr	179,700	-	199,700
6.1.91	30.00 m span to four lane dual carriageway		nr	199,700	-	239,600
	Roadbridges					
	Roadbridges including all excavation, reinforcement, formwork, concrete,					
	bearings, expansion joints, deck water proofing and finishing's, parapets etc.					
	RC bridge with precast beams					
6.1.92	10.00 m span	deck area	m²		1,054.00	
6.1.93	15.00 m span	deck area	m²		998.00	
	RC bridge with prefabricated steel beams					
6.1.94	20.00 m span	deck area	m²		1,045.00	
6.1.95	30.00 m span	deck area	m²		978.00	
	Underpass					
	Provision of underpasses to new roads, constructed as part of a road					
	building programme					
	Precast concrete pedestrian underpass					
6.1.96	3.00 m wide x 2.50 m high		m	3,840	-	4,518
	Precast concrete vehicle underpass					
6.1.97	7.00 m wide x 5.00 m high		m	10,729	-	13,440
6.1.98	14.00 m wide x 5.00 m high		m		27,335	
	Bridge type structure vehicle underpass					
6.1.99	7.00 m wide x 5.00 m high		m	19,011	-	23,435
6.1.100	14.00 m wide x 5.00 m high		m		46,495	
	Roundabouts					
6.1.101	Roundabout on existing dual carriageway; including perimeter road,		nr	349,500	-	514,500
	drainage and lighting, signs and disruption while under construction					
	Guard rails and parking bollards etc.					
6.1.102	Open metal post and rail fencing 1.00 m high		m	129.00	-	150.00
6.1.103	Galvanised steel post and rail fencing 2.00 m high		m	144.00	-	189.00
6.1.104	Steel guard rails and vehicle barriers		m	45.90	-	70.00
	Parking bollards					
6.1.105	precast concrete		nr	104.00	-	122.00
6.1.106	steel		nr	168.00	-	220.00
6.1.107	cast iron		nr	195.00	-	269.00
6.1.108	Vehicle control barrier; manual pole		nr	904.00	-	969.00
6.1.109	Galvanised steel cycle stand		nr	38.00	-	50.00
6.1.110	Galvanised steel flag staff		nr	1,016	-	1,289

Item nr	SPECIFICATIONS	Unit	ALL AREAS £ range £		
6.1	**SITE WORK - cont'd**				
	surface area (unless otherwise described)				
	Street Furniture				
	Reflected traffic signs 0.25 m² area				
6.1.111	on steel post	nr	92.00	-	168.00
	Internally illuminated traffic signs				
6.1.112	dependent on area	nr	199.00	-	269.00
	Externally illuminated traffic signs				
6.1.113	dependent on area	nr	489.00	-	1,289
	Lighting to pedestrian areas and estates				
6.1.114	roads on 4.00 m - 6.00 m columns with up to 70 W lamps	nr	222.00	-	325.00
	Lighting to main roads				
6.1.115	10.00 m - 12.00 m columns with 250 W lamps	nr	509.00	-	622.00
6.1.116	12.00 m - 15.00 m columns with 400 W high pressure sodium lighting	nr	649.00	-	782.00
6.1.117	Benches - hardwood and precast concrete	nr	190.00	-	260.00
	Litter bins				
6.1.118	precast concrete	nr	190.00	-	220.00
6.1.119	hardwood slatted	nr	77.00	-	104.00
6.1.120	cast iron	nr	327.00		
6.1.121	large aluminium	nr	574.00		
6.1.122	Bus stops	nr	346.00		
6.1.123	Bus stops including basic shelter	nr	800.00		
6.1.124	Pillar box	nr	289.00		
6.1.125	Telephone box	nr	3,162		
	Playground equipment				
	Modern swings with flat rubber safety seats:				
6.1.126	four seats; two bays	nr	1,285		
6.1.127	Stainless steel slide, 3.40 m long	nr	1,422		
6.1.128	Climbing frame - igloo type 3.20 m x 3.75 m on plan x 2.00 m high	nr	1,478		
6.1.129	Seesaw comprising timber plank on sealed ball bearings 3960 mm x 230 mm x 70 mm thick	nr	1,026.00		
6.1.130	Wickstead "Tumbleguard" type safety surfacing around play equipment	m²	86.60		
6.1.131	Bark particles type safety surfacing 150 mm thick on hardcore bed	m²	12.00		
	Fencing and screen walls, ancillary building etc				
	Chain link fencing; plastic coated				
6.1.132	1.20 m high	m	16.00	-	19.00
6.1.133	1.80 m high	m	23.00	-	25.80
	Timber fencing				
6.1.134	1.20 m high chestnut pale facing	m	18.00	-	21.00
6.1.135	1.80 m high cross-boarded fencing	m	46.00	-	57.00
	Screen walls; one brick thick; including foundations etc.				
6.1.136	1.80 m high facing brick screen wall	m	231.00	-	289.00
6.1.137	1.80 m high coloured masonry block boundary wall	m	258.00	-	325.00
6.1.138	Squash courts, independent building, including shower	nr	69,882	-	81,788
	Demolish existing buildings				
6.1.139	of brick construction	m²	4.90	-	8.70

Item nr	SPECIFICATIONS	Unit	ALL AREAS £ range £
6.20	**EXTERNAL SERVICES** **gross internal area** (unless otherwise described)		
	Service runs all laid in trenches including excavation Water main		
6.2.1	75 mm uPVC main in 225 mm diameter ductile iron pipe as duct	m	48.00
	Electric main		
6.2.2	600/1000 volt cables. Two core 25 mm diameter cable including 100 mm diameter clayware duct	m	31.00
	Gas main		
6.2.3	150 mm diameter ductile or cast iron gas pipe	m	48.00
	Telephone		
6.2.4	British Telecom installation in 100 mm diameter uPVC duct	m	19.00
6.2.5	External lighting (per m² of lighted area)	m²	2.40 - 3.70
	Connection areas The privatisation of telephone, water, gas and electricity has complicated the assessment of service connection charges. Typically, service connection charges will include the actual cost of the direct connection plus an assessment of distribution costs from the main. The latter cost is difficult to estimate as it depends on the type of scheme and the distance from the mains. In addition, service charges are complicated by discounts that may be offered. For instance, the electricity boards will charge less for housing connections if the house is all electric. However, typical charges for an estate of 200 houses might be as follows		
6.2.6	Water	house	527.00 - 1,073
	Electric		
6.2.7	all electric	house	269.00
6.2.8	gas/electric	house	527.00
	Extra cost of		
6.2.9	sub-station	nr	13,458 - 19,953
6.2.10	Gas	house	527.00 - 678.00
	Extra cost of		
6.2.11	governing station	nr	13,458
6.2.12	Telephone	house	173.00
6.2.13	Sewerage	house	405.00 - 527.00

Item nr	SPECIFICATIONS	Unit	ALL AREAS

6.3   DRAINAGE

gross internal area (unless otherwise described)

comprising:

Overall £/m² allowances
Comparative pipework
Comparative manholes

Overall £/m² allowances

Item nr	SPECIFICATIONS	Unit	£ range £
6.3.1	Site drainage (per m² of paved area)	m²	6.80 - 18.00
6.3.2	Building drainage (per m² of gross floor area)	m²	6.80 - 15.00
6.3.3	Drainage work beyond the boundary of the site and final connection	nr	1,633 - 10,353
	Drains; hand excavation; grade bottom, earthwork support, laying and jointing pipe, backfill and compact, disposal of surplus soil; land drain, clay field drain, pipes, nominal size		0.75m £
6.3.4	75 mm diameter	m	26.00
6.3.5	100 mm diameter	m	28.00
6.3.6	150 mm diameter	m	29.00
	Land drain, vitrified clay perforated sub-soil pipes, nominal size		
6.3.7	100 mm diameter	m	29.00
6.3.8	150 mm diameter	m	35.00
6.3.9	225 mm diameter	m	41.00
	Machine excavation, grade bottom, earthwork support, laying and jointing pipes and accessories, backfill and compact, disposal of surplus soil (excluding beds, benchings and coverings)		
	Vitrified clay pipes and fittings, socketted, cement and sand joints, nominal size		1.00m £
6.3.10	100 mm diameter	m	21.00
6.3.11	150 mm diameter	m	24.00
6.3.12	225 mm diameter	m	36.00
6.3.13	300 mm diameter	m	55.00
6.3.14	450 mm diameter	m	102.00
	Vitrified clay pipes and fittings, "Hepseal" socketted, with push fit flexible joints, nominal size		
6.3.15	100 mm diameter	m	24.00
6.3.16	150 mm diameter	m	29.00
6.3.17	225 mm diameter	m	45.00
6.3.18	300 mm diameter	m	69.00
6.3.19	450 mm diameter	m	140.00
	Class M tested concrete centrifugally spun pipes and fittings, flexible joints, nominal size		
6.3.20	300 mm diameter	m	43.00
6.3.21	450 mm diameter	m	59.00
6.3.22	600 mm diameter	m	77.00
6.3.23	900 mm diameter	m	-
6.3.24	1200 mm diameter	m	-
	Cast iron "Timesaver" drain pipes and fittings, mechanical coupling joints, nominal size		
6.3.25	75 mm diameter	m	50.00
6.3.26	100 mm diameter	m	54.00
6.3.27	150 mm diameter	m	81.00
	uPVC pipes and fittings, lip seal coupling joints, nominal size		
6.3.28	100 mm diameter	m	17.00
6.3.29	160 mm diameter	m	22.00

AVERAGE DEPTH

1.00 m £	1.25 m £	1.50 m £	1.75 m £	2.00 m £	Item nr
34.00	45.00	65.00	77.00	89.00	6.3.4
36.00	46.00	67.00	79.00	90.00	6.3.5
39.00	48.00	69.00	81.00	94.00	6.3.6
39.00	48.00	69.00	81.00	94.00	6.3.7
42.00	52.00	75.00	85.00	96.00	6.3.8
48.00	61.00	81.00	94.00	103.00	6.3.9

AVERAGE DEPTH OF DRAIN

1.50 m £	2.00 m £	2.50 m £	3.00 m £	3.50 m £	
26.00	31.00	41.00	48.00	65.00	6.3.10
29.00	37.00	45.00	52.00	69.00	6.3.11
41.00	48.00	57.00	65.00	69.00	6.3.12
63.00	67.00	75.00	83.00	89.00	6.3.13
107.00	113.00	127.00	133.00	140.00	6.3.14
29.00	37.00	45.00	52.00	69.00	6.3.15
35.00	39.00	48.00	55.00	75.00	6.3.16
50.00	55.00	65.00	73.00	102.00	6.3.17
74.00	81.00	90.00	96.00	102.00	6.3.18
146.00	151.00	163.00	171.00	179.00	6.3.19
48.00	55.00	63.00	71.00	77.00	6.3.20
69.00	73.00	85.00	92.00	98.00	6.3.21
87.00	92.00	103.00	113.00	121.00	6.3.22
148.00	155.00	171.00	181.00	190.00	6.3.23
-	238.00	254.00	267.00	277.00	6.3.24
55.00	62.00	71.00	77.00	94.00	6.3.25
58.00	63.00	75.00	81.00	98.00	6.3.26
89.00	92.00	102.00	109.00	126.00	6.3.27
23.00	29.00	39.00	44.00	61.00	6.3.28
29.00	34.00	44.00	50.00	69.00	6.3.29

Item nr	SPECIFICATIONS	Unit	1.00 m £
6.3	**DRAINAGE - cont'd**		
	gross internal area (unless otherwise described)		
	uPVC "Ultra-Rib" ribbed pipes and fittings, sealed ring push fit joints, nominal size		
6.3.30	150 mm diameter	m	19.00
6.3.31	225 mm diameter	m	30.00
6.3.32	300 mm diameter	m	41.00

Item nr		Unit	BED 100 mm thick £
	Pipe beds, benching and coverings granular filling, pipe size		
6.3.33	100 mm diameter	m	2.00
6.3.34	150 mm diameter	m	2.20
6.3.35	225 mm diameter	m	2.60
6.3.36	300 mm diameter	m	3.00
6.3.37	450 mm diameter	m	3.70
6.3.38	600 mm diameter	m	4.00
	In situ concrete 10.00 N/mm² - 40 mm aggregate (1:3:6), pipe size		
6.3.39	100 mm diameter	m	4.10
6.3.40	150 mm diameter	m	4.10
6.3.41	225 mm diameter	m	4.80
6.3.42	300 mm diameter	m	5.70
6.3.43	450 mm diameter	m	7.30
6.3.44	600 mm diameter	m	8.10
6.3.45	900 mm diameter	m	9.70
6.3.46	1200 mm diameter	m	13.00
	In situ concrete 20.00 N/mm² - 20 mm aggregate (1:2:4), pipe size		
6.3.47	100 mm diameter	m	4.10
6.3.48	150 mm diameter	m	4.10
6.3.49	225 mm diameter	m	5.00
6.3.50	300 mm diameter	m	5.80
6.3.51	450 mm diameter	m	7.50
6.3.52	600 mm diameter	m	8.30
6.3.53	900 mm diameter	m	10.00
6.3.54	1200 mm diameter	m	13.30

Brick Manholes

Excavate pit in firm ground, partial backfill, partial disposal, earthwork support, compact base of pit, plain in situ concrete 20.00 N/mm² - 20 mm aggregate (1:2:4) base, formwork, one brick wall of engineering bricks PC £175.00/1000 in cement mortar (1:3) finished fair face, vitrified clay channels, plain insitu concrete 25.00 N/mm² - 20 mm aggregate (1:2:4) cover and reducing slabs, fabric reinforcement, formwork step irons, cast iron cover and frame, depth from cover to invert

Item nr		Unit	600 mm x 450 mm £
6.3.55	0.75 m	nr	329.00
6.3.56	1.00 m	nr	403.00
6.3.57	1.25 m	nr	484.00
6.3.58	1.50 m	nr	557.00
6.3.59	1.75 m	nr	635.00

with reducing slab and brick shaft internal size 600 mm x 450 mm; depth from cover to invert

Item nr		Unit	
6.3.60	2.00 m	nr	-
6.3.61	2.50 m	nr	-
6.3.62	3.00 m	nr	-
6.3.63	3.50 m	nr	-
6.3.64	4.00 m	nr	-

1.50 m £	2.00 m £	AVERAGE DEPTH OF DRAIN 2.50 m £	3.00 m £	3.50 m £	Item nr
24.00	29.00	39.00	47.00	64.00	6.3.30
35.00	41.00	50.00	57.00	61.00	6.3.31
48.00	52.00	61.00	69.00	75.00	6.3.32

BED 150 mm thick £	BED AND BENCHING 100 mm thick £	150 mm thick £	BED AND COVERING 100 mm thick £	150 mm thick £	
3.00	4.00	4.40	5.80	8.60	6.3.33
3.30	4.20	4.80	7.10	9.70	6.3.34
3.70	5.40	6.40	9.70	12.50	6.3.35
4.00	6.20	8.00	11.60	14.80	6.3.36
5.30	9.30	11.10	17.00	21.00	6.3.37
6.30	12.10	13.90	21.00	25.00	6.3.38
5.70	7.60	8.50	10.60	16.00	6.3.39
6.50	8.50	9.40	12.40	18.00	6.3.40
7.30	10.20	11.90	18.00	23.00	6.3.41
8.10	11.90	15.00	21.00	27.00	6.3.42
10.50	18.00	21.00	30.00	38.00	6.3.43
12.20	23.00	27.00	39.00	46.00	6.3.44
15.40	37.00	43.00	59.00	75.00	6.3.45
19.00	55.00	61.00	81.00	106.00	6.3.46
5.80	7.80	8.70	10.90	16.00	6.3.47
6.70	8.70	9.60	12.70	18.00	6.3.48
7.50	10.40	12.20	18.00	24.00	6.3.49
8.30	12.20	16.00	22.00	28.00	6.3.50
10.80	18.00	22.00	31.00	39.00	6.3.51
12.50	23.00	28.00	40.00	47.00	6.3.52
15.80	38.00	44.00	61.00	77.00	6.3.53
19.00	56.00	62.00	83.00	109.00	6.3.54

INTERNAL SIZE OF MANHOLE

750 x 450 mm £	900 x 600 mm £	900 x 900 mm £	900 x 1500 mm £	1200 x 1800 mm £	
359.00	442.00	511.00	685.00	860.00	6.3.55
441.00	536.00	622.00	822.00	1,026.00	6.3.56
525.00	636.00	736.00	965.00	1,197	6.3.57
609.00	732.00	847.00	1,102.00	1,361	6.3.58
689.00	829.00	956.00	1,241	1,528	6.3.59
-	-	1,058.40	1,348	1,638	6.3.60
-	-	1,267	1,592	1,921	6.3.61
-	-	1,428	1,760	2,101	6.3.62
-	-	1,582	1,925	2,274	6.3.63
-	-	1,738	2,088	2,445	6.3.64

Item nr   SPECIFICATIONS   Unit

6.3   **DRAINAGE - cont'd**

                              gross internal area (unless otherwise described)

         Concrete manholes
         Excavate pit in firm ground, disposal, earthwork support, compact base of
         pit, plain insitu concrete 20.00 N/mm² - 20 mm aggregate (1:2:4) base,
         formwork, reinforced precast concrete chamber and shaft rings, taper
         pieces and cover slabs bedded jointed and pointed in cement;mortar (1:3)
         weak mix concrete filling to working space, vitrified clay channels, plain
         insitu concrete 25.00 N/mm² - 20 mm aggregate (1:1:5:3) benchings, step
         irons, cast iron cover and frame; depth from cover to invert

6.3.65   0.75 m   nr
6.3.66   1.00 m   nr
6.3.67   1.25 m   nr
6.3.68   1.50 m   nr
6.3.69   1.75 m   nr

         with taper piece and shaft 675 mm diameter, depth from cover to invert
6.3.70   2.00 m   nr
6.3.71   2.50 m   nr
6.3.72   3.00 m   nr
6.3.73   3.50 m   nr
6.3.74   4.00 m   nr

| INTERNAL DIAMETER OF MANHOLE | | | Item nr |
1350 mm £	1500 mm £	1800 m £	
557.00	658.00	864.00	6.3.65
627.00	734.00	956.00	6.3.66
696.00	813.00	1,056.00	6.3.67
769.00	890.00	1,150	6.3.68
835.00	965.00	1,242	6.3.69
1,024.00	1,211	1,453	6.3.70
1,169	1,323	1,655	6.3.71
1,297	1,465	1,837	6.3.72
1,418	1,600	2,012	6.3.73
1,536	1,738	2,185	6.3.74

Spon's Estimating Costs Guide to Roofing

Bryan Spain

Especially written for contractors and small businesses carrying out small works, Spon's Estimating Costs Guide to Roofing contains accurate information on thousands of rates, each broken down to labour, material overheads and profit.

This is the first book to include typical project costs for slating and tiling, sheeting, cladding and other coverings, rooflights, underfelt and battens, repairs and alterations, and different sized houses.

More than just a price book, it gives easy-to-read, professional advice on setting up and running a business including help on producing estimates faster, and keeping estimates accurate and competitive.

Suitable for any size firm from one-man-band to established business, this book contains valuable commercial and cost information that contractors can't afford to be without.

March 2005: 216x138 mm: 304 pages
PB: 0-415-34412-3: £24.99

To Order: Tel: +44 (0) 1264 343071 Fax: +44 (0) 1264 343005, or
Post: Taylor and Francis Customer Services, Thomson Publishing Services, Cheriton House, Andover, Hants, SP10 5BE, UK Email: book.orders@tandf.co.uk

For a complete listing of all our titles visit :
www.sponpress.com

Taylor & Francis
Taylor & Francis Group plc

Cost Limits and Allowances

Information given under this heading is based upon the cost targets currently in force for buildings financed out of public funds, i.e., hospitals, schools and public authority housing. The information enables the cost limit for a scheme to be calculated and is not intended to be a substitute for estimates prepared from drawings and specifications.

The cost limits are generally set as target costs based upon the user accommodation. However ad-hoc additions can be agreed with the relevant Authority in exceptional circumstances.

The documents setting out cost targets are almost invariably complex and cover a range of differing circumstances. They should be studied carefully before being applied to any scheme; this study should preferably be undertaken in consultation with a Chartered Quantity Surveyor.

HOSPITAL BUILDINGS

The index level for all business' cases for all health buildings is now set at a Median Index of Public Sector Building Tender Prices (MIPS) Variation of Price (VOP) index level of 385 with a Firm Price (FP) differential allowance of 2.6% increase on the VOP level, that is, a Firm Price (FP) index level of 395. The effective date for these increased allowances was 1 October 2003.

Both the Cost Allowances (DCAGs) and the Equipment Cost Allowance Guides (ECAGs) are now included in version 1.0 of the Health Capital Investment (HCI) document, issued in March 1997. This supersedes previous publications including version 13 of the Concise 4D/DCAG database.

"Quarterly Briefing" is now the official document for the notification of all new/revised DCAGs and ECAGs. Users should check Briefings issued from and including volume 13 no. 3 to ensure that all revisions to the HCI have been identified.

The NHS Estates has recently completed research into alternative indices for its Equipment Price Index, this was due to concerns that the index did not reflect market conditions as it had not been effectively maintained over the past few years. The result has been the development of a new equipment price index which reflects more accurately the market indicators for equipment.

The new index is a combination of various sources of information. This includes taking into consideration equipment-specific indices issued by the NHS Executive, namely the Health Service Cost Index, the retail price index and a general construction materials index. The combination of all this produces a new index series which reflects price movement and inflationary effects specifically associated with equipment.

The new equipment price index is set at 1997 = 100.

The ECAGs in the HCI document result from a complete revision of existing cost guidance and therefore supersede all previous equipment cost guidance.

During the calculation of capital costs for business cases, consideration must be given to the date when the equipment is likely to be purchased in relation to the construction tender index base date. This is the base date that the capital costs are adjusted to once a business case has been approved. Most equipment is likely to be purchased near the end of a building contract and will therefore have a later base date than the construction date.

Further advice can be obtained from NHS Estates (see Useful Addresses for Further Information on page 983).

EDUCATIONAL BUILDINGS (Procedures and Cost Guidance)

In January 1986 the then Department of Education and Science introduced new procedures for the approval of educational building projects.

In its Administrative Memorandum 1/86 and subsequent letter AB13/12/028, dated 12 November 1991, the Department currently requires detailed individual approval only for projects costing £2 million and over. Minor works i.e., costing less than £200,000, require no approval except where the authority requires such or where statutory notices are involved. Projects of £200,000, up to £2 million require approval which will be given automatically upon the submission of particulars of the scheme and performance data relating to it.

EDUCATIONAL BUILDINGS

The Department for Education and Employment publishes information on costs and performance data for school building projects.

Building Guide Costs

The Building Guide Costs are intended to provide reasonable and achievable target costs for use in the cost planning of new schools and extensions. The values relate to median values between middle and lower quartile costs in LEA projects.

The Building Guide Costs relate to a DTI PUBSEC indicative index of 160 at Q1 2005 national average price levels.

The values exclude the cost of:

- 'Abnormal' substructure costs (i.e. the proportion of the total substructure costs over £78/m² at Q1 2005 prices).
- External works.
- Furniture and fittings whether built-in or loose.
- Equipment, whether fixed or loose.
- ICT infrastructure or hardware.
- Professional Fees and VAT.

If used as the basis for project cost planning, the values should be adjusted to take account of tender date, location and contract size factors. Other factors affecting cost will include design, specification and site conditions. The guide values for primary and secondary extensions are intended to relate to projects providing an average mix of accommodation types. Actual costs may therefore be higher in schemes providing disproportionately more specialist accommodation.

The Building Guide Costs may be adjusted to reflect tender price movements by reference to DETR's PUBSEC index. It is suggested that adjustments for location and contract size may be made by reference to factors published by the RICS's Building Cost Information Service.

The table below provides indicative unit costs for both the primary and secondary sectors. The Department intends to use these values for reference when scrutinising cost standards in grant-aided school projects, PFI Outline Business Cases, Academies and Targeted Capital Funding.

Building Guide Costs per m² at Q1 2005 prices
(Relating to DETR PUBSEC indicative index 160)
(NOTE: DETR PUBSEC indicative index 1995 = 100)

Primary School Projects	£1,226/m²
Secondary School Projects	£1,226/m²

HOUSING ASSOCIATION SCHEMES

Grant rates 2004/05 and 205/06 and other current literature is available from The Housing Corporation, 149 Tottenham Court Road, London, W1P 7BN. Tel: 0207 393 2000. Fax: 0207 393 2111 Email: enquiries@housingcorp.gsx.gov.uk . With the permission of the Housing Corporation and for the benefit of readers, the main TCI system has been reproduced here in full

The Housing Corporation advises associations of:

    (i)   the Total Cost Indicators, and grant rates effective from 1 April 2004.

    (ii)   the grant rates applicable for 2004/05 and 2005/06 approvals for mixed and publicly funded schemes for rent and housing for sale schemes approved under the Housing Act 1988 and funded by the Housing Corporation or by local authorities.

Please direct enquiries about the contents of these Guidance Notes to Regional offices of the Corporation.

TOTAL COST INDICATORS 2004/05 AND 2005/06 GUIDANCE NOTES

INTRODUCTION

These guidance notes are designed to explain the use of Total Cost Indicators (TCI), grant rates, and administrative allowances in the Social Housing Grant (SHG) funding framework. They are intended to help registered social landlords complete scheme submissions. The notes are effective from 1 April 2004.

FUNDAMENTAL CHANGES FROM 2003/04 TCI

Two-year applicability
The Corporation has invited new bids for the two-year period 2004/05 and 2005/06. Therefore the TCI framework outlined in these TCI guidance notes and the accompanying TCI tables will form the basis of assessment for both 2004/05 and 2005/06. No intermediate adjustments are planned.

TCI enhancements for individual local authorities
Following detailed discussions with Government Departments, including H M Treasury, concerning the need for additional outputs and the desire to maintain a more stable cost framework, it has been decided to retain the 2003/04 TCI tables as the basis for future adjustments. Cost groupings will remain unchanged and TCI base tables, key and supplementary multipliers and key and supplementary on-costs are published at unchanged levels. The opportunity has been taken to correct a number of minor errors contained in the 2003/04 TCI tables, but otherwise the tables remain as last year.

However, to take account of forecast cost movements in 2004/05, that may differ not only by cost group but also by local authority, the TCI base tables 1.4 and 1.5 are subject to specific uplifts of between +5% and +15%. The relevant enhancement percentages applicable to individual local authorities are contained within table 1.12.

Homebuy
The principle changes are as follows:
1. Value Limits no longer apply to Homebuy purchases
2. Two new categories of Homebuy have been introduced to complement the traditional Homebuy option, namely:
   - • Key Worker Homebuy (Market Purchase).
   - • London Challenge Key Teacher Homebuy (Market Purchase).
3. Following piloting within the 2003/04 Challenge Fund programme, a related option of Newbuild Homebuy has been mainstreamed to operate within the TCI framework.
4. The eligibility criteria, operating procedures and allowances vary according to the category.

VPG and RTA discount levels
The discount levels remain unchanged. The relevant cost group headings have been amended to reflect the fact that the unchanged six cost groups now apply only to VPG/RTA discount levels and no longer apply to Homebuy.

HOUSING ASSOCIATION SCHEMES

FUNDAMENTAL CHANGES FROM 2003/04 TCI – cont'd

LA DIYSO
Withdrawn.

Administrative allowances and expenses
These remain unchanged and fixed. The local authority enhancements to the TCI base tables do not apply to administrative allowances and expenses.

EXPLANATION OF TCI

A key objective of the funding system is to achieve value for money in return for grant, and to ensure the correct level of grant is paid. TCI form the basis of this system, and are divided into unit type and cost group area categories.

TCI's apply equally to units funded with Social Housing Grant (SHG) by the Housing Corporation, or those sponsored by a local authority.

TCIs represent the basis for a cost evaluation of SHG funded units. TCI are also used to calculate the maximum level of grant or other public subsidy payable.

Key and supplementary multipliers are applied to the base TCIs to allow for scheme variations as outlined in the multiplier tables (tables 1.6 to 1.9 and table 1.12).

TYPES OF ACCOMMODATION

Different types of accommodation other than self-contained housing for general needs are classified as follows:

Accommodation for older people

i.   Category 1 - self-contained accommodation for the more active older person, which may (optional) include an element of support and/or additional communal facilities;

ii. Category 2 - self-contained accommodation for the less active older person, which includes an element of support and the full range of communal facilities;

     The term 'sheltered' is used generally to describe Category 1 and Category 2 schemes;

iii. Frail older people - extra care accommodation, which may be either shared or self-contained, for the frail older person. Includes the full range of communal facilities, plus additional special features, including wheelchair user environments and supportive management.

Shared accommodation

Accommodation predominantly for single persons, which includes a degree of sharing between tenants of some facilities (e.g. kitchens, bathrooms, living room) and may include an element of support and/or additional communal facilities.

Supported housing

Accommodation, which may be either shared or self-contained, designed to meet the needs of particular user groups requiring intensive housing management (see the Housing Corporation's 'The Guide to Supported Housing'). Such accommodation may also include additional communal facilities.

HOUSING ASSOCIATION SCHEMES

Accommodation for wheelchair users

Accommodation, which may be either shared or self-contained, designed for independent living by people with physical disabilities and wheelchair users. Where such accommodation is incorporated within schemes containing communal facilities, these facilities should be wheelchair accessible.

Communal facilities

Ancillary communal accommodation, the range of which comprises:

    i.   Common room - consisting of common room/s of adequate size to accommodate tenants and occasional visitors, chair storage and kitchenette for tea-making

    ii.   Associated communal facilities - consisting of warden's office, laundry room and   guest room.

TREATMENT OF COMBINED SUPPORTED HOUSING AND GENERAL NEEDS SCHEMES

Arrangements exist which allow the combination of supported housing and general needs units within a single scheme.

TEMPORARY HOUSING

Temporary Social Housing (TSH) Grant is a term used to describe SHG paid to registered social landlords (RSLs) to cover the cost of bringing properties into temporary use.

Properties are eligible for TSH Grant if they are available for use by the RSL for a period of time covered by a lease or licence for not less than two years and not more than 29 years.

A capital grant contribution will be available towards initial acquisition costs or periodic lease charges up to a grant maximum. The maxima are based upon the Housing Corporation's own assessment of what constitutes a reasonable contribution to the capitalised lease value. This is calculated using capitalised lease premium factors.

The *TSH multipliers and capitalised lease premium factor tables for 2004/05* (tables 1.09 and 1.10) *are* included in this guidance.

THE COMPOSITION OF TCI

TCI comprise the following elements:

Acquisition
    i.   Purchase price of land/property.
Works
    i.   Main works contract costs (including where applicable adjustments for additional claims and fluctuations, but excluding any costs defined as on-costs below) (see note below).
    ii.   major site development works rehabilitation (where applicable). These include piling, soil stabilisation, road/sewer construction, major demolition;
    iii. major pre-works (rehabilitation) where applicable;
    iv. statutory agreements, associated bonds and party wall agreements (including all fees and charges directly attributable to such works) where applicable;
    v.   additional costs associated with complying with archaeological works and party wall agreement awards (including all fees, charges and claims attributable to such works) where applicable;
    vi. home loss and associated costs. This applies to new build only;
    vii. VAT on the above, where applicable.
On-Costs
    i.   Legal fees, disbursements and expenses;
    ii.   stamp duty;
    iii. net gains/losses via interest charges on development period loans;

HOUSING ASSOCIATION SCHEMES

THE COMPOSITION OF TCI – cont'd

iv.   building society or other valuation and administration fees;

v.   fees for building control and planning permission;

vi.   fees and charges associated with compliance with European Community directives, and the Housing Corporation's requirements relating to energy rating of dwellings and Housing Quality Indicators;

vii.   in-house or external consultants' fees, disbursements and expenses (where the development contract is a design and build contract) (see below);

viii. insurance premiums including building warranty and defects/liability insurance (except contract insurance included in works costs);

ix.   contract performance bond premiums;

x.   borrowing administration charges (including associated legal and valuation fees);

xi.   an appropriate proportion of the RSL's development and administration costs (formerly Acquisition and Development allowances), excluding Co-operative Promotional Allowance (CPA) and Special Projects Promotion Allowances (SPPA) and including an appropriate proportion of any abortive scheme costs;

xii.   furniture, loose fittings and furnishings;

xiii. home loss and disturbance payments for rehabilitation;

xiv. preliminary minor site development works (new build), pre-works (rehabilitation), and minor works (off-the-shelf) and minor works and repairs in connection with existing satisfactory purchases;

xv.   marketing costs - for sale schemes only;

xvi. post completion interest - for sale schemes only;

xvii. legal, administrative and related fees and costs associated with negotiating and arranging leases for TSH only;

xviii. VAT on the above, where applicable.

Note:

Where the development contract is design and build, the on-costs are deemed to include the builder's design fee element of the contract sum. Therefore the amount included by the builder for design fees should be deducted from the works cost element submitted by the RSL to the Housing Corporation.

Similarly, other non-works costs that may be included by the builder such as fees for building and planning permission, building warranty and defects/liability insurance, contract performance bond and energy rating of dwellings should also be deducted from the works cost element submitted by the RSL to the Housing Corporation.

The Housing Corporation will subsequently check compliance through its compliance audit framework.

EXPLANATION OF ON-COSTS

TCI are inclusive of on-costs contained in the relevant on-cost table. The on-costs vary according to TCI cost group and the general purpose of the scheme. TCI levels are set with the assumption that the RSL's development and administrative costs will be contained within the percentages in the relevant on-cost table.

In order to allow a proper comparison between the total eligible costs and the relevant TCI it is necessary to add the percentage on-cost (from the relevant table) to the estimated eligible final costs of acquisition and works.

Major repairs schemes and adaptation schemes are not measured against TCIs. However, on-costs (from the relevant table) should be added to such schemes. Supplementary on-costs may not be used in any circumstances in connection with major repairs or adaptation schemes.

SELECTION OF ON-COSTS

One key on-cost will apply per scheme. To this should be added any appropriate supplementary on-cost. Supplementary on-costs may be used when the accommodation is designed to meet the relevant standards set out in the Housing Corporation publication Scheme Development Standards (latest version, August 2003) including the enhancements, applicable from April 2004, notified in the Guide to the Allocation Process (GTAP) 2004/05.

HOUSING ASSOCIATION SCHEMES

The appropriate key or supplementary on-cost is determined by the predominant dwelling type in a scheme. Predominance is established, where necessary, by the largest number of persons in total. Where two key on-costs or two supplementary on-costs are equally applicable (e.g. supported housing and shared), the higher should be used.

TRANCHES

For units developed under the Housing Act 1996, a set percentage of approved grant can be paid once a unit reaches certain key development stages. These grant payments are known as tranches.

The key stages are:
    i.   exchange of purchase contracts (ACQ);
    ii.   start on site of main contract works (SOS); this is deemed to be the date when the contractor took possession of the site/property in accordance with the signed main building contract;
    iii.   practical completion of the scheme (PC).

Where a *public subsidy* is given by way of discounted land, (acquisition public subsidy), the whole subsidy is deducted from the first tranche; any excess balance should be deducted from the second tranche. This is to ensure that grant is not paid in advance of need. In other circumstances any other public subsidy will be deducted from each tranche on a pro-rata basis. In the case of *land inclusive packages* the first and second tranches are paid together at start on site stage.

Tranche details for Special Project Promotion Allowances (SPPA) and Co-op Promotion Allowances (CPA), together with further guidance relating to tranches for management contracting arrangements, can be found in the Capital Funding Guide.

The grant on outstanding mortgages for re-improvement schemes will be paid in accordance with the tranche percentage for the scheme. All tranche payments may be paid directly to RSLs rather than via solicitors.

THE USE OF THE TCI BASE TABLE

The unit size in square metres shown in the *TCI base table 2004/05 self-contained accommodation* (table 1.4) relates to the total floor area of the unit. The probable occupancy figure in the tables is only a guideline figure. The number of occupants is derived from the total number of bed spaces provided.

The TCI for a unit where the total floor area exceeds 120m^2 will be the cost of a unit of 115 - 120m^2 plus for each additional 5m^2 or part thereof, the difference between the cost of a 110 - 115m^2 unit, and the cost of a 115 - 120m^2 unit. For practical purposes the unit size calculation limit has been set at a 345 – 350m^2 unit.

In selecting the appropriate TCI floor area band the actual floor area should first be rounded to the nearest whole number. This rounded number must then be used to select the TCI floor area band.

                  For example
                  actual floor area = 40.2m²
                  actual floor area rounded = 40m²
                  selected floor area band = >35 – 40m²

                  You must not make the *wrong* assumption that 40.2m² falls into the range ">40 – 45m²"
                  because 40.2m² must be first rounded to 40m² which falls into the range ">35 – 40m²"

For self-contained accommodation

Self-contained units provide each household, defined as a tenancy, with all their basic facilities behind their own lockable front door.

For self-contained units the base TCI is determined by its total floor area and the cost group in which it is located. The dwelling floor area is determined by the area of each unit for the private use of a single household. Communal areas or any facilities shared by two or more households should be excluded. The total floor area of self-contained accommodation is measured to the finished internal faces of the main containing walls on each floor of the

HOUSING ASSOCIATION SCHEMES

THE USE OF THE TCI BASE TABLE – cont'd

accommodation and includes the space, on plan, taken up by private staircases, partitions, internal walls (but not 'party' or similar walls), chimney breasts, flues and heating appliances. It includes the area of tenants' internal and/or external essential storage space. It excludes:

  i.   any space where the height to the ceiling is less than 1.50m (e.g. areas in rooms with sloping ceilings, external dustbin enclosures);
  ii. any porch, covered way; etc., open to the air;
  iii. all balconies (private, escape and access) and decks;
  iv. non-habitable basements, attics, thermal buffer zones, conservatories or sheds;
  v.   external storage space in excess of 2.50m^2;
  vi. all space for purposes other than housing (e.g. garages, commercial premises etc.).

TCIs for Frail older persons dwellings should always be calculated as *self-contained* units even if they have some characteristic which are more typical of shared accommodation.

For shared accommodation
Shared accommodation is defined as one household (i.e. one tenancy or licence) which shares facilities (i.e. bathroom, kitchen) with other households. Each household sharing such accommodation may comprise more than one person. The base TCI for shared accommodation should be calculated separately to any self-contained accommodation in the scheme. The base TCI for shared accommodation is calculated on a per bed space basis and may include any staff with a residential tenancy for shared accommodation. Staff sleepover accommodation which is not subject to a tenancy is not regarded as a bed space for TCI purposes. The relevant base TCI cost for the cost group from the *TCI base table 2004/05: shared accommodation* (table 1.5) is used.

For TSH shared accommodation
The relevant floor area, for TCI and capitalised lease premium calculation purposes only, should be taken as the overall building gross floor area measured to the finished internal faces of the main containing walls all as otherwise described for self-contained units above, divided by the number of people sharing. This calculation will result in the correct band size per person sharing which will then be used to select the base figure from the TCI base table: self-contained (table 1.4). This figure should then be multiplied by the number of people sharing prior to applying the relevant TSH key and supplementary multipliers or capitalised lease premium factor.

SELECTION OF KEY MULTIPLIERS

Only one key multiplier can be used per unit. (See table 1.6)

New build acquisition and works is the basic key multiplier, hence its neutral value.

The *off-the-shelf* multiplier is used where new dwellings to a standard suitable for social housing letting are purchased, following inspection, from contractors/developers or their agents. The cost of any minor works required should be set against the on-cost allowance.

The *existing satisfactory* multiplier is used where existing dwellings of a standard and in a condition suitable for social housing letting are purchased, following inspection, from the second-hand property market. The cost of any minor works required should be set against the on-cost allowance.

The *purchase and repair* multiplier is used where existing dwellings are purchased, following inspection, from the property market which necessitate a degree of repair to bring them to a standard and condition suitable for social housing but not full rehabilitation. Purchase and repair classification will apply where the estimated repair/improvement costs of each dwelling exceed 1,500 but are less than £10,000.

The *works only* multiplier is used for accommodation which involves the development of land or property already in the RSL's ownership and for which no acquisition costs (other than basic legal charges) apply.

The *re-improvement* multiplier is used for dwellings which have already received some form of public/grant subsidy

HOUSING ASSOCIATION SCHEMES

and are now being rehabilitated. Re-improvement schemes are generally expected to be submitted no less than 15 years after a rehabilitation or 30 years after construction. It should be noted that the outstanding mortgage of the original works can be considered an eligible cost and will attract the grant rate applicable to the new scheme as a whole. The re-improvement key multiplier is linked to that of the Rehabilitation works only (vacant) multiplier rather than the Rehabilitation works only (tenanted) multiplier in order to reflect the average cost of provision..

The *TSH improved and unimproved vacant* multiplier is used for accommodation with a lease of between 2 & 29 yrs.

SELECTION OF SUPPLEMENTARY MULTIPLIERS

Table 1.7 is used for acquisition and works, off-the-shelf, existing satisfactory and purchase and repair schemes. Works only and re-improvement schemes types use the table 1.8. None of these supplementary multipliers are applicable to TSH schemes. Supplementary multipliers for TSH schemes are in table 1.9.

Supplementary multipliers can be applied to new build and rehabilitation units when the accommodation is designed to meet the relevant standards set out in the Housing Corporation publication Scheme Development Standards (August 2003) including the enhancements, applicable from April 2004, notified in the Guide to the Allocation Process (GTAP) 2004/05.

More than one supplementary multiplier can be used per unit. However certain combinations of multipliers are invalid. Multipliers for sheltered, frail older people, supported housing and extended families cannot be combined. The matrix on (table 1.11) gives a comprehensive list of valid combinations of multipliers.

The main reason for combinations of multipliers being invalid is that the combination of those multipliers would lead to a duplication of the financial provision for the facilities accounted for in the multipliers. e.g. category 2 includes allowance for new lifts or single storey. This means that in these circumstances the other relevant multiplier does not apply i.e. a new lift or single storey multiplier cannot be used with a category 2 multiplier.

The *supported housing* multiplier and on-costs will only apply to schemes approved within the funding framework introduced in 1995. A scheme which is developed within this framework must be eligible to receive SHMG whether or not SHMG is actually being claimed for the scheme. Applications for approval of capital only supported housing schemes which utilise the supported housing multiplier must be accompanied by form TS1 (revenue budget). This multiplier should only be used where it is the RSL's plan to use the accommodation to provide supported housing in the long term.

Supported housing schemes with shared facilities cannot be combined with either of the three common room multipliers of the supplementary multiplier table.

The supported housing multiplier cannot be used for staff units.

The appropriate *shared* supplementary multiplier is determined by the total number of bed spaces provided within all of the households sharing facilities in the scheme. Where a cluster (i.e. more than one) of shared accommodation is provided the appropriate shared supplementary multiplier is determined by the total number of bed spaces contained within the households comprising each independent and self sufficient shared accommodation arrangement. The *TCI base table: shared accommodation (table 1.5)* is deemed to include all communal and ancillary facilities.

The shared multiplier does not apply to either sheltered or frail older people schemes.

The *extended families* multiplier is used when a self-contained dwelling is to cater for eight or more persons and additional or duplicate facilities i.e. kitchen and/or sanitary fittings/equipment are provided. The additional space requirement is accounted for in the size band selection. Where significant additional facilities are not provided the RSL should contact the relevant local office of the Corporation to receive confirmation that the extended families multiplier may be applied.

The *served by new lifts* multiplier is used when new vertical passenger lift provision is incorporated for access to dwelling entrances and communal accommodation. The multiplier does not apply to dwellings with entrances at ground floor level unless, exceptionally, the scheme includes essential communal accommodation provided at a level other than at ground floor level.

HOUSING ASSOCIATION SCHEMES

SELECTION OF SUPPLEMENTARY MULTIPLIERS – cont'd

The *wheelchair with individual carport* multiplier should be used only with individual self-contained dwellings designed in accordance with the relevant standards set out in the Housing Corporation publication Scheme Development Standards. Where non-individual self-contained wheelchair user dwellings are provided e.g. on some category 2 schemes, or where a waiver for non-compliance with the carport provisions has been obtained from the local office, the wheelchair without individual carport multiplier should be used. The wheelchair multipliers are intended to cover the costs of providing housing to suit a range of wheelchair users.

The *wheelchair* multiplier does not allow for any fixed additional equipment for people with disabilities; these needs should be met via the adaptations funding framework.

The *parent with children refuges* multiplier applies to shared accommodation specifically designed to meet the needs of parent with children, including vulnerable women with babies and women and children at risk of domestic violence. The TCI is calculated on a per bed space basis with children counted as full bed spaces. The provision of additional bunk-bed spaces should be disregarded for TCI calculation purposes.

The *housing for sale* multiplier is used for all sale schemes. It cannot be used with the supported housing or shared multipliers.

The *rehabilitation pre-1919 properties* multiplier is used where the scope of the refurbishment or conversion work is carried out on a property or properties originally constructed prior to 1919. It cannot be used in connection with existing satisfactory or purchase and repair multipliers.

The *no VAT rehabilitation* multiplier is used when the scope of the refurbishment or conversion work is such that the relevant local Customs and Excise office determines that VAT is not chargeable on the works.

The *rural housing* multiplier is used for schemes identified by rural investment codes R, G and F. Rural areas mainly comprise those with 1,000 or less inhabitants. Exceptionally, the limit may be extended to 3,000 inhabitants on a case by case basis by the relevant regional office of the Housing Corporation. (See the Housing Corporation's Guide to the Allocations Process, for details of population settlements, the Housing Corporation's Rural Settlements Gazetteer, last published in 1998).

The *national park* multiplier may be applied to any scheme within a formally designated national park or formally designated area of outstanding beauty. It may be used in conjunction with the rural housing multiplier. A listing of the recognised areas is set out in table 1.13.

The *sustainability* multiplier has been introduced to encourage RSLs towards greater sustainability. In order to qualify for the 1.01 multiplier, two separate aspects must be addressed:

i.   greening - in pursuit of the government's stated policy of increasing energy efficiency and reducing levels of CO_2 in the atmosphere, an 'Eco-Home rating of 'Good' (second level) must be certified;

ii.   security - Secured by Design certification must be obtained for the scheme.

The *adaptability* multiplier is intended to encourage RSLs to design homes with lofts that may be readily adapted to provide additional habitable space. In order to qualify for the 1.02 multiplier the following features must be present:

i.   a clear loft area of a size and height that will satisfy planning requirements to accommodate a single bedroom;

ii.   loft floor joists size for floor loading;

iii. loft floor trimmed for new staircase;

iv.   landing layout and size that will accommodate a new access to the converted loft;

HOUSING ASSOCIATION SCHEMES

    v.   a bedroom sized gable window, dormer window or opening roof light.

The *construction clients' charter* multiplier is intended to recognise the additional expense involved in setting up and maintaining 'charter' status as supported by the Government and encouraged for all agencies and associated organisations in receipt of public funds. In order to qualify for the supplementary on-cost and associated multiplier, the RSL must be able to satisfy and comply with either the RSL group 'Clients' Charter' or the new 'Mini-Charter' criteria as appropriate. The 'Mini-Charter' is intended for RSLs with small or occasional development programmes. Details of qualifying criteria and useful links are set out in the Guide to the Allocation Process (GTAP) 2003/2004 (see also www.clientsuccess.org).

The P&R/ESP multiplier is intended to address the extremes of imbalance between base TCI and dwelling prices. The levels of the P&R and ESP key multipliers are linked to the TCI/dwelling price differences in each cost group. HOUSING ASSOCIATION SCHEMES – cont'd

SELECTION OF SUPPLEMENTARY MULTIPLIERS – cont'd

The supplementary multiplier adjusts TCI's at an individual local authority level. The P&R/ESP multipliers for each local authority area is set out in table 1.12.

The *TSH* supplementary multiplier is used for all schemes with a lease length of between two and 29 years requiring works, (see table 1.9) and it can only be used with the TSH shared supplementary multiplier. It does not apply to improved TSH schemes.

Note: Where a RSL is in any doubt concerning the appropriateness of the application of any supplementary multiplier, it is advised to seek advice from the relevant local office of the Corporation. RSLs should also ensure that relevant information relating to the appropriateness of the application of supplementary multipliers is maintained on file for compliance audit purposes.

CALCULATION OF MAXIMUM GRANT CONTRIBUTION TO LEASE COSTS

The factors in table 1.10 are used to calculate maximum grant contributions for lease premiums outside the normal TCI framework. Whilst the factors are applied to the appropriate figures in the TCI base table and the relevant TSH key multiplier to determine the maximum contribution, any grant paid is additional to that paid in respect of works costs, which is subject to separate value for money assessment using the TCI multipliers. The grant payment will be calculated according to the actual cost of the lease premium.

The above factors should be used only in conjunction with the *TCI base table for 2004/05: self-contained accommodation* (table 1.4) and the relevant TSH key multiplier. The resultant value reflects the maximum grant contribution towards any capitalised lease premium payable to acquire the lease. No other factors or supplementary multipliers apply. The on-costs associated with setting up the lease are included within the TCI element of eligible costs. The different principles underlying the calculation of TCI for self-contained accommodation and for shared accommodation apply equally to the calculation of capitalised lease premiums.

HOUSING ASSOCIATION SCHEMES

GRANT RATES 2003/2004 GUIDANCE NOTES

INTRODUCTION

In its 'Guide to Social Rents' published in December 2000, the Government set out the formula for calculating restructured (or target) rents. Rents will be set partly in relation to a property's value (30% weight) and partly in relation to local earnings (70% weight), with the latter component multiplied by a bedroom weighting factor. Restructured rents on newly provided property will be phased in accordance with individual RSL's rent plans.

Grant rates are based on scheme specific rents. The Corporation provides a grant rate calculator which will enable RSLs to calculate the maximum eligible grant rate for each bid.

The calculator is made available to RSLs on an Excel spreadsheet which can be downloaded from the HC website.

EXPLANATION OF GRANT RATES

Grant rates apply equally to units funded with Social Housing Grant (SHG) by the Housing Corporation and to those sponsored by a local authority.

Grant rates represent the maximum proportion of scheme costs which will be funded by any form of public subsidy including SHG. (Public subsidy in this context is defined in general 6 of the capital Funding Guide). Where a scheme gets public subsidy from sources other than SHG, the maximum amount of SHG payable is reduced pound for pound.

The grant percentages determined by the calculator represent the maxima which may be paid. Grant paid to RSLs will be based upon the lower of the amount allocated in response to bids or the amount produced by the calculator.

REVISIONS TO THE GRANT RATE CALCULATOR

The grant rate calculator has been adapted for 2004/05 and 2005/06 to enable both social rent and intermediate grant rate calculations using one and the same model. The differences between the calculations is explained in the 'Guide to the Allocation Process' available on the Corporation's website.

COST GROUP AREAS

The local authority area in which a scheme is located defines the cost group for the scheme. A list of the local authority areas in each cost group is included in table 1.12.

SCHEMES FOR RENT

The calculator will provide a maximum eligible grant rate for each unit type included within a bid base on values, incomes, TCI and standard outgoings (management, maintenance, void, major repairs and loan costs). These rates for each unit type will be aggregated to produce a maximum eligible grant rate for each bid.

SCHEMES FOR SALE

For all shared ownership schemes, prospective rents, as if renting, are needed from which the calculator will produce maximum eligible grant rates for rent. The calculator then applies the appropriate factor to the result from table 2.1 to calculate the grant appropriate to the sale scheme.
Home buy value limits, Voluntary Purchase Grant and Right to Acquire discount amounts, and Local Authority Do-it-Yourself Shared Ownership value limits are shown in tables 2.2, 2.3 and 2.4.

GRANT CALCULATIONS AND COST OVER-RUNS

All schemes

Projects above TCI for rent or sale will be subject to value for money assessment. Schemes will not be approved at more than 110% of TCI.

HOUSING ASSOCIATION SCHEMES

Schemes for rent

For schemes for rent the maximum grant percentage is fixed at grant confirmation stage. Maximum grant entitlement calculated at this stage is estimated eligible cost x grant rate. The costs are reviewed at practical completion, and grant eligibility recalculated as eligible outturn cost x the original grant rate. For RSLs following the scheme contract funding route grant will not be paid on an outturn cost greater than 110% of TCS of the estimate at confirmation or 110% of TCI, whichever is the lower. RSLs following   the programme contract funding route will calculate grant eligibility on cost over-runs as above, but these will be funded from their grant pot or from their own resources, rather than by allocation of additional Housing Corporation resources.

Schemes for sale

For housing for sale schemes maximum grant eligibility is calculated at grant confirmation as:

Estimated eligible cost x grant rate x LCHO factor = grant in £

The grant is fixed at grant confirmation; it is not recalculated at practical completion.

Temporary Social Housing

Grant for Temporary Social Housing remains based on 100% for non-relifed and 70% for relifed shared unimproved properties. Please see section TSH-2 Grant Confirmation Properties whose life is extended (Re-lifed) in the Capital Funding Guide.

ADMINISTRATIVE ALLOWANCES

Position for 2004/05 and 2005/06

Administrative allowances and expenses remain at 2003/04 levels. The local authority enhancement percentages do not apply to administrative allowances and expenses.

HOUSING ASSOCIATION SCHEMES

Table 1.1: Key on-costs 2004/05 and 2005/06 by cost group

Key on-costs	A1 & A2 %	A3 %	A4 %	B1 %	B2 %	B3 %	C1 %	C2 %	C3 %	D1 %	D2 %	E %
a) New build												
i) acquisition and works	11	12	12	12	13	13	14	15	15	16	16	17
ii) off-the-shelf	8	8	8	8	8	8	8	8	8	8	8	8
iii) works only	17	17	17	17	17	17	17	17	17	17	17	17
b) Rehabilitation												
i) acquisition and works (vacant)	11	11	12	12	13	13	14	15	15	16	17	17
ii) acquisition and works (tenanted)	13	14	14	15	16	16	17	18	19	20	21	21
iii) existing satisfactory	9	9	9	9	9	9	9	9	9	9	9	9
iv) purchase and repair	10	10	10	10	10	10	10	10	10	10	10	10
v) RH works only (vacant)	22	22	22	22	22	22	22	22	22	22	22	22
vi) RH works only (tenanted)	26	26	26	26	26	26	26	26	26	26	26	26
vii) Re-improvements	22	22	22	22	22	22	22	22	22	22	22	22
viii) TSH (unimproved vacant)	21	21	21	21	21	21	21	21	21	21	21	21
ix) TSH (improved vacant)	10	10	10	10	10	10	10	10	10	10	10	10
c) Major repairs and miscellaneous works	25	25	25	25	25	25	25	25	25	25	25	25
d) Adaptation works	13	13	13	13	13	13	13	13	13	13	13	13

Table 1.2: Supplementary on-costs 2004/05 and 2005/06

Supplementary on-costs (all cost groups)	Purchase & Repair and Acquisition & Works %	Works only and re-improvements %	Off-the-Shelf existing satisfactory %
a) Sheltered with common room or communal facilities	2	3	1
b) Frail older persons	4	6	3
c) i) Supported housing	4	6	3
ii) Supported housing with Room or common facilities	5	7	4
d) Shared	5	7	5
e) Construction Clients' Charter	1	1	0
f) Housing for sale	4	6	5
g) Community self build	4	0	0
h) i) TSH shared unimproved	7		
ii) TSH shared improved	5		

HOUSING ASSOCIATION SCHEMES

Table 1.3: Grant payments for tranches 2004/05 and 2005/06
Tranche percentages

Scheme type	Cost groups	Acquisition & Works			Works only re-improvement		Off-the-shelf/ existing satis.	Purchase & repair	
		(i)	(ii)	(iii)	(i)	(ii)	(i)	(i) + (ii)	(iii)
Housing for rent									
Mixed funded: New build	All	40	40	20	65	35	100		
Mixed funded: Rehabilitation	All	50	30	20	60	40	100	80	20
100% SHG: New build	As, Bs & Cs	30	35	35	50	50	100		
100% SHG: New build	Ds & Es	20	35	45	45	55	100		
100% SHG: Rehabilitation	As, Bs & Cs	50	20	30	40	60	100	80	20
100% SHG: Rehabilitation	Ds & Es	45	20	35	35	65	100	80	20
TSH unimproved					65	35			
TSH improved							100		
Housing for sale									
Mixed funded: New build and rehabilitation	All	50	45	5	95	5	100	95	5

Table 1.4: TCI base table 2004/05 and 2005/06: self-contained accommodation

Total unit costs		All self-contained accommodation (including all frail older persons and TSH) £ per unit Cost Group											
Unit floor area	Probable Occupancy (persons)	A1 & A2	A3	A4	B1	B2	B3	C1	C2	C3	D1	D2	E1
Up To 25m²	1	£78,400	£70,100	£65,200	£60,600	£57,300	£53,100	£49,900	£47,300	£43,900	£41,800	£39,700	£36,900
Exceeding/not exceeding													
25-30m²	1 and 2	£89,200	£79,300	£73,400	£67,800	£63,900	£59,100	£55,200	£52,100	£48,300	£45,600	£43,200	£40,100
30-35m²	1 and 2	£100,000	£88,500	£81,600	£75,100	£70,600	£65,100	£60,600	£56,900	£52,600	£49,400	£46,600	£43,200
35-40m²	1 and 2	£110,800	£97,600	£89,800	£82,400	£77,300	£71,100	£65,900	£61,700	£56,900	£53,300	£50,100	£46,400
40-45m²	2	£121,600	£106,800	£98,000	£89,700	£84,000	£77,000	£71,100	£66,400	£61,200	£57,100	£53,600	£49,600
45-50m²	2	£132,400	£116,000	£106,200	£97,000	£90,600	£83,000	£76,600	£71,200	£65,500	£60,900	£57,100	£52,800
50-55m²	2 and 3	£143,200	£125,100	£114,500	£104,300	£97,300	£89,000	£81,900	£76,000	£69,800	£64,700	£60,600	£55,900
55-60m²	2 and 3	£154,000	£134,300	£122,700	£111,600	£104,000	£95,000	£87,200	£80,800	£74,100	£68,500	£64,100	£59,100
60-65m²	3 and 4	£164,800	£143,500	£130,900	£118,900	£110,600	£101,000	£92,500	£85,500	£78,400	£72,300	£67,600	£62,300
65-70m²	3 and 4	£175,600	£152,600	£139,100	£126,200	£117,300	£106,900	£97,900	£90,300	£82,700	£76,100	£71,100	£65,500
70-75m²	3,4 and 5	£186,400	£161,800	£147,300	£133,500	£124,000	£112,900	£103,200	£95,100	£87,000	£79,900	£74,500	£68,600
75-80m²	3,4 and 5	£197,200	£171,000	£155,500	£140,800	£130,700	£118,900	£108,500	£99,900	£91,300	£83,700	£78,000	£71,800
80-85m²	4,5 and 6	£208,000	£180,100	£163,700	£148,100	£137,300	£124,900	£113,900	£104,600	£95,600	£87,600	£81,500	£75,000
85-90m²	4,5 and 6	£218,800	£189,300	£171,900	£155,400	£144,000	£130,900	£119,200	£109,400	£99,900	£91,400	£85,000	£78,100
90-95m²	5 and 6	£229,600	£198,500	£180,200	£162,700	£150,700	£136,800	£124,500	£114,200	£104,200	£95,200	£88,500	£81,300
95-100m²	5 and 6	£240,400	£207,600	£188,400	£169,900	£157,400	£142,800	£129,800	£119,000	£108,500	£99,000	£92,000	£84,500
100-105m²	6 and 7	£251,200	£216,800	£196,600	£177,200	£164,000	£148,800	£135,200	£123,700	£112,800	£102,800	£95,000	£87,700
105-110m²	6 and 7	£262,000	£226,000	£204,800	£184,500	£170,700	£154,800	£140,500	£128,500	£117,100	£106,600	£99,000	£90,800
110-115m²	6,7 and 8	£272,700	£235,100	£213,000	£191,800	£177,400	£160,800	£145,800	£133,300	£121,400	£110,400	£102,400	£94,000
115-120m²	6,7 and 8	£283,500	£244,300	£221,200	£199,100	£184,100	£166,700	£151,200	£138,100	£125,700	£114,200	£105,900	£97,200

Note:
In selecting the appropriate TCI floor area band the actual floor area should first be rounded to the nearest whole number.
This rounded figure must then be used to select the TCI floor area band.
For example:
Actual floor area = 40.2m²
Actual floor area rounded = 40m²
Selected floor area band = >35-40m²
You must not make the wrong assumption that 40.2m² falls into the range 40-45m² because 40.2m² must be first rounded to 40m² which falls in the 35-4

HOUSING ASSOCIATION SCHEMES

Table 1.5: TCI base table 2004/05 and 2005/06 shared accommodation

Total unit costs	All shared accommodation (except TSH) £ per person sharing Cost Group											
TCI per person	A1 & A2	A3	A4	B1	B2	B3	C1	C2	C3	D1	D2	E1
Each person bed space	£115,400	£100,000	£90,900	£82,400	£76,400	£69,600	£63,500	£61,200	£53,400	£49,000	£45,700	£42,000

Table 1.6: Key multiplier 2004/05 and 2005/06 by cost group
Note: only one of the following to be used

Scheme type	TCI calc. Form Line no.	Cost group											
		A1 & A2	A3	A4	B1	B2	B3	C1	C2	C3	D1	D2	E1
a) New build													
i) acquisition and works	0010	1.00	1.00	1.00	1.00	1.00	1.00	1.00	1.00	1.00	1.00	1.00	1.00
ii) off-the-shelf	0020	1.00	1.00	1.00	1.00	1.00	1.00	1.00	1.00	0.97	0.90	0.90	0.90
iii) works only	0090	0.46	0.50	0.53	0.58	0.60	0.64	0.68	0.73	0.76	0.83	0.86	0.89
b) Rehabilitation													
i) acquisition and works (vacant)	0100	1.18	1.16	1.17	1.17	1.16	1.15	1.15	1.15	1.15	1.14	1.15	1.15
i) acquisition and works (tenanted)	0105	1.08	1.08	1.08	1.08	1.07	1.07	1.07	1.06	1.07	1.09	1.09	1.09
ii) existing satisfactory	0120	1.08	1.24	1.17	1.20	1.15	1.07	1.01	0.97	0.95	0.94	0.94	0.94
iii) purchase and repair	0110	1.09	1.25	1.18	1.21	1.16	1.08	1.02	0.98	0.96	0.95	0.95	0.95
iv) works (vacant)	0125	0.43	0.47	0.50	0.54	0.57	0.60	0.64	0.69	0.72	0.78	0.81	0.83
iv) works only (tenanted)	0130	0.44	0.48	0.51	0.56	0.58	0.62	0.66	0.71	0.74	0.80	0.84	0.86
v) re-improvements	0135	0.43	0.47	0.50	0.54	0.57	0.60	0.64	0.69	0.72	0.78	0.81	0.83
c) TSH													
i) vacant improved	0030	1.18	1.16	1.17	1.17	1.16	1.15	1.15	1.15	1.15	1.14	1.15	1.15
ii) vacant unimproved	0035	1.18	1.16	1.17	1.17	1.16	1.15	1.15	1.15	1.15	1.14	1.15	1.15

HOUSING ASSOCIATION SCHEMES

Table 1.7: Supplementary multipliers for acquisition and works, off-the-shelf, existing satisfactory and purchase and repair schemes only 2004/05 and 2005/06

Scheme type	TCI calc. Form Line no.	Cost group											
		A1 & A2	A3	A4	B1	B2	B3	C1	C2	C3	D1	D2	E
Sheltered Cat 1	0140	1.00	1.00	1.00	1.00	1.00	1.00	1.00	1.00	1.00	1.00	1.00	1.00
Sheltered Cat 2	0170	1.24	1.26	1.28	1.3	0.31	1.33	1.35	1.37	1.4	1.4	1.42	1.42
Frail elderly	0180	1.38	1.41	1.44	1.46	1.49	1.51	1.54	1.57	1.63	1.62	1.65	1.66
Special needs	0186	1.14	1.15	1.16	1.17	1.17	1.18	1.19	1.2	1.22	1.22	1.22	1.23
Extended general family	0195	1.07	1.08	1.08	1.09	1.1	1.1	1.11	1.12	1.13	1.14	1.15	1.15
Shared 2-3	0200	1.00	1.00	1.00	1.00	1.00	1.00	1.00	1.00	1.00	1.00	1.00	1.00
Shared 4-6	0210	0.88	0.88	0.88	0.88	0.88	0.88	0.88	0.88	0.88	0.88	0.88	0.88
Shared 7-10	0220	0.79	0.79	0.79	0.79	0.79	0.79	0.79	0.79	0.79	0.79	0.79	0.79
Shared 11+	0235	0.74	0.74	0.74	0.74	0.74	0.74	0.74	0.74	0.74	0.74	0.74	0.74
Served by new lifts	0245	1.06	1.06	1.06	1.07	1.07	1.08	1.08	1.09	1.09	1.1	1.1	1.1
Single storey	0095	1.21	1.2	1.2	1.19	1.18	1.18	1.17	1.16	1.15	1.14	1.13	1.12
Common room only	0250	1.07	1.07	1.07	1.07	1.07	1.07	1.08	1.08	1.08	1.08	1.09	1.09
Associated communal facilities	0260	1.04	1.04	1.05	1.05	1.05	1.05	1.06	1.06	1.07	1.07	1.07	1.07
Common room and associated facilities	0270	1.11	1.11	1.12	1.12	1.12	1.12	1.14	1.14	1.15	1.15	1.16	1.16
Wheelchair with individual carport	0380	1.28	1.28	1.27	1.27	1.27	1.27	1.27	1.26	1.26	1.26	1.26	1.26
Wheelchair without individual carport	0385	1.07	1.07	1.08	1.08	1.09	1.09	1.1	1.11	1.11	1.12	1.13	1.13
Rural housing	0430	1.11	1.12	1.13	1.14	1.15	1.15	1.17	1.18	1.19	1.21	1.21	1.22
Construction 'Clients' Charter'	0460	1.01	1.01	1.01	1.01	1.01	1.01	1.01	1.01	1.01	1.01	1.01	1.01
Housing for sale	5100	1.03	1.03	1.03	1.03	1.03	1.03	1.03	1.03	1.03	1.03	1.03	1.03
Parents with children refuges	0420	0.75	0.75	0.75	0.75	0.75	0.75	0.75	0.75	0.75	0.75	0.75	0.75
Pre 1919 rehabilitation	0310	1.05	1.06	1.06	1.06	1.07	1.07	1.08	1.08	1.09	1.1	1.1	1.1
No VAT rehabilitation	0320	0.94	0.94	0.93	0.93	0.92	0.92	0.91	0.9	0.9	0.89	0.88	0.88
National Parks	0440	1.14	1.15	1.15	1.16	1.17	1.17	1.18	1.19	1.2	1.21	1.22	1.23
Adaptability – loft	0470	1.02	1.02	1.02	1.02	1.02	1.02	1.03	1.03	1.03	1.03	1.03	1.04
Sustainability	0450	1.01	1.01	1.01	1.01	1.01	1.02	1.02	1.02	1.02	1.02	1.02	1.02
P&R multiplier	0480	Please refer to Table 1.12 for individual local authority multiplier for this scheme type											
Community self build	0490	1.04	1.04	1.04	1.04	1.04	1.04	1.04	1.03	1.03	1.03	1.03	1.03

Notes: Shared categories refer to bed spaces per scheme/cluste; Shared categories cannot be used with 'frail older persons'

'Served with new lifts' cannot be used with 'frail older persons' or 'sheltered category 2'

'Single storey' is applicable to new build only and cannot be used with frail older person', 'sheltered category 2' or 'wheelchair with carport'

'Common room' is applicable to 'sheltered category 1 and 'self-contained supported housing' only

'Pre 1919 rehabilitation' cannot be used with 'ESP' or 'purchase and repair'

'Wheelchair without individual carport' needs a waiver from the local Corporation office when used

HOUSING ASSOCIATION SCHEMES

Table 1.8: Supplementary multipliers for works only re-improvement schemes only 2004/05 and 2005/06

Scheme type	TCI calc. Form Line no.	Cost group											
		A1 & A2	A3	A4	B1	B2	B3	C1	C2	C3	D1	D2	E1
Sheltered Cat 1	0140	1.00	1.00	1.00	1.00	1.00	1.00	1.00	1.00	1.00	1.00	1.00	1.00
Sheltered Cat 2	0170	1.48	1.49	1.48	1.50	1.49	1.48	1.48	1.49	1.48	1.46	1.47	1.47
Frail elderly	0180	1.77	1.77	1.76	1.76	1.77	1.75	1.73	1.75	1.76	1.72	1.73	1.74
Special needs	0186	1.28	1.28	1.28	1.28	1.27	1.26	1.26	1.26	1.27	1.25	1.25	1.26
Extended general family	0195	1.14	1.15	1.14	1.15	1.16	1.15	1.15	1.16	1.16	1.16	1.17	1.17
Shared 2-3	0200	1.00	1.00	1.00	1.00	1.00	1.00	1.00	1.00	1.00	1.00	1.00	1.00
Shared 4-6	0210	0.76	0.77	0.79	0.80	0.81	0.82	0.84	0.84	0.85	0.86	0.86	0.86
Shared 7-10	0220	0.58	0.60	0.64	0.65	0.67	0.69	0.71	0.73	0.75	0.76	0.76	0.76
Shared 11+	0235	0.48	0.51	0.55	0.57	0.59	0.62	0.65	0.66	0.69	0.70	0.71	0.71
Served by new lifts	0245	1.12	1.11	1.10	1.12	1.11	1.12	1.11	1.12	1.11	1.12	1.11	1.11
Single storey	0095	1.42	1.38	1.35	1.31	1.28	1.26	1.23	1.21	1.18	1.16	1.15	1.14
Common room only	0250	1.14	1.13	1.12	1.12	1.11	1.10	1.11	1.10	1.10	1.09	1.10	1.10
Associated communal facilities	0260	1.08	1.08	1.09	1.08	1.08	1.07	1.08	1.08	1.08	1.08	1.08	1.08
Common room and associated facilities	0270	1.22	1.21	1.21	1.20	1.19	1.18	1.19	1.18	1.18	1.17	1.18	1.18
Wheelchair with individual carport	0380	1.56	1.53	1.47	1.45	1.42	1.40	1.37	1.34	1.31	1.30	1.29	1.29
Wheelchair without individual carport	0385	1.14	1.13	1.14	1.13	1.14	1.13	1.14	1.14	1.13	1.14	1.15	1.15
Rural housing	0430	1.22	1.23	1.22	1.23	1.24	1.22	1.23	1.24	1.23	1.24	1.24	1.25
Construction 'Clients' Charter'	0460	1.02	1.02	1.02	1.02	1.02	1.01	1.01	1.01	1.01	1.01	1.01	1.01
Housing for sale	5100	1.06	1.06	1.05	1.05	1.05	1.04	1.04	1.04	1.04	1.03	1.03	1.03
Parents with children refuges	0420	0.50	0.53	0.57	0.59	0.61	0.63	0.66	0.67	0.70	0.71	0.72	0.72
Pre 1919 rehabilitation	0310	1.11	1.11	1.10	1.10	1.11	1.10	1.11	1.10	1.11	1.12	1.11	1.11
No VAT rehabilitation	0320	0.88	0.89	0.88	0.88	0.87	0.88	0.88	0.87	0.88	0.87	0.86	0.88
National Parks	0440	1.28	1.28	1.26	1.27	1.27	1.25	1.24	1.25	1.24	1.24	1.25	1.26
Adaptability – loft	0470	1.04	1.04	1.03	1.03	1.03	1.03	1.04	1.04	1.04	1.03	1.03	1.05
Sustainability	0450	1.02	1.02	1.02	1.02	1.03	1.03	1.03	1.03	1.03	1.02	1.02	1.02

Notes: Shared categories refer to bed spaces per scheme/cluster; Shared categories cannot be used with 'frail older persons'

'Served with new lifts' cannot be used with 'frail older persons' or 'sheltered category 2'

'Single storey' is applicable to new build only and cannot be used with frail older person', 'sheltered category 2' or 'wheelchair with carport'

'Common room' is applicable to 'sheltered category 1 and 'self-contained supported housing' only

Pre 1919 rehabilitation' cannot be used with 'ESP' or 'purchase and repair'

Wheelchair without individual carport' needs a waiver from the local Corporation office when used

'Parent with children' refuges' is applicable to 'shared general needs' and 'shared supported housing' only

Cost Limits and Allowances

HOUSING ASSOCIATION SCHEMES

Table 1.9: Supplementary multipliers (inclusive of on-costs) for temporary housing (TSH) 2004/05 and 2005/06

TSH term (years)	TCI calc. Form Line no.	Cost group											
		A1 & A2	A3	A4	B1	B2	B3	C1	C2	C3	D1	D2	E1
	4000												
29		0.36	0.39	0.42	0.46	0.48	0.51	0.54	0.59	0.61	0.67	0.69	0.71
28		0.35	0.39	0.41	0.45	0.47	0.50	0.54	0.58	0.60	0.66	0.68	0.70
27		0.35	0.38	0.41	0.44	0.47	0.50	0.53	0.57	0.60	0.65	0.67	0.69
26		0.34	0.38	0.40	0.44	0.46	0.49	0.52	0.57	0.59	0.64	0.66	0.68
25		0.34	0.37	0.40	0.43	0.46	0.48	0.52	0.56	0.58	0.63	0.66	0.67
24		0.33	0.36	0.38	0.42	0.44	0.47	0.50	0.54	0.57	0.61	0.64	0.65
23		0.32	0.35	0.37	0.41	0.43	0.46	0.49	0.53	0.55	0.60	0.62	0.63
22		0.31	0.34	0.36	0.40	0.42	0.44	0.47	0.51	0.53	0.58	0.60	0.62
21		0.30	0.33	0.35	0.39	0.40	0.43	0.46	0.50	0.52	0.56	0.58	0.60
20		0.29	0.32	0.34	0.37	0.39	0.42	0.45	0.48	0.50	0.55	0.57	0.58
19		0.28	0.31	0.33	0.36	0.38	0.40	0.43	0.47	0.49	0.53	0.55	0.56
18		0.28	0.30	0.32	0.35	0.37	0.39	0.42	0.45	0.47	0.52	0.53	0.55
17		0.27	0.30	0.31	0.34	0.36	0.38	0.41	0.44	0.46	0.50	0.52	0.53
16		0.26	0.29	0.30	0.33	0.35	0.37	0.40	0.43	0.45	0.49	0.50	0.52
15		0.25	0.28	0.30	0.32	0.34	0.36	0.39	0.42	0.43	0.47	0.49	0.50
14		0.22	0.24	0.26	0.28	0.30	0.31	0.34	0.36	0.38	0.41	0.42	0.44
13		0.19	0.21	0.22	0.24	0.26	0.27	0.29	0.32	0.33	0.36	0.37	0.38
12		0.17	0.18	0.19	0.21	0.22	0.24	0.25	0.27	0.29	0.31	0.32	0.33
11		0.14	0.16	0.17	0.19	0.20	0.21	0.22	0.24	0.25	0.27	0.28	0.29
10		0.13	0.14	0.15	0.16	0.17	0.18	0.19	0.21	0.22	0.24	0.24	0.25
9		0.12	0.14	0.15	0.16	0.17	0.18	0.19	0.21	0.21	0.23	0.24	0.25
8		0.12	0.13	0.14	0.16	0.16	0.17	0.18	0.20	0.21	0.23	0.24	0.24
7		0.12	0.13	0.14	0.15	0.16	0.17	0.18	0.20	0.21	0.23	0.23	0.24
6		0.12	0.13	0.14	0.15	0.16	0.17	0.18	0.20	0.20	0.22	0.23	0.24
5		0.10	0.11	0.12	0.13	0.14	0.14	0.15	0.17	0.17	0.19	0.20	0.20
4		0.09	0.10	0.10	0.11	0.12	0.12	0.13	0.14	0.15	0.16	0.17	0.17
3		0.07	0.08	0.08	0.09	0.09	0.10	0.10	0.11	0.12	0.13	0.13	0.14
2		0.05	0.06	0.06	0.07	0.07	0.08	0.08	0.09	0.09	0.10	0.10	0.11
TSH (shared) term (years)	4001												
2-29		1	1	1	1	1	1	1	1	1	1	1	1

HOUSING ASSOCIATION SCHEMES

Table 1.10: Capitalised leased premium factors for temporary housing (TSH) 2004/05 and 2005/06

TSH term (years)	TCI calc. Form Line no.	Cost group											
		A1 & A2	A3	A4	B1	B2	B3	C1	C2	C3	D1	D2	E
	N/a												
29		0.26	0.25	0.24	0.23	0.21	0.20	0.19	0.17	0.16	0.13	0.12	0.12
28		0.26	0.25	0.23	0.22	0.21	0.20	0.18	0.16	0.15	0.13	0.12	0.11
27		0.25	0.24	0.23	0.21	0.20	0.19	0.18	0.16	0.15	0.13	0.12	0.11
26		0.25	0.23	0.22	0.21	0.20	0.19	0.17	0.15	0.15	0.12	0.11	0.11
25		0.24	0.23	0.22	0.20	0.19	0.18	0.17	0.15	0.14	0.12	0.11	0.11
24		0.23	0.22	0.21	0.20	0.19	0.18	0.16	0.14	0.14	0.11	0.11	0.10
23		0.23	0.22	0.21	0.19	0.18	0.17	0.16	0.14	0.13	0.11	0.10	0.10
22		0.22	0.21	0.20	0.19	0.18	0.17	0.15	0.13	0.13	0.11	0.10	0.10
21		0.21	0.20	0.19	0.18	0.17	0.16	0.15	0.13	0.12	0.11	0.10	0.09
20		0.21	0.20	0.19	0.18	0.17	0.16	0.15	0.13	0.12	0.10	0.09	0.09
19		0.20	0.19	0.18	0.17	0.16	0.15	0.14	0.12	0.12	0.10	0.09	0.09
18		0.20	0.18	0.18	0.17	0.16	0.15	0.14	0.12	0.11	0.10	0.09	0.08
17		0.19	0.18	0.17	0.16	0.15	0.14	0.13	0.12	0.11	0.09	0.09	0.08
16		0.19	0.18	0.17	0.16	0.15	0.14	0.13	0.12	0.11	0.09	0.08	0.08
15		0.18	0.17	0.16	0.15	0.15	0.14	0.13	0.11	0.11	0.09	0.08	0.08
14		0.17	0.17	0.16	0.15	0.14	0.13	0.12	0.11	0.10	0.09	0.08	0.07
13		0.17	0.16	0.15	0.14	0.14	0.13	0.12	0.11	0.10	0.09	0.08	0.07
12		0.16	0.15	0.15	0.14	0.13	0.12	0.11	0.10	0.10	0.08	0.07	0.07
11		0.16	0.15	0.14	0.13	0.13	0.12	0.11	0.10	0.09	0.08	0.07	0.07
10		0.15	0.14	0.14	0.13	0.12	0.12	0.11	0.09	0.09	0.08	0.07	0.07
9		0.14	0.14	0.13	0.12	0.12	0.11	0.10	0.09	0.09	0.07	0.07	0.06
8		0.14	0.13	0.13	0.12	0.11	0.11	0.10	0.09	0.08	0.07	0.06	0.06
7		0.13	0.13	0.12	0.11	0.11	0.10	0.09	0.08	0.08	0.07	0.06	0.06
6		0.13	0.12	0.11	0.11	0.10	0.10	0.09	0.08	0.07	0.06	0.06	0.06
5		0.10	0.09	0.09	0.08	0.08	0.08	0.07	0.06	0.06	0.05	0.05	0.04
4		0.08	0.07	0.07	0.07	0.06	0.06	0.05	0.05	0.05	0.04	0.04	0.03
3		0.06	0.06	0.06	0.05	0.05	0.05	0.04	0.04	0.04	0.03	0.03	0.03
2		0.05	0.05	0.04	0.04	0.04	0.04	0.03	0.03	0.03	0.02	0.02	0.02

Cost Limits and Allowances

HOUSING ALLOWANCE SCHEMES

Table 1.11 : Valid combination of supplementary multipliers 2004/05 and 2005/06 (X INDICATES A VALID COMBINATION)

	CAT 1 0140	CAT 2 0170	FF 0180	SN 0186	ExFm 0195	SH23 0200	SH46 0210	SH 7-10 0220	SH11+ 0235	LIFT 0245	SS 0095	CR 0250	FAC 0260	CR&FC 0270	1919 0310	VAT 0320	WC+C 0360	WC 0385	PWCR 0420	HFS 5100	RH 0430	NP 0440	SUS 0450	CCC 0460	ADA 0470	P&R 0480	CSB 0490
CAT 1 0140																											
CAT 2 0170																											
FF 0180																											
SN 0186																											
ExFm 0195																											
SH23 0200																											
SH46 0210																											
SH 7-10 0220																											
SH11+ 0235																											
LIFT 0245																											
SS 0095																											
CR 0250																											
FAC 0260																											
CR&FC 0270																											
1919 0310																											
VAT 0320																											
WC+C 0360																											
WC 0385																											
PWCR 0420																											
HFS 5100																											
RH 0430																											
NP 0440																											
SUS 0450																											
CCC 0460																											
ADA 0470																											
P&R 0480																											
CSB 0490																											

HOUSING ASSOCIATION SCHEMES

Table 1.11 : Valid combination of supplementary multipliers 2004/05 and 2005/06 – cont'd

Key:

CAT 1	Category 1
CAT 2	Category 2
FE	Frail older person
SN	Supported housing
ExFam	Extended families
SH 23	Shared 2-3 bed spaces
SH 46	Shared 4-6 bed spaces
SH 710	Shared 7-10 bed spaces
SH 11+	Shared 11+ bed spaces
LIFT	Served by new lifts
SS	Single Storey
SUS	Sustainability
CCC	Construction 'Clients' Charter'
ADA	Adaptability
CR	Common room
FAC	Common room associated communal facilities only
CR&FC	Common room and communal facilities
1919	Rehab pre-1919 properties
VAT	No VAT rehabilitation
WC&C	Wheelchair and individual carport
WC	Wheelchair without individual carport
PWCR	Parent with children refuges
HFS	Housing for sale
RH	Rural housing
NP	National parks
P&R	Purchase & repair
CSB	Community self build

Notes:

It is valid to combine each supplementary multiplier singularly with each key multiplier with the following xceptions:
  the 'housing for sale' multiplier cannot be combined with the 'rehabilitation re-improvement' key multiplier;
  the 'single storey' multiplier can only be combined with the 'new build acquisition works', 'new build off-the-shelf' and 'new build works only' key multipliers;
  the 'rehabilitation pre-1919' multiplier cannot be combined with the 'existing satisfactory' or 'purchase and repair' key multipliers.
  the 'P&R' supplementary multiplier may only be used in conjunction with the 'housing for sale' multiplier in circumstances outlined in the Capital Funding Guide (sale-1 paragraph 2).
TSH is not included in this matrix.

HOUSING ASSOCIATION SCHEMES

Table 1.12: TCI grouping, ESP and P&R supplementary multipliers and Home buy and VPG/RTA groupings 2004/05 and 2005/06

In alphabetical order – commencing with the London authorities

LA code	LA name	TCI grouping	P&R multiplier*	VPG/RTA grouping**	LA Enhance - ment***
202	City of London	A1	1.00	H1	7%
203	Barking and Dagenham	B3	0.95	H3	5%
204	Barnet	A2	1.15	H1	5%
205	Bexley	A4	0.90	H1	5%
206	Brent	A3	1.05	H1	7%
207	Bromley	A2	1.00	H1	5%
208	Camden	A2	1.15	H1	7%
209	Croydon	A3	0.85	H1	5%
210	Ealing	A3	0.95	H1	5%
211	Enfield	A2	1.15	H1	5%
212	Greenwich	B1	1.00	H1	7%
213	Hackney	A3	1.00	H1	7%
214	Hammersmith	A2	1.15	H1	7%
215	Haringey	A3	1.00	H1	5%
216	Harrow	A3	1.00	H1	5%
217	Havering	B1	0.90	H2	5%
218	Hillingdon	A3	0.85	H1	5%
219	Hounslow	A2	1.00	H1	5%
220	Islington	A2	1.15	H1	7%
221	Kensington and Chelsea	A1	1.15	H1	7%
222	Kingston upon Thames	A4	1.15	H1	5%
223	Lambeth	A2	1.10	H1	7%
224	Lewisham	A4	1.00	H1	7%
225	Merton	A3	1.15	H1	5%
226	Newham	A4	0.90	H2	5%
227	Redbridge	B1	0.95	H1	5%
228	Richmond upon Thames	A3	1.10	H1	5%
229	Southwark	A2	1.00	H1	7%
230	Sutton	A3	0.85	H1	5%
231	Tower Hamlets	A4	1.15	H1	7%
232	Waltham Forest	B1	1.00	H1	5%
233	Wandsworth	A3	1.15	H1	7%
234	Westminster	A1	1.15	H1	7%
272	Adur	C2	1.15	H2	5%
638	Allerdale	D2	0.90	H6	7%
594	Alnwick	D2	1.00	H5	11%
482	Amber Valley	D1	0.85	H6	10%
273	Arun	B2	0.90	H3	6%
474	Ashfield	D2	0.90	H6	9%
251	Ashford	C1	1.00	H3	5%
316	Aylesbury Vale	B3	1.00	H2	6%
348	Babergh	C3	1.00	H4	9%
551	Barnsley	E1	0.90	H6	7%
639	Barrow-in-Furness	D1	0.85	H6	7%
355	Basildon	C1	1.00	H2	10%
279	Basingstoke and Deane	B1	0.95	H2	6%
475	Bassetlaw	D1	0.85	H6	9%
701	Bath & NESomerset	B1	0.85	H3	9%

HOUSING ASSOCIATION SCHEMES

LA code	LA name	TCI grouping	P&R multiplier*	VPG/RTA grouping**	LA Enhance - ment***
331	Bedford	C2	1.10	H3	9%
595	Berwick upon Tweed	D2	0.90	H6	10%
515	Birmingham	C2	1.00	H3	8%
451	Blaby	C3	0.95	H5	11%
624	Blackburn	D2	0.90	H6	7%
625	Blackpool	D1	0.85	H6	9%
596	Blyth Valley	E1	0.90	H6	9%
483	Bolsover	D2	0.90	H6	8%
606	Bolton	D1	0.90	H5	8%
460	Boston	D2	0.90	H6	8%
401	Bournemouth	B2	0.85	H3	9%
294	Bracknell Forest	B2	1.00	H2	6%
555	Bradford	E1	1.00	H5	7%
357	Braintree	C1	1.00	H3	10%
341	Breckland	D1	0.90	H5	9%
356	Brentwood	B2	1.05	H1	11%
531	Bridgnorth	C3	1.10	H3	7%
706	Brighton and Hove	B1	1.00	H1	6%
436	Bristol	B2	0.95	H2	9%
342	Broadland	C3	0.95	H5	9%
501	Bromsgrove	C2	0.85	H4	8%
321	Broxbourne	B1	1.00	H1	12%
476	Broxtowe	D1	0.95	H5	10%
626	Burnley	D2	0.90	H6	7%
607	Bury	D2	0.95	H5	8%
556	Calderdale	E1	0.90	H6	7%
335	Cambridge	A4	1.15	H1	14%
522	Cannock Chase	C3	0.85	H6	7%
252	Canterbury	B2	0.85	H3	6%
429	Caradon	D1	1.00	H4	7%
640	Carlisle	D2	1.00	H5	7%
430	Carrick	C3	1.15	H3	7%
597	Castle Morpeth	D2	1.00	H5	12%
358	Castle Point	C1	1.00	H3	10%
452	Charnwood	C2	0.90	H5	13%
359	Chelmsford	B3	1.00	H2	11%
441	Cheltenham	B3	1.05	H2	9%
311	Cherwell	B3	1.00	H3	6%
616	Chester	C3	1.00	H4	10%
484	Chesterfield	D1	0.90	H5	9%
581	Chester-le-Street	D2	0.90	H6	15%
274	Chichester	B1	0.95	H1	6%
318	Chiltern	B1	1.00	H1	6%
627	Chorley	C3	0.85	H5	10%
402	Christchurch	B2	0.90	H2	9%
360	Colchester	C2	1.00	H3	9%
617	Congleton	D2	1.00	H4	9%
641	Copeland	D2	0.90	H6	7%
467	Corby	D2	0.90	H6	9%
442	Cotswold	C1	1.15	H2	8%
516	Coventry	D1	1.00	H4	7%
560	Craven	D2	1.10	H3	8%
275	Crawley	B3	1.05	H2	6%
618	Crewe and Nantwich	D1	1.00	H5	9%
322	Dacorum	A3	1.00	H1	15%

HOUSING ASSOCIATION SCHEMES

Table 1.12: TCI grouping, ESP and P&R supplementary multipliers and Home buy and VPG/RTA groupings 2004/05 and 2005/06 – cont'd

LA code	LA name	TCI grouping	P&R multiplier*	VPG/RTA grouping**	LA Enhance - ment***
582	Darlington	D1	0.85	H5	14%
253	Dartford	C1	1.00	H3	5%
468	Daventry	C2	0.95	H4	11%
485	Derby	D1	0.85	H5	10%
490	Derbyshire Dales	C3	1.00	H4	10%
583	Derwentside	D1	0.85	H6	10%
552	Doncaster	D1	0.85	H6	8%
254	Dover	C2	1.05	H3	5%
517	Dudley	C3	1.00	H4	8%
584	Durham	D1	1.00	H4	15%
585	Easington	D2	0.90	H6	10%
336	East Cambridgeshire	C1	1.05	H2	10%
419	East Devon	C1	1.00	H3	8%
408	East Dorset	B3	1.00	H2	9%
280	East Hampshire	B2	1.00	H2	6%
323	East Hertfordshire	B2	1.00	H1	12%
461	East Lindsey	D2	0.90	H6	7%
469	East Northamptonshire	C1	0.85	H5	12%
708	East Riding	D2	0.90	H6	8%
523	East Staffordshire	D2	1.00	H5	7%
266	Eastbourne	C1	1.15	H1	6%
281	Eastleigh	B3	1.00	H2	6%
642	Eden	D1	1.00	H4	7%
619	Ellesmere Port and Neston	D2	0.90	H6	7%
300	Elmbridge	B1	1.15	H1	6%
361	Epping Forest	B1	1.15	H1	12%
301	Epsom and Ewell	B2	1.15	H1	6%
486	Erewash	D1	0.90	H5	10%
420	Exeter	C1	1.00	H3	8%
282	Fareham	B3	1.00	H2	6%
337	Fenland	D1	1.00	H4	7%
349	Forest Heath	C2	1.00	H4	9%
443	Forest of Dean	C3	1.05	H3	7%
628	Fylde	C2	0.85	H5	11%
589	Gateshead	D2	0.95	H5	14%
477	Gedling	D1	0.95	H5	10%
444	Gloucester	C2	1.00	H3	8%
283	Gosport	C1	1.00	H3	6%
256	Gravesham	C2	1.00	H3	5%
343	Great Yarmouth	D2	0.95	H5	7%
302	Guildford	B1	1.10	H1	6%
620	Halton	C3	0.85	H6	14%
561	Hambleton	C3	1.00	H4	10%
453	Harborough	C1	0.85	H4	15%
362	Harlow	C1	1.15	H1	9%
562	Harrogate	C2	1.10	H3	10%
284	Hart	A4	1.00	H1	6%
577	Hartlepool	D2	0.90	H6	10%
267	Hastings	C3	1.15	H3	5%
285	Havant	B3	0.95	H3	6%

HOUSING ASSOCIATION SCHEMES

LA code	LA name	TCI grouping	P&R multiplier*	VPG/RTA grouping**	LA Enhance - ment***
712	Herefordshire	C1	0.85	H4	9%
324	Hertsmere	A3	1.00	H1	15%
487	High Peak	C3	1.00	H4	10%
454	Hinckley and Bosworth	C3	0.95	H5	12%
276	Horsham	B2	1.00	H1	6%
338	Huntingdon	C1	1.00	H3	10%
629	Hyndburn	E1	0.90	H6	7%
350	Ipswich	C2	1.00	H4	10%
707	Isle of Wight	C3	1.00	H4	5%
447	Isles of Scilly	A2	1.00	H1	10%
409	Kennet	B3	1.00	H3	8%
431	Kerrier	D2	1.10	H4	7%
470	Kettering	C2	0.85	H5	10%
347	Kings Lynn and West Norfolk	D1	0.90	H5	8%
574	Kingston upon Hull	D2	0.90	H6	7%
557	Kirklees	D2	0.90	H5	8%
601	Knowsley	D2	0.90	H6	9%
630	Lancaster	C3	0.95	H5	11%
558	Leeds	D1	1.00	H4	9%
455	Leicester	C3	0.85	H5	11%
269	Lewes	B2	0.85	H3	6%
524	Lichfield	C2	1.00	H4	7%
462	Lincoln	D2	0.90	H5	8%
602	Liverpool	C3	0.85	H5	15%
332	Luton	C2	1.00	H3	9%
621	Macclesfield	C2	1.10	H3	10%
257	Maidstone	B3	1.00	H3	6%
363	Maldon	C2	1.10	H3	9%
713	Malvern Hills District	C1	1.00	H3	9%
608	Manchester	C2	1.00	H4	10%
478	Mansfield	D2	0.90	H6	9%
456	Melton	C2	0.85	H5	13%
414	Mendip	D1	1.00	H4	7%
333	Mid Bedfordshire	C1	1.10	H2	10%
425	Mid Devon	C2	1.00	H4	7%
351	Mid Suffolk	C3	1.00	H4	9%
277	Mid Sussex	B2	1.00	H1	6%
579	Middlesbrough	D2	0.90	H6	10%
319	Milton Keynes	C1	0.95	H3	6%
303	Mole Valley	B2	1.15	H1	6%
286	New Forest	B2	1.00	H2	6%
479	Newark	D1	0.90	H5	10%
590	Newcastle upon Tyne	C3	1.00	H4	15%
525	Newcastle under Lyme	D2	0.90	H6	7%
432	North Cornwall	D1	1.15	H3	7%
421	North Devon	C2	1.00	H4	7%
403	North Dorset	C1	1.00	H3	9%
488	North East Derbyshire	D1	1.00	H5	9%
709	North East Lincolnshire	E1	0.90	H6	7%
325	North Hertfordshire	B3	1.15	H1	10%
463	North Kesteven	D1	0.85	H6	8%

HOUSING ASSOCIATION SCHEMES

Table 1.12: TCI grouping, ESP and P&R supplementary multipliers and Home buy and VPG/RTA groupings 2004/05 and 2005/06 – cont'd

LA code	LA name	TCI grouping	P&R multiplier*	VPG/RTA grouping**	LA Enhance - ment***
710	North Lincolnshire	E1	0.90	H6	7%
344	North Norfolk	D1	0.95	H5	9%
532	North Shropshire	D2	1.00	H5	7%
440	North Somerset	C1	1.00	H2	8%
591	North Tyneside	D1	1.00	H5	15%
510	North Warwickshire	C3	1.00	H5	7%
457	North West Leicestershire	C3	0.85	H5	10%
410	North Wiltshire	B3	0.95	H3	9%
471	Northampton	C1	0.90	H4	13%
345	Norwich	C1	0.85	H4	11%
480	Nottingham	C3	0.85	H5	10%
511	Nuneaton and Bedworth	C3	0.85	H5	7%
458	Oadby and Wigston	C3	1.00	H4	11%
609	Oldham	D1	0.85	H5	9%
533	Oswestry	D1	0.85	H6	7%
312	Oxford	A2	0.95	H1	7%
631	Pendle	D2	0.90	H6	7%
433	Penwith	D1	1.05	H3	7%
339	Peterborough	C3	1.00	H4	9%
422	Plymouth	C3	1.00	H4	7%
404	Poole	B2	0.85	H3	9%
287	Portsmouth	C1	1.00	H3	6%
632	Preston	C3	0.85	H5	10%
405	Purbeck	C1	1.00	H3	8%
296	Reading	A4	0.90	H1	6%
578	Redcar and Cleveland	E1	0.90	H6	10%
505	Redditch	C3	1.00	H4	8%
304	Reigate and Banstead	B2	1.10	H1	6%
434	Restormel	D1	1.05	H4	7%
633	Ribble Valley	C3	1.00	H4	10%
563	Richmondshire	D2	1.05	H4	9%
610	Rochdale	D1	0.90	H5	9%
364	Rochford	C1	1.00	H2	10%
634	Rossendale	D2	1.00	H5	7%
270	Rother	C1	1.00	H3	5%
553	Rotherham	E1	0.90	H6	7%
512	Rugby	C3	0.95	H5	7%
305	Runnymede	B2	1.05	H1	6%
481	Rushcliffe	C3	1.00	H4	11%
288	Rushmoor	B2	1.00	H1	6%
459	Rutland	C1	0.95	H4	14%
564	Ryedale	D1	1.00	H4	9%
611	Salford	D1	0.85	H6	9%
411	Salisbury	B3	1.00	H2	9%
518	Sandwell	D1	0.90	H5	7%
566	Scarborough	D2	0.95	H5	8%
586	Sedgefield	D2	0.90	H6	11%

HOUSING ASSOCIATION SCHEMES

LA code	LA name	TCI grouping	P&R multiplier*	VPG/RTA grouping**	LA Enhance - ment***
415	Sedgemoor	D1	1.05	H4	7%
604	Sefton	D1	0.95	H5	10%
565	Selby	D2	1.10	H4	7%
259	Sevenoaks	B2	1.05	H1	6%
554	Sheffield	D2	1.00	H4	8%
260	Shepway	C3	1.05	H3	5%
534	Shrewsbury and Atcham	D1	1.00	H4	7%
297	Slough	B2	1.00	H1	6%
519	Solihull	B2	0.95	H2	9%
334	South Bedfordshire	C2	1.05	H3	9%
317	South Bucks	B1	1.10	H1	6%
340	South Cambridgeshire	B3	1.15	H1	11%
489	South Derbyshire	D2	0.90	H6	8%
702	South Gloucestershire	B2	0.85	H3	9%
423	South Hams	C3	1.15	H2	7%
464	South Holland	D2	0.90	H6	8%
465	South Kesteven	D1	0.95	H5	9%
643	South Lakeland	C3	1.00	H4	10%
346	South Norfolk	C3	0.95	H5	9%
472	South Northamptonshire	B3	0.85	H4	15%
313	South Oxfordshire	B2	1.00	H1	6%
635	South Ribble	C3	0.85	H5	10%
535	South Shropshire	D1	1.00	H4	7%
418	South Somerset	C2	1.00	H4	8%
526	South Staffordshire	C2	0.85	H5	8%
592	South Tyneside	D2	1.00	H5	15%
289	Southampton	B3	1.00	H3	6%
365	Southend-on-Sea	C2	1.00	H3	9%
306	Spelthorne	B2	1.15	H1	6%
326	St Albans	A3	1.15	H1	15%
352	St Edmundsbury	C1	1.00	H3	10%
603	St Helens	C3	0.85	H6	13%
527	Stafford	D1	0.90	H5	7%
528	Staffordshire Moorland	D2	0.90	H6	7%
327	Stevenage	C1	1.15	H1	10%
612	Stockport	C1	1.00	H3	13%
580	Stockton-on-Tees	D2	0.90	H6	11%
529	Stoke-on-Trent	D2	0.90	H6	7%
513	Stratford upon Avon	B1	1.00	H1	10%
445	Stroud	C2	1.00	H3	7%
353	Suffolk Coastal	C3	1.00	H4	9%
593	Sunderland	D1	1.00	H5	15%
307	Surrey Heath	B2	1.05	H1	6%
261	Swale	C2	1.10	H3	6%
412	Swindon	C1	1.00	H3	9%
613	Tameside	D1	0.85	H6	9%
530	Tamworth	D1	1.00	H5	7%
308	Tandridge	B2	1.00	H1	6%
416	Taunton Deane	C1	1.00	H3	8%

HOUSING ASSOCIATION SCHEMES

Table 1.12: TCI grouping, ESP and P&R supplementary multipliers and Home buy and VPG/RTA groupings 2004/05 and 2005/06 – cont'd

LA code	LA name	TCI grouping	P&R multiplier*	VPG/RTA grouping**	LA Enhance - ment***
587	Teesdale	D2	0.90	H5	14%
424	Teignbridge	C1	0.95	H4	8%
366	Tendring	D1	1.05	H3	7%
290	Test Valley	C1	1.00	H3	6%
446	Tewkesbury	C2	1.00	H4	8%
262	Thanet	C2	1.00	H3	5%
711	The Medway Towns	C2	1.00	H3	5%
536	The Wrekin	D1	0.95	H5	7%
328	Three Rivers	A3	1.05	H1	15%
367	Thurrock	C2	1.10	H3	9%
263	Tonbridge and Malling	B2	1.00	H2	6%
426	Torbay	C2	1.00	H4	8%
427	Torridge	C3	1.00	H4	7%
614	Trafford	B3	0.85	H3	14%
264	Tunbridge Wells	B3	1.00	H2	6%
598	Tynedale	D1	1.00	H5	12%
368	Uttlesford	B2	1.00	H1	12%
314	Vale of White Horse	B3	1.00	H2	6%
622	Vale Royal	C3	1.00	H4	10%
559	Wakefield	D1	0.85	H5	9%
520	Walsall	C3	0.85	H5	7%
599	Wansbeck	D2	0.90	H6	9%
623	Warrington	C3	0.85	H6	14%
514	Warwick	B3	1.05	H1	9%
329	Watford	A3	0.90	H1	15%
354	Waveney	D2	0.95	H5	7%
309	Waverley	B1	1.10	H1	6%
271	Wealden	C1	1.15	H2	6%
588	Wear Valley	D2	0.90	H6	12%
473	Wellingborough	C3	0.90	H5	10%
330	Welwyn Hatfield	B1	1.00	H1	12%
295	West Berkshire	B1	0.95	H2	6%
428	West Devon	C3	1.15	H2	7%
406	West Dorset	B3	1.00	H3	9%
636	West Lancashire	C2	0.90	H5	13%
466	West Lindsey	E1	0.90	H6	7%
315	West Oxfordshire	B1	0.90	H2	6%
417	West Somerset	C3	1.00	H4	7%
413	West Wiltshire	C1	0.95	H3	9%
407	Weymouth and Portland	C1	0.85	H3	9%
615	Wigan	D1	0.90	H5	9%
291	Winchester	A4	1.00	H1	6%
298	Windsor and Maidenhead	B1	1.15	H1	6%
605	Wirral	D2	0.90	H6	9%
310	Woking	B1	1.00	H1	6%
299	Wokingham	B2	1.05	H1	6%
521	Wolverhampton	D2	0.90	H5	7%
507	Worcester City	C2	1.00	H3	8%

HOUSING ASSOCIATION SCHEMES

LA code	LA name	TCI grouping	P&R multiplier*	VPG/RTA grouping**	LA Enhance - ment***
278	Worthing	C1	1.10	H2	6%
508	Wychavon	C2	1.00	H3	8%
320	Wycombe	B1	0.90	H2	6%
637	Wyre	C3	0.85	H5	10%
509	Wyre Forest	C2	0.90	H4	8%
567	York	C3	1.05	H3	10%

Notes

* The P&R supplementary multiplier applies to ESP and P&R schemes only. It does not apply to OTS.

** RTA Cost Groups remain as at 2003/04 for 2004/05.

*** The specified LA enhancement percentages should be applied to inflate the TCI base table values.

HOUSING ASSOCIATION SCHEMES

Table 1.13: National parks and areas of outstanding beauty in England applicable for 2004/05 and 2005/06 TCI purposes

National parks	Areas of outstanding beauty
The Broads	Arnside and Silverdale
Dartmoor	Blackdown Hills
Exmoor	Cannock Chase
Lake District	Chichester Harbour
The New Forest	Chilterns
North Yorkshire Moor	Cornwall
Northumberland	Cotswolds
Peak District	Cranbourne Chase and West Wiltshire Downs
Yorkshire Dales	Debham Vale
	Dorset
	East Devon
	East Hampshire
	Forest of Bowland
	High Weald
	Howardian Hills
	Isle of Wight
	Isles of Scilly
	Kent Downs
	Lincolnshire Wolds
	Malvern Hills
	Mendip Hills
	Nidderdale
	Norfolk Coast
	North Devon
	North Pennines
	Northumberland Coast
	North Wessex Downs
	Quantock Hills
	Shropshire Hills
	Solway Coast
	South Devon
	South Hampshire Coast
	Suffolk Coast and Heaths
	Surrey Hills
	Sussex Downs
	Tamar Valley
	Wye Valley

HOUSING ASSOCIATION SCHEMES

Table 2.1: Low cost home ownership (LCHO) factors 2004/05 and 2005/06

Sale programme	Priority investment areas	Other areas
Shared ownership	58%	50%
Shared ownership for the elderly	68%	60%
Improvement for outright sale	33%	

Table 2.2: Home buy value limits and on-cost allowance 2004/05 and 2005/06

The principal changes are as follows:
1. Value limits no longer apply to Homebuy purchases
2. Two new categories of Homebuy have been introduced to complement the traditional Homebuy option, namely:
> Key Worker Homebuy (Market Purchase)
> London Challenge Key Teacher Homebuy (Market Purchase)
3. Following piloting within the 2003/04 Challenge Fund programme, a related option of Newbuild Homebuy has been mainstreamed to operate within the TCI framework.
4. The eligibility criteria, operating procedures and allowances vary according to category.

On-cost allowances (%)

Homebuy (traditional)	2.5%	Applied to the actual purchase price* (*Note: there is a cap of £2,563 on this allowance)
Key Worker Homebuy	3%	Applied to the actual purchase price** (**Note: there is a cap of £3,075 on this allowance)
London Challenge Key Teacher Homebuy	3%	Applied to the actual purchase price** (**Note: there is a cap of £3,075 on this allowance)
Newbuild Homebuy	5%	Applied to the land and works costs as defined in the TCI Guidance Notes.

Table 2.3: Voluntary purchase grant (VPG) and right to acquire (RTA) discount amounts 2004/05 and 2005/06

	Home buy cost groups					
	H1	H2	H3	H4	H5	H6
VPG and RTA discount amounts £	16,000	13,500	11,000	10,000	9,000	9,000

The RTA discount amounts, and the local authorities that they apply to, are set by Statutory Instrument, the Housing Right to Acquire Discount Order (2002 No 1091) and may be varied by subsequent orders. The indicative RTA discount levels for 2003/04 are set out above. The current intention is that the TA discount levels should reflect those for VPG. Any discrepancies should be reported to the Corporation.

HOUSING ASSOCIATION SCHEMES

Table 3.1: Administrative Allowances and expenses 2004/05 and 2005/06

Note 1: All allowances set below have been fixed at those applicable for 2003/04
Note 2: The LA enhancements set out in table 1.12 do not apply to the allowances and expenses set out here.

	£	IMS code	£ (VAT enhanced)	IMS code
Special project promotion				
• London				
Agency Schemes				
First project	12,026	A010	13,538	A020
Second and subsequent projects	8,018	A050	9,026	A060
Directly managed schemes				
First project	10,864	A090	12,230	A100
Second and subsequent projects	7,216	A130	8,123	A140
• Outside London				
Agency schemes				
First project	8,738	A030	9,836	A040
Second and subsequent projects	5,823	A070	6,555	A080
Directly managed schemes				
First project	7,865	A110	8,854	A120
Second and subsequent projects	5,244	A150	5,903	A160
Co-operative promotion				
• London				
Per new primary co-op project	8,980	A170	10,109	A180
For second and subsequent schemes:				
New build	5,990	A210	6,743	A220
Rehabilitation	1,347	A250	1,516	A260
• Outside London				
Per new primary co-op project	8,141	A190	9,164	A200
For second and subsequent schemes:				
New build	5,427	A230	6,109	A240
Rehabilitation	1,221	A270	1,374	A280
Property disposal deductible administration expenses				
• All areas				
Stair casing sales	449	A900	n/a	
Right to buy sales (house)	701		n/a	
Right to buy sales (flats)	1,576		n/a	
Voluntary and Statutory Purchase Grants (house)	701	A940	n/a	
Voluntary and Statutory Purchase Grants (flat)	1,576	A950	n/a	
Recovery of tenant's discount	103		n/a	
Move on allowances for RSF				
• All areas	543		611	

Property Insurance

The problem of adequately covering by insurance the loss and damage caused to buildings by fire and other perils has been highlighted in recent years by the increasing rate of inflation.

There are a number of schemes available to the building owner wishing to insure his property against the usual risk. Traditionally the insured value must be sufficient to cover the actual cost of reinstating the building. This means that in addition to assessing the current value an estimate has also to be made of the increases likely to occur during the period of the policy and of rebuilding which, for a moderate size building, could amount to a total of three years. Obviously such an estimate is difficult to make with any degree of accuracy, if it is too low the insured may be penalized under the terms of the policy and if too high will result in the payment of unnecessary premiums.

There are variations on the traditional method of insuring which aim to reduce the effects of over estimating and details of these are available from the appropriate offices. For the convenience of readers who may wish to make use of the information contained in this publication in calculating insurance cover required the following may be of interest.

1 PRESENT COST

The current rebuilding costs may be ascertained in a number of ways:

(a)   where the actual building cost is known this may be updated by reference to tender prices (page 702);
(b)   by reference to average published prices per square metre of floor area (page 711). In this case it is important to understand clearly the method of measurement used to calculate the total floor area on which the rates have been based;
(c)   by professional valuation;
(d)   by comparison with the known cost of another similar building.

Whichever of these methods is adopted regard must be paid to any special conditions that may apply, i.e., a confined site, complexity of design, or any demolition and site clearance that may be required.

2 ALLOWANCE FOR INFLATION

The "Present Cost" when established will usually, under the conditions of the policy, be the rebuilding cost on the first day of the policy period. To this must be added a sum to cover future increases. For this purpose, using the historical indices on pages 701 - 702, as a base and taking account of the likely change in building costs and tender climate the following annual average indices are predicted for the future.

Year	Cost Index	Tender Index
1995	401	265
1996	411	267
1997	421	283
1998	439	313
1999	460	332
2000	489	359
2001	507	384
2002	536	412
2003	567	429
2004	600	442
2005	644 (F)	469 (F)
2006	679 (F)	491 (F)
2007	705 (F)	517 (F)
2008	731 (F)	544 (F)

3 FEES

To the total of 1 and 2 above must be added an allowance for fees.

4 VALUE ADDED TAX (V.A.T.)

To the total of 1 to 3 above must be added Value Added Tax. Historically, relief may have been given to total reconstruction following fire damage etc. Since the 1989 Finance Act, such work, except for self-contained dwellings and other residential buildings and certain non-business charity buildings, has attracted V.A.T. and the limit of insurance cover should be raised to follow this.

5 EXAMPLE

An assessment for insurance cover is required in the fourth quarter of 2004 for a property which cost £200,000 when completed in 1976.

Present Cost
Known cost at mid 1976   £200,000.00

Predicted tender index fourth quarter 2005	=	477
Tender index fourth quarter 1976	=	100
Increase in tender index	=	377%
applied to known cost	=	£754,000.00

Present cost (excluding any allowance for demolition)   =   £954,000.00

Allowance for inflation
Present cost at day one of policy   £954,000.00

Predicted tender index fourth quarter 2006	=	500
Predicted tender index fourth quarter 2005	=	477
Increase in tender index	=	4.82%
applied to present cost	= say	£ 46,000.00

Anticipated cost at expiry of policy   =   £1,000,000.00

Assuming that total damage is suffered on the last day of the currency of the policy and that Planning and documentation would require a period of twelve months before re-building could commence, then a further similar allowance must be made.

Predicted tender index fourth quarter 2007	=	528
Predicted tender index fourth quarter 2006	=	500
Increase in tender index	=	5.6%
applied to cost at expiry of policy	= say	£ 56,000.00

Anticipated cost at tender date   =   £1,056,000.00

Assuming that reconstruction would take one year, allowance must be made for the increases In costs which would directly or indirectly be met under a building contract.

Predicted tender index fourth quarter 2008	=	740
Predicted tender index fourth quarter 2007	=	715
Increase in tender index	=	3.50%

This is the total increase at the end of the one year period.
The amount applicable to the contract would be about half,   say   £ 18,500.00

Estimated cost of reinstatement   =   £1,074,500.00

SUMMARY OF EXAMPLE

Estimated cost of reinstatement	=	£1,074,500.00
Add professional fees at, say 16%	=	£172,000.00
	s/t	£1,246,500.00
Add for V.A.T., currently at 17½% say	=	£218,150.00
Total insurance cover required	=	**£1,464,650.00**

Spon's Estimating Costs Guide to Finishings
Painting and Decorating, Plastering and Tiling

Bryan Spain

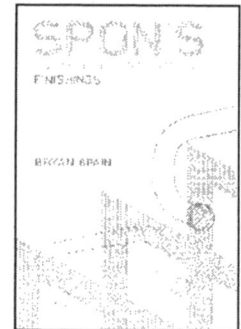

Especially written for contractors and small businesses carrying out small works, Spon's Estimating Costs Guide to Finishings contains accurate information on thousands of rates, each broken down to labour, material overheads and profit.

This is the first book to include typical project costs for painting and wallpapering, plasterwork, floor and wall tiles, rendering, and external work.

More than just a price book, it gives easy-to-read, professional advice on setting up and running a business including help on producing estimates faster, and keeping estimates accurate and competitive.

Suitable for any size firm from one-man-band to established business, this book contains valuable commercial and cost information that contractors can't afford to be without.

March 2005: 216x138 mm: 288 pages
PB: 0-415-34411-5: £24.99

To Order: Tel: +44 (0) 1264 343071 Fax: +44 (0) 1264 343005, or
Post: Taylor and Francis Customer Services, Thomson Publishing Services, Cheriton House, Andover, Hants, SP10 5BE, UK Email: book.orders@tandf.co.uk

For a complete listing of all our titles visit :
www.sponpress.com

Taylor & Francis
Taylor & Francis Group plc

The Aggregates Tax

The Aggregates Tax came into operation on 1 April 2002 in the UK, except for Northern Ireland where it is being phased in over five years from 2003.

It is currently levied at the rate of £1.60 per tonne on anyone considered to be responsible for commercially exploiting 'virgin' Aggregates in the UK and should naturally be passed by price increase to the ultimate user.

All materials falling within the definition of 'Aggregates' is liable for the levy unless it is specifically exempted.

It does not apply to clay, soil, vegetable or other organic matter.

The hope is that this will :-

- Encourage the use of alternative materials that would otherwise be disposed of to landfill sites.
- Promote development of new recycling processes, such as using waste tyres and glass
- Promote greater efficiency in the use of virgin aggregates
- Reduce noise + vibration, dust + other emissions to air, visual intrusion, loss of amenity + damage to wildlife habitats

The intention is for part of the revenue from the levy to be recycled to business and communities affected by Aggregates extraction, through :-

- A 0.1 percentage point cut in employers' national insurance contributions
- A new £35 million per annum 'Sustainability Fund' to reduce the need for virgin materials and to limit the effects of extraction on the environmental where it takes place. A number of key priorities were identified with a promise to give effect to them through existing programmes. Following a mid-term review in December 2003, this fund was extended for a further three years.

Definition

'Aggregates' means any rock, gravel or sand which is extracted or dredged in the UK for aggregates use. It includes whatever substances are for the time being incorporated in it or naturally occur mixed with it.

'Exploitation' is defined as involving any one or a combination of any of the following :-

- Being removed from its original site
- Becoming subject to a contract or other agreement to supply to any person
- Being used for construction purposes
- Being mixed with any material or substance other than water, except in permitted circumstances

Incidence

It is a tax on primary Aggregates production – i.e. 'virgin' Aggregates won from a source and used in a location within the UK territorial boundaries (land or sea). The tax is not levied on aggregates which are exported nor on Aggregates imported from outside the UK territorial boundaries.

It is levied at the point of sale.

Exemption from tax

An 'aggregate' is exempt from the levy if it is a/an :

- Material which has previously been used for construction purposes
- Aggregate that has already been subject to a charge to the Aggregates levy
- Aggregate which was previously removed from its originating site before the commencement date of the levy
- Aggregate which is being returned to the land from which it was won
- Aggregate won from a farm land or forest where used on that farm or forest
- Rock which has not been subjected to an industrial crushing process

Exemption from tax – continued

- Aggregate won by being removed from the ground on the site of any building or proposed building in the course of excavations carried out in connection with the modification or erection of the building and exclusively for the purpose of laying foundations or of laying any pipe or cable
- Aggregate won by being removed from the bed of any river, canal or watercourse or channel in or approach to any port or harbour (natural or artificial), in the course of carrying out any dredging exclusively for the purpose of creating, restoring, improving or maintaining that body of water
- Aggregate won by being removed from the ground along the line of any highway or proposed highway in the course of excavations for improving, maintaining or constructing the highway + otherwise than purely to extract the aggregate
- Drill cuttings from petroleum operations on land and on the seabed
- Aggregate resulting from works carried out in exercise of powers under the New Road and Street Works Act 1991, the Roads (Northern Ireland) Order 1993 or the Street Works (Northern Ireland) Order 1995
- Aggregate removed for the purpose of cutting of rock to produce dimension stone, or the production of lime or cement from limestone.
- Aggregate arising as a waste material during the processing of the following industrial minerals:
  - ball clay
  - barytes
  - calcite
  - china clay
  - coal, lignite, slate or shale
  - feldspar
  - flint
  - fluorspar
  - fuller's earth
  - gems and semi-precious stones
  - gypsum
  - any metal or the ore of any metal
  - muscovite
  - perlite
  - potash
  - pumice
  - rock phosphates
  - sodium chloride
  - talc
  - vermiculite

However, the levy is still chargeable on any aggregates arising as the spoil or waste from or the by-products of the above exempt processes. This includes quarry overburden.

Anything that consists 'wholly or mainly' of the following is exempt from the levy (note that 'wholly' is defined as 100% but 'mainly' as more than 50%, thus exempting any contained aggregates amounting to less than 50% of the original volumes :

- clay, soil, vegetable or other organic matter
- coal, slate or shale
- china clay waste and ball clay waste

Relief from the levy either in the form of credit or repayment is obtainable where :
- it is subsequently exported from the UK in the form of aggregate
- it is used in an exempt process
- where it is used in a prescribed industrial or agricultural process
- it is waste aggregate disposed of by dumping or otherwise, e.g. sent to landfill or returned to the originating site

Environment Act 1995

Provides for planning permissions for minerals extraction (which includes aggregates) to be reviewed and updated on a regular basis by the mineral planning authorities.

Minerals planning guidance notes were to be updated to ensure that all mineral operators provide local benefits that clearly outweigh the likely impacts of mineral extraction.

The Rural White Paper published in November 2000

This set out the government's 'vision of a countryside that is sustainable economically, socially and environmentally' apart from economic support, action was proposed to deal with a number of environmental threats, one is to reduce the environmental impact (such as damage to biodiversity and visual intrusion) of aggregate extraction by imposing an Aggregates levy.

Finance Act 2001

This provides for a levy being charged on aggregate which is subject to commercial exploitation. It places the levy under the care and management of the Commissioners of Customs & Excise.

Impact

The British Aggregates Association suggests that the additional cost imposed by quarries is more likely to be in the order of £2.65 per tonne on mainstream products, applying an above average rate on these in order that by-products and low grade waste products can be held at competitive rates, as well as making some allowance for administration and increased finance charges.

With many gravel aggregates costing in the region of £7.50 to £9.50 per tonne, there is a significant impact on construction costs.

Avoidance

An alternative to using new aggregates in filling operations is to crush and screen rubble which may become available during the process of demolition and site clearance as well as removal of obstacles during the excavation processes.

Example :   Assuming that the material would be suitable for fill material under buildings or roads, a simple cost comparison would be as follows (note that for the purpose of the exercise, the material is taken to be 1.80 t/m³ and the total quantity involved less than 1,000 m³) :-

Importing fill material :		£/m³	£/tonne
Cost of 'new' aggregates delivered to site		17.10	9.50
Addition for Aggregates Tax		2.88	1.60
Total cost of importing fill materials	£	19.98	11.10

Disposing of site material :		£/m³	£/tonne
Cost of removing materials from site materials	£	9.50	5.28

Crushing site materials :	£/m³	£/tonne
Transportation of material from excavations or demolition to stockpiles	1.25	.69
Transportation of material from temporary stockpiles to the crushing plant	1.00	.56
Establishing plant and equipment on site; removing on completion	.75	.42
Maintain and operate plant	3.75	2.08
Crushing hard materials on site	5.50	3.05
Screening material on site	.75	.42
Total cost of crushing site materials £	13.00	7.22

From the above it can be seen that potentially there is a great benefit in crushing site materials for filling rather than importing fill materials.

Setting the cost of crushing against the import price would produce a saving of £6.98 per m³. If the site materials were otherwise intended to be removed from the site, then the cost benefit increases by the saved disposal cost to £16.48 per m³.

Even if there is no call for any or all of the crushed material on site, it ought to be regarded as a useful asset and either sold on in crushed form or else sold with the prospects of crushing elsewhere.

Specimen Unit rates	unit³	£
Establishing plant and equipment on site; removing on completion		
Crushing plant	trip	£500
Screening plant	trip	£250
Maintain and operate plant		
Crushing plant	week	£3,000
Screening plant	week	£750
Transportation of material from excavations or demolition places to temporary stockpiles	m³	£1.25
Transportation of material from temporary stockpiles to the crushing plant	m³	£1.00
Breaking up material on site using impact breakers		
mass concrete	m³	£5.50
reinforced concrete	m³	£6.50
brickwork	m³	£2.50
Crushing material on site		
mass concrete ne 1000m³	m³	£5.50
mass concrete 1000 - 5000m³	m³	£5.00
mass concrete over 5000m³	m³	£4.50
reinforced concrete ne 1000m³	m³	£6.50
reinforced concrete 1000 - 5000m³	m³	£6.00
reinforced concrete over 5000m³	m³	£5.50
brickwork ne 1000m³	m³	£5.00
brickwork 1000 - 5000m³	m³	£4.50
brickwork over 5000m³	m³	£4.00
Screening material on site	m³	£0.75

Capital Allowances

Introduction

Capital Allowances provide tax relief by prescribing a statutory rate of depreciation for tax purposes in place of that used for accounting purposes. They are utilised by government to provide an incentive to invest in capital equipment, including commercial property, by allowing the majority of taxpayers a deduction from taxable profits for certain types of capital expenditure, thereby deferring tax liabilities.

The capital allowances most commonly applicable to real estate are those given for capital expenditure on both new and existing industrial buildings, and plant and machinery in all commercial buildings.

Other types of allowances particularly relevant to property are hotel and enterprise zone allowances, which are in fact variants to industrial buildings allowances code. Enhanced rates of allowances are available to small and medium sized enterprises and on certain types of energy saving plant and machinery, whilst reduced rates apply to items with an expected economic life of more than 25 years.

The Act

The primary legislation is now contained in the Capital Allowances Act 2001. Amendments to the Act have been made in each subsequent Finance Act.

The Act is arranged in 12 Parts and was published with an accompanying set of Explanatory Notes.

Plant and Machinery

The Finance Act 1994 introduced major changes to the availability of Capital Allowances on real estate. A definition was introduced which precludes expenditure on the provision of a building from qualifying for plant and machinery, with prescribed exceptions.

List A in Section 21 of the 2001 Act sets out those assets treated as parts of buildings:-

- *Walls, floors, ceilings, doors, gates, shutters, windows and stairs.*
- *Mains services, and systems, for water, electricity and gas.*
- *Waste disposal systems.*
- *Sewerage and drainage systems.*
- *Shafts or other structures in which lifts, hoists, escalators and moving walkways are installed.*
- *Fire safety systems.*

Similarly, List B in Section 22 identifies excluded structures and other assets.

Both sections are, however, subject to Section 23. This section sets out expenditure, which although being part of a building, may still be expenditure on the provision of Plant and Machinery.

List C in Section 23 is reproduced below:

LIST C EXPENDITURE UNAFFECTED BY SECTIONS 21 AND 22

Sections 21 and 22 do not affect the question whether expenditure on any item in List C is expenditure on the provision of Plant or Machinery

1. Machinery (including devices for providing motive power) not within any other item in this list.
2. Electrical systems (including lighting systems) and cold water, gas and sewerage systems provided mainly –
    (a) to meet the particular requirements of the qualifying activity, or
    (b) to serve particular Plant or Machinery used for the purposes of the qualifying activity.
3. Space or water heating systems; powered systems of ventilation, air cooling or air purification; and any floor or ceiling comprised in such systems.
4. Manufacturing or processing equipment; storage equipment (including cold rooms); display equipment; and counters, checkouts and similar equipment.
5. Cookers, washing machines, dishwashers, refrigerators and similar equipment; washbasins, sinks, baths, showers, sanitary ware and similar equipment; and furniture and furnishings.
6. Lifts, hoists, escalators and moving walkways.
7. Sound insulation provided mainly to meet the particular requirements of the qualifying activity.
8. Computer, telecommunication and surveillance systems (including their wiring or other links).
9. Refrigeration or cooling equipment.
10. Fire alarm systems; sprinkler and other equipment for extinguishing or containing fires.
11. Burglar alarm systems.
12. Strong rooms in bank or building society premises; safes.
13. Partition walls, where moveable and intended to be moved in the course of the qualifying activity.
14. Decorative assets provided for the enjoyment of the public in hotel, restaurant or similar trades.
15. Advertising hoardings; signs, displays and similar assets.
16. Swimming pools (including diving boards, slides and structures on which such boards or slides are mounted).
17. Any glasshouse constructed so that the required environment (namely, air, heat, light, irrigation and temperature) for the growing of plants is provided automatically by means of devices forming an integral part of its structure.
18. Cold stores.
19. Caravans provided mainly for holiday lettings.
20. Buildings provided for testing aircraft engines run within the buildings.
21. Moveable buildings intended to be moved in the course of the qualifying activity.
22. The alteration of land for the purpose only of installing Plant or Machinery.
23. The provision of dry docks.
24. The provision of any jetty or similar structure provided mainly to carry Plant or Machinery.
25. The provision of pipelines or underground ducts or tunnels with a primary purpose of carrying utility conduits.
26. The provision of towers to support floodlights.
27. The provision of –
    (a) any reservoir incorporated into a water treatment works, or
    (b) any service reservoir of treated water for supply within any housing estate or other particular locality.
28. The provision of –
    (a) silos provided for temporary storage, or
    (b) storage tanks.
29. The provision of slurry pits or silage clamps.
30. The provision of fish tanks or fish ponds.
31. The provision of rails, sleepers and ballast for a railway or tramway.
32. The provision of structures and other assets for providing the setting for any ride at an amusement park or exhibition.
33. The provision of fixed zoo cages.

Case Law

The fact that an item appears in List C does not automatically mean that it will qualify for capital allowances. It only means that it may potentially qualify.

Guidance about the meaning of plant has to be found in case law. The cases go back a long way, beginning in 1887. The current state of the law on the meaning of plant derives from the decision in the case of Wimpy International Ltd v Warland and Associated Restaurants Ltd v Warland in the late 1980s. The Judge in that case said that there were three tests to be applied when considering whether or not an item is plant.

1. Is the item stock in trade? If the answer yes, then the item is not plant.
2. Is the item used for carrying on the business? In order to pass the business use test the item must be employed in carrying on the business; it is not enough for the asset to be simply used in the business. For example, product display lighting in a retail store may be plant but general lighting in a warehouse would fail the test.
3. Is the item the business premises or part of the business premises? An item cannot be plant if it fails the premises test, i.e. if the business use is as the premises (or part of the premises) or place on which the business is conducted. The meaning of part of the premises in this context should not be confused with the law of real property. The Inland Revenue's internal manuals suggest there are four general factors to be considered, each of which is a question of fact and degree:
    *   Does the item appear visually to retain a separate identity
    *   With what degree of permanence has it been attached to the building
    *   To what extent is the structure complete without it
    *   To what extent is it intended to be permanent or alternatively is it likely to be replaced within a short period

    There is obviously a core list of items that will usually qualify in the majority of cases. However, many other still need to be looked at on a case-by-case basis. For example, decorative assets in a hotel restaurant may be plant but similar assets in an office reception area would almost certainly not be.

Refurbishment Schemes

Building refurbishment projects will typically be a mixture of capital costs and revenue expenses, unless the works are so extensive that they are more appropriately classified a redevelopment. A straightforward repair or a "like for like" replacement of part of an asset would be a revenue expense, meaning that the entire amount can be deducted from taxable profits in the same year.

Where capital expenditure is incurred that is incidental to the installation of plant or machinery then Section 25 of the 2001 Act allows it to be treated as part of the expenditure on the qualifying item. Incidental expenditure will often include parts of the building that would be otherwise disallowed, as shown in the Lists reproduced above. For example, the cost of forming a lift shaft inside an existing building would be deemed to be part of the expenditure on the provision of the lift.

Rate of Allowances

Capital Allowances on plant and machinery are given in the form of writing down allowances at the rate of 25% per annum on a reducing balance basis. For every £100 of qualifying expenditure £25 is claimable in year 1, £18.75 in year 2 and so on until either the all the allowances have been claimed or the asset is sold. In addition to the basic rate, enhanced rates are available to certain types of business and on certain classes of asset.

Capital expenditure on plant and machinery by a small and medium sized enterprise attracts a 40% first year allowance. In subsequent years allowances are available at the 25% rate mentioned above. The definition of small and medium sized enterprise is broadly one that meets at least 2 of the following criteria:

- Turnover not more than £22.8m
- Assets not more than £11.4m
- Not more than 250 employees

First year allowances are not generally available on the provision of plant and machinery for leasing.

The Enhanced Capital Allowances Scheme

The scheme is one of a series of measures introduced to ensure that the UK meets its target for reducing greenhouse gases under the Kyoto Protocol. 100% first year allowances are available on products included on the Energy Technology List published on the DETR website at www.eca.gov.uk and other technologies supported by the scheme. All businesses will be able to claim the enhanced allowances, but only investments in new and unused Machinery and Plant can qualify. Leased assets only qualify from 17 April 2002.

There are currently sixteen technologies covered by the scheme.

- Air-to-air energy recovery.
- Automatic monitoring and targeting.
- Boilers.
- Combined heat and power e.g. utilisation of the heat produced as a waste by-product in power stations.
- Compact heat exchangers.
- Compressor air equipment.
- Heat pumps for space heating.
- HVAC zone controls.
- Lighting.
- Motors.
- Pipe work Insulation.
- Refrigeration equipment.
- Solar thermal systems.
- Thermal screens.
- Variable Speed Drives.
- Warm air and radiant heaters.
- Radiant and warm air heaters
- Solar heaters
- Energy-efficient refrigeration equipment

The Finance Act 2003 introduced a new category of environmentally beneficial plant and machinery qualifying for 100% first-year allowances. The Water Technology List includes six categories of sustainable water use products, namely water meters, flow controllers, leak detection equipment, low flush toilets, efficient taps and rainwater-harvesting equipment.

Buildings and structures as defined above and long life assets as discussed below cannot qualify.

Long Life Assets

A reduced writing down allowance of 6% per annum is available on plant and machinery that is a long-life asset. A long-life asset is defined as plant and machinery that can reasonably be expected to have a useful economic life of at least 25 years.

The useful economic life is taken as the period from first use until it is likely to cease to be used as a fixed asset of any business. It is important to note that this likely to be a shorter period than an item's physical life.

Plant and machinery provided for use in a building used wholly or mainly as dwelling house, showroom, hotel, office or retail shop or similar premises, or for purposes ancillary to such use, cannot be long-life assets.

In contrast plant and machinery assets in buildings such as factories, cinemas, hospitals and so on are all potentially long-life assets.

Industrial Building Allowances

An industrial building (or structure) is defined in Sections 271 and 274 of the 2001 Act and includes buildings used for the following qualifying purposes:

- Manufacturing
- Processing
- Storage
- Agricultural contracting
- Working foreign plantations
- Fishing
- Mineral extraction

The following undertakings are also qualifying trades:

- Electricity
- Water
- Hydraulic power
- Sewerage
- Transport
- Highway undertakings
- Tunnels
- Bridges
- Inland navigation
- Docks

The definition is extended to include buildings provided for the welfare of workers in a qualifying trade and sports pavilions provided and used for the welfare of workers in any trade. Vehicle repair workshops and roads on industrial estates may also form part of the qualifying expenditure.

Retail shops, showrooms, offices, dwelling houses and buildings used ancillary to a retail purpose are specifically excluded.

Writing Down Allowances

Allowances are given on qualifying expenditure at the rate of 4% per annum on a straight-line basis over 25 years. The allowance is given if the building is being used for a qualifying purpose on the last day of the accounting period. Where the building is used for a non-qualifying purpose that year's allowance is lost.

A purchaser of used industrial building will be entitled to allowances equal to, in very simple terms, the original construction cost after adjustment for any periods of non-qualifying use. The allowances will be spread equally over the remaining period to the date twenty-five years after first use. The only exception to this rule is where the purchaser acquires the building unused from a property developer when the allowances will be based on the purchase price.

Hotel Allowances

Industrial Building Allowances are also available on capital expenditure incurred on constructing a "qualifying hotel". The building must not only be a "hotel" in the normal sense of the word, but must also be a "qualifying hotel" as defined in Section 279 of the 2001 Act, which means satisfying the following conditions:

- The accommodation is in buildings of a permanent nature
- It is open for at least 4 months in the season (April to October)
- It has 10 or more letting bedrooms
- The sleeping accommodation consists wholly or mainly of letting bedrooms
- The services that it provides include breakfast and an evening meal (i.e. there must be a restaurant), the making of beds and cleaning of rooms.

A hotel may be in more than one building and swimming pools, car parks and similar amenities are included in the definition.

Enterprise Zones

A 100% first year allowance is available on capital expenditure incurred on the construction (or the purchase within two years of first use) of any commercial building within a designated enterprise zone, within ten years of the site being so designated. Like other allowances given under the industrial buildings code the building has a life of twenty-five years for tax purposes.

The majority of enterprise zones had reached the end of their ten-year life by 1993. However, in certain very limited circumstances it may still be possible to claim these allowances up to twenty years after the site was first designated.

Flats Over Shops

Tax relief is available on capital expenditure incurred on or after 11 May 2001 on the renovation or conversion of vacant or underused space above shops and other commercial premises to provide flats for rent.

In order to qualify the property must have been built with 1980 and the expenditure incurred on, or in connection with:

- Converting part of a qualifying building into a qualifying flat.
- Renovating an existing flat in a qualifying building if the flat is, or will be a qualifying flat.
- Repairs incidental to conversion or renovation of a qualifying flat, and
- The cost of providing access to the flat(s).

The property must not have more than 4 storeys above the ground floor and it must appear that, when the property was constructed, the floors above the ground floor were primarily for residential use. The ground floor must be authorised for business use at the time of the conversion work and for the period during which the flat is held for letting. Each new flat must be a self-contained dwelling, with external access separate from the ground-floor premises. It must have no more than 4 rooms, excluding kitchen and bathroom. None flats can be "high value" flats, as defined in the legislation. The new flats must be available for letting as a dwelling for a period of not more than 5 years.

An initial allowance of 100 per cent is available or, alternatively, a lower amount may be claimed, in which case the balance may be claimed at a rate of 25 per cent per annum in subsequent a years. The allowances may be recovered if the flat is sold or ceases to be let within 7 years

Business premises renovation allowance

The Business Premises Renovation Allowance (BPRA) was first announced in December 2003. The idea behind the scheme is to bring long-term vacant properties back into productive use by providing 100 per cent capital allowances for the cost of renovating and converting unused premises in disadvantaged areas. The legislation is included in Finance Act 2005 and subject to EU state aid approval BPRA will be introduced later in 2005 and run for five years.

The legislation is identical in many respects to that for flat conversion allowances. The scheme will apply to properties within one of the 1,997 currently designated Enterprise Areas and will apply to the same buildings that previously qualified for SDLT relief. A list of areas and a postcode search tool are available on the Inland Revenue's stamp duty website.

BPRA will be available to both individuals and companies who own or lease business property that has been unused for 12 months or more. Allowances will be available to a person who incurs qualifying capital expenditure on the renovation of business premises.

Agricultural Buildings

Allowances are available on capital expenditure incurred on the construction of buildings and works for the purposes of husbandry on land in the UK. Agricultural building means a building such as a farmhouse or farm building, a fence or other works. A maximum of only one-third of the expenditure on a farmhouse may qualify.

Husbandry includes any method of intensive rearing of livestock or fish on a commercial basis for the production of food for human consumption, and the cultivation of short rotation coppice. Over the years the Courts have held that sheep grazing and poultry farming are husbandry, and that a dairy business and the rearing of pheasants for sport are not. Where the use is partly for other purposes the expenditure can be apportioned.

The rate of allowances available and the way in which the system operates is very similar to that described above for industrial buildings. However, no allowance is ever given if the first use of the building is not for husbandry. A different treatment is also applied following acquisition of a used building unless the parties to the transaction elect otherwise.

Other Capital Allowances

Other types of allowances include those available for capital expenditure on Mineral Extraction, Research and Development, Know-How, Patents, Dredging and Assured Tenancy.

Davis Langdon Crosher & James

Spon's Estimating Costs Guide to Minor Landscaping, Gardening and External Works

Bryan Spain

Especially written for contractors and small businesses carrying out small works, Spon's Estimating Costs Guide to Small Landscaping Work, Gardening and External Works contains accurate information on thousands of rates, each broken down to labour, material overheads and profit.

This is the first book to focus on garden maintenance work on blocks of flats and individual houses, schools and sports fields, garden makeovers, laying patios and paths, small land drainage schemes on farmland, and small-scale local authority maintenance work.

More than just a price book, it gives easy-to-read, professional advice on setting up and running a business including help on producing estimates faster, and keeping estimates accurate and competitive.

Suitable for any size firm from one-man-band to established business, this book contains valuable commercial and cost information that contractors can't afford to be without.

March 2005: 216x138 mm: 304 pages
PB: 0-415-34410-7: £24.99

Land Remediation

The purpose of this section is to review the general background of ground contamination, the cost implications of current legislation and to consider the various remedial measures and to present helpful guidance on the cost of Land Remediation.

It must be emphasised that the cost advice given is an average and that costs can vary considerably from contract to contract depending on individual Contractors, site conditions, type and extent of contamination, methods of working and various other factors as diverse as difficulty of site access and distance from approved tips.

We have structured this Unit Cost section to cover as many aspects of Land Remediation works as possible.

The introduction of the Landfill Directive in July 2004 has had a considerable impact on the cost of Remediation works in general and particularly on the practice of Dig and Dump. The number of Landfill sites licensed to accept Hazardous Waste has drastically reduced and inevitably this has led to increased costs.

Market forces will determine future increases in cost resulting from the introduction of the Landfill Directive and the cost guidance given within this section will require review in light of these factors.

Statutory framework

In July 1999 new contaminated land provisions, contained in Part IIa of the Environmental Protection Act 1990 were introduced. A primary objective of the measures is to encourage the recycling of brownfield land.

Under the Act action to re-mediate land is required only where there are unacceptable actual or potential risks to health or the environment. Sites that have been polluted from previous land use may not need re-mediating until the land use is changed. In addition, it may be necessary to take action only where there are appropriate, cost-effective remediation processes that take the use of the site into account.

The Environment Act 1995 amended the Environment Protection Act 1990 by introducing a new regime designed to deal with the remediation of sites which have been seriously contaminated by historic activities. The regime became operational on 1 April 2000. Local authorities and/or the Environment Agency will regulate seriously contaminated sites which will be known as 'special sites'. The risks involved in the purchase of potentially contaminated sites are high, particularly considering that a transaction can result in the transfer of liability for historic contamination from the vendor to the purchaser.

The contaminated land provisions of the Environmental Protection Act 1990 are only one element of a series of statutory measures dealing with pollution and land remediation that have been and are to be introduced. Others include:

- Groundwater regulations, including pollution prevention measures

- An integrated prevention and control regime for pollution

- Selections of the Water Resources Act 1991, which deals with works notices for site controls,   restoration and clean up.

The contaminated land measures incorporate statutory guidance on the inspection, definition, remediation, apportionment of liabilities and recovery of costs of remediation. The measures are to be applied in accordance with the following criteria:

- The standard of remediation should relate to the present use

- The costs of remediation should be reasonable in relation to the seriousness of the potential harm

- The proposals should be practical in relation to the availability of remediation technology, impact of site constraints and the effectiveness of the proposed clean-up method.

Liability for the costs of remediation rests with either the party that 'caused or knowingly permitted' contamination, or with the current owners or occupiers of the land.

Apportionment of liability, where shared, is determined by the local authority. Although owners or occupiers become liable only if the polluter cannot be identified, the liability for contamination is commonly passed on when land is sold.

The ability to forecast the extent and cost of remedial measures is essential for both parties, so that they can be accurately reflected in the price of the land. If neither the polluter nor owner can be found, the clean up is funded from public resources.

The EU Landfill Directive

The Landfill (England and Wales) Regulations 2002 came into force on 15 June 2002. These new regulations implement the Landfill Directive (Council Directive 1999/31/EC), which aims to prevent, or to reduce as far as possible, the negative environmental effects of landfill. The regulations will have a major impact on waste regulation and the waste management industry in the UK.

The Scottish Executive and the Northern Ireland Assembly will be bringing forward separate legislation to implement the Directive within their regions.

In summary, the Directive requires that:

- Sites are to be classified into one of three categories: hazardous, non-hazardous or inert, according to the type of waste they will receive.
- Higher engineering and operating standards will be followed.
- Biodegradable waste will be progressively diverted away from landfills.
- Certain hazardous and other wastes, including liquids, explosive waste and tyres will be prohibited from landfills.
- Pre-treatment of wastes prior to landfilling will become a requirement.

On 15 July 2004 the co-disposal of hazardous and non-hazardous waste in the same landfill site ended and in July 2005 new waste acceptance criteria will be introduced which will also prevent the disposal of materials contaminated by coal tar.

The effect of this Directive has been to dramatically reduce the hazardous disposal capacity post July 2004, resulting in a **SIGNIFICANT** increase in remediating costs. There are now less than 20 commercial landfills licensed to accept hazardous waste as a direct result of the implementation of the Directive! There are no sites in Wales and only limited capacity in the South of England. This has significantly increased travelling distance and cost for disposal to landfill. The increase in operating expenses incurred by the landfill operators has also resulted in higher tipping costs.

There is likely to be a marked slowdown in brownfield development in the UK in the short to medium term with higher remediation costs, longer clean-up programmes and a lack of viable treatment options for some wastes.

The UK Government established the Hazardous Waste Forum in December 2002 to bring together key stakeholders to advise on the way forward on the management of hazardous waste.

Effect on Disposal Costs

Exactly how and to what extent disposal costs will increase is a matter of much speculation and concern within the waste industry. One major landfill operator has stated, "The price (gate price) will be what the market dictates!" Although most landfills are reluctant to commit to future tipping prices, during the 2nd half of 2004 gate prices for the disposal of hazardous waste increased between 200% and 300%!

For most projects to remain viable there is an increasing need to treat soil in-situ by bioremediation, soil washing or other alternative long-term remediation measures. Waste untreatable on-site such as coal tar will remain a problem. Development costs and programmes need to reflect this change in methodology.

Types of hazardous waste

- Sludges, acids and contaminated wastes from the oil and gas industry
- Acids and toxic chemicals from chemical and electronics industries
- Pesticides from the agrochemical industry
- Solvents, dyes and sludges from leather and textile industries
- Hazardous compounds from metal industries
- Oil, oil filters and brake fluids from vehicles and machines
- Mercury-contaminated waste from crematoria
- Explosives from old ammunition, fireworks and airbags
- Lead, nickel, cadmium and mercury from batteries
- Asbestos from the building industry
- Amalgam from dentists
- Veterinary medicines

Source: Sepa

Land remediation techniques

There are two principal approaches to remediation - dealing with the contamination in situ or off site. The selection of the approach will be influenced by factors such as: initial and long term cost, timeframe for remediation, types of contamination present, depth and distribution of contamination, the existing and planned topography, adjacent land uses, patterns of surface drainage, the location of existing on-site services, depth of excavation necessary for foundations and below-ground services, environmental impact and safety, prospects for future changes in land use and long-term monitoring and maintenance of in situ treatment.

In situ techniques

A range of in situ techniques is available for dealing with contaminants, including:

- Dilution - the reduction of the concentrations of contaminants to below trigger levels by on-site mixing with cleaner material.

- Clean cover - a layer of clean soil is used to segregate contamination from receptor. This technique is best suited to sites with widely dispersed contamination. Costs will vary according to the need for barrier layers to prevent migration of the contaminant.

- On-site encapsulation - the physical containment of contaminants using barriers such as slurry trench cut-off walls. The cost of on-site encapsulation varies in relation to the type and extent of barriers required.

There are also in situ techniques for treating more specific contaminants, including:

- Bio-remediation - for removal of oily, organic contaminants through natural digestion by micro-organisms. The process is slow, taking from one to three years, and is particularly effective for the long-term improvement of a site, prior to a change of use.

- Soil washing - involving the separation of a contaminated soil fraction or oily residue through a washing process. The dewatered contaminant still requires disposal to landfill. In order to be cost effective, 70 - 90% of soil mass needs to be recovered.

- Vacuum extraction - involving the extraction of liquid and gas contaminants from soil by vacuum.

- Thermal treatment - the incineration of contaminated soils on site. The uncontaminated soil residue can be recycled. By-products of incineration can create air pollution and exhaust air treatment may be necessary.

- Stabilisation - cement or lime, is used to physically or chemically bound oily or metal contaminants to prevent leaching or migration. Stabilisation can be used in both in situ and off-site locations.

Off-site techniques

Removal for landfill disposal has, historically, been the most common and cost-effective approach to remediation in the UK, providing a broad spectrum solution by dealing with all contaminants. As discussed above, the implementation of the Landfill Directive has resulted in other techniques becoming more competitive for the disposal of hazardous waste. .

If used in combination with material-handling techniques such as soil washing, the volume of material disposed at landfill sites can be significantly reduced. The disadvantages of the technique include the fact that the contamination is not destroyed, there are risks of pollution during excavation and transfer; road haulage may also cause a local nuisance.

Cost drivers

Cost drivers relate to the selected remediation technique, site conditions and the size and location of a project.

The wide variation of indicative costs of land remediation techniques shown below is largely because of differing site conditions.

Indicative costs of land remediation techniques (excluding landfill tax)		
Remediation technique	**Unit**	**Rate (£/unit)**
Removal – non-hazardous Removal - hazardous	disposed material (m³) disposed material (m³)	80 - 150 135 - 355
Clean cover	surface area of site (m²)	25-60
On-site encapsulation	encapsulated material (m³)	30-95
Bio-remediation	treated material (tonne)	35-100
Soil washing	treated material (tonne)	50-100
Soil flushing	treated material (tonne)	70-130
Vacuum extraction	treated material (tonne)	60-130
Thermal treatment	treated material (tonne)	900-1,450

Factors that need to be considered include:

- Waste classification of the material

- Underground obstructions, pockets of contamination and live services

- Ground water flows and the requirement for barriers to prevent the migration of contaminants

- Health and safety requirements and environmental protection measures

- Location, ownership and land use of adjoining sites

- Distance from landfill tips, capacity of the tip to accept contaminated materials, and transport restrictions

Other project related variables include size, access to disposal sites and tipping charges; the interaction of these factors can have a substantial impact on overall unit rates.

Cost drivers – **cont'd**

The tables below set out the costs of remediation using *dig-and-dump* methods for different sizes of project, differentiated by the disposal of non-hazardous and hazardous material. Variation in site establishment and disposal cost accounts for 60 - 70% of the range in cost.

Variation in the costs of land remediation by removal: Non-hazardous Waste			
Item	Disposal Volume (less than 3000 m³) (£/m³)	Disposal Volume (3000 - 10 000 m³) (£/m³)	Disposal Volume (more than 10 000 m³) (£/m³)
General items and site organisation costs	55 - 90	25 - 40	7 - 20
Site investigation and testing	5 - 10	2 - 6	2 - 5
Excavation and backfill	18 - 35	12 - 25	10 - 20
Disposal costs (including tipping charges but not landfill tax)	20 - 35	20 - 35	20 - 35
Haulage	15 - 30	15 - 30	15 - 30
Total (£/m³)	**113 - 200**	**76 - 136**	**54 - 110**
Allowance for site abnormals	*0 - 10 +*	*0 - 15 +*	*0 - 10 +*

Variation in the costs of land remediation by removal: Hazardous Waste			
Item	Disposal Volume (less than 3000 m³) (£/m³)	Disposal Volume (3000 - 10 000 m³) (£/m³)	Disposal Volume (more than 10 000 m³) (£/m³)
General items and site organisation costs	55 - 90	25 - 40	7 - 20
Site investigation and testing	5 - 10	2 - 6	2 - 5
Excavation and backfill	18 - 35	12 - 25	10 - 20
Disposal costs (including tipping charges but not landfill tax)	70 – 170	70 - 170	70 - 170
Haulage	20-100	20 - 100	20 - 100
Total (£/m³)	**168 - 405**	**129 -341**	**109 - 315**
Allowance for site abnormals	*0 - 10 +*	*0 - 15 +*	*0 - 10 +*

The strict health and safety requirements of remediation can push up the overall costs of site organisation to as much as 50% of the overall project cost. A high proportion of these costs are fixed and, as a result, the unit costs of site organisation increase disproportionally on smaller projects.

Haulage costs are largely determined by the distances to a licensed tip. Current average haulage rates, based on a return journey range from £1.55 to £2.75 per mile. Short journeys to tips, which involve proportionally longer standing times, typically incur higher mileage rates, up to £6.00 per mile. The volatility of oil prices will also have a major impact on haulage rates.

A further source of cost variation relates to tipping charges. The table below summarises typical tipping charges for 2005, exclusive of landfill tax:

Typical 2005 tipping charges (excluding landfill tax)	
Waste classification	**Charges (£/tonne)**
Non-hazardous wastes	12 - 15
Hazardous wastes	35 - 85
Contaminated liquid	20 - 60
Contaminated sludge	45 - 75

Tipping charges fluctuate in relation to the grades of material a tip can accept at any point in time. This fluctuation is a further source of cost risk. Furthermore, tipping charges in the North of England are generally less than in the rest of the country.

In addition, a special waste regulation charge of £16.76 per load, equivalent to 88p per tonne, is also payable. This charge does not apply to non-hazardous wastes.

Landfill tax, increased on 1 April 2005 to £18 a tonne for active waste, is also payable, although exemptions are currently available for the disposal of historically contaminated material (refer also to *'Landfill Tax'* section).

Tax Relief for Remediation of Contaminated Land

The Finance Act 2001 included provisions that allow companies (but not individuals or partnerships) to claim tax relief on capital and revenue expenditure on the "remediation of contaminated land" in the United Kingdom. The relief is available for expenditure incurred on or after 11 May 2001.

A company is able to claim an additional 50% deduction for "qualifying land remediation expenditure" allowed as a deduction in computing taxable profits, and may elect for the same treatment to be applied to qualifying capital expenditure.

The Relief

Qualifying expenditure may be deducted at 150% of the actual amount expended in computing profits for the year in which it is incurred.

For example, a property trading company may buy contaminated land for redevelopment and incurs £250,000 on qualifying land remediation expenditure that is an allowable for tax purposes. It can claim an additional deduction of £125,000, making a total deduction of £375,000. Similarly, a company incurring qualifying capital expenditure on a fixed asset of the business is able to claim the same deduction provided it makes the relevant election within 2 years.

What is Remediation?

Land remediation is defined as the doing of works including preparatory activities such as condition surveys, to the land in question, any controlled waters affected by the land, or adjoining or adjacent land for the purpose of: -

- Preventing or minimising, or remedying or mitigating the effects of, any harm, or any pollution of controlled waters, by reason of which the land is in a contaminated state; or
- Restoring the land or waters to their former state.

Definitions

Contaminated land is defined as land that, because of substances on or under it, is in such a condition that: -

- Harm is or may possibly be caused; or
- Controlled waters are or likely to be polluted.

Land includes buildings on the land, and expenditure on asbestos removal is expected to qualify for this tax relief. It should be noted that the definition is not the same as that used in the Environmental Protection Act Part 11A.

Harm is defined as meaning: -

- Harm to the health of living organisms;
- Interference with the ecological systems of which any living organisms form part;
- Offence to the senses of human beings;
- Damage to property.

Pollution of controlled waters is defined as the entry into such waters of any poisonous, noxious or polluting matter or any solid waste matter. Nuclear sites are specifically excluded.

Conditions

In order to become qualifying, the expenditure must be in land that was in a contaminated state when it was acquired. The land must not have been contaminated by the company, or by a connected company.

Spon's Middle East Construction Costs Handbook
2nd Edition

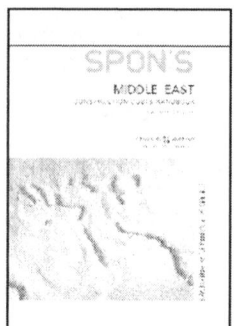

Franklin and Andrews

The indispensable guide to building costs in Bahrain, Egypt, Iran, Iraq, Jordan, Kuwait, Lebanon, Oman, Qatar, Saudi Arabia, Syria, Turkey and the UAE. Features detailed information across all sectors and by individual country, plus comparative information.

July 2005: 234x156 mm: 384 pages
HB: 0-415-36315-2: £170.00

To Order: Tel: +44 (0) 1264 343071 Fax: +44 (0) 1264 343005, or
Post: Taylor and Francis Customer Services, Thomson Publishing Services, Cheriton House, Andover, Hants, SP10 5BE, UK Email: book.orders@tandf.co.uk

For a complete listing of all our titles visit:
www.sponpress.com

Taylor & Francis
Taylor & Francis Group plc

The Landfill Tax

The Tax

The Landfill tax came into operation on 1 October 1996. It is levied on operators of licensed landfill sites at the following rates:

£2 per tonne	-	Inactive or inert wastes. Included are soil, stones, brick, plain and reinforced concrete, plaster and glass.
£18 per tonne	-	All other taxable wastes. Included are timber, paint and other organic wastes generally found in demolition work, builders skips etc.

From 1 April 2005 the rate of for "all other taxable wastes" was increased from £15 to £18 per tonne, whilst the rate for "inactive or inert wastes" remained at £2 per tonne.

Mixtures containing wastes not classified as inactive or inert will not qualify for the lower rate of tax unless the amount of non-qualifying material is small and there is no potential for pollution. Water can be ignored and the weight discounted.

Calculating the Weight of Waste

There are two options:

*   If licensed sites have a weighbridge, tax will be levied on the actual weight of waste.

*   If licensed sites do not have a weighbridge, tax will be levied on the permitted weight of the lorry based on an alternative method of calculation based on volume to weight factors for various categories of waste.

Effect on Prices

The tax is paid by Landfill site operators only. Tipping charges reflect this additional cost.

As an example, Spon's A & B rates for mechanical disposal will be affected as follows:

* Inactive waste	Spon's A & B 2006 net rate	£12.36 per m³
	Tax, 2 t per m³ (unbulked) @ £2.00	£ 4.00 per m³
	Spon's rate including tax (page 114)	£16.36 per m³

Effect on Prices - cont'd

*   Active waste   Active waste will normally be disposed of by skip and will probably be mixed
                                              inactive waste. The tax levied will depend on the weight of the materials in the
                                              skip which can vary significantly.

Exemptions

The following disposals are exempt from Landfill Tax:

*   dredgings which arise from the maintenance of inland waterways and harbours.
*   naturally occurring materials arising from mining or quarrying operations.
*   waste resulting from the cleaning up of historically contaminated land, although to obtain an exemption it is necessary
    to first obtain a contaminated land certificate from Customs and Excise.
*   waste removed from one site to be used on another or to be recycled or incinerated.

An additional exemption was introduced from the 1st October 1999 for inert waste used to restore landfill sites and to fill
working and old quarries with a planning condition or obligation in existence to fill the void.

For further information contact the National Advisory Service, Telephone: 0845 010 9000 and select option 3

Revisions to Part L of the Building Regulations

Introduction

The revised Part L of the Building Regulations was published on 31 October 2001. The main thrust of the revisions is to control carbon emissions from buildings created by their environmental services. 46% of the UK's carbon emissions relate to the occupation of buildings. The Kyoto protocol set targets for a reduction in the production of six greenhouse gases to 12½% below their 1990 output by 2008-2012. In addition the Government has also set a target for the reduction of carbon dioxide production to 20% below 1990 levels by 2010. The revisions to Part L is one of the Government's principal tools in promoting their post-Kyoto environmental agenda. Much of the impact of the new Part L will be felt by house builders, as domestic housing produces almost 59% of the UK's building related carbon output, and it is the prime target of the new regulations. However, the regulations also set challenging targets for non-domestic buildings which will affect designers, constructors and clients. A phased programme of revisions to Part L is also planned as part of an on-going process to increase the performance of buildings to meet the 2010 carbon production targets.

Cost Implications

It is likely that the revisions to Part L will have a significant effect on the costs of simple buildings, where the costs of the envelope comprise a high proportion of the overall cost.

Most of the additional cost of compliance will be associated with enhancements to the thermal performance of the envelope. Buildings with a high ratio of wall and roof area to floor area will incur particularly high costs associated with improved fabric insulation. Window blinds, often installed as part of a tenant's fit-out may also be required as part of the base-build to provide enhanced solar control.

One of the results of improved thermal performance of buildings is the reduction of heating and cooling loads. As a result, any additional services costs will be offset, in whole or in part, by savings on the sizing of heating and cooling plant. Savings on the services installation will not offset the increased cost of fabric and solar control however.

The rates within the 'Prices for Measured Works' and the 'Approximate Estimating' sections of Spon's Architects' and Builders' Price Book 2005 have been adjusted to take into account the implications of buildings complying with the revised Part L Regulations.

Spon's African Construction Cost Handbook
2nd Edition

Franklin and Andrews

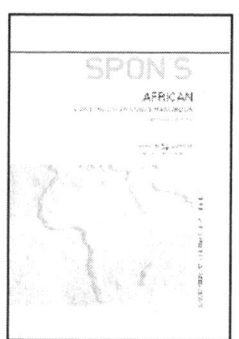

The indispensable guide to building costs in thirteen African countries including Algeria, Cameroon, Chad, Cote d'Ivoire, Gabon, The Gambia, Ghana, Kenya, Liberia, Nigeria, Senegal, South Africa and Zambia. Features detailed information across all sectors and by individual country, plus comparative information.

July 2005: 234x156 mm: 368 pages
HB: 0-415-36314-4: £170.00

To Order: Tel: +44 (0) 1264 343071 Fax: +44 (0) 1264 343005, or
Post: Taylor and Francis Customer Services, Thomson Publishing Services, Cheriton House, Andover, Hants, SP10 5BE, UK Email: book.orders@tandf.co.uk

For a complete listing of all our titles visit:
www.sponpress.com

Taylor & Francis
Taylor & Francis Group plc

Value Added Tax

Introduction

Value Added Tax (VAT) is a tax on the consumption of goods and services. The UK adopted VAT when it joined the European Community in 1973. The principal source of European law in relation to VAT is the EC Sixth Directive 77/388 which is currently restated and consolidated in the UK through the VAT Act 1994 and various Statutory Instruments as amended by subsequent Finance Acts. The tax is administered in the UK by HM Revenue & Customs.

VAT Notice 708: Buildings and construction (July 2002) gives an interpretation of the law in connection with construction works from the point of view of HM Revenue & Customs. VAT tribunals and court decisions since the date of this publication will affect the application of the law in certain instances. The Notice is available on HM Revenue & Customs website at www.hmrc.gov.uk.

The scope of VAT

VAT is payable on:

- Supplies of goods and services made in the UK
- By a taxable person
- In the course or furtherance of business; and
- Which are not specifically exempted or zero-rated.

Rates of VAT

There are three rates of VAT:

- A standard rate, currently 17.5%
- A reduced rate, currently 5%; and
- A zero rate.

Additionally some supplies are exempt from VAT and others are outside the scope of VAT.

Recovery of VAT

When a taxpayer makes taxable supplies he must account for VAT at the appropriate rate of either 17.5% or 5%. This VAT then has to be passed to HM Revenue & Customs. This VAT will normally be charged to the taxpayer's customers.

As a VAT registered person, the taxpayer can reclaim from HM Revenue & Customs as much of the VAT incurred on their purchases as relates to the standard-rated, reduced-rated and zero-rated onward supplies they make. A person cannot however reclaim VAT that relates to any non-business activity or to any exempt supplies they make.

At predetermined intervals the taxpayer will pay to HM Revenue & Customs the excess of VAT collected over the VAT they can reclaim. However if the VAT reclaimed is more than the VAT collected, the taxpayer can reclaim the difference from HM Revenue & Customs.

Example

X Ltd constructs a block of flats. It sells long leases to buyers for a premium. X Ltd has constructed a new building designed as a dwelling and will have granted a long lease. This sale of a long lease is VAT zero-rated. This means any VAT incurred in connection with the development that which X Ltd will have paid (e.g. payments for consultants and certain preliminary services) will be reclaimable. For reasons detailed below the builder employed by X Ltd will not have charged VAT on his construction services.

Taxable Persons

A taxable person is an individual, firm, company etc who is required to be registered for VAT. A person who makes taxable supplies above certain value limits is required to be registered. The current registration limit is £60,000 for 2005-06. The threshold is exceeded if at the end of any month the value of taxable supplies in the period of one year then ending is over the limit, or at any time, if there are reasonable grounds for believing that the value of the taxable supplies in the period of 30 days than beginning will exceed £60,000.

A person who makes taxable supplies below these limits is entitled to be registered on a voluntary basis if they wish, for example in order to recover VAT incurred in relation to those taxable supplies.

In addition, a person who is not registered for VAT in the UK but acquires goods from another EC member state, or make distance sales in the UK, above certain value limits may be required to register for VAT in the UK.

VAT Exempt Supplies

If a supply is exempt from VAT this means that no tax is payable – but equally the person making the exempt supply cannot normally recover any of the VAT on their own costs relating to that supply.

Generally property transactions such as leasing of land and buildings are exempt unless a landlord chooses to standard-rate its supplies by a process known as electing to waive exemption – more commonly known as opting to tax. This means that VAT is added to rental income and also that VAT incurred, on say, an expensive refurbishment, is recoverable.

Supplies outside the scope of VAT

Supplies are outside the scope of VAT if they are:

- Made by someone who is not a taxable person
- Made outside the UK; or
- Not made in the course or furtherance of business

In course or furtherance of business

VAT must be accounted for on all taxable supplies made in the course or furtherance of business with the corresponding recovery of VAT on expenditure incurred.

If a taxpayer also carries out non-business activities then VAT incurred in relation to such supplies is not recoverable.

In VAT terms, business means any activity continuously performed which is mainly concerned with making supplies for a consideration. This includes:

- Any one carrying on a trade, vocation or profession;
- The provision of membership benefits by clubs, associations and similar bodies in return for a subscription or other consideration; and
- Admission to premises for a charge.

It may also include the activities of other bodies including charities and non-profit making organisations.

Examples of non-business activities are:

- Providing free services or information;
- Maintaining museums, or particular historic sites;
- Publishing religious or political views.

Construction Services

In general the provision of construction services by a contractor will be VAT standard rated at 17.5%, however, there are a number of exceptions for construction services provided in relation to certain residential and charitable use buildings.

The supply of building materials is VAT standard rated at 17.5%, however, where these materials are supplied as part of the construction services the VAT liability of those materials follows that of the construction services supplied.

Zero-rated construction services

The following construction services are VAT zero-rated including the supply of related building materials.

The construction of new dwellings

The supply of services in the course of the construction of a building designed for use as a dwelling or number of dwellings is zero-rated other than the services of an architect, surveyor or any other person acting as a consultant or in a supervisory capacity.

The following conditions must be satisfied in order for the works to qualify for zero-rating:

1. The work must not amount to the conversion, reconstruction or alteration of an existing building;
2. The work must not be an enlargement of, or extension to, an existing building except to the extent that the enlargement or extension creates an additional dwelling or dwellings;
3. The building must be designed as a dwelling or number of dwellings. Each dwelling must consist of self-contained living accommodation with no provision for direct internal access from the dwelling to any other dwelling or part of a dwelling;
4. Statutory planning consent must have been granted for the construction of the dwelling, and construction carried out in accordance with that consent;
5. Separate use or disposal of the dwelling must not be prohibited by the terms of any covenant, statutory planning consent or similar provision.

The construction of a garage at the same time as the dwelling can also be zero-rated as can the demolition of any existing building on the site of the new dwelling

A building only ceases to be an existing building (see points 1. and 2. above) when it is:

1. Demolished completely to ground level; or when
2. The part remaining above ground level consists of no more than a single façade (or a double façade on a corner site) the retention of which is a condition or requirement of statutory planning consent or similar permission.

The construction of a new building for 'relevant residential or charitable' use

The supply of services in the course of the construction of a building designed for use as a relevant residential or charitable building is zero-rated other than the services of an architect, surveyor or any other person acting as a consultant or in a supervisory capacity.

A 'relevant residential' use building means:

1. A home or other institution providing residential accommodation for children;
2. A home or other institution providing residential accommodation with personal care for persons in need of personal care by reason of old age, disablement, past or present dependence on alcohol or drugs or past or present mental disorder;
3. A hospice;
4. Residential accommodation for students or school pupils
5. Residential accommodation for members of any of the armed forces;
6. A monastery, nunnery, or similar establishment; or
7. An institution which is the sole or main residence of at least 90% of its residents.

The construction of a new building for 'relevant residential or charitable' use – continued

A 'relevant residential' purpose building does not include use as a hospital, a prison or similar institution or as an hotel, inn or similar establishment.

A 'relevant charitable' use means use by a charity:

1.　Otherwise than in the course or furtherance of a business; or
2.　As a village hall or similarly in providing social or recreational facilities for a local community.

Non qualifying use which is not expected to exceed 10% of the time the building is normally available for use can be ignored. The calculation of business use can be based on time, floor area or head count subject to approval being acquired from HM Revenue & Customs.

The construction services can only be zero-rated if a certificate is given by the end user to the contractor carrying out the works confirming that the building is to be used for a qualifying purpose i.e. for a 'relevant residential or charitable' purpose. It follows that such services can only be zero-rated when supplied to the end user and, unlike supplies relating to dwellings, supplies by sub contractors cannot be zero-rated.

The construction of an annex used for a 'relevant charitable' purpose

Construction services provided in the course of construction of an annexe for use entirely or partly for a 'relevant charitable' purpose can be zero-rated.

In order to qualify the annexe must:

1.　Be capable of functioning independently from the existing building;
2.　Have its own main entrance; and
3.　Be covered by a qualifying use certificate.

The conversion of a non-residential building into dwellings or the conversion of a building from non-residential use to 'relevant residential' use where the supply is to a 'relevant' housing association

The supply to a 'relevant' housing association in the course of conversion of a non-residential building or non-residential part of a building into:

1.　A building or part of a building designed as a dwelling or number of dwellings; or
2.　A building or part of a building for use solely for a relevant residential purpose,

of any services related to the conversion other than the services of an architect, surveyor or any person acting as a consultant or in a supervisory capacity are zero-rated.

A 'relevant' housing association is defined as:

1.　A registered social landlord within the meaning of Part I of the Housing Act 1996
2.　A registered housing association within the meaning of the Housing Associations Act 1985 (Scottish registered housing associations), or
3.　A registered housing association within the meaning of Part II of the Housing (Northern Ireland) Order 1992 (Northern Irish registered housing associations).

If the building is to be used for a 'relevant residential' purpose the housing association should issue a qualifying use certificate to the contractor completing the works.

The construction of a permanent park for residential caravans

The supply in the course of the construction of any civil engineering work 'necessary for' the development of a permanent park for residential caravans of any services related to the construction can be VAT zero-rated. This includes access roads, paths, drainage, sewerage and the installation of mains water, power and gas supplies.

Certain building alterations for "handicapped" persons

Certain goods and services supplied to a "handicapped" person, or a charity making these items and services available to "handicapped persons" can be zero-rated. The recipient of these goods or services needs to give the supplier an appropriate written declaration that they are entitled to benefit from zero rating.

The following services (amongst others) are zero-rated:

1.   the installation of specialist lifts and hoists and their repair and maintenance
2.   the construction of ramps, widening doorways or passageways including any preparatory work and making good work
3.   the provision, extension and adaptation of a bathroom, washroom or lavatory; and
4.   emergency alarm call systems

Approved alterations to protected buildings

A supply in the course of an 'approved alteration' to a 'protected building' of any services other than the services of an architect, surveyor or any person acting as consultant or in a supervisory capacity can be zero-rated.

A 'protected building' is defined as a building that is:

1.   designed to remain as or become a dwelling or number of dwellings after the alterations; or
2.   is intended for use for a 'relevant residential or charitable purpose' after the alterations; and which is;
3.   a listed building or scheduled ancient monument.

A listed building does not include buildings that are in conservation areas but not on the statutory list, or buildings included in non-statutory local lists.

An 'approved alteration' is an alteration to a 'protected building' that requires and has obtained listed building consent or scheduled monument consent. This consent is necessary for any works that affect the character of a building of special architectural or historic interest.

It is important to note that 'approved alterations' do not include any works of repair or maintenance or any incidental alteration to the fabric of a building that results from the carrying out of repairs or maintenance work.

A 'protected building' that is intended for use for a 'relevant residential or charitable purpose' will require the production of a qualifying use certificate by the end user to the contractor providing the alteration services.

Listed Churches are 'relevant charitable' use buildings and where 'approved alterations' are being carried out zero-rate VAT can be applied. Additionally since April 1 2001, listed places of worship can apply for a grant for repair and maintenance works equal to the difference between the VAT paid at 17.5% on the repair and maintenance works and the amount that would have been charged if VAT had been 5%.

With effect from 1 April 2004, it has been possible to reclaim the full amount of VAT paid on eligible works carried out on or after 1 April 2004. Information relating to the scheme can be obtained from the website at www.lpwscheme.org.uk.

DIY Builders and Converters

Private individuals who decide to construct their own home are able to reclaim VAT they pay on goods they use to construct their home by use of a special refund mechanism made by way of an application to HM Revenue & Customs. This also applies to services provided in the conversion of an existing non-residential building to form a new dwelling.

The scheme is meant to ensure that private individuals do not suffer the burden of VAT if they decide to construct their own home.

Charities may also qualify for a refund on the purchase of materials incorporated into a building used for non-business purposes where they provide their own free labour for the construction of a 'relevant charitable' use building.

Reduced-rated construction services

The following construction services are subject to the reduced rate of VAT of 5%, including the supply of related building materials.

A changed number of dwellings conversion

In order to qualify for the 5% rate there must be a different number of 'single household dwellings' within a building than there were before commencement of the conversion works. A 'single household dwelling' is defined as a dwelling that is designed for occupation by a single household.

These conversions can be from 'relevant residential' purpose buildings, non-residential buildings and houses in multiple occupation.

A house in multiple occupation conversion

This relates to construction services provided in the course of converting a 'single household dwelling', a number of 'single household dwellings', a non-residential building or a 'relevant residential' purpose building into a house for multiple occupation such as a bedsit accommodation.

A special residential conversion

A special residential conversion involves the conversion of a 'single household dwelling', a house in multiple occupation or a non-residential builidng into a 'relevant residential' purpose building such as student accommodation or a care home.

Renovation of derelict dwellings

The provision of renovation services in connection with a dwelling or 'relevant residential' purpose building that has been empty for three or more years prior to the date of commencement of construction works.can be carried out at a reduced rate of VAT of 5%.

Installation of energy saving materials

The supply and installation of certain energy saving materials including insulation, draught stripping, central heating and hot water controls and solar panels in a residential building or a building used for a relevant charitable purpose.

Grant-funded of heating equipment or connection of a gas supply

The grant funded supply and installation of heating appliances, connection of a mains gas supply, supply, installation, maintenance and repair of central heating systems, and supply and installation of renewable source heating systems, to qualifying persons.   A qualifying person is someone aged 60 or over or is in receipt of various specified benefits.

Installation of security goods

The grant funded supply and installation of security goods to a qualifying person.

Building Contracts

Design and build contracts

If a contractor provides a design and build service relating to works to which the reduced or zero rate of VAT is applicable then any design costs incurred by the contractor will follow the VAT liability of the principal supply of construction services.

Management contracts

A management contractor acts as a main contractor for VAT purposes and the VAT liability of his services will follow that of the construction services provided. If the management contractor only provides advice without engaging trade contractors his services will be VAT standard rated.

Construction Management and Project Management

The project manger or construction management is appointed by the client to plan, manage and co-ordinate a construction project. This will involve establishing competitive bids for all the elements of the work and the appointment of trade contractors. The trade contractors are engaged directly by the client for their services. The VAT liability of the trade contractors will be determined by the nature of the construction services they provide and the building being constructed.

The fees of the construction manager or project manager will be VAT standard rated. If the construction manager also provides some construction services these works may be zero or reduced rated if the works qualify.

Liquidated and Ascertained Damages

Liquidated damages are outside of the scope of VAT as compensation. The employer should not reduce the VAT amount due on a payment under a building contract on account of a deduction of damages. In contrast an agreed reduction in the contract price will reduce the VAT amount.

Davis Langdon Crosher & James

Spon's Manual for Educational Premises

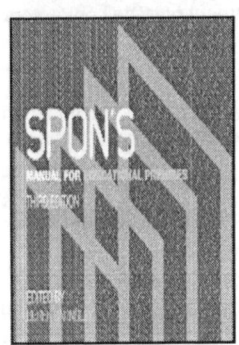

Derek Barnsley

Spon's Manual for Educational Premises is an essential reference book for planning, building, remodelling, repairing, maintaining and managing a wide range of both modern and historic educational premises.

It contains clear, practical guidance for local authorities, head teachers and governing boards responsible for planning, costing, commissioning, supervising and paying for building work and maintenance services. The book is equally essential for architects, surveyors and other professionals and contractors carrying out work in the educational sector.

The third edition has been revised to respond to the evolution of new teaching methods and technology, the development of vocational training and to meet new mandatory regulations relating to children who require special care. The book focuses on cost and performance, including PFI and PPP criteria, but with added emphasis on economic planning to improve standards in design and performance to meet detailed educational needs.

January 2004: 297x210 mm: 464 pages
HB: 0-415-28077-X: £200.00

To Order: Tel: +44 (0) 1264 343071 Fax: +44 (0) 1264 343005, or
Post: Taylor and Francis Customer Services, Thomson Publishing Services, Cheriton House, Andover, Hants, SP10 5BE, UK Email: book.orders@tandf.co.uk

For a complete listing of all our titles visit:

www.sponpress.com

Taylor & Francis
Taylor & Francis Group plc

PART V

Tables and Memoranda

This part of the book contains the following sections:

Understanding the Building Regulations

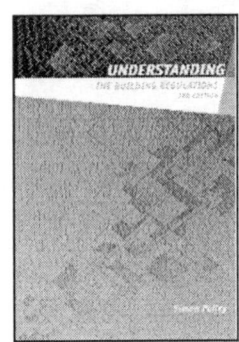

Simon Polley

In this third edition of the bestselling guide, Simon Polley outlines the latest changes to the building regulations with coverage of the updated Parts A, B, C, E, H, J, L and M together with the new Part P. Written by a leading industry practitioner, Understanding the Building Regulations is a clear, well presented, jargon-free and practical pocket reference. Ideal as an introductory text for students, this is also of everyday use for professionals.

Preface. Acknowledgements. Introduction. The Building Regulations 2000. Approved Document to support Regulation 7: Materials and Workmanship. Approved Document A: Structure. Approved Document B: Fire Safety. Approved Document C: Site Preparation and Resistance to Moisture. Approved Document D: Toxic Substances. Approved Document E: Resistance to the Passage of Sound. Approved Document F: Ventilation. Approved Document G: Hygiene. Approved Document H: Drainage and Waste Disposal. Approved Document K: Protection from Falling Collision and Impact. Document L: Conservation of Fuel and Power. Approved Document M: Access and Facilities for Disabled People. Approved Document N: Glazing - Safety in Relation to Impact, Opening and Cleaning. Further Information. Index.

May 2005: 234x156 mm
PB: 0-415-34917-6: £18.99

To Order: Tel: +44 (0) 1264 343071 Fax: +44 (0) 1264 343005, or
Post: Taylor and Francis Customer Services, Thomson Publishing Services, Cheriton House, Andover, Hants, SP10 5BE, UK Email: book.orders@tandf.co.uk

For a complete listing of all our titles visit :
www.sponpress.com

Tables and Memoranda

CONVERSION TABLES

	Unit		Conversion factors		

Length

Millimetre	mm	1 in	= 25.4 mm	1 mm	= 0.0394 in
Centimetre	cm	1 in	= 2.54 cm	1 cm	= 0.3937 in
Metre	m	1 ft	= 0.3048 m	1 m	= 3.2808 ft
		1 yd	= 0.9144 m		= 1.0936 yd
Kilometre	km	1 mile	= 1.6093 km	1km	= 0.6214 mile

Note:
1 cm	= 10 mm	1 ft	= 12 in
1 m	= 1 000 mm	1 yd	= 3 ft
1 km	= 1 000 m	1 mile	= 1 760 yd

Area

Square Millimetre	mm^2	$1\ in^2$	$= 645.2\ mm^2$	$1\ mm^2$	$= 0.0016\ in^2$
Square Centimetre	cm^2	$1\ in^2$	$= 6.4516\ cm^2$	$1\ cm^2$	$= 1.1550\ in^2$
Square Metre	m^2	$1\ ft^2$	$= 0.0929\ m^2$	$1\ m^2$	$= 10.764\ ft^2$
		$1\ yd^2$	$= 0.8361\ m^2$	$1\ m^2$	$= 1.1960\ yd^2$
Square Kilometre	km^2	$1\ mile^2$	$= 2.590\ km^2$	$1\ km^2$	$= 0.3861\ mile^2$

Note:
$1\ cm^2$	$= 100\ mm^2$	$1\ ft^2$	$= 144\ in^2$
$1\ m^2$	$= 10\ 000\ cm^2$	$1\ yd^2$	$= 9\ ft^2$
$1\ km^2$	$= 100$ hectares	1 acre	$= 4\ 840\ yd^2$
		$1\ mile^2$	$= 640$ acres

Volume

Cubic Centimetre	cm^3	$1\ cm^3$	$= 0.0610\ in^3$	$1\ in^3$	$= 16.387\ cm^3$
Cubic Decimetre	dm^3	$1\ dm^3$	$= 0.0353\ ft^3$	$1\ ft^3$	$= 28.329\ dm^3$
Cubic Metre	m^3	$1\ m^3$	$= 35.3147\ ft^3$	$1\ ft^3$	$= 0.0283\ m^3$
		$1\ m^3$	$= 1.3080\ yd^3$	$1\ yd^3$	$= 0.7646\ m^3$
Litre	l	1 l	= 1.76 pint	1 pint	= 0.5683 l
			= 2.113 US pt		= 0.4733 US l

Note:
$1\ dm^3$	$= 1\ 000\ cm^3$	$1\ ft^3$	$= 1\ 728\ in^3$
$1\ m^3$	$= 1\ 000\ dm^3$	$1\ yd^3$	$= 27\ ft^3$
1 l	$= 1\ dm^3$		

1 pint	= 20 fl oz
1 gal	= 8 pints

Neither the Centimetre nor Decimetre are SI units, and as such their use, particularly that of the Decimetre, is not widespread outside educational circles.

Mass

Milligram	mg	1 mg	= 0.0154 grain	1 grain	= 64.935 mg
Gram	g	1 g	= 0.0353 oz	1 oz	= 28.35 g
Kilogram	kg	1 kg	= 2.2046 lb	1 lb	= 0.4536 kg
Tonne	t	1 t	= 0.9842 ton	1 ton	= 1.016 t

Note:
1 g	= 1000 mg		1 oz	= 437.5 grains
1 kg	= 1000 g	1 lb	= 16 oz	1 ton
1 t	= 1000 kg	1 stone	= 14 lb	

1 cwt	= 112 lb
= 20 cwt	

CONVERSION TABLES

Force	Unit	Conversion factors			
Newton	N	1 lbf	= 4.448 N	1 kgf	=9.807 N
Kilonewton	kN	1 lbf	= 0.004448 kN	1 ton f	=9.964 kN
Meganewton	MN	100 tonf	= 0.9964 MN		

Pressure and stress

Kilonewton per square metre	kN/m^2	1 lbf/in^2	= 6.895 kN/m^2
		1 bar	= 100 kN/m^2
Meganewton per MN/m^2		1 tonf/ft^2	= 107.3 kN/m^2 = 0.1073
square metre	MN/m^2	1 kgf/cm^2	= 98.07 kN/m^2
		1 lbf/ft^2	= 0.04788 kN/m^2

Coefficient of consolidation (Cv) or swelling

Square metre per year	m^2/year	1 cm^2/s	= 3 154 m^2/year
		1 ft^2/year	= 0.0929 m^2/year

Coefficient of permeability

Metre per second	m/s	1 cm/s	= 0.01 m/s
Metre per year	m/year	1 ft/year	= 0.3048 m/year
			= 0.9651 x (10)^{8}m/s

Temperature

Degree Celsius $^\circ$C $^\circ$C $= \dfrac{5}{9}$ x ($^\circ$F - 32) $^\circ$F $= \dfrac{(9 \times {}^\circ C)}{5} + 32$

FORMULAE

Two dimensional figures

Figure	Area
Square	(side)^2
Rectangle	Length x breadth
Triangle	½ (base x height)
	or $\sqrt{(s(s - a)(s-b)(s-c))}$ where a, b and c are the lengths of the three sides, and s $= \dfrac{a + b + c}{2}$
	or $a^2 = b^2 + c^2 - (2b\ c\cos A)$ where A is the angle opposite side a
Hexagon	2.6 x (side)^2
Octagon	4.83 x (side)^2
Trapezoid	height x ½ (base + top)
Circle	3.142 x radius^2 or 0.7854 x diameter^2 (circumference = 2 x 3.142 x radius or 3.142 x diameter)

FORMULAE

Two dimensional figures

Figure	Area
Sector of a circle	½ x length of arc x radius
Segment of a circle	area of sector - area of triangle
Ellipse	3.142 x AB (where A = ½ x height and B = ½ x length)
Bellmouth	$\frac{3}{14}$ x radius^2.

Three dimensional figures

Figure	Volume	Surface Area
Prism	Area of base x height	circumference of base x height
Cube	(side)^3	6 x (side)^2
Cylinder	3.142 x radius^2 x height	2 x 3.142 x radius x (height - radius)
Sphere	$\frac{4}{3}$ x 3.142 x radius^3	4 x 3.142 x radius^2
Segment of a sphere	$\frac{(3.142 \times h) \times (3 \times r^2 + h^2)}{6}$	2 x 3.142 x r x h
Pyramid	1/3 of area of base x height	½ x circumference of base x slant height
Cone	1/3 x 3.142 x radius^2 x h	3.142 x radius x slant height
Frustrum of a pyramid	1/3 x height [A + B + √(AB)] where A is the area of the large end and B is the area of the small end	½ x mean circumference x slant height
Frustrum of a cone	(1/3 x 3.142 x height (R^2 + r^2 + R x r)) where R is the radius of the large end and r is the radius of the small end	3.142 x slant height x (R + r)

Other formulae

Formula	Description
Pythagoras' two theorum	$A^2 = B^2 + C^2$ where A is the hypotenuse of a right-angled triangle and B and C are the adjacent sides
Simpson's Rule	Volume $= \frac{x}{3}$ [(y$_1$ + y$_n$) + 2(y$_3$ + y$_5$) + 4(y$_2$ + y$_4$)] The volume to be measured must be represented by an odd number of cross-sections (y$_1$ -y$_n$) taken at fixed intervals (x), the sum of the areas at even numbered intermediate cross-sections (y$_2$, y$_4$, etc.) is multiplied by 4 and the sum of the areas at odd numbered intermediate cross-sections (y$_3$, y$_5$, etc.) is multiplied by 2, and the end cross-sections (y$_1$ and y$_n$) taken once only. The resulting *weighted average* of these areas is multiplied by 1/3 of the distance between the cross-sections (x) to give the total volume.

FORMULAE

Other formulae

Formula	Description
Trapezoidal Rule	(0.16 x [Total length of trench] x [area of first section x 4 times area of middle section + area of last section])

Note: Both Simpson's Rule and Trapezoidal Rule are useful in accurately calculating the volume of an irregular trench, or similar longitudinal earthworks movement, e.g. road construction.

DESIGN LOADINGS FOR BUILDINGS

Note: Refer to BS 6399: Part 1: 1996 Code of Practice for Dead and Imposed Loads min. loading examples.

Definitions

Dead load: The load due to the weight of all walls, permanent partitions, floors, roofs and finishes, including services and all other permanent construction.

Imposed load: The load assumed to be produced by the intended occupancy or use, including the weight of moveable partitions, distributed, concentrated, impact, inertia and snow loads, but excluding wind loads.

Distributed load: The uniformly distributed static loads per square metre of plan area which provide for the effects of normal use. Where no values are given for concentrated load it may be assumed that the tabulated distributed load is adequate for design purposes.

Note: The general recommendations are not applicable to certain atypical usages particularly where mechanical stacking, plant or machinery are to be installed and in these cases the designer should determine the loads from a knowledge of the equipment and processes likely to be employed.

The additional imposed load to provide for partitions, where their positions are not shown on the plans, on beams and floors, where these are capable of effective lateral distributional of the load, is a uniformly distributed load per square metre of not less than one-third of the weight per metre run by the partitions but not less than 1 kN/m².

Floor area usage	Distributed load KN/m^2	Concentrated load $kN/300\,m^2$
Industrial occupancy class (workshops, factories)		
Foundries	20.0	-
Cold storage of storage height	5.0 for each metre with a minimum of 15.0	9.0
Paper storage, for printing plants	4.0 for each metre of storage height	9.0
Storage, other than types listed separately	2.4 for each metre of storage height	7.0
Type storage and other areas in printing plants	12.5	9.0

DESIGN LOADINGS FOR BUILDINGS

Floor area usage load	Distributed load kN/m²	Concentrated load kN/300m²
Industrial occupancy class (workshops, factories) - cont'd		
Boiler rooms, motor rooms, fan rooms and the like, including the weight of machinery	7.5	4.5
Factories, workshops and similar buildings	5.0	4.5
Corridors, hallways, foot bridges, etc. subject to loads greater than for crowds, such as wheeled vehicles, trolleys and the like	5.0	4.5
Corridors, hallways, stairs, landings, footbridges, etc.	4.0	4.5
Machinery halls, circulation spaces therein	4.0	4.5
Laboratories (including equipment), kitchens, laundries	3.0	4.5
Workrooms, light without storage	2.5	1.8
Toilet rooms	2.0	-
Cat walks	-	1.0 at 1 m centres
Institutional and educational occupancy class (prisons, hospitals, schools, colleges)		
Dense mobile stacking (books) on mobile trolleys	4.8 for each metre of stack height but with a minimum of 9.6	7.0
Stack rooms (books)	2.4 for each metre of stack height but with a minimum of 6.5	7.0
Stationery stores	4.0 for each metre of storage height	9.0
Boiler rooms, motor rooms, fan rooms and the like, including the weight of machinery	7.5	4.5
Corridors, hallways, etc. subject to loads greater than from crowds, such as wheeled vehicles, trolleys and the like	5.0	4.5

DESIGN LOADINGS FOR BUILDINGS

Floor area usage load	Distributed load kN/m^2	Concentrated load kN/300m^2
Institutional and educational occupancy class (prisons, hospitals, schools, colleges) - cont'd		
Drill rooms and drill halls	5.0	9.0
Assembly areas without fixed seating, stages gymnasia	5.0	3.6
Bars	5.0	-
Projection rooms	5.0	-
Corridors, hallways, aisles, stairs, landings, foot-bridges, etc.	4.0	4.5
Reading rooms with book storage, e.g. libraries	4.0	4.5
Assembly areas with fixed seating	4.0	-
Laboratories (including equipment), kitchens, laundries	3.0	4.5
Corridors, hallways, aisles, landings, stairs, etc. not subject to crowd loading	3.0	2.7
Classrooms, chapels	3.0	2.7
Reading rooms without storage	2.5	4.5
Areas for equipment	2.0	1.8
X-ray rooms, operating rooms, utility rooms	2.0	4.5
Dining rooms, lounges, billiard rooms	2.0	2.7
Dressing rooms, hospital bedrooms and wards	2.0	1.8
Toilet rooms	2.0	-
Bedrooms, dormitories	1.5	1.8
Balconies	same as rooms to which they give access but with a minimum of 4.0	1.5 per metre run concentrated at the outer edge
Fly galleries	4.5 kN per metre run distributed uniformly over the width	-

DESIGN LOADINGS FOR BUILDINGS

Floor area usage load	Distributed load kN/m^2	Concentrated load kN/300 m^2
Offices occupancy class (offices, banks)		
Stationery stores	4.0 for each metre of storage height	9.0
Boiler rooms, motor rooms, fan rooms and the like, including the weight of machinery	7.5	4.5
Corridors, hallways, etc. subject to loads greater than from crowds, such as wheeled vehicles, trolleys and the like	5.0	4.5
File rooms, filing and storage space	5.0	4.5
Corridors, hallways, stairs, landings, footbridges, etc.	4.0	4.5
Offices with fixed computers or similar equipment	3.5	4.5
Laboratories (including equipment), kitchens, laundries	3.0	-
Banking halls	3.0	4.5
Offices for general use	2.5	2.7
Toilet rooms	2.0	-
Balconies	Same as rooms to which they give access but with a minimum of 4.0	1.5 per metre run concentrated at the outer edge
Cat walks	-	1.0 at 1 m centre
Public assembly occupancy class (halls, auditoria, restaurants, museums, libraries, non-residential clubs, theatres, broadcasting studios, grandstands)		
Dense mobile stacking (books) on mobile trucks	4.8 for each metre of stack height but with a minimum of 9.6	7.0
Stack rooms (books)	2.4 for each metre of stack height but with a minimum of 6.5	7.0
Boiler rooms, motor rooms fan rooms and the like, including the weight of machinery	7.5	4.5
Stages	7.5	4.5

DESIGN LOADINGS FOR BUILDINGS

Floor area usage load	Distributed load kN/m^2	Concentrated load kN/300m^2

Public assembly occupancy class (halls, auditoria, restaurants, museums, libraries, non-residential clubs, theatres, broadcasting studios, grandstands) - cont'd

Floor area usage	Distributed load kN/m^2	Concentrated load kN/300m^2
Corridors, hallways, etc. subject to loads greater than from crowds, such as wheeled vehicles, trolleys and the like. Corridors, stairs, and passage ways in grandstands	5.0	4.5
Drill rooms and drill halls	5.0	9.0
Assembly areas without fixed seating dance halls, gymnasia, grancstands	5.0	3.6
Projection rooms, bars	5.0	-
Museum floors and art galleries for exhibition purposes	4.0	4.5
Corridors, hallways, stairs, landings, footbridges, etc.	4.0	4.5
Reading rooms with book storage, e.g. libraries	4.0	4.5
Assembly areas with fixed seating	4.0	-
Kitchens, laundries	3.0	4.5
Chapels, churches	3.0	2.7
Reading rooms without book storage	2.5	4.5
Grids	2.5	-
Areas for equipment	2.0	1.8
Dining rooms, lounges, billiard rooms	2.0	2.7
Dressing rooms	2.0	1.8
Toilet rooms	2.0	-
Balconies	Same as rooms to which they give access but with a minimum of 4.0	1.5 per metre run concentrated at the outer edge
Fly galleries	4.5 kN per metre run distributed uniformly over the width	
Cat walks	-	1.0 at 1 m centres

DESIGN LOADINGS FOR BUILDINGS

Floor area usage load	Distributed load kN/m^2	Concentrated load kN/300 m^2
Residential occupancy class		
Self contained dwelling units and communal areas in blocks of flats not more than three storeys in height and with not more than four self-contained dwelling units per floor accessible from one staircase		
All usages	1.5	1.4
Boarding houses, lodging houses, guest houses, hostels, residential clubs and communal areas in blocks of flats other than type 1		
Boiler rooms, motor rooms, fan rooms and the like including the weight of machinery	7.5	4.5
Communal kitchens, laundries	3.0	4.5
Corridors, hallways, stairs, landings, footbridges etc.	3.0	4.5
Dining rooms, lounges, billiard rooms	2.0	2.7
Toilet rooms	2.0	-
Bedrooms, dormitories	1.5	1.8
Balconies	Same as rooms to which they give access but with a minimum of 3.0 at the outer edge	1.5 per metre run concentrated
Cat walks	-	1.0 at 1 m centres
Hotels and Motels		
Boiler rooms, motor rooms, fan rooms and the like, including the weight of machinery	7.5	4.5
Assembly areas without fixed seating, dance halls	5.0	3.6
Bars	5.0	-
Assembly areas with fixed seating	4.0	-
Corridors, hallways, stairs, landings, footbridges, etc.	4.0	4.5
Kitchens, laundries	3.0	4.5
Dining rooms, lounges, billiard rooms	2.0	2.7
Bedrooms	2.0	1.8

DESIGN LOADINGS FOR BUILDINGS

Floor area usage load	Distributed load kN/m^2	Concentrated load kN/300m^2
Hotels and Motels – cont'd		
Toilet rooms	2.0	-
Balconies	Same as rooms to which they give 1.5 per metre run concentrated access but with a minimum of 4.0 at the outer edge	
Cat Walks	-	1.0 at 1 m centres
Retail occupancy class (shops, departmental stores, supermarkets)		
Cold storage	5.0 for each metre of storage height with a minimum of 15.0	9.0
Stationery stores	4.0 for each metre of storage height	9.0
Storage, other than types separately	2.4 for each metre of storage height	7.0
Boiler rooms, motor rooms, fan rooms and the like, including the weight of machinery	7.5	4.5
Corridors, hallways, etc. subject to loads greater than from crowds, such as wheeled vehicles, trolleys and the like	5.0	4.5
Corridors, hallways, stairs, landings, footbridges, etc.	4.0	4.5
Shop floors for the display and sale of merchandise	4.0	3.6
Kitchens, laundries	3.0	4.5
Toilet rooms	2.0	-
Balconies	Same as rooms to which they give 1.5 per metre run concentrated access but with a minimum of 4.0 at the outer edge	
Cat walks	-	1.0 at 1 m centres
Storage occupancy class (warehouses)		
Cold storage	5.0 for each metre of storage height with a minimum of 15.0	9.0
Dense mobile stacking (books) on mobile trucks	4.8 for each metre of storage height with a minimum of 15.0	7.0
Paper storage, for printing plants	4.0 for each metre of storage height	9.0

DESIGN LOADINGS FOR BUILDINGS

Floor area usage load	Distributed load kN/m²	Concentrated load kN/300 m²
Stationery stores	4.0 for each metre of storage height	9.0
Storage, other than types listed separately, warehouses	2.4 for each metre of storage height	7.0
Motor rooms, fan rooms and the like, including the weight of machinery	7.5	4.5
Corridors, hallways, foot-bridges, etc. subject to loads greater than for crowds, such as wheeled vehicles, trolleys and the like	5.0	4.5
Cat walks	-	1.0 at 1 m centres

Vehicular occupancy class (garages, car parks, vehicle access ramps)

Motor rooms, fan rooms and the like, including the weight of machinery	7.5	4.5
Driveways and vehicle ramps, other than in garages for the parking only of passenger vehicles and light vans not exceeding 2500 kg gross mass	5.0	9.0
Repair workshops for all types of vehicles, parking for vehicles exceeding 2500 kg gross mass including driveways and ramps	5.0	9.0
Footpaths, terraces and plazas leading from ground level with no obstruction to vehicular traffic, pavement lights	5.0	9.0
Corridors, hallways, stairs, landings, footbridges, etc. subject to crowd loading	4.0	4.5
Footpaths, terraces and plazas leading from ground level but restricted to pedestrian traffic only	4.0	4.5
Car parking only, for passenger vehicles and light vans not exceeding 2500 kg gross mass including garages, driveways and ramps	2.5	9.0
Cat walks	-	1.0 at 1 m centres

PLANNING PARAMETERS

Definitions

*   For precise definitions consult the Code of Measuring Practice published by the Royal Institution of Chartered Surveyors and the Incorporated Society of valuers and Auctioneers.

General definitions

Plot ratio *
Ratio of GEA to site area where the site area is expressed as one.

Gross external area (GEA) *
Gross area on each floor including the external walls of all spaces except open balconies and fire escapes, upper levels of atria and areas less than 1.5 m (5ft) such as under roof slopes, open covered ways or minor canopies, open vehicle parking areas, terraces and party walls beyond the centre line. Measured over structural elements and services space such as partitions and plant rooms. Roof level plant rooms may be excluded from the planning area

Site area *
Total area of the site within the site title boundaries measured on the horizontal plane.

Gross site area *
The site area, plus any area of adjoining roads enclosed by extending the side boundaries of the site up to the centre of the road, or to 6 m (20 ft) out from the frontage, whatever is the less.

Gross internal floor area (GIFA)/ Gross internal area (GIA) *
Gross area measured on the same basis as GEA, but excluding external wall thickness, and for rating GIA, excluding areas with a headroom of less than 1.5 m, except under stairs.

Net internal floor area (NIFA) *
Net usable area measured to the internal finish of the external walls excluding all auxiliary and ancillary spaces such as WC's and lobbies, ducts, lift, tank and plant space etc, staircases, lift wells and major access circulation, fire escape corridors and lobbies, major switchroom space and areas used by external authorities, internal structural walls and columns, car parking and areas with less than 1.5 m headroom, such as under roof slopes, corridors used in common with other occupiers or of a permanent essential nature such as fire corridors, smoke lobbies, space occupied by permanent air-conditioning, heating or cooling apparatus and surface mounted ducting causing space to be unusable.

Cubic content *
The GEA multiplied by the vertical height from the lowest basement floor or average ground to the average height of the roof.

Internal cube
The GIFA of each floor multiplied by its storey height.

Ceiling height *
The height between the floor surface and the underside of the ceiling.

Building frontage *
The measurement along the front of the building from the outside of the external walls or the centre line of party walls.

External wall area
The wall area of all the enclosed spaces fulfilling the functional requirements of the buildings measured on the outer face of the external walls and overall windows and doors etc.

Wall to floor ratio
The factor produced by dividing the external wall area by the GIFA.

PLANNING PARAMETERS

Window to external wall ratio
The factor produced by dividing the external windows and door area by the external wall area.
Circulation (C)
Circulation and ancillary area measured on plan on each floor for staircases, lift lobbies, lift wells, lavatories, cleaners' cupboards usually represented as the allowances for circulation and ancillary space as a percentage of NIFA.

Plant area
Plant rooms and vertical duct space.

Retail definitions

Sales area *
NIFA usable for retailing excluding store rooms unless formed by non-structural partitions.

Storage area *
NIFA not forming part of the sales area and usable only for storage.

Shop frontage *
Overall external frontage to shop premises including entrance and return shop frontage, but excluding recesses, doorways and the like of other accommodation.

Overall frontage *
Overall measurement in a straight line across the front of the building and any return frontage, from the outside of external walls and / or the entire line or party walls.

Shop width *
Internal measurement between inside faces of external walls at shop front or other points of reference.

Shop depth *
Overall measurement from back of pavement or forecourt to back of sales area measured over any non-structural partitions.

Built depth *
Overall external ground level measurement from front to rear walls of building.

Zone A
Front zone of 6 m in standard retail units 6 m x 24 m.

Housing definitions

Number of persons housed
The total number for whom actual bed spaces are provided in the dwellings as designed.

Average number of persons per dwelling
The total number of persons housed divided by the total number of dwellings.

Density
The total number of persons housed divided by the site in hectares or acres.
The total number of units divided by the site area in hectares or acres.

PLANNING PARAMETERS

Functional units

As a "rule of thumb" guide to establish a cost per functional unit, or as a check on economy of design in terms of floor area, the following indicative functional unit areas have been derived from historical data. For indicative unit costs see "Building Prices per Functional Units" (Part IV - Approximate Estimating) on page 707.

Car parking	- surface	20 - 22 m^2/car
	- multi storey	23 - 27 m^2/car
	- basement	28 - 37 m^2/car
Concert Halls		8 m^2/seat
Halls of residence m^2/bedroom	- college/polytechnic	25 - 35
	- university	30 - 50
m^2/bedroom		
Hospitals	- district general	65 - 85 m^2/bed
	- teaching	120 + m^2/bed
	- private	75 - 100 m^2/bed
Hotels	- budget	28 - 35 m^2/bedroom
	- luxury city centre	70 - 130 m^2/bedroom
Housing		**Gross internal floor area**
Private developer:	1 Bedroom Flat	45 - 50 m^2
	2 Bedroom Flat	55 - 65 m^2
	2 Bedroom House	55 - 65 m^2
	3 Bedroom House	70 - 90 m^2
	4 Bedroom House	90 - 100 m^2
Offices	- high density open plan	20 m^2/person
	- low density cellular	15 m^2/person
Schools	- nursery	3 - 5 m^2/child
	- secondary	6 - 10 m^2/child
	- boarding	10 - 12 m^2/child
Theatres	- small, local	3 m^2/seat to
	- large, prestige	7 m^2/seat

Typical planning parameters

The following are indicative planning design and functional criteria derived from historical data for a number of major building types.

Gross internal floor areas (GIFA)

Offices

Feasibility assessment of GIFA for:

Curtain wall office	GEA x 0.97
Solid wall office	GEA x 0.95

These measures apply except for thick stone façades - take measurements on site.

PLANNING PARAMETERS

Typical dimensions measured on plan between the internal finishes of the external walls for:

Speculative offices	13.75 m
Open plan offices	15.25 m
Open plan / cellular offices	18.3 m

Retail

Typical gross internal floor areas:

Food courts, comprising	232 to 372 m^2
Kiosks	37 m^2
Services - per seat	1.1 to 1.5 m^2
Seating area in mall - per seat	1.2 to 1.7 m^2
Retail Kiosks	56 to 75 m^2
Small specialist shops	465 to 930 m^2
Electrical goods	930 to 1 395 m^2
DIY	930 to 4 645 m^2
Furniture / carpets	1858 to 5 575 m^2
Toys	3715 to 4 645 m^2
Superstores	3715 to 5 575 m^2
Department stores within shopping centres	5575 to 27 870 m^2
Specialist shopping centres	5574 to 9 290 m^2

Leisure

Standard sizes:

Large sports halls	Medium sports halls	Small sports halls
36.5 x 32 x 9.1 m	29 x 26 x 7.6 - 9.1 m	29.5 x 16.5 x 6.7 - 7.6 m
32 x 26 x 7.6 - 9.1 m	32 x 23 x 7.6 - 9.1 m	26 x 16.5 x 6.7 - 7.6 m
	32 x 17 x 6.7 - 7.6 m	22.5 x 16.5 x 6.7 - 7.6 m

Community halls
17.2 x 15.6 x 6.7 m
17 x 8.5 x 6.7 m

Court sizes:

badminton	13.4 x 6.1 m	volleyball	18 x 9 m
basketball	26+2 x 14+1 m	tug of war	35 (min) x 5 m (min)
handball	30 - 40 x 17 - 20 m	bowls	4.5 x 32 m (min) per rink
hockey	36 - 44 x 18 - 22 m	cricket nets	3.05 (min) x 33.5 m per
net			
women's lacrosse	27 - 36 x 15 - 21m	snooker	3.7 x 1.9 m table size
men's lacrosse	46 - 48 x 18 - 24m	ice hockey	56.61 x 26 - 30.5 m
netball	30.50 x 15.25 m	racquets	18.288 x 9.144 m
tennis	23.77 x 10.97 m	squash	9.754 x 6.4 x 5.64 m

PLANNING PARAMETERS

Leisure - cont'd

Typical swimming pool dimensions:

Olympic standard	50 m x 21 m (8 lanes) water depth 1.8 m (constant)
ASA, national and county	25 or 33.3 m long with width multiple of 2.1 m wide
championship standard	lanes minimum water depth 900 mm
	1 m springboard needs minimum 3 m water depth
Learner pool	width 7.0 - 7.5 m
	depth 600 - 900 mm
Toddlers pool	450 mm depth
Leisure pool	informal shape: will sometimes encompass 25 m in one direction to accommodate roping-off for swimming lanes; water area from 400 - 750 m^2
Splash pool	minimum depth 1.05 m
Changing cubicles	minimum dimensions: 914 x 1057 mm

Note: For 25 m pool developments the ratio of water area to gross floor area may average 1:3. For free form leisure pool developments, a typical ratio is 1:5.5.

Multiplex space planning data:

Ideal number of screens	10 (minimum six)
Average area per screen	325 m^2
Typical dimensions:	71 x 45 m (10 screens)
	66 x 43 m (8 screens)
	plus 20 m^2 food area

Housing

Typical densities	Persons per hectare	Units per hectare
Urban	200	90
Suburban	150	55
Rural	110	35

Typical gross internal floor areas for housing associations / local authorities schemes:

	(m^2)
Bungalows	
one-bed	48
two-bed	55 - 65
Houses	
one-bed	44
two-bed	62 - 80
three-bed	75 - 95
four-bed	111 - 145
Flats	
bedsitters	23
one-bed	35 - 63
two-bed	55 - 80
three-bed	75 - 100

PLANNING PARAMETERS

Gross internal floor areas for private developments are much more variable and may be smaller or larger than the indicative areas shown above, depending on the target market. Standards for private housing are set out in the NHBC's Registered House Builders Handbook. There are no floor space minima, but heating , kitchen layout, kitchens and linen storage, WC provisions, and the number of electrical socket outlets are included.

Average housing room sizes - net internal floor areas:

		Living room (m²)	Kitchen (m²)	Bathroom (m²)	Main bedroom (m²)	Average bedroom size (m²)
Bungalows						
	one-bed	15.0	6.0	3.5	11.0	-
	two-bed	17.0	9.0	3.5	12.5	10.0
Houses						
	one-bed	14.5	6.5	3.5	11.0	-
	two-bed	17.5	9.5	4.5	10.0	9.0
	three-bed	17.5	13.5	7.0	13.0	10.5
	four-bed	22.5	12.5	8.0	17.5	12.5
Flats						
	bedsitters	18.0	-	3.0	-	-
	one-bed	13.5	7.5	4.5	10.0	-
	two-bed	17.0	10.0	5.5	13.5	11.5
	three-bed	23.0	3.5	5.5	14.0	14.0

Storage accommodation for housing

NHBC requirements are that in every dwelling, enclosed domestic storage accommodation shall be provided as follows:

Area of dwelling (m²)	Minimum volume of storage (m³)
less than 60	1.3
60 - 80	1.7
over 80	2.3

Hotels

Typical gross internal floor areas per bedroom: m²

Five star, city centre hotel	60+
Four star, city centre / provincial centre hotel	45 to 55
Three star, city / provincial hotel	40 to 45
Three / two star, provincial hotel	33 to 40
Three / two star bedroom extension	26 to 30

Indicative space standards (unit):

Suites including bedroom, living room bathroom and hall (nr)	55 to 65

Double bedrooms including bathroom and lobby (nr)

large	30 to 35
average	25 to 30
small	20 to 25
disabled	3 to 5 m² extra

PLANNING PARAMETERS

Hotels - cont'd

Restaurant (seat)	
first class	1.85
speciality/grill	1.80
Coffee shop (seat)	1.80
Bar (customer standing)	0.40 to 0.45
Food preparation/main kitchen/storage	40% to 50% of restaurant and bar areas
Banquet (seat)	1.40
Catering to banquets	10 % to 25 % of banquet area
Function/meeting rooms (person)	1.50
Staff areas (person)	0.40 to 0.60
Staff restaurant and kitchen (seat)	0.70 to 0.90
Service rooms (floor)	30 to 50
General storage and housekeeping	1.5 to 2% of bedroom and circulation areas
Front hall, entrance areas, lounge	2 to 3% average (up to 5%) of total hotel area
Administrative areas	Allowances based on number of accounts staff. Additional area if self accounting 15 to 25 per cent for bedroom floors depending on number of storeys, layout and operating principles, 20 to 25 per cent for public areas
Plant rooms and ducts	4 to 5 % of total hotel area for non-air-conditioned areas, 7 to 8% for air conditioned areas

Typical internal bedroom dimensions:

Bedroom including bathroom	
five star	8.0 m x 4.0 m
four star	7.5 m x 3.75 m
three/two star	7.0 m x 3.5 m
Typical corridor width	1.4 m to 1.6 m

PLANNING PARAMETERS

Circulation (C)

Figures represent net area which is gross area less space to be set aside for staircases, lift lobbies, lift wells, lavatories, cleaners' cupboards, service risers, plant space, etc.

Typical NIFA to GIFA areas:	**Percentage of GIFA**

Offices

2 to 4 storey	82 - 87
5 to 9 storey	76 - 82
10 to 14 storey	72 - 76
15 to 19 storey	68 - 72
20 + storeys	65 - 68

Adjustments	
for fancoil air-conditioned offices	deduct 2 - 3
for VAV air-conditioned offices	deduct 6 - 7

Flats

Staircase access	85
Enclosed balcony	83
Internal corridor and lobby	80

Typical sales to gross internal areas

Retail

Superstores	45 - 55
Department stores	50 - 60
Retail warehouses	75 - 85

Wall and Window to floor ratios

Typical ratios based on historic data:

Legend:	(1) W/F	- External wall to gross floor area (GIFA) ratio
	(2) W/W	- External window to external wall ratio
	(3) IW/F	- Internal wall to gross floor area (GIFA) ratio

Building types	(1) W/F	(2) W/W	(3) IW/F
Industrial			
warehouse	0.45	0.04	-
factory	0.60	0.14	-
nursery	0.70	0.14	-
Offices			
open	0.80	0.35	0.30
cellular	0.80	0.35	1.10

PLANNING PARAMETERS

Plant area   **Percentage of GIFA**

Industrial 3 - 5

Offices   4 - 11

                                                                          **Percentage of treated
                                                                                    floor area**

Leisure

all air, low velocity	4.0 - 6.0
induction	2.0 - 3.0
fan coil	1.5 - 2.5
VAV	3.0 - 4.5
versatemp	1.5 - 2.0
boiler plant	0.8 - 1.8
(excluding hws cylinders)	
oil tank room	1.0 - 2.0
refrigeration plant (excluding cooling towers)	1.0 - 2.0
supply and extract ventilation	3.0 - 5.0
electrical (excluding input substation or standby generation)	0.5 - 1.5
lift rooms	0.2 - 0.5
toilet ventilation	0.3 - 1.0

Other key dimensions

Structural grid and cladding rail spacing for industrial buildings

Typical economic dimensions   **m**

spans	18
column spacing	6 - 7.5
purlin spacing	1.8

Wall to core for offices

Typical dimensions measured on plan between
 the internal finish of external wall to finish of core   7.3

Floor to floor heights

Typical dimensions, measured on section

Industrial
top of ground slab to top of first floor slab	3.9 - 4.5
top of first floor slab to underside of beams / eaves	3.4 - 3.7

Minimum dimensions; floor finish to floor finish

Offices
speculative centrally heated	3.3
speculative air-conditioned	3.8
trading floors air-conditioned	4.7

Hotels
bedrooms	2.7 - 3
public areas	3.5 - 3.6

PLANNING PARAMETERS

Floor to underside of structure heights

Industrial
Minimum internal clear height

minimum cost stacking warehouse/light industrial	5 - 5.5
minimum height for storage racking	7.5
turret trucks used for stacking	9
automatic warehouse with stacker cranes	15 - 30

Clearance for structural members, sprinklers and lighting in addition to the above

Retail
Clear height from floor to underside of beams / eaves:

shop sales area	3.3 - 3.8
shop non-sales area	3.2 - 3.6
retail warehouse	4.75 - 5.5

Leisure
Specified by each sport's governing body

badminton/tennis to county standard	7.6
badminton/tennis/ trampolining to international standard	9.1
pool hall from pool surround	8.4 - 8.9

Floor to underside of structure heights

Industrial floor to eaves height
Typical dimensions measured on section:

low bay warehouse	6
high bay warehouse	9 - 18

Floor to ceiling height

Typical dimensions measured on section:
Industrial

top of ground slab to underside of first floor slab	3.7 - 4.3
top of first floor finish to ceiling finish	2.75 - 3

Minimum dimensions measured on section from floor finish to ceiling finish:
Offices

Speculative offices	2.6
Trading floors	3

Leisure

Multiple cinemas	6
Fitness/dance studios	5 - 6
Snooker room	3
Projectile room	3
Changing rooms	3.5

Houses

Ground floor	2.1 - 2.55
First floor	2.35 - 2.55
Flats	2.25 - 2.65
Bungalows	2.4

Hotels

Bedrooms	2.5
Lounges	2.7
Meeting rooms	2.8
Restaurant / coffee shop / bar	3

PLANNING PARAMETERS

Raised floor areas	**mm**
Minimum clear void for:	
Speculative offices	100 - 200
Trading floors	300

Note: one floor box per 9 m^2

Suspended ceilings	**mm**
Minimum clear voids (beneath beams)	
Mechanically ventilated offices	300
Fan coil air-conditioned offices	450
VAV air-conditioned offices	550
Trading floors	760

Typical floor loadings

For more precise floor loadings according to usage refer to section on **DESIGN LOADINGSFOR BUILDINGS** earlier in this section.

Typical loadings (based on minimum uniformly distributed loads plus 25% for partition loads) are:

	KN/m^2
Industrial 24 - 37	
Offices	5 - 7
Retail warehouse / storage	24 - 29
Shop sales areas	6
Shop storage	12
Public assembly areas	6
Residential dwelling units	2 - 2.5
Residential corridor areas	4
Hotel bedrooms	3
Hotel corridor areas	4
Plant rooms	9
Car parks and access ramps	3 - 4

PLANNING PARAMETERS

Fire protection and means of escape

BS 5588: Fire Precautions in the Design and Construction of Building: includes details of:
    angle between escape routes
    disposition of fire resisting construction
    permitted travel distances

The Building Regulations fire safety approved document B 1992 provides advice on interpretation of the Building Regulations and is still the relevant controlling legislation for fire regulations, although the Loss Prevention Council have recently produced an advisory note, the *Code of Practice for the Construction of Buildings* which argues for a higher performance than the mandatory regulations.

Some minimum periods of fire resistance in minutes for elements of a structure are reproduced hereafter, based on Appendix A Table A2 of the Building Regulations fire safety approved document B, but refer to the relevant documentation to ensure that the information is current.

Building group   **Minimum fire resistance in minutes**

	Basement storey		Ground and Upper storey			
	<10m deep	>10m deep	<5m high	>20m high	<30m high	>30m high
Industrial						
not sprinklered	120	90	60	90	120	not allowed
sprinklered	90	60	30*	60	60	120#
Offices						
not sprinklered	90	60	30*	60	90	not allowed
sprinklered	60	60	30*	30*	60	120#
Shop, commercial and leisure						
not sprinklered	90	60	60	60	90	not allowed
sprinklered	60	60	30*	60	60	120#
Residential dwelling houses						
	-	30*	30*	60	-	-

    *   Increase to a minimum of 60 minutes for compartment walls separating buildings
    #   Reduce to 90 minutes for elements not forming part of the structural frame

Section 20
Applies to buildings in the Greater London area - refer to *London Building Acts (Amendment) Act 1939: Section 20, Code of Practice*. Major cost considerations include 2 hour fire resistance to reinforced concrete columns, possible requirement for sprinkler installation in offices and / or basement car parks, automatic controls and smoke detection in certain ventilation trucking systems, 4 hour fire resistance to fire fighting lift/stair/lobby enclosures and requirements for ventilated lobbies with a minimum floor area of 5.5 m^2 to fire fighting staircases.

Sprinkler installations

Sprinkler installations should be considered where any of the following are likely to occur:

♦   rapid fire spread likely, for example warehouses with combustible goods/packaging
♦   large un-compartmented areas
♦   high financial or consequential loss arising from fire damage

Refer to BS 5306: Part 2: 1990 for specification of sprinkler systems and associated Technical Bulletins from the Fire Officers Committee.

PLANNING PARAMETERS

Sanitary provisions

For the provisions of sanitary appliances refer to BS 6465: Part 1: 1994, which suggests the following minimum requirements (refer to the relevant documentation to ensure information is correct).

Factories (table 5)	Males	Females
WC's	1 per 25 persons or part thereof	1 per 25 persons or part thereof
Urinals	As required	Not applicable
Baths or showers	As required	As required

	Male and Female
Wash basins	1 per 20 persons; for clean processes 1 per 10 persons; for dirty processes 1 per 5 persons; for injurious processes

Housing (table 1)	2 - 4 person	5 person	6 person and over

One level, e.g. bungalows and flats

	2 - 4 person	5 person	6 person and over
WC's	1	1	2
Bath	1	1	1
Wash basin *	1	1	1
Sink and drainer	1	1	1

On two or more levels, e.g. houses and maisonettes

	2 - 4 person	5 person	6 person and over
WC's	1	2	2
Bath	1	1	1
Wash basin *	1	1	1
Sink and drainer	1	1	1

* in addition, allow one extra wash basin in every separate WC compartment which does not adjoin a bathroom.

Tables 2 and 3 deal with sanitary provisions for elderly people

Office building and shops (table 4)	Number per male and per female staff
WC's (no urinals) and wash hand basins	1 for 1 to 15 persons 2 for 16 to 30 persons 3 for 31 to 50 persons 4 for 51 to 75 persons 5 for 76 to 100 persons add 1 for every additional 25 persons or part thereof
Cleaners' sink	At least 1 per floor

For WC's (urinals provided), urinals, incinerators, etc. refer to BS 6465: Part 1: 1984. One unisex type WC and one smaller compartment for each sex on each floor where male and female toilets are provided - refer to BS 5810: 1979 and Building Regulations 1985 Schedule 2 (shortly to be replaced by part M).

PLANNING PARAMETERS

Swimming pools (table 11)

	For spectators Males	Females	For bathers Males	Females
WC's places	1 for 1 - 200 persons 2 for 201 - 500 persons 3 for 501 - 1000 persons Over 1000 persons, 3 plus 1 for every additional 500 persons or part thereof	1 for 1 - 100 persons 2 for 101 - 250 persons 3 for 251 - 500 persons Over 500 persons, 3 plus 1for every additional 400 persons or part thereof	1 per 20 changing places	1 per 10 changing
Urinals	1 per 50 persons	n/a	1 per 20 changing places	n/a
Wash basins places	1 per 60 persons	1 per 60 persons	1 per 15 changing places	1 per 15 changing
Showers places	n/a	n/a	1 per 8 changing places	1 per 8 changing

Refer also to BS 6465: Part 1: 1994 for sanitary provisions for schools, leisure, hotels and restaurants, etc.

Minimum cooling and ventilation requirements

General offices	40 W/m^2
Trading floors	60 W/m^2
Fresh air supply	
offices/dance halls	8 - 12 litres/person/second
bars	12 - 18 litres/person/second

Recommended design values for internal environmental temperatures and empirical values for air infiltration and natural ventilation allowances

	Temperature $^\circ$C (winter	Air infiltration rate (changes per hour)	Ventilation allowance (W/m^3 degrees C)
Warehouses			
working and packing spaces	16	0.5	0.17
storage space	13	0.25	0.08
Industrial			
production	16	0.5	0.17
offices	20	1.0	0.33
Offices	20	1.0	0.33
Shops			
small	18	1.0	0.33
large	18	0.5	0.17
department store	18	0.25	0.08
fitting rooms	21	1.5	0.50
store rooms	15	0.5	0.17

PLANNING PARAMETERS

Recommended design values for internal environmental temperatures and empirical values for air infiltration and natural ventilation allowances - cont'd

	Temperature °C (winter	Air infiltration rate (changes per hour)	Ventilation allowance (W/m³ degrees C)
Housing			
living rooms	21	1.0	0.33
bedrooms	18	0.5	0.17
bed sitting rooms	21	1.0	0.33
bathrooms	22	2.0	0.67
lavatory, cloakrooms	18	1.5	0.50
entrance halls, staircases, corridors	16	1.5	0.50
Hotels			
bedrooms (standard)	22	1.0	0.33
bedrooms (luxury)	24	1.0	0.33
public rooms	21	1.0	0.33
corridors	18	1.5	0.50
foyers	18	1.5	0.50

Typical design temperatures and mechanical ventilation allowances for leisure buildings

	Air temperature °C	Mechanical airchange rates (changes per hour)
Leisure buildings		
ice rink	below 25(heating temperature in winter:-8)	6
sports hall	16 - 21	3
squash courts	16 - 21	3
bowls halls	16 - 21	3
activity rooms	16 - 21	3
function room/bar	21 ± 2	2 - 4
fitness / dance studio	16 - 21	3 - 6
snooker room	16 - 21	3 - 6
projectile room	16 - 21	3 - 6
changing rooms	22	10
swimming pools	28	4 - 6
bar and cafe areas	23	2 - 4
administration areas	21	2 - 4

	Pool water temperature °C	
Swimming pools		
main pool	27	Ventilation rates must be related to the
splash pool	27	control of condensation. The criteria is
learners pool	28 – 30	the water area and the recommended basis
diving pool	27	is 20 litres/per m² of water surface,
leisure pool	29	plus a margin (say 20 per cent) to allow
jacuzzi pool	35	for the effect of wet surrounds.

PLANNING PARAMETERS

Typical lighting levels

Lighting levels for a number of common building types are given below. For more precise minimum requirements refer to the IES Code.

	Lux
Industrial building - production/assembly areas	100 - 1000(varies)
Offices	500
Conventional shops with counters or wall displays and self-service shops	500
Supermarkets	500
Covered shopping precincts and arcades	
main circulation paces	100 - 200
lift, stairs, escalators	150
external covered walkways	30
Sports buildings	
multi use sports halls	500
squash courts	500
dance / fitness studio	300
snooker room	500 on table
projectile room	300 generally
	1000 on target
Homes	
living rooms	
general	50
casual reading	150
bedrooms	
general	50
bedhead	150
studios	
desk and prolonged reading	300
kitchens	
working areas	300
bathrooms	100
halls and landings	150
stairs	100
Hotels	
internal corridors	200
guest room sleep area; stair wells	300
guest room activity area; housekeeping areas	500
meeting / banquet facilities	800

Electrical socket outlets (NHBC)

	Desirable provision	Minimum provision
Homes		
working area of kitchen	4	4
dining area	2	1
living area	5	3
first or only double bedroom	3	2
other double bedrooms	2	2
single bedrooms	2	2
hall and landing	1	1
store/workshop/garage	1	-
single study bedrooms	2	2
single bed sitting rooms in family dwellings	3	3
single bed sitting rooms in self contained bed sitting room dwellings	5	5

PLANNING PARAMETERS

Lifts
Performance standard to be not less than BS 5655: Lifts and service Lifts.

Industrial
Typical goods lift - 1000 kg

Offices
Dependant on number of storeys and planning layout, usually based on:

	Number of lifts
< 4 storeys	1
> = 4 storeys and < 10 000m^2 GIA	2
> = 4 storeys and > 10 000m^2 GIA	3

Hotels
Dependant on number of bedrooms, number of storeys and planning layout.
Typical examples
120 bed hotel on 3 floors	two 6 - 8 person lifts and service lift
200 bed hotel on 10 floors	four 13 person lifts and fireman's lift and service lift

Car park

Typical car space requirements   **One car space per**

Industrial 45 - 55m^2 GIA

Offices
medium tech	28 - 37 m^2 GIFA
high tech 19 - 25 m^2 GIFA	

Retail
superstores	8 - 10 m^2 GIFA
shopping centres/out of town retailing	18 - 23 m^2 GIFA
furniture/DIY stores	20 - 30 m^2 GIFA

Leisure
swimming pools	
patrons	10 m^2 pool area
staff	2 nr staff
leisure centres	
patrons	10 m^2 activity area

Residential   1 - 2 dwellings
                                               (depending on garage space,
                                                standard of dwelling, etc)

Goods and reception and service vehicles

Typical goods reception bay suitable for two 15 m articulated lorries with 1.5 m clearance either side. Loading bays must be level and have a clear height of 4.73 m. Approach routes should have a clear minimum height of 5.03 m. Minimum articulated lorry turning circle 13 m.

Typical design load for service yard 20 KN/m².

PLANNING PARAMETERS

Recommended sizes of various sports facilities

Archery (Clout)   7.3 m firing area — Range 109.728 (Women), 146.304 (Men)
182.88 (Normal range)

Baseball — Overall 60 m x 70 m

Basketball — 14 m x 26 m

Camogie — 91 - 110 m x 54 - 68 m

Discus and Hammer — Safety cage 2.74 m square
Landing area 45 arc (65° safety) 70 m radius

Football, American
57.94 m — Pitch 109.80 m x 48.80 m overall 118.94 m x

Football, Association — NPFA rules
Senior pitches 96 - 100 m x 60 - 64 m
Junior pitches 90 m x 46 - 55 m
International 100 - 110 m x 64 - 75 m

Football, Australian Rules — Overall 135 - 185 m x 110 - 155 m

Football, Canadian — Overall 145.74 m x 59.47 m

Football, Gaelic — 128 - 146.40 m x 76.80 - 91.50 m

Football, Rugby League — 111 - 122 m x 68 m

Football, Rugby Union — 144 m max x 69 m

Handball — 91 - 110 m x 55 - 65 m

Hockey — 91.50 m x 54.90 m

Hurling — 137 m x 82 m

Javelin — Runway 36.50 m x 4.27 m
Landing area 80 - 95 m long, 48 m wide

Jump, High — Running area 38.80 m x 19 m
Landing area 5 m x 4 m

Jump, Long — Runway 45 m x 1.22 m
Landing area 9 m x 2.75 m

Jump, Triple — Runway 45 m x 1.22 m
Landing area 7.30 m x 2.75 m

Korfball — 90 m x 40 m

Lacrosse — (Mens) 100 m x 55 m (Womens) 110 m x 73 m

Netball — 15.25 m x 30.48 m

Pole Vault — Runway 45 m x 1.22 m Landing area 5 m x 5 m

PLANNING PARAMETERS

Recommended sizes of various sports facilities - cont'd

Polo	275 m x 183 m
Rounders	Overall 19 m x 17 m
400m Running Track	115.61 m bend length x 2 84.39 m straight length x 2 Overall 176.91 m long x 92.52 m wide
Shot Putt	Base 2.135 m diameter Landing area 65° arc, 25 m radius from base
Shinty	128 - 183 m x 64 - 91.50 m
Tennis	Court 23.77 m x 10.97 m Overall minimum 36.27 m x 18.29 m
Tug-of-war	46 m x 5 m

SOUND INSULATION

Sound reduction requirements as Building Regulations (E1/2/3)

The Building Regulations on airborne and impact sound (E1/2/3) state simply that both airborne and impact sound must be reasonably reduced in floors and walls. No minimum reduction is given but the following tables give example sound reductions for various types of constructions.

Sound reductions of typical walls	Average sound reduction (dB)
13 mm Fibreboard	20
16 mm Plasterboard	25
6 mm Float glass	30
16 mm Plasterboard, plastered both sides	35
75 mm Plastered concrete blockwork (100 mm)	44
110 mm half brick wall, half brick thick, plastered both sides	43
240 mm Brick wall one brick thick, plastered both sides	48
Timber stud partitioning with plastered metal lathing both sides	35
Cupboards used as partitions	30
Cavity block wall, plastered both sides	42
75 mm Breeze block cavity wall, plastered both sides	50
100 mm Breeze block cavity wall, plastered both sides including 50 mm air-gap and plasterboard suspended ceiling	55
As above with 150 mm Breeze blocks	65
19 mm T & G boarding on timber joists including plasterboard ceiling and plaster skim coat	32
As above including metal lash and plaster ceiling	37
As above with solid sound proofing material between joists approx 98 kg per sq metre	55
As above with floating floor of T & G boarding on batten and soundproofing quilt	75

SOUND INSULATION

Impact noise is particularly difficult to reduce satisfactorily. The following are the most efficient methods of reducing such sound.

1)   Carpet on underlay of rubber or felt;
2)   Pugging between joists (e.g. Slag Wool); and
3)   A good suspended ceiling system.

Sound requirements

Housing

NHBC requirements are that any partition between a compartment containing a WC and a living-room or bedroom shell have an average sound insulation index of not less than 35 dB over the frequency range of 100 - 3150 Hz when tested in accordance with BS2750.

Hotels

Bedroom to bedroom or bedroom to corridor 48dB

THERMAL INSULATION

Thermal properties of various building elements

Thickness (mm)	Material	(m^2k/W) R	(W/m^2K) U - Value
n/a	Internal and external surface resistance	0.18	-
	Air-gap cavity	0.18	-
103	Brick skin	0.12	-
	Dense concrete block		
100	ARC conbloc	0.09	11.11
140	ARC conbloc	0.13	7.69
190	ARC conbloc	0.18	5.56
	Lightweight aggregate block		
100	Celcon standard	0.59	1.69
125	Celcon standard	0.74	1.35
150	Celcon standard	0.88	1.14
200	Celcon standard	1.18	0.85
	Lightweight aggregate thermal block		
125	Celcon solar	1.14	0.88
150	Celcon solar	1.36	0.74
200	Celcon solar	1.82	0.55
	Insulating board		
25	Dritherm	0.69	1.45
50	Dritherm	1.39	0.72
75	Dritherm	2.08	0.48
13	Lightweight plaster "Carlite"	0.07	14.29
13	Dense plaster "Thistle"	0.02	50.00
	Plasterboard		
9.5	British gypsum	0.06	16.67
12.7	British gypsum	0.08	12.50
40	Screed 0.10	10.00	
150	Reinforced concrete	0.12	8.33
100	Dow roofmate insulation	3.57	0.28

THERMAL INSULATION

Resistance to the passage of heat

Provisions meeting the requirement set out in the Building Regulations (L2/3):

		Minimum U - Value
a)	**Dwellings**	
	Roof	0.35
	Exposed wall	0.60
	Exposed floor	0.60
b)	**Residential, Offices, Shops and Assembly Buildings**	
	Roof	0.06
	Exposed wall	0.60
	Exposed floor	0.60
c)	**Industrial, Storage and Other Buildings**	
	Roof	0.70
	Exposed wall	0.70
	Exposed floor	0.70

TYPICAL CONSTRUCTIONS MEETING THERMAL REQUIREMENTS

External wall, masonry construction:

Concrete blockwork	U - Value
200 mm lightweight concrete block, 25 mm air-gap, 10 mm plasterboard	0.68
200 mm lightweight concrete block, 20 mm EPS slab, 10 mm plasterboard	0.54
200 mm lightweight concrete block, 25 mm air-gap, 25 mm EPS slab,10 mm plasterboard	0.46

Brick/Cavity/Brick

105 mm brickwork, 50 mm UF foam, 105 mm brickwork, 3 mm lightweight plaster	0.55

Brick/Cavity/Block

105 mm brickwork, 50 mm cavity, 125 mm Thermalite block, 3 mm lightweight plaster	0.59
105 mm brickwork, 50 mm cavity, 130 mm Thermalite block, 3 mm lightweight plaster	0.57
105 mm brickwork, 50 mm cavity, 130 mm Thermalite block, 3 mm dense plaster	0.59
105 mm brickwork, 50 mm cavity, 100 mm Thermalite block, foilbacked plasterboard	0.55
105 mm brickwork, 50 mm cavity, 115 mm Thermalite block, 9.5 mm plasterboard	0.58
105 mm brickwork, 50 mm cavity, 115 mm Thermalite block, foilbacked plasterboard	0.52
105 mm brickwork, 50 mm cavity, 125 mm Theramlite block, 9.5 mm plasterboard	0.55
105 mm brickwork, 50 mm cavity, 100 mm Thermalite block, 25 mm insulating plasterboard	0.53
105 mm brickwork, 50 mm cavity, 125 mm Thermalite block, 25 mm insulating plasterboard	0.47

TYPICAL CONSTRUCTIONS MEETING THERMAL REQUIREMENTS

Brick/Cavity/Block - cont'd	U-Value
105 mm brickwork, 25 mm cavity, 25 mm insulation, 115 mm Thermalite block, lightweight plaster	0.44
Render, 100 mm "Shield" block, 50 mm cavity, 100 mm Thermalite block, lightweight plaster	0.50
Render, 100 mm "Shield" block, 50 mm cavity, 115 mm Thermalite block, lightweight plaster	0.47
Render, 100 mm "Shield" block, 50 mm cavity, 125 mm Thermalite block, lightweight plaster	0.45

Tile hanging

	U-Value
10 mm tile on battens and felt, 150 mm Thermalite block, lightweight plaster	0.57
25 mm insulating plasterboard	0.46
10 mm tile on battens and felt, 190 mm Thermalite block, lightweight plaster	0.47
25 mm insulating plasterboard	0.40
10 mm tile on battens and felt, 200 mm Thermalite block, lightweight plaster	0.45
25 mm insulated plasterboard	0.38
10 mm tile on battens, breather paper, 25 mm air-gap, 50 mm glass fibre quilts, 10 mm plasterboard	0.56
10 mm tile on battens, breather paper, 25 mm air-gap, 75 mm glass fibre quilts, 10 mm plasterboard	0.41
10 mm tile on battens, breather paper, 25 mm air-gap, 100 mm glass fibre quilts, 10 mm plasterboard	0.33

Pitched roofs

Slate or concrete tiles, felt, airspace, Rockwool flexible slabs laid between rafters, plasterboard

		U-Value
Slab	40 mm thick	0.62
	50 mm thick	0.52
	60 mm thick	0.45
	75 mm thick	0.38
	100 mm thick	0.29

Concrete tiles, sarking felt, rollbatts between joists, plasterboard

		U-Value
Insulation	100 mm thick	0.31
	120 mm thick	0.26
	140 mm thick	0.23
	160 mm thick	0.21

TYPICAL CONSTRUCTIONS MEETING THERMAL REQUIREMENTS

Pitched roofs - cont'd   **U-Value**

Steel frame Rockwool insulation sandwiched between steel exterior
profiled sheeting and interior sheet lining

Insulation	60 mm thick	0.53
	80 mm thick	0.41
	100 mm thick	0.34

Steel frame, steel profiled sheeting, Rockwool insulation over purlins
and plasterboard lining

Insulation	60 mm thick	0.51
	80 mm thick	0.38
	100 mm thick	0.32
	120 mm thick	0.27
	140 mm thick	0.24
	160 mm thick	0.21

Flat roofs

Asphalt, Rockwool roof slabs, 25 mm timber boarding, timber joists
and 9.5 mm plasterboard

Insulation	30 mm thick	0.68
	40 mm thick	0.57
	50 mm thick	0.49
	60 mm thick	0.44
	70 mm thick	0.39
	80 mm thick	0.35
	90 mm thick	0.32
	100 mm thick	0.29

Asphalt, Rockwool roof slabs on 150 mm dense concrete deck and
screed with 16 mm plaster finish

Insulation	40 mm thick	0.68
	50 mm thick	0.57
	60 mm thick	0.49
	70 mm thick	0.43
	80 mm thick	0.39
	90 mm thick	0.35
	100 mm thick	0.32

Asphalt, Rockwool roof slabs on 150 mm dense concrete deck and
screed with suspended plasterboard ceiling

Insulation	40 mm thick	0.60
	50 mm thick	0.52
	60 mm thick	0.45
	70 mm thick	0.40
	80 mm thick	0.36
	90 mm thick	0.33
	100 mm thick	0.30

TYPICAL CONSTRUCTIONS MEETING THERMAL REQUIREMENTS

Flat roofs - cont'd　　　　　　　　　　　　　　　　　　　　　　**U-Value**

Steel frame, asphalt on insulation slabs on troughed steel decking

Insulation	50 mm thick	0.59
	60 mm thick	0.51
	70 mm thick	0.45
	80 mm thick	0.39
	90 mm thick	0.35
	100 mm thick	0.33

Steel frame, asphalt on insulation slabs on troughed steel decking
including suspended plasterboard ceiling

Insulation	40 mm thick	0.67
	50 mm thick	0.57
	60 mm thick	0.49
	70 mm thick	0.43
	80 mm thick	0.38
	90 mm thick	0.34
	100 mm thick	0.32

WEIGHTS OF VARIOUS MATERIALS

Material		kg/m³	Material		kg/m³

Aggregates

Material		kg/m³	Material		kg/m³
Ashes		610	Lime:	Chalk (lump)	704
Cement	(Portland)	1600		Ground	961
Chalk		2406		Quick	880
Chippings	(stone)	1762	Sand:	Dry	1707
Clinker	(furnace)	800		Wet	1831
	(concrete)	1441	Water		1000
Ballast or stone 2241			Shale/Whinstone		2637
Pumice		640	Broken stone	1709	
Gravel		1790	Pitch		1152

Metals

Material		kg/m³	Material	kg/m³
Aluminium		2559	Lead	11260
Brass		8129	Tin	7448
Bronze		8113	Zinc	7464
Gunmetal		8475		
Iron:	Cast	7207		
	Wrought	7687		

Stone and brickwork

Blockwork:			Brickwork:	
	Aerated	650	Common Fletton	1822
	Dense concrete	1800	Glazed brick	2080
	Lightweight concrete	1200	Staffordshire Blue	2162
	Pumice concrete	1080	Red Engineering	2240
			Concrete	1841

WEIGHTS OF VARIOUS MATERIALS

Material	kg/m³	Material	kg/m³
Stone and brickwork - cont'd			
Stone:			
Artificial	2242	Granite	2642
Bath	2242	Marble	2742
Blue Pennant	2682	Portland	2170
Cragleith	2322	Slate	2882
Darley Dale	2370	York	2402
Forest of Dean	2386	Terra-cotta	2116

Wood

	kg/m³		kg/m³
Blockboard	500 - 700	Jarrah	816
Cork Bark	80	Maple	752
Hardboard:		Mahogany:	
Standard	940 - 1000	Honduras	576
Tempered	940 - 1060	Spanish	1057
Wood chipboard:		Oak:	
Type I	650 - 750	English	848
Type II	680 - 800	American	720
Type III	650 - 800	Austrian & Turkish	704
Type II/III	680 - 800	Pine:	
Laminboard	500 - 700	Pitchpine	800
Timber:		Red Deal	576
Ash	800	Yellow Deal	528
Baltic spruce	480	Spruce	496
Beech	816	Sycamore	530
Birch	720	Teak:	
Box	961	African	961
Cedar	480	Indian	656
Chestnut	640	Moulmein	736
Ebony	1217	Walnut:	
Elm	624	English	496
Greenheart	961	Black	720

MEMORANDA FOR EACH TRADE

EXCAVATION AND EARTHWORK

Transport capacities

Type of vehicle	Capacity of vehicle m³ (solid)
Standard wheelbarrow	0.08
2 ton truck (2.03 t)	1.15
3 ton truck (3.05 t)	1.72
4 ton truck (4.06 t)	2.22
5 ton truck (5.08 t)	2.68
6 ton truck (6.10 t)	3.44
2 cubic yard dumper (1.53 m³)	1.15
3 cubic yard dumper (2.29 m³)	1.72
6 cubic yard dumper (4.59 m³)	3.44
10 cubic yard dumper (7.65 m3)	5.73

MEMORANDA FOR EACH TRADE

Planking and strutting

Maximum depth of excavation in various soils without the use of earthwork support

Ground conditions	Metres (m)
Compact soil	3.65
Drained loam	1.85
Dry sand	0.30
Gravelly earth	0.60
Ordinary earth	0.90
Stiff clay	3.00

It is important to note that the above table should only be used as a guide. Each case must be taken on its merits and, as the limited distances given above are approached, careful watch must be kept for the slightest signs of caving in.

Baulkage of soils after excavation

Soil type	Approximate bulk of 1m³ after excavation
Vegetable soil and loam	25 - 30%
Soft clay	30 - 40%
Stiff clay	10 - 15%
Gravel	20 - 25%
Sand	40 - 50%
Chalk	40 - 50%
Rock, weathered	30 - 40%
Rock, unweathered	50 - 60%

CONCRETE WORK

Approximate average weights of materials

Materials Percentage of	Weight per m³ voids (%)	(kg)
Sand	39	1660
Gravel 10 - 20 mm	45	1440
Gravel 35 - 75 mm	42	1555
Crushed stone	50	1330
Crushed granite		
(over 15 mm)	50	1345
(n.e. 15 mm)	47	1440
"All-in" ballast	32	1800

MEMORANDA FOR EACH TRADE

CONCRETE WORK - cont'd

Common mixes for various types of work per m³

Recommended mix	Class of work suitable for:	Cement (kg)	Sand (kg)	Coarse Aggregate (kg)	No. of 50 kg bags of of cement per m³ of combined aggregate
1:3:6	Roughest type of mass concrete such as footings, road haunchings 300 mm thick	208	905	1509	4.00
1:2.5:5	Mass concrete of better class than 1:3:6such as bases for machinery, walls below ground.	249	881	1474	5.00
1:2:4	Most ordinary uses of concrete such as mass walls above ground, road slabs etc. and general reinforced concrete work	304	889	1431	6.00
1:1.5:3	Watertight floors, pavements, and walls tanks, pits, steps, paths, surface of two course roads, reinforced concrete where extra strength is required	371	801	1336	7.50
1:1:2	Work of thin section such as fence posts and small precast work	511	720	1206	10.50

Bar reinforcement

Cross-sectional area and mass

Nominal sizes (m)	Cross-sectional area (mm²)	Mass per metre run (kg)
6*	28.3	0.222
8	50.3	0.395
10	78.5	0.616
12	113.1	0.888
16	201.1	1.579
20	314.2	2.466
25	490.9	3.854
32	804.2	6.313
40	1256.6	9.864
50*	1963.5	15.413

*   Where a bar larger than 40 mm is to be used the recommended size is 50 mm. Where a bar smaller than 8 mm is to be used the recommended size is 6 mm.

MEMORANDA FOR EACH TRADE

Fabric reinforcement

Preferred range of designated fabric types and stock sheet sizes

Fabric reference	Longitudinal wires			Cross wires			
	Nominal wire size (mm)	Pitch (mm)	Area (mm²/m)	Nominal wire size (mm)	Pitch (mm)	Area (mm²/m)	Mass (kg/m²)
Square mesh							
A393	10	200	393	10	200	393	6.16
A252	8	200	252	8	200	252	3.95
A193	7	200	193	7	200	193	3.02
A142	6	200	142	6	200	142	2.22
A98	5	200	98	5	200	98	1.54
Structural mesh							
B1131	12	100	1131	8	200	252	10.90
B785	10	100	785	8	200	252	8.14
B503	8	100	503	8	200	252	5.93
B385	7	100	385	7	200	193	4.53
B283	6	100	283	7	200	193	3.73
B196	5	100	196	7	200	193	3.05
Long mesh							
C785	10	100	785	6	400	70.8	6.72
C636	9	100	636	6	400	70.8	5.55
C503	8	100	503	5	400	49.0	4.34
C385	7	100	385	5	400	49.0	3.41
C283	6	100	283	5	400	49.0	2.61
Wrapping mesh							
D98	5	200	98	5	200	98	1.54
D49	2.5	100	49	2.5	100	49	0.77

Stock sheet size   4.8 m x 2.4 m, Area 11.52 m²

Average weight kg/m³ of steelwork reinforcement in concrete for various building elements

Substructure	kg/m³ concrete		
Pile caps	110 - 150	Plate slab	150 - 220
Tie beams	130 - 170	Cant slab	145 - 210
Ground beams	230 - 330	Ribbed floors	130 - 200
Bases	125 - 180	Topping to block floor	30 - 40
Footings	100 - 150	Columns	210 - 310
Retaining walls	150 - 210	Beams	250 - 350
Raft	60 - 70	Stairs	130 - 170
Slabs - one way	120 - 200	Walls - normal	40 - 100
Slabs - two way	110 - 220	Walls - wind	70 - 125

Note: For exposed elements add the following % :

Walls 50%, Beams 100%, Columns 15%

MEMORANDA FOR EACH TRADE

BRICKWORK AND BLOCKWORK

Number of bricks required for various types of work per m^2 of walling

Description	Brick size	
	215 x 102.5 x 50 mm	**215 x 102.5 x 65 mm**
Half brick thick		
Stretcher bond	74	59
English bond	108	86
English garden wall bond	90	72
Flemish bond	96	79
Flemish garden wall bond	83	66
One brick thick and cavity wall of two half brick skins		
Stretcher bond	148	119

Quantities of bricks and mortar required per m^2 of walling

	Unit	No of bricks required	Mortar required (cubic metres)		
Standard bricks			**No frogs**	**Single frogs**	**Double frogs**
Brick size 215 x 102.5 x 50 mm					
half brick wall (103 mm)	m^2	72	0.022	0.027	0.032
2 x half brick cavity wall (270 mm)	m^2	144	0.044	0.054	0.064
one brick wall (215 mm)	m^2	144	0.052	0.064	0.076
one and a half brick wall (322 mm)	m^2	216	0.073	0.091	0.108
Mass brickwork	m^3	576	0.347	0.413	0.480
Brick size 215 x 102.5 x 65 mm					
half brick wall (103 mm)	m^2	58	0.019	0.022	0.026
2 x half brick cavity wall (270 mm)	m^2	116	0.038	0.045	0.055
one brick wall (215 mm)	m^2	116	0.046	0.055	0.064
one and a half brick wall (322 mm)	m^2	174	0.063	0.074	0.088
Mass brickwork	m^3	464	0.307	0.360	0.413
Metric modular bricks				**Perforated**	
Brick size 200 x 100 x 75 mm					
90 mm thick	m^2	67	0.016	0.019	
190 mm thick	m^2	133	0.042	0.048	
290 mm thick	m^2	200	0.068	0.078	
Brick size 200 x 100 x 100 mm					
90 mm thick	m^2	50	0.013	0.016	
190 mm thick	m^2	100	0.036	0.041	
290 mm thick	m^2	150	0.059	0.067	
Brick size 300 x 100 x 75 mm					
90 mm thick	m^2	33	-	0.015	
300 x 100 x 100 mm					
90 mm thick	m^2	44	0.015	0.018	

Note: Assuming 10 mm thick joints.

MEMORANDA FOR EACH TRADE

Mortar required per m² blockwork (9.88 blocks/m²)

Wall thickness	75	90	100	125	140	190	215
Mortar m³/m²	0.005	0.006	0.007	0.008	0.009	0.013	0.014

Standard available block sizes

Block	Length x height Co-ordinating size	Work size	Thicknesses
A	400 x 100 400 x 200	390 x 90 440 x 190	(75, 90, 100,140 & 190 mm (
	450 x 225	440 x 215	(75, 90, 100140, 190, & 215 mm
B	400 x 100 400 x 200	390 x 90 390 x 190	(75, 90, 100 (140 & 190 mm
	450 x 200 450 x 225 450 x 300 600 x 200 600 x 225	440 x 190 440 x 215 440 x 290 590 x 190 590 x 215	((75, 90, 100 (140, 190, & 215 mm ((
C	400 x 200 450 x 200 450 x 225 450 x 300 600 x 200 600 x 225	390 x 190 440 x 190 440 x 215 440 x 290 590 x 190 590 x 215	(((60 & 75 mm (((

ROOFING

Total roof loadings for various types of tiles/slates

		Slate/Tile	Roof load (slope) kg/m² Roofing underlay and battens	Total dead load kg/m²
Asbestos cement slate (600 x 300)		21.50	3.14	24.64
Clay tile	interlocking	67.00	5.50	72.50
	plain	43.50	2.87	46.37
Concrete tile	interlocking	47.20	2.69	49.89
	plain	78.20	5.50	83.70
Natural slate (18" x 10")		35.40	3.40	38.80

		Slate/Tile	Roof load (plan) kg/m²	Total dead load kg/m²
Asbestos cement slate (600 x 300)		28.45	76.50	104.95
Clay tile	interlocking	53.54	76.50	130.04
	plain	83.71	76.50	60.21
Concrete tile	interlocking	57.60	76.50	134.10
	plain	96.64	76.50	173.14

MEMORANDA FOR EACH TRADE

ROOFING - cont'd

Tiling data

Product		Lap (mm)	Gauge of battens	No. slates per m²	Battens (m/m²)	Weight as laid (kg/m²)
CEMENT SLATES						
Eternit slates	600 x 300 mm	100	250	13.4	4.00	19.50
(Duracem)		90	255	13.1	3.92	19.20
		80	260	12.9	3.85	19.00
		70	265	12.7	3.77	18.60
	600 x 350 mm	100	250	11.5	4.00	19.50
		90	255	11.2	3.92	19.20
	500 x 250 mm	100	200	20.0	5.00	20.00
		90	205	19.5	4.88	19.50
		80	210	19.1	4.76	19.00
		70	215	18.6	4.65	18.60
	400 x 200 mm	90	155	32.3	6.45	20.80
		80	160	31.3	6.25	20.20
		70	165	30.3	6.06	19.60
CONCRETE TILES/SLATES						
Redland Roofing						
Stonewold slate	430 x 380 mm	75	355	8.2	2.82	51.20
Double Roman tile	418 x 330 mm	75	355	8.2	2.91	45.50
Grovebury pantile	418 x 332 mm	75	343	9.7	2.91	47.90
Norfolk pantile	381 x 227 mm	75	306	16.3	3.26	44.01
		100	281	17.8	3.56	48.06
Renown inter-locking						
tile	418 x 330 mm	75	343	9.7	2.91	46.40
"49" tile	381 x 227 mm	75	306	16.3	3.26	44.80
		100	281	17.8	3.56	48.95
Plain, vertical tiling	265 x 165 mm	35	115	52.7	8.70	62.20
Marley Roofing						
Bold roll tile	420 x 330 mm	75	344	9.7	2.90	47.00
		100	-	10.5	3.20	51.00
Modern roof tile	420 x 330 mm	75	338	10.2	3.00	54.00
		100	-	11.0	3.20	58.00
Ludlow major	420 x 330 mm	75	338	10.2	3.00	45.00
		100	-	11.0	3.20	49.00
Ludlow plus	387 x 229 mm	75	305	16.1	3.30	47.00
		100	-	17.5	3.60	51.00
Mendip tile	420 x 330 mm	75	338	10.2	3.00	47.00
		100	-	11.0	3.20	51.00
Wessex	413 x 330 mm	75	338	10.2	3.00	54.00
		100	-	11.0	3.20	58.00
Plain tile	267 x 165 mm	65	100	60.0	10.00	76.00
		75	95	64.0	10.50	81.00
		85	90	68.0	11.30	86.00
Plain vertical	267 x 165 mm	35	110	53.0	8.70	67.00
tiles (feature)		34	115	56.0	9.10	71.00

MEMORANDA FOR EACH TRADE

Slate nails, quantity per kilogram

	Type			
Length	**Plain wire**	**Galvanised wire**	**Copper nail**	**Zinc nail**
28.5 mm	325	305	325	415
34.4 mm	286	256	254	292
50.8 mm	242	224	194	200

Metal sheet coverings

Thicknesses and weights of sheet metal coverings

Lead to BS 1178

BS Code No	3	4	5	6	7	8
Colour Code	Green	Blue	Red	Black	White	Orange
Thickness (mm)	1.25	1.80	2.24	2.50	3.15	3.55
kg/m^2	14.18	20.41	25.40	28.36	35.72	40.26

Copper to BS 2870

Thickness (mm)		0.60	0.70
Bay width			
Roll (mm)		500	650
Seam (mm)		525	600
Standard width to form bay	600	750	
Normal length of sheet	1.80	1.80	

Zinc to BS 849

Zinc Gauge (Nr)	9	10	11	12	13	14	15	16
Thickness (mm)	0.43	0.48	0.56	0.64	0.71	0.79	0.91	1.04
Density kg/m^2	3.1	3.2	3.8	4.3	4.8	5.3	6.2	7.0

Aluminium to BS 4868

Thickness (mm)	0.5	0.6	0.7	0.8	0.9	1.0	1.2
Density kg/m^2	12.8	15.4	17.9	20.5	23.0	25.6	30.7

MEMORANDA FOR EACH TRADE

ROOFING - cont'd

Type of felt	Nominal mass per unit area (kg/10m)	Nominal mass per unit area of fibre base (g/m²)	Nominal length of roll (m)
Class 1			
1B fine granule surfaced bitumen	14	220	10 or 20
	18	330	10 or 20
	25	470	10
1E mineral surfaced bitumen	38	470	10
1F reinforced bitumen	15	160 (fibre) 110 (hessian)	15
1F reinforced bitumen, aluminium faced	13	160 (fibre) 110 (hessian)	15
Class 2			
2B fine granule surfaced bitumen asbestos	18	500	10 or 20
2E mineral surfaced bitumen asbestos	38	600	10
Class 3			
3B fine granule surfaced bitumen glass fibre	18	60	20
3E mineral surfaced bitumen glass fibre	28	60	10
3E venting base layer bitumen glass fibre	32	60*	10
3H venting base layer bitumen glass fibre	17	60*	20

* Excluding effect of perforations

MEMORANDA FOR EACH TRADE

WOODWORK

Conversion tables (for timber only)

Inches	Millimetres	Feet	Metres
1	25	1	0.300
2	50	2	0.600
3	75	3	0.900
4	100	4	1.200
5	125	5	1.500
6	150	6	1.800
7	175	7	2.100
8	200	8	2.400
9	225	9	2.700
10	250	10	3.000
11	275	11	3.300
12	300	12	3.600
13	325	13	3.900
14	350	14	4.200
15	375	15	4.500
16	400	16	4.800
17	425	17	5.100
18	450	18	5.400
19	475	19	5.700
20	500	20	6.000
21	525	21	6.300
22	550	22	6.600
23	575	23	6.900
24	600	24	7.200

Planed softwood
The finished end section size of planed timber is usually 3/16" less than the original size from which it is produced. This however varies slightly depending upon availability of material and origin of the species used.

Standards (timber) to cubic metres and cubic metres to standards (timber)

Cubic metres	Cubic metres standards	Standards
4.672	1	0.214
9.344	2	0.428
14.017	3	0.642
18.689	4	0.856
23.361	5	1.070
28.033	6	1.284
32.706	7	1.498
37.378	8	1.712
42.050	9	1.926
46.722	10	2.140
93.445	20	4.281
140.167	30	6.421
186.890	40	8.561
233.612	50	10.702
280.335	60	12.842
327.057	70	14.982
373.779	80	17.122

Standards (timber) to cubic metres and cubic metres to standards (timber)

Tables and Memoranda

MEMORANDA FOR EACH TRADE

WOODWORK - cont'd

1 cu metre = 35.3148 cu ft = 0.21403 std

1 cu ft = 0.028317 cu metres

1 std = 4.67227 cu metres

Basic sizes of sawn softwood available (cross sectional areas)

Thickness (mm)   **Width (mm)**

Thickness (mm)	75	100	125	150	175	200	225	250	300
16	X	X	X	X					
19	X	X	X	X					
22	X	X	X	X					
25	X	X	X	X	X	X	X	X	X
32	X	X	X	X	X	X	X	X	X
36	X	X	X	X					
38	X	X	X	X	X	X	X		
44	X	X	X	X	X	X	X	X	X
47*	X	X	X	X	X	X	X	X	X
50	X	X	X	X	X	X	X	X	X
63	X	X	X	X	X	X	X		
75		X	X	X	X	X	X	X	X
100		X		X		X		X	X
150				X		X			X
200						X			
250								X	
300									X

* This range of widths for 47 mm thickness will usually be found to be available in construction quality only.

Note: The smaller sizes below 100 mm thick and 250 mm width are normally but not exclusively of European origin. Sizes beyond this are usually of North and South American origin.

MEMORANDA FOR EACH TRADE

Basic lengths of sawn softwood available (metres)

1.80	2.10	3.00	4.20	5.10	6.00	7.20
	2.40	3.30	4.50	5.40	6.30	
	2.70	3.60	4.80	5.70	6.60	
		3.90			6.90	

Note: Lengths of 6.00 m and over will generally only be available from North American species and may have to be recut from larger sizes.

Reductions from basic size to finished size by planning of two opposed faces

		Reductions from basic sizes for timber			
Purpose		**15 - 35 mm**	**36 - 100 mm**	**101 - 150 mm**	**over 150 mm**
a)	Constructional timber	3 mm	3 mm	5 mm	6 mm
b)	Matching interlocking boards	4 mm	4 mm	6 mm	6 mm
c)	Wood trim not specified in BS 584	5 mm	7 mm	7 mm	9 mm
d)	Joinery and cabinet work	7 mm	9 mm	11 mm	13 mm

Note: The reduction of width or depth is overall the extreme size and is exclusive of any reduction of the face by the machining of a tongue or lap joints.

Maximum spans for various roof trusses

Maximum permissible spans for rafters for Fink trussed rafters

Basic size (mm)	Actual size (mm)	Pitch (degrees)								
		15 (m)	**17.5** (m)	**20** (m)	**22.5** (m)	**25** (m)	**27.5** (m)	**30** (m)	**32.5** (m)	**35** (m)
38 x 75	35 x 72	6.03	6.16	6.29	6.41	6.51	6.60	6.70	6.80	6.90
38 x 100	35 x 97	7.48	7.67	7.83	7.97	8.10	8.22	8.34	8.47	8.61
38 x 125	35 x 120	8.80	9.00	9.20	9.37	9.54	9.68	9.82	9.98	10.16
44 x 75	41 x 72	6.45	6.59	6.71	6.83	6.93	7.03	7.14	7.24	7.35
44 x 100	41 x 97	8.05	8.23	8.40	8.55	8.68	8.81	8.93	9.09	9.22
44 x 125	41 x 120	9.38	9.60	9.81	9.99	10.15	10.31	10.45	10.64	10.81
50 x 75	47 x 72	6.87	7.01	7.13	7.25	7.35	7.45	7.53	7.67	7.78
50 x 100	47 x 97	8.62	8.80	8.97	9.12	9.25	9.38	9.50	9.66	9.80
50 x 125	47 x 120	10.01	10.24	10.44	10.62	10.77	10.94	11.00	11.00	11.00

MEMORANDA FOR EACH TRADE

WOODWORK - cont'd

Sizes of internal and external doorsets

Description	Size (mm)	Internal Permissible deviation	External Size (mm)	Permissible deviation
Co-ordinating dimension: height of door leaf height sets	2100		2100	
Co-ordinating dimension: height of ceiling height set	2300 2350 2400 2700 3000		2300 2350 2400 2700 3000	
Co-ordinating dimension: width of all door sets S = Single leaf set D = Double leaf set	600 S 700 S 800 S&D 900 S&D 1000 S&D 1200 D 1500 D 1800 D 2100 D		900 S 1000 S 1200 D 1500 D 1800 D 2100 D	
Work size: height of door leaf height set	2090	± 2.0	2095	± 2.0
Work size: height of ceiling height set	2285) 2335) 2385) ± 2.0 2685) 2985)		2295) 2345) 2395) ± 2.0 2695) 2995)	
Work size: width of all door sets S = Single leaf set D = Double leaf set	590 S) 690 S) 790 S&D) 890 S&D) 990 S&D) ± 2.0 1190 D) 1490 D) 1790 D) 2090 D)		895 S) 995 S) 1195 D) 1495 D) ± 2.0 1795 D) 2095 D)	
Width of door leaf in single leaf sets F = Flush leaf P = Panel leaf	526 F) 626 F) 726 F&P) ± 1.5 826 F&P) 926 F&P)		806 F&P) 906 F&P) ± 1.5	

MEMORANDA FOR EACH TRADE

Description	Internal		External	
	Size (mm)	Permissible deviation	Size (mm)	Permissible deviation
Width of door leaf	362 F	)	552 F&P	)
in double leaf sets	412 F	)	702 F&P	) ± 1.5
F = Flush leaf	426 F	)	852 F&P	)
P = Panel leaf	562 F&P	) ± 1.5	1002 F&P	)
	712 F&P	)		
	826 F&P	)		
	1012 F&P	)		
Door leaf height for all door sets	2040	± 1.5	1994	± 1.5

STRUCTURAL STEELWORK

Tables showing the mass and surface area per metre run for various steel members

Size (mm)	Mass (kg/m)	Surface area per m run (m^2)
Universal beams		
914 x 419	388	3.404
	343	3.382
914 x 305	289	2.988
	253	2.967
	224	2.948
	201	2.932
838 x 292	226	2.791
	194	2.767
	176	2.754
762 x 267	197	2.530
	173	2.512
	147	2.493
686 x 254	170	2.333
	152	2.320
	140	2.310
	125	2.298
610 x 305	238	2.421
	179	2.381
	149	2.361
610 x 229	140	2.088
	125	2.075
	113	2.064
	101	2.053
533 x 210	122	1.872
	109	1.860
	101	1.853
	92	1.844
	82	1.833

MEMORANDA FOR EACH TRADE

STRUCTURAL STEELWORK - cont'd

Tables showing the mass and surface area per metre run for various steel members - cont'd

Size (mm)	Mass (kg/m)	Surface area per m run (m^2)
Universal beams - cont'd		
457 x 191	98	1.650
	89	1.641
	82	1.633
	74	1.625
	67	1.617
457 x 152	82	1.493
	74	1.484
	67	1.474
	60	1.487
	52	1.476
406 x 178	74	1.493
	67	1.484
	60	1.476
	54	1.468
406 x 140	46	1.332
	39	1.320
356 x 171	67	1.371
	57	1.358
	51	1.351
	45	1.343
356 x 127	39	1.169
	33	1.160
305 x 165	54	1.245
	46	1.235
	40	1.227
305 x 127	48	1.079
	42	1.069
	37	1.062
305 x 102	33	1.006
	28	0.997
	25	0.988
254 x 146	43	1.069
	37	1.060
	31	1.050
254 x 102	28	0.900
	25	0.893
	22	0.887
203 x 133	30	0.912
	25	0.904

MEMORANDA FOR EACH TRADE

Tables showing the mass and surface area per metre run for various steel members - cont'd

Size (mm)	Mass (kg/m)	Surface area per m run (m²)
Universal columns		
356 x 406	634	2.525
	551	2.475
	467	2.425
	393	2.379
	340	2.346
	287	2.312
	235	2.279
356 x 368	202	2.187
	177	2.170
	153	2.154
	129	2.137
305 x 305	283	1.938
	240	1.905
	198	1.872
	158	1.839
	137	1.822
	118	1.806
	97	1.789
254 x 254	167	1.576
	132	1.543
	107	1.519
	89	1.502
	73	1.485
203 x 203	86	1.236
	71	1.218
	60	1.204
	52	1.194
	46	1.187
152 x 152	37	0.912
	30	0.900
	23	0.889
Joists		
254 x 203	81.85	1.193
254 x 114	37.20	0.882
203 x 152	52.09	0.911
152 x 127	37.20	0.722
127 x 114	29.76	0.620
127 x 114	26.79	0.635
114 x 114	26.79	0.600
102 x 102	23.07	0.528

MEMORANDA FOR EACH TRADE

STRUCTURAL STEELWORK - cont'd

Tables showing the mass and surface area per metre run for various steel members - cont'd

Size (mm)	Mass (kg/m)	Surface area per m run (m²)
Joists - cont'd		
89 x 89	19.35	0.460
76 x 76	12.65	0.403

Circular hollow sections - outside dia (mm)	Mass (kg/m)	Surface area per m run (m²)	Thickness (mm)
21.30	1.43	0.067	3.20
26.90	1.87	0.085	3.20
33.70	1.99	0.106	2.60
	2.41	0.106	3.20
	2.93	0.106	4.00
42.40	2.55	0.133	2.60
	3.09	0.133	3.20
	3.79	0.133	4.00
48.30	3.56	0.152	3.20
	4.37	0.152	4.00
	5.34	0.152	5.00
60.30	4.51	0.189	3.20
	5.55	0.189	4.00
	6.82	0.189	5.00
76.10	5.75	0.239	3.20
	7.11	0.239	4.00
	8.77	0.239	5.00
88.90	6.76	0.279	3.20
	8.38	0.279	4.00
	10.30	0.279	5.00
114.30	9.83	0.359	3.60
	13.50	0.359	5.00
	16.80	0.359	6.30
139.70	16.60	0.439	5.00
	20.70	0.439	6.30
	26.00	0.439	8.00
	32.00	0.439	10.00
168.30	20.10	0.529	5.00
	25.20	0.529	6.30
	31.60	0.529	8.00
	39.00	0.529	10.00

MEMORANDA FOR EACH TRADE

Tables showing the mass and surface area per metre run for various steel members - cont'd

Size (mm)	Mass (kg/m)	Surface area per m run (m²)	Thickness (mm)
Circular hollow sections- outside diameter (mm) - cont'd			
193.70	23.30	0.609	5.00
	29.10	0.609	6.30
	36.60	0.609	8.00
	45.30	0.609	10.00
	55.90	0.609	12.50
	70.10	0.609	16.00
219.10	33.10	0.688	6.30
	41.60	0.688	8.00
	51.60	0.688	10.00
	63.70	0.688	12.50
	80.10	0.688	16.00
	98.20	0.688	20.00
273.00	41.40	0.858	6.30
	52.30	0.858	8.00
	64.90	0.858	10.00
	80.30	0.858	12.50
	101.00	0.858	16.00
	125.00	0.858	20.00
	153.00	0.858	25.00
323.90	62.30	1.020	8.00
	77.40	1.020	10.00
	96.00	1.020	12.50
	121.00	1.020	16.00
	150.00	1.020	20.00
	184.00	1.020	25.00
406.40	97.80	1.280	10.00
	121.00	1.280	12.50
	154.00	1.280	16.00
	191.00	1.280	20.00
	235.00	1.280	25.00
	295.00	1.280	32.00
457.00	110.00	1.440	10.00
	137.00	1.440	12.50
	174.00	1.440	16.00
	216.00	1.440	20.00
	266.00	1.440	25.00
	335.00	1.440	32.00
	411.00	1.440	40.00

MEMORANDA FOR EACH TRADE

STRUCTURAL STEELWORK - cont'd

Tables showing the mass and surface area per metre run for various steel members - cont'd

Size (mm)	Mass (kg/m)	Surface area per m run (m²)	Thickness (mm)
Square hollow sections			
20 x 20	1.12	0.076	2.00
	1.35	0.074	2.50
30 x 30	2.14	0.114	2.50
	2.51	0.113	3.00
40 x 40	2.92	0.155	2.50
	3.45	0.154	3.00
	4.46	0.151	4.00
50 x 50	4.66	0.193	3.20
	5.72	0.191	4.00
	6.97	0.189	5.00
60 x 60	5.67	0.233	3.20
	6.97	0.231	4.00
	8.54	0.229	5.00
70 x 70	7.46	0.272	3.60
	10.10	0.269	5.00
80 x 80	8.59	0.312	3.60
	11.70	0.309	5.00
	14.40	0.306	6.30
90 x 90	9.72	0.352	3.60
	13.30	0.349	5.00
	16.40	0.346	6.30
100 x 100	12.00	0.391	4.00
	14.80	0.389	5.00
	18.40	0.386	6.30
	22.90	0.383	8.00
	27.90	0.379	10.00
120 x 120	18.00	0.469	5.00
	22.30	0.466	6.30
	27.90	0.463	8.00
	34.20	0.459	10.00
150 x 150	22.70	0.589	5.00
	28.30	0.586	6.30
	35.40	0.583	8.00
	43.60	0.579	10.00
	53.40	0.573	12.50
	66.40	0.566	16.00

MEMORANDA FOR EACH TRADE

Tables showing the mass and surface area per metre run for various steel members - cont'd

Size (mm)	Mass (kg/m)	Surface area per m run (m²)	Thickness (mm)
Square hollow sections - cont'd			
180 x 180	34.20	0.706	6.30
	43.00	0.703	8.00
	53.00	0.699	10.00
	65.20	0.693	12.50
	81.40	0.686	16.00
200 x 200	38.20	0.786	6.30
	48.00	0.783	8.00
	59.30	0.779	10.00
	73.00	0.773	12.50
	91.50	0.766	16.00
250 x 250	48.10	0.986	6.30
	60.50	0.983	8.00
	75.00	0.979	10.00
	92.60	0.973	12.50
	117.00	0.966	16.00
300 x 300	90.70	1.180	10.00
	112.00	1.170	12.50
	142.00	1.170	16.00
350 x 350	106.00	1.380	10.00
	132.00	1.370	12.50
	167.00	1.370	16.00
400 x 400	122.00	1.580	10.00
	152.00	1.570	12.50
Rectangular hollow sections			
50 x 30	2.92	0.155	2.50
	3.66	0.153	3.20
60 x 40	4.66	0.193	3.20
	5.72	0.191	4.00
80 x 40	5.67	0.232	3.20
	6.97	0.231	4.00
90 x 50	7.46	0.272	3.60
	10.10	0.269	5.00
100 x 50	6.75	0.294	3.00
	7.18	0.293	3.20
	8.86	0.291	4.00
100 x 60	8.59	0.312	3.60
	11.70	0.309	5.00
	14.40	0.306	6.30

MEMORANDA FOR EACH TRADE

STRUCTURAL STEELWORK - cont'd

Tables showing the mass and surface area per metre run for various steel members - cont'd

Size (mm)	Mass (kg/m)	Surface area per m run (m²)	Thickness (mm)
Rectangular hollow sections - cont'd			
120 x 60	9.72	0.352	3.60
	13.30	0.349	5.00
	16.40	0.346	6.30
120 x 80	14.80	0.389	5.00
	18.40	0.386	6.30
	22.90	0.383	8.00
	27.90	0.379	10.00
150 x 100	18.70	0.489	5.00
	23.30	0.486	6.30
	29.10	0.483	8.00
	35.70	0.479	10.00
160 x 80	18.00	0.469	5.00
	22.30	0.466	6.30
	27.90	0.463	8.00
	34.20	0.459	10.00
200 x 100	22.70	0.589	5.00
	28.30	0.586	6.30
	35.40	0.583	8.00
	43.60	0.579	10.00
250 x 150	38.20	0.786	6.30
	48.00	0.783	8.00
	59.30	0.779	10.00
	73.00	0.773	12.50
	91.50	0.766	16.00
300 x 200	48.10	0.986	6.30
	60.50	0.983	8.00
	75.00	0.979	10.00
	92.60	0.973	12.50
	117.00	0.966	16.00
400 x 200	90.70	1.180	10.00
	112.00	1.170	12.50
	142.00	1.170	16.00
450 x 250	106.00	1.380	10.00
	132.00	1.370	12.50
	167.00	1.370	16.00

MEMORANDA FOR EACH TRADE

Tables showing the mass and surface area per metre run for various steel members - cont'd

Size (mm)	Mass (kg/m)	Surface area per m run (m^2)
Channels		
432 x 102	65.54	1.217
381 x 102	55.10	1.118
305 x 102	46.18	0.966
305 x 89	41.69	0.920
254 x 89	35.74	0.820
254 x 76	28.29	0.774
229 x 89	32.76	0.770
229 x 76	26.06	0.725
203 x 89	29.78	0.720
203 x 76	23.82	0.675
178 x 89	26.81	0.671
178 x 76	20.84	0.625
152 x 89	23.84	0.621
152 x 76	17.88	0.575
127 x 64	14.90	0.476

Angles - sum of leg lengths	Thickness (mm)	Mass (kg/m)	Surface area per m run (m^2)
50	3	1.11	0.10
	4	1.45	0.10
	5	1.77	0.10
80	4	2.42	0.16
	5	2.97	0.16
	6	3.52	0.16
90	4	2.74	0.18
	5	3.38	0.18
	6	4.00	0.18
100	5	3.77	0.20
	6	4.47	0.20
	8	5.82	0.20
115	5	4.35	0.23
	6	5.16	0.23
	8	6.75	0.23

MEMORANDA FOR EACH TRADE

STRUCTURAL STEELWORK - cont'd

Tables showing the mass and surface area per metre run for various steel members - cont'd

Angles - sum of leg lengths	Thickness (mm)	Mass (kg/m)	Surface area per m run (m²)
120	5	4.57	0.24
	6	5.42	0.24
	8	7.09	0.24
	10	8.69	0.24
125	6	5.65	0.25
	8	7.39	0.25
200	8	12.20	0.40
	10	15.00	0.40
	12	17.80	0.40
	15	21.90	0.40
225	10	17.00	0.45
	12	20.20	0.45
	15	24.80	0.45
240	8	14.70	0.48
	10	18.20	0.48
	12	21.60	0.48
	15	26.60	0.48
300	10	23.00	0.60
	12	27.30	0.60
	15	33.80	0.60
	18	40.10	0.60
350	12	32.00	0.70
	15	39.60	0.70
	18	47.10	0.70
400	16	48.50	0.80
	18	54.20	0.80
	20	59.90	0.80
	24	71.10	0.80

MEMORANDA FOR EACH TRADE

PLUMBING AND MECHANICAL INSTALLATIONS

Dimensions and weights of tubes

Outside diameter (mm)	Internal dia (mm)	Weight per m (kg)	Internal dia (mm)	Weight per m (kg)	Internal dia (mm)	Weight per m (kg)
Copper to EN 1057:1996						
	Table X		**Table Y**		**Table Z**	
6	4.80	0.0911	4.40	0.1170	5.00	0.0774
8	6.80	0.1246	6.40	0.1617	7.00	0.1054
10	8.80	0.1580	8.40	0.2064	9.00	0.1334
12	10.80	0.1914	10.40	0.2511	11.00	0.1612
15	13.60	0.2796	13.00	0.3923	14.00	0.2031
18	16.40	0.3852	16.00	0.4760	16.80	0.2918
22	20.22	0.5308	19.62	0.6974	20.82	0.3589
28	26.22	0.6814	25.62	0.8985	26.82	0.4594
35	32.63	1.1334	32.03	1.4085	33.63	0.6701
42	39.63	1.3675	39.03	1.6996	40.43	0.9216
54	51.63	1.7691	50.03	2.9052	52.23	1.3343
76.1	73.22	3.1287	72.22	4.1437	73.82	2.5131
108	105.12	4.4666	103.12	7.3745	105.72	3.5834
133	130.38	5.5151	-	-	130.38	5.5151
159	155.38	8.7795	-	-	156.38	6.6056

MEMORANDA FOR EACH TRADE

PLUMBING AND MECHANICAL INSTALLATIONS - cont'd

Dimensions and weights of tubes - cont'd

Nominal size (mm)	Outside diameter max (mm)	min (mm)	Wall thickness (mm)	Weight (kg/m)	Weight screwed and socketted (kg/m)
Steel pipes to BS 1387					
Light gauge					
6	10.1	9.7	1.80	0.361	0.364
8	13.6	13.2	1.80	0.517	0.521
10	17.1	16.7	1.80	0.674	0.680
15	21.4	21.0	2.00	0.952	0.961
20	26.9	26.4	2.35	1.410	1.420
25	33.8	33.2	2.65	2.010	2.030
32	42.5	41.9	2.65	2.580	2.610
40	48.4	47.8	2.90	3.250	3.290
50	60.2	59.6	2.90	4.110	4.180
65	76.0	75.2	3.25	5.800	5.920
80	88.7	87.9	3.25	6.810	6.980
100	113.9	113.0	3.65	9.890	10.200
Medium gauge					
6	10.4	9.8	2.00	0.407	0.410
8	13.9	13.3	2.35	0.650	0.654
10	17.4	16.8	2.35	0.852	0.858
15	21.7	21.1	2.65	1.220	1.230
20	27.2	26.6	2.65	1.580	1.590
25	34.2	33.4	3.25	2.440	2.460
32	42.9	42.1	3.25	3.140	3.170
40	48.8	48.0	3.25	3.610	3.650
50	60.8	59.8	3.65	5.100	5.170
65	76.6	75.4	3.65	6.510	6.630
80	89.5	88.1	4.05	8.470	8.640

MEMORANDA FOR EACH TRADE

Nominal size (mm)	Outside diameter max (mm)	min (mm)	Wall thickness (mm)	Weight (kg/m)	Weight screwed and socketted (kg/m)
Medium gauge - cont'd					
100	114.9	113.3	4.50	12.100	12.400
125	140.6	138.7	4.85	16.200	16.700
150	166.1	164.1	4.85	19.200	19.800
Heavy gauge					
6	10.4	9.8	2.65	0.493	0.496
8	13.9	13.3	2.90	0.769	0.773
10	17.4	16.8	2.90	1.020	1.030
15	21.7	21.1	3.25	1.450	1.460
20	27.2	26.6	3.25	1.900	1.910
25	34.2	33.4	4.05	2.970	2.990
32	42.9	42.1	4.05	3.840	3.870
40	48.8	48.0	4.05	4.430	4.470
50	60.8	59.8	4.50	6.170	6.240
65	76.6	75.4	4.50	7.900	8.020
80	89.5	88.1	4.85	10.100	10.300
100	114.9	113.3	5.40	14.400	14.700
125	140.6	138.7	5.40	17.800	18.300
150	166.1	164.1	5.40	21.200	21.800
Stainless steel pipes to BS 4127					
8	8.045	7.940	0.60	0.1120	
10	10.045	9.940	0.60	0.1419	
12	12.045	11.940	0.60	0.1718	
15	15.045	14.940	0.60	0.2174	
18	18.045	17.940	0.70	0.3046	
22	22.055	21.950	0.70	0.3748	
28	28.055	27.950	0.80	0.5469	

MEMORANDA FOR EACH TRADE

PLUMBING AND MECHANICAL INSTALLATIONS – cont'd

Maximum distances between pipe supports

Pipe material onto	BS nominal pipe size		Pipes fitted vertically	Pipes fitted horizontally
	inch	mm	support distances in	low gradients support
distances			metres	in metres
Copper	0.50	15.0	1.90	1.3
	0.75	22.0	2.50	1.9
	1.00	28.0	2.50	1.9
	1.25	35.0	2.80	2.5
	1.50	42.0	2.80	2.5
	2.00	54.0	3.90	2.5
	2.50	67.0	3.90	2.8
	3.00	76.1	3.90	2.8
	4.00	108.0	3.90	2.8
	5.00	133.0	3.90	2.8
	6.00	159.0	3.90	2.8
muPVC	1.25	32.0	1.20	0.5
	1.50	40.0	1.20	0.5
	2.00	50.0	1.20	0.6
Polypropylene	1.25	32.0	1.20	0.5
	1.50	40.0	1.20	0.5
PVC	-	82.4	1.20	0.5
	-	110.0	1.80	0.9
	-	160.0	1.80	1.2

Litres of water storage required per person in various types of building

Type of building	Storage per person (litres)
Houses and flats	90
Hostels	90
Hotels	135
Nurse's home and medical quarters	115
Offices with canteens	45
Offices without canteens	35
Restaurants, per meal served	7
Boarding school	90
Day schools	30

MEMORANDA FOR EACH TRADE

Cold water plumbing - thickness of insulation required against frost

Bore of tube	Pipework within buildings declared thermal conductivity (W/m degrees C)		
	Up to 0.040	0.041 to 0.055	0.056 to 0.070
(mm)	Minimum thickness of insulation (mm)		
15	32	50	75
20	32	50	75
25	32	50	75
32	32	50	75
40	32	50	75
50	25	32	50
65	25	32	50
80	25	32	50
100	19	25	38

Cisterns

Capacities and dimensions of galvanised mild steel cisterns from BS 417

Capacity (litres)	BS type	Dimensions (mm)		
		length	width	depth
18	SCM 45	457	305	305
36	SCM 70	610	305	371
54	SCM 90	610	406	371
68	SCM 110	610	432	432
86	SCM 135	610	457	482
114	SCM 180	686	508	508
159	SCM 230	736	559	559
191	SCM 270	762	584	610
227	SCM 320	914	610	584
264	SCM 360	914	660	610
327	SCM 450/1	1220	610	610
336	SCM 450/2	965	686	686
423	SCM 570	965	762	787
491	SCM 680	1090	864	736
709	SCM 910	1170	889	889

Capacities of cold water polypropylene storage cisterns from BS 4213

Capacity (litres)	BS type	Maximum height (mm)
18	PC 4	310
36	PC 8	380
68	PC 15	430
91	PC 20	510
114	PC 25	530
182	PC 40	610
227	PC 50	660
273	PC 60	660
318	PC 70	660
455	PC 100	760

MEMORANDA FOR EACH TRADE

HEATING AND HOT WATER INSTALLATIONS

Storage capacity and recommended power of hot water storage boilers

Type of building		Storage at 65°C (litres per person)	Boiler power to 65°C (kW per person)
Flats and dwellings			
(a)	Low rent properties	25	0.5
(b)	Medium rent properties	30	0.7
(c)	High rent properties	45	1.2
Nurses homes		45	0.9
Hostels		30	0.7
Hotels			
(a)	Top quality - upmarket	45	1.2
(b)	Average quality - low market	35	0.9
Colleges and schools			
(a)	Live-in accommodation	25	0.7
(b)	Public comprehensive	5	0.1
Factories		5	0.1
Hospitals			
(a)	General	30	1.5
(b)	Infectious	45	1.5
(c)	Infirmaries	25	0.6
(d)	Infirmaries (inc. laundry facilities)	30	0.9
(e)	Maternity	30	2.1
(f)	Mental	25	0.7
Offices		5	0.1
Sports pavilions		35	0.3

Thickness of thermal insulation for heating installations

Size of tube (mm)	Up to 0.025	Declared thermal conductivity 0.026 to 0.040	0.041 to 0.055	0.056 to 0.070
		Minimum thickness of insulation		
LTHW Systems				
15	25	25	38	38
20	25	32	38	38
25	25	38	38	38
32	32	38	38	50
40	32	38	38	50
50	38	38	50	50
65	38	50	50	50
80	38	50	50	50

MEMORANDA FOR EACH TRADE

Size of tube (mm)	Up to 0.025	Minimum thickness of insulation		
		0.026 to 0.040	0.041 to 0.055	0.056 to 0.070
LTHW Systems - cont'd				
100	38	50	50	63
125	38	50	50	63
150	50	50	63	63
200	50	50	63	63
250	50	63	63	63
300	50	63	63	63
Flat surfaces	50	63	63	63

**MTHW Systems
and condensate**

		Declared thermal conductivity		
15	25	38	38	38
20	32	38	38	50
25	38	38	38	50
32	38	50	50	50
40	38	50	50	50
50	38	50	50	50
65	38	50	50	50
80	50	50	50	63
100	50	63	63	63
125	50	63	63	63
150	50	63	63	63
200	50	63	63	63
250	50	63	63	75
300	63	63	63	75
Flat surfaces	63	63	63	75

**HTHW Systems
and steam**

15	38	50	50	50
20	38	50	50	50
25	38	50	50	50
32	50	50	50	63
40	50	50	50	63
50	50	50	75	75
65	50	63	75	75
80	50	63	75	75
100	63	63	75	100
125	63	63	100	100
150	63	63	100	100
200	63	63	100	100
250	63	75	100	100
300	63	75	100	100
Flat surfaces	63	75	100	100

MEMORANDA FOR EACH TRADE

HEATING AND HOT WATER INSTALLATIONS - cont'd

Capacities and dimensions of copper indirect cylinders (coil type) from BS 1566

Capacity (litres)	BS Type	External diameter (mm)	External height over dome (mm)
96	0	300	1600
72	1	350	900
96	2	400	900
114	3	400	1050
84	4	450	675
95	5	450	750
106	6	450	825
117	7	450	900
140	8	450	1050
162	9	450	1200
206	9 E	450	1500
190	10	500	1200
245	11	500	1500
280	12	600	1200
360	13	600	1500
440	14	600	1800

		Internal diameter (mm)	Height (mm)
109	BSG 1M	457	762
136	BSG 2M	457	914
159	BSG 3M	457	1067
227	BSG 4M	508	1270
273	BSG 5M	508	1473
364	BSG 6M	610	1372
455	BSG 7M	610	1753
123	BSG 8M	457	838

Energy costs (July 2001)

GAS SUPPLIES

The last year has seen the wholesale gas market remain somewhat volatile. Suppliers source their gas from this market unless they have a related company producing gas when they can purchase using the transfer pricing mechanism, which is again market based and is equally volatile. The volatility has invoked a continuing increase in the wholesale price of gas and such increases continue to be reflected in the price that the end-user has to pay.

The reasons suggested for the present situation include heavy buying by suppliers in European markets and the link of such markets with oil prices. Another reason is that a new system has been introduced to allocate and price the capacity suppliers require to put their gas into the network from the producers. This capacity has been restricted due to maintenance of the system which has forced entry capacity prices to rise. The suppliers are indicating that rates have reached their peak and will gradually recover in the next few months but not to levels experienced in the last year.

Domestic Markets

This sector refers to individual supply points, which do not consume more than 73,250 kw/hrs (2,500 therms) per annum. Suppliers must supply at their published rates, although there are exceptions to this for bulk purchasing schemes, which can reduce prices by approximately 3%. By contracting with an independent supplier, savings can still be achieved over British Gas Tariffs. Care must be exercised when selecting a supplier, look beyond the savings as some supply contracts contain onerous risk clauses. A typical "all-in" supply rate would be 1.30 p/kw hr for a domestic property. This shows an increase on last year.

MEMORANDA FOR EACH TRADE

Energy costs (July 2001) - cont'd

GAS SUPPLIES – cont'd

Commercial
This sector refers to all other gas supplies. During the last 12 months the price of gas in this sector has continued to increase. For a typical supply consuming 1,000,000 kw/annum, rates approaching 1.2 p/kw are not uncommon.

ELECTRICITY SUPPLIES

In contrast with the significant downtrend last year the market has somewhat levelled out.

Over 100 KVA Supplies
For supplies in this sector of the market there are many options to choose from regarding the charging structure. A typical contract for a supply site with an annual expenditure of £50,000 can expect an "all-in" rate in the region of 4.5 p/kw hr dependent on the load factor. Supplies in this sector require half hourly meters with the associated telephone line in order to collect the half hourly consumption data.

Under 100 KVA Supplies (Non Domestic)
This sector of the market completed its deregulation in 1999. All consumers can purchase their electricity from any authorised supplier, generally a Regional Electricity Company (REC) or Generator, although there are other independent companies in the market place. As suppliers in this market place have established themselves, their pricing structures have matured, many no longer just offering discounts off the local REC's tariff, but offering a pricing structure to meet the consumer's needs. However, the process of changing supplier has not in some cases been the smooth process that was intended with some suppliers experiencing extreme difficulties in managing the transfer process. In extreme cases the industry regulator OFGEM has suspended some suppliers from taking on further business until they, OFGEM, are satisfied the companies in question have the ability to manage the process.

Supply rates achieved vary from region to region, but a typical average rate for a day night supply with an annual expenditure of £500 remains at around 6 p/kw hr.

Domestic Tariff Supplies
Again this sector of the market completed its deregulation process in 1999. Generally the principle is the same as the "Under 100 KVA" market except that the typical discounts are lower, a typical discount being 15% off the host REC tariff.

GENERALLY

For users who are able to group purchase their fuels (eg. schools, health trusts, local authorities, housing associations and any other organisation with multiple supplies) further savings can be achieved. Advice on how to go about this or energy purchasing in general can be obtained from the editor's, Davis Langdon & Everest's, Cambridge office, Tel: 01223 351 258, Fax: 01223 321 002 who have considerable experience in both purchasing energy and the establishment of bulk purchasing schemes.

CLIMATE CHANGE LEVY

This levy, which is a tax on industrial and commercial use of energy is designed to encourage businesses to use less energy and so reduce carbon dioxide emissions. It came into effect on 1st April 2001 and applies to electricity, natural gas, coal, coke and liquid petroleum gas (LPG) but is not levied on standard charges.

The rates for 2001 – 2002 are as follows:

Electricity	0.43 p/kWh
Natural Gas, Coal, Coke	0.15 p/kWh
Liquid Petroleum Gas (LPG)	0.07 p/kWh

which could add 8% - 15% to the energy bills of most businesses. VAT is charged on the levy. Energy supplies are responsible for collecting this levy from customers.

MEMORANDA FOR EACH TRADE

HEATING AND HOT WATER INSTALLATIONS - cont'd

Energy costs (July 2000) - cont'd

CLIMATE CHANGE LEVY – cont'd

National insurance contributions

The Government has reduced the level of employer's National Insurance contributions by the same amount it expects the levy to raise – so, supposedly, there will be no increase in taxation, but the impact is likely to vary company to company, or even sector by sector. The reduction in employers' National Insurance contributions is 0.30%.

Exemptions

Where a taxable commodity (electricity, gas, coal etc.) is used for non energy purpose, e.g. coal is used as a raw material to make carbon filters, the levy is not due. Additionally, where an organisation uses a taxable commodity to produce another taxable commodity, this is also exempt from the levy, e.g. burning gas in a power station to produce electricity. Further, in certain circumstances combined Heat and Power Plants (CHP) are exempt from the levy, and if VAT is paid at the reduced level, i.e. 5% (domestic rate) on any supplies these are not levied.

For further information you may care to access the Customs and Excise website http//www.hmce.gov.uk. A Climate Change Levy Helpdesk also exists on Tel: 0161 827 0332, Fax: 0161 827 0356. Again the Cambridge Office of Davis Langdon & Everest are happy to advise.

MEMORANDA FOR EACH TRADE

VENTILATION AND AIR-CONDITIONING

Typical fresh air supply factors in typical situations

Building type floor area	Litres of fresh air per second per person	Litres of fresh air per second per m^2
General offices	5 - 8	1.30
Board rooms	18 - 25	6.00
Private offices	5 - 12	1.20 - 2.00
Dept. stores	5 - 8	3.00
Factories	20 - 30	0.80
Garages	-	8.00
Bars	12 - 18	-
Dance halls	8 - 12	-
Hotel rooms	8 - 12	1.70
Schools	14	-
Assembly halls	14	-
Drawing offices	16	-

Note: As a global figure for fresh air allow per 1000 m^2 1.20 m^3/second.

Typical air-changes per hour in typical situations

Building type	Air changes per hour
Residences	1 - 2
Churches	1 - 2
Storage buildings	1 - 2
Libraries	3 - 4
Book stacks	1 - 2
Banks	5 - 6
Offices	4 - 6
Assembly halls	5 - 10
Laboratories	4 - 6
Internal bathrooms	5 - 6
Laboratories - internal	6 - 8
Restaurants/cafes	10 - 15
Canteens	8 - 12
Small kitchens	20 - 40
Large kitchens	10 - 20
Boiler houses	15 - 30

MEMORANDA FOR EACH TRADE

GLAZING

Float and polished plate glass

Nominal thickness (mm)	Tolerance on thickness (mm)	Approximate weight (kg/m²)	Normal maximum size (mm)
3	+ 0.2	7.50	2140 x 1220
4	+ 0.2	10.00	2760 x 1220
5	+ 0.2	12.50	3180 x 2100
6	+ 0.2	15.00	4600 x 3180
10	+ 0.3	25.00)	
12	+ 0.3	30.00)	6000 x 3300
15	+ 0.5	37.50	3050 x 3000
19	+ 1.0	47.50)	
25	+ 1.0	63.50)	3000 x 2900

Clear sheet glass

Nominal thickness (mm)	Tolerance on thickness (mm)	Approximate weight (kg/m²)	Normal maximum size (mm)
2 *	+ 0.2	5.00	1920 x 1220
3	+ 0.3	7.50	2130 x 1320
4	+ 0.3	10.00	2760 x 1220
5 *	+ 0.3	12.50)	
6 *	+ 0.3	15.00)	2130 x 2400

Cast glass

Nominal thickness (mm)	Tolerance on thickness (mm)	Approximate weight (kg/m²)	Normal maximum size (mm)
3	+ 0.4		
	- 0.2	6.00)	
4	+ 0.5	7.50)	2140 x 1280
5	+ 0.5	9.50	2140 x 1320
6	+ 0.5	11.50)	
10	+ 0.8	21.50)	3700 x 1280

Wired glass

(Cast wired glass)

Nominal thickness (mm)	Tolerance on thickness (mm)	Approximate weight (kg/m²)	Normal maximum size (mm)
6	+ 0.3	-)	
	- 0.7	)	3700 x 1840
7	+ 0.7	-)	

(Polished wire glass)

Nominal thickness (mm)	Tolerance on thickness (mm)	Approximate weight (kg/m²)	Normal maximum size (mm)
6	+ 1.0	-	330 x 1830

*   The 5 mm and 6 mm thickness are known as *thick drawn sheet*. Although 2 mm sheet glass is available it is not recommended for general glazing purposes.

MEMORANDA FOR EACH TRADE

DRAINAGE

Width required for trenches for various diameters of pipes

Pipe diameter (mm)	Trench n.e. 1.50 m deep	Trench over 1.50 m deep
n.e. 100 mm	450 mm	600 mm
100 - 150 mm	500 mm	650 mm
150 - 225 mm	600 mm	750 mm
225 - 300 mm	650 mm	800 mm
300 - 400 mm	750 mm	900 mm
400 - 450 mm	900 mm	1050 mm
450 - 600 mm	1100 mm	1300 mm

Weights and dimensions of typically sized uPVC pipes

Nominal size	Mean outside diameter (mm)		Wall thickness	Weight kg per metre
Standard pipes	min	max		
82.40	82.40	82.70	3.20	1.20
110.00	110.00	110.40	3.20	1.60
160.00	160.00	160.60	4.10	3.00
200.00	200.00	200.60	4.90	4.60
250.00	250.00	250.70	6.10	7.20

Perforated pipes

Heavy grade as above

Thin wall

82.40	82.40	82.70	1.70	-
110.00	110.00	110.40	2.20	-
160.00	160.00	160.60	3.20	-

Vitrified clay pipes

Product	Nominal diameter	Effective pipe length	Limits of bore load		Crushing strength per metre length	Weight kg/pipe (/m)
	(mm)	(mm)	min	max	(kN/m)	
Supersleve	100	1600	96	105	35.00	15.63 (9.77)
Hepsleve	150	1600	146	158	22.00 (normal)	36.50 (22.81)
Hepseal	150	1500	146	158	22.00	37.04 (24.69)
	225	1750	221	235	28.00	95.24 (54.42)
	300	2500	295	313	34.00	196.08 (78.43)
	400	2500	394	414	44.00	357.14 (142.86)

MEMORANDA FOR EACH TRADE

DRAINAGE – cont'd

Vitrified clay pipes – cont'd

Product	Nominal diameter (mm)	Effective pipe length (mm)	Limits of bore load min	max	Crushing strength per metre length (kN/m)	Weight kg/pipe (/m)
Supersleve	100	1600	96	105	35.00	15.63 (9.77)
Hepseal	450	2500	444	464	44.00	500.00 (200.00)
	500	2500	494	514	48.00	555.56 (222.22)
	600	3000	591	615	70.00	847.46 (282.47)
	700	3000	689	719	81.00	1111.11 (370.37)
	800	3000	788	822	86.00	1351.35 (450.35)
	1000	3000	985	1027	120.00	2000.00 (666.67)
Hepline	100	1250	95	107	22.00	15.15 (12.12)
	150	1500	145	160	22.00	32.79 (21.86)
	225	1850	219	239	28.00	74.07 (40.04)
	300	1850	292	317	34.00	105.28 (56.90)
Hepduct	90	1500	-	-	28.00	12.05 (8.03)
(Conduit) 150	100	1600	-	-	28.00	14.29 (8.93)
	125	1250	-	-	22.00	21.28 (17.02)
	150	1250	-	-	22.00	28.57 (22.86)
	225	1850	-	-	28.00	64.52 (34.88)
	300	1850	-	-	34.00	111.11 (60.06)

USEFUL ADDRESSES FOR FURTHER INFORMATION

ACOUSTICAL INVESTIGATION & RESEARCH
ORGANISATION LTD (AIRO)
Duxon's Turn
Maylands Avenue
Hemel Hempstead
Hertfordshire
HP2 4SB
Tel: 01442 247 146
Fax: 01442 256 749
E-mail: airo@bcs.org.uk
Web: www.airo.co.uk

ALUMINIUM FEDERATION LTD (ALFED)
Broadway House
Calthorpe Road
Five Ways
Birmingham
West Midlands
B15 1TN
Tel: 0121 456 1103
Fax: 0870 138 9714
E-mail: alfed@alfed.org.uk
Web: www.alfed.org.uk

ALUMINIUM FINISHING ASSOCIATION
Broadway House
Calthorpe Road
Five Ways
Birmingham
West Midlands
B15 1TN
Tel: 0121 456 1103
Fax: 0870 138 9714
E-mail: alfed@alfed.org.uk
Web: www.alfed.org.uk

ALUMINIUM ROLLED PRODUCTS
MANUFACTURERS ASSOCIATION
Broadway House
Calthorpe Road
Five Ways
Birmingham
West Midlands
B15 1TN
Tel: 0121 456 1103
Fax: 0870 138 9714
E-mail: info@alfed.org.uk
Web: www.alfed.org.uk

AMERICAN HARDWOOD EXPORT COUNCIL (AHEC)
3 St. Michaels Alley
London
EC3V 9DS
Tel: 0207 626 4111
Fax: 0207 626 4222
E-mail: info@ahec.co.uk
Web: www.ahec-europe.org

ANCIENT MONUMENTS SOCIETY (AMS)
Saint Ann's Vestry Hall
2 Church Entry
London
EC4V 5HB
Tel: 0207 236 3934
Fax: 0207 329 3677
E-mail: office@ancientmonumentssociety.org.uk
Web: www.ancientmonumentssociety.org.uk

APA - THE ENGINEERED WOOD ASSOCIATION
Claridge House
29 Barnes, High Street
London
SW13 9LW
Tel: 0845 123 3721
Fax: 0208 282 1660
E-mail: cdp@apa-europe.org
Web: apa-europe.org

ARCHITECTURAL ADVISORY SERVICE CENTRE
(POWDER/ANODIC METAL FINISHES)
Barn One
Barn Road
Conswick
Buckinhamshire
HP27 9RW
Tel: 01844 342 425
Fax: 01844 274 781
E-mail: daveparsons@aasc.org.uk

ARCHITECTURAL ASSOCIATION (AA)
34 - 36 Bedford Square
London
WC1B 3ES
Tel: 0207 887 4000
Fax: 0207 414 0782

ARCHITECTURAL CLADDING ASSOCIATION (ACA)
60 Charles Street
Leicester
Leicestershire
LE1 1FB
Tel: 0116 253 6161
Fax: 0116 251 4568
Email: aca@britishprecast.org
Web: www.britishprecast.org/aca

ASBESTOS INFORMATION CENTRE (AIC)
PO Box 69
Widnes
Cheshire
WA8 9GW
Tel: 0151 420 5866

USEFUL ADDRESSES FOR FURTHER INFORMATION

ASBESTOS REMOVAL CONTRACTORS'
ASSOCIATION (ARCA)
Friars House
6 Parkway
Chelmsford,
Essex
CM2 ONF
Tel: 01245 259 744
Fax: 01245 490 722

ASSOCIATION OF INTERIOR SPECIALISTS
Olton Bridge
245 Warwick Road
Solihull
West Midlands
B92 7AH
Tel: 0121 707 0077
Fax: 0121 706 1949
E-mail: info@ais-interiors.org.uk
Web: www.ais-interiors.org.uk

BOX CULVERT ASSOCIATION (BCA)
60 Charles Street
Leicester
Leicestershire
LE1 1FB
Tel: 0116 253 6161
Fax: 0116 251 4568
E-mail: cjb@britishprecast.org
Web: www.britishprecast.org

BRITISH ADHESIVES & SEALANTS
ASSOCIATION(BASA)
33 Fellowes Way
Stevenage
Hertfordshire
SG2 8BW
Tel: 01438 358 514

BRITISH AGGREGATE CONSTRUCTION
MATERIALS INDUSTRIES LTD (BACMI)
156 Buckingham Palace Road
London
SW1W 9TR
Tel: 0207 730 8194

BRITISH APPROVALS FOR FIRE EQUIPMENT (BAFE)
Thames House
29 Thames Sreet
Kingston upon Thames
Surrey
KT1 1PH
Tel: 0208 541 1950
Fax: 0208 547 1564
E-mail: bafe@abft.org.uk
Web: www.bafe.org.uk

BRITISH APPROVALS SERVICE FOR CABLES
(BASEC)
23 Presley Way
Crownhill
Milton Keynes
Buckinghamshire
MK8 0ES
Tel: 01908 267 300
Fax: 01908 267 255
E-mail: mail@basec.org.uk
Web: www.basec.org.uk

BRITISH ARCHITECTURAL LIBRARY (BAL)
Royal Institute of British Architects
66 Portland Place
London
W1N 4AD
Tel: 0906 302 0400
Fax: 0207 307 3812

BITISH ASSOCIATION OF LANDSCAPE INDUSTRIES
(BALI)
Landscape House
National Agricultural Centre
Stoneleigh Park
Warwickshire
CV8 2LG
Tel: 0870 770 4971
Fax: 0870 770 4972
E-mail: contact@bali.co.uk
Web: www.bali.co.uk

BRITISH   BATHROOM   COUNCIL   (BATHROOM
MANUFACTURERS ASSOCIATION)
Federation House
Station Road
Stoke-on-Trent
Staffordshire
ST4 2RT
Tel: 01782 747 123
Fax: 01782 747 161
E-mail: info@bathroom-association.org.uk
Web: www.bathroom-assciation.org

BRITISH BOARD OF AGREMENT (BBA)
PO Box 195
Bucknalls Lane
Garston
Watford
Hertfordshire
WD25 9BA
Tel: 01923 665 300
Fax: 01923 665 301
E-mail: info.bba.stal.co.uk
Web: www.bbacerts.co.uk

USEFUL ADDRESSES FOR FURTHER INFORMATION

BRITISH CABLES ASSOCIATION (BCA)
37a Walton Road
East Molesey
Surrey
KT8 0DH
Tel: 0208 941 4079
Fax: 0208 783 0104
E-mail: admin@bcauk.org
Web: www.bcauk.org

BRITISH CARPET MANUFACTURERS ASSOCIATION
LTD (BCMA)
PO Box 1155
MCF Complex
60 New Road
Kidderminster
Worcestershire
DY10 1AQ
Tel: 01562 755 568
Fax: 01562 865 4055
E-mail: info@carpetfederation.com
Web: www.carpetfoundation.com

BRITISH CEMENT ASSOCIATION (BCA), CENTRE
FOR CONCRETE INFORMATION
Century House
Telford Avenue
Crowthorne
Berkshire
RG45 6YS
Tel: 01344 762 676
Fax: 01344 761 214

BRITISH CERAMIC CONFEDERATION (BCC)
Federation House
Station Road
Stoke-on-Trent
Staffordshire
ST4 2SA
Tel: 01782 744 631
Fax: 01782 744 102
E-mail: bcc@ceramfed.co.uk
Web: www.ceramfed.co.uk

BRITISH CERAMIC RESEARCH LTD (BCR)
Queens Road
Penkhull
Stoke-on-Trent
Staffordshire
ST4 7LQ
Tel: 01782 845 431
Fax: 01782 412 331
Web: www.ceram.co.uk

BRITISH CERAMIC TILE COUNCIL (BCTC TILE
ASSOCIATION)
Federation house
Station Road
Stoke On Trent
ST4 2RT
Tel: 01782 747 147
Fax: 01782 747 161
E-mail: tiles@netcentral.co.uk

BRITISH COMBUSTION EQUIPMENT
MANUFACTURERS ASSOCIATION (BCEMA)
58 London Road
Leicester
LE2 0QD
Tel: 0116 275 7111
Fax: 0116 275 7222
E-mail: bcema@btconnect.com
Web: bcema.co.uk

BRITISH CONCRETE MASONRY ASSOCIATION
(BCMA)
Grove Crescent House
18 Grove Place
Bedford
MK40 3JJ
Tel/fax: 01234 353 745

BRITISH CONSTRUCTIONAL STEELWORK
ASSOCIATION LTD (BCSA)
4 Whitehall Court
Westminster
London
SW1A 2ES
Tel: 0207 839 8566
Fax: 0207 976 1634
Web: www.steelconstruction.org

BRITISH CONTRACT FURNISHING ASSOCIATION
(BCFA)
Suite 2/4
The Business Design Centre
52 Upper Street
Islington Green
London
N1 0QH
Tel: 0207 226 6641
Fax: 0207 288 6190

BRITISH DECORATORS ASSOCIATION (BDA)
32 Coton Road
Nuneaton
Warwickshire
CV11 5TW
Tel: 01203 353 776
Fax: 01203 354 4513

USEFUL ADDRESSES FOR FURTHER INFORMATION

BRITISH ELECTROTECHNICAL APPROVALS
BOARD (BEAB)
1 Station View
Guildford
Surrey
GU1 4JY
Tel: 01483 455 466
Fax: 01483 455 477
E-mail: info@beab.com
Web: www.beab.co.uk

BRITISH FIRE PROTECTION SYSTEMS ASSOCIATION
LTD (BFPSA)
Thames House
29 Thames Street
Kingston-upon-Thames
Surrey
KT1 1PH
Tel: 0208 549 5855
Fax: 0208 547 1564
Web: www.bfpsa.org.uk

BRITISH FURNITURE MANUFACTURERS
FEDERATION
LTD (BFM Ltd)
30 Harcourt Street
London
W1H 2AA
Tel: 0207 724 0851
Fax: 0207 723 0622

BRITISH GEOLOGICAL SURVEY (BGS)
Keyworth Headquarters
Kingsley Drive
Dunham Centre
Nottingham
Nottinghamshire
NG12 5GG
Tel: 0115 936 3100
Fax: 0115 936 3200
E-mail: enquiries@bgs.ac.ukc.uk
Web: www.thebgs.co.uk

BRITISH INSTITUTE OF ARCHITECTURAL
TECHNOLOGISTS (BIAT)
397 City Road
London
EC1V 1NH
Tel: 0207 278 2206
Fax: 0207 837 3194
Web: www.biat.org.uk

BRITISH LAMINATED FABRICATORS ASSOCIATION
6 Bath Place
Rivington Street
London
EC2A 3JE
Tel: 0870 444 1500
Fax: 0207 457 5000
Web: www.bpf.co.uk

BRITISH LIBRARY BIBLIOGRAPHIC SERVICE AND
DOCUMENT SUPPLY
Boston Spa
Wetherby
West Yorkshire
LS23 7BQ
Tel: 0870 444 1500
Fax: 0207 457 5000
E-mail: nbs-info@bl.uk
Web: www.bl.uk

BRITISH LIBRARY ENVIRONMENTAL INFORMATION
SERVICE
96 Euston Road
London
NW1 2DB
Tel: 0870 444 1500
Fax: 0207 457 5000
E-mail: stms@bl.uk
Web: www.bl.uk/environment

BRITISH NON-FERROUS METALS FEDERATION
Broadway House
60 Calthorpe Road
Edgbaston
Birmingham
West Midlands
B15 1TN
Tel: 0121 456 6110
Fax: 0121 456 2274
Email: copperuk@compuserve.com

BRITISH PLASTICS FEDERATION (BPF)
Plastics & Rubber Advisory Service
6 Bath Place
Rivington Street
London
EC2A 3JE
Tel: 0207 457 5000
Fax: 0207 457 5045

USEFUL ADDRESSES FOR FURTHER INFORMATION

BRITISH PRECAST CONCRETE FEDERATION LTD
60 Charles Street
Leicester
Leicestershire
LE1 1FB
Tel: 0116 253 6161
Fax: 0116 251 4568
E-mail: birpre@aol.com
Web: www.britishprecast.org.uk

BRITISH PROPERTY FEDERATION (BPF)
35 Catherine Place
London
SW1E 6DY
Tel: 0207 828 0111
Fax: 0207 824 3442

BRITISH RUBBER MANUFACTURERS'
ASSOCIATION LTD (BRMA)
6 Bath Place
Rivington Street
London
EC2A 3JE
Tel: 0207 457 5040
Fax: 0207 972 9008
E-mail: mail@brma.co.uk
Web: www.brma.co.uk

BRITISH STANDARDS INSTITUTION (BSI)
389 Chiswick High Road
London
W4 4AL
Tel: 0208 996 9000
Fax: 0208 996 7400

BRITISH WATER
1 Queen Anne's Gate
London
SW1H 9BT
Tel: 0207 957 4554
Fax: 0207 957 4565
E-mail: info@britishwater.co.uk
Web: www.britishwater.co.uk

BRITISH WOOD PRESERVING & DAMP PROOFING
ASSOCIATION (BWPDA)
6 Office Village
Romford Road
London
E15 4ED
Tel: 0208 519 2588
Fax: 0208 519 3444

BRITISH WOODWORKING FEDERATION
55 Tufton Street
London
SW1 3QL
Tel: 0870 458 6939
Fax: 0870 458 6949
Email: bwf@bwf.org.uk
Web: www.bwf.org.uk

BUILDING CENTRE
The Building Centre
26 Store Street
London
WC1E 7BT
Tel: 0207 692 4000
Fax: 0207 580 9641
E-mail: information@buildingcentre.co.uk
Web: www.buildingcentre.co.uk

BUILDING COST INFORMATION SERVICE LTD (BCIS)
Royal Institution of Chartered Surveyors
3 Cadogan Gate
London
SW1X 0AS
Tel: 0207 695 1500
Fax: 0207 695 1501
E-mail: bcis@bcis.co.uk
Web: www.bcis.co.uk

BUILDING EMPLOYERS CONFEDERATION (BEC)
55 Tufton Street
Westminster
London
SW1P 3QL
Tel: 0870 89 89 090
Fax: 0870 89 89 095
E-mail: enquiries@thecc.org.uk
Web: www.thecc.org.uk

BUILDING MAINTENANCE INFORMATION (BMI)
Royal Institution of Chartered Surveyors
3 Cadogan Gate
London
SW1X OAS
Tel: 0207 695 1500
Fax: 0207 695 1501
E-mail: acowan@bcis.co.uk
Web: www.bcis.co.uk

USEFUL ADDRESSES FOR FURTHER INFORMATION

BUILDING RESEARCH ESTABLISHMENT (BRE)
BRE Garston
Watford
WD5 9XX
Tel: 01923 664 000
E-mail: enquiries@bre.co.uk
Web: www.bre.co.uk

BUILDING RESEARCH ESTABLISHMENT:
SCOTLAND (BRE)
Kelvin Road
East Kilbride
Glasgow
G75 0RZ
Tel: 01355 233 001
Fax: 01355 241 895
Web: www.bre.co.uk

BUILDING SERVICES RESEARCH AND
INFORMATION ASSOCIATION Ltd
Old Bracknell Lane West
Bracknell
Berkshire
RG12 7AH
Tel: 01344 465 600
Fax: 01344 465 626
E-mail: bsria@bsria.co.uk
Web: www.bsria.co.uk

BUILT ENVIRONMMENT RESEARCH GROUP
c/o Disabled Living Foundation
380 - 384 Harrow Road
London
W9 2HU
Tel: 0207 289 6111
Fax: 0207 273 4340
Email: advise@dlf.org.uk
Web: www.dlf.org.uk

CATERING EQUIPMENT MANUFACTURERS
ASSOCIATION (CEMA)
Carlyle House
235 Vauxhall Bridge Road
London
SW1V 1EJ
Tel: 0207 233 7724
Fax: 0207 828 0667

CHARTERED INSTITUTE OF BUILDING (CIOB)
Englemere
Kings Ride
Ascot
Berkshire
SL5 8BJ
Tel: 01344 630 700
Fax: 01344 630 777

CHARTERED INSTITUTION OF BUILDING
SERVICES ENGINEERS (CIBSE)
Delta House
222 Balham High Road
London
SW12 9BS
Tel: 0208 675 5211
Fax: 0208 675 5449
Web: www.cibse.org

CLAY PIPE DEVELOPMENT ASSOCIATION (CPDA)
Treetops House
Billingdon
Chesham
HP5 2XL
Tel: 01494 791 456
Fax: 01494 792 378
E-mail: cpda@aol.com

CLAY ROOF TILE COUNCIL
Federation House
Station Road
Stoke-on-Trent
Staffordshire
ST4 2SA
Tel: 01782 744 631
Fax: 01782 744 102
E-mail: crtc@ceramfed.co.uk

COLD ROLLED SECTIONS ASSOCIATION (CRSA)
National Metal Forming Centre
47 Birmingham Road
West Bromwich
West Midlands
B70 6PY
Tel: 0121 601 6350
Fax: 0121 601 6373
E-mail: crsa@crsauk.com
Web: www.crsauk.com

COMMONWEALTH ASSOCIATION OF ARCHITECTS
(CAA)
PO BOX 508
Edgware
HA8 9XZ
Tel: 44 20895 10550
E-mail: inof@comarchitect.org
Web: www.comarchitect.org

USEFUL ADDRESSES FOR FURTHER INFORMATION

CONCRETE SOCIETY ADVISORY SERVICE
Riverside House
4 Meadows Business Park
Station Approach
Blackwater, Camberley
Surrey
GU17 9AB
Tel: 01276 607 140
Fax: 01276 607 141
Web: www.concrete.org.uk

CONCRETE BRIDGE DEVELOPMENT GROUP
Riverside House
4 Meadows Business Park
Station Approach
Blackwater, Camberley
Surrey
GU17 9AB
Tel: 01276 607 140
Fax: 01276 607 141
Web: www.cconcrete.org.uk

CONCRETE LINTEL ASSOCIATION
60 Charles Street
Leicester
Leicestershire
LE1 1FB
Tel: 0116 253 6161
Fax: 0116 251 4568
E-mail: birpre@aol.com
Web: www.britishprecast.org.uk

CONCRETE PIPE ASSOCIATION (CPA)
60 Charles Street
Leicester
Leicestershire
LE1 1FB
Tel: 0116 253 6161
Fax: 0116 251 4568
E-mail: birpre@aol.com
Web: www.britishprecast.org.uk

CONCRETE REPAIR ASSOCIATION (CRA)
Association House
235 Ash Road
Aldershot
Hampshire
GU12 4DD
Tel: 01252 321 302
Fax: 01252 333 901
E-mail: info@associationhouse.org.uk
Web: www.concreterepair.org.uk

CONCRETE SOCIETY Ltd
3 Eatongateuse
112 Windsor Road
Slough
Berks
SL1 2JA
Tel: 01753 693 313
Fax: 01753 692 333

CONFEDERATION OF BRITISH INDUSTRY (CBI)
Centre Point
103 New Oxford Street
London
WC1A 1DU
Tel: 0207 379 7400
Fax: 0207 240 1578

CONSTRUCT - CONCRETE STRUCTURES GROUP
LTD
Riverside House
4 Meadows Business Park
Station Approach
Blackwater, Camberley
Surrey
GU17 9AB
Tel: 01276 38444
Fax: 01276 38899
E-mail: enquiries@construct.org.uk
Web: www.construct.org.uk

CONSTRUCTION EMPLOYERS FEDERATION LTD
(CEF)
143 Malone Road
Belfast
Northern Ireland
BT9 6SU
Tel: 01232 877 143
Fax: 01232 877 155

CONSTRUCTION INDUSTRY RESEARCH &
INFORMATION ASSOCIATION (CIRIA)
Classic House
174-180 Old Street
London
EC1V 9BP
Tel: 0207 549 3300
Fax: 0207 253 0523
E-mail: enquiries@ciria.org.uk
Web: www.ciria.org.uk

CONSTRUCTION PLANT-HIRE ASSOCIATION (CPA)
28 Eccleston Street
London
SW1P 3AU
Tel: 0207 730 7117

USEFUL ADDRESSES FOR FURTHER INFORMATION

CONTRACT FLOORING ASSOCIATION (CFA)
4c Saint Mary's Place
The Lace Market
Nottingham
Nottinghamshire
NG1 1PH
Tel: 0115 941 1126
Fax: 0115 941 2238
E-mail: info@cfa.org.uk
Web: www.cfa.org.uk

CONTRACTORS MECHANICAL PLANT ENGINEERS
(CMPE)
3 Hillview
Hornbeam
Waterlooville
Hampshire
PO8 9EY
Tel: 023 9236 5829
Fax: 023 9236 5829

COPPER DEVELOPMENT ASSOCIATION
Verulam Industrial Estate
224 London Road
Saint Albans
Hertfordshire
AL1 1AQ
Tel: 01727 731 205
Fax: 01727 731 216
E-mail: copperdev@compuserve.com
Web: www.cda.org.uk

CORUS RESEARCH DEVELOPMENT AND
TECHNOLOGY
Swinden Technology Centre
Moorgate
Rotherham
South Yorkshire
S60 3AR
Tel: 01709 820 166
Fax: 01709 825 337

COUNCIL FOR ALUMINIUM IN BUILDING (CAB)
191 Cirencester Road
Charlton Kings
Cheltenham
Gloucestershire
GL53 8DF
Tel: 01242 578 278
Fax: 01242 578 283

DRY STONE WALLING ASSOCIATION OF GREAT
BRITAIN (DSWA)
Westmorland County Showground
Lane Fram
Crooklands, Milnthorpe
Cumbria
LA7 7NH
Tel: 01539 567 953
E-mail: information@dswa.org.uk
Web: www.dswa.org.uk

ELECTRICAL CONTRACTORS ASSOCIATION (ECA)
ESCA House
34 Palace Court
Bayswater
London
W2 4HY
Tel: 0207 313 4800
Fax: 0207 221 7344
E-mail: electricalcontractors@eca.co.uk
Web: www.eca.uk

ELECTRICAL CONTRACTORS ASSOCIATION
OF SCOTLAND (SELECT)
The walled Gardens
Bush Estate
Midlothian
Scotland
EH26 0SB
Tel: 0131 445 5577
Fax: 0131 445 5548
E-mail: admin@select.org.uk
Web: www.select.org.uk

ELECTRICAL INSTALLATION EQUIPMENT
MANUFACTURERS ASSOCIATION LTD (EIEMA)
Beama Installation Ltd
Westminster Tower
3 Albert Embankment
London
SE1 7SL
Tel: 0207 793 3013
Fax: 0207 793 3003
E-mail: cac@beama.org.uk
Web: www.eiema.org.uk

EUROPEAN LIQUID ROOFING ASSOCIATION
(ELRA)
Fields House
Gower Road
Haywards Heath
West Sussex
RH16 4PL
Tel: 01444 417 458
Fax: 01444 415 616

USEFUL ADDRESSES FOR FURTHER INFORMATION

FACULTY OF BUILDING
Central Office
35 Hayworth Road
Sandiacre
Nottingham
Nottinghamshire
NG10 5LL
Tel: 0115 949 0641
Fax: 0115 949 1664
E-mail: mail@faculty-of-building.co.uk
Web: www.faculty-of-building.co.uk

FEDERATION OF MANUFACTURERS OF
CONSTRUCTION EQUIPMENT & CRANES
Ambassador House
Brigstock Road
Thornton Heath
Surrey
CR7 7JG
Tel: 0208 665 5727
Fax: 0208 665 6447
E-mail: cea@admin.co.uk
Web: www.coneq.org.uk

FEDERATION OF MASTER BUILDERS
Gordon Fisher House
14 - 15 Great James Street
London
WC1N 3DP
Tel: 0207 242 7583
Fax: 0207 404 0296

FEDERATION OF PILING SPECIALISTS
Forum Court
83 Coppers Cope Road
Beckenham
Kent
BR3 1NR
Tel: 0208 663 0947
Fax: 0208 663 0949
E-mail: fps@fps.org.ik
Web: www.fps.org.uk

FEDERATION OF PLASTERING & DRYWALL
CONTRACTORS
Construction House
56 - 64 Leonard Street
London
EC2A 4JX
Tel: 0207 608 5092
Fax: 0207 608 5081
Web: www.fpdc.org

FENCING CONTRACTORS ASSOCIATION
Warren Road
Trellech
Monmouthshire
NP5 4PQ
Tel: 07000 560 722
Fax: 01600 860 614

FINNISH PLYWOOD INTERNATIONAL
PO BOX 99
Welwyn Garden City
Herts
AL6 0HS
Tel: 01438 798 746
Fax: 01438 798 305

FLAT ROOFING ALLIANCE
Fields House
Gower Road
Haywards Heath
West Sussex
RH16 4PL
Tel: 01444 440 027
Fax: 01444 415 616

FURNITURE INDUSTRY RESEARCH ASSOCIATION
(FIRA INTERNATIONAL LTD)
Maxwell Road
Stevenage
Hertfordshire
SG1 2EW
Tel: 01438 777 700
Fax: 01438 777 800
E-mail: info@fira.co.uk
Web: www.fira.co.uk

GLASS & GLAZING FEDERATION (GGF)
44 - 48 Borough High Street
London
SE1 1XB
Tel: 0870 024 4255
Fax: 0870 024 4266
E-mail: info@ggf.org.uk
Web: www.ggf.org.uk

HEATING & VENTILATING CONTRACTORS'
ASSOCIATION
ESCA House
34 Palace Court
Bayswater
London
W2 4JG
Tel: 0207 313 4900
Fax: 0207 727 9268

USEFUL ADDRESSES FOR FURTHER INFORMATION

HOUSING CORPORATION HEADQUARTERS
Maple House
149 Tottenham Court Road
London
W1N 7BN
Tel: 0845 230 7000
Fax: 0207 393 2111
E-mail: enquiries@housingcorp.gsx.gov.uk
Web: www.housingcorp.gov.uk

INSTITUTE OF ACOUSTICS
77A Saint Peter' Street
Saint Albans
Hertfordshire
AL1 3BN
Tel: 01727 848 195
Fax: 01727 850 553
E-mail: ioa@ioa.org.uk
Web: www.ioa.org.uk

INSTITUTE OF ASPHALT TECHNOLOGY
Paper Mews Place
290 High Street
Dorking
Surrey
RH4 1QT
Tel: 01306 742792
Fax: 01306 888902
Web: www.instofasphalt.org
Email: secretary@instoasphalt.demon.co.uk

INSTITUTE OF MAINTENANCE AND BUILDING
MANAGEMENT
Keets House
30 East Street
Farnham
Surrey
GU9 7SW
Tel: 01252 710 994
Fax: 01252 737 741
Email: imbm.@btconnect.com
Web: www.imbm.org.uk

INSTITUTE OF MATERIALS
Headquarters
1 Carlton House Terrace
London
SW1Y 5DB
Tel: 0207 451 7300
Fax: 0207 839 1702
Web: www.materials.org.uk

INSTITUTE OF PLUMBING
64 Station Lane
Hornchurch
Essex
RM12 6NB
Tel: 01708 472 791
Fax: 01708 448 987
E-mail: info@iphe.org.ukk
Web: www.plumbers.org.uk

INSTITUTE OF WASTES MANAGEMENT
9 Saxon Court
St Peter's Gardens
Northampton
NN1 1SX
Tel: 01604 620 426
Fax: 01604 621 339
E-mail: technical@iwm.co.uk
Web: www.iwm.co.uk

INSTITUTE OF WOOD SCIENCE
Stocking Lane
Hughenden Valley
High Wycombe
Buckinghamshire
HP14 4NU
Tel: 01494 565 374
Fax: 01494 565 395
E-mail: info@iwsc.org.uk
Web: www.iwsc.org.uk

INSTITUTION OF CIVIL ENGINEERS (ICE)
1 Great George Street
London
SW1P 3AA
Tel: 0207 222 7722
Fax: 0207 222 7500

INSTITUTION OF INCORPORATED ENGINEERS
Savoy Hill House
Savoy Hill
London
WC2R 0BS
Tel: 0207 836 3357
Fax: 0207 497 9006

INSTITUTION OF STRUCTURAL ENGINEERS (ISE)
11 Upper Belgrave Street
London
SW1X 8BH
Tel: 0207 235 4535
Fax: 0207 235 4294

USEFUL ADDRESSES FOR FURTHER INFORMATION

INTERPAVE (THE PRECAST CONCRETE PAVING
& KERB ASSOCIATION)
60 Charles Street
Leicester
Leicestershire
LE1 1FB
Tel: 0116 253 6161
Fax: 0116 251 4568

JOINT CONTRACTS TRIBUNAL LTD
9 Cavendish Place
London
W1G 0GD
Tel: 0207 630 8650
Fax: 0207630 8670
Email: spanform@jctltd.co.uk
Web: www.jctltd.co.uk

KITCHEN SPECIALISTS ASSOCIATION
12 TopBarn Business Centre
Holt Heath
Worcester
Worcestershire
WR6 6NH
Tel: 01905 621 787
Fax: 01905 621 887
Web: www.kbsa.co.uk

LIGHTING ASSOCIATION LTD
Stafford Park 7
Telford
Shropshire
TF3 3BQ
Tel: 01952 290 905
Fax: 01952 290 906
E-mail: enquiries@lightingasscociation.com
Web: http://www.lightingassociation.com/

MASTIC ASPHALT COUNCIL LTD
PO BOX e House
Hastings
Kent
TN35 4WL
Tel: 01424 814 400
Fax: 01424 814 446

METAL CLADDING & ROOFING MANUFACTURERS
ASSOCIATION
18 Mere Farm Road
Prenton
Birkenhead
Merseyside
CH43 9TT
Tel: 0151 652 3846
Fax: 0151 653 4080
E-mail: mcrma@compuserve.com
Web: www.mcrma.co.uk

NATIONAL HOUSE-BUILDING COUNCIL (NHBC)
Ash house
Linford Wood
Milton Keynes
MK14 6ET
Tel: 01494 434 477
Fax: 01494 728 521
E-mail: sts@nhbc.co.uk
Web: www.nhbc.co.uk

NATURAL SLATE QUARRIES ASSOCIATION
26 Store Street
London
WC1E 7BT
Tel: 0207 323 3770
Fax: 0207 323 0307
Email: enquiries@constprod.org.uk
Web: www.constprod.org.uk

NHS ESTATES
Departments of Health
1 Trevelyan Square
Boar Lane
Leeds
West Yorkshire
LS1 6AE
Tel: 0113 254 7000
Fax: 0113 254 7299

ORDNANCE SURVEY
Romsey Road
Southampton
SO16 4GU
Tel: 08456 050 504
Fax: 02380 792 615
E-mail: custiomerservices@ordnancesurvey.co.uk
Web: www.ordnancesurvey.co.uk

PIPELINE INDUSTRIES GUILD
14 - 15 Belgrave Square
London
SW1X 8PS
Tel: 0207 235 7938
Fax: 0207 235 0074
E-mail: hqsec@pipeguild.co.uk
Web: www.pipeguild.co.uk

PLASTIC PIPE MANUFACTURERS SOCIETY
89 Cornwall Street
Birmingham
West Midlands
B3 3BY
Tel: 0121 236 1866
Fax: 0121 262 3370

USEFUL ADDRESSES FOR FURTHER INFORMATION

PRECAST FLOORING FEDERATION
60 Charles Street
Leicester
Leicestershire
LE1 1FB
Tel: 0116 253 6161
Fax: 0116 251 4568
E-mail: info@pff.org.uk
Web: www.pff.org.uk

PRESTRESSED CONCRETE ASSOCIATION
60 Charles Street
Leicester
Leicestershire
LE1 1FB
Tel: 0116 253 6161
Fax: 0116 251 4568
E-mail: pca@britishprecast.org
Web: www.britishprecast.org

PROPERTY CONSULTANTS SOCIETY LTD
107a Tarrant Street
Arundel
West Sussex
BN18 9DP
Tel: 01903 883 787
Fax: 01903 889 590
E-mail: pcs@propco.freeserve.co.uk

QUARRY PRODUCTS ASSOCIATION
Gillingham House
38-44 Gillingham Street
London
SW1 V1HU
Tel: 0207 963 8000
Fax: 0207 963 8001
E-mail: info@qpa.org
Web: www.qpa.org

READY-MIXED CONCRETE BUREAU
Century House
Telford Avenue
Crowthorne
Berkshire
RG45 6YS
Tel: 01344 725 732
Fax: 01344 774 976
E-mail: speed@qpa.org
Web: www.rcb.org.uk

REINFORCED CONCRETE COUNCIL
Riverside House
4 Meadows Business Park
Station Approach
Camberley
Berkshire
GU17 9AB
Tel: 01276 607140
Fax: 01276 607141
Web: www.rcc-info.org.uk
Email: rcc@bca.org.uk

ROYAL INCORPORATION OF ARCHITECTS IN
SCOTLAND (RIAS)
15 Rutland Square
Edinburgh
Scotland
EH1 2BE
Tel: 0131 229 7545
Fax: 0131 228 2188
E-mail: info@rias.org.uk
Web: www.rias.org.uk

ROYAL INSTITUTE OF BRITISH ARCHITECTS (RIBA)
66 Portland Place
London
W1N 4AD
Tel: 0207 580 5533
Fax: 0207 255 1541

ROYAL INSTITUTION OF CHARTERED SURVEYORS
(RICS)
12 Great George Street
Parliament Square
London
SW1P 3AD
Tel: 0207 222 7000
Fax: 0207 222 9430
Web: www.rics.org.uk

ROYAL TOWN PLANNING INSTITUTE
(RTPI)
26 Portland Place
London
W1N 4BEL
Tel: 0207 636 9107
Fax: 0207 323 1582
E-mail: online@rtpi.org.uk

USEFUL ADDRESSES FOR FURTHER INFORMATION

RURAL DESIGN AND BUILDING ASSOCIATION
ATSS House
Station Road East
Stowmarket
Suffolk
IP12 41RQ
Tel: 01449 676 049
Fax: 01449 770 028
E-mail: secretary@rdba.org.uk
Web: www.rdba.org.uk

SCOTTISH BUILDING EMPLOYERS FEDERATION
Carron Grange
Carron Grange Avenue
Stenhousemuir
Scotland
FK5 3BQ
Tel: 01324 555 550
Fax: 01324 555 551
E-mail: info@scottish-building.co.uk
Web: www.scottish-building.co.uk

SCOTTISH HOMES- Community Scotland
Thistle House
91 Haymarket Terrace
Edinburgh
Scotland
EH12 5HE
Tel: 0131 313 0044
Fax: 0131 313 2680
Web: www.communitiescotland.gsi.gov.uk
SCOTTISH NATURAL HERITAGE
Communications Directorate
12 Hope Terrace
Edinburgh
EH9 2AS
Tel: 0131 447 4784
Fax: 0131 446 2277
Web: www.snh.org.uk

SINGLE PLY ROOFING ASSOCIATION
177 Bagnall Road
Basford
Nottinghamshire
NG6 8SJ
Tel: 0115 703 332

SMOKE CONTROL ASSOCIATION
2 Waltham Court
Milley Lane
Hare Hatch
Reading
Berkshire
RG10 9TH
Tel: 0118 940 3416
Fax: 0118 940 6258
Web: www.feta.co.uk
Email: info@feta.co.uk

SOCIETY FOR THE PROTECTION OF
ANCIENT BUILDINGS (SPAB)
37 Spital Square
London
E1 6DY
Tel: 0207 377 1644
Fax: 0207 247 5296
E-mail: info@spab.org.uk
Web: www.spab.org.uk

SOCIETY OF GLASS TECHNOLOGY
Don Valley House
Saville Street East
Sheffield
South Yorkshire
S4 7UQ
Tel: 0114 263 4455
Fax: 0114 263 4411
E-mail: info@sgt.org
Web: www.sgt.org

SOIL SURVEY AND LAND RESEARCH INSTITUTE
Cranfield University
Silsoe Campus
Bedford
Bedfordshire
MK45 4DT
Tel: 01525 863 000
Fax: 01525 863 253
E-mail: nsri@cranfield.ac.uk
Web: www.cranfield.ac.uk/sslrc

SOLAR ENERGY SOCIETY
c/o School of Engineering
Oxford Brookes University
Gipsy Lane
Headington, Oxford
OX3 0BP

SPORT ENGLAND
3rd Floor
Victoria House
Bloomsbury Square
London
WC1B 4SE
Tel: 0845 850 8508
Fax: 020 7383 5740
Web: www.sportengland.org
Email: info@sportengland.org

SPON'S A&B PRICE BOOK EDITOR
David Wood FRICS
327 Brighton Road
Worthing
BN11 2HP
Tel: 01903 214901

USEFUL ADDRESSES FOR FURTHER INFORMATION

SPORT SCOTLAND
Caledonia House
South Gyle
Edinburgh
Scotland
EH12 9DQ
Tel: 0131 317 7200
Fax: 0131 317 7202
E-mail: info@sportscotland.org.uk
Web: www.sportscotland.org.uk

SPORTS COUNCIL FOR WALES
Welsh Institute of Sport
Sophia Gardens
Cardiff
CF11 9SW
Tel: 02920 300 500
Fax: 02920 300 600
Web: www.sports-council-wales.co.uk
Email: scw@scw.co.uk

SPORTS TURF RESEARCH INSTITUTE (STRI)
Saint Ives Estate
Bingley
West Yorkshire
BD16 1AU
Tel: 01274 565 131
Fax: 01274 561 891
E-mail: info@stri.co.uk
Web: www.stri.co.uk

SPRAYED CONCRETE ASSOCIATION
Association House
235 Ash Road
Aldershot
Hampshire
GU12 4DD
Tel: 01252 321 302
Fax: 01252 333 901

STAINLESS STEEL ADVISORY SERVICE
Room 2.04
The Innovation Centre
217 Portabella
Sheffield
South Yorkshire
S1 4DP
Tel: 0114 224 2240
Fax: 0114 273 0444
Email: ssas@materials.org.uk

STEEL CONSTRUCTION INSTITUTE
Silwood Park
Ascot
Berkshire
SL5 7QN
Tel: 01344 623 345
Fax: 01344 622 944
E-mail: reception@steel-sci.com
Web: www.steel-sci.org

STEEL WINDOW ASSOCIATION
The Building Centre
26 Store Street
London
WC1E 7BT
Tel: 0207 637 3571
Fax: 0207 637 3572
E-mail: info@steel-window-association.co.uk
Web: www.steel-window-association.co.uk

STONE FEDERATION GREAT BRITAIN
18 Mansfield Street
London
W1M 9FGX
Tel: 0207 580 5404
Fax: 0207 636 5984

SUSPENDED ACCESS EQUIPMENT
MANUFACTURERS ASSOCIATION
18 Mansfield Street
London
W1M 9FGX
Tel: 0207 580 5404
Fax: 0207 636 5984

SWIMMING POOL & ALLIED TRADES ASSOCIATION
(SPATA)
Spata House
1a Junction Road
Andover
Hampshire
SP10 3QT
Tel: 01264 356210
Fax: 01264 332628
Web: www.spata.co.uk
Email: admin@spata.co.uk

USEFUL ADDRESSES FOR FURTHER INFORMATION

THERMAL INSULATION CONTRACTORS
ASSOCIATION
Tica House
Allington Way
Yarm Road Business Park
Darlington
County Durham
DL1 4QB
Tel: 01325 466 704
Fax: 01325 487 691
E-mail: enquiries@tica-acad.co.uk
Web: www.tica-acad.co.uk

TIMBER RESEARCH & DEVELOPMENT
ASSOCIATION (TRADA)
Stocking Lane
Hughenden Valley
High Wycombe
Buckinghamshire
HP14 4ND
Tel: 01494 569 600
Fax: 01494 565 487
E-mail: information@trada.co.uk
Web: www.trada.co.uk

TIMBER TRADE FEDERATION
4th Floor
Clareville House
26-27 Oxenden Street
London
SW1Y 4EL
Tel: 0207 839 1891
Fax: 0207 930 0094
E-mail: ttf@ttf.co.uk
Web: www.ttf.co.uk

TOWN & COUNTRY PLANNING ASSOCIATION
(TCPA)
17 Carlton House Terrace
London
SW1Y 5AS
Tel: 0207 930 8903
Fax: 0207 930 3280
E-mail: tcpa@tcpa.org.uk
Web: tcpa.org.uk

TREE COUNCIL
71 Newcomen Street
London
SE1 1WT
Tel: 0207 7407 9992
Fax: 0207 7407 9908
Email: info@treecouncil.org.uk
Web: www.treecouncil.org.uk

TRUSSED RAFTER ASSOCIATION
31 Station Road
Sutton
Retford
Nottinghamshire
DN22 8PZ
Tel: 01777 869281
Fax: 01777 869281
Web: www.tra.org.uk
Email: info@tra.org.uk

TWI (FORMERLY THE WELDING INSTITUTE)
Granta Park
Great Abington
Cambridge
Cambridgeshire
CB1 6AL
Tel: 01223 891 162
Fax: 01223 892 588
E-mail: twi@twi.co.uk
Web: www.twi.co.uk

UK STEEL ASSOCIATION: REINFORCEMENT
MANUFACTURING PRODUCT GROUP
Broadway House
Tothill Street
London
SW1H 9NQ
Tel: 0207 222 7777
Fax: 0207 222 2782

UNDERFLOOR HEATING MANUFACTURERS'
ASSOCIATION
Belhaven House
67 Walton Road
East Moseley
Surrey
KT8 0DB
Tel: 0208 941 7177
Fax: 0208 941 815
Web: www.uhma.org.uk

VERMICULITE INFORMATION SERVICE
1A Guildford Business Park
Guildford
Surrey
GU2 8XG
Tel: 01483 242 100
Fax: 01483 242 101
E-mail: info@palabora.co.uk
Web: www.palabora.co.uk

USEFUL ADDRESSES FOR FURTHER INFORMATION

WALLCOVERING MANUFACTURERS ASSOCIATION
James House
Bridge Street
Leatherhead
Surrey
KT22 7EP
Tel: 01372 360 660
Fax: 01372 376 069
E-mail: Alison.brown@bcf.co.uk

WATER RESEARCH CENTRE
Henley Road
Medmenham
Marlow
Buckinghamshire
SL7 2HD
Tel: 01491 636 500
Fax: 01491 636 501
E-mail: solutions@wrcplc.co.uk
Web: www.wrcplc.co.uk

WATER SERVICES ASSOCIATION
1 Queen Anne's Gate
London
SW1H 9BT
Tel: 0207 957 4567
Fax: 0207 344 1866
Email: info@wtaer.org.uk

WATERHEATER MANUFACTURERS ASSOCIATION
15 Edge Lanedge
Stetford
Manchester
M32 8HN
Tel: 0161 865 8915
Fax: 0161 866 8242

WELDING MANUFACTURERS' ASSOCIATION
Westminster Tower
3 Albert Embankment
London
SE1 7SL
Tel: 0207 793 3041
Fax: 0207 582 8020
Email: wma@beama.org.uk
Web: www.WMA.uk.com

WOOD PANEL INDUSTRIES FEDERATION
Grantham
LincolnshireHertfordshire
NG31 6LR
Tel: 01476 563 707
Fax: 01476 579 314
E-mail: enquiries@wpif.org.uk

ZINC DEVELOPMENT ASSOCIATION
42 Weymouth Street
London
W1N 3LQ
Tel: 0207 499 6636
Fax: 0207 493 1355

DAVIS LANGDON

Maximising value and reducing risk for clients investing in
infrastructure, construction and property

managed
solutions

DAVIS LANGDON

EUROPE & MIDDLE EAST
office locations

ENGLAND

DAVIS LANGDON

LONDON
Mid City Place
71 High Holborn
London WC1V 6QS
Tel: (020) 7061 7000
Fax: (020) 7061 7061
Email: neill.morrison@davislangdon.com

BIRMINGHAM
75-77 Colmore Row
Birmingham
B3 2HD
Tel: (0121) 710 1100
Fax: (0121) 710 1399
Email: david.daly@davislangdon.com

BRISTOL
St Lawrence House
29/31 Broad Street
Bristol BS1 2HF
Tel: (0117) 927 7832
Fax: (0117) 925 1350
Email: alan.francis@davislangdon.com

CAMBRIDGE
36 Storey's Way
Cambridge
CB3 0DT
Tel: (01223) 351 258
Fax: (01223) 321 002
Email: laurence.brett@davislangdon.com

LEEDS
No 4 The Embankment
Victoria Wharf
Sovereign Street
Leeds LS1 4BA
Tel: (0113) 243 2481
Fax: (0113) 242 4601
Email: duncan.sissons@davislangdon.com

LIVERPOOL
Cunard Building
Water Street
Liverpool L3 1JR
Tel: (0151) 236 1992
Fax: (0151) 227 5401
Email: andrew.stevenson@davislangdon.com

MAIDSTONE
11 Tower View
Kings Hill
West Malling
Kent ME19 4UY
Tel: (01732) 840 429
Fax: (01732) 842 305
Email: nick.leggett@davislangdon.com

MANCHESTER
Cloister House
Riverside
New Bailey Street
Manchester M3 5AG
Tel: (0161) 819 7600
Fax: (0161) 819 1818
Email: paul.stanion@davislangdon.com

MILTON KEYNES
Everest House
Rockingham Drive
Linford Wood
Milton Keynes
MK14 6LY
Tel: (01908) 304 700
Fax: (01908) 660 059
Email: kevin.sims@davislangdon.com

NORWICH
63 Thorpe Road
Norwich NR1 1UD
Tel: (01603) 628 194
Fax: (01603) 615 928
Email: michael.ladbrook@davislangdon.com

OXFORD
Avalon House
Marcham Road
Abingdon
Oxford OX14 1TZ
Tel: (01235) 555 025
Fax: (01235) 554 909
Email: paul.coomber@davislangdon.com

PETERBOROUGH
Clarence House
Minerva Business Park
Lynchwood
Peterborough PE2 6FT
Tel: (01733) 362 000
Fax: (01733) 230 875
Email: stuart.bremner@davislangdon.com

PLYMOUTH
1 Ensign House
Parkway Court
Longbridge Road
Plymouth PL6 8LR
Tel: (01752) 827 444
Fax: (01752) 221 219
Email: gareth.steventon@davislangdon.com

SOUTHAMPTON
Brunswick House
Brunswick Place
Southampton SO15 2AP
Tel: (023) 8033 3438
Fax: (023) 8022 6099
Email: chris.tremellen@davislangdon.com/
peter.boote@davislangdon.com

**DAVIS LANGDON
LEGAL SUPPORT**
Mid City Place
71 High Holborn
London WC1V 6QS
Tel: (020) 7061 7000
Fax: (020) 7061 7061
Email: mark.hackett@davislangdon.com

**DAVIS LANGDON
CONSULTANCY**
Mid City Place
71 High Holborn
London WC1V 6QS
Tel: (020) 7061 7007
Fax: (020) 7061 7005
Email: john.connaughton@davislangdon.com

**DAVIS LANGDON
SCHUMANN SMITH**
Southgate House
St Georges Way
Stevenage
Hertfordshire SG1 1HG
Tel: (01438) 742 642
Fax: (01438) 742 632
Email: nick.schumann@schumannsmith.com

**DAVIS LANGDON
MOTT GREEN & WALL**
Mid City Place
71 High Holborn
London WC1V 6QS
Tel: (020) 7061 7777
Fax: (020) 7061 7009
Email: general@mottgreenwall.co.uk

**DAVIS LANGDON
CROSHER & JAMES**
Mid City Place
71 High Holborn
London WC1V 6QS
Tel: (020) 7061 7077
Fax: (020) 7061 7078
Email: tony.llewellyn@crosherjames.com

BIRMINGHAM
102 New Street
Birmingham B2 4HQ
Tel: (0121) 632 3600
Fax: (0121) 632 3601
Email: clive.searle@crosherjames.com

CARDIFF
4 Piershead Street
Capital Waterside
Cardiff
CF10 4QP
Tel: (029) 2049 7497
Fax: (029) 2049 7111
Email: michael.murraym@crosherjames.com

EDINBURGH
39 Melville Street
Edinburgh
EH3 7JF
Tel: (0131) 220 4225
Fax: (0131) 220 4226
Email: ian.mcfarlane@crosherjames.com

GLASGOW
Monteith House
11 George Square
Glasgow
G2 1DY
Tel: (0141) 248 0333
Fax: (0141) 248 0313
Email: fraserk@nbwcrosherjames.com

MANCHESTER
Cloister House
Riverside
New Bailey Street
Manchester M3 5AG
Tel: (0161) 819 7600
Fax: (0161) 819 1818
Email: sharmas@nbwcrosherjames.com

SOUTHAMPTON
Brunswick House
Brunswick Place
Southampton SO15 2AP
Tel: (023) 8068 2800
Fax: (023) 8033 6360
Email: reesd@nbwcrosherjames.com

SCOTLAND

DAVIS LANGDON

GLASGOW
Monteith House
11 George Square
Glasgow G2 1DY
Tel: (0141) 248 0300
Fax: (0141) 248 0303
Email:
sam.mackenzie@davislangdon.com

EDINBURGH
39 Melville Street
Edinburgh
EH3 7JF
Tel: (0131) 240 1350
Fax: (0131) 240 1399
Email: erland.rendall@davislangdon.com

WALES

CARDIFF
4 Pierhead Street
Capital Waterside
Cardiff CF10 4QP
Tel: (029) 2049 7497
Fax: (029) 2049 7111
Email: paul.edwards@davislangdon.com

IRELAND

DAVIS LANGDON PKS

DUBLIN
24 Lower Hatch Street
Dublin 2
Ireland
Tel: (00 353 1) 676 3671
Fax: (00 353 1) 676 3672
Email: mwebb@dlpks.ie

GALWAY
Heritage Hall
Kirwan's Lane
Galway, Ireland
Tel: (00 353 91) 530 199
Fax: (00 353 91) 530 198
Email: joregan@dlpks.ie

LIMERICK
8 The Crescent
Limerick
Ireland
Tel: (00 353 61) 318 870
Fax: (00 353 61) 318 871
Email: cbarry@dlpks.ie

SPAIN

DAVIS LANGDON EDETCO

BARCELONA
C/Muntaner, 479, 12°
Barcelona 08021
Spain
Tel: (00 34 93) 418 6899
Fax: (00 34 93) 211 0003
Email: fmonells@barcelona.edetco.com

GIRONA
C/Salt 10
Girona 17005
Spain
Tel: (00 34 97) 223 8000
Fax: (00 34 97) 224 2661
Email: girona@girona.edetco.com

FRANCE

DAVIS LANGDON
5 Rue St Germain l'Auxerrois
75001 Paris
France
Tel: (00 33 1) 5340 9480
Fax: (00 33 1) 5340 9481
Email: andrew.richardson@dleparis.com

POLAND

DAVIS LANGDON
Warsaw Trade Tower
ul. Chlodna 51, 26th Floor
00-867 Warsaw, Poland
Tel: (00 48 22) 455 39 00
Fax: (00 48 22) 455 39 01
Email: warsaw@davislangdon-polska.pl

RUSSIA

DAVIS LANGDON
Office 5
Myasnitskaya
Moscow, 101000
Russia
Tel: (00 7 095) 933 7810
Fax: (00 7 095) 933 7811
Email: stephen.thomas@davislangdon.com

MIDDLE EAST

DAVIS LANGDON
PO Box 13-5422-Shouran
Beirut
Lebanon
Tel: (00 9611) 780 111
Fax: (00 9611) 809 045
Email: DLL.MI@cyberia.net.lb

ARABIAN GULF

DAVIS LANGDON

BAHRAIN
3rd Floor Building 256
Road No 3605
Area No 336
PO Box 640, Manama
State of Bahrain
Arabian Gulf
Tel: (00 973) 1782 7567
Fax: (00 973) 1772 8257
Email: david.galbraith@davislangdon-bahrain.com

UNITED ARAB EMIRATES
PO Box 7856
Office 410
Oud Metha Office Building
Dubai, UAE
Tel: (00 9714) 32 42 919
Fax: (00 9714) 32 42 838
Email: neil.taylor@davislangdon-dubai.com

QATAR
PO Box 3206, Doha
State of Qatar
Tel: (00 974) 4580 150
Fax: (00 974) 4697 905
Email: david.craig@davislangdon-qatar.com

EGYPT
35 Misr Helwan Road
Maadi 11431
Cairo
Egypt
Tel: (00 20 2) 526 2319
Fax: (00 20 2) 527 1338
Email: dlegypt@link.net

Index

References in brackets after page numbers refer to SMM7 and the Common Arrangement of Work sections.

Project Planning Control

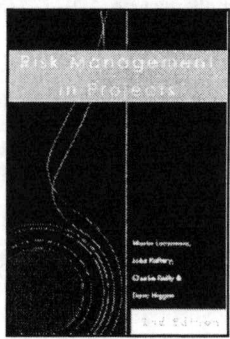

David G. Carmichael

Project management is widely used in the construction industry and is central to planning and controlling time, costs and resources. This book enables readers to perform more effectively, to understand project planning and control procedures and to gain an insight into the associated skills. Numerous case examples from diverse industries and exercises support and illustrate important concepts. The result is a new perspective for project managers: planning can be shown to be a systems synthesis or an inverse problem, and this provides a way to reach a satisfactory solution, avoiding the time-consuming or impractical search for the optimal solution.

September 2005: 234x156 mm: 304 pages
HB: 0-415-34726-2: £60.00

To Order: Tel: +44 (0) 1264 343071 Fax: +44 (0) 1264 343005, or
Post: Taylor and Francis Customer Services, Thomson Publishing Services, Cheriton House, Andover, Hants, SP10 5BE, UK Email: book.orders@tandf.co.uk

For a complete listing of all our titles visit :
www.sponpress.com

Taylor & Francis
Taylor & Francis Group plc

CD-Rom Single-User Licence Agreement

We welcome you as a user of this Taylor & Francis CD-ROM and hope that you find it a useful and valuable tool. Please read this document carefully. **This is a legal agreement** between you (hereinafter referred to as the "Licensee") and Taylor and Francis Books Ltd. (the "Publisher"), which defines the terms under which you may use the Product. **By breaking the seal and opening the package containing the CD-ROM you agree to these terms and conditions outlined herein. If you do not agree to these terms you must return the Product to your supplier intact, with the seal on the CD case unbroken.**

1. **Definition of the Product**
   The product which is the subject of this Agreement, *Spon's Architects' and Builders' Price Book 2006 on CD-ROM* (the "Product") consists of:
1.1 Underlying data comprised in the product (the "Data")
1.2 A compilation of the Data (the "Database")
1.3 Software (the "Software") for accessing and using the Database
1.4 A CD-ROM disk (the "CD-ROM")

2. **Commencement and licence**
2.1 This Agreement commences upon the breaking open of the package containing the CD-ROM by the Licensee (the "Commencement Date").
2.2 This is a licence agreement (the "Agreement") for the use of the Product by the Licensee, and not an agreement for sale.
2.3 The Publisher licenses the Licensee on a non-exclusive and non-transferable basis to use the Product on condition that the Licensee complies with this Agreement. The Licensee acknowledges that it is only permitted to use the Product in accordance with this Agreement.

3. **Multiple use**
   For more than one user or for a wide area network or consortium, use is only permissible with the purchase from the Publisher of a multiple-user licence and adherence to the terms and conditions of that licence.

4. **Installation and Use**
4.1 The Licensee may provide access to the Product for individual study in the following manner: The Licensee may install the Product on a secure local area network on a single site for use by one user.
4.2 The Licensee shall be responsible for installing the Product and for the effectiveness of such installation.
4.3 Text from the Product may be incorporated in a coursepack. Such use is only permissible with the express permission of the Publisher in writing and requires the payment of the appropriate fee as specified by the Publisher and signature of a separate licence agreement.
4.4 The CD-ROM is a free addition to the book and no technical support will be provided.

5. **Permitted Activities**
5.1 The Licensee shall be entitled:
   5.1.1 to use the Product for its own internal purposes;
   5.1.2 to download onto electronic, magnetic, optical or similar storage medium reasonable portions of the Database provided that the purpose of the Licensee is to undertake internal research or study and provided that such storage is temporary;
   5.1.3 to make a copy of the Database and/or the Software for back-up/archival/disaster recovery purposes.
5.2 The Licensee acknowledges that its rights to use the Product are strictly set out in this Agreement, and all other uses (whether expressly mentioned in Clause 6 below or not) are prohibited.

6. **Prohibited Activities**
   The following are prohibited without the express permission of the Publisher:
6.1 The commercial exploitation of any part of the Product.
6.2 The rental, loan, (free or for money or money's worth) or hire purchase of this product, save with the express consent of the Publisher.
6.3 Any activity which raises the reasonable prospect of impeding the Publisher's ability or opportunities to market the Product.
6.4 Any networking, physical or electronic distribution or dissemination of the product save as expressly permitted by this Agreement.
6.5 Any reverse engineering, decompilation, disassembly or other alteration of the Product save in accordance with applicable national laws.
6.6 The right to create any derivative product or service from the Product save as expressly provided for in this Agreement.
6.7 Any alteration, amendment, modification or deletion from the Product, whether for the purposes of error correction or otherwise.

7. General Responsibilities of the License

7.1 The Licensee will take all reasonable steps to ensure that the Product is used in accordance with the terms and conditions of this Agreement.

7.2 The Licensee acknowledges that damages may not be a sufficient remedy for the Publisher in the event of breach of this Agreement by the Licensee, and that an injunction may be appropriate.

7.3 The Licensee undertakes to keep the Product safe and to use its best endeavours to ensure that the product does not fall into the hands of third parties, whether as a result of theft or otherwise.

7.4 Where information of a confidential nature relating to the product of the business affairs of the Publisher comes into the possession of the Licensee pursuant to this Agreement (or otherwise), the Licensee agrees to use such information solely for the purposes of this Agreement, and under no circumstances to disclose any element of the information to any third party save strictly as permitted under this Agreement. For the avoidance of doubt, the Licensee's obligations under this sub-clause 7.4 shall survive the termination of this Agreement.

8. Warrant and Liability

8.1 The Publisher warrants that it has the authority to enter into this agreement and that it has secured all rights and permissions necessary to enable the Licensee to use the Product in accordance with this Agreement.

8.2 The Publisher warrants that the CD-ROM as supplied on the Commencement Date shall be free of defects in materials and workmanship, and undertakes to replace any defective CD-ROM within 28 days of notice of such defect being received provided such notice is received within 30 days of such supply. As an alternative to replacement, the Publisher agrees fully to refund the Licensee in such circumstances, if the Licensee so requests, provided that the Licensee returns the Product to the Publisher. The provisions of this sub-clause 8.2 do not apply where the defect results from an accident or from misuse of the product by the Licensee.

8.3 Sub-clause 8.2 sets out the sole and exclusive remedy of the Licensee in relation to defects in the CD-ROM.

8.4 The Publisher and the Licensee acknowledge that the Publisher supplies the Product on an "as is" basis. The Publisher gives no warranties:

    8.4.1 that the Product satisfies the individual requirements of the Licensee; or

    8.4.2 that the Product is otherwise fit for the Licensee's purpose; or

    8.4.3 that the Data are accurate or complete of free of errors or omissions; or

    8.4.4 that the Product is compatible with the Licensee's hardware equipment and software operating environment.

8.5 The Publisher hereby disclaims all warranties and conditions, express or implied, which are not stated above.

8.6 Nothing in this Clause 8 limits the Publisher's liability to the Licensee in the event of death or personal injury resulting from the Publisher's negligence.

8.7 The Publisher hereby excludes liability for loss of revenue, reputation, business, profits, or for indirect or consequential losses, irrespective of whether the Publisher was advised by the Licensee of the potential of such losses.

8.8 The Licensee acknowledges the merit of independently verifying Data prior to taking any decisions of material significance (commercial or otherwise) based on such data. It is agreed that the Publisher shall not be liable for any losses which result from the Licensee placing reliance on the Data or on the Database, under any circumstances.

8.9 Subject to sub-clause 8.6 above, the Publisher's liability under this Agreement shall be limited to the purchase price.

9. Intellectual Property Rights

9.1 Nothing in this Agreement affects the ownership of copyright or other intellectual property rights in the Data, the Database of the Software.

9.2 The Licensee agrees to display the Publishers' copyright notice in the manner described in the Product.

9.3 The Licensee hereby agrees to abide by copyright and similar notice requirements required by the Publisher, details of which are as follows:

"© 2006 Taylor & Francis. All rights reserved. All materials in *Spon's Architects' and Builders' Price Book 2006* are copyright protected. © 2003 Adobe Systems Incorporated. All rights reserved. No such materials may be used, displayed, modified, adapted, distributed, transmitted, transferred, published or otherwise reproduced in any form or by any means now or hereafter developed other than strictly in accordance with the terms of the licence agreement enclosed with the CD-ROM. However, text and images may be printed and copied for research and private study within the preset program limitations. Please note the copyright notice above, and that any text or images printed or copied must credit the source."

9.4 This Product contains material proprietary to and copyedited by the Publisher and others. Except for the licence granted herein, all rights, title and interest in the Product, in all languages, formats and media throughout the world, including copyrights therein, are and remain the property of the Publisher or other copyright holders identified in the Product.

10. Non-assignment

This Agreement and the licence contained within it may not be assigned to any other person or entity without the written consent of the Publisher.

11. Termination and Consequences of Termination.

11.1 The Publisher shall have the right to terminate this Agreement if:

    11.1.1 the Licensee is in material breach of this Agreement and fails to remedy such breach (where capable of remedy) within 14 days of a written notice from the Publisher requiring it to do so; or

    11.1.2 the Licensee becomes insolvent, becomes subject to receivership, liquidation or similar external administration; or

    11.1.3 the Licensee ceases to operate in business.

11.2 The Licensee shall have the right to terminate this Agreement for any reason upon two month's written notice. The Licensee shall not be entitled to any refund for payments made under this Agreement prior to termination under this sub-clause 11.2.

11.3 Termination by either of the parties is without prejudice to any other rights or remedies under the general law to which they may be entitled, or which survive such termination (including rights of the Publisher under sub-clause 7.4 above).

11.4 Upon termination of this Agreement, or expiry of its terms, the Licensee must:

    11.4.1 destroy all back up copies of the product; and

    11.4.2 return the Product to the Publisher.

12. General

12.1 **Compliance with export provisions**

The Publisher hereby agrees to comply fully with all relevant export laws and regulations of the United Kingdom to ensure that the Product is not exported, directly or indirectly, in violation of English law.

12.2 **Force majeure**

The parties accept no responsibility for breaches of this Agreement occurring as a result of circumstances beyond their control.

12.3 **No waiver**

Any failure or delay by either party to exercise or enforce any right conferred by this Agreement shall not be deemed to be a waiver of such right.

12.4 **Entire agreement**

This Agreement represents the entire agreement between the Publisher and the Licensee concerning the Product. The terms of this Agreement supersede all prior purchase orders, written terms and conditions, written or verbal representations, advertising or statements relating in any way to the Product.

12.5 **Severability**

If any provision of this Agreement is found to be invalid or unenforceable by a court of law of competent jurisdiction, such a finding shall not affect the other provisions of this Agreement and all provisions of this Agreement unaffected by such a finding shall remain in full force and effect.

12.6 **Variations**

This agreement may only be varied in writing by means of variation signed in writing by both parties.

12.7 **Notices**

All notices to be delivered to: Spon's Price Books, Taylor & Francis Books Ltd., 2 Park Square, Milton Park, Abingdon, Oxfordshire, OX14 4RN, UK.

12.8 **Governing law**

This Agreement is governed by English law and the parties hereby agree that any dispute arising under this Agreement shall be subject to the jurisdiction of the English courts.

If you have any queries about the terms of this licence, please contact:

Spon's Price Books
Taylor & Francis Books Ltd.
2 Park Square, Milton Park, Abingdon, Oxfordshire, OX14 4RN
Tel: +44 (0) 20 7017 6000
Fax: +44 (0) 20 7017 6702
www.sponpress.com

Multiple-user use of the Spon Press CD–ROM

To buy a licence to install your Spon Press Price
Book CD–ROM on a secure local area network or a
wide area network, and for the supply of network key
files, for an agreed number of users please contact:

Spon's Price Books
Taylor & Francis Books Ltd.
2 Park Square, Milton Park, Abingdon, Oxfordshire, OX14 4RN
Tel: +44 (0) 207 7017 6000
Fax: +44 (0) 207 7017 6072
www.sponpress.com

Number of users	Licence cost
2–5	£360
6–10	£840
11–20	£1600
21–30	£2850
31–50	£4200
51–75	£6600
76–100	£9000
Over 100	Please contact Spon for details

CD-ROM Installation Instructions

System requirements

Minimum

- Pentium processor
- 32 MB of RAM
- 10 MB available hard disk space
- CD-ROM drive
- Microsoft Windows 95/98/2000/NT/ME/XP
- SVGA screen
- Internet connection

Recommended

- Pentium 266 MHz processor
- 256 MB of RAM
- 100 MB available hard disk space
- CD-ROM drive
- Microsoft Windows 2000/NT/XP
- XVGA screen
- Internet connection

Microsoft ® is a registered trademark and Windows™ is a trademark of the Microsoft Corporation.

Installation

How to install *Spon's Architects' and Builders' Price Book 2006 CD-ROM*

Windows 95/98/2000/NT

Spon's Architects' and Builders' Price Book 2006 CD-ROM should run automatically when inserted into the CD-ROM drive. If it fails to run, follow the instructions below.

- Click the **Start** button and choose **Run.**
- Click the **Browse** button.
- Select your CD-ROM drive.
- Select the Setup file (setup.exe) then click **Open.**
- Click the OK button.
- Follow the instructions on screen.
- The installation process will create a folder containing an icon for *Spon's Architects' and Builders' Price Book 2006 CD-ROM* and also an icon on your desktop.

How to run the *Spon's Architects' and Builders' Price Book 2006 CD-ROM*

- Double click the icon (from the folder or desktop) installed by the Setup program.
- Follow the instructions on screen.

The CD-ROM is a free addition to the book and no technical support will be provided. For help with the use of the CD-ROM please visit www.pricebooks.co.uk